船舶建造

（第二版）

林源民 著

上海浦江教育出版社

ⓒ 林源民 2024

内容简介

  本书在英国法的框架下比较全面地分析了常见的船舶建造合同的条款,不仅涉及合同条款的磋商和订立,而且还包括合同条款的具体履行要求以及违约后果。本书引用了较多的案例,希望有助于读者对相关问题有一个比较切合实际的理解。

图书在版编目(CIP)数据

船舶建造:汉、英/林源民著. —2 版. —上海:上海浦江教育出版社有限公司,2024.1
ISBN 978-7-81121-849-7

Ⅰ.①船… Ⅱ.①林… Ⅲ.①造船—经济合同—经济纠纷—案例—英国—汉、英 Ⅳ.①D956.13

中国国家版本馆 CIP 数据核字(2024)第 010900 号

CHUANBO JIANZAO(DI-ER BAN)
船舶建造(第二版)

上海浦江教育出版社出版发行
社址:上海海港大道 1550 号上海海事大学校内 邮政编码:201306
电话:(021)38284910(12)(发行) 38284923(总编室) 38284910(传真)
E-mail:cbs@shmtu.edu.cn URL:http://www.pujiangpress.com
上海盛通时代印刷有限公司印装
幅面尺寸:170 mm×228 mm 印张:60.25 字数:1 048 千字
2024 年 1 月第 2 版 2024 年 7 月第 2 次印刷
策划编辑:蔡则齐 责任编辑:蔡则齐 封面设计:赵宏义
定价:258.00 元

第一版序

2007年,我第一次应邀为上海海事大学EMBA班讲授"造船合同管理"课程,并为此编写了讲稿。"造船合同管理"授课内容主要是从造船合同的磋商、订立直至履行的整个过程解释相关合同条款,介绍相关案例和事例,分析船厂的合同地位。2011年,我第二次应邀为上海海事大学在福州讲授该课程,于是利用这一机会对原来的讲稿进行比较大的改动。本书是在第二个讲稿的基础上写成的。

本书是一本关于法律的书,而且是关于英国法律的书。除非另有说明,书中提到的法律均指英国法。之所以写英国法,是因为船舶建造合同适用的几乎都是英国法。但本书对船舶建造的实务操作同样有意义,因为法律本来就无法与实务分得清清楚楚。

如果说本书有特点的话,首先,本书在引用法律条文、合同规定以及法院判决时均采用了英文原文,目的是避免自己理解和翻译的错误给读者造成误解;其次,本书使用了不少案例,希望有助于读者对自己的实际工作或争议有一个大致的判断,因为可预见性是普通法的一个特征;再次,本书比较分析了常见的船舶建造合同标准格式,从而使读者可以了解合同条款的不同措辞可能带来的不同后果;最后,本书准备了索引,以方便读者查阅。

我应当感谢曾给我机会参与争议解决的船厂,没有船厂的信任,本书的写作显然是不可能完成,甚至是无法开始的。

我还想感谢我的三位学生,林孜清、翁建山和朱夔俊,他们对初稿进行了阅读和纠错。三位学生没有分工,而是各自读完全书,因此浪费了他们不少的时间。林孜清同学还准备了本书的案例目录,翁建山同学则为本书准备了其他目录。

林源民

2013年6月30日于上海

第二版序

《船舶建造》一书的第一版出版于 2013 年，距今已有 11 年了，修订应当是合适的。第二版对第一版的调整和修改主要包括：纠错，包括谬误、语法错误和笔误等；段落编号的调整；第一版引用的文献有新版的，第二版予以了更新；增加了新的判例；索引也有更改。此外，第二版增加了第 25 章（海工装备建造）。

我要感谢出版社的于杰，他的认真给我留下深刻的印象，还要感谢赵婉婷，她为全书的格式进行了校对，浪费了她不少时间。

林源民

2024 年 5 月 19 日于上海

目　录

第一版序
第二版序

第1章　绪　论 ··· 1
　Ⅰ　合同概述 ··· 1
　　合同的定义 ··· 1
　　合同定义的问题 ··· 3
　Ⅱ　船舶建造合同的性质 ·· 4
　　英国法 ··· 4
　　船舶建造合同在中国法的地位 ··· 7
　　确定船舶建造合同性质的意义 ··· 10
　Ⅲ　英国法的适用 ··· 11
　　历史的原因 ··· 12
　　法律的原因 ··· 12
　　语言的原因 ··· 12
　Ⅳ　英国1979年《货物买卖法》 ··· 13
　　《货物买卖法》简介 ·· 13
　　成文法的适用和排除 ··· 14
　　买卖合同的定义 ··· 14
　　　出售协议 ··· 15
　　　出售 ··· 15
　　　区分出售协议和出售的意义 ··· 16
　　特定货物和未确定货物 ·· 16
　　　特定货物 ··· 16
　　　未确定货物 ·· 17

　　　　区分特定货物和未确定货物的意义 …………………………………… 17
　现有货物和未来货物 ……………………………………………………………… 18
　　现有货物 ……………………………………………………………………… 18
　　未来货物 ……………………………………………………………………… 18
　　区分现有货物和未来货物的意义 …………………………………………… 19
　绝对的买卖和有条件的买卖 ……………………………………………………… 19
　凭描述进行的买卖 ………………………………………………………………… 19
　　凭描述买卖的种类 …………………………………………………………… 20
　　关于货物描述的性质 ………………………………………………………… 20
　　关于船舶的描述 ……………………………………………………………… 21
　　买方对货物描述的依赖 ……………………………………………………… 23
　　船舶建造合同的特征 ………………………………………………………… 24

Ⅴ　买卖合同的默示保证 ………………………………………………………………… 24
　所有权默示保证 …………………………………………………………………… 25
　　卖方的权利及享有权利的时间 ……………………………………………… 25
　　"不受干扰的占有" …………………………………………………………… 26
　　船舶建造合同 ………………………………………………………………… 27
　货物符合描述默示保证 …………………………………………………………… 27
　　默示条款 ……………………………………………………………………… 28
　　不符合描述的情形 …………………………………………………………… 28
　　船舶建造合同对船舶的描述 ………………………………………………… 29
　货物质量默示保证 ………………………………………………………………… 30
　　买者自负原则 ………………………………………………………………… 30
　　"在业务经营中" ……………………………………………………………… 31
　　可销售质量 …………………………………………………………………… 32
　　令人满意的质量 ……………………………………………………………… 33
　　应当考虑的因素 ……………………………………………………………… 38
　　令人满意质量的例外 ………………………………………………………… 39
　　责任的排除及其效力 ………………………………………………………… 40
　货物适合用途的默示保证 ………………………………………………………… 42

Ⅵ　船舶建造合同的标准格式 …………………………………………………………… 49
　标准格式合同 ……………………………………………………………………… 49

船舶建造合同标准格式介绍 ······················· 49
　　　　SAJ 格式 ···································· 49
　　　　AWES 格式 ··································· 51
　　　　Norwegian 格式 ······························· 51
　　　　MARAD 格式 ·································· 52
　　　　NEWBUILDCON 格式 ···························· 52
　　　　CSTC 格式 ··································· 54
　　　　CMAC 格式 ··································· 54
　　标准格式合同的作用 ····························· 55

第 2 章　合同的洽谈和订立

Ⅰ　合同的洽谈 ·· 57
　　谈判概述 ·· 57
　　技术洽谈 ·· 57
　　　　规格书 ·· 58
　　　　图纸 ·· 59
　　　　厂商表 ·· 60
　　商务洽谈 ·· 61
　　了解和信任 ······································ 62
　　专业知识和专业人员 ······························ 62
　　洽谈的费用及其承担 ······························ 63

Ⅱ　合同的成立 ·· 69
　　意思表示一致 ···································· 69
　　客观标准 ·· 70

Ⅲ　要约 ·· 71
　　要约的定义 ······································ 71
　　创立法律关系的意图 ······························ 72
　　交易的邀请 ······································ 73
　　要约应包含合同主要条款 ·························· 76
　　要约的撤回 ······································ 77
　　问题单 ·· 79

Ⅳ 接受 … 79
接受的定义 … 79
接受必须是明确肯定的 … 80
接受生效的时间 … 81
传统的接受生效时间 … 82
对接受生效时间的质疑 … 83
瞬间通信条件下接受生效的时间 … 83
接受在收到时生效原则的确立 … 86
电子邮件的接受时间 … 87
以行为表示的接受 … 88
沉默 … 89
反要约 … 89
格式之战 … 93

Ⅴ 意向书 … 96
意向书的性质 … 96
意向书没有约束力的情形 … 97
意向书具有要约性质的情形 … 99

Ⅵ 招标 … 100
招标邀请和要约 … 100
招标人谨慎行事的义务 … 102
欺诈性陈述 … 105
合理报酬 … 106

Ⅶ 合同形式 … 107
法律对合同形式的要求 … 107
货物买卖合同的形式 … 108
船舶建造合同的形式 … 108
以合同为准 … 110
电子方式订立的合同 … 113

Ⅷ 洽谈合同的协议 … 113
概述 … 113
不可执行性 … 114
"尽最大努力" … 115

Ⅸ 对价 ············ 116
  对价的定义 ············ 116
  利益的获得 ············ 117
  对价的合适性 ············ 118
  合同变更的对价 ············ 119
  合同解除后的对价问题 ············ 120
Ⅹ 合同条款 ············ 122
  条件 ············ 122
  保证 ············ 124
  中间条款 ············ 125
  陈述成为合同条款 ············ 126
  关于履行时间的规定 ············ 126
Ⅺ 合同当事人 ············ 127
  船厂 ············ 128
  联合建造人 ············ 128
  船东 ············ 129
  指定买方 ············ 130
  转售船东 ············ 130
  质保受让人 ············ 131
Ⅻ 新建船经纪人 ············ 131
  法律地位 ············ 131
  商业代理人 ············ 132
  唯一经纪人 ············ 134
  业务素质及作用 ············ 134
  佣金 ············ 135
    获得佣金的权利 ············ 136
    船厂的违约 ············ 137

第3章 船舶描述及船级 ············ 139
Ⅰ 船舶描述 ············ 139
  船号 ············ 139
    船号的特定性 ············ 140

	船号的唯一性	142
	船舶尺寸和吨位	143
	船舶特征	146
	建造标准	149
II	船级社	150
	概述	150
	船级社的职能和服务	150
	法定检验	151
	入级检验	152
	国际船级社协会	152
	成员船级社	153
	共同行动	153
	船级社的责任	154
	谨慎义务	154
	免责与责任限制	157
	技术问题决定权	159
III	船舶入级	160
	船级的意义	160
	船舶入级的程序	163
	船级符号	164
	符合船级社规范	165
	双重船级	167
IV	船舶登记	167
	船舶的国籍	167
	船旗国的职责	169
	船舶登记的法律效力	170
	船舶登记的条件	170
	船舶登记的办理	171
	在建船舶的登记	173
	中国法	173
	英国法	174
	在建船舶抵押登记	175

	V 船级社的监造 ·································	175
	船级社和船厂的关系 ·······························	175
	船舶监造的必要性 ·································	176
	监造协议 ···	176
	VI NEWBUILDCON 格式的新规定 ······················	177
	有害物质清单 ·····································	177
	保护涂层 ···	179
	原产地 ···	180
	VII 船舶建造的分包 ·································	181
	概念 ···	181
	船厂分包的权利 ···································	182
	分包商的选择 ·····································	183
	分包商的地位 ·····································	184
	分包商的谨慎之责 ·································	185
	分包商的责任限制 ·································	186

第4章 价格及支付方式 ································· 187

I 合同价格 ·· 187
    固定价格 ··· 187
    货币的选择 ······································· 188
    虚假合同价格 ····································· 189
II 合同价格的支付 ····································· 191
    支付方式 ··· 191
        分期支付 ····································· 191
        电汇支付 ····································· 194
    支付时间的约定 ··································· 195
        法律关于支付时间的规定 ····················· 196
        银行工作日 ··································· 197
    预付款和定金 ····································· 198
    交船款的支付 ····································· 202
    提前支付 ··· 202

- Ⅲ 支付条件 …… 203
  - 收到还款保函 …… 203
  - 收到付款通知 …… 204
  - 收到节点证书 …… 205
    - 节点的真实达到 …… 207
    - 船东监造代表的会签 …… 208
- Ⅳ 抵销 …… 208
  - 抵销的概念 …… 208
  - 抵销权的排除 …… 209
  - 标准格式的规定 …… 210
  - 约定的明确性 …… 211
  - 排除的效力 …… 213
- Ⅴ 约定赔偿 …… 215
  - 特征 …… 215
  - 赔偿与惩罚 …… 216
  - 标准格式的规定 …… 222
  - 有经验当事人的约定 …… 223
  - 约定赔偿的数额 …… 224
    - 实际损失超过约定数额 …… 224
    - 确定数额的时间 …… 225
  - 约定赔偿的名称 …… 225
  - 约定赔偿和过错 …… 226
  - 约定赔偿的支付 …… 227
  - 船东支付约定赔偿 …… 229
- Ⅵ 合同价格的调整 …… 230
  - 概述 …… 230
  - 交船日保证 …… 230
    - 提前交船奖励 …… 232
  - 航速保证 …… 235
    - 航速保证的独立性 …… 237
  - 油耗保证 …… 238
  - 载重吨保证 …… 241

	货舱容积保证	243
	关于建造保证	243
	因建造不符合约定引起的调整	244
VII	合同价格的重新谈判	245
	船厂要求加价的机会	245
	加价的对价	245
	减价的机会	247
VIII	还款保函	247
	概念	247
	保证合同	248
	还款保函的性质	249
	"主债务人"	250
	见索即付保函	251
	法院的解释	252
	还款保函的有效期	255
	还款保函的转让	256
	标准格式规定的问题	256
	仲裁止付条款	259
	担保人的责任解除	261
IX	付款保函	264
	性质和作用	264
	母公司保函	265
	标准格式的规定	265
	付款保函的无条件性	266
	付款保函准据法	269
X	安慰函	270
	概念	270
	安慰函的措辞	270
	承担义务的意愿	272
	不受约束的表示	273
	船舶建造中的安慰函	274

第5章 设计、审图和监造 275
Ⅰ 船舶设计 275
概述 275
Design 和 Engineering 276
船舶设计的阶段 276
- 概念设计阶段 276
- 初步设计阶段 277
- 合同设计阶段 277
- 功能设计阶段 277
- 过渡设计阶段 277
- 工作站信息准备阶段 278

关于设计的约定 278
- SAJ 格式 278
- AWES 格式 279
- Norwegian 格式 280
- NEWBUILDCON 格式 280

设计和工艺 281
船东的设计 282
第三人的设计 283
- 船厂的责任 283
- 明显的设计缺陷 286

Ⅱ 审图 287
船级社审图 288
- 船级社审图的延误 288

船东审图 288
- 额外审图时间 291
- 船东代表审图 291
- 船东的审图意见 292
- 不构成修改和变更的情形 292
- 不明确的意见 293

视为批准的情形 295
审图争议 296

  审图与船厂的责任 …………………………………… 298
 Ⅲ 监造代表 …………………………………………………… 301
  监造代表的指派 …………………………………… 301
  监造代表的授权 …………………………………… 302
  监造代表的职责 …………………………………… 304
  船厂的协助 ………………………………………… 304
  监造代表和船厂的关系 …………………………… 305
  船东的雇主责任 …………………………………… 306
   免责约定的有效性 …………………………… 307
   船厂的代理 …………………………………… 308
   过失和重大过失 ……………………………… 310
   NEWBUILDCON 格式的规定 ……………… 313
  监造代表的更换 …………………………………… 315
  监造代表和船级社的联系 ………………………… 317
 Ⅳ 船舶检验 ………………………………………………… 317
  船东代表的检验 …………………………………… 317
   项目和时间的约定 …………………………… 319
   查看船舶的权利 ……………………………… 320
   重复测试或检验 ……………………………… 321
   通知缺陷的义务 ……………………………… 321
   争议的解决 …………………………………… 323
  船级社的检验 ……………………………………… 324
  建造进程报告 ……………………………………… 324

第 6 章 修 改 ………………………………………………… 326
 Ⅰ 概述 ……………………………………………………… 326
 Ⅱ 船东的修改 ……………………………………………… 326
  船东修改的原因 …………………………………… 326
  标准格式的规定 …………………………………… 327
  修改的约定 ………………………………………… 330
  费用的约定 ………………………………………… 332
  获得修改费用的权利 ……………………………… 334

合理报酬 ··· 335
修改费用的支付 ··· 336
船东的修改和约定赔偿 ································· 336
合同交船日的顺延 ······································· 338
　　不能顺延交船日的情形 ···························· 339
　　顺延交船日的条件 ································· 339
　　修改造成延误 ······································· 341
减少工作量的修改请求 ································· 341
关于修改的争议 ··· 342
Ⅲ 船厂提出的修改 ··· 343
Ⅳ 船级规范等变更导致的修改 ······························ 345
概述 ·· 345
船厂的义务和权利 ······································· 346
船厂继续履行合同的义务 ······························ 348
建造合同的倒签 ··· 350
　　保护涂层性能标准 ································· 350
　　倒签合同的性质 ··································· 351
　　公共政策 ··· 352
　　倒签合同的影响 ··································· 353
Ⅴ 材料的替代 ·· 354
Ⅵ 修改费用的支付 ·· 356

第7章 试 航 ·· 358
Ⅰ 概述 ··· 358
系泊试验 ·· 358
　　倾斜试验 ··· 359
航行试验 ·· 360
试验大纲 ·· 360
　　船厂的试航 ·· 361
Ⅱ 试航通知 ··· 361
船厂发出试航通知的义务 ······························ 361
数个试航通知 ·· 363

		试航的延期	365
		船东代表的签证	366
		其他通知	367
	Ⅲ	试航的天气状况	367
		天气状况对试航的影响	367
		船厂决定试航的天气状况	367
		试航的延迟	368
	Ⅳ	试航的进行	370
		试航方式	370
		Performance 的含义	371
		参加试航的人员	371
		船厂的代表	371
		船东的代表	372
		船级社的代表	374
		厂商的代表	374
		试航成本及其分摊	374
		消耗品的处置	377
		船舶的临时登记	378
	Ⅴ	接受和拒绝	379
		船东是否接受船舶的表态	379
		船东权利的放弃	380
		船东接受船舶的意义	381
		船舶不符合合同要求	383
		船东拒绝接受船舶的权利	384
		客观原因	386
		Delivery Defects	387
		船东解除合同的权利	389
		争议的解决	391
		船东错误拒绝船舶	391
	Ⅵ	试航后的建造工作	392

第8章 交 船 393

I 交船概述 393
　　交付的意义及要求 393
　　"交船"和"船舶交接" 394
　　可交接状态 395

II 交船日期 397
　　合同交船日 397
　　交船日规定的性质 398
　　合同规定的解释 402
　　违约的构成 403
　　不确定的交船日 404
　　提前的交船 405
　　新的协议 406
　　交船地点 407

III 交船款的支付 409
　　交船款的特殊性 409
　　标准格式的规定 409
　　交船款支付的安排 412
　　交船款支付的争议 413

IV 船舶的交接 414
　　"接受"和"接船" 414
　　建造合同的规定 415
　　交接的程序和安排 417
　　交接备忘录 418

V 交船文件 419
　　测试报告 420
　　设备和备件清单 420
　　消耗品清单 420
　　证书 421
　　建造人证书 421
　　无负担保证 422
　　图纸 422

  商业发票 …………………………………………………… 422
  无登记证书 …………………………………………………… 422
  卖据 …………………………………………………………… 423
  IMO 有害物质清单 …………………………………………… 423
  其他文件 ……………………………………………………… 425
  授权委托书 …………………………………………………… 425
Ⅵ 所有权的转移 …………………………………………………… 425
  所有权的意义 ………………………………………………… 425
  拥有船舶所有权的惯例 ……………………………………… 427
    船厂抵押船舶 …………………………………………… 428
  所有权转移的时间 …………………………………………… 428
    船舶完成建造后转移 …………………………………… 428
    船东登记船舶的意义 …………………………………… 429
    在指定之前不转移 ……………………………………… 430
    随当事人意愿转移 ……………………………………… 431
    当事人意愿的确定 ……………………………………… 434
    逐步转移的约定 ………………………………………… 436
    "指定"的解释 …………………………………………… 438
  《货物买卖法》规定的适用 …………………………………… 440
  所有权的回转 ………………………………………………… 441
  建造合同的规定 ……………………………………………… 442
  所有权的保留 ………………………………………………… 443
  船厂的留置权 ………………………………………………… 444
  船舶抵押 ……………………………………………………… 445
  所有权转移的准据法 ………………………………………… 445
  中国法的规定 ………………………………………………… 447
Ⅶ 风险的转移 ……………………………………………………… 447
  普通法原则 …………………………………………………… 447
  建造合同的规定 ……………………………………………… 448
  违约与风险的转移 …………………………………………… 449
Ⅷ 提交船舶 ………………………………………………………… 450
  "提交船舶"的概念 …………………………………………… 450

　　　　船厂的责任 ……………………………………………………… 451
　Ⅸ　船舶离厂 …………………………………………………………… 452
　　　　建造合同的规定 …………………………………………………… 452
　　　　合理期限 …………………………………………………………… 454
　　　　船舶留在船厂的安排 ……………………………………………… 455
　　　　　　船东已支付交船款 ………………………………………… 455
　　　　　　船东未支付交船款 ………………………………………… 455

第9章　不可抗力 ……………………………………………………… 456
　Ⅰ　不可抗力概述 ……………………………………………………… 456
　　　　来源 ………………………………………………………………… 456
　　　　英国法 ……………………………………………………………… 457
　Ⅱ　不可抗力的特征 …………………………………………………… 459
　　　　实际发生 …………………………………………………………… 459
　　　　无法预见 …………………………………………………………… 459
　　　　无法避免或克服 …………………………………………………… 460
　　　　导致履行不可能 …………………………………………………… 461
　Ⅲ　不可抗力的后果 …………………………………………………… 461
　　　　合同的解除 ………………………………………………………… 461
　　　　自动解除 …………………………………………………………… 464
　　　　履行推迟 …………………………………………………………… 465
　Ⅳ　不可抗力条款 ……………………………………………………… 467
　　　　SAJ 格式 …………………………………………………………… 467
　　　　NEWBUILDCON 格式 …………………………………………… 468
　　　　AWES 格式 ………………………………………………………… 469
　　　　Norwegian 格式 …………………………………………………… 470
　　　　条款的解释 ………………………………………………………… 470
　　　　举证之责 …………………………………………………………… 472
　　　　免责的条件 ………………………………………………………… 473
　　　　　　没有疏忽或过失 …………………………………………… 474
　　　　　　已采取合理措施 …………………………………………… 475
　　　　　　损害确已发生 ……………………………………………… 476

V 不可抗力事件 …… 477
天灾 …… 477
地震等 …… 478
台风等 …… 478
水灾 …… 479
坏天气 …… 480
异常天气 …… 481
火灾和爆炸 …… 481
罢工和停工 …… 482
一般性质 …… 485
战争 …… 485
类似战争行动等 …… 487
革命、叛乱等 …… 489
君主或统治者行为 …… 492
政府征用、控制和要求 …… 493
瘟疫和流行病 …… 493
停电 …… 493
公共设施的中断 …… 494
运输迟延等 …… 494
船厂或船舶的毁坏 …… 495
碰撞和搁浅 …… 495
材料或设备短缺 …… 496
其他原因 …… 496

VI 不可抗力通知 …… 499
标准格式 …… 499
前提条件 …… 501
通知的解释 …… 505

VII 合同解除 …… 508
船东的合同解约权 …… 508
船东解约的后果 …… 510
船东作出选择的义务 …… 511

第10章 延误及延期 ... 513
Ⅰ 建造中的延误 ... 513
概述 ... 513
可允许延误的定义 ... 513
可允许延误的种类 ... 514
不可抗力事件 ... 515
审图延误 ... 515
监造代表的延误 ... 515
修改引起的延误 ... 516
船东供应品引起的延误 ... 516
建造款支付延误 ... 516
船东原因造成的延误 ... 517
完工和延误 ... 517
共同延误 ... 519
因果关系 ... 519
可以延期的原因 ... 520
违约方对违约负责 ... 521
整体索赔 ... 522
分摊 ... 524
Ⅱ 关键路径 ... 526
概述 ... 526
关键路径法的局限性 ... 527
关键路径在中国的应用 ... 529
影响关键路径的延误 ... 529
Ⅲ 阻碍原则 ... 530
概述 ... 530
延误责任的承担 ... 531
延误和约定赔偿 ... 532
合法行为和原因 ... 533
船舶建造合同和阻碍原则 ... 534
Ⅳ 延误通知 ... 535
概述 ... 535

标准格式的规定 ································· 535
　　　　SAJ 格式 ··································· 535
　　　　CSTC 格式 ·································· 536
　　　　NEWBUILDCON 格式 ························ 536
　　　　AWES 格式 ································· 537
　　　　Norwegian 格式 ······························ 537
　　　通知作为前提条件 ································· 538
　　　前提条件的成立 ··································· 539
　　　不利于制定人原则 ································· 541
　　　通知的内容 ······································· 542
　Ⅴ　交船的延期 ······································· 543
　　　概述 ··· 543
　　　延期条款的作用 ··································· 544
　　　标准格式的规定 ··································· 545
　　　　SAJ 格式 ··································· 545
　　　　Norwegian 格式 ······························ 546
　　　　NEWBUILDCON 格式 ························ 547
　　　对船舶建造的影响 ································· 547
　　　船厂的举证之责 ··································· 548
　Ⅵ　延误解约权 ······································· 549
　　　概述 ··· 549
　　　不可抗力解约权 ··································· 549
　　　解约的日期 ······································· 552
　　　作出选择的义务 ··································· 554
　　　解约权的丧失 ····································· 555

第 11 章　质量保证 ······································· 557
　Ⅰ　质保条款 ··· 557
　　　概述 ··· 557
　　　产品责任 ··· 558
　　　质量保证 ··· 558

Ⅱ 船舶交接的意义 ······ 559
船厂义务的终止 ······ 559
标准格式的规定 ······ 560
合理性要求 ······ 563
合同要求的符合 ······ 565

Ⅲ 质保范围 ······ 566
标准格式的规定 ······ 566
缺陷 ······ 567
缺陷导致的损坏 ······ 568

Ⅳ 质保期限 ······ 570
标准格式的规定 ······ 570
质保期限内的缺陷 ······ 571
期限的延长 ······ 572

Ⅴ 质保通知 ······ 574
标准格式的规定 ······ 574
质保义务的前提 ······ 575

Ⅵ 修理和替换 ······ 577
SAJ 格式 ······ 577
AWES 格式 ······ 578
Norwegian 格式 ······ 578
CSTC 格式 ······ 580
NEWBUILDCON 格式 ······ 581

Ⅶ 间接损失 ······ 583
特征 ······ 583
结果性损失 ······ 584
事实问题的认定 ······ 586
建造合同规定 ······ 587
第三人的修理或替换 ······ 589
其他原因 ······ 590
责任排除的效力 ······ 590
排除责任的无效 ······ 594

Ⅷ	质保的转让 ··	595
	转让的意义 ··	595
	非正常情况转让 ···	595
	转售中的转让 ···	597
Ⅸ	质保工程师 ··	597
	概述 ··	597
	船厂的权利 ··	597
	船厂的义务 ··	598
	费用 ··	599
	船东的过失责任 ···	600

第 12 章　船东的解约 ·· 603

Ⅰ	概述 ··	603
	"解约"的表述 ···	603
	解约方式 ···	605
	标准格式 ···	605
Ⅱ	根据合同约定解约 ··	606
	不符合保证事项 ···	606
	交船延迟 ···	607
	担保人破产 ··	608
	中止建造 ···	609
	未提供还款保函 ···	610
	破产或重组 ··	610
Ⅲ	根据法律规定解约 ··	612
	违反默示保证 ···	612
	船舶不适航 ··	612
	船厂毁约 ···	613
	实际履行 ···	615
Ⅳ	解约的后果 ··	617
	解约的不可逆转 ···	617
	建造款返还 ··	617
	利息 ··	618

其他费用返还 ··· 619
船东供应品返还 ··· 620
处置船舶的权利 ··· 621
船舶建造的继续 ··· 621
Ⅴ 责任的解除 ··· 623
按合同约定解约 ··· 623
按法律规定解约 ··· 626
Ⅵ 减损义务 ··· 627
法律义务 ·· 627
合同义务 ·· 628

第 13 章 船东的违约 ··· 630
Ⅰ 违约的构成 ··· 630
违约的定义 ·· 630
船东的支付义务 ··· 631
违约后果的约定 ··· 631
Ⅱ 利息和费用 ··· 633
违约利息 ·· 633
支付利息的约定 ··· 635
违约费用 ·· 637
Ⅲ 顺延和中止 ··· 638
概述 ·· 638
合同交船日顺延 ··· 639
中止建造的权利 ··· 640
中止建造和合同交船日顺延 ··· 641
Ⅳ 船厂的解约 ··· 642
支付的违约 ·· 642
违约通知和解约通知 ··· 643
船厂权利的排除 ··· 645
因破产而解约 ··· 646
Ⅴ 解约的结果 ··· 647
建造款的保留 ··· 647

	到期款的支付	647
	尚未到期的款项	649
	船东供应品的归属	651
	船舶的处置	651
	船厂的选择	652
	完成建造后出售	653
	未完成建造的出售	654
	出售船舶的义务	655
	余额的处置	658
	额外支付义务	659
	担保人的义务	660

第14章 保 险 …… 662
  Ⅰ 建造风险 …… 662
    概述 …… 662
    建造人保险 …… 663
    协会建造人保险条款 …… 663
    保险利益 …… 664
    合同义务 …… 664
  Ⅱ 保险单 …… 665
    保险标的物 …… 665
    保险价值 …… 666
    被保险人 …… 668
      被保险人的名称 …… 669
    保险期限 …… 672
      期限的开始 …… 672
      期限的结束 …… 673
      期限的延伸 …… 674
  Ⅲ 承保风险 …… 675
    一切险承保风险 …… 675
    延迟交船 …… 676
    潜在缺陷 …… 677

设计缺陷 …………………………………………………… 677
焊接缺陷 …………………………………………………… 679
船舶下水的费用 …………………………………………… 679
污染风险 …………………………………………………… 679
航行风险 …………………………………………………… 680
碰撞风险 …………………………………………………… 681
保赔保险风险 ……………………………………………… 682
共同海损和救助 …………………………………………… 684
承保风险的约定 …………………………………………… 685
Ⅳ 除外责任 ……………………………………………………… 686
法定除外责任 ……………………………………………… 686
固有缺陷和潜在缺陷 ………………………………… 687
约定除外责任 ……………………………………………… 688
地震和火山爆发 ……………………………………… 689
碰撞 …………………………………………………… 689
保赔保险 ……………………………………………… 690
战争 …………………………………………………… 691
罢工 …………………………………………………… 692
恶意行为 ……………………………………………… 692
核风险 ………………………………………………… 693
除外责任的承保安排 ……………………………………… 694
Ⅴ 船舶的损失 …………………………………………………… 695
部分损失 …………………………………………………… 695
全损 ………………………………………………………… 695
实际全损 ……………………………………………… 695
推定全损 ……………………………………………… 698
协议全损 ……………………………………………… 700
索赔通知 …………………………………………………… 700
Ⅵ 船厂的施救义务 ……………………………………………… 701
施救义务概述 ……………………………………………… 701
施救费用的承担 …………………………………………… 703
施救费用超过施救所得 …………………………………… 703

Ⅶ	保险赔偿的应用	704
	部分损失	704
	全损	705
	合同交船日的调整	709
Ⅷ	保险义务的终止	709

第15章　争议和仲裁 … 711

Ⅰ	仲裁概述	711
	解决争议的方式	711
	仲裁的优点	712
	英国1996年《仲裁法》	713
	仲裁协议	714
	争议和分歧	715
	开始仲裁的前提	717
Ⅱ	仲裁适用的法律	718
	概述	718
	合同准据法	720
	准据法的约定	720
	没有准据法约定	721
	仲裁协议准据法	722
	仲裁程序法	723
	仲裁本座	724
	仲裁程序法的约定	725
Ⅲ	仲裁的开始	727
	争议范围	727
	"关于合同的"	728
	机构仲裁和临时仲裁	728
	"一事不再理"原则	730
	电子邮件	732
	仲裁开始的时间	733
	开始仲裁的时限	733
	时限的延长	736

		仲裁开始的方式	736
		法院的参与	736
	Ⅳ	仲裁庭的组成	738
		仲裁员的指定	738
		仲裁庭组成的时间	739
		独任仲裁员	740
		小额仲裁	740
	Ⅴ	技术争议的解决	741
		概述	741
		专家裁定	743
	Ⅵ	调解	745
		概述	745
		建造合同争议的调解	746
	Ⅶ	仲裁裁决	747
		概述	747
		裁决通知	748
		仲裁费用	749
		合同交船日的改变	751
	Ⅷ	仲裁裁决的上诉	752
		上诉的权利	752
		法律问题	752
		允许上诉的理由	753
		明显的错误	754
		普遍公共重要性	754
		上诉的放弃	757

第 16 章 转让和变更 ········ 758

	Ⅰ	转让	758
		概述	758
		诉权的转让	759
		转让的限制	760
		船舶建造合同权利的转让	761

　　　　转让的区分 ································· 763
　　　　转让的通知 ································· 764
　　　　船东的履约责任 ···························· 766
　　　　转让的费用 ································· 766
　　　　索赔权的保留 ······························ 767
　　Ⅱ 针对受让人的抵销 ························· 768
　　　　概述 ··· 768
　　　　关联性 ······································ 769
　　　　船舶建造合同约定 ························· 769
　　Ⅲ 合同变更 ····································· 770
　　　　概述 ··· 770
　　　　合同变更的必要性 ························· 771
　　　　合同变更协议 ······························ 772
　　　　船厂的权利 ································· 772

第17章 税收和规费 ································· 773
　　Ⅰ 船厂所在国税收和规费 ··················· 773
　　　　概述 ··· 773
　　　　税收和规费的分担 ························· 773
　　　　出口退税 ···································· 775
　　Ⅱ 其他税收和规费 ···························· 775
　　　　船东的责任 ································· 775
　　　　关于税负的约定 ···························· 776

第18章 专利、商标和版权 ························ 778
　　Ⅰ 知识产权 ····································· 778
　　　　概述 ··· 778
　　　　专利 ··· 779
　　　　商标 ··· 780
　　　　商号 ··· 781
　　Ⅱ 船舶建造中的知识产权 ··················· 781
　　　　专利 ··· 781

　　　　船厂的合同义务 …………………………………………………… 781
　　　　责任范围及期限 …………………………………………………… 783
　　Ⅲ　知识产权的保护 …………………………………………………… 784
　　　　第三人的知识产权 ………………………………………………… 784
　　　　船厂的知识产权 …………………………………………………… 784
　　　　船舶的处置 ………………………………………………………… 785
　　　　NEWBUILDCON 格式 …………………………………………… 785

第 19 章　船东供应品 ………………………………………………………… 788
　　Ⅰ　原因 ………………………………………………………………… 788
　　Ⅱ　船东的责任 ………………………………………………………… 789
　　　　建造合同规定 ……………………………………………………… 789
　　　　船厂的拒绝 ………………………………………………………… 790
　　　　提供迟延 …………………………………………………………… 791
　　　　继续建造的权利 …………………………………………………… 792
　　　　责任抑或权利 ……………………………………………………… 793
　　Ⅲ　船厂的责任 ………………………………………………………… 794
　　　　保管和安装义务 …………………………………………………… 794
　　　　船东供应品的质量 ………………………………………………… 795
　　　　联合检验 …………………………………………………………… 795
　　　　船舶建造人险 ……………………………………………………… 795

第 20 章　通　知 ……………………………………………………………… 797
　　Ⅰ　概述 ………………………………………………………………… 797
　　Ⅱ　地址 ………………………………………………………………… 797
　　　　收件人 ……………………………………………………………… 797
　　　　形式要求 …………………………………………………………… 798
　　　　通知的生效 ………………………………………………………… 799
　　　　联合卖方的通知 …………………………………………………… 800
　　Ⅲ　语言 ………………………………………………………………… 801

第 21 章 合同的生效 ··· 802
 I 合同的条件 ··· 802
  概述 ··· 802
  条件的分类 ··· 803
 II 合同的生效 ··· 804
  SAJ 格式 ··· 804
  CSTC 格式 ··· 804
  NEWBUILDCON 格式 ····································· 806
 III 合同的失效 ··· 806
 IV 当事人的行为 ··· 806
  因自己过错主张利益 ······································· 806
  解释问题 ··· 810
  主观意志 ··· 811

第 22 章 解 释 ·· 813
 I 概述 ··· 813
  缔约的情形 ··· 813
  解释的原则 ··· 814
 II 文件间的关系 ··· 816
  概述 ··· 816
  建造合同特征 ··· 816
 III 整体协议 ··· 818
  概述 ··· 818
  缔约前的承诺 ··· 819
  误述 ··· 819

第 23 章 选择权 ·· 823
 I 选择权概述 ··· 823
  一般选择权 ··· 823
  标准格式中的选择权 ······································· 824
 II 船舶建造选择权 ·· 824
  要约的特征 ··· 824

		单方的选择	825
	Ⅲ	选择权的给予	826
		原因	826
		影响	826
	Ⅳ	选择权的行使	827

第 24 章		其他规定	829
	Ⅰ	设计和图纸费用	829
	Ⅱ	第三人权利	829
	Ⅲ	当事人住所地	830
	Ⅳ	责任限制	831

第 25 章		海工装备建造	832
	Ⅰ	概述	832
		海洋工程	832
		海工装备	833
		海工装备建造合同的特征	834
		合同价格	834
		设计	835
		采购	835
		保函	836
		付款期数及比例	836
		更改	837
		责任限制	838
		船东提供设备	838
		船东的解约权	839
		LOGIC 标准格式	839
	Ⅱ	中止建造与解约	841
		概述	841
		决定的效力	841
		中止建造	842
		解除合同	844

- Ⅲ 更改 ·· 846
  - 船东的权利 ··· 846
  - 船厂提出更改的程序 ··· 847
  - 加账和交付日期的顺延 ·· 848
  - 无法达成一致的情形 ··· 850
  - 更改费用的支付 ·· 850
- Ⅳ 相互赔偿条款 ··· 851
  - 概述 ·· 851
  - 身份与过错 ··· 851
  - 约定范围的措辞 ·· 852
  - 偏袒与任意 ··· 854
  - 明确的约定 ··· 855
  - 整体的解释 ··· 857
  - 重大疏忽和故意不当行为 ·· 859
  - 不公平合同条款 ·· 861
  - LOGIC 格式 ··· 861
  - 保赔保险 ·· 862
- Ⅴ 健康、安全与环境条款 ·· 863
  - 概述 ·· 863
  - ISO 14001 ·· 863
  - ISO 45001 ·· 864
  - 中国的健康、安全与环境 ·· 865
  - 法定责任和合同责任 ··· 865
  - LOGIC 格式 ··· 866
- Ⅵ 反腐败条款 ·· 868
  - 概述 ·· 868
  - 国际商会规则 ··· 868
  - 经合组织公约 ··· 869
  - 联合国公约 ··· 870
  - 腐败行为 ·· 871
  - LOGIC 格式 ··· 873
  - 船厂的地位 ··· 875

案例	876
英国成文法	896
其他法律	899
国际公约及文件	900
标准格式	901
参考文献	908
索引	911

第1章 绪 论

Ⅰ 合同概述

合同的定义

除了少数成文法外,英国合同法实际上就是普通法,然而普通法似乎并没有一个统一的合同的定义。我们可以将各种关于合同的定义大致分为相互间有着相当明显区别的两大类。第一类定义强调合同是由一个或数个允诺(promise)组成的,即合同是允诺。例如,*Anson's Law of Contract* 便对合同进行了如下定义:①

> A contract consists of an actionable promise or promises. Every such promise involves at least two parties, a promisor and a promisee, and an outward expression of common intention and of expectation as to the declaration or assurance contained in the promise.

1.1

英国法权威百科全书 *Halsbury's Laws of England* 也将合同解释为是一个或数个允诺:②

1.2

> Whilst it is probably impossible to give one absolute and universally correct definition of a contract, the most commonly accepted definition is "a promise or set of promises which the law will enforce". The expression "contract" may, however, be used to describe any or all of the following: (1)that series of promises or acts themselves constituting the contract; (2)the document or documents constituting or evidencing that series of promises or acts, or their performance; (3)the legal relations resulting from that series.

---

① J. Beatson et al, *Anson's Law of Contract*, 30th edn Oxford University Press 2016, p.31.
② *Halsbury's Laws of England*, 5th edn Contract Volume 22(2019)para.1.

1.3　美国法的合同定义同样将合同视为允诺，例如 Restatement Second of Law of Contracts 将合同定义为：①

> A contract is a promise or set of promises for the breach of which the law gives a remedy or the performance of which the law in some way recognises as a duty.

1.4　合同的第二类定义则是强调当事人之间的协议（agreement），即合同是协议。例如在 The Law of Contract 一书中，合同的定义是：②

> A contract is an agreement giving rise to obligations which are enforced or recognised by law. The factor which distinguishes contractual from other legal obligations is that they are based on the agreement of the contracting parties. This proposition remains generally true, even though it is subject to a number of important qualifications.

1.5　A Restatement of the English Law of Contract 也把合同视为有法律约束力的协议：③

> A contract is an agreement that is legally binding because-
> (a) it is supported by consideration or made by deed;
> (b) it is certain and complete;
> (c) it is made with the intention to create legal relations; and
> (d) it complies with any formal requirement needed for the agreement to be legally binding.

1.6　法律辞典也都将合同视为协议，例如在 Jowitt's Dictionary of English Law 中，合同被描述为：④

> ...an agreement to do or to abstain from doing some act which is intended to give rise to legal relations.

1.7　Oxford Dictionary of Law 的定义更为简洁，把合同称之为有约束力的协议：⑤

> [Contract is] a legally binding agreement.

---

① s.1 of the American Law Institute's *Restatement Second of the Law of Contracts*.
② G H Treitel, *The Law of Contract*, 11th edn Sweet & Maxwell 2003, p.1.
③ Andrew Burrows et al, *A Restatement of the English Law of Contract*, Oxford University Press 2016, p.5.
④ Daniel Greenberg, *Jowitt's Dictionary of English Law*, 3rd edn Sweet & Maxwell 2010, p.534.
⑤ Elizabeth A Martin, *Oxford Dictionary of Law*, 5th edn Oxford University Press 2002, p.114.

传统的合同定义是把合同视为协议,而把合同视为允诺的则应当是19世纪 1.8
以后出现的情形。而且这种情形似乎并不是普通法自身发展的结果。① 我们可
以清楚地看到,强调合同是允诺明显与普通法中的对价要求相矛盾。即使允诺是
有约束力的,但实际上法律并不执行所有允诺,而只是执行得到对价支持的允诺。
没有对价支持的允诺(gratuitous promise)通常无法得到法律的执行。

合同定义的问题

1834 年出版的第 2 版 *Chitty on Contracts* 采用的是第二类定义,即将合同视 1.9
为协议,然而 1989 年出版的第 26 版 *Chitty on Contracts* 则开始采用了第一类定
义,即合同是允诺。从第 27 版起,*Chitty on Contracts* 编者放弃了在这两种定义中
作出选择的方式,而是列出合同的两种不同的定义并给予评论。自 2008 年出版
的第 30 版起,*Chitty on Contracts* 介绍了两种合同定义后指出,两种定义都存在各
自的问题,将合同视为允诺的定义的问题是:②

> However, analysis of contracts in terms of an enforceable promise or sets of enforceable promises is not entirely satisfactory. First, outside the context of consideration, in general neither courts nor parties to contracts describe the relationships which they create in terms of promises, but rather in terms of agreements, and for the courts this is clearest in the context of the rules as to offer and acceptance which when satisfied form that agreement. Moreover, as will be described later, the doctrine of consideration to which the "promise theory" is so closely related, it somewhat under siege: from the legislature, since the enactment of the Contracts(Rights of Third Parties)Act 1999 has limited its traditional domain, and from the courts, notably in the decision in *Williams* v *Roffey Bros & Nicholls(Contractors)Ltd*.③ Secondly, definition of contracts in terms of sets of promises does not give full force to the interrelationship of the obligations of the parties which exists in many contracts, an interrelationship which can be seen particularly in the availability of the remedy of terminate his own obligations by reason of the failure of the other party to perform his side of the bargain.

---

① Hugh Beale, *Chitty on Contracts*, 31st edn Sweet & Maxwell 2012, para.1-17.
② Hugh Beale, *Chitty on Contracts*, 33rd edn Sweet & Maxwell 2019, para.1-20, see also 35th edn 2023, para.1-051.
③ [1991] 1 QB 1.

1.10　　*Chitty on Contracts* 认为将合同视为协议存在如下问题:①

> However, an understanding of modern contracts as agreements does not fit easily with two recognised types of contract. First, in the case of a unilateral contract where A promises to do something if B does something else, the performance by B of the condition is enough for A to be bound. Here, analysis in terms of doing something of value in return for a promise fits more naturally than does the construction of an acceptance by B's performance of the condition of A's promise. Secondly, promises contained in deeds are enforceable by the person in whose favour they are made, whether or not that person is aware of them and so while a deed may give contractual force to an agreement, agreement is unnecessary for the enforcement of the promises which it contains.

Ⅱ　船舶建造合同的性质

1.11　　船舶建造合同一般是指由船厂按照约定的技术规范和要求在约定的时间内完成船舶的建造、配备、测试和交接,而由船东按照约定的数额和方式分期支付建造款并接船的合同。虽然船舶建造合同在不同的法律体系里具有不同的法律性质,但通常可以将船舶建造合同笼统地归纳为两种,即具有买卖合同性质的合同和具有承揽合同性质的合同。

英国法

1.12　　传统上,船舶建造合同在英国法中被视为货物买卖合同的一种。在 20 世纪初的 *Reid v Macbeth & Gray* 一案中,②船舶建造合同规定:

> The vessel as she is constructed, and all her engines, boilers, and machinery, and all materials from time to time intended for her or them, whether in the building-yard, workshop, river, or elsewhere, shall immediately as the same proceeds become the property of the purchasers, and shall not be within the ownership, control, or disposition of the builders, but the builders shall at all times have a lien thereon for their unpaid purchase-money.

---

① Hugh Beale, *Chitty on Contracts,* 33rd edn Sweet & Maxwell 2019, para.1 – 20, see also 35th edn 2023, para.1 – 052.
② [1904] AC 223.

船舶建造合同还规定,船厂在建造中有违约行为或在交付时有违约行为的, 1.13
船东有权占有船舶及其主机、锅炉、机器以及所有将用于该船舶的材料,并有权和
其他船厂订立合同完成船舶的建造。船东有权使用船厂的场地、车间、机器以及
工具等,因此产生的费用从尚未支付的购船款中扣除。船厂在船舶建造全部完成
之前破产了,在破产当日船厂订购的钢板和铁板还在火车站。那些钢板和铁板在
供应商处就已经通过了劳氏船级社的检验,钢板和铁板上也已标注了船号以及在
船上的使用位置。

苏格兰最高民事法院认为船东对材料以及其他产品享有权利。但是上议院 1.14
则推翻了该判决,上议院认为买方无权获得材料,理由是双方订立的合同是船舶
买卖合同,而不是材料的买卖合同。上议院的 Lord Davey 说:①

> There is only one contract—a contract for the purchase of the ship. There is no contract for the sale or purchase of these materials separating; and unless you can find a contract for the sale of these chattels within the meaning of the Sale of Goods Act, it appears to me that the sections of that Act have no application whatever to the case.

五十多年后,高院的 Diplock 法官在 *McDougall* v *Aeromarine of Emsworth Ltd* 1.15
一案中也指出:②

> I say "a contract for the sale of goods" because it seems well settled by authority that, although a shipbuilding contract is, in form, a contract for the construction of the vessel, it is in law a contract for the sale of goods.

到了 20 世纪 80 年代,法院开始意识到船舶建造合同和一般货物买卖合同的 1.16
差异,并开始注意到船舶建造合同与建设合同的相似性,例如上议院的 Dilhorne
法官在 *Hyundai Heavy Industries Co Ltd* v *Papadopoulos and Others* 一案中便对船
舶建造合同的买卖性质提出了质疑,他说:③

> [Shipbuilding contract] was not just for the sale of a ship. As I have said it was a contract to "build, launch, equip and complete" a vessel and "to deliver and sell" her. The contract price included "all costs and expenses for designing and supplying all necessary drawings for the

---

① [1904] AC 223 at 232.
② [1958] 2 Lloyd's Rep 345 at 355.
③ [1980] 2 Lloyd's Rep 1 at 5.

Vessel ..." It was a contract which was not simply one of sale but which so far as the construction of the vessel was concerned, resembled a building contract.

1.17   到了 20 世纪 90 年代，法院开始强调船舶建造合同与一般建设合同之间的差异。在 *Stocznia Gdanska SA v Latvian Shipping Co* 一案中，上议院的 Lord Goff 指出了建造物所有权的归属在两个不同合同中的差异，即在船舶建造合同中是船厂拥有在建船舶的所有权，他说：①

The situation was therefore different from that under an ordinary building contract, where the building as it is erected belongs to the building owner as the owner of the land on which it is being built.

1.18   Lord Goff 还进一步分析了船舶建造合同的性质，他认为船舶建造合同并不是一个简单的出售船舶的合同，他是这样说的：②

... the anterior question has to be asked: is the contract in question simply a contract for the sale of a ship? Or is it rather a contract under which the design and construction of the vessel formed part of the yard's contractual duties, as well as the duty to transfer the finished object to the buyers? ... I am satisfied that the present case falls into the latter category. This was what the contracts provided in their terms.

1.19   将船舶建造合同视为货物买卖合同是英国法的一个比较特殊的特征，但实际上船舶建造合同因其建造周期长、技术复杂、风险较大等特点与一般的货物买卖合同相去甚远。Simon Curtis 在 *The Law of Shipbuilding Contracts* 一书中说：③

However, a significant proportion of the content of most shipbuilding contracts is directed towards the regulation of a substantial and complex construction project, in which each party assumes long-term obligations to the other and bears significant commercial risks. Although the ultimate purpose of such a contract is to transfer legal title to a good (i.e. a ship) in return for payment of an agreed price, the nature and extent of the commitments assumed by both parties in order to achieve this objective are more akin to those of a non-marine construction project than to a mere agreement of sale and purchase.

---

① [1998] 1 WLR 574 at 587.
② [1998] 1 WLR 574 at 588.
③ Simon Curtis et al, *The Law of Shipbuilding Contracts*, 5th edn informa 2020, p.2.

在司法实践中，英国法院在审理船舶建造合同争议时不仅适用货物买卖的判例，同时也适用大量建设合同的判例。 1.20

船舶建造合同在中国法的地位

我国法律把合同分为"有名合同"和"无名合同"。① 有名合同并不包括船舶建造合同，在有名合同中与船舶建造合同有某些类似特征的则有买卖合同、承揽合同和建设工程合同。买卖合同是指出卖人转移标的物的所有权于买受人，买受人支付价款的合同；②承揽合同是承揽人按照定作人的要求完成工作，交付工作成果，定作人给付报酬的合同。承揽合同包括加工、定作、修理、复制、测试、检验等工作。③ 而建设工程合同是指承包人进行工程建设，发包人支付价款的合同。建设工程合同包括工程勘察、设计、施工合同。④ 1.21

在我国，"船舶建造合同"或"造船合同"不仅不是有法律明确规定其性质和特征的有名合同，甚至也不是可以在法律词典或法律大百科全书里找到定义或解释的词语。将合同进行分类应当是大陆法系国家的一个主要特征，我国学术界也曾对船舶建造合同的法律性质进行过讨论。从这些讨论来看，对船舶建造合同的性质似乎存在着几种不同的观点。 1.22

第一种观点认为船舶建造合同具有承揽合同的性质：⑤ 1.23

> 在我国，一般的观点认为船舶建造合同是承揽合同。船舶建造合同是建造合同的一种，而所谓建造合同是承揽人按定作人的要求进行建造，交付建造成果，由定作人给付报酬的合同，明显属于承揽合同的范畴，适用有关承揽合同的法律规定。

第二种观点认为船舶建造合同具有建设工程合同的性质：⑥ 1.24

> 笔者认为，应将造船合同界定为建设工程合同，理由如下：
>
> 第一，英美法系将造船合同界定为买卖合同，是适合于该法系缺少成文法、体系较灵活、注重个案解决的特点的；大陆法系将造船合同界定为建设工程合同，是适合于该法系依赖成文法、体系较严谨、注重法典的

---

① 《中华人民共和国民法典》将有名合同称为"典型合同"。
② 《中华人民共和国民法典》第五百九十五条。
③ 《中华人民共和国民法典》第七百七十条。
④ 《中华人民共和国民法典》第七百八十八条。
⑤ 周平.论建造中船舶的物权问题[J].海商法研究,2000(1):30.
⑥ 罗国强.造船合同法律规制与中国《海商法》的修改[J].学术论坛,2008(2):89.

抽象性和逻辑性的特点的……我国的法律体系与大陆法系较为接近,在我国,成文法是唯一的立法形式,注重逻辑性、抽象性和严谨性的法典为法官提供明确的指引,法官没有造法权而只能严格依据法律判案,因而造船合同在我国应被界定为某一种具体类型的合同。

第二,如果要把造船合同划入某一具体类型的合同的话,那么它应该被划归建设工程合同一类。建设工程合同是由承包人进行工程设计、施工等建设,发包人支付报酬的合同,该类合同的标的物一般都是不动产和大型设备。笔者认为造船合同符合建设工程合同的特征:首先,合同标的是船舶这样造价一般在几百万美元以上的大型设备;其次,船厂对合同义务的履行并不仅限于交付船舶,还包括设计和建造船舶,也就是说,船东通过造船合同所购得的,不仅有作为最终产品的实物船舶,还包括船厂在设计建造船舶中所付出的劳动以及对有关知识产权的运用;最后,船东为了监督合同的适当履行,通常会派代理人到造船现场进行监理,这也是建设工程合同所独有的。

综上,把造船合同界定为建设工程合同,既符合成文法系国家的普遍作法,又适合我国法律体系现状。在这一建设工程合同中,船厂是承包人,船东是发包人。

1.25　第三种观点则认为船舶建造合同是买卖合同的一种:①

从以上的论述来看,将造船合同看成买卖合同已基本成为共识,但在建船舶的所有权安排却是不尽相同。

1.26　还有一种观点则认为不能简单地将船舶建造合同进行单一性归类,而应当根据当事人的意思表示作出判断。无法根据当事人意思进行判断的,则应将船舶建造合同定性为买卖和承揽的混合合同:②

鉴于实践中船舶建造合同在价款支付、材料提供、船舶所有权及风险转移等各方面表现出的复杂性与多样性,笔者认为,船舶建造合同的法律属性具有非单一性、无法简单地加以类型化的特征。应首先以当事人的意思表示为判断标准,确定船舶建造合同的属性。在缺乏明示的意思表示的情况下,可借助材料的提供、船舶的设计、船舶建造过程的监督

---

① 张敏,刘征宇.买卖性造船合同下的所有权安排[J].中国海商法年刊,2006(1):330.
② 单红军,于诗卉.非单一性:船舶建造合同法律属性之特征[J].中国海商法年刊,2010(12):85.

检查等因素,推定出当事人的意思表示,确定合同的目的以及主要特征。如果仍无法推定出当事人的意思表示,能否从实用主义角度出发,将船舶建造合同定性为买卖合同?笔者认为,如果仍无法推定出当事人的意思表示,则合同的属性为买卖和承揽的混合合同。此时,可借鉴《日本民法》第559条中的但书规定,针对具体争议的类型确定其法律属性。如果该争议的属性不同于买卖,则不能一概准用买卖合同的规定,也不能将合同直接定性为买卖合同。

承揽合同(contract for work),亦称加工承揽合同,通常是指承揽方承担标的物意外灭失或工作条件意外恶化造成损失的风险,完成定作人所交付的工作,并将该项工作成果交付定作人,定作人在验收工作成果后给付约定报酬的合同。承揽合同包括加工、定作、修理、复制、测试以及检验等工作。① 将船舶建造合同视为承揽合同并适用关于承揽的法律恐怕是不妥当的,因为两者实际上存在着本质上的区别。首先,标的物的所有权归属不同。在船舶建造合同中在建船舶的所有权通常归船厂所有,船舶所有权只有在船舶交付时才会随船舶转移至船东。然而在承揽合同中,承揽人拥有工作成果似乎并不符合承揽合同的特征。相反,承揽人对工作成果享有留置权恰恰证明了承揽人对工作成果并不享有所有权,因为对自己拥有所有权的东西实施留置权应当是没有意义的。② 其次,支付报酬的方式不同。在船舶建造实践中,船东通常按照船舶建造合同的规定采用分期的方式向船厂支付建造款,只有最后一期在接船时支付。然而在承揽合同中,虽然工作报酬也可以约定分期支付,但通常是由定作人在承揽人完成了工作后才支付工作报酬的。最后,解除合同的权利不同。法律允许定作人在承揽合同开始履行后随时解除承揽合同,③定作人解除承揽合同所应承担的责任是赔偿承揽人因此遭受的损失。然而在船舶建造合同中船东并没有随时解除合同的权利,船东错误解约将构成违约,应当承担违约损害赔偿责任,而且其赔偿责任并不局限于船厂的损失。在绝大多数情况下,船厂有权继续完成船舶建造并可向船东索取合同价款的全部以及其他损失和费用。

1.27

建设工程合同(building contract),亦称基本建设合同,通常是指承包人按期

1.28

---

① 中国大百科全书.法学[M].北京:中国大百科全书出版社,2006:34.
② 《中华人民共和国民法典》第七百八十三条规定,定作人未向承揽人支付报酬或者材料费等价款的,承揽人对完成的工作成果享有留置权。
③ 《中华人民共和国民法典》第七百八十七条规定,定作人可以随时解除承揽合同,造成承揽人损失的,应当赔偿损失。

完成并交付发包人所委托的基本建设工作,而发包人按期进行验收和支付工程价款或报酬的合同。建设工程合同属于承揽合同的特殊类型,法律对建设工程合同没有特别规定的,适用法律对承揽合同的相关规定。① 建设工程合同包括工程勘察、设计以及施工合同。② 虽然船舶建造确有类似于建设工程之处,但将船舶建造合同视为建设工程合同并适用关于建设工程合同的法律同样是不妥当的。首先,由于建设工程合同实际上是承揽合同之一种,上述关于船舶建造合同与承揽合同的区别同样也适用于船舶建造合同与建设工程合同的区别,因此船舶建造合同同样不应被视为建设工程合同。其次,合同内容不同。从建设工程所包括的工程勘察、设计以及施工来看,建设工程合同涉及的是基本建设,即建筑和其他基础设施项目,而船舶建造显然不是基建项目。最后,验收标准不同。建设工程必须符合国家颁发的施工验收规范和质量检验标准,③而在船舶建造合同中,虽然船舶建造会涉及国家的相关标准,但在船东接受船舶时通常不涉及国家规范和标准,而是合同的规定。而且在船舶建造合同中,所谓的验收并不是在船舶建造完毕后的一次性行为,而是分散于船舶建造整个过程的行为。

1.29　　买卖合同(contract of sale)是当事人一方(出卖人)应将其出卖的财产交付他方(买受人)所有,买受人应接受此项财产并支付约定价款的合同。④ 船舶建造合同与货物买卖合同的相似之处是船厂即出卖人在交船之前拥有船舶所有权,但是两者依然存在明显的差异,因此将船舶建造合同视为货物买卖合同同样是不合适的。

确定船舶建造合同性质的意义

1.30　　在大陆法国家里,有名合同是指法律明确规定其特征和内容并赋予一定名称的合同;无名合同则是指法律没有规定其特征、内容以及名称,由当事人自由创设的合同。由于法律规定了有名合同的特征和内容,因此将一个无名合同认定为某一有名合同就可以解决该合同的性质以及法律适用的问题,这应当是在大陆法国家里确定船舶建造合同的意义。英国合同法主要是普通法,法律没有对合同进行

---

① 《中华人民共和国民法典》第八百零八条规定。
② 中国大百科全书.法学[M].北京:中国大百科全书出版社,2006:166;《中华人民共和国民法典》第七百八十八条。
③ 《中国大百科全书》总编辑委员会.《中华人民共和国民法典》第七百九十九条规定,建设工程竣工后应根据国家颁发的施工验收规范和质量检验标准进行验收。
④ 中国大百科全书.法学[M].北京:中国大百科全书出版社,2006:341;《中华人民共和国民法典》第五百九十五条。

类似于大陆法中的有名合同和无名合同的区分。然而,可以肯定有名合同是无法包含社会生活中所有交易关系特征的,无名合同在数量上和种类上大大超过有名合同。将合同分为有名合同和无名合同实际上已经说明了这一点。大量无名合同的存在表明在社会生活中交易关系的复杂性以及当事人合意内容的复杂性。而且,契约自由原则允许当事人在不违反社会基本道德原则和强制性法律规定的前提下自由决定合同的类型和内容。将一个无名合同认定为一特定有名合同从某种意义上说可能违反了契约自由原则,因为当事人事实上是在有名合同存在的情况下自主创设无名合同的。当事人的真实意图可能是不订立法律有明文规定的有名合同。根据一个无名合同的某一特征而将其认定为一特定的有名合同的做法难免会违背当事人的真实意图,而且这种做法无疑会导致无谓的争议,因为根据某些特征或条文,一个无名合同可以被认定为两个甚至两个以上的有名合同。而将一个无名合同认定为具有两种或两种以上有名合同特征的做法实际上已经不再强调法律将合同分为有名和无名两种的意义了。

就船舶建造合同而言,船厂按照规格书和船东的要求建造船舶这一特征或许符合承揽合同的基本性质,而船东按照约定支付建造款并最终接船似乎又是买卖合同性质的体现。但是,无论是把船舶建造合同认定为承揽合同还是买卖合同,其结果同样是在没有解决任何问题的情况下制造了新的问题,例如在将船舶建造合同认定为承揽合同的情况下,遇到的问题是船东是否可以随时解除船舶建造合同,以及在建船舶的所有权归属问题。如果将船舶建造合同认定为买卖合同,我们会发现作为买方的船东实际上参与了船舶建造的整个过程。 1.31

Ⅲ 英国法的适用

当今世界,在各国签署的船舶建造合同绝大多数均约定英国法为合同准据法,并且还规定将双方关于合同解释、效力、履行等的争议提交伦敦仲裁解决。这种情况即使在船东和船厂均不是英国公司或与英国有关的公司的情况下依然比比皆是。英国法在船舶建造领域得到最为普遍的适用已是不争之事实,究其原因可以简单归纳为历史、法律和语言三个方面。实际上这三个方面的原因并非各自独立,而是相互影响、相互关联的。 1.32

历史的原因

1.33　1588年英国击败西班牙无敌舰队后,开始了对北美洲的殖民。1600年起英国通过东印度公司开始了在印度的扩张。从17世纪初到18世纪中叶,英国和法国进行了四次战争,英国凭借强大的海军力量,在海外夺取了法国在印度、加拿大和密西西比河以东的大片领土,一跃成为殖民大国。以1763年英国与法国和西班牙签订《巴黎条约》为标志,英国取代西班牙,成为世界头号殖民强国。随着英国殖民活动的推进,英国法开始逐渐渗入英国的殖民地,成为当地的法律或对当地法律产生了不同程度的影响。第一次世界大战以后,随着英国势力逐渐遭到削弱,英国各殖民地的人民纷纷要求独立。1931年英国国会通过《威斯敏斯特法令》(Statute of Westminster 1931),创设了"英联邦"。英联邦成员国包括:澳大利亚、巴哈马、孟加拉国、加拿大、印度、新西兰、巴基斯坦等。英国始终保持着对英联邦成员国的影响。在英联邦成员国家施行的法律都是普通法或以普通法为基础的法律,英语也是英联邦的官方语言。

法律的原因

1.34　英国是普通法国家,其法律的基本特征是采用判例形式,人们可以通过各种法律报告查阅英国法的具体内容。从判例中可以比较直观地了解英国法的原则及其具体的要求。而且,英国法院的判例得到了相当完整的保留,更由于英语的作用,英国法的判例顺利地流传到英国境外,为外国人所了解。相反,人们尤其是外国人对大陆法国家法律的了解往往停留在对法律条文的认识,不如对英国法的理解来得更加直观。因此,适用英国法相对而言比适用其他国家的法律更具有可预见性。此外,英国拥有一大批相当优秀的法律人才,既包括法官,也包括出庭律师。这就为英国法的适用提供了保障。实际上,在英国进行商业诉讼或仲裁的当事人中已鲜有英国的当事人。法律服务已经成为英国为整个世界提供的具有相当强竞争力的服务。

语言的原因

1.35　英语虽然不是使用人最多的语言,但毫无疑问是世界上使用地域最为广泛的语言。尤其是在国际商业交往中英语更是成为了国际商业的"官方语言"。就船舶建造而言,无论是在日本还是在韩国,乃至中国,船舶建造合同鲜有例外地均采用英语订立。在我国船舶建造实践中,即使双方均为国内企业的船舶建造合同依然会采用英语订立并适用英国法。在船舶建造合同采用英语订立的情况下,适用英国法并通过伦敦仲裁解决争议似乎也就顺理成章了。

Ⅳ 英国 1979 年《货物买卖法》

《货物买卖法》简介

当船舶建造合同约定英国法为准据法时,除了普通法外,成文法同样也适用,其中值得一提的是 1979 年《货物买卖法》(Sale of Goods Act 1979)。1979 年《货物买卖法》于 1980 年 1 月 1 日起生效,它汇集了关于货物买卖的法律,适用于整个英国。1979 年《货物买卖法》取代了 1893 年《货物买卖法》以及部分其他成文法。1979 年《货物买卖法》是具有溯及力的法律,适用于 1894 年 1 月 1 日后订立的所有货物买卖合同,即 1893 年《货物买卖法》开始生效之时。① 1979 年《货物买卖法》自颁布以来已经有了三次修订,分别是 1994 年《货物买卖(修订)法》(Sale of Goods(Amendment) Act 1994);1994 年《货物买卖和供应法》(Sale and Supply of Goods Act 1994);以及 1995 年《货物买卖(修订)法》(Sale of Goods(Amendment) Act 1995)。② 1.36

1979 年《货物买卖法》适用于所有种类的货物买卖合同,包括商业买卖(commercial sales)和私人间的买卖(private sales);商人间的买卖(merchants' sales)和零售买卖(retail sales);新货物买卖(sales of new goods)和二手货买卖(sales of second-hand goods)。③ 1979 年《货物买卖法》规定:④ 1.37

> The rules of the common law, including the law merchant, except in so far as they are inconsistent with the provisions of this Act, and in particular the rules relating to the law of principal and agent and the effect of fraud, misrepresentation, duress or coercion, mistake, or other invalidating cause, apply to contracts for the sale of goods.

1979 年《货物买卖法》汇集的仅仅是关于货物买卖的法律,因此关于合同以及动产的一般法律,包括商人法,只要不与 1979 年《货物买卖法》的规定有冲突的 1.38

---

① s.1(1).
② Michael Bridge, *Benjamin's Sale of Goods*, 12th edn Sweet & Maxwell 2024, para.1-005.
③ Michael Bridge, *Benjamin's Sale of Goods*, 12th edn Sweet & Maxwell 2024, para.1-006.
④ s.62(2).

同样也适用于货物买卖合同。① 此外,1979 年《货物买卖法》还规定了其他特定普通法规则适用的情形,例如关于合同当事人买卖货物的行为能力;②因履行不能的免责;③以及买方或卖方在没有对价情况下可以获得利息、特殊损害以及金钱赔偿的权利。④

成文法的适用和排除

1.39　根据契约自由的原则,只要不违反 1977 年《不公平合同条款法》(Unfair Contract Terms Act 1977)的规定,合同当事人可以排除法律规定的适用。为此,1979 年《货物买卖法》作出了如下规定:⑤

> Where a right, duty or liability would arise under a contract of sale of goods by implication of law, it may (subject to the Unfair Contract Terms Act 1977) be negatived or varied by express agreement, or by the course of dealing between the parties, or by such usage as binds both parties to the contract.

1.40　1977 年《不公平合同条款法》对 1979 年《货物买卖法》第 15(1)条的适用进行了限制,在某种程度上甚至否定了当事人排除或改变 1979 年《货物买卖法》规定的货物买卖合同默示条款的权利。例如按照 1977 年《不公平合同条款法》第 6(1)条的规定,当事人不能通过合同排除或限制 1979 年《货物买卖法》第 12 条关于货物买卖合同默示条款规定的适用。除此之外,1979 年《货物买卖法》的不少规定也无法通过当事人的合同约定予以排除或限制,例如第 16 条关于未确定货物之所有权在确定之前不发生转移的规定,又如第 5(3)条关于出售未来货物的是出售协议的规定,这些都不能通过当事人的协议予以改变。⑥

买卖合同的定义

1.41　1979 年《货物买卖法》给货物买卖合同下了如下定义:⑦

---

① Michael Bridge, *Benjamin's Sale of Goods*, 12th edn Sweet & Maxwell 2024, para.1-007.
② s.3.
③ s.7.
④ s.54.
⑤ s.55(1).
⑥ Michael Bridge, *Benjamin's Sale of Goods*, 12th edn Sweet & Maxwell 2024, para.1-015.
⑦ s.2(1).

A contract of sale of goods is a contract by which the seller transfers or agrees to transfer the property in goods to the buyer for a money consideration, called the price.

从上述定义可以看出,买卖合同是卖方向买方转让或同意转让货物所有权,以换取价款对价的合同。英国法将货物买卖区分为"出售"(sale)和"出售协议"(agreement to sell)。买卖合同既包括出售协议,也包括出售。① 买卖合同可以是出售协议,也可以是出售,但不能两者兼之。

出售协议

作为买卖合同之一的"出售协议",其特征是货物所有权在合同订立之后,或者在某些条件成就之时才发生转移的买卖合同。② 出售协议只是一份协议而已,无法给买方创设任何以所有或占有为依据的权利,而只能对违约主张索赔。在通常情况下,出售协议的标的物由卖方占有,除非卖方的行为构成对出售协议的违反,买方不能予以干涉。

出售

1979年《货物买卖法》并没有给"出售"下一个直截了当的定义,但是第2(4)条规定:

Where under a contract of sale the property in the goods is transferred from the seller to the buyer the contract is called a sale.

第2(6)条又规定:

An agreement to sell becomes a sale when the time elapses or the conditions are fulfilled subject to which the property in the goods is to be transferred.

从上述两条规定来看,出售至少应当包括两种情形:其一,出售应当是指货物所有权在合同订立时即从卖方转移至买方的买卖合同;其二,出售应当是出售协议规定的所有权发生转移的期限届满或条件成就时的买卖合同。

---

① s.61(1).
② s.2(5).

区分出售协议和出售的意义

1.47　英国法区分"出售"和"出售协议"的意义在于前者不仅是一个合同,而且还是一份权利转移证书;而后者只是一个合同而已。Benjamin's Sale of Goods 对此作出相当明确的解释:①

> When a party to an agreement to sell defaults, the remedy of the other party is normally an action for damages; on the other hand, where there is a sale, the seller may sue for the price, and the buyer may assert the remedies of an owner for wrongful interference with the goods not only against the seller, but in appropriate circumstances also against third party.

1.48　由此可见,在出售中的卖方一旦违约,买方不仅可以就货物本身获得所有权上的救济,同时也可以作为合同权利向卖方主张违约损害赔偿。此外,在出售协议中,卖方通常要承担交付前货物毁坏或变质的风险。而在出售中,承担这一风险的就应当是买方了。

1.49　在船舶建造合同中,由于在合同订立之时作为合同标的物的船舶并不存在,从而不会产生船舶所有权转移的结果。因此,船舶建造合同应当不是"出售",而是一个"出售协议"。

特定货物和未确定货物

1.50　1979 年《货物买卖法》将货物区分为特定货物(specific goods)和未确定货物(unascertained goods),这是 1979 年《货物买卖法》对货物的另一个重要的分类。

特定货物

1.51　按照 1979 年《货物买卖法》第 61(1)条的规定,特定货物是指:

> ... goods identified and agreed on at the time a contract of sale is made and includes an undivided share, specified as a fraction or percentage, of goods identified and agreed on as aforesaid.

1.52　所谓特定货物是指在订立买卖合同时就已特定的,即已被识别的和约定的货物。特定货物是买卖合同当事人指定的用以履行合同的独一无二的货物,买卖合

---

① Michael Bridge, *Benjamin's Sale of Goods*, 12th edn Sweet & Maxwell 2024, para.1 – 028.

同当事人可以通过文字描述指定用于履行合同的货物。在买卖合同订立以后再被识别和约定的则不构成1979年《货物买卖法》意义上的特定货物。

有时,货物在订立买卖合同时尚不存在,但是这并不影响该未来货物依然是特定货物。在这个问题上,船舶建造合同中的船舶应当是一个明显的例子。在船东和船厂订立船舶建造合同之时船舶并不存在,但作为合同标的物,船舶依然是特定的。在 Reardon Smith Line Ltd v Yngvar Hansen-Tangen[①] 一案中,法院认为对船舶的描述,即"Yard No. 354"和"Built by Osaka Shipbuilding Co Ltd"已经使船舶成为特定货物。

1.53

未确定货物

1979年《货物买卖法》并没有为未确定货物下定义,但是有一点则是明确的,即未确定货物不是特定货物。未确定货物是指在买卖合同订立时尚未被识别和约定的货物。未确定货物有三种主要类型:第一种是种类物或者是某一特定形态或种类的货物,例如100吨大麦,或福特Fiesta汽车;第二种是尚不存在的,但卖方将要制造或生产的或者将要以其他方式获取的货物;第三种则是特定货物中尚未识别部分的货物,例如在卖方的仓库中储存的1,000吨或数量不确定的货物中的100吨货物。

1.54

与未确定货物相对应的是确定货物。1979年《货物买卖法》在第16条中提到了货物必须确定,在第17(1)条和第52(1)条中又分别提到了"specific or ascertained goods",但是1979年《货物买卖法》并没有为确定货物下定义。在 In Re Wait 一案中,上诉法院的 Atkin 法官则认为:[②]

1.55

> "Ascertained" probably means identified in accordance with the agreement after the time a contract of sale is made, and I shall assume that to be the meaning.

区分特定货物和未确定货物的意义

区分特定货物和未确定货物的意义同样在于货物所有权的转移。按照1979年《货物买卖法》的规定,特定货物的所有权在买卖合同订立之时自卖方转移至

1.56

---

① [1976] 1 WLR 989.
② [1927] 1 Ch 606 at 630.

买方,①但是买卖合同中未确定货物的所有权只有在货物确定后才发生转移。②按照1979年《货物买卖法》第52条的规定,法院可以命令当事人实际履行买卖合同,让卖方向买方交付特定的或确定的货物,但是法院不能根据1979年《货物买卖法》或衡平法命令当事人实际履行买卖未确定货物的合同。③

现有货物和未来货物

1.57　1979年《货物买卖法》还将货物区分为现有货物和未来货物,第5(1)条规定:

> The goods which form the subject of a contract of sale may be either existing goods, owned or possessed by the seller, or goods to be manufactured or acquired by him after the making of the contract of sale, in this Act called future goods.

1.58　作为货物买卖合同标的物的货物既可以是现有货物,也可以是未来货物。

现有货物

1.59　现有货物是指卖方在订立买卖合同时就已经拥有或占有的货物,即使货物实际上确实存在,但只要卖方并不拥有或占有,就1979年《货物买卖法》而言,该货物并非现有货物,而是未来货物。

未来货物

1.60　未来货物是指卖方在买卖合同订立后生产或获得的货物。④ 未来货物可能是已经实际存在的货物,由于该货物尚未被卖方拥有或占有,因此就1979年《货物买卖法》而言属于未来货物。未来货物可以分为五大类:第一类是卖方将要制造的,无论是采用已经存在的还是尚未存在的材料;第二类是将要成为或可能成为卖方财产的货物,无论是通过买卖还是其他方式;第三类是可以期待会作为卖方财产而存在的货物,例如来自奶牛的牛奶;第四类是附属于或组成土地的,但未来将要与土地分离的物质,例如将会产生的矿物或将要砍伐的木材等;第五类则是卖方在未来将要种植的农作物。

---

① s.18, r.1.
② s.16.
③ *In Re Wait* [1927] 1 Ch 606 at 630.
④ s.5(1).

区分现有货物和未来货物的意义

1.61 货物关于现有和未来以及确定和未确定的分类对货物所有权的转移具有重要的意义,货物的不同分类和货物所有权发生转移的时间存在密切的关系。未确定货物的所有权在货物确定之前不转移至买方;①而出售特定货物或已确定货物的,货物所有权按照当事人的意图发生转移。②

1.62 以此为标准,由于船舶在船舶建造合同订立时尚未开始建造,因此船舶建造合同就应当是买卖未来货物的合同。

绝对的买卖和有条件的买卖

1.63 按照1979年《货物买卖法》第2(3)条的规定,买卖合同可以是绝对的,也可以是有条件的。在货物买卖合同的标的物为未来货物时,买卖合同是绝对的还是有条件的将会导致不同的结果。作为卖方,他可以和买方订立绝对的买卖合同,出售自己尚未拥有或占有的未来货物。在这种情况下,卖方在无法交付货物时就应当承担履行不能的后果。若卖方虽已占有货物但无法转移所有权则构成对1979年《货物买卖法》关于有权出售货物的默示保证的违反。③

1.64 相反,如果买卖合同是有条件的,即卖方交付货物以取得货物或货物确实存在为条件的,在卖方因未取得货物或货物确实不存在而无法交付货物时,买方并没有索赔的权利。1979年《货物买卖法》第5(2)条针对此种情形作出了如下规定:

> There may be a contract for the sale of goods the acquisition of which by the seller depends on a contingency which may or may not happen.

凭描述进行的买卖

1.65 按照1979年《货物买卖法》第13(1)条的规定,双方可以根据对货物的描述进行货物的买卖。

---

① s.16.
② s.17.
③ s.12(1).

凭描述买卖的种类

1.66　凭描述的买卖通常可以分为两种,第一种是某一种类或类别的未确定货物或未来货物的买卖,或者是买卖合同的描述适用的其他货物;第二种则是买方全部或至少部分依赖卖方的描述而决定购买的特定货物的买卖。所有未确定货物的买卖都属于凭描述买卖,大多数未来货物的买卖也属于凭描述买卖。在订立买卖合同时买方看见且要求的,由第三人拥有的但卖方将要获得的特定物的买卖则通常不是凭描述买卖。然而,买方在订立买卖合同时尚未看见货物而仅依赖卖方对货物描述的买卖依然属于凭描述买卖。① 在实践中,不通过对货物进行描述而进行的货物买卖相对而言并不多见。

关于货物描述的性质

1.67　在通过对货物进行描述而进行的买卖中需要解决的问题是哪些内容或词语构成了对货物的描述。并非所有词语都构成对货物的描述。对货物的描述很有可能仅构成合同前导致双方缔约的陈述,而不是买卖合同的条款。关于货物描述的陈述一旦被引入合同,需要解决的问题是,合同中关于货物描述的内容是一项保证,还是一项条件。如果只是一项保证,作出此项保证的一方若违反该保证的,对方只能主张损害赔偿;如果合同中关于货物的描述构成合同条件条款,一旦违反,对方不仅可以主张损害赔偿,而且还可以解除合同。

1.68　如何识别买卖合同中关于货物描述的性质应当是合同解释的问题,在这个问题上,上议院的 Lord Diplock 在 *Ashington Piggeries Ltd* v *Christopher Hill Ltd* 一案中发表了他自己的观点,他说:②

> The "description" by which unascertained goods are sold is, in my view, confined to those words in the contract which were intended by the parties to identify the kind of goods which were to be supplied. It is open to the parties to use a description as broad or narrow as they choose. But ultimately the test is whether the buyer could fairly and reasonably refuse to accept the physical goods proffered to him on the ground that their failure to correspond with that part of what was said about them in the contract makes them goods of a different kind from those he had agreed to buy. The key to sect.13 is identification.

---

① Michael Bridge, *Benjamin's Sale of Goods*, 12th edn Sweet & Maxwell 2024, para.11－007 & 11－008.
② [1971] 1 Lloyd's Rep 245 at 277.

关于船舶的描述

1.69 法院曾认为关于船舶载重吨的陈述只是一项保证,而不是条件。在 *T & J Harrison and Others v Knowles & Foster* ①一案中,被告向原告出售两艘船并向原告提供了该两艘船的具体描述,包括每艘船载重吨为 460 吨。原告同意购买该两艘船。被告关于船舶细节的陈述还写明:"not accountable for errors in description"。双方于 1915 年 12 月 9 日签署了一份合同备忘录,但备忘录并没有关于船舶描述的内容。原告在接船后发现两艘船的载重吨只有 360 吨,于是原告对被告提起诉讼,主张被告违反了买卖合同的条件或保证。高院的 Bailhache 法官认为,关于船舶载重吨的陈述是善意作出的,被告的陈述与船舶的实际状况只是程度的区别,而不是种类的区别。被告的陈述构成合同的一部分,但被告的陈述只是一项保证而不是条件。高院最终判决被告无需承担责任。

1.70 原告提起了上诉,但是上诉法院驳回了原告的上诉。上诉法院认为关于船舶载重吨的陈述并不构成合同的条款。上诉法院的 Scrutton 法官说:②

> I agree with the result arrived at by Bailhache J, but I arrive at that result by a different road. A statement may form part of a contract which the party making it promises to be true, or it may be an innocent representation of fact which he does not promise to be true, but which, if it was it was untrue in a material particular, and formed part of the inducement to enter into the contract, may give rise to a claim to rescind, but does not give rise to a claim for damages. It is a question of intention whether a representation amounts to a warranty. In my opinion the particulars formed no part of the contract between the parties.

1.71 然而在 *Couchman v Hill* ③一案中,我们似乎可以看到法院对 *T & J Harrison and Others v Knowles & Foster* 一案的判决作出了纠正。在该案中通过拍卖买卖的是一头小母牛,出售小母牛的被告将其描述为"尚未交配过"。拍卖的条件中注明了对所有拍卖物品描述的错误、瑕疵和缺点均不负责。在交易时原告要求被告和拍卖人确认小母牛尚未交配过并且得到了没有交配过的确认。事后原告发现小母牛怀有小牛犊,而且因为过早怀有小牛犊而死亡。原告起诉要求被告赔偿

---

① [1918] 1 KB 608.
② [1918] 1 KB 608 at 610.
③ [1947] KB 554.

因违反保证而产生的损失,但郡法院却认为关于没有交配过的确认由于拍卖条件中的免责规定而不再有价值。郡法院判决被告胜诉。

1.72　　原告提起了上诉,上诉法院认为被告和拍卖人对原告的确认构成了一个保证的要约,该保证要约的效力强于拍卖条件的规定。原告的竞买小母牛的行为已经构成对该要约的接受,而且关于小母牛的描述构成条件,一旦被违反,原告有权视其为保证并可以获得损害赔偿。上诉法院的 Scott 法官指出:①

> There was a good deal of discussion as to whether the description "unserved" constituted a warranty or a condition. I have, in what I have said so far, deliberately refrained from expressing a view thereon, but as a matter of law, I think every item in a description which constitutes a substantial ingredient in the "identity" of the thing sold is a condition, although every such condition can be waived by the purchaser, who thereupon becomes entitled to treat it as a warranty and recover damages. I think there was here an unqualified oral condition, the breach of which the plaintiff was entitled to treat as a breach of warranty and recover the damages claimed.

1.73　　在 *Reardon Smith Line Ltd* v *Yngvar Hansen-Tangen* 一案中,上议院引用了 *Couchman* v *Hill* 一案中 Scott 法官的判决,上议院的 Lord Wilberforce 认为描述是否构成对标的物"特征"的描述是认定描述是否构成条件的因素,他是这样说的:②

> I find to be excessively technical and due for fresh examination in this House. Even if a strict and technical view must be taken as regards the description of unascertained future goods(eg commodities) as to which each detail of the description must be assumed to be vital, it may be, and in my opinion is, right to treat other contracts of sale of goods in a similar manner to other contracts generally so as to ask whether a particular item in a description constitutes a substantial ingredient of the "identity" of the thing sold, and only if it does to treat it as a condition (see *Couchman* v *Hill* [1947] KB 554, 559, per Scott LJ).

1.74　　至此,上议院确立了货物买卖合同中关于标的物描述内容的性质,即关于标的物的描述并非始终是保证。如果关于标的物的描述构成识别标的物实质性要

---

① [1947] KB 554 at 559.
② [1976] 1 WLR 989 at 998.

素,关于标的物的描述就构成合同的条件条款。

买方对货物描述的依赖

凭描述进行的买卖是指买方依赖卖方对货物的描述而与卖方订立的货物买卖合同。在 *Harlingdon and Leinster Enterprises Ltd* v *Christopher Hull Fine Art Ltd*① 一案中,买卖双方都是伦敦的美术品商人,买卖标的物是一幅画。卖方声称该画的作者是 Gabriele Münter。买方的雇员查看了画,卖方则表示对画知之甚少,更不知道 Gabriele Münter 是何人。买方后来发现该幅画是赝品,于是起诉要求卖方返还价款,理由是画的买卖构成 1979 年《货物买卖法》第 13(1) 条规定的凭描述买卖,而卖方违反了 1979 年《货物买卖法》第 14(2) 条默示的条款,即画是具有可销售质量的。

1.75

高院认为买方并没有依赖该画系出自 Gabriele Münter 之手的描述,因此画的买卖并不是凭描述的买卖,而且法院认为买方并未证明该画不具有可销售质量,最终法院判决买方败诉。买方于是提起上诉,但遭到上诉法院的驳回。上诉法院认为关于画系出于 Gabriele Münter 之手的描述对画的买卖并没有太大的影响,双方并没有将此作为合同的条款,因此买卖并不是凭描述买卖。卖方也没有违反货物应当具有可销售质量的默示条款。上诉法院的 Nourse 法官说:②

1.76

> In theory it is no doubt possible for a description of goods which is not relied on by the buyer to become an essential term of a contract for their sale. But in practice it is very difficult, and perhaps impossible, to think of facts where that would be so. The description must have a sufficient influence in the sale to become an essential term of the contract and the correlative of influence is reliance. Indeed, reliance by the buyer is the natural index of a sale by description .... For all practical purposes, I would say that there cannot be a contract for the sale of goods by description where it is not within the reasonable contemplation of the parties that the buyer is relying on the description.

在该幅画是否具有可销售质量的问题上,Nourse 法官则指出:③

1.77

It is true that the painting was defective in that it was not the work of the

---

① [1991] 1 QB 564.
② [1991] 1 QB 564 at 574.
③ [1991] 1 QB 564 at 576.

> artist by whom it appeared to have been painted.... But it was not one which made it unsaleable. The evidence was that it could have been resold for £50 to £100. Admittedly that would have been a very long way below the £6,000 which the plaintiffs paid for it. But the question whether goods are reasonably fit for resale cannot depend on whether they can or cannot be resold without making a loss. Nor did the defect make the painting unfit for aesthetic appreciation. It could still have been hung on a wall somewhere and been enjoyed for what it was, albeit not for what it might have been.

1.78 但是上诉法院的 Stuart-Smith 法官则持不同意见,他认为画家的名字构成了对画的描述,他还引用了 *Couchman* v *Hill* 一案中 Scott 法官的判决以及在 *Leaf* v *International Galleries* 中 Denning 法官的判词,①Stuart-Smith 法官说:②

> Be that as it may, the nub of his conclusion is that Mr. Runkel did not rely on the description but on his own judgment as to the authorship of the painting. For my part I have great difficulty in understanding how the concept of reliance fits into a sale by description. If it is a term of the contract that the painting is by Münter, the purchaser does not have to prove that he entered into the contract in reliance on this statement. This distinguishes a contractual term or condition from a mere representation which induces a purchaser to enter into a contract. In the latter case the person to whom the representation is made must prove that he relied on it as a matter of fact.

船舶建造合同的特征

1.79 综上,我们可以看出,船舶建造合同是通过对船舶进行描述而对未来的和特定的货物进行买卖的绝对的出售协议。虽然船舶是特定物,但除非船东和船厂另有约定,船舶的所有权在船舶建造完毕交付时才由船厂转移至船东。

V 买卖合同的默示保证

1.80 1979 年《货物买卖法》规定了三项货物买卖合同的默示保证。下文对这三项默示保证做一简单的介绍。

---

① [1950] 2 KB 86 at 89.
② [1991] 1 QB 564 at 579.

所有权默示保证

1979 年《货物买卖法》第 12 条有如下规定: 1.81

(1) In a contract of sale, other than one to which subsection (3) below applies, there is an implied term on the part of the seller that in the case of a sale he has a right to sell the goods, and in the case of an agreement to sell he will have such a right at the time when the property is to pass.

(2) In a contract of sale, other than one to which subsection (3) below applies, there is also an implied term that—
   (a) the goods are free, and will remain free until the time when the property is to pass, from any charge or encumbrance not disclosed or known to the buyer before the contract is made, and
   (b) the buyer will enjoy quiet possession of the goods except so far as it may be disturbed by the owner or other person entitled to the benefit of any charge or encumbrance so disclosed or known.

(3) This subsection applies to a contract of sale in the case of which there appears from the contract or is to be inferred from its circumstances an intention that the seller should transfer only such title as he or a third person may have.

卖方的权利及享有权利的时间

作为货物买卖合同的卖方必须有权出售货物,但这一权利并非一定要在订立合同之时就存在。至于卖方应当何时有权出售货物则取决于货物买卖合同的性质。如果买卖合同是一个出售,卖方在订立货物买卖合同之时就应当有权出售货物;而如果买卖合同是一个出售协议的,卖方则应当在货物所有权发生转移之时有权出售货物。如果在货物所有权应当发生转移之时卖方无法转移的即构成对这一默示条款的违反。 1.82

1979 年《货物买卖法》第 12(1) 条规定属于合同的条件条款。卖方违反的,买方可以解除买卖合同并要求损害赔偿,也可以不继续履行合同并要求损害赔偿。[1] 同时,卖方有权出售货物是一个绝对的责任,即无论卖方是否知情或是否有过错,只要卖方无权出售货物的即构成对这一绝对责任的违反。 1.83

---

[1] Sale of Goods Act 1979, s.12(5A).

"不受干扰的占有"

1.84 　　按照 1979 年《货物买卖法》第 12(2) 条的规定,卖方出售的货物在所有权上必须是清洁的,没有任何负担或障碍;买方可以不受干扰地占有货物。"charge or encumbrance"应当是指具有财产性质的权利,上诉法院的 Robert Goff 法官在 *Athens Cape Naviera SA* v *Deutsche Dampfschiffahrtgesellschaft "Hansa" Aktiengesellschaft (The Barenbels)* 一案中对 encumbrances 进行了解释,他说:①

> The word "encumbrances" refers, we incline to think, to proprietary and possibly also possessory rights over the ship: the expression would, for example, certainly embrace a ship's mortgage, and possibly also a possessory lien.

1.85 　　就"不受干扰地占有"而言,作为买卖合同的卖方,不仅要保证自己对出售的货物享有完全的所有权,而且还要保证买方在货物所有权转移后可以不受干扰地占有货物,否则同样不符合第 12(2) 条的规定。上诉法院的 Scrutton 法官在 *Niblett Ltd* v *Confectioners' Materials Co Ltd* 一案中对这一问题给予非常明确的说明,他认为享有权利就是指可以不受影响地行使权利,否则就等于没有权利。他说:②

> The [sellers] impliedly warranted that they had then a right to sell them. In fact they could have been restrained by injunction from selling them, because they were infringing the rights of third person. If a vendor can be stopped by process of law from selling, he has not the right to sell.

1.86 　　根据 1977 年《不公平合同条款法》的规定,1979 年《货物买卖法》第 12(2) 条的规定构成买卖合同中的保证条款,一旦卖方违反这一条款,买方只能主张损害赔偿,而不能解除买卖合同。③ 同样根据 1977 年《不公平合同条款法》的规定,1979 年《货物买卖法》第 12(1) 条和第 12(2) 条规定的买卖合同默示条款是无法通过合同或当事人协议予以排除或限制的。④

---

① [1985] 1 Lloyd's Rep 528 at 532.
② [1921] 3 KB 387 at 398.
③ Sale of Goods Act 1979, s.12(5A).
④ Unfair Contract Terms Act 1977, s.6(1).

船舶建造合同

在船舶建造中，船厂在订立船舶建造合同之时对将要建造的船舶尚未享有任何权利，因为在那时船舶实际上并不存在。但是 1979 年《货物买卖法》规定的是卖方可以按照买卖合同的规定在约定的时候转移货物的所有权，因此船厂必须做到的是在交船时自己对船舶享有完整的权利。如果船厂在船舶建造合同规定的交船日依然无法转让船舶所有权的，船厂就应当承担相应的责任。船东可以视船厂的行为构成毁约，船东不仅可以要求船厂退还所有船东已经支付的建造款，还可以要求船厂赔偿其因此产生的损失和费用。

1.87

有时船厂为了为船舶建造融资而在在建船舶上设定了抵押，并且在船舶登记机关办理了所有权的临时登记和抵押权的登记。在这种情况下，船厂务必在交船之前注销船舶所有权的临时登记以及船舶抵押权的登记。船厂不仅要保证自己有权处置建造完毕的船舶，而且还要保证船东在接船后所享有的所有权不会因为船厂的原因而受到影响。此种影响的一个例子是：由于船厂没有支付专利费用导致专利所有人对使用其专利的船舶采取法律行动。正如上诉法院的 Atkin 法官在 *Niblett Ltd v Confectioners' Materials Co Ltd* 一案中所说的：①

1.88

> The right to pass the property is one thing ..., but the existence of a title superior to that of the vendor, so that the possession of the vendee may be disturbed, is another thing; and there was a title superior to that of the vendor, so that the possession of the vendee could be disturbed, unless title means no more than ability to pass the property, in which case it does not exhaust all the contingencies whereby the possession of the vendee can be disturbed. The owners of the patent had no right or ability to pass the property, but they had a right to disturb the possession of the defendant in that case.

货物符合描述默示保证

1979 年《货物买卖法》第 13(1) 规定，双方可以根据对货物的描述进行买卖。凭描述买卖货物的买卖合同有一默示条款，即卖方交付的货物必须符合买卖合同对货物的描述：

1.89

> Where there is a contract for the sale of goods by description, there is an

---

① [1921] 3 KB 387 at 402.

implied term that the goods will correspond with the description.

1.90 如果货物是通过样品和描述进行买卖的,卖方交付的货物不仅要符合样品,而且也应当符合描述:①

> If the sale is by sample as well as by description it is not sufficient that the bulk of the goods corresponds with the sample if the goods do not also correspond with the description.

1.91 上述默示条款构成买卖合同中的条件条款,因为1979年《货物买卖法》第13(1A)条有如下规定:

> As regards England and Wales and Northern Ireland, the term implied by subsection(1)is a condition.

默示条款

1.92 如果买卖合同中有关于货物的描述,卖方交付的货物应当符合买卖合同的描述似乎已不再是一项默示条款了。但把其视为默示条款是有意义的,因为默示条款构成合同的条件。上诉法院的 Greer 法官在 *Andrews Bros(Bournemouth)Ltd* v *Singer & Co Ltd* 一案中对此作出了解释:②

> It may be right to say that the descriptive terms of the contract, though they are express terms, are not expressly made conditions of the contract, and by using the expression "implied condition" in s.13, those responsible for the statute did not mean to say that the obligation to supply the thing described is not an express obligation; they merely meant to say that the description is not a mere term or a mere warranty but is a condition of the contract by implication of law.

不符合描述的情形

1.93 卖方实际交付的货物不符合买卖合同的描述可能有两种情况,第一种是不完全符合,例如卖方交付的货物虽然其本身符合买卖合同的描述,但其包装则不符合买卖合同的描述;第二种则是完全不符合,例如买卖合同买卖的是新车,但卖方交付的则是二手车。在第一种不符合的情况下,如果交付的货物应当符合合同描

---

① s.13(2).
② [1934] 1 KB 17 at 25.

述是买卖合同的条件条款的,不完全符合同样构成对 1979 年《货物买卖法》第 13 (1)条的违反,买方有权拒绝接受货物。在第二种不符合的情况下,由于是完全不符合,无疑构成了对第 13(1)条的违反,买方可以拒绝接受货物。1979 年《货物买卖法》第 13(1)条规定的默示条款不仅适用于未确定货物的买卖,同时也适用于特定货物的买卖。就后者而言,无论买方订立合同时是否看见过货物,买方均基于卖方对货物的描述而订立合同。一旦实际货物不符合描述,即使卖方能够证明实际货物具有令人满意的质量且符合买方订立合同的用途也无济于事。①

然而值得注意的是,除非另有约定,买方并不可以因存在任何与合同描述不符之处就可以拒绝接收货物。在 *Ashington Piggeries Ltd* v *Christopher Hill Ltd* ② 一案中,上议院的 Lord Diplock 说:③

1.94

> The "description" by which unascertained goods are sold is, in my view, confined to those words in the contract which were intended by the parties to identify the kind of goods which were to be supplied. It is open to the parties to use a description as broad or narrow as they choose. But ultimately the test is whether the buyer could fairly and reasonably refuse to accept the physical goods proffered to him on the ground that their failure to correspond with that part of what was said about them in the contract makes them goods of a different kind from those he had agreed to buy.

船舶建造合同对船舶的描述

在船舶建造合同中,船东和船厂是通过描述买卖船舶的。但是船舶建造合同的哪些内容构成对船舶的描述在不同的船舶建造合同中则可能有所不同。在 *Britain Steamship Co Ltd* v *Lithgows Ltd*④ 一案中,规格书中关于主机的描述是:

1.95

> Power: continuous service output 16,800 b.h.p.; r.p.m. continuous service output 110

船东在船舶试航后接受了船舶。在实际营运中,主机转速也确实达到了每分钟 110 转。但是由于船舶的主机接二连三发生问题,为了保证安全船舶只能将主

1.96

---

① Hugh Beale, *Chitty on Contracts*, 35rd edn Sweet & Maxwell 2023, para.47‑089.
② [1971] 1 Lloyd's Rep 245.
③ [1971] 1 Lloyd's Rep 245 at 277.
④ 1975 SC 110.

机转速保持在每分钟 100 转的状况下航行。主机是根据船东的要求订购的。船东主张船舶不符合合同的描述。针对这一主张,简易程序审判中的 Lord Maxwell 认为上述描述出现在规格书中,是主机技术数据的一部分。这些描述并不是建造完成后船舶或其性能的描述,而且船东并没有主张船舶不符合上述技术数据。Lord Maxwell 说:①

> The express contractual provisions as to the performance of the completed vessel, the manner in which that performance is to be demonstrated and tested and the remedies for failure are to be found, as I read the contract, in clause 12 of the agreement and possibly also in the reference in the rather obscure hull specification to the "vessel" being able to obtain $15\frac{1}{2}$ knots in certain conditions. In addition to these express provisions there may be implied conditions under section 14(2) of the 1893 Act or otherwise as to the reliability and durability of the vessel. But in my opinion conditions relating to these matters are not to be found in a list of technical data relating to the engine as such and not purporting to relate to the performance of the completed vessel.

货物质量默示保证

1.97　普通法中有一项关于货物买卖的基本原则,即"买者自负"(caveat emptor)原则,其基本含义是,除非买卖合同另有明确约定,卖方原则上无需保证关于货物的质量及其特定的用途。

买者自负原则

1.98　1979 年《货物买卖法》第 14(1)条以成文法的形式引入了普通法的这一基本原则:②

> Except as provided by this section and section 15 below and subject to any other enactment, there is no implied term about the quality or fitness for any particular purpose of goods supplied under a contract of sale.

1.99　但是 1979 年《货物买卖法》第 14(2)条又规定:

> Where the seller sells goods in the course of a business, there is an

---

① 1975 SC 110 at 118.
② 实际上这一规定在 1893 年《货物买卖法》中就有了,见第 14 条。

implied term that the goods supplied under the contract are of satisfactory quality.

显然,第 14(2)条的规定与第 14(1)条是不一致的;由于第 14(2)条的规定,第 14(1)条即普通法的"买者自负"这一基本原则实际上已经不复存在了。

"在业务经营中"

鉴于第 14(2)条对买卖作出了限定,即"在业务经营中"(in the course of a business)。因此只有在符合这一限定的情况下,关于卖方交付的货物应当具有令人满意质量的默示条款才适用,因此关于"in the course of a business"的解释也就变得相当重要。"in the course of a business"几乎包含了各种交易方式,它既可以是以营利为目的一次性买卖;也可以是构成经营业务之一部分的买卖;还可以是附属于所经营的业务但又有一定规律性的买卖。①

在 Stevenson v Rogers② 一案中,被告是一个有 20 年左右捕鱼经历的人,他将自己的渔船出售给了原告,打算再建一艘新船。高院认为被告实际上是在处置已不符合其要求的船舶,而不是作为卖方按照 1979 年《货物买卖法》第 14 条规定的"in the course of a business"出售船舶。并且原告也未能证明该船的出售构成作为渔民的经营中不可分割的一部分。高院认为被告的船舶出售是"经营已不再需要设备的零星出售",并不符合 1979 年《货物买卖法》第 14(2)条规定"在业务经营中"的规定。原告提起上诉,上诉法院接受了原告的上诉并推翻了一审的判决。上诉法院认为,在原告和被告之间的买卖合同中有一默示条款,船舶具有可销售质量。而且,对第 14(2)条应当作宽泛的解释,因此在卖方和买方之间的买卖确实构成被告经营的一部分。上诉法院的 Potter 法官说:③

> It seems to me clear that, free of any constraints imposed by the decisions to which we have been referred, this court, making use of the tools of construction now available to it, should construe the words of section 14(2) of the Act of 1979 at their wide face value…. Given the removal of that requirement, there is on the face of it no reason or warrant (at any rate in a civil rather than a criminal context) to reintroduce some implied qualification, difficult to define, in order to narrow what appears to be the wide scope and apparent purpose of the

---

① Per Potter J in *Stevenson v Roger* [1999] QB 1028 at 1033.
② [1999] QB 1028.
③ [1999] QB 1028 at 1039.

words, which is to distinguish between a sale made in the course of a seller's business and a purely private sale of goods outside the confines of the business(if any) carried on by the seller.

1.103　在买卖是否构成被告经营组成部分问题上，Potter 法官认为：①

I acknowledge that it seems a most curious result that the sale by a seller of the very asset without which he could not carry on his business, with the intention of purchasing a replacement for the purpose of continuing that business, should not be regarded as a sale made in the course of a business.

1.104　就船舶建造合同而言，作为卖方的船厂为作为买方的船东建造并交付船舶无疑是其经营的一部分，因此，除非船舶建造合同另有约定，卖方建造并交付的船舶应当具有令人满意的质量。有时贸易公司会参与船舶建造合同的订立。这时，船厂是建造人，贸易公司是卖方，船东是买方。然而在船厂和贸易公司之间往往还会签署一份代理协议，实际上贸易公司是作为船厂的代理人负责设备的采购和进口以及船舶的出口，有时贸易公司还会负责船舶建造所需的融资安排。这种安排应当适用的是 1979 年《货物买卖法》第 14(5) 条的规定，该条的内容是：

The preceding provisions of this section apply to a sale by a person who in the course of a business is acting as agent for another as they apply to a sale by a principal in the course of a business, except where that other is not selling in the course of a business and either the buyer knows that fact or reasonable steps are taken to bring it to the notice of the buyer before the contract is made.

1.105　因此，在上述情况下，无论船厂是以何种身份订立船舶建造合同，其行为都将构成"在业务经营中"。其所建造的船舶都应当具有令人满意的质量。

可销售质量

1.106　按照 1893 年《货物买卖法》的规定，当货物通过描述的方式出售时，货物应当具有"可销售质量"，第 14 条的内容如下：

Where goods are bought by description from a seller who deals in goods

---

①　[1999] QB 1028 at 1042.

of that description(whether he be the manufacturer or not), there is an implied condition that the goods shall be of merchantable quality; provided that if the buyer has examined the goods, there shall be no implied condition as regards defects which such examination ought to have revealed . . . .

在 *Rasbora Ltd* v *JCL Marine Ltd*①一案中,原告与被告船厂订立了一艘摩托艇的船舶建造合同,该合同的第 16 条规定:

1.107

It is agreed that the Company's liability for warranty of the craft is limited to the terms and conditions set out in the Warranty Certificate given to the Purchaser on acceptance of the Craft. Any implied condition or warranty is expressly excluded, and the Company shall not be liable for any loss, damage, expense or injury howsoever arising, except as accepted under the terms and conditions of the Warranty Certificate.

船东接船后不到两天,摩托艇由于电器部分的缺陷而着火并最终导致全损。高院的 Lawson 法官说:②

1.108

To a material and substantial extent that safety and the safeguarding against fire risk depends upon the electrical installations and circuits on [the boat] being properly designed and installed. In the respects which I have previously indicated there was a serious failure on the defendants' part in respect of the design and installation of the works of electrical engineering on [the boat] and, as I have found, it was this failure which led to the loss of the boat and jeopardising the lives of those aboard her . . . . I am entitled to take into account that the defects found led to the total loss of [the boat] at sea within about 27 hours of her delivery by the defendants. I have no doubt at all that [the boat] was not of merchantable quality . . . .

令人满意的质量

1994 年《货物买卖和供应法》对 1979 年《货物买卖法》的第 14 条作出了修改,增加了一些新的规定。③ 由于第 14(2)条规定卖方出售的货物必须具有"令

1.109

---

① [1977] 1 Lloyd's Rep 645.
② [1977] 1 Lloyd's Rep 645 at 650.
③ Sale and Supply of Goods Act 1994, s.1.

人满意的质量",取代了1893年《货物买卖法》中的"可销售质量"一词,新增加的第14(2A)条对令人满意的质量进行了解释。第14(2A)条的内容如下:

> For the purposes of this Act, goods are of satisfactory quality if they meet the standard that a reasonable person would regard as satisfactory, taking account of any description of the goods, the price(if relevant) and all the other relevant circumstances.

1.110　"令人满意"显然是很难定义的,因为非常主观。"合理人士"同样不好定义。"合理人士"应当是站在买方的立场,拥有相关知识的人士;而不应当是对交易及其背景并不熟悉的合理的第三人旁观者。Auld 法官在 *Bramhill* v *Edwards* 一案中对"合理人士"作出了解释,他说:①

> ... although the test is objective, the reasonable buyer must be attributed with knowledge of all relevant background facts.

1.111　而且,"令人满意"还应当有依据。在 *Cammell Laird & Co Ltd* v *Manganese Bronze and Brass Co Ltd* 一案中,②船厂需为船东建造两艘油轮,于是向螺旋桨供应商订造螺旋桨。螺旋桨的采购合同约定:

> ... to be to the entire satisfaction of the owners' representative and ourselves ....

1.112　船厂认为由于自己对螺旋桨不满意,因此有权拒绝接受螺旋桨供应商提供的螺旋桨。但是高院的 Roche 法官则拒绝接受船厂援引的先例,他说:③

> I think that those cases have no application to a case like the present, where there is an agreement to do something and to do that to the satisfaction of the buyer or of a certain named person. That, I think, is a contract to do the thing which is agreed to be done to the satisfaction of a certain person, and that person's satisfaction, probably if it is *bona fide,* and certainly if it is reasonable, is the test of whether the contract has been performed; but the person who has to be satisfied has no right to add another term to the contract and say: "I am not satisfied with this delivery, although it complies with the contract, because I am not satisfied about something else which is not in the contract."

---

① [2004] 2 Lloyd's Rep 653 at 660.
② (1932) 43 Ll L Rep 466.
③ (1932) 43 Ll L Rep 466 at 477.

Roche 法官的观点在上诉中得到了上诉法院的支持,上诉法院的 Scrutton 法官说:①

1.113

> In my opinion that decision is right. Admittedly a reasonable construction must be placed upon the stipulation in question. It would be absurd to suppose that the parties had intended that the respondents should be at liberty to reject the propeller, after it had been made in all respects according to their specification, because, for instance, its pitch ratio proved to be too low or because its diameter proved too large for the aperture which had been provided for it.

在 *McDougall* v *Aeromarine of Emsworth Ltd* ②一案中,船舶建造合同约定建造一艘赛艇,并规定赛艇的建造应符合买方的合理满意。船厂向船东交付船舶时,船舶实际上尚未建造完成,赛艇顶部拼接处不符合规定,而且不水密。有的木料出现了收缩和开裂,木板的固定也不够牢靠。船东拒绝接受赛艇。船厂对存在的问题进行修补后再一次交船,但是赛艇依然存在不少问题。法院最终判定赛艇的建造没有符合买方的合理满意,因此买方有权拒绝接受赛艇。但是 Diplock 法官又说:③

1.114

> ... it does not follow that because ... the buyer is reasonably dissatisfied with her, he is entitled to treat the defects then existing as a beach of condition, so as to enable him to treat the contract as repudiated .... The buyer is entitled to refuse to accept delivery of the vessel in its existing state, but, if the defect is one that can be remedied, and remedied within a time which will still permit the seller to deliver within the period of delivery permitted by the contract, the buyer is not ... entitled to treat the contract as repudiated by the seller ....

1994 年《货物买卖(修订)法》修改了 1979 年《货物买卖法》第 14(2)条,增加了新的内容。新增加的第 14(2B)条对"令人满意质量"作出了进一步的规定,这些新规定应当有助于理解"质量"一词:

1.115

> For the purposes of this Act, the quality of goods includes their state and condition and the following (among others) are in appropriate cases

---

① (1933) 45 Ll L Rep 89 at 110.
② [1958] 2 Lloyd's Rep 345.
③ [1958] 2 Lloyd's Rep 345 at 357.

aspects of the quality of goods-
- (a) fitness for all the purposes for which goods of the kind in question are commonly supplied,
- (b) appearance and finish,
- (c) freedom from minor defects,
- (d) safety, and
- (e) durability.

1.116　第14(2B)条中的"适合于通常提供的特定种类货物的所有目的"一句虽然规定了"所有目的",但这些目的应局限于货物出售的目的,而不应当包括该货物可能使用的所有目的。在 *Balmoral Group Ltd v Borealis(UK) Ltd* ①一案中,原告是旋转模塑油桶的制造商,向被告购买聚乙烯纤维聚合物。原告生产的油桶出现大量问题,一旦煤油或柴油装入油桶后就会造成永久性脆性破损,导致油桶无法使用。凡是承受压力较大的地方都会发生永久性脆性破损,主要原因是环境压力裂痕,与材料无关。原告起诉,要求被告赔偿损失,理由是被告提供的货物不具有令人满意的质量。但是法院驳回了原告起诉,理由是原告并没有能够证明被告提供的货物不具有令人满意的质量。被告提供的货物并无瑕疵或制造存在错误,可以适合一般的旋转模塑。问题是货物是否符合建造长期储存油类油桶的特定目的。原告已告知被告其购买聚乙烯纤维聚合物是为了通过转塑机制造绿色油桶。虽然原告可以合理地期待被告供应适合于制作绿色油桶的聚合物,但原告不能合理地期待被告提供符合其设计或具备转塑属性的聚合物。对此,高院的 Christopher Clarke 法官指出:②

> Section 14(2)of the Sale of Goods Act 1979 is primarily directed towards substandard goods. Although there is an overlap between sections 14(2) and(3)the function of 14(2)is to establish a general standard which the goods in question are required to reach, and not to ensure that they attain some higher standard of fitness for a particular purpose made known to the seller. In appropriate cases the question as to whether goods are of satisfactory quality may be determined by considering whether they are fit for all purposes for which goods of the kind in question are commonly supplied .... For a material that has a very wide range of possible uses, and which is to be used and transformed by a specialist manufacturer for his own particular purposes, that seems to

---

① [2006] 2 CLC 220.
② [2006] 2 CLC 220 at 264.

me somewhat too wide a test, particularly when polyethylene although commonly supplied for oil tanks is not, in respect of some grades, suitable for that purpose . . . .

In my judgment Balmoral have not established that borecene was of unsatisfactory quality. The material supplied was not defective or incorrectly manufactured. Borecene was suitable for rotomoulding generally. The question is whether it was suitable for the particular purpose of constructing above ground static tanks to be used for storing oil over long periods. That is something that falls within the reach of section 14(3).

"外观和外表"是针对买方是消费者的情形,例如新车身上的划痕,虽然此种划痕并不影响车的功能,却不符合外观质量的要求。此外,"无细小缺陷"应当与"外观和外表"有类似之处。所谓的"缺陷"应当与货物是否具有令人满意的质量无关,与货物是否适合其用途也无关。换言之,即使货物具有令人满意的质量且符合其用途,同样也可能由于不满足"无细小缺陷"的要求而不符合第14(2B)条的规定。这些规定应当不适用于船舶建造合同。在 Rogers v Parish(Scarborough) Ltd 一案中,原告花了14,000英镑从被告处买了一辆路虎汽车,但是作为新车卖出的路虎被发现有不少缺陷,包括发动机、齿轮箱、车身以及油封等。六个月后,缺陷依然存在,原告退还了汽车。在此后的诉讼中,原告认为被告违反了合同的明示条款,即汽车是新的且具有1979年《货物买卖法》第14条规定的可销售质量。一审法院认为被告对汽车的描述是恰当的,也没有任何导致汽车无法上路、无法使用或不适合路虎汽车正常目的的缺陷,汽车具有可销售质量并适合其目的。法院驳回了原告的起诉。

1.117

原告于是上诉,上诉法院接受了原告的上诉。上诉法院认为不能仅仅因为缺陷尚未毁损货物的工作状况就认定货物具有可销售质量。上诉法院的 Mustill 法官说:①

1.118

Starting with the purpose for which "goods of that kind" are commonly bought, one would include in respect of any passenger vehicle not merely the buyer's purpose of driving the car from one place to another but of doing so with the appropriate degree of comfort, ease of handling and reliability and, one might add, of pride in the vehicle's outward and interior appearance. What is the appropriate degree and what relative

---

① [1987] QB 933 at 944.

weight is to be attached to one characteristic of the car rather than another will depend on the market at which the car is aimed.

To identify the relevant expectation one must look at the factors listed in the subsection. The first is the description applied to the goods. In the present case the vehicle was sold as new. Deficiencies which might be acceptable in a secondhand vehicle were not to be expected in one purchased as new. Next, the description "Range Rover" would conjure up a particular set of expectations, not the same as those relating to an ordinary saloon car, as to the balance between performance, handling, comfort and resilience. The factor of price was also significant. At more than £14,000 this vehicle was, if not at the top end of the scale, well above the level of the ordinary family saloon. The buyer was entitled to value for his money.

With these factors in mind, can it be said that the Range Rover as delivered was as fit for the purpose as the buyer could reasonably expect? The point does not admit of elaborate discussion. I can only say that to my mind the defects in engine, gearbox and bodywork, the existence of which is no longer in dispute, clearly demand a negative answer.

1.119　　"安全"应当是一项毋庸置疑的要求,尽管严格意义上说安全可能并不是货物的质量指标。"耐用"作为一项货物的质量指标是指在交付时货物应当具有合理的使用寿命,否则货物就不能视为具有令人满意的质量。确定货物是否耐用则应当考虑买卖合同对货物的描述、价格等各种因素。就船舶建造合同而言,安全显然是船厂必须满足的要求,但船舶的安全性实际上是通过船舶的设计和建造符合船级社规范以及船旗国要求而实现的。在船舶的设计和建造符合船级社规范和船旗国要求的情况下,耐用,即船舶的使用寿命通常就不再是问题了。

应当考虑的因素

1.120　　第14(2A)条提到了两项应当考虑到因素,即"对货物的描述"以及"价格"(若有关的话)。买卖合同中对货物的描述无疑会对货物是否具有令人满意的质量产生影响,例如货物是作为废弃物出售的,合理人士就不应当期望该货物仍然具有良好的工作状况。而价格显然与货物的质量是有关系的,它可以成为货物质量的标识。在买卖合同约定二手货物价格的情况下,合理人士就不应当对不符合新货物质量标准的货物表示不满。但是这也可能有例外,买卖合同约定的价格可能远远高于市场价格,但这并不意味着合理人士可以就此对货物质量提出更高的要求。在 BS Brown and Son Ltd v Craiks Ltd 一案中,上议院的 Dilhorne 子爵便指出:①

> ... it is not enough just to show that there is a difference between the contract price and that which the goods would fetch if sold for a different use. The buyer might have agreed to pay too high a price. But if the contract price was so far above the price that the goods would have fetched if sold for another purpose as to indicate that goods for that other purpose were unsaleable at anything approaching the contract price then it might be held that the goods were not of merchantable quality.

除了对货物的描述和价格外,其他应当考虑的因素分别列明于第14(2C)条、第14(2D)条、第14(2E)条以及第14(2F)条。② 1.121

令人满意质量的例外

新增加的第14(2C)条规定的是卖方应当提供具有令人满意质量货物的几个例外情形: 1.122

> The term implied by subsection(2)above does not extend to any matter making the quality of goods unsatisfactory-
> (a) which is specifically drawn to the buyer's attention before the contract is made,
> (b) where the buyer examines the goods before the contract is made, which that examination ought to reveal, or
> (c) in the case of a contract for sale by sample, which would have been apparent on a reasonable examination of the sample.

第14(2C)条规定的例外情形共有三项,任何一项都构成卖方保证货物具有令人满意质量的例外。 1.123

"已告知买方的缺陷"与货物描述有关,即买卖合同对货物的描述应当受到"已告知买方的缺陷"的影响。一旦卖方已经将货物的缺陷告诉了买方且买方没有提出异议的,买方就不能就该缺陷向卖方主张权利。"已告知买方的缺陷"并不限于卖方已经告知了买方的情形,还包括买方从其他渠道获得此类信息的情形。当然,关于卖方是否已经将货物的缺陷告知了买方的问题,负有举证之责的 1.124

---

① [1970] 1 WLR 750 at 760.
② 但这些条文中列出的其他应当考虑的因素均与船舶建造合同无涉。

应当是卖方。

1.125　"订立合同前检查货物应当发现的"是1893年《货物买卖法》便有的,该法第14(2)条的规定如下:

> Where goods are bought by description from a seller who deals in goods of that description(whether he be the manufacturer or not), there is an implied condition that the goods shall be of merchantable quality; provided that if the buyer has examined the goods, there shall be no implied condition as regards defects which such examination ought to have revealed.

1.126　显而易见,两者的措辞有所不同,主要区别是:1893年《货物买卖法》的措辞只是提及检查,并没有规定检查的时间;1979年《货物买卖法》的措辞似乎是强调检查应当发生在买卖合同订立之前。"可以发现的缺陷"是指买方通过检查应当发现的缺陷,这就意味着即使由于各种原因买方在这种检查中没有发现货物质量缺陷的,卖方也无需承担货物质量缺陷的责任。同理,若主张这一例外情形的,卖方应当负有举证之责。

1.127　"合理检查样品可以发现的"无疑是适用于凭样品进行的买卖。这一例外情形与"订立合同前检查货物应当发现的"不同。前者是指实际发生的对货物进行的检查,而后者则并不一定要存在对样品的合理检查。只要合理的检查能够发现的缺陷就不是卖方应当为此负责的缺陷。

1.128　根据第14(6)条的规定,关于卖方出售的货物应当具有令人满意质量货物的默示保证在买卖合同中属于条件条款。第14(6)条的规定是:

> As regards England and Wales and Northern Ireland, the terms implied by subsections(2)and(3)above are conditions.

责任的排除及其效力

1.129　有时买卖合同会明确规定卖方的免责,但是此种免责条款未必始终有效。在 *Rasbora Ltd* v *JCL Marine Ltd* [①]一案中,被告和原告订立合同,由被告为原告建造一艘汽艇,编号410。船舶建造合同第15条规定:

> The Purchaser acknowledges that he has read the Terms of Business of the Company and undertakes to be bound by them.

---

① [1977] 1 Lloyd's Rep 645.

船舶建造合同第 16 条规定:

1.130

It is agreed that the Company's liability for warranty of the craft is limited to the terms and conditions set out in the Warranty Certificate given to the Purchaser on acceptance of the Craft. Any implied condition or warranty is expressly excluded, and the Company shall not be liable for any loss, damage, expense or injury howsoever arising, except as accepted under the terms and conditions of the Warranty Certificate.

质保证书规定,被告将替换或修理任何由他们造成的且他们认为因有问题的材料或工艺引起的缺陷。但是接船后才 27 个小时,船舶便着火并沉入河中,遭受全损。原告起诉,认为被告违反了 1893 年《货物买卖法》第 14(2)条规定的默示保证,汽艇是由于有缺陷的电气安装和电路而遭全损,因此它不具有可销售质量。被告则认为他们可以援引船舶建造合同第 16 条的规定。

1.131

高院也认为汽艇不具有可销售质量,高院的 Lawson 法官说:①

1.132

On these findings I have to answer the question whether the fire caused as I found supports the view that 410 was not of merchantable quality. I am entitled to take into account that the defects found led to the total loss of 410 at sea within about 27 hours of her delivery by the defendants. I have no doubt at all that 410 was not of merchantable quality having regard to the definition of the term provided by s.1(a) of the 1893 Sale of Goods Act as amended.

对于船舶建造合同第 16 条的规定,Lawson 法官认为:②

1.133

If, however, I am wrong on the last point, I would still find that JCL's exclusion clause was ineffective to oust the implied term of merchantability because I would have been satisfied having regard to the provisions of s.55(4) and (5) of the Sale of Goods Act and to the fact as found that it would not be fair or reasonable to allow the defendants to rely on the exclusion. Briefly put, the defendants were responsible for electrical engineering defects which caused the total loss of 410 within 27 hours of her being handed over, a situation in which, if the exclusion clause applied, the buyer would be left without any remedy at all.

---

① [1977] 1 Lloyd's Rep 645 at 650.
② [1977] 1 Lloyd's Rep 645 at 651.

货物适合用途的默示保证

1.134　按照1979年《货物买卖法》的规定,除了货物必须具有令人满意质量外,当卖方知道买方购买货物的用途时,卖方出售的货物还必须合理地适合该用途。货物应当合理地适合其用途这一默示条款同样也是买卖合同的条件条款。该法的规定是:①

> Where the seller sells goods in the course of a business and the buyer, expressly or by implication, makes known-
> (a) to the seller, or
> (b) where the purchase price or part of it is payable by instalments and the goods were previously sold by a credit-broker to the seller, to that credit-broker,
> any particular purpose for which the goods are being bought, there is an implied term that the goods supplied under the contract are reasonably fit for that purpose, whether or not that is a purpose for which such goods are commonly supplied, except where the circumstances show that the buyer does not rely, or that it is unreasonable for him to rely, on the skill or judgment of the seller or credit-broker.

1.135　"在业务经营中"及其含义在前文关于1979年《货物买卖法》第14(2)条的内容中已经进行了讨论。"明示或默示地使卖方知道"可以包括很多种方式,例如买卖合同规定、信函往来、声明、要求以及通知等。在 *Cammell Laird & Co Ltd v Manganese Bronze and Brass Co Ltd* ②一案中,船厂为船东建造两艘油轮,船号分别是972和973。船厂向螺旋桨供应商(即本案中的被告)订造了两个四叶螺旋桨。螺旋桨采购合同包括如下内容:

> ... to be to the entire satisfaction of the owners' representative and ourselves.

1.136　船厂向螺旋桨供应商提供了一些图纸以及他们要求的细节,但要求的细节并不完全。螺旋桨是按照经船级社批准的设计和图纸制造的。装在972轮上的螺旋桨在主机尚未达到全速时会发出很大的噪声,而主机达到全速时该螺旋桨的工作状况则令人相当满意。船级社拒绝为船舶入级,船东也拒绝接受船舶。第二个

---

① s.14(3).
② (1932) 43 Ll L Rep 466.

螺旋桨装上973轮后,在主机尚未达到全速时依然有噪声,但不足以使船东和船厂拒绝接受船舶。船厂又把安装在973轮上的螺旋桨拆下安装在972轮上,螺旋桨在主机所有转速运行中均没有噪声的问题。但是船厂没有将安装在972轮上的螺旋桨装在973轮上试过。两艘船的柴油机型号不同,螺旋桨供应商按照相同的设计和图纸制造了一个替代螺旋桨,但是噪声过大的问题依然存在。螺旋桨供应商于是根据相同的图纸又制造了第二个替代螺旋桨。第二个替代螺旋桨装上后,问题得到了解决。

船厂起诉要求螺旋桨供应商赔偿其所遭受的延误的损失以及因此产生的费用。船厂的理由是:(1)螺旋桨供应商没有满足螺旋桨应当令船厂满意这一条件;(2)1893年《货物买卖法》第14条规定的例外情形应当适用,即螺旋桨应当适合其特定用途,而且船厂已经使螺旋桨供应商知道螺旋桨的用途,并对其能力和判断力给予了信任。螺旋桨供应商则认为法律上并不存在螺旋桨应当令船厂满意这一默示保证,应当适用的是1893年《货物买卖法》第14条的一般规则,即在货物买卖合同中没有货物质量或适合任何特定用途的默示保证或条件。第14条规定的例外情形不适用。

1.137

在一审中,双方的证人给出了相互矛盾的证词,高院采纳了船厂证人的证词而拒绝了螺旋桨供应商证人的证词。最后高院判决船厂胜诉,高院的 Roche 法官认为船厂已经使螺旋桨供应商知道了螺旋桨的用途,即用于柴油主机。Roche 法官说:①

1.138

> I hold that there was in this case, as in that case, a making known to the seller by implication of the particular purpose for which the goods were required, that is to say, for use as a propeller on a steamship, and that making known of the purpose was done in such a manner, and in such a way, as to show that the buyer relied upon the skill and judgment of the seller, and that there consequently was this warranty.

Roche 法官认为螺旋桨并不适合船舶,螺旋桨供应商因而违反了1893年《货物买卖法》第14(1)条规定的货物应当适合其用途的默示保证:②

1.139

> ... As the matter stands, it is proved that this propeller was not suitable upon this ship. The defendants have never tried it on any other ship, and I find that the propeller was not fit for use as a propeller at all, as it

---

① [1977] 1 Lloyd's Rep 645 at 651.
② (1932) 43 Ll L Rep 466 at 478.

turned out.

1.140　螺旋桨供应商对高院的判决提起了上诉,上诉法院推翻了高院的判决,判决螺旋桨供应商胜诉。上诉法院认为案件与 1893 年《货物买卖法》第 14(1) 条无关,上诉法院的 Scrutton 法官认为船厂并没有明示或默示将螺旋桨的特定用途告诉螺旋桨供应商,即用于特定船舶和一个特定规格且有其敏感期的柴油机。螺旋桨供应商并不知道规格和敏感期。船厂也没有向螺旋桨供应商表明在螺旋桨是否适合主机的问题上其对后者能力和判断力的依赖,实际上船厂并没有对螺旋桨供应商有此依赖。因此螺旋桨采购合同中并不存在螺旋桨应当合理适合其用途的默示条件。上诉法院的 Scrutton 法官是这样说的:①

> ... It must be proved that there was buyer's reliance on the skill of the seller, and that his reliance was known to the seller; that is, that as a reasonable man he must have known that the buyer was relying on the seller's skill and judgment and not on his own .... The questions are questions of degree; in some cases the reliance is obvious, in others doubtful, in other obviously absent. The reliance need not be exclusive—the buyer may also consider advice of his own experts—but the reliance on the seller must be "a substantial and effective inducement," and the seller must be aware of its existence and operation.

1.141　但是上诉法院的 Greer 法官则持不同的观点,他认为螺旋桨供应商一开始提供的螺旋桨以及后来提供的替代螺旋桨均不是令船厂满意的螺旋桨。他认为船厂已经部分明示地部分默示地将螺旋桨的特定用途告诉了螺旋桨供应商,从而表明了对螺旋桨供应商的能力和判断力的依赖。因此,螺旋桨供应商违反了合同的默示条款。他说:②

> The propeller that they first supplied was one which did not, in fact, satisfy either the plaintiffs or the owners' representative, or, if it is necessary to go beyond the owners' representative, the owners themselves. This was, in my judgment, a clear breach of contract, and the defendants are responsible for such damages as are recoverable in law as damages for the proposition that the words of an agreement fall to be interpreted according to their natural meaning.

---

① (1933) 45 Ll L Rep 89 at 95.
② Ibid.

在船厂是否依赖螺旋桨供应商的能力和判断力问题上，Greer 法官说：① 　　1.142

> It is obvious that a shipbuilder in ordering a propeller, whether he trusts to the seller's skill and judgment or to his own, must prescribe the size of the propeller that he requires, and that the prescription of size in the case of a propeller necessarily involves the length from the centre of the boss to the tip, the width of the various parts of the propeller, and the maximum thickness which is at a line near the centre of the propeller, and inasmuch as he will be known to be responsible for the speed, he must necessarily prescribe the pitch and the circumference. The reset of the essentials required for a good propeller he, in this case, left to be determined by the skilled propeller maker …. Further, though the extreme thickness of the blade was specified by the buyer, the rate at which that thickness was to be reduced between the thickest point and the fine edge was left to the defendants to decide, and this necessarily includes the thickness of each blade within a few inches from the edge …. The effect of all this evidence is that there were many important matters relevant to the quality of the propeller when finished and tendered by the defendants that the plaintiffs left to the defendants' skill and judgment.

船厂对上诉法院的判决提起了上诉，上议院采纳了上诉法院 Greer 法官的意见，推翻了上诉法院的判决。上议院认为鉴于船东并不是船厂和螺旋桨供应商之间采购合同的当事人，采购合同势必会将一些问题留给螺旋桨供应商，根据他们的能力和判断力予以解决。大家都知道螺旋桨将作为船舶的一部分用于船上，而船舶则必须符合船东的要求。在螺旋桨是否令人满意的问题上，上议院的 Lord Tomlin 说：② 　　1.143

> In fact it was not till each propeller was fitted to its ship and the ship was given its trial that the owners were in a position to express any satisfaction or dissatisfaction. In my judgment the language of the clause in question is apt to provide for and does provide for just such a position. The owners admittedly after the trials were dissatisfied and expressed dissatisfaction. Further, in my opinion it is the proper inference from all the facts that the source of the trouble lay in the region of the matters left to the skill and judgment of the respondents and that, even if the

---

① （1933）45 Ll L Rep 89 at 124.
② [1934] AC 402 at 412.

satisfaction clause was to operate only in respect of these matters, the owners were still entitled to express dissatisfaction .... I think therefore that the conditions of the clause were not fulfilled and that the respondents are liable in damages to the appellants for breach of it.

1.144　虽然此案三审出现了不同的判决，但值得注意的是，上诉法院判决船厂败诉是建立在认定船厂没有将螺旋桨的特定用途告诉螺旋桨供应商且没有依赖螺旋桨供应商的能力及判断力这一基础之上的，而这一认定实际上是事实问题，而非法律问题。换言之，三审法院在法律问题上并没有不一致。

1.145　在 *Bristol Tramways & Carriage Co Ltd* v *Fiat Motors Ltd* ①一案中，原告向被告订购一批公交车和公交车底盘，被告知道公交车的特定用途，即在布里斯托尔附近的山区运送旅客。被告同时也知道原告向他们订购是对他们的信任，意在避免原告遇到过的因其他制造商的原因而导致的公交车问题。然而，公交车交货后不适合在当地运送旅客，原告起诉要求被告赔偿，法院判原告胜诉，被告提起了上诉。上诉法院认为公交车和底盘均不适合在山区运载旅客。Cozens-Hardy 法官说：②

> I think, therefore, that on the findings of fact by the learned judge there was an implied condition that the goods should be reasonably fit for the purpose. I also think that the case may be brought within sub-s.2, namely, that there was an implied condition that the goods should be of merchantable quality. In the face of Mr. Preen's report of October 25, 1907, which comes from the defendants' custody, I cannot doubt that the goods sold were not of merchantable quality within the fair meaning of those words, and I see no reason to doubt the finding of the learned judge that the slight inspection by the representatives of the plaintiffs of one of the complete omnibuses was not of such a nature as sufficed to disclose the defects.

1.146　关于采购合同中"to be to the entire satisfaction of the owners' representative and ourselves"一句的含义，无论是一审的 Roche 法官，还是上诉审的 Scrutton 法官都认为：只要螺旋桨的制造符合规格书且使用了良好的材料和工艺，船厂就不能以采购合同以外的问题为由对螺旋桨的质量表示不满意。但是上议院似乎有不同的观点，上议院认为一审和上诉审都忽视了采购合同规定货物应当令

---

① [1910] 2 KB 831.
② [1910] 2 KB 831 at 837.

合同外第三人满意这一事实,而第三人可能并不了解采购合同的内容。上议院的 Lord Russell of Killowen 认为,实际上原告仅凭这一点就已经可以胜诉了。他说:①

> I can see no ground for so limiting the clause as regards a stranger to the contract. In terms there is an obligation on the respondents to make a propeller which will satisfy a third person. No doubt the third person must act in good faith and not capriciously. But that is only to say in other words, that he must in fact be dissatisfied with the propeller before it can be alleged that the express term has been broken. I can find no justification for modifying the absolute nature of this term of the contract. Even if its operation were limited to satisfaction in respect of matters not specifically covered by the contract, the facts of this case fall within it, because, as indicated above, the cause of the noise must be some feature or property not covered by the specified particulars and details.

Lord Russell of Killowen 继续说:②

> Nor can I see any ground for limiting the operation of the clause to satisfaction with the propeller as a manufactured article, and saying that it does not include satisfaction with the propeller in operation. But even so limited, the clause would apply here. The owner is dissatisfied with the propeller, not with its propelling; the dissatisfaction is with the propeller because it contains some feature or property which results in excessive noise. The dissatisfaction is with the propeller because, as manufactured, it contains that undesirable feature or property.

然而,在 *Britain Steamship Co Ltd* v *Lithgows Ltd* 一案中,船东主张的是船舶不符合"特殊用途",因为船舶主机的马力和转速没有达到船舶建造合同规定的要求。针对第一主张,法院认为根据船东的陈述,"用途"是指将船舶"作为一散货船使用",然而船东并没有证明船舶不能如此使用。Lord Maxwell 认为主机的马力和转速并不构成建造船舶的"目的",他说:③

> Commercial men do not buy ships for the "purpose" of getting a machine which will produce a particular power or speed of operation.

---

① [1934] AC 402 at 416.
② Ibid.
③ (1933) 45 Ll L Rep 89 at 112.

They may require that their ship's engine shall have particular power or speed of operation because that is what they believe is required in order that the ship may fulfill its purpose, but the horse-power and speed of operation are themselves matters of quality, not purpose.

1.149　此外,卖方承担货物不符合买方购买货物"特定目的"的责任应当以卖方知晓该特定目的为前提。在 *Slater and Others* v *Finning Ltd* ①一案中,船东将自己的一艘捕鱼船加长并更换了卡特彼勒主机。此后主机轴承出了问题,船东找到了经营海上机械的被告。被告建议更换凸轮轴,并提供且安装了凸轮轴。但是问题并没有得到解决,于是被告又提供了第二套、第三套凸轮轴并进行了安装。问题依然没有得到解决。最终船东卖了主机并重新安装了一台采用不同设计的新的卡特彼勒主机。旧主机经过大修(但没换凸轮轴)安装到了另一艘捕鱼船上后始终没有发生任何凸轮轴的问题。于是原告对被告起诉,根据《货物买卖法》第14(3)条的规定,要求被告赔偿其损失。

1.150　一审法院的 Lord Weir 驳回了船东的起诉,理由是凸轮轴本身是符合船舶用途的,问题并非由凸轮轴引起。船东上诉,苏格兰最高民事法院驳回了上诉。船东于是上诉至上议院,主张根据第14(3)条的规定承诺提供符合特定船舶用途设备的卖方应承担因船舶特殊性带来的风险。上议院认为:凸轮轴必须符合的特定用途是适合船舶的主机,但被告并不知道凸轮轴有扭力共振过度的趋势,因此被告并无利用其技能解决该问题的义务,被告亦没有违反默示义务。上议院的 Lord Keith 说:②

> As matter of principle, therefore, it may be said that where a buyer purchases goods from a seller who deals in goods of that description there is no breach of the implied condition of fitness where the failure of the goods to meet the intended purpose arises from an abnormal feature or idiosyncrasy, not made known to the seller, in the buyer or in the circumstances of the use of the goods by the buyer. That is the case whether or not the buyer is himself aware of the abnormal feature or idiosyncrasy.

---

① [1997] AC 473.
② [1997] AC 473 at 483.

Ⅵ 船舶建造合同的标准格式

标准格式合同

标准格式合同通常是指由一方事先起草的包括所有合同主要条款的书面合同文本。作为一般原则,普通法视标准格式合同为一般的合同,对合同签署方具有约束力,即使一方当事人实际上并没有看过或理解合同的内容,合同对签署方依然具有约束力。然而,如果合同条文或内容出现歧义的,法院则应作对提供合同一方不利的解释(*contra proferentem*),理由是提供合同文本的一方理应有能力和机会消除歧义。在船舶建造业,采用标准格式订立船舶建造合同的做法比较常见。在实践中的具体做法是以某一标准格式合同为基础,双方在此基础上通过协商作出必要的取舍和修改。

1.151

船舶建造合同标准格式介绍

下文是对一些比较常见的船舶建造合同标准格式的简单介绍。

1.152

SAJ 格式

SAJ 格式是日本造船人协会于 1974 年 1 月推出的船舶建造合同标准格式。日本造船人协会的日文名称为"日本造船工業会"。该协会成立于 1947 年,成立之时为非社团法人,自 1951 年起改为社团法人。目前该协会共有十七个会员造船企业,它们分别是:

1.153

株式会社 IHI(IHI Corporation) ;①
今治造船株式会社(Imabari Shipbuilding Co Ltd) ;②
株式会社大岛造船所(Oshima Shipbuilding Co Ltd) ;③
尾道造船株式会社(Onomichi Dockyard Co Ltd) ;④
川崎重工業株式会社(Kawasaki Heavy Industries Ltd) ;⑤

---

① 网址: www. ihi. co. jp/index-e. html.
② 网址: www. imazo. co. jp.
③ 网址: www. osy. co. jp.
④ 网址: www. onozo. co. jp.
⑤ 网址: www. khi. co. jp.

佐世保重工業株式会社(Sasebo Heavy Industries Co Ltd);①

ジャパン マリンユナイテッド株式会社(Japan Marine United Corporation);②

株式会社新来島サノヤス造船(Shin Krushima Sanoyas Shipbuilding Co Ltd);③

株式会社新来島どっく(Shin Krushima Dockyard Co Ltd);④

株式会社新来島豊橋造船(Shin Kurushima Toyohashi Shipbuilding Co Ltd);⑤

住友重機械工業株式会社(Sumitomo Heavy Industries Ltd);⑥

常石造船株式会社(Tsuneishi Shipbuilding Co Ltd);⑦

内海造船株式会社(Naikai Zosen Corporation);⑧

株式会社名村造船所(Namura Shipbuilding Co Ltd);⑨

函館どつく株式会社(The Hakodate Dock Co Ltd);⑩

株社会社三井E&S(Mitsui E&S);⑪

三菱重工業株式会社(Mitsubishi Heavy Industries Ltd)。⑫

除了上述17个企业会员外,日本造船人协会还有一个团体会员,即日本中小型造船工业会(The Cooperative Association of Japan Shipbuilders)。⑬

1.154　　SAJ格式通常被认为是偏向船厂利益的船舶建造合同标准格式,例子包括船厂可以将船舶建造的任何部分进行分包;⑭船舶建造因任何船厂无法控制的原因或事件而迟延的,无论船厂在订立合同时是否可以预见,船厂均可以顺延交船日。⑮ 这应当是日本造船业当时在世界上的地位使然。但是可能由于起草的疏忽,SAJ格式也有明显对船厂不利,同时也是不公平的条款。⑯

---

① 网址: www.ssk-sasebo.co.jp.
② 网址: www.jmuc.co.jp.
③ 网址: www.sanoyas.skdy.co.jp.
④ 网址: www.skdy.co.jp.
⑤ 网址: www.toyozo.jp.
⑥ 网址: www.shi.co.jp.
⑦ 网址: www.tsuneishi.com.
⑧ 网址: www.naikaizosen.co.jp.
⑨ 网址: www.namura.co.jp.
⑩ 网址: www.hakodate-dock.co.jp/jp/index.html.
⑪ 网址: www.mes.co.jp.
⑫ 网址: www.mhi.co.jp.
⑬ 网址: www.cajs.or.jp.
⑭ Article I.4.
⑮ Article VIII.1.
⑯ SAJ格式第VIII条关于延误以及延误通知的内容明显不利于船厂的利益,见本书第10章相关讨论。

SAJ 格式在日本、韩国、新加坡、中国得到比较广泛的使用。在这些国家进行的船舶建造,船厂和船东大多以 SAJ 标准格式为基础开始磋商他们自己的船舶建造合同。中国船厂与船东订立的船舶建造合同具有相当明显的 SAJ 格式的痕迹。 1.155

AWES 格式

AWES 格式是西欧船舶建造人和修理人联合会(Association of West European Shipbuilders and Shiprepairers)于 1972 年制定的船舶建造合同标准格式,最近一次修改是在 1999 年 5 月。虽然 AWES 格式实际上得到使用的地区主要在欧洲,例如德国、法国、意大利以及希腊等,但由于这是一份最早的国际性船舶建造合同标准格式,对此后制定的标准格式例如 SAJ 格式产生了不小的影响。与 SAJ 格式相同,AWES 格式也是由代表船厂利益的造船厂联合会制定的,因此 AWES 格式是相对比较倾向于保护船厂利益的合同格式。例如 AWES 格式也规定,船厂有权将船舶建造之部分分包给第三者。① AWES 格式还规定,只要不影响船舶的功能特征,船厂有权对规格书、图纸做出修改从而适合船厂的当地条件和设施,当地可获得的材料和设备,生产方式的改进或其他因素。② 1.156

Norwegian 格式

Norwegian 格式是挪威船东协会(Norwegian Shipowners Association)③于 2000 年制定并颁布的船舶建造合同标准格式。虽然 Norwegian 格式在挪威得到采用是显而易见的,但在挪威以外的船舶建造合同中使用 Norwegian 格式的实际上并不多见。值得一提的是,Norwegian 格式与其他大多数格式不同,它是经过代表船东利益的挪威船东协会和代表船厂利益的挪威船舶建造人销售和营销组织④以及挪威船舶建造人协会通过协商达成一致的标准合同格式。因此 1.157

---

① Article 1(e).
② Article 3(b).
③ 挪威船东协会由挪威的航运和海洋开发公司组成,关注国内和国际政策、雇主问题、资格和招募、环境问题、海上安全以及创新。协会于 1909 年 9 月 15 日成立于挪威南部城市 Kristiania,当时名称为 The Norwegian Shipowner Association。1984 年改为现在的名称。协会总部设在奥斯陆,共有 160 个成员。协会网址:www.rederi.no。
④ 挪威船舶建造人销售和营销组织是由船厂组成的从事集体销售和营销的组织,成立于 1945 年,当时名为 West Norway Shipbuilders Association。1990 年改组为纯粹销售和营销机构并改为现在的名称。成员船厂通过同一渠道进行销售和推广。在有项目时,每个船厂在投标时各自独立并充分竞争。挪威船舶建造人销售和营销组织为其客户提供免费的服务,所需资金由成员船厂承担。挪威船舶建造人销售和营销组织网站:www.nssm.no。

Norwegian 格式应当是在船东和船厂之间形成的一种平衡,与其他标准格式相比较,Norwegian 格式应当也确实体现了此种平衡。

MARAD 格式

1.158　　MARAD 格式是美国海事资助局制定颁布的船舶建造合同标准格式。海事资助局从属于美国海事局(United States Maritime Administration,"MARAD"),而后者则是美国运输部的一个机构。海事资助局的主要职能是负责洽谈船舶建造合同并向航运公司提供经营差额资助。按照 1936 年《商船法》(Merchant Marine Act 1936)第 501 条的规定,只要符合法律规定的要求,任何美国公民均可申请建造差额资助以支持美国建造的船舶投入美国对外商业运营。MARAD 格式正是用于按照 1936 年《商船法》授权的联邦船舶融资计划进行的船舶建造。按照 MARAD 格式的规定,适用美国海事资助局补贴的船舶建造应当符合下列条件:①

1.159　　第一,作为美国公民的船厂已向海事资助局提出了建造差额资助的申请且所建船舶将用于美国的对外商业。

1.160　　第二,海事资助局已确认:(1)符合美国对外商业要求的规格书及图纸,有助于推进和发展美国对外商业,并在战争时期或国家紧急状态下适合美国国防或军事用途;(2)船东拥有从事所建新船营运或维持所需的能力、经验、财务资源以及其他条件;(3)提供所申请的资助已经过合理的计算。

1.161　　第三,海事资助局将船舶建造的图纸和规格书提交海军部并获得海军部的批准。

1.162　　第四,海事资助局已批准了最低的投标,并已和船厂就部分船价的支付订立了合同。

1.163　　MARAD 格式除了美国以外,在加拿大和一些南美国家也得到了采用。

NEWBUILDCON 格式

1.164　　NEWBUILDCON 格式是指国际海事组织于 2007 年推出的船舶建造合同标准格式。与其他标准格式不同的是,NEWBUILDCON 格式是在现有各种船舶建造合同标准格式及其实际在船舶建造中使用的合同基础上起草的。NEWBUILDCON 格式的制定与国际海事组织的其他标准格式有相同之处,也采用了方格条款和文字条

---

① 参见 MARAD 格式引言部分的内容。

款相结合的方式。与其他标准格式相比,NEWBUILDCON 格式对条文的排列重新进行了安排,例如 SAJ 格式关于解约(包括船东的解约和船厂的解约)的规定散见于各个条款,而 NEWBUILDCON 格式把船舶建造合同的解除专列一条(第 39 条)。该条不仅规定船东的解约,也规定船厂的解约,例如船东可以解约的情形包括:还款保函担保人破产、船厂不履行合同、不可抗力导致的延误超过 180 天、因船厂的原因导致的延误超过 180 天、船舶建造不符合合同约定(包括航速,耗油,载重吨位等)以及还款保函不符合合同约定等。

虽然国际海事组织在严格意义上并不是一个纯粹的船东组织,但 NEWBUILDCON 格式似乎是一个比较偏袒船东利益的标准格式。首先,按照 NEWBUILDCON 格式关于分包的规定,船厂可以将部分建造工作分包给规格书或厂商表(Maker's List)中列出的分包商,除了较小的工作外,船厂将其分包给规格书或厂商表列明分包商以外分包人的必须获得船东的书面同意,①这一规定对船厂的设计、采购以及建造可能会构成比较大的限制,而且也未必符合当今船舶建造的实际做法。其次,按照 NEWBUILDCON 格式关于修改或变更的规定,船东有权在任何时候对规格书、图纸等进行修改,而船厂只有在船东提出的修改或变更是重大的情况下才有权主张交船日的推延,在双方无法就修改或变更达成一致的情况下,船东有权要求船厂实施自己提出的修改或变更要求,而将修改或变更问题作为一个纠纷予以处理。② 再次,在使用 NEWBUILDCON 格式情况下,船东在交船之前有权将船舶建造合同进行转让,所谓的转让实际上是船舶建造合同当事人的变更,③虽然船舶建造合同的条款并未发生变化,但船东单方面有权更换合同当事人应当是不利于船厂的。而且此种合同当事人的变更还可能引起付款担保和还款担保的更改。

1.165

NEWBUILDCON 格式颁布之时依然是新建船市场处于急剧上升的阶段,不难想象在 2008 年时 NEWBUILDCON 格式不太可能得到大多数船厂的青睐。但时过境迁,在新建船市场自 2008 年年底起滑至低谷后,船东应当有机会推动 NEWBUILDCON 格式的采用。虽然国际海事组织对这一格式充满了希望,但其是否会得到市场的采纳还将拭目以待。

1.166

---

① Clause 19.
② Clause 24.
③ Clause 34(b).

CSTC 格式

1.167　CSTC 格式是指由原中国船舶工业总公司（以下简称"中船总"）制定的船舶建造合同标准格式。CSTC 格式在中国船舶建造业得到比较广泛的采用，不仅是中船总系统的船厂大多采用 CSTC 格式，不少非中船总系统的船厂也采用 CSTC 格式。可以说 CSTC 格式对中国船厂的船舶建造合同产生了相当大的影响。从条文的排列来看，CSTC 格式应当是在 SAJ 格式上起草的。与 SAJ 格式的不同之处主要有：第 II 条（合同价格及支付条件）增加了关于付款保证和还款保证的内容；把 SAJ 格式第 XVII 条关于船东供应品的相关内容放在第 V 条修改和变更之内；在第 X 条增加了关于违约通知的内容；在第 XIII 条（争议与仲裁）增加了关于将技术争议提交船级社解决的内容。

1.168　CSTC 格式具有两个比较明显的特征：第一，CSTC 格式可能是众多标准格式中唯一由船东、出口商以及船厂作为共同卖方签署的船舶建造合同，但从 CSTC 格式的具体内容来看，这种安排似乎仅仅是为了适应当时中船总订立船舶建造合同的特征，并没有实质性的意义。第二，CSTC 格式可能是第一个规定还款保函的船舶建造合同的标准格式。第三，从内容来看，CSTC 格式与 SAJ 格式基本相同，同样具有比较倾向于保护船厂利益的特征。

CMAC 格式

1.169　CMAC 格式又称"上海格式"，是中国海事仲裁委员会组织起草并于 2010 年推出的船舶建造合同标准格式。上海格式应当是在 NEWBUILDCON 格式基础上起草的，其中最明显的一个特征是上海格式也采用了方格条款和文字条款相结合的方式。另外，在格式条文的基础上增设了"节"，与 NEWBUILDCON 的"Section"相同。这两个格式各有六节，每节的名称也相同，分别是：第一节船舶，第二节财务，第三节生产，第四节交船，第五节法律，第六节杂项。①

1.170　上海格式有中文和英文两种，但是第 30 条（通知和语言）第 2 款则有如下规定：

　　本合同的全部文件和通知、通讯、说明书、图纸等书面资料均应使用中文或英文书写，视具体情况选定。两种语言均具有同等法律效力，如

---

① NEWBUILDCON 格式的六个 Section 则分别是: Section 1-Vessel, Section 2-Financial, Section 3-Production, Section 4-Delivery, Section 5-Legal, Section 6-Sundry.

发生不一致情况时,以中文为准。本合同双方无义务将其译为其他种类语言。

上述条文应当存在比较明显的问题。首先,"两种语言均具有同等法律效力"一句实际上是不考虑两种语言可能存在的矛盾和歧义的,所谓的"具有同等法律效力"是以两者没有矛盾和歧义为前提的,而此种前提实际上并不存在;其次,由于有"以中文为准"的规定,"两种语言均具有同等法律效力"一句其实已不再有任何意义了;第三,上海格式应当是用于中国船厂的,而且是用于中国船厂为外国船东建造船舶的合同,在此前提下,让不懂中文的外国船东接受一份以中文起草的合同应当是无法想象的;第四,如果"本合同全部文件"包括本合同本身,似乎意味着船舶建造合同可以使用中文制定,而以中文制定船舶建造合同在为外国船东建造船舶的实践中应当是难以实现的,如果合同只有英文文本,那么第30条的规定也就没有意义了,即使合同同时有中文本和英文本,"以中文为准"一句马上让只看得懂英文本的外国船东感到英文本的不可靠性,如果"本合同全部文件"不包括本合同,上述问题的似乎同样有可能发生,即除非合同只有一个英文本,否则一样会发生中文本优于英文本的情形;最后,关于通知等可以中文或英文书写且无义务进行翻译的规定近乎可笑。在采用上海格式情况下,中国的船厂在收到国外船东用英文写来的信函或电邮时可以用中文与其联系。一旦两种文字有歧义的则以中文为准。不难想象,上海格式要在世界范围内得到广泛采用恐怕是很难指望的。①

1.171

标准格式合同的作用

使用标准格式订立船舶建造合同的一个明显优点是避免了从无到有起草一个船舶建造合同的麻烦,因为标准格式通常已经考虑到了缔约双方在磋商合同时可能遇到的问题。采用标准格式不仅能节省时间,而且还能避免一些不必要的摩擦。但是任何的标准格式都未必符合特定缔约双方具体的意愿。虽然同为船舶建造合同,由于船东和船厂的经济实力、市场地位以及缔约当时的市场状况在不同的船舶建造合同中有可能会有相当大的差别,这就需要缔约双方在标准格式的基础上根据具体的情况作出取舍、修改和调整。因此标准格式的作用是为缔约双方确立了一个合同条文的基础,而标准格式也正是在合同当事人不断使用中逐步

1.172

---

① 关于作者对上海格式的意见请参见拙文"关于'上海格式'的若干意见",《海大法律评论 2010—2011》,上海浦江教育出版社 2011 年,第 28 页。

得到完善。

1.173　　不少船厂都制定了自己的船舶建造合同标准格式,希望在和船东订立船舶建造合同时可以得到采用。但此种想法可能有些不切实际,因为船舶建造业是一个几乎完全受制于市场的行业,船东或者船厂是否可以采用自己选择的标准格式或者自己起草的合同文本几乎无一例外地取决于缔约当时的市场状况。当船舶建造业处于卖方市场时,船舶建造合同的格式乃至于船舶建造的质量都可能不会成为一个问题。但是在航运市场萎缩、船东的经营变得异常困难时,所有不是问题的问题都将成为问题,而且是极其重要的问题。2008年金融危机后发生的大量的船东和船厂之间争议应当是一个极好的例证。在2004至2008年间订立的船舶建造合同的付款方式大多是分为五期支付,每期为合同价格的20%,而在2008年之后订立的船舶建造合同的付款方式的特征是,第一第二期的建造款数额越来越小,而船东在接船时支付的那期建造款则越来越大,有的甚至到了合同价格的70%~80%。

1.174　　在船舶建造业低迷期间,船厂即使有经过缜密思考、反复斟酌、来回推敲的处处保护船厂利益的合同文本也未必有用得上的机会。因此,问题可能并不是船厂是否应当有自己起草的船舶建造合同文本或标准格式,或者船舶建造合同使用船东的标准格式还是船厂的标准格式,而是船厂是否真正了解船舶建造合同的内容,以及船舶建造合同内容是否有利于保护船厂的利益。

第 2 章　合同的洽谈和订立

I　合同的洽谈

谈判概述

2.1　谈判（negotiation）其实是决策过程，通常是有不同利益诉求的两方或多方通过交流实现各自目标的过程。*Negotiation-Theory and Strategy* 一书是这样定义谈判的：①

> Negotiation is an interactive communication process by which two or more parties who lack identical interests attempt to coordinate their behavior or allocate scarce resources in a way that will make them both better off than they could be if they were to act alone.

2.2　"谈判"与"讨价还价"（bargaining）差不多是同义词。讨价还价未必一定是指价格的磋商，但几乎可以肯定是利益的磋商。商业谈判是谈判的一种，其本质与一般谈判并无二致，只是商业谈判的目的是为了追求商业利益而已。船舶建造合同的洽谈属于商业谈判的一种。

2.3　说到谈判似乎一定会涉及"谈判技巧"。其实商业谈判往往是在两方或多方专业人员之间进行的，双方各自知道自己的商业目的。谈判技巧恐怕没有太大的作用，即使有用也不会涉及谈判的根本。商业谈判是否成功取决于谈判各方的商业利益是否实现。与其关心技巧，还不如熟悉自己的目标并在谈判前做好充分的准备。

技术洽谈

2.4　除了极个别例外，②船厂通常是在有船东下订单的情况下才会开始建造船舶

---

① Russell Karobkin, *Negotiation-Theory and Strategy*, Wolters Kluwer, 2009, p.1.
② 在实践中也确有船厂在没有船东下订单的情况下建造船舶的情形，但这往往是船厂的一种市场投机行为。

的。与一般的货物买卖合同相比,船舶建造合同的洽谈相对复杂一些,所需时间也比较长一些。船东在与船厂初次接触时通常会向船厂提供船舶的基本信息,包括船舶种类、载重吨、航速以及船舶的计划航区。双方的洽谈基于这些基本信息展开。在实践中,船舶建造合同的洽谈主要包括技术洽谈和商务洽谈。

2.5 　　船舶建造合同的技术洽谈通常包括:建造规范、船级标准、设计要求、设备选择以及专利问题等。如果船厂建造的船舶是首制船(leading ship)[①],或者船东希望采用自己的新技术或新设计,技术洽谈就可能更为复杂。由于这种技术洽谈往往没有现存的图纸和技术规范可供参考,因此双方可能需要较长的时间才能完成此种技术洽谈。相反,若双方洽谈的是采用船厂已经建造过的标准船型,则洽谈就会相对简单。从事技术洽谈的一般是船厂和船东的技术人员,有时还会涉及船级社甚至船旗国的代表。下面是与船舶建造合同技术洽谈有关的主要文件与内容。

规格书

2.6 　　规格书(specification),也有称为"技术规格书"(technical specification),是船舶建造合同技术部分的重要文件,是船厂和船东之间关于技术问题的协议。规格书的内容比较繁杂,通常有几百页。规格书的基本目的是和总布置图等一起解决船舶及其设备的设计、材料、预制、安装、检验以及工艺等的所有问题,包括船舶基本特征的简单描述、主要尺寸、载重吨和货舱容积、航速和动力要求、稳性要求、工艺质量和标准、检验和证书、生活区细节、试航条件、设备和属具等。规格书没有包含的问题则适用船厂的标准做法。如果建造的是一艘首制船,规格书的洽谈就可能是一项相当繁重的工作。

2.7 　　规格书的内容相当多,以一艘普通散货船的规格书为例,通常会由以下几个部分组成。一般部分,这部分的主要内容是:各种用词的定义、船舶的一般描述、船舶的尺寸及基本特征、适用于船舶的国际公约的相关规定、船旗国的规定以及船级社的规范和规则、船舶证书、船舶的稳性计算及其要求、船型和船体结构以及船模试验、船舶检验以及测试和试验。船体和油漆部分,这部分的内容主要是:船体包括主船体、上层建筑和甲板以及烟囱等、表面处理和油漆包括油漆厚度等。生活区部分,这部分的主要内容是:生活区分类、家具和装饰、舷窗、门和阶梯、空调以及通风等。舾装部分,这部分的主要内容是:锚机和绞车包括锚和锚链、操舵

[①] "首制船"通常是指其结构和特征是船厂第一次实施建造的船舶。

系统包括舵机和舵、货舱及舱盖、救生设施、航行设备、消防设施以及管路系统。机械部分,这部分的主要内容是:机械的主要特征、发电机、蒸汽机、辅助机械、各种设备和舾装、绝缘和油漆、机舱管系、自动化监控和遥控系统、备件以及工具。电器部分,这部分的主要内容是:布线、主电源、副电源、动力、照明系统、航行灯号和信号、航海仪器以及无线电设备。规格书的作用是详细描述并解释船厂按照船舶建造合同规定应当交付的船舶。在通常情况下,规格书没有提及但船级社或船旗国有要求的项目,船厂有义务提供或完成。但规格书没有提及而船东要求超过船级社要求的则构成船舶建造合同的修改。

另外,规格书中会约定船舶建造所适用的标准。如果船舶是在中国境内建造的,船厂可以也应当接受的标准是中国的相关标准,例如中国工业标准、中国造船标准、中国造船质量标准、中国冶金标准以及中国机械和电器标准。如果中国没有相关标准,或中国标准不适用时,可以考虑接受国际标准组织的标准。 2.8

图纸

"图纸"一词在英文中的表述主要有两个,即 plans 和 drawings。虽然 plans 和 drawings 都可以解释为"图纸",但两者似乎并不是始终可以随意互用的同义词。Plans 通常是指比较整体或全面的图纸,例如 plot plan(布局图)。总布置图在英语中是 general arrangement plan,虽然在建筑中会有 general arrangement drawings 的用法,但在船舶建造中通常不会用 drawing 来描述总布置图。相反,drawings 则往往是指比较具体或详细的图纸,例如 detailed drawing(明细图), electrical drawings(电气图)等。Plans 用作图纸时往往是指平面图,例如 floor plan(平面图),很少会见到 floor drawing;而二维图或三维图则更多用 drawings 来表示,例如 3D drawing,似乎不会用 plans 予以替代。 2.9

图纸中最为重要的是总布置图,它是船舶设计及其他工作的基础。总布置图通常是作为船舶建造合同文件之一签署的。总布置图是显示船舶总体布置的图纸,它反映了船舶的技术特征和性能,是一份重要的全船基本图纸。总布置图的作用是:首先,总布置图表明了船舶上层建筑的型式和舱室、设备、门窗以及通道等的布置情况;其次,总布置图为其他设计和计算提供了依据,例如全船重量和重心位置的计算,船舶设备设计和结构设计等均离不开总布置图;再次,总布置图为其他图纸的绘制提供了依据,例如各类设备和系统布置图的绘制;最后,总布置图是具体施工的指导性图纸,机械和设备的相互关系发生矛盾时均以总布置图中的布置为准。由于船舶的总布置往往会反映船东的生活区标准,因此总布置图通常 2.10

由船厂和船东共同完成。

2.11　中横剖面图（midship section）顾名思义是船体中段范围内的典型横向剖视图。中横剖面图是船舶建造的另一份重要图纸。它是体现船体结构基本情况的全船结构图样，因此是校核和绘制其他结构图样的重要依据。通过阅读中横剖面图可以了解船体各部分结构的相对位置以及船体构件的布置、尺寸、结构形式和相互连接方式。中横剖面图的内容包括：横向构件——肋板、肋骨、横梁和支柱的尺寸、结构形式和相互连接方式；纵向构件——纵桁材、旁桁材、舷侧纵桁和甲板纵桁、纵骨等；外板、内底板和甲板的横向排列及其宽度；上层建筑纵向围壁的位置和板厚及扶强材的尺寸和结构形式；舱口的宽度及舱口围板的尺寸和结构形式；双层底、船舱及各层甲板间的高度以及梁拱高等。

厂商表

2.12　厂商表（maker list）是指列明主机及主要设备的制造商或供应商的文件。原则上，厂商表是由船东提供的。除非是普通设备或产品，船厂通常很难选择或决定制造商或供应商。厂商表表明了船东对制造商或供应商的偏好，但与制造商或供应商签约的通常是船厂，即船东选择的制造商或供应商在合同关系上是船厂的分包商。换言之，船厂应当对由船东选择的制造商或供应商的违约或过错向船东承担责任。如果船厂以往的经历表明船东选择的制造商或供应商存在问题的话，船厂应当在签约前就把问题提出来。如果船东接受了船厂的意见，问题就能得到解决。如果船东坚持自己的选择，船厂应当有机会做出相应的保留。

2.13　厂商表有可能针对同一设备列出两个或两个以上的制造商或供应商。在此种情况下，船厂可以在列明的制造商和供应商中根据具体情况作出选择。如果船东对船厂的选择提出异议，船厂恐怕未必能够坚持自己的选择，因为船东作为相关设备的最终用户，其选择应当得到尊重。如果存在价差的话，船厂可以就额外成本或费用的承担与船东协商。由于较大的供应商几乎在世界各地都有分公司或派驻机构，同一品牌的设备可能会在不同国家或地区制造。如果厂商表明确载明制造商或供应商的所在地，船厂只能向厂商表列明的制造商或供应商订制或采购船舶建造所需的设备。

2.14　如果厂商表列明的制造商或供应商因各种原因无法提供船厂所需的设备或产品的，船厂可以从其他制造商或供应商处订制或采购，但船厂选择的制造商或供应商依然需要获得船东的许可。如果可以，船厂应尽可能地与船东针对各种情形及其处理方式作出约定。

商务洽谈

　　船舶建造合同的商务洽谈是指双方就技术部分以外的合同内容的洽谈,这些内容主要包括:价格及其支付方式、还款保函和付款保函、审图和监造、交船日为、试航安排、质量保证、建造保险以及争议解决等。从事商务谈判的一般是船厂和船东的商务人员。与技术洽谈相比,商务洽谈可能相对比较复杂一点。技术洽谈只有在建造首制船的情况下才会涉及到纯技术问题,如果所建造的船舶是成型船舶且有标准图纸的,技术洽谈应当是比较简单的。即使建造的是首制船,对船厂来说,是否能够按照船东的要求建造船舶并不是一个无法或很难确定的问题。相对而言,商务洽谈则不同。船厂做出的承诺往往要在合同实际履行中才会发现所做承诺是否可以切实履行。例如以简单的建造期或交船日为例,负责商务洽谈的经营人员恐怕很难自作主张,往往需要得到船厂负责生产的人员的确认。即使负责生产的人员确认的建造周期,经营人员还应当明确建造周期的计算是否已经考虑到了各种意外因素可能产生的影响。不考虑各种意外因素影响的建造周期恐怕是没有太大的实际意义。

2.15

　　在我国的船舶建造实践中应当存在着轻视或忽视商务洽谈重要性的倾向。船厂往往只关心价格及其支付方式、交船日期,而不重视商务洽谈的其他方面,例如可允许延误的定义等。不少船厂对船东提供的合同文本缺乏深入细致的理解,不清楚船厂在合同履行过程中可能遇到的风险。有的船厂在对合同的商务条款都不熟悉甚至不了解的情况下就签署船舶建造合同,在市场比较好的时候尤为如此。从船厂在履行合同中遇到的实际问题和纠纷来看,几乎无一例外地都涉及建造合同的商务条款。

2.16

　　商务洽谈之所以重要的理由主要有两点。首先,商务洽谈是技术洽谈内容得以实现的保障。在技术洽谈中船厂遇到的问题是船厂是否有能力在满足技术要求的前提下完成船舶的建造,而船厂完成船舶建造的能力往往又受到各种因素的影响,这就要求船厂在洽谈合同商务条款时做出相应的约定。其次,商务洽谈也是船厂实现船舶建造合同商业目的的保障,合同的签订只是船厂实现商业目的的开始,能否最终实现预期的商业目的在很大程度上受到合同商务条款的影响。船厂实现其合同商业目的显然是以合同顺利履行船舶顺利交接为前提,而合同条款尤其是商务条款如何订立则会在很大程度上关系到船舶能否按照约定顺利交接。

2.17

了解和信任

2.18　虽然技术日新月异,但船舶建造的周期依然比较长。加之船舶建造涉及的资金比较大,因此在建造周期中发生的市场供需的变化、贸易特征的改变以及汇率波动等都会给船东和船厂带来相当大的影响,有时甚至是颠覆性的影响。对第一次交船的船东和船厂来说,由于相互间缺乏信任,双方在建造合同洽谈中不得不小心翼翼且处处提防对方。相对而言,如果船东和船厂之前有过船舶建造的经历或其他类似的业务往来,船舶建造合同的洽谈和订立对双方来说都会变得相对简单。由于已有往来,各自对对方已经有了基本的信任,对各自的管理方式和商务特征相对熟悉。双方的谈判,无论是商务还是技术都会变得比较简单。因此,无论是船厂还是船东,通常都愿意致力于与对方建立长期的合作关系。

2.19　航运市场是一个较为特殊的市场,无论是船东还是船厂都没有影响市场的能力。当航运市场处在卖方市场时,船厂便占据了合同洽谈的相对优势。相反,当市场处于买方市场时,船厂则面临着巨大的市场压力。船厂和船东建立起长期的良好关系后,在市场中处于劣势地位的一方就有机会获得对方的支持。当造船业趋于低迷时,船东可以通过继续向船厂订造船舶给船厂提供有力的支持。相反,当造船业供求发生变化,需求大幅度上升时,船厂则可以优先考虑为与自己有长期合作关系的船东建造船舶。

专业知识和专业人员

2.20　这里的"专业知识"是指与船舶建造合同洽谈有关的专业知识,这些专业知识包括:船舶设计和建造、技术规范的特点和变化、市场信息的掌握和运用、风险管理和控制、商务知识、谈判技巧以及相关的法律知识和经验。"专业人员"则是指具有上述知识和经验的人员。从众多的实例来看,绝大多数发生争议的船舶建造合同在商务条款上都存在不同程度的缺陷和问题。因此,下文所讨论的"专业知识"主要是指船舶建造合同洽谈所需的商务知识。

2.21　在实践中,船厂通常会将遇到的问题简单地分为"技术问题""商务问题"和"法律问题"三大类。技术人员负责技术问题,商务人员负责商务问题,而法务人员则对法律问题负责。实际上将问题进行如此分类并不妥当,很多时候根本就无法以此种标准进行归类。船舶建造合同中的条款并不都具有明显的法律特征,但可以肯定的是,船舶建造合同几乎所有条款均与法律密不可分。同一合同条款既会导致商业后果,同时也会导致法律后果。因此在船舶建造合同洽谈期间很难甚至无法清晰地区分技术问题、商务问题和法律问题。

应当避免的一种现象是由船厂的商务人员负责与船东代表的谈判,然后在洽谈基本完成之后将双方谈好的船舶建造合同交由船厂的法务人员或律师予以审核。所谓的"审核"往往是在船舶建造合同即将签署之前进行的程序。除非船厂的法务人员或律师本身具有较为丰富的船舶建造的相关知识和经验,否则提出"专业意见"只能是一种不切实际的奢望。在实践中,不少法务人员或律师对船舶建造合同的所谓"审核"其实只是停留在合同条款是否违反我国法律的判断,或者对合同的准据法或仲裁地发表无关痛痒的意见。毫无疑问,这种做法显然是不可取的。作为船厂负责商务洽谈的专业人员应当受过专业的法律培训,或者船厂应当选拔具有法律背景的人员从事商务洽谈工作。一旦商务人员在自己的商务专业基础上配备了法律武器后,他们在商务谈判中就会胸有成竹,得心应手。很多问题在船舶建造合同形成初稿之前就可以解决了。商务人员提出合同条款增减或修改的建议可能遇到的阻力无疑将远远小于由船厂法务人员提出的相同或类似建议可能遇到的阻力。 2.22

我国大多数船厂都有法务部或专业法务人员的设置,专门负责船厂的法律事务。这些法务人员均有法律专业的学位,但船舶建造商务谈判的知识和经验只能是在漫长的船厂工作实践中逐渐取得。船厂的法务人员只有在具有充分的商务实践的基础上才可能发挥其法律的专业技能,而法务人员获得商务谈判经验的唯一方法就是参与商务谈判。此外,船厂应当对船舶建造合同有充分细致的了解。任何经营都会面临风险,船舶建造也不例外。然而,最大的风险莫过于对船舶建造合同缺乏应有的了解,即不知道是否存在风险及其性质。在市场好的时候,虽然船舶建造合同存在许多明显不利于船厂的条款和规定,但是这些风险都被上扬的航运市场掩盖了。一旦航运市场出现下滑,船舶建造合同中不利于船厂的条款和规定都将成为船厂面临的真实风险。 2.23

洽谈的费用及其承担

船舶建造合同的洽谈,尤其是首制船或建造有特殊性能船舶合同的洽谈通常会产生一定的成本和费用,有时甚至会产生数额不小的成本和费用。船厂最终和船东签署船舶建造合同的,这些费用通常都可以得到补偿,但并不是所有的洽谈最终都会以双方签署船舶建造合同告终。如果由于各种原因,最终船厂未能和船东签署船舶建造合同的,除非双方另有约定,为船舶建造合同的洽谈和订立而产生的成本和费用通常应当由船厂自己承担。在 *Regalian Properties* 2.24

plc v London Docklands Development Corp 一案中，雇主给承包商的函包括如下内容：

> SUBJECT TO CONTRACT
> Further to your submission of 11 June 1986 in respect of the above I am pleased to inform you that the Corporation's Board has accepted your company's offer for this site, subject to(1)Contract; (2)The District Valuer's certificate of market value; (3)Your scheme achieving the desired design quality and the obtaining of detailed planning consent.

2.25　承包商为此产生了费用，但雇主和承包商最终并没有签署合同。衡平法院认为，除非合同已经订立，否则任何一方都不受约束，因洽谈产生的费用应由产生一方自己承担。Rattee 法官说：①

> Each party to such negotiations must be taken to know ... that pending the conclusion of a binding contract any cost incurred by him in preparation for the intended contract will be incurred at his own risk, in the sense that he will have no recompense for those costs if no contract results.

2.26　但是，如果船厂产生的费用并不是为了自己准备船舶建造合同的订立和履行，而是因为根据船东的要求在船舶建造合同正式签署之前就已经开始设计或其他工作的，问题就不同了。在大多数情况下，即使双方最终并没有签署船舶建造合同，但船厂因开始工作而产生的合理费用可以得到船东的补偿（quantum meruit）。正如高院的 Robert Goff 法官在 British Steel Corporation v Cleveland Bridge and Engineering Co Ltd 一案中所说的：②

> In most cases where work is done pursuant to a request contained in a letter of intent, it will not matter whether a contract did or did not come into existence; because if the party who has acted on the request is simply claiming payment, his claim will usually be based upon a *quantum meruit*, and it will make no difference whether that claim is contractual or quasi-contractual. Of course, a *quantum meruit* claim (like the old actions for money had and received, and for money paid) straddles the boundaries of what we now call contract and restitution; so the mere framing of a claim as a *quantum meruit* claim, or a claim for a

---

① [1995] 1 WLR 212 at 231.
② [1984] 1 All ER 504 at 509.

reasonable sum, does not assist in classifying the claim as contractual or quasi-contractual.

问题在于一方获得合理报酬的依据是什么。传统上有两种观点:一种观点认为之所以可以获得合理报酬是因为合同已经在双方之间成立了;另一种观点则认为获得合理报酬并不建立在已有合同成立,而是基于恢复原状。在 *British Steel Corporation* v *Cleveland Bridge and Engineering Co Ltd* 一案中,①当双方进行复杂的合同谈判期间,雇主向承包商发出了有如下内容的意向书:

2.27

> We are pleased to advise you that it is [our] intention to enter into a subcontract with your company, for the supply and delivery of the steel castings which form the roof nodes on this project .... We understand that you are already in possession of a complete set of our node detail drawings and we request that you proceed immediately with the works pending the preparation and issuing to you of the official form of subcontract.

承包商按照雇主的要求开始并完成了一部分工作,最终双方未能就一些重要问题达成协议,于是谈判失败了。法院认为承包商根据雇主要求完成的工作并不构成一个可执行的合同,但是雇主应当为承包商根据其要求完成的工作支付合理的报酬。高院的 Robert Goff 法官说:②

2.28

> For these reasons, I reject the solution of the "if" contract. In my judgment, the true analysis of the situation is simply this. Both parties confidently expected a formal contract to eventuate. In these circumstances, to expedite performance under that anticipated contract, one requested the other to commence the contract work, and the other complied with that request. If thereafter—as anticipated—a contract was entered into, the work done as requested will be treated as having been performed under that contract; if, contrary to their expectation, no contract was entered into, then the performance of the work is not referable to any contract of which the terms can be ascertained, and the law simply imposes an obligation on the party who made the request to pay a reasonable sum for such work as has been done pursuant to that request, such an obligation sounding in quasi-contract or, as we now say, in restitution.

---

① [1984] 1 All ER 504.
② [1984] 1 All ER 504 at 510.

2.29　　即使雇主默示要求承包商开始工作,承包商同样有权获得合理的报酬。在 *Marston Construction Co Ltd v Kigass Ltd* 一案中,雇主明确告知唯一中标的承包商只有在获得保险赔偿的前提下才会开始改造项目。雇主清楚地知道承包商必须在合同正式签署之前开始准备工作。双方明确约定在 1987 年 1 月 16 日签署合同,1987 年 2 月 2 日开工。雇主明确要求承包商在合同正式签订之前开始一小部分设计工作,但又默示要求承包商完成一些普通的准备工作。Peter Bowsher 法官认为无论雇主的请求是明示的还是默示的,承包商都有权获得合理数额的支付。①

2.30　　在 *Whittle Movers Ltd v Hollywood Express Ltd* ②一案中,被告是招标的雇主,而原告则是成功中标的承包商。招标文件明确规定以订立正式书面合同为准。招标文件第 2.6.3 条规定:

> Following the non-binding Letter of Intent referred to in 2.4 above, a formal contract incorporating the terms of the successful Tender Response will be finalised, and once signed this Tender contract will supersede all prior documents and discussions in respect of the supply of logistics including this Tender and the Tender Response.

2.31　　在双方正式签署合同之前,承包商已经开始工作,但最终合同未能签成。高院认为,双方之间的长期合同并没有成立,但是在双方之间已经成立一个临时合同,雇主应当按照双方在长期合同洽谈中使用的价格支付承包商已经完成的工作。雇主不服高院的判决,提起了上诉。上诉法院也认为在双方之间并不存在长期合同,因为不存在任何放弃正式合同要求的情形。上诉法院同时也认为在雇主和承包商之间并不存在所谓的临时合同。上诉法院的 Waller 法官适用了 Goff 法官在 *British Steel Corporation v Cleveland Bridge and Engineering Co Ltd* 一案中的判决,他从三个方面阐述了应当适用不当得利的原则而不应主张双方之间已经成立合同的主张,他说:③

> First, while parties are negotiating a contract under which they will, if the contract is concluded, enter into reciprocal obligations binding each other as to future performance, it is highly unlikely that by conduct they will conclude in the interim an executory contract containing terms still

---

① (1989) 15 Con LR 116.
② [2009] 2 CLC 771.
③ [2009] 2 CLC 771 at 783.

the subject of negotiation(see 510b-f). Second it is more likely that they will have entered into what Goff J refers to as an "if" contract i.e. a contract under which if one party supplies, the other agrees to pay a reasonable remuneration. Third even an "if" contract will not have been entered into if important terms such as those relating to standard of performance are still under negotiation, and in such cases the proper answer is no contract but a restitutionary remedy to the extent that one party has been unjustly enriched(see page 511).

2.32 Waller 法官认为,在当事人之间找出一个可以执行的合同不仅是困难的,而且是没有必要的,他说:①

> In my view not only was there no necessity to find some executory contract, there was a difficulty and thus no necessity in finding even what Goff J called an "if" contract because terms as to performance were still under negotiation. All negotiations were subject to contract and no binding arrangement was to come into existence until a formal document was signed.

2.33 然而,从最新的判例来看这一原则似乎又有了变化。在 *RTS Flexible Systems Ltd.v Molkerei Alois Müller GmbH &Co.K.G. (UK Productions)*②一案中,原告是承包商,被告是雇主。2005 年 2 月 21 日,雇主给承包商发出了意向书,该意向书包括如下内容:

> Project: Build, delivery, complete installation and commissioning by RTS ... of the Automated Pot Mixing Lines 1 & 2 and the De-Palletising Cell('the Equipment') for the Repack line('Repack Line') within the Repack facility in Market Drayton of ... Müller ....
>
> Thank you for your mail dated 16 February 2005 setting out your offer (number FS04014-Issue J) to supply the Equipment to Müller ("the Offer").
>
> Please accept this letter of intent as confirmation of our wish to proceed with the Project as set out in the Offer subject to the following terms:
> (i)   The agreed price for the engineering, build, delivery, installation and commissioning as set out in the Offer is GBP 1,682,000 ....
> (ii) RTS is now to commence all work required in order to meet

---

① [2009] 2 CLC 771 at 784.
② [2010] 1 WLR 753.

Müller's deadlines set out in the Offer to allow commencement of full production by Müller on the Repack Lines by 30 September 2005. Delivery of line also to be in accordance with the timetable set out in the Offer.

(iii) That the full contractual terms will be based on Müller's amended form of MF/1 contract and the full terms and the relevant technical specifications will be finalised, agreed and then signed within 4 weeks of the date of this letter. Prior to agreement on the full contractual terms, only Müller shall have the right to terminate this supply project and contract. However, should Müller terminate, Müller undertakes to reimburse RTS for the reasonable demonstrable out of pocket expenses incurred by RTS up to the date of termination. Müller will not be liable for any loss of profits (whether direct or indirect), loss of contracts, loss of anticipated savings, data, goodwill and revenue or any other indirect or consequential loss arising from such termination. No further legal rights or remedies shall be available to RTS upon such termination.

Please confirm your acceptance of the above by signing below where indicated.

2.34　一般条件的第48条规定：

48.1. This contract may be executed in any number of counterparts provided that it shall not become effective until each party has executed a counterpart and exchanged it with the other.

2.35　2005年7月5日合同可以签署了，双方没有签署合同，但项目依然在继续。项目完成后，承包商收到了70%的合同款。双方发生了争议，雇主拒绝支付剩余合同款。承包商要求雇主支付合同款，理由是根据意向书的条件，合同继续有效，或者在意向书失效后有权获得合理报酬。法院需要解决的首要问题是在雇主和承包商之间是否存在合同；若有合同存在，合同的条款又是什么。高院认为在意向书的期限届满后双方存在一个新的合同，但是该新合同不适用MF/1规定的条件。承包商提起上诉，上诉法院的 Waller 法官作出了和 *Whittle Movers Ltd* v *Hollywood Express Ltd* 一案相同的判决，即在雇主和承包商之间并不存在合同。但是最高法院却有自己的看法，最高法院的 Lord Clarke 说：①

For the reasons we have given, we have reached a different conclusion

---

① [2010] 1 WLR 753 at 784.

from both the judge and the Court of Appeal. It was agreed in the course of the argument that the court would reach its conclusions on the issues of principle before it and that the parties would subsequently have an opportunity to make submissions on the form of the order. However, subject to submissions on the precise form of order, including the precise formulation of the declarations to be made, our conclusion is that the appeal should be allowed, the order of the Court of Appeal set aside and declarations made(1)that the parties reached a binding agreement on or about 25 August on the terms agreed on or before 5 July as subsequently varied on 25 August and(2)that that binding agreement was not subject to contract or to the terms of clause 48.

从上述判例来看,法院现在似乎倾向于认定有合同的存在,并因此认为已经实际实施工作的一方可以获得合理数额的报酬。 2.36

II 合同的成立

意思表示一致

一个合同的有效成立取决于各种因素。合同成立的第一个前提或条件是合同当事人就特定事宜已经达成一致,此种一致通常体现在一方的要约得到了另一方的接受,即双方的意思表示一致(consensus ad idem)。*Chitty on Contracts* 是这样解释合同成立的条件的:① 2.37

> The first requirement for the formation of a contract is that the parties should have reached agreement. Generally speaking, the law regards an agreement as having been reached when an offer made by one of the parties (the offeror) is accepted by the other to whom the offer is addressed(the offeree or acceptor).

合同的成立以合同双方的意思表示一致为前提,而对合同是否成立的判断其实是对相关文件或文字等的解释。此种判断或解释绝非易事,正如上议院的 Lord Cairns 在 *Brogden* v *Metropolitan Railway Co* 一案中所指出的:② 2.38

> My Lords, there are no cases upon which difference of opinion may

---

① Hugh Beale, *Chitty on Contracts*, 35th edn Sweet & Maxwell 2023, para.4－001.
② (1877) 2 App Cas 666 at 672.

more readily be entertained, or which are always more embarrassing to dispose of, than cases where the court has to decide whether or not, having regard to letters and documents which have not assumed the complete and formal shape of executed and solemn agreements, a contract has really been constituted between the parties. But, on the other hand, there is no principle of law better established than this, that even although parties may intend to have their agreement expressed in the most solemn and complete form that conveyancers and solicitors are able to prepare, still there may be a consensus between the parties far short of a complete mode of expressing it, and that consensus may be discovered from letters or from other documents of an imperfect and incomplete description; I mean imperfect and incomplete as regards form.

客观标准

2.39　在判断当事人是否已经达成一致时，法院通常会适用客观标准，而不考虑当事人实际的主观想法。一旦当事人在客观上已就特定事宜达成一致的，任何一方均不得再以自己主观并未同意为由提出异议。正如王座法院的 Blackburn 法官在 *Smith* v *Hughes* 一案中所说的：①

If, whatever a man's real intention may be, he so conducts himself that a reasonable man would believe that he was assenting to the terms proposed by the other party, and that other party upon that belief enters into the contract with him, the man thus conducting himself would be equally bound as if he had intended to agree to the other party's terms.

2.40　一百多年后，上诉法院的 Steyn 法官在 *G Percy Trentham Ltd* v *Archital Luxfer Ltd* 一案中也认为，关键的是诚实人士的合理期待，他说：②

The first is the fact that English law generally adopts an objective theory of contract formation. That means that in practice our law generally ignores the subjective expectations and the unexpressed mental reservations of the parties. Instead the governing criterion is the reasonable expectations of honest men.

2.41　在 2006 年，高院的 Langley 法官在 *Covington Marine Corporation* v *Xiamen*

---

① [1871] LR6 QB 597 at 607.
② [1993] 1 Lloyd's Rep 25 at 27.

Shipbuilding Industry Co Ltd 一案中则对这一客观原则进行了归纳,他说:①

(i) The question whether or not the letters do constitute a binding agreement is one of law or mixed fact and law.

(ii) Subject only to actual knowledge on the part of the Buyers that no offer was in fact intended to be made, both alleged offer and acceptance have to be viewed objectively, the one to determine whether the offeror intended to be bound if the offer were accepted, the other to determine whether the offer or, in this case, one of the alternatives proposed, has been accepted.

(iii) Both are to be considered in their commercial context and viewed commercially rather than literally where the two might give different answers.

2.42 在适用客观标准的情况下,当事人的主观意图已不再重要,重要的是当事人对外的表达,即另一方当事人作为一个合理的人对其所表达的意图进行客观的判断。

Ⅲ 要约

要约的定义

2.43 *Chitty on Contracts* 对要约作了如下定义:②

An offer is an expression of willingness to contract on specified terms made with the intention that it is to become binding as soon as it is accepted by the person to whom it is addressed.

2.44 要约应当是明确的且肯定的,发出要约的人(offeror)通过要约向受要约人(offeree)传达了自己的缔约意图,即受法律约束的意愿。要约一旦得到接受就将在要约人和接受人之间成立合同。一般的对事实的陈述或对信息的提供并不构成要约,即使接受也不会成立合同。*Harvey v Facey* ③ 一案是一个例子,在该案中,原告向被告发报称:

---

① [2006] 1 CLC 624.
② Hugh Beale, *Chitty on Contracts*, 35th edn Sweet & Maxwell 2023, para.4-003.
③ [1893] AC 552.

Will you sell us Bumper 1893 Hall Pen? Telegraph lowest cash price – answer paid.

2.45 被告回复说：

Lowest price for Bumper Hall Pen £ 900.

2.46 原告又回复道：

We agree to buy Bumper Hall Pen for the sum of nine hundred pounds asked by you. Please send us your title deed in order that we may get early possession.

2.47 虽然原告接受了被告的价格，但枢密院认为在原告和被告之间并没有成立合同，Lord Morris 是这样说的：①

> The first telegram asks two questions. The first question is as to the willingness of LM Facey to sell to the appellants; the second question asks the lowest price, and the word "Telegraph" is in its collocation addressed to that second question only. LM Facey replied to the second question only, and gives his lowest price. The third telegram from the appellants treats the answer of LM Facey stating his lowest price as an unconditional offer to sell to them at the price named. Their Lordships cannot treat the telegram from LM Facey as binding him in any respect, except to the extent it does by its terms, viz., the lowest price. Everything else is left open, and the reply telegram from the appellants cannot be treated as an acceptance of an offer to sell to them; it is an offer that required to be accepted by LM Facey. The contract could only be completed if LM Facey had accepted the appellant's last telegram.

创立法律关系的意图

2.48 并非所有的允诺都可以成立合同，只有当要约人发出的要约具有受法律约束的意图时才可能成立合同。如果当事人并没有创设法律关系的意图，通过接受成立的协议同样不会创设法律关系。没有创设法律关系意图的情形往往出现在社交或家事中，在商业活动中则一般不会出现。上诉法院的 Scrutton 法官在 *Rose and Frank Co v J R Grompton & Bros. Ltd* 一案指出：②

---

① [1893] AC 552 at 555.
② [1923] 2 KB 261 at 288.

Now it is quite possible for parties to come to an agreement by accepting a proposal with the result that the agreement concluded does not give rise to legal relations. The reason of this is that the parties do not intend that their agreement shall give rise to legal relations. This intention may be implied from the subject-matter of the agreement, but it may also be expressed by the parties. In social and family relations such an intention is readily implied, while in business matters the opposite result would ordinarily follow.

2.49 在协议涉及商业活动时,法院通常会认定当事人有缔约意图,正如 Megaw 法官在 *Edwards v Skyways Ltd* 一案中所说的:①

Where the subject-matter of the agreement is some domestic or social relationship or transaction ... the law will often deny legal consequences to the agreement, because of the very nature of the subject-matter. Where the subject-matter of the agreement is not domestic or social, but is related to business affairs, the parties may, by using clear words, show that their intention is to make the transaction binding in honour only, and not in law; and the courts will give effect to the expressed intention.

In the present case, the subject-matter of the agreement is business relations, not social or domestic matters. There was a meeting of minds-an intention to agree. There was, admittedly, consideration for the company's promise. I accept the propositions of counsel for the plaintiff that in a case of this nature the onus is on the party who asserts that no legal effect was intended, and the onus is a heavy one.

交易的邀请

2.50 在订立合同的磋商中,一方当事人正式发出要约之前有可能已经和对方开始了通信往来,例如一方当事人要求对方提供与合同标的物有关的信息,或向对方发出交易的邀请(invitation to treat)。从 *Harvey v Facey* 一案中不难看出,要区分要约和交易的邀请并不是简单的事情。一个基本的标准是看作出陈述的一方是否有缔约的意图。通常情况下,广告不是要约而是交易的邀请或要约的邀请(invitation to offer)。船厂制定并散发的宣传册不是要约,船厂的价目表也同样也不是要约。船厂经常会参加海事推介会或类似活动,并设立自己的展台介绍自

---

① [1964] 1 WLR 349 at 354.

已制造的船舶,即使在不同的船舶上标上价格同样也不构成要约,船厂并不受这些价格的约束。船东要求船厂报价也只是交易的邀请,而船厂根据船东的要约作出的回复是否构成要约则要看回复的具体内容。

2.51　在 Gibson v Manchester City Council① 一案中,原告是租户,被告是业主。1970 年 11 月,被告向原告发出了表格和小册子,详细提供了如何购买其租用房屋的内容。原告填写了表格并寄回给了被告要求被告告知房屋的价格:

> Please inform me of the price of buying my council house. I am ... interested in obtaining a mortgage from the corporation to buy the house. Please send ... me details about the monthly repayments based on the following methods ....

2.52　1971 年 2 月 10 日被告回复称:

> I refer to your request for details of the cost of buying your council house. The corporation may be prepared to sell the house to you at the purchase price of £2,725 less 20 per cent. =£2,180(freehold).
>
> > Maximum mortgage the corporation may grant: £2,177 repayable over 20 years.
> > Annual fire insurance:　　　　　　　　£2.45
> > Monthly repayment charge, calculated by:
> > 　(i) flat rate repayment method　£19.02
>
> If you wish to pay off some of the purchase price at the start and therefore require a mortgage for less than the amount quoted above, the monthly instalment will change; in these circumstances, I will supply new figures on request. The above repayment figures apply so long as the interest rate charged on home loans is $8\frac{1}{2}$ per cent. The interest rate will be subject to variation by the corporation after giving not less than three months' written notice, and if it changes, there will be an adjustment to the monthly instalment payable. This letter should not be regarded as firm offer of a mortgage.
>
> If you would like to make formal application to buy your council house, please complete the enclosed application form and return it to me as soon as possible.

2.53　原告填了表并于 1971 年 3 月 5 日将表格寄回给了被告,但原告并没有在价

---

① [1979] 1 WLR 294.

格一栏填写,并且在信里要求被告考虑通外房屋小径上的缺陷。1971年3月12日被告回复说:

> Dear Sir, I refer to your letter concerning certain repairs to the path. Account is taken of the general condition of the property at the time of the survey and valuation and the price is fixed accordingly, allowing for such defects as there may be. I regret I cannot authorise repairs of this nature at this stage.

3月18日,原告写信要求被告: 2.54

> Ref. your letter of March 12 .... In view of your remarks I would be obliged if you will, carry on with the purchase as per my application already in your possession.

被告在由其负责保养的房屋清单中删除了原告居住的房屋,原告则对房屋开始了工作。1971年5月,被告由于政治控制的变更决定不再向租户出售房屋了,并且认为双方并没有订立合同。但是曼彻斯特郡法院的 Bailey 法官则认为在原告和被告之间已经成立了房屋买卖合同。原告于3月18日寄出的信以及申请表已经构成对被告2月10日要约的接受,因此被告应当实际履行。被告上诉,但上诉法院驳回了被告的上诉。上诉法院的 Lord Denning 说:① 2.55

> We have had much discussion as to whether Mr. Gibson's letter of March 18, 1971, was a new offer or whether it was an acceptance of the previous offer which had been made. I do not like detailed analysis on such a point. To my mind it is a mistake to think that all contracts can be analysed into the form of offer and acceptance. I know in some of the text books it has been the custom to do so: but, as I understand the law, there is no need to look for a strict offer and acceptance. You should look at the correspondence as a whole and at the conduct of the parties and see therefrom whether the parties have come to an agreement on everything that was material. If by their correspondence and their conduct you can see an agreement on all material terms—which A was intended thenceforward to be binding—then there is a binding contract in law even though all the formalities have not been gone through ....

但是 Geoffrey Lane 法官则持不同意见,他认为2月10日的信并不是一个要 2.56

---

① [1978] 1 WLR 520 at 523.

约,因为该封信的内容中包含了不少不确定的用词。Geoffrey Lane 法官说:①

> It is largely a matter of impression, but, although to Lord Denning MR and Ormrod LJ it appears perfectly plain that that was a firm offer, to me it appears equally plain that it was not. First of all, the words used "may be" in the first paragraph and "may grant a mortgage" a little lower down and finally the expression "If you would like to make a formal application to buy your council house" are strange words to use if this was indeed a formal offer on behalf of the council. It is, in my judgment, no more than one would expect of a letter coming from the city treasurer. It is a letter setting out the financial terms on which it may be the council will be prepared to consider a sale and purchase in due course.

2.57 被告上诉至上议院。上议院认为,针对一些特殊的合同很难采用通常的要约和接受的分析方式予以分析,应当通过对来往的信函进行整体的考虑。Lord Diplock 这样说:②

> My Lords, the application form and letter of March 18, 1971, were relied on by Mr. Gibson as an unconditional acceptance of the corporation's offer to sell the house; but this cannot be so unless there was a contractual offer by the corporation available for acceptance, and, for the reason already given I am of opinion that there was none.

2.58 一封信或一封电邮是否构成要约并不在于是否使用了"要约"字样;虽然明确写明"接受"的文件有可能实际上是一个"要约"。因此判断一封信或一封邮件是否构成要约或接受应当取决于其具体内容,而非其名称。

要约应包含合同主要条款

2.59 另外,要约必须包含合同必须有的关键内容,如果要约缺少能够成立合同的关键内容,要约即使得到受要约人的接受,依然不会成立对双方均有约束力的合同。上议院的 Lord Buckmaster 在 *May and Butcher, Limited* v *The King* 一案中对此予以了说明,他说:③

> In my opinion there never was a concluded contract between the parties.

---

① [1978] 1 WLR 520 at 529.
② [1979] 1 WLR 294 at 297.
③ [1934] 2 KB 17 at 20.

It has long been a well recognized principle of contract law that an agreement between two parties to enter into an agreement in which some critical part of the contract matter is left undetermined is no contract at all. It is of course perfectly possible for two people to contract that they will sign a document which contains all the relevant terms, but it is not open to them to agree that they will in the future agree upon a matter which is vital to the arrangement between them and has not yet been determined.

在同一案件中,Dunedin 子爵也对此发表了他的观点,他说的是:① 2.60

I am of the same opinion. This case arises upon a question of sale, but in my view the principles which we are applying are not confined to sale, but are the general principles of the law of contract. To be a good contract there must be a concluded bargain, and a concluded contract is one which settles everything that is necessary to be settled and leaves nothing to be settled by agreement between the parties. Of course it may leave something which still has to be determined, but then that determination must be a determination which does not depend upon the agreement between the parties.

要约的撤回

普通法的基本原则是,除非要约被接受,否则要约人可以随时撤回要约。即 2.61
使要约人在要约中已经明确规定了要约的有效期限,要约人依然可以在有效期届满之前撤回要约。在 *Routledge* v *Grant*② 一案中,被告向原告出售一栋房屋并同意原告在六周内给出确定答复。法院认为,只要原告没有接受要约,被告可以在六周内随时撤回自己的要约。Best 法官说:③

... if six weeks are given on one side to accept an offer, the other has six weeks to put an end to it. One party cannot be bound without the other. One party cannot be bound without the other.... If they are to be considered as making the offer till it is accepted, the other may say, "make no further offer, because I shall not accept it;" and to place them on an equal footing, the party who offers should have the power of retracting as well as the other of rejecting: therefore I cannot bring

---

① [1934] 2 KB 17 at 21.
② (1828) 4 Bing 653.
③ *Routledge* v *Grant*(1828) 4 Bing 653 at 660.

myself to admit that a man is bound when he says, "I will sell you goods upon certain terms, receiving your answer in course of post."

2.62 虽然要约人可以随时撤回要约,但要约人撤回要约的通知必须在传递至受要约人后才能生效。① 在 *Byrne & Co v Leon Van Tienhoven & Co*② 一案中,原告是在纽约的买方,被告则是在卡迪夫的卖方。在1879年,信件在两地的传递需要10天或11天的时间。10月1日,卖方通过信函向买方发出要约并要求买方在当月15日之前电报回复。该函于10月11日送到买方,买方于当天通过电报接受了卖方的要约。但是在买方接受要约之前即10月8日,卖方又向买方发出了撤销要约的函,该函于10月20日送递至买方。买方认为合同已经成立并于同日通过电报要求卖方履行合同。

2.63 民事法庭的 Lindley 法官在肯定了有有效期规定的要约依然可以随时被撤回的原则的基础上,提出了两个问题:即要约的撤回在传递至受要约人之前是否有任何效力,以及寄出撤回通知是否构成传递至受要约人。在此之前英国法院未曾对这两个问题作出过任何判决。针对第一个问题,Lindley 法官认为没有通知到对方的撤回不是撤回。针对第二个问题,虽然他意识到受要约人在发出接受的函时要约即视为已被接受而无需等到要约人实际收到受要约人的接受,但是 Lindley 法官认为这一原则是建立在要约人将邮局视为代理的假设之上。Lindley 法官认为这一原则不应当适用于要约的撤回,撤回要约的通知必须在传递至受要约人后才生效,他说:③

> But this principle appears to me to be inapplicable to the case of the withdrawal of an offer. In this particular case I can find no evidence of any authority in fact given by the plaintiffs to the defendants to notify a withdrawal of their offer by merely posting a letter; and there is no legal principle or decision which compels me to hold, contrary to the fact, that the letter of the 8th of October is to be treated as communicated to the plaintiff on that day or on any day before the 20th, when the letter reached them. But before that letter had reached the plaintiffs they had accepted the offer, both by telegram and by post; and they had themselves resold the tin plates at a profit. In my opinion the withdrawal by the defendants on the 8th of October of their offer of the 1st was

---

① Hugh Beale, *Chitty on Contracts*, 35th edn Sweet & Maxwell 2023, para.4-116.
② (1880) 5 CPD 344.
③ (1880) 5 CPD 344 at 348.

inoperative; and a complete contract binding on both parties was entered into on the 11th of October, when the plaintiffs accepted the offer of the 1st, which they had no reason to suppose had been withdrawn.

普通法中关于要约、接受以及要约撤回生效时间的规定在今天可能只有学术意义上的价值了。在当今国际商业活动中，随着通信技术的快速发展，使用信函相互传递各自缔约意图已经变得无法想象了。当前使用最为广泛的通信方式应当是电子邮件等利用电子手段提供信息交换的通信方式。虽然这种被称为瞬间通信(instantaneous communication)的电子邮件未必真正会在几秒钟之内将信息传达至世界各地，但在使用电子邮件的今天应当已不太可能发生 *Byrane* 一案中的情形了。绝大多数船舶建造合同的洽谈往往也是通过电子邮件的方式进行的，因此上述案例的实用价值并不大。

2.64

问题单

船东在正式与船厂就船舶建造进行接触之前往往会对目标船厂有一个初步的评估。之所以称之为初步评估主要是因为船东与目标船厂通常没有直接的接触，而是通过新造船经纪人或其他船东的介绍来进行。在完成初步评估且对目标船厂有缔约倾向时，船东往往会准备一份问题单，列出船东希望船厂作出答复的问题。船厂对船东的问题单作出了答复，船东就能更进一步了解船厂的具体相关情况。问题单里的问题通常涉及：船厂的组织结构情况（有时船东会要求船厂提供相关的文件）、船厂股东的基本情况、财务状况及相关数据（有时船东会要求船东提供最新的财务报表）、船厂的设施、设备及其建造能力、船舶建造的经历和经验、船厂的设计和制图程序、船厂的管理及质量体系、船厂员工及其保险情况、船厂现有的订单情况及其建造进程等其他情况。问题单通常不构成船东的要约。

2.65

Ⅳ 接受

接受的定义

接受是指收到要约的人对要约表示同意的意思表示，在 *Chitty on Contracts* 中，接受的定义是：①

2.66

---

① Hugh Beale, *Chitty on Contracts*, 35th edn Sweet & Maxwell 2023, para.4－032.

> An acceptance is a final and unqualified expression of assent, whether by words or conduct, to the terms of an offer.

2.67　接受必须是无条件的,只有无条件的接受才会成立一个对双方都有约束力的合同。如果要约规定了接受方式,只有符合规定接受方式的接受才是有效的接受。如果要约未规定接受方式,则接受可以采用口头或书面等明示方式,也可以采用行为的方式。接受应当是对要约条件表示最终的、无条件的同意。有时双方的洽谈过程比较长,各自在来往的信件或邮件中可能作出了让步,或者提出了新的要求等。在这种情况下,确定要约何时得到接受并不是一件简单的事。法院通常会对所有的来往信件或邮件进行分析,从而确定双方是否已经就合同的主要条款达成一致。如果已经达成一致了,合同即已成立。如果没有达成一致,合同就不存在。

接受必须是明确肯定的

2.68　由于合同是在要约得到接受之时成立的,因此接受就必须是明确的和肯定的,否则就不构成接受。在 *Peter Lind & Co Ltd* v *Mersey Docks & Harbour Board*① 一案中,被告要求原告为集装箱码头的建造投两个标,一个是采用固定价格的投标;另一个是价格随人工和材料价格变动而变化的投标。1970 年 3 月 26 日,雇主接受了承包商的报价,但雇主只是说接受"your tender"。接着雇主按照固定价格的投标准备了签署正式合同所需的文件并要求承包商开始工作。1970 年 4 月 15 日,雇主通知承包商称:

> Further to my letter dated 26th March, 1970, I am arranging for the necessary documents to be prepared for a formal contract to be entered into between the Board and yourselves on the basis of the fixed price tender.

2.69　承包商按照雇主的要求开始了工作但拒绝签署正式合同,承包商主张雇主并没有接受固定价格的投标,承包商可以以成本增加为由提高合同价格。高院的 Cooke 法官对 3 月 26 日以及 4 月 15 日函进行了分析,Cooke 法官认为 3 月 26 日的函并不构成一个接受,他说:②

> It seems to me that an acceptance, in order to be unequivocal, must be

---

① [1972] 2 Lloyd's Rep 234.
② [1972] 2 Lloyd's Rep 234 at 240.

unequivocal to the businessman as well as to the lawyer. I do not think that the first paragraph of the Board's letter of Mar. 26 combines those qualities; and if the paragraph had stood alone, I should not have regarded it as an unequivocal acceptance of the fixed price offer.

But, of course, the paragraph does not stand alone and the letter must be considered as a whole. In the second paragraph the defendants say that the plaintiffs' letter of Feb. 19 to the stores and purchasing manager is receiving consideration. It seems to me that there are at any rate two meanings which that paragraph may bear. One is: "We are still considering but have not yet decided whether to agree to your withdrawing the fixed price offer". Another is: "We are still considering but have not yet decided whether the figure named in your fixed price offer should be increased, and if so by how much, to take account of the factors mentioned in your letter of Feb. 19". On either interpretation the paragraph is inconsistent with contractual finality. Taking the letter of Mar. 26 as a whole, I think it left the parties in the position of still being in negotiation on the question of price.

2.70 Cooke 法官在对 4 月 15 日的函进行了分析后也认为该函同样不构成接受,他说:①

I come now to the defendants' letter of Apr. 15 informing the plaintiffs that formal contractual documents are being prepared on the basis of the fixed price tender. It is, I think, impossible to regard that letter as an acceptance of the plaintiffs' fixed price offer because that offer had by its terms expired on Mar. 29, 1970.

2.71 要约的接受不能有改变,否则便构成反要约,而不是接受。"镜像原则"(mirror image rule)的要求是只有当接受是要约的镜像时合同才成立。接受要约的一方若改变要约的内容或增加新的内容,按照镜像原则,合同并不成立。

接受生效的时间

2.72 由于合同是在要约得到接受之时成立的,因此接受生效的时间至关重要。在普通法中,关于接受生效时间的规定随着通信技术的发展经历了自己的发展历程。

---

① Ibid.

传统的接受生效时间

2.73　与要约生效的时间不同,普通法中传统的接受时间是受要约人发出接受之时,这一原则应当是在 Adams v Lindsell ①一案中确立的。在该案中,被告是一个羊毛商人,1817 年 9 月 2 日被告给羊毛制造商的原告写信说:

> We now offer you eight hundred tods of wether fleeces, of a good fair quality of our country wool, at 35s. 6d. per tod, to be delivered at Leicester, and to be paid for by two months' bill in two months, and to be weighed up by your agent within fourteen days, receiving your answer in course of post.

2.74　但是被告将该封信寄错了地方,原告一直到 9 月 5 日下午 7:00 才收到该封信。收到信的当天,原告写信回复并接受了被告的要约。被告在 9 月 9 日收到原告的接受,但是被告由于在 9 月 8 日没有收到原告的接受而将羊毛出售给了第三人。Burrough 法官认为延误是由于被告的疏忽造成的,因此被告应当对损失承担责任。法院认为如果合同要在接受传递至要约人之后才成立,合同就可能无法通过信件成立了。如果被告在要约被原告接受后依然不受约束而必须在收到接受后才受约束,那么原告在收到被告已经接受要约的通知之前也不应当受约束。这样就可能没完没了了。因此,法院认为合同是在要约得到接受之时成立的。Burrough 法官说:②

> The defendants must be considered in law as making, during every instant of the time their letter was travelling, the same identical offer to the plaintiffs; and then the contract is completed by the acceptance of it by the latter. Then as to the delay in notifying the acceptance, that arises entirely from the mistake of the defendants, and it therefore must be taken as against them, that the plaintiffs' answer was received in course of post.

2.75　在 Henthorn v Fraser ③一案中,被告作为业主的代理人向原告出售房屋,要约规定原告可以在 14 天内接受要约。在原告收到要约的当天,业主向原告发函撤回要约。当天 15:50,原告发出了接受要约的函,然而在 17:00,原告又收到了

---

① (1818) 1 B & Ald 681.
② (1818) 1 B & Ald 681 at 683.
③ [1892] 2 Ch 27.

业主的撤回通知。衡平法院认为双方的合同已在原告发出接受要约通知,即 15:50 就成立了。因为发信原则(postal rule)把邮局视为要约人的代理人,受要约人发出接受通知视为接受已经传递至要约人。衡平法院的 Lord Herschell 在该案中说:①

> I should prefer to state the rule thus: Where the circumstances are such that it must have been within the contemplation of the parties that, according to the ordinary usages of mankind, the post might be used as a means of communicating the acceptance of an offer, the acceptance is complete as soon as it is posted.

对接受生效时间的质疑

区别对待撤回要约通知生效的时间和接受生效的时间从一开始就曾受到过质疑。在 Household Fire Insurance Co v Grant ②一案中,衡平法院的大多数法官一致认为对要约的接受应当在交付邮局之时生效。但是 Bramwell 法官则对这一原则提出了质疑,他说:③

2.76

> It is impossible to hold, if I offer my landlord to sell him some hay and he writes accepting my offer, and in the same letter gives me notice to quit, and posts his letter which, however, does not reach me, that he has communicated to me his acceptance of my offer, but not his notice to quit. Suppose a man has paid his tailor by cheque or banknote, and posts a letter containing a cheque or banknote to his tailor, which never reaches, is the tailor paid? If he is, would he be if he had never been paid before in that way? ... The question then is, is posting a letter which is never received a communication to the person addressed, or an equivalent, or something which dispenses with it? ... My answer beforehand to any argument that may be urged is, that it is not a communication, and that there is no agreement to take it as an equivalent for or to dispense with a communication.

瞬间通信条件下接受生效的时间

就接受在受要约人发出信函之时生效的原则而言,虽然把邮局视为要约人的

2.77

---

① [1892] 2 Ch 27 at 33.
② [1879] 4 Ex D 216.
③ [1879] 4 Ex D 216 at 234.

代理人可以在理论上排除一些障碍,但这一原则同样存在不少问题,例如要约人并不知情,即使在要约的有效期届满后向其他人另行发出相同的要约同样会面临第一个要约已经得到接受的困境。从上述判词中可以看出,接受在发出之时生效的原则并非适用于所有情形。随着瞬间通信方式越来越多的使用,以发信作为接受生效时间的做法亦开始显得不合时宜。

2.78　　在 *Entores Ltd* v *Miles Far East Corp* ①一案中,法院鉴于当时已经在商业中使用电传没有适用发信原则,而是认为通过电传发出的接受只有在传递至要约人后才生效。在该案中,原告是一家英国公司,被告是一家在荷兰阿姆斯特丹有分公司的美国公司。合同是通过电传的方式在伦敦的原告与在荷兰的分公司之间订立的。1954年9月8日,荷兰公司发出的电传是:

> Offer for account our associates Miles Far East Corporation Tokyo up to 400 tons Japanese cathodes sterling 240 longton c.i.f. shipment Mitsui Line September 28 or October 10 payment by letter of credit. Your reply Telex Amsterdam 12174 or phone 31490 before 4 p.m. invited.

2.79　　英国公司回复称:

> Accept 100 longtons cathodes Japanese shipment latest October 10 sterling £23910s. longton c.i.f. London/Rotterdam payment letter of credit stop please confirm latest tomorrow.

2.80　　荷兰公司回复:

> We received O.K. Thank you.

2.81　　1954年9月9日,英国公司通过电传说:

> Regarding our telephone conversation a few minutes ago we note that there is a query on the acceptance of our bid for 100 tons payment in sterling and you are ascertaining that your Tokyo office will confirm the price to be longton we therefore await to hear from you further.

2.82　　1954年9月10日,英国公司又通过电传称:

> Is the price for the sterling cathodes understood to be for longton by Japan as you were going to find this out yesterday?

---

① [1955] 2 QB 327.

荷兰公司的回复是： 2.83

Yes, price £23910s. for longton.

双方的争议是,合同是在哪里成立的。上诉法院的 Denning 法官首先对通过 2.84
信函订立的合同与通过电传订立的合同予以了区分,他说:①

> When a contract is made by post it is clear law throughout the common law countries that the acceptance is complete as soon as the letter is put into the post box, and that is the place where the contract is made. But there is no clear rule about contracts made by telephone or by Telex. Communications by these means are virtually instantaneous and stand on a different footing.

Denning 法官首先以口头方式订立合同为例,他说当他口头向河对岸或院子 2.85
另一边的另一个人发出要约时头上飞过一架飞机,他因而没有听到那个人的回
答。在那一刻合同并不成立。如果那人希望订立合同,那人就必须等飞机飞过以
后再说一遍,以便让他能够听见。他只有在听到那人的回答以后才受合同的约
束。接着,Denning 法官又以电话方式订立合同为例,他假设自己在电话里向另
一个人发出要约,由于电话在对方回答时突然断了,他没能听到那人的接受。在
那一刻合同依然不成立。虽然那人并不知道电话断线的确切时间,但他应当知道
电话通话中断了。如果那人希望订立合同就必须再一次接通电话重复自己的接
受。合同并不是在第一次电话通话时成立的,而是在第二次电话通话时成立的。
如果那人不再通话,合同便不会成立。合同只有在他听到了那人的回答后才成
立。最后,Denning 法官以电传方式订立合同为例,他假设在伦敦办公室里的一
名职员在电传机上发出了要约,该要约马上在曼彻斯特办公室里的电传机上记录
了下来。曼彻斯特办公室里的一名职员在电传机上发出了接受。如果线路在发
出接受时中断,电传就会停止。在那一刻显然没有合同成立。在曼彻斯特办公室
里的职员必须再发一次电传,完成他接受要约的发报。但是有可能发生的是,虽
然线路没有中断,但报文仍然没有发至伦敦,有可能伦敦办公室里的电传机的油
墨用完了。在这种情况下,在曼彻斯特办公室里的职员并不知道,但在伦敦办公
室里的职员则会发现问题并立即发出电传告诉对方自己没有收到对方的电文。
这样,在曼彻斯特办公室里的职员就会再发一遍接受报文。合同只有在伦敦办公
室收到曼彻斯特的接受报文时才会成立。在上述三个例子中,发出接受的一方知

---

① [1955] 2 QB 327 at 332.

道或者有理由知道自己的接受并没有传递到对方。因此他必须重复接受。然而，如果他不知道接受没有传递至对方或者知道接受已经传递至对方，例如发出要约的人在电话中没有听到对方接受的答复，但他不再要求对方重复；或者职员在发现电传机油墨已用完时也不要求对方再一次发出电文，在这种情况下，发出接受的一方可以合理地相信自己的接受应当传递至要约人。但若要约人没有任何过失但没有收到接受，而发出接受的人又合理地相信接受已经传递至对方。在这种情况下，Denning 法官认为合同不成立。他说：①

> My conclusion is that the rule about instantaneous communications between the parties is different from the rule about the post. The contract is only complete when the acceptance is received by the offeror: and the contract is made at the place where the acceptance is received.

接受在收到时生效原则的确立

2.86　在 *Brinkibon Ltd v Stahag Stahl Und Stahlwarenhandels GmbH* 一案中，上诉人认为法院应当对 *Entores* 一案的判决予以重新考虑，但是上议院确认了 *Entores* 一案的判决，上议院的 Lord Wilberforce 说：②

> In *Entores Ltd* v *Miles Far East Corporation* [1955] 2 QB 327 the Court of Appeal classified them with instantaneous communications. Their ruling, which has passed into the textbooks, including *Williston on Contracts*, 3rd ed (1957), appears not to have caused either adverse comment, or any difficulty to business men. I would accept it as a general rule. Where the condition of simultaneity is met, and where it appears to be within the mutual intention of the parties that contractual exchanges should take place in this way, I think it a sound rule, but not necessarily a universal rule.

2.87　Lord Wilberforce 认为通过电话或无线电通信方式缔约的，合同应当在受要约人将接受传递至要约人之时成立，他说：③

> Now such review as is necessary must be made against the background of the law as to the making of contracts. The general rule, it is hardly

---

① [1955] 2 QB 327 at 333.
② [1983] 2 AC 34 at 42.
③ [1983] 2 AC 34 at 41.

necessary to state, is that a contract is formed when acceptance of an offer is communicated by the offeree to the offeror .... In the common case of contracts, whether oral or in writing *inter praesentes*, there is no difficulty; and again logic demands that even where there is not mutual presence at the same place and at the same time, if communication is instantaneous, for example by telephone or radio communication, the same result should follow.

电子邮件的接受时间

2.88 在 *David Baxter Edward Thomas, Peter Sandford Gander* v *BPE Solicitors* 一案中,高院的 Blair 法官认为 Lord Wilberforce 在 *Brinkibon* 一案中的判决同样适用于通过电子邮件订立合同的情形。他说:①

> Contrary to the claimants' submissions, in my view the same principle applies to communication by email, at least where the parties are conducting the matter by email ....

2.89 在如何确定电子邮件收到时间的问题上,Blair 法官的观点是:②

> Once one sets aside the "postal rule" as inapplicable to email communications, the question whether an email acceptance is effective when it arrives, or at the time when the offeror could reasonably be expected to have read it, is not a straightforward one, and does not appear to be settled by authority. On the basis that it must be resolved by reference to the intentions of the parties, by sound business practice and in some cases by a judgment where the risks should lie (*Brinkibon* at page 42), the answer does however appear to me to be clear in the present case. In the context in which the 18:00 email was sent—that is a transaction which (as the earlier emails show) could have been completed that evening—I do not consider that 18:00 was outside working hours. The email was available to be read within working hours, despite the fact that [the recipient] had in fact gone home. For that reason, I would have held that ... as a matter of law such acceptance would have been effective upon the receipt of the email at or about 18:00.

---

① [2010] EWHC 306 at [86], see also *Damian Ratilal Chunilal* v *Merrill Lynch International Incorporated* [2010] EWHC 1467.
② [2010] EWHC 306 at [90].

2.90　如前所述,电子邮件在船舶建造合同洽谈中得到相当广泛的采用,实际上几乎已没有不采用电子邮件进行洽谈的船舶建造合同了。电子邮件的使用不仅停留在船舶建造合同的洽谈阶段,而且也在船舶建造合同履行阶段得到广泛的采用,包括从设计图纸的传递到变更项目的磋商,乃至船东驻厂代表与船厂项目经理的日常联系等。

以行为表示的接受

2.91　虽然在大多数情况下合同双方会通过书信洽谈并订立合同,但是要约同样可以通过行为来接受。在 G Percy Trentham Ltd v Archital Luxfer Ltd and Others ① 一案中,原告是一个从事设计和建造的承包商,被告则是一个分包商。原告承包的工程分为两个阶段,每个阶段都有被告负责的工作。被告首先向原告发出了要约,要约的条件是适用被告自己的条款和条件。原告没有接受被告的要约,而是发出了自己的反要约,该反要约的规定虽然列出了被告的工作范围和价格,但规定适用原告自己的条款和条件。另外还规定:

> ... subject to (a) Form of sub-contract being entered into ... (b) the signing and immediate return of the attached acknowledgment slip.

2.92　实际上既没有格式,也没有确认回折。后来双方又约定合同为固定费用合同。被告完成了约定的工作,原告则支付了约定的报酬。但双方始终没有签署过任何书面合同。原告以工程有缺陷为由与被告开始了合同之诉,但被告否认合同已经成立。上诉法院的 Steyn 法官认为,在合同已经履行完毕后再主张合同没有成立的做法应当是很难接受的。合同可以通过行为而成立。Steyn 法官说: ②

> In a case where the transaction was fully performed the argument that there was no evidence upon which the Judge could find that a contract was proved is implausible. A contract can be concluded by conduct .... The argument that there was insufficient evidence to support a finding that a contract was concluded is wrong .... I am, in any event, satisfied that in this fully executed transaction a contract came into existence during performance even if it cannot be precisely analysed in terms of offer and acceptance. And it does not matter that a contract

---

① [1993] 1 Lloyd's Rep 25.
② [1993] 1 Lloyd's Rep 25 at 29.

came into existence after part of the work had been carried out and paid for. The conclusion must be that when the contract came into existence it impliedly governed pre-contractual performance.

沉默

前文讨论的是受要约人通过行为接受要约,虽然以行为接受的方式可以理解为是一种沉默,但这里讨论的沉默是指受要约人既没有以语言表示接受或拒绝,也没有通过行为表示接受或拒绝的情形。一般的原则是沉默不构成接受,即使要约明确规定可以通过沉默接受,或者规定在一定期限内没有拒绝的则视为接受,但沉默依然不构成接受。这一原则的理由是要约人不能给受要约人创设回复要约的义务。而且,沉默通常是比较含糊的,并不明确。在 *Jayaar Impex Ltd* v *Toaken Group Ltd* 一案中,高院的 Rix 法官说:①

2.93

> If it were otherwise, the sellers would be imposing on the buyers the obligation to negate the sellers' offer to vary fundamentally the parties' contract; whereas in principle the sellers, if in doubt about whether their offer to amend had been accepted in the absence of a signed and returned document, should have been querying the matter with the buyers expressly rather than relying on silence.

在船舶建造合同的洽谈中,因一方沉默导致双方纠纷的情形应当不会多见,因为船舶建造合同从开始洽谈直到合同成立的整个过程几乎不可能仅通过信函或电子邮件完成,双方几乎肯定会见面。在绝大多数情况下,船舶建造合同一般都会采用书面的正式合同文本由双方代表签署成立。

2.94

反要约

受要约人在收到要约后可以接受,也可以拒绝。一旦要约被拒绝就不复存在了,受要约人不能再次接受该要约。但是由于受要约人并没有回复要约的义务,因此不愿接受要约的受要约人通常不会对要约作出拒绝的表示。有时,受要约人在整体上愿意接受要约,但不愿意接受要约的某些条件,例如在船舶建造合同中,船厂接受船东提出的船价,但是不愿接受合同规定的交船日或者可允许延误的计算方式等;或者受要约人愿意就要约人提出的交易按照自己的方式和条件继续进

2.95

---

① [1996] 2 Lloyd's Rep 437 at 445.

行洽谈,例如船东希望采用固定价格的方式,而船厂则希望采用材料加人工的方式。这时受要约人就可以针对相关条件提出自己的意见。受要约人提出的意见通常被称为反要约,反要约是指在进行磋商的双方当事人中的一方就对方提出的要约作出修改的一种意思表示。

2.96 　　与拒绝要约相同,反要约由于对要约的内容进行了修改、删除或增加,因此构成了对要约的拒绝。在 *Hyde v Wrench*① 一案中,被告向原告发出要约,出售自己的农场,报价1,000英镑,原告还价950英镑但遭到被告的拒绝。两天后,原告向被告表示愿意以1,000英镑的价格购买农场,但被告对此不感兴趣。双方于是开始诉讼,Lord Langdale 认为:②

> Under the circumstances stated in this bill, I think there exists no valid binding contract between the parties for the purchase of the property. The Defendant offered to sell it for £1,000, and if that had been at once unconditionally accepted, there would undoubtedly have been a perfect binding contract; instead of that, the Plaintiff made an offer of his own, to purchase the property for £950, and he thereby rejected the offer previously made by the Defendant. I think that it was not afterwards competent for him to revive the proposal of the Defendant, by tendering an acceptance of it; and that, therefore, there exists no obligation of any sort between the parties; the demurrer must be allowed.

2.97 　　只要受要约人提出了与要约的规定不同的条件,无论受要约人是否将其回复称为接受,该回复只能是反要约,而不是接受。除非得到要约人的同意,否则就无法再接受该要约了。③ 附条件的接受,或对要约内容进行任何实质性修改的接受,或增加新的内容的接受都不是法律意义上的接受,都不会导致成立对双方都有约束力的合同。上述接受实际上是一个反要约,其法律结果是向要约人发出了一个新的要约。从本质上讲,反要约其实就是一个要约,一旦得到对方的接受就可以成立对双方均有约束力的合同。

2.98 　　然而,接受必须和要约一致并不是指逐字逐句的完全一致,只要没有相反的意思就应当是一致的。如果在回复要约时使用了"we hereby confirm"等字眼的则很有可能构成接受。在 *Anangel Atlas Compania Naviera SA and Others* v

---

① (1840) 3 Beavan 334.
② (1840) 3 Beavan 334 at 337.
③ Hugh Beale, *Chitty on Contracts*, 35th edn Sweet & Maxwell 2023, para.4–122.

Ishikawajima-Harima Heavy Industries Co Ltd(No.2) ①一案中,原告是船东,被告是船厂。原告是被告的长期客户。1984—1985 年间,航运市场萧条,原告寻求被告降低合同价格以及合同的其他变更且得到了船厂的帮助。其他船东也向船厂提出了类似的要求并也得到了一定的满足。7 月 16 日,船东向船厂发函,内容如下:

> This letter is intended to serve as a confirmation of the general agreement established between Buyers and Builders in connection with the delivery status of the captioned vessels.
>
> The standard of construction and outfitting of the aforesaid vessels shall be at least equal to that applied to other vessels of this series built and delivered to the respective Buyers during the contract and construction period covered by the four contracts under reference.
>
> The Builder hereby confirms that the net contract prices of the captioned vessels (Hulls 2866/7/8/9) as agreed upon between the contracting parties are not more than the said net contract price of sisterships built by I.H.I. and delivered to the respective other Buyers.
>
> As a condition of the Delivery & Acceptance of Hull 2869 by the Buyer of said vessel it has been mutually agreed upon between Buyers and Builders that in the event the Builder shall build and sell any of the sisterships (excluding resales) to other Buyers at lower net contract prices and the equivalent of corresponding payment terms that the net prices received by Builders from the respective Buyers of Hulls 2866/7/8/9 with deliveries within mid 1986 the Builder shall reimburse the respective Buyers of Hulls 2866/7/8/9 in the equivalent of the difference in said net contract prices. Such payments shall be made by IHI to the respective Buyers within 90 days after the date of said alternate deliveries to other Buyers, in a manner to be mutually agreed upon in writing in advance of said due payment.
>
> It is hereby likewise agreed upon between the parties hereto that the Builder shall at Builders cost incorporate any new and/or additional features in the said four vessels which additional features are also provided in the aforesaid other new vessels by the Builder without extra cost to the respective Buyers.

---

① [1990] 2 Lloyd's Rep 526.

2.99　　7月18日,船厂回复称:

With reference to your letter of 16th July 1985 on the captioned subject, we would like to express to you our deep appreciation for your continued co-operation and assistance extended to us for construction of the vessels, IHI Hulls Nos. 2866/7 and 2868/9. We hereby confirm to you the following for the sake of good order:

(a) The standard of construction and outfitting of the said vessels are at least equal to those applied to other vessels of the series built and delivered to respective buyers during the contract and construction period for the aforesaid four(4)vessels.

(b) The respective net contract prices for the captioned four(4)vessels as agreed upon between the contracting parties are not more than the net contract price of the sisterships built by us and delivered to respective Buyers.

(c) Subject to the buyer's taking delivery of Hull 2869 from us on 25th July, 1985, we agree that in the event we shall build and sell any of the sisterships to other buyers at lower net contract prices than the net prices received by us from the respective buyers of Hulls 2866/7/8/9 and for deliveries by 30th June, 1986, we shall re-imburse the respective buyers of Hulls 2866/7/8/9 in the equivalent of the difference in the said net contract prices, provided however that such re-imbursement shall not be made in the case where resales and deliveries of the sisterships are compelled and effected owing to contractual default by any original buyer(s)of such sistership(s)and further in calculation of the differ-ence in the net contract prices, actual payment terms applied to such sisterships shall be taken into account in comparison with the payment terms applied to Hulls 2866/7/8/9.

Settlement of the reimbursement, if any, shall be made in such manner as will be agreed upon between the respective buyers of Hulls 2866/7/8/9 and us after respective deliveries of such sisterships to other buyers.

(d) We shall incorporate at our cost any new and/or additional features in the said four vessels if and when such new and/or additional features shall have been provided in the aforesaid sisterships by us without extra cost to respective other buyers.

This undertaking shall not be applied to the case where such new and/or additional features are specifically forced to facilitate the resale of the sisterships, necessitated by the original buyers' contractual default.

(e) All the provisions of above(a), (b), (c)and(d) are final and binding upon both principal parties to the respective contracts under reference herein under the British laws as practiced in London, England, as of the date hereof, despite any provisions of the said contracts.

双方的争议是,船东认为自己的第一封信是一个要约,而船厂的第二封信则是一个接受。船厂则认为第二封信其实是一个反要约,因为至少有四处是与第一封信不一致的。第一,船东信中的"such payments"在船厂的回复中被改为了"settlement of the reimbursement",这是一个重要的不同之处,但是法院认为"reimbursement"意味着"payment",而且船东也使用了相同的字。第二,船东提及的"condition of the delivery"与船厂提及的不同,船东没有指明特定的日期,而船厂则特指 7 月 25 日,但法院认为船东提及交船显然可以理解为是指 7 月 25 日。第三,船厂提到的"compelled and effective owing to contractual default by any original buyer"一句的含义显然要比船东的"resales"更为广泛,但法院认为船厂并没有给"resales"一字增加任何内容。第四,船厂在(d)段中增加了"resales"实际上增加了船东信中所没有的新的内容,但是法院则认为船东信中的倒数第二段中的"likewise"具有完全相同的作用。高院的 Hirst 法官认为合同已经成立,他说:①

2.100

> In my judgment the position is precisely the opposite, seeing that in the first paragraph IHI state expressly, with reference to Mr. Campbell's letter, that they –
>
>> ... hereby confirm ... the following for the sake of good order ...
>
> This is the clearest possible objective indication of an intention to accept, and cannot possibly be explained away, as Mr. Hunt argued, on the footing that they are doing no more than confirm a different version of the understanding referred to in the first paragraph of Mr. Campbell's letter. It follows that I hold that the IHI letter was indeed an acceptance of Mr. Campbell's offer . . . .

格式之战

有时交易双方均有自己的标准条款和条件,而且还可能各自坚持使用自己的

2.101

---

① [1990] 2 Lloyd's Rep 526 at 542.

条款和条件。在这种情况下,双方关于合同的洽谈可能仅仅针对合同的一些基本条款,例如价格条款等。洽谈双方通过各自的标准格式洽谈合同条款的,通常被称为"格式之战"。*Butler Machine Tool Co Ltd* v *Ex-Cell-O Corporation(England) Ltd* ①是一个典型的格式之战案例。在该案中,卖方原告于1969年5月23日向买方被告发出要约,报了价格和交货期。报价单的背面是卖方的合同条款,其中的价格变更条款规定合同价格以交货当日的价格为准。卖方的合同条款有如下内容:

> All orders are accepted only upon and subject to the terms set out in our quotation and the following conditions. These terms and conditions shall prevail over any terms and conditions in the buyer's order.

2.102 其中的价格变更条款规定:

> Prices are based on present day costs of manufacture and design and having regard to the delivery quoted and uncertainty as to the cost of labour, materials etc. during the period of manufacture, we regret that we have no alternative but to make it a condition of acceptance of order that goods will be charged at prices ruling upon date of delivery.

2.103 1969年5月27日,买方在收到报价后向卖方订货,买方的订单有如下内容:

> Please supply on terms and conditions as below and overleaf.

2.104 买方订单列出了订购的货物,但是与卖方的报价有些不同:(1)增加了安装费用;(2)交货期有所不同。在买方订单的最后有一张可以撕下的纸,上面写着:

> Acknowledgment: Please sign and return to Ex-Cell-O. We accept your order on the terms and conditions stated thereon—and undertake to deliver by—Date—signed.

2.105 其中交货期和签署处均为空白,由卖方填写。1969年6月5日,卖方写信给买方称:

> We have pleasure in acknowledging receipt of your official order dated May 27 covering the supply of one Butler Double Column Plane-Miller. This being delivered in accordance with our revised quotation of May 23 for delivery in 10/11 months, ie March/April 1970. We return herewith

---

① [1979] 1 WLR 401,并见 *Tekdata Interconnections Ltd* v *Amphenol Ltd* [2009] 2 CLC 866.

duly, completed your acknowledgment of order form.

2.106 卖方在确认条上填写了1970年3月或4月为交货期。在卖方交货时价格上涨了,于是卖方要求买方支付额外的数额。买方拒绝支付额外费用,买方说:

> We did not accept the sellers' quotation as it was. We gave an order for the self-same machine at the self-same price, but on the back of our order we had our own terms and conditions. Our terms and conditions did not contain any price variation clause.

2.107 高院的 Thesiger 法官认为,在买卖双方之间的合同包含了价格变更条款。但是上诉法院推翻了 Thesiger 法官的判决,上诉法院的 Lord Denning 说:①

> If those documents are analysed in our traditional method, the result would seem to me to be this: the quotation of May 23, 1969, was an offer by the sellers to the buyers containing the terms and conditions on the back. The order of May 27, 1969, purported to be an acceptance of that offer in that it was for the same machine at the same price, but it contained such additions as to cost of installation, date of delivery and so forth that it was in law a rejection of the offer and constituted a counter-offer.... The letter of the sellers of June 5, 1969, was an acceptance of that counter-offer, as is shown by the acknowledgment which the sellers signed and returned to the buyers. The reference to the quotation of May 23 referred only to the price and identity of the machine.

2.108 在谈及如何在各种格式中确认构成合同条款时,Lord Denning 说:②

> [I]t will be found that in most cases when there is a "battle of forms," there is a contract as soon as the last of the forms is sent and received without objection being taken to it....

2.109 格式之战有一个"最后一枪原则"(last shot rule),其含义是在格式之战中放最后一枪,即最后提出己方条件和条款且未遭另一方当事人明确反对的一方获胜。但在 *TRW Ltd* v *Panasonic Industry Europe GmbH*③ 格式之战中获胜的却不是放最后一枪的一方。这是一个关于法律适用和管辖权条款的案例。首先提出

---

① [1979] 1 WLR 401 at 404.
② [1979] 1 WLR 401 at 404, 405.
③ [2021] EWHC 19(TCC),并见 Hugh Beale, *Chitty on Contracts*, 35ᵗʰ edn Sweet & Maxwell 2023, para. 4-045.

适用己方条件和条款的被告明确对法律和管辖权条款的适用作了保留,法院认为除非缔约另一方对法律适用条款和管辖权条款明确提出反对,否则"最后一枪"并不能改变对方条件和条款中对法律适用和管辖权条款的适用。

V 意向书

2.110　船舶建造合同洽谈所需时间的长短可能会受到各种因素的影响,船舶设计比较复杂的,尤其是采用新技术的船舶建造合同就可能需要较长时间的谈判。为了谈判,船东和船厂都必须投入较多的人力、物力,然而任何一方均无订立合同的义务。在这种情况下,船东和船厂会签署一份意向书,表明双方当事人将认真磋商合同的订立。

意向书的性质

2.111　意向书通常被认为是不具有合同约束力的文件,只是表明了当事人有在将来订立合同的意向而已,但是英国普通法中也有不少将意向书视为对当事方有约束力的合同的案例。在很大程度上,意向书的实际性质往往取决于对当事人之间的来往信函以及行为进行适当的解释。对于意向书是否构成有约束力合同的问题并没有一个直截了当的答案,而必须根据具体案件的具体情况作出判断。① 在 *A C Controls Limited* v *British Broadcasting Corporation* 一案中,高院的 Thornton 法官对相关先例进行了总结后将意向书的效力归纳为以下几种:②

1. A document called or treated by the parties as a letter of intent may, on analysis, give rise to a binding contract, if that is the effect of the language of the parties when objectively construed. That contract is one in which, pending the entering into of a formal contract governing the whole of the project, the parties have assumed reciprocal obligations towards each whose content is defined by the terms of the document.

2. Alternatively, the document may, on an objective construction of its terms, give rise to an "if" contract whereby one party makes a standing offer to the other that if it carries out the defined performance of services, that other party will be remunerated for that performance.

---

① *British Steel Corporation* v *Cleveland Bridge and Engineering Co Ltd* [1971] 9 BLR 20.
② [2002] EWHC 3132(TCC) at [35].

However, no obligation to perform is created and the reciprocal obligation to remunerate is limited by the express and implied terms of the offer.

3. It is possible for a contract to come into being without the conclusion of the formalities of the signing and execution of a formal contract documents if a transaction is fully performed and all obstacles to the formation of a contract are removed in the negotiations and during the performance of the contract.

4. In construing and giving effect to the language of a letter of intent, it is necessary to take into account the factual background out of which the letter of intent arose.

由上可见,虽然被认为或视为意向书的文件有可能是一个有约束力的合同,或者是构成一个"如果"合同,即一方当事人向对方发出了一个始终有效的要约,只要对方实施了规定的服务就可以获得该服务的报酬。如果交易已经全部完成且所有关于合同形式的障碍均已在洽谈和履行中被消除,合同则有可能在无需完成签署的情况下就已经成立。 2.112

"意向书"并不是一个专门术语,并没有自己特定的含义。意向书的性质应当根据具体情况作出判断。正如在 *ERDC Group Limited* v *Brunel University* 一案中,Humphrey Lloyd 法官所说的:① 2.113

> Letters of intent come in all sorts of forms. Some are merely expressions of hope; others are firmer but make it clear that no legal consequences ensue; others presage a contract and may be tantamount to an agreement "subject to contract"; others are contracts falling short of the full-blown contract that is contemplated; others are in reality that contract in all but name. There can therefore be no prior assumptions, such as looking to see if words such as "letter of intent" have or have not been used. The phrase "letter of intent" is not a term of art. Its meaning and effect depend on the circumstances of each case.

意向书没有约束力的情形

如前所述,在通常情况下意向书并不是具有约束力的合同,在 *Alldridge* 2.114

---

① [2006] EWHC 687(TCC) at [27].

(*Builders*) *Ltd* v *Grandactual Limited* ①一案中,被告是雇主,打算将自己在伦敦的物业改造成餐馆,原告是受被告邀请参加改建项目的承包商。雇主向受邀的承包商提供了招标须知和一般条件、招标书、规格书和图纸等,承包商则向雇主发出了费率表。7月14日,承包商致函雇主称:

> Dear Sirs,
>
> Re Texas Embassy Cantina
>
> We enclose priced specifications for various aspects of the work. (1) General Building and demolition works fully priced, (2) Wall and floor finishes ONLY finished plaster and screed as priced; at present we have allowed for rendering for tiling. It is difficult to price the other sections without a visit to the site but we thought that the initial sections would assist you in programming the works. We are quite prepared to work on site with other contractors to expedite the works.
>
> Yours faithfully,
> Allridge (Builders) Limited
> A. R. Davis

2.115　8月10日,雇主的代理代表雇主致函承包商称:

> Dear Sirs,
>
> RE: TEXAS EMBASSY CANTINA
>
> On behalf of Grandactual Limited of 19/21 Great Tower Street, London EC3R 5AQ, we hereby write this letter of intent to enter into a contract with yourselves for the wall and floor finishes packages at the Texas Embassy Cantina, 1 Cockspur Street, London SW1, in accordance with your quote of 8 July 1994. Please proceed with the works as instructed.
>
> Yours faithfully,
> M. E. SIMMS for and on behalf of
> BLAIR EASTWICK ARCHITECTURE

2.116　双方没有签署正式合同,承包商开始了工作。双方发生了争议,法院需要解决的首要问题包括:费率表、招标文件以及10月8日的意向书是否已经在双方之间构成了合同。法院虽然认为在承包商和雇主之间已经成立了合同,但并不是因

---

① (1996) 55 Con LR 91.

为意向书的存在。高院的 David Blunt 法官说：①

> ... My answer in relation to the second preliminary issue is in the affirmative, but is subject to the qualification that in my judgment the tender drawings included version D as well as version C of the drawings numbered 1188/GA01-03, that the contract was further evidenced not only by the Schedule of Rates but also by the Schedule of Works, and that the contract was not evidenced by the letter of intent or fax dated 10. 8. 94.

意向书具有要约性质的情形

2.117 虽然意向书通常并不是具有约束力的合同，但是文件法律效力的认定取决于该文件的具体内容和措辞，而非文件的名称。如果意向书的内容构成了一个要约，对方就可以"接受"意向书。在 *Wilson Smithett & Cape (Sugar) Ltd* v *Bangladesh Sugar and Food Industries Corporation*② 一案中，被告是招标人，原告是竞标人。双方经过磋商后，原告向被告发出了要约函，规定了最后的接受日期。被告在规定的有效期最后一天向原告发出了包括下列文字的意向书：

> We are pleased to issue this letter of intent to you for supply of the following materials .... All other terms and conditions will be as per your ... offer dated 12. 6. 1981 except any overage insurance premium on vessels over fifteen years old to be borne by the seller .... You are advised to submit security deposit/performance bond in the form of bank guarantee as per enclosed specimen for ten per cent of the total c & f value of the material within seven days from the date of issue of this letter of intent. Bank guarantee direct from the principal will not be accepted unless the same is endorsed by a local bank. Formal purchase contract will be signed on receipt of necessary security deposit/performance bond from you.

2.118 原告按照意向书要求出具了履约担保。被告因不再需要招标的商品了，决定不和原告成交。原告起诉要求被告履行合同。高院的 Leggatt 法官认为意向书实际上是一个合同，他说：③

---

① Ibid.
② [1986] 1 Lloyd's Rep 378.
③ [1986] 1 Lloyd's Rep 378 at 382.

It appears to me quite plain that . . . this document was intended to have contractual significance and indeed effect. I do not regard the reference to performance bond as constituting a condition. No failure to accord with such a condition is relied upon by way of defence. The evidence, as will appear, as to the details of the performance bond is inconclusive, but, as will also appear, in any event there was the plainest possible acceptance by the defendants of that form of performance bond which was subsequently provided within the time limited by the plaintiffs.

2.119　为了避免不必要的问题和风险，除非双方确有真实的缔约意图，否则应当在意向书中予以明确，例如可以写明"本意向书不应视为当事人之间的生效合同"等类似字样。

VI　招标

2.120　招标也是船东建造船舶的一种方式。船东的招标往往是有的放矢的，通常是在了解了投标船厂的基本情况后进行的。船东一般通过经纪人、与投标船厂有过交易的船东以及问题单等方式在开始招标前对投标船厂进行相关情况的初步了解。招标文件是船舶建造投标中的重要文件，招标文件一般包括投标函、标书、投标保证金以及履约保函等。标书是招标文件中的关键文件，它通常包括下列内容：技术文件和商务文件、合同格式及条款、船厂情况及其经历介绍、财务报表、质量体系认证证书、管理和质量体系文件、建造工期的安排、采购计划及其安排、设计和制图程序、检验和检查的计划、分包项目以及分包商情况、项目组织架构及其人员、付款安排、现金流计划及控制、文件控制和管理、建造保险的安排及其条款等。

招标邀请和要约

2.121　根据船东的要求而提供标书通常构成船厂发出的要约，然而船东对投标的接受是否构成对船厂的要约的接受则要视具体情况而定。除非明确约定在签订正式船舶建造合同之前双方不存在有约束力的合同关系，船东对船厂投标的接受一般构成对要约的接受。双方各自使用的措辞有可能影响文件的性质。招标邀请在绝大多数情况下只是一个要约邀请或交易邀请而已，船东要求船厂投标的邀请也一样，船厂按照船东的要求进行投标并不导致船舶建造合同的成立。这是由招标的性质所决定的，正如 Willes 法官在 *Spencer and Others* v *Harding and Others*

一案中所说的：①

> In advertisements for tenders for buildings it is not usual to say that the contract will be given to the lowest bidder, and it is not always that the contract is made with the lowest bidder. Here there is a total absence of any words to intimate that the highest bidder is to be the purchaser. It is a mere attempt to ascertain whether an offer can be obtained within such a margin as the sellers are willing to adopt.

但在个别情形下，如果船东的招标邀请具有特别措辞，例如：价格最低者中标等，船东的招标邀请就有可能构成一个要约，即一旦船厂按照船东的要求投标就可立即在双方之间成立船舶建造合同。在 *Harvela Investments Ltd* v *Royal Trust Co of Canada(CI) Ltd* ② 一案中，被告出售股票并向两个人发出了投标的邀请，原告是收到邀请的两人之一。邀请书的内容是：

2.122

> We have before us two similar offers but subject to differing terms and conditions and value. Accordingly we invite you to submit to the Royal Trust Company of Canada(CI) Ltd. the registered holder of the shares referred to below any revised offer which you may wish to make by sealed tender or confidential telex to be submitted to our London solicitors, Messrs. Bischoff & Co., ... by 3 pm London time Wednesday 16 September 1981 .... Tenders are to be submitted on the following terms: 1. That tenders are a single offer for all shares held by us. 2. That payment of the agreed purchase price shall be within 30 days of 16 September 1981. (The date of actual payment hereafter called the "closing date.") 3. Payment shall be in full on the closing date without any deduction. 4. The closing shall take place at Messrs. Bischoff's office, payment being by banker's draft payable at sight drawn on the head office of a London clearing bank in Canadian dollars. 5. In the event that closing shall not take place within 30 days other than by reason of any delay on our part interest shall be payable by the purchaser on the full purchase price at a rate higher by 4 per cent, than the Bank of Montreal prime rate from time to time for Canadian dollar loans. We hereby agree subject to acceptance by us of any offer made by you: ... (c)We confirm that if any offer made by you is the highest offer received by us we bind ourselves to accept such offer provided that

---

① (1870) LR 5 CP 561 at 564.
② [1986] AC 207.

such offer complies with the terms of this telex ....

2.123　　上议院认为,邀请函要求投标人报价,并且规定卖方接受最高价格,因此被告应当接受原告的要约。Lord Templeman 说:①

> The court is not concerned to define the word "offer" in isolation, without regard to its context and by reference to the widest possible meaning which can be culled from the weightiest available dictionary. The mere use by the vendors of the word "offer" was not sufficient to invoke all the frustrating dangers and uncertainties which inevitably follow from uncontrolled referential bids. The task of the court is to construe the invitation and to ascertain whether the provisions of the invitation, read as a whole, create a fixed bidding sale or an auction sale. I am content to reach a conclusion which reeks of simplicity, which does not require a draftsman to indulge in prohibitions, but which obliges a vendor to specify and control any form of auction which he seeks to combine with confidential bidding. The invitation required [bidders] to name their price and bound the vendors to accept the higher price. The invitation was not difficult to understand and the result was bound to be certain and to accord with the presumed intentions of the vendors discernible from the express provisions of the invitation .... The vendors were bound to accept Harvela's offer.

招标人谨慎行事的义务

2.124　　如果招标邀请明确规定了程序,该程序就有可能构成招标人考虑所有符合要求投标的义务。在 *Blackpool and Fylde Aero Club Ltd* v *Blackpool Borough Council* ②一案中,被告招标,招标文件明确规定:

> The council do not bind themselves to accept all or any part of any tender. No tender which is received after the last date and time specified shall be admitted for consideration.
>
> Successful tenderers will be required to execute an agreement prepared by the town clerk for the time being of the council. A specimen form of agreement may be examined on application to the airport director and it will be assumed that tenderers are aware of the covenants and conditions

---

① [1986] AC 207 at 233.
② [1990] 1 WLR 1195.

contained therein.

被告要求所有投标必须在 1983 年 3 月 17 日 12:00 时之前收到,原告的标书是在 3 月 17 日 11:00 时投入市政厅的信箱。通常市政厅的职员会在 12:00 时取出信箱的信件,但是 17 日那天没有取出,因此原告的标书一直到第二天,即 3 月 18 日才被取出,信封上打上了 3 月 18 日的日戳。一共有三个投标人,被告在没有考虑原告标书的情况下将标发给了其他投标人,并通知了中标人。被告又写信给原告告知其标书由于晚交而未予以考虑。原告回复称自己的标书是在截止时间之前递交的。被告最后发现了问题,并于 3 月 30 日致函原告: 2.125

> Due to an error in the administration of the terms of tender for the above concession I regret to inform you that the tenders recently received have been declared invalid.

招标文件经过修改后被告又重新招了一次标,3 月 31 日,被告通知包括原告在内的投标人称: 2.126

> I trust that you will appreciate that the only course of action open to us is to go through the formalities of seeking tenders for a second time.

这时,第一次招标时中标的人主张自己的投标已经得到接受,被告有义务履行合同,并且威胁被告将提起诉讼。被告于是决定不再考虑在第二次招标中收到的投标,而选择履行与第一次招标时中标人的合同。原告以违约和侵权对被告提起了诉讼。高院认为明确要求他人投标的在适当情况下有可能导致招标人考虑标书的默示义务,被告在招标文件中关于在截止日之后不再接受标书的规定意味着被告负有考虑在截止日之前送交的标书的合同义务。被告提起上诉,被告认为投标的邀请历来只是对要约的邀请,招标人没有义务和投标人订立合同。 2.127

上诉法院维持了一审法院的判决,上诉法院认为招标的程序显然是有利于招标人的。他可以决定邀请多少人参加投标,他也无需告诉投标人还有哪些其他人投标。而投标人则会为了投标而花费不小的人力和物力准备标书等,除非中标,否则没有人会承担此种费用。招标人并不需要承诺从事招标的项目,他也并非一定要接受最高的或最低的标书,甚至没有接受任何标书的义务。但上诉法院的 Bingham 法官认为投标人应当可以获得最起码的保护。只要投标人的投标符合招标人规定的要求,招标人应当考虑投标人的投标。他认为招标的邀请构成了要 2.128

约,而投标则构成了接受。他说:①

> [T]he invitee is in my judgment protected at least to this extent: if he submits a conforming tender before the deadline he is entitled, not as a matter of mere expectation but of contractual right, to be sure that his tender will after the deadline be opened and considered in conjunction with all other conforming tenders or at least that his tender will be considered if others are. Had the club, before tendering, inquired of the council whether it could rely on any timely and conforming tender being considered along with others, I feel quite sure that the answer would have been "of course". The law would, I think, be defective if it did not give effect to that.
>
> It is of course true that the invitation to tender does not explicitly state that the council will consider timely and conforming tenders. That is why one is concerned with implication. But the council do not either say that they do not bind themselves to do so, and in the context a reasonable invitee would understand the invitation to be saying, quite clearly, that if he submitted a timely and conforming tender it would be considered, at least if any other such tender were considered.
>
> I readily accept that contracts are not to be lightly implied. Having examined what the parties said and did, the court must be able to conclude with confidence both that the parties intended to create contractual relations and that the agreement was to the effect contended for .... I think it plain that the council's invitation to tender was, to this limited extent, an offer, and the club's submission of a timely and conforming tender an acceptance.

2.129　上诉法院的 Stocker 法官则对招标书构成要约的理由予以了说明,他认为,既然招标人规定了明确的要求,招标人就应当有义务考虑所有符合要求的投标。他说:②

> Of particular significance, in my view, was the requirement that tenders be submitted in the official envelope supplied and endorsed ... by the council. The purpose of this requirement must surely have been to preserve the anonymity of the tenderer and, in conjunction with the council's standing orders, to prevent any premature leak of the nature

---

① [1990] 1 WLR 1195 at 1202.
② [1990] 1 WLR 1195 at 1204.

and amount of such tender to other interested or potentially interested parties. Such a requirement, as a condition of the validity of the tender submitted, seems pointless unless all tenders submitted in time and in accordance with the requirements are to be considered before any award of the concession is made. There can be no doubt that this was the intention of both parties, as exemplified by the council's actions when their error with regard to the time of receipt of the club's tender was appreciated. Such a common intention can, of course, exist without giving rise to any contractual obligations, but the circumstances of this case indicate to me that this is one of the fairly rare exceptions to the general rule . . . . I therefore agree that in all the circumstances of this case there was an intention to create binding legal obligations if and when a tender was submitted in accordance with the terms of the invitation to tender, and that a binding contractual obligation arose that the club's tender would be before the officer or committee by whom the decision was to be taken for consideration before a decision was made or any tender accepted. This would not preclude or inhibit the council from deciding not to accept any tender or to award the concession, provided the decision was bona fide and honest, to any tenderer. The obligation was that the club's tender would be before the deciding body for consideration before any award was made. Accordingly, in my view, the conclusion of the judge and his reasons were correct.

欺诈性陈述

如果船东实际上并没有与船厂缔约的意图,而只是为了了解市场情况而进行招标,船东就有可能为此承担赔偿责任。这是因为船东的招标行为实际上构成了"欺诈性陈述"。在 *Richardsons v Sylvester*① 一案中,被告登了广告出售农场,但实际上农场并不能出售。原告看了广告后打算购买农场并为此产生了费用。郡法院认为原告没有诉因,但是王座法院则认为被告的广告有欺诈性陈述,原告可以起诉。王座法院的 Blackburn 法官说:②

2.130

> It must be taken upon the statement of the plaintiff that the advertisement was issued with some indirect motive, and that the farm was not to be let. This amounts to a false representation. It was a false statement

---

① (1873-74) LR 9 QB 34.
② (1873-74) LR 9 QB 34 at 36.

knowingly made and published in order to be read by persons who would be likely to be tenants of farms, and the natural consequence would be that a person who was desirous of becoming a tenant would, upon reading the advertisement, incur expense in looking at the farm.

Then, if there is a false representation knowingly made to the plaintiff, and he acts on it and is injured, he has a cause of action.

合理报酬

2.131 船厂如果根据船东的指示完成了部分工作,即使双方最终未能订立船舶建造合同,船厂依然有机会获得相应的补偿。在这种情况下,船厂获得的并不是损害赔偿,而是对工作支付的合理报酬。在 William Lacey(Hounslow) Ltd v Davis① 一案中,被告的物业在战争中遭到破坏,被告要求包括原告在内的三家承包商投标。原告的投标价格最低,被告向原告表示其有可能中标。由于被告的重建需要获得相关的许可,被告要求原告先进行结构方面的计算。原告还提供了重建的费用估计,因此原告实际实施的工作明显超过投标所需的一般工作范围。由于原告的工作,被告获得了较多的战争赔偿。但是被告最终出售了该物业并取消了重建计划,于是原告起诉要求被告赔偿因其违约而造成的损失,或者支付原告完成的投标所需范围以外工作的合理报酬。法院认为,由于在双方之间并不存在有约束力的合同,因此原告不能要求违约的损害赔偿。但是由于被告从原告的工作中获益,被告应当向原告支付合理的报酬。高院的 Barry 法官说:②

> It is perhaps justifiable to surmise that these facts, especially the reconstruction plans and the increase in the "permissible amount", had at least some influence on the price of the damaged building which the defendant obtained when it was ultimately sold by him. The work itemised in the schedule which does not relate to estimation, as I think, falls even more clearly outside the type of work which any builder would be expected to do without charge when tendering for a building contract.

2.132 法院之所以作出这一判决是因为雇主已经表示愿意为承包商完成的工作支付合理报酬,Barry 法官是这样说的:③

---

① [1957] 1 WLR 932.
② [1957] 1 WLR 932 at 935.
③ Ibid.

I have, therefore, come to the conclusion that ... the court should imply a condition or imply a promise that the defendant should pay a reasonable sum to the plaintiffs for the whole of these services which were rendered by them .... The plaintiffs are entitled to a fair remuneration for the work which they have done, but they cannot, in my view, quantify their charges by reference to professional scales.

Ⅶ 合同形式

法律对合同形式的要求

2.133 法律针对特定合同规定了形式要求,这些形式要求在成文法中得到了确认。法律规定特定合同形式要求的目的有以下四个方面:①

First, they may serve as clear evidence of a transaction and of its terms. Secondly, they may have a cautionary effect, thereby deterring hasty, premature or ill-considered contracts being made. Thirdly, they may have a "channelling" function, offering "a legal framework into which a party may fit his actions". Thus, formalities may mark off transactions from one another and create a standardised form of transaction. Fourthly, formal requirements may be used as a device to protect the weaker parties to contracts.

2.134 成文法规定的特殊合同包括:可流通票据、消费者信用、雇佣以及保证等。法律针对这些合同规定的形式要求各不相同,例如为期超过三年的租赁应当采用契据的形式。② 即使采用书面形式,不同的成文法也规定了不同的具体要求,例如转让土地的合同应当采用书面的形式订立,或有书面的备忘录证明之。③ 有的成文法甚至规定了书面形式的具体要求。④ 当事人实际订立的合同若不符合成文法规定的形式则可能导致合同无效的后果,例如不符合法定格式和措辞的卖据就是无效的;⑤或者导致合同无法执行,例如当事人不能凭非书面形式的买卖土地或土

---

① Law of Property Act 1925 s.52.
② Ibid.
③ Law of Property Act 1925 s.40.
④ Unsolicited Goods and Services(Amendment) Act 1975, s.1.
⑤ Bills of Sale Act(1878) Amendment Act 1882, s.9.

地利益合同在法院提起诉讼;①或只能通过法院的命令才可以对债务人执行。②

货物买卖合同的形式

2.135　　1979年《货物买卖法》对货物买卖合同没有规定形式要求,货物买卖合同可以采取书面方式订立,可以采取口头方式订立,也可以部分采用书面部分采用口头的方式订立,甚至还可以通过行为推定。该法的规定是:③

> Subject to this and any other Act, a contract of sale may be made in writing (either with or without seal), or by word of mouth, or partly in writing and partly by word of mouth, or may be implied from the conduct of the parties.

2.136　　虽然法律对货物买卖合同几乎没有形式上的要求,但除了日常生活中的买卖活动,商业买卖通常采用书面的形式订立。

船舶建造合同的形式

2.137　　虽然法律对形式没有要求,但在实践中以口头方式订立船舶建造合同的做法应当是相当罕见的。几乎所有的船舶建造合同均采用双方签署正式合同文本的方式订立。除非双方明确约定,签署合同并不当然成为合同成立的前提条件。在 *Okura & Co Ltd v Navara Shipping Corporation SA* ④一案中,船厂和船东于1976年9月3日签署了船舶建造合同,由船厂为船东在广岛建造一艘载重16,000吨的船舶。船舶建造合同规定船厂应当在1977年9月交船,交船延迟的,合同价格将作出调整。延迟超过150天的,船东有权解除合同。船厂因遭遇财务困难延迟了交船。150天的期限于1978年2月27日届满,第二天船东便解除了船舶建造合同。双方接着开始在降低造价的基础上重新洽谈船舶建造合同。5月2日,船厂向船东发出了如下要约:

> (1) delivery date/time of vessel to be within 35 consecutive days from date of Navara's declaration of acceptance of vessel ....
>
> (10) All other terms and conditions as contained in shipbuilding contract dated 3.9.76 to apply in full except article 6 item 4(a) third line to read

---

① Law of Property Act 1925, s.40.
② Consumer Credit Act 1974, s.65.
③ s.4(1).
④ [1982] 2 Lloyd's Rep 537.

"within three days".

5月3日,船东回复船厂并提出了一个反要约,首先将35个连续日修改为20个连续日(后来又调整至25个连续日),其次将船厂的(10)改为: 2.138

... all other terms and conditions as contained in shipbuilding contract dated 3.9.76 to apply in full.

5月4日,船厂回复称: 2.139

Thanks for your telex and telephone call during holiday of 3-5-78. Before we go back to buyer on firm basis we would like to point out that delivery of vessel within 20 days from the date of buyer's declaration of acceptance of vessel is found to be mathematically impossible .... Builder now intends commencing their work right after the declaration of buyer, thus leaving only 7 consecutive days to complete unfinished items .... Besides we have not received to date the list of unfinished items from buyer. We happen to have a copy of the list as composed by Mr. Marlas and addressed to Mr. Todani of Builder dated 27-2-78, 0335 hours. We do not believe that there is any other document in existence, but any event please confirm. Will call you to discuss at 10:00 hours your time.

5月4日晚上,船东又发电传给船厂: 2.140

Confirming numerous telephonic exchanges sale confirmed basis buyers telex offer yesterday except clause 1, line 1 reads "25 days" instead of "20 days".

5月8日,船东又给船厂发了电传,包括未完成项目的清单。5月10日,船东将备忘录草稿寄给船厂,该备忘录包括下列条款: 2.141

(10) The parties hereto agree that there shall be no extension of time for delivery of the vessel due to force majeure and that the provisions of article 8(1) of the contract shall not apply to this agreement.

5月18日,船厂回复船东并要求船东删除该条款,船东拒绝删除该条款,但洽谈继续在船东和船厂之间进行。到了7月,船舶已不再可能出售给船东了。船厂在7月底退还了船东支付的预付款。船厂要求法院确认船厂和船东在船东解除船舶建造合同后未达成任何协议。船东则主张双方已经于5月初达成了协议,而船厂又违反了该协议。法院拒绝接受船厂认为双方没有达成最终协议的观点, 2.142

法院认为双方已经于 5 月 4 日达成了协议,但又认为 5 月 4 日达成的协议是不可执行的。高院的 Neill 法官说:①

> In my judgment the parties agreed all the essential terms on May 4 and a binding contract came into existence at that time. A written memorandum recording the terms was no doubt necessary for, among other things, the obtaining of Japanese government approval .... The signing of the memorandum of agreement was not, however, a condition precedent to the formation of a binding contract.

2.143　案件上诉至上诉法院,上诉法院认为在 5 月 4 日双方并没有成立有约束力的协议。所有的一切都是暂定的,只有在签署协议后双方才受约束。因为 5 月 4 日的电传本身并没有约束力,此后双方签署的文件才具有约束力。而该文件虽然已经起草,但从未获得双方的签署。上诉法院的 Lord Denning 说:②

> The Judge held that there was a binding agreement. I do not agree with him. Everything was provisional only. The parties were not to be bound unless and until they signed an agreement. Item 3 of the telex said, "within 15 consecutive days after signing of this agreement". Article XIX of the original contract said that it would become effective when the agreement was signed. Item 11 of the telex clearly contemplated that there should be a memorandum of agreement in mutually acceptable terms. It is a matter simply of the construction of the document. The telex itself was not binding. It was a preliminary to a future document which was to be binding when signed. The future document was drafted but it was never signed. It was never agreed by the parties.

以合同为准

2.144　在不少情况下,洽谈合同的双方会约定双方的洽谈以合同为准。在有此种约定时,即使双方实际上已经就合同的主要条款达成了一致,双方之间的合同也只有在正式合同签署后才真正生效。在正式合同签署之前,双方协议是不完整的。在 *Kingston-upon-Hull(Governors)* v *Petch*③ 一案中,原告的招标书中有如下内容:

---

① 　[1981] 1 Lloyd's Rep 561 at 567.
② 　[1982] 2 Lloyd's Rep 537 at 541.
③ 　(1854) 10 Ex 610.

> P. S. – All contractors will have to sign a written contract after acceptance of tender.

被告投了标,原告接受了被告的投标并通知了被告。但当天被告写信告知原告不打算提供其已在标书中承诺的物品。法院需要解决的问题是原告和被告之间是否存在有约束力的合同。被告认为自己的投标只是一个建议而已,因此自己可以撤销该建议。原告则认为合同已经成立,被告应当受约束。就原告是否可以获得赔偿的问题,财税法庭的 Parker 法官认为:① 　　2.145

> The defendant is entitled to judgment. It was clearly the intention of the parties that there should be no binding engagement until a written contract had been executed. The tender, though accepted, was not a contract.

在 Confetti Records v Warner Music UK 一案中,衡平法院的 Lewison 法官对"subject to contract"作出了解释,他说:② 　　2.146

> In my judgment, the words "subject to contract", at least in the field of land law, do have a definite and ascertained legal meaning. They are relied on everyday to prevent contracts coming into existence … although the phrase may have originated in the context of sales and leases of land, it has a more general application in commerce generally.
>
> In the ordinary way, once negotiations have begun "subject to contract" that label governs all subsequent communications between the parties unless the label is expunged by express agreement or necessary implication.

在 Christie, Owen and Davies Ltd v Stockton ③一案中,原告是代理,被告是业主。业主委托代理出售其房产和业务: 　　2.147

> Please offer by private treaty the within described premises and business. I approve and confirm your commission and terms as printed below.

代理的佣金合同规定: 　　2.148

> Christie & Co. 's commission is payable by the owner in respect of any

---

① (1854) 10 Ex 610 at 613.
② [2003] EWCH 1274 at [66] & [100].
③ [1953] 1 WLR 1353.

completed transaction pertaining to the within described premises or to such other premises belonging to the owner which may be subsequently sold to their applicant. Should the owner withdraw after having accepted an offer to purchase by a person able and willing to enter into a formal contract then [the agents] shall be paid their commission.

2.149 代理为业主介绍一个潜在的买家,业主和买家在一次会议中约定,买家同意购买业主的业务,但以合同为准。虽然双方没有使用"以合同为准"的字眼,但双方的一致约定是要约和接受均以合同为准。当天业主电话告知代理已经同意向该潜在买家出售业务。接着业主和潜在买家的律师开始洽谈合同条款,并就此达成了一致。但是业主的律师却通知潜在买家的律师说:

Our client instructs us he is not proposing to proceed with the proposed sale to your client and asking for the return of the documents.

2.150 这时潜在买家虽然已经签署了合同,但并未和业主进行交换。原告要求被告支付佣金。法院认为代理要获得佣金就必须证明业主已经订立了合同,该合同虽然是有效的,但由于没有做成书面的,因此无法执行。王座法院的 Slade 法官指出:①

Therefore, quite apart from other considerations, I should hold the word "offer", in the agency contract that I have to consider, to mean "an offer capable of being turned into a contract by acceptance." Equally, I should regard the words "after having accepted an offer" as meaning "after that offer had been turned into a contract by acceptance," albeit (there being no memorandum), an unenforceable contract.

2.151 接着 Slade 法官对"以合同为准"作出了解释:②

Where you have an agreement made subject to contract there are four possible outcomes of that so-called agreement. The first is a completed transaction; the second is a legally enforceable contract, but one which at the time that the agent issues his writ claiming commission, for example, has not yet actually proceeded to completion; the third one is a contract which is not legally enforceable; and the fourth one is a state of affairs which has never passed beyond the realm of negotiations .... With regard to the fourth outcome, where nothing has proceeded beyond

---

① [1953] 1 WLR 1353 at 1357.
② [1953] 1 WLR 1353 at 1358.

the stage of negotiation, it is, of course, open to a principal and agent to arrive at any agreement they choose, and many attempts have been made by highly reputable estate agents like the plaintiffs in the present case to hit on a form of phraseology which will prevent a person who has had the benefit of their services and has gone right up to the point of being about to put his pen to sign a contract, from either caprice or, more likely, because at the last moment he receives a better offer, discarding any moral obligation he may have incurred and merely resiling from the negotiations in order to get more money.

电子方式订立的合同

越来越多的合同包括船舶建造合同都由双方通过电子方式进行磋商、洽谈并订立。电子方式的采用对传统的法定合同形式及其认定提出了挑战。为了适应现代通信方式,2000年《电子通信法》(Electronic Communications Act 2000)作出了如下规定:① 2.152

Subject to subsection(3), the appropriate Minister may by Power to modify order made by statutory instrument modify the provisions of

(a) any enactment or subordinate legislation, or
(b) any scheme, licence, authorisation or approval issued, granted or given by or under any enactment or subordinate legislation,

in such manner as he may think fit for the purpose of authorising or facilitating the use of electronic communications or electronic storage (instead of other forms of communication or storage) for any purpose mentioned in subsection(2).

由此可见,政府可以通过修改立法、规定以及许可等其认为合适的方式允许或方便电子通信以及储存方式的采用。 2.153

Ⅷ 洽谈合同的协议

概述

前文讨论的是合同的形式问题,本节将要讨论的是当事人通过协议约定就另 2.154

---

① s.8(1).

一合同进行磋商的情形。约定磋商或同意磋商的协议恐怕没有太大的意义,负有磋商的义务并不意味着合同最终的订立。约定磋商的协议多半是当事人有意愿磋商某一特定合同意愿的表示,至于未来是否会有合同的订立则取决于当事人的磋商结果。由此可见,约定磋商协议的最大问题是其不确定性。

不可执行性

2.155　在 *Courtney & Fairbairn Ltd v Tolaini Brothers(Hotels) Ltd and Another*① 一案中,被告打算建一个酒店,需要资金和建筑商。原告是一个建筑商并可以为被告找到资金。双方约定由原告为被告寻找资金,找到资金的就由原告负责建造。为此原告写信给被告:

> I think I should mention, at this point, that my commercial interest in this matter is that of a building contractor .... Accordingly I would be very happy to know that, if my discussions and arrangements with interested parties lead to an introductory meeting, which in turn leads to a financial arrangement acceptable to both parties you will be prepared to instruct your quantity surveyor to negotiate fair and reasonable contract sums in respect of each of the three projects as they arise. (These would, incidentally be based upon agreed estimates of the net cost of work and general overheads with a margin for profit of 5 per cent) which, I am sure you will agree, is indeed reasonable ....

2.156　被告的答复是:

> In reply to your letter of April 10, I agree to the terms specified therein, and I look forward to meeting the interested party regarding finance.

2.157　原告为被告找到了资金,被告指定质量检验人和原告洽谈建造价格,但最终未能谈成。被告最后委托了其他建筑商建造酒店,但使用了通过原告获得的资金。原告起诉,主张被告违约。一审法院认为原告的信函构成了一个可执行的合同,合同价格为合理成本加5%利润。被告上诉,上诉法院的 Lord Denning 认为,约定订立合同的合同并不是法律认可的合同,他说:②

> It seems to me that a contract to negotiate, like a contract to enter into a contract, is not a contract known to the law .... I think we must apply

---

① [1975] 1 WLR 297.
② [1992] 2 WLR 174.

the general principle that when there is a fundamental matter left undecided and to be the subject of negotiation, there is no contract. So I would hold that there was not any enforceable agreement in the letters between the plaintiff and the defendants.

在 Walford and Others v Miles and Another① 一案中,卖方和买方口头约定就买卖进行洽谈,卖方同意若买方提供由买方银行出具的"安慰函"的,卖方就停止与其他买方的洽谈。买方提供了"安慰函",该函确认在谈判成功后提供融资,但规定以签订合同为条件。卖方后来终止了和买方的谈判,将标的物出售给了第三人。买方起诉卖方主张卖方违反了口头合同,并要求赔偿。高院认为卖方行为构成毁约,但上诉法院则推翻了一审法院的判决,认为双方的约定只是一个同意洽谈的协议。上议院驳回了买方的上诉,上议院的 Lord Ackner 说:②

> The reason why an agreement to negotiate, like an agreement to agree, is unenforceable, is simply because it lacks the necessary certainty. The same does not apply to an agreement to use best endeavours ... the concept of a duty to carry on negotiations in good faith is inherently repugnant to the adversarial position of the parties when involved in negotiations. Each party to the negotiations is entitled to pursue his (or her) own interest, so long as he avoids making misrepresentations. To advance that interest he must be entitled, if he thinks it appropriate, to threaten to withdraw from further negotiations or to withdraw in fact, in the hope that the opposite party may seek to reopen the negotiations by offering him improved terms.

"尽最大努力"

即使当事人在约定洽谈合同的协议中使用了"尽最大努力"(exercise best endeavour)的字眼,同样是不可执行的。在 Scandinavian Trading Tranker Co AB v Flota Petrolera Ecuatoriana (The Scaptrade) 一案中,高院的 Lloyd 法官认为尽最大努力并不是一项合同义务,他说:③

> Finally, I should mention what seems to me to be the weakest ground of

---

① [1992] 2 AC 128.
② [1992] 2 AC 128 at 138.
③ [1981] 2 Lloyd's Rep 425 at 432.

all, namely, that the plaintiffs were in breach of an implied term to use their best endeavours to reach a mutually acceptable conclusion.... But here, so far as the discussions in Quito are concerned, there was no contract at all; for an agreement to seek a mutually acceptable conclusion is like an agreement to agree, or an agreement to negotiate. It is a thing writ in water. It confers no rights or obligations of any kind;

2.160 在 *Little* v *Courage Ltd* 一案中，上诉法院的 Millett 法官也认为尽最大努力并不构成可执行的法律义务，他说的是：①

An undertaking to use one's best endeavours to agree is no different from an undertaking to agree, to try to agree or to negotiate with a view to reaching agreement; all are equally uncertain and incapable of giving rise to an enforceable legal obligations.

IX 对价

2.161 作为英国法的基本原则之一，允诺只有在以契据（deed）方式作出或有对价（consideration）支持的情况下才有约束力。对价是合同有效成立的前提，即使是有法律约束力的允诺依然需要有对价的支持，否则依然是无效的。②

对价的定义

2.162 传统的对价定义强调"有价值的东西"，对价可以是某种权利或利益，也可以是某种忍耐和克制，即没有实施本可实施的行为等，正如 Lush 法官在 *Currie* v *Misa* 一案中所说的：③

A valuable consideration, in the sense of the law, may consist either in some right, interest, profit, or benefit accruing to the one party, or some forbearance, detriment, loss, or responsibility, given, suffered, or undertaken by the other ....

2.163 在 *Guiness Mahon & Co Ltd* v *Kensington & Chelsea Royal BC* 一案中，上诉法

---

① (1995) 70 R&CR 469.
② Hugh Beale, *Chitty on Contracts*, 35th edn Sweet & Maxwell 2023, para. 6-001.
③ (1875) LR 10 Ex 153 at 162.

院的 Waller 法官对对价的定义进行了归纳:①

> In English law the expression "consideration" has at least three possible meanings. Its primary meaning is the "advantage conferred or detriment suffered" (*Midland Bank Trust Co Ltd* v *Green* [1981] AC 513, 531) which is necessary to turn a promise not under seal into a binding contract. In the context of failure of consideration, however, it is, in the very well known words of Viscount Simon LC in *Fibrosa Spolka Ackyjna* v *Fairbairn Lawson Combe Barbour Ltd* [1943] AC 32, 48: "generally speaking, not the promise which is referred to as the consideration, but the performance of the promise." Then there is the older and looser, and potentially very confusing, usage of "consideration" as equivalent to the Roman law "*causa*" reflected in the traditional conveyancing expression, "in consideration of natural love and affection" see Professor Birks's textbook, p 223. Professor Birks appears, at least superficially, to have moved his position in the last part of his more recent article, 23 WALR 195, 233–234.

简而言之,对价是一方当事人获得的利益或好处,或另一方当事人所遭受的损失或不利。对价要么是对接受允诺人的某种损害,即提供价值,要不就是对做出允诺人的某种利益,即收受利益。通常情况下,此种损害或利益其实是同一件事,只是从不同利益角度看待而已。买方支付价款购买是卖方同意交付货物的对价,支付对价可以视为是对买方的一种损害,或者是对卖方的一种利益。相反,卖方交付货物就是买方同意支付价款的对价,因此交付货物同样可以视为是对卖方的一种损害,或者是对买方的一种利益。但这里的利益与合同一方当事人通过交易获得的利益是两码事。所谓的对价是针对允诺而言的,并不是针对合同而言的。法律关心的是针对允诺的对价,而不是针对合同的对价。

2.164

利益的获得

传统上,对价的定义强调的是对接受允诺的人有某种损害或者对作出允诺的人有某种利益。因此只要接受允诺的人受到某种损害即可,即使做出允诺的人并没有获得任何利益也无所谓。适用于船舶建造合同,船厂的银行为船厂的利益向船东提供还款保函,保证在船东按照船舶建造合同规定解除合同时可以获得预付款的返还。在这种情况下,船厂的银行虽然没有获得任何来自船东的利益,但依

2.165

---

① [1999] QB 215 at 236.

然受还款保函的约束。在 *Gill & Duffus SA v Rionda Futures Ltd* ①一案中,原告和一买家订立了买卖古巴糖的合同,被告担保买家履行买卖合同。运载古巴糖的船舶在途中遇到问题,导致了共同海损。船舶驶抵卸货港后,买家拒绝支付货款。原告凭被告的担保提出了索赔但遭被告的拒绝,被告提出了各种理由,其中包括担保没有对价的支持。高院的 Clarke 法官认为担保是有对价支持的,即原告同意接受买方替代被告。Clarke 法官说:②

> In my judgment the correct legal analysis of the contractual position based on those facts is that the plaintiffs agreed to sell the sugar to Rionda on May 8. On May 9 the plaintiffs agreed to substitute the buyers for Rionda on terms that the guarantors agreed to guarantee the buyers' obligations under the contract. That agreement was made between the plaintiffs, Rionda, the buyers and the guarantors. The consideration for the guarantee was the promise by the plaintiffs to accept the buyers in substitution for Rionda and the promise by the guarantors to guarantee the buyers' liability in return for the promise on the part of the plaintiffs. I therefore reject the submission that there was no consideration for the guarantee.

2.166 然而这一观点逐渐演变成只要作出允诺的人获得利益即可,即使接受允诺的人没有受到损害也同样可以满足对价的要求。在 *Sandeman Coprimar SA v Transitos y Transportes Integrales SL* 一案中,上诉法院的 Lord Phillips 在讨论对价时仅仅提到"利益"而没有提及"损害"。他说:③

> There will be ... no difficulty in identifying consideration, at least if the terms are capable of resulting in benefit to each of the parties.

对价的合适性

2.167 一个允诺若没有对价的支持就不具有合同的效力,但是作为一项原则,法院并不关心对价是否"足够"。在 *Hill v Haines* 一案中,上诉法院的 Rix 法官说:④

> The doctrine is used in essence to distinguish the obligatory promise from the merely voluntary: the concept is based on the idea of

---

① [1994] 2 Lloyd's Rep 67.
② [1994] 2 Lloyd's Rep 67 at 82.
③ [2003] 2 CLC 551 at 572.
④ [2008] 1 Ch 416 at 432.

reciprocity: that something of value in the eye of the law must be given for a promise in order to make it enforceable as a contract ..., the adequacy of consideration is not weighed, as long as there is some value in the eye of the law ....

然而,法律不关心对价是否"足够"的原则依然还有不少例外,Lord Denning 在 *Lloyds Bank Ltd* v *Bundy* 一案中对这些例外情形予以了说明,他说:①

Yet there are exceptions to this general rule: There are cases in our books in which the courts will set aside a contract, or a transfer of property, when the parties have not met on equal terms—when the one is so strong in bargaining power and the other so weak—that, as a matter of common fairness, it is not right that the strong should be allowed to push the weak to the wall. Hitherto those exceptional cases have been treated each as a separate category in itself. But I think the time has come when we should seek to find a principle to unite them. I put on one side contracts or transactions which are voidable for fraud or misrepresentation or mistake. All those are governed by settled principles. I go only to those where there has been inequality of bargaining power, such as to merit the intervention of the court.

合同变更的对价

对价不仅适用于合同的订立,同时也适用于合同的变更或修改。因此,任何对船舶建造合同的修改也同样必须得到对价的支持,否则此种修改就可能是无效的。在 *Anangel Atlas Compania Naviera SA and Others* v *Ishikawajima-Harima Heavy Industries Co Ltd* (*No.* *2*)② 一案中,原告船东是被告船厂的长期客户。1984—1985 年间,航运市场萧条,原告要求被告降低合同价格并变更合同其他条款并且得到了船厂的帮助,双方约定原告可以享有不差于船厂给予任何其他船东的条件。其他船东也向船厂提出了类似的要求也得到了一定的满足。在原告发现船厂向其他船东提供的条件优于船厂给自己的条件后要求船厂提供相同的条件。船厂拒绝了原告的要求,理由之一是双方的协议没有对价的支持。船厂认为双方在船舶建造合同成立之后签署的协议只是对之前规定得不够清楚的问题进行调整,这种协议显然不具有对价。而且,协议完全是为了船东的利益订立的。

---

① [1975] QB 326 at 336.
② [1990] 2 Lloyd's Rep 526.

但是高院的 Hirst 法官则认为船东和船厂已经成立了协议，而且该协议是有对价支持的。他说：①

> In my judgment this last argument of [shipyard] is basically unsound. Where parties clarify a previous ill-defined understanding in precise terms, defining both its scope and limitations, there is clearly consideration moving from both sides, and it is immaterial that the main beneficiaries of the agreement themselves volunteered the limitations. Prior to the exchange of letters the understanding was unquestionably vague and ill-defined.

合同解除后的对价问题

2.170　按照英国法的规定，除非船舶建造合同采用契据的方式制作，否则没有对价的船舶建造合同是无效的合同。但是在船舶建造合同中，对价是否存在的衡量规则与一般的货物买卖合同有所不同。如上所述，在一般的货物买卖合同中，卖方交付货物是其收取货款的对价，反之，买方支付的货款也正是其收受货物的对价。然而在船舶建造合同中，似乎并不能简单地将船东支付建造款理解为是接受船舶的对价，而船厂建造船舶则是收取建造款的对价。

2.171　在 *Stocznia Gdanska SA v Latvian Shipping Co*② 一案中，船东没有在船舶建造合同规定的时间内支付建造款，船厂于是解除了船舶建造合同。船厂对船东提起诉讼，要求船东支付尚未支付的建造款。船东的观点是，在船厂解除了船舶建造合同后就不再有权要求船东支付建造款，因为这一主张没有任何对价的支持。船东一旦支付了建造款就应当有权要求船厂立即返还，因为船东支付建造款的对价已不复存在了。实际上船厂花时间和金钱造船仅仅是为了他们自己的利益，因为船厂拥有船舶的所有权。船厂则认为，按照船舶建造合同的规定，船厂不仅仅要在完成建造后将船舶的所有权转移至船东，船厂还必须按照规格书进行设计、建造、完成和交付。船舶建造合同并不是一个简单的买卖合同，而是一个既包括工作也包括材料的合同。船厂对船舶建造合同的履行始于根据规格书进行设计，然后再将设计转化为船舶。在这之后才会发生完工船舶的所有权转移。

2.172　船厂的观点最终得到了法院的支持，法院认为应当衡量的不是船东是否获得

---

① [1990] 2 Lloyd's Rep 526 at 544.
② [1998] 1 WLR 574.

任何特定的利益,而是船厂是否履行了船舶建造合同针对船东支付应当履行的义务。上议院的 Lord Goff of Chieveley 说:①

> I start from the position that failure of consideration does not depend upon the question whether the promisee has or has not received anything under the contract like, for example, the property in the ships being built … in the present case. Indeed, if that were so, in cases in which the promisor undertakes to do work or render services which confer no direct benefit on the promisee, for example where he undertakes to paint the promisee's daughter's house, no consideration would ever be furnished for the promisee's payment. In truth, the test is not whether the promisee has received a specific benefit, but rather whether the promisor has performed any part of the contractual duties in respect of which the payment is due. The present case cannot, therefore, be approached by asking the simple question whether the property in the vessel or any part of it has passed to the buyers. That test would be apposite if the contract in question was a contract for the sale of goods (or indeed a contract for the sale of land) *simpliciter* under which the consideration for the price would be the passing of the property in the goods (or land). However before that test can be regarded as appropriate, the anterior question has to be asked: is the contract in question simply a contract for the sale of a ship? Or is it rather a contract under which the design and construction of the vessel formed part of the yard's contractual duties, as well as the duty to transfer the finished object to the buyers? If it is the latter, the design and construction of the vessel form part of the consideration for which the price is to be paid, and the fact that the contract has been brought to an end before the property in the vessel or any part of it has passed to the buyers does not prevent the yard from asserting that there has been no total failure of consideration in respect of an instalment of the price which has been paid before the contract was terminated, or that an instalment which has then accrued due could not, if paid, be recoverable on that ground.

Lord Goff of Chieveley 继续说:②

2.173

> For this was not a simple contract of sale. The contract required the plaintiffs to design and construct the vessels. That was part of the

---
① [1998] 1 WLR 574 at 587.
② [1998] 1 WLR 574 at 600.

benefit which the buyers were to receive under the contract. When the contracts were rescinded, construction of the vessels had reached the point at which the second instalment had already fallen due. Even though the buyers have not enjoyed the whole of the benefit for which they contracted, which included the completion and delivery of the vessels, their enjoyment of part of the benefit is sufficient to defeat any claim to recover back the second instalment.

X 合同条款

2.174 普通法传统上将合同条款分为两类，一类是条件，一类是保证。由于条件条款和保证条款之间的关系并不是非此即彼的关系，于是合同条款出现了第三类，即中间条款。

条件

2.175 条件可以是指合同条款，例如常见的"条款与条件"。但条件更多用来指合同条款的性质，属于条件的合同条款又被称为条件条款。如果一方违反的是合同的条件，另一方有权选择不再继续履行合同义务。但无论该方当事人是否选择解除合同，他均有权要求违约一方赔偿其因违约而遭受的损失。*Chitty on Contracts* 写道：①

> Today, the most commonly used sense of the word "condition" is that of an essential stipulation of the contract which one party guarantees is true or promises will be fulfilled. The word condition has therefore broken free from its historical roots and can no longer be confined to an obligation which must be performed as a condition precedent to the liability of the other party.

2.176 一方当事人在对方违反合同的条件时可以解除合同，这是因为合同的条件往往是比较根本性的条款，违反条件通常会导致订立合同的目的无法实现。正如 Fletcher Moulton 法官在 *Wallis, Son & Wells* v *Pratt & Haynes* 一案中所指出的：②

---

① Hugh Beale, *Chitty on Contracts*, 35th edn Sweet & Maxwell 2023, para.28 – 014.
② [1910] 2 KB 1003 at 1012.

[Conditions] go so directly to the substance of the contract or, in other words, are so essential to its very nature that their non-performance may fairly be considered by the other party as a substantial failure to perform the contract at all.

一方当事人违反合同条件的,另一方当事人有权解除合同,但并没有义务解除合同。他可以视该条件为保证并要求对方赔偿因违约而导致的损失。上议院的 Lord Loreburn 在 *Wallis, Son & Wells v Pratt & Haynes* 上诉审中是这样说的:①

If a man agrees to sell something of a particular description he cannot require the buyer to take something which is of a different description, and a sale of goods by description implies a condition that the goods shall correspond to it. But if a thing of a different description is accepted in the belief that it is according to the contract, then the buyer cannot return it after having accepted it; but he may treat the breach of the condition as if it was a breach of warranty, that is to say, he may have the remedies applicable to a breach of warranty. That does not mean that it was really a breach of warranty or that what was a condition in reality had come to be degraded or converted into a warranty. It does not become degraded into a warranty *ab initio*, but the injured party may treat it as if it had become so, and he becomes entitled to the remedies which attach to a breach of warranty.

Lord Denning 在 *Wickman Machine Tool Sales Ltd* v *L Schuler AG* 一案中对"condition"一词的各种用法进行了说明,在讨论"condition"作为合同条款的用法时,他说:②

I must turn to the third meaning of "condition." It is the meaning given to it by lawyers as a term of art. A "condition" in this sense is a stipulation in a contract which carried with it this consequence: if the promisor breaks a "condition" in any respect, however slight, it gives the other party a right to be quit of his future obligations and to sue for damages: unless he, by his conduct, waives the condition, in which case he is bound to perform his future obligations, but can sue for the damages he has suffered. A "condition" in this sense is used in contrast to a "warranty". If a promisor breaks a warranty in any respect,

---

① [1911] AC 394 at 395, see Sale of Goods Act 1979, s.11(2).
② [1972] 2 WLR 840 at 851.

however serious, the other party is not quit of his future obligations. He has to perform them. His only remedy is to sue for damages.

2.179　然而,合同当事人可以通过合同约定合同的某一条款具有条件的性质,一方一旦违反该条款,对方就可以解除合同。在这种情况下,被当事人视为条件的条款未必是法律意义上的条件。船舶建造合同就是一个例子,船舶建造合同通常会规定船东未按约定支付建造款的,船厂有权解除合同;而船厂未能在约定期限内交船的,船东也有权解除合同。然而,按照普通法的规定,支付时间和交船时间其实并不是合同的条件。

保证

2.180　与"条件"相比,保证(warranty)一词的使用更为随意,正如 Lord Greene 在 *Finnegan v Allen* 一案中所指出的:①

> Warranty is one of the most ill-used expressions in the legal dictionary .... This is one of those cases where the word "warranty" has been used, as it so frequently is, to try to manufacture a cause of action by calling something a warranty which on its face is clearly not contractual. Warranty is something collateral or incidental to some contract, but in this case there is no contract alleged to which it is incidental or collateral.

2.181　在很多早年的案例中,"保证"被当作"条件"解,而现在"保证"则常常被简单地当作合同的担保或允诺解。然而,究其本意,"保证"应当是指合同的条款,违反该条款会产生损害赔偿,但不会产生视合同已被拒绝履行的权利。作为合同条款,"保证"是指那些不如条件的重要的合同条款。

1979 年《货物买卖法》也给"保证"下过定义,该定义是:②

> Warranty (as regards England and Wales and Northern Ireland) means an agreement with reference to goods which are the subject of a contract of sale, but collateral to the main purpose of such contract, the breach of which gives rise to a claim for damages, but not to a right to reject the goods and treat the contract as repudiated.

---

① [1943] 1 KB 425 at 430.
② Sale of Goods Act 1979, s.61(1).

中间条款

将合同条款分为条件条款和保证条款这一传统分类法的一个明显优点是明确,即任何一个合同条款,要么是条件,要么就是保证。然而问题是,一旦对方违反了合同的条件,无过失的另一方往往就会解除合同,而不关心违约造成的真正后果。有时解除合同的一方甚至没有因对方的违约遭受任何损失。针对上述情况,法院逐渐开始采取不再严格按传统方式区分合同条款的态度,而是在传统的合同条款分类中创设了一类新的合同条款,从而对解除合同的权利进行了限制。法院这样做的用意在于鼓励合同的履行,而不是合同的解除。新的合同条款的名称是中间条款(intermediate term)或无名条款(innominate term),中间条款的法律效力主要取决于其违约的后果。如果违约的后果并未触及合同的根本,对方就不能解除合同,而只能要求损害赔偿。只有在违约后果导致订立合同的意义不复存在时,另一方才可以解除合同。上诉法院的 Diplock 法官在 *Hongkong Fir Shipping Co Ltd v Kawasaki Kisen Kaisha Ltd* 一案中拒绝将船东提供适航船舶的义务视为合同的条件,Diplock 法官意识到很多合同条款都非常复杂,无法简单地将他们概括为条件还是保证。他说:①

2.182

> There are, however, many contractual undertakings of a more complex character which cannot be categorized as being "conditions" or "warranties".... Of such undertakings all that can be predicated is that some breaches will and others will not give rise to an event which will deprive the party not in default of substantially the whole benefit which it was intended he should obtain from the contract; and the legal consequences of a breach of such undertaking, unless provided for expressly in the contract, depend upon the nature of the event to which the breach gives rise and do not follow automatically from a prior classification of the undertaking, as a "condition" or a "warranty".

在 *Cehave MV v Bremer Handelgesellschaft MBH(The Hansa Nord)* 一案中,上诉法院的 Roskill 法官从缔约的目的在于履行这一基本原则出发,认为法院只有在有判例或成文法明确规定的情况下才可以将合同条款解释为条件:②

2.183

---

① [1962] 2 QB 26 at 70.
② [1975] 2 Lloyd's Rep 445 at 457.

In my view, a Court should not be over ready, unless required by statute or authority so to do, to construe a term in a contract as a "condition" any breach of which gives rise to a right to reject rather than as a term any breach of which sounds in damages. I deliberately avoid the use of the word "warranty" at this juncture. In principle contracts are made to be performed and not to be avoided according to the whims of market fluctuation and where there is a free choice between two possible constructions. I think the Court should tend to prefer that construction which will ensure performance and not encourage avoidance of contractual obligations.

陈述成为合同条款

2.184 合同一旦成立,规定合同当事人权利义务的便是合同的条款。虽然合同往往通过当事人的陈述而成立,但并非所有陈述都会成为合同条款。有些陈述只是引导或导致合同的成立,有些陈述则是规定了当事人的权利和义务,只有规定当事人权利义务的陈述才会成为合同条款。但是确定哪些陈述是导致合同订立的陈述,哪些陈述最终成为合同条款并非易事。法院采用的标准是看是否有证据表明当事人的一方或双方具有将陈述视为合同责任的意图。正如上议院的 Lord Moulton 在 *Heilbut, Symons & Co* v *Buckleton* 一案中所说的:①

> There is [something] which can by any possibility be taken as evidence of an intention on the part of either or both of the parties that there should be a contractual liability in respect of the accuracy of the statement.

2.185 在很多情况下,合同是通过由一方提供的标准格式而订立的。而标准格式往往是在双方洽谈过程中,甚至是在洽谈将近结束时才由一方向另一方提供的。收到标准格式的一方未必会对标准格式的条款进行逐字逐句的分析。然而,作为一项原则,一方当事人一旦签署了合同就将受合同条款的约束。

关于履行时间的规定

2.186 在不少判例中都有如何看待合同中关于履行时间的规定,即将这种规定视为合同的条件条款,还是中间条款。在普通法中,合同中关于履行时间的规定往往

---

① [1913] AC 30 at 51.

被视为合同的本质，即合同的条件。正如上诉法院的 Lord Romilly 在 *Parkin* v *Thorold* 一案中所说的：①

> At law, time is always of the essence of the contract. When any time is fixed for the completion of it, the contract must be completed on the day specified, or an action will lie for the breach of it.

然而，普通法也有认为履行时间不是合同的本质的判例。在 *Martindale* v *Smith* 一案中，Lord Denman 认为，除非明示作出相反的规定，否则在动产买卖中时间并不是合同的核心，他说：②

2.187

> In a sale of chattels, time is not of the essence of the contract, unless it is made so by express agreement, than which nothing can be more easy, by introducing conditional words into the bargain.

在 *United Scientific Holdings Ltd* v *Burnley BC* 一案中，Lord Simon of Glaisdale 对以前的判例进行了分析并在此基础上得出他的观点，他说：③

2.188

> In my view the modern law in the case of contracts of all types is correctly summarised in *Halsbury's Laws of England*, 4th ed., vol.9, para.481, p.338:
>
>> Time will not be considered to be of the essence unless: (1) the parties expressly stipulate that conditions as to time must be strictly complied with; or (2) the nature of the subject matter of the contract or the surrounding circumstances show that time should be considered to be of the essence . . . .

从上述案例中可以看出，船舶建造合同中关于履行时间的规定通常是构成合同条件条款的，尤其是在船厂和船东作出明确约定或者是根据具体情况可以认定时间构成合同本质的情形时。

2.189

XI 合同当事人

船舶建造合同最基本的当事人应当是船厂和船东。船厂又被称为"卖方"或"建造人"，船东则又被称为"买方"。除了船东和船厂，船舶建造合同还往往涉及

2.190

---

① (1852) 16 Beav 59 at 65.
② [1841] 1 QB 389 at 395.
③ [1978] AC 904 at 944.

其他各有关方，例如指定买方和转售船东等。

船厂

2.191　在船舶建造合同中，船厂通常被描述为英文中的"Sellers"或"Builders"；"Shipyard"或"Yard"。作为卖方或建造人订立船舶建造合同的船厂一般都是拥有实际资产的实体企业。很少会有一空壳公司作为卖方或建造人与船东订立船舶建造合同的，这是因为作为买方的船东一般不会接受一个没有船台、船坞或其他建造设备的公司作为卖方或建造人与自己订立合同。与一个没有建造设施或设备的"船厂"订立建造合同恐怕是没有意义的，因为建造合同是否能够得到切实履行在缔约之初就已经是个问题了。

2.192　船厂的资质、设施和设备、建造能力、管理水平以及船舶建造经验往往是船东比较关心的事项。在船东与船厂初次打交道时，船东通常会在订立合同时甚至开始洽谈之前就会对船厂进行访问，并对船厂的设施和管理水平进行实地考察，从而确保船厂具有建造船舶的能力和实力。

联合建造人

2.193　有时船舶建造合同会出现"联合卖方"或"联合建造人"，即合同有两个卖方或建造人。在中国船厂建造船舶的船东大多遇到过卖方为两个人的情形。出现这一情形的原因可能主要有两大类。第一类原因是出于卖方对船舶建造管理的要求。船厂，尤其是拥有数家船厂的集团性企业希望由集团控制船舶建造合同的洽谈、磋商、订立和管理，由集团统一负责所有船舶建造合同的洽谈和订立，而集团属下的各个船厂只是负责船舶的实际建造和交接。CSTC格式的卖方一栏就包括贸易公司和船厂两个当事人，这一特征正是由中船总当时的经营模式所决定的。CSTC格式可能也是国际上唯一的卖方为联合卖方的船舶建造合同标准格式。

2.194　如果第一类原因是卖方的一个选择，那么第二类原因则多半是出于一种无奈。第二类原因又可以分为两种，第一种是政策限制所致。在我国，为国外船东建造船舶传统上被视为是对外经营，然而并不是所有企业都有对外经营权。中小型船厂以及民营船厂通常都不享有对外经营权。在这种情况下，船厂不得不找到享有对外经营权的贸易公司和自己一起作为卖方与国外船东订立船舶建造合同。第二种则是能力限制所致。虽然随着改革开放的深入，中小型船厂以及民营船厂都不再受对外经营权的困扰，但它们依然不具备充分的融资能力，银行一般不愿意为此类船厂提供融资服务。船舶建造合同的另一个卖方或建造人实际上就是一个可以获得银行融资的贸易公司。这种贸易公司在船舶建造合同中的作用和功能是：替船厂解决融资问题，作为船厂的出口代理进行境外的采购，并负责资金的管理和使用等。

在卖方有两个人的船舶建造合同中，负责船舶建造的通常是船厂，负责采购、设备进口以及船舶出口等的则是贸易公司。除非船舶建造合同另有约定，否则船厂和贸易公司对合同的履行应当承担连带责任。① 然而，由作为联合卖方的贸易公司承担船舶建造的合同责任实际上并不可取。首先，贸易公司获取的仅仅是代理费用，而代理费用类似于经纪人的佣金，因此利润和风险不成比例；其次，贸易公司大多不是船舶建造的专业公司，对船舶建造知之甚少，并且也很难控制船厂的建造进程。

2.195

船东

船东（shipowner）是指与船厂订立船舶建造合同的人。"船东"可能是一个使用比较随意的词。航运业为了规避风险而普遍采用一艘船一个船东的习惯做法，即所谓的单船公司。船舶的真正所有人为自己的船舶分别设立不同的公司作为登记船东拥有这些船舶，而自己则往往作为这些船舶的管理人或代理人实际从事这些船舶的经营。当我们使用"船东"这一概念时应当是指"登记船东"，即在船舶登记机关作为船舶所有人进行登记的人。换言之，所谓"船东"其实已经不再是指船舶的真正所有人了，而是船舶的名义上的所有人。相反，真正的船舶所有人则成为船舶的"管理人"或"代理人"了。

2.196

在船舶建造实践中，与船厂洽谈船舶建造业务以及船舶建造合同条款的往往是实际船东，即船舶的最终受益人。然而与船厂订立船舶建造合同的则几乎无一例外是实际船东在提供方便旗登记服务的国家为拥有该船舶而注册成立的一家空壳公司。所谓的"空壳公司"是指已完成注册地国家的公司注册法律程序，拥有公司应当具备的相关文件，但没有实际办公地点，没有实际雇员的公司。这些公司在接船之前没有资产，通常也不从事任何实际经营。

2.197

这些作为船舶建造合同一方的船东事实上完全由实际船东或最终受益人控

2.198

---

① 实际上在绝大多数情况下贸易公司会与船东另行订立代理协议，约定双方在船舶建造项目中的权利义务以及贸易公司的报酬。但是由于这是贸易公司和船东之间的协议，并不能改变贸易公司在船舶建造合同中作为联合卖方应当承担的合同义务。

制，他们既没有独立的决策权，也没有独立的管理权，甚至没有一个独立的办公室。一旦这些船东在船舶建造合同中违约，船厂直接向实际船东或最终受益人主张权利的机会并不很大。正如 Staughton 法官在 Atlas Maritime Co SA v Avalon Maritime LTd(The Coral Rose)一案中所说的：①

> The creation or purchase of a subsidiary company with minimal liability, which will operate with the parent's funds and on the parent's directions but not expose the parent to liability, may not seem to some the most honest way of trading. But it is extremely common in the international shipping industry, and perhaps elsewhere. To hold that it creates an agency relationship between the subsidiary and the parent would be revolutionary doctrine.

指定买方

2.199　有些船舶建造合同有指定买方的规定，即作为买方的船东可以指定第三人作为船舶的买方。一旦船东指定了买方，该买方也就成为船舶建造合同的当事人之一。应当注意的是，船东指定买方的做法与合同当事人的变更不同。船东在指定了买方后依然对船舶建造合同的履行承担义务，即买方的指定并不解除船东履行船舶建造合同的义务。然而，在合同当事人发生变更的情况下，除非另有约定，否则原合同当事人就不再继续负有履行合同的义务。

2.200　船东在船舶建造合同中保留指定第三人作为船舶买方的权利通常是因为船舶有可能在建造过程中就会被转让。有时甚至在船东订立船舶建造合同之时就已经有了受让的对象。船舶建造合同中关于指定买方的规定确保船舶的真正买方可以在船厂交船时实际接船，由船旗国和船级社颁发的船舶相关证书都将指定买方记载为船舶所有人。如果船舶建造合同没有关于船东指定买方的规定，船东转卖船舶无疑会遇到不少麻烦。除非可以得到船厂的配合，否则船东只能按照船舶建造合同的规定在接船后才能开始船舶的转卖。

转售船东

2.201　船东在接船之前将在建船舶进行转售比较少见。在这种情况下，真正接船的是转售船东，而不再是与船厂订立船舶建造合同的原船东了。由于船舶建造合同

---

① [1991] 1 Lloyd's Rep 563 at 571.

的当事人发生了变更,因此船东转售在建船舶必须获得船厂的同意。① 通常有两种做法,第一种做法是由船厂、原船东以及转售船东三方订立船舶建造合同变更协议,约定由转售船东取代原船东成为船舶建造合同的当事人,转售船东自成为船舶建造合同当事人之时起负有履行船舶建造合同的义务并享有船舶建造合同的权利。在船舶交接时,接船的不再是和船厂订立船舶建造合同的船东,而是转售船东了。另一种做法则是在转售船东替代原船东成为船舶建造合同当事人的同时,原船东继续负有履行船舶建造合同的义务。具体的转售特征通常取决于相关方的约定。

质保受让人

船厂在船舶交接完毕,船舶所有权转移至船东后,依然对船东承担着通常为期一年的质保义务。质保义务同样是船舶建造合同的义务。理论上,船厂提供的质保既包括船体,也包括设备。船体的质保由船厂自己负责,而设备的质保实际上是由设备供应商向船厂提供的。除非另有相反约定,质保通常可以转让,船厂可以将设备供应商提供的质保转让给船东。船厂需要做到的只是通知船东和供应商而已。就设备供应商而言,其合同义务并没有发生任何变化,只是履行对象变成作为最终用户的船东了。 2.202

XII 新建船经纪人

经纪人是撮合相关当事人达成协议之人。经纪人的报酬是佣金。不同的行业有不同的经纪人。新建船经纪人是航运经纪人之一,专门从事船舶建造的经纪业务。新建船经纪人一般不会同时从事其他航运经纪业务,例如租船经纪业务、二手船买卖经纪业务、保险经纪业务等;而其他航运经纪人一般也不会涉足新建船经纪业务。 2.203

法律地位

普通法中,经纪人就是代理人,因此新建船经纪人在本质上也就是代理人。普通法中的经纪人往往是指货物买卖等交易的代理人。普通法关于经纪人的定 2.204

---

① 关于船舶建造合同的转让及变更参见本书第16章。

义可以在 *Milford v Hughes* 一案中找到,在该案中,Alderson B 法官说:①

> The Law Dictionary defines brokers to be "those that contrive, make, and conclude bargains and contracts between merchants and tradesmen, for which they have a fee or reward."

2.205 　　在同案中,Rolf B 法官也指出:②

> It seems to me, that to make it a case of brokerage, it must relate to goods and money, and not merely to personal contracts for work and labour.

2.206 　　*Bowstead & Reynolds on Agency* 关于经纪人的定义是:③

> A broker is an agent whose ordinary course of business is to negotiate and make contracts for the sale and purchase of goods and other property, of which he is not entrusted with the possession or control.

2.207 　　我们可以从法院对经纪人以及代销商进行的比较中看出经纪人的基本特征及其法律地位。在 *Baring v Corrie* 一案中,Lord Ellenborough 将经纪人与代销商进行了下列比较:④

> Now the distinction between a broker and factor is not merely nominal, for they differ in many important particulars. A factor is a person to whom goods are consigned for sale by a merchant, residing abroad, or at a distance from the place of sale, and he usually sells in his own name, without disclosing that of his principal; the latter, therefore, with full knowledge of these circumstances, trusts him with the actual possession of the goods, and gives him authority to sell in his own name. But the broker is in a different situation; he is not trusted with the possession of the goods, and he ought not to sell in his own name. The principal, therefore, who trusts a broker, has a right to expect that he will not sell in his own name.

商业代理人

2.208 　　"商业代理人"是欧盟理事会采用的法律用语,根据 1972 年《欧洲共同体法》

---

① (1846) 16 Meeson and Welsby 174 at 177.
② Ibid.
③ Peter Watts et al, *Bowstead & Reynolds on Agency*, 22nd edn Sweet & Maxwell 2021, para.1－039(10).
④ (1818) 2 B & Ald 137 at 143.

（European Communities Act 1972）适用于英国。① 1993 年《商业代理人（理事会命令）条例》（The Commercial Agents (Council Directive) Regulations 1993）关于商业代理人的定义是：②

> A commercial agent means a self-employed intermediary who has continuing authority to negotiate the sale or purchase of goods on behalf of another person ("the principal") or to negotiate and conclude the sale or purchase of goods on behalf of and in the name of that principal.

在 *Bell Electric Ltd* v *Aweco Appliance Systems GmbH & Co KG* 一案中，高院的 Elias 法官认为商业代理人不仅可以是自然人，同时也可以是法人。他说：③ 2.209

> In my judgment this argument is wholly unsustainable. The directive in terms in the preamble refers to the need to remove restrictions on the freedom of establishment and the freedom to provide services and it is clear that under European Union law, the rules relating to such principles apply both to legal as well as to natural persons: see e. g. *EC Commission* v *UK* [1991] ECR 1-4585. Moreover, there have been numerous other cases where legal persons have been commercial agents, and in none of them has the point apparently ever been taken that they do not fall under the terms of the regulations.

商业代理人并非普通法固有的概念，商业代理人在英国的适用比较有限，正如 *Chitty on Contracts* 所指出的：④ 2.210

> Although the notion of a commercial agent was unfamiliar in Great Britain, a body of case law under the Commercial Agents Regulations has developed. The Regulations "govern the relations between commercial agents and their principals". *Commercial agent* is defined as "a self-employed intermediary who has continuing authority to negotiate the sale or purchase of goods on behalf of another person (the "principal"), or to negotiate and conclude the sale or purchase of goods on behalf of and in the name of that principal".

---

① s.2(1). 随着英国的脱欧，欧盟的法律不再适用于英国。
② r.2(1).
③ [2002] CLC 1246 at 1259.
④ Hugh Beale, *Chitty on Contracts*, 35rd edn Sweet & Maxwell 2023, para.22‑022. See all.

2.211　除非有明确授权,新建船经纪人不能代表委托他的船东或船厂签署船舶建造合同。在实践中,新建船经纪人代表其委托人签署船舶建造合同的情形并不多见。

唯一经纪人

2.212　船东的经纪人就是船东的代理人,船厂的经纪人也就是船厂的代理人。在船舶建造合同中有时船厂和船东各有代表自己的经纪人,有时船舶建造合同的洽谈中只有一名新建船经纪人。在这种情况下就需要对该唯一的经纪人的法律地位进行认定。唯一的经纪人可能是代表船东的,也可能是代表船厂的。这就需要对具体的事实有所了解,例如该唯一的经纪人是否接受了任何一方的委托。如果没有正式委托的,就要看该经纪人的具体言行来判断其法律地位。如果唯一的经纪人是同时代表船厂和船东的,就可能存在利益冲突的问题。

2.213　作为一方代理人的经纪人对其委托人负有严格的诚信义务,正如上诉法院的Millett法官在 *Bristol and West Building Society* v *Mothew* 一案中所指出的:①

> The distinguishing obligation of a fiduciary is the obligation of loyalty. The principal is entitled to the single-minded loyalty of his fiduciary. This core liability has several facets. A fiduciary must act in good faith; he must not make a profit out his trust; he may not act for his own benefit or the benefit of a third person without the informed consent of his principal.

2.214　按照上述判决,经纪人并非绝对不可以同时代表双方进行交易,问题在于必须得到船厂和船东的同意。是否获得的船厂和船东的同意显然是一个事实问题,很难列出一个可以适用于各种情形的原则。但是委托人的同意应当是明确的,而不是推定的,主张自己已获得授权的经纪人负有举证之责。如果经纪人有利益的还应当明确告知自己的委托人。②

业务素质及作用

2.215　新建船经纪人应当熟悉船舶建造业务及其具体程序,了解不同船舶的不同建造特征以及建造周期等。新建船经纪人不仅应当详细了解新建船市场,包括市场水平及走向、订单情况以及交船情况等;同时还应当了解其他航运市场,例如二手

---

① [1998] 1 Ch 1 at 18.
② *Hurstanger* v *Wilson* [2007] 1 WLR 2351.

船买卖市场和运费市场等。新建船经纪人不仅应当了解船厂的情况,包括地理位置、管理特征、船位使用情况、建造能力以及手持订单等;同时还应当了解船东的情况,例如船东船队中船舶的特征及其船龄等情况、营运和管理特征以及发展目标等。此外,新建船经纪人还应当具备较强的沟通能力和危机处理能力。

一个合格的新建船经纪人能够为委托人带来有价值的服务。他们不仅能为船厂和船东牵线搭桥,而且还能起草船舶建造合同的条款或对合同条款及其影响和履行后果发表比较专业的意见。新建船经纪人的作用主要体现在如下三个方面。首先,新建船经纪人有助于船东和船厂相互了解对方。由于经纪人的专业知识和特殊地位,相信经纪人也是一种商业习惯。而且,不通过经纪人,船厂尤其是规模较小或历史较短的船厂想要了解市场,尤其是有建造新船意向的船东是比较困难的。同样,想要建造新船的船东要了解船厂也不容易。新建船经纪人一般会与船厂或船东保持长期的密切联系,随时会为船厂或船东提供情况和信息。其次,新建船经纪人能够协助船厂或船东进行船舶建造合同的谈判。在正式谈判之前,新建船经纪人可以给船东或船厂提供市场情况,包括:船舶的市场建造价、已成交的价格、同类船舶的订单情况、同类船舶交船情况以及船厂的建造情况等。有时新建船经纪人甚至可能为其委托人进行谈判。最后,新建船经纪人可以成为船厂和船东之间冲突的缓冲器。由于有经纪人的存在,船东和船厂之间的谈判一般不会出现让双方都觉得很被动、尴尬,甚至无法挽回的局面。此外,一些不方便当面提出的问题或建议可以通过经纪人来转达。经纪人还可以为双方试探对方对某一敏感问题的立场等。谈判或履约过程中的冲突和争议似乎很难避免,在这种情况下,经纪人就可以成为一种缓冲或润滑剂,避免矛盾的进一步加剧。 2.216

佣金

佣金是经纪人通过向其委托人提供经纪服务而获取的报酬。佣金数额通常为合同价格的一个百分比。当然,经纪人也可以和委托人约定一个确定的数额。佣金一般由船厂支付,支付方式可以通过协议规定。经纪人通常会和船厂另行订立佣金协议,约定佣金的数额以及支付方式。在可以约定的情况下,一个比较可取的方式是船厂按照船东支付的各期建造款向经纪人分期支付佣金。新建船经纪人在船厂收到船东支付的建造款后就有权获得约定的佣金数额。如果有几个经纪人参与船舶建造合同的洽谈,经纪人相互间还会约定各自的佣金数额及其支付方式。大多数佣金协议都会约定,新建船经纪人获得佣金的前提是船厂收到船东的付款。 2.217

获得佣金的权利

2.218　经纪人获得佣金的前提是自己的参与是交易成功的"有效原因",高院的 Field 法官在 *Berezovsky and Another* v *Edmiston & Co Ltd and Another(The Darius)* 一案中是这样说的:①

> Entitlement to a commission dependent on the eventuation of a transaction has been subject to the "effective cause" test since at least the decision of the Court of Appeal in *Millar, Son & Co* v *Radford* (1903) 19 TLR 575 .... In my judgment, it is open to a broker operating in the superyacht market to establish that he was the effective cause of the eventual sale notwithstanding that the eventual buyer whom he alerted to the availability of the vessel chooses not to negotiate through the introducing broker. Whether the introducing broker was indeed the effective cause of the sale will depend on the facts of the individual case.

2.219　除非另有约定,否则经纪人收取佣金并不以佣金协议的签订为前提条件。只要经纪人的工作取得成效,他就可以获得佣金。即使委托人在最后阶段放弃使用经纪人,经纪人同样可以获得佣金,正如高院的 Devlin 法官在 *Allan* v *Leo Lines Ltd* 所说的:②

> One cannot look at the final end of the negotiations and see which was the more effective force in bringing about a particular figure. If it were otherwise it would make an agent's position hopeless. It is well known that in these matters there is a term to be implied that a principal will not do anything which might prevent his agent from earning commission ... and I cannot believe it to be the law that if an agent works very hard at bringing the parties close together so that only a thousand pounds or two separates them, the principal is entitled to say, "I propose to deal with the matter myself because I think I should be more effective than you in clinching the final figure, " and when he has done that to say, "No, you never arranged a sale at this figure. The best you could do was £1,000 less than I was willing to take. " All these points, in my judgment, therefore fail ....

---

① [2011] 1 Lloyd's Rep 419 at 426.
② [1957] 1 Lloyd's Rep 127 at 133.

即使没有关于佣金具体数额或百分比的约定,只要经纪人确实是交易成功的 "有效原因",经纪人就可以获得合理数额的佣金。①

船厂的违约

船舶建造合同的履行并非始终一帆风顺,即使船东和船厂签署了船舶建造合同,也不等于合同最终会得到顺利的履行。市场的变化往往给船舶建造合同的履行带来各种不确定因素。船东或船厂在履行过程中解除合同的情形也时有发生。当船舶建造合同最终未能得到履行时,经纪人是否依然可以获得佣金就会成为问题甚至是争议。除非另有约定,船厂有一项默示义务,即不能以自己的违约行为剥夺经纪人获得佣金的权利。上诉法院的 Templeman 法官在 *Alpha Trading Ltd* v *Dunnshaw-Patten Ltd* 一案中对此予以了明确的说明:②

> In my judgment, it is necessary to imply a term which prevents a vendor, in these circumstances, from playing a dirty trick on the agent with impunity after making use of the services provided by that agent in order to secure the very position and safety of the vendor. It is necessary to imply a term which prevents the vendor from acting unreasonably to the possible gain of the vendor and the loss of the agent. In my judgment, the term proper to be implied in the present circumstance is that the vendors will not deprive the agents of their commission by committing a breach of the contract between the vendors and the purchaser which releases the purchaser from its obligation to pay the purchase price.

如果船东在支付了几期建造款后根据船舶建造合同的规定解除了合同并获得了建造款的全部还款,在这种情况下船厂显然已经没有任何收入了,船厂是否依然有义务支付新建船经纪人的佣金的问题可能会涉及到船东的解约是否合理。如果船东的解约是由于船厂违约引起的,经纪人应当可以获得其佣金,因为这是在船舶建造合同得到履行的情况下的结果。在 *George Moundreas & Co SA* v *Navimpex Centrala Navala*③ 一案中,经纪人为船厂争取到了 16 艘船的船舶建造合同的订立。合同订立以后,经纪人又与船厂订立了 16 份佣金协议。佣金协议约定船厂只有在收到船东付款后才需支付佣金。最终由于船厂违约,船东解除了

---

① *Berezovsky and Another* v *Edmiston & Co Ltd and Another* (*The Darius*) [2011] 1 Lloyd's Rep 419.
② [1981] 1 Lloyd's Rep 122 at 129.
③ [1985] 2 Lloyd's Rep 515.

16 个合同中的 14 个合同,但新建船经纪人要求船厂支付佣金。Saville 法官认为,虽然佣金协议规定佣金应当在相关款项支付后才需支付,但是协议有一个默示条款,即船厂不违反船舶建造合同从而剥夺经纪人按照协议规定收取佣金的权利,因此船厂应当支付佣金。高院的 Saville 法官是这样说的:①

> In my judgment the commission agreement contained an implied term that Navimpex would not break the shipbuilding contract so as to deprive the brokers of the commission due under the commission agreements . . . .

---

① [1985] 2 Lloyd's Rep 515 at 517.

第 3 章 船舶描述及船级

I 船舶描述

3.1　船舶建造合同对船舶的基本描述通常包括船号、船舶种类以及船舶特征等。对船舶进行描述的内容不仅体现在合同条款中,也体现在规格书和图纸等文件中。船舶建造合同条款中关于船舶的描述一般都比较简单,具体细节往往规定在规格书中。

船号

3.2　船号(hull number, yard number)是船厂为船舶编制的用于识别船舶的标志。船东也可能为自己的船舶编号,但是船厂为船舶编制的船号与船东为船舶编制的船号是不同的。船厂为船舶编制的船号仅仅适用于船舶在建阶段,而船东为船舶编制的船号则是在船舶建造完毕后才开始使用。本书讨论所涉及的船号是指船厂为在建船舶编制的标志。有的船号只有数字,例如:"2045";有的船号则既包括数字,也包括字母,例如:"NSH115"等。船号是船舶交船前在船厂使用的"船名"。

3.3　船舶建造合同标准格式一般都有关于船号的规定,例如 SAJ 格式关于船号的规定是:①

> The VESSEL shall have the BUILDER's Hull No. _____ and shall be constructed, equipped and completed in accordance with the provisions of this Contract and the Specifications and the General Arrangement Plan (hereinafter collectively called the "Specifications") signed by each of the parties hereto for identification and attached hereto and made an integral part thereof.

---

① Article I.1.

3.4　NEWBUILDCON 格式的规定也相当简单:①

The Vessel shall be constructed at the Shipyard and shall have the Builder's Hull Number stated in Box 6.

3.5　两者的区别是 NEWBUILDCON 格式实际上强调了船舶应当在船厂建造,而 SAJ 格式并没有这一明确要求。Norwegian 格式不仅规定船舶应当在船厂建造,而且还规定了建造船舶船厂的地址:②

The Vessel shall be built at the Builder's yard at .... and shall have the Builder's Hull No. .... and be designed, constructed, equipped, completed and delivered by the Builder in accordance with the provisions of the Contract.

3.6　当合同约定船舶应当在船厂建造,船厂应当明白任何由其他船厂或分包方在其他地方完成工作的都必须得到船东的许可。从船舶建造实践来看,船厂自己完成所有建造工作的情形并不多见。因此船厂应避免只能在自己船厂进行建造的约定。

船号的特定性

3.7　船号是特定的,即一个特定的船号用于特定的船舶。使用特定船号的不仅有船厂,而且还包括船东和船级社。有观点认为船号仅仅是一个标签而已,并不构成必须严格履行的前提条件。只要船厂建造的船舶符合合同约定的技术要求,船东通常无权以船号不同为由拒绝接船。持这种观点的依据是 *Reardon Smith Line Ltd v Yngvar Hansen-Tangen and Sanko Steamship Co Ltd(The "Diana Prosperity")* 一案。③ 在该案中,船东为筹款,将订造的船舶进行出租。租约规定船舶由大阪船厂建造,船号为 354。租船人又将船舶进行转租。由于大阪船厂无法建造 45,000 吨以上的船舶,于是委托了大岛船厂建造。大阪船厂拥有大岛船厂的 50%股份。合同约定大岛船厂应在大阪船厂的监督下在大岛船厂建造船舶,船号为大岛 4,但 354 作为大阪建造船号继续出现在各种文件中。在船舶建造完毕交船时,转租租船人拒绝接船,理由是船舶建造人发生了变化。一审法院认为由于船舶是由大岛船厂建造的,因此不符合租约的规定,但是租船人无权拒

---

① Clause 2(a).
② Article II.1, para.1.
③ [1976] 2 Lloyd's Rep 60.

绝接受船舶。租船人和转租租船人上诉,上诉法院驳回了上诉。上诉法院的 Denning 法官说:①

> In the present case I cannot regard the description "built by the Osaka Company Hull No. 354" as a strict condition precedent which was to be exactly fulfilled. It is sufficient that the vessel to be delivered will be in substance the vessel described in the charter-party. I think it will be. The vessel to be delivered will, on our assumptions, be physically identical in every respect with the vessel contracted for.

租船人和转租租船人上诉至上议院,上议院认为租船人和转租租船人无权拒绝接受船舶。关于船号问题,上议院认为船号并不构成对船舶描述的一部分;关于建造人,上议院认为由于大阪船厂计划、组织并指导了建造,因此船舶依然可视为是由大阪船厂建造的。上议院的 Lord Wilberforce 说:② 3.8

> The fact is that the vessel always was Osaka Hull No. 354—though also Oshima No. 4—and equally it can fairly be said to have been "built" by Osaka Shipbuilding Co Ltd as the company which planned, organised and directed the building and contractually engaged with Sculptor to build it, though also it could be said to have been built by Oshima Shipbuilding Co. Ltd. For the purpose of the identificatory clause, the words used are quite sufficient to cover the facts. No other vessel could be referred to: the reference fits the vessel in question.

值得注意的是,*The Diana Prosperity* 一案涉及的是租约,而不是船舶建造合同。在租约争议中法院需要解决的问题是船东交给租船人的船是不是租约约定的船。无论该船的船号是大阪354还是大岛4,实际上是同一艘船。法院的判决是可以理解的,因为作为租船人应当关心的是船东交付的船舶是否符合租约的要求,以及船舶的状况是否符合租船人订立租约的目的。船舶的船号乃至建造人与租船人并不存在必然的关系。因此 *The Diana Prosperity* 一案不应当理解为船号是可以随意变更的。如果在船舶建造合同中船号或船厂发生变化或不符合合同约定,法院就完全有可能做出截然不同的判决。实际上,Denning 法官在 *The Diana Prosperity* 上诉审中已经提到了这个问题。他是这样说的:③ 3.9

---

① [1976] 2 Lloyd's Rep 60 at 72.
② *Reardon Smith Line Ltd v Yngvar Hansen-Tangen and Sanko Steamship Co Ltd* (The "Diana Prosperity") [1976] 2 Lloyd's Rep 621 at 627.
③ [1976] 2 Lloyd's Rep 60 at 72.

> The charterers will get exactly the vessel they bargained for, suitable in every way for the work they required of her. The only misdescription is one of nomenclature. That might be of some importance between a buyer and seller ....

船号的唯一性

3.10　船号的唯一性是指特定的在建船舶只有一个确定的船号,特定的船号也只适用于特定的在建船舶。属于特定船舶的船号不能随意用于其他船舶。在 *Stocznia Gdanska SA v Latvian Shipping Co Latreefer Inc and Others* 一案中,①船厂和船东约定由船厂建造六艘技术规格相同的冷冻船。船舶建造合同规定船东应当在船厂发出安放龙骨通知后的5天内支付第二期建造款,该通知应同时得到船级社的确认。船东在收到船厂的通知后没有支付第一艘和第二艘船的安放龙骨建造款,于是船厂解除了第一艘和第二艘船的船舶建造合同。接着船厂又利用第一艘和第二艘船的分段作为第三艘和第四艘船的分段再一次安放龙骨并要求船东支付第三艘和第四艘船的第二期建造款。在遭到船东拒绝后船厂又解除了第三艘和第四艘船的船舶建造合同。然后,船厂又以同样方式要求船东支付第五艘和第六艘船的第二期建造款,但也遭到船东的拒绝。船厂又相应解除了第五艘和第六艘船的船舶建造合同。

3.11　船厂此后对船东提起诉讼,要求船东支付所有六艘船的第二期建造款。高院认为船厂只能获得第一艘和第二艘船的第二期建造款。而就另外四艘船而言,由于并没有安放龙骨,因此船厂不能要求船东支付第二期建造款。船厂提起了上诉,上诉法院维持了原审法院的判决。船厂又将案件上诉至上议院,上议院也认为船厂只能得到两艘船的第二期建造款。上议院认为只有在得到船东同意的情况下,船厂才可以使用其他合同的分段。上诉法院的 Goff 法官说:②

> In truth, what the yard was doing was to appropriate to contracts 3 and 4 (and subsequently to contracts 5 and 6) sections which had been joined as part of the construction of a vessel being built under a different contract. There was nothing to stop them doing that, if the buyers agreed. In normal circumstances, it might well be possible to obtain such agreement; but in a case such as the present, there was no chance

---

① [1998] 1 Lloyd's Rep 609.
② [1998] 1 Lloyd's Rep 609 at 617.

of it being obtained. Moreover, if the yard's argument is right, they were entitled to do this as of right in a case where the contracts in question were with different buyers. In such a case it would be most surprising if the yard could so proceed without first obtaining the consent of the second buyer.

上诉法院的 Lloyd 法官则从船东权利的角度进一步指出,船厂只有在得到船东许可的情况下才可以将合同已解除的分段用作其他合同的分段,他说:①   3.12

One can test the position by assuming that vessels 3-6 had been sold to a different purchaser. Would the purchaser of vessel 3 have been obliged to accept sections which had already been constructed in the workshop and joined on the berth in respect of another vessel? Clearly not. I agree that under cl.11.01 the property in the two sections would have remained in the plaintiffs. But under cl.6.01(b) the purchaser of vessel 3 would have been entitled to appoint a supervisor to supervise every aspect of the construction of the vessel. Thus the purchaser of vessel 3 could in theory have objected to the keel sections of hull 1 being appropriated to his contract, since his supervisor would not have had any opportunity to inspect, for example, the integrity of the welding. No doubt the purchaser would in practice have accepted the keel sections of hull 1 by agreement. But on the facts as they are, the buyers never agreed to the keel sections for hulls 1 and 2 being renumbered 3-6.

从上述判例不难看出,在船厂同时建造数艘技术规格完全相同的船舶时,一旦其中一艘或数艘的合同因延误或其他原因遭到解除的,除非得到船东的同意,船厂不能将被解约的船舶作为其他同类船舶继续建造。甚至是在同一船东的情况下船厂依然不能随意更换或者调换船号。因为虽然船舶的技术规范相同,但它们毕竟是不同的船舶建造合同的标的物。   3.13

船舶尺寸和吨位

船舶尺寸通常是船舶描述的组成部分。货船尺寸的大小会影响载货量,客轮的尺寸则会影响包括生活区的上层建筑的尺寸。船长与航速以及船型有关;船宽与船舶横稳性相关;船的型深则与船舶的强度有关;排水量与船舶的载重量有关。船舶尺寸的各因素相互间同样有关联,例如型深的增加通常会导致船长的增加;   3.14

---

① [1998] 1 Lloyd's Rep 609 at 629.

船型的改变会导致航速的变化。

3.15　在合同条款中关于船舶尺寸的内容主要有以下几种：总长、两柱间长、型宽、型深和结构吃水。例如 SAJ 格式的船舶尺寸就包括下列内容：①

　　　　Length, overall　　　　　　　　　　　................................
　　　　Length, between perpendiculars　　................................
　　　　Breadth, moulded　　　　　　　　　................................
　　　　Depth, moulded　　　　　　　　　　................................
　　　　Designed loaded draft, moulded　 ....

3.16　船舶的总长(length overall)经常被缩写成 LOA，是指船舶首尾两端之间最长的距离。两柱间长(length between perpendiculars)又被称为垂线间长，即艏垂线和艉垂线之间的距离，经常被缩写成 LBP。艏垂线(forward perpendicular, FP)是通过设计水线首部端点所作的垂线，而艉垂线(after perpendicular, AP)则是艉柱后缘或舵杆中心线。两段的距离沿夏季载重线测量而得。艏垂线和艉垂线的中间即为船中间(amidships)。型宽(breadth moulded, moulded beam)是船舶最宽两侧之间的距离，对于金属壳板的船，其宽度是在船长中点处量到两线的肋骨型线。② 型深(depth moulded)是指船侧从龙骨基线至上甲板横梁的垂直距离。如果船舶中央横剖面的底部具有凹形，或装有加厚的龙骨翼板时，垂直距离便是从船底平坦部分向内引伸与龙骨侧面相交的一点量起。具有圆弧形舷边的船舶，型深是量到甲板型线和船舷外板型线相交之点。当上甲板为阶形甲板，并且其升高部分延伸超过决定型深的一点时，型深应量到此甲板较低部分的引伸虚线，此虚线平行于甲板升高部分。③ 型吃水(draft moulded)，又称设计满载吃水(designed loaded draft)是指在船中点处由龙骨上缘至夏季载重水线的垂直距离。设计吃水也是船舶装载设计载重量货物情况下达到的吃水深度。干舷(freeboard)是指夏季载重线或和干舷甲板之间的距离。吨位(tonnage)与船舶大小有关，是指船舶内部密封处所的体积，每吨为 100 立方英尺。

3.17　NEWBUILDCON 格式的咨询意见稿中关于船舶尺寸的内容包括：总长、两柱间长、总吨和净吨、型宽、型深、设计吃水、结构吃水以及载重吨，但是最终的 NEWBUILDCON 格式关于船舶尺寸的内容则比较简单：④

---

① Article I.2.
② 1969 年《国际船舶吨位丈量公约》附则 I，第二条第 3 项。
③ 1969 年《国际船舶吨位丈量公约》附则 I，第二条第 2 项。
④ Box 4A.

(i) LOA(m)
(ii) Length between perpendiculars(m)
(iii) Deadweight capacity DWT(mts)
(iv) Mean draft in salt water(m)

3.18 总吨(gross tonnage)经常被缩写为 GT。总吨不是重量概念,而是体积概念。总吨又被称为总登记吨(gross registered tonnage),缩写为 GRT。总吨是船舶所有围蔽处所的总容积与系数 K_1 的乘积,①总吨代表了船舶的总容积。船舶总吨反映了船舶的大小及其收益能力,而且还有助于确定船舶人员配备规则、安全规则、登记费用、港口税以及保险费等。

3.19 净吨(net tonnage)又被称为容积净吨,被缩写为 NT。净吨是指从总吨中扣除那些不用于载货空间后所剩余的有效容积,也就是船舶可以用来装载货物的容积折合成的吨数。净吨是根据船舶各载货处所的总容积、系数 K_2 和 K_3 以及船舶的型深和型吃水等数据计算出来的。② 净吨主要用于船舶的报关和结关,是船舶向港口交纳各种税收和费用的依据,也是作为船舶通过运河时交纳运河费的依据。

3.20 结构吃水(scantling draft)是指船体结构强度所能承受的最大限度的吃水。船舶之所以既有设计吃水又有结构吃水是因为设计船舶时需要进行两个重要计算,即稳性计算和结构计算。进行稳性计算的目的是保障船舶在运营过程中的稳性安全,而进行结构计算则是为了保障船舶运营过程中的结构安全。在进行稳性计算时需要有一个标准,这个标准就是满载吃水的设计吃水,在该吃水状态下考核航速。但有时船舶装载密度大的货物,如钢板,货物重心很低,即使装载超过了设计吃水,从稳性方面来讲也是安全的,于是就有了一个新的说法,即重载。重载时虽然稳性没问题,但按照设计吃水核算的结构在重载时却是不安全的。于是在船舶最开始设计的时候就定义了一个结构吃水,按照结构吃水进行结构计算,这样以后运营过程中即使重载超过设计吃水,只要没超过结构吃水船舶也是安全的。一般散货船、干货船、工程船的两种吃水都不一样,结构吃水通常要比设计吃水大。

3.21 载重吨(deadweight ton)是指船舶可以装载货物的重量,船舶载重吨是船舶满载排水量减去空船排水量得出的值。由于世界海区不同、经纬度不同、盐度不同以及季节不同,船舶的载重吨也会有所不同,因此船舶往往有热带淡水、

---
① 1969 年《国际船舶吨位丈量公约》附则 I,第三条。
② 1969 年《国际船舶吨位丈量公约》附则 I,第四条。

淡水、热带、夏季、冬季、北大西洋冬季等不同的载重吨。装运木材的船舶还有木材载重吨。船舶的载重吨往往是船舶分类的标准，例如：散货船的好望角型、巴拿马型、灵便型等都是以船舶的载重吨为标准进行划分的。载重量是货物重量与燃油、物料、压载水、淡水、船员等重量的总和，即满载排水量和空船排水量的差。

3.22　海水平均吃水（mean draft in salt water）是指船舶的艏吃水和艉吃水的平均值。艏吃水是指船舶首柱与水线的交点至龙骨底线的垂直距离，艉吃水则是指尾柱与水线的交点至龙骨底线的垂直距离。当有横倾时则指左右舷测量值平均值。当船舶倾斜不大时，通常可用平均吃水来进行有关的性能计算。当船舶倾斜较大时，平均吃水则不能代表船舶的吃水状况进行有关计算，具体运用时，应根据计算的精确要求而定。在平均吃水已知的情况下，可利用船舶静水力曲线和载重量表查取船舶的排水量和载重量。

船舶特征

3.23　SAJ 格式中关于船舶特征的内容包括：[①]

```
Gross tonnage                      ................
Propelling Machinery               ................
Deadweight, guaranteed             ................
Trial speed, guaranteed            ................
Fuel consumption, guaranteed       ................
```

The details of the above particulars as well as the definitions and method of measurements and calculations are as indicated in the Specifications.

3.24　船舶特征也是船舶描述的组成部分，建造合同条款中关于船舶特征的内容主要有：动力装置、载重吨、航速、油耗等。动力装置是保证船舶正常航行、提供各种能量、保障人员正常生活以及完成各种作业的动力设备。动力装置是船舶的一个重要组成部分，是一整套系统，包括主动力装置、辅助动力装置以及其他辅机和设备等。主动力装置主要有蒸汽机、汽轮机、柴油机、燃气轮机和核动力装置等五类。辅助动力装置是用于提供除推进装置以外的各种能量，供船舶航行、作业以及生活需要，包括为全船提供电力、照明和其他动力的装置，如发电机组、副锅炉等。船上最基本的辅机和设备有：甲板机械、舵机、锚机以及起货机等辅助机械。

---

① Article I.2, AWES 的规定基本相同，见 Article 1(a)。

各种管路系统,如用于调节船舶压载的压载水系统;用于排除舱底积水的舱底水排出系统;为全船提供压缩空气的压缩空气系统;用于灭火的消防系统等。机舱自动化设备,用于保证实现动力装置远距离操纵与集中控制,改善工作条件,提高工作效率。机舱自动化设备包括自动控制与调节系统,自动操纵系统以及集中监测系统。全船系统,用于保证船舶生命力和安全,为船员和旅客提供生活服务的取暖、空调、通风以及冷藏等系统。

虽然 SAJ 格式使用了"保证载重吨",但这里是否使用"保证"两字并没有什么实际意义,因为在 SAJ 格式第Ⅲ条(合同价格调整)中已经对载重吨不符合"保证载重吨"的后果作出了规定。 3.25

保证试航航速是指船舶在海上试航过程中达到的航速。航速是船舶在单位时间内所航行的里程,单位时间通常是一小时,而距离则以海里表示。船舶在一小时内完成的海里数称之为"节"。最大航速指主动力装置以最大功率运转时达到的速度,而全速指主动力装置以额定总功率运转时达到的速度。最大航速一般有两个,一个是最大前行航速,是指根据设计船舶在海上航行可以实现的最快速度。[1] 另一个是最大后退航速,是指船舶在海上航行可以实现的最大倒退航速的估计值。[2] 与上述"保证载重吨"中的"保证"相同,"保证航速"中的"保证"两字并没有给"航速"带来更多的含义,因为 SAJ 格式第Ⅲ条已经规定了船舶航速低于保证航速的后果。 3.26

保证油耗是指船舶在额定功率和航速情况下单位时间内燃油消耗量。船舶油耗量通常以天为单位进行计算。耗油的除了主机外,还有辅机和锅炉等。油耗显然是与航速有着极为密切的联系,在一般情况下,航速的提升会伴随油耗的上升。另外,与上述"保证载重吨"中的"保证"相同,"保证油耗"中的"保证"两字并没有给"油耗"带来更多的含义。SAJ 格式第Ⅲ条也规定了油耗超过保证油耗的后果。 3.27

NEWBUILDCON 格式的规定相对比较详细一点:[3] 3.28

The Vessel shall have the dimensions and characteristics as stated in Box 4 and the Specification. These shall be defined, measured and calculated in accordance with the Specification or, if omitted from the Specification, in accordance with the following:

---

[1] 1974 年《国际海上人命安全公约》第Ⅱ-1 章,A 部分,规则第 3-14 条。
[2] 1974 年《国际海上人命安全公约》第Ⅱ-1 章,A 部分,规则第 3-15 条。
[3] Clause 2(b), see also Norwegian Article Ⅱ.2, CSTC Article Ⅰ.3.

(i) Speed – The Vessel's average speed on a sea trial undertaken in both directions over a measured distance of one(1)nautical mile, with clean hull, in weather with wind speed and sea state not exceeding Beaufort Wind Force Scale 3 and Douglas Sea State Scale 2 respectively on a draft as stated in Box 4D(i) shall be at least the number of knots stated in Box 4D(ii). During such a sea trial the engine's output in kilowatts shall be as stated in Box 4D(iii) corresponding to the percentage of the engine's maximum continuous power output stated in Box 4D(iv) at the approximate revolutions per minute stated in Box 4D(v).

(ii) Fuel Consumption – The fuel consumption of the main engine on the test bed using fuel of the type and specification stated in Box 4C(vii) shall not exceed the number of grams per kilowatt/hour stated in Box 4C(iv) when the engine develops the number of kilowatts with an effective calorific value of the number of kilocalories per kilogram stated in Box 4C(ii) and Box 4C(vii) respectively.

(iii) Deadweight – The Vessel's deadweight shall be the number of metric tons stated in Box 4A(iii) on international summer freeboard, corresponding to a mean draft in saltwater(specific gravity 1.025) as stated in Box 4A(iv). The specified deadweight shall include fuel, provisions, stores, freshwater, crew and passengers in addition to spare parts not less than the requirements of the Classification Society.

(iv) Propulsion – The Vessel's propulsion machinery shall be of the type and with maximum continuous power in kilowatts at the number of revolutions per minute as stated in Box 4C(i), 4C(ii) and 4C(iii).

(v) Cargo Capacity – The Vessel's cargo capacity shall be the capacities stated in Box 4B1 and 4B2.

(vi) Other matters – The Vessel shall meet the technical requirements stated in Box 4E.

3.29 针对航速,NEWBUILDCON 格式明确规定了实现航速的条件,即不同方向,超过一海里,干净船壳,风速不超过蒲氏风二级,道氏浪二级,吃水不超过约定等。其实在采用 SAJ 格式时规格书同样会对船舶载重吨、航速、耗油等测定作出相当详细的条件的规定。NEWBUILDCON 格式只是将部分通常在规格书内的内容写入了船舶建造合同的条款。实际上 SAJ 格式在船舶特征后也规定"上述特征的细节以及定义和衡量及计算方式见规格书"。①

建造标准

NEWBUILDCON 格式在关于船舶描述的内容后有下列内容：② 3.30

> The Builder shall design, construct, test and survey, launch, equip, complete, sell and deliver the Vessel to the Buyer all in accordance with good international shipbuilding and marine engineering practice ....

上述规定提及的"良好国际造船和海洋工程做法"并非是指有特定含义或标 3.31
准的做法。船厂的义务是按照船舶建造合同的规定以及相关适用的质量标准或
工艺标准进行船舶设计、建造、检验和测试。

Norwegian 格式也有关于建造标准的规定：③ 3.32

> The Vessel shall be designed and built in accordance with first class shipbuilding practice in Western Europe for new vessels of similar type and characteristics as the Vessel.

有的船舶建造合同还会用"最佳"取代"良好"。显而易见，"最佳"的含义不 3.33
仅优于"良好"，而且应当超过"一流"。"最佳"应当解释为"最好"，可以有其他
同样符合"最佳"要求的标准，但不应当有比"最佳"更好的标准。船厂的建造标
准是否符合"最佳"的要求还存在一个何为"最佳"的问题。④ 虽然船舶建造合同
中的类似规定是否真正构成严格的合同义务并不十分清楚，但船厂不顾实际情况
在船舶建造合同中作出此种承诺应当是不可取的。如果船舶是在中国建造的，船
舶建造合同就应当适用中国的建造标准和船厂的实际做法。船舶建造合同采用
如下措辞应当是比较合适的：

> All workmanship entering into the construction of the vessel to be in accordance with the Chinese ship building standards and Builder's standard practice. All work to be carried out according to Specification and plans and to the requirement of Classification Society and also regulatory bodies mentioned hereinafter.

---

① Article I.2. Norwegian 在第 II.2 也规定："The further details of the above main particulars, as well as definitions and methods of measurements and calculation shall be as described in the Specification".
② Clause 1(a).
③ Article II.2.
④ SAJ 和 AWES 都没有关于建造标准的规定。

3.34　我国与船舶建造有关的标准主要有以下各项：
1. 中国工业标准
2. 中国造船标准
3. 中国造船质量标准
4. 中国冶金标准

3.35　不少中国船厂其实也都有自己的质量标准，即使船舶建造合同没有约定，此种质量标准也同样适用于船厂的所有船舶建造工程。

II　船级社

概述

3.36　"船级"的英文是 classification，有"分类"的含义。在船级社刚出现时，船舶的船级具有"分类"的含义，是船级社根据船体和设备状况对船舶进行分类的结果。例如劳氏船级社曾将船体的建造及状况分为 A，E，I，O 和 U 五大类，将设备分为 G（good），M（middling）和 B（bad）3 种。此 3 种分类后被 1 至 3 所替代。"A1"代表了船舶的最高级别。其他的船级社则有不同的分类标准和方式，例如德国船级社曾对符合全部规范和规则的船舶赋予"100 A 5"的符号。"100"指符合所有要求；"5"是指该船级的有效期为五年。这一做法的痕迹至今依稀可见，例如美国船级社的"A1"，法国船级社的"I"，中国船级社的"H CSA 5/5"，挪威船级社的"1A1"，德国船级社的"100 A5"，英国船级社的"100 A1"等等。现在船舶入级都必须符合船级社规定的最低入级要求，因此字母的数字只有区别船舶种类和特定功能的意义，而不再有等级高低的含义了。符合船级社船级要求的船舶就有船级，不符合的就没有船级。具有特殊设备或特殊功能的船舶不仅有船级，还有"入级标志"（class notation），例如从事散装原油或冷冻货物运输的船舶都有标明其设备或功能的入级标志。特别设备或功能的丧失并不当然导致船级的丧失，例如 AUT 通常是表明船舶具有自动操舵功能的入级标志。即使船舶由于种种原因不再有自动操舵功能，船级社便会撤销该标识，但并不因此撤销船舶的船级。

船级社的职能和服务

3.37　船级社已经有 200 多年的历史了。几乎所有的船舶都需按照船级社的要求完成建造。虽然船级社之间的竞争非常激烈，但船级社本质上是非盈利性组织。船级社根据国际公约的要求制定并实施各种关于船舶设计、建造、结构和保养等技术规范和标准，以保障海上航行的人命和保护海洋环境。船级社的职能既有公共职能，也有私人职能。所谓的公共职能是指船级社经常接受政府或政府机构的委托，对申请在该国登记或希望保留在该国登记的船舶进行检验，确认船舶符合船旗国关于船舶建造、保养和营运的规定。所谓的私人职能是指船级社接受船东和其他当事人的委托，对船舶进行检验从而确定是否符合关于船舶建造、保养和营运的标准，并提出为符合标准必须完成的工作的建议。船级社还经常提供技术服务和意见，并接受保险人、潜在买方和租船人等的委托，提供船舶估价、船舶状况评估以及对损害进行调查等服务。但是与船东或经营人不同，船级社并不对船舶的日常营运、保养和船舶状况直接控制，也不了解这些情况。① 船级社只能对船舶的状况发表意见和建议。

船级社提供的服务主要是对船舶与海上设施进行入级服务、检验服务以及其他服务。船级社提供的服务主要包括两个方面，一是提供法定服务，二是提供船级服务。前者是船级社根据有关船旗国的授权按照有关国际公约的规定和要求对船舶进行法定检验并签发各种法定证书又称航行证书；后者则是船级社根据自己的规则和要求对船舶进行船级检验并签发各种船级证书。 3.38

法定检验

虽然按照国际法原则，拥有商船队是任何主权国家的国际法权利，但是按照有关国际公约对本国船队进行全面有效的检验和发证则需要拥有强大的技术、人力和财力基础。不少国家虽有自己的商船队，但并不具有相应的技术资源，因此需要通过授权本国的或其他国家的船级社对船舶进行检验和发证。不少船旗国授权船级社代为行使检验和发证的职能，是因为这些船旗国提供船舶登记服务的目的主要是增加政府的财政收入。尽管船旗国授权船级社代其行使职能，但船旗国仍须承担国际公约规定的船旗国的全部责任和义务。国际公约一般都允许缔约国授权他人实施检验并签发证书，但此种签发应注明系授权签发，例如1974年《国际海上人命安全公约》便规定：② 3.39

---

① Marc Rich & Co AG and Others v Bishop Rock Marine Co Ltd, Bethmarine Co Ltd and Nippon Kaiji Kyoki (The Nicholas H) [1992] 2 Lloyd's Rep 481 at 497.

② 第Ⅰ章，B部分，规则第十三条。

> A Contracting Government may, at the request of the Administration, cause a ship to be surveyed and, if satisfied that the requirements of the present regulations are complied with, shall issue or authorize the issue of certificates to the ship and, where appropriate, endorse or authorize the endorsement of certificates on the ship in accordance with the present regulations. Any certificate so issued shall contain a statement to the effect that it has been issued at the request of the Government of the State the flag of which the ship is entitled to fly, and it shall have the same force and receive the same recognition as a certificate issued under regulation 12.

3.40　　船级社的法定服务是接受船旗国政府的委托和授权，代为行使船旗国政府的职能，对悬挂该国国旗的船舶建造进行法定检验并签发相关证书。船级社具有其他类似组织难以比拟的人力资源、专业知识和技术技能，因此它们有能力从事有关国际公约或规则规定的船舶检验、记录以及对船舶进行技术评估等。

入级检验

3.41　　船级社还提供船级检验服务，即为船舶和海上设施的入级和船级保持提供检验，签发入级证书和必要的文件等。就新建船而言，船级社的入级服务在设计阶段就已经开始并持续至船舶建造全部完成。符合船级社要求的船舶都会得到相关的船级证书。船级证书证明特定船舶的设计和建造符合船级社的要求，适合从事特定的营运。船级服务还包括对船用工业产品进行检验，包括船用材料、高压容器、船用主机和辅机、发电设备、轴系与传动装置、起货设备、集装箱、系泊设备、消防设备、救生设备、舾装设备、航行设备和电气设备等等。

国际船级社协会

3.42　　国际船级社协会（International Association of Classification Societies，IACS）是世界主要海运国家的船级社之间的非政府间国际组织，其宗旨是加强各船级社之间的联系，讨论和解决共同关心的问题，商定特定的问题，如海上防污染，海上安全等的统一立场。①

---

① 有关国际船级社协会的情况可访问其网站：www.iacs.org.uk

成员船级社

国际船级社协会成立于 1968 年 9 月 11 日,总部设在英国伦敦,在世界各地的分支机构超过 1,500 个。国际船级社协会目前共有 12 个会员船级社,包括美国船舶检验局(American Bureau of Shipping,ABS)①、法国船级社(Bureau Veritas,BV)②、中国船级社(China Classification Society,CCS)③、克罗地亚船级社(Croatian Register of Shipping,CRS)④、挪威德劳船级社(DNV GL)⑤、印度船级社 (Indian Register of Shipping,IRS)⑥、韩国船级社(Korean Register of Shipping,KR)⑦、英国劳氏船级社(Lloyd's Register of Shipping,LR)⑧、日本船级社(Nippon Kaiji Kyokai,NK)⑨、波兰船级社(The Polish Register of Shipping,PRS)⑩、意大利船级社(Registro Italiano Navale,RINA)⑪以及俄罗斯船级社(Russian Maritime Register of Shipping,RS)⑫。目前世界商船队中差不多有 90%以上的船舶均在上述 12 个船级社入级,受制于该 12 个船级社制定的船舶设计、建造以及营运的规则和标准。

3.43

国际船级社协会的最高权力机构是理事会(Council),理事会设一名主席,两名副主席,理事会会员由各会员船级社委派的一名代表组成。理事会每年召开两次会议,讨论和决定国际船级社的政策、方针和战略。理事会主席由各会员船级社代表轮流担任,任期两年。理事会主席负责协调各会员船级社的活动,并担任协会的正式发言人。

3.44

共同行动

船级社有各自的船级规范和规则,这些规范和规则在不同的船级社之间各不相同。但随着国际船级社协会的成立,虽然船级社依然各自颁布船级规范和规

3.45

---

① 美国船舶检验局成立于 1862 年,其网址为:www. eagle. org
② 法国船级社成立于 1828 年,其网址为:www. veritas. com
③ 中国船级社成立于 1956 年,于 1988 年 5 月成为国际船级社协会正式会员,其网址为:www. ccs. org. cn
④ 克罗地亚船级社成立于年 1949 年,其网址为:www. crs. hr
⑤ 挪威德劳船级社是原成立于 1864 年的挪威船级社与成立于 1867 年的德国劳氏船级社于 2013 年合并后组成的船级社,其网址为:www. dnvgl. com
⑥ 印度船级社成立于 1975 年,其网址为:www. irclass. org
⑦ 韩国船级社成立于 1960 年,其网址为:www. krs. co. kr
⑧ 英国船级社成立于 1760 年,其网址为:www. lr. org
⑨ 日本船级社成立于 1899 年,其网址为:www. classnk. or. jp
⑩ 波兰船级社成立于 1932 年,其网址为:www. prs. pl
⑪ 意大利船级社成立于 1861 年,其网址为:www. rina. org
⑫ 俄罗斯船级社成立于 1913 年,其网址为:www. rs-head. spb. ru

则，但相互间的差异却越来越小。与此同时，船级社协会越来越多地颁布适用于所有会员船级社的规范和规则，从而在成员船级社之间形成了统一的规范和规则。

3.46　　2006 年 1 月国际船级社协会分别颁布了《散货船共同结构规范》(Common Structural Rules for Bulk Carriers) 和《双壳油船共同结构规范》(Common Structural Rules for Double Hulls Oil Tankers)，两个规范的最新一版均为 2012 年 7 月。《散货船共同结构规范》适用于在 2006 年 4 月 1 日或之后签订的船舶建造合同建造的散货船，所谓的"签订合同"是指船东和船厂签署船舶建造合同的日期。而"散货船"则是指长度超过 90 米，船体结构为单舷侧和双舷侧的全球航行不受限制的船舶，具体而言是指在货物长度区域通常具有单层甲板、双层底、底边舱和顶边舱以及单舷侧或双舷侧结构，且主要用于运输散装干货的海上自航船舶，但不包括矿砂船和兼装船。该规范也适用于至少有一个货舱具有底边舱和顶边舱的混合型散货船。对于货舱内没有底边舱或顶边舱的船舶，其结构强度应符合共同结构规范的强度标准。①《双壳油船共同结构规范》适用于在 2006 年 4 月 1 日或之后签订的船舶建造合同建造的长度在 150 米及以上的双壳油船。②

船级社的责任

3.47　　船级社的地位在包括船舶建造的航运业中比较独特，发挥着非常重要的作用。对各相关方都会产生相当的影响。船级社有可能因其过失或疏忽给他人带来伤害和损失，船级社是否应当承担责任，若应承担责任，其责任基础又是什么是值得讨论的问题。③

谨慎义务

3.48　　谨慎义务(duty of care)一般是指个人或组织负有的避免自己实施的能合理预见到可能给他人带来损害的作为或不作为的法律责任。例如制造商负有的避免自己的产品给消费者带来伤害的义务，又如医生和律师避免自己的执业给病人或委托人带去伤害或损害的义务等。船级社的谨慎义务通常是指避免船级社或

---

① Chapter 1, Section 1, Rule 1.1.2.
② Chapter 1, Section 1, Rule 1.1.1.
③ 关于船级社的责任的讨论可参见 Jürgen Basedow et al, *Third-Party Liability of Classification Societies-A comparative perspective*, Springer 2005, Nicolai Lagoni, *The Liabilities of Classification Societies*, Springer 2007.

其人员可能给第三方造成的损害的作为或不作为。

就英国法而言,*Mariola Marine Corporation* v *Lloyd's Register of Shipping*(*The Morning Watch*) 一案应当是英国第一个涉及船级社对第三方是否负有谨慎义务的判例。① 在该案中,劳氏船级社接受打算出售其游艇的船东的请求对游艇进行了特验,船东对锈蚀进行了修理。劳氏船级社出具了临时证书称游艇通过特检并同意其他修理项目推迟至游艇改装时完成。船东于是告诉买家游艇已通过特检,但船东既没有完成其他项目的修理,也没有向买家出示临时证书。买家在改装游艇时发现了多处锈蚀。买家认为这些锈蚀非常严重,可以导致游艇不适航,验船师在检验时理应发现。于是买家向劳氏船级社提出了索赔。法院需要解决的问题是:船级社是否对船东以外的有可能信任船级社证书的人负有谨慎义务。高院认为虽然劳氏船级社应能合理地预见到临时证书对游艇买家的影响,但劳氏船级社并不知道有人打算购买游艇,因此对原告并不负有谨慎义务。

3.49

在 *Marc Rich & Co AG* v *Bishop Rock Marine Co Ltd*(*and ClassNK*)(*The Nicholas H*)一案中,船舶在运货自智利去意大利和前苏联的途中发现船体有裂缝。日本船级社的验船师建议进行永久性修理,但船东为了赶时间只进行了临时性修理。验船师接受了临时性修理,同意船舶保留船级,但要求船舶在卸货后进行永久性修理。船舶在运货途中因临时性焊缝开裂而进水,最终随货物一起沉没。由于有责任限制,货主无法从船东处获得全额的赔偿,于是向日本船级社提出了索赔。货主一审获胜,但在上诉审中败诉,上诉法院的判决得到了上议院的多数确认。

3.50

在该案中,法院需要解决的问题是船级社是否对货主负有谨慎义务。Lord Steyn 认为船级社对货主并不负有谨慎义务。他说:②

3.51

> ... the recognition of a duty would be unfair, unjust and unreasonable, as against the shipowners who would ultimately have to bear the costs of holding classification societies liable, such consequence being at variance with the bargain between shipowners and cargo-owners based on an internationally agreed contractual structure. It would also be unfair, unjust and unreasonable towards classification societies, notably because they act for the collective welfare and unlike shipowners they would not have the benefit of any limitation provisions.

---

① [1990] 1 Lloyd's Rep 547 QB.
② [1995] 2 Lloyd's Rep 299(HL) at 316 – 317.

3.52　上议院的这一判决应当是在全面考虑了各种因素后作出的,而且似乎更多考虑的并非法律因素,而是政策因素。上议院多数意见认为一旦认定船级社对货主负有谨慎义务,船级社的所有检验恐怕都将适用。这不仅会给船级社带来巨大的压力,而且会给航运业造成巨大的负面影响。上议院多数意见考虑的政策因素主要有:船级社是为公共利益行使某种政府职能,没有了船级社,相关的职能和服务就必须由政府来行使和提供;船级社不是追逐利益的机构,而是为公众服务的非营利性机构;航运业有责任限制制度,一旦船级社承担责任且不能限制其责任,现有的责任限制制度则可能名存实亡了。基于这些原因,上议院多数意见认为让船级社对第三方货主负有谨慎义务不公平、不公正且不合理。

3.53　Lord Lloyd 是上议院唯一持不同意见的法官。他担心多数意见有可能导致法律关于疏忽的规定将失去统一的适用标准。他说:①

> Otherwise there is a risk that the law of negligence will disintegrate into a series of isolated decisions without any coherent principle at all, and the retreat from Anns [*Anns v Merton London Borough Council*, [1978] AC 728] will turn into a rout.

3.54　在认定船级社对第三方货主负有谨慎义务是否会打开责任大闸的问题上,Lord Lloyd 的回答是否定的,他是这样说的:②

> I would only add at this point that if concern is felt that a decision in favour of the cargo-owners would open a wide field of liability, I would reply "not so". There is an obvious, sensible and readily defensible line between the surveyor in the present case, where the cargo was on board, and the joint venture was in peril, and a surveyor called in to carry out a periodic survey.

3.55　针对责任限制制度,Lord Lloyd 还以船厂修船为例来说明其观点。他说:③

> How then does the position of a surveyor, called in by shipowners because the vessel is leaking, differ from that of the ship repairer? The answer is that it differs not at all. If it is fair, just and reasonable to hold a shiprepairer liable to an unlimited extent for damage to cargo on

---

①　[1995] 2 Lloyd's Rep 299(HL) at 309.
②　[1995] 2 Lloyd's Rep 299(HL) at 308.
③　[1995] 2 Lloyd's Rep 299(HL) at 306.

board caused by his negligence, even though the damage does not occur until after the vessel has sailed, why should it not be fair, just and reasonable in the case of a surveyor? Suppose in case of the inspection cover, the surveyor negligently tells the fitter that four bolts are sufficient to secure the cover, instead of the usual six, how could it be fair, just and reasonable that the surveyor should not be liable? On what principle would the fitter be liable in such circumstances, when he acts unadvised, but not the surveyor who advises him?

免责与责任限制

简而言之,免责是指责任的完全免除,责任限制则是指在一定范围内承担责任。绝大多数船级社出具的证书或报告中都会有免责条款或责任限制条款。与上文提及的针对第三人的谨慎义务不同,免责或责任限制是针对合同相对方的,与第三人无涉。如果第三人凭1999年《合同(第三人权利)法》获得合同权利,除非免责或责任限制条款无效,否则不仅免责或责任限制的约定适用,而且针对第三人的谨慎义务都有可能也不复存在了。 3.56

下面是劳氏船级社使用的免责声明: 3.57

In providing services, information or advice neither Lloyd's Register of Shipping (hereinafter referred to as LR) nor any of its officers, employees or agents warrants the accuracy of any information or advice supplied. Except as set out herein, neither LR nor any of its officers, employees or agents (on behalf of each of whom LR has agreed this clause) shall be liable for any loss, damage or expense whatever sustained by any person due to any act, omission or error of whatsoever nature and howsoever caused in any information or advice given in any way whatsoever by or on behalf of LR, even if held to amount to a breach of warranty. Nevertheless, if any person, who is party to the agreement pursuant to which LR provides any service, uses LR's services or relies on any information or advice given by or on behalf of LR and suffers loss, damage or expense thereby which is proved to have been due to any negligent act, omission or error of LR, then LR will pay compensation to such person for his proved loss up to but not exceeding the amount of the fee (if any) charged by LR for that particular service, information or advice.

3.58　上述条款似乎既具有免责条款的性质,又有责任限制条款的特征。按照英国法的规定,合同中的免责条款只要合理通常是有效的。一旦免责条款有效,免除的不仅是合同责任,而且还包括侵权责任。免责条款必须是明确的且没有歧义,否则便是无效的。① 否定合同主要目的或免除一方当事人所有权利义务的免责条款通常是无效的。虽然与免责条款相比船级社的责任限制条款被认定有效的概率比较高,但并非所有责任限制条款都是有效的。就上述条款限制赔偿数额而言,1977 年《不公平合同条款法》有如下规定:②

> Where by reference to a contract term or notice a person seeks to restrict liability to a specified sum of money, and the question arises (under this or any other Act) whether the term or notice satisfies the requirement of reasonableness, regard shall be had in particular (but without prejudice to subsection (2) above in the case of contract terms) to –
>
> (a) the resources which he could expect to be available to him for the purpose of meeting the liability should it arise; and
>
> (b) how far it was open to him to cover himself by insurance.

3.59　因此,船级社限制赔偿数额是否有效还要取决于具体合同的具体情形。另外,按照 1977 年《不公平合同条款法》的规定,合同当事人不能凭合同条款或通知免除或限制自己在因疏忽引起的人身伤亡事件中的责任,即使是其他损失,合同当事人也只能在合同免责条款或免责通知符合合理要求的情况下才可以主张免责:③

> (1) A person cannot by reference to any contract term or to a notice given to persons generally or to particular persons exclude or restrict his liability for death or personal injury resulting from negligence.
>
> (2) In the case of other loss or damage, a person cannot so exclude or restrict his liability for negligence except in so far as the term or notice satisfies the requirement of reasonableness.
>
> (3) Where a contract term or notice purports to exclude or restrict liability for negligence a person's agreement to or awareness of it is not of itself to be taken as indicating his voluntary acceptance of any risk.

---

① Hugh Beale, *Chitty on Contracts*, 35th edn Sweet & Maxwell 2023, para.18 – 008.
② s.11(4).
③ Unfair Contract Terms Act 1977, s.2.

技术问题决定权

大多数船舶建造合同都规定关于船舶建造是否符合船级规范或规则的问题由船级社决定,而且船级社的决定对双方均有约束力。SAJ 格式便有类似的规定:①

3.60

> Decision of the Classification Society as to compliance or non-compliance with the classification shall be final and binding upon both parties hereto.

从上述规定来看,船厂和船东似乎约定将相互间关于船舶建造是否符合船级规范的争议提交给船级社解决了。严格意义上这并不是一个争议解决条款,而是针对特定问题,即船舶建造是否符合船级规范和规则的认定。上述条文既没有涉及双方应如何指定船级社相关人员,也没有规定船级社的哪些人以及多少人可以对船舶建造是否符合船级规范和规则的问题作出认定。② 要求船级社决定船舶建造是否符合船级规范和规定似乎是恰当的,但又好像是多余的。因为船舶建造是否符合船级社的规定只能由船级社来决定,而且也只能由船舶建造合同规定的船级社来决定。船级社参与了船舶建造的整个过程,船级社实际上是通过对各个具体项目的检验对船厂的建造是否符合船级社规定作出决定的。

3.61

NEWBUILDCON 格式也有类似的规定,但该格式的规定在范围上则比 SAJ 格式更为广泛。该格式的规定是:③

3.62

> The final decisions of the Classification Society or Regulatory Authorities shall be binding on the Parties as to the Vessel's compliance with their respective applicable laws, rules, regulations and requirements.

上述条文中的"laws, rules, regulations and requirements"应当包括船级社的规范和规则。按照 NEWBUILDCON 格式的规定,船舶需要符合的不仅仅是船级社的规定,而且还包括所有适用的法律、规则和要求。对船舶是否符合这些规定和要求作出认定的不仅仅是船级社,还包括船旗国在内的船舶监管当局。

3.63

---

① Article I.3, para.2, see also AWES Article 1(d).
② 关于船级社参与船厂和船东技术问题争议解决请参见本书第 15 章第 V 节。
③ Clause 3(b).

3.64　CSTC 格式有两处分别规定了船级社可以作出有约束力决定的情形,第一种情形是:①

Decisions of the Classification Society as to compliance or noncompliance with Classification rules and regulations shall be final and binding upon the parties hereto.

3.65　这一规定与 SAJ 格式的相关规定是一致的。第二种情形则是:②

Should there be any dispute between the BUILDER and the BUYER in such calculations and/or measurements, the decision of the Classification Society shall be final.

3.66　上述规定应当是船级社在船厂和船东就船舶的航速、油耗以及载重吨等是否符合船舶建造合同规定产生争议时作出的决定是最终的。这似乎涉及到争议的解决,而 CSTC 格式的争议和仲裁条款实际上已经作出了相应的规定了。③　就船厂而言,船级社就船舶建造是否符合船级社的要求作出认定的意义在于一旦船厂和船东就某一项目是否符合船级社的规定发生争议,只要该项目通过船级社的检验,除非船级社的检验有误,否则船厂就可以继续船舶的建造,而无需等待船东的检验意见。

3.67　在实践中,除非是对自己负责监造的船舶技术问题发表意见,船级社一般不愿意在船厂与船东的争议中扮演定夺是非的角色。即使是对自己负责监造船舶的技术问题发表意见,船级社的位置似乎也有些尴尬。船厂是与船级社有监造协议的相对方,而船东则是将船级社选为船舶建造完毕后的入级船级社。而且,船厂应当明白,虽然与船级社签署监造协议的是船厂,而对船级社做出选择的是船东,并非船厂。

Ⅲ　船舶入级

船级的意义

3.68　可以说船舶入级的做法源于海上保险。当时,海上保险人为了确保船舶的基本良好状况将入级设定为承保船舶的条件之一。这一要求延续至今,船壳保险人依然仅对入级的船舶进行承保。协会船级条款(Institute Classification Clause)就

---

① Article I.2, para.5.
② Article I.6, para.4.
③ Article XIII.2.

有如下规定:①

> This insurance and the marine transit rates as agreed in the policy or open cover apply only to cargoes and/or interests carried by mechanically self-propelled vessels of steel construction classed with a Classification Society which is:
>
> 1.1 a Member or Associate Member of the International Association of Classification Societies(IACS), or
>
> 1.2 a National Flag Society as defined in Clause 4 below, but only where the vessel is engaged exclusively in the coastal trading of that nation(including trading on an inter-island route within the archipelago of which that nation forms part).

保赔协会对入会船舶同样有入级的要求,例如汽船保赔协会的保险条款对船舶的船级做出了详细的规定:② 3.69

> The Member shall ensure that from the time when a ship is entered in the Club and throughout the period of the ship's entry that:
>
> a The ship is and remains classed with a Classification Society approved by the Managers in respect of the entered ship;
>
> b Any incident or condition in respect of which that Classification Society might make recommendations as to repairs or other action to be taken is promptly reported to that Classification Society;
>
> c All rules, recommendations and requirements of the Classification Society relating to the entered ship are complied with within the time or times specified by the Society;
>
> d If requested by the Managers, any overdue recommendations or conditions are immediately notified to them, together with any extensions granted by the Classification Society and certified by the Society;
>
> e The Managers are authorised to inspect any documents and obtain any information relating to the maintenance of Class of the entered ship in the possession of any Classification Society with which the

---

① Institute Classification Clause 01/01/2001.
② Class 1 Rules, Protection and Indemnity 2020/2021 of Steamship Mutual 2020/2021, Rule 26(i); see also Class 5, The Protecting and Indemnity Rules 2020/2021 of the London P&I Club, Rule 8.1.

ship is or has at any time been classed and such Classification Society or Societies are where necessary authorised to disclose and make available such documents and information to the Managers upon request by them and for whatsoever purpose the Managers may consider necessary;

    f   If at any time after acceptance for entry or during the period of entry, the Classification Society with which the ship is classed is proposed to be changed, the Managers are to be given not less than 14 days notice in advance, and in any event as much notice in advance as is possible of the proposed change of Classification Society, stating the identity of the Classification Society to which the ship is to be transferred, and all outstanding recommendations of the ship's existing Classification Society;

...

3.70　除了船舶本身的保险,船级在货物保险、货物运输、租船和船舶买卖中都起着重要的作用。货物保险人对运送货物的船舶,托运人对承运人提供的船舶,租船人对出租人出租的船舶,买方对卖方出售的船舶等都有船级要求。①

3.71　此外,船舶入级也是国际公约的要求。《国际海上人命安全公约》明确规定船舶必须按照船级社关于结构、机器和电器设备的要求进行设计、建造和保养:②

In addition to the requirements contained elsewhere in the present regulations, ships shall be designed, constructed and maintained in compliance with the structural, mechanical and electrical requirements of a classification society which is recognized by the Administration in accordance with the provisions of regulation XI/1, or with applicable national standards of the Administration which provide an equivalent level of safety.

3.72　按照《国际海上人命安全公约》颁发的法定证书,例如货船构造安全证书(Cargo Ship Safety Construction Certificate)和货船设备安全证书(Cargo Ship Safety Equipment Certificate)等也以船舶有船级为前提。

3.73　没有船级的船舶显然是很难通过港口国检验的。即使有船级,若提供船级的船级社不是国际船级社协会的成员船级社,船舶的营运同样会面临港口国检验的

---

① Class 1 Rules, Protection and Indemnity 2020/2021 of Steamship Mutual 2020/2021, Rule 26(i); see also Class 5, The Protecting and Indemnity Rules 2020/2021 of the London P&I Club, Rule 8.1.
② SOLAS, Part A-1, Regulation 3-1.

问题。

虽然几乎所有船舶都有船级,但实际上船东并没有安排船舶入级的法律义务。就船东而言,船舶入级是船舶从事营运的前提条件。没有船级的船舶不具有挂靠世界各地港口必须具备的船舶证书;保险人通常不会同意承保没有船级的船舶;没有船级的船舶无法在市场上找到租船人。① 船东对船舶船级的陈述通常是一项条件,如果船舶没有入级或者在租期内丧失船级,租船人就有机会解除租约。

3.74

船舶入级的程序

船舶的船级通常是通过一整套证书予以证明的,船舶证书是对船舶符合法律、规范、规则和要求的确认。船舶船级包括三个组成部分,第一是船级社设定标准;第二是船级社通过批准规格书和图纸、对船舶实施检验和测试,核实船舶符合标准;第三则是通过签发检验报告、船级证书等确认船舶符合标准。船舶符合船级社规范要求的,船级社将为船舶颁发"入级证书"。但是入级证书并不意味着船舶具有安全性,适于航行或达到预期用途。因为入级检验所适用的船级社规范并没有包括影响船舶安全的所有项目,也不包括船舶的操作;船级社也没有对船舶的设计、建造和使用进行全过程的控制,而只是进行"关键路径"的控制。② 在船舶建造中,船级社只对部分项目进行检验,参加测试。

3.75

只有符合入级条件的船舶才可入级。船级社的监造在船舶开始建造之前就已经开始。船舶的设计、船舶建造使用的材料等都必须经过船级社的批准。船级社将根据相关国际公约、船旗国的规定和要求对船舶建造实施全面的监督和检验,包括:设计、材料、船体结构和船舶设备等。船舶建造完毕后,船级社将根据船舶建造的情况以及船级社驻厂代表对船舶建造整个过程的监督,为船舶签发各种船舶证书。入级条件因船舶不同而异,通常包括:船舶的船体、船舶机械、船舶设备符合船级社规范;船舶完整稳性符合主管机关的要求,或不低于国际海事组织有关决议及修正案的规定或国际海事组织特殊船型的有关标准;船舶的分舱和破舱稳性符合国际海事组织有关公约的要求,或不低于国际海事组织有关公约及修正案的规定或国际海事组织特殊船型的有关标准,例如中国船级社的《钢质海船入级与建筑规范》便有如下规定:③

3.76

---

① 例如在航运市场常用的 NYPE 期租格式合同就有关于船舶船级的内容,船东必须对船舶的船级进行陈述,并保证在租期内保持船舶的船级,见 NYPE 46 Line 5, Line 37; NYPE 93 Line 12, Clause 6.
② 关于关键路径请参见本书第 10 章第 Ⅱ 节。
③ 第一章,第一节,入级条件。

凡船舶的船体(包括设备)和船舶机械(包括电气设备)符合本社《钢质海船入级与建造规范》(以下简称《规范》)或等效要求且船舶完整稳性和分舱及破舱稳性(如有要求时)符合主管机关的要求,或虽无主管机关的批准,但船舶的完整稳性和分舱及破舱稳性(如有要求时)不得低于国际海事组织有关决议、公约及其修正案的标准,或国际海事组织特殊船型(如适用时)的有关标准,本社将授予相应的船级,并载入本社的船舶录。

3.77　具体而言,船级社提供的新建船入级服务主要有下列几个方面:(1)设计图纸审核,即由船级社审核船舶的所有设计图纸及其他有关结构以确定其符合船级社的规范;此种审核包括船体结构、电气系统、管路、主机和辅机、螺旋桨等;(2)建造阶段检验,即船级社的验船师会在船舶建造过程中常驻现场监督建造的整个过程,从而确保船舶建造是按照已批准的图纸进行,所使用的材料和部件经过批准,以及建造运用了良好的工艺并遵守船级社的规范;(3)船级社的检验人还会亲临有关材料的制造地对材料和部件按船级社规范进行检测。

船级符号

3.78　船级符号是指船舶船体、轮机、电气装置以及消防等机器设备的主要特征均符合船级社规范或等效标准规定的表述。入级符号具有强制性。入级符号往往还伴有附加标志,附加标志是船舶不同特点的分级表述,加注在入级符号之后的附加标志有强制性和非强制性之分。附加标志表述的内容主要是:船舶类型、航行限制、特殊性能、货物特征、特殊检验、特殊设备等。

3.79　船舶的入级符号通常由符号、字母和数字组成。以 DNV 的入级符号为例,所有入级 DNV 的船舶都会有一个入级符号。该入级符号包括:建造符合、船级主要特征、航行区域符号以及基本设计符号。船舶的入级符号包含两种不同的要求,一种是强制性要求,另一种是选择性要求。船舶的入级标志也可能有一个附加图案,其目的是明确与入级符号有关的特定要求或限制。下面是挪威船级社的入级符号:

✠R0 1A1 Bulk Carrier ESP TMON E0 VCS‑2 PLUS

3.80　在这个入级符号中,✠(马耳他十字)是建造符号,即表明该船是在 DNV 监督下完成建造的。没有这一符号的则表明船舶是在有资质的船级社的监督下完成建造的,且在此后获得 DNV 船级的。

  1A1 是船级主要特征,船舶的主要特征表明该船的船体、机器、安装和设备符合钢质船规范的要求。1A1 表示该船每 5 年应当进行一次特检。1A2 则是特殊设计的钢质船或者是轻合金船,该船每 3 年应当进行一次特检。 3.81

  Bulk Carrier ESP 表明的是船型,即该船是散货船,这一入级符号既包括散货船的共同结构规范,也包括散货船的增强检验计划。增强检验计划是 SOLAS IX,Reg.1.6 以及 IACS URZ11 定义的散货船的强制性的入级符号。 3.82

  ESP 是 Enhanced Survey Programme 的缩写,即"增强检验计划",这是强制性的检验要求。 3.83

  CSR 是 Common Structure Rules,即共同结构规范的缩写,主要船型的补充船级符号。 3.84

  R0 是选择性入级符号,表明船舶的航行区域的限制。航行区域限制采用海里,代表离开港口或安全锚泊地的最大距离。航行区域限制涉及到载重线公约定义的区域、地区以及季节。R0 代表冬季 250 海里、夏季没有限制、热带没有限制。 3.85

  TMON 是选择性入级符号,表明船舶的检验周期。 3.86

  E0 VCS－2 是选择性入级符号,表明船舶设备和系统符号。 3.87

  PLUS 是选择性入级符号,表明船舶设计的特征。 3.88

  船舶的入级符号及其具体内容和特征通常约定在规格书中,船舶建造合同通常只约定船舶将按照某一特定船级社的规范建造。 3.89

符合船级社规范

  鉴于船舶必须获得船级才能从事营运,因此船级对船舶而言至关重要。要获得船级,船舶就必须符合船级社规范的规定。SAJ 格式在规定了船舶建造应当符合船舶建造合同后又规定了船舶建造应当符合船级社规范的要求:① 3.90

> The VESSEL, including its machinery, equipment and outfittings, shall be constructed in accordance with the rules(the edition and amendments thereto being in force as of the date of this Contract) of and under special survey of ....
> (herein called the "Classification Society"), and shall be distinguished in the register by the symbol of ....

---

① Article I.3, para.1.

3.91 船舶应当符合船级社规定的要求是不言自明的。船级社授予船舶的船级符号实际上是对船舶特征、类型和性能等的总结和认可。船舶建造不仅应当符合船级社的规范、规则和要求,同时还要符合国际海事组织以及船旗国等的法律、规则、规定以及要求等。对此,SAJ 格式规定:①

> The VESSEL shall also comply with the rules, regulations and requirements of other regulatory bodies as described in the Specifications in effect as of the date of this Contract.

3.92 上文中的"other regulatory bodies"应当是指船旗国以及对船舶享有管辖权的国家当局,例如船舶停靠港口的当局等。由于船舶将投入国际营运,因此也应当符合船舶挂靠港所在国的法律规定。

3.93 相比之下,NEWBUILDCON 的相关规定就比较明确一些:②

> The Vessel shall be designed, constructed, surveyed, tested and delivered in compliance with the applicable laws, rules, regulations and requirements of the Classification Society stated in Box 8, and the Regulatory Authorities:
> (i) in force as of the date of this Contract stated in Box 1, or
> (ii) if not in force as of the date of this Contract, which are ratified and promulgated on or before the date of this Contract and which will be compulsory for the Vessel on or before the delivery of the Vessel in accordance with Clause 28(Delivery).
>
> All such laws, rules, regulations and requirements of the Classification Society and the Regulatory Authorities shall be complied with without qualification (see Clause 26(Changes in Rules and Regulations)).

3.94 上文中的"Regulatory Authorities"与 SAJ 格式中的"regulatory bodies"应当同义,均指船旗国当局。NEWBUILDCON 格式对船舶应当符合的规定进行了区分,即(1)在船舶建造合同订立之时已经生效的相关规定;以及(2)在船舶建造合同订立之时或之前已经通过但尚未生效,而在合同规定的船舶交船日或之前将强制实施的。这一规定应当比 SAJ 格式的规定更为明确且更为合理。按照 SAJ 格式的规定,船舶应当符合的仅仅是在船舶建造合同订立之时已经生效的相关规定和要求。严格地说,即使在船舶建造合同订立之时已经通过了对船舶建造的新的要求,但只要这些新的要求在船舶建造合同订立之时尚未生效的,船厂就无需适用。

---

① Article I.3, para.3.
② Clause 3(a).

在采用 NEWBUILDCON 格式时,由于该条文将相关规定或要求生效的时间限制在船舶建造合同规定的交船日或之前,这也就意味着船厂应当承担船舶是否符合交船时生效的相关规定或要求的风险。

还有一种情况是,船级社的新规定或新要求在船舶建造合同订立之后制定但又在船舶交付之前开始强制实施了。除非船舶建造合同另有约定,否则该等新规定或新要求适用于船厂建造的船舶。因为船厂的合同义务之一是设计、建造并交付一艘符合国际公约、相关法律以及船舶规范的船舶。 3.95

双重船级

有时船东会选择将同一艘船向两个船级社申请入级。在这种情况下,船舶建造就将同时适用两个船级社的规范和要求,接受两个船级社代表的监督和检验。在这种情况下,两个船级社可以联合也可以分别成立审图和检验工作组,负责建造船舶的入级、审图、检验和发证事宜。但为了高效地开展工作,两个船级社往往会签署协议,对图纸审批、建造检验等具体工作的原则、内容以及分工等作出约定。还会订立联合检验工作协议,协调相互间的工作。在船舶同时按照两个船级社要求建造的情况下,两个船级社通常会和船厂共同订立三方协议,对图纸审批和检验程序等作出特别的规定。船舶申请双重船级的,无论两个船级社如何分工,所有图纸都必须同时获得两个船级社的批准才能用于船舶建造;所有用于船舶建造的产品和设备等均必须同时持有两个船级社颁发的产品或设备证书。 3.96

Ⅳ 船舶登记

船舶虽然是动产,但绝大多数国家都对船舶适用不动产法律规则,例如:登记、抵押和转移等。船舶登记是指将船舶登记于一国的公开记录,从而明确了船舶的国家属性。① 船舶拥有其登记所在国的国籍。 3.97

船舶的国籍

可以说公海上的航行自由是以船舶拥有国籍为前提的。1982 年《联合国海洋法公约》第 90 条规定: 3.98

---

① Edward Watt et al, *Ship Registration-Law and Practice*, 3rd edn informa 2019, para.1－1.

> 每个国家,不论是沿海国或内陆国,均有权在公海上行驶悬挂其旗帜的船舶。

3.99　根据公海自由这一国际法的基本原则,有国籍的船舶有权进入公海。虽然法律并没有明文禁止无国籍的船舶进入公海航行,但在公海上航行的无国籍船舶不受国际法的保护。一国依其主权,可以拒绝无国籍船舶进入其港口。所以船舶国籍是船舶从事国际航运的必要条件。船舶通过登记取得国籍,即在船舶完成登记后就拥有登记国的国籍,有权悬挂该国国旗航行。① 绝大多数国家都规定内河、沿海运输只能由悬挂本国国旗的船舶经营,完成登记的船舶便可享有从事登记国内河、沿海的排他经营权。《中华人民共和国海商法》便规定:②

> 中华人民共和国港口之间的海上运输和拖航,由悬挂中华人民共和国国旗的船舶经营。

3.100　船旗是船舶国籍的体现,拥有国籍的船舶都可以悬挂国籍国的旗帜。船舶行驶或停泊在需要识别国籍的地方时,例如行驶或停泊在一国水域或港口等,船舶应当悬挂国旗。③ 船舶航行只能悬挂一国国旗,并只受该国的专属管辖。1982年《联合国海洋法公约》对此作了明确的规定:④

> 船舶航行应仅悬挂一国的旗帜,而且除国际条约或本公约明文规定的例外情形外,在公海上应受该国的专属管辖。除所有权确实转移或变更登记的情形外,船舶在航程中或在停泊港内不得更换其旗帜。

3.101　国际法并没有关于船舶悬挂一国国旗权利的规定,但国际法要求国家通过国内法规定要求悬挂该国国旗的船舶应当满足的条件,例如1958年在日内瓦通过的《公海公约》(Convention on the High Seas, 1958)⑤就规定了每个国家应当确定允许船舶拥有该国国籍的条件,船舶在该国领土登记的条件,以及船舶享有悬挂该国国旗权利的条件。⑥

3.102　1982年《联合国海洋法公约》则有了更进一步的规定:⑦

---

① 参阅1969年《国际船舶吨位丈量公约》第三条第一款,1966年《国际载重线公约》第四条第一款。
② 第四条。
③ 船舶在公海行驶时是否始终需要展示国旗似乎并不是一个明确的问题。
④ 第九十二条。
⑤ 该公约于1962年9月30日起生效。
⑥ 第五条第一款。
⑦ 第九十一条第一款。

每个国家应确定对船舶给予国籍、船舶在其领土内登记及船舶悬挂该国国旗的权利的条件……

船旗国的职责

从维护公海秩序出发,不悬挂任何一国国旗的船舶不受任何保护,公海上的航行自由是悬挂一国国旗的船舶才能享受的自由。对于船舶国籍以及船旗的重要性,《奥本海国际法》有简单明确的解释:① 3.103

> 下述的国际法规则是被普遍承认的:第一,每一个具有海商旗的国家都必须制定规则,规定哪些船舶可以悬挂它的旗帜,并且必须对这种船舶发给正式证件,准许它们使用它的旗帜;第二,每一个国家都有权惩罚未经准许而悬挂它的旗帜的外国船舶;第三,在公海上,一切船舶以及船上的人和货物都被认为是在船旗国权力之下的;第四,每一个国家都有权在公海上惩罚海盗行为,即使是外国人所犯的海盗行为,而且为了消灭海盗起见,一切国家的军舰可以要求一切有嫌疑的船舶展示它们的旗帜。

船旗国对在该国登记船舶的要求基本上就是相关国际公约作出的规定和要求。这些相关的国际公约包括 1966 年《国际船舶载重线公约》、1969 年《国际船舶吨位丈量公约》、1972 年《国际避碰公约》、1973 年《国际防止船舶造成污染公约》、1974 年《国际海上人命安全公约》等。符合这些国际公约规定和要求的,船旗国就会接受申请并授予申请船舶该国的国籍。船舶的法定证书或航行证书实际上就是按照相关国际公约规定的要求在对船舶进行检验后签发的,这些证书包括:船舶登记证书、国际吨位证书、国际载重线证书、最低安全配员证书、国际防止油污证书、货船安全结构证书、货船安全设备证书、货船安全无线电证书以及客船安全证书等。 3.104

作为接受船舶登记的船籍国对悬挂其旗帜的船舶负有国际法上的义务,1982 年《联合国海洋法公约》对此种义务做出了明确的规定。② 按照公约的规定,船舶登记国的义务主要包括两个方面:第一是对悬挂该国国旗的船舶有效地实施行政、技术及社会事项的管辖和控制;第二是对悬挂该国国旗的船舶采取各项为保 3.105

---

① 《奥本海国际法》第 9 版,上卷第二分册,[英] 詹宁斯,瓦茨修订,王铁崖等译,王铁崖校订,中国大百科全书出版社 1989 年,第 160 页。
② 第九十四条。

证海上安全所必需的措施。

3.106　就第一方面而言,船舶登记国的具体义务包括制作并保持一本船舶登记册,载列悬挂该国国旗的船舶的名称及其他详细情况,并且根据其国内法的规定,就行政、技术和社会事项对该船及其船长、高级船员和普通船员行使管辖权。就第二方面而言,船舶登记国的具体义务则包括:对船舶的构造、装备、适航条件、船员的资格以及配备、船员的劳动条件和训练、船舶的信号使用、通信的维持和碰撞的防止、船舶定期检验、船舶图书和文件的配备等制定并实施必要的安全措施。

船舶登记的法律效力

3.107　船舶登记的法律效力可以从公法和私法两方面来考察。公法把船舶视为浮动的领土,其所体现的是船旗国的主权;而私法则把船舶看作是财产,一种可移动的,法律保护其所有人权益的财产。从国际公法上来看,船舶登记具有以下法律效力:①

(a) the allocation of a vessel to a specific State and its subjection to a single jurisdiction for the purposes, for example, of safety regulation, crewing and discipline on board;
(b) the conferment of the right to fly the national flag;
(c) the right to diplomatic protection and consular assistance by the flag State;
(d) the right to naval protection by the flag State;
(e) the right to engage in certain activities within the territorial waters of the flag State – for example, coastal fishing or trading between the ports of the flag State(cabotage);
(f) in case of war, for determining the application of the rules of war and neutrality to a vessel.

3.108　从私法上来看,船舶登记具有以下两个法律效力:一是形成对登记所有人的权利的保护;另一则是对船舶抵押权人利益的保护。

船舶登记的条件

3.109　1982年《联合国海洋法公约》规定,每个国家应当确定对船舶给予国籍、船舶

---

① NP Ready, *Ship Registration*, Lloyd's of London Press Ltd 1991, p.8.

在其领土内登记及船舶悬挂该国国旗权利的条件。① 早在 1905 年国际常设仲裁法院在 *Muscat Dhows between Great Britain and France*② 一案中就已确立了这一国际法原则。在该案中,国际常设仲裁法院认为主权国家有权决定同意船舶悬挂该国国旗并规定船舶享有此种权利的规则。这一国际法原则在 *Lauritzen* v *Larsen* 一案中也得到了美国最高法院的确认:③

> Under international maritime law, each state may determine for itself the conditions on which it will grant to a merchant ship its nationality as evidence to world by ship's papers and its flag, and the regularity and validity of registration can be questioned only by the registering state.

各国对申请在该国登记的船舶都规定了明确的要求,但这些要求不尽相同,有的比较严格,有的则比较宽松。英国法规定了申请登记的船舶应当符合如下条件:④

3.110

(1) A ship is entitled to be registered if –
    (a) it is owned, to the prescribed extent, by persons qualified to own British ships; and
    (b) such other conditions are satisfied as are prescribed under subsection(2)(b)below;
(and any application for registration is duly made).

(2) It shall be for registration regulations –
    (a) to determine the persons who are qualified to be owners of British ships, or British ships of any class or description, and to prescribe the extent of the ownership required for compliance with subsection(1)(a)above;
    (b) to prescribe other requirements designed to secure that, taken in conjunction with the requisite ownership, only ships having a British connection are registered.

船舶登记的办理

船舶建造合同通常有关于船舶登记的规定,例如 SAJ 格式就有如下规定:⑤

3.111

---

① 第九十一条第一款。
② Hague Court Reports 1916, p.93.
③ (1953) 345 US 571.
④ Merchant Shipping Act, 1995, s.9.
⑤ Article I.5.

> The VESSEL shall be registered by the BUYER at its own cost and expense under the laws of .... with its home port of .... at the time of its delivery and acceptance and acceptance and acceptance.

3.112　上述条文规定了船东可以登记船舶的时间，即交船之时。因为船舶的所有权在交付之前始终由船厂享有，船东在接船后才对船舶享有所有权，才能办理船舶的所有权登记。但在实践中船东并不是在接船后或接船时才办理船舶登记的，而是早在船舶交付之前就已经在其选择的船旗国为船舶办理了临时的登记手续。船舶的临时登记与船舶建造或建造合同无甚关联。前文已阐明无国籍船舶得不到适当的保护，也无法安全地从事国际航行，保险人也不会提供保险，这就意味着船东必须自己承担在船厂接船后航次的全部风险。船舶的临时登记则能解决船东的这一困境，它可以确保离开船厂后的航行是正常的，可以得到船籍国的保护，可以获得适当的保险，可以从事国际航行和国际营运。由此可见，船舶的临时登记在效力上可以说等同于船舶的永久登记，两者的区别在于效力期间。一国船舶登记机关同意船东的临时登记申请是因为船东尚无法提供可以完成永久登记的文件，例如船舶所有权证明等。船舶临时登记证书通常会有三个月至一年不等的有效期，除非船舶的临时登记在此期间转化成永久登记，船舶的临时登记在载明有效期届满之时即告失效。

3.113　船舶登记其实是交船后的事宜，并不是船东或船厂在船舶建造合同中的合同义务。因此船舶建造合同并非一定要就船舶登记作出规定。船厂需要知道的是船舶未来的船旗国，因为船舶的建造必须符合船旗国的规定和要求。在实践中，船舶建造应当符合的规定和要求在规格书中会有比较详细的描述。AWES 格式和 CSTC 格式也有类似的规定。①

3.114　对此，Norwegian 格式关于船厂应当协助船东办理船舶登记的规定比较适当，而且从字面来看，协助实际上还构成了船厂的一项合同义务。该格式规定的是：②

> The Builder shall provide, deliver and pay for all certificate necessary for the approval of the Vessel, as further set out in the Contract, together with all documents reasonably required by the Buyer necessary

---

① AWES Article 1(c), para.2, CSTC Article I.8.
② Article II.5.

for the registration of the Vessel in _____.

The Vessel shall be registered by the Buyer at its own cost and expense.

船东在办理船舶登记时需要提供船舶的相关细节、文件及证书等,这些细节、文件和证书的提供都需要船厂的协助。在实践中,双方在交船前就已经开始了船舶登记的办理。船厂会按照船东的要求向船东提供必要的信息、文件和证书。在提供证书和文件问题上,船厂应当注意的是并非任何文件和证书均可以在交船前提供,有些文件和证书只能在交船时提供,例如建造人证书和交接备忘录。建造人证书是船厂提供的各种文件中一份相当重要的文件,也是船东为船舶办理登记手续必不可少的文件。船舶登记机关在接受船舶登记申请时都必须确认申请人拥有所有权。建造人证书证明船舶是新建的,没有任何所有权的登记。持有建造人证书的船东就是建造人在证书中描述的船舶所有人。 3.115

在建船舶的登记

中国法

船舶登记是指船东对船舶享有的所有权的登记,但由于船舶所有权通常是在船舶交付时才从船厂转移至船东,因此在建船舶的登记是指船厂对尚处在建造过程中的船舶进行的登记。在建船舶的登记与交船以后的船舶登记不同,前者实际上只是一种临时登记。这一临时登记在船舶交付给船东之前必须注销。在建船舶登记通常是指船厂对在建船舶进行所有权登记,其目的是为了对船舶进行抵押并完成抵押权登记,从而解决船厂的融资问题。中国法律允许对尚在建造中的船舶进行登记,《中华人民共和国船舶登记条例》规定在建船舶可以办理所有权登记:[①] 3.116

> 船舶所有人申请船舶所有权登记,应当向船籍港船舶登记机关交验足以证明其合法身份的文件,并提供有关船舶技术资料和船舶所有权取得的证明文件的正文、副本。
>
> ……
>
> 就新造船舶申请船舶所有权登记的,应当提供船舶建造合同和交接文件。但是,就建造中的船舶申请船舶所有权登记的,仅需提供船舶建

---

① 第十三条。

造合同;就自造自用船舶申请船舶所有权登记的,应当提供足以证明其所有权取得的文件。

3.117 　　一旦在建船舶完成了所有权登记,登记为所有权人的船厂就可以对在建船舶设定船舶抵押。对在建船舶设置抵押的,船厂和为船厂融资的银行或金融机构应当在船厂所在地的船舶登记机关办理抵押权登记。① 我国法律针对在建船舶抵押规定了一些条件,只有满足这些条件后才可对在建船舶设定抵押。这些条件包括:②第一,作为抵押人的船厂应当符合国家关于船厂资质的要求,换言之,并非所有船厂都可以对由其建造的船舶设定抵押。而所谓的资质要求应当至少包括船厂的经营范围包括船舶建造。第二,作为抵押权人必须是具备发放贷款资格的金融机构,因此企业间或民间的借贷或资金支持可能无法通过抵押得到保障。第三,船厂对在建船舶拥有所有权。几乎所有标准格式都规定船舶在交接之前由船厂拥有。第四,作为抵押物的在建船舶应当符合"建造中船舶"的定义,如为分段建造的,应该已经完成至少一个以上的船舶分段并仍然处于建造阶段;如为整体建造的,应该已经安放龙骨并处于建造阶段的船舶才构成"在建船舶"。第五,作为抵押物的在建船舶所担保的债权不能超过申请抵押权登记时的在建船舶评估价格,而评估价格则是指由具备资产评估资质的机构对在建船舶评估的价格。这一要求可以说在很大程度上弱化了对在建船舶设定抵押的积极意义,因为在申请抵押之时的在建船舶应当是价值最低的时候,然而随着建造进程的推移,在建船舶的价值才会越来越大。

英国法

3.118 　　在英国法中,在建船舶并不构成法律意义上的船舶,因为英国法强调船舶是从事航行的,1995 年《商船法》(Merchant Shipping Act 1995) 有如下规定:③

　　Ship includes every description of vessel used in navigation.

3.119 　　由此可见,按照英国法,尚处于建造中的船舶并不符合法律上船舶的定义,船东因而无法对在建船设定抵押。

---

① 《建造中船舶抵押权登记暂行办法》第三条。
② 《建造中船舶抵押权登记暂行办法》第四条。
③ s.313(1).

在建船舶抵押登记

中国法允许对在建船舶进行所有权登记并允许对在建船舶设定抵押,对我国船厂无疑是有积极意义的。我国船厂尤其是中小型船厂一般都会在在建船舶上设定抵押,因为银行一般只会在成为在建船舶抵押权人后才会同意为船厂提供还款保函或其他融资。按照我国法律规定,船舶抵押未经登记的不得对抗第三人,①而船舶抵押权的登记显然必须以船舶所有权的登记为前提。由于抵押权是一种影响所有权的权利,希望将在建船舶抵押的船厂应当确保船舶建造合同中没有任何禁止或妨碍对在建船舶设定抵押的规定。

3.120

V 船级社的监造

船级社的监造是指船级社按照船级规范和船籍国要求对船舶建造的整个过程,包括设计、材料、设备、施工、检验以及测试等所有环节进行审核、监督以及测试等的整个过程。

3.121

船级社和船厂的关系

虽然船厂和船级社之间存在合同关系,但与船厂有合同关系的船级社实际上并不是船厂的选择,而往往是船东在和船厂订立船舶建造合同之前就已经确定了的。有观点认为船级社是由船厂雇用的并仅代表船厂。② 船级社的监造费用虽然是由船厂支付的,但似乎很难因此认定在船厂和船级社之间存在雇用和被雇用的关系,更无法认定船级社是代表船厂的。首先,船级社在船舶建造过程中起着监督的作用,但船级社并不是代表船厂对船舶建造进行监督的,船级社根据船旗国的要求以及船级规范的规定对船舶违造进行监督和检验。不属于船旗国或船级规范的项目,即使是按照船舶建造合同船厂必须完成的项目,也不构成船级社监造和检验的内容或对象。船级社监造的内容、程序及方式等均有明确的规定和要求,船厂并不能通过磋商予以增减或改变。其次,船厂应当没有机会通过雇用合同要求船级社放弃按照船旗国规定的或船级社规范规定的要求对项目进行监督和检验;船厂同样也很难通过合同要求船级社对船旗国规定和船级社规范规定

3.122

---

① 《中华人民共和国海商法》第十三条规定:"设定船舶抵押权,由抵押权人和抵押人共同向船舶登记机关办理抵押权登记;未经登记的,不得对抗第三人"。

② Simon Curtis et al, *The Law of Shipbuilding Contracts*, 5th edn informa 2020, p.30.

以外的项目进行监督和检验。虽然在船厂和船级社之间确有合同存在,但在监造协议中,双方也无法通过契约自由订立具有雇佣特征的其他条款。再次,船厂对船级社做出的关于船舶设计或建造的意见或检验结果通常没有提出异议的权利;同样道理,船东也不能将船级社的言行和立场视为船厂的言行和立场。最后,船舶建造合同通常会约定在船厂和船东就技术问题发生争议时应当将双方的争议提交船级社解决,船级社一旦做出决定对双方都有约束力。如果船级社是代表船厂的,就会有利益上的冲突,因而无法接受双方的委托对技术问题做出独立的决定。从船级社的实际作用和地位来判断,不难看出船级社实际上代表的应当是船舶的船旗国以及作为技术权威第三者的船级社本身。船级社对船舶建造实施监督和检验的依据是船旗国以及船级社本身的相关规定和要求,并不受其与船厂的协议所影响。

船舶监造的必要性

3.123　　前文已经提及船舶只有在符合船级社规范并获得由船级社赋予的船级符号以及由船级社颁发的各类证书后才能从事营运。船级社对船舶建造过程的监督是为了确保船舶的设计、建造以及设备等符合船级社规范的要求。随着国际社会对海上人命安全以及海洋防污染的重视,大量的关于航行安全以及海洋环境防污染的国际公约获得了通过,各个船级社之间对船舶在人命安全和海洋环境防污染问题上已经达成了高度的一致。换言之,不同船级社的要求已趋于同一化,差异可能仅仅体现在执行的力度上。

3.124　　船舶的建造不仅要符合船东选定的船级社的各项要求,而且还必须满足船旗国的所有要求。这包括船舶必须符合船旗国所加入的国际公约对船舶规定的要求。这些公约主要包括:1966 年《国际船舶载重线公约》、1969 年《国际船舶吨位丈量公约》、1972 年《国际海上避碰规则》、1973 年《国际防止船舶造成污染公约》以及 1974 年《国际海上人命安全公约》。此外,船舶还应当满足有关当局对船舶的要求,例如巴拿马和苏伊士运河当局对船舶的要求。又如美国公共卫生署对船舶的要求等。船级社的监造正是船舶建造符合船旗国要求的保障。

监造协议

3.125　　在船舶开始建造之前,船厂通常会与船级社订立一份监造协议。按照监造协议的规定,船级社提供的服务通常包括:审核并批准图纸;在船厂对船舶的建造包括机器、电器等的安装实施监督；参加测试、检验和试航；签发船级证书；将船舶登记于船级社。

船级社为自己的监造收取费用，监造费用由船厂承担且构成建造成本的一部分。标准合同对此均有规定，例如 SAJ 格式便规定：①

3.126

All fees and charges incidental to the classification and with respect to compliance with the above referred rules, regulations and requirements shall be for account of the Builder.

船级社收取的监造费用通常包括新船入级费用、图纸审核费用、破坏性稳性试验费用、船舶检验和一次试航的费用（如果需要重新检验和试航的，船级社将另行收费）、船舶证书的费用以及其他费用。但除非另有约定，监造费用通常不包括船级社验船师的额外交通费用和加班费等。如果建造周期超过约定期限过长，或者试航次数超过约定次数等，船级社也可能会另行加收费用。

3.127

Ⅵ NEWBUILDCON 格式的新规定

NEWBUILDCON 格式在关于船舶描述及船级的规定部分新增加了关于"有害物质清单""保护涂层"以及"原产地"的内容。下文将对这些新内容及其作用做一个简单的介绍和评价。

3.128

有害物质清单

NEWBUILDCON 格式的规定是：②

3.129

The Builder shall, in accordance with the IMO Guidelines on Ship Recycling, Resolution A.962(23), with amendments in force as of the date of this Contract:

(a) Endeavour to take due account of the Vessel's ultimate disposal when designing and constructing the Vessel by:
(1) Using materials which can be recycled safely and in an environmentally sound manner; and
(2) By minimizing the use of materials known to be potentially hazardous to health and the environment.

---

① Article I.3, para.4, see also Norwegian Article II.3, para.2, NEWBUILDCON Clause 3(c).
② Clause 4.

(b) In consultation with equipment manufacturers provide the Buyer with a Green Passport Statement of Compliance issued by the Classification Society containing information including the Vessel's hull number and main particulars and listing any and all materials known to be potentially hazardous utilised in the construction of the Vessel, its equipment and systems.

The list of the materials known to be potentially hazardous shall contain the location and the approximate quantity/volume of each identified material on board the Vessel.

3.130　　上述条文给船厂施加了两项义务,其依据是国际海事组织第 A.962(23)号决议通过的《国际海事组织拆船指南》(IMO Guidelines on Ship Recycling)。第一项义务是,考虑到船舶的最终处置,船舶建造应尽可能使用安全且环境无害化的材料,并尽可能避免使用已知的对人身和环境有潜在危害的材料;第二项义务则是向船东提供由船级社签发的确认船舶符合上述规定的绿色通行证。

3.131　　自 20 世纪 80 年代起,世界拆船业逐渐移向亚洲,随之而来的是大量的安全与环境污染问题。针对这些问题,国际海事组织颁布了《IMO 拆船指南》并于 2003 年 12 月得到了成员国的采纳。① 与此同时,国际劳工组织和其他国际组织也开始致力于解决拆船带来的安全与环境的问题。国际海事组织在海上环境保护委员会第 53 届会议上决定就拆船带来的安全与环境问题制定国际公约,并在第 54 届海上环境保护委员会会议上颁布了公约的初稿,经过数番修改后最终于 2009 年,即在 NEWBUILDCON 推出后,在香港通过了《香港国际安全及环境无害化拆船公约》(Hong Kong International Convention for the Safe and Environmentally Sound Recycling of Ships)(以下简称为《香港公约》),而"绿色通行证"(Green Passport)的概念也被"有害物质清单"(Inventory of Hazardous Materials(IHM))而取代。

3.132　　按照《香港公约》的规定,在每艘新船上均应存放一份有害物质清单。该清单应经主管机关或者经授权的任何个人或组织结合国际海事组织制定的指南予以验证。该有害物质清单应至少将公约附录 1 和 2 所述的船舶结构和设备中包含的有害物质及其位置和大约数量作为清单的第 I 部分列出,并且说明船舶符合第 4 条规定。② 有害物质清单并非一成不变,而将随着知识、经验以及立法的发

---

① 国际海事组织大会 A.962(23)决议通过了《拆船指南》,A.980(24)决议通过了《拆船指南》的修订。
② 《香港公约》第五条。

展而发生变化。有害物质清单的作用并不服务于正在使用船舶的船东,而是为了将来的船舶拆解人的利益,便于船舶拆解人了解船舶上的有害物质。国际海事组织为了配合《香港公约》的顺利实施,于2009年通过了MEPC 179(59)号决议,制定了《有害物质清单制定编制指南》(Guidance for the Development of the Inventory of Hazardous Materials),该指南提供了制定有害物质清单的建议,提供了相应的模板,为造船厂、拆船厂、修船厂、设备供应商、船东和船舶管理公司的清单制定提供了参考和依据。2011年海上环境保护委员会又通过了MEPC 197(62)号决议,制定了新的《有害物质清单制定编制指南》,同时废除了2009年的《指南》。海上环境保护委员会邀请各成员国尽快或在《香港公约》生效后适用2011年的《指南》。

《香港公约》在NEWBUILDCON格式推出之时实际上还未生效,①《香港公约》中使用了"新船"(newbuilds)的概念,所谓的"新船"是指《香港公约》生效时或生效后签订的建造合同所建造的船舶;或者无建造合同的则在《香港公约》生效时或生效6个月后安放龙骨或处于类似建造阶段的船舶;或在《香港公约》生效时或生效30个月后交付的船舶。② 因此《香港公约》实际上至今并不适用于开始建造的新船。在《香港公约》正式生效之前开始适用其相关规定未必合适,也未必符合船东的利益。 3.133

保护涂层

本节讨论的"保护涂层"是指国际海事组织于2006年制定的关于船舶海水压载舱及散货船双舷侧处所保护涂层性能标准(Performance Standard for Protective Coatings),简称为"PSPC"。NEWBUILDCON格式对保护涂层作出了如下规定:③ 3.134

> The Vessel's double-side skin spaces and dedicated seawater ballast tanks shall be coated in accordance with the Specification. In any event the minimum coating standard shall be in accordance with the requirements of the IMO Performance Standard for Protective Coatings

---

① 按照《香港公约》的规定,该公约应当在不少于15个国家签署公约并对批准、接受或认可无保留,或已交存必要的批准、接受、认可或加入文件;所述国家的商船总吨位合计不少于世界商船总吨位的40%;以及所述国家在过去10年的最大年度总拆船量合计不少于该国商船总吨位的3%以后的24个月才生效。
② 《香港公约》附录第一条第四款。
③ Clause 5.

for dedicated seawater ballast tanks in all types of ships and double-side skin spaces of bulk carriers (IMO PSPC, Resolution MSC.215(82)) and, where applicable, in accordance with the IACS Common Structural Rules for Bulk Carriers and for Oil Tankers or subsequent modifications or replacement applicable in accordance with Clause 3(a)(Classification, Rules and Regulations).

3.135　　上述条文实际上规定了船厂的三个义务：第一，船厂对船舶的双舷侧处所及专用海水压载舱实施的涂层应当符合规格书规定的要求；第二，涂层的标准至少应当符合国际海事组织规定的《所有类型船舶专用海水压载舱及散货船双舷侧处所保护涂层性能标准》；第三，在适用的情况下应当符合国际船级社协会的《散货船结构共同规范》及其修订文件。

3.136　　第一项义务的规定与否应当没有太大的区别，因为即使没有规定，船厂依然有义务确保双舷侧处所及专用海水压载舱的涂层符合规格书的规定。第二项规定船厂的涂层应当符合的标准适用于2008年7月1日及以后签订的建造合同所建造的500总吨以上适于国际航行的所有类型的新造船，或在2009年1月1日以后安放龙骨或处于类似建造阶段，或在2012年7月1日以后交付的船舶。因此在NEWBUILDCON格式推出之时该标准已经开始实施，即使该格式没有第二项义务的规定，船厂依然负有按照国际海事组织规定的涂层标准对船舶实施涂层的义务。第三项义务规定的油轮和散货船的结构共同规范实际上已经于2006年4月1日起开始实施，即在NEWBUILDCON格式推出之前就已经开始实施了，因此即使格式没有规定第三项义务，船厂依然必须严格遵守国际船级社协会的结构共同规范，否则船舶就无法获得证书。

原产地

3.137　　NEWBUILDCON格式关于原产地的规定是：①

If so requested by the Buyer, the Builder shall identify the country of originof all the main components listed in the Maker's List and Specification.

3.138　　原产地要求旨在明确相关设备或部件的生产地，从而帮助船东了解相关设备或部件的实际制造地。经常遇到的情况是，同一设备或部件在不同国家或地区都

---

① Clause 6.

可以采购到,即使是同一品牌的设备或部件也可以在不同的国家或地区生产。船东对相关设备或部件提出原产地要求往往出于对特定国家或地区生产的相关设备或部件的质量比较有信心,也可能是因为船东所在国对特定国家或地区的采购有限制。

NEWBUILDCON 格式只是要求船厂向船东告知其采购设备或部件的实际生产地。在实践中,厂商表有时仅规定船厂应当采购的设备的品牌,有时不仅规定船厂应当采购的品牌,而且还会规定船厂应当在特定国家或地区进行采购。

3.139

VII 船舶建造的分包

概念

分包是指船厂将自己在船舶建造合同中承担的部分建造工作交由第三人完成的做法。分包在船舶建造中比较常见。船厂将自己的工作进行分包可能是出于专业的原因,例如船厂除保留施工设计外,一般会将绝大部分设计工作通过分包交由专业的设计公司完成;也可能是出于降低成本的考虑,例如将部分分段通过分包交由第三人完成。有船舶建造合同标准格式给分包商下过定义,例如 Norwegian 格式的分包商定义是:①

3.140

> Any person (not being a servant or employee of the Builder) or company, with whom the Builder has entered into a contract for the design, construction, manufacture or supply of any item, equipment, work or service for the Vessel.

从上述定义可以看出,分包商几乎包括了所有为了船舶建造与船厂订立合同的第三方。分包商可以是为船厂提供基本设计或详细设计的设计公司,也可以是为船厂制作分段或其他工作的船厂或工厂,而且还可以是为船厂提供材料、设备等的供应商或制造厂商。分包商的工作根据其性质可以在船厂的场地完成,也可以在自己的场地完成。

3.141

分包与采购或分包商与供应商应当是有区别的。分包通常是指一方替另一方完成指定的工作,完成工作的一方即为分包商。采购则是指产品的购买。船厂

3.142

---

① Article I. NEWBUILDCON 的分包商的定义与此相同。

为了完成船舶建造是不可能没有采购的,供应商是为船厂提供产品的一方。两者的本质区别应当是分包商是通过劳动服务为船厂的船舶建造提供了帮助,而供应商则是通过产品为船厂的船舶建造提供帮助的。

船厂分包的权利

3.143　船厂是否可以将建造工作进行分包以及如何分包往往是船舶建造合同约定的问题。虽然船厂原则上有权分包和对外采购,但是不同船舶建造合同会对船厂的此种权利作出各种不同的限制。SAJ 格式和 AWES 格式中关于分包的内容明显对船厂有利,例如 SAJ 格式规定:①

> The BUILDER may, at its sole discretion and responsibility, subcontract any portion of the construction work of the VESSEL.

3.144　按照 SAJ 格式的规定,船厂几乎可以将整艘船的建造工作分包给他认为合适的人,且无需获得船东的同意。这样的规定应当是一个极端,在实践中并不多见。很少船东会接受此种分包安排。AWES 格式也有类似的规定:②

> The Contractor has the right to subcontract part of the work to third parties.

3.145　CSTC 格式对 SAJ 格式的规定进行了调和,该格式关于分包的规定是:③

> The SELLER may, at its sole discretion and responsibility, subcontract any portion of the construction work of the VESSEL to experienced subcontractors, but delivery and final assembly into the VESSEL of any such work subcontracted shall be at the BUILDER's Shipyard.

3.146　CSTC 格式增加了"experienced"一词,即分包商必须是"有经验的"。所谓的"有经验的"在实践中应当不难满足。只要有过船舶建造经历的船厂似乎都可以成为有经验的船厂。

3.147　Norwegian 格式在分包问题上则与 SAJ 格式和 AWES 格式有着明显的不同。该格式在分包问题上给船厂设置了明确的限制:④

> The hull and major sections thereof are to be built by the Builder at the

---

① Article I.4.
② Article 1(e).
③ Article I.7.
④ Article II.4, para.1.

Yard set out in Article II, clause 1, unless the Buyer consents otherwise, such consent not to be unreasonably withheld. Save as aforesaid, the Builder may, at its sole discretion and responsibility, subcontract any portion of the construction of the Vessel. Builder shall remain fully liable for the due performance of such work as if done by the Builder at the Builder's yard.

3.148 毫无疑问,Norwegian 格式给船厂的分包规定了较多的限制。除非得到船东的同意,否则船体的主要分段必须由船厂在自己的场地内完成。虽然规定船东不能不合理地拒绝船厂的分包要求,但这一规定实际上并不会有太大的实际意义,因为船东要求船厂自己建造船舶似乎并不是一个不合理的要求。

3.149 NEWBUILDCON 格式关于船厂分包的规定比较简单,即以规格书或厂商表规定的厂商为限。除非是次要的工作,船厂向规格书或厂商表规定的厂商以外的人进行分包或采购的都应当获得船东的许可:①

The Builder shall employ the sub-contractors as set out in the Specification or Maker's List. Except for minor work, the Builder shall not employ other sub-contractors without the Buyer's approval, which shall not be unreasonably withheld.

分包商的选择

3.150 作为合同组成部分的厂商表有可能会对分包及分包商产生影响。在绝大多数船舶建造合同中都会有厂商表,列明了船厂可以缔约的第三方,既包括供应商,也包括分包商。在有厂商表列明船厂可以使用分包商时,船厂可以在列明的分包商中按照自己的意愿作出选择。AWES 格式考虑了船东和船厂各自的利益,作出了比较仔细的规定。作为原则,船厂可以自由选择厂商表列出的供应商或分包商,船东有不同意见的且涉及价格差异的,可以最终决定船厂应选择的供应商或分包商,但应当承担额外的成本。AWES 格式的规定是:②

There is attached to the Specifications a Makers' List of major items on which the PURCHASER and CONTRACTOR agree on one or more suppliers and/or subcontractors. The CONTRACTOR shall be free to choose any of the proposed suppliers and/or subcontractors. Should the

---

① Clause 19.
② Article 2(b)para.3.

PURCHASER prefer a particular supplier and/or subcontractor other than the one actually chosen by the CONTRACTOR (whether or not originally proposed by the CONTRACTOR) and should the PURCHASER's preference involve a cost change the CONTRACTOR shall quote the amount of such cost change to the PURCHASER who shall then have the option to notify the CONTRACTOR within .... days from the date of receipt of such notice by the PURCHASER of the CONTRACTOR's chosen(selected) suppliers and/or subcontractors or within .... days from despatch on the CONTRACTOR's notice, whichever is the sooner, that it insists on its preference, and in such case the amount of the cost change shall be added to or deducted from the contract price. Failing any action by the PURCHASER or in case of dissent, the CONTRACTOR shall, subject to the CONTRACTOR's guarantee liability under Article 12 hereof, be free to use any of the suppliers and/or subcontractors proposed.

3.151 由于船舶建造合同大多采用一揽子价格,分包商或供应商的选择对船东而言比较简单,择优选之即可。船东的选择可能会给船厂带来成本上的压力。船厂可能遇到的情形是,虽然都是厂商表列明的供应商,但价格有高有低。在确保质量的前提下船厂显然会倾向于要价较低的供应商采购,但若船东坚持要船厂的要价较高的供应商采购时,船厂恐难有很好的理由拒绝。

分包商的地位

3.152 分包商虽然直接参与船舶建造,但由于与分包商有直接合同关系的是船厂而不是船东,因此分包商通常对船东并不直接承担责任。[①] 相反,即使船厂指派的分包商是规格书或厂商表列明的厂商,船厂依然必须对分包的工作或采购的设备等的质量、方式和交付等对船东承担合同义务。一旦船东指定的厂家或供应商提供的设备存在质量问题或者交付迟延,船厂仍需为此种质量问题和交付迟延对船东承担责任。因为船东的指定实际上只是一种推荐而已,与厂商订立合同的依然是船厂。如果船厂根据以往经验认为船东指定厂商提供的设备或产品存在质量问题,或有拖延交付的情况,船厂应当设法作出保留。

3.153 AWES 格式还规定船东与分包商的接触应当通过船厂进行:[②]

---

① 如果船厂将分包商提供的质保转让给船东的,分包商将对船东承担直接的责任。
② Article 2(b)para.4.

It is agreed that all contact with the CONTRACTOR's supplier concerning supplies intended for the VESSEL under this CONTRACT shall be made through the CONTRACTOR.

3.154 上述规定的出发点应当是船厂为了保护自己的权利和利益,但此种规定并没有什么实际意义,也不会给船厂提供实实在在的保护。在当今的造船实践中,上述条款已经很难见到了。船厂应当明白的是船东,尤其是大船东都与主要供应商保持着良好的关系。虽然与供应商签约的是船厂,但主要分包商其实是船东的选择结果。

分包商的谨慎之责

3.155 船东虽然与分包商没有合同关系,但为船舶提供设备的分包商对船东依然负有谨慎之责。分包商提供的设备若有缺陷的,船东除了可以依据船舶建造合同向船厂主张权利外,还有机会直接向分包商主张损害赔偿。在 *Diamante Sociedad de Transportes SA v Todd Oil Burners Ltd(The Diamantis Pateras)* 一案中,①原告船东和一家船厂订立了船舶建造合同,由船厂为船东建造一艘船舶。按照船舶建造合同的规定,船厂应当安装由船东分包商设计和生产的燃油设备。在船舶海试过程中,船东的总管和轮机长发现炉膛内火焰又短又浓,于是向船厂指出了这一现象。但是分包商的代表告诉他们说这是正常的现象。在船舶投入营运一年左右后,锅炉的右舷炉内发现有折裂并进行了修理。船级社的验船师建议对锅炉进行检查,并在检查后建议更换炉膛。船舶于是进行了修理并发现由于折裂需要更换所有的炉膛。船东向分包商提出了索赔,要求赔偿修理费用以及因此产生的营运利润损失。争议的焦点之一是分包商对船东是否负有谨慎之责。船东认为分包商对自己负有谨慎职责,由于炉膛的设计和制造有缺陷,分包商因此违反了该谨慎之责。但是分包商认为:自己对船东不负有任何责任,并且否认自己有任何疏忽。

3.156 高院的 Lawrence 法官认为分包商对船东负有谨慎之责,他说:②

It is true that in certain instances foresight may not be the sole criterion; but plainly in this present case the plaintiffs must have been reasonably in the contemplation of the defendants when the defendants were complying with the order from the shipbuilders; and, indeed, this fact

---

① [1966] 1 Lloyd's Rep 179.
② [1966] 1 Lloyd's Rep 179 at 187.

was admitted by the managing director of the defendants when he gave his evidence.

A consideration of modern authorities leads me to the conclusion that the opportunity of intermediate examination is a matter which goes now rather to the question of causation than to the issue of whether or not a duty of care is imposed on the defendants. In any event, on the facts of this case, it was the defendants who had an opportunity for such examination and adjustment of burners; and although the plaintiffs also may be said to have had an equal opportunity thereafter, I think it is reasonable that the plaintiffs' superintendent, Mr. Robertson, and the chief engineer should have relied on the adjustments and assurances of the representatives of the defendants. In short, I hold that the defendants did in the circumstances of this case owe a duty of care to the plaintiffs, and, subject to the facts, the action is well founded.

分包商的责任限制

3.157　　虽然船厂与分包商订立的分包合同通常也会规定分包商的违约责任,但此种责任往往有一个责任限制,例如不超过合同金额的10%。一旦分包商违反分包合同导致船厂违反船舶建造合同时,分包商按照分包或采购合同应当承担的赔偿金额,这对船厂可能要承担的船舶建造合同违约责任而言显然是杯水车薪。

3.158　　分包合同规定的责任限制通常是有效的,但若分包商的违约是故意的或恶意的,在适用英国法的情况下,船厂应当有机会主张分包合同中关于责任限制的规定无效。

第 4 章　价格及支付方式

I　合同价格

　　毫无疑问,合同价格是船舶建造合同的重要条款之一。合同价格通常包括:设计、材料和设备、建造和监造、检验和测试、船级社费用、船旗国费用、试航、证书、人力和管理等所有完成船舶建造所需的成本和费用。但合同价格不包括船东供应品,也不包括船东的登记费等费用。

固定价格

　　与一般的建造合同不同,船舶建造合同的价格绝大多数均采用固定价格(lump sum)的方式。即合同价格不会因成本、材料和人力的变化而变化。SAJ 格式的价格条款是:[①]

> The purchase price of the VESSEL is ....
> ....
> .... Japanese Yen
> (¥...).
> net receivable by the BUILDER (herein called the "Contract Price"), which is exclusive of the BUYER's Suppliers as provided in Article XVII hereof and shall be subject to upward or downward adjustment, if any, as hereinafter set forth in this Contract.

　　上述条文中的"subject to upward or downward adjustment"是指合同价格的调整,因为在建造过程中有可能发生建造项目增减或者设备调整的情况。这些项目的增减和设备的调整等通常会导致建造成本发生变化,因此合同价格将根据这些变化而调整。"net receivable"是指船厂收到的实际数额,因此船东应当承担汇款

---

① Article II.1.

所需的费用。AWES 格式的相关规定比较明确：①

> Expenses for remitting payments and any other expenses connected with such payments shall be for the account of the PURCHASER.

4.4　在约定固定价格的情况下，由于船舶建造往往会经历一个比较长的时间周期，在这期间船厂有可能由于市场变化导致成本增加而遭受损失。但这并不构成船厂要求提高合同价格的理由。正如上议院的 Lord Reid 在 *Davis Contractors Ltd v Fareham Urban District Council* 一案中所说的：②

> In a contract of this kind the contractor undertakes to do the work for a definite sum and he takes the risk of the cost being greater or less than he expected.

4.5　从理论上来讲，合同价格取决于成本和利润。就成本而言，影响船舶建造合同价格的因素主要有：船舶的基本规范和技术要求、材料和设备的市场价格以及劳动力和管理人员的成本。如果建造合同约定的货币与船厂采购使用的货币不同的话，船厂还会受汇率变化的影响。

货币的选择

4.6　传统上，船舶建造合同通常只会约定一种货币作为合同价格的计价币种，例如 SAJ 格式使用日元计价。这也从某种程度上反映了当时日本在世界造船业的地位。美元通常是船舶建造合同计价货币的选择。使用哪一种货币可能并不在于币种本身，而在于所使用的货币与使用人之间的关系。对船东而言，选择美元作为船舶建造合同的货币应当是比较合理的，因为船东经营的收入和成本乃至融资基本都采用美元。如果船舶建造合同按照 SAJ 格式的规定采用日元，船东就会遇到营运收入和造船支出不相吻合的问题。如果船东融资也采用美元的话，问题可能会更大。一旦美元和日元的汇率发生较大的波动，船东就可能因此而遭受巨大的损失。

4.7　就船厂而言也一样，船厂希望船舶建造合同采用的币种与自己采购合同的币种是一致的，从而避免因汇率波动可能带来的不利影响。我国船厂的采购通常不局限于单一货币。钢板通常是在国内采购，因此会用人民币计价，而主机和不少

---

① Article 7(c), para.3.
② [1956] AC 696 at 723.

设备则往往是在全球范围内采购,最有可能使用的货币是美元和欧元。在这种情况下,美元和人民币以及欧元的汇率变化就可能带来风险。随着美元在国际金融界日趋疲软,欧洲的供应商也越来越多地使用欧元计价,这就造成了船厂收入的计价货币和成本的计价货币不一致的情况。就国内的采购而言,如果人民币与美元相比日益坚挺,船厂因美元和人民币的汇率变化而遭受损失几乎是注定的。为了应对国际金融格局的变化,我国船厂的船舶建造合同也有采用两种货币计价的做法,即合同价格由美元部分和欧元部分组成。这种做法显然能尽可能缩小船厂因美元和欧元汇率变化带来的不利影响。而就使用人民币采购而言,船舶建造合同也有特别的条款约定在美元和人民币的汇率差达到约定百分比时,由双方共同承担因此引起的汇差损失。

虚假合同价格

如果船舶建造合同记载的合同价格是一方当事人为了实现某一目的而虚设的,船舶建造合同就有可能因此被认为无效或不可执行。这是公共政策的要求。当事人的合同行为应当合法且符合公共政策要求。如果当事人的选择带有非法目的,法院就可能认定合同无效或不可执行。正如 Lord Truro 在 *Egerton* v *Bronlow* 一案中指出的,任何人都不能从事任何有可能危及公众利益的行为。他说:①   4.8

> Public policy, in relation to this question, is that principle of the law which holds that no subject can lawfully do that which has a tendency to be injurious to the public, or against the public good, which may be termed, as it sometimes has been, the policy of the law, or public policy in relation to the administration of the law.

Swinfen Eady 法官在 *Reversionary and General Securities Co Ltd* v *Hall* 一案中也认为违反公共政策的合同是无效的:②   4.9

> When questions arise as to conditions or provisions being void as being against the public good or against public policy, great caution is necessary in considering them; at different times very different views have been entertained as to what is injurious to the public .... If, however, it be clearly established that the condition is against public

---

① (1853) 4 HL Cas 1 at 196.
② [1908] 1 Ch 383 at 386.

policy, it is certainly void.

4.10 在 *Mitsubishi Corporation v Aristidis I Alafouzos*① 一案中,作为原告的日本船厂和一希腊公司订立了船舶建造合同,约定由船厂为船东建造一艘散货船。被告是希腊公司的实际拥有人。合同价格为四十亿日元,由船东分期支付。合同约定适用英国法,争议提交伦敦仲裁解决。虽然合同价格是四十亿日元,但实际上船东和船厂另行签署了补充协议,约定了较低的合同价。在签署船舶建造合同时,被告作为担保人向船厂提供了担保,保证希腊船东履行船舶建造合同,该担保有如下内容:

> I ... as a primary obligor and not as a surety merely ... irrevocably and unconditionally guarantee to you ... the due and faithful performance and fulfillment by the Buyer of all the terms and conditions in the Contract ... including but not limited to prompt payment when due of the price of the vessel ... to you ....

4.11 在船东逾期未支付第二期和第三期建造款时,船厂要求担保人履约。担保人认为合同价格是一项欺诈性误述,因而该合同违反了英国的公共政策,目的是骗取日本政府的建造许可和出口许可。高院也认为该船舶建造合同是不可执行的,Styen 法官说:②

> ... in an age in which commercial fraud is increasing, it seems imperative that the Court should refuse to allow a party to rely on a contract which was drafted or structured to deceive third parties, and the fact that what is alleged to have happened in this case is by no means unknown in the shipbuilding trade makes the stringent application of that public policy in this area a matter of the first importance.

4.12 船厂的一个观点是,欺骗行为发生在英国境外,因此不构成英国法下的犯罪或侵权。但是 Steyn 法官认为这一情形并不能改变他的判决,他说:③

> That difference does not in my judgment amount to a material distinction. It would be extraordinary if public policy, in the context of international business transactions, condemned such conduct in this country but allowed the coercive power of the state to be enlisted if the

---

① [1988] 1 Lloyd's Rep 191.
② [1988] 1 Lloyd's Rep 191 at 194.
③ [1988] 1 Lloyd's Rep 191 at 195.

deception was practised abroad. I hold, without hesitation, that the public conscience does not permit our Courts to show a larger tolerance to the enforcement of a deceiving transaction if it took place abroad.

Ⅱ 合同价格的支付

4.13 按照船舶建造合同的约定,支付合同价格可以说是船东在船舶建造合同中的最主要的义务。船舶建造合同通常会要求船东按照合同的签订以及船舶建造的节点分期支付合同价格。

支付方式

4.14 支付方式主要包括两个内容,一是分期支付,一是电汇支付。

分期支付

4.15 由于合同价格数额较大且建造周期较长,船舶建造合同通常都会规定分期支付合同价格。采用分期支付的方式有利于减轻船厂建造船舶的资金压力,正如 Lord Alverstone 在 *Workman Clark & Co Ltd v Lloyd Brazileno* 一案中所说的:①

> The object of provisions for payment by instalments appears to be to put the contractor, who has to incur great expense in labour and materials during the progress of the work, in funds to meet these expenses.

4.16 至于如何分期以及分几期支付则由船厂和船东通过协商决定,而市场因素会对此种协商有相当大的影响。按照 SAJ 格式的规定,船东应当分四期支付合同价格:②

> The Contract Price shall be paid by the BUYER to the BUILDER in installations as follows:
>
> (a) 1st Installment:
>   The sum of .... Japanese Yen(¥......) shall be paid upon issuance by the Japanese Government of the Export License for the VESSEL.
> (b) 2nd Installment:

---

① [1908] 1 KB 968 at 971.
② Article Ⅱ.3.

The sum of .... Japanese Yen(￥......)
shall be paid upon keel-laying of the VESSEL.
(c) 3rd Installment:
The sum of .... Japanese Yen(￥......)
shall be paid upon launching of the VESSEL.
(d) 4th Installment:
The sum of .... Japanese Yen(￥......)
plus any increase or minus any decrease due to adjustments of the Contract Price hereunder, shall be paid upon delivery of the VESSEL.

4.17 　　四期支付分别是：第一期在船厂获得船舶出口许可后支付；第二期在铺龙骨时支付；第三期在船舶下水时支付；而第四期则在交船时支付。"日本政府批准船舶出口"反映的是 SAJ 格式制定之初的情况，该条款已不再适用。SAJ 格式应当是所有标准格式中关于支付的规定最为简单的格式。随着船舶建造实践的变化，船舶建造合同关于支付的规定也相应发生了不小的变化，付款的分期数也不再是四期了，例如 2000 年的 Norwegian 格式便规定合同价格分为六期支付：①

The Original Contract Price shall—subject to notices being given under this Article III clause 3—be paid in installations as follows:

(a) 1st Instalment:
The sum of ....
shall be paid three(3) Banking Days after the Date of the Contract.
(b) 2nd Installment:
The sum of ....
shall be paid within .... Banking Days after ....
(c) 3rd Instalment:
The sum of ....
shall be paid within .... Banking Days after ....
(d) 4th Installment:
The sum of ....
shall be paid within .... Banking Days after ....
(e) 5th Installment:
The sum of ....
shall be paid within .... Banking Days after ....
(f) Instalment on Delivery and Acceptance:

---

① Article III.3, para.1.

The sum of ....
plus and increase or minus any decrease due to adjustments of the
Contract Price hereunder, shall subject to the other provisions of the
Contract, be paid upon Delivery and Acceptance of the Vessel.

4.18　在船舶建造合同中,船东支付建造款的时间通常与船舶建造的节点挂钩。所谓节点是指船舶建造过程中比较关键的时间段,例如:签约、开工、上船台、下水、交船。签约是指船东和船厂签署船舶建造合同,签约后支付的建造款通常是船东支付的第一期款。船东和船厂大多都会约定签署船舶建造合同的时间和地点,船厂甚至还会为签约举行仪式。船东在签约后支付的第一期建造款也因此被称为"签约款"。有时船舶建造合同的签署并不意味着合同的生效,合同只有在满足双方约定的条件后才生效,例如:船厂开出还款保函,或者双方董事会批准合同等等。在这种情况下,船东的第一期款则应在船舶建造合同生效后支付,因此也被称为"生效款"。

4.19　开工(steel cutting)是指船厂正式开始船舶的建造。通常船厂会为正式开工举行仪式,并邀请船东和船级社的代表出席。其实,所谓的开工实际上是割一块分段使用的钢板。因此开工的形式意义往往大于其实际意义,有时开工时所割的钢板甚至有可能并不是开工船舶所用的钢板。船舶建造正式开工后,船东通常会支付建造款,由于是在开工后支付的,因此也被称为"开工款"。

4.20　上船台(keel laying)是指将船舶的分段吊上船台并进行焊接合拢。上船台也被称为"铺龙骨",英文是"keel laying"。但是随着船舶建造的现代化,大量分段的采用,所谓的龙骨其实都已分散在预制的相关分段中,实际上已不再有真正意义上的铺龙骨了。由于不存在铺设龙骨这一过程,因此何为铺龙骨就取决于船厂和船东的约定,有的船舶建造合同会约定"第一个分段和第二个分段在船台上合拢后";而有的船舶建造合同并不要求分段的合拢,而是规定第一个分段被吊至船台之上就视为是铺龙骨。倘若双方没有对上船台或铺龙骨作出约定,争议就有可能产生。在这种情况下,1974年《国际海上人命安全公约》的规定应当有助于问题的解决。该公约对何为铺龙骨作出了规定:①

The assembly of that ship has commenced comprising at least 50 tonnes or one per cent of the estimated mass of all structural material, whichever the less.

---

① 第Ⅱ-1章,A部分,规则第1.2.2条。

4.21　　船舶按照合同规定上船台后,船东应当支付建造款。这部分价款也被称为"上船台款"或"铺龙骨款",也有将其称之为"合拢款"。

4.22　　下水(launching)是指船舶在完成了船体建造后,从船台或船坞中移至水中继续建造的过程。下水大多指船舶从船台移至水中的过程,而船舶从船坞中移至水中的过程一般被称为"出坞"(undocking)。绝大部分舾装工作均在船舶下水后完成。船舶下水后,船东也应当支付建造款,该期建造款也因此被称为"下水款"。

4.23　　交船(delivery)是指船厂在完成船舶建造后按照船舶建造合同的规定将船舶交给船东,而船东则按照船舶建造合同的规定接收船舶的过程。交船并不仅仅是船舶本身的交接,还包括船舶文件的交接,这些文件包括证明船舶所有权的文件和证明船舶船级的文件。船舶的交船意味着船舶建造合同的履行完毕。船东在接船时支付的建造款通常是最后一期建造款,因此这一期建造款也被称为"交船款"或"尾款"。

4.24　　按照上述各个节点支付五期建造款是船舶建造款支付的一个基本特征。按照 CSTC 格式的规定,船东应分别按照船舶建造合同生效、开工、上船台、下水以及交船五期支付合同价款。① 从上述规定来看,船东支付的五期建造款中除了尾款外均为预付款,只有尾款才是在接船时支付的。区分交船前支付的建造款和交船时支付的建造款的意义在于,船厂通常会出具还款保函保证交船前建造款的返还,而还款保函不包括船东在接船时支付的那期建造款。如果船东向船厂出具付款保函的,一般也仅包括交船前支付的建造款中的第二期至第四期,而不包括交船时支付的建造款。

电汇支付

4.25　　针对交船前的各期建造款的支付,船舶建造合同基本都会规定采用电汇的方式。不同的标准格式都有类似的规定,例如 SAJ 格式有如下规定:②

(a) 1st Installment:
Upon receipt of a cable notice from the BUILDER of issuance by the Japanese Government of the Export License for the VESSEL, the BUYER shall remit the amount of this Installment by telegraphic transfer to The .... Bank

---

① Article II.3.
② Article II.4.

Ltd. , Tokyo, Japan (herein called "........................ Bank") for the account of the BUILDER.
(b) 2nd Installment:
Upon receipt of a cable notice from the BUILDER of keel-laying of the VESSEL having been made, the BUYER shall remit the amount of this Installment by telegraphic transfer to .... Bank for the account of the BUILDER.
(c) 3rd Installment:
Upon receipt of a cable notice from the BUILDER of launching of the VESSEL having been made, the BUYER shall remit the amount of this Installment by telegraphic transfer to .... Bank for the account of the BUILDER.
...

NEWBUILDCON 格式同样也规定付款应当采用电汇的方式:① 4.26

Payment of sums due in accordance with the provisions of this Contract shall be made, in the case of payments to the Builder, by electronic transfer to the Builder's account stipulated in Box 12 ....

电汇简而言之是指两家处于不同国家的银行通过电话或计算机快速汇款的方法。款项在国与国之间电汇时会涉及多家银行,这些银行构成一个网络,称之为银行结算系统(SWIFT)。② 相关银行相互间是"代理银行"关系,代理银行在进行电汇时通常都会收取一定的费用,收费标准在各银行间并不统一。银行间的电汇以前采用电报的方式办理汇款,随着被电子方式取代,电汇也就变成了"电子汇款"(electronic funds transfer, EFT)。 4.27

支付时间的约定

SAJ 格式对交船款之前的各期建造款的支付均没有规定时限,Norwegian 格式规定船东应在三个银行工作日内支付,③NEWBUILDCON 格式则针对不同的交船前的建造款规定了不同的时间限制:④ 4.28

The Contract Price shall be paid by the Buyer to the Builder by Instalments, when due and payable in accordance with Box 11 and this

---
① Clause 15(d)(ii).
② SWIFT 是 Society for Worldwide Interbank Financial Telecommunication 的缩写。
③ Article III.3.
④ Clause 15(a).

Clause, the pre-delivery Instalments being paid as advances and not deposits as follows:

(i) Unless otherwise stated in Box 11 the first Instalment shall be due and payable by the Buyer five (5) Banking Days after the Refund Guar-antee has been provided in accordance with Clause 14(b) (Buil-der's Refund Guarantee).

(ii) The Builder shall give the Buyer invoices for each Instalment under this Contract. With the exception of the first and Final Instalment the Builder shall give the Buyer an invoice to cover the sum due to it not less than ten(10) Banking Days prior to the due date of each Instalment.

(iii) All Instalments other than the first and Final Instalment shall be payable within four(4) Banking Days of the due date thereof.

...

4.29 根据上述规定,船东在收到还款保函后有不少于 5 个银行工作日的时间安排第一期建造款的支付;除了第一期和最后一期款外,船东在收到船厂的发票后至少有 14 个银行工作日的时间安排其他建造款的支付。

法律关于支付时间的规定

4.30 根据 1979 年《货物买卖法》的规定,除非合同另有规定,关于支付时间的规定并不构成买卖合同的本质。① 合同中其他关于时间的规定是否构成合同本质则应根据合同条款确定。② 在 *Raineri v Miles* 一案中,上议院的 Dilhorne 子爵认为,在货物买卖合同中,支付时间并不是合同的核心问题,他这样说道:③

> The time of payment in a contract for the sale of goods is not of the essence of the contract unless made so by express agreement.

4.31 在该案中,Lord Fraser of Tullybelton 也认为,违反合同关于时间的规定并不构成对前提条件的违反,他说:④

> The principle which in my opinion emerges from the authorities to which I have referred is that breach of a contractual stipulation as to time which is not of the essence of a contract will not be treated as a breach of a

---

① s.10(1).
② s.10(2).
③ [1981] AC 1050 at 1078.
④ [1981] AC 1050 at 1093.

condition precedent to the contract, that is as a breach which would entitle the innocent party to treat the contract as terminated or which would prevent the defaulting party from suing for specific performance. Nevertheless it is a breach of the contract and entitles the injured party to damages if he has suffered damage.

换言之,合同规定的船东支付建造款的时间并不意味着关于支付时间的规定具有合同条件条款的性质。只有当合同明确约定支付时间具有条件条款性质时,船东违反支付时间条款才会使船厂享有解除船舶建造合同的选择权。 4.32

银行工作日

银行工作日是指银行营业的日子,船舶建造合同有时会对"银行工作日"作出定义,即明确约定在计算银行工作日时应当考虑的地点,例如 NEWBUILDCON 格式就将"银行工作日"定义为:① 4.33

"Banking Day" means a day on which banks are open in the places stated in Box 2 and Box 3 and, where a remittance is in US dollars, in New York.

NEWBUILDCON 格式的方格 2 是"船厂",方格 3 则是"船东"。虽然填入方格 2 的是船厂的真实地址,但填入方格 3 的往往是船东在提供方便旗船舶登记的国家或地区设立的空壳公司的地址。几乎可以肯定,建造款不可能从该地由该公司汇出。当船东通过融资造船时,支付建造款的应当是融资银行。原则上,除非船舶建造合同另有规定,"银行工作日"应当是指与付款和收款有关的银行所在地的银行营业的日子,包括汇款地的银行工作日、收款地的银行工作日、支付货币涉及地的银行工作日。只有在所有相关地点的银行均营业的日子才是船舶建造合同规定的"银行工作日"。 4.34

根据 NEWBUILDCON 格式的规定,船东应当支付建造款之日若不是银行工作日的,则可顺延至下一个工作日:② 4.35

Payment Procedures
(i) If the date on which any payment is due in accordance with the provisions of this Contract does not fall on a Banking Day, payment shall be made on the next Banking Day.

---

① Definitions.
② Clause 15(d).

(ii) ...

4.36 　　上述 NEWBUILDCON 格式的规定只提及"到期日",而不是最后一个到期日。通常船东可以在几个银行工作日内完成建造款的支付。就第一期和最后一期以外的各期建造款而言,NEWBUILDCON 格式规定船东在收到船厂的发票后有 14 个银行工作日安排建造款的支付。假设船东应当支付建造款的最后一天不是银行工作日,船东按照上述规定就可以在下一个银行工作日安排支付。但如果没有这一规定的话,船东就应当在前一个银行工作日而不是后一个银行工作日安排建造款的支付。在 *Astro AMO Compania Naviera SA* v *Elf Union SA and First National City Bank(The Zographia M)* 一案中,高院的 Ackner 法官认为在应当安排支付的最后一日是节假日时,付款人应当在前一个银行工作日,而不是后一个银行工作日安排支付。他说:①

> ... I ... am not persuaded that the obligation to pay in advance of a certain date, which must mean before a certain date, means after that date where there is some practical difficulty, such as a bank being closed, which prevents payment being made on the very last day before that date.

4.37 　　同样,在 *Mardorf Peach & Co Ltd* v *Attica Sea Carriers Corporation of Liberia (The Laconia)* 一案中,租金的到期日是一个星期天,但是上议院的 Lord Salmon 认为租船人应当在星期五就安排支付租金,他说:②

> Punctual payment cannot be made on the day after it falls due, but I cannot see any reason in the present case why it could not be made before that day. If the hire is to be paid to the owners' bank semi-monthly in advance and an instalment happens to fall due on a Sunday when the banks are closed, then as the banks are also closed on Saturday, payment, in my view, should be tendered on the previous Friday.

预付款和定金

4.38 　　大多数船舶建造合同都会规定船东支付的建造款具有预付款的性质,SAJ 格

---

① [1976] 2 Lloyd's Rep 382 at 393.
② [1977] 1 Lloyd's Rep 315 at 323.

式便有如下规定:①

> The payments made by the BUYER prior to the delivery of the VESSEL shall be in the nature of advances to the BUILDER. In the event that the BUYER shall exercise its right of rescission of this Contract under and pursuant to any of the provisions of this Contract specifically permitting the BUYER to do so, then the BUYER shall notify the BUILDER in writing or by cable confirmed in writing, and such rescission shall be effective as of the date notice thereof is received by the BUILDER.

4.39　上述"payments"应当不仅包括船东按照合同约定支付的各期建造款,而且还应当包括其他所有款项,例如船东因提出修改而支付的修改费用等。Norwegian 格式也有类似的规定:②

> The payment of any sums under this Contract by the Buyer prior to delivery of the Vessel shall be by way of advances to the Builder. In the event that the Buyer shall exercise its right of cancelling the Contract under and pursuant to any of the provisions of the Contract specifically permitting the Buyer to do so, then the Buyer shall notify the Builder in writing or by telefax confirmed by registered mail, and such cancellation shall be effective as of the date notice thereof is received by the Builder.

4.40　NEWBUILDCON 格式不仅规定船东支付的建造款具有预付款的性质,而且还特别说明建造款不是定金:③

> The Contract Price shall be paid by the Buyer to the Builder by Instalments, when due and payable in accordance with Box 11 and this Clause, the pre-delivery Instalments being paid as advances and not deposits as follows....

4.41　预付款是指支付一方提前支付未来可能但未必一定要支付的款项。由于船东支付的款项具有预付款的性质,因此即使船厂收到了款项并且已经用于船舶建造,在船东按照船舶建造合同的规定解除合同时,船厂依然有义务返还已经收到的建造款。在 *Bronester v Priddle* 一案中,上诉法院的 Holroyd Pearce 法官完全同意一审法院对预付款作出的解释,他这样说道:④

---

① Article X.1.
② Article XII.1, paras.1 & 2.
③ Clause 15(a).
④ [1961] 3 All ER 471 at 475.

> The learned judge ... set out his point of view very clearly in the following words: "It seems to me that 'advance' means: 'I will pay now what I may have to pay in the future. I am paying before due time. If, after the advance, some event in the future upon which payment becomes due does not occur, you can recover it back.' There are to be found cases where a tenant has paid rent in advance before due time to the landlord. That was held to be a loan by the tenant to the landlord. It was not rent because it was not due; it was in the nature of a loan. When someone says: 'I am going to make you an advance', I think they are saying: 'We will let you have it as a loan or on an implied understanding that if the event does not occur which makes it legally payable, we must have it back'." I accept the learned judge's very clear reasoning in his judgment.

4.42　定金与预付款不同,定金的支付往往是为了保证合同的切实履行,因此一旦支付定金的一方没有切实履行合同的,就无法要求对方返还定金。但是违约方若已支付了作为预付款的分期付款,则有机会要求对方返还预付款。在 *Howe* v *Smith* 一案中,财税法院的 Cotton 法官在分析了之前的判例后对定金作出了如下说明:①

> What is the deposit? The deposit, as I understand it, and using the words of Lord Justice James, is a guarantee that the contract shall be performed. If the sale goes on, of course, not only in accordance with the words of the contract, but in accordance with the intention of the parties in making the contract, it goes in part payment of the purchase-money for which it is deposited; but if on the default of the purchaser the contract goes off, that is to say, if he repudiates the contract, then, according to Lord Justice James, he can have no right to recover the deposit.... In order to enable the vendor so to act, in my opinion there must be acts on the part of the purchaser which not only amount to delay sufficient to deprive him of the equitable remedy of specific performance, but which would make his conduct amount to a repudiation on his part of the contract.

4.43　*Harrison* v *Holland & Hannen & Cubitts Ltd*② 是一个涉及到定金和预付款问题的案例,在该案中买卖土地的合同在第3条有如下规定:

---

① (1884) 27 Ch D 89 at 95.
② [1921] 3 KB 297.

... the purchasers having on the signing hereof paid to the vendors the sum of 50,000*l* as a deposit and in part payment of the said purchase money, shall pay the sum of 100,000*l* further on account of the purchase price within fourteen days from the date hereof and shall pay the balance of the purchase money.

合同的第 20 条则有下列规定：

... if the purchasers fail to comply with the stipulations hereof their deposit of 50,000*l*, but not the said sum of 100,000*l*, shall be forfeited and the vendors may resell the property in such manner as they think fit and any deficiency arising on the resale and all expenses attending the same or any attempted resale shall be paid by the purchasers to the vendors as liquidated damages.

买方在支付了 50,000 英镑定金和 100,000 英镑第二期款之后没有支付最后一期款，卖方遂将土地进行了转卖。双方的争议是卖方是否有权保留 100,000 英镑的第二期款。Lush 法官认为卖方不仅无权没收 100,000 英镑，而且也不能保留该 100,000 英镑，因为该笔钱并不是定金。他说：①

In the present case the parties have expressly provided, although that was not necessary, that the deposit of 50,000*l* should be forfeited if the purchasers made default, but as to the 100,000*l* they have expressly provided that it shall not be forfeited. The 100,000*l* is not called a deposit; it is expressly stated to be in part payment of the purchase money, and so it is not money paid as a guarantee for the due performance of the contract. It is therefore not forfeitable. But the question remains, can the vendors claim to retain it until the lapse of a reasonable time, so that, if within that time they resell the property at a loss which is not capable of being made good out of the deposit of 50,000*l*, they can satisfy their loss out of so much of the 100,000*l* as with the 50,000*l* will make up the whole loss suffered? In my opinion the vendors have no such right. I am unable to see how such a right can be extracted from clause 20, or, apart from that clause, how it can be supported on any principle of law.

在船舶建造合同中约定船东在接船前支付的所有建造款均为预付款性质而不是定金，其目的是船东希望保留索回已支付建造款的权利，例如船东在按照合

---

① [1921] 3 KB 297 at 300.

同约定可以解除合同时可以要求船厂返还所有已经收到的建造款。①

交船款的支付

4.47　交船款是船舶建造合同规定的最后一期建造款。交船款的支付与船东之前支付的各期建造款不同，最后一期款并不具有预付款的性质，因此也不是还款保函所担保的款项。就船厂而言，交船款之前任何一期建造款的支付出现延迟甚至拒付，都会给船厂带来影响或损失，但未必是根本性的，毕竟船厂始终控制着在建船舶。然而交船款的支付会直接影响到船厂对船舶的控制，一旦失去对船舶的控制，船东违约造成的影响或损失就有可能变得无法控制。就船东而言，交船款的支付与船舶所有权和占有权的获得是互为条件的。而在此之前，船舶始终在船厂的控制之下，船东之前支付的各期建造款均不涉及船舶占有权和所有权的转移。因此交船款的支付方式类似于二手船买卖的支付方式，即通过银行的安排进行支付。②

提前支付

4.48　在实践中有些船舶建造合同会规定船东可以提前支付约定的各期建造款。有些标准格式也有关于提前支付的规定，例如按照 SAJ 格式的规定，船东提前支付建造款不仅要得到船厂的同意，而且还要获得日本政府的批准：③

> Prepayment of any installment due on or before delivery of the VESSEL shall be subject to mutual agreement between the parties hereto and also subject to approval of the Japanese Government.

4.49　SAJ 格式之所以有此规定是由于日本也曾经历过对外汇进行管制的时期。CSTC 格式虽然允许船东提前支付建造款，但同样也对船东提前支付规定了不少条件：④

> The BUYER shall have the right to make prepayment of any and all instalments before delivery of the VESSEL, by giving to the SELLER at least thirty (30) days prior written notice, without any price adjustment of the VESSEL for such prepayment.

---

① 关于船东按照船舶建造合同约定解约请参见本书第 12 章第 II 节，第 25 章第 II 节。
② 关于最后一期款的支付请参见本书第 8 章第 III 节。
③ Article II.5.
④ Article II.5.

这里规定的书面通知应当是相当明确的,即除非提前 30 天向船厂发出书面通知,否则船东不能提前支付建造款。在船舶建造实践中船东提前支付建造款的做法相当少见,理由比较简单。首先,船东以自有资金建造船舶的,从船东的利益出发应当是越晚支付越好,没有理由提前支付尚未到期的建造款;其次,如果船东是通过银行融资建造船舶的,一旦贷款协议按照船舶建造合同的支付节点作出规定后,船东也无法提前任何一期由融资银行安排支付的建造款;最后,即使船东有其自身的原因希望提前支付建造款,似乎也没有理由提前支付最后一期建造款。 4.50

Ⅲ 支付条件

在当今的造船业,似乎所有的船舶建造合同都规定了船东支付建造款的条件。只有在条件得到满足的情况下,船东才有支付的义务。船舶建造合同规定的支付条件可以简单归纳为:船厂已经提供还款保函,船厂提供了付款通知、发票以及由船级社出具的节点证书等。 4.51

收到还款保函

船东在收到还款保函后才有支付建造款的义务应当是一个合理的规定,因为船厂提供还款保函实际上正是为了确保船东在按照船舶建造合同规定解约时可以获得其所支付的建造款的返还。Norwegian 格式的规定是:① 4.52

> The Buyer's obligation to pay the first and subsequent instalments, excluding the instalment payable on Delivery and Acceptance, shall be subject to the Builder providing the Buyer with refund guarantee(s) from a bank or other security, satisfactory to the Buyer, securing the repayment obligation of the Builder if the contract is lawfully cancelled.

虽然 NEWBUILDCON 格式也有关于还款保函的规定,②但该格式似乎仅针对第一期建造款作出了还款保函的规定。很显然,NEWBUILDCON 格式是以船厂针对所有预付款金额一次性提供还款保函为前提的,若船厂分期向船东提供还款保函的,在采用 NEWBUILDCON 格式时,船东在支付第二期至交船款前一期 4.53

---

① Article Ⅲ.3, para.5.
② Clause 15(a).

的建造款之前同样可以要求船厂提供还款保函。在实践中,船厂可以针对每一期建造款提供还款保函,也可以针对除交船款外的所有建造款一次性提供还款保函。对船厂而言,分期提供还款保函有助于船厂减少因要求银行提供还款保函而产生的费用。

收到付款通知

4.54　虽然船舶建造合同都会规定船东应当在船舶建造达到某一节点时支付建造款,但是船东的支付义务依然以收到船厂的付款通知为前提条件,例如 SAJ 格式便规定船东应当在收到船厂发出的通知后支付建造款。① AWES 格式则规定船厂应当提前 10 天通知船东支付建造款:②

> Except for the first instalment the CONTRACTOR shall notify the PURCHASER at least ten(10) days in advance of the estimated dates of the instalment payment falling due.

4.55　Norwegian 格式的相关规定似乎更为明确:③

> The instalments under 3(b) to 3(f)(both inclusive) unless payable on specific dates, shall under no circumstances fall due until 14 days from receipt of written notice from the Builder ....

4.56　上述规定涉及第二期至第五期的建造款。在船舶建造合同没有规定支付建造款具体日期而是规定节点的情况下,这一规定实际上有可能改变船东支付建造款的实际时间。在采用 Norwegian 格式的上述规定时,第 III.3 条第 1 段中应当填入船东在节点后支付建造款的银行工作日天数。如果填入的是 5 个银行工作日,除非船厂在节点达到之前 14 天就发出付款通知,否则船东似乎就有可能在 5 个银行工作日之后才有支付的义务。

4.57　NEWBUILDCON 格式的规定如下:④

> The Contract Price shall be paid by the Buyer to the Builder by Instalments, when due and payable in accordance with Box 11 and this Clause, the pre-delivery Instalments being paid as advances and not deposits as follows:

---

① Article II.4.
② Article 7(c), para.1.
③ Article III.3, para.3.
④ Clause 15(a).

(i) ...
(ii) The Builder shall give the Buyer invoices for each Instalment under this Contract. With the exception of the first and Final Instalment the Builder shall give the Buyer an invoice to cover the sum due to it not less than ten(10) Banking Days prior to the due date of each Instalment.
(iii) All Instalments other than the first and Final Instalment shall be payable within four(4)Banking Days of the due date thereof.
...

  根据上述条款的规定,船厂应当在建造款到期日之前不少于 10 个银行工作日向船东提供发票。① 建造款到期日不太可能是一个具体的日历日,双方一般会采用建造节点作为付款日期,例如"铺龙骨"或"下水"等并将其填入 NEWBUILDCON 格式的方格 11。如果船厂希望船东在约定节点付款,就应当提前 10 个银行工作日向船东发出付款通知。如果船厂提供发票 10 个银行工作日后约定的建造节点实际上并没有发生的话,船东应当是没有付款义务的。如果约定的建造节点实际上发生在 10 个银行工作日期间,船东的付款义务也应当在 10 个银行工作之后才产生。上述条款提及的 4 个银行工作日应当是指船东可以在建造款到期日后的 4 个银行工作日内支付。如果在约定的建造款到期日没有收到发票的话,船东应当没有在 4 个银行工作日内完成建造款支付的义务。 4.58

收到节点证书

  大多数船舶建造合同都会规定除了第一期和最后一期建造款外,船东支付其他各期建造款的前提条件是收到节点证书,例如 CSTC 格式便有如下规定:② 4.59

The Contract Price shall be paid by the BUYER to the SELLER in instalments as follows:
(a) ...
(b) 2nd Instalment:
  The sum of United States Dollars _____
  (US $ _____), representing _____ percent(_____%) of the Contract Price shall become due and payable and be paid by the

---

① 船厂提供发票具有要求船东付款通知的作用,实践中,船厂在提供发票时也往往会发出要求付款的通知。
② Article II.3.

BUYER within three (3) New York business days after the cutting the first steel plate of the Vessel in the BUILDER's workshop. The SELLER shall notify with a telex or telefax notice along with a certificate certified by the BUYER's authorised party to this effect to the BUYER stating that the 1st steel plate has been cut in its workshop. The SELLER shall send to the BUYER a telex or telefax demand for payment of this instalment as soon as the cutting of the steel is made.

(c) 3rd Instalment:

The sum of United States Dollars＿＿＿＿＿＿＿＿＿＿＿＿＿＿＿＿＿ (US $ ＿＿＿＿＿＿), representing ＿＿＿ percent (＿＿＿%) of the Contract Price shall become due and payable and be paid by the BUYER within three (3) New York business days after the keel-laying of the first section of the VESSEL. The keel-laying shall be notified by the SELLER with a telex or telefax notice along with a certificate certified by the BUYER's authorised party to this effect to the BUYER stating that the keel-laying has been carried out. The SELLER shall send to the BUYER a telex or telefax demand for payment of this instalment as soon as the keel-laying is carried out.

(d) 4th Instalment:

The sum of United States Dollars＿＿＿＿＿＿＿＿＿＿＿＿＿＿＿＿＿ (US $ ＿＿＿＿＿＿), representing ＿＿＿ percent (＿＿＿%) of the Contract Price shall become due and payable and be paid by the BUYER within three (3) New York business days after the launching of the VESSEL. The launching of the VESSEL shall be notified by the SELLER with a telex or telefax notice along with a certificate certified by the BUYER's authorised party to this effect to the BUYER stating that the launching of the VESSEL has been carried out. The SELLER shall send to the BUYER a telex or telefax demand for payment of this instalment as soon as the VESSEL is launched.

(e) ...

4.60　按照上述规定，船东只有在收到开工、上船台以及下水的节点证书后才有义务支付各期建造款。而且，不少船舶建造合同还规定船厂应当提供由船级社出具的建造节点证书。船级社通常会根据监造协议的约定接受邀请参加船厂为船舶建造各节点举行的仪式并出具相应的节点证书。

节点的真实达到

节点证书是证明船舶建造已经达到一定阶段的文件,因此船舶的建造节点必须实际达到或完成,否则船厂发出的付款通知就可能是无效的。在 *Stocznia Gdanska SA v Latvian Shipping Co , Latreefer Inc and Others*① 一案中,船东和船厂订立了六个船舶建造合同,由船厂建造六艘冷冻船。合同第5.02(6)条有如下规定: 4.61

> ... within five(5)banking days after the seller has given notice by telex to the purchaser of keel-laying of the vessel meaning that the first and second sections of the vessel's hull have been joined on the berth where the vessel is being constructed, such a notice to be confirmed simultaneously by the classification society.

第一和第二艘船的两个分段合龙后,船厂向船东发出了节点通知。船东没有在规定的期限内支付建造款,船厂于是解除了第一和第二个船舶建造合同。接着船厂通过更改编号又将相同的分段分别用于第三和第四艘,以及第五和第六艘船,并且又分别向船东发出了第三至第六艘船的合龙款的节点通知。船东认为针对第三至第三艘船的节点通知是无效的,因为按照合同规定第一和第二两个分段应当在建造第三至第六艘船的船台上合拢,但事实上在第一和第二两个分段是在建造第一和第二艘船的船台上合龙的。 4.62

上议院也认为船厂针对第三至第六艘船发出的付款通知是无效的,理由是在船厂向船东发出通知时实际上并没有分段合龙的事实。上议院认为付款通知应当是一个事实的通知,即两个分段已经合龙,但是船厂针对第三至第六艘船发出的付款通知并不是一个事实的通知。上议院的 Lord Goff of Chieveley 说:② 4.63

> In truth, what the yard was doing was to appropriate to contracts 3 and 4 (and subsequently to contracts 5 and 6)sections which had been joined as part of the construction of a vessel being built under a different contract. There was nothing to stop them doing that, if the buyers agreed. In normal circumstances, it might well be possible to obtain such agreement; but in a case such as the present, there was no chance of it being obtained. Moreover, if the yard's argument is right, they were entitled to do this as of right in a case where the contracts in question were with different buyers. In such a case it would be most

---

① [1998] 1 WLR 574.
② [1998] 1 WLR 574 at 583.

surprising if the yard could so proceed without first obtaining the consent of the second buyer.

船东监造代表的会签

4.64　船舶建造合同通常会约定节点证书应当由船东的监造代表会签，并将此作为船东支付建造款的条件之一。这一规定的作用是船东可以确保船厂所说的建造节点确实已达到或完成。如果双方关于节点没有约定或虽有约定但不够明确，船厂收取建造款就有可能因此受到影响。但是，如果关于节点的约定是明确的，船东的这一保留便不会有太大的实际意义。船东的监造代表会签节点证书既是一项权利，同时也是一项义务。只要相关的建造节点已经达到或已完成，船厂收取建造款的权利并不会因为船东的监造代表拒绝在节点证书上签字而受到影响。换言之，船东的监造代表在这种情况下负有在节点证书上会签的义务，不能随意拒绝签字。在 Frederick Leyand & Co Ltd(J Russell & Co) v Compania Panamena Europea Navegacion Ltada① 一案中，船舶修理合同规定船东应在船东的检验人出具证明工程已令人满意地完成的证书后支付船舶修理款。船厂完成了相关工程后，船东的检验人以需要详细费用资料为由拒绝出具该证书。船厂于是对船东提起了诉讼，一审法院判决船厂胜诉。船东上诉，但上诉法院支持了一审法院的判决，Scott 法官说：②

> I agree with the learned Judge that the provision as to the surveyor's certificate, which I have quoted, is limited to questions of quality, and excludes all questions of amount from the scope of the surveyor's inquiry and decision, which is rightly restricted to topics within the special expert cognisance.

Ⅳ　抵销

抵销的概念

4.65　抵销是普通法规定的一项权利。如果 A 针对 B 享有一定数额的索赔，而 B 对 A 也享有一个一定数额金钱的交叉索赔，B 在其交叉索赔范围内就可以免除其

---

①　(1943) 76 Ll L Rep 113.
②　[1934] Ch 431 at 437.

支付 A 的索赔的义务,并且可以将其交叉索赔作为一项针对 A 提起的意在执行其索赔之诉讼的抗辩,B 有权在其交叉索赔范围内对 A 的索赔进行抵销。① 上诉法院的 Lord Hanworth 在 *Re Bankruptcy Notice(No 171 of 1934)* 一案中对"抵销"作出了如下说明:②

> With regard to the word "set-off," that is a word well known and established in its meaning; it is something which provides a defence because the nature and quality of the sum so relied upon are such that it is a sum which is proper to be dealt with as diminishing the claim which is made, and against which the sum so demanded can be set off.

抵销权的排除

4.66 当事人可以通过合同约定排除抵销的适用,正如 Lord Salmon 在 *Gilbert Ash (Northern) Ltd* v *Modern Engineering(Bristol) Ltd* 一案中所说的:③

> The parties to building contracts or sub-contracts, like the parties to any other type of contract are, of course, entitled to incorporate in their contract any clause they please. There is nothing to prevent them from extinguishing, curtailing or enlarging the ordinary rights of set off, provided they do so expressly or by clear implication.

4.67 高院的 Hirst 法官在 *Hong Kong and Shanghai Banking Corp* v *Kloeckner & Co AG* 一案中也指出当事人可以排除抵销的权利,他说:④

> I hold that as a matter of law the [parties] are entitled to rely on the clause excluding any right of set-off against the letter of undertaking, and that this effectively debars the set-off which [the other parties] seek to maintain.

4.68 一旦当事人对抵销的排除作出了明确的约定,法院通常就不会予以干涉。在 *Continental Illinois National Bank & Trust Company of Chicago* v *Papanicolaou*⑤ 一案中,贷款合同有如下规定:

---

① *Halsbury's Laws of England*, 5th edn - Civil Procedure Volume 12(2015) para.382.
② (1943) 76 Ll L Rep 113 at 122.
③ [1974] AC 689 at 723.
④ [1990] 2 QB 514 at 521.
⑤ [1986] 2 Lloyd's Rep 441.

> Notwithstanding anything to the contrary contained in this Agreement and/or any of the Security Documents all payments by the Borrower under this Agreement and the Security Documents shall be made without set-off or counterclaim and without deductions or withholdings whatsoever in dollars to CINB's account at . . . .

4.69　担保合同则有如下规定：

> All amounts payable by the Guarantor hereunder(whether on account of principal or interest or otherwise) shall be paid in full free of set-off or counterclaim and without any withholding or deductions whatsoever on account of any present or future taxes or charges or otherwise save and except for taxes on the overall gross receipts or net income of CINB.

4.70　上诉法院的 Parker 法官认为法院不应干涉当事人的安排，他说：①

> Indeed the present cases make it the more necessary that the Court should not interfere, for here the parties have specifically provided both in the loan agreement and the guarantees that payment should be made free of any set off or counterclaim.

标准格式的规定

4.71　船厂在开始建造之前一般会根据各期建造款的数额和支付时间对建造资金作出安排，每一期建造款都会有特定的用途。因此船厂显然既不希望船东拖延建造款的支付，也不希望船东在支付建造款时有任何抵销或扣减。要实现这一目的，船厂就应当与船东在船舶建造合同中就抵销权的排除作出约定。标准格式间也有排除抵销权利的规定，例如 SAJ 格式便有如下规定：②

> No payment under this Contract shall be delayed or withheld by the BUYER on account of any dispute or disagreement of whatever nature arising between the parties hereto.

4.72　与 SAJ 格式不同，AWES 格式规定似乎比较明确：③

> The PURCHASER shall not delay any payment in case of any disagreement as to the amount of . . . liquidated damages or premiums or

---

① [1986] 2 Lloyd's Rep 441 at 445.
② Article II.4, para.2.
③ Article 7(f).

in the event of other exceptions or claims the PURCHASE may have asserted or may intend to assert against the CONTRACTOR, whether in connection with this CONTRACT or otherwise without prejudice to the PURCHASER's right to apply subsequently to Arbitration. The right of retention or set-off with counterclaims of the PURCHASER is excluded.

NEWBUILDCON 格式关于抵销有如下规定：① 4.73

The Buyer shall not be entitled to retain or set-off any amount against any payment due to the Builder under this Contract except in relation to the final instalment as specifically provided in this Contract.

从上述规定的句式来看，除了最后一期建造款外，船东不能主张任何数额的抵销。同意船东在支付最后一期时主张抵销基本上等同于双方在最后一期根据建造过程中的实际情况对约定的合同价格进行调整。 4.74

约定的明确性

当事人关于排除抵销权的约定应当是明确的，否则就是无效的。*Gilbert-Ash (Northern) Ltd v Modern Engineering (Bristol)*②是一个关于如何解释建造分包合同条款的案件，该案中的建造合同第 27 条规定，总包人应当在雇主的建筑师确定数额后的 14 天内向分包人支付。总包人在支付时可以扣减(1)分包合同规定的保留金；(2)总包人因分包人完成工作延误而获得的数额；(3)特定的现金折扣。但是分包合同的条款则不同，分包合同第 14 条有如下规定： 4.75

> ... if the sub-contractor fails to comply with any of the conditions of this sub-contract the contractor reserves the right to suspend or withhold payment ... the contractor also reserves the right to deduct from any payments certified as due ... the amount of any bona fide contra accounts and/or other claims which he, the contractor, may have against the sub-contractor in connection with this or any other contract.

虽然上诉法院认为当事人已经约定排除了抵销权，但上议院则认为分包合同并没有排除抵销的权利。Reid 法官说：③ 4.76

---

① Clause 17.
② [1974] AC 689.
③ [1974] AC 689 at 696.

It is now admitted, and in my view properly admitted, that at common law there is a right of set off in such circumstances: but that right can be excluded by contract. So the sole question in the appeal is whether by their contract with the sub-contractors the contractors have agreed that sums which they receive from the employers earmarked as due to the sub-contractors on architects' interim certificates must be paid over immediately without any right of set off.

4.77　　Reid 法官认为分包合同第 14 条并不具有排除普通法规定的抵销权利的效力，为此他说：①

So I turn to the fourth sentence. I do not see how it can be limited to sums which have either been found to be due or agreed. It refers to *bona fide* contra accounts. The words '*bona fide*' would be quite unnecessary and, indeed, meaningless, if the scope of this provision were limited to sums adjudged or agreed to be due. They must imply a claim which the contractor believes to be genuine but which may still be in dispute and contra accounts are generally itemised accounts not yet agreed. Even if 'other claims' could be read as claims *ejusdem generis* with contra accounts, that would not help the sub-contractor because in this case the claim in respect of bad workmanship and delay are worked out in great detail. It is true that this provision goes a very long way if that is its meaning, because it would allow deduction of all detailed claims outstanding under other contracts. But if the sub-contractor chooses to agree to that, that is his affair.

4.78　　在 *BOC Group plc* v *Cention LLC & Anor*② 一案中，原告将其拥有的子公司"Delta"的全部股本出售给第二被告，合同约定价款分三期支付。作为买家的第二被告的合同义务由第一被告担保履行。买卖合同的第2.7条有如下规定：

The Purchaser's obligations to make payments of the deferred instalments of the Initial Consideration and (subject to the express terms thereof) the Further Consideration shall be absolute and unconditional and shall not be affected by transfer of any of the equity interest in Delta, the transfer of any or all of Delta's assets or business, the dissolution of Delta, the termination of the business of Delta (or any part thereof), the success or failure of any research projects undertaken by

---

①　[1974] AC 689 at 698.
②　[1999] CLC 497.

Delta, the future commercialization or otherwise of any products, Delta's future business or technological or technical successes or by any other matter whatsoever.

在合同履行过程中,被告认为原告的行为违反了自己的保证且构成毁约,被告因此有权解除合同并可向原告索赔损失。原告要求被告支付第三期款,被告则认为有权抵销。原告认为第2.7条已经明确规定,买家的支付义务是"绝对的且无条件的""不受任何其他因素的影响",虽然没有直接提及"抵销",但实际上已经构成了对抵销权利的明示排除。被告则认为第2.7条使用的文字并不足以排除被告的抵销权利。高院的 Rix 法官认为第2.7条并没有排除被告的抵销权利,他说:[1]

4.79

> It is clear, therefore, that if the parties in this case wished to exclude all rights of set-off, there was no difficulty in finding clear, simple and direct language to do so. In the absence, however, of any express exclusion of rights of set-off in s.2.7, of particular interest are a small number of cases in which the courts have held that rights of set-off have been successfully excluded without specific reference to set-off *eo nomine*.

排除的效力

即使船舶建造合同明确排除了抵销权的适用,此种约定依然有可能被认为是对权利的放弃而受成文法的禁止。*Stewart Gill Ltd* v *Horatio Myer & Co Ltd*[2] 是一个关于货物供应的案例,在该案中原告同意向被告供应一套双轨的高架传送带系统并在被告的场地安装和测试。合同规定的支付方式是签约支付15%,工程进展后支付75%,完工支付5%,完工后30天支付5%。当原告要求被告支付合同款项时,被告拒绝支付,理由是因原告违约而引起的交叉索赔可以抵销原告的请求。原告则认为,由于合同的规定,被告原本可以有的抵销权利已经被排除了。合同的第12.4条有如下规定:

4.80

> The customer shall not be entitled to withhold payment of any amount due to the company under the contract by reason of any payment credit set off counterclaim allegation of incorrect or defective goods or for any

---

[1] [1999] CLC 497 at 502.
[2] [1992] QB 600.

other reason whatsoever which the customer may allege excuses him from performing his obligations hereunder.

4.81　被告主张,合同第12.4条规定违反了1977年《不公平合同条款法》的规定,因而是无效的。被告最终得到上诉法院的支持。上诉法院认为该条规定不合理,不应得到执行。上诉法院的 Lord Donaldson 说:①

> Now clause 12.4 can perhaps be said to make the enforcement of the plaintiffs' liability subject to a condition that the defendants shall not have sought to set off their own claims against their liability to pay the price and this might well be said to be onerous. However, I do not think it necessary to pursue this, because it is quite clear that clause 12.4 excludes the defendants' "right" to set off their claims against the plaintiffs' claim for the price and further excludes the remedy which they would otherwise have of being able to enforce their claims against the plaintiffs by means of a set-off.... It also excludes or restricts the procedural rules as to set-off.... Thus far, therefore, the defendants can bring themselves within the section.

4.82　但是,如果排除抵销的约定在特定行业中是普遍的,通行的,法院则可能因此认为此种约定是合理的,因而是有效的。例如 *Schenkers Ltd* v *Overland Shoes Ltd*② 一案中,合同的23(A)条规定:

> The Customer shall pay to the Company in cash or as otherwise agreed all sums immediately when due, without reduction or deferment on account of any claim, counterclaim or set-off.

4.83　上诉法院认为合同中排除抵销权的规定是行业习惯,当事人双方都是了解的,并没有违反1977年《不公平合同条款法》的规定。上诉法院的 Phil 法官是这样说的:③

> In my judgment, the plaintiffs have satisfied the burden upon them of establishing that cl.23(A) in the circumstances satisfies the requirement of reasonableness. The clause was in common use and well known in the trade following comprehensive discussions between reputable and representative bodies mindful of the considerations involved. It reflects a

---

① [1992] QB 600 at 606.
② [1998] 1 Lloyd's Rep 498.
③ [1998] 1 Lloyd's Rep 498 at 507.

general view as to what is reasonable in the trade concerned. It was sufficiently well known that any failure by the defendant's officers, in the course of long and substantial dealings, to put their minds to the clause cannot be relied on to establish that it was unfair or unreasonable to include it in the contracts.... In a situation in which there was no significant inequality of bargaining position, the customs of the trade were an important factor. The parties were well aware of the circumstances in which business was conducted, the heads of expenditure to be incurred and the risks involved.

V 约定赔偿

特征

4.84　约定赔偿（liquidated damages）是指合同当事人根据对违约可能产生损失的估计予以确定的，在一方违约时另一方可获得的且无需考虑实际损失的赔偿数额。与约定赔偿相对的是"未约定赔偿"（unliquidated damages）即是指赔偿数额由法院予以确定的情形。并非当事人的所有约定赔偿都是有效的，只有采用符合法律规定要求的方式约定的赔偿才是有效的。①

4.85　虽然违约方应当承担因其违约给对方带来的所有损失，但是并非始终可以计算出违约导致另一方的具体的实际损失。在这个问题上，*Australian Steamship Proprietary Ltd* v *John Lewis & Sons Ltd* ②一案应当是一个明显的例子。在该案中，被告船厂为原告船东建造一艘运煤船，但是船厂建造的船舶在不少方面均不符合规格书的要求，包括船舶的吃水高于保证吃水，载重吨低于保证载重吨。仲裁员认为船厂应当在过高吃水和载重吨不足两个方面赔偿船东的损失。在估计过高吃水可能造成的损失时应当考虑降低吃水的成本，而在估计载重吨不足可能造成的损失时则应考虑船舶预计寿命内运费的净损失。在考虑上述两种损失时还应考虑船舶灭失的可能性或出售或没有货运的情形。船厂要求提供证据证明船舶在交船后曾运载过超过保证载重吨的货物，而且也曾在超过船舶保证吃水的装卸港之间航行。双方在法院的争议是，船厂是否可以提供关于船舶在交船后的

---

① Hugh Beale, *Chitty on Contracts*, 35th edn Sweet & Maxwell 2023, para.30－205.
② (1933)47 Ll L Rep 132.

状况的证据。高院的 Lord Hewart 说：①

> We have listened with care to the arguments on both sides and have arrived at the conclusion that the answer to the question, viz., whether upon the true construction of pars. 3 and 5 of the interim award the evidence referred to is relevant to the assessment of damages, and we think it is.

4.86 由于计算损失所应考虑的各种因素有可能导致计算根本无法进行，因而事先在合同中约定赔偿应当是一种可以解决这一实际问题的方法。正如 Halsbury 伯爵在 *Clydebank Engineering & Shipbuilding Co Ltd v Don Jose Ramos Izquierdo y Castaneda* 一案中所说的：②

> The very reason why the parties do in fact agree to such a stipulation is that sometimes, although undoubtedly there is damage and undoubtedly damages ought to be recovered, the nature of the damage is such that proof of it is extremely complex, difficult, and expensive.

4.87 一旦合同当事人的约定赔偿是有效的，违约一方就应当承担约定赔偿，无论其违约实际上给对方造成了什么损失。正如上议院的 Dilhorne 子爵在 *Suisse Atlantique Societe d'Armement SA v NV Rotterdamsche Kolen Centrale* 一案中所说的：③

> An agreed damage clause is for the benefit of both; the party establishing breach by the other need prove no damage in fact; the other must pay that, no less but no more.

赔偿与惩罚

4.88 约定赔偿应当是对可能发生的损失作出的估计，而不应当是违约的惩罚。如果约定赔偿构成惩罚，当事人的约定就是无效的。在 1891 年 *Law v Redditch Local Board* 一案中，上诉法院的 Kay 法官说道：④

> In early times it was decided by Courts of Equity that, where a sum of money was agreed to be paid as a penalty for non-performance of a

---

① (1933)47 Ll L Rep 132 at 134.
② [1905] AC 6 at 11.
③ [1966] 1 Lloyd's Rep 529 at 556.
④ [1892] 1 QB 127 at 133.

collateral contract, equity would not allow the whole sum to be recovered; but, where the damages for non-performance of such contract could be estimated, would cut down the penalty to the amount of the actual damages sustained.

4.89 合同当事人的约定赔偿是否构成惩罚在很大程度上取决于约定赔偿之目的, 如果目的是阻却违约, 约定赔偿就很有可能构成惩罚; 如果目的是赔偿损失, 约定赔偿就很可能是有效的。Colman 法官在 *Lordsvale Finance Plc* v *Bank of Zambia* 一案中这样说道:①

> ... whether a provision is to be treated as a penalty is a matter of construction to be resolved by asking whether at the time the contract was entered into the predominant contractual function of the provision was to deter a party from breaking the contract or to compensate the innocent party for breach. That the contractual function is deterrent rather than compensatory can be deduced by comparing the amount that would be payable on breach with the loss that might be sustained if breach occurred.

4.90 如果赔偿数额过度或显失公平, 约定赔偿就可能被法院认为是一种罚款, 因而是无效的。② 衡量的标准是: 所约定的数额是否为当事人对违约可能造成的损失的真实估计。在 *Clydebank Engineering & Shipbuilding Co Ltd* v *Don Jose Ramos Izquierdo y Castaneda*③ 一案中, 西班牙政府与原告船厂订立船舶建造合同, 由原告为西班牙政府建造四艘鱼雷艇驱逐舰。船舶建造合同规定:

> The penalty for later delivery shall be at the rate of 500l. per week for each vessel not delivered by the contractors in the contract time.

4.91 四艘驱逐舰的交船都晚于合同规定的交船期, 西班牙政府支付了建造款, 但要求船厂支付每艘船每星期 500 英镑共计 67,500 英镑的罚金。苏格兰最高民事法院第二法庭认为合同规定的数额是约定赔偿, 西班牙政府有权获得。这一判决得到了上议院的支持, 上议院的 Halsbury 伯爵说:④

> It is obvious on the face of it that the very thing intended to be provided

---

① *Lordsvale Finance Plc* v *Bank of Zambia* [1996] QB 752 at 762.
② *Dunlop Pneumatic Tupe Co Ltd* v *New Garage and Motor Co Ltd* [1915] AC 79.
③ [1905] AC 6.
④ [1905] AC 6 at 11.

against by this pactional amount of damages is to avoid that kind of minute and somewhat difficult and complex system of examination which would be necessary if you were to attempt to prove the damage. As I pointed out to the learned counsel during the course of his argument, in order to do that properly and to have any real effect upon any tribunal determining that question, one ought to have before one's mind the whole administration of the Spanish Navy—how they were going to use their torpedo-boat destroyers in one place rather than another, and what would be the relative speed of all the boats they possessed in relation to those which they were getting by this agreement. It would be absolutely idle and impossible to enter into a question of that sort unless you had some kind of agreement between the parties as to what was the real measure of damages which ought to be applied.

4.92　在 *Philips Hong Kong Ltd* v *The Attorney-General of Hong Kong*① 一案中，香港政府和原告订立了建造高速公路的合同，合同第29.1条规定：

If the Contractor shall fail to complete the Works or any Section thereof or shall fail to achieve a Specified Degree of Completion within the time prescribed by Clause 27 or extended time, or shall fail to complete or shall unduly delay the Tests on Completion then the Contractor shall pay to the Employer the sum or sums stated in the Appendix to the Form of Tender as liquidated damages for such default and not as a penalty for every day or part of a day which shall elapse between the time prescribed by Clause 27 or extended time, as the case may be, and the date of completion of the Works or the relevant Section thereof or the relevant Specified Degree of Completion.

4.93　虽然香港高院的 Mayo 法官承认有证据表明香港政府在洽谈合同时就已经花了大量的时间和精力，试图对工程未能在约定期限内完成可能造成的损失进行了量化，但是他最终还是认为第29条构成惩罚性条款。上诉法院则认为第29条规定的是约定赔偿。案件最终上诉至枢密院，枢密院支持了上诉法院的判决。枢密院认为上诉人若要证明合同的约定赔偿实际上是一种惩罚就必须能够推翻他们自己同意的合同约定，证明约定的数额远远大于香港政府实际遭受的损失。枢密院 Lord Woolf 认为，除非构成过度，否则即使约定赔偿的数额大于实际遭受

---

① [1993] HKLR 269.

的损失也不影响约定的数额是基于当事人真实的估计作出的,他说:①

> Except possibly in the case of situations where one of the parties to the contract is able to dominate the other as to the choice of the terms of a contract, it will normally be insufficient to establish that a provision is objectionably penal to identify situations where the application of the provision could result in a larger sum being recovered by the injured party than his actual loss. Even in such situations so long as the sum payable in the event of non-compliance with the contract is not extravagant, having regard to the range of losses that it could reasonably be anticipated it would have to cover at the time the contract was made, it can still be a genuine pre-estimate of the loss that would be suffered and so a perfectly valid liquidated damage provision.

在 *Oresundsvarvet Aktiebolag* v *Marcos Diamantis Lemos (The Angelic Star)*② 一案中,原告船厂和一船东订立了船舶建造合同,由船厂为该船东建造一艘散货船。船舶建造合同适用贷款协议的相关规定,其中第 13 条规定: 4.94

> The loan, together with all other monies due to the Lenders by the Owners, shall immediately become payable and the Lenders shall forthwith be put in funds to cover all existing and future liability under any outstanding bills drawn in connection with the loan, and the security for the loan and such monies shall become enforceable in spite of the conditions contained in the contract or the security documents about payment by instalments, if any of the following events were to happen.

上诉法院认为,关于一旦发生任何违约即构成长期贷款及其利息必须立刻偿还的规定应当构成惩罚。但上诉法院的 John Donaldson 法官认为上述条款并没有构成惩罚,他说:③ 4.95

> But I do not so read condition 13. "The loan" is the capital sum. "All other monies due to the lenders by the owners" cannot be construed as "all other monies which would otherwise become due by the owners in the future". It means "all other monies due at the time of the happening of an event of default". The mere fact that the capital sum becomes immediately repayable upon a failure to comply with the conditions upon

---

① [1993] HKLR 269 at 279.
② [1988] 1 Lloyd's Rep 122.
③ [1988] 1 Lloyd's Rep 122 at 125.

which credit was extended cannot constitute a penalty. The provision that the lenders shall forthwith be put in funds to cover all existing and future liability under any outstanding bills drawn in connection with the loan is intended to safeguard the shipbuilders against their potential liability as drawers should the bills have been negotiated and the purchaser, as acceptor, fail to honour the bills upon maturity. This again is not a penalty provision.

4.96 同样道理,在船舶建造合同中有约定赔偿时,如果船厂的行为虽然构成了对承诺的违反,但违反是微小的话,船舶建造合同中的约定赔偿也不应适用,否则就有可能构成惩罚。在 *Cenargo Ltd* v *Empresa Nacional Bazan de Construcciones Navales Militarres SA*① 一案中,船东和船厂订立了船舶建造合同,建造两艘滚装船。合同约定了在船舶有缺陷时的赔偿,但没有约定具体的缺陷程度。船东发现滚装船的卡车甲板有缺陷,但仅需花很少费用就能轻易使其符合合同要求。船东主张适用合同约定的损害赔偿,但船厂认为在更正缺陷的费用远远小于约定赔偿的情况下不能适用合同约定的损害赔偿。一审法院判决可以适用约定的损害赔偿,但上诉法院推翻了一审法院的判决,Longmore 法官说:②

> There is a danger that, if a liquidated damages clause is held to apply to trifling breaches of contract which result in a trifling loss, the whole clause might be struck down as a penalty clause .... I do not consider that the parties in this case, when agreeing liquidated damages in relation to trailer carrying capacity, could have had in mind defects in design or workmanship which could be rectified without incurring major expense, even if it could be said that until such defects were rectified the vessel's spaces were, in breach of contract, not fully available.

4.97 法院认定约定赔偿条款为惩罚条款的案例并不多,在 *Cooden Engineering Co* v *Stanford*③ 一案中,汽车租赁合同第 11 条规定:

> If the hirer shall have made any incorrect or untrue statement or suppressed any information in the said hire purchase proposal, or shall fail to make any payment under this agreement on the day on which it is due or demanded, as the case may be, or shall die, the owners may by 24 hours' previous notice in writing determine the hiring ... and on any

---

① [2002] CLC 1151.
② [2002] CLC 1151 at 1197.
③ [1953] 1 QB 86.

such determination by notice or otherwise the full balance then remaining unpaid of the sum mentioned together with all costs, charges, and expenses whatsoever which the owners may incur or for which they may become liable ... or which they may be required to pay in order to regain possession of the vehicle, shall at once become payable to and be recoverable by them. All moneys payable under the provisions of this clause by the hirer to the owner shall carry interest at the rate of 10 per cent, per annum . . . .

一审法院认为第 11 条并不是惩罚条款,因而判决车主可以获得约定的赔偿。 4.98
但是上诉法院则认为第 11 条构成惩罚条款,上诉法院的 Jenkins 法官说:①

Therefore, ignoring the exceptional and improbable case I have mentioned, I think the sum payable on determination under clause 11 can, in point of amount, fairly be brought within the intention though not strictly within the letter of the first test of a penalty given by Lord Dunedin in *Dunlop Pneumatic Tyre Co Ld* v *New Garage and Motor Co Ld* in paragraph 4(a)as being a sum which is "extravagant and unconscionable in amount in comparison with" the greatest loss that could conceivably be proved to have followed from the breach.

我们可以从 Halsbury 伯爵在 *Clydebank Engineering and Shipbuilding* 4.99
Company, *Limited and Others* v *Don Jose Ramos Yzquierdo Y Castaneda and Others*
一案中举的例子看出构成惩罚条款的基本特征,他在该案中说:②

For instance, if you agreed to build a house in a year, and agreed that if you did not build the house for 50*l*, you were to pay a million of money as a penalty, the extravagance of that would be at once apparent.

如果合同约定了一个适用于几种不同情形的数额,该数额就有可能构成惩 4.100
罚,正如上议院的 Lord Watson 在 *Lord Elphinstone* v *The Monkland Iron and Coal*
Company Limited and Liquidators 一案中所说的:③

When a single slump sum is made payable by way of compensation, on the occurrence of one or more or all of several events, some of which may occasion serious and others but trifling damage, the presumption is

---
① [1953] 1 QB 86 at 109.
② [1905] AC 6 at 10.
③ [1886] 11 App Cas 332 at 342.

that the parties intended the sum to be penal, and subject to modification.

标准格式的规定

4.101　约定赔偿相当广泛地运用于各种合同,船舶建造合同也不例外。SAJ 格式在合同价格调整条款内便有关于约定赔偿的内容:①

> The Contract Price shall be subject to adjustment, as hereinafter set forth, in the event of the following contingencies(it being understood by both parties that any reduction of the Contract Price is by way of liquidated damages and not by way of penalty).

4.102　加入"is by way of liquidated damages and not by way of penalty"字样的目的是为了排除衡平法的适用。然而,当事人明确表示约定的数额是损害赔偿而不是惩罚并不影响法院将其视为惩罚,从而认定其无效。在法院看来,因违约而需支付的数额有可能是惩罚,因行使权利而需支付的数额则可能是约定赔偿。在 *Astley v Weldon* 一案中,Heath 法官说:②

> Where articles contain covenants for the performance of several things, and then one large sum is stated at the end to be paid upon breach of performance, that must be considered as a penalty. But where it is agreed that, if a party do such a particular thing, such a sum shall be paid by him, there the sum stated may be treated as liquidated damages.

4.103　NEWBUILDCON 格式的规定有些别出心裁。虽然该格式没有类似于 SAJ 格式的上述内容,但是该格式把类似的内容加入了每一项具体规定之内,例如该格式针对船舶油耗标准便有如下规定:③

> If the excess fuel consumption is greater than 2%(two percent) of the specified fuel consumption the Contract Price shall be reduced by the amount stated in Box 14(i) for each whole percentage in excess of 2% as liquidated damages up to a maximum amount as stated in Box 14(ii).

4.104　除了分别对交船日以及船舶的具体性能作出约定赔偿的规定外,NEWBUILDCON 格式还专门作出了供选择的条款,以便船东可以根据具体情况

---

① Article III, para.1.
② 2 B&P 346.
③ Clause 9(b).

针对船舶的具体性能作出关于约定赔偿的规定。①

有经验当事人的约定

如果订立合同双方均为有经验的公司,合同中关于约定赔偿条款通常会得到法院的支持。在 *Steria Limited v Sigma Wireless Communications Limited* ②一案中,被告是承包商,原告是分包商。分包合同第7.1条规定: 4.105

> If the Sub-Contractor fails to complete the Sub-Contract Works or any part thereof within the time for completion or any extension thereof granted under Clause 6(Completion), there shall be deducted from the Sub-Contract Price, or the Sub-Contractor shall pay to the Contractor as and for liquidated damages, the percentage (stated in the Sixth Schedule) of the Sub-Contract Value of that part of the Sub-Contract Works as cannot in consequence of the delay be put to the use intended for each week between such time for completion and the actual date of completion, but in no case shall the total amount to be deducted or so paid exceed the maximum percentage of the Sub-Contract Price stated in the Sixth Schedule hereto. Such deduction or payment shall be in full satisfaction of and to the exclusion of any other remedy of the Contractor against the Sub-Contractor in respect of the Sub-Contractor's failure to complete within the time for completion of the Sub-Contract Works.

在分包合同第7.1条是有效的约定赔偿还是惩罚的问题上,承包商和分包商有分歧。高院的 Stephen Davies 法官认为,如果约定赔偿与实际遭受的损失没有显著的差别,合同关于约定赔偿的规定不应视为是一种惩罚,他说:③   4.106

> In such circumstances, in my judgment: (ⅰ) there is no substantial discrepancy between the liquidated damages provisions of the sub-contract and the level of damages likely to be suffered by Sigma; (ⅱ) on the facts of this case I am unable to conclude that the clause was – objectively considered as at the date the contract was entered into – intended to bedeterrent rather than compensatory. Overall, this being a commercial contract entered into between two substantial and experienced companies with knowledge of the difficulties which can occur where after the event one party seeks to recover general damages

---

① Clause 12.
② [2008] BLR 79.
③ [2008] BLR 79 at 99.

from the other for delay, I am not prepared to strike down the clause as penal.

约定赔偿的数额

4.107 　　约定赔偿的数额通常由船东和船厂根据具体情况来确定，就船厂交船延误约定赔偿而言，影响约定数额的因素大致包括船型和船价等。一般的散货船交船延误的约定赔偿每天大约为数千美元，船型大的，约定赔偿数额也就相应大一些。海工项目的约定赔偿数额通常比较大，从几万美元到十几万甚至几十万美元不等。每天的赔偿数额大致与船舶一天的市场租金相当。这种对违约可能造成的损失的估计通常不会太复杂，正如上议院的 Halsbury 伯爵在 *Clydebank Engineering & Shipbuilding Co Ltd* v *Don Jose Ramos Izquierdo y Castaneda* 一案中所说的：①

> ... I suppose there would not be very much difficulty in finding out what the ordinary use of a vessel of this size and capacity and so forth would be, what would be the hire of such a vessel, and what would therefore be the equivalent in money of not obtaining the use of that vessel according to the agreement during the period which had elapsed between the time of proper delivery and the time at which it was delivered in fact.

4.108 　　当然，船舶建造合同中约定赔偿数额也可能会受到其他因素的影响，包括造船市场等，因此约定的数额和市场租金并不一定相等或接近。相比较而言，船舶建造合同中关于船舶航速、油耗和载重吨等保证的约定赔偿的计算则很难找到比较可靠的依据。由于船舶的使用寿命接近甚至超过 20 年，要在这样一段时间内估计出由于船厂建造的船舶不符合合同约定可能在未来带来的损失应当是极其困难的。但是除非约定的数额是船东单方面坚持的，且与当时可能估计的未来损失存在很大的差异，否则船厂应当很难有机会以数额过高为由主张船舶建造合同约定赔偿无效。

实际损失超过约定数额

4.109 　　实际损害超过约定赔偿的并不当然影响约定赔偿数额的有效。在 *Cellulose*

---

① [1905] AC 6 at 12.

Acetate Silk Co v *Widnes Foundry*① 一案中，合同规定，若工程未能在约定时间内完成的，承包人应以罚款的方式每星期支付 20 英镑。工程实际延迟了 30 个星期，买方拒付工程款。承包人起诉要求买方支付，买方则提出反索赔要求承包人承担因延迟造成的损失。买方认为合同约定的每星期 20 英镑因是惩罚而归无效，承包人应承担迟延造成的实际损失 5,850 英镑。一审法院认为承包人应当按照实际损失承担赔偿，但上诉法院则认为承包人仅需承担 600 英镑的延误损失。上议院支持了上诉法院的判决，Lord Atkin 说：②

> I entertain no doubt that what the parties meant was that in the event of delay the damages and the only damages were to be 20*l*. a week, no less and no more .... Except that it is called a penalty, which on the cases is far from conclusive, it appears to be an amount of compensation measured by the period of delay. I agree that it is not a pre-estimate of actual damage. I think it must have been obvious to both the parties that the actual damage would be much more than 20*l*. a week; but it was intended to go towards the damage, and it was all that the sellers were prepared to pay.

确定数额的时间

当事人对违约可能造成的损失作出估计的时间显然是在订立合同之时，换言之，确定约定赔偿的数额是否真实反映了实际损失同样应以合同订立之时为准作出判断。对此，上议院的 Lord Dunedin 在 *Dunlop Pneumatic Tyre Company Ltd* v *New Garage Motor Company Ltd* 就曾说过：③

4.110

> ... the question whether a sum stipulated is penalty or liquidated damages is a question of construction to be decided upon the terms and inherent circumstances of each particular contract, judged of as at the time of making the contract, not as at the time of the breach.

约定赔偿的名称

不少船舶建造合同的约定赔偿条款都会有一个说明，即约定的数额是双方约

4.111

---

① [1933] AC 20.
② [1933] AC 20 at 25.
③ 在我国造船业，约定赔偿通常被称为"罚款"，船厂无需支付约定赔偿的期间则被称为"免罚期"。从严格意义上来说，约定赔偿并不具有"罚款"的性质。

定的损害赔偿，而不是惩罚。前文提及的 SAJ 格式的条款便有这一说明，Norwegian 格式也有相同的语句：①

> The Contract Price shall be subject to adjustments, as hereinafter set forth, in any of the events set out in this Article IV (it being understood by both parties that any reduction of Contract Price is by way of liquidated damages and not by way of penalty) and the Builder shall not in any way be responsible or liable for any other consequences by way of damages or otherwise as a consequence of any of the matters hereinafter set forth in this Article IV, except for the Buyer's right to cancel in accordance with the provisions of the Contract.

4.112　但是船舶建造合同中的这种说明实际上并没有太大的意义，因为条款性质的确定在于其具体规定，而不是其名称。在上文提及的 *Clydebank Engineering & Shipbuilding Co Ltd v Don Jose Ramos Izquierdo y Castaned* 一案中，虽然合同使用了"惩罚"的字样，但是上议院的 Halsbury 伯爵说：②

> It cannot, I think, be denied indeed, I think it has been frankly admitted by the learned counsel—that not much reliance can be placed upon the mere use of certain words. Both in England and in Scotland it has been pointed out that the Court must proceed according to what is the real nature of the transaction, and that the mere use of the word "penalty" on the one side, or "damages" on the other, would not be conclusive as to the rights of the parties.

约定赔偿和过错

4.113　主张约定赔偿的一方对损害的发生应当是没有过错的，除非另有约定，有过错的一方不能主张约定赔偿。在 *Holme v Guppy* 一案中，原告与被告订立合同，由原告为被告完成建造一个酿酒厂所需的木工活，合同约定原告应当在四个半月内完成工作。逾期的，每星期支付 40 英镑作为约定赔偿。由于被告的原因，原告在合同订立四个星期后才开始工作，结果在约定截止日后五个星期原告才完成所有工作。但是财税法院认为，被告既不能获得四个星期的约定赔偿，也不能获得一个星期的约定赔偿。③

---

① Article IV, para.1.
② [1905] AC 6 at 9.
③ (1838)M&W 387.

在 *Astilleros Canarios SA* v *Cape Hatteras Shipping Co Inc and Hammerton Shipping Co SA(The Cape Hatteras)*①一案中,船舶修理合同规定船厂未能在约定时间完成修理的应当支付每天 12,000 美元的罚款,实际上船厂完成修理所需的时间超过了合同约定日期 92 天,但造成这一延误也有可以归责于船东的原因。高院的 Staughton 法官认为船厂无需支付约定赔偿,他说:② 4.114

> In my judgment, the conduct of the defendants in requiring the crankshaft to be returned without repair when it was first taken to Barcelona, even if it was in all respects lawful, did delay the overall progress of the repairs covered by the contract. So did the defendants' conduct at a later stage in requiring the crankpins to be ground, eventually in Barcelona. Accordingly, the principle established by the authorities, that no liquidated damages for delay can be claimed if completion was in part delayed by conduct of the employer, is applicable in the present case. Had the parties wished to avoid that result, they could and should have inserted in the contract a term that the agreed date for completion should be extended in the event of delay caused by the defendants.

约定赔偿的支付

船舶建造合同一般都会明确规定约定赔偿应当在交船时进行计算,这是因为在大多数情况下,交船时可以比较准确地计算出约定赔偿的数额。AWES 格式便有如此规定:③ 4.115

> Any amounts for liquidated damages or any premiums under Article 5 and 6 shall be calculated and determined on delivery of the VESSEL and the balance(of one over the other) shall be paid to the party entitled thereto on the VESSEL's delivery, provided that, if the balance exceeds 10 percent of the CONTRACT price in paragraph(a) of this Article then the payment shall be equal to 10 percent of this said price.

根据上述规定,约定赔偿应当在船舶交接时支付,实际做法就是在船东应当支付的交船款中进行扣减或者增加。 4.116

---

① [1982] 1 Lloyd's Rep 518.
② [1982] 1 Lloyd's Rep 518 at 526.
③ Article 7(e), para.1.

4.117　NEWBUILDCON 格式也规定约定赔偿应当在最后一期建造款中扣除：①

> Any amounts for liquidated damages under Clause 8 (Speed Deficiency), Clause 9 (Excessive Fuel Consumption), Clause 10 (Deadweight Deficiency), Clause 11 (Cubic Capacity Deficiency), Clause 12 (Other Deficiencies) and Clause 13 (Late Delivery for non-permissible delays) shall be calculated and determined before delivery and may be deducted from the Final Instalment.

4.118　大多数建造缺陷都可以在交船时计算出船厂应当支付的约定赔偿的具体数额，例如交船延误、航速不足或油耗过高等。因为在交船时已经知道了船舶的航速和油耗。但并非所有缺陷都可以在交船时计算出应当支付的约定赔偿的具体数额。在交船时无法准确计算出约定赔偿数额的，船东并不因此丧失向船厂索赔约定赔偿的权利，船东在接船后依然可以向船厂提出约定赔偿的索赔。在 *Cenargo Ltd* v *Empresa Nacional Bazan de Construcciones Navales Militares SA*② 一案中，合同第Ⅲ.5 条规定：

> In this Clause 5 "trailers" refers to fully laden trailers with a mean carrying capacity of thirty (30) mt. (a) If the actual trailer carrying capacity of the Vessel is less than 146 Units of 13 metres each the Builder shall pay to the Buyer as liquidated damages One hundred and fifty thousand United States Dollars ($ 150,000) for each trailer unit by which the Vessel is deficient but excluding the first one (1) in respect of which deficiency no liquidated damages shall be payable. If the deficiency in trailer carrying capacity is ten (10) or more the Buyer as an alternative to receiving the aforementioned liquidated damages may rescind the Contract. (b) ...

4.119　在船舶交接之时并没有也无法对集装箱拖架进行测试，因为拖架的载重能力只有在船舶投入营运之后才能准确地测定。船东实际上也是在接船几个月后才向船厂提出索赔的。对于约定赔偿数额是否应当在交船时计算确定并由船厂在交船时向船东支付。Longmore 法官认为，合同并没有排除船东在接船后提出约定赔偿的权利，而且在船舶实际投入营运才能知道实际损害的情况下要求船东在接船时提出索赔是不公平的，他说：③

---

① Clause 15(c).
② [2002] CLC 1151.
③ [2002] CLC 1151 at 1198.

I cannot detect any provision in the contract positively excluding a claim for liquidated damages once delivery is made and it would not be fair for the builders to seek to do so if, in fact, it was a possibility that a genuine claim for deficiency in trailer carrying capacity would not emerge until the vessel had been successfully operated. If there had been a good claim in this case, I would not have held that it was barred by virtue of the fact that art. II provides for liquidated damages to be calculated, determined and paid on delivery. The only barring clause is art.X.5 and that, as the judge said, is not apt to bar claims for breaches of express contractual obligations.

船东支付约定赔偿

*Azimut-Benetti Spav Healey*① 是涉及船东按照船舶建造合同约定向船厂支付约定赔偿的案例。在该案中,原告船厂于 2008 年 9 月 25 日与一家在马恩岛设立的公司订立了船舶建造合同,为船东建造一艘 60 米长的游艇。被告是船东的股东。合同约定的交船日为 2011 年 11 月 30 日。被告作为担保人担保船东履行船舶建造合同。船舶建造合同的第 16 条规定,如果船东未能在 45 天内支付合同规定的任何款项,船厂有权解除合同。第16.3条的内容是: 4.120

> Upon lawful termination of this Contract by the Builder it will be entitled to retain out of the payments made by the Buyer and/or recover from the Buyer an amount equal to 20% of the Contract Price by way of liquidated damages as compensation for its estimated losses (including agreed loss of profit) and subject to that retention the Builder will promptly return the balance of sums received from the Buyer together with the Buyer's Supplies if not yet installed in the Yacht.

船东没有按照船舶建造合同的规定支付建造款,船厂解除了合同并对被告提起了诉讼,要求法院根据简易程序作出判决。被告拒绝承担责任,理由是船舶建造合同第 16.3 条是一惩罚性条款。第 16.3 条规定的合同价格 20%的约定赔偿不是对船厂在解除合同情况下可能遭受的损失的真实预估,因此是不可执行的。原告认为该条款具有明显的商业和赔偿的性质。高院的 Blair 法官认为第 16.3 条并不是惩罚条款,他说:② 4.121

---

① [2011] 1 Lloyd's Rep 473.
② [2011] 1 Lloyd's Rep 473 at 480.

In my judgment, the evidence clearly shows that the purpose of the clause was not deterrent, and that it was commercially justifiable as providing a balance between the parties upon lawful termination by the builder.

VI 合同价格的调整

概述

4.122 　　船舶建造合同通常会针对交船日、航速、耗油和载重吨等方面规定船厂的合同义务，即由船厂向船东保证在约定的交船日交船，并且保证建造完毕的船舶性能符合合同的约定。从法律上说，关于船舶交船日以及船舶性能保证的条款并不构成合同的条件条款，即船舶不符合保证性能的，船东未必可以解除合同。但是这并不影响当事人双方在合同中约定一方当事人可以解除合同的情形，一旦约定的情形出现，该方当事人就有权按约定解除合同。几个常见的船舶建造合同标准格式都有关于船舶性能保证的条款。

交船日保证

4.123 　　船舶建造合同通常会规定交船日，①一般称之为"合同交船日"。合同交船日并不是船厂应当向船东交船的最后一日，而往往是可以交船的第一日。这可能是鉴于船舶建造周期较长，在整个建造过程中有可能遇到各种在合同订立时无法或很难预料的但会影响船舶建造的进度的情形。虽然船厂无需在合同交船日交船，但船厂在合同交船日之后交船就有可能要承担约定赔偿。不少船舶建造合同还会根据时间的长短约定不同数额的赔偿，交船拖延时间越长，船厂需要支付的约定赔偿数额也就越高。换言之，船舶建造合同规定的约定赔偿实际上是船厂延长交船期所需支付的代价。

4.124 　　船厂未能在合同交船日交船其实已经构成了违约，只是双方对该违约的后果已经做出约定而已。船东不能解除船舶建造合同，而只能要求船厂支付约定赔偿。只有到船舶建造合同约定的船厂可以延迟交船的期限届满之后，船东才可以解除合同。不同的船舶建造合同会有不同长短的延迟交船的期限。其中 AWES

---

① 有些船舶建造合同则是规定一个期限，例如 24 个月或两年等，自合同签署日或合同生效日起算。

格式可能是规定最长延迟交船期的标准格式:①

> Should the delay in delivery for causes for which the CONTRACTOR is liable exceed 360 days from the date set forth under paragraph(a)above as extended for permissible extensions under the terms of this CONTRACT, the PURCHASER, as an alternative to receiving the above mentioned liquidated damages, shall have the option to terminate this CONTRACT with the consequences provided for in Article 11.

根据上述规定,船厂可以在合同交船日后的 360 天交船,一旦延误构成可允许延误的,船厂则可以在合同交船日 360 天之后交船。SAJ 格式规定的期限为 210 天,该期限应当是我国造船业使用最为常见的船厂可以延迟交船的期限。SAJ 格式的规定是:②   4.125

> No adjustment shall be made and the Contract Price shall remain unchanged for the first thirty (30) days of delay in delivery of the VESSEL beyond the Delivery Date as defined in Article VII thereof (ending as of twelve o'clock midnight of the thirtieth (30th) day of delay).

按照上述规定,船厂交船迟于合同交船日后 30 天内的无需支付任何约定赔偿。自第 31 天起则应向船东支付约定赔偿,而且约定赔偿的数额也将随着延误时间增加而增加。应当支付约定赔偿的天数共计为 180 天,换言之,只要愿意支付约定赔偿,船厂就可以在合同交船日后的 210 天内交船。船东只有当 210 天的期限届满后才有权解除船舶建造合同。NEWBUILDCON 格式把 210 天的期限缩短至 180 天:③   4.126

> If delivery takes place more than 30 days after the Delivery Date then for each day thereafter the Contract Price shall be reduced by the amount stated in Box 18 per day as liquidated damages up to a maximum delay of 180 days (comprising a 30 day grace period plus 150 days).

> If the delay exceeds 180 days the Buyer shall have the option to terminate this Contract in accordance with Clause 39(a)(iii)(Suspension and Termination).

---

① Article 6(c), para.2.
② Article III.1(a).
③ Clause 13, see also Norwegian Article IV.1(a).

4.127　上述所称之天数是指由于船厂的原因或过失造成交船延误的天数。如果交船延误是由于船东的原因或过失造成的,船厂则无需支付约定赔偿。相反,合同交船日可以顺延。应当注意的是,交船的延迟是以船舶建造合同约定的交船日即合同交船日为依据的,但是合同交船日实际上并不是一个固定的日期,而是根据合同的规定在发生特定情况时可以顺延的日期,例如一旦发生不可抗力事件,合同交船日就会顺延;又如船东支付建造款有延迟的,合同交船日也可顺延。

4.128　在有宽限期规定的情况下,船舶建造合同中关于交船日的约定应当不是一个很大的问题。在实践中依然有不少船厂无法按时交船且遭船东解约。究其原因,可以作如下归纳:首先,交船计划不可靠。船厂在确定合同交船日时缺乏周密可靠的计划,没有充分考虑建造过程中可能遇到的各种影响建造进程的困难。一艘在建船舶出问题而无法及时下水有可能会影响到其他等待上船台船舶的建造进程,从而产生多米诺骨牌效应。其次,执行力薄弱。在有明确计划情况下,船厂未能切实地执行计划。无论是人力还是物力的投入都无法确保计划得以贯彻执行。事实告诉我们,导致船期拖延的往往不是什么难以克服的技术难题,而是琐碎小事,包括部门之间的扯皮。最后,对弃船风险缺乏真正的认识。不少船厂始终没有把船东的弃船作为一种切实的风险予以应对,而是抱侥幸心理。殊不知,船东弃船多半缘于市场因素,是市场迫使船东作出弃船的决定。而且,一旦发生弃船往往是全面的,而不是个别的。虽然船厂依然拥有船舶,但是在船东纷纷选择弃船的时候也就是无法合理出售船舶的时候,船厂会因此面临巨大的风险。

提前交船奖励

4.129　与在合同交船日之后交船应当承担约定赔偿的责任相似,船厂在约定合同交船日之前交船的也有可能因此获得奖励。SAJ格式的规定是:①

> If the BUYER requests in writing that the delivery of the VESSEL be made earlier than the Delivery Date, and if the delivery of the VESSEL is made, in response to such request of the BUYER, more than thirty (30) days earlier than the Delivery Date, then, in such event, beginning with the thirty-first (31st) day prior to the Delivery Date, the Contract Price of the VESSEL shall be increased by adding thereto

---

① Article III.1(d).

¥................. for each full day (it being understood that the BUILDER's acceptance of such BUYER's request for early delivery shall be in no way construed as change or alteration of the Delivery Date under this Contract.

从上述规定可以看出,船厂提前交船有如下几个特征:第一,船厂提前交船是以船东提出书面要求为条件的;第二,提前 30 天交船是没有奖励的,奖励自第 31 天开始起算;第三,船厂提前交船并不意味着合同交船日的变更。CSTC 格式也有关于提前交船的规定,而且规定得比较详细:①

4.130

If the SELLER notifies the BUYER by telex that the delivery of the VESSEL shall be made earlier than the specified Delivery Date as defined in Article VII of the Contract and such notification being given not less than _____ (_____) months prior to the newly planned delivery date, a certain amount of bonus shall be given by the BUYER to the SELLER as follows: -

In the event that the delivery shall be made within fifteen(15)days earlier than the specified Delivery Date, the Contract Price shall remain unchanged. In the event that the delivery shall be made more than fifteen(15)days earlier than the specified Delivery Date, then a bonus shall be added to the Contract Price at rate of United States Dollars _____ _____ (U. S. $ _____)per day for each full day earlier than the 15th day earlier than the Delivery Date.

The total increase of the Contract Price for the earlier delivery shall be added to the fifth instalment of the Contract Price, however, shall not be more than the sum of United State Dollars _____ (U. S. $ _____).

For the purpose of determining the increase of the Contract Price under this Paragraph 1(e), the SELLER shall not be entitled to the bonus contemplated under Paragraph 1(e) of this Article for the period between the Delivery Date defined in Article VII and the date to which the delivery of the VESSEL is extended by reason of the permissible delays.

与 SAJ 格式不同,按照 CSTC 格式的规定,提前交船应当是船厂的权利,只是应当事先书面通知船东而已。只要按照约定事先向船东发出了提前交船的通知,船厂就可以获得提前交船的奖金。但只有提前超过 15 天的,船厂才可以获得提

4.131

---

① Article III.1(e).

前交船的奖金,而且受最高数额的限制。按照上述最后一段的规定,交船日顺延的,船厂就不能获得提前交船奖励。从船东方面来说,船舶是在合同交船日之后交付的,因而不存在提前交船的情形。然而从船厂方面来说,合同交船日的顺延意味着不能在合同交船日交付并不是船厂的原因或过失。如果是船东的原因,例如审批图纸延误或提出修改要求等导致船厂无法在合同交船日之前交付船舶。但只要是在可顺延期限届满之前交付船舶的就应当构成提前交船,因为船厂完成建造所用的时间依然少于合同约定的时间。

4.132　　AWES 格式则使用了"working day"的概念,即船东只需针对节省的工作日支付奖金:①

> Should the VESSEL be completed before the Delivery Date set forth under paragraph(a), the PURCHASER shall subject to the proviso contained in Article 7(e) pay to the CONTRACTOR a premium equal to .... for each working day of earlier delivery, beginning on the .... day after completion.

4.133　　如果 working days 是指周六、周日以及节假日之外的工作日,将提前交船的天数分为"工作日"和"非工作日"应当是没有意义的,对船厂来说恐怕是不公平的。提前就是提前,无所谓工作日或非工作日。如果船东出租船舶,提前租期意味着船东至少可以提前收到租金。租船人按天支付租金,不区分工作日和非工作日。仅奖励提前天数中的 working days 只是表明船东不愿意奖励提前交船而已。

4.134　　船厂在建造完毕的情况下希望提前交船应当是可以理解的,但实际上船东并不始终愿意船厂提前交船,有时船厂提前交船不仅不会给船东带来好处,反而造成各种麻烦。提前接船意味着船东必须提前支付交船款。如果船东是通过融资建造船舶的,是否可以提前接船就成为融资银行是否可以提前支付的问题了。但在贷款或融资已经作出具体安排后,融资银行并不是随时可以拿出钱来支付交船款的。如果船东已经将船舶出租,尤其是以长期期租的方式出租了,提前接船也就意味着租船人同样愿意提前接船。除非租船人愿意提前接船,否则船东就要设法为船舶在出租前安排营运。因此,船厂希望提前交船的一般还要符合一定的条件,例如船厂应当在一定天数之前通知船东,约定的提前交船的日期通常不能再改以及放弃提前交船的奖励等。

---

① Article 6(c), para.3.

航速保证

船舶的航速对船东至关重要,直接关系到船舶的营运能力。在期租租约中都有关于船舶航速的规定,船舶航速达不到合同规定的保证航速,租船人就可以向船东提出航速索赔,甚至可以解除租约。船舶建造合同通常会对船舶的航速作出比较具体的规定,例如 SAJ 格式有下列规定:①

4.135

(a) The Contract Price shall not be affected or changed by reason of the actual speed, as determined by the trial run, being less than three-tenths(3/10) of one (1) knot below the guaranteed speed of the VESSEL.

(b) However, commencing with and including such deficiency of three-tenths(3/10) of one (1) knot in actual speed below the guaranteed speed of the VESSEL, the Contract Price shall be reduced as follows(but disregarding fractions of one-tenth(1/10) of a knot):
For Three-tenths(3/10) of a knot ... a total sum of ￥..........
For Three-tenths(4/10) of a knot ... a total sum of ￥..........
For Three-tenths(5/10) of a knot ... a total sum of ￥..........
For Three-tenths(6/10) of a knot ... a total sum of ￥..........
For Three-tenths(7/10) of a knot ... a total sum of ￥..........
For Three-tenths(8/10) of a knot ... a total sum of ￥..........
For Three-tenths(9/10) of a knot ... a total sum of ￥..........
For One(1) knot ... a total sum of ￥..........................

(c) If the deficiency in actual speed of the VESSEL upon trial run is more than one(1) full knot below the guaranteed speed of the VESSEL, then the BUYER may, at its option, reject the VESSEL and rescind this Contract in accordance with the provisions of Article X hereof, or may accept the VESSEL as a reduction in the Contract Price as above provided for one(1) full know only, that is, at a total reduction of ￥............................

SAJ 格式关于航速的规定比较简单,航速低于船舶建造合同规定但小于一节的,船厂支付约定赔偿;超过一节的,船东可以拒绝接受船舶并解除船舶建造合同。AWES 格式和 Norwegian 格式与 SAJ 格式的基本相同,但没有规定具体的数值,而是留待船厂和船东通过磋商予以规定。②

4.136

---

① Article III.2.
② AWES Article 5(a), see also Norwegian Article IV.2.

4.137　NEWBUILDCON 格式有如下规定:①

If the speed of the Vessel as stated in Box 4D(ii) is not achieved in the manner stated in the Specification or Clause 2(b)(i) the following shall apply:

(a) There shall be no adjustment of the Contract Price except to the extent provided in Sub-clause 8(b).
(b) If the reduction in speed is greater than 2/10ths of a knot, the Contract Price shall be reduced by the amount stated in Box 13(i) for each whole 1/10th of a knot reduction in speed in excess of 2/10th of a knot as liquidated damages up to the maximum amount stated in Box 13(ii).
(c) If the reduction in speed would entitle the Buyer to a reduction in the Contract Price greater than the maximum amount stated in Box 13(ii), the Buyer shall have the option to terminate this Contract in accordance with Clause 39(a)(iv)(Suspension and Termination).

4.138　船舶的航速通常是在试航过程中予以确定的,在试航中测得的航速又称为试航航速(trial speed)。船舶建造合同或规格书会规定在船舶试航时测定航速的特定条件,这些条件包括排水量、主机额定工况、横倾情况、推进器位置、水面的情况、试航区风力和波浪等。船舶的试航航速即为船舶的交船航速。如果船舶试航时的实际情况与船厂和船东约定的情况有所不同,所测得的航速还要根据模型测试进行修正。通常规格书会对确定船舶航速的条件作出明确规定,但 NEWBUILDCON 格式则在合同文本本身增加了关于确定船舶航速的条件:②

The Vessel shall have the dimensions and characteristics as stated in Box 4 and the Specification. These shall be defined, measured and calculated in accordance with the Specification or, if omitted from the Specification, in accordance with the following:

(i) Speed – The Vessel's average speed on a sea trial undertaken in both directions over a measured distance of one (1) nautical mile, with clean hull, in weather with wind speed and sea state not exceeding Beaufort Wind Force Scale 3 and Douglas Sea State Scale 2 respectively on a draft as stated in Box 4D(i) shall be at least the number of knots stated in Box 4D(ii). During such a sea trial the engine's output in kilowatts shall be as stated in Box 4D(iii) corresponding to the

---

① Clause 8.
② Clause 2(b).

percentage of the engine's maximum continuous power output stated in Box 4D(iv) at the approximate revolutions per minute stated in Box 4D(v).

(ii) ...

虽然上述规定是在规格书没有作出相应规定的情况下才适用的,但即使规格书已经有了相应的规定,只要与上述规定有冲突的,仍应以上述规定为准。① 4.139

航速保证的独立性

一旦船厂在船舶建造合同中作出了船舶性能的保证,船舶就必须符合船厂作出的保证,否则船厂就应当承担责任。在 *Admiralty Commissioners* v *Cox and King*②一案中,原告海军部与被告船厂订立建造一艘快艇的船舶建造合同,快艇的主机由海军部提供,由船厂安装。船舶建造合同规定: 4.140

> With the above loads you must be prepared to guarantee a speed of 40 knots subject to a penalty of Pounds Sterling 20 for each 1/10 of a knot below 40 knots. If the speed should be below 38 knots the boat may be rejected by the Admiralty. The speed is to be taken as the mean of means of six consecutive runs alternatively with and against the tide in the usual Admiralty manner on an approved measured course.

船舶建造合同还规定: 4.141

> The speed mentioned in the specification is to be obtained on the trials with the boat in the condition specified in the hull specification and with screw propeller of such form, pitch and dimensions as may be approved by the Commissioners.

海军部提供了主机,船厂安装了主机并完成了建造。但是由于海军部提供的主机已部分生锈,生锈的原因是排气管的内壁没有镀锌。在开始正式测试快艇航速之前排气管已经穿孔了。船厂意识到快艇不可能在正式测试中达到合同保证的数据,因此始终没有进行正式的测试。海军部于是对船厂提起诉讼,拒绝接受快艇并要求船厂返还海军部已经支付的所有建造款,理由是快艇已不可能达到合同保证的 38 节的航速。船厂则认为海军部拒绝对由其提供的主机进行整修是错误的,因此无权获得建造款的返还。一审法院的 MacKinnon 法官认为海军部有 4.142

---

① NEWBUILDCON 的方格部分规定,合同文本和规格书等发生冲突的,以合同文本为准。
② (1927) 27 Ll L Rep 223.

权拒绝快艇,船厂应当返还快艇的建造款。船厂对这一判决提起了上诉。上诉法院维持了一审的判决,Bankes 法官说:①

> If that were the only reference in the contract to this particular guarantee, it seems to me quite plain that with this language the guarantee is that the vessel will attain this speed of 38 knots – that is the guarantee; and the method of ascertaining whether it will or will not, or one method of ascertaining whether it will or will not, is this official trial.
>
> But, of course, although parties may agree that one means of ascertaining whether the vessel comes up to the guarantee is an official trial, it does not prevent the party who gives the guarantee saying: "Oh, it is no good having that trial: I admit it" – and it does not lie in the mouth of the man who makes the admission afterwards to say: "Oh, but you cannot rely upon the clause in the contract entitling you to recover the money if the vessel does not come up to the guaranteed speed, because there has been no official trial, " when the fact is that there was no official trial in substance because he was prepared to admit that it was of no use having it.

油耗保证

4.143　　船舶油耗反映的是船舶主机的效能。船舶的油耗和船舶的航速是与主机功效有关的两个相互关联的问题,也可以说是一个问题的两个方面。对船东而言,船舶的油耗和航速同样重要。在航速不发生变化的前提下,油耗的高低是船东关心的问题。因此,在船舶建造合同中,除了有船舶航速的保证外还有船舶油耗的保证。SAJ 格式对油耗保证作出了如下规定:②

> (a) The Contract Price shall not be affected or changed by reason of the fuel consumption of the VESSEL, as determined by .... trial as per the Specifications, being more than the guaranteed fuel consumption of the VESSEL, if such excess is not more than .... percent (...%) over the guaranteed fuel consumption.

---

① (1927) 27 Ll L Rep 223 at 224.
② Article III.3.

(b) However, commencing with and including an excess of .... percent(...%) in the actual fuel consumption over the guaranteed fuel consumption of the VESSEL, the Contract Price shall be reduced by the sum of ¥ .... for each full one percent (1%) increase in fuel consumption above said .... percent (...%) over the guaranteed fuel consumption of the VESSEL.

(c) If such actual fuel consumption exceeds .... percent (...%) of the guaranteed fuel consumption of the VESSEL, the BUYER may, at its option, reject the VESSEL and rescind this Contract in accordance with the provisions of Article X hereof, or may accept the VESSEL at a reduction in the Contract Price as above specified for .... percent (...%) only, that is, at a total reduction of ¥ ....

SAJ格式实际并没有规定任何数值,而是留待船东和船厂确定。在实践中,船厂通常会在船舶建造合同中对油耗作出保证。与船舶的航速一样,船舶油耗的确定同样取决于一系列条件,包括额定主机工况、输出功率以及吃水状况等,常见的船舶油耗保证的措辞是:

4.144

> The Seller guarantees that the fuel oil consumption of the Main Engine is not to exceed 171.0 grams/(kW * hour) at 85% of MCR output at shop trial based on diesel fuel oil having a lower calorific value of 42,700 kJ per kilogram.

油耗是指主机的油耗,而主机通常是由船厂采购而不是由船厂制造的,因此在船舶建造合同中关于主机油耗的保证其实是主机供应商在采购合同中作出的油耗保证。船舶的油耗一般由主机生产商在出厂之前通过主机的台架试验予以确定的。NEWBUILDCON格式关于油耗的保证则规定得比较详细:①

4.145

> If the fuel consumption of the Vessel's main engine on the test bed using the fuel specified in Box 4C(vii)exceeds the figure stated in Box 4C(iv) the following shall apply:
>
> (a) There shall be no adjustment of the Contract Price except to the extent provided in Sub-clause 9(b).

---

① Clause 9.

(b) If the excess fuel consumption is greater than 2% (two percent) of the specified fuel consumption the Contract Price shall be reduced by the amount stated in Box 14(i) for each whole percentage in excess of 2% as liquidated damages up to a maximum amount as stated in Box 14(ii).

(c) If the excess fuel consumption would entitle the Buyer to a reduction in the Contract Price greater than the maximum amount stated in Box 14(ii), the Buyer shall have the option to:

(i) accept the main engine at a reduction in the Contract Price corresponding to the maximum amount stated in Box 14(ii) or

(ii) reject the main engine and either:

(1) require the Builder to rectify the deficiency and repeat the trial or replace the main engine with one that conforms to the requirements of the Contract. (The time taken to rectify the deficiency and repeat the trial or replace the main engine in accordance with this Sub-clause shall not be a Permissible Delay) or

(2) terminate this Contract forthwith in accordance with Clause 39(a)(v)(Suspension and Termination).

4.146 NEWBUILDCON 可能是唯一将计算约定赔偿起点规定为2%的标准格式。在我国，船舶建造合同中一般约定超过5%才开始计算约定赔偿。与其他标准格式不同，NEWBUILDCON 格式进一步规定了在油耗超过约定最高值时船东可以享有选择权。在这种情况下，船东可以选择接受主机并获得约定赔偿，也可以选择拒绝接受主机并要求船厂整改后再一次试航，或者要求船厂更换符合合同要求的主机。当然，船东也可以选择解除合同。NEWBUILDCON 格式的这一规定无疑为船东带来较大的灵活度，船东可以根据当时的市场作出选择。如果市场处在上升期或看好，船东可以在获得约定赔偿的前提下接受船舶，也可以要求船厂更换主机后接受船舶。这一选择同样不影响船东获得约定赔偿。如果市场低落或不看好，船东就可以选择解除合同。由于合同规定了船东的权利，相对而言便是船厂的义务。如果船东要求船厂就油耗问题进行改进，船厂无疑是应当接受的。

4.147 与船舶的航速保证相同，NEWBUILDCON 格式也规定了确定船舶油耗的条件：①

---

① Clause 2(b).

The Vessel shall have the dimensions and characteristics as stated in Box 4 and the Specification. These shall be defined, measured and calculated in accordance with the Specification or, if omitted from the Specification, in accordance with the following:

(i) ...

(ii) Fuel Consumption – The fuel consumption of the main engine on the test bed using fuel of the type and specification stated in Box 4C(vii) shall not exceed the number of grams per kilowatt/hour stated in Box 4C(iv) when the engine develops the number of kilowatts with an effective calorific value of the number of kilocalories per kilogram stated in Box 4C(ii) and Box 4C(vii) respectively.

(iii) ...

4.148　同样道理,虽然上述规定是在规格书没有作出相应规定情况下适用的,但即使规格书已经有了相应的规定,只要与上述规定有冲突的则应以上述规定为准。

载重吨保证

4.149　船舶的载重吨与船舶吃水有关,通常是根据船舶夏季吃水计算所得。船舶载重吨同样是船东较为关心的,因为它直接关系到船舶的运载能力。SAJ格式关于船舶载重吨保证有如下规定:①

(a) In the event that the actual deadweight of the VESSEL as determined in accordance with the Specifications is less than or in excess of the guarantee deadweight of the VESSEL, the Contract Price shall be either reduced by the sum of ￥................ for each full long ton of such deficiency being more than .... (............) long tons, up to a maximum reduction of ￥............, or increased by the sum of ￥.......................... for each full long ton of such excess being more than .... (...........) long tons, as the case may be (in both cases disregarding fractions of one (1) long ton).

(b) In the event of such deficiency in the actual deadweight of the VESSEL being .... (...........) long tons or more, then, the BUYER may, at its option, reject the VESSEL and rescind this Contract in accordance

---

① Article III.4.

> with the provisions of Article X hereof or accept the VESSEL at a reduction in the Contract Price as above provided for .... (............) long tons only, that is, as a total reduction of ¥.........................

4.150　根据上述规定,船舶实际载重吨小于保证载重吨且达到一定限额的,船厂应当承担约定赔偿的责任。但若船舶实际载重吨大于保证载重吨时,船厂则可以获得奖励。如果船舶实际载重吨小于保证载重吨的数值超过约定数值的,船东就有权解除合同,或者接受船舶并主张相应的约定赔偿。

4.151　NEWBUILDCON 格式关于载重吨保证的规定与上述 SAJ 格式的规定大致相同。船舶实际载重吨低于合同保证载重吨但未达到约定数额时,船厂应当承担支付约定赔偿的责任;超过约定数值的,船东则有权拒绝接受船舶并解除船舶建造合同。① 但是 NEWBUILDCON 格式没有考虑船舶载重吨超过保证载重吨的情形。与船舶的航速保证相同,NEWBUILDCON 格式也规定了确定船舶载重吨的条件:②

> The Vessel shall have the dimensions and characteristics as stated in Box 4 and the Specification. These shall be defined, measured and calculated in accordance with the Specification or, if omitted from the Specification, in accordance with the following:
>
> (iii) Deadweight – The Vessel's deadweight shall be the number of metric tons stated in Box 4A(iii) on international summer freeboard, corresponding to a mean draft in saltwater(specific gravity 1.025) as stated in Box 4A(iv). The specified deadweight shall include fuel, provisions, stores, freshwater, crew and passengers in addition to spare parts not less than the requirements of the Classification Society.
>
> (iv) ...

4.152　这一规定实际上采用了《国际海上人命安全公约》的概念:③

> ... the difference in tones between the displacement of a ship in water of a specific gravity of 1.025 at the load waterline corresponding to the

---

① Clause 10.
② Clause 2(b).
③ 第Ⅱ-1章,A 部分,规则第 2.20 条。规则第 2.21 条将"Lightweight"定义为"the displacement of the ship in tonnes without cargo, fuel, lubricating oil, ballast water, fresh water and feed water in tanks, consumable stores, and passengers and crew and their effects."

assigned summer freeboard and the lightweight of the ship.

货舱容积保证

船舶的容积与载重吨一样都与船舶的货载有关,两者的区别是前者考虑的是货物的体积,而后者考虑的则是货物的重量。散货船的船舶建造合同大多会有关于船舶容积的保证条款。SAJ 格式没有关于船舶容积的保证条款,Norwegian 格式则有如下内容:①   4.153

> If the cubic capacity (............... m^3/cbft) stipulated in the Contract with pertaining specifications is not attained, and the reduction exceeds ....% of the stipulated cubic capacity, the Contract Price shall be reduced by .... for each m^3/cbft of the reduction in excess of the said per cent.
>
> If the reduction in cubic capacity is more than ....% of the stipulated capacity, the Buyer may cancel this Contract.

上述规定比较常见,NEWBUILDCON 格式也有相似的规定。② 而 AWES 格式不仅针对船舶实际容积低于合同要求的情形作出了规定,而且也针对船舶实际容积大于合同规定的情形作出了规定:③   4.154

> Should the VESSEL's capacity be in excess of .... percent of the specified capacity, the PURCHASER shall pay to the CONTRACTOR a premium equal to .... for each cubic metre of capacity in excess of .... percent of the specified capacity, disregarding fractions of a cubic metre.

关于建造保证

除了对船舶性能做出保证外,船舶建造合同还有一个一般的保证,即保证船舶将符合某一特定标准完成建造。Norwegian 格式可能是第一个有类似保证的标准格式。④ NEWBUILDCON 格式应当继承了这一特征,也做出了类似的规定。⑤   4.155

---

① Article IV.5.
② Clause 11.
③ Article 5(c), para.4.
④ Article II.1, para.3.
⑤ Clause 1(a),本书第 3 章已有相关介绍。

比较两者不难看出，Norwegian 格式实际上设定了一个比较高的标准。"first class shipbuilding practice in Western Europe"并不是一个笼统的概念，而是相当明确的标准。如果船东可以证明船舶建造不符合一流西欧船厂的习惯做法，就有权要求船厂对特定项目进行返工。相反，NEWBUILDCON 格式的一般保证则相对比较合理。首先，"good"一字的含义是具有特定功能所需的质量，而该质量标准并不是特定的；其次，"in accordance with the terms and conditions of this Contract"一句实际上是对适用国际标准的一种限制，即只有在符合合同规定的情况下才可以适用合同外的质量标准。

因建造不符合约定引起的调整

4.156　　如果船东建造的船舶不完全符合合同或规格书的规定，虽然船东未必有权拒绝接船，但应当有机会根据不符的具体情况主张合同价格的调整。在 *Mondel v Steel*① 一案中，被告船厂为原告船东建造船舶，船舶建造合同约定船厂应按合同以及规格书的规定建造船舶。船厂建造的船舶有很多处都不符合规格书的要求，船东以船舶存在缺陷导致修理产生费用为由拒绝支付余款。船东认为自己针对船厂的索赔类似于交叉诉讼，因此可以抵销船厂的支付建造款的请求。但是法院虽然认为船东有权对合同价格进行扣减，因为船厂建造的船舶不符合船厂的保证，但这并不是抵销。Parker 法官说：②

> It must however be considered, that in all these cases of goods sold and delivered with a warranty, and work and labour, as well as the case of goods agreed to be supplied according to a contract, the rule which has been found so convenient is established; and that it is competent for the defendant, in all of those, not to set-off, by a proceeding in the nature of a cross action, the amount of damages which he has sustained by breach of the contract, but simply to defend himself by shewing how much less the subject-matter of the action was worth, by reason of the breach of contract; and to the extent that he obtains, or is capable of obtaining, an abatement of price on that account, he must be considered as having received satisfaction for the breach of contract, and is precluded from recovering in another action to that extent; but no more.

---

① (1841) 8 M & W 858.
② (1841) 8 M & W 858 at 871.

VII 合同价格的重新谈判

合同价格的重新谈判可能是船舶建造合同所特有的,这一特征可能是变化无常的航运市场决定的。在船东和船厂签订了船舶建造合同后,市场有可能会发生剧烈变化,例如运费剧烈下降、钢材价格的大幅度上升或者汇率发生变化等。然而船舶建造合同往往采用固定价格,不会有价格调整条款。在这种情况下,船厂继续建造船舶必将面临亏损的结局。作为造船业特有的一种惯例,船厂在这种情况下大多会向船东提出重新洽谈合同价格的请求。

4.157

船厂要求加价的机会

船厂是否可以对合同价格进行上调在很大程度上取决于当时航运市场的情况。如果当时的航运市场低迷,船厂上调合同价格的请求几乎注定是无法实现的。相反,如果在船厂提出上调合同价格之时,航运市场正处在上升时期,船东多半会同意船厂的加价请求。船厂的加价请求只是小幅度减少船东的利润空间而已,拒绝船厂的加价请求则有可能导致船厂无法交船。即使在法律上船东胜券在握,诉讼中获胜并不当然给船东带来利润。面对这样的商业现实,船东一般不会断然拒绝船厂的加价请求。

4.158

加价的对价

船东同意船厂的加价请求实际上构成了双方对船舶建造合同的修改,此种修改属于协议修改。按照英国法的规定,只有得到对价支持的合同修改才是可执行的。针对缺乏对价的价格调整,船东有机会主张此种加价的无效性。在 *North Ocean Shipping Co Ltd* v *Hyundai Construction Co Ltd and Hyundai Shipbuilding and Heavy Industries Co Ltd*① 一案中,原告船东和被告现代船厂订立建造一艘26万吨油轮的船舶建造合同,合同价格为 30,950,000 美元,分五期支付。船东在船舶建造合同签订后支付了第一期建造款。随后美元对韩元的汇率剧烈下滑。船厂要求船东在合同价格基础上增加 10% 建造款,但遭到船东的拒绝。船厂主张汇率的变化是无法预期的,因此构成不可抗力,继续履行合同已不再公平。最后船东同意加价 10%,船厂也同意增加担保信用证的金额。

4.159

---

① [1979] 1 Lloyd's Rep 89.

4.160　船舶交付后,船东要求船厂返还多付部分,理由是额外数额是在被迫的情况下支付或错误支付的。船东开始了与船厂的仲裁。仲裁庭作出了船厂胜诉的裁决,但要求法院对船东是否有权获得多付数额的返还做出决定。高院认为船厂要求加价10%没有合法的理由,但对价是存在的。由于合同是在被迫的情形下成立的,因此合同是可撤销的,但并不是无效的。由于船东在没有做出保留的情况下支付了加价后的建造款,其行为构成了对可撤销合同的确认。Mocatta法官是这样说的:①

> I have come to the conclusion that the important points here are that since there was no danger at this time in registering a protest, the final payments were made without any qualification and were followed by a delay until July 31, 1975, before the owners put forward their claim, the correct inference to draw, taking an objective view of the facts, is that the action and inaction of the owners can only be regarded as an affirmation of the variation in June, 1973, of the terms of the original contract by the agreement to pay the additional 10 per cent. In reaching this conclusion I have not, of course, overlooked the findings in par.45 of the special case, but I do not think that an intention on the part of the owners not to affirm the agreement for the extra payments not indicated to the yard can avail them in view of their overt acts.

4.161　由此可见,如果船东在支付额外部分款项时作出了适当的保留,他们就有机会以缺乏对价为由获得该部分款项的返还。就船厂而言,船东的加价并没有增加工作量,但船厂承诺按期完成船舶建造同样可以构成船东加价的对价。在 *Williams v Roffey Bros. and Nicholls(Contractors) Ltd*② 一案中,被告将部分工作分包给原告,原告由于价格过低而发生财务困难。被告担心迟延交付会在主合同中承担罚款,于是向原告口头同意增加合同价格。但被告没有全部支付承诺的数额,原告对其提起了诉讼。法院支持了原告的诉请。被告提起了上诉,被告认为原告所做的实际上是其按照合同规定应当做的,并没有任何额外的工作,因此加价是没有对价的。上诉法院认为原告的加价是有对价支持的,上诉法院的 Glidewell 法官说:③

> It is therefore my opinion that on his findings of fact in the present case,

---

① [1979] 1 Lloyd's Rep 89 at 99.
② [1991] 1 QB 1.
③ [1991] 1 QB 1 at 16.

the judge was entitled to hold, as he did, that the defendants' promise to pay the extra £10,300 was supported by valuable consideration, and thus constituted an enforceable agreement.

Russell 法官也说：① 4.162

A gratuitous promise, pure and simple, remains unenforceable unless given under seal. But where, as in this case, a party undertakes to make a payment because by so doing it will gain an advantage arising out of the continuing relationship with the promisee the new bargain will not fail for want of consideration.

减价的机会

船厂和船东对船舶建造合同规定的价格重新进行谈判的情形并不仅仅局限于船厂要求提高合同价格，同样也适用于船东要求降低合同价格。2008年年底开始的金融危机导致航运市场"一泻千里"，不少种类的船舶市场价已经不足船舶建造合同的一半了。船东开始意识到，按照船舶建造合同规定的价格接船意味着巨额的亏损。在这种情况下，船东同样会和船厂洽谈合同价格下调的可能性。在实践中，大多数船厂通常也会考虑到船东面临的困难而同意下调合同价格。在船东单方面要求下调合同价格时，同样存在调整后的合同价格是否会因缺乏对价支持而无效或可撤销的问题。但是，如果双方在调整合同价格的同时也变更了船舶建造合同其他条款的内容，船厂以缺乏对价支持为由主张合同价格调整无效的机会应当不是很大。假设在降低合同价格的同时，船舶的合同交船日也相应推迟到话，合同价格的调整就应当是有对价支持的。 4.163

VIII 还款保函

概念

还款保函是指由船厂向船东提供的，通常是由银行出具的以船东为受益人，保证在船东可以主张返还预付款时向船东支付的担保。船舶建造合同的一个基本特征是船舶所有权通常在船舶交接时才由船厂转移至船东。换言之，船东在支 4.164

---

① [1991] 1 QB 1 at 19.

付建造款时并不拥有船舶或其任何部分。一旦船厂破产或遭遇其他不幸而无法完成船舶建造,遭受损失的是船东。因此,还款保函对船东而言是一种保障,即船东支付的所有预付款可以得到返还。

保证合同

4.165　还款保函在普通法中具有保证合同(contract of suretyship)的性质。保证合同的保证人承担的责任可以是支付一定数额的金钱,也可以是履行某种义务。保证合同可以分为两类,一类是担保合同(contract of guarantee),另一类则是补偿合同(contract of indemnity),两者之间有不少相似点。"担保"一词也经常被用来指"补偿"。William Blackburne 法官在 *Vossloh Aktiengesellschaft* v *Alpha Trains (UK) Limited* 一案中给保证合同下了如下定义:①

> A contract of suretyship is in essence a contract by which one person, the surety, agrees to answer for some existing or future liability of another, the principal (or principal debtor), to a third party, the creditor, and by which the surety's liability is in addition to, and not in substitution for, the liability of the principal.

4.166　William Blackburne 法官还分别给担保合同和补偿合同下了定义,担保合同的定义是:②

> A contract of guarantee, in the true sense, is a contract whereby the surety (the guarantor) promises the creditor to be responsible for the due performance by the principal of his existing or future obligations to the creditor if the principal fails to perform them or any of them.

4.167　在担保合同中,担保人承担的责任可能仅限于履行某一特定义务,若债务人因任何原因不再有义务的,担保人也不再负有任何义务。因此担保人的责任是有条件的,即债务人未履行其义务,且条件已满足。在担保合同中担保人的责任始终是从属性的或辅助性的,对债权人承担主要责任的是债务人。只有当债务人未履行其义务时,担保人才有责任履行担保义务。而且,担保人的责任以债务人对债权人承担的责任为限。换言之,一旦债务人的义务无效或不可执行或不复存在,担保人同样不再有任何责任。

---

① [2011] 2 All ER 307 at [21].
② [2011] 2 All ER 307 at [23].

补偿合同则与担保合同有着不同的特征,补偿合同的特征是给予补偿承诺的人负有主要责任,除非他与债务人承担连带责任,否则他的责任完全独立于债务人和债权人之间产生的责任。给予补偿承诺的人一旦作出了补偿便对债务人享有追索权。William Blackburne 法官给补偿合同下了如下定义:①

4.168

> In contrast to the contract of guarantee is the contract of indemnity. In one sense all contacts of guarantee (strictly so called) are contracts of indemnity (as indeed are many contracts of insurance) since, in its widest sense, an indemnity is an obligation imposed by operation of law or by agreement of the parties. In the narrower sense in which, in the current context, the expression occurs, a contract of indemnity denotes a contract where the person who gives the indemnity undertakes his indemnity obligation by way of security for the performance of an obligation by another.

船厂向船东提供的还款保函通常具有担保合同性质。出具还款保函的银行向船东作出保证,一旦船厂不履行船舶建造合同规定的义务,担保银行将对船东承担履行合同义务的责任。但是担保银行保证履行合同义务仅仅局限于返还船东已经支付的所有预付款及按照约定利率计算的利息。由于船舶建造中使用的还款保函并没有标准的格式或措辞,因此还款保函的性质也只能根据具体情况予以认定,正如上诉法院的 Tuckey 法官在 *Caja de Ahorros del Mediterraneo & ors* v *Gold Coast Ltd* 一案中所说的:②

4.169

> ... [R]efund guarantees are a common feature of the shipbuilding industry. However, as the judge notes, there is no standard practice in relation to such guarantees; they can either be in the form of independent performance bonds (or stand-by letters of credit) or true 'see to it' guarantees.

还款保函的性质

如前所述,在船舶建造中使用的还款保函并没有固定的格式或措辞,有些还款保函明确写明担保人承担"主债务人"的责任,有些则没有如此规定;有些还款保函通过日期规定还款保函的有效期,有些则通过事件规定有效期;虽然大多数

4.170

---

① [2011] 2 All ER 307 at [25].
② [2002] CLC 397 at 400.

还款保函有仲裁止付条款,但也有没有仲裁支付条款的还款保函。因此,还款保函的性质取决于还款保函所采用的格式及其措辞。

"主债务人"

4.171　绝大多数还款保函一般都会写上担保人是作为"主债务人而不是作为保证人承担责任"(as a primary obligor and not merely as a surety)。但是,还款保函的性质似乎并不因此而发生变化,正如 Fisher 法官在 *Heald v O' Connor* 一案中所说的:①

> The only straw for the plaintiff to clutch is the phrase "as a primary obligor and not merely as a surety" but that, in my judgment, is merely part of the common form of provision to avoid the consequences of giving time or indulgence to the principal debtor and cannot convert what is in reality a guarantee into an indemnity.

4.172　还款保函明确规定担保人以主债务人的身份担保的,担保人的还款义务似乎不再取决于船东发出的请求,除非在船舶建造合同中船厂的还款义务同样以收到支付请求为条件。正如 David Richards 法官在 *TS & S Global Limited v John Fithian-Franks, Anthony Charles Hayes, Frank David Simpson, Robert Edward Poskitt, Ian Fifthian-Franks* 一案中所说的:②

> In my judgment, the decision in *MS Fashions v BCCI* cannot be distinguished on this basis. It is clear, I think, from the judgment of Dillon LJ that because [guarantors] had covenanted to pay as principal debtors, their position was equated with that of a primary debtor, who is under an immediate obligation to pay without the need for a demand even though the contract provides for payment on demand.

4.173　NEWBUILDCON 格式可能是唯一一个不仅在附录中含有还款保函的格式和措辞,而且在合同正文部分也对还款保函作出了规定的标准格式。该格式的还款保函有如下文字:③

> ... at the request of the Builder we irrevocably and unconditionally guarantee(but as primary obligor and not by way of secondary liability

---

① [1971] 1 WLR 497 at 503.
② [2007] EWHC 1401 at [26].
③ Annex A(iii).

only) that if the Builder becomes liable under the Contract to repay any part of any Instalment we shall, upon receipt by us from you of a Demand for the same . . . .

4.174 从上述规定来看,只要船厂应当返还船东支付的预付款,船东就可以要求还款保函银行支付,而无需等到付款期届满船厂依然没有支付时才可以要求还款保函银行支付。

见索即付保函

4.175 根据2010年《国际商会见索即付保函统一规则》(ICC Uniform Rules for Demand Guarantee(URDG 758))的规定,见索即付保函(demand guarantee)的定义是:①

A demand guarantee (also called independent, autonomous or first demand guarantee) is an irrevocable undertaking issued by the guarantor upon the instructions of the applicant to pay the beneficiary any sum that may be demanded by that beneficiary up to a maximum amount determined in the guarantee, upon presentation of a demand complying with the terms of the guarantee.

4.176 见索即付保函的一个基本特征是一旦受益人按照保函规定提出支付请求,担保人就有义务支付。作为出具还款保函的银行不能以船舶建造合同的规定为由拒绝履行见索即付保函的付款义务。正如 URDG 758 所规定的:②

A guarantee is by its nature independent of the underlying relationship and the application, and the guarantor is in no way concerned with or bound by such relationship. A reference in the guarantee to the underlying relationship for the purpose identifying it does not change the independent nature of the guarantee. The undertaking of a guarantor to pay under the guarantee is not subject to claims or defences arising from any relationship other than a relationship between the guarantor and the beneficiary.

4.177 作为见索即付保函,一旦受益人提出的付款请求在形式上符合担保要求,担保人就有支付义务,而不论船厂和船东对船舶建造合同是否存在争议。应当注意

---

① Georges Affaki et al, *Guide to ICC Uniform Rules for Demand Guarantees URDG* 758, International Chamber of Commerce, 2011, p.1.
② Article 5(a).

的是,《国际商会见索即付保函统一规则》并非法律,只有在当事人约定适用时才适用于担保和保函。① 在还款保函适用《见索即付保函统一规则》的情况下,保函是否构成见索即付保函取决于还款保函的具体措辞。还款保函规定适用《见索即付保函统一规则》并不当然使还款保函成为见索即付保函。相反,即使不适用《见索即付保函统一规则》,还款保函依然可能构成见索即付保函。在 Gold Coast Ltd v Caja de Ahorros del Mediterraneo & Others 一案中,上诉法院的 Tuckey 法官便根据该案中还款保函的特征认定其为见索即付保函:②

> The instrument has all the appearances of a first demand guarantee. It describes itself as a guarantee, but this is simply a label; it does not use the language of guarantee. Rather the obligation, which is expressed to be an "irrevocable and unconditional undertaking", is that the banks "will pay" on a first written demand. The only express condition of payment is contained in condition 1. This requires a certificate but makes no reference to arbitration or underlying liability under the shipbuilding contract. The instrument contains its own dispute resolution provisions.

4.178　综上,在船舶建造合同中使用的还款保函是否具有见索即付保函的性质,还是只是一份从属性的担保,保函的名称并不起关键的作用,应当根据还款保函的具体格式和措辞予以确定。

法院的解释

4.179　在 Rainy Sky SA and Others v Kookmin Bank ③ 一案中,原告是六家与一家韩国船厂订立船舶建造合同的船东,被告是根据船厂的请求向原告提供还款保函的银行。每一份船舶建造合同均规定船厂在破产时应返还船东支付的所有预付款。银行提供担保均有如下内容:

> ADVANCE PAYMENT BOND
> (1) We refer to the shipbuilding contract dated (the Contract) entered into between Jinse Shipbuilding Co Ltd of Pusan, Korea (the

---

① Article 1(a) of URDG 758: "The Uniform Rules for Demand Guarantees ("URDG") apply to any demand guarantee or counter-guarantee that expressly indicates it is subject to them. They are binding on all parties to the demand guarantee or counter-guarantee except so far as the demand guarantee or counter-guarantee modifies or excludes them."
② [2002] 1 Lloyd's Rep 617 at 622.
③ [2012] 1 Lloyd's Rep 34.

Builder) and yourselves for the construction and delivery of a new-built Vessel to be delivered before …

(2) Pursuant to the terms of the Contract, you are entitled, upon your rejection of the Vessel in accordance with the terms of the Contract, your termination, cancellation or rescission of the Contract to repayment of the pre-delivery instalments of the Contract Price paid by you prior to such termination and the value of the Buyer's Supplies delivered to the Shipyard (if any), together with interest thereon at the rate of seven per cent (7%) per annum from the respective dates of payment by you of such instalments to the date of remittance by telegraphic transfer of such refund.

(3) In consideration of your agreement to make the pre-delivery instalments under the Contract we hereby, as primary obligor, irrevocably and unconditionally undertake to pay to you, your successors and assigns, on your first written demand, all such sums due to you under the Contract.

(4) Payment by us under this Bond shall be made without any deduction or withholding and promptly upon receipt by us of a written demand stating that the Builder has failed to fulfil the terms and conditions of the Contract and as a result of such failure, the amount claimed is due to you and specifying in what respects the Builder has so failed and the amount claimed.

船舶建造合同的第 X.5 条是关于返还预付款的规定,该规定的措辞如下: 4.180

The payments made by the Buyer to the Builder prior to the delivery of the Vessel shall constitute advances to the Builder. If the Vessel is rejected by the Buyer in accordance with the terms of this Contract, or if the Buyer terminates, cancels or rescinds this Contract pursuant to any of the provisions of this Contract specifically permitting the Buyer to do so, the Builder shall forthwith refund to the Buyer in US dollars, the full amount of total sums paid by the Buyer to the Builder in advance of delivery together with interest thereon as herein provided within thirty (30) banking days of acceptance of rejection.

船舶建造合同的第 XII.3 条则是关于船厂违约的规定,其内容如下: 4.181

If the Builder shall apply for or consent to the appointment of a receiver, trustee or liquidator, shall be adjudicated insolvent, shall apply to the courts for protection from its creditors, file a voluntary petition in bankruptcy or take advantage of any insolvency law, or any action shall be taken by the Builder having an effect similar to any of the foregoing or the equivalent thereof in any jurisdiction, the Buyer may by notice in writing to the Builder require the Builder to refund immediately to the Buyer the full amount of all sums paid by the Buyer to the Builder on account of the Vessel and interest thereon at seven percent(7%) per annum on the amount to be refunded to the Builder, computed from the respective date such sums were paid by the Buyer to the date of remittance of the refundable amount to the Buyer and immediately upon receipt of such notice the Builder shall refund such amount to the Buyer. Following such refund the Builder may, but shall not be obliged to, by notice in writing to the Buyer given within ten (10) business days terminate this contract. If the Builder does not so terminate the Contract the Buyer's obligation to pay further instalments prior to delivery of the Vessel under Article X paragraphs 2(a), (b), (c)and(d) shall be suspended and the full Contract price shall be paid to the Builder on delivery of the Vessel in the manner contemplated by Article X paragraph 2(e).

4.182　　船东支付了第一期建造款。2008年船厂遭遇了金融危机并于2009年根据韩国法律进入"债务解决程序"。船东援引船舶建造合同第XII.3条的规定,要求船厂立即返还所有预付款以及7%的利息。船厂没有返还预付款,于是船东要求银行支付。双方的争议是银行的担保责任仅仅局限于担保约定的事项,还是船舶建造合同约定的所有事项。一审的Simon法官认为担保第3段中的"such sums"是指任何情形应当返还的预付款,包括船舶建造合同第XII.3条规定的情形。银行上诉,上诉法院则认为银行仅需在担保约定的情形发生时承担担保责任,上诉法院的Patten法官说:①

> When one comes then to consider the operative words of para.3 the question is whether "all such sums due to you under the Contract" refer back to pre-delivery instalments becoming repayable in any circumstances under the contract or to their becoming repayable under the provisions referred to in para.2. The reference to pre-delivery instalments occurs in both paragraphs. The judge adopted the first of these alternatives by construing "such sums" as a reference to the pre-delivery instalments mentioned in the first line of para.3 so as to read the words in dispute as meaning "all (pre-delivery instalments) due to you under the Contract". But the difficulty about this construction is that it

---

① [2011] 1 Lloyd's Rep 233 at 242.

robs para.2 of any purpose or effect. If the purpose of the bond was to provide a guarantee for the repayment of the pre-delivery instalments regardless of the circumstances in which they came to be repayable, para.2 could have been omitted in its entirety.

船东上诉，最高法院认为对担保第3段的两种解释都有各自的理由，在这种情况下，法院应当考虑商业的常识，采纳一个合理的人应当有的判断。最后最高法院认为银行应当针对破产的情形承担担保责任。最高法院的 Lord Clarke 说：① 4.183

> In these circumstances I would, if necessary, go so far as to say that the omission of the obligation to make such re-payments from the bonds would flout common sense but it is not necessary to go so far. I agree with the judge and Sir Simon Tuckey that, of the two arguable constructions of para [3] of the bonds, the buyers' construction is to be preferred because it is consistent with the commercial purpose of the bonds in a way in which the bank's construction is not.

上述判例实际上为合同条款的解释设定了一个新的原则，即在两种解释都可以成立的情况下应当采纳更符合商业常识的解释。银行的担保虽然没有明确把船厂破产作为自己承担担保责任的情形，但提供担保本身应当是对受益人的一种全面的保障。 4.184

还款保函的有效期

还款保函一般都会有有效期。没有有效期的保函应当是始终有效的保函。还款保函通常会通过两种方式规定有效期，一种是以船舶的交接作为还款保函有效期的届满，另一种则是确定一个还款保函失效的具体日期。两者同时规定的则一般以先到者为准，即一旦船舶交接完毕，即使还款保函规定的失效日尚未来临，还款保函照样无效。同理，虽然船舶尚未交接，一旦规定的失效日到来的，还款保函也照样失效。 4.185

还款保函的有效期通常是可以延长的。在船舶建造合同履行中有可能遇到各种在订立合同时没有预见到的情形，这些未预见到的情形一旦对船舶建造的进程造成影响，船厂和船东往往会根据具体情况以补充协议的方式约定合同交船日的推迟。随着合同交船日的推迟，由船厂提供的还款保函有可能在船舶 4.186

---

① [2012] 1 Lloyd's Rep 34 at 45.

交接之前就已经失效了,这就需要延长还款保函的有效期,从而保证船东享有还款保函赋予的利益。在这种情况下,船厂就要向出具还款保函的银行申请延长还款保函有效期。不少还款保函都规定,一旦船厂和船东就船厂是否应当返还预付款问题开始仲裁的,还款保函的有效期即自动延长至仲裁程序最终结束后的 30 天。还款保函有此种规定的,其有效期在仲裁程序开始后就自动延长了。

还款保函的转让

4.187　如果船东通过融资建船,几乎肯定需要转让还款保函。船东的融资银行为了确保自己的贷款能够得到偿还,往往会要求船东将船舶建造合同和还款保函一并转让给自己。① 除非明确规定不可转让,还款保函一般都是可以转让的。还款保函的转让并不需要得到出具还款保函银行的同意,还款保函受让方所要做的只是向出具还款保函的银行发出通知即可。如前所述,还款保函实际上是随着船舶建造合同的转让而转让的,如果船东仅仅转让船舶建造合同而不转让还款保函,船东的融资银行的利益显然不能得到切实的保障。

4.188　船东转让了还款保函后一般会通知船厂以及出具还款保函的银行。在有融资安排情况下,按照船舶建造合同规定支付建造款的并不是船东,而是船东的融资银行。船东的融资银行不愿意看到船舶建造合同由于船东的违约而被船厂解除,因此船东的融资银行会要求船厂确认:在船东违约且船厂按照合同可以解除合同的情形时,船厂应当将船东的违约情况通知船厂的融资银行,并承诺给予船东的融资银行一段时间纠正船东的违约或代为船东履行。船厂应当注意的是:一旦船厂在转让通知的确认书上签署后其按照船舶建造合同享有的解约权的行使就此发生了改变。

标准格式规定的问题

4.189　在常用的标准格式中,似乎只有 CSTC 格式和 NEWBUILDCON 格式有关还款保函的规定。但无论是 CSTC 格式还是 NEWBUILDCON 格式关于船厂提供还款保函的规定似乎都有问题。CSTC 格式规定的是:②

　　　　As security to the BUYER, the SELLER shall deliver to the BUYER,

---

① 关于船舶建造合同的转让请参见本书第 16 章第 I 节。
② Article II.7, para.2.

concurrently with this Contract being signed, a Refund Guarantee to be issued by the Bank of China, Head Office, Banking Department, Beijing, the People's Republic of China in the form as per Exhibit "A" annexed hereto.

按照 CSTC 格式的规定,船厂应当在双方签署船舶建造合同之时便提供由银行出具的还款保函。然而按照 CSTC 格式的生效条款的规定,船舶建造合同应当在列明的 5 个条件同时得到满足时才开始生效,这些条件是:(1)合同和规格书已经签署;(2)船厂收到船东支付的第一期建造款;(3)船厂收到船东提供的付款保函;(4)船东收到船厂提供的还款保函;(5)船厂和船东的董事会批准。① 对照合同生效条款不难看出,船厂不应当在签署船舶建造合同时便提供还款保函。按照合同生效条款的规定,提供还款保函是船舶建造合同生效应当满足的条件之一,因此船厂提供还款保函不是合同义务。但是从上述规定来看,船厂在签署合同时提供还款保函似乎又是一项合同义务,因为上述规定使用了"shall"一字。船厂提供还款保函势必产生费用,而在船舶建造合同尚未正式生效之时产生费用可能会造成浪费。② 4.190

作为 NEWBUILDCON 格式附件的还款保函便有如下内容:③ 4.191

... this Guarantee shall remain in force until the first to occur of (a) due delivery of the Vessel to, and acceptance of the Vessel by, you (b) the payment to you by the Builder or by us of all sums secured by this Guarantee, and (c) three-hundred (300) days after the Contractual Date of Delivery. However, notwithstanding the foregoing, if within twenty-eight (28) days after our receipt of a Demand we receive a written notice from you or the Builder that your claim for the repayment of any sums referred to in the Demand has been disputed and that such dispute will be resolved in accordance with the Contract, the period of validity of this Guarantee shall be extended until thirty (30) days after the dispute has been finally determined in accordance with paragraph 5 below.

上述内容在 NEWBUILDCON 格式的正文中也可以找到:④ 4.192

The Parties shall ensure that any guarantee issued on their behalf shall:

---

① Article XVIII.
② 关于船舶建造合同生效条款请参见本书第 21 章。
③ Annex A(iii).
④ Clause 14(c).

(i) ...
(ii) ...
(iii) in the case of the Refund Guarantee(sub-clause 14(b)), remain in force until either
  (1) a date at least 300 days after the Contractual Date of Delivery stated in Box 10 or 30 days after the final resolution of any dispute under Clause 42(Dispute Resolution), whichever is the later; or
  (2) delivery of the Vessel to, and acceptance of the Vessel by, the Buyer whichever is the sooner.

4.193　NEWBUILDCON 格式关于还款保函的规定如下:①

To secure the Builder's obligation to refund the Buyer's pre-delivery instalments pursuant to this Contract the Builder shall, within the number of days stated in Box 19(b)(i) after the signing of this Contract and before the date for payment of the first instalment in accordance with Clause 15(a)(i)(Payments – Instalments), provide the Buyer with a Refund Guarantee issued by the bank or party named in Box 32 substantially in the form and substance set out in Annex A(iii)(Refund Guarantee), failing which the Buyer shall have the option to terminate this Contract in accordance with Clause 39(a)(ix)(Suspension and Termination).

4.194　按照上述规定,船厂应当在方格 19(b)(i)中规定的船舶建造合同签署完毕后的天数内提供还款保函,未能在约定天数内提供还款保函的,船东便有权利解除合同。与 CSTC 格式一样,NEWBUILDCON 格式也有合同生效条款,该条款规定船舶建造合同应当在方格 25 内规定的条件得到满足后生效,若方格 25 没有规定条件的,船舶建造合同则应按方格 1 规定的日期生效。② 假设方格 19(b)(i)中填入了 5 天,而在方格 25 内则规定船厂提供还款保函为船舶建造合同的生效条件之一,按照上述 NEWBUILDCON 的规定,船厂应当在签约后的 5 天内提供还款保函,否则船东就可以解除船舶建造合同。然而,按照方格 25 的规定,船厂提供还款保函实际上是船舶建造合同生效的条件之一,即合同在船厂提供还款保函后依然尚未生效。如果船厂是在方格19(b)(i)规定的五天后的一天,即第 6 天提供还款保函的,船东可以解除船舶建造合同,但其所解除的其实是一个尚未生效的

---

① Clause 14(b)。
② Clause 44(a)。

船舶建造合同。

仲裁止付条款

绝大多数还款保函都会有仲裁止付条款，即一旦船厂或船东就船厂是否应当返还预付款或船东是否可以获得预付款返还开始了仲裁，出具还款保函的银行就不再有义务向船东支付还款保函的数额，一直到最终的仲裁裁决或法院判决作出且要求船厂返还预付款时为止。 4.195

如果还款保函中没有仲裁止付条款的，担保银行在仲裁庭作出船厂应当返还预付款的裁决之前就有支付义务了。即使还款保函中有关于仲裁的规定，但若此种规定不明确的，则无法起到阻止还款担保银行返还预付款义务的作用。在 *Gold Coast Ltd* v *Caja de Ahorros del Mediterraneo and Others*① 一案中，原告船东是船舶建造合同的受让人，被告是西班牙船厂。按照船舶建造合同的规定，船厂应当为船东建造一艘 22,000 吨的不锈钢化学品船。船东支付建造款的义务以收到还款保函为前提条件。船东将船舶建造合同和还款保函转让给了自己的融资银行。船舶建造合同第 11.1 条规定： 4.196

> If, in accordance with any of the provisions of this contract the buyer declares the contract in default and/or rescinds the contract then, subject to any arbitration under art.15, at the buyer's option, either
>
> (a) the builder shall be liable to repay to the buyer all monies paid by the buyer for or on account of the contract price together with interest thereon ... from the date when such monies were paid by the buyer to the builder up to the date of the repayment thereof ... or
>
> (b) make a demand under the refund guarantee(s); or ...

还款保函则有如下规定： 4.197

> In consideration of your payment ... of the ... instalment ... under the Shipbuilding Contract we do hereby irrevocably and unconditionally undertake ... that we will pay to you within five(5)days of your written demand ... amounts due to you under this Guarantee ....
>
> This Guarantee is subject to the following conditions:
> (1) We shall pay any amounts payable under this Guarantee upon receipt of a certificate issued by LLOYDS BANK PLC stating the

---

① [2002] 1 Lloyd's Rep 617.

amount of the instalment paid to the builder under the agreements, the date of such payment that you have become entitled to a refund pursuant to the agreements and that the builder has not made such refund.

(2) This Guarantee shall become null and void upon ... (c) 1 July 2000, provided that ... if arbitration proceedings have been commenced ... under Article 15 of the Shipbuilding Contract, then the Guarantee will remain in full force and effect until 21 days after the publication of the final award ....

(3) Any variation amendment to or waiver given in respect of the Agreement will not limit, reduce or exonerate our liability under this Guarantee ....

4.198 由于船厂交船延误，船东按照第11条的规定解除了船舶建造合同。船厂认为船东无权解除合同，双方于是开始了仲裁。在仲裁期间，船东向担保银行出示了由劳氏银行出具的证书，要求返还已付的建造款。担保银行认为由于仲裁程序尚未结束，船东无权获得还款。但是法院认为船东可以获得还款，因为劳氏银行出具的证书已经满足了担保函的要求。法院不接受船厂提出的船舶建造合同中"subject to arbitration"一句意味着船东应当在通过仲裁解决争议后才能要求返还预付款的主张。被告上诉，上诉法院驳回了被告的上诉，同样认为船东可以获得建造款的返还。针对还款保函中关于仲裁的规定，上诉法院的Tuckey法官说：①

> Reference to arbitration in condition 2, which deals with the duration of the obligation assumed by the instrument and not the obligation itself, is perfectly explicable on the basis that this is a necessary provision in the event of Lloyds deciding that it is unable to issue the certificate until after any dispute has been resolved by arbitration.

4.199 针对船舶建造合同中关于仲裁的内容，Tuckey法官说：②

> The reference to arbitration in art.11(1) does not, I think, help the defendant banks either. The article does not say "subject to any arbitration award", as the defendant banks must contend and, if it did, it would not make sense. If the buyer's options under art.11(1) were all conditional upon an arbitration award, none of them could accrue until such time as an award was

---

① [2002] 1 Lloyd's Rep 617 at 622.
② Ibid.

made, in which case there would be no dispute to refer to arbitration in the first place. It is the contract which creates rights and obligations. Once these have accrued any dispute about them can be referred to arbitration, but until that has happened there is nothing to arbitrate. Mr. Boyd, QC for the buyer, suggests that the words "subject to arbitration" in art.11 were intended to have the same meaning as the opening words in art.10, that is to say, that the options afforded to the buyer under art.11 are without prejudice to the builder's rights to go to arbitration. I think he is right about this.

不难看出,还款保函中的仲裁止付条款实际上改变了还款保函见索即付的性质,因为担保银行支付的实质条件已经满足了。仲裁是在船厂和船东之间针对船舶建造合同进行的,不应涉及还款保函。 4.200

担保人的责任解除

还款保函的提供是以船舶建造合同为依据的,即还款担保人是以船舶建造合同的条款为基础提供还款保函的。一旦船舶建造合同在还款保函担保人不知情的情况下发生影响其利益的重要改变,还款保函担保人就无需继续承担担保责任。这一原则应当来自17世纪的 *Pigot's Case* 一案,在该案中法院指出,契据的关键内容经权利人或任何第三人修改的,对义务人便不再有效:① 4.201

> When any deed is altered in a point material, by the plaintiff himself, or by any stranger, without the privity of the obligee, be it by interlineation, addition, rasing, or by drawing of a pen through a line, or through the midst of any material word, that the deed thereby becomes void.

当然,导致担保人免责的改变必须是重要的,否则担保人依然应当承担担保责任。在 *Raiffeisen Zentralbank Osterreich AG* v *Crossseas Shipping Ltd & Ors*② 一案中,担保人签署担保时,"接受送达人"一栏是空白的,银行的职员在担保人签署了担保后填入了接受送达的代理人的名称、地址等内容。担保人以此为由拒绝承担担保责任。法院认为在担保人签署后填入送达代理人并不构成重要改变。上诉法院的 Potter 法官说:③ 4.202

---

① (1614) 11 Co Rep 26b at 27b.
② [2000] 1 WLR 1135.
③ [2000] 1 WLR 1135 at 1148.

... it seems to me that, to take advantage of the rule, the would-be avoider should be able to demonstrate that the alteration is one which, assuming the parties act in accordance with the other terms of the contract, is one which is potentially prejudicial to his legal rights or obligations under the instrument.

4.203　　在 *Holme v Brunskill*① 一案中，原告同意出租自己的农场，包括一个牧场和700头羊。被告向原告提供了担保，保证在租期届满后将700头羊完好无损地归还。在租期届满之前原告通知承租人终止租赁，承租人反对终止租赁并与原告订立协议，归还牧场但保留农场并且降低了租金。租期届满时，原告发现羊群的数目减少了，质量也差了。原告于是凭担保向被告起诉。上诉法院的Cotton法官认为，如果当事人在没有征询担保人意见的情况下变更了合同条款且此种变更系重要变更的，法院可以让担保人自己决定是否继续担保。他说：②

The true rule in my opinion is, that if there is any agreement between the principals with reference to the contract guaranteed, the surety ought to be consulted, and that if he has not consented to the alteration, although in cases where it is without inquiry evident that the alteration is unsubstantial, or that it cannot be otherwise than beneficial to the surety, the surety may not be discharged; yet, that if it is not self-evident that the alteration is unsubstantial, or one which cannot be prejudicial to the surety, the Court, will not, in an action against the surety, go into an inquiry as to the effect of the alteration, or allow the question, whether the surety is discharged or not, to be determined by the finding of a jury as to the materiality of the alteration or on the question whether it is to the prejudice of the surety, but will hold that in such a case the surety himself must be the sole judge whether or not he will consent to remain liable notwithstanding the alteration, and that if he has not so consented he will be discharged.

4.204　　但是上诉法院的Brett法官则持不同意见，Brett法官认为，即使变更的重要规定，担保人是否免责依然应当根据具体情况予以确定，他说：③

The proposition of law as to suretyship to which I assent is this, if there is a material alteration of the relation in a contract, the observance of

---

① (1878) 3 QBD 495.
② (1878) 3 QBD 495 at 505.
③ (1878) 3 QBD 495 at 508.

which is necessary, and if a man makes himself surety by an instrument reciting the principal relation or contract, in such specific terms as to make the observance of specific terms the condition of his liability, then any alteration which happens is material; but where the surety makes himself responsible in general terms for the observance of certain relations between parties in a certain contract between two parties, he is not released by an immaterial alteration in that relation or contract.

在 Bank of Baroda v Patel① 一案中,原告银行向一家名为 ANY 的企业提供融资,被告为此提供了担保。按照融资协议,银行不时向 ANY 提供了一些外汇业务服务,但 ANY 并没有英国出口信贷担保局的保险,也不知道自己应当有此保险。银行也没有要求 ANY 安排出口信贷担保局的保险,最终导致 ANY 对银行的责任大幅度加重。银行要求被告支付所欠数额。但被告认为,鉴于银行放弃了出口信贷担保局的保险且没有通知被告,因此被告已无需承担担保责任。高院的 Potter 法官驳回了银行的主张,Potter 法官认为银行和 ANY 的行为已经构成对融资安排的改变,被告无需承担担保责任了。他说:② 4.205

> It seems to me that there is a short answer to those contentions. First, whether or not, in other contexts, it might properly be dubbed a waiver rather than a variation, the operation of the facility by the bank at the request of ANY without ECGD cover in respect of particular transactions, when both parties were well aware of the terms of the facility, amounts in broad terms to an agreement so to operate it and in effect as a variation of the terms of the facility. Even were that not so, I consider that operation of the facility in that manner should be regarded as conduct by the bank as creditor to the prejudice of its surety sufficient to discharge the defendant from liability.

从上述案例中不难看出,如果船东和船厂对船舶建造合同作出重要修改且没有得到还款保函银行同意的,还款保函银行就有机会无需承担还款保函规定的责任。至于何为重要修改则是事实问题,应当根据具体案件的具体事实作出判断。但凡是在船舶建造合同中增加或加重还款保函银行担保责任的修改都应当构成重要修改。 4.206

---

① [1995] 1 Lloyd's Rep 391.
② [1995] 1 Lloyd's Rep 391 at 396.

IX 付款保函

4.207　付款保函是指由船东在船舶建造合同订立后向船厂提供的通常由银行出具的,保证船东切实履行付款义务的保函。船舶建造合同通常会以附件的形式将付款保函的格式和措辞附于合同文本之后。

性质和作用

4.208　和还款保函一样,付款保函的性质同样取决于保函的措辞。前文关于还款保函的内容绝大部分也适用于付款保函。在船舶建造合同中,船东最主要的合同义务就是按照约定支付建造款并在船厂交船时接船。其中接船既是船东的义务,同时也是船东的权利。就船厂而言,最为关心的正是船东按照约定履行支付各期建造款的义务,因此船东提供的付款保函也可以被视为是一份履行担保,①保证船东将按船舶建造合同的约定履行。作为 NEWBUILDCON 格式附件的付款保函规定了对船东履约的保证:②

> In consideration of you entering into the Contract, agreeing to construct the Vessel in accordance with the terms of the Contract, and agreeing to accept this Guarantee pursuant to the Contract, at the request of the Buyer we irrevocably and unconditionally guarantee (but as primary obligor and not by way of secondary liability only) performance by the Buyer of all its liabilities and responsibilities under the Contract, including but not limited to due and punctual payment of any instalment of the contract price by the Buyer to you under the Contract ....

4.209　如前所述,在绝大多数情况下,作为船舶建造合同的买方通常是在提供方便旗登记的国家注册成立的空壳公司,在接船之前往往没有任何资产。除非船厂在合同生效时收到较大数额的建造款,否者就将面临自己已经投入大量资金而船东拒绝或无法支付建造款的局面。一旦市场发生大幅度的跌落,船厂就将遭受巨大的损失。

---

① 相比之下,船厂向船东提供的还款保函严格意义上并不是一份履约担保,因为还款保函银行承诺的只是返还船厂收到的所有预付款及其利息,还款保函银行并不承担因船厂违约而引起的损害赔偿。
② Annex A(ii).

母公司保函

虽然就担保性质而言,付款保函应当是银行出具的保函,但在实践中也不时可以看见由船东的母公司提供的付款保函。船东母公司提供的付款保函和银行提供的付款保函的最明显区别正是商业信用和银行信用的区别。所谓的"母公司"应当是指作为船舶建造合同买方的控股公司,但是应当注意的是"母公司"未必就比"子公司"更为可靠。如前所述,船舶建造合同中的买方几乎无一例外都是在提供方便旗登记的国家注册成立的空壳公司。虽然不可靠,但在接船后至少有船舶作为该公司的资产,而其母公司则可能是什么都没有的一个空壳公司。因此,是否可以接受由母公司提供的付款保函并不取决于该母公司和船舶建造合同买方的关系,而是该母公司的资信是否可靠。

4.210

标准格式的规定

在标准格式中,CSTC 格式和 NEWBUILDCON 格式都有关于付款保函的规定。其中 CSTC 格式规定的是:①

4.211

> The BUYER shall, concurrently when this Contract being signed, deliver to the SELLER an irrevocable and unconditional Letter of Guarantee in the form annexed hereto as Exhibit "B" in favour of the SELLER issued by a first class international bank(hereinafter called the "Guarantor") acceptable to Bank of China and the SELLELR. This guarantee shall secure the BUYER's obligation for the payment of all 2nd, 3rd and 4th instalments of the Contract Price.

与还款保函的问题一样,按照 CSTC 格式生效条款的规定,船东向船厂提供付款保函其实是船舶建造合同的生效条件之一。② 因此在签署船舶建造合同时船东可以但没有义务提供付款保函。

4.212

NEWBUILDCON 格式关于付款保函的规定则是:③

4.213

> To secure the Buyer's obligation to pay the instalments of the Contract Price prior to delivery the Buyer shall, within the number of days stated in Box 19(a)(i)after the signing of this Contract, deliver to the Builder an irrevocable and unconditional guarantee issued by the bank or party

---

① Article II.6.
② Article XVIII.
③ Clause 14(a).

stated in Box 31 substantially in the form and substance set out in Annexes A(i)(Instalments) or A(ii)(Performance) as stated in Box 19(a)(ii), failing which the Builder shall have the option to terminate this Contract in accordance with Clause 39(b)(iv)(Suspension and Termin-ation).

4.214　上述规定可能存在的问题与 NEWBUILDCON 格式关于还款保函规定可以存在的问题相类似。

付款保函的无条件性

4.215　作为履约保函的付款保函通常是无条件的,即为见索即付保函。除非有欺诈,船厂无需证明船东已经违约或满足其他条件而只需按照付款保函的规定提出付款请求,付款保函银行就有支付的义务。正如高院的 Kerr 法官在 *RD Harbottle (Mercantile) Ltd* v *National Westminster Bank Ltd* 一案中所说的:①

> It is only in exceptional cases that the courts will interfere with the machinery of irrevocable obligations assumed by banks. They are the life-blood of international commerce. Such obligations are regarded as collateral to the underlying rights and obligations between the merchants at either end of the banking chain. Except possibly in clear cases of fraud of which the banks have notice, the courts will leave the merchants to settle their disputes under the contracts by litigation or arbitration as available to them or stipulated in the contracts. The courts are not concerned with their difficulties to enforce such claims; these are risks which the merchants take. In this case the plaintiffs took the risk of the unconditional wording of the guarantees. The machinery and commitments of banks are on a different level. They must be allowed to be honoured, free from interference by the courts. Otherwise, trust in international commerce could be irreparably damaged.

4.216　上诉法院的 Lord Denning 在 *Edward Owen Engineering Ltd* v *Barclays Bank International Ltd & Umma Bank* 一案中也表达了类似的观点,他说的是:②

> A bank which gives a performance guarantee must honour that guarantee according to its terms. It is not concerned in the least with the relations between the [creditor] and the customer; nor with the question whether the [creditor] has performed his contracted obligation or not; nor with

---

① [1978] 1 QB 146 at 155.
② [1978] 1 QB 159 at 171.

the question whether the [creditor] is in default or not. The bank must pay according to its guarantee, on demand, if so stipulated, without proof or conditions. The only exception is when there is a clear fraud of which the bank has notice.

最新的判例应当是上诉法院在 Shanghai Shipyard Co Ltd v Reignwood International Investment(Group) Company Limited 一案,①在该案中的被告是一家香港公司,向原告提供了一份履约保函。该保函有如下内容:

1. In consideration of [the Builder] entering into [the Contract] with [the Buyer] ... for the construction of [the Vessel], [the Guarantor] hereby IRREVOCABLY, ABSOLUTELY and UNCONDITIONALLY guarantee[s] in accordance with the terms hereof, as the primary obligor and not merely as the surety, the due and punctual payment by [the Buyer] of the Final [I]nstalment of the Contract Price amounting to ... US $ 170,000,000 ....

...

3. [The Guarantor] also IRREVEOCABLY, ABSOLUTELY and UNCONDITIONALLY guarantee[s], as primary obligor and not merely as surety, the due and punctual payment by [the Buyer] of interest on the Final Instalment guaranteed hereunder at the rate of ... (5%) per annum from and including the first day after the default until the date of full payment by [the Guarantor] of such amount guaranteed hereunder.

4. In the event that [the Buyer] fails to punctually pay the Final Instalment guaranteed hereunder in accordance with the Contract or [the Buyer] fails to pay any interest thereon, and any such default continues for a period of fifteen(15)days, then, upon receipt by [the Guarantor] of [the Builder's] first written demand, [the Guarantor] shall immediately pay to [the Builder] or [the Builder's] assignee all unpaid Final [I]nstalment, together with the interest as specified in paragraph (3)hereof, without requesting [the Builder] to take any further action, procedure or step against [the Buyer] or with respect to any other security which you may hold.

In the event that there exists dispute between [the Buyer] and the Builder as to whether:

4.217

---

① [2021] EWCA Civ 1147.

(i) [The Buyer] is liable to pay to the Builder the Final Instalment; and
(ii) The Builder is entitled to claim the Final Instalment from [the Buyer],

and such dispute is submitted either by [the Buyer] or by [the Builder] for arbitration in accordance with Clause 17 of the Contract, [the Guarantor] shall be entitled to withhold and defer payment until the arbitration award is published. [The Guarantor] shall not be obligated to make any payment to [the Builder] unless the arbitration award orders [the Buyer] to pay the Final Instalment. If [the Buyer] fails to honour the award, then [the Guarantor] shall pay you to the extent the arbitration award orders.

...

7. Our obligations under this guarantee shall not be affected or prejudiced by:
   (a) any dispute between you as the Builder and the Owner under the Contract; or
   (b) the Builder's delay in the construction and/or delivery of the Drillship due to whatever causes; or
   (c) any variation or extension of their terms thereof; or
   ......

4.218　被告没有按照约定支付最后一期建造款,原告解除了建造合同并要求被告支付最后一期建造款。被告认为其担保人责任以买方有义务支付为条件,而且在仲裁裁决公布前没有义务支付。高院需要解决的是两个首要问题:一是担保人的责任是见索即付还是以买方负有付款义务为条件;二是担保人的责任是否以仲裁开始为条件。高院的 Robin Knowles 法官认为:担保人的责任以买方负有付款义务为条件;担保人在仲裁结果公布之前可以拒绝支付。

4.219　原告提起上诉,上诉法院改判了高院的判决,上诉法院认为:担保人的责任是见索即付;担保人的支付义务不以仲裁裁决为条件。上诉法院的 Lord Popplewell 结合了担保中的不同文字得出他的结论。这些文字包括:"absolutely and unconditionally","as primary obligor and not merely as the surety","upon receipt by us of your first written demand","upon receipt by us of your first written demand we shall immediately pay to you..."。针对第 7(a)条,Lord Popplewell 是

这样说的:①

> Clause 7(a), which expressly provides that obligations on the Guarantor are to be unaffected by any dispute under the Building Contract. Were clause 4 not to contain the proviso in its second half, this would in my view put beyond argument that the instrument is not a surety guarantee: a surety guarantee would make the Guarantor's obligation dependent upon the very thing which clause 7(a)provides is not to affect or prejudice the obligation. The proviso to clause 4 does nothing to alter that conclusion. It is a carve out of what is otherwise a demand guarantee, modifying the parties' rights and obligations in the event that it is triggered in accordance with its terms(which is the second issue).

付款保函准据法

付款保函通常会规定准据法以及管辖权条款。鉴于船舶建造合同一般都会规定英国法为准据法,伦敦仲裁为解决争议的方式,付款保函也可以考虑采用相同的准据法,尽可能保证结果的一致性。有的付款保函干脆约定适用船舶建造合同中的准据法条款和争议解决条款。在 *Mitsubishi Corporation v Aristidis I Alafouzos*② 一案中,船舶建造合同规定英国法为准据法。船东提供的付款保函有下列内容: 4.220

> I ... as a primary obligor and not as a surety merely ... irrevocably and unconditionally guarantee to you ... the due and faithful performance and fulfillment by the Buyer of all the terms and conditions in the Contract ... including but not limited to prompt payment when due of the price of the ... vessel to you ....

但是付款保函没有关于准据法的规定,Steyn 法官认为付款保函的准据法是英国法,他的理由是:③ 4.221

> Here I take into account three factors. First, not only is the shipbuilding contract governed by English law, but it is in every sense of the word an English contract. It provides for all notices and communications to be given in the English language. It provides for technical disputes to be

---

① [2021] EWCA Civ 1147 at [37].
② [1988] 1 Lloyd's Rep 191.
③ [1988] 1 Lloyd's Rep 191 at 196.

resolved by the Lloyds' Register of Shipping Society, and, as I have said, it provides for London arbitration. Secondly, there is a very close relationship between the buyers and the guarantor. Indeed the buyers are in reality simply a nominee company of the guarantor. It is therefore not a case of a guarantee given by an independent bank or financial institution where, depending on the circumstances, the guarantee might arguably not be governed by the proper law of the principal contract. Thirdly, as is shown by the terms of the shipbuilding contract, it is a transaction which involves a complex bundle of reciprocal rights and obligations. This factor tends to make a ruling that the accessory contract is governed by a proper law other than the one governing the principal transaction commercially unattractive. Making due allowance for the fact that the guarantee was negotiated and signed in Greece, and taking into account the cumulative effect of the factors which I have listed, I am satisfied that the proper law of the guarantee is English law.

X 安慰函

概念

4.222 安慰函通常是指由合同以外的第三人向合同的权利人提供的，表明合同义务人有能力且有意愿履行合同义务的书面文件。安慰函一般由合同义务人的母公司或关联公司提供，出具安慰函的目的通常是给接受安慰函的一方以安慰。安慰函经常用在银行贷款中，由借款人的母公司向银行出具安慰函。安慰函往往是作为担保函的替代而提供的，出具安慰函的原因包括：出具人不希望承担法律责任，或者出具人没有能力出具保函等。

安慰函的措辞

4.223 与意向书相类似，安慰函是否具有合同约束力同样不取决于其名称，而是取决于安慰函的措辞。如果安慰函的措辞实际上包含了合同成立的要素，即使使用了"安慰函"的字样，依然有可能构成有约束力的合同。通常情况下，安慰函并不构成有合同约束力的文件，其原因主要是因为出具安慰函的一方并没有缔约的意图。一个比较典型例子是 *Kleinwort Benson Ltd* v *Malaysian Mining Berhad*[①] 一

---

① [1988] 1 WLR 799.

案,在该案中被告是一家在马来西亚注册的公司,该公司在英国成立了一家完全由其控股的公司并作为伦敦金属交易所的成员从事戒指交易。原告是一家商业银行,为该英国公司提供多种货币的现金贷款并且接受了由被告提供的一份安慰函。该安慰函有如下措辞:

> We refer to your recent discussions with [the subsidiary] as a result of which you propose granting [the subsidiary]: (a)banking facilities of up to £5 million; and(b)spot and forward foreign exchange facilities with a limitation that total delivery in cash will not on any one day exceed £5 million.
>
> (1) We hereby confirm that we know and approve of these facilities and are aware of the fact that they have been granted to [the subsidiary] because we control directly or indirectly [the subsidiary].
>
> (2) We confirm that we will not reduce our current financial interest in [the subsidiary] until the above facilities have been repaid or until you have confirmed that you are prepared to continue the facilities with new shareholders.
>
> (3) It is our policy to ensure that the business of [the subsidiary] is at all times in a position to meet its liabilities to you under the above arrangements.

英国公司最终破产了,被告拒绝承担任何责任并主张自己在安慰函中并没有任何缔约的意图。高院判决被告应当承担责任。高院的 Hirst 法官说:① 4.224

> The wording of the crucial paragraph is unequivocal and categorical. Far from being expressed other than in the language of contract, as Mr. Stamler submitted, I think that the phraseology is fully apt to express a legal obligation. I see no magic in the opening words "we confirm that we will not ..." in paragraph(2), or their omission from paragraph (3): put another way, I do not think that any greater strength would have been added to paragraph(3)if it had begun "We confirm that it is our policy ..." Thus I reject Mr. Stamler's argument based on comparison of the various paragraphs and consider the wording of the crucial paragraph completely apt to constitute a contractual undertaking.

被告不服,提起了上诉。上诉法院推翻了高院的判决。针对安慰函中 4.225

---

① [1988] 1 WLR 799 at 809.

"ensure that"一句,上诉法院的 Ralph Gibson 法官说:①

> The statement in paragraph 3, however, was not, it was submitted, a contractual promise and was not intended to have legal effect as such. It was nevertheless ... not devoid of legal significance; it was a representation of fact as to the policy of the defendants at the time that the statement was made; and the plaintiffs were entitled to rely upon it as a statement of the current policy of the defendants. If it were shown to have been untrue to the knowledge of the defendants at the time when it was made, the plaintiffs would have had a claim in deceit, but there has been no suggestion of that nature.

承担义务的意愿

4.226　如果安慰函明确表示了出具人愿意承担合同义务的,安慰函就会对出具人产生合同约束力。在 *Chemco Leasing SpA* v *Rediffusion Plc*② 一案中,被告向原告出具的安慰函包含如下内容:

> We confirm to you that the share capital of [borrower] is owned 99.91% by CMC which is in turn 100% owned by the undersigned Rediffusion Limited. Therefore Rediffusion Limited will be in a position to exercise sufficient control over the administration and management of [borrower] to ensure that its obligations to Chemco are maintained.
>
> We assure you that we are not contemplating our interest in [borrower] and undertake to give Chemco prior notification should we dispose of our interest during the life of the leases. If we dispose of our interest we undertake to take over the remaining liabilities to Chemco of [borrower] should the new shareholders be unacceptable to Chemco.

4.227　在一审中,高院的 Staughton 法官驳回了原告的起诉。Staughton 法官认为被告无需因安慰函承担责任。但是上诉法院的 Parker 法官则认为安慰函对被告具有合同约束力,他说:

> It is common ground that the intention of the final paragraphs of the letters were to confer a "put option" on the plaintiffs in the event that they found the new shareholders unacceptable, i.e., it was an offer to

---

① [1989] 1 WLR 379 at 385.
② [1987] FTLR 201.

take over the remaining liabilities in such an event. It follows that ... the defendants could be under no liability unless and until the offer was accepted, and thus that the plaintiffs could not succeed unless they proved acceptance. This can be put on the alternative but, as I think, less accurate basis that it was an implied term of the letters that the plaintiffs should give notice to the defendants that the new shareholders were unacceptable. This was accepted by the plaintiffs.

不受约束的表示

4.228 一旦出具人在安慰函中明确表示了其不受约束的意图,即使在安慰函中尚有足以使之被解释为有合同约束力的措辞,该安慰函通常也不应被解释为具有合同约束力。在 Re Altantic Computer Plc(in administration)①一案中,银行向一家公司提供融资,该公司的母公司向银行出具了一份安慰函,该安慰函的措辞包括如下内容:

> We hereby confirm that Atlantic Medical Ltd is wholly owned by Atlantic Computers plc. We confirm that we are aware of the facility detailed below and which your bank has granted to Atlantic Medical Ltd.
>
> In consideration of the bank granting such credit, we undertake that without the prior consent of the bank: (a)that the beneficial ownership of Atlantic Medical Ltd will be maintained by this company during the currency of the facility now to be made available by the bank; (b)that the moneys owing by Atlantic Medical Ltd to the parent company will not be repaid in priority to any moneys owing or contingently owing by Atlantic Medical Ltd to the bank; (c) that if Atlantic Medical Ltd is unable to meet its commitment, the parent company will take steps to make arrangements for Atlantic Medical Ltd's present, future or contingent obligations to the bank both for capital and interest to be met.
>
> This document is not intended to be a guarantee and, in the case of para.(c)above, it is an expression of present intention by way of comfort only.

4.229 Chadwick 法官认为由于最后一点内容,该安慰函并不构成一份担保。他是这样说的:②

---

① [1995] BCC 696.
② [1995] BCC 696 at 697.

If it were not for the final paragraph in the letter of comfort, I should have no real doubt that Atlantic Computers had accepted an obligation to ensure that AML's present, future and contingent obligations in relation to the hire-purchase facilities described were met. Although not strictly a guarantee, in that the obligation could be fulfilled without direct payment by Atlantic Computers to [bank] – for example by the parent company putting its subsidiary in funds sufficient to enable AML to meet its commitments – the obligation which Atlantic Computers had assumed would, I think, have been that of a surety.

But para.(c) does not stand alone. It is qualified by the final paragraph in the letter. In particular, it is made clear in that final paragraph that para.(c) is intended to take effect as 'an expression of present intention by way of comfort only'.

If para.(c) is to take effect only as an expression of present intention, it can contain no contractual promise as to the future policy or intentions of Atlantic Computers. It must be treated as nothing more than a warranty that, at the relevant date, 30 December 1986 or 31 March 1987 as the case may be, Atlantic Computers did intend that, if in future AML was unable to meet its commitment to [bank], then the parent would stand behind its subsidiary. That warranty may or may not have given comfort to [bank]; but as is made clear by the final paragraph, it was not intended to do more than give such comfort as [bank] might derive from an expression of present intention.

船舶建造中的安慰函

4.230　　在船舶建造中，通常的做法是船厂向船东提供由银行出具的还款保函，而船东则向船厂提供同样由银行出具的付款保函。但是，银行保函并不是始终可以获得的。在市场低迷时，例如在2008年金融危机后，很少银行愿意为船舶建造项目提供银行保函了。在这种情况下，母公司保函或母公司安慰函开始得到采用。就船厂而言，在绝大多数情况下，是否可以接受船东母公司出具的安慰函等同于是否可以接受船东付款没有担保的做法。如前所述，只要各期建造款的支付时间及其相应数额安排好，即使没有付款担保，船厂依然可以在将风险处于可控状态下接受订单。

第 5 章　设计、审图和监造

I　船舶设计

概述

设计,简而言之是指为实现特定目的而进行的策划、计划或制图的过程。设计一个非常宽泛的概念,包括服装设计、建筑设计、工业设计、艺术设计、平面设计、立体设计等等。就船舶建造而言,设计是指制定符合法律、船级规范以及船东要求并利用现有建造技术和习惯的建造依据的过程。*Introduction to Naval Architecture* 一书有一个非常简单的定义:[1]

5.1

> Design is a process of synthesis bringing together a wide range of disciplines and analysis methods.

Ship Design and Construction 一书给船舶设计下的定义是:[2]

5.2

> Design can be defined as the activity involved in producing the drawings (or 3-D computer models), specifications and other data needed to construct an object, in this case a ship.

船舶是为船东建造的,船舶设计的最根本的目的是以最低的成本最大限度地满足船东的要求。[3]

5.3

> The key requirement of a new ship is that it can trade profitably, so economics is of prime importance in designing a merchant ship. An owner requires a ship that will give the best possible returns for the

---

[1] Eric C Tupper, *Introduction to Naval Architecture*, 5th edn Butterworth Heinemann, 2013, p.377.
[2] Thomas Lamb, *Ship Design and Construction*, The Society of Naval Architects and Marine Engineers, 2003, p.5 - 1.
[3] J Eyres et al, *Ship Construction*, 7th edn Elsevier, 2012, p.4.

owner's initial investment and running costs. The final design should be arrived at taking into account not only present economic considerations, but also those likely to develop within the life of the ship.

Design 和 Engineering

5.4　　Design 在中文中是"设计",而 engineering 在中文中通常是"工程"。两者虽非同义词,但却经常有互用的现象。Design 通常是指针对物品、建筑或系统的结构和功能而制作的计划或设想,其特征是一个从无到有的过程,而 engineering 则常常用来指运用科学技术解决具体问题的过程。从某种意义上说,engineering 往往在 design 基础上的展开。

5.5　　我们可以把 design 视为艺术,会说"设计艺术"(art of design),但我们恐怕不会说 art of engineering。这是因为 design 从无到有的特征具有艺术特征,而 engineering 给我们的感觉应当精雕细琢。有些用法似乎已成为固定搭配,例如我们说 architectural design 或 furniture design,但不会说 architectural engineering 或 furniture engineering;我们可能说 civil engineering 或 electrical engineering,但不会说 civil design 或 electrical design。Engineering 和 design 放在一起构成 engineering design,即工程设计,是指在设计新方案、新产品等过程中所采取的一系列步骤。

船舶设计的阶段

5.6　　船舶设计按照不同标准可以分成不同的阶段,实践中不同的船舶设计阶段还有不同的名称,时常引起误会。有的人把船舶设计分为三个阶段,即概念设计、初步设计和合同设计。有的人则把船舶设计分为两个阶段,即基本设计和生产设计。基本设计又包括概念设计、初步设计、合同设计以及功能设计,后两个设计阶段又被称为体系设计阶段。生产设计则包括过渡设计和工作站信息准备。对设计进行阶段划分的意义在于不同设计阶段的工作性质各不相同且各自基本独立,对前一阶段工作的复核不仅可以独立完成,而且还有利于下一阶段工作的准备和开始。下文对不同的船舶设计阶段作简单的介绍。

概念设计阶段

5.7　　概念设计(concept design)是一个创造性的设计阶段。设计者从分析需求出发,确定实现船舶功能所需要的总体对象,通过初步的评价和优化后得出最为合理的技术系统。概念设计阶段又被称为成本及可行性研究阶段（cost and feasibility study phase），是船舶设计的基础。这一阶段的主要目标是搞清船东的要求并完成满足船东要求的概念设计。在这一阶段，设计师与船东通常会有接触和交流。

初步设计阶段

初步设计（preliminary design）是船舶设计真正开始的阶段。这一阶段的主要工作是对船舶进行全面的技术规划，包括布置和结构及其尺寸、配置关系以及技术条件等。船舶结构的合理性、工艺性、经济性和可靠性等都取决于船舶的初步设计阶段。初步设计阶段的目标是：确定并量化船舶性能、船舶尺寸及形状、船舶整体配置、船舶动力装置的选择、船体结构配置、船员配置、制定建造策略等。

5.8

合同设计阶段

合同设计（contract design）是满足合同要求的过程。这一设计阶段的工作目标是：确认船舶的功能、船舶建造的成本以及建造的标准。上述目标的实现需要更为详细的设计投入。设计者应针对船舶的每个系统完成替代系统的设计概念、提供系统选项、完成系统规格及图纸。船型及总布置将在这一阶段得到进一步的细化，船舶内部空间的布置图也将在这一阶段完成。

5.9

功能设计阶段

功能设计（functional design）将进一步细化并最终完成合同设计工作。所有的设计计算，包括详细的轮机及电器设计的计算将在这一阶段完成，系统配置制图也将随之完成。如果在之前阶段尚有未完成的遗留设计决策也将在这一阶段完成。设计者还应当在这一阶段完成管系、电器、电缆等的型号和尺寸等图解，典型分段的管系及通风管路的标识、采购的技术规则以及供应商的选择等。在这一阶段，设计者还应当完成与船东以及船旗国主管机关的沟通并获得其对设计的认可。

5.10

过渡设计阶段

过渡设计（transition design）阶段是随着分段和区域设计布置的结束而完成所有设计信息从系统到分段的过渡的阶段。在这一阶段，负责船舶建造的船厂会完成船舶建造的程序及其具体操作，例如工作区块的划分，分段制作阶段的工作

5.11

内容和船台上工作内容的划分，分段的搭载、设备的吊装和安装等。结构设计工作也在这一阶段完成包括每一分段的结构图纸。建模工作也应当在这一阶段完成。

工作站信息准备阶段

5.12　在工作站信息准备（workstation/zone information preparation）阶段，所有船舶建造的生产和其他部门需要的图纸、数据及其他信息应已准备就绪，包括图纸、草图、部件清单等等。特定区块的生产已被分解成数个工作包，每一个工作包均有自己的工作目标。每个工作包仅包含完成该项工作所需的信息，没有多余且无用的信息。

关于设计的约定

5.13　大多数船舶建造合同都是设计和建造合同，即船厂既负责船舶的设计，同时也负责船舶的建造。但这一做法也有例外。有时船东希望船舶采用新设计，而该新设计实际上是船东和设计公司共同开发的，或者是设计公司根据船东的意图专门完成的。在这种情况下，船东可能希望船厂按照自己提供的设计完成船舶建造。如果船东分别与设计公司和船厂订立船舶设计合同和船舶建造合同，设计公司和船厂各自承担自己的合同义务，而船东则需同时面对设计公司和船厂。对船东来说，这显然是不可取的。常见的做法是船东指定设计公司，但由船厂与该设计公司签订设计委托合同。

5.14　即使在约定由船厂负责设计和建造的船舶建造合同中，船厂依然将大部分设计工作，尤其是基本的概念设计和结构设计等转委托给专业的设计公司完成，而船厂自己只是负责施工设计。在这种情况下，虽然船厂并不直接负责船舶的设计，但船厂依然要对船舶设计承担合同责任，即船厂要对设计公司的疏忽和过错对船东承担合同责任。

5.15　在船舶建造合同的洽谈中，双方几乎肯定会对船舶建造设计义务的归属做出约定。船东和船厂还可以将全部的船舶建造设计进行分割，由船厂和船东共同完成。有意思的是，船舶建造合同的标准格式似乎都没有明确规定设计义务的归属。

SAJ 格式

5.16　SAJ 格式关于设计的内容很不清晰。SAJ 格式的前言有"build""launch"

"equip"及"complete",但没有提及"设计":

> In consideration of the mutual covenants herein contained, the BULDER agrees to build, launch, equip and complete at its ＿＿＿＿＿ (hereinafter called the "Shipyard") and sell and deliver to the BUYER one(1) .... more fully described in Article I hereof ....

而 Article I 中也仅有"constructed""equipped"以及"completed",同样没有"设计"。但 SAJ 格式的第 XXI 条则有如下规定: 5.17

> It is hereby mutually confirmed that the Contract Price includes the expenses amounting to ￥＿＿＿＿ for design and supply of drawings as the technical services required to be rendered by the BULDER under this Contract.

前言部分仅仅说"船厂同意建造、下水、装备及完成……"并没有包括设计。因此就该部分规定而言,除非双方另有约定,船厂的合同责任应当不包括设计。第 I 条也仅提及"建造""装备"和"完成",依然没有包括"设计"。第 XXI 条虽然有"合同价格包括数额为＿＿＿＿的设计和提供图纸的费用……"但是"设计"和"提供图纸"其实是受后面的"按照本合同"一句的限制,即合同价格包括了船厂按照合同规定应当完成的设计和提供图纸的费用。但这里的设计可以是指通常由船厂自己完成的施工设计。 5.18

SAJ 格式第 IV.1(a)条也有关于设计的内容: 5.19

> The BUILDER shall submit to the BUYER three(3)copies of the plans and drawings to be submitted thereto for its approval at its address as set forth in Article XVIII hereof ....

这一条规定的船厂义务是:向船东提供三套图纸,图纸是指概念设计的图纸还是施工设计的图纸并不明确,图纸制定是由第三方完成还是由船厂完成也不明确。由于合同价格已经包含船厂设计以及提供图纸的费用,因此可以说在使用 SAJ 格式时,除非双方另有约定,船厂负有设计的合同义务。 5.20

AWES 格式

AWES 格式规定的船厂合同义务似乎也没有包括设计:[1] 5.21

---

[1] Article 1(a), para.1.

> The CONTRACTOR undertakes to build at the CONTRACTOR's yard ... and to deliver to the PURCHASER ....

5.22　上述规定没有提及设计,但是与 SAJ 格式相类似,AWES 格式同样也规定了船厂应当向船东送审图纸:①

> The CONTRACTOR shall send to the PURCHASER (or its Representative) for approval three copies of the drawings and the technical information of machinery and equipment, for which such approval is required by the Specifications ....

5.23　虽然"图纸"一词是指船舶建造所需的所有图纸还是仅指施工图纸并不十分明确,但或许可以根据规格书的具体内容予以确定。即使规格书没有规定船厂负责船舶设计,船厂似乎很难仅凭这一规定主张自己除了制作施工图纸外没有其他设计义务。因为需要向船东送审的通知往往是基本设计的图纸,而施工图纸其实通常不需要获得船东的审批。

Norwegian 格式

5.24　与上述两个格式不同,Norwegian 格式明确规定了船厂的设计义务:②

> In consideration of the mutual covenants herein contained, the Builder agrees to design, build, launch, equip, complete, sell and deliver to the Buyer at the Builder's shipyard the "Vessel" as hereinafter described ....

> The Vessel shall be built at the Builder's yard ... and be designed, constructed, equipped, completed and delivered by the Builder in accordance with the provisions of the Contract.

5.25　船舶建造合同对设计作出明确约定无疑是可取的,在实践中,绝大多数船舶建造合同均有与上述 Norwegian 格式相似的规定。

NEWBUILDCON 格式

5.26　NEWBUILDCON 格式有专门的关于批准的条款,其中关于图纸审批的规定是:③

---

① Article 2(b), para.1.
② Preamble, Article II.1, para.3.
③ Clause 20(b), para.1.

The Builder shall dispatch to the Buyer a total of three(3)full sets of the Plans and Drawings for the Buyer's approval and shall also submit such other technical information as the Buyer may reasonably require, not less than thirty(30)running days before any construction works commence. The Builder shall give notice to the Buyer advising the date of dispatch of the Plans and Drawings and the Buyer shall give notice to the Builder confirming receipt thereof. The Buyer shall within fourteen(14)running days of receipt send to the Builder one(1)set of the Plans and Drawings with the Buyer's approval or approval with comments, amendments or reservations.

5.27　船舶建造合同规定了设计义务归属的应当按合同规定办理,若船舶建造合同没有对设计义务归属作出规定或规定不明的,船厂是否负有设计的合同义务应按合同和规格书等合同文件的内容予以确定。在实践中,无法确定由船厂还是船东负责船舶设计的情况应当不会多见。可能出现的问题是船厂和船东约定各自负责一部分设计工作,例如船东负责船舶的基本设计,而船厂则负责施工设计。在通常情况下,除非另有约定,船舶设计的合同责任应当由船厂承担,因为船厂毕竟是负责船舶建造的一方。

设计和工艺

5.28　工艺通常是指将各种原材料或半成品等进行加工处理且最终使之成为制成品的方法与过程。船舶建造工艺则是指船厂对钢板、其他材料、主机和其他设备等进行切割、焊接、组装和安装而最终完成船舶建造的方法与过程。由于船舶建造无法避免设计阶段,因此设计也可能会被视为是工艺的一部分。由于船厂对船舶建造的工艺负责,因此船厂也应当对设计负责。在 *Aktiebolaget Gotaverken* v *Westminster Corporation of Monrovia and Another* 一案中,①船东的一艘油轮在船厂修理和改装,船厂提供的舱口盖和舱口围存在设计缺陷,但是合同并没有规定船东可以此为由提出索赔,作为合同一部分的一般条件第 11 条(责任)的第 3 款有如下规定:

> If the material used or the work performed by the shipyard is not in accordance with the contract and the customer has given notice in due time(see [reg.] 13), this entails no further liability for the shipyard except that the shipyard shall, without charge, undertake repairs or

---

① [1971] 2 Lloyd's Rep 505.

replacement of the material or otherwise take the necessary steps to correct faults or deficiencies existing at the delivery.

5.29　一般条件第 13 条(索赔)又有如下内容:

Claims on account of asserted defects or deficiencies of material or workmanship shall always be given immediately after such defects or deficiencies have been discovered.

5.30　高院的 Donaldson 法官认为由于英语并不是一般条件起草人的母语,因此应当以商业的观点而不是太过于注重法律的观点来看待。他认为第 13 条和第 11(3)条显然是有联系的。第 13 条指的是材料或工艺的缺陷或不足,而第 11(3)条中的"If the material used or the work performed by the shipyard is not inaccordance with the contract…"指的是"workmanship"而不是"work"。但这并没有将设计排除在条款之外。Donaldson 法官说:①

The contract, as varied, required Gotaverken to supply watertight hatch covers. This required good workmanship both in the design and the execution, and if there were design errors, I see no reason why these should not be characterized and attract liability as bad workmanship. The alternative view would be that Gotaverken escaped all liability … which seems an improbably result for the parties to have intended.

船东的设计

5.31　根据船厂是否负责设计,船舶建造合同可以分成两大类,一类是由船厂负责船舶的设计和建造,另一类则是由船东负责设计,船厂负责施工设计、图纸制作及建造。如果船舶建造合同是由船厂负责设计和建造的,即使船东提供了设计,船厂依然负有设计的合同义务。在 *Adyard Abu Dhabi* v *SD Marine Services* 一案中,②船舶建造合同第 I.1 条规定:

The vessel … shall be designed, constructed, launched, equipped, completed and delivered by the Builder in accordance with the provisions of this Contract and the specifications and General Arrangement Plan which contemporaneously herewith have for the purposes of identification been signed by each of the parties hereto and

---

① [1971] 2 Lloyd's Rep 505 at 512.
② [2011] EWHC 848(Comm).

which are made an integral part hereof which specifications and General Arrangement Plan are hereinafter respectively called the "specifications" and "Plan" and together are called the "Specifications".

实际上规格书和总布置图包含一项由船东在船舶建造合同订立之前就已经完成的设计,船厂并没有参与该设计。船厂认为船厂接受的合同义务是"按照之前已经完成的合同设计进行设计",即船厂的义务只是负责更为具体的设计以及其他采购和建造所需的图纸,从而对合同设计进行"填补空白"而已。船舶建造合同并没有赋予船厂改变规格书或总布置图设计的权利或义务。 5.32

船东则认为,虽然船舶的基础设计已经体现在规格书和总布置图中,但是船舶建造合同依然是"设计和建造合同"。符合船舶建造合同的要求所需的设计依然是船厂的责任。高院的 Hamblen 法官接受了船东的观点,他说:① 5.33

So far as material, the only design developments which were not the responsibility of [shipyard] were those set out in Article V, namely those resulting from variations requested by [shipowner] or a change in Class or other regulatory requirements. In so far as the design had to be developed in order to meet Class or other regulatory requirements which were not the result of any change thereto, that was the risk and responsibility of [shipyard].

第三人的设计

当船舶设计由船东委托第三人负责的情况下,船东是否要对第三人的设计负责是一个应当根据具体情况予以确定的问题。 5.34

船厂的责任

如果设计是由第三人完成的,船舶建造合同约定船舶按该第三人设计建造的,船舶建造只要符合该设计,船厂就无需对该设计的缺陷负责。在 *Dixon Kerly Ltd v Robinson* 一案中,②船厂和船东订立船舶建造合同,约定由船厂为船东建造一艘游艇。船厂致函给船东并寄去了由第三人提供的、船级社首次入级的、船厂正在建造的新设计,包括图纸和规格书等。船厂向船东表示船舶将按该设计建 5.35

---

① [2011] EWHC 848(Comm) at [72].
② [1965] 2 Lloyd's Rep 404.

造。船舶建造完毕后交给了船东，由于船东没有付清尾款，船厂起诉要求船东付清尾款。船东则认为自己对船厂享有反索赔，理由包括船厂违反了船舶建造合同的明示条款，即船舶应当按照船厂提供的图纸和规格书建造，船舶的吃水不超过 4 英尺 4 英寸，而船舶的实际吃水是超过 4 英尺 10 英寸。

5.36　　法院认为船厂的义务仅仅是按照提供的图纸建造船舶，而按照图纸和规格书的规定，船舶吃水不可能少于 4.4 英尺。由于设计人对船舶吃水的估计并不构成船舶建造合同的一部分，因此船厂无需对船舶的设计负责。高院的 Thompson 法官说：①

> The defendant was, as I have said, buying a boat which was in course of being built and the promise made was associated with perfectly true statements as to who had designed her and what else he had been associated with. The promise made was to build generally according to the designer's specification and in accordance with his drawings .... In my judgment that is not something for which the plaintiffs are responsible ....

5.37　　但是，即使船舶建造合同规定由船厂按照船东提供的图纸建造，如果船东提供的图纸有错且船厂可以发现该错误的，船厂按照图纸施工所造成的损失或浪费则未必可以从船东处获得赔偿。在 *Alexander Thorn* v *The Mayor and Commonalty of London* 一案中，②建造的是桥梁，图纸和规格书是由业主的工程师提供的，业主要求承包商听从其工程师的指示。规格书包含下列规定：

> 36. Drawings lettered A, & C, are plans and sections of the existing bridge, and of the works executed thereon. They give all the information possessed respecting the foundations. These plans are believed to be correct, but their accuracy is not guaranteed, and the contractor will not be entitled to charge any extra should the work to be removed prove more than indicated on these drawings.
>
> 54. The contractor must satisfy himself as to the nature of the ground through which the foundations have to be carried; all the information given on this subject is believed to be correct, but is not guaranteed.
>
> 63. The foundations of the piers will be put in by means of wrought iron caissons, as shewn on drawing No.7.

---

① [1965] 2 Lloyd's Rep 404 at 412.
② (1876) 1 App Cas 120.

64. The casing of the lower part of which caissons will be left permanently in the work. The upper part, which is formed of buckle plates, is to be removed. The whole of the interior girder framing must be removed as the building proceeds, the work being made good close up to the underside of each girder before removal thereof.

66. The whole of the iron used in the caissons shall be of good quality capable of bearing a tensible strain of 18 tons per square inch. Plates and bars will be selected at random by the engineer, which must be cut to the required form, and submitted to such tests as the engineer may direct.

77. All risk and responsibility involved in the sinking of these caissons will rest with the contractor, and he will be bound to employ divers or other efficient means for removing and overcoming any obstacles or difficulties that may arise in the execution of the works.

5.38 承包商按照规格书的规定进行了沉箱的施工,但结果表明沉箱没有任何价值,原因是沉箱无法抵御外来水的压力,桥柱只能采用其他方式建造。承包商要求赔偿因沉箱施工造成的损失,理由是业主已向承包商默示保证桥梁将按照图纸和规格书建造,图纸也表明沉箱可以抵御水流的压力。承包商是在此种情形下与业主订立建造合同的,由于图纸和规格书的错误,承包商为此产生了额外费用。但是财税法院认为业主并没有向承包商作出过类似的保证,并判决业主胜诉。财税上诉法院维持了财税法院的判决。承包商于是向上议院提起了上诉。上议院也同样认为业主并没有向承包商默示保证按照图纸和规格书就能够完成桥梁的建造并最终驳回了承包商的上诉,Lord Chancellor 说:①

> If this contractor is entitled to remuneration for the services he performed, it must be sought, or ought to have been sought, in a way different from the present. Damages as for a breach of warranty he is, in my opinion, in no respect entitled to; and therefore I move your Lordships that the judgment of the Court below be affirmed, and the appeal dismissed with costs.

5.39 上议院的 Lord Chelmsford 认为承包商订立合同时过于疏忽,只要仔细检查,承包商实际上可以发现沉箱存在的问题。他说:②

---

① (1876) 1 App Cas 120 at 129.
② (1876) 1 App Cas 120 at 132.

If the Plaintiff had considered, as he was bound to do, the terms of the specification, he would either have abstained from tendering for the work, or he would have asked the Defendants to protect him from the loss he was likely to sustain if the plan of working described in the specification should turn out to be an improper one. It is unnecessary to speculate upon what the answer would have been to such an application. But I think we may fairly assume that if the Defendants had been asked for an express warranty to the effect alleged in the declaration, they would have refused to give it.

明显的设计缺陷

5.40　　与此相类似，如果由第三人完成的设计存在比较明显的缺陷，而且是船厂能够发现的缺陷，在这种情况下，船厂若按照有缺陷的设计建造船舶依然有可能为此承担责任。在 *Brunswick Construction Ltd v Nowlan* 一案中，[1]业主聘用了建筑师设计了一栋房屋，又聘用了承包商按照设计建造房屋。虽然建造合同规定业主的工程师应当对施工进行监督和指导，但实际上并没有人对施工进行监督。建造完毕的房屋有严重的缺陷，屋顶和墙均没有通风，导致木材的腐蚀。原因是设计本身没有足够的通风。业主要求承包商承担责任，但承包商则认为自己的责任仅限于建造的工艺，并不扩展至设计缺陷。加拿大的最高法院认为：承包商是在没有监造的情况下进行施工的，因此应被视为业主完全依赖承包商的技能和专注。承包商的经验应当能够发现设计中通风的缺陷，在知道业主依赖设计的情况下，承包商有义务向业主提出实施设计将会导致通风不足的危险性。承包商应当建造具有正常功能的建筑物，这一一般的义务应当优先于承包商按照特定设计施工的义务，因此承包商虽然是按照业主指定的设计建造，但依然应当对房屋的缺陷负责。

5.41　　然而，如果设计和图纸均由业主提供，而且承包商也没有保证其建造一定符合特定功能，在这种情况下，承包商应当无需承担设计缺陷的责任。在 *Sunnyside Nursing Home v Builders Contract Management* 一案中，[2]业主招标建造公寓，业主的建筑师和工程师按照中标人选择的结构体系完成了详细图纸的制作。在建造中发现图纸有问题，双方争执的焦点是应当由业主还是承包商承担图纸缺陷的责任。法院认为承包商并没有保证建造具有特定功能的建筑物，而且业主自己聘请

---

[1]　21 BLR 27.
[2]　(1986) 2 Const LJ 240.

建筑师和工程师表明其并没有依赖承包商,因此承包商不应对设计缺陷承担责任。

负有设计义务的一方应当就设计问题对船东承担合同责任,有时还甚至有可能对船东以外的人承担设计责任。在 The Amoco Cadiz 一案中,①负责油轮设计的是西班牙的 Astilleros Espanoles SA 船厂,该船厂是当时有能力设计和建造超大型油轮油船的少数的几个船厂之一。包括舵机图纸等在内的各种图纸都经过了船东和美国船级社的批准。规格书关于舵机的规定是一般性的,船厂送审的与舵机有关的图纸仅有一份,即舵机的总布置图。没有图纸表明螺柱、法兰、安全阀或舵机其他组成部分的细节,船厂也没有向船东提供舵机的设计计算。1978 年 3 月 16 日,舵手发现舵机有故障。虽然舵角显示的是左满舵,但实际上是处在右满舵的状况。船长试图修理舵机但未获成功。12 小时后油轮在法国沿海搁浅,大量的原油泄漏至海中。油轮的舵机是船厂设计并制造的,并且通过了美国船级社的检验。经过调查发现,导致舵机故障的原因是固定液压管的法兰上的螺栓发生断裂。船厂的设计存在问题,法兰装配以及螺栓的测试等显示低于不符合要求的规格,最终导致法兰上螺栓的断裂。美国伊利诺伊斯州北区的地区法院认为船厂由于存在过失,因此也应当承担油污赔偿责任。船级社已经批准船厂设计的事实并不能减轻船厂应负的责任。Frank McGarr 法官说:② 5.42

> The Amoco parties' third-party claims against Astilleros, seeking indemnity or contribution from Astilleros in the event of the finding of the liability of one or more of the Amoco parties, are granted. Astilleros is found to be liable to the Amoco parties in an amount to be later determined.... Amoco is entitled to damages against Astilleros to the extent that its own liability was contributed to by the negligence and fault of the shipbuilder.

Ⅱ 审图

审图通常是指在由船厂负责设计的情况下船级社和船东对船厂制作图纸的合规性和可行性进行审核的过程。审图的意义在于确保船舶建造符合船级规范和船舶建造合同及规格书的要求。船舶建造的一个明显特征是:虽然实际实施船 5.43

---

① [1984] 2 Lloyd's Rep 304.
② [1984] 2 Lloyd's Rep 304 at 339.

舶建造的是船厂，但整个建造过程，包括设计阶段的工作进行始终处于船级社以及船东的监督之下，而图纸审核则是此种监督的开始。

船级社审图

5.44　用于船舶建造的图纸只有在经过船级社审核和批准后才能投入使用，这不仅包括船厂制作的图纸，也包括船东或设计公司等制作的图纸。船级社对图纸进行审核的依据是船级社的规范和船旗国的要求，船级社通常仅对与船级规范以及船旗国要求有关项目的图纸进行审核，而不会审核与船舶建造合同和规格书有关但不属于船级规范和船旗国要求范畴的图纸。虽然船东也会对关系到船级规范和船旗国要求的图纸进行审核，也能对图纸发表自己的意见，但船东的审核意见并不是最终的，只有船级社的审核意见才是对船厂有约束力的意见。有时相关图纸还必须获得船籍国主管机关甚至是第三国有关机关的审核。①

船级社审图的延误

5.45　虽然在船舶建造实践中并不常见，但船级社审图同样有可能会发生延误。由于船级社在对船舶建造实施监造时的地位比较特殊，即使在船厂和船级社之间存在着合同关系，由船厂委托船级社对船舶的设计和建造实施全面的监督，或者从某种程度上来说，船级社可以被视为是船厂的分包商。即使按照船厂和船级社的监造协议船级社在审图中的延误构成对该协议的违反且船级社应当为此承担责任，除非建造合同另有约定，船厂似乎很难以此为由主张可允许延误并要求顺延合同规定的交船日。

5.46　船厂应当注意的是在船舶建造合同中关于船东送审图纸的时间应当与船厂与船级社签署的监造协议相互吻合，以免发生船东退审图纸的时限已过而船级社的退审图纸时限尚未届满。在这种情况下，船厂就不得不等到船级社退审图纸后才可以施工。因此浪费的时间并不能视为可允许延误，而应由船厂自己承担。

船东审图

5.47　船东对图纸进行审核的依据是船舶建造合同以及规格书的相关规定，出于对实务的考虑，船东的审图往往会受其自身偏好或其管理特征的影响。船东的审图

---

① 例如：按照澳大利亚海事安全局颁布的货物装卸设备修正案的规定，货舱通道的布置图必须提交安全局指定的公司审核。

通常可以分为两个阶段,第一阶段是由船厂将图纸递交船东审核,第二阶段则是由船厂将图纸递交船东的驻厂代表审核。船舶建造合同通常都会对船厂送审图纸作出规定,例如 SAJ 格式的规定是:①

> The BUILDER shall submit to the BUYER three(3)copies each of the plans and drawings to be submitted thereto for its approval at its address as set forth in Article XVIII hereof. The BUYER shall, within fourteen (14) days after receipt thereof, return to the BUILDER one(1)copy of such plans and drawings with the BUYERS's approval or comments written thereon, if any. A list of the plans and drawings to be so submitted to the BUYER shall be mutually agreed upon between the parties hereto.

5.48 上述规定中的审图是指船东驻厂代表驻厂之前的船东审图,船厂需要按照船舶建造合同约定的地址将图纸送交船东审核。SAJ 格式规定的船东审图时间为 14 天。AWES 格式关于船厂向船东送审图纸的规定相对而言比 SAJ 格式更为详细,AWES 格式规定的是:②

> The CONTRACTOR shall send to the PURCHASER (or its Representative) for approval three copies of the drawings and the technical information of machinery and equipment, for which such approval is required by the Specifications. One of the three copies so submitted shall be returned, either approved, or supplemented with remarks and amendments, to reach the CONTRACTOR within … Days from the date of receipt by the PURCHASER or within … days after dispatch by the CONTRACTOR, whichever is the sooner, and if this is not done within this time limit the drawings and technical information shall be regarded as approved, unless additional time is specifically requested in writing by the PURCHASER and agreed in writing by the CONTRACTOR.

5.49 AWES 格式不仅规定了船东在约定期限内没有对船厂送审的图纸发表意见的情形及其后果,而且还规定了船东可以要求延长审图期限的情形。按照上述规定,船东要求延长审图期限应当获得船厂的书面同意,但这一规定却没有太大的实际意义,因为很难想象船厂可以拒绝延长船东的审图时间,问题是额外时间应由谁来承担。由于双方已经约定了船东审图的时间,原则上额外时间不能视为船

---

① Article IV.1(a).
② Article 2(b), para.1.

厂的时间。另外，AWES 格式对船东未能在约定期限内完成审图的情形作出了规定，即船东视为已批准船厂送审的图纸。

5.50　　NEWBUILDCON 格式关于图纸送审的规定更为详细和具体：①

The Builder shall dispatch to the Buyer a total of three(3)full sets of the Plans and Drawings for the Buyer's approval and shall also submit such other technical information as the Buyer may reasonably require, not less than thirty(30)running days before any construction works commence. The Builder shall give notice to the Buyer advising the date of dispatch of the Plans and Drawings and the Buyer shall give notice to the Builder confirming receipt thereof. The Buyer shall within fourteen(14)running days of receipt send to the Builder one(1)set of the Plans and Drawings with the Buyer's approval or approval with comments, amendments or reservations.

In the event that the Buyer needs additional time to consider the Plans and Drawings submitted pursuant to this Clause, it shall request the same in writing of the Builder whose agreement shall not be unreasonably withheld ....

5.51　　NEWBUILDCON 格式至少有下列几个与其他标准格式不同之处。第一，船东审图的时间增加到 30 天。第二，这可能是第一个要求船厂在开工前不少于 30 天向船东送审图纸的标准格式，这一要求的意义恐怕在于船东对船厂开工时间的限制。因为开工在实践中往往是船东的一个付款节点，而开工大多是形式开工，即割一块无关紧要的钢板而已。如果开工是指实际开始建造，一旦船东按照约定在收到图纸后的 14 天内完成审核且没有变更或修改的，不允许船厂马上开工应当是没有意义的。第三，要求船厂在向船东送审图纸后发出告知送审日期的通知且船东应确认收到通知的规定似乎来自 Norwegian 格式，②其用意应当是在船厂以邮寄或快递的方式向船东发出送审图纸的情形下可以通过传真方式告知船东图纸已经寄出。如果采用电子方式送审图纸，或者是向船东在船厂的驻厂代表送审图纸，这一规定可能就不再有意义了。如果船东应当确认的话，也应当确认收到图纸而不是确认收到通知。

---

① Clause 20(b), para.1&2.
② Norwegian Article V.1(a): "... The Builder shall send a notice by telefax(or by such other electronic means as the parties may agree) to the Buyer giving the date of dispatch of such plans and drawings, and the Buyer shall confirm receipt of such plans and drawings."

额外审图时间

船东由于各种原因无法在约定时间内完成审图就会产生额外的审图时间,SAJ 格式和 Norwegian 格式都没有关于额外审图时间的规定。当船东未能在约定时间内完成审图时,按照 SAJ 格式和 CSTC 格式的规定,图纸即可视为自动获得船东批准,①而 Norwegian 格式则规定船厂应当书面要求船东在 3 天内归还图纸,只有当船东未能在 3 天内归还时,才能视图纸已经获得船东批准。②

5.52

船东未能在约定的时间内完成审图应当是一种违约。虽然在船东提出要求额外时间完成审图时船厂通常不能也不会拒绝此种要求,但除非船舶建造合同另有约定,因此产生的额外时间应当视为可允许延误,③船厂可以以此为由顺延合同交船日。当船东未能在约定时间内完成审图,无论是由于图纸存在问题,还是由于船东提出了额外的新的设计要求,作为原则,因此造成的时间浪费均应由船东承担。因为船舶建造合同约定的船东审图时间并不是以船厂送审的图纸没有问题为前提的。

5.53

船东代表审图

船舶建造合同通常会约定在合同签署后,船东应当指派其监造代表驻船工作。一旦船东的监造代表开始驻厂,审图就将由船东的监造代表负责,船厂无需再向船东送审图纸,可以直接向船东的监造代表送审图纸。除非双方另有约定,否则船厂向船东监造代表送审图纸视同船厂向船东送审图纸。船东监造代表对图纸的审批则视同船东对图纸的审批。船东的监造代表一般会在船厂开始建造船舶之时进驻船厂,那时船厂应当已经完成了向船级送审图纸的工作并且也已经收到船级社的退审了。因此,这里提及的图纸一般都不再是需要船级社审批的图纸。如果有需要船级社审批的图纸,船厂在向船东驻厂代表送审同时还应当按照自己与船级社的监造协议约定向船级社送审。

5.54

SAJ 格式有如下规定:④

5.55

When and if the Representative shall have been sent by the BUYER to the shipyard in accordance with Paragraph 2 of this Article, the

---

① SAJ Article 4.1(c); CSTC Article IV.2, para.3.
② Article V.1(d).
③ 关于可允许延误请参见本书第 10 章第 I 节。
④ Article IV.1(b).

BUILDER may submit the remainder, if any, of the plans and drawings in the agreed list, to the Representative for its approval, unless otherwise agreed upon between the parties hereto. The Representative shall, within seven(7)days after receipt thereof, return to the BUILDER one(1)copy of such plans and drawings with his approval or comments written thereon, if any. Approval by the Representative of the plans and drawings duly submitted to him shall be deemed to be the approval by the BUYER for all purposes of this Contract.

5.56　　SAJ格式根据船厂送审图纸的对象不同分别适用不同的审图时间限制，船东应当在14天内完成审图，而船东的驻厂代表则应当在7天内完成审图。通常情况下，船东指派的监造代表应当有权代表船东审图、并参加各种检验和试验等。船东代表在现场审图的时间短于船东审图的时间，这可能是考虑了图纸相对比较简单的缘故。

船东的审图意见

5.57　　船东的审图意见可以大致分为两种：一种是批准船厂提供的图纸且没有任何意见；另一种则是船东对图纸提出了修改意见。有时船东在批准图纸时会加上："以船级社批准为条件"(subject to approval of the Class)或者"批注：以满足船级规范为条件"(comments: subject to Class rules are satisfied)。虽然使用了"subject"和"comments"，但实际上这并不构成船东对船厂图纸的修改。至于"以船级社批准为条件"或"以满足船级规范为条件"等字眼并不构成船东的审图意见，即使不加也无妨。

5.58　　针对船厂的送审图纸提出修改意见的一般又有两种情形，一是船东认为船厂送审的图纸有问题，不符合合同或规格书的要求；另一则是船厂送审的图纸符合合同和规格书的要求，但船东希望对此作出调整或改动，从而符合自己新的要求。第一种情形有可能由于双方的表述和理解导致争议，此种争议可以通过双方的协商予以解决，也可以适用建造合同约定的争议解决机制予以解约。第二种情形则构成变更，双方需要对此作出时间和费用的约定。

不构成修改和变更的情形

5.59　　船东发现船厂送审的图纸不符合船舶建造合同或规格书规定的要求通常会在图纸上进行批注。在这种情况下，船厂应当按照船东的意见和建议重新开始或

修正自己的设计,正如 AWES 格式对此作出的规定:①

> If the drawings and technical information are returned to the CONTRACTOR within the said time limit supplemented with remarks and amendments by the PURCHASER and if the said remarks and amendments are not of such a nature or extent as to constitute modifications under Article 3 hereof, then the CONTRACTOR shall start or continue production on the basis of the corrected or amended drawings and technical information ....

上述 AWES 格式的规定不仅包括船东纠正船厂送审的图纸不符合合同或规格书要求的情形,同时也包括了船东对船厂送审的且符合合同及规格书要求的图纸作出的微小改动,这些意见或改动只是一种说明或澄清,并不构成对图纸乃至船舶建造合同规定的修改。NEWBUILDCON 格式也有类似的规定:② 5.60

> The Builder shall take due note of the Buyer's comments, amendments or reservations(if any) on Plans and Drawings submitted pursuant to this Clause and, if such comments amendments or reservations are not of such a nature or extent as to constitute a modification or change of the specification within the meaning of Clause 24(Modifications and Changes), then the Builder shall commence or continue construction of the Vessel in accordance with the corrected or amended Plans and Drawings.

不明确的意见

还有一种情形是船东对图纸发表了意见,但是船东的意见不够明确。针对这种情况,Norwegian 格式作出了如下规定:③ 5.61

> If Buyer's comments on the plans and drawings are unclear or unspecified, the Builder may by fax notice to the Buyer request a clarification, failure by the Buyer or its Representative to respond to this request within 3 Working Days of receipt of such notice shall entitle the Builder to place its own reasonable interpretation on such remarks, comments or amendments when implementing the same.

---

① Article 2(b)para.2.
② Clause 20(c).
③ Article V.1(b).

5.62 上述条文使用了 may,即船厂发现船东对图纸的意见不清楚或不特定时,船厂可以要求船东予以澄清,但船厂似乎并没有义务要求船东澄清。如果船厂选择不要求船东澄清,船厂便要对自己的决定承担责任。相反,如果船厂选择要求船东澄清,从上述规定来看,似乎船东同样没有义务作出澄清。如果船东不予以澄清,船厂实际上又回到了自己选择不要求船东澄清的地位,即按照自己对船东意见的理解行事并对自己的行为承担责任。因此,Norwegian 格式的上述规定似乎没有太大的实际意义,相反会有可能会造成不必要的争议。

5.63 NEWBUILDCON 格式规定可能来自于 Norwegian 格式,因为两者比较相似:①

> In the event that the Buyer's comments, amendments or reservations are unclear, unspecified or illegible, the Builder may give notice requesting clarification. If the Buyer fails to respond to the request to provide clarification within five (5) running days of receipt of the Builder's notice, the Builder shall determine whether and to what extent it can adopt the comments, amendments or reservations.

5.64 按照上述规定,船厂在遇到船东审图意见不明确或不确定的情况下同样可以要求船东澄清,船东若未能在收到通知后的 5 天内作出澄清的,船厂应当自行决定如何接受船东的审图意见、变更和保留。这一规定似乎是为争议的产生埋下了伏笔。在审图意见不明确时,船厂是可以而不是应当要求船东澄清,但无论是否要求澄清,船厂都必须承担后果。双方不仅会对船东的审图意见是否明确发生争议,甚至还会对船厂是否应当要求船东澄清发生争议。NEWBUILDCON 格式似乎并没有规定船东在收到船厂的要求澄清的通知后有义务向船厂澄清,而是规定在船东没有作出澄清的情况下,船厂应当自己决定如何行事。毫无疑问,船厂依然必须对自己的决定负责。如果船厂作出的选择或决定符合船东意愿,船东应当不会有意见。相反,如果船厂作出的选择或决定不符合船东的意愿,争议势必又会产生。从船厂的利益出发,一旦遇到含糊、不确定或有歧义时都应当主动与船东进行沟通,通过交换意见和协商尽可能及时解决问题,避免在未来产生重大争议。

---

① Clause 20(b)para.2,SAJ、AWES 以及 CSTC 则没有相似的规定。

视为批准的情形

SAJ 格式规定了船东应当完成审图的时间限制,若船东在规定时间内没有完成审图的,船厂就可以视图纸已获得船东的批准:①

5.65

In the event that the BUYER or the Representative shall fail to return the plans and drawings to the BUILDER within the time limit as hereinabove provided, such plans and drawings shall be deemed to have been automatically approved without any comment.

由于有了视为批准的约定,一旦船东未能在约定期限届满时退还船厂送审图纸的,船厂就不应当继续等待船东退还图纸,而应当将自己提交的图纸视为已获得船东的批准并开始施工或继续建造。如果船厂继续等待船东退还图纸,由此浪费的时间不能视为可允许延误而顺延合同交船日。CSTC 格式也规定,除非船东通知船厂,否则在约定的审图时间届满时,船厂送审的图纸即视为自动获得船东的批准。② AWES 格式也有"视为批准"的规定:③

5.66

... if this is not done within this time limit the drawings and technical information shall be regarded as approved ...

NEWBUILDCON 格式关于"视为批准"的规定是:④

5.67

In the event that the Buyer fails to return any Plans and Drawings to the Builder with approval or approval with comments, amendments or reservations, if any, within the time limit stated above, such Plansand Drawings shall be deemed to have been approved by the Buyer.

与上述提及的格式不同,Norwegian 格式规定了在这种情况下船厂的催促义务:⑤

5.68

In the event that the Buyer fails to return the plans and drawings to the Builder within the time limit specified in(a)above, the Builder shall by fax to the Buyer request the return of same within 3 days, failing which the Builder shall have the right to consider such plans and drawings as

---

① Article IV.1(c).
② Article IV.2 para.3.
③ Article 2(b), para.1.
④ Clause 20(e).
⑤ Article V.1(d).

approved by the Buyer.

5.69　在船舶建造合同有上述规定时,船东未能在约定时间内完成审图的,船厂并不当然有权视图纸已获批准,而应当向船东发出通知,要求船东在3天内退还送审图纸。只有在3天后船东依然没有退还图纸或发表审图意见的情况下,船厂才可以视图纸已获批准。

审图争议

5.70　如前所述,船东的审图意见或建议未构成对船舶建造合同规定的修改时,船厂应当按照船东的意见或建议实施。相反,如果船东的意见和建议构成对合同的修改,船舶建造合同关于修改的规定应当适用。① 实际上问题可能并非如此简单,船厂和船东有可能就船厂的图纸是否符合合同及规格书的要求,或者船东的意见是否构成修改等产生争议。在这种情况下,船东和船厂之间的争议就有可能需要通过约定的争议解决方式予以解决了。SAJ格式没有针对此种情形作出规定,但AWES格式则有如下规定:②

> ... In case of any dispute concerning the drawings and/or technical information which can not be solved by negotiations the dispute shall be referred to experts assessment in accordance with Art.15(b) of the CONTRACT. Any delay caused by such dispute shall be Permissible Delay(see art.6(e)).

5.71　按照上述规定,船厂和船东首先应当就双方的争议进行磋商以期达成一致的解决方案。双方无法通过协商解决争议的,则应共同指定一位专家对争议作出决定。有意思的是,由于指定专家解决双方争议而导致的时间延误不加区分的均被视为可允许延误,而实际上专家完全有可能认为船厂对图纸或船东意见的理解是错误的。因此,造成实际浪费的应当是船厂。允许船厂可以凭借自己的错误而顺延合同交船日应当是不合理的。另外,在船舶建造合同有上述规定时,无论是船厂还是船东似乎都没有理由拒绝将争议提交专家解决。

5.72　AWES格式第15(b)条的规定是:

> ... should any dispute arise between the parties in regard to the construction of the VESSEL, engines materials or workmanship it shall

---

① 关于修改,见本书第6章。
② Article 2(b)para.2.

forthwith be referred to an expert nominated by agreement between the parties hereto or failing such agreement by the .... and his decision shall be final and binding upon both parties hereto.

然而上述规定可能缺乏较强的可操作性。一旦双方发生了争议,共同选定一位专家绝非易事。尤其是当我国船厂为外国船东建造船舶时,由于双方的文化乃至对专家认识上的差异,几乎无法找到可以得到双方共同认同的专家。而在船舶建造合同订立之时便确定双方无法就专家人选达成一致时解决争议的方法只不过把问题提前而已,很难想象船厂和船东在订立合同之初就可以填入双方都接受的个人或机构。 5.73

Norwegian 格式也对船厂与船东就审图发生争议的情形作出了规定:① 5.74

If the Builder and the Buyer fail to agree whether such comments or remarks are of such a nature or extent as to constitute modification or change under Article VI hereof, the Builder shall nevertheless proceed with the construction based on the Buyer's comments if so requested by the Buyer. If it is established by mutual agreement or by arbitration as per Article XIX, that the comments, remarks or amendments constitute a modification or change under Article VI, the Builder shall be entitled to an appropriate adjustment of the Contract Price, Delivery Date and/or the characteristics of the Vessel. Article VI clause 1, first paragraph to apply.

与 AWES 格式相比,Norwegian 格式至少就船东的意见或建议是否构成修改规定了解决争议的方式,即船厂应当按照船东的意见或建议开始或继续船舶的建造,一旦通过协商或仲裁表明船东的意见或建议构成修改的,船厂便有权适用船舶建造合同中关于修改的规定,要求调整合同价格、合同交船日等。 5.75

NEWBUILDCON 格式也有类似的规定,但该格式的规定比较复杂。格式的争议解决条款规定了四种解决争议的方式,分别是:船级社或主管机关对争议作出决定,专家对争议作出决定,仲裁以及调解。② 当船厂认为船东的意见或建议构成修改的,船厂应当按照船舶建造合同中关于修改的规定向船东发出通知。③ 5.76

---

① Article V.1(c).
② Clause 42.
③ Clause 20(d).

If the Builder considers the comments, amendments or reservations to the Plans and Drawings are of the nature or extent that constitutes a modification or change under Clause 24(Modifications and Changes), the Builder shall notify the Buyer accordingly and proceed in accordance with Clause 24(Modifications and Changes). If the Buyer disagrees the matter shall be resolved in accordance with Clause 24(e).

5.77 如果船东不同意船厂观点的,船东依然可以指示船厂按照其意见实施,双方的争议则根据合同关于争议解决条款的规定予以解决:①

If the Buyer does not accept the Builder's notice as provided in Clause 20(d)(Approvals) or if in the Buyer's opinion the Builder's proposal for modifications and/or changes under this Clause is unreasonable, the Buyer may, by giving notice to the Builder, order the Builder to proceed with the requested modifications and/or change but the consequences of implementing such modifications and/or changes shall be decided in accordance with Clause 42(Dispute Resolution).

审图与船厂的责任

5.78 船舶建造合同有时会约定船东审图并不解除船厂应当按照合同、规格书以及船级社规范的要求等建造船舶的义务,换言之,船厂并不会由于船东批准了船厂提供的不符合合同、规格书或船级社规范要求的图纸而免除自己的设计责任。船厂应当注意的是,即使船舶建造合同没有类似的约定,只要没有相反的约定,无论船东是否批准了船厂的设计和图纸,船厂依然要对自己的设计和图纸的错误负责。船东审图从其作用上来说是对船厂设计的确认,而不是纠错。在 *Cenargo Ltd* v *Empresa Nacional Bazan de Construcciones Navales Militares SA*② 一案中,建造两艘滚装船的船舶建造合同规定了容纳货物拖车的空间,即146个位置,每个位置长13米。船舶建造合同第5条规定:

Deficiency in Trailer Carrying Capacity.
In this Clause 5 "trailers" refers to fully laden trailers with a mean carrying capacity of thirty(30) mt.

(a) If the actual trailer carrying capacity of the Vessel is less that 146 Units of 13 metres each the Builder shall pay to the Buyer as

---

① Clause 24(e).
② [2002] CLC 1151.

liquidated damages One hundred and fifty thousand United States Dollars($150,000) for each trailer unit by which the Vessel is deficient but excluding the first one (1) in respect of which deficiency no liquidated damages shall be payable. If the deficiency in trailer carrying capacity is ten (10) or more the Buyer as an alternative to receiving the aforementioned liquidated damages may rescind the Contract.

5.79 船舶建造合同第 IV.7 条还规定：

The above approvals and/or inspections do not diminish the Builder's responsibilities for the construction of the Vessel.

5.80 交船时船舶只能容纳 140 个拖车位置。船厂认为自己是按照图纸建造的，而图纸已经得到了船东的批准，船东不得翻供。但是法院认为合同的明示约定排斥了禁止翻供的抗辩，高院的 Andrew Smith 法官说：①

I consider that this rebuts [shipbuilder's] case of estoppel by convention. Article IV, cl.7 shows the parties' intention that [shipbuilder] should not cease to be responsible for the vessels' capacity because [owner] gave approval to plans of this kind. Since this is how the contracts distribute responsibility, it does not seem to me unconscionable for [owner] to assert their case against [shipbuilder].

5.81 因此，除非另有约定，船东批准船厂递交的图纸并不意味着船厂无需承担设计和制图错误的责任。船厂的合同义务是按照船级规范以及合同和规格书的要求设计船舶，只要船厂的设计不符合船级规范或合同和规格书，船厂就应当承担责任。如果船厂的设计错误违反了船级规范，即使船东放弃对错误的追究，船厂也无法通过船级社的检验。Norwegian 格式可能是唯一明确规定船东审图不影响船厂船舶建造合同义务的标准格式，Norwegian 格式的规定是：②

The Buyer's approval or non approval of drawings shall not affect any of the Builder's obligations hereunder, including the Builder's obligation to deliver the Vessel fully approved by the Regulatory Bodies, or the Builder's responsibility under Article X hereof.

5.82 NEWBUILDCON 格式在这个问题上的规定不仅包括船厂的义务，而且还包

---

① [2002] CLC 1151 at 1161.
② Article V.1(e).

括船东义务：①

> The Buyer's approval or deemed approval of any Plans and Drawings shall not affect the obligations of the Builder to design, construct and deliver, or the obligations of the Buyer to take delivery of, and pay for, the Vessel in accordance with the other provisions of this Contract; nor shall it diminish the Builder's responsibility in respect of its obligations under this Contract nor shall it constitute any acceptance by the Buyer or any responsibility for any defect in the Vessel.

5.83　关于船东接船和付款的义务不因此受影响的规定似乎有些费解。假设获得船东批准的图纸存在错误，该错误虽违反了规格书，但依然符合船级规范的要求，船东接船付款义务不受影响意味着船东不能要求船厂纠正其错误吗？合同应当强调的是船厂的义务不受船东批准图纸的影响，而不是船东的义务不受此影响。

5.84　普通法中有"共识禁止反言"（estoppel by convention），即指交易双方均以推定的事实或法律行事，这里的推定可能是双方分享的或一方作出而另一方同意的。在这种情况下，如果允许当事人推翻，就会造成不公正的后果，故当事人双方不得否认该推定的真实性。② 在 *Republic of India v India Steamship Co Ltd (The Indian Endurance and The Indian Grace) (No 2)* 一案中，上议院的 Lord Steyn 认为"共识禁止反言"的成立并不一定要求当事人的约定为条件，他是这样说的：③

> It is settled that an estoppel by convention may arise where parties to a transaction act on an assumed state of facts or law, the assumption being either shared by them both or made by one and acquiesced in by the other. The effect of an estoppel by convention is to preclude a party from denying the assumed facts or law if it would be unjust to allow him to go back on the assumption . . . . It is not enough that each of the two parties acts on an assumption not communicated to the other. But it was rightly accepted by counsel for both parties that a concluded agreement is not a requirement for an estoppel by convention.

5.85　当船厂向船东送审图纸时，双方都应当明白其目的是让船东确认船厂的图纸

---

① Clause 20(f).
② Hugh Beale, *Chitty on Contracts*, 35th edn Sweet & Maxwell 2023, para.7–016.
③ [1989] AC 878 at 913. See also *Mears Ltd v Shoreline Housing Partnership Ltd* [2015] EWHC 1396 (TCC).

是否符合合同以及规格书的要求。当船东退还图纸并表示批准时，双方也都应当明白船东的批准意味着船厂的图纸符合合同及规格书的要求。船东受其批准的约束应当是顺理成章的。然而，在这种情形下，双方似乎很难有船厂的错误已经得到船东认可的共识。在正常情况下，船厂不可能故意埋下一个错误并试图蒙混过关，因为这样做对船厂恐怕是没有利益的。相反，无论是船厂的送审还是船东的退审，双方的共识应当是船厂送审的图纸是符合合同及规格书要求且没有错误的。因此，船厂无法利用"共识禁止反言"的原则主张自己的错误已经得到船东的认可。

或许有一种情况可以适用"共识禁止反言"原则。如果船厂的图纸修改了规格书的要求，并且将自己的修改明确告知了船东，在这种情况下如果船东批准了图纸就应当视为船东已经接受了船厂的修改。此后，船东不能再以船厂图纸不符合规格书要求为由提出任何主张了。

5.86

III 监造代表

船东除了对船厂的图纸进行审批外，通常还可以指派专门人员进入船厂，对船舶建造的整个过程进行监督。

5.87

监造代表的指派

指定监造代表并派驻船厂参与船舶建造的整个过程是船东在船舶建造合同中的一项权利，为此 SAJ 格式有如下规定：①

5.88

> The BUYER may send to and maintain at the Shipyard, at the BUYER's own cost and expense, one representative who shall be duly authorized in writing by the BUYER (herein called the "Representative") to act on behalf of the BUYER in connection with modifications of the Specifications, adjustments of the Contract Price, approval of the plans and drawings, attendance to the tests and inspections relating to the VESSEL, its machinery, equipment and outfitting, and any other matters for which he is specifically authorized by the BUYER.

指派代表在船厂对船舶建造的整个过程进行监督无疑是符合船东利益的。由于有了自己的代表在船厂，船东就可以了解船舶建造的具体细节以及实际发生

5.89

---

① Article IV.2.

的各种问题。应当注意上述规定使用了 may，因此船东没有义务指派监造代表驻厂参与船舶建造。换言之，船东可以放弃这一权利而不指定任何代表驻厂，这一行为并不构成对船舶建造合同的违反。船厂在没有船东监造代表在厂的情况下依然负有按照合同和规格书规定建造船舶的义务，只是没有船东代表的参与而已。船厂不能以船东代表不在场为由停止建造并主张可允许延误。而且，即使没有船东监造代表的参与，船级社的验船师依然会全程参与所有涉及船级规范的船舶建造过程。

5.90 虽然船东通常会指派多名驻厂的监造代表，但未必会给每一名驻厂代表相同的授权。严格意义上说，只有有授权的监造人员才是船东的"代表"，其他人员只是船东监造代表的助手而已。船厂在与船东监造代表接洽时应当注意其授权。

5.91 在监造人员的人数问题上，Norwegian 格式有明确的规定：①

> ... The Representative shall have as many assistants as he may require, but any and all approvals must be given by the Representative and be in writing.

5.92 按照上述规定，船东指派驻厂的监造代表可以携带任意数量的助手。但在实践中，船东委派的驻厂代表并不会很多，尤其是在船舶建造的开始阶段。无论是从必要性还是从成本上来说，船东都没有必要派遣过多人员驻厂。

5.93 相比之下，NEWBUILDCON 格式的规定比较合理：②

> The Buyer may, at its own cost and expense, have one representative present at the Shipyard throughout the construction together with a reasonable number of assistants and, as appropriate, officers and crew ....

监造代表的授权

5.94 船东在指定其驻厂监造代表时往往会通知船厂其监造代表的授权范围，船东的监造代表抵达船厂后也会向船厂提供一份由船东签字的授权委托书。除非船东代表的授权委托书另有规定，船东的监造代表可以全权代表船东。如果船东指派一个以上监造代表的，通常也会明确各人的授权范围。船厂应当熟悉授权委托书的内容。如果船厂认为船东的监造代表的授权委托书有较大的限制或其他可

---

① Article V.2.
② Clause 22(a).

能会影响船厂和船东监造代表顺利沟通的情形的,应当要求船东予以澄清或更改船东监造代表的授权范围。

按照 SAJ 格式的规定,船东指派的驻厂监造代表的职责主要包括以下几个方面:修改规格书;调整合同价格;审批图纸;参加各种机器、设备和舾装的测试和检验以及其他经船东特别授权的事宜。这些授权是必不可少的,否则船东指派驻厂监造代表的意义就会成问题。但是 Norwegian 格式则有不同的规定:①

5.95

> ... Unless otherwise advised by the Buyer in writing, the Representative shall have no general authority to change the Contract or to approve plans and drawings. The Representative shall, however, be authorised to sign Change Order Forms (Article VI clause 1) on behalf of Buyer, unless otherwise advised by Buyer in writing ....

上述规定应当有比较明显的偏袒船东的倾向。船东的监造代表虽有修改和变更的签字权,但是没有改变合同价格的权利,这就意味着船东的监造代表可以提出修改的要求,但无权同意因此引起的合同价格的调整。规定船东监造代表无权批准图纸有些费解,似乎是说所有的由船东监造代表签署的修改均不涉及图纸或图纸的修改。这一规定可能并不符合船东的自身利益。船东监造代表应当有处理所有与修改有关的事宜的授权,包括批准设计和图纸、同意合同价格和交船日的调整等。

5.96

NEWBUILDCON 格式的相关规定是:②

5.97

> ... The Buyer shall notify the Builder in advance in writing of:
> (i) the names of the Buyer's Representative, assistants and, as appropriate, officers and crew; and
> (ii) the scope of the Buyer's Representative's authority which, in particular, shall include the extent to which the Buyer's Representative has authority to approve plans, drawings and calculations, agree modifications and invoices and attendance at and approval of tests, trials and inspections relating to the Vessel at the Shipyard and/or premises of Sub-contractors; and
> (iii) any other information reasonably required by the Builder to facilitate access to the Shipyard and/or premises of Sub-contractors.

---

① Article V.2.
② Clause 22(a).

5.98　　　NEWBUILDCON 格式区别对待船东的监造代表和船员，船员既不是监造代表，也不是监造代表的助手，但此种区分没有太大的实际意义。在实践中船员通常是在试航时才会参与，在此之前的建造活动一般与船员无关。

监造代表的职责

5.99　　　船东的监造代表在船厂期间是代表船东工作的，船舶建造合同规定的一些船东的合同义务实际上是由船东监造代表履行的。对此，SAJ 格式作出了原则性的规定：①

> The BUYER shall undertake and assure that the Representative shall carry out his duties hereunder in accordance with the normal shipbuilding practice of the BUILDER and in such a way as to avoid any unnecessary increase in building cost, delay in the construction of the VESSEL, and/or any disturbance in the construction schedule of the BUILDER.

5.100　　　Norwegian 格式的规定与 SAJ 格式的规定基本一致，只是把 SAJ 格式中特指的"船厂的正常建造实践"改为了更为宽泛的"正常建造实践"。② 这一规定可以说是船东在船舶建造合同中的一项义务，但是由于缺乏明确的适用标准，船厂似乎很难凭借这一规定主张船东的违约并要求合同交船日的顺延。因为所谓的"正常建造实践"应当是没有统一的定义，而"避免船舶建造成本的不必要增加和船舶建造的延误"同样没有明确的适用标准。但若双方对正常建造实践作出约定的话，情形可能就不一样了，例如建造合同载明船厂全年无休，星期六和星期日照常工作。除非船东的监造代表有适当的理由，否则就应当根据船厂的作息时间工作。

船厂的协助

5.101　　　船东指派驻厂代表的，船厂应当为船东代表提供各种方便，SAJ 格式的规定是：③

> The BUILDER shall furnish the Representative and his assistant(s) with adequate office space, and such other reasonable facilities according to

---

① Article IV.6 para.1.
② Article V.6 para.1.
③ Article IV.4.

the BUILDER's practice at, or in the immediate vicinity of, the Shipyard as may be necessary to enable them to effectively carry out their duties.

按照 Norwegian 格式的规定,船东监造代表的办公室可以安排在船厂之外:①   5.102

The Builder shall furnish the Representative and his assistant(s) with adequate office space, and such other reasonable facilities according to the Builder's practice at, or in the immediate vicinity of, the shipyard as may be necessary to enable them to effectively carry out their duties ....

船厂应当为船东的监造代表提供其在船厂工作的设施和设备等,这些设施和设备通常包括独立的办公室、电脑、网络、住处以及至船厂或分包商工作场所的交通等。船厂通常还应当支付船东监造代表在船厂的电话费和宽带使用费等。船东的监造代表可以不受限制地自由出入船厂及其分包商的工作场所。值得注意的是,按照 SAJ 格式的规定,船厂似乎可以在船厂以外地点为船东的监造代表提供办公室以及必要的办公室设施。但船东监造代表的办公室不在船厂内势必会给监造代表的工作带来不少麻烦,在实践中这种情形应当并不多见。   5.103

监造代表和船厂的关系

船东有可能指派自己的雇员常驻船厂,但并非所有船东都能做到这一点。有些船东会委托专业的船舶监造公司对船舶建造进行全面监督。一旦船东指派了驻厂代表,船东和船厂之间的联系主要发生在船东代表和船厂之间。这一关系对船舶建造具有相当重要的意义。由于船东的监造代表和船厂的作息时间未必相同,而且除了重大的法定节假日以外,船厂通常没有其他休息时间了。为了避免各自作息时间的差异,船舶建造合同应当规定船东的监造代表须按照船厂的作息时间安排工作。   5.104

船舶建造合同有时还会约定船东监造代表参加检验和试验的具体程序,例如船厂应当提前几天通知,船东监造代表应当在规定的时间内参加并完成检验和试验。一旦船东监造代表未能按照约定时间参加检验或试验的,船厂有机会顺延合同交船日,或者将船东监造代表的行为视为放弃监造。   5.105

---

① Article V.4.

船东的雇主责任

5.106　船东指派的驻厂监造代表在船厂工作期间显然会面临各种受伤甚至更大不幸的风险。作为惯例,虽然船东的监造代表在船厂工作,但船舶建造合同通常都会规定,船东的监造代表系船东的雇员,而非船厂的雇员。除非船东监造代表遭受的人身伤亡因船厂的重大过失造成,否则船厂对船东的监造代表无需承担任何责任。对此,SAJ 格式有如下规定:①

> The Representative and his assistant(s) shall at all times be deemed to be the employees of the BUYER and not of the BUILDER. The BUILDER shall be under no liability whatsoever to the BUYER, the Representative or his assistant(s) for personal injuries, including death, suffered during the time when he or they are on the VESSEL, or within the premises of either the BUILDER or its subcontractor, or are otherwise engaged in and about the construction of the VESSEL, unless, however, such personal injuries, including death, were caused by a gross negligence of the BUILDER, or of any of its employees or agents or subcontractors. Nor shall the BUILDER be under any liability whatsoever to the BUYER, the Representative or his assistant(s) for damage to, or loss or destruction of property in Japan of the BUYER or of the Representative or his assistant(s), unless such damage, loss or destruction were caused by a gross negligence of the BUILDER, or of any of its employees or agents or subcontractors.

5.107　虽然措辞与 SAJ 格式的不同,但 Norwegian 格式规定的雇主责任在本质上与 SAJ 格式的规定是相同的。按照该格式的规定,船东的代表及其助手应被视为船东的雇员,除非船厂有"重大过失",否则无需对船东代表及其助手的人身伤亡以及财产损失承担责任。

5.108　Norwegian 格式不仅针对人身伤亡的责任归属作出了规定,而且还针对财产的毁损作出了类似的规定:②

> The Buyer, the Representative and his assistant(s) shall be under no liability whatsoever to the Builder, the Builder's employees or Subcontractors, and the Builder shall keep the Buyer, the Representative or his assistant(s) harmless, for personal injuries, including death, un-

---

① Article IV.5, CSTC Article IV.4.
② Article V.5 para.2.

less such personal injuries including death were caused by gross negligence of the Representative or his assistant(s). Nor shall the Buyer be under any liability whatsoever to the Builder, the Builder's employees or Subcontractors for damage to, or loss or destruction of property of the Builder, its employees or Subcontractors unless such damage, loss or destruction were caused by gross negligence of the Representative or his assistant(s).

免责约定的有效性

船舶建造合同约定的当事人之间的责任划分未必是有效的。此种约定有可能因违反成文法而无效,1977 年《不公平合同条款法》便有如下规定:①   5.109

(1) A person cannot by reference to any contract term or to a notice given to persons generally or to particular persons exclude or restrict his liability for death or personal injury resulting from negligence.
(2) In the case of other loss or damage, a person cannot so exclude or restrict his liability for negligence except in so far as the term or notice satisfies the requirement of reasonableness.
(3) Where a contract term or notice purports to exclude or restrict liability for negligence a person's agreement to or awareness of it is not of itself to be taken as indicating his voluntary acceptance of any risk.

在 EE Caledonia Ltd v Orbit Valve Co Europe② 一案中,被告同意提供服务工程师在平台上对一些阀进行检修,原告是平台的所有人之一。服务合同第 10 条有如下规定: 5.110

... (b) Company's and Contractor's Employees and Property. Each party hereto shall indemnify ... the other, provided that the other party has acted in good faith, from and against any claim, demand, cause of action, loss expense or liability ... arising by reason of any injury to or death of any employee ... of the indemnifying party, resulting from or in any way connected with the performance of this Order.

检修工作大致需要 10 天的时间,期间服务工程师居住在平台上。一天,当服务工程师工作完毕后走回自己的居住之处时平台着火,服务工程师不幸身亡。着   5.111

---

① s.2.
② [1993] 2 Lloyd's Rep 418.

火的原因是原告的雇员违反规定,与服务工程师无关。服务工程师的家属对原告提起诉讼,原告与索赔人达成了和解,接着向被告提起诉讼,按照合同的赔偿条款要求补偿。高院的 Hobhouse 法官认为,法律规定的原则是任何人均不能免除对自己的疏忽应当承担的责任,他说:①

> The question remains one of the construction of the contract applying the established principles of construction. These include the principle that the parties to a contract are not to be taken to have agreed that a party shall be relieved of the consequences of its negligence without the use of clear words showing that that was the intention of the contract. The law therefore presumes that a man will not readily be granted an indemnity against a loss caused by his own negligence. While an indemnity clause may be regarded as the obverse of an exempting clause, when considering the meaning of such a clause one must, I think, regard it as even more inherently improbable that one party should agree to discharge the liability of the other for acts for which he is responsible.

船厂的代理

5.112　不仅船东的驻厂代表不是船厂的雇员,所有船东的代表都不应被视为船厂的雇员或代理,即使是参加试航的船东代表同样不是船厂的雇员或代理人。在 *Hobson* v *Bartram & Sons Ltd* 一案中,②原告是船厂分包商的一名管子工,该分包商负责的是船上冷冻设备的安装,被告是一家为阿根廷政府建造船舶的船厂。船舶建造合同包含下列规定:

> 3. The vessel, including engines, boilers, machinery outfit and equipment as she is constructed and all materials, wherever situated, appropriated to this contract shall immediately after payment of the first instalment, as the work proceeds, become the property of the purchasers, and shall not be within the ownership or disposition of the builders; but the builders shall at all times have a lien thereon for any unpaid purchase money and interest thereon, and for their charges for any additions, alterations or extra work.
>
> 9. ... In the event of a sea trial trip being carried out in accordance with Clause 6 to purchasers' account the engine-builders, for the

---

① [1993] 2 Lloyd's Rep 418 at 422.
② (1950) 83 Ll L Rep 313.

purpose of such trial, shall supply the attendants, fuel and engine consumable stores for the propelling machinery. The builders shall provide pilotage, and towage and the purchasers shall provide the crew necessary for the safe handling and navigation of the vessel, whilst proceeding to or from and during the trial.

5.113　船舶开始试航时，冷冻设备的安装尚未完成，于是原告和其他分包商的雇员也上船继续冷冻设备的安装。原告实际上并不是参加试航的人员，而是为了安装冷冻设备而受邀上船的人员。船东也派了部分船员参加试航，船员参加试航的目的并不是试航本身，而是为了熟悉船舶。原告在靠近舱口的二层舱甲板上工作。原告离开自己的工作地点去用午餐时有一盏灯亮着，舱盖也已封住了。原告必须经过舱口盖才能用餐地点。等原告用完餐回来时，那盏灯不在了，舱口盖也挪走了，也没有设置绳索或护栏等。结果原告从舱口摔了下去并受了重伤。灯和舱盖实际上都是被在船上的阿根廷船员移走的，其目的是为了了解情况。他们拿走了灯，挪开了舱盖后下去检查货舱。

5.114　原告以受邀人的身份将船厂作为邀请人提起了诉讼，认为作为邀请人的船厂违反了其对受邀人所负有的谨慎之责。高院认为，除非将阿根廷船员视为船厂的代理人，否则船厂就没有违反作为邀请人对受邀人所负的谨慎之责。最终高院认为船东的船员受制于船厂总体指挥，船东的船员检查货舱是试航的组成部分之一，因此船厂应当负责。高院的 Oliver 法官说：①

> Turning once more to the question of agency, the situation to be examined is the position of the Argentino crew *que* the defendants during the trial; not at any other time. Considering the number of ships which must have undergone similar trials during the last century or so, it seems rather unusual that there should be no authority establishing the relationship between the buyer's crew and the builders during such a trial as this, but none has been discovered. I have come to the conclusion that, inasmuch as both the defendants and the Argentine Government were equally interested in the success of the trials, or otherwise, the Argentino crew were, *pro tem.*, under the orders of the defendants, and their examination of all parts of the ship was an integral part of the trial, and they were agents of the defendants when they went below to make their examination.

---

① (1950) 83 Ll L Rep 313 at 318.

5.115　但高院的判决被上诉法院推翻了。上诉法院的 Tucker 法官认为:船东的船员"与任何在买卖完成之前检查货物的买方代理处于完全相同的地位",他说:①

> I am of a contrary opinion. It seems to me that there is nothing in this case to show that the Argentino sailors were at any time during this trial the agents of the defendants. They were there on behalf of the Argentine Government, who were the intending purchasers of the ship, to satisfy themselves and their Government with regard to the performance of the vessel before they took delivery of it. They were in exactly the same position as the agents of any purchaser who goes to inspect goods before the actual purchase is completed. It is quite true that there is a common interest in the success of the trial between the builders of the ship and the purchasers, but that is not sufficient to make the servants of the purchasers the agents or servants of the builders. It is quite true that the defendants' manager, who was in charge of the ship, admitted that he had a control for certain purposes over these men. Every captain of a ship (and this man was in the position of a captain) necessarily has control in a certain sense over all the acts of the persons on a ship, but that does not make them for all purposes his agents.

过失和重大过失

5.116　按照上述 SAJ 格式的规定,船厂就船东的监造代表或其他雇员在船厂遭受人身伤亡向船东承担责任的前提是船厂或其雇员或其代理或分包商有重大过失。然而,"过失"和"重大过失"在英国法中似乎并没有明确差异,法院一般不愿意区分"gross negligence"和"simple negligence"之间的差异。在 *Hinton v Dibber* 一案中,王座法院的 Lord Denman 便说:②

> It is believed, however, that in none of the numerous cases upon this subject is any such attempt made: and it may well be doubted whether between "gross negligence" and negligence merely any intelligible distinction exists.

5.117　Crompton 法官在 *Beal v South Devon Rly* 一案中也认为,一旦未能实施合理

---

① Ibid.
② (1842) 2 QB 646 at 661.

的谨慎、技能和职责就构成"重大过失",他说的是:①

> The authorities are numerous, and the language of the judgments various, but for all practical purposes the rule may be stated to be, that the failure to exercise reasonable care, skill and diligence is gross negligence.

在 Grill v General Iron Screw Collier Co 一案中,民事法庭的 Willes 法官指出,所谓的"重大过失"实际上就是未能实施应实施的谨慎,"重大"一词只是描述,而不是定义:② 5.118

> Confusion has arisen from regarding negligence as a positive instead of a negative word. It is really the absence of such care as it was the duty of the defendant to use. A bailee is only bound to use the ordinary care of a man, and so the absence of it is called gross negligence. A person who undertakes to do some work for reward to an article must exercise the care of a skilled workman, and the absence of such care in him is negligence. Gross, therefore, is a word of description, and not a definition, and it would have been only introducing a source of confusion to use the expression gross negligence, instead of the equivalent, a want of due care and skill in navigating the vessel ....

在 Pentecost v London District Auditor 一案中,Lord Goddard 也对"重大过失"发表了自己的意见,他认为在过失杀人罪以外的其他任何情形使用"重大过失"都是一种误解。Lord Goddard 也认为过失就是对义务的违反,至于违反是可原谅的还是严重的并不是问题,任何程度的违反都是可以起诉的。他说的是:③ 5.119

> The use of the expression "gross negligence" is always misleading. Except in the one case of the law relating to manslaughter, the words "gross negligence" should never be used in connexion with any matter to which the common law relates, and for this reason: negligence is a breach of duty. If there is a duty and there has been a breach of it which causes loss, it matters not whether it is a venial breach or a serious one: a breach of a legal duty in any degree which causes loss is actionable. The question whether it is venial or gross is quite immaterial.

---

① (1864) 3 H&C 337 at 341.
② (1866) LR 1 CP 600 at 612.
③ [1951] 2 KB 759 at 766.

5.120 在 *Tradigrain SA v Intertek* 一案中，上诉法院也认为"重大疏忽"并不是一个区别于"简单疏忽"的概念，上诉法院的 Moore-Bick 法官是这样说的：①

> The term "gross negligence", although often found in commercial documents, has never been accepted by English civil law as a concept distinct from simple negligence, witness the assent of several judges to the assertion that gross negligence is "ordinary negligence with a vituperative epithet"(per Willes J. in Grill v General Iron Screw Collier Co. (1866) L. R. 1 C. P. 600, 612 referring to a dictum of Rolfe B. in Wilson v Brett (1843) 11 M. & W. 113; see also Armitage v Nurse [1998] Ch. 241, 254 per Millett L. J.). It is a concept recognised by German law, however, and it was common ground between the parties that the expression "gross negligence" in the 'waiver of recourse' clause should be construed as importing that concept.

5.121 但是在 *Red Sea Tankers Ltd and Others v Paopachristidis and Others* 一案中，高院的 Mance 法官则认为"重大过失"与一般的因未实施适当技能或谨慎而构成的过失相比更为根本，重大过失将使当事人丧失援引免责条款的权利。Mance 说：②

> "Gross" negligence is clearly intended to represent something more fundamental than failure to exercise proper skill and/or care constituting negligence. But, as a matter of ordinary language and general impression, the concept of gross negligence seems to me capable of embracing not only conduct undertaken with actual appreciation of the risks involved, but also serious disregard of or indifference to an obvious risk . . . .
>
> As to authority, I was not referred to the criminal field, where "gross negligence" features in the law of manslaughter. In essence, the position there is that a breach of a duty of care will amount to manslaughter if its seriousness in all the circumstances is such that a jury considers that it should be characterized as a crime . . . . The analogy in the civil field would be to explain gross negligence as conduct so seriously negligent that the defendant should not be entitled to rely on the exemption clause. The test involves an element of circularity, but Lord Mackay in *Adamoko* said that it was "necessarily a question of

---

① [2007] EWCA Civ 154 [23].
② [1997] 2 Lloyd's Rep 547 at 586.

degree, and an attempt to specify that degree more closely is … extra likely to achieve only a spurious precision". Although, in the present context, the question cannot be left to a jury and it will be necessary to attempt to identify and evaluate various factors bearing on the decision, the question whether any negligence in the present case was "gross" appears to me ultimately still very much a matter of degree and judgment.

NEWBUILDCON 格式的规定

NEWBUILDCON 格式也有关于船厂和船东雇主责任的规定,但是该格式并没有针对船东的监造代表和船厂的质保工程师分别作出相关责任的规定,而是统一规定了船厂和船东各自的雇主责任:①

5.122

> (f) Responsibility for death and personal injury
> Each Party to this Contract shall accept responsibility and liability for the death and personal injury of its Personnel, unless the death or personal injury was inflicted by the other Party or its Sub-contractors with the intent to cause such death or injury, or recklessly and with knowledge that such death or injury would probably result.
>
> Each Party further agrees to indemnify and hold harmless the other Party, as regards both liability and legal costs, in the event of claims relating to or resulting from death or personal injury of its Personnel against the Party who is not responsible for them under this Sub-clause 37(f).
>
> (g) Responsibility for damage to or loss of property
> Unless otherwise provided in this Contract, each Party shall accept responsibility and liability for damage to or loss of its property and the property belonging to its Personnel unless such damage or loss was caused by the other Party or its Sub-contractors with the intent to cause such damage or loss, or recklessly and with knowledge that such damage or loss would probably result.
>
> Each Party further agrees to indemnify and hold harmless the other Party, as regards both liability and legal costs, in the event of claims relating to or resulting from damage to or loss of property against the Party who is not responsible for them under this Sub-clause 37(g).

---

① Clause 37(f), (g).

5.123　相比较而言，NEWBUILDCON 格式的规定比较恰当，该格式主要有如下几个特点：首先，关于责任的规定是整体的，而不局限于任何一种特定情形，因此其适用范围比较广泛；其次，关于责任的规定不仅包括人身伤亡，也包括财产的损坏和灭失；最后，该格式放弃了其他标准格式使用的"重大过失"的概念，而采用了"有意"（intent）和"鲁莽"（recklessly）两个均有先例解释的用词。

5.124　Pennycuick 法官在 Lloyds Bank Ltd v Marcan 一案中曾对"有意"一词作出过解释，他说：①

> The word "intent" denotes a state of mind. A man's intention is a question of fact. Actual intent may unquestionably be proved by direct evidence or may be inferred from surrounding circumstances. Intent may also be imputed on the basis that a man must be presumed to intend the natural consequences of his own act.

5.125　而 Devlin 法官在 Reed(Albert E) & Co Ltd v London and Rochester Trading Co Ltd 一案中则对"鲁莽"一词作出了解释：②

> The term "recklessly", I think, does not really give rise to much difficulty. It means something more than mere negligence or inadvertence. I think it means deliberately running an unjustifiable risk. There is not anything necessarily criminal, or even morally culpable, about running an unjustifiable risk; it depends in relation to what risk is run; it may be a big matter or it may be a small matter.

5.126　由于 recklessly 一词后面接着"明知有可能"发生此种人身伤亡或财产损失的鲁莽，因此无论是船厂还是船东承担对方雇员人身伤亡或财产损失的可能性应当是比较小的。

5.127　根据 NEWBUILDCON 格式的上述规定，任何一方均应对自己雇员的人身伤亡承担责任，除非此种人身伤亡是由于对方的故意或明知结果会发生而依然鲁莽行事的行为造成的。言下之意，即使雇员的人身伤亡是由于对方的疏忽造成的，责任仍有可能由自己承担。但合同关于一方承担另一方责任的约定应当可以得到法院的认可。在 Hancock Shipping Co Ltd v Deacon & Trysail(Private) Ltd and Another(The Casper Trader)③ 一案中，原告是船东，被告是一家专门提供随船修理

---

① [1973] 2 All ER 359 at 367.
② [1954] 2 Lloyd's Rep 463 at 465.
③ [1991] 2 Lloyd's Rep 550.

技师的新加坡公司,被告为原告提供17名随船技师。合同第9(3)条有如下规定:

> ... (the Contractor) agrees to defend, indemnify and hold harmless MIPGB, Hancock Shipping Company Limited, the vessel, its Owners, masters, Officers and Crew (hereinafter collectively referred to as "Indemnitees") from and against any loss, costs (including but not limited to court costs and fees and expenses of legal Counsel), claims, damages, liability and/or judgments (hereinafter collectively referred to as "losses") arising out of any loss of property, personal injury, or death suffered by Contractor or any of the Contractor's Employees while performing services under this agreement, including but not limited to, any such losses suffered by the Indemnitees while the Contractor's personnel are on board or in transit to the vessel howsoever caused and whether or not caused by or through the fault or negligence of the Indemnitees or any of them ....

由于主机在供油中出现的一系列疲劳断裂,船上发生了火灾,最终导致推定全损。高院认为无论损失是否由于接受赔偿方的过失或疏忽造成的,上述条款中关于"使对方不受损害"的约定均应适用。Steyn 法官说:① 5.128

> The third issue raises the question whether the defendants might have been entitled, in this case, to rely on an argument of circuity of action. In that regard, it seems to me that if the hold harmless provision had not contained any reference to negligence that argument may well run in this case but there is such a reference to negligence. The concluding words make clear that the hold harmless agreement applies whether or not the losses are caused by or through the fault or negligence of the indemnitees or any of them.

监造代表的更换

船东更换驻厂监造代表可能有各种原因,原因之一是船厂的抱怨。船东派遣的监造代表与船厂的相关人员在工作上存在沟通困难且此种困难已直接影响到船舶建造的顺利进行时,船厂往往会提出更换驻厂监造代表的要求。例如 SAJ 格式就有关于更换监造代表的规定:② 5.129

---

① [1991] 2 Lloyd's Rep 550 at 552.
② Article IV.6 para.2; CSTC Article IV.7; Norwegian Article V.6 para.2.

> The BUILDER has the right to request the BUYER to replace the Representative who is deemed unsuitable and unsatisfactory for the proper progress of the VESSEL's construction. The BUYER shall investigate the situation by sending its representative(s) to the Shipyard if necessary, and if the BUYER considers that such BUILDER'S request is justified, the BUYER shall effect such replacement as soon as conveniently arrangeable.

5.130　船厂的权利只是提出请求而已,船东的义务则是对此进行调查。"不合适"并不是有明确含义的用词,而"不令人满意"则是较为主观的判断。鉴于船厂和船东利益的对立,船东通常不会仅凭船厂的要求而更换监造代表。因此在实践中,除非出现极端情形,否则船厂要求船东更换监造代表并非易事。

5.131　AWES格式没有关于船厂要求船东更换监造代表的规定,但是AWES格式规定,如果船东指派船舶建造合同约定之外的公司或人员进驻船厂的则须事先获得船厂的书面同意:①

> Should the PURCHASER elect to use as the Representative to firms or persons other than or in addition to its full time employees, different or inaddition to the ones established in the provisions of this contract, admittance of such firms or persons and their duties shall be subject to the CONTRACTOR's prior written approval, which shall not be unreasonably withheld.

5.132　按照NEWBUILDCON格式的规定,只有在船厂可以证明船东监造代表的行为已经影响到船舶建造的正常进程时,船厂才可以提出更换监造代表的请求:②

> The Builder shall have the right to request the Buyer to replace the Buyer's Representative or any assistants but only if the Builder shows that they are carrying out their duties in an unreasonable manner detrimental to the proper progress of the construction of the Vessel, in which case the Buyer shall make proper replacement as soon as possible.

5.133　同样道理,除了极端情形,船东监造代表的行为是否构成对船舶建造正常进程的影响依然是一个事实问题,缺乏可操作性的标准。

---

① Article 2(a)para.5.
② Clause 22(c).

监造代表和船级社的联系

与其他的标准格式不同,NEWBUILDCON 格式有关于船东监造代表与对船舶建造负责监督的船级社联系的规定:①　　　　　　　　　　　　　　5.134

The Buyer's Representative shall have the right to communicate directly with the Classification Society, provided such communication does not unreasonably interfere with the Builder's communication with the Classification Society.

显然,船厂拒绝船东监造代表和船级社直接联系缺乏令人满意的理由。即使船厂可以阻止船东监造代表和船级社发生联系,也阻止不了船东和船级社发生联系。一个比较合理的做法应当是,船东监造代表与船级社的所有联系均应告知船厂,船东监造代表与船级社的书面来往均应抄送给船厂。　　　　　　　　　　　　　　5.135

IV　船舶检验

这里的船舶检验是指船级社、船舶的主管当局以及船东在船舶建造过程中对在建船舶实施的各种测试和检验。SAJ 格式有相应的规定:②　　　　　　　　　5.136

The necessary inspections of the VESSEL, its machinery, equipment and outfittings shall be carried out by the Classification Society, other regulatory bodies and/or an inspection team of the BUILDER throughout the entire period of construction, in order to ensure that the construction of the VESSEL is duly performed in accordance with this Contract and the Specifications . . . .

船东代表的检验

船东对船舶的检验是以船舶建造合同为依据的,因此船舶建造合同一般会就船东或其监造代表检验船舶作出比较详细的规定。SAJ 格式的规定是:③　　　　　5.137

. . . The Representative shall have, during construction of the VESSEL, the right to attend such tests and inspections of the VESSE, its

---

① Clause 22(d).
② Article IV.3 para.1.
③ Ibid.

machinery and equipment as are mutually agreed between the BUYER and BUILDER. The BUILDER shall give a notice to the Representative reasonably in advance of the date and place of such tests and inspections to be attended by him for his convenience. Failing of the Representative to be present at such tests and inspections after due notice to him as above provided shall be deemed to be a waiver of this right to be present.

5.138　从上述规定来看,船东的监造代表有权参加船舶、机器以及设备的测试或检验。当然,这里使用的"参加"一词是指所有的测试或检验均由船厂而不是船东监造代表具体实施。但船东有权了解整个过程以及测试和检验的结果。在船舶建造过程中,船级社参加测试或检验的均为涉及船级规范的项目,船级社不会对船级规范以外的项目进行测试和检验。船东参加的则是所有的项目,既包括涉及船级规范的项目,也包括不涉及船级规范的合同约定项目。如果测试或检验的项目涉及船级规范,船厂通常会同时向船级社和船东发出检验通知。船级社代表和船东代表会同时对参加报检项目的测试或检验。涉及船级规范的项目,有权作出决定的是船级社代表。虽然船东的监造代表可以发表自己的意见,但对于相关项目是否符合船级规范的要求以船级社代表的意见为准。

5.139　船东通过其监造代表参加对在建船舶进行的测试和检验是船舶建造合同赋予船东的一项权利,而不是义务。由于这是一项船东的权利,船厂应当按照船舶建造合同的约定向船东的监造代表报检。如果由于船厂没有报检而遗漏的项目,船东有权要求船厂重新施工。也正是由于这是一项权利,船东可以放弃对船舶的建造过程进行检验。在船厂正常报检的情况下船东的监造代表拒绝检验或不对船厂已完成项目进行检验的,船厂可以视该项目已通过船东监造代表的测试或检验。① 如果该项目涉及船级规范的,只要在通过船级社代表的检验后就可以继续船舶的建造。除非船舶建造合同另有规定,船厂等待船东监造代表检验的时间并不构成可允许延误,而应当由船厂自己承担。

5.140　AWES 格式关于船舶检验的规定如下:②

The PURCHASER shall have the right to have the VESSEL and all engines, machinery, outfit and equipment intended therefore inspected

---

① AWES Article 2(a)para.4.
② Article 2(a)para.1.

during construction by one or more(up to a maximum of …) authorised representative(s)(jointly the "Representative") to whom the CONTRACTOR shall grant free access for such purposes during working hours to the VESSEL and to the Shipyard and workshops, save and except areas which are controlled for purposes of national security ….

虽然 AWES 格式使用的是"the right to have the Vessel inspected",与 SAJ 格式中的"the right to attend tests and inspections"不同,但实质上应当是相同的。在所有测试和检验中,进行实际操作的是船厂的工作人员,船东的监造代表实际上并不进行任何实际操作。

项目和时间的约定

按照 SAJ 格式的规定,船厂和船东应当约定检验的时间和项目。实际做法通常是船厂在完成某一需要船东检验的建造项目后会安排船东监造代表进行检验,具体的程序是由船厂向船东监造代表发出测试或检验的通知,告知检验的项目、时间和地点,俗称"报检"。

船东要求改变检验时间或项目就有可能产生时间的延误。此种延误是否可以视为可允许延误则应根据具体情况予以判断。原则上船厂通知船东监造代表检验的时间应当是合理的,而是否合理则需要根据船厂报检的项目多寡、报检和检验时间的长短以及船厂在驻厂监造代表及其助手人数作出判断。虽然船厂的建造往往不受周末周日乃至普通节假日的影响,但除非船舶建造合同另有约定,原则上船东监造代表应当有权拒绝在周末或节假日参加测试或检验。在这个问题上,AWES 格式的规定应当是比较合理的:①

The PURCHASER's Representative whose name, duties and extent of authority are to be made known in advance, shall observe the works' rules prevailing at the CONTRACTOR's and the SUBCONTRACTOR's premises ….

如果建造项目的测试或检验由于船东监造代表的原因而被延误,而且此种延误实际影响到船舶建造的进程的,船厂就有机会将因此浪费的时间视为可允许延误,主张合同交船日的顺延。相反,虽然船厂原定的检验安排被延误,但原因不能归责于船东监造代表的,例如报检项目过多,船东监造代表无法在船厂规定的时

5.141

5.142

5.143

5.144

---

① Article 2(a)para.3.

间内完成等,因此引起的延误则应当计算为船厂的正常建造期限。

查看船舶的权利

5.145　船东的监造代表除了在接到船厂的通知后参加船舶的测试和检验外,还有权随时查看船舶,这是参加船舶测试和检验以外的权利。SAJ 格式没有相关的规定,但 Norwegian 格式则有如下规定:①

> Whilst the Vessel is under construction and until Delivery and Acceptance, the Representative and his assistants shall during all working hours be given free access to the Vessel, its engines and accessories, and to any other place where work is being done, or materials are being processed or stored in connection with the construction of the Vessel, including the yards, workshops and offices of the Builder, and the premises of the Subcontractors of the Builder who are doing work or storing materials in connection with the Vessels construction.

5.146　上述规定的实际意义就是船东的监造代表及其助手只要在工作时间内就可以随意在船厂内活动,船厂必须有理由才可以拒绝船东监造代表及其助手在船厂内的自由活动。船东监造代表及其助手可以自由去的地方包括船台、车间、仓库以及办公室等。虽然船厂可以允许船东代表在船厂范围内自由活动,但未必可以在船舶建造合同内承诺船东的监造代表可以随意去分包商的场地。相比之下,AWES 格式的规定则比较合理:②

> The CONTRACTOR will obtain for the PURCHASER's right of access to subcontractor's premises as far as possible.

5.147　而按照 CSTC 格式的规定,船东监造代表可以随意去的地方甚至没有时间的限制,CSTC 格式的规定是:③

> ... At all times, during the construction of the VESSEL until delivery thereof, the Supervisor shall be given free and ready access to the VESSEL, her engines and accessories, and to any other place where the work is being done, or the materials are being processed or stored, in connection with the construction of the VESSEL, including the yards, workshops, stores of the BUILDER, and the premises of subcontractors

---

① Article V.3 para.2; NEWBUILDCON, Clause 23(c).
② Article 2(a)para.1.
③ Article IV.3 para.3.

of the BUILDER, who are doing work, or storing materials in connection with the VESSEL's construction . . . .

5.148 虽然上述规定使用了"is being done",但未必就能解释为船东监造代表只能去"正在工作"的场所,而且"are being stored"显然不能理解为有任何活动正在进行。

重复测试或检验

5.149 在船舶建造过程中,船东的监造代表对已经测试或检验完毕的项目进行重复测试或检验的情形绝非罕见。出现这种情形的原因可能是船东在建造期间更换了监造代表或其助手,新的监造代表或其助手有可能会提出重新测试或检验的要求;也可能是船东的监造代表发现之前的测试或检验可能存在问题,从而提出再一次测试或检验的请求。

5.150 原则上,船东的监造代表不能要求重新测试或检验已通过其测试或检验的项目,船厂应当可以拒绝重新测试或检验的要求。如果船东监造代表坚持重复测试或检验的就应当对因此引起的时间、费用甚至损失承担责任。

通知缺陷的义务

5.151 船东的监造代表在测试或检验过程中或在其自行检查中有可能发现或认为船舶建造不符合合同或规格书规定的情形,SAJ 格式规定了船东监造代表在这种情况下通知船厂的义务:①

In the event that the Representative discovers any construction or material or workmanship which is not deemed to conform to the requirements of this Contract and/or the Specifications, the Representative shall promptly give the BUILDER a notice in writing as to such non-conformity. Upon receipt of such notice from the Representative, the BUILDER shall correct such non-conformity, if the BUILDER agrees to his view . . . .

5.152 按照本条的规定,船东的监造代表在发现船舶的建造、材料或工艺不符合船舶建造合同或规格书的要求时,有义务以书面的方式及时向船厂提出。船厂接受船东监造代表意见的则应在收到通知后予以更正。然而 NEWBUILDCON 格式

---

① Article IV.3 para.2.

则有不同的规定：①

> Neither the Buyer's Representative's and/or assistants' inspection and/or attendance at any inspection, test or trial, nor the Buyer's Representative's and/or assistants' failure to notify the Builder of any non-conformity shall relieve the Builder from its obligations under this Contract or be deemed to be or construed as a waiver of any objection to, or any acceptance of, faulty design, construction, material and/or workmanship, or any admission that any materials or workmanship are of the standard required for due performance of this Contract.

5.153　上述规定可能是针对SAJ格式中关于通知义务的。按照上述规定，即使船东监造代表没有将其在自己的检查中或者参加船厂组织的测试或检验中发现的船舶建造缺陷通知船厂的，船厂并不因此可以免除自己的合同责任，也不影响船东事后对有缺陷的设计、建造、材料以及工艺等主张权利。此种规定应当存在不合理之处。在实践中，船东的监造代表在完成船厂报检项目的测试或检验后通常会发表意见，这些意见包括：接受、有保留的接受或拒绝接受等。换言之，船东应当对已完成的测试或检验项目发表意见。如果船东的监造代表在其所参加的测试或检验中发现了船舶建造的缺陷或问题，但在检验意见一栏里填上"接受"，却允许船东事后拒绝接受该项目应当是不合理的。虽然船东监造代表的检验并不免除船厂合同责任的观点是可以成立的，而且也是合理的，但这是以船东的监造代表未能在检验中发现问题为前提的。一旦船东监造代表发现问题就应当向船厂提出，即使没有SAJ格式的规定，船东依然应当向船厂提出其所发现的问题，否则就可能因放弃而无法在事后提出相关的主张。

5.154　另一种情形则是船东的监造代表不是在参加船厂安排的测试或检验时发现问题或缺陷，而是在自己进行的检验或检查中发现了问题或缺陷。如果船东的监造代表选择不将自己发现的问题或缺陷通知船厂，其结果与船东的监造代表在参加由船厂安排的测试或检验时发现问题或缺陷而不告知船厂的情形应当是相同的，即监造代表事后不能就早已发现的问题或缺陷提出任何主张。正如Lord Kinnear在*Nelson* v *William Chalmers & Co Ltd*一案中所说的：②

---

① Clause 23(d).
② 1913 SC 441 at 451.

... [T]he [owner] not only had sufficient opportunity to satisfy himself that the contract was being fulfilled, but by an express stipulation he undertook to do so. If he had neglected this duty or if, on inspection, he was satisfied, or had concealed his dissatisfaction so as to allow the contractors to go on with the work on the understanding that so far as already seen it was sufficient, he would in my opinion have lost his right to object to the vessel on the ground of disconformity to contract.

但是在 Aktiebolaget Gotaverken v Westminster Corporation of Monrovia and Anther①一案中,情形则似乎有所不同,在该案中的船舶改装合同规定: 5.155

Claims on account of asserted defects or deficiencies of material or workmanship shall always be given immediately after such defects or deficiencies have been discovered.

高院则认为,虽然"立即通知"是船东的一项义务,但船东违反这一义务并不因此丧失索赔权利,只是应当承担因此产生的额外费用,高院的 Donaldson 法官是这样说的:②   5.156

The second paragraph of the regulations which provides that claims " shall always be given immediately after" discovery, places an obligation on owners, the breach of which sounds in damages, but does not bar a claim. If, for example, the owners know that the engine bed-plates are defective but allow the engines to be installed before saying anything, they may be liable in respect of the additional cost of remedial work.

争议的解决

在船东监造代表向船厂发出监造缺陷的书面通知后,船厂同意船东监造代表意见的,就应当及时更正船东监造代表发现的缺陷。但是,如果船厂不同意船东监造代表的意见,按照 SAJ 格式的规定就应当适用争议和仲裁条款。SAJ 格式有如下规定:③   5.157

Notwithstanding the preceding provisions of this Paragraph, it is recognized that in the event of any dispute or difference of opinion arising

---

① [1971] 2 Lloyd's Rep 505.
② [1971] 2 Lloyd's Rep 505 at 513.
③ Article XIII.1 para.8.

in regard to the construction of the VESSEL, her machinery or equipment, or concerning the quality of materials or workmanship thereof or thereon, such dispute may be referred to the Classification Society upon mutual agreement of the parties hereon as far as the Classification Society agrees to determine such dispute. The decision of the Classification Society shall be final and binding upon the parties hereto.

5.158　约定由船级社对船厂和船东在技术问题上产生的争议作出决定似乎是可取的。这种解决争议的方式与仲裁相比无疑更为方便和快捷，而且可以避免不必要的法律费用的产生。但是，如前所述，船级船由于自己的地位的特殊，一般不愿意接受船厂或船东的共同委托解决争议。

船级社的检验

5.159　船级社检验是指船级社驻厂代表按照船级规范、国际公约、船旗国以及其他相关国家法律的要求，根据船舶的用途、技术状况和航行区域等对船舶及其相关产品，用度量、检查、试验和测量等方式对照经过批准的图纸进行比较的过程。这里的船级社检验也就是船级社的入级检验的一部分，即建造中船舶的测试和检验。船级社的测试和检验项目通常要少于船舶建造合同规定的检验项目。

5.160　船级社对在建船舶的测试和检验的主要内容包括：原材料的检验，船体、机械、电器和冷藏等所用材料的测试，船体的建造检验，船舶舾装检验，管系制造及安装检验，轴系及螺旋桨制造及安装检验，主机和辅机的安装检验，系泊试验以及船用产品的检验等。如果提供钢材以及设备和装置的供应商已取得船级社颁发的船用产品证书，船级社通常就不再进行测试和检验了。

5.161　船级社的检验人员对船舶建造进行测试和检验的依据并不是船舶建造合同，而是船级规范、国际公约以及相关国家的规定等。由于船东的监造代表可以参加船舶建造所有的测试和检验，因此他们也可以参加船级社对在建船舶进行的测试和检验。在完成涉及船级规范的建造项目后，船厂不仅应当向船级社报检，也应当同时向船东的监造代表报检。但是关于此类项目的检验应当只有一次，即由船级社的验船师实施的检验。如果船东的监造代表没有参加检验的，船厂无需再一次进行报检或检验。

建造进程报告

5.162　CSTC格式可能是唯一的规定船东可以要求船厂提供船舶建造进程报告的

标准格式:①

> The BUYER is entitled to require the BUILDER to report the condition of progress as to the construction of the VESSSEL whenever the BUYER requires during the construction of the VESSEL.

船舶建造进程报告,顾名思义,是指记录特定时间内船舶建造活动细节的文件。如果进程报告是每月提供的,在一份进程报告中就应当包含上一个月所发生的与船舶建造有关的事件和活动。进程报告内容将随着船舶建造的不同阶段而有所不同,例如在开始阶段的进程报告通常包含的内容有计划进度和实际进度的差异及其原因、采购的安排和执行、供应商的确定、船厂的图纸送审以及船东的退审及意见等;在船舶下水后的建造进程报告则会更多地涉及舾装工程,例如设备的安装、船厂的报检及船东的检验意见、试航的安排以及测试和检验项目的约定等。除了记录船舶建造的整个过程外,进程报告还应当记载意外事件的发生以及船厂和船东的应对措施、双方就报检项目和建造质量而产生的争议及其双方的立场和应对的措施等,例如项目经理和船东的监造代表之间的会议及其主要内容以及具体实施状况等。 5.163

船舶建造合同规定船厂应当定期向船东提供船舶建造进程报告并非罕见。但我国不少船厂对船舶建造进程报告的理解可能有问题,似乎都不太愿意接受这一规定,觉得这一要求对船厂是一种"限制"。其实不然,对船东而言,船厂定期向船东提供建造进程报告对船东而言无疑是船厂管理水准的体现;对船厂而言,建造进程报告同样有利于船厂管理体系的健全,计划的可靠以及执行力的贯彻。建造进程报告有助于船厂清晰了解船舶建造的实际状况,从而便于控制和调整。对于证据的保留同样也有相当大的作用。 5.164

---

① Article IV.6.

第 6 章 修 改

I 概述

6.1 　　虽然船舶建造应当按照双方订立的船舶建造合同以及规格书和图纸的要求进行,但是在建造过程中,合同、规格书、图纸等有可能发生变化或修改。本章讨论的修改就是指在船舶建造过程中发生的针对设计、图纸以及建造等进行的变动和修改。对船舶进行的修改通常是局部的,一般不会影响船舶特性和基本特征。[①] 在船舶建造过程中发生修改应当比较常见,相反在整个建造过程中没有任何修改的情形则不多见。相比较而言,海工设备建造发生的修改无论从修改的复杂程度还是修改所涉及的金额均远远大于普通商船建造中发生的修改。有的海工设备修改所产生的费用甚至超过合同价格。

6.2 　　从修改的原因来看可以将修改分为三种:船东提出的修改;船厂提出的修改以及规范和主管当局要求变更导致的修改。其中最为常见的应当是船东提出的修改。虽然船舶的建造规范代表了完整的船舶及其建造方式,但在船舶建造合同履行过程中,船东一般还会提出一些新的修改请求。无论是出于何种原因的修改从本质上来说都构成对船舶建造合同的变更,具体的变更可能包括对规格书、合同价格、合同交船日以及其他条款的变更。

II 船东的修改

船东修改的原因

6.3 　　船东是实际使用船舶的人,因此对船舶有自己独特的理解和要求。船东通过

[①] 有时也会有影响甚至改变船舶基本特征和功能的修改,此种修改实际上是船厂和船东对已经订立的船舶建造合同的变更,不是本章讨论的内容。

长期对船舶进行营运和管理会逐渐形成具有自己特色的营运和管理模式,这些营运和管理模式往往会对船舶提出特定的要求。同样的船舶在不同的船东手上所从事的营运也会有其独有的特征,这些营运特征同样也会对船舶建造提出特定的要求。这些特定的要求不仅涉及船舶的结构,而且还可能涉及船舶的机械和设备的特征。虽然船东对自己打算建造的船舶有自己独特的要求,但是绝大多数船舶建造合同均采用已定型的船型,不一定能满足船东的特殊要求。在这种情况下,船东若有特殊的要求,修改几乎是不可避免的。

6.4 船东的修改可以发生在船舶建造的整个过程之中,在收到船厂送审的图纸后,船东在审图时就可以对船厂的设计提出修改意见了,在那时提出修改请求无疑是最方便也是最经济的。在船东批准图纸且船厂正式开工后,船东的修改依然会发生。有时,相关工程或项目全部完成后船东依然会提出修改请求。除非是微小项目,凡是越接近完工的修改越有可能带来麻烦和费用。

6.5 船东提出修改的原因主要有以下几种:(1)船厂的设计不符合船东的特定要求和营运习惯;(2)船东因船级规范或国际公约的实施而作出的选择;(3)船东或船东的监造代表改变主意;(4)因船东监造代表的更换而导致的设计或建造要求的不同;(5)由于船东或船东监造代表的错误引起的修改。①

标准格式的规定

6.6 常用的船舶建造合同的标准格式都有关于船东修改的规定,但是相互存在着较大的差异,因此做一个简单的比较有助于对不同格式规定的理解。SAJ 格式关于船东修改的规定是:②

> The Specifications may be modified and/or changed by written agreement of the parties hereto, provided that such modifications and/or changes or an accumulation thereof will not, in the BUILDER's judgment, adversely affect the BUILDER's planning or program in relation to the BUILDER's other commitments, and provided, further, that the BUYER shall first agree, before such modifications and/or changes are carried out, to alterations in the Contract Price, the Delivery Date and other terms and conditions of this Contract and Specifications occasioned by or resulting from such modifications and/or changes.

---

① 这里的船东修改是以船厂的设计和建造符合合同和规格书要求为前提。
② Article V.1, para.1.

6.7　从上述规定来看,船东提出对规格书的修改应当是一种权利,但是此种权利是受限制的,这些限制包括:第一,船厂和船东应当订立书面协议对规格书进行修改;第二,船东提出的修改请求不影响船厂的其他工作,由于有"in the BUILDER's judgment"一句,因此是否影响船厂的其他工作应当由船厂作出判断。换言之,只要有合理的理由,船厂是可以拒绝船东提出的修改或变更规格书的请求的;第三,船东应先就修改引起的合同价格、合同交船日、规格书及其他船舶建造合同相关条款的变动表示接受。

6.8　一般说来,除非船东提出的修改请求确实会影响到船厂的其他建造项目的正常进行,或者是船厂技术能力所不可及的,船厂通常没有理由拒绝船东提出的修改请求。但是,一旦接受船东的修改请求将会影响船厂其他船舶建造的安排,船厂就应当谨慎考虑是否接受船东的修改请求,因为接受修改请求可能意味着船厂会面临在其他合同中的违约。

6.9　AWES 格式的修改条款与 SAJ 的有些许差异:①

The PURCHASER may request the CONTRACTOR in writing to make modifications to the Specifications and the CONTRACTOR will agree to carry out such modifications provided that such modifications or an accumulation of such modifications will not in the CONTRACTOR's judgment adversely affect the CONTRACTOR's planning or programme in relation to the CONTRACTOR's other commitments and provided that the CONTRACTOR and the PURCHASER fully agree expressly and in writing with 10 days from the dispatch of the CONTRACTOR's notification upon the (a) adjustment of price, (b) adjustment of Delivery Date, (c) adjustment of deadweight and/or grain/bale capacity, (d) adjustment of speed requirements and (e) any other adjustment of the CONTRACT and/or Specifications.

6.10　AWES 格式规定了船东修改的一个条件,即双方应当在船厂发出通知后的 10 天内就合同价格、合同交船日、载重吨或舱容、航速,以及合同和规格书的调整达成书面协议。AWES 格式关于调整船舶航速、载重吨或舱容等的规定显然是考虑到船东的修改请求有可能会对船舶建造合同已经约定的船舶特征及船厂已经作出的性能保证产生影响。

6.11　Norwegian 格式中关于船东修改的规定有如下内容:②

---

①　Article 3(a), para.1.
②　Article VI.1, para.1.

The work to be performed by the Builder under the Contract can be modified or changed by request from the Buyer provided that such modifications or changes will not adversely affect the Builder's other commitments, and provided further that the parties shall first agree to possible adjustment in Contract Price, the Delivery Date and such other terms and conditions occasioned by or resulting from such modification or change . . . .

6.12 很显然,在对船东修改作出规定时,Norwegian 格式与 SAJ 格式以及 AWES 格式并没有太大的差异。① 相比之下,NEWBUILDCON 格式关于船东修改的规定则与 SAJ 和 AWES 格式有比较明显的差异。NEWBUILDCON 格式规定的是:②

(a) The Buyer shall have the right at any time to request reasonable modifications or changes in the Specification and/or Plans and Drawings. The Buyer shall request such modifications and/or changes in writing, giving sufficient particulars, documentation and details fully to describe the modifications and/or changes requested.

(b) The Builder shall, as soon as possible after receipt of the written request for modifications or changes give the Buyer a written proposal of the consequences of implementing such modifications and/or changes. These consequences may include changes in the Contract Price, Delivery Date, capacity, draft, speed, fuel consumption, or any other provisions of this Contract. If in the Builder's reasonable judgment, such modifications and/or changes will adversely affect the Builder's planning or programme in relation to the Builder's other commitments, the Builder shall notify the Buyer that it declines to give such a proposal for the requested modifications and/or changes or part thereof.

(c) The Builder shall use reasonable efforts to minimise the extra costs, delay or other negative impact on the Vessel's capacity, performance or other factors caused by the Buyer's request. The Builder's proposal shall be reasonable for such work.

(d) On the basis of the Builder's proposal the Buyer may elect in writing to agree to the necessary adjustments to this Contract, in which case the Builder shall build the Vessel in accordance with this

---

① CSTC 关于船东修改的规定也与 SAJ 和 AWES 基本相似。
② Clause 24.

Condition so amended.

(e) If the Buyer does not accept the Builder's notice as provided in Clause 20(d)(Approvals) or if in the Buyer's opinion the Builder's proposal for modifications and/or changes under this Clause is unreasonable, the Buyer may, by giving notice to the Builder, order the Builder to proceed with the requested modifications and/or changes but the consequences of implementing such modifications and/or changes shall be decided in accordance with Clause 42 (Dispute Resolution).

(f) If the Buyer elects not to maintain the request for modifications and/or changes, the Buyer shall notify the Builder accordingly.

(g) If the Buyer does not respond within seven (7) running days after receipt of the Builder's notice in Sub-clause (b), the Buyer shall be deemed to have withdrawn the request for modifications and/or changes.

6.13　不难看出，NEWBUILDCON 格式的规定比较倾向于保护船东的利益，而且还可以看出 NEWBUILDCON 格式的起草参照了海洋工程合同中关于船东修改的相关规定。按照第 24(b) 条的规定，船厂有义务在收到船东的书面修改请求后向船东发出实施修改的建议，包括对合同价格以及合同交船日的调整。但是如果船厂认为船东的修改请求将对船厂的其他船舶建造带来不利影响的，船厂还是可以拒绝船东的修改请求的。在船厂提供了实施修改的建议后，船东可以按照第 24(d) 条的规定选择接受；也可以按照第 24(e) 条的规定拒绝接受船厂的建议。但即使船东拒绝船厂针对船东修改请求作出的建议，依然可以向船厂发出通知，要求船厂实施船东提出的修改，因此产生的争议适用合同的争议解决条款。船东提出的修改请求无论大小都构成对已经生效的船舶建造合同的变更，合同变更的一个基本原则是以合意为基础，即只有在合同当事人一致同意的情况下才能变更合同。然而按照上述规定，无论结果如何，船东可以单方面按照自己的意愿变更船舶建造合同和规格书。

修改的约定

6.14　按照 SAJ 格式的规定，船东提出的修改是否得以实施取决于船厂与船东的书面协议。① 此种书面协议并不一定是正式的由双方签署的书面协议，只要是有书

---

① Article V.1, para.1.

面文件显示的双方意思表示的一致即可,为此,SAJ 格式还针对书面协议作出了规定:①

> Such agreement may be effected by exchange of letters signed by the authorised representatives of the parties hereto or by cables confirmed by such letters manifesting agreements of the parties hereto which shall constitute amendments to this Contract and/or the Specifications.

根据上述规定,如果双方的协议采用信函交换方式订立,信函应当由获得授权代表的签署。然而在当今船舶建造实践中已经很少采用有签字的信函进行交流了,最为常见的是双方通过电子邮件交流。除非双方另有约定,只要来往的邮件能够证明双方关于修改的协议,即使没有签署也不应影响此种协议的有效性。实际上最为常见的做法是船东或其监造代表将船东的修改请求以电子邮件或口头的方式通知船厂,船厂若同意修改的,则大多会通过邮件告诉船东或其监造代表修改所需的费用及时间,并同时将修改后的图纸或设计等交由船东或其监造代表确认,船东或其监造代表接受船厂修改方案的则会予以确认。 6.15

在不少情况下,船厂往往会在船东确认之前就开始实施船东提出的修改,此种做法应当避免。在得到船东确认之前实施的任何工作都可能是白费的,甚至有可能给船厂带来麻烦。除非船舶建造合同另有约定,船厂并没有合同义务实施船东提出的修改请求,至少在船东确认船厂的方案和建议之前没有任何义务实施船东的修改请求。这一点 SAJ 格式已经作出了规定,而 AWES 格式则进一步明确了这一点:② 6.16

> The PURCHASER will keep modifications to Specifications to a minimum. The CONTRACTOR has the right to continue production on the basis of the Specifications until agreement has been reached as above stated.

与 SAJ 格式不同的是,AWES 格式没有关于双方应当签署协议的规定。这一特征应当比较符合当今船厂和船东实际进行联系的方式,因此只要能证明书面协议的存在,是否签字并不重要。CSTC 格式也有与此类似的规定:③ 6.17

---

① Article V.1, para.2.
② Article 3(a), para.2.
③ Article V.1.

... If due to whatever reasons, the parties hereto shall fail to agree on the adjustment of the Contract Price or extension of time of delivery or providing additional security to the SELLER or modification of any terms of this Contract which are necessitated by such modifications and/or changes, then the SELLER shall have no obligation to comply with the BUYER's request for any modifications and/or changes.

6.18 Norwegian 格式中关于船东修改的规定有如下内容：①

... Such agreement shall be effected either by way of exchanges of letters duly signed by authorised representatives of the parties, or by signed change order form, or by minutes of meeting or similar signed by authorised representatives of the parties, which shall constitute the necessary amendments to the Contract ....

6.19 相比之下，Norwegian 格式关于船东修改的规定比较复杂。上述第一段规定了几种双方就船东的修改达成协议的方式，包括由授权代表签署的信函、变更单、会议纪要以及其他经签署的文件。仅就双方关于船东的修改的协议以及协议的效力而言，上述规定并没有太大的意义。

费用的约定

6.20 确定因实施船东提出的修改请求而产生费用的最好的方式应当是双方通过信函或邮件予以确认。修改费用的确定其实也应当是船厂和船东关于船东修改达成的协议的重要内容之一。但是，在实践中依然有不少船厂在确定费用之前就已经开始甚至完成了船东的修改请求的情形。按照 Norwegian 格式的相关规定，如果双方在船东修改请求开始实施或实施完毕时仍然没有确定修改费用，则修改费用可以按照单价或预算价或船厂习惯做法予以确定：②

... Possible increase or decrease in the Contract Price shall be calculated in accordance with unit price (inclusive of administration costs) or budget prices if such prices are available, otherwise as per the Builder's customary price for such work.

6.21 船厂获得修改费用是以双方就修改达成协议为前提的，而上述规定只是为双

---

① Article VI.1, para.1.
② Article VI.1, para.1.

方就修改费用达成一致提供了指引而已。Norwegian 格式中还有如下内容：①

> If modifications or changes are made without such written agreement as aforesaid, or if the Builder fails to notify the Buyer in writing without undue delay that there are modifications or changes which will require an increase in the Contract Price, delayed delivery, changes in the Vessel's characteristics or other changes in the Contract, the Builder will not be entitled to any increase in the Contract Price, adjustment of Delivery Date or other adjustments, and the Contract will remain unchanged.

上述规定实际上包含了两种情形：一是船厂在没有协议的情况下完成了船东提出的修改；二是船厂未能及时通知修改将导致合同价格的上升、合同交船日的推迟以及船舶特征等的改变。这两种情形的后果是相同的，即船厂无权要求提高合同价格，无权要求推迟交船，也无权要求作出其他变动，船舶建造合同将不发生变化。就第一种情形而言，"are made"应当可以作"完成"解，即关于修改的书面协议在船厂完成了修改后依然没有成立或订立。若作此解，只要在船东提出的修改实施完毕之前，船厂都有机会设法和船东就修改达成书面协议。这一规定的意义在于船东在协议问题上掌握了主动。但是，"are made"似乎也可以作"are started to be made"，即已经开始实施但尚未完成。若按此解，一旦开始实施船东提出的修改请求，船厂便丧失了权利。 6.22

就第二种情形而言，"未能及时通知"一句中的"及时"（without undue delay）一词似乎比较费解。如果这里的"及时"是指船厂意识到船东提出的修改有可能涉及合同价格的变化，或合同交船日的延误，或船舶特征的改变等以后的及时，即在修改完成之前的及时，那么在第一种情形中对"are made"作出"完成"的解释也就没有意义了，因为一旦船厂没有及时通知船东修改可能带来的影响，船厂即丧失了获得修改费用和推迟交船日的权利。如果"及时"可以理解为在完成船东提出的修改请求之前的任何时候，那么在第一种情形中对"are made"作出"are started to be made"的解释并不会因此不成立。相反，把"are made"作为"完成"的解释倒是没有意义了，因为船厂在修改完成之前没有通知船东修改可能带来的影响已经使船厂丧失了获得修改费用和推迟交船日的权利了。 6.23

在上述情形下，船厂不能获得修改费用，也不能推迟交船日已成定局，但"合同保持不变"一句似乎意味着船东还能以船厂实施了船东提出的修改后船舶建造 6.24

---

① Article VI.1, para.2.

不符合合同或规格书要求为由提出索赔。因此，Norwegian 格式的上述规定对船厂来说应当是比较糟糕的。

获得修改费用的权利

6.25　　即使船舶建造合同没有明确约定船东的修改导致合同价格的调整，但船厂的权利并不因此丧失。*Vosper Thornycroft Ltd* v *Ministry of Defence*① 一案是一个比较典型的例子，在该案中，海军向原告船厂订造了一艘护卫舰，船舶建造合同的第 6 条规定：

> In the event of exceptional dislocation and delay arising during the construction of the vessel due to modifications ... or any other cause beyond the Contractors control, the effect thereof shall be assessed by mutual agreement between the Ministry and the Contractor, failing which the Ministry may pay for the vessel on an "actual cost" basis, subject to cost investigation by the Ministry, plus a fair and reasonable sum for profit.

6.26　　船舶由于非船厂的原因延误了交接，海军支付了 200 万英镑作为修改的成本和利润，但船厂另外要求索赔 400 万英镑。双方对如何确定船厂索赔数额产生了争议。船厂认为应当赋予"影响"一词简单的日常的含义，即是指"引起或产生某一结果或后果的事"。由于船舶在船厂多放置了两年三个月，船厂损失的是在这期间船厂通过建造船舶可以获得的利润，因此船厂可以获得此种利润的赔偿。海军则认为船厂获得额外建造款的权利是以双方达成协议为条件的，由于没有协议，船厂不能要求海军支付。海军还认为对"影响"的解释必须仅限于建造成本在船厂提供的基本成本基础上的增加。Ackner 法官接受了船厂对"影响"一词的解释，他说：②

> Moreover, since the restriction placed on damages recoverable for breach of contract is to ensure, as far as possible, that the innocent party should be placed, so far as money can do it, in the same position as he would have been had the contract been performed, I see nothing repugnant in a construction of this proviso which achieves the same effect. In all fairness, why should not the Ministry pay for the effects which have resulted naturally and reasonably from the dislocation and

---

① [1976] 1 Lloyd's Rep 58.
② [1976] 1 Lloyd's Rep 58 at 62.

delay which they have imposed upon the plaintiffs? Why should the plaintiffs be expected to bear the loss?

合理报酬

有些船舶建造合同没有针对船东的修改作出规定,或者合同虽规定因修改增加的费用由双方协商确定,但船厂和船东实际上并没有进行协商或虽经协商但没能达成一致。在这种情况下就会产生应当如何确定船厂可以获得的修改费用数额的问题,按照普通法的规定,这时应当适用"合理数额"原则。在 *Serck Controls Limited* v *Drake & Schull Engineering Limited* 一案中,Hicks 法官对"合理数额"原则的适用范围进行了说明,他说:①   6.27

> A *quantum meruit* claim may, however, arise in a wide variety of circumstances, across a spectrum which ranges at one end from an express contract to do work at an unquantified price, which expressly or by implication must then be a reasonable one, to work (at the other extreme) done by an uninvited intruder which nevertheless confers on the recipient a benefit which for some reason, such as estoppel or acquiescence, it is unjust for him to retain without making restitution to the provider.

合理不仅适用于没有合同的情形,同时也适用于有合同的情形。在 *ERDC Group Limited* v *Brunel University* 一案中,Humphrey Lloyd 法官进一步阐述了确定"合理数额"的方式,他说:②   6.28

> It has rightly been said that there are no hard and fast rules for the assessment of a *quantum meruit*. All the factors have to be considered. This is not a case in which there was no contract. In such circumstances the assessment of a *quantum meruit* is usually based on actual cost (which will include on and off site overheads, with in the latter case some estimates or extrapolations being required), provided that it was reasonable (which can frequently be checked by the use of standard rates and prices such as Spon) and was reasonably and not unnecessarily incurred, plus an appropriate addition for profit.

从上述两个判例可以看出,除非船舶建造合同另有明确约定或者船厂已明示   6.29

---

① 73 Con LR 100 at [34].
② [2006] EWHC 687 at [42].

放弃，作为原则，船厂应当有权获得因实施船东提出的修改而产生的费用。

修改费用的支付

6.30　SAJ 格式不仅规定在对技术规范进行修改时，船东应首先和船厂就费用问题以及合同条款的修改达成一致，而且还规定了因修改产生的费用应当在船东支付最后一期建造款时，即支付交船款时一并支付。①

6.31　AWES 格式有专门针对支付因修改而产生费用的规定：②

The sums due for modifications under Article 3 of this CONTRACT shall be paid as follows:
(i) 50% on the date of agreement for modifications under Paragraph(a) and(d) of Article 3 or for modifications under paragraph(c) of Article 3 when the Statement of the adjustment of price is made by the CONTRACTOR as the case may be.
(ii) 50% on the date of delivery of the VESSEL as part of the delivery instalment.

6.32　毫无疑问，AWES 格式的上述规定对船厂是有利的，尤其是在船东提出的修改涉及较大金额的情况下。因为船厂在与船东就修改达成协议之时就可以获得 50% 的修改费用，剩下的 50% 在交船时收取应当也不会给船厂带来太大的风险。

船东的修改和约定赔偿

6.33　船舶建造合同规定的约定赔偿是以合同规定的工作量为依据的，如果船东增加了工作量，合同交船日就不再约束船厂。船厂在合同交船日后交船，船东也没有获得约定赔偿的权利。在 *Dodd v Churton*③ 一案中，建造合同规定了完工日并且规定了承包商未能在完工日完成工作应当向雇主支付的约定赔偿。合同第 4 条规定，雇主可以变更工作，既可以增加工作，也可以减少工作。结果雇主增加了工作，从而导致承包商无法在约定的完工日完工。承包商要求雇主支付合同余款，而雇主则要求承包商支付约定赔偿。法院认为，由于雇主增加了工作，因此放弃了获得约定赔偿的权利。雇主不服判决并提起了上诉，上诉法院的 Lord Esher 说：④

---

① Article II.3(d).
② Article 7(d).
③ [1897] 1 QB 562.
④ [1897] 1 QB 562 at 566.

It was, no doubt, part of the original contract that the building owner should have a right to call upon the builder to do that extra work, and if he did give an order for it, the builder could not refuse to do it. The principle is laid down in *Comyns's Digest,* Condition L(6), that, where one party to a contract is prevented from performing it by the act of the other, he is not liable in law for that default; and, accordingly, a well recognised rule has been established in cases of this kind, beginning with *Holme v Guppy*, to the effect that, if the building owner has ordered extra work beyond that specified by the original contract which has necessarily increased the time requisite for finishing the work, he is thereby disentitled to claim the penalties for non-completion provided by the contract. The reason for that rule is that otherwise a most unreasonable burden would be imposed upon the contractor.

船东有时会在较晚时才向船厂提出修改的请求,但只要在合同交船日之前提出,合同交船日就不再约束船厂,船厂可以根据船东的修改要求主张顺延合同交船日。但有时船东提出修改请求时合同交船日已过,如果按照船舶建造合同的规定船厂已应支付约定赔偿,船东获得约定赔偿的权利则不会因其提出修改请求而受影响。在 *Balfour Beatty Building Ltd* v *Chestermount Properties Ltd*① 一案中,承包商未能在建设合同规定的完工日之前完成工作,雇主在完工日后又向承包商发出了变更要求。实际完工后,雇主要求承包商支付约定赔偿,但是承包商则认为由于雇主提出了变更要求,承包商就不再受时间约束,因此承包商无需支付任何约定赔偿。仲裁员认为在已经产生延误情况下延期应当是净延期,即有明确期限的延期。仲裁员的裁决得到法院的支持,Colman 法官认为除非延期的时间和延误的时间相等,否则承包商应当支付约定赔偿,他说:②

6.34

> It will be perfectly obvious that, unless the amount of time by which he postpones the completion date corresponds with the amount of delay time caused by the relevant event, the contractor will become potentially or actually liable for an amount of liquidated damages commensurate with a period which does *not* correspond with the amount of delay beyond the previously fixed completion date attributable to events of which he takes the risk under the contract. Having regard to the purpose of the completion date/adjustment of time/liquidated damages regime under the contract, it would need clear words to introduce alongside that

---

① (1933) 9 Const LR 117.
② See Powell-Smith & Furmston's *Building Contract Casebook* 4th edn, Blackwell 2006, p.399.

regime a requirement that the architect should depart from the requirement of co-extensiveness between (i) the period of postponement of the completion date, and (ii) the period of delay caused by the relevant event. No such words are present . . . .

合同交船日的顺延

6.35　经常发生的事是，不仅船东提出的修改请求造成船厂的额外成本或费用，即涉及到合同价格的调整，而且完成船东的修改也可能需要额外的时间，即涉及合同交船日的调整。这在实践中应当是比较常见的。然而，有不少船厂似乎只关心针对船东提出的修改收取费用，并没有对实施修改可能产生的合同交船日的顺延有足够的关注。其实，调整合同价格和调整合同交船日具有相同重要的作用，更何况所有修改费用的实际获得一般都是以船厂按时交付船舶为前提的。只有在船舶按时交接的情形下，船厂才可能获得修改费用。一旦船厂未能在约定的期间内向船东交付船舶，所有的修改成本或费用都将化为乌有。

6.36　因实施船东提出的修改而产生的额外时间通常构成可允许延误，即船厂可以根据具体天数顺延合同交船日。这对船厂来说无疑是有意义的，即使船厂可以在约定的最后期限内交船，也同样有助于船厂减少因延迟交船而需支付的约定赔偿的数额。然而并非所有的可允许延误都可以自动顺延合同交船日，船厂只有凭借那些实际上对船舶建造的关键路径产生影响的可允许延误才可以顺延合同交船日。① 与一般的可允许延误不同的是，一旦船厂和船东约定了因实施船东提出的修改而花费了时间，船厂就可以直接顺延合同交船日，无需证明此种修改是否实际上影响了船舶建造的关键路径。因为此种约定实际上就是对船舶建造合同规定的合同交船日作出了修改。

6.37　如果船厂在与船东就合同交船日顺延问题达成一致之前就已开始实施并完成了船东提出的修改请求，除非船舶建造合同另有明确约定或船厂已明示放弃了主张顺延合同交船日的权利，船厂应当依然有权主张合同交船日的顺延。只是在这种情况下船厂负有比较严格的举证之责，而且只有在证明了确实存在对船舶建造的关键路径实际造成影响的可允许延误后才可以顺延合同交船日。

---

① 关于关键路径请参见本书第10章第Ⅱ节。

不能顺延交船日的情形

如果船舶建造合同明确约定合同交船日是不能延期的,即使船东提出了修改的请求,船厂有可能依然无法推迟合同交船日。在 *Hull Central Dry Dock & Engineering Works Ltd v Ohlson Steamship Ltd*① 一案中,原告是船厂,被告是船东,双方订立了船舶修理合同,由船厂在 40 天内完成船舶的修理,如果船厂延迟完成船舶修理则应当支付罚金。此外,船舶修理合同还有如下规定: 6.38

> No extension of time will be allowed unless it is clearly and mutually agreed that extra repairs cannot be carried out concurrently with the contract work.

在船舶修理过程中,船东又增加一些新的修理项目,结果船厂未能在约定的 40 天内完成船舶的修理。Bailhache 法官认为,由于双方并没有就延期达成协议,因此船厂不能延长约定的修理时间,而应当支付约定的罚金,他说: 6.39

> This is a contract to do a particular work in a given time with a penalty clause if it is not done. Now if the contract contains nothing more than that, I understand the law to be this. That if in such circumstances the owner of a ship, or a person for whom a house is to be built, gives orders for extras, and if those orders will necessarily mean an extension of the time required to do the work either because they are given late or because the orders involve work of such a character that it could not be done in time, in either case, in the absence of any clause to the contrary, the penalty clause goes altogether. The contract then becomes a contract to do the whole of the work within a reasonable time; and if that were the position in this case the plaintiffs would be perfectly right.

顺延交船日的条件

如果船舶建造合同对船厂顺延合同交船日规定了条件,船厂只有在满足了规定的条件后才有权顺延合同交船日。在 *City Inn Ltd v Shepherd Construction Ltd*② 一案中,建设合同规定了完工日,但是工程未能在完工日或之前完成。双方对承包商是否可以主张延期发生了争议。建设合同第13.8.1条规定: 6.40

---

① (1924) 19 Ll L Rep 54.
② [2003] BLR 468.

Where, in the opinion of the Contractor, any instruction, or other item which, in the opinion of the Contractor, constitutes an instruction issued by the Architect, will require an adjustment to the Contract Sum and/or delay the Completion Date, the Contractor shall not execute such instruction (subject to Clause 13.8.4) unless he shall have first submitted to the Architect, in writing, within 10 working days ... details of:

1. initial estimate of the adjustment ....
2. initial estimate of the additional resources ....
3. initial estimate of the length of any extension of time to which he considers he is entitled under Clause 25 and the new Completion Date ....
4. initial estimate of the amount of any direct loss and/or expense to which he may be entitled ....

6.41　建设合同的第13.8.5条又规定：

If the Contractor fails to comply with any one or more of the provisions of Clause 13.8.1, where the Architect has not dispensed with such compliance under Clause 13.8.4, the Contractor shall not be entitled to any extension of time ....

6.42　雇主认为承包商无权顺延完工日，理由是承包商未能按照建设合同第13.8.1条的规定向雇主提供相关细节，因此无权顺延完工日。但是承包商认为自己有权顺延完工日，建设合同第13.8.5条因系惩罚条款而无效。苏格兰最高民事法院（Court of Session）外庭（Outer House）的Lord Ordinary[①]认为第13.8.1条规定的并不是承包商的一项选择权而是一项义务，承包商没有按照该条规定向雇主提供细节不仅使自己丧失了按照合同顺延完工日的权利，同时也剥夺了建筑师根据承包商提供的细节决定是否撤销其指示的机会。因此承包商的行为构成违约。Lord Ordinary还认为第13.8.5条并不是惩罚条款，承包商应当支付约定赔偿。

6.43　苏格兰最高民事法院内庭（Inner House）第二分庭（Second Division）虽然认为Lord Ordinary的判决是正确的，但是基于不同的理由。Clerk法官认为承包商并没有违约，因为第13.8条规定的并不是承包商的义务，而是权利。他说：

---

① 苏格兰最高民事法院分为内庭（Inner House）和外庭，内庭是外庭的上诉庭，外庭的独任法官均称为Lord Ordinary。

If the contractor receives such an instruction, he has to consider its likely effects, and in particular its likely effect on the duration of the building period. He may, for reasons of his own, decide to accept the instruction without resistance and hope that he will be able to complete the work, as varied by the instruction, within the building period. But if he wishes an extension of time, he must comply with the conditions precedent that cl.13.8 provides for in these specific circumstances(cf cl. 13.8.5). In particular, he must serve notice on the architect of his estimate of inter alia the probable cost .... But if the contractor fails to take the steps specified in cl.13.8.1, then unless the architect waives the requirements of the clause under cl.13.8.4, the contractor will not be entitled to an extension of time on account of that particular instruction.

修改造成延误

6.44　即使船东向船厂提出了修改的请求，除非另有约定，船厂并非当然可以顺延合同交船日。船厂只有在船东的修改请求确实影响了船舶建造以及交船安排情况下才可以顺延合同交船日。如果关键路径因船东的修改请求受到影响，即使双方没有就延误的具体时间作出约定，船厂依然可以顺延合同交船日。高院的 Hamblen 法官在 *Adyard Abu Dhabi v SD Marine Services* 一案中对此予以了说明，他说：①

If, for example, a two day variation was instructed the day before the sea trials date, and was a variation of a type which would need to be completed before sea trials, then, if there was an extension of time clause [shipyard] would be entitled to a one day extension of time, or, if there was no such clause, [shipyard] could rely on the prevention principle.

减少工作量的修改请求

6.45　虽然船东提出的修改请求大多会导致工作量和成本的增加，而且还有可能会影响到船舶是否可以在合同交船日交接，但是船东的修改请求也可能是放弃或取消某一已经约定的项目，从而导致船厂合同工作量的减少。除非能够证明船东的修改请求将给船厂的其他建造项目带来不利的影响，否则船厂应当没有理由拒绝

---

① [2011] EWHC 848 at [259].

船东减少工作量的修改请求。

6.46　　船东提出减少工作量修改请求可能产生的另一个问题是：船东有没有权利要求对合同价格作出相应的调整。在船舶建造合同没有对此作出约定时，合同价格似乎没有减少的理由。首先，船舶建造合同采用的是固定价格，其基本特征是合同价格不因发生影响合同价格的因素而受影响，船厂承担了成本价格或汇率差可能带来的风险；其次，减少工作量的请求是船东单方面提出的，构成对船舶建造合同的变更，除非有相反的表示，船厂同意此种变更并不意味着同意调整合同价格；最后，船东减少工作量未必一定产生船厂建造成本的节省。在已经周密安排的情况下，工期的提前同样有可能对船舶建造构成一种不利的影响。因为船厂可能面临比较尴尬的局面，即完成其他工作时间不够，而维持原计划又势必造成时间的浪费。

6.47　　在有合同约定情况下，船东是否可以凭借工作量减少主张价格调整则是如何解释合同的问题。在采用 SAJ 格式情形下船东应当有机会主张合同价格的调整。SAJ 格式的关于合同价格的条款有如下规定：①

　　　　[Contract Price] shall be subject to upward or downward adjustment, if any, as hereinafter set forth in this Contract.

6.48　　根据上述规定，合同价格是可以按照合同的规定进行上下调整的，而 SAJ 格式关于修改的条款则有如下规定：②

　　　　... and provided, further, that the BUYER shall first agree, before such modifications and/or changes are carried out, to alterations in the Contract Price ....

6.49　　虽然上述规定明显是指合同价格的增加，但"变动"显然并不仅仅是指上升或增加，而同样包括"下降"和"减少"。因此，船东是否有机会主张合同价格的减少取决于双方在船东减少船厂合同工作量时的约定。

关于修改的争议

6.50　　船厂和船东不仅会因为船东提出的修改涉及合同价格的调整或合同交船日的调整而发生争议，而且还可能针对船东请求是否构成对船舶建造合同规定的修改产生争议。在审图阶段就可能发生此种争议，例如：船东对船厂送审的图纸提

---

① Article II.1.
② Article V.1, para.1.

出了修改意见,在船东看来之所以提出修改意见是因为船厂送审的图纸不符合合同或规格书的要求,但船厂则可能认为自己的图纸符合合同和规格书的要求,船东提出的修改意见构成了对船舶建造合同的修改。在建造阶段,船东和船厂同样有可能因船厂的建造是否符合合同或规格书发生类似的争议。此种争议多半是由于双方对合同或规格书的规定在理解上存在分歧,有时船厂的理解是对的,有时船东的理解是对的。有时甚至会发生双方的理解都对的情形,因为合同和规格书可能由于表述问题存在两种甚至两种以上正确的理解。

虽然不少船舶建造合同都规定将技术争议提交船级社解决,但船级社一般都不愿意牵涉到船厂与船东的争议之中。而且,如果合同或规格书的规定确实可以有两种或甚至两种以上解释的,船级社的意见其实也解决不了船厂和船东的争议。在这种情况下,最好的方法应当是由当事人双方通过协商解决。协商不成的,也可以约定在不影响船舶建造的前提下指定仲裁员就特定问题作出快速仲裁。 6.51

Ⅲ 船厂提出的修改

虽然船厂也可以提出修改的请求,但在实践中船厂提出修改请求的情形并不多见。按照 SAJ 格式的规定,船厂可以改进生产方式等理由提出对规格书进行修改的请求:① 6.52

> The BUILDER may make minor changes to the Specifications, if found necessary for introduction of improved production methods or otherwise, provided that the BUILDER shall first obtain the BUYER's approval which shall not be unreasonably withheld.

虽然船厂可以提出修改的请求,但与船东的修改应当是不同的。"微小"一词已经决定了船厂提出的修改的性质,即使是为了实施新设计、使用新材料或采用新的工艺,此种修改也只能是微小的。此外,船厂提出修改应当事先征得船东的同意。虽然上述规定还使用了"否则"一字,但是船厂因其他原因修改规格书的可能性应当不是很大。 6.53

AWES 格式的规定与 SAJ 格式有所不同,AWES 格式规定:② 6.54

---

① Article V.1 para.3.
② Article 3(b).

The CONTRACTOR may seek the PURCHASER's approval to make changes to the Specifications. These proposed changes will be dealt with in the manner as described in paragraph(a)of this Article.

The CONTRACTOR is entitled to make minor changes to the Specifications and drawings, not affecting the VESSEL's performance characteristics if such changes are found necessary to suit the Shipyard's local conditions and facilities, the availability of materials and equipment, the introduction of improved production methods or otherwise.

6.55　　AWES 格式将船厂的修改分成了两种。上述第一段规定的是需要事先获得船东同意的船厂修改,这些修改并不以"微小"为条件。第二段规定的才是 SAJ 格式中关于船厂修改的内容。这种修改似乎是无需事先得到船东同意的,但应当符合两个条件:第一,修改应当是微小的;第二,修改不影响船舶性能特征。至于船厂提出此种修改的原因则多于 SAJ 格式的规定,包括为了适应当地条件和设施、材料和设备的特征以及新的生产方式引入等。在满足上述条件的情况下,船厂可以修改规格书和图纸。即使船舶建造合同没有要求船厂提出的修改应事先征得船东的同意,但是在实践中这种做法显然是不值得提倡的。一旦船厂确有修改规格书或图纸的需要,比较妥当的做法依然是设法事先征得船东的书面同意。①

6.56　　Norwegian 格式中关于船厂修改的规定与 AWES 格式的规定的第二段相似,只是增加了船厂应当事先征得船东同意的内容。② NEWBUILDCON 格式关于船厂的修改有如下规定:③

> The Builder shall have the right to make minor modifications and/or changes to the Specification and/or plans if so required by virtue of the Builder's local conditions or facilities, the availability of materials and equipment, the introduction of improved methods or for any other reason of a similar nature provided that the Builder shall first obtain the Buyer's written approval, which shall not be unreasonably withheld or delayed.
>
> Such modifications and/or changes shall satisfy the requirements of the Classification Society and the Regulatory Authorities and shall not

---

① CSTC 似乎没有关于船厂修改的内容。
② Article VI.1, para.3.
③ Clause 25.

relieve the Builder from its obligation to otherwise deliver the Vessel in accordance with this Contract. Any savings obtained shall be credited to the Buyer and the Buyer shall not be obliged to pay any extra for, or suffer any delay in delivery or other adverse consequences of, such modification and/or changes.

6.57　NEWBUILDCON 格式的规定与 Norwegian 格式的规定基本相同,只是增加了一些新的内容。首先,船厂的修改必须符合船级社及主管当局的规定;其次,船厂的修改并不解除其按照船舶建造合同交船的义务;最后,修改导致成本或费用增加的由船厂负担,若有节省的则归船东所有。第一和第二的两项规定应当是不言自明的。

Ⅳ　船级规范等变更导致的修改

概述

6.58　由于船舶的设计和建造都必须符合船级社的船级规范以及主管当局规定的要求,因此船级社的船级规范或主管当局的要求的变化势必影响在建船舶的建造。船级社规范或主管当局要求的变化可能导致在建船舶的设计或建造发生修改,此种修改是船舶建造合同当事人之外的原因引起的。船级社规范是指船级社针对船舶入级、维持、海上安全和环境保护等的规定、规则和要求;而这里的"主管当局"是指国际组织、船旗国以及与船舶营运有关的港口国。主管当局要求的变化是指新的国际公约的通过、现有的国际公约的修订、船旗国针对船舶的法律、法令,条例等的变化。国际海事组织的《船舶专用海水压载舱及散货船双舷侧处所保护涂层性能标准规则》就是一个比较典型的例子。

6.59　船级社规范或主管当局要求在船舶建造过程中发生变化是比较正常的,但船级社规范和主管当局要求的变化大都有一个特征,即新规范或新要求的通过或颁布离实际实施往往有一个时间段。新的规定或新的要求一般从船东的自愿遵循开始慢慢走向强制实施。换言之,在第一阶段新规定和新要求往往是选择性的,由船东作出是否遵循的决定。但到了第二阶段,新规定或新要求的遵循就不再是选择性的,而是强制性的。船舶是否符合新规定或新要求将直接影响到船舶是否可以获得航行证书和船级证书。船舶建造合同规定的船舶的设计和建造符合船级社规范的既包括在船舶建造合同订立之时已经开始生效实施的规定和要求,同时也包括在船舶交接时已经开始生效实施的规定和要求。①

船厂的义务和权利

6.60　SAJ 格式有如下关于船级社规范或主管当局要求变化的规定:②

In the event that, after the date of this Contract, any requirements as to class, or as to rules and regulations to which the construction of the VESSEL is required to conform are altered or changed by the Classification Society or the other regulatory bodies authorised to make such alterations or changes, the following provisions shall apply.

(a) If such alternations or changes are compulsory for the VESSEL, either of the parties hereto, upon receipt of such information from the Classification Society or such other regulatory bodies, shall promptly transmit the same to the other in writing, and the BUILDER shall thereupon incorporate such alterations or changes into the construction of the VESSEL, provided that the BUYER shall first agree to adjustments required by the BUILDER in the Contract Price, the Delivery Date and other terms and conditions of this Contract and the Specifications occasioned by or resulting from such alterations or changes.

(b) If such alterations or changes are not compulsory for the VESSEL, but the BUYER desires to incorporate such alterations or changes into the construction of the VESSEL, then the BUYER shall notify the BUILDER of such intention. The BUILDER may accept such alterations or changes, provided that such alterations or changes will not, in the judgment of the BUILDER, adversely affect the BUILDER's planning or program in relation to the Builder's other commitments, and provided, further, that the BUYER shall first agree to adjustments required by the BUILDER in the Contract Price, the Delivery Date and other terms and conditions of this Contract and the Specifications occasioned by or resulting from such alterations or changes.

6.61　上述规定区分了两种情形，即新规定或新要求强制适用于和非强制适用于在建船舶的情形。新规定或新要求强制适用于在建船舶的，无论是船厂还是船东均有义务保证船舶符合新规定和新要求。即使双方尚未就因船舶符合新规定或新

---

① SAJ, Article I.3.
② Article V.2, para.1.

要求而产生的成本或费用以及交船日的调整达成一致,船厂也必须按照新规定或新要求完成船舶的建造。船厂也不能以新规定或新要求会给其他建造项目带来不利影响为由拒绝。即使船东不愿意适用新规定或新要求,船厂也不能按照船东的意愿,即按照原来的规定和要求完成船舶建造,否则船厂就承担了到时因不符合新规定或新要求而无法获得船舶航行证书或船级证书的风险。如果双方无法就合同价格及合同交船日的调整达成协议,船厂也应当搁置争议,按新规定或新要求继续船舶的建造。作为原则,船东应当承担因此引起的合理的成本或费用的增加。

6.62 在船级社规范或主管当局的新要求尚未强制实施的情形下,船厂应当根据船东的意愿行事。如果船东不打算对在建船舶适用新规定或新要求,船厂就应当按照已经约定的合同和规格书的规定继续船舶的建造。如果船东决定对在建船舶适用新规定或新要求,这其实构成了船东对合同的修改,对于这种修改则应当适用船舶建造合同中关于船东修改的规定。从上述规定可以看出,船东的此种请求同样是以不影响船厂其他建造项目为条件。在这个问题上,NEWBUILDCON 格式则明确规定应当适用合同关于船东修改的规定:①

> If such changes are not compulsory but the Buyer requires the changes to be incorporated, Clause 24(Modifications and Changes) shall apply.

6.63 应当注意的一个问题是,根据上述 SAJ 格式规定中的"after the date of this Contract"应当是指船级社规范或主管当局要求的变化发生在船舶建造合同订立之后的情形。而"date of this Contract"也应当解释为船厂和船东签署船舶建造合同的日期,而不是双方约定的合同日期。也就是说,在船舶建造合同订立之时已经存在的,但尚未生效或实施的船级社规范或主管当局要求不受上述规定的影响。假设船级社某一规定在船舶建造合同订立时已经存在,但尚未生效或实施,而是在船舶建造合同约定的交船日或之前就已开始强制实施了,船舶就应当符合该规定,合同中关于船级社规范变化的规定并不适用于此种情形。在这个问题上,Norwegian 格式作出了相应的规定:②

> If, after the Date of Contract, there are any changes in the rules, regulations and requirements(including official changed application of the rules) of Class or Regulatory Bodies, the following shall apply:

---

① Clause 26(c).
② Article VI.2.

(a) The Builder shall as soon as possible notify the Buyer thereof, and the Builder shall be obliged – except as otherwise agreed – to carry out the required changes in accordance with the provisions set out below, provided always that any changes in such rules, regulations or requirements which are published on or before the Date of Contract, and which apply mandatory to the Vessel on or before the Contract Delivery Date shall not give to the Builder a right to claim any adjustments of the price, delivery date or other contract terms.

6.64 上述规定明确了凡是在船舶建造合同订立之时已经公布的,以及在船舶建造合同规定的交船日之前强制适用于船舶的船级社规范或主管当局的规定或要求,船厂不仅有义务执行,而且不能主张任何的合同价格调整、合同交船日调整以及其他任何合同条款的调整。这里的"Date of Contract"同样是指船厂和船东订立船舶建造合同的日期,而不是船舶建造合同使用的日期。

6.65 因实施新规定或新要求而产生的额外的建造时间应当视为可允许延误。对此 AWES 格式作出了明确的规定:①

... Any such adjustment of the Delivery Date shall constitute Permissible Delay.

6.66 而且,AWES 格式还规定因考虑和解释新规定或新要求而产生的时间也同样视为可允许延误:②

The adjustment of the Delivery Date shall include any adjustment needed by reason of delay caused by the interpretation or consideration of modifications, deletions or addition.

船厂继续履行合同的义务

6.67 NEWBUILDCON 格式关于船级社规范或主管当局要求改变而引起的修改有如下规定:③

If such changes will be compulsory for the Vessel at the time of delivery, the Builder shall, unless the Buyer at its sole discretion seeks and obtains a waiver from the Classification Society or Regulatory

---

① Article 3(c), para.1.
② Article 3(c), para.2.
③ Clause 26(b).

Authorities (as appropriate), incorporate such modifications and/or changes into the construction of the Vessel. The Parties shall endeavour to agree on such adjustments to the Contract Price, Delivery Date or other Contract terms as are a direct consequence and the matter shall be decided in accordance with Clause 42(Dispute Resolution).

在新规定或新要求强制实施情况下,船东可能依然希望从船级社或主管当局获得豁免,或者船厂和船东无法就合同价格和合同交船日的调整达成协议,船厂可能不得不暂时中止船舶建造。然而,船厂继续建造船舶的合同义务并不会因此而免除,除非另有明确的约定,否则任何时间浪费都可能由船厂来承担。在 Adyard Abu Dhabi v SD Marine Services① 一案中,船舶建造合同第V.2.1条有如下规定: 6.68

(a) In the event that, after the Effective Date of the Contract, any requirements as to class, or as to rules and regulations to which the construction of the Vessel is required to conform are altered or changed by the Classification Society or the other regulatory bodies authorized to make such alterations or changes, the following provisions shall apply:
...
(b) if such alterations or changes are compulsory for the Vessel, the Builder, unless otherwise instructed by the Buyer, shall thereupon incorporate such alterations or changes into the construction of the Vessel, provided that the Buyer shall first agree to reasonable adjustments required by the Builder in the Contract Price, Delivery Date and other terms and conditions of this Contract and the Specifications occasioned by or resulting from such alterations or changes.
(c) ...

双方的争议是船东是否可以船舶未按时试航为由解除船舶建造合同。船厂认为船东无权解约,因为船舶无法按时试航的原因是船东提出了各种英国海事与海岸警卫署颁布的新设计。而船东则认为所谓的新设计并不是合同规定的修改。船厂认为,按照第 V.2.1(b)条的规定,船东可以选择先同意船厂因变更或改变而提出的关于合同价格、交船日以及其他条款和规格书的调整,船东也可以作出其他指示,否则船厂就无法继续船舶的建造。因为船厂按照原来的规格书建造将构成违约,而按照新规定建造船舶则没有船东的指示,且双方没 6.69

---
① [2011] EWHC 848(Comm) at [242].

有就合同价格等条款的调整达成一致。船东则认为,在双方未能就合同价格以及其他合同条款的调整达成一致的情况下,船厂并不能因此停止建造,因为船厂建造船舶的合同义务依然存在。在这种情况下,船厂可以选择实施新规定或新要求,而保留要求延期交船或增加合同价格的权利;船厂同样也可以选择不实施新规定或新要求。

6.70　　高院的 Hamblen 法官认为,该船舶建造合同起草得不够好,存在歧义,但是在合同有歧义时,法院倾向于采纳有利于合同继续履行的解释,即船东的解释,他说:①

> Having carefully considered the parties' arguments on construction it has to be acknowledged that the contract is not particularly well drafted and that there is a degree of ambiguity. However, I have no doubt that the construction advanced by [shipowner] is to be preferred for the reasons given by it and in particular:
> (1) It involved construing the contract as a whole giving effect to its provisions in a complementary and coherent manner.
> (2) It avoids the unsatisfactory consequence of the parties being in a contractual "limbo".
> (3) It is inherently unlikely that the parties would have intended there to be such a "limbo", particularly in an obviously foreseeable situation such as a failure to agree an adjustment.

建造合同的倒签

6.71　　船舶建造合同"倒签"泛指船厂和船东在签署船舶建造合同时使用实际签署日以前的日期作为合同日期,但这里则特指船厂和船东为了避免新的船级规范或主管当局的规定或要求的适用而采用相关规范开始适用之前的日期。在实践中这种情况时有发生,较为典型的可能是针对保护涂层性能标准适用的"倒签"。

保护涂层性能标准

6.72　　所谓的保护涂层性能标准是指所有类型船舶专用海水压载舱及散货船双舷侧处所保护涂层性能标准。国际海事组织于 2006 年 12 月 8 日通过了 MSC.215(82)号决议,对保护涂层性能标准作出了规定,旨在解决由于保护涂层失效以及

---

① [2011] EWHC 848(Comm) at [255].

由此产生的未受保护的钢板快速腐蚀等情形导致海水压载舱的整体结构遭受破坏的问题。根据修订后的1974年《国际海上人命安全公约》的规定,保护涂层性能标准适用于2008年7月1日或之后签订的船舶建造合同建造,或在没有船舶建造合同情况下于2009年1月1日之后铺放龙骨或处于类似建造阶段的,或在2012年7月1日之后交付的,不小于500总吨的所有类型船舶专用海水压载舱以及船长不小于150米的散货船双舷侧处所。①

国际船级社协会制定的分别适用于油船和散货船的《共同结构规范》也采纳了保护涂层性能标准,并作为船舶入级的强制性要求。《共同结构规范》适用于2006年12月8日或之后签订船舶建造合同建造的船长90米或以上散货船以及船长150米或以上的双壳油船,因此船级社通过《共同结构规范》的规定提前适用了保护涂层性能标准。由于国际船级社协会的《共同结构规范》是强制性的,因此船舶要想在国际船级社协会成员船级社入级就必须符合保护涂层性能标准。 6.73

倒签合同的性质

在《国际海上人命安全公约》和国际船级社协会的《共同结构规范》共同适用保护涂层性能标准的情形下,2006年12月8日以前订立的船舶建造合同建造的船舶无须符合保护涂层性能标准,在2006年12月8日以后订立的船舶建造合同建造的船舶都必须符合保护涂层性能标准。② 在实践中不少船舶建造合同虽然是在2006年12月8日之后签署的,但为了规避保护涂层性能标准的适用,船舶建造合同都选择了2006年12月8日之前的日期作为合同日期。有些甚至是在2008年7月1日之后签署的船舶建造合同也使用了2006年12月8日之前的日期作为合同日期。 6.74

倒签船舶建造合同或者使用2006年12月8日之前的日期作为船舶建造合同的日期并不能避免《共同结构规范》和《国际海上人命安全公约》的适用,因为无论是《共同结构规范》还是《国际海上人命安全公约》规定的均为船舶建造合同订立的日期,而不是船舶建造合同使用的合同日期。实际上国际船级社协会已经对船舶建造合同的日期作出了定义:③ 6.75

---

① SOLAS Chapter II, Part A-1, Regulation 3-2.
② 虽然从理论上来说,由于共同结构规范是国际船级社协会的规定,适用于该协会的成员船级社,但差不多90%以上的船队均在国际船级社协会成员船级社入级。而且,即使非国际船级社协会成员船级社对保护涂层性能标准不作要求,船舶在实际营运中同样会遇到各种障碍。
③ IACS Procedural Requirement 2004/Rev.4 2007 No.29.

The date of "contract for construction" of a vessel is the date on which the contract to build the vessel is signed between the prospective owner and the shipbuilder . . . .

公共政策

6.76 合同日期应当是合同当事人的一个选择,法律并没有强制当事人采用签约当天作为合同的日期。然而,当事人的这一选择无疑应当合法且符合最基本的公共政策的要求。如果当事人的选择带有非法的目的,就将违反公共政策,法院就会认定该合同不可执行。① 在 *Scott v Brown Doering McNab & Co*② 一案中,几个人为了招引他人购买一家公司的股份而签订了一份购买该公司股份的协议,从而造成该公司股份确有市场的假象。法院认为该协议是非法的,因而是无法执行的。Lindley 法官说:③

> *Ex turpi causa non oritur actio.* This old and well-known legal maxim is founded in good sense, and expresses a clear and well-recognised legal principle, which is not confined to indictable offences. No Court ought to enforce an illegal contract or allow itself to be made the instrument of enforcing obligations alleged to arise out of a contract or transaction which is illegal, if the illegality is duly brought to the notice of the Court, and if the person invoking the aid of the Court is himself implicated in the illegality.

6.77 Smith 法官也说:④

> If two or more persons agree to cheat and defraud others by means of deceit and fraud, there can be no doubt that each and all are indictable for a criminal conspiracy at common law. It has been held that it is a criminal conspiracy for two or more to agree by false rumours to endeavour to raise the price of the public funds on a particular day: *Bex v Berenger*(3 M&S 67) It has also been held in *Beg v Aspinall*(1 QBD 730) that an agreement by two or more to cheat and defraud by means of false pretences those who might buy shares in a company was an indictable conspiracy. False pretences here do not mean such false

---

① 参见本书第 4 章,第 4.9 – 4.11 段。
② [1892] 2 QB 724.
③ [1892] 2 QB 724 at 733.
④ [1892] 2 QB 724 at 728.

pretences as would support an indictment for obtaining money or goods by false pretences.

在 Alexander v Rayson① 一案中，被告同意从原告处租入一套房，租金是每年 1,200 英镑。该数额还包括原告的一些其他服务。原告向被告提供了两套文件，一套是房屋以及其他服务的租约，租金是每年 450 英镑；另一套则是原告提供其他服务的协议，合同价格为每年 750 英镑。除了一台冰箱外，协议规定的其他服务和租约规定的其他服务基本上是相同的。每年 1,200 英镑的租金按季支付。后来被告终止了租金的支付，理由是原告没有按照约定履行其义务。原告起诉要求被告支付租金。被告认为该协议因违反公共政策而不可执行，因为原告以较低的租金欺骗了当地政府。一审法院认为协议并没有违反公共政策。但上诉法院则认为协议违反了公共政策，因而是不能执行的。上诉法院的 Scott 法官说：②

6.78

> It is settled law that an agreement to do an act that is illegal or immoral or contrary to public policy, or to do any act for a consideration that is illegal, immoral or contrary to public policy, is unlawful and therefore void. But it often happens that an agreement which in itself is not unlawful is made with the intention of one or both parties to make use of the subject matter for an unlawful purpose, that is to say a purpose that is illegal, immoral or contrary to public policy. The most common instance of this is an agreement for the sale or letting of an object, where the agreement is unobjectionable on the face of it, but where the intention of both or one of the parties is that the object shall be used by the purchaser or hirer for an unlawful purpose. In such a case any party to the agreement who had the unlawful intention is precluded from suing upon it. *Ex turpi causa non oritur actio*. The action does not lie because the Court will not lend its help to such a plaintiff. Many instances of this are to be found in the books.

倒签合同的影响

为了规避保护涂层性能标准的适用而倒签船舶建造合同的做法有可能构成欺诈，欺诈的对象包括：船旗国当局、港口国当局、相关航运当事人以及船级社。如果船旗国知道船舶建造合同是在保护涂层性能标准开始实施后订立的，而船舶

6.79

---

① [1936] 1 KB 169.
② [1936] 1 KB 169 at 177.

建造并不符合保护涂层性能标准，就不会为船舶颁发相关的航行证书。船厂和船东倒签船舶建造合同的行为也形成了对有关主管当局的欺骗，因为在保护涂层性能标准强制实施后，建造的船舶不符合保护涂层性能标准的几乎是无法投入国际航运经营，船舶挂靠港所在国的主管当局有权力同时也有职责禁止此类船舶的营运。遭受船厂和船东倒签船舶建造合同的行为欺诈的还有航运界相关当事人，包括保险人、船舶的经营人和承租人等。这些相关当事人都是以船舶符合《共同结构规范》和《国际海上人命安全公约》规定为前提的，而实际上船舶并不符合相关的规定。虽然船级社也可能成为船厂和船东的欺诈对象，但与前述几个对象相比，船级社应当有机会知道船舶建造合同的真实签署日期，尤其是针对 2008 年 7 月 1 日以后签署的船舶建造合同。因为船舶的开工、采购乃至合同价格等还是能够反映船舶建造合同确切的签署日期的。

6.80　　综上，为了规避相关国际公约或船级规范的适用而倒签船舶建造合同的行为构成对公共政策的违反，因而是非法的，船舶建造合同也因此是不可执行的。由于此种欺骗是由船厂和船东共同实施的，因此有可能构成共谋。

V　材料的替代

6.81　　材料的替代是指双方约定的供应商无法提供或无法及时提供船舶建造合同或规格书规定的材料，船厂采用其他材料替代约定材料的情形。材料的替代从本质上说与前面提及的修改应当是不同的。虽然合同或规格书的修改同样有可能导致材料的更换，而材料的替代则未必会导致合同或规格书的修改。

6.82　　SAJ 格式关于材料的替代有如下规定：①

> In the event that any of the materials required by the Specifications or otherwise under this Contract of the VESSEL cannot be procured in time or are in short supply to maintain the Delivery Date of the VESSEL, the BUILDER may, provided that the BUYER shall so agree in writing supply other materials capable of meeting the requirements of the Classification Society and of the rules, regulations and requirements with which the construction of the VESSEL must comply. Any agreement as to such substitution of materials shall be effected in the manner provided in Paragraph 1 of this Article, and shall, likewise,

---

① Article VI.3.

include alterations in the Contract Price and other terms and conditions of this Contract occasioned by or resulting from such substitution.

从上述规定来看,材料的替代是由于无法采购而造成的。但是在实践中发生使用替代材料的可能性应当不会太大。船厂和船东约定的厂商表通常会针对同一材料或设备列出两个或两个以上的供应商。除非是极为特殊的材料,否则船厂无法采购到的可能性很小。按照上述规定,船厂使用替代材料应当以船东同意为条件。如果船厂使用的替代材料同样符合船级社规范和船旗国规定的,船东应当没有理由拒绝材料的替代。① 另外,"材料"一词似乎并不应当包括"机械"和"设备"。若确如此,所谓的"材料"其实主要就是指钢板了。在船舶建造国发生钢板短缺而必须进口的可能性应当不会太大。 6.83

Norwegian 格式关于材料替代的规定中有船东不能不合理地拒绝船厂使用替代材料的内容:② 6.84

If any of the materials required by the Specifications or the Maker's List cannot be procured in time or are in short supply, the Builder may, in order to maintain the Delivery Date and subject to the Buyer's approval, which shall not unreasonably be withheld and which shall be provided without under delay, supply other materials capable of meeting the requirements of the Classification Society or Regulatory Bodies. No extra charges shall be made to the Buyer and except that any savings shall be credited to the Buyer, the Contract shall remain unaltered.

关于船东不能不合理拒绝船厂使用替代材料且应当及时同意的规定有其合理性。与 SAJ 格式不同,Norwegian 格式还规定,替代材料的采购成本若高于原采购成本的由船厂承担;替代材料的采购成本若低于原采购承担的,节省的费用则归船东所有。这一规定可能未必合理,至少有明显的倾向性。虽然船舶建造合同的价格在某种程度上反映了材料的成本,但是船舶建造合同的价格是针对符合合同以及规格书要求的船舶。为此,船厂承担了成本等于或甚至高于合同价格的风险。因此,只要船舶符合合同和规格书规定的要求,任何合同价格的降低都缺乏正当理由。 6.85

NEWBUILDCON 格式没有专门针对材料替代的规定,但是该格式把材料的 6.86

---

① 船厂若无法采购到合同或规格书规定的材料甚至有可能构成不可抗力事件,因为按照 SAJ 的规定,"材料短缺"也是不可抗力事件之一,见 Article VIII.1。
② Article VI.3.

替代视为船厂提出的修改的原因之一,与其他导致船厂提出修改的原因一起作出了规定。①

> The Builder shall have the right to make minor modifications and/or changes to the Specification and/or plans if so required by virtue of the Builder's local conditions or facilities, the availability of materials and equipment, the introduction of improved methods or for any other reason of a similar nature provided that the Builder shall first obtain the Buyer's written approval, which shall not be unreasonably withheld or delayed.

6.87 如前所述,材料的替代未必引起船舶建造合同或规格书的变动或修改。然而上述规定第一段提及的船东不应不合理拒绝其实是针对船厂提出的修改规格书或图纸请求的,换言之,上述规定应当不适用于不涉及规格书或图纸修改的材料的替代。另外,与 Norwegian 格式一样,NEWBUILDCON 格式也规定了额外采购成本由船厂负担,而船东则可以享有任何采购成本的节省。

VI 修改费用的支付

6.88 通常情况下,因修改而产生或减少的费用往往由船东在支付最后一期建造款时结算。如果应当由船东支付的,船东在支付最后一期建造款时一并支付;如果应当扣减的,也由船东在支付最后一期建造款时予以扣减。针对因修改产生或减少费用的结算,NEWBUILDCON 格式有如下规定:②

> The sums due or refundable as a result of modifications and changes, and changes in Rules and Regulations under Clause 24 (Modifications and Changes) and Clause 26 (Changes in Rules and Regulations) shall be added to or deducted from the Final Instalment.

6.89 与此相比,AWES 格式的规定则似乎更有利于船厂,该格式的规定是:③

> The adjustments of price made under paragraphs (a), (b) and (c) above shall be paid by the PURCHASER in accordance with paragraph (d) of Article 7 in so far as they cause an increase in the price. If the

---

① Clause 25, para.1.
② Clause 15(b)(i).
③ Article 3(d).

adjustments cause a reduction in price such adjustment shall be credited by the CONTRACTOR to the PURCHASER against the payments by the PURCHASER.

AWES 格式的第 7 条是价格和付款条款,该条则有如下规定:[1]   6.90

The sums due for modifications under Article 3 of this CONTRACT shall be paid as follows:
(i) 50% on the date of agreement for modifications under Paragraph(a) and (b) of Article 3 or for modifications under paragraph (c) of Article 3 when the Statement of the adjustment of price is made by the CONTRACTOR as the case may be.
(ii) 50% on the date of delivery of the VESSEL as part of the delivery instalment.

上述 AWES 格式的规定无疑有利于船厂的资金周转,在船东提出修改或因船级社规范或主管当局法律变化而引起修改涉及较大金额时尤为如此。   6.91

---

[1] Article 7(d).

第7章 试　航

Ⅰ　概述

7.1　试航是船舶建造基本完成之后对船舶进行的一次综合性测试。虽然船东和船级社参与了船舶建造的整个过程，包括图纸的审核和船舶建造的每一个阶段和步骤，但船舶的状况及其功能以及是否符合船级社和主管当局的要求，是否符合船舶建造合同以及规格书的要求必须通过试航才能得到证实。由于船舶试航会包括一段海上航行，因此也有将船舶试航称为"海试"。中国船级社针对试航制定了《海船系泊及航行试验通则》。[1]

系泊试验

7.2　系泊试验(mooring test)又称"码头试验"(dockside test)，是船舶在开始海上试航前在码头完成的试验，也是船舶海试的一个准备阶段。系泊试验的目的是通过各种检查和测试保证船舶的完整性和可靠性，系泊试验的内容包括对主机、辅机、锚机、舵机、锅炉以及其他设备的试验。

7.3　系泊试验是在船舶的船体工程和动力装置安装完毕，船厂根据设计图纸和试验规程的要求，对主机、辅机以及各种设备和系统进行的试验。系泊试验的目的是检查船体、机械设备、电器设备及动力装置的制造、安装的完整性和可靠性，以便对不符合要求的地方重新调整，使船舶具备适航条件。船舶在进行系泊试验时基本上处于一种静止状态，凡是需要验证功效的机械设备一般都会在系泊实验中进行测试。由于码头的水深以及堤岸等的限制，主机的系泊试验是在航速为零的状态下进行各种工况试验的。无法验证主机、轴系以及各种服务于主机的辅机、舵机和锚机等在全工况运转下的性能和功能是系泊试验的局限性。相对而言，对

---

[1] GB/T 3471—2011.

于那些不受航行状态限制的设备,如柴油发电机、汽轮发电机、空气压缩机和通风设备等则可在系泊试验中进行满负荷试验,从而减少试航中的测试项目。

系泊试验的内容包括:锚设备及锚机试验、舵装置及舵机试验、救生设备试验、系缆装置及拖曳设备试验、起货设备试验、机舱行车试验、机械升降机试验、舷梯装置及舷梯试验、门窗舱口盖等开启关闭装置包括水密舱盖试验、信号设备试验、灭火系统试验、探火及失火报警系统试验、舱底系统及油污水分离器试验、危险及可燃气体探测系统试验、压载系统试验、生活及排水系统试验、通风系统试验、冷藏系统试验、空调系统试验、传令设备试验、惰性气体系统试验、主辅机冷却系统试验、主辅机滑油系统试验、主辅机燃油系统试验、燃油及滑油离心分油机试验、空气压缩机及压缩空气系统试验、液压系统试验、燃油锅炉试验、主推进系统试验、柴油发电机组及配电板试验、应急柴油发电机组及配电板试验、电动机及起动器试验、充放电板及蓄电池组试验、主照明及应急照明试验、交流高压设备试验、机舱自动化实验、无线电通信设备试验、助航设备试验、船内通讯系统试验等。集装箱船或油船的系泊试验还应包括集装箱导轨架或非导轨架集装箱堆装试验和油船各系统的试验等。

倾斜试验

船舶的倾斜试验(inclining test)是确定船舶重量和重心位置的试验。在船舶设计阶段通常是通过分配计算方法求取空船重量和重心位置,然而这个重量和重心位置与船舶建成后的实际重量和重心位置往往会出现一定的偏差,而倾斜试验就可以正确地获得船舶的重量和重心位置。船舶倾斜试验是通过船舶横倾来获得船舶完工后的实际重量和重心高度。船舶倾斜试验可以确保船舶稳性。国际海事组织专门制定了船舶完整稳性规则,即《关于国际海事组织文件包括的所有船舶的完整稳性规则》,国际海事组织通过决议建议采用倾斜试验来确定船舶的稳性。[1]

倾斜试验在航行试验之前进行,通常在建造完毕或基本完毕后进行。进行倾斜试验的船舶处于正常航行状态,但不装载货物、物料、消耗品等,即处于空船状态。倾斜试验通常在水面相对平静的水域进行,也可以在坞内进行。船舶应当保持漂浮和自由横倾状态。为保证试验的准确性,船上的水舱和油舱均应清除。用于倾斜的压载舱则应灌满,从而避免自由液面可能带来的影响。

---

[1] IMO 决议第 A.749(18)号,第 2 章,第2.1.3.15条。

航行试验

7.7 在顺利完成了系泊试验后,船舶就可以开始海上航行试验。船舶在开始试航前应当满足各项基本要求,这些基本要求包括:船舶的油水已装载完毕且船舶吃水满足要求;航海仪器、消防及救生设备已备齐;船舶已获得临时登记证书、试航证书以及最低安全配员证书等。航行试验前应获得船级社颁发的试航证书。如果在系泊试验中发现故障或缺陷的,应当在消除这些故障或缺陷后再开始航行试验。

7.8 海上航行试验是全面的,涵盖船体部分、轮机部分以及电器部分,这些试验主要包括:船舶性能试验(包括测速试验、停船试验、回转性试验、航行稳定性试验、侧向推进器试验、Z型操纵试验、溺水救生试验等)、助航设备试验(包括磁罗经试验、电罗经试验、双曲向定位仪试验、导航雷达试验、自动雷达标绘仪实验、卫星导航接收机试验、计程仪实验、测深仪试验等)、主推进系统试验(包括主柴油机运转试验、轴系部分试验、液力耦合器试验、螺旋桨及其操纵装置试验、轴系制动装置试验等)、废弃锅炉试验、海水淡化装置试验、柴油发电机组运行试验、其他辅助设备及系统运行试验、抛锚试验、操舵试验(包括主操舵装置的操舵试验、辅助操舵装置试验、自动舵操舵试验、应急电源操舵试验等)、电话及警铃试验、断电试验、瘫船试验、机舱自动化试验、船体振动试验(包括船体总振动试验、上层建筑振动试验、局部振动试验、抛锚激振试验、激振机试验等)、机械设备振动试验(包括机械设备试验、机械振动试验等)、轴系振动试验(包括扭转振动试验,纵向振动试验、回旋振动试验等)、船舶噪声试验等。

7.9 鉴于系泊试验和航行试验的关系,系泊试验越仔细越全面,航行试验就会相应地越顺利。

试验大纲

7.10 在系泊试验开始前,船厂应当按照船级社的要求制定试验大纲。试验大纲既包括系泊试验,也包括航行试验。试验大纲应当列明系泊试验和航行试验的所有项目。由于试验及其具体项目涉及船东的利益,因此船厂制定的试验大纲需要得到船东的认可。此外,试验大纲还需要得到船级社的批准。船级社的批准依据便是相应的船级规范和要求。在试验开始后,船厂和船东以及船级社代表会按照试验大纲的规定对各个项目逐一进行测试和试验。

船厂的试航

有些船舶的技术含量可能比较高,涉及到技术问题可能比较复杂,尤其是首制船,船厂有可能会在正式试航之前先进行一次类似的试航,通常称之为"船厂试航"。但是船厂自己进行的试航并不是正式的试航。试航即使成功也不意味着船东必须接受船舶,当然试航不成功的也并不因此构成合同试航的失败。船厂对船舶进行试航的原因可能是由于船舶的设计和设备等对船厂而言是陌生的,船厂对此缺乏经验。通过自己的试航,船厂可以对船舶的功能尤其是特殊性能有所了解,从而可以在交船之前有充分的时间对可能存在或出现的问题或缺陷进行及时的补救和更正。船厂在进行船厂试航时有时也会邀请船东代表参加试航,但船厂的试航并非一定要在有船东代表参加的情况下进行。由于船厂试航并不是一次合同规定的正式试航,因此船厂通常不会邀请船级社委派代表参加船厂试航。出于同一理由,船级社一般也不会愿意指派验船师参加船厂自己进行的试航。 7.11

按照 AWES 格式的规定,船厂有权进行自己的试航:① 7.12

The CONTRACTOR shall be entitled to conduct preliminary sea trials.
The CONTRACTOR shall have the right to repeat any trial whatsoever.

上文提及的"preliminary sea trials"虽然没有明指,但应当可以理解为至少包括船厂自己的试航。而且,船厂自己进行的试航还不受次数的限制。 7.13

II 试航通知

试航通知是指船厂在开始船舶试航前向船东发出的关于试航时间和地点的书面通知。 7.14

船厂发出试航通知的义务

船舶建造合同都会规定船厂应当在试航前向船东发出书面的试航通知,例如 SAJ 格式便有如下规定:② 7.15

The Buyer shall receive from the Builder at least fourteen (14) days prior notice in writing or by cable confirmed in writing of the time and place

---

① Article 4(c), paras.4&5.
② Article VI.1.

of the trial run of the Vessel, and the Buyer shall promptly acknowledge receipt of such notice. The Buyer shall have its representative on board the Vessel to witness such trial run. Failure in attendance of the representative of the Buyer at the trial run of the Vessel for any reason whatsoever after due notice to the Buyer as above provided shall be deemed to be a waiver by the Buyers of its right to have its representative on board the Vessel at the trial run, and the Builder may conduct the trial run without the representative of the Buyer being present, and in such case the Buyer shall be obliged to accept the Vessel on the basis of a certificate of the Builder that the Vessel, upon trial run, is found to conform to this Contract and the Specifications.

7.16　　船厂在试航开始前向船东发出试航通知应当是合理的,因为船东需要时间安排或聘请合适的人员和船员参加试航,而参加试航的人员和船员可能也需要时间对自己的工作以及试航作出准备。14 天的时间应当是比较合理的,但是参加试航的人员若没有中国的签证,14 天时间可能未必够这些人员申请到中国的签证。如果船东觉得时间不够的,可以要求船厂延长试航通知的时间。实际上船厂在发出正式试航通知之前一般都会与船东的监造代表就试航的日期进行过交流。NEWBUILDCON 格式规定的通知时间也是 14 天,①AWES 格式没有规定具体天数,而是留待双方确定。② Norwegian 格式规定的通知的期限更短,只有 7 天。③

7.17　　上述规定中"the Buyer shall promptly acknowledge receipt of such notice"给船东设定了一项合同义务。④ 在实践中,确认收到船厂的试航通知对船东来说应当不成问题。如果时间不合适的,船东势必会说出自己的看法。如果船东没有确认已收到船厂的试航通知,只要船厂能够证明自己已经向船东发出了试航通知,船东不委派代表参加试航将被视为船东放弃参加试航的权利。船厂可以在没有船东代表参与的情况下完成船舶的试航。试航成功的,即试航结果表明船舶符合船级规范、船舶建造合同和规格书的要求,船东就必须接受船舶。上述规定中的"证书"是指船厂确认船舶符合合同和规格书要求的证书,当然船厂的证书必须得到船级社的确认。Norwegian 格式对此作出了明确的规定:⑤

---

① Clause 27(a), para.1.
② Article 4(a).
③ Article VII.1, para.1.
④ AWES 也有相同的规定,Article 4(a).
⑤ Article VII.1, para.2.

The Builder may after due notice conduct the sea trial without the Representative of the Buyer being present, provided a representative of the Classification Society is present, and in such case the Buyer shall be obligated to accept the results of the sea trial on the basis of a certificate of the Builder confirmed by the Classification Society and/or Regulatory Bodies stating the results of the sea trial.

然而,NEWBUILDCON 格式则明确规定,若试航是在没有船东代表参加情况下进行的则必须有船级社指派的代表参加:① 7.18

If neither the Buyer's Representative nor any authorised assistants attend the sea trials for any reason after such notice to the Buyer, such absence shall be deemed to be a waiver by the Buyer of its right to be present. The Builder may then conduct the sea trials without the Buyer's Representative being on board, provided that a representative of the Classification Society and Regulatory Authorities is present. In such circumstances, the results and conditions of the sea trials shall be as confirmed in writing by the Classification Society and/or Regulatory Authorities.

按照上述规定,船厂自己实施的试航必须有船级社指派的代表参加才是有效的。但这仅仅是指涉及到船级规范或船旗国要求部分的建造项目,而不是船舶建造合同的全部。船级社指派的验船师参加船舶试航的目的是确认船舶各部分及各方面是否符合船级规范以及船旗国的要求,验船师通常只会参与涉及船级规范及船旗国要求的项目的测试或试验并对项目是否符合船级规范及船旗国要求作出确认,但船级社一般不会对船舶是否符合船舶建造合同或者规格书发表意见。 7.19

船东在收到试航通知后没有指派代表参加试航就应当接受试航结果。虽然船级社会指派验船师参加船厂的试航,但船级社的验船师通常不会参与不涉及船级规范或船旗国要求项目的测试或试验。非船级或非船旗国项目的测试或试验实际上是船厂自行完成的,但船东依然有义务接受测试或试验的结果。这应当是船东放弃权利的结果。 7.20

数个试航通知

在试航通知规定上,CSTC 格式有些与众不同,该格式规定船厂应当发出两 7.21

---

① Clause 27(a), para.2.

个试航通知:①

> The BUYER and the Supervisor shall receive from the SELLER at least thirty(30)days notice in advance and seven(7)days definite notice in advance in writing or by telex confirmed in writing, of the time and place of the VESSEL's sea trial as described in the Specifications (hereinafter referred to as "the Trial Run")and the BUYER and the Supervisor shall promptly acknowledge receipt of such notice ....

7.22　按照上述约定,船厂应当给船东发两个通知,一个是30天的大致通知,②另外一个是7天的确定通知。此种规定恐怕是来自关于交船通知的约定。船厂分别发大致通知和确定通知对船东而言无疑是受欢迎的,因为船东可以根据大致通知和确定通知作出不同的准备。然而,这种做法对船厂来说可能存在操作上的问题。首先,30天的大致通知可能过长了。即使是船厂负责生产的部门实际上也未必能在30天之前就知道船舶可以在30天后试航。在试航前30天,船舶可能还没有开始或还没有完成船舶的系泊试验,而系泊试验是否成功将直接影响到船舶是否可以试航。虽然船厂可以连续给船东发数个大致通知,但是都应当提前30天,因此对船厂而言没有太大的意义。其次,大致通知和确定通知的间隔时间太长。虽然船厂可以发数个大致通知,但是船厂不能发数个确定通知,之所以称之为"确定通知"是因为通知里的日期是不能更改的。而且最后一个大致通知确定的试航日必须和确定通知的试航日是同一日。换言之,船厂在发出了一个大致通知后可以选择继续向船东发出为期30天的大致通知,除非在发了大致通知23天以后船厂可以确定7天后船舶能够出海试航,否则船厂就必须再发一个30天的大致通知。船厂实际上很难在30天的大致通知和7天的确定通知之间作出选择。

7.23　如果船舶建造合同选择由船厂发出两个以上试航通知的,船厂应当尽可能避免约定提前30天或更早发出通知。相比较而言,10天或者更短的时间对船厂而言应当较有把握。当然,船厂也可以参照二手船买卖中交船通知的规定方式,在船舶建造合同中约定两个或两个以上大致通知,例如:船厂应当向船东发出30天、20天以及10天的大致通知和7天的确切通知。这样船厂在试航通知问题上

---

① Article VI.1.
② 虽然CSTC针对30天的通知仅用了notice一字,并没有明确其为大致通知,但由于CSTC针对7天的通知使用了definite notice的字样,因此30天的试航通知应当是大致通知,换言之,船厂可以发一个以上的30天的试航通知。

可能就会相对灵活一些。原则上,确切通知的时间越短则越便于船厂掌握。

试航的延期

大多数标准格式都规定船东代表在收到通知后没有出席试航的即视为船东放弃了参加试航的权利。但是 CSTC 格式则有不同的规定:①   7.24

> The BUYER's representatives and/or the Supervisor shall be on board the VESSEL to witness such Trial Run, and to check upon the performance of the VESSEL during the same. Failure of the BUYER's representatives to be present at the Trial Run of the VESSEL, after due notice to the BUYER and the Supervisor as provided above, shall have the effect to extend the date for delivery of the VESSEL by the period of delay caused by such failure to be present. However, if the Trial Run is delayed more than seven(7)days by reason of the failure of the BUYER's representatives to be present after receipt of due notice as provided above, then in such event, the BUYER shall be deemed to have waived its right to have its representatives on board the VESSEL during the Trial Run, and the BUILDER may conduct such Trial Run without the BUYER's representatives being present, and in such case the BUIYER shall be obliged to accept the VESSEL on the basis of a certificate jointly singed by the BUILDER and the Classification Society certifying that the VESSEL, after Trial Run subject to minor alterations and corrections as provided in this Article, if any, is found to conform to the Contract and Specifications and is satisfactory in all respects....

按照上述规定,船东在收到船厂的试航通知后不参加试航的,因此耽误的时间可以顺延合同交船日。换言之,船厂并不能在船东缺席的情况下进行试航。只有在船东代表收到船厂的试航通知后 7 天以上依然没有出现的,船厂才可以视船东放弃了指派代表参加试航的权利,才可以在没有船东代表参与的情况下进行船舶的试航。这一规定给船厂造成的应当是更多的麻烦而不是便利。首先,顺延合同交船日应当没有太大的意义,因为船厂在等船东代表期间恐怕什么也干不了。其次,由于船厂只有在等待了 7 天以上船东代表仍未出现时才可以视船东已放弃了参加试航的权利,因此船东代表在 7 天内任何一天出现的都不构成违约,都有权参加试航。这时的问题是:船级社代表以及主机和设备生产商是否也同意与船厂一起等待船东代表的到来?除非有约定,无论是船级社代表还是生产商代表应   7.25

---

① Ibid.

当是没有合同义务与船厂一起等待船东代表的。再其次,假设船东代表在收到船厂的试航通知后第 8 天仍没有出现或回复,船厂就可以在没有船东代表参与的情况下开始试航了。如果船级社代表和生产商代表依然在等待,船厂就有可能在第 9 天开始试航了。如果他们在此之前已离开了,船厂同样无法开始试航。最后,如果船厂不得不另行约定试航的时间,船东知道新的试航时间和地点且要求参加的,船厂是否可以拒绝船东的要求呢? 从上述规定来看,船厂似乎有权拒绝,因为在第 8 天后船东就可以被视为已经放弃了指派代表参加试航的权利。如果在这种情况下,船东要求以观察员身份参加试航,船厂是否可以拒绝呢? 这时,问题就会变得较为复杂,而此种复杂性可能正是由于上述规定引起的。

船东代表的签证

7.26　CSTC 格式还针对参加试航的船东代表的中国签证问题作出了如下规定:①

> The SELLER hereby warrants that the necessary visa for the BUYER's representatives to enter China will be issued in order on demand and without delay otherwise the Trial Run shall be postponed until after the BUYER's representatives have arrived at the BUILDER's Shipyard and any delays as a result thereof shall not count as a permissible delay under Article VIII thereof. However, should the nationalities and other personal particulars of the BUYER's representatives be not acceptable to the SELLER in accordance with its best understanding of the relevant rules, regulations and/or Laws of the People's Republic of China then prevailing, then the BUYER shall, on the SELLER's telex demand, effect replacement of all or any of them immediately. Otherwise the Delivery Date as stipulated in Article VII hereof shall be extended by the delays so caused by the BUYER . . . .

7.27　"Warrant"在这里的含义应当是"保证"或"担保"。按照上述规定,船厂保证船东参加试航的代表可以获得进入中国的签证,否则试航将延期,直至船东参加试航的代表到达船厂。因此引起的时间损失不视为可允许延误而由船厂承担。这一规定似乎有些离谱,作为船厂实际上既没有义务,也没有能力保证船东参加试航的代表一定能够获得进入中国的签证。船厂自己对船东指派参加试航的人员是否可以获得进入中国的签证进行判断应当是没有任何意义的。

---

① Ibid.

其他通知

船厂在给船东发出试航通知时也会对船级社以及主机和设备的生产商发出船舶试航的通知,因为船级社和生产商也会参加船舶试航。因此船厂应当在事先就针对试航时间在各参加试航的人员之间进行安排和协调,从而确保各有关方均会同时参加船舶试航。 7.28

Ⅲ 试航的天气状况

天气状况对试航的影响

虽然船舶在营运中可能遭遇各种天气状况,包括恶劣天气,但是船舶在海上的试航应当在特定的良好天气状况下进行。在良好天气状况下进行船舶的海上试航应当有两个目的:一是安全目的,另一则是效果目的。安全目的是指确保海上航行的安全,由于参加试航的船舶是第一次进行海上航行,主机、辅机和其他设备虽已经过各种形式的测试,但是真正在海上实际状况中进行使用是第一次。而且船舶在试航时并未完成全部建造,有可能发生各种无法合理预期的情形。安全问题是船厂必须考虑的问题,而选择良好天气进行船舶的海上试航应能最大程度保障船舶以及船上人员的安全。 7.29

至于效果目的,船厂在船舶建造合同中保证的船舶性能是指在特定情况下船舶应当具有的性能,例如 NEWBUILDCON 格式便规定试航气候情况为不超蒲福风力 3 级,道格拉斯海浪 2 级。① 航速就是指船舶在特定风力和海况的情况下一小时内航行的距离。因此选择最接近保证性能所对应的天气状况进行船舶的海上试航无疑能最好地确定船舶的实际性能和状况。作为船舶建造合同组成部分的规格书通常会规定船舶进行海上试航的天气条件,但是选择一个完全符合合同约定的船舶试航的天气状况即使是可能的话也应当是没有必要的,因为只要是在类似的天气状况下进行试航,相关的船舶性能都能通过调整而获得。 7.30

船厂决定试航的天气状况

SAJ 格式对试航的天气要求作出了规定:② 7.31

---

① Clause 2(b)(i).
② Article Ⅵ.2, para.1.

> The trial run shall be carried out under the weather condition which is deemed favourable enough by the judgment of the BUILDER. In the event of unfavourable weather on the date specified for the trial run, the same shall take place on the first available day thereafter that the weather condition permits. It is agreed that, if during the trial run of the VESSEL, the weather should suddenly become so unfavourable that orderly conduct of the trial run can no longer be continued, the trial run shall be discontinued and postponed until the first favourable day next following, unless the BUYER shall assent in writing to acceptance of the VESSEL on the basis of the trial run already made before such discontinuance has occurred.

7.32　上述规定主要有三个内容。首先,天气状况是否适合船舶的试航由船厂决定,即只有在船厂认为天气适合试航时才可以进行试航。这一约定的理由应当是:船舶在试航阶段依然是船厂的财产,船厂必须对自己的财产负责,因此有权按照自己的判断决定是否进行试航。由于决定试航时间的是船厂,因此船厂在船舶出海试航前应当对试航水域以及船厂码头至试航水域的天气和海况有准确的了解。其次,一旦约定的试航时间的天气状况不允许船舶出海试航的,船舶的试航应当在下一个良好天气日进行。最后,天气状况在试航过程中变坏,不再适合船舶继续试航的,除非船东书面同意根据试航已经获得的数据接受船舶,船厂可以决定放弃或中止试航。当然,这里所说的船东放弃是指船东放弃尚未完成的确认船舶是否符合合同及规格书要求的测试或试验,而不是涉及船舶入级或船旗国要求的测试和试验。在这种情况下,即使船东放弃试航可能也没有意义,因为船级社不会也不可以放弃涉及船级项目或船旗国要求的项目的测试和试验。

试航的延迟

7.33　由于天气原因不得不推迟或中止试航而产生的时间损失应当视为可允许延误,因为时间的浪费不能归责于船厂。SAJ 格式对此作出了规定:①

> Any delay of trial run caused by such unfavourable weather condition shall operate to postpone the Delivery Date by the period of delay involved and such delay shall be deemed as a permissible delay in the delivery of the VESSEL.

---

① Article VI.2, para.2.

AWES 格式也有类似的规定:①　　　　　　　　　　　　　　　　　　　　　　7.34

> The trial run shall be carried out under favourable weather conditions. Any delay in delivery caused by delay of the trial run due to unfavourable weather conditions shall be Permissible Delay.

虽然上述规定与前文提及的 SAJ 格式的相关规定似乎相类似,但两者应当是 7.35
有比较根本的区别。SAJ 格式规定的是海上试航因天气原因而发生的延误,例如
原定的海上试航由于一场大暴雨而不得不推迟了 10 天再进行,海上试航就有 10
天的延误。按照 SAJ 格式的规定,船厂能够利用这 10 天顺延合同交船日。而且,
SAJ 格式也明确规定该 10 天的延误应视为可允许延误,而可允许延误的一个基
本特征便是可以顺延合同交船日。然而,AWES 格式规定则与 SAJ 格式有所不
同,按照 AWES 格式的规定,只有当船舶海上试航因天气原因而产生的延误实际
上导致了船舶交接延误时才可以被视为可允许延误,从而顺延合同交船日。船舶
海上试航发生延误有可能但未必会导致船舶交接的延误。因此,SAJ 格式和
AWES 格式在这个问题上的区别是,按照 SAJ 格式的规定,只要船舶的海上试航
发生延误,无论此种延误是否最终影响到船舶的交接,船厂都可以顺延合同交船
日;然而按照 AWES 格式的规定,只有当船舶海上试航的延误导致船舶交接的延
误时,船厂才能顺延合同交船日。

CSTC 格式的规定与 SAJ 格式的规定大致相同。② NEWBUILDCON 格式也 7.36
同样规定试航的延误即为可允许延误,只是措辞有所不同而已:③

> The sea trials shall be conducted in weather conditions as described in this Contract and/or Specification. If the sea trials are interrupted or prevented by weather conditions in excess of the stated conditions, any resulting delay in delivery of the Vessel shall be deemed a Permissible Delay in accordance with Clause 34(Permissible Delays). In such an event, the sea trials shall be discontinued or postponed until the first favourable day thereafter when weather conditions permit.

NEWBUILDCON 格式与 AWES 格式的相同之处是:试航的延误只有在导致 7.37
交船延误的情况下才可以视为可允许延误。

---

① Article 4(b).
② Article VI.1.
③ Clause 27(b).

Ⅳ 试航的进行

试航方式

7.38　船舶在海上试航时应当进行各种项目的测试或试验,如何进行各种项目的测试或试验则往往取决于船舶建造合同的规定。SAJ 格式针对船舶试航作出了如下规定:①

> ... The trial run shall be conducted in the manner prescribed in the Specifications, and shall prove fulfilment of the performance requirements for the trial run as set forth in the Specifications. The course of trial run shall be determined by the BUILDER.

7.39　即使船舶建造合同没有约定,船舶在海上航行的线路依然由船厂决定。这可能是因为船厂比船东更了解相关水域的状况。而且,船厂在决定船舶行驶路线以及试航水域时负有的合同义务是:船厂选定的路线和水域适合船舶的试航,并且能够体现船舶的设计功能和具体性能。CSTC 格式也规定船舶的航行线路由船厂决定。②

7.40　下面是 NEWBUILDCON 格式的规定:③

> The sea trials shall be conducted in the presence of representatives from the Classification Society and Regulatory Authorities and in the manner described in this Contract. The sea trials shall be of sufficient scope and duration to enable the Parties to verify and establish that the Vessel conforms in all respects with the performances requirements of this Contract. The Builder shall have the right to repeat any sea trials, subject to appropriate notice to the Buyer.

7.41　NEWBUILDCON 格式除了规定试航应当按照合同约定进行外,还规定试航的范围和持续时间应当足以确认船舶在各方面均符合合同规定的性能要求。此外,船厂可以重复海上试航,但都应给船东发出通知。这里所提及的第一次试航以后的试航应当是指进行第一次试航尚未完成项目的测试或试验的试航,而不应是指船厂自己的试航。但是鉴于在试航时船舶通常是船厂的财产,船东应当只有

---

① Article Ⅵ.3(a).
② Article Ⅵ.2(a), para.2.
③ Clause 27(c)(i).

在获得船厂邀请的情况下才能参加船厂试航。

Performance 的含义

Performance 通常指"性能"或"工作状况",例如船舶试航时的状况。在 *McDougall v Aeromarine of Emsworth Ltd*① 一案中,原告是船厂,被告是船东,双方订立了船舶建造合同,约定由被告为原告建造一艘赛艇。船舶建造合同的第6条有如下规定: 7.42

> The builders shall be deemed to have completed the construction and fitting out of the craft in accordance with the requirements of the annexed specification at the conclusion of the trial run provided that the performance of the craft during such trial run is to the reasonable satisfaction of the purchaser such satisfaction to be indicated by the signature of the purchaser to the memorandum endorsed on the back hereof.

法院认为 performance 是指材料和工艺标准符合规格书的要求,即使船舶的内部舾装尚未完成也不影响船舶的 performance。Diplock 法官说:② 7.43

> I construe the expression [performance of the craft] widely and as including the standard of workmanship and materials and the compliance of the craft with the specification. To read the words "performance of the craft" in a narrower sense would result in the seller being deemed to have fulfilled his contract even if the interior fittings were incomplete so long as the vessel sailed well.

参加试航的人员

参加试航的人员一般有:船厂的代表,包括负责船舶操纵的船员;船东的代表,包括船舶交接时接船的船员;船级社的代表以及主机和设备等的生产商的代表。 7.44

船厂的代表

船舶进行海上航行必须有船员,因此船厂必须为试航船舶配备船员。AWES 7.45

---

① [1958] 2 Lloyd's Rep 345.
② [1958] 2 Lloyd's Rep 345 at 357.

格式、①Norwegian 格式、②CSTC 格式、③NEWBUILDCON 格式都对此作出了规定,其中 NEWBUILDCON 格式的规定如下:④

> The Builder shall provide sufficient crew necessary for the safe navigation of the Vessel.

7.46　虽然在船舶试航中,无论是航行距离还是航行时间都比较有限,而且船舶试航时通常也没有货载,但是由于试航同样是在海上航行,因此船舶试航时也必须符合法定的最低配员要求。根据我国《船舶港内安全作业监督管理办法》的规定,船舶在试航、试车时应配备足够的合格船员。⑤ 船厂通常没有完整的合格船员,因此船厂一般会为了试航临时招聘合格船员。

7.47　除了操纵船舶的船员外,船厂还会派遣船厂的其他技术人员和管理人员上船参加试航。这些人员的任务主要是负责和船东指派参加试航的代表、船级社指派的参加试航的代表以及主机和设备生产厂商的代表进行沟通,与上述人员共同确认船舶是否符合船级规范、船旗国及主管当局的要求,以及船舶建造合同和规格书的规定。

船东的代表

7.48　按照 1979 年《货物买卖法》的规定,作为货物的买方有权对卖方提交的货物是否符合合同规定进行检查:⑥

> ... Unless otherwise agreed, when the seller tenders delivery of goods to the buyer, he is bound on request to afford the buyer a reasonable opportunity of examining the goods for the purpose of ascertaining whether they are in conformity with the contract.

7.49　因此,检查货物是买方的一项法定权利。即使货物已经交付给了买方,只要买方没有对货物进行过检查,买方就不能被视为已经接受了货物。对此,1979 年《货物买卖法》是这样规定的:⑦

---

① Article 4(c), para.6.
② Article VII.3, para.2.
③ Article VI.2(a), para.1.
④ Clause 27(c)(ii).
⑤ 《船舶港内安全作业监督管理办法》第十条。
⑥ s.34(2).
⑦ s.34(1).

Where goods are delivered to the buyer, and he has not previously examined them, he is not deemed to have accepted them until he has had a reasonable opportunity of examining them for the purpose of ascertaining whether they are in conformity with the contract.

7.50　由于船舶建造的特殊性,船东对船舶的检查和试验实际上贯穿于整个船舶建造过程。相反,船东在船舶交接时则不会对船舶进行全面的检查,而是依赖由船级社颁发的和代表船旗国颁发的各类证书。贯穿于整个船舶建造过程中的检查和检验一般都是针对特定的材料和建造项目,相对缺乏完整性,而船东在试航中对船舶进行的检验和测试则是比较完整和系统的。参加船舶试航也是船东对船舶整体状况进行了解和核实的重要手段,同时也往往是唯一的机会。

7.51　参加试航是船东的合同权利,船舶建造合同都会规定船东的此项权利。在实践中,船东一般会派遣自己的技术代表全程参加船舶的试航,并从船体、轮机以及电气等部分负责核实船舶是否符合船舶建造合同以及规格书的要求。代表船东参加船舶试航的技术代表有可能是船东自己的雇员,也可能是船东外聘的人员。由于是权利,因此船东可以放弃参加试航的机会,大多数船舶建造合同的标准格式都规定了船东丧失参加船舶试航权利的情形。参加试航的船东代表还可能包括船员,这些船员往往是船东接船后接管船舶的船员。但是参加试航的船东船员只能了解和熟悉船舶,并不能实际对船舶进行操纵,在试航的整个过程中,船舶是由船厂派遣的船员实际控制和操纵的。

7.52　无论是 SAJ 格式、AWES 格式,还是 Norwegian 格式或 CSTC 格式提及船东代表参加试航时都使用了"见证"一词,即表明船东指派参加船舶试航的技术代表是以证人或观察员的身份参加试航的,他们既不参与船舶的操纵,也不实际操作任何一项测试或试验。当然,船东代表在试航中的"证人"或"观察员"的身份并不仅仅停留在对事实进行确认的作用上。除了不实际动手外,船东指派参加船舶试航的代表可以发表意见或提出具体的试验或测试的要求乃至具体方法。如果在试航之前船厂和船东已有争议或纠纷的,船舶试航时的情况就可能比较紧张。为了避免不必要的争议,船厂在试航前应尽可能详细地与船东针对试航中要进行测试和试验的机械、设备以及项目等作出约定。此种约定不仅要包括将要进行测试和试验的机械和设备,还应当包括测试和试验的性质和程序。船厂在试航中应尽可能地满足船东代表提出的要求和建议。每做完一个项目的试验或测试,双方应当就试验和测试结果当场签署相关的文件,从而确定当时的试验和测试的结果。双方应尽可能避免在试航结束后重新根据回忆签署相关的试航文件。相关文件的措辞应当既明确又准确,如果双方对某一项目的具体问题有不同看法的,只要有可能就应当设法立即解决,而不要拖至试航之后再解决。

船级社的代表

7.53　船级社作为船舶的发证机关显然应当参加船舶的试航,实际上也只有在参加了船舶试航后才能确定船舶是否符合船级规范和船旗国主管当局的要求,船级社才能决定是否为船舶颁发航行证书和船级证书。AWES 格式、Norwegian 格式①以及 NEWBUILDCON 格式都规定,②船舶试航应当在有船级社代表在场的情况下进行,其中 AWES 格式的规定如下:③

> The trial run shall be carried out in the presence of representatives from the Classification Society and/or Regulatory Bodies, and shall be conducted in a manner and to an extent prescribed in the Specifications and shall prove the VESSEL's proper functioning and fulfillment of the performance requirements for the trials set forth in this CONTRACT and the Specifications.

7.54　船级社代表参加船舶试航的项目是特定的,即涉及船舶是否符合船级规范和船旗国要求的项目。因此,船级社代表通常不会参与船东代表参与的关于船舶是否符合船舶建造合同以及规格书规定的试验和测试。

厂商的代表

7.55　主机以及主要设备的生产商通常也会指派代表参加船舶的试航,生产商代表参加试航的目的是确定其所制造或提供的设备符合船级规范以及生产商与船厂之间的采购合同的要求。因此,生产商代表只会参加与由其制造和出售设备的测试或试验。

试航成本及其分摊

7.56　船舶在试航时的所有权依然属于船厂并由船厂实际控制,风险也依然由船厂承担。船厂对船舶进行试航的目的是向船东证明其所建造的船舶符合船级规范、

---

① Article VII, 3, para.1.
② Clause 27(c)(i).
③ Article 4(c), para.1.

船旗国要求、船舶建造合同以及规格书的要求,可以说试航是船舶建造的组成部分。因此,因试航产生的成本和费用也应当由船厂承担。对此,SAJ 格式有如下规定:①

> All expenses in connection with the trial run are to be for the account of the BUILDER and the BUILDER shall provide at its own expense the necessary crew to comply with conditions of safe navigation. The trial run shall be conducted in the manner prescribed in the Specifications, and shall prove fulfillment of the performance requirements for the trial run as set forth in the Specifications. The course of trial run shall be determined by the BUILDER.

7.57 船厂通常要承担船级社代表参加试航代表的费用,由于船厂与船级社已经订立了监造协议,因此相关费用已经包含在监造费用之中。但如果船级社代表需要参加一次以上试航的,除非另有约定,船厂一般需要另行支付额外的船级社代表参加试航的费用。船厂通常不负担船东指派试航代表的费用,为此 AWES 格式作出了明确的规定:②

> All expenses except those of the PURCHASER's Representative and its assistant(s) in connection with the trial run shall be for the account of the CONTRACTOR, including without limitation all necessary crew.

7.58 除了上述费用,船舶试航还可能产生的成本和费用主要包括:船员费用、燃油、润滑油、机油、伙食、消耗供应和淡水等。这些费用均为试航费用,由船厂承担。船厂通常只负责提供船员配备、伙食、消耗供应和淡水等,而船东则负责提供燃油和润滑油等。SAJ 格式就有如下规定:③

> Notwithstanding the foregoing, fuel oil, lubricating oil and greases necessary for the trial run of the VESSEL shall be supplied by the BUYER at the Shipyard prior to the time of the trial run, and the BUILDER shall pay the BUYER upon delivery of the VESSEL the cost of the quantities of fuel oil, lubricating oil and greases consumed during the trial run at the original purchase price. In measuring the consumed quantity, lubricating oils and greases remaining in the main engine, other machinery and their pipes, stern tube and the like, shall be

---

① Article VI.3(a).
② Article 4(c), para.6.
③ Article VI.3(b).

excluded. The quantity of fuel oil, lubricating oils and greases supplied by the BUYER shall be in accordance with the instruction of the BUILDER.

7.59 船舶建造合同规定由船东供应试航所需的燃油、润滑油以及机油应当符合船东的利益。大多数船东对自己拥有或经营的船舶所使用的燃油和润滑油等均有自己的偏好，并且会有自己选定的供应商。相反，就试航而言船厂通常对所使用的燃油和润滑油等没有太多特殊的要求。因此船舶建造合同约定由船东供应试航所需的燃油和润滑油等实际上使船东可以根据自己的意愿进行采购。由于船厂应当承担试航成本，因此船厂必须向船东支付试航所消耗的燃油和润滑油等的费用。按照上述 SAJ 格式的规定，在主机或其他机器及其管路、管道内的润滑油等不应被视为是试航所消耗的。这一规定无疑是合理的，因为在这些处所的油类在接船后实际上可以为船东所用。CSTC 格式在这个问题上对润滑油进行了区分，分别由船厂和船东供应：①

The BUILDER shall provide the VESSEL with the required quantities of water, fuel oil and greases with exception of lubrication oil and hydraulic oil which shall be supplied by the BUYER for the conduct of the Trial Run or Trial Runs as prescribed in the Specifications. The fuel oil and greases supplied by the SELLER, and lubricating oil and hydraulic oil supplied by the BUYER shall be in accordance with the applicable engine specifications, and the cost of the quantities of water, fuel oil, lubricating oil, hydraulic oil and greases consumed during the Trial Run or Trial Runs shall be for the account of the BUILDER.

7.60 在船东负责供应燃油和润滑油等的情况下，有些船舶建造合同会规定把船东提供的试航用的燃油和润滑油等视为船东供应品，从而适用合同关于船东供应品的规定。一旦船东供应燃油和润滑油等有延误导致船舶试航延误的，因此浪费的时间可以视为可允许延误，船厂可以根据延误的天数顺延合同交船日。然而，NEWBUILDCON 格式则作出了相反的规定：②

All expenses in connection with the sea trial, including the provision of bunkers, lubricating oil, grease, fresh water and stores needed to undertake the sea trials shall be for the Builder's cost and expense. Together with the Final Instalment, the Buyer shall reimburse the

---

① Article VI.2(b).
② Clause 27(c)(iii).

Builder at cost price for any quantities of bunkers and unbroached lubricating oil, grease, fresh water and stores remaining on board at delivery.

根据上述规定,船厂应当自行采购船舶试航所需的燃油、润滑油等,而由船东在支付最后一期建造款时按照船厂的采购价格支付试航后仍然遗留在船上的燃油和润滑油等。按照上述 NEWBUILDCON 格式的规定,船东似乎无需为遗留在主机或其他机器及其管路、管道内的润滑油支付价款了,因为船东仅需支付尚未开桶的润滑油的采购价格。 7.61

消耗品的处置

船厂为了试航会为船舶供应各种消耗品,例如伙食和淡水等。在试航结束后这些在船上的消耗品有可能仍有剩余。虽然船厂应当负责试航期间消耗品的供应并承担费用,但船东则可以在接船后继续使用在船上的试航剩余的消耗品。因此有的船舶建造合同会对这些消耗品的处置作出约定。SAJ 格式关于消耗品处置有如下规定:① 7.62

Should any fresh water or other consumable stores furnished by the BUILDER for the trial run remain on board the VESSEL at the time of acceptance thereof by the BUYER, the BUYER agrees to buy the same from the BUILDER at the original purchase price thereof, and payment by the BUYER shall be effected upon delivery of the VESSEL.

上述规定的消耗品是指船东接受船舶之时遗留在船上的消耗品,但是船东作出接受船舶的表态往往是试航结束以后的事,离船舶交接可能仍有一段时间。因此以船东表示接受船舶之时作为时间点计算在船上的消耗品不是很恰当。相比较而言,NEWBUILDCON 格式的规定则比较合理:② 7.63

... Together with the Final Instalment, the Buyer shall reimburse the Builder at cost price for any quantities of bunkers and unbroached lubricating oil, grease, fresh water and stores remaining on board at delivery.

---

① Article Ⅵ.6.
② Clause 27(c)(ⅲ).

船舶的临时登记

7.64　船舶的试航通常是在一国领海上进行的,而商船在一国领海航行就必须符合该国法律的规定。各国针对商船在本国领海航行都有明确的规定。在一国领海航行的船舶都必须拥有国籍并悬挂国旗,例如《中华人民共和国海上交通安全法》规定,船舶必须持有船舶国籍证书,或船舶登记证书,或船舶执照。① 因此船舶在试航前就必须获得国籍,无论是中国国籍还是外国国籍。由于船舶试航阶段通常依然是船厂的财产,因此船厂在对船舶进行试航之前都会对船舶进行临时登记,从而取得船舶国籍。

7.65　船舶在我国水域进行试航的,作为船舶登记主管机关的海事局会向船厂颁发船舶的临时国籍证书、船员最低安全配员证书、以及船舶的临时电台执照。临时国籍证书只记载了船舶的主要尺寸及主机的种类和功率,通常没有船舶的 IMO 编号,船名也往往采用船厂的船号。临时国籍证书的有效期也比较短,一般不会超过 3 个月。通常船舶的国籍证书的颁发以船舶已经进行了有效的所有权登记为前提,②但船东若是国外法人的话就无法在中国就船舶所有权进行登记,因为《中华人民共和国船舶登记条例》规定,只有在中国境内有住所或主要营业所的中国公民和在中国设立的主要营业所在中国境内的中国企业法人可以登记为悬挂中国旗船舶的船东,若中国企业法人有外商出资的,中方投资人的出资额不得低于 50%。③ 虽然船厂可以登记为船舶的所有人,为船舶申请中国国籍从而可以在海上进行试航,但这样做就意味着船东所接的船舶已经有过登记,这往往是船东不愿意接受的。由于船舶在试航成功后将交给船东在其他国家办理所有权的登记,因此我国允许试航船舶在没有进行所有权登记的情况下获得中国国籍,以便船舶进行海上的试航。④

7.66　试航船舶一般不会行驶很远,船员最低安全配员通常适用沿海船舶的最低安全配员要求。⑤ 由于对部分船员给予了豁免,因此船员最低安全配员证书一般会对航行时间进行限制,船舶的连续航行一般不能超过 36 小时。临时电台执照的

---

① 第五条。
② 《中华人民共和国船舶登记条例》第十五条规定:"船舶所有人申请船舶国籍,除应当交验依照本条例取得的船舶所有权等级证书外……"
③ 《中华人民共和国船舶登记条例》第二条。
④ 《〈中华人民共和国船舶登记条例〉若干问题的说明》第十六条第三款规定:"在船舶所有人申请办理临时船舶国籍证书时,可不以船舶已取得船舶所有权登记证书为必需的前提条件。"
⑤ 在我国,船员最低安全配员标准主要三种,分别是:从事国际航线、国内沿海航线以及国内内河航线运输的船舶,见《中华人民共和国船舶最低安全配员规则》第十二条的规定。

申请是为了确保在试航过程中可以使用船舶无线电。按照《中华人民共和国无线电管理条例》的规定,船舶上的无线电台必须领取电台执照并报国家无线电管理机构或者地方无线电管理机构备案。①

Ⅴ 接受和拒绝

7.67　船舶海上试航的结束意味着船舶建造在技术上已基本完成,接下来的建造工作更多的是扫尾和补漏。而且,可以进行海上试航的船舶已经具备了船舶建造合同以及规格书所规定的特征和性能,尚未完成的建造项目应当不会影响船舶在试航时所应取得的状况和性能。实际上,无论是船厂还是船东在船舶试航完毕后都已经对该船舶是否符合交船条件形成了自己的判断。因此,船东应当对船舶是否符合船舶建造合同以及规格书的要求作出表态,即表示是否接受船舶。

船东是否接受船舶的表态

7.68　按照 SAJ 格式的规定,船厂应当在试航结束且认为试航符合船舶建造合同及规格书要求的情况下向船东发出书面通知,要求船东确认是否接受船舶,而船东则应当在 3 天内书面通知船厂是否接受船舶:②

> Upon completion of the trial run, the BUILDER shall give the BUYER a notice by cable confirmed in writing of completion of the trial run, as and if the BUILDER considers that the results of the trial run indicate conformity of the VESSEL to this Contract and the Specifications. The BUYER shall, within three(3)days after receipt of such notice from the BUILDER, notify the BUILDER by cable confirmed in writing of its acceptance or rejection of the VESSEL.

7.69　除非整个船舶建造合同的履行始终一帆风顺且船舶的试航完全满足了船级社代表和船东代表的要求,否则要求船东在 3 天内作出是否接受船舶的决定可能有欠公平。除非实际情况一目了然,否则船东可能需要更长的时间对是否接受船舶作出最终的决定。首先,船东在作出是否接受船舶的决定之前都希望知道船级社对船舶试航状况乃至船舶的整体状况的态度,这应当是无可非议的。船厂是否

---

① 第十四条。
② Article Ⅵ.4(a)。

可以成功交船不仅需要船东的配合，更重要的是要确保船舶符合船级规范及船旗国主管当局的规定，否则即使船东接受，船厂也无法成功交船。其次，如果在试航中有问题发生，船东也自然希望在有关问题得到解决或已有结论的情况下才对是否接受船舶作出决定。最后，试航报告是船东决定接受还是拒绝船舶的重要依据，船东应当在收到记录船舶试航整个过程及各个试验或测试项目的结果和数据后再作出决定。但是船厂未必能够在试航结束后的 3 天内向船东提供完整的试航报告。Norwegian 格式规定的时间期限更短，仅为收到船厂的通知以及测试结果后的 48 个小时；①NEWBUILDCON 格式规定的是 5 天；②CSTC 格式规定的期限最长，为 6 个工作日；③AWES 格式没有规定船东在此种情况下应当作出决定的时限，而只是规定船东应当在收到船厂通知以及测试结果后书面通知船厂是否接受船舶。④

7.70 　　对船东而言，除非一切令其满意，否则作出接受或拒绝接受船舶的决定并非易事。如果船东的决定是接受船舶，船厂显然欢迎此种决定，但船东也就放弃了就某些问题提出异议的机会。如果船东的决定是拒绝船舶，船东可能面临的风险是拒绝船舶的理由是否成立。船东拒绝船舶通常还应当给出具体的理由，⑤船东拒绝船舶实际上就是解除船舶建造合同，如果其所凭借的缺陷等不足以构成船东解约的理由，船东的解约就可能构成毁约，船厂可以以此为由解除船舶建造合同。

船东权利的放弃

7.71 　　如果船东未能在约定的时间内对是否接受船舶作出表态的，按照 SAJ 格式的规定，船厂可以视船东已接受了船舶：⑥

> In the event that the BUYER fails to notify the BUILDER by cable confirmed in writing of the acceptance of or the rejection together with the reason therefor of the VESSEL within the period as provided in the above Sub-paragraph (a) or (b), the BUYER shall be deemed to have accepted the VESSEL.

---

① Article Ⅶ.4(a).
② Clause 27(d)(i).
③ Article Ⅵ.4(a).
④ Article 4(d), para.1.
⑤ Norwegian Article Ⅶ.4(c); AWES Article 4(d); NEWBUILDCON Article 27(d)(iii).
⑥ Article Ⅵ.4(d), CSTC 也有类似的视为放弃的规定，见 Article Ⅵ.4(c).

7.72 然而在实践中船东在约定时间内不对是否接受船舶表态的情形应当是绝无仅有的。即使船东决定接受船舶,通常也会向船厂作出明确的表示。

船东接受船舶的意义

7.73 船东一旦接受了船舶就是最终的,换言之,船东不能对此反悔。为此,SAJ 格式有如下规定:①

> Acceptance of the VESSEL as above provided shall be final and binding so far as conformity of the VESSEL to this Contract and the Specifications is concerned and shall preclude the Buyer from refusing formal delivery of the VESSEL as hereinafter provided, if the BUILDER complies with all other procedural requirements for delivery as provided in Article VII hereof.

7.74 船东接受船舶表明船舶建造符合建造合同规定的技术状况和性能。除非发生意外,船东在船厂交船时不能以船舶的技术状况或性能不符合建造合同规定为由拒绝接船。AWES 格式以及 CSTC 格式也有类似的规定。② Norwegian 格式的规定有所不同:③

> Acceptance of the Vessel as provided above, shall be final and binding and shall preclude the Buyer from refusing formal delivery on basis of any alleged deficiency in any part or parts of the Vessel which were tested during the sea trial, provided all other procedural requirements for delivery have been met.

7.75 按照上述规定,船东似乎可以以那些在试航中没有经过测试或试验的项目存在缺陷为由拒绝接受船厂的交船,但无需测试或试验的项目即使存在不符合建造合同的规定,船东通常只能主张赔偿,而不能拒绝接船。在 China Shipbuilding Corporation v Nippon Yusen Kabukishi Kaisha and another(Seta Maru, Saikyo and Suma)④一案中,船厂同意为船东建造三艘散货船,三个船舶建造合同的内容基本相同,其中第 VI.4 条规定:

---

① Article VI.5.
② AWES Article 4(e); CSTC Article VI.6.
③ Article VII.5.
④ [2000] 1 Lloyd's Rep 367.

Method of Acceptance or Rejection (a) Upon telex notification by the Builder of the completion of the trials of the vessel the Buyer shall within six(6)days thereafter notify by telex the builder of its acceptance ... (c)In the event the Buyer fails to notify by telex the Builder of its acceptance .... of the vessel ... the Buyer shall be deemed to have accepted the vessel.

7.76 船舶建造合同第 VI.5 条则规定：

Subject to the provisions of Article IX hereof the Buyer's notification under this Article VI. 4 shall be final and binding so far as conformity of the vessel to this contract and the specifications is concerned and shall preclude the Builder from refusing formal delivery of the vessel ....

7.77 船东在试航后并没有向船厂表示接受船舶，但船东此后接受了船厂交付的三艘船，并且在每艘船交船时均与船厂签署了交接备忘录。第一、第二艘船在过了质保期后被发现船舶的焊接有问题，于是船东在质保期内对第三艘进行了检验并也发现了焊接的问题。船东向船厂提出了索赔，船厂在仲裁中提出一个首要问题，希望仲裁庭首先予以考虑，即船厂是否应当承担责任。仲裁庭认为，由于船厂和船东并没有按照第 VI.4 条的规定相互交换电传，船东就不能依赖第 VI.5 条的规定，即船东接受船舶构成对船舶建造符合建造合同和规格书要求的确认。只有在按照第 VI.4 条的规定发出了电传的情况下才可能满足第 VI.5 条的要求。但是法院认为仲裁员的观点是错的，高院的 Thomas 法官认为第 VI.4 条规定的通知并不是第 VI.5 条生效的条件，实际上第 VI.5 条已经规定了视为船东接受的情形。Thomas 法官认为第 VI.5 条是"不可拒绝条款"，他说：①

The provision in art.VI.5 that acceptance was to be regarded as final and binding as regards conformity with the contract and specifications was made for the purpose of ensuring that the buyers could not thereafter refuse delivery. Article VI.5 made this clear by stating that the buyers were precluded from refusing formal delivery. It was a nonrejection clause. There were in the 1970s and 1980s numerous instances known throughout the shipbuilding industry where refusal of delivery was made on the basis that there was some noncompliance with the contract or specifications; this provision was designed to exclude that possibility and prevent rejection, once the procedures in art.VI.4 had been complied

---

① [2000] 1 Lloyd's Rep 367 at 374.

with or acceptance made. It did no more than that.

船东在船舶试航后作出了接受船舶的表示意味着船东因此丧失了以船舶建造不符合建造合同或者规格书为由拒绝船舶的权利,Thomas 法官将这一条款称为"不得拒绝条款"。但这一条款并不影响船东的其他权利。Thomas 法官是这样说的:① 7.78

> Article VI.5 did not exclude any rights other than the right to reject; if there were latent defects, art.VI.5 did not affect the buyers' rights when they were discovered ....
>
> Furthermore, even if the provision affected the buyers' rights other than the right to reject, it only had evidential effect and could only take effect as an estoppel ....

船舶不符合合同要求

船舶的航行试验有可能成功,也有可能不成功。试航不成功通常是指试航结果表明船舶或设备不符合船舶建造合同或规格书的要求。SAJ 格式对此作出的规定是:② 7.79

> However, should the results of the trial run indicate that the VESSEL or any part or equipment thereof, does not conform to the requirements of this Contract and/or the Specifications, or if the BUILDER is in agreement to non-conformity as specified in the BUYER's notice of rejection, then, the BUILDER shall take necessary steps to correct such non-conformity. Upon completion of correction of such non-conformity, the BUILDER shall give the BUYER a notice thereof by cable confirmed in writing. The BUYER shall, within two (2) days after receipt of such notice from the BUILDER, notify the BUILDER of its acceptance or rejection of the VESSEL.

上述规定涉及两种情形,一是指船厂在试航结束后认为船舶试航的结果不符合合同及规格书的要求。在此种情形下船厂要求船东表态是否接受船舶已不再有意义。另一是船厂在试航结束后认为试航结果符合合同及规格书的要求,但船东则认为试航结果不符合合同及规格书的要求并拒绝接受船舶,而船厂又同意了 7.80

---

① [2000] 1 Lloyd's Rep 367 at 375.
② Article VI.4(b).

船东拒绝接受船舶的理由。在这两种情形下船厂应当做的是采取措施纠正试航中发现的不符点。只有在纠正了所有的不符点后,船厂才能向船东发出通知,要求或再一次要求船东表态是否接受船舶。

7.81 如果不符点需要通过试航才能确认的,船厂还必须再一次对船舶进行试航,SAJ 格式没有对再次试航作出规定,但 AWES 格式有关于再次试航的规定:①

> ... If necessary, the CONTRACTOR shall for its own account carry out a further trial run to ascertain that the VESSEL conforms to the terms of the CONTRACT ....

船东拒绝接受船舶的权利

7.82 船东在收到船厂的通知后应当对是否接受船舶作出明确的表态,船东的这一表态将直接影响到船舶建造合同的履行。船东表示接受船舶的,如前所述,船东就要受这一表态的约束。虽然船东可以拒绝接受船舶,但船东拒绝接受船舶的应当给出理由。SAJ 格式的规定是:②

> In any event that the BUYER rejects the VESSEL, the BUYER shall indicate in its notice of rejection in what respect the VESSEL or any part or equipment thereof does not conform to this Contract and/or the Specifications.

7.83 从上述规定来看,船东拒绝接受船舶的理由是船舶或其设备不符合船舶建造合同或规格书的规定。但是不符合合同或规格书规定的情形应当存在程度上的差异,是否意味着只要有任何不符点,无论该不符点与安全、船舶性能、船舶的经营是否有关,船东都可以拒绝接受船舶?相比较而言,AWES 格式的规定似乎明确一些:③

> If the PURCHASER for any reason rejects the VESSEL, the PURCHASER shall in its notice of rejection give particulars of the reason in such detail as can reasonably be expected. The PURCHASER shall be obliged to take delivery of the VESSEL if it is in conformity

---

① Article 4(d), para.2; see also Norwegian, Article VII.4(b), NEWBUILDCON, Clause 27(d)(ii) and CSTC, Article VI.4(b).
② Article VI.4(c).
③ Article 4(d), para.3.

with the CONTRACT, unless there are any deficiencies or conditions or recommendations imposed by the Classification Society and/or Regulatory Bodies preventing the VESSEL to carry out its intended operation. If the deficiencies or the conditions/recommendations are of minor importance and do not prevent safe operation of the VESSEL, the CONTRACTOR may require the PURCHASER to take delivery of the VESSEL provided the CONTRACTOR undertakes for its own account to remedy the deficiency or fulfill the requirement as soon as possible, however latest by the end of the guarantee period.

7.84 按照上述规定,船东只有在船舶存在影响其运行的缺陷或不符合船级规范或船旗国条件的情况下才可以拒绝接受船舶。换言之,船舶试航结果符合船级社规范和船旗国要求的,船东就不能拒绝接受。当然,船舶试航一旦无法满足船级社规范或船旗国主管当局要求的,船东是否拒绝接受船舶可能也不再有太大的意义了,因为在这种情况下船厂实际上是无法向船东交船的。在船舶虽有缺陷但不影响船舶安全营运的情况下,只要船厂采取了相应的补救和整改措施,船东依然应当接受船舶。

7.85 Norwegian 格式针对这个问题作出的规定是:①

The Buyer shall not be obliged to take delivery of the Vessel if it is not fully in conformity with the Contract, or if there are any conditions or recommendations imposed by the Classification Society and/or Regulatory Bodies. However, if the deficiencies or the conditions/recommendations are of minor importance, and the Builder is unable to rectify the matter within a reasonable time, the Builder may nevertheless require the Buyer to take delivery of the Vessel, provided:
(i) The Builder undertakes for its own account to remedy the deficiency or fulfil the requirement as soon as possible, and
(ii) The Builder shall indemnify the Buyer for any loss incurred as a consequence thereof, including loss of time.

7.86 按照上述规定的第一句,如果船舶不完全符合合同规定的,船东没有义务接船。仅就这一句而言,只要有任何不符点,船东都可以拒绝接船。根据上述规定的第二句,如果不符点的重要性不大且船厂无法在合理时间内对不符点进行补正的,船厂依然可以交船。这里的重要性不大应当是一个事实问题,在不同的案件中可能会有不同的解释,缺乏明确的标准和操作性。

---

① Article VII.4(d).

客观原因

7.87 船舶建造合同通常会赋予船东在发现船舶不符合合同或规格书规定时拒绝接受船舶的权利。但是这种情形与合同约定卖方提供买方满意的货物的情形并不相同。后一种情形明显带有主观因素,而前者提及的不符合合同或规格书的缺陷则应当是客观的,而不是主观的。*Docker v Hyams*① 是一个关于游艇买卖的案件,在该案中原告是卖方,被告是买方。船舶买卖合同的第 5 条有如下内容:

> After the completion of ... survey, if any material defect or defects in the yacht or her machinery shall have been found, the Purchaser may give notice to the Vendor or the Brokers of his rejection of the yacht by indicating the nature of the defect or defects. On receipt of notification of such defect or defects, the Vendor shall forthwith either indicate his willingness to make good such defect or defects without delay, or make a mutually agreed cash allowance in lieu. If the Vendor shall decline to make good the defect or defects or if the parties hereto fail to agree the amount of the cash allowance in lieu either party may by notice in writing to the other cancel this agreement.

7.88 买方在检验了游艇后通知卖方拒绝接受船舶。双方在游艇是否存在缺陷的问题上产生了争议。上诉法院的 Harman 法官认为,"缺陷"应当是客观事实,与主观意见无关。而事实问题应当由仲裁庭或法庭作出认定。他说:②

> ... I think, that where the condition is that something is to be done to A's approval or to his satisfaction then he is the judge, and as long as he is honest he need not be reasonable. But they are not quite the same, as I see it, as this case, which talks of a "defect" being "found". That removes the matter from the subjective of opinion to the objective of fact, and I think, therefore, that the cases, well illustrating as they do the point, are no compelling reason to reject the vendor's plea here that on the true construction of this contract it is a matter of objective fact and that if, on the truth being ascertained, by arbitration or otherwise, there were no such defects, there was no ground for serving notice of rejection and therefore the question ought to be answered as the Judge

---

① [1969] 1 Lloyd's Rep 487.
② [1969] 1 Lloyd's Rep 487 at 491.

answered it - that it does matter whether defects exist or do not exist, and if they do not exist then the notice was not capable of being a good notice.

Delivery Defects

7.89　NEWBUILDCON 格式在试航后船东是否接受船舶问题上有比较特别的规定。下面是 NEWBUILDCON 格式第 27 条(海试)中关于船东在海试结束后接受或拒绝船舶的相关规定内容：①

Method of Acceptance or Rejection
(i) Upon completion of the sea trials the Builder shall give the Buyer the results of the sea trials in writing. If the Builder considers that the results thereof demonstrate that the Vessel conforms to the requirements of this Contract, the Builder shall give the Buyer notice of when delivery will take place. Such notice shall state where and when the Vessel will be ready for delivery, which will be at least fifteen(15)running days after the notice is given. Within five(5)running days after receipt of this notice and the trial results, the Buyer shall notify the Builder in writing of its acceptance for delivery or rejection of the Vessel.
(ii) If the results of the sea trials demonstrate that the Vessel or any part or equipment thereof does not conform to the requirements of this Contract, or if the Buyer rejects the Vessel for other reasons which the Builder accepts as valid, the Builder shall take all necessary steps to rectify such non-conformity. If necessary the Builder shall for its own cost and expense carry out a further sea trial in accordance with this Clause to ascertain that the Vessel complies with the terms of this Contract. Upon demonstration by the Builder that the deficiencies have been corrected, the procedure set out in this Sub-clause(d)shall apply.
(iii) If the Buyer gives notice of rejection under (i)above or rejects the Vessel under (ii) above, the Buyer shall state in which respects the Vessel does not conform to the requirements of this Contract (hereinafter "Delivery Defects").
(iv) If the Delivery Defects are of minor importance and do not affect Class or the operation of the Vessel in its intended trade but the

---

① Clause 27(d).

Builder is unable to rectify the matter within a reasonable time and in any event before the accrual of the Buyer's right to terminate in accordance with Clause 39 (Suspension and Termination), the Buildermay nevertheless require the Buyer to take delivery of the Vessel, on condition that the Builder first:

(1) undertakes to remedy the Delivery Defects for its own cost and expense as soon as possible; and

(2) agrees in writing to indemnify the Buyer for any loss incurred as a consequence thereof, including loss of time; and

(3) provides the Buyer with a guarantee issued by the party named in Box 32 (or if Box 32 is not filled in, a bank guarantee from a first class bank) substantially in the form and substance set out in Annex A(iv) for a sum which the Buyer reasonably requests to cover (1) and (2) above, failing agreement such sum to be resolved in accordance with Clause 42 (Dispute Resolution);

whereupon the Buyer shall accept delivery of the Vessel.

(v) If the Builder disputes the rejection of the Vessel by the Buyer, the dispute shall be resolved in accordance with Clause 42 (Dispute Resolution).

7.90　　按照第27(d)(i)条的规定,试航结束后如果船厂认为试航结果符合建造合同规定的应当向船东发出交船通知,船东则应在收到通知后的5天内作出接受或拒绝船舶的决定。按照第27(d)(ii)条的规定,如果试航结果不符合建造合同规定的要求或船东以船厂接受的其他原因拒绝船舶,船厂应当采取必要的措施纠正不符合合同规定的缺陷。如果船厂证明缺陷已经得到纠正,第27(d)条的规定方才适用。该条并没有涉及不符合建造合同规定是如何确定的,即是船东自己的观点还是第三方例如船级社的观点。如果是船级社认为试航结果不符合建造合同规定的,船厂显然是不能交船的。采取措施纠正缺陷也是必然的。但如果仅仅是船东的观点且没有得到船厂认可的话,双方就可能会因此产生争议。只要船东认为不符合船厂就应当采取措施予以纠正,这样的规定可能有失公平。相比之下,SAJ格式的规定可能更为合适。按照SAJ格式的规定,船东主张船舶不符合建造合同规定的,船厂只有在认同船东的主张才应当采取措施予以纠正。①

---

① SAJ Article VI.4(b).

7.91　按照第27(d)(iii)条的规定,如果船东按照第27(d)(i)条规定发出拒绝船舶的通知或者按照第27(d)(ii)条规定拒绝船舶,船东均应说明船舶不符合建造合同规定之处。此种不符之处被称为 Delivery Defects。由于两个字的首字母都采用了大写,因此 Delivery Defects 应当是专用词汇,但 NEWBUILDCON 格式实际上并没有 Delivery Defects 的定义。但从第27(d)(iii)条来看,Delivery Defects 应当就是不符合合同规定的缺陷,而且有可能是船东单方面认为的不符合合同规定的缺陷。这些缺陷有可能成立,也有可能不成立。但无论船东主张的缺陷是否成立,船厂都应采取措施予以纠正,这构成船厂的合同义务。

7.92　第27(d)(iv)条是针对特定的 Delivery Defects 作出的规定,特定的 Delivery Defects 是指并不十分重要且不影响船级和船舶正常运行,而船厂又无法在船东可以解约之日前的予以纠正的 Delivery Defects。在这种情况下,船厂可以要求船东接船,但应当承诺尽快纠正缺陷,同意赔偿船东因此遭受的损失,包括时间损失,提供银行担保。如果 Delivery Defects 不影响船舶和船舶的正常运行,船东其实是不能拒绝船舶的。拒绝船厂意味着船东解除了建造合同,建造不符合合同规定虽然构成船厂的违约,但除非另有约定,此种建造缺陷并不赋予船东解约的权利。

7.93　NEWBUILDCON 格式第27(d)条应当是针对试航后船东接受或拒绝船舶一事作出的规定。接受是指船东确认船舶建造符合合同约定,拒绝则是指船东以船舶建造不符合合同约定为由拒绝船舶,即船东不再继续履行建造合同。然而 NEWBUILDCON 格式并没有针对船东此种拒绝作出规定,而是针对那些不影响船东接船的缺陷作出了规定。

船东解除合同的权利

7.94　船东在试航后拒绝接受船舶与船东解除船舶建造合同应当是两回事。拒绝接受船舶是指船东认为在试航后船舶依然存在缺陷和问题,这些缺陷和问题不符合船舶建造合同的要求。因此船东有权在船厂解决了所有缺陷和问题后再接受船舶。而解除合同则是指船东不再继续履行船舶建造合同了,因此只有在船厂的行为构成毁约的情况下,船东才可以解除船舶建造合同。*McDougall* v *Aeromarine of Emsworth Ltd*[①] 一案中,原告是船东,被告是船厂。双方订立了船舶建造合同,由船厂为船东建造一艘赛艇。船舶建造合同的第5条规定:

---

① [1958] 2 Lloyd's Rep 345.

Upon completion of the craft the builders will notify the purchaser in writing that the craft is ready for acceptance trials to be run and the purchaser or his authorized agent will present himself within twenty-eight days of the date of such notice to accompany the builders or their representative upon a trial run of not less than one hour's duration ....

7.95 船舶建造合同的第 6 条规定：

The builders shall be deemed to have completed the construction and fitting out of the craft in accordance with the requirements of the annexed specification at the conclusion of the trial run provided that the performance of the craft during such trial run is to the reasonable satisfaction of the purchaser such satisfaction to be indicated by the signature of the purchaser to the memorandum indorsed on the back hereof.

7.96 在船舶试航时，船东发现了很多缺陷和问题，船东没有签署表示接受船舶的备忘录。船东要求船厂对发现的缺陷和问题进行纠正，船厂也表示将解决所有的缺陷和问题。Diplock 法官认为船东按照合同第 5 条和第 6 条的规定有权拒绝无法合理地使船东满意的船舶，他说：①

In my view, the effect of Clauses 5 and 6 of the contract is to entitle the buyer to refuse delivery if he is not reasonably satisfied of the performance of the craft when tendered by the seller for delivery at the conclusion of the acceptance trials ....

7.97 但是 Diplock 法官认为船舶存在的缺陷和问题未必使船东有权以船厂已违反了船舶建造合同的条件为由而解除合同。他是这样说的：②

But it does not follow that, because when the vessel is first tendered by the seller for acceptance trials the buyer is reasonably dissatisfied with her, he is entitled to treat the defects then existing as a breach of condition, so as to enable him to treat the contract as repudiated .... The buyer is entitled to refuse to accept delivery of the vessel in its existing state, but, if the defect is one that can be remedied, and remedied within a time which will still enable the seller to deliver within the period of delivery permitted by the contract, the buyer is not, in my

---

① [1958] 2 Lloyd's Rep 345 at 357.
② Ibid.

view, entitled to treat the contract as repudiated by the seller by reason of the existence of such defects at the time when the vessel is first tendered for acceptance.

从上述案例可以看出,即使船舶交船时存在着足以使船东有权拒绝接受船舶的缺陷或问题,但是船东未必可以以此为由解除船舶建造合同,因为船厂并没有构成毁约。

争议的解决

船舶的试航结果是否符合船级规范和船旗国的要求并不是一个经常会导致船厂和船东之间争议的问题,在这个问题上船级社是可以也应当作出最终结论的机构。然而,船舶试航结果是否符合船舶建造合同或规格书要求的问题则并非如此简单。如前所述,船级社一般只关心船舶涉及船级规范和船旗国要求的项目,而不会关心船舶是否符合船舶建造合同及规格书的要求。因此,船厂和船东就船舶是否符合合同及规格书要求发生争议也就不奇怪了。一旦发生此类争议,除非能通过相互间的协商解决,否则就会适用船舶建造合同的争议解决条款了。SAJ格式就对此作出了规定:①

The BUILDER may dispute the rejection of the VESSEL by the BUYER under this Paragraph, in which case the matter shall be submitted for final decision by arbitration in accordance with Article XIII hereof.

其他标准格式,包括 AWES 格式,②Norwegian 格式,③CSTC 格式,④以及 NEWBUILDCON 格式都有类似的规定。由于不同的船舶建造合同的争议解决条款又有不同的规定,所以争议的解决方式和程序等也会有所不同。例如按照 NEWBUILDCON 格式的争议解决条款的规定,一旦发生船舶是否符合合同或规格书规定的争议时,一方可以书面通知对方并将争议提交独立的第三人解决。⑤

船东错误拒绝船舶

如果船东拒绝接受船舶缺乏正当理由,即拒绝是错误的,船东就可能承担因

---

① Article VI.4(e).
② Article 4(d), para.4.
③ Article VII.4(e).
④ Article VI.4(d).
⑤ Clause 42(b).

此而引起的后果。如果船东拒绝接受船舶并要求船厂对由其提出的缺陷或问题作出补正后再交船,船东可能应承担由此产生的时间和费用的损失;如果船东拒绝接受船舶并解除船舶建造合同的,船东则可能承担毁约责任。船厂在这种情况下可以拒绝船东的毁约,坚持要求船东履约,即接受船舶。船厂也可以接受船东的毁约,并按照船舶建造合同的规定处置船舶并主张损害赔偿。

VI 试航后的建造工作

7.102　虽然船舶在试航结束后并不马上交接,但在正常情况下试航之后的建造工作基本上是整理、补遗和补正性的。一旦试航成功,船舶就可以在此后的较短时间内,差不多两至三周左右的时间内交接。通常情况下,船厂在船舶试航成功后还至少会有以下两方面的工作需要完成:一方面是船厂在船舶试航前就已经安排在试航后完成的工作,这些是船厂在试航前就已经知道的工作,这些工作主要是各项扫尾工作或补遗工作;另一方面的工作则是船舶的试航带来的工作,这些是船厂在试航前并不知道也没有作出相应安排的工作。

7.103　试航带来的工作包括:船厂在船舶试航中发现的需要完成的工作或需要解决的缺陷或问题;船东指派参加试航的代表在试航中发现的且船厂在交船前需要解决的问题,如短缺的物件或工具等;船级社的验船师在船舶试航后向船厂提出的需要在船级社颁发航行证书和船级证书之前予以消除的缺陷或问题等。船东指派参加试航的代表和船级社指派参加试航的代表一般会将他们发现的问题列成清单,要求船厂在交船之前完成。如果这些清单列明的工作都是扫尾和补遗性质的,船厂应当不需要很长时间就能完成。否则,船厂就应当和船东的监造代表协商具体后续工作的实施计划和施工程序。

7.104　船东提供的清单甚至有可能构成新的修改,这时就要适用船舶建造合同关于修改的规定。双方还需要就合同交船日以及合同价格的调整重新达成一致。

第 8 章 交 船

I 交船概述

交付的意义及要求

8.1 船舶试航成功后就将面临交船。"Delivery"在中文中的表述应当是"交付""给付""交割"等，交船只是"delivery"的一种表现形式。作为"交付"或"给付"，"delivery"的定义是：①

> The Sale of Goods Act 1979 s.61(1) defines delivery as the "voluntary transfer of possession from one person to another". The words "delivery" and "deliver" are not, however, used in a single consistent sense in the Act. A tender of delivery is not the same thing as an actual delivery. For example, with respect to the seller's duty to deliver the goods, it is normally sufficient for the seller, further to the presumptive rule of delivery at the seller's place of business in s.29(2), to place the goods specified by the contract at the disposition of the buyer in a deliverable state without any reciprocal act on the part of the buyer.

8.2 高院的 Pearson 法官在 *Christie & Vesey Ltd v Maatschappij Tot Exploitatie Van Schepen en Andere Zaken Helvetia NV* 一案中对"delivery"进行了解释，他说：②

> The word "delivery" can have different meanings. One meaning – the original, proper meaning, I suppose – is the handing over under the Sale of Goods Act, 1893, the transferring of possession from the seller to the buyer.

---

① Michael Bridge, *Benjamin's Sale of Goods*, 12th edn Sweet & Maxwell 2024, para.8 – 002
② [1960] 1 Lloyd's Rep 540 at 549.

8.3　按照成文法的规定,船舶的"交付"可以是虚拟的,因为"交付"强调的是所有权的转移,而不是物的转移。上述规定显然不是针对根据船舶建造合同进行的船舶交付,因为船舶的交付都是实际的,既不是虚拟的,也不是象征性的。1979年《货物买卖法》也有关于"delivery"一词的定义:①

> "Delivery" means voluntary transfer of possession from one person to another; except that in relation to sections 20A and 20B above it includes such appropriation of goods to the contract as results in property in the goods being transferred to the buyer.

8.4　虽然在船舶建造中,船舶所有权往往随船舶的交接自船厂一方转移至船东一方,但是船舶所有权并非只能随船舶一起发生转移,因此交船和船舶所有权转移没有必然的关系。从上述1979年《货物买卖法》的规定也可以看出,交船强调的是船舶占有的转移。

"交船"和"船舶交接"

8.5　"交船"一词既可以指"船舶交接",也可以指"提交"或"交付"。"船舶交接"强调的是买卖双方的行为,即由船厂的交与船东的接共同组成。"提交"和"交付"强调的则是船厂交船的单方面行为。"交船"的第一种含义需要船厂和船东双方的行为才可以完成,而"交船"的第二种含义则无需船东的参与,而只是船厂按照船舶建造合同的规定将已处于可交接状态的船舶向船东交付。第一种含义的"交船"需要船厂和船东的共同行为才能完成,而第二种含义的"交船"则是船厂自己就可以完成的。无论船东是否接受都不影响船厂"交船"的完成。

8.6　1979年《货物买卖法》有关于交付的规定:②

> It is the duty of the seller to deliver the goods, and of the buyer to accept and pay for them, in accordance with the terms of the contract of sale.

8.7　这里的"deliver"是指上述第二种"交船"的含义,即船厂单方面履行船舶建造合同义务的行为。而前文提及的1979年《货物买卖法》中关于"delivery"一词的定义则应是指上述第一种"交船"的含义,即船厂和船东共同的完成船舶交接的

---

① s.61(1).
② s.27.

行为。船厂单方面"交船"的行为既可能导致船舶占有发生转移,也可能不导致船舶占有及其所有权和风险发生转移。

可交接状态

交船前船舶必须处于可交接状态,只有处于可交接状态的船舶才能交接。船舶在试航成功且得到船东接受后,通常就已经处于可交接状态了。1979年《货物买卖法》对"可交接状态"作出了规定:① 8.8

> Goods are in a deliverable state within the meaning of this Act when they are in such a state that the buyer would under the contract be bound to take delivery of them.

就船舶而言,所谓"可交接状态"应当是指船舶已经按照船舶建造合同以及规格书规定的要求建造完毕,并且通过了船东和船级社以及船旗国的检验。船舶是否建造完毕应当是一个事实问题,但建造完毕并不是指船舶建造没有任何缺陷。在这个问题上,虽然 Westminster Corporation v J Jarvis and Son and Another② 并不是一个船舶建造的案件,但有助于我们理解"建造完毕"的概念。在该案中,原告是雇主,被告是承包人。承包人受雇于雇主建造一个多层停车场。合同规定了承包人应当完成工程的日期,此外合同的第23条还规定: 8.9

> Upon it becoming reasonably apparent that the progress of the works is delayed, the contractor shall forthwith give written notice of the cause of the delay to the architect . . . and if in the opinion of the architect . . . the completion of the works is likely to be or has been delayed . . . (g) by delay on the part of nominated sub-contractors . . . the architect . . . shall . . . make . . . a fair and reasonable extension of time for completion of the works . . . .

分包商按照其与承包人的分包合同规定,在6月20日完成了打桩的分包工作并离开了工地,但是差不多在一个月以后分包商的工作被发现存在缺陷,原因是分包商的工艺有问题或者是分包商使用的材料有问题。于是分包商开始对其工作进行了补正,补正工作一直到9月29日才结束,结果导致承包人无法按时完成工程。双方的争议是承包人是否可以顺延其与雇主之间的合同的完工日。一审的 Donaldson 法官认为延误只能发生在工作正在继续的情况下,由于分包商已 8.10

---

① s.61(5).
② [1970] 1 WLR 637.

经按期完成他们的工作,因此不存在分包商的延误。但是上诉法院则认为分包商是在 9 月 29 日完成工作的,因此存在延误。上议院推翻了上诉法院的判决,维持了一审法院 Donaldson 法官的判决,上议院的 Lord Hodson 说:①

> I agree with the contention that delay relates to the time when performance is due. From the contractor's point of view it matters not why the work has not been done on time. Dilatoriness is not in itself relevant. The short answer, however, to the sub-contractor's main contention is that ... delay does not, for practical purposes, run after there is such completion as will enable the contractor to take over himself .... The discovery of the latent defects in the piles showed that the subcontractor was in breach, not that it was in delay. It did not return in order to fulfil its contract but to remedy the breach. Time had already run out.

8.11 　上议院的 Dilhorne 子爵认为承包商是否可以顺延完工日取决于分包商何时完成他们的工作。如果分包商是在 6 月 22 日完成工作的就没有延误;如果分包商是在 9 月 29 日完成工作的就有延误。按照合同第 15(a)条的规定,一旦工程实际完成,建筑师就应当签发证书,但合同并没有对"实际完成"作出定义。Dilhorne 子爵对 practically completed 进行了解释,他说:②

> One would normally say that a task was practically completed when it was almost but not entirely finished, but "practical completion" suggests that that is not the intended meaning and that what is meant is the completion of all the construction work that has to be done .... Completion under the contract is not postponed until defects which became apparent only after the work had been finished have been remedied. This interpretation is supported by the fact that the defects liability period runs from the date in the practical completion certificate. This contract provided for a defects liability period of 12 months.

8.12 　由上文可见,在船舶建造合同中,船舶在交船时尚有一些工作没有完成,即使已完成的工作存在一些缺陷,这些都不影响船厂向船东交船。一旦在交船后发现缺陷,虽然船厂应当按照船舶建造合同中质量保证条款对缺陷进行修理或更换,但这并不影响船厂交船的成立。

---

① [1970] 1 WLR 637 at 643.
② [1970] 1 WLR 637 at 646.

II 交船日期

合同交船日

船舶建造合同规定交船日一般有两种办法,一是将一个特定的日期规定为交船日;另一则是规定建造期限以及开始起算该期限的日期,建造期限届满之日即为最后交船日。相比而言,大多数船舶建造合同采用前一种方式规定交船日。船舶建造合同规定的交船日又称为"合同交船日"。SAJ格式规定:① 8.13

> The VESSEL shall be delivered by the BUILDER to the BUYER at the Shipyard on or before ...., ..., except that, in the event of delays in the construction of the VESSEL or any performance required under this Contract due to causes which under the terms of this Contract permit postponement of the date for delivery, the aforementioned date for delivery of the VESSEL shall be postponed accordingly. The aforementioned date, or such later date to which the requirement of delivery is postponed pursuant to such terms, is herein called the "Delivery Date".

从上述SAJ格式的规定可以看出,合同交船日既不是一个确定的日期,也不是一个固定的日期。如果发生任何可以顺延交船的情形,合同交船日就会随之推迟。而因此推迟的日期依然称作为"合同交船日"。其他标准格式也有类似的规定,②其中AWES格式的规定是:③ 8.14

> ... The Delivery Date as set out above shall be subject to extension by the cumulative amount of all Permissible Delays as provided for in this CONTRACT.

NEWBUILDCON格式则采用不同的方式对合同交船日的调整作出了规定。该格式的交船条款有如下规定:④ 8.15

> Subject to Clause 27(d) (Sea Trials – Method of Acceptance or Rejection)

---

① Article VII.1.
② Norwegian Article VIII.1, CSTC Article VII.1.
③ Article 6(a), para.1.
④ Clause 28.

the Vessel shall be delivered to the Buyer on or after the Delivery Date at the Shipyard or at a safe place in the immediate vicinity thereof in a clean and orderly condition ready for service, upon . . . .

8.16　虽然在这一条中没有关于合同交船日调整或顺延的规定，但是该格式的定义条款中的下列内容应能说明"合同交船日"并不是固定的：

"Delivery Date" means the Contractual Date of Delivery as may be adjusted in accordance with the terms of this Contract.

"Permissible Delays" means delays to the construction and/or delivery of the Vessel and which entitle the Builder to extend the Delivery Date in accordance with Clause 34(Permissible Delays).

8.17　船舶建造和交付因合同约定的可允许延误的原因延误的，船厂便可以顺延合同交船日。在实践中有可能造成船舶建造及交付延误的情况大致包括：不可抗力事件、船东审批图纸的延误、船东提出变更和修改造成的延误、船东支付建造款的延误、船东提供供应品的延误以及其他因船东的原因导致的交船日推迟。因船东原因致使船舶建造和交船发生延误的均构成可允许延误。在实践中，很少有船舶是在合同交船日交接的，船厂大多是在合同交船日之后交船。合同交船日和实际交船日往往不是同一日。

交船日规定的性质

8.18　作为成文法，1893年《货物买卖法》对合同中关于支付时间的性质作出了规定：①

Unless a different intention appears from the terms of the contract stipulations as to time of payment are not deemed to be of the essence of a contract of sale. Whether any other stipulation "as to time is of the essence" of the contract or not depends on the terms of the contract.

8.19　上述规定允许合同当事人自己就关于履行时间的规定是否构成合同的条件条款作出约定，在当事人没有约定履行时间规定的性质时，则应根据合同条款予以确定。按照1893年《货物买卖法》的规定，除非与该法的明文规定有冲突，普通法依然适用于货物买卖合同：②

---

① s.10(1).
② s.61(2).

The rules of the common law, including the law merchant, save in so far as they are inconsistent with the express provisions of this Act, and in particular the rules relating to the law of principal and agent and the effect of fraud, misrepresentation, duress or coercion, mistake, or other invalidating cause, shall continue to apply to contracts for the sale of goods.

在 Hartley v Hymans 一案中, McCardie 法官对 1893 年《货物买卖法》的上述条文提出了批评:①   8.20

It is curious that s.10 of the Sale of Goods Act, 1893, deals so ambiguously with this point .... Now the common law and the law merchant did not make the question whether time was of the essence depend on the terms of the contract, unless indeed those terms were express on the point. It looked rather to the nature of the contract and the character of the goods dealt with. In ordinary commercial contracts for the sale of goods the rule clearly is that time is *prima facie* of the essence with respect to delivery .... In *Paton & Sons* v *Payne & Co* ((1897) 35 SLR 112), however, it was held by the House of Lords that in a contract for the sale and delivery of a printing machine time was not of the essence.

在 *Compagnie Commerciale Sucres et Denrees* v *C Czarnikow Ltd*② 一案中, 货物买卖合同适用的规则 14 有如下内容: 8.21

(1) In cases of f.a.s., f.o.b., and free stowed in hold (f.o.b. stowed) contracts the seller shall have the sugar ready to be delivered to the buyer at any time within the contract period.

(2) The buyer, having given reasonable notice, shall be entitled to call for delivery of the sugar between the first and last working day inclusive of the period of delivery.

(3) If the vessel (or vessels) has presented herself in readiness to load within the contract period but has failed to be presented within five calendar days of the date contained in the notice above calling for delivery of the sugar the buyer shall be responsible for any costs incurred by the seller by reason of such delay exceeding the five calendar days.

---

① [1920] 3 KB 475 at 483.
② [1990] 1 WLR 1337.

(4) If the vessel(or vessels) has presented herself in readiness to load within the contract period, but loading has not been completed by the last working day of the period, the seller shall be bound to deliver and the buyer bound to accept delivery of the balance of the cargo or parcel up to the contract quantity."

8.22　争议主要是两个问题:第一,规则 14 是否规定了卖方在船舶抵达装港且收到通知后负有立即将货物准备就绪装船的义务;第二,如果是的话,该义务是否为合同的条件条款。仲裁员的回答都是肯定的,一审法院的 Gatehouse 法官的回答是否定的;上诉法院的多数法官对第一个问题的回答是肯定的,而对第二个问题的回答则是否定的。上议院的 Lord Ackner 认为规则 14 规定了卖方的一项明示的义务,违反该义务就构成对合同条件条款的违反。Lord Ackner 在对规则 14 作出了解释以后指出:①

This clearly was a mercantile contract and rule 14(1) can properly be described as a "time clause." It imposes an obligation to have the goods called forward available for loading at a definite point of time – at the expiration of the notice given under clause 7 and as soon as the vessel presents herself ready to load within the contract period. The performance by the sellers of their obligations under rule 14(1) does not involve questions of degree....

8.23　Lord Ackner 接着说:②

Rule 14(1) was crucially important to the buyers since it removed the risk that the absence or insufficiency of cargo would be a cause of delay. Since it must be rare, if ever, for it to be in the sellers' interest to load a vessel very slowly, the rule ensures to a very large extent that loading will be promptly commenced and speedily carried out and thus enable the buyers punctually to perform their own obligations to their customers. The rule tends to provide certainty which is such an indispensable ingredient of mercantile contracts.

8.24　综上,普通法对合同中关于履行时间规定的性质应当取决于对相关条款的解释以及合同的特征等。在 *Lindvig* v *Forth Shipbuilding & Engineering Company*

---

① [1990] 1 WLR 1337 at 1347.
② [1990] 1 WLR 1337 at 1348.

Ltd① 一案中,船舶建造合同规定:

> The contractor undertakes to build the vessel to her proper turn, bearing the Forth Shipbuilding Company's number 67, and to deliver the vessel in October, 1920.

但由于合同同时又规定,船厂迟延交船的应每星期支付 100 英镑,Roche 法官并不认为上述条款构成船舶建造合同的条件条款,他说:② 8.25

> ... this clause as to the date of delivery is not a condition of the contract so as to entitle the plaintiff in the event of non-performance of the term as to delivery, to treat the contract as broken in such an essential as to entitle him to treat it as repudiated and rescinded.

在 *McDougall* v *Aeromarine of Emsworth Ltd* 一案中,船舶建造合同规定: 8.26

> The builders will use their best endeavours to complete the construction and fitting out by the first day of May 1957 but owing to the effect of delays and shortages such delivery date cannot be guaranteed.

虽然船厂并没有保证在交船日或之前交船,但是高院的 Diplock 法官则认为船厂在交船日前后合理时间内交船是合同的条件条款,他说:③ 8.27

> By Sect. 10 of the Sale of Goods Act, 1893, whether this stipulation as to time of delivery is a condition or a warranty depends on the terms of the contract. In my view, the obligation to deliver within a reasonable time of May 1, 1957, is a condition .... Where a purchaser buys a yacht for use for his own pleasure from the beginning of a particular yachting season, I think it must, as a matter of common sense, be of the essence of the contract that he should receive delivery in time to make substantial use of it during that season.

由于绝大多数船舶建造合同都会在规定一个合同交船日的同时再允许船厂在合同交船日之后的一段时间内交船,因此船舶建造合同中的合同交船日就不再是一个具有关键意义的时间规定了。 8.28

---

① (1921) Ll L Rep 253.
② (1921) Ll L Rep 253 at 255.
③ [1958] 2 Lloyd's Rep 345 at 358.

合同规定的解释

8.29 　　有时船舶建造合同的规定并没有反映当事人的真正意思表示,有时则没有引起船厂和船东应有的注意。在这种情况下,条款的含义可能需要通过解释予以确定,至于当事人主观是如何考虑的也就不再那么重要了。在 *Harland & Wolff Ltd* v *Lakeport Navigation Co Panama SA*① 一案中,船舶建造合同的交船延误条款有如下规定:

> 4(1)Delayed Delivery
>
> (a) No adjustment shall be made, and the basic purchase price shall remain unchanged, for the first thirty(30) days delay in delivery beyond the delivery date as defined in Clause 10 hereof …
>
> (b) If the delivery of the Vessel is delayed more than thirty(30) days then, in such event beginning at midnight of the thirtieth(30th) day after delivery is required under this Agreement, the basic purchase price shall be reduced by deducting therefrom as follows for the delay in delivery of the Vessel beyond the said thirty days allowance,
>
> | | | |
> |---|---|---|
> | a For the first forty-five | (45) days | £2,000 per diem |
> | b For the second forty-five | (45) days | £2,500 per diem |
> | c For the last thirty | (30) days | £3,000 per diem |
>
> ……
>
> (c) For the purposes of sub-paragraphs(a)and(b)herein, credit shall be given for extension of delivery date by reason of permissible delays, as hereinafter provided.
>
> (d) But if in any event the delay in delivery, inclusive of Force Majeure delays but exclusive of any delay for which the Buyer is responsible continues for a period of more than One Hundred and Fifty(150) days after the date of delivery set forth in this Agreement, then in such event the Buyer may, at its option, cancel this Agreement by serving upon the Builder written notice of cancellation. The Buyer may serve such written notice by cable or telex to that effect …

8.30 　　合同的第 10 条是交船日条款,该条规定:

> The Builder shall use due diligence to construct complete and deliver the

---

① 　[1974] 1 Lloyd's Rep 301.

Vessel on the delivery date specified herein and subject to any extension of the delivery date as may be permitted in accordance with the relevant provisions of this Agreement the Vessel ... shall be delivered ... on or before February 28, 1973.

合同的第 11 条是不可抗力条款。船舶建造因各种原因发生了延误,船厂根据第 11 条的规定主张推迟合同交船日,船东也没有表示反对。船厂未能在 1973 年 2 月 28 日完成船舶建造,150 天的期限在 1973 年 7 月 28 日届满,船厂依然未能完成船舶建造。船东要求船厂尽快完成船舶建造,但是双方对第 4(1)(d)条的解释发生了争议。船东认为由于有"... after delivery date set forth in this Agreement"一句,150 天期限应当自 1973 年 2 月 28 日经可允许延误调整后的日期起算,因此不会在 1973 年 7 月 28 日届满。船厂则认为"set forth in this Agreement"的交船日与第 4(1)(a)和(b)条中提及的交船日是相同的,因此只能是 1973 年 2 月 28 日,而不可能是调整后的日期。Ackner 法官接受了船厂的观点,他认为"set forth"通常是指"written out in"而不应是"calculated in accordance with"。Ackner 法官说:①

8.31

> While it is true that by accepting Feb. 28 as the appropriate date for cl. 4(1)(d) it may result in the 150 days thereafter ending before the 150 days provided for under sub-pars.(a)plus(b). But this is *nihil ad rem* since sub-cl.(a) and (b) both exclude force majeure delays while sub-par.(d) includes it. Accordingly I conclude that the period of 150 days provided by cl.4(1)(d) had expired on July 29, 1973.

违约的构成

除非合同另有规定,如果船厂未能在合同规定的交船日交船就构成违约,但此种违约并不足以使船东有权拒绝接船。在 *Raineri v Miles* 一案中,房屋买卖合同规定了交割日,但并没有明确规定时间事关重要。上议院的 Lord Fraser of Tullybelton 说:②

8.32

> The principle which in my opinion emerges from the authorities to which I have referred is that breach of a contractual stipulation as to time which is not of the essence of a contract will not be treated as a breach of a

---

① [1974] 1 Lloyd's Rep 301 at 310.
② [1981] AC 1050 at 1093.

condition precedent to the contract, that is as a breach which would entitle the innocent party to treat the contract as terminated or which would prevent the defaulting party from suing for specific performance. Nevertheless it is a breach of the contract and entitles the injured party to damages if he has suffered damage.

8.33 普通法的地位是清楚的,即使时间并不是合同的关键,只要船厂未能在约定的日期交船即构成违约,应当承担损害赔偿。只是绝大多数船舶建造合同都有因延迟而须支付的损害赔偿的规定,而且一般还有 30 天宽限期,因此船厂也就无需承担其他损害赔偿了。

不确定的交船日

8.34 船舶建造合同一般都会规定一个确定的或可以确定的交船日。如果船舶建造合同规定交船日是大约的或虽有确定日期但船厂并不保证交船的交船日,船厂就应当在合理的时间内交船。在 *McDougall* v *Aeromarine of Emsworth Ltd* ① 一案中,船舶建造合同的第 3 条规定:

> The builders will use their best endeavours to complete the construction and fitting out by the first day of May 1957 but owing to the effect of delays and shortages such delivery date cannot be guaranteed.

8.35 高院的 Diplock 法官认为,虽然船厂没有保证在约定日期交船,但是船厂的义务是在该日期的合理期限内交船。他说:②

> A clause in this form, in my view, places upon the seller a duty to deliver within a reasonable time of the specified date. What is a reasonable time from the specified date is a question of fact depending upon all the circumstances of the case as they exist up to the time when delivery is or ought to be made.

8.36 在该案中,船东建造赛艇的目的是为了参加 1957 年的赛艇季节的活动,Diplock 法官认为合理期间应当在 1957 年 9 月起结束,因为那时已经是应当交船的日期后 3 个月了,且 1957 年赛艇季节已经过去了五分之四了。而且,Diplock 法官认为船厂在合理期限内依然没有交船的就构成对船舶建造合同条件条款的

---

① [1958] 2 Lloyd's Rep 345.
② [1958] 2 Lloyd's Rep 345 at 357.

违反,船东可以视船舶建造合同已被毁约。他说:①

> The defendants' failure to tender the yacht for delivery in accordance with the contract by Sept. 5 was itself, I think, a breach of condition which the plaintiff was entitled to treat as rescinding the contract. Their intimation, for that was what their offer amounted to, that they could not complete it before the end of the 1957 yachting season was *a fortiori*, in my opinion, a wrongful repudiation of the contract by the defendants, as was their intimation that they would only complete the contract upon terms different from those of the original contract.

提前的交船

大多数船舶建造合同在规定合同交船日时都会在合同交船日之前加上"on or before"的字样。② 这其实是允许船厂在合同交船日之前交船。在实践中可以看到有船舶建造合同在规定了船厂可以在合同交船日或之前交船的同时又规定船厂不可以在特定日期或期限之前交船。在合同允许船厂在合同交船日之前交船的情况下,打算提前交船的船厂就应当按照合同的规定向船东发出通知。在船东通过融资建造船舶的情形下,无论船东是否愿意在合同交船日之前接船,船东实际上都未必可以作出决定。因为在合同交船日之前交船意味着融资银行有可能要提前准备支付最后一期款。 8.37

Norwegian格式虽然在合同交船日之前仅使用了"on",但Norwegian格式实际上又明确允许船厂在合同交船日之前交船,只是不能在合同交船日前2周交船而已:③ 8.38

> ... Unless otherwise agreed, the Vessel shall not be delivered earlier than maximum 2 weeks prior to the Contract Delivery Date.

与SAJ等格式不同,Norwegian格式已经明确了船厂在合同交船日之前交船的合同权利,只要船厂的交船不早于合同交船日前两周,船东不能拒绝接受船舶。在标准格式中,NEWBUILDCON格式应当是唯一明确规定不允许船厂单方面在合同交船日之前交船的标准格式,因为该格式交船条款的规定与大多数标准格式 8.39

---

① [1958] 2 Lloyd's Rep 345 at 359.
② SAJ Article VII.1, AWES Article 6(a), para.1, CSTC Article VII.1, para.1.
③ Article VIII.2.

不同，不是采用"on or before"，而是使用了"on or after"。①

> ... the Vessel shall be delivered to the Buyer on or after the Delivery Date ...

8.40　因此船舶建造合同在有上述规定的情况下，除非征得船东的同意，否则船厂不能在合同交船日之前交船。

新的协议

8.41　船舶建造合同的标准格式都有一条款，规定在船东按照合同规定可以解约时没有解约的，船厂可以提出新的交船日，而船东则应当在约定时间内作出是接受新的交船日还是解除合同的决定。SAJ 的规定如下：②

> ... The BUILDER may, at any time after the accumulated time of the aforementioned delays justifying rescission by the BUYER, demand in writing that the BUYER shall make an election, in which case the BUYER shall, within twenty (20) days after such demand is received by the BUYER either notify the BUILDER of its intention to rescind this Contract, or consent to a postponement of the Delivery Date to a specific future date, it being understood and agreed by the parties hereto that, if any further delay occurs on account of causes justifying rescission as specified in this Article, the BUYER shall have the same right of rescission upon the same terms as hereinabove provided.

8.42　船厂是否可以推迟交船完全取决于船东，而船东则有可能根据当时的市场情况作出规定。一旦船东决定接受船厂的推迟交船，船厂就可以在该新交船日或之前交船。但是这一新交船日并不是"合同交船日"，因此船厂不再享有之前约定的交船日后的宽限期。一旦船厂无法在新的交船日交船的，船东就可以解除船舶建造合同。但是，除非另有约定，在新的交船日之前发生的所有按照合同可以顺延合同交船日的可允许延误则依然可以顺延新的交船日。

8.43　NEWBUILDCON 格式也有关于船厂要求船东作出是否解约决定的规定，而且规定得更为明确：③

> The Builder may at any time after the right to terminate has occurred

---

① Clause 28.
② Article VIII.4.
③ Clause 39(a)(iii), para.2.

give notice requesting that the Buyer either agrees to a new delivery date or terminates this Contract. Such new delivery date shall be a reasonable estimate by the Builder of the date when the Vessel will be ready for delivery. Within fifteen(15) days of the Builder's request, the Buyer shall notify the Builder of its decision. If the Buyer does not terminate this Contract then the new delivery date shall be deemed to be the Delivery Date provided it does not occur later than thirty(30) days prior to the expiry of the Refund Guarantee(Clause 14(b)(Guarantees – Builder's Refund Guarantee)). Notwithstanding Clause 34(a)(i)(Permissible Delays – Force majeure events) and this Clause 39(a)(iii)(1),(2)or(3) but subject to Clause 34(a)(ii)(Permissible Delays) – Other events), if the Vessel is not delivered by that date, the Buyer shall have the right to terminate this Contract. The Builder's right to request the Buyer to agree a new delivery date shall operate on each and every occasion the events stated in this Sub – clause(a)(iii) give rise to the Buyer's option to terminate.

交船地点

8.44 在绝大多数情况下,船舶都会在船厂的码头或者锚地交接。SAJ格式就规定应当在船厂交船:①

The VESSEL shall be delivered by the BUILDER to the BUYER at the Shipyard ....

8.45 这里的Shipyard似乎并没有明确的定义,因此可以解释为在船厂交船。Norwegian格式也有类似的规定:②

The Vessel shall be delivered at the Builder's yard or in the vicinity thereof ....

8.46 NEWBUILDCON格式的规定是:③

... the Vessel shall be delivered to the Buyer ... at the Shipyard or at a safe place in the immediate vicinity thereof ....

---

① Article VII.1, see also CSTC Article VII.1, para.1.
② Article VIII.1.
③ Clause 28.

8.47 　　与其他标准格式不同,AWES格式没有把交船地局限于船厂:①

> The VESSEL shall be delivered to the PURCHASER at the Shipyard or other agreed place on or before .... (the "Delivery Date") ....

8.48 　　然而,有些在长江沿线甚至内河的船厂由于水深等原因往往需要离开长江到海上进行试航,因此一般不会再回船厂交接,而是在海边或长江口寻找合适的交船地点和船东交接船舶。在这种特殊情况下,船舶建造合同应当明确规定船舶交船地点。

8.49 　　如果船舶建造合同没有规定交船地点的,船舶应当在船厂交接。1979年《货物买卖法》便有如下规定:②

> Apart from any such contract, express or implied, the place of delivery is the seller's place of business if he has one, and if not, his residence; except that, if the contract is for the sale of specific goods, which to the knowledge of the parties when the contract is made are in some other place, then that place is the place of delivery.

8.50 　　交船地点一旦确定,除非得到船东的同意,船厂不能随意变更。如果船厂不是在船舶建造合同规定的地点交船,船东有权拒绝接船。在 *Wackerbarth* v *Masson* 一案中,买卖糖的合同规定原告应当将货物交至被告指定的船,但被告要求原告交给他本人或交至仓库。Lord Ellenborough 说:③

> The delivery for which the plaintiff undertook was – on board a ship to be named by the defendant .... But the defendant requires a *tertium quid*. Instead of naming a ship, he demanded to have the sugars weighed off and delivered into his own hands, or transferred to his own name in the warehouse – keeper's books. The seller might have been exposed to some risk, or might have lost some advantage by agreeing to this; and he had a right to refuse, as it was not the mode of delivery for which he had stipulated.

---

① Article 6(a), para.1.
② s.29(2).
③ (1812) 3 Camp 270 at 271.

III 交船款的支付

按照船舶建造合同的规定,船东应当支付各期建造款。建造款在实践中通常被分为交船款和其他各期建造款,因为交船款,即最后一期款具有其他各期所不具有的特殊性。① 8.51

交船款的特殊性

与其他各期建造款相比,交船款的特殊性主要有以下几点:首先,交船款并不是预付款,因此不是还款保函担保的款项;其次,交船款的支付将直接导致船厂丧失船舶所有权和占有权,其他各期款项的支付均不会有此结果;最后,交船款支付以后,船厂要想实现自己向船东主张的任何索赔都可能会遇到各种困难。按照1979年《货物买卖法》的规定,除非另有约定,付款和交船应当具有同时履行性:② 8.52

> Unless otherwise agreed, delivery of the goods and payment of the price are concurrent conditions, that is to say, the seller must be ready and willing to give possession of the goods to the buyer in exchange for the price and the buyer must be ready and willing to pay the price in exchange for possession of the goods.

这一规定无疑适用于交船和交船款的支付,因此交船款的支付和交船具有和一次性付款的货物买卖合同中的支付相同的性质。"对流条件"即意味着合同双方同时履行,类似于一般商品买卖中的"一手交钱,一手交货"。 8.53

标准格式的规定

鉴于交船款的特殊性,船舶建造合同通常会对交船款的支付作出特别安排。SAJ格式针对交船款的支付规定了两种方式,一是由船东在交船前7天开出以船厂为受益人的信用证,另一则是将现金存入船厂指定的银行:③ 8.54

> 4th Installment:
> The BUYER shall, at least seven(7)days prior to the scheduled delivery

---

① 关于其他各期建造款的支付请参见本书第4章第II节。
② s.28.
③ Article II.4(d).

date of the VESSEL, either cause a prime bank acceptable to the BUILDER to issue anirrevocable letter of credit in favour of the BUILDER through, or to made cash deposit with .... Bank, covering the amount of this Installment as adjusted, available or releasable to the BUILDER against a signed copy of the Protocol of Delivery and Acceptance of the VESSEL as set forth as Paragraph 3 of Article VII hereof.

8.55 在现在的实践中,由船东开立以船厂为受益人的信用证的做法并不多见,绝大多数船舶建造合同都会规定,船东应当在接船前将交船款存入船厂指定银行的账户。船厂指定的银行其实就是在船舶交接时会为双方提供服务的银行。CSTC格式便有比较详细的规定:①

That BUYER shall, at least three (3) New York business days prior to the scheduled date of delivery of the VESSEL, make an irrevocable cash deposit in the name of the BUYER with Bank of China, Head Office, Banking Department, Beijing, the People's Republic of China, for a period of thirty (30) days and covering the amount of this instalment (as adjusted in accordance with the provisions of this Contract), with an irrevocable instruction that the said amount shall be released to the SELLER against presentation by the SELLER to the said Bank of China, Head Office, Banking Department, Beijing, the People's Republic of China, of a copy of the Protocol of Delivery and Acceptance signed by the BUYER's authorised representative and the SELLER. Interest, if any, accrued from such deposit, shall be for the benefit of the BUYER.

8.56 上述 CSTC 格式规定的用意应当是明确的,即船厂在交船之前就希望得到船东会按照船舶建造合同约定支付交船款的保障。此种保障对船厂而言无疑是必要的。上述规定中有几个问题值得讨论。第一个是"irrevocable cash deposit"的问题。"irrevocable cash deposit"应当是指"不可撤销的存款",这里的 deposit 不应做"押金"解。不知银行是否可以将现金做"不可撤销的存款",因为从性质上看,"不可撤销的存款"似乎与一般的"定期存款"没什么不同,即都是在一定时间不提取的存款。第二个是"不可撤销的"问题。即使银行可以做此种"不可撤销的存款",对船厂可能也没有太大的意义。船东将尾款等汇入船厂指定的银行账户明显表明其有接船意图,因而船东在接船前突然撤回存款的可能性应当不大。

---

① Article II.4(e), para.1.

即使船东撤回了存款,船厂也不会因此面临很大的风险,因为船舶始终在船厂的实际控制之下。更何况,船舶交易不成功的原因可能是多方面的,未必一定可以归责于船东。如果交接失败的原因在于船厂,不允许船东撤回资金同样是不合理的。船东应当有机会就此提出索赔。第三个是"New York business day"问题。约定适用"纽约工作日"显然是因为交易货币是美元,而且美元的汇款都要经过纽约。但是如果汇款地不是工作日的话就无法汇款,即使纽约银行开门营业也无济于事。因此工作日的约定还应当考虑付款人和收款人的银行所在地的银行工作日。此外,

  NEWBUILDCON 格式针对交船款的支付也作出了比较详细的规定:①   8.57

(a) The Final Instalment shall be adjusted in accordance with this Contract and notified by the Builder to the Buyer not later than seven(7) Banking Days prior to the notified date of delivery(see Clause 27(d) (Sea Trials – Method of Acceptance or Rejection)). Not later than two (2)Banking Days prior to the notified date of delivery the amount of the Final Instalment, as adjusted, shall be deposited with the Builder's Bank as set out in Box 12, with irrevocable instructions that, subject to sub-clause(c)below, the amount shall be released to the Builder against presentation by the Builder of a copy of the Protocol of Delivery and Acceptance of the Vessel signed by the Builder and the Buyer. Interest, if any, accruing on such deposit shall be for the benefit of the Buyer.

(b) If the Buyer does not agree the amount of the Final Instalment as adjusted and notified by the Builder, the Buyer shall notify the Builder within five(5)running days. Thereafter the Buyer may take delivery of the Vessel on payment of the Final Instalment as adjusted(or such other amount as the Builder may agree) but without prejudice to the Buyer's rights and remedies under this Contract and the dispute shall be resolved in accordance with Clause 42(Dispute Resolution).

(c) If the Protocol of Delivery and Acceptance is not so presented within seven(7)days following the date for delivery of the Vessel as notified by the Builder in accordance with Clause 27(d)(Sea Trials – Method of Acceptance or Rejection), the Buyer shall have the right to withdraw the said deposit plus accrued interest. However, if and when a new date for delivery of the Vessel is notified to the Buyer by the Builder in accordance with Clause 27(d)(Sea Trials – Method of Acceptance or

---

① Clause 30.

Rejection), the Buyer shall make a further cash deposit for the Final Instalment in accordance with the same terms and conditions as set out above.

8.58　除了船东是否应当发出不可撤销付款指令存在与 CSTC 格式一样的问题外，上述(a)规定的应当是比较公平且符合实际做法的付款方式。上述(b)应当是针对尾款数额发生变化且双方对调整后数额有争议的情形。在海洋工程船舶或设备建造合同中尾款数额发生变化比较常见，而且数额往往很大，但在商船建造中尾款数额发生变化的并不多见。即使有变化，数额通常也比较小，双方为此开始仲裁的可能性应当不是很大。上述(c)是针对船舶未能在预定日期交付情形作出的规定。

8.59　Norwegian 格式对船厂在交船时无法确定具体数额的情形作出了规定：①

...If the Builder is unable to present a final account at delivery, the Buyer may require the Vessel to be delivered in return for a bank guarantee or other security, satisfactory to the Builder, for the reasonably estimated balance owed to the Builder. Costs of such guarantee to be for Builder's account.

8.60　上述规定的实际意义不太大，虽然由于修改、存油、伙食等原因双方有可能对最后一期款的具体数额会产生争议，但船厂在交船时无法确定最后一期款数额的情形应当很少出现。

交船款支付的安排

8.61　交船款的支付通常已不再是简单的船东向船厂支付，而是涉及银行参与的付款安排，从某种程度上说船东交船款的支付已具有银行信用的特征。在双方约定的交船日船东其实并没有向船厂汇出任何款项，而是给银行发出了不可撤销的付款指示。虽然是不可撤销的付款指示，但是银行的付款是有条件的，即银行只能在看到双方签署并交换了交接备忘录后才可以将约定的款项汇入船厂在该银行的账号。在正式交接当天，双方的代表在相互核对所有文件后便可以签署交接备忘录。在双方交换交接备忘录的同时，银行参加交接的代表凭船东签署的不可撤销的付款指示向船厂确认约定的数额将如数汇入船厂的账户。

---

① Article III.3, para.6.

就船东而言，船东派遣的船员已经实际占有并控制了船舶，而船东派遣 8.62
的参加交接的代表则已经掌握了所有代表船舶所有权的文件以及所有船舶
营运必备的证书。船东在这种情况下支付约定的交船款应当不再有风险了。
就船厂而言，虽然在交接当时船厂并没有收到船东支付的交船款，但由于船
东已经将钱款汇入了银行，且船东已经作出了不可撤销的付款指示，因此船
厂收款实际上是有保障的，因为船东已经无法取消或撤销其要求银行付款的
指示了。

交船款支付的争议

绝大多数船舶建造合同都会规定加减账放在船东支付交船款时计算并支付， 8.63
因此船厂和船东不太可能就之前的各期建造款的数额发生争议，容易引起双方争
议的应当是交船款的数额和支付。Norwegian 格式对此作出了规定：①

> In the event of any dispute concerning the payment on delivery of the
> Vessel, including the question of the Buyer's right to offset any claim it
> may have, the Buyer may be paying the entire amount demanded by the
> Builder require the Builder to provide a bank guarantee or other security
> satisfactory to the Buyer for the disputed amount. The Builder cannot in
> such case refuse to deliver the Vessel. If the Builder does not wish to
> issue security for the disputed part of the claim, the Buyer is entitled to
> take delivery of the Vessel against payment of the undisputed amount
> and provide a bank guarantee or other security satisfactory to the Builder
> for the disputed part of the claim. Security which has been issued by a
> party pursuant to this sub-clause terminates automatically unless the
> other party has brought legal action pursuant to Article XIX below
> within 3 months from date of issue of the security. The costs of security
> shall be shared proportionately between the parties according to the final
> outcome of the dispute.

虽然针对双方有争议的数额提供担保不失为一个可取的方法，但要求船厂 8.64
提供此种担保似乎并不切合实际。船厂在交船后其实已经很难对船舶有所控
制，而作为船舶登记船东的单船公司显然存在可信性的问题，因此船厂的担忧
并非空穴来风。相反，船东从船厂获得赔偿的可行性则远远高于船厂从单船公
司获得赔偿的可行性。更何况关于交船款争议的数额在绝大多数情况下并不

---

① Article III.3, para.7.

会是一个巨大的数额。一个比较可取的方法应当是由船东支付无争议的那部分数额并对有争议的数额提供担保。按照上述规定，船东支付所有数额并不是一项义务，而是权利。即船东希望接船时可以选择支付所有数额而接船，若船东因市场原因或其他原因不希望接船时就无需支付所有数额。船东一旦选择支付所有数额，船厂似乎是有义务提供担保的，否则就意味着放弃争议而同意船东接船了。

8.65　　NEWBUILDCON 格式也针对交船款支付产生争议作出了规定：①

If the Buyer does not agree the amount of the Final Instalment as adjusted and notified by the Builder, the Buyer shall notify the Builder within five(5) running days. Thereafter the Buyer may take delivery of the Vessel on payment of the Final Instalment as adjusted(or such other amount as the Builder may agree) but without prejudice to the Buyer's rights and remedies under this Contract and the dispute shall be resolved in accordance with Clause 42(Dispute Resolution).

8.66　　相比较而言，NEWBUILDCON 格式的规定比较合理。船东在不放弃争议的情况下，只要支付了船厂主张的数额就可以接船。其实，即使船厂要求船东支付的交船款的数额没有依据且是错误的，船东在绝大多数情况下没有权利拒绝接船。因为拒绝接船会构成船东的违约。即使船厂由于要求船东支付不合理的数额构成违约，只要这种违约不构成毁约，船东只能主张损害赔偿，而不能拒绝履行船舶建造合同。

Ⅳ　船舶的交接

"接受"和"接船"

8.67　　在船舶试航成功后，除非船东表示拒绝接受船舶，在船厂正式交船时，船东通常都会接船。这里的"接受"和"接船"具有不同的含义。"接受"是指船东对船舶试航结果的肯定，表示在船厂交船时船东不会以通过试航的项目不符合合同或规格书的规定为由而拒绝接受船舶，"接受"是一种意思表示。"接船"则是指船东在船厂向其交付船舶时，按照船舶建造合同的规定接收船舶，它是相对于"交船"而言的，而且是以交船为前提的。在船厂按照合同交船时，接船是船东的一项重

---

① Clause 30(b).

要义务。大多数船舶建造合同都会明确规定船东的这一合同义务。①

通常情况下,船东一旦在船舶试航完成后接受了船舶,就会在船厂交船时接船。但是"接受"和"接船"并不始终是同时发生的,船东在试航结束后接受了船舶的,依然有可能会在船厂交船时拒绝接船,例如船东在接船时发现船舶存在违反船级规范或船旗国要求的缺陷,或者存在影响安全或正常运行的重大缺陷,在这种情况下,船东虽然已经明确表示接受船舶,但依然可以拒绝接船。

8.68

建造合同的规定

标准格式似乎都只是原则性地对船舶交接作出了规定,这些规定并没有涉及船舶交接的详细内容和步骤,例如 SAJ 格式的规定是:②

8.69

> Provided that the BUYER shall have fulfilled all of its obligations stipulated under this Contract, delivery of the VESSEL shall be effected forthwith by the concurrent delivery by each of the parties hereto to the other of the Protocol of Delivery and Acceptance, acknowledging delivery of the VESSEL by the BUILDER and acceptance thereof by the BUYER.

上述规定中的第一个 delivery 是指"船舶交接",即是包括船厂交船和船东接船的整个交接过程。第二个 delivery 是指"提交",即船厂和船东相互向对方提交已经签署完毕的交接备忘录。第三个 delivery 则是指"交船",即船厂向船东交付船舶的行为。从上述规定来看,船舶的交接是以船厂和船东相互交换交接备忘录体现的。

8.70

Norwegian 格式关于船舶交接的规定与 SAJ 格式的规定基本相同,但多了下面的内容:③

8.71

> ... Both parties have the right to make reservations or notes in the Protocol, or in a separate document signed by the parties "for acknowledgement of receipt only".

虽然该条款规定无论是船厂还是船东都可以在交接备忘录上或在独立的文件上注明"仅确认收到",但是行使这一权利的后果及其对船舶交接的影响并不

8.72

---

① SAJ Preamble, Norwegian Preamble, CSTC Preamble, AWES Article 6(a), para.2.
② Article VII.2.
③ Article VIII.2.

清楚。"保留"和"说明"的含义是不同的。"保留"通常是指对权利的保留,而"说明"一般只是指对某一问题的解释而已。就保留权利而言,只要作出保留的一方按照船舶建造合同的规定与对方进行并完成了船舶的交接,船舶交接本身就应当是完整且有效的。任何一方是否对权利作出了保留不影响船舶交接的完成和有效性。就说明而言问题可能更为简单。任何说明都是单方面的,因此不会影响船舶交接的完成及其有效性。按照Norwegian格式的规定,所谓的保留和说明似乎就是"仅确认收到"而已。"仅确认收到"虽然毫无疑问构成了一种说明,但未必就可以解释为对某种特定权利的保留。

8.73　按照Norwegian格式的规定,船舶交接也是在船厂和船东相互交换签署完毕的交接备忘录之时完成的。因此,无论是船厂还是船东,只要签署了交接备忘录并且与对方进行了交换,船舶交接就已经完成。如果船厂或者船东在与对方交换了交接备忘录后另行再向对方提交一份文件,声明仅确认收到由对方签署的交接备忘录,船舶交接的完成及其效力应当不会受这样一份文件的影响。

8.74　如果船厂或船东不是在独立的文件上注明"仅确认收到"对方的交接备忘录,而是在交接备忘录上注明"仅确认收到",船舶交接的完成及其效力似乎也不会因此受到影响。实际上,此种注明似乎只能出现在一份交接备忘录上,而且是作出此种注明的一方所持有的那份交接备忘录上。而在自己持有的文件上注明"仅确认收到"应当没有太大的意义。然而希望作出保留或说明的一方却很难在给对方的交接备忘录上注明"仅确认收到",因为该份交接备忘录并不是那一方所收到的,而是对方所收到的。

8.75　从实际出发,在交船时希望对自己权利作出保留的一方完全可以作出针对性明确的保留,而无需通过注明"仅确认收到"的方式。如果船东认为船厂要求支付的最后一期款的数额有错,但为了不影响船舶交接的进行或者为了避免自己违约而同意支付船厂要求的数额,同时又不愿放弃权利的,船东可以明确向船厂保留自己对最后一期款数额的异议。此种保留既可以在交接备忘录上作出,也可以通过邮件或信函等作出。但是只要船东实际支付了船厂要求的数额并且得到了船厂的接受,船舶交接本身的完成和效力就不应当受到船东保留的影响。

交接的程序和安排

虽然大多数船舶建造合同都会针对交船款的支付作出特殊的规定,但是很少有船舶建造合同对船厂和船东应当如何交接船舶作出具体的规定。在实践中的做法似乎也各不相同。船舶建造合同中的船舶交接与二手船买卖中的船舶交接有很多相似之处。 8.76

一个比较常见的程序和安排是:在船厂向船东发出交船通知后,双方可以就船东在接船时应当支付的交船款的数额达成一致。由于在船舶建造过程中有可能发生船东要求的修改,从而对合同价格进行了上调。只要双方对加账的数额没有争议,交船款数额的相应调整应当是相当简单的。除了因修改而发生的合同价格的调整外还会有各种其他原因引起的合同价格的调整,例如在船东为试航提供的润滑油和机油等的情况下,船厂应当向船东支付为试航而消耗的润滑油和机油等的价格,这将导致合同价格的下调;又如在船厂为试航而提供的燃油、物料和淡水等的情况下,船东应当为交船时船上所剩的燃油、物料和淡水支付价格,这将导致合同价格的上调。在船舶交接时船东支付的交船款不作任何调整的情形并不多见。 8.77

船舶建造合同通常会有船厂指定银行以及银行账号等内容,除非船厂通知船东这些信息另有变化,否则船东可以在双方就交船款数额进行协商之时,如果时间允许也可以在双方就交船款数额达成一致之后在船厂指定的银行开立自己的账户,并在交船前将约定的数额或自己估计的数额汇入在船厂指定银行开立的自己的账户。在约定交船的一天,船东应当向船厂指定的银行发出不可撤销的付款指示。虽然是不可撤销的付款指示,但是银行只有在约定的条件成就时,即看到双方签署并交换了交接备忘录后才可以将款项汇入船厂在该银行的或其他银行的账户。① 8.78

在船舶交接的前一天或前两天,双方的代表通常会对物品和文件进行核对和确认。物品主要是指船上的物品,包括备件等,而文件则既有在船上交接的文件,如随船的船舶证书和文件,又有在岸上交接的文件,如船厂的交船文件以及双方代表的授权委托书等。在船舶正式交接之前对物品和文件进行核对和确认能确保船舶交接的顺利进行。 8.79

---

① 如果船厂为了获得建造资金或让银行同意开立还款保函而曾对在建船舶设定过抵押,船厂还应当在船舶交接前撤销船舶的抵押。

8.80　在船舶交接当天,船东的船员开始登船并与船厂在船上的代表办理物品和文件的正式交接。由于之前已经经过了双方的核对和确认,因此物品和文件的正式交接比较简单,只是简单地清点而已,无需对所有的物品和文件逐一审查和核对。与此同时,双方在岸上的代表也开始清点交船文件包括由船东代表签署的不可撤销的付款指示。在文件核对无误后,双方的交接代表可以约定一个船舶交接的时间,并将其填入交接备忘录。在双方交换了签署完毕的交接备忘录后,参加船舶交接的银行代表会向船厂确认款项的支付。在船上的船厂的人员开始离船并将船舶交由船东的代表占有和控制。

8.81　船舶的交接可以分为两个部分,即实际交接和法律交接。实际交接是指船舶本身的交接,由船厂的代表将船舶交由船东代表实际控制,这是实际占有的转移。而法律交接则是指文件的交接,船厂代表将代表船舶所有权的文件,例如建造人证书等交付给船东代表,从而完成法律意义上的所有权转移。

交接备忘录

8.82　交接备忘录(Protocol of Delivery and Acceptance)是证明双方按照船舶建造合同的规定交付和接收船舶的文件。交接备忘录的内容主要包括船舶交接的日期和具体时间以及双方对船舶已按合同规定交接的确认。交接备忘录由双方授权的代表签署,可以按照需要制作数份交接备忘录的正本。虽然 SAJ 格式,AWES 格式以及 Norwegian 格式都要求船厂在向船东提供交船文件时一并提供交接备忘录,①但交接备忘录其实并不是交船文件,而是双方确认交船的文件。交接备忘录可以由船厂提供,也可以由船东提供。大多数交船文件都是由船厂自己制作和签发的,说明或证明各种事实或情形的文件。交船文件一般都无需船东的签署,但是交接备忘录则是需要由双方签署的文件。船舶交接完毕后,不仅船东持有交接备忘录,船厂同样也持有交接备忘录。交接备忘录是一份重要的文件,因为交接备忘录有船舶交接具体时间的记载,船东在为船舶办理船舶登记、船舶保险时都需要交接备忘录。NEWBUILDCON 格式没有把交接备忘录视为应当由船厂提供的交船文件之一,而是在交接部分规定双方应当在交接时签署交接备忘录。②

---

① SAJ Article VII.3, AWES Article 6(b), Norwegian Article VIII.3.
② Article 28(a).

V 交船文件

船厂交船时不仅包括船舶本身,还要向船东提交各种交船文件。SAJ 格式规定了船厂在交船时应当向船东提供下列文件:①

Upon delivery and acceptance of the VESSEL, the BUILDER shall deliver to the BUYER the following documents, which shall accompany the PROTOCOL OF DELIVERY AND ACCEPTANCE.
(a) PROTOCOL OF TRIALS of the VESSEL made pursuant to the Specifications.
(b) PROTOCOL OF INVENTORY of the equipment of the VESSEL, including spare parts and the like, all as specified in the Specifications.
(c) PROTOCOL OF STORERS OF CONSUMABLE NATURE referred to under Paragraph 3(b) of Article VI hereof, including the original purchase price thereof.
(d) ALL CERTIFICATES including the BUILDER'S CERTIFICATE required to be furnished upon delivery of the VESSEL pursuant to this Contract and the Specifications. It is agreed that if, through no fault on the part of the BUILDER, the classification and/or other certificates are not available at the time of delivery of the VESSEL, provisional certificates shall be accepted by the BUYER, provided that the BUILDER shall furnish the BUYER with the formal certificates as promptly as possible after such formal certificates have been issued.
(e) DECLARATION OF WARRANTY of the BUILDER that the VESSEL is delivered to the BUYER free and clear of any liens, charges, claims, mortgages, or other encumbrances upon the BUYER's title thereto, and in particular, that the VESSEL is absolutely free of all burdens in the nature of imposes, taxes or charges imposed by the Japanese governmental authorities charges, as well as of all liabilities of the BUILDER to its subcontractors, employees and crew, and of all liabilities arising from the operation of the VESSEL in trial runs, or otherwise, prior to delivery.
(f) DRAWING AND PLANS pertaining to the VESSEL as stipulated in the Specifications.

---

① Article VII.3.

(g) COMMERCIAL INVOICE.

8.84　其他标准格式也规定了船厂在交船时应当向船东提供的交船文件,下面结合常用标准格式的规定对交船文件做一简单的介绍。

测试报告

8.85　测试报告包括船舶的试航报告以及其他设备和系统的测试和试验报告,这一文件的作用是向船东证明船舶符合船舶建造合同、规格书、船级规范以及船旗国等要求。船舶的试航报告并非是指船厂在试航结束后自己制作并向船东提供的报告,所谓的试航报告实际上是由各种测试或试验结果组成的文件。关于船舶设备和系统的测试报告在船舶试航完毕和设备及系统测试完毕后就已经由船厂向船东提供了,这些报告是船东决定是否接受船舶的重要依据。[1] 测试报告通常是由船厂制作的。此外,船级社通常也不会向船厂或船东确认试航的成功或失败。船级社在试航结束后没有对任何项目提出异议或问题,或者要求再一次试航的,试航就应当是成功的。

设备和备件清单

8.86　船舶的设备和备件清单列明了船舶的各项设备和备件,所有的设备和备件不仅要符合船级规范及船旗国的要求,还应当符合船舶建造合同以及规格书的规定。通常船厂和船东的代表会在交船前根据设备和备件清单对船厂的设备和备件进行清点和确认。

消耗品清单

8.87　消耗品是指在船舶正常运行中会不断消耗的物品,主要包括燃油、润滑油、机油、物料、伙食和淡水等。消耗品清单会列明交船时船上的所有消耗品。这些消耗品如果是船厂提供的,船东应当按照约定付钱购买。如果消耗品是船东订购的,船厂则应为交船前已经实际消耗掉消耗品付钱购买。按照 SAJ 格式的规定,船厂还应当提供消耗品的价格。[2] NEWBUILDCON 格式针对消耗品清单的规定是针对船厂采购情形的,因为该格式规定船厂应提供需要船东付款的消耗品

---

[1]　CSTC 还特别规定船厂应当提供载重吨和倾斜试验报告,见 Article Ⅶ.3(e)。
[2]　SAJ Article Ⅶ.3(c)。

清单。①

证书

证书是由船级社自己或代表船旗国制作颁发以及由设备厂商制作并签署的 8.88
文件,包括船舶的航行证书、船级证书以及设备和其他证书。船舶建造合同或规
格书一般会详细列明船厂在交船时应当提供的所有证书。大多数标准格式都规
定,如果非因船厂过失或原因而无法提供某些船级社或其他正式证书的,船东应
当接受临时证书。② 有些船舶建造合同还会规定船厂提供的证书均不得有批注
或限制,例如按照 NEWBUILDCON 格式的规定,船厂在提供临时证书时应当保
证临时证书不会影响船东办理船舶登记、营运,否则船厂应当承担船东因此遭受
的所有损失。③ 这是应当引起船厂重视的规定,因为有时船级社颁发的证书可能
会有批注或建议,例如船舶在出厂后第一次进坞时应当完成某项测试等。此种批
准或建议并不影响船舶的船级,但却不符合船舶建造合同要求。

CSTC 格式在证书问题上还规定船舶应当符合船舶建造合同订立时已生效 8.89
的规则和规定,④但实际上船舶不仅要符合在船舶建造合同订立时已经生效的规
则和规定,而且还要符合在船舶建造合同订立时尚未生效,但在船厂交船已经生
效且强制适用于船舶的新规范和规定。

建造人证书

建造人证书是一份相当重要的文件,通常会记载船舶的特征,包括:总吨和净 8.90
吨、建造年份和建造地点、IMO 号、船东名称等。建造人证书的签发意味着船舶
在交接前没有经过所有权登记,建造人证书是船舶所有权的凭证。建造人证书是
船舶登记机关确定船舶所有权以及新建船性质的依据,没有建造人证书,新建船
就无法完成永久登记。建造人证书在 SAJ 格式、AWES 格式以及 Norwegian 格式
中是作为证书之一规定的,⑤而在 NEWBUILDCON 格式中则是一份独立的交船
文件。⑥

---

① Clause 29(c)。
② SAJ Article Ⅶ.3(d)、NEWBUILDCON Clause 29(e)、AWES Article 6(b)、Norwegian Article Ⅷ.3(e)。CSTC 格式还特别规定船厂应当提供载重吨和倾斜试验报告,见 Article Ⅶ.3(e)。
③ NEWBUILDCON Clause 29(e)。
④ Article Ⅶ.3(g)。
⑤ SAJ Article Ⅶ.3(d)、AWES Article 6(b)、Norwegian Article Ⅷ.3(e)。
⑥ NEWBUILDCON Clause 29(g)。

无负担保证

8.91　虽然船厂交付的是刚完成建造的船,但由于船厂为了融资曾对在建船设定过抵押,船厂的债权人也可以对在建船采取行动或实施保全等,一艘新建船同样有可能负有债务。船东显然不希望自己接受的船负有任何债务。无负担保证中的"负担"(encumbrance 或 incumbrance)是指针对土地或其他财产的所有权之外的权利,包括租赁、留置、抵押等。由于这些权利影响到土地或其他财产的价值,故而称其为"负担"。无负担保证是船厂向船东确认并保证船舶没有任何留置权、债务、索赔、抵押、政府税款或费用以及其他负担的文件。

图纸

8.92　图纸是指船舶建造合同和规格书规定的所有图纸,船上通常会保留一套完整的船舶图纸。船舶的正常维护、保养和修理都离不开图纸。图纸一般是由船厂或船东委托的设计人以及船厂制作的。除了各种图纸,船厂还会提供与设备或系统有关的使用或操作手册和指南等。

商业发票

8.93　商业发票通常会载明船舶的基本特征以及价格,其作用主要是证明船舶的建造价格。商业发票由船厂在交船时提供,因此商业发票载明了船东支付的所有款项,即船东实际支付的用于船舶建造的所有款项的总金额。有的船东只需要一张发票,记载船东支付的总金额;有的船东只需要记载船价的发票;有的船东则希望船厂提供两张商业发票,一张记载的是船价,即合同价,另一张记载的是燃油、滑油等金额。NEWBUILDCON 格式规定商业发票的金额应当包括船东支付的交船款以及因船东提出的修改而产生的额外费用。①

无登记证书

8.94　有的船东仍然希望船厂出具一份无登记证书,例如 NEWBUILDCON 格式规定的交船文件便包括无登记证书。② 提供无登记证书的目的是证明船舶在交接前没有经过任何登记,从某种意义上说船厂提供的建造人证书应当已经证明了船

---

① NEWBUILDCON Clause 29(i).
② NEWBUILDCON Clause 29(h).

厂交付的船舶是没有经过任何登记的新建船。无登记证书一般由船厂制作并签署,但有时船东会要求船厂提供一份律师出具的法律意见证明船舶没有经过任何登记。

卖据

Norwegian 格式,CSTC 格式以及 NEWBUILDCON 格式均将卖据(bill of sale)作为船厂应当提交的交船文件之一。卖据是证明所有权的文件,由船舶所有人出具,用于船舶所有权的转移。卖据与建造人证书虽然都是船舶所有权的证明,但两者的性质并不相同。船厂出具建造人证书是证明船舶未曾有过所有权登记,因此持有建造人证书的人就是该船的所有人。卖据则是船舶所有人签发的,证明其对卖据所描述的船舶拥有完全的所有权。因此持有卖据的人就享有卖据所描述的船舶的所有权。在船舶建造中使用的卖据和通常在二手船买卖中使用的卖据有所不同。前者在英文中被成为"大卖据"(grand bill of sale),而后者则被称为"普通卖据"(ordinary bill of sale)。大卖据是针对两种情形的转移船舶所有权的文件,一是在海上的船舶所有权发生转移的情形,另一则是船舶所有权由建造人转移至买方的情形。普通卖据则意味着船舶由原来的船东转移至新的船东。在实践中,船厂提供的卖据都不会将船厂记载为船舶所有人。

8.95

IMO 有害物质清单

IMO 有害物质清单是 NEWBUILDCON 格式规定的交船文件之一,这一交船文件应当源于该格式关于船舶描述的一项要求。①

8.96

为了推动《香港公约》的实施,欧洲议会和理事会于 2013 年通过了第 1257/2013 法规。② 按照该法规的规定,"有害物质"(hazardous material)系指对人体健康和/或环境造成危害的任何材料或物质。③ 该法规适用于所有悬挂欧盟成员国旗帜的商船,④悬挂其他国家旗帜的船舶停靠欧盟成员国港口或锚地的都应随船携带符合该法规规定的有害物质清单,即至少列明船舶结构或设备中的有害物质及其位置和大概数量。⑤

8.97

---

① NEWBILDCON Clause 4.
② Regulation(EU) No 1257/2013 of the European Parliament and of the Council of 20 November 2013 on ship recycling and amending Regulation(EC) No 1013/2006 and Directive 2009/16/EC.
③ Article 3(4).
④ Article 2(1).
⑤ Articles 5(1), 12(1).

8.98　　　　国际海事组织第 68 届环保会通过了 2015 年《有害物质清单编制指南》(2015 Guidelines for the Development of the Inventory of Hazardous Materials)。① 2015 年的《指南》详细列出了有害物质清单应当列明的有害物质,这些有害物质共分为四大类,即禁止使用的有害物质(A 表)、控制使用的有害物质(B 表)、潜在有害项目(C 表)以及潜在含有有害物质的常规消耗品(D 表)。A 表禁止使用的有害物质包括石棉、多氯联苯、消耗臭氧材料、含有机锡化合物作为杀生物剂的防污底系统、全氟辛烷磺酸及其衍生物;B 表控制使用的有害物质包括镉和镉化合物、六价铬和六价铬化合物、铅和铅化合物、汞和汞化合物、多溴化联(二)苯、多溴二苯醚、多氯化联萘(超过三个氯原子)、放射性物质、某些短链氯化石蜡、溴化助燃剂;C 表潜在有害项目包括液体中的煤油、石油溶剂、润滑油、液压油、防粘剂、燃料添加剂、发动机冷却剂添加剂、防冻液、锅炉和给水处理和试验试剂、脱离子剂再生化学品、蒸发器定量和除锈酸、涂料稳定剂/锈稳定剂、溶剂/稀释剂、涂料、化学制冷剂、电池电解液、酒精、甲基化酒精、燃油、油脂、废油、舱底水和/或机器上安装的后处理系统产生的废水、油性液体货油舱残余物、压载水、原始污水、处理的污水、非油性液体货物残余,气体中的乙炔、丙烷、丁烷、氧气、二氧化碳、全氟化碳、甲烷、氢化氟烃、一氧化二氮、六氟化硫、燃料气体、干货残余物、医疗废弃物/传染性废弃物、焚烧炉灰渣、垃圾、燃料舱残余物、油性固体货油舱残余、油性或化学污染的碎、电池、农药/杀虫剂喷雾、灭火器、化学清洁器(包括电气设备清洁器、除积炭器)、清洁剂/漂白剂(可能是液体)、各种药品、消防服和人员保护设、干舱残余物、货物残余物、包含表 A 或表 B 所列物质的备件;D 表潜在含有有害物质的常规消耗品包括电子和电气设备(电脑、冰箱、打印机、扫描仪、电视机、收音机、照相机、摄像机、电话、消费电池)、照明设备(荧光灯、细丝灯泡、灯)、非船舶特定家具、内饰和类似设备(椅子、沙发、桌子、床、窗帘、地毯、垃圾桶、床单、枕头、毛巾、床垫、储物架、装饰、浴室设施、玩具、非结构相关或作为结构一部分的艺术品)等。

8.99　　　　2015 年《指南》的附录还分别列出了 有害物质清单标准格式(附录一)、符合《香港公约》的有害物质清单符合证明格式(附录二)以及符合欧盟 1257/2013 号法规的有害物质清单符合证明格式(附录三)。

---

①　国际海事组织第 68 届环保会 MEPC.269(68)号决议通过的 2015 年《有害物质清单编制指南》取代了第 62 届环保会 MEPC.197(62)决议通过的 2011 年《有害物质清单编制指南》。

其他文件

除了船舶建造合同列明的交船文件,船东还可能要求船厂提供其他文件,这些文件一般是指船东选择的船舶登记机关要求的或者其他船舶主管机关甚至船舶的承租人可能要求的而必须由船厂出具或提供的文件。船东需要船厂提供其他文件的,应当尽可能早地通知船厂,以便船厂可以按船东要求提供相关的文件。 8.100

除了希望船厂提供特定的文件外,船东还会对文件的措辞和形式有自己的要求,例如在船东已将船舶转卖给第三人的情况下就希望船厂的交船文件是针对船舶买家的,从而方便该买家办理船舶登记。船东也可能要求某些文件,例如建造人证书等文件办理公证和认证手续。在实践中的做法是,船厂在交船前先向船东提供自己制作的交船文件的草稿,由船东对交船文件发表意见或确认。船东可以提出修改意见并提出对交船文件的形式要求以及公证认证的要求。 8.101

授权委托书

在船舶交接中,船厂和船东的意思和行为需要通过个人予以表达或实施,因此就会产生具体表达意思和实施行为的个人是否有权代表船厂或船东表达意思或实施行为的问题。授权委托书是证明代理人享有授权的文件。授权委托书是指船厂或船东制作的列明代表自己的代理人的姓名、身份证明文件及其授权范围的文件。授权委托书并不是交船文件之一,似乎所有的标准格式列明的交船文件均不包括授权委托书,但每一次船舶交接却又离不开授权委托书。授权委托书是证明交船文件乃至交易真实的文件。授权委托书是由船厂和船东制作并由船厂和船东的董事签署的文件,授权委托书通常需要经过公证和认证方可使用。 8.102

VI 所有权的转移

所有权的意义

绝大多数船舶建造合同都会规定船舶的所有权在交船前归船厂所有,只有当 8.103

船厂向船东交船时所有权才自船厂转移至船东。对此,SAJ 格式作出了如下规定:①

> Title to and risk of loss of the VESSEL shall pass to the BUYER only upon delivery and acceptance thereof having been completed as stated above; it being expressly understood that, until such delivery is effected, title to and risk of loss of the VESSEL and her equipment shall be in the BUILDER, excepting risks of war, earthquakes and tidal waves.

8.104 上述规定中使用的"title"有比较多的用法,包含了不同的含义。正如 Kindersley 法官早在 17 世纪的案例,*Felkin v Lord Herbert* 一案中所说的:②

> "Title" is an ambiguous word; it may mean the title to real estate or property: properly and technically used, it is the title of the plaintiff to get the relief he asks . . . .

8.105 就财产权而言"title"是指普通法上的一种权利,此种普通法上的权利既包括财产权(*jus proprietatis*),也包括"占有权"(*jus possidendi*)。而这里的财产权正是以所有权为基础的权利,这种权利是:③

> The highest right a man can have to anything, being that right which one has to lands or tenements, goods or chattels which does not depend on another's courtesy . . . . Property is of two kinds, real property and personal property. Property in realty is acquired by entry, conveyance, or devise; and in personalty, by many ways, but most usually be gift, bequest, or sale . . . .

8.106 1979 年《货物买卖法》也为"property"下了定义:④

> "property" means the general property in goods, and not merely a special property.

8.107 这里"general property"指完整的和完全的所有权,而"special property"则是指不完整的、受限制的所有权。享有船舶所有权不仅意味着可以不受他人

---

① Article VII.5.
② (1861) 30 LJ Ch 798 at 799, see David Hay *Words and Phrases Legally Defined*, 4th edn LexisNexis, 2007, p.1251.
③ Daniel Greenberg, *Jowitt's Dictionary of English Law*, 3rd edn Sweet & Maxwell, 2010, p.1821.
④ s.61(1).

干扰地占有船舶,并且可以处置船舶。这一权利对船厂无疑是有相当大的利益。因为我国法律与英国法不同,"船舶"不仅是指已经建造完毕的船舶,而且还包括建造中的船舶。在建船舶是指已安放龙骨或处于相似建造阶段的船舶。① 按照《中华人民共和国海商法》的规定,船厂可以对在建船舶设定船舶抵押权。② 因此,除非船舶建造合同另有约定,船厂可以在船舶上船台后就可以对在建船舶设定抵押,从而获得船舶建造所需的资金。船厂凭船舶建造合同就可以完成对在建船舶抵押权的设定。③ 对于小型船厂而言,提供还款保函的银行也往往会要求对在建船舶设定抵押权作为其承担还款保函责任的担保。

拥有船舶所有权的惯例

尽管船厂和船东可以在船舶建造合同中作出不同的约定,但船厂在交船前对船舶拥有所有权应当是造船业的一个惯例。船厂对船舶拥有的所有权通常基于整艘船舶及其所有机器和设备等。船舶建造合同的标准格式无一例外地都规定船舶的所有权在船舶交付给船东之前始终归船厂所有。之所以形成这个惯例可能是由于:首先,在船东拥有在建船舶所有权的情况下同时拥有拒绝接受船舶的权利存在明显的冲突;其次,在船东拥有在建船舶所有权时的建造款就不应当具有预付款的性质,船东要求返还建造款的权利就有可能因为船厂的破产而受到不利的影响。 8.108

当然,法律并没有对在建船舶的归属作出强制性的规定,船厂和船东可以在船舶建造合同中按照自己的意愿对在建船舶所有权的归属作出约定。实践中也确有船舶建造合同约定在建船舶以及建造船舶的所有材料和设备等均归船东所有,船东在按照合同或法律规定拒绝接受船舶的权利不受影响。在船东对在建船舶拥有所有权的情况下,船厂对船舶享有的只能是留置权了。只要船东仍有任何款项未支付的,船厂可以对船舶实施留置。在这种情况下,船厂享有的留置权与船舶修理合同中的留置权基本相似。 8.109

由于船厂对在建船舶拥有所有权,因此船厂可以通过对在建船舶设定抵押获得船舶建造所需的资金。当然这以船舶建造合同没有相反约定为前提。例如 8.110

---

① 《〈中华人民共和国船舶登记条例〉若干问题的说明》第八条。
② 《中华人民共和国海商法》第十四条第一款。
③ 《中华人民共和国船舶登记条例》第二十条。

AWES 格式便明确规定船厂不得擅自对在建船舶设定抵押：①

> During construction the VESSEL shall be the CONTRACTOR's property and the CONTRACTOR undertakes not to dispose of the VESSEL and not to allow any mortgage or lien being registered on the VESSEL except with the PURCHASER's prior written consent.

8.111　根据上述规定，船厂若要对在建船舶设定抵押必须事先得到船东的书面同意。船东可以拒绝船厂的要求且无须提供任何理由。

船厂抵押船舶

8.112　在船厂对在建船舶享有所有权的前提下，船厂有权对在建船舶进行抵押应当是不言而喻的。因此，作为原则，除非船舶建造合同另有规定，船厂对在建船舶设定抵押无需征得船东的同意或许可，甚至无需通知船东。在这个问题上，Norwegian 格式可能是唯一明确规定船厂可以对在建船舶设定抵押，并且规定船东应当予以协助：②

> The Builder may mortgage the Vessel and its materials (excluding Buyer's Supply if possible) as security for the construction financing, including the provision of refund guarantee(s), for the Vessel. The Buyer shall if necessary give its consent for that purpose. Any such mortgage shall be cancelled and deleted from the relevant registry at the latest on Delivery and Acceptance.

所有权转移的时间

8.113　在船舶所有权转移的问题上，普通法似乎经历了一个变化的过程。

船舶完成建造后转移

8.114　在 *Mucklow v Mangles*③ 一案中，船舶建造合同约定由船厂为船东建造一艘驳船。在驳船开始建造之前，船东便支付了一定数额的建造款。随着建造的进行，买方继续支付建造款并在驳船建造完毕之前支付了所有的建造款。驳船的船尾已经漆上了船东的名称。船厂破产，船东和船厂受托人就船舶的归属发生了争

---

① Article 8(b), para.1.
② Article XI.1, para.2.
③ [1808] 1 Taunt 318.

议。法院认为,如果合同的标的是合同订立时尚不存在的动产,即使买方预先支付了所有价款,在该动产建造完毕且交付之前买方也不拥有该动产的所有权。Mansfield 法官对建造合同和买卖合同进行了区分,他说:①

> ... the bankrupt was under a contract to finish the barge: that is quite a different thing from a contract of sale, and until the barge was finished we cannot say that it was so far [owner]'s property, that he could have taken it away.

Heath 法官同样也从标的物的性质出发,认为所有权只有在船舶建造完成之后才会发生转移:② 8.115

> A tradesman often finishes goods, which he is making in pursuance of an order given by one person, and sells them to another. If the first customer has other goods made for him within the stipulated time, he has no right to complain; he could not bring trover against the purchaser for the goods so sold. The painting of the name on the stern in this case makes no difference. If the thing be in existence at the time of the order, the property of it passes by the contract, but not so, where the subject is to be made.

船东登记船舶的意义

但是在 *Woods v Russsell*③ 一案中,法院则认为船舶的所有权在船舶建造完毕之前就已经发生了转移。在该案中,船舶建造合同约定由船厂为船东建造一艘船,合同价款分四期支付,第一期在安放龙骨时支付,第二期在铺木板时支付,第三期和第四期则是在下水之时支付。船厂签发证书同意船东将船舶登记在自己的名下,船东在将船舶登记在自己名下之日支付了第三期款,当时船舶尚未下水。几天后船厂不幸破产。船东派遣船员实际占有了未完成的船舶、船厂制造的舵和船厂为船舶购买的绳索。 8.116

法院认为船厂签发证书同意船东登记船舶意味着船厂同意船舶所有权在登记完成之时转移至船东;由于舵和绳索将用于船舶,因此其所有权随船舶转移至船东;但船舶依然在船厂的占有中,船东在没有支付第四期款的情况下占有船舶 8.117

---

① [1808] 1 Taunt 318 at 319.
② [1808] 1 Taunt 318 at 320.
③ (1822) 5 B & Ald 942.

是错误的,船厂就第四期款对船舶享有留置权。Abbott 法官说:①

> This ship is built upon a special contract, and it is part of the terms of the contract, that given portions of the price shall be paid according to the progress of the work .... The payment of these instalments appears to us to appropriate specifically to the defendant the very ship so in progress, and to vest in the [shipowner] a property in that ship, and that, as between him and the builder, he is entitled to insist upon the completion of that very ship, and that the builder is not entitled to require him to accept any other .... [The builder] signed the certificate to enable the [shipowner] to have the ship registered in his name, and by that act consented, as it seems to us, that the general property in the ship should be considered from that time as being in the [shipowner].

8.118 在 Woods v Russsell 一案中,法院没有适用 Mucklow v Mangles 一案的判决,理由是在 Mucklow v Mangles 中建造款没有按照船舶建造的进度支付。而且,在 Mucklow v Mangles 一案中只是船尾油漆上了船东的名称,而在 Woods v Russsell 中,船厂则签发了同意船东登记船舶的证书。

在指定之前不转移

8.119 Atkinson v Bell 一案涉及的并不是船舶建造合同,而是制造精纺机的合同。精纺机制造专利持有人按照被告的要求委托一家制造商按照专利持有人的设计制造精纺机。制造商在精纺机制造完毕后破产了。制造商的破产受托人此后要求被告提取精纺机但遭被告拒绝。被告认为精纺机的所有权从未转移至自己一方。法院援引了 Mucklow v Mangles 一案的判决,认为精纺机的所有权在精纺机制造完成之前不发生转移。Bayley 法官说:②

> [I]f you employ a man to build a house on your land, or to make a chattel with your materials, the party who does the work has no power to appropriate the produce of his labour and your materials to any other person. Having bestowed his labour at your request on your materials, he may maintain an action against you for work and labour. But if you employ another to work up his own materials in making a chattel, then he may appropriate the produce of that labour and materials to any other

---

① (1822) 5 B & Ald 942 at 946.
② (1828) 8 B & C 277 at 283.

person.

在上述案例中,精纺机实际上在制造商破产之前就已经制造完毕了,法院依然作出精纺机所有权没有发生转移的判决应当是受了被告和制造商之间不存在直接的合同关系这一事实的影响。Holroyd 法官认为制造商从未对精纺机进行过指定(appropriation),他说:①

8.120

> I have entertained great doubt during the argument, whether a verdict might not be sustained on the count for work and labour and materials found. I think it will not lie for goods bargained and sold, because there was no specific appropriation of the machines assented to by the purchaser, and the property in the goods, therefore, remained in the maker. Then as to work and labour, the work was done, and the labour bestowed on the materials of the maker in manufacturing an article which never became the property of the defendants. I am of opinion, therefore, that the work was done for the bankrupt, and not for the defendants.

随当事人意愿转移

在 Wood v Bell② 一案中,原告是船东,被告则是破产船厂的受托人。船厂和船东订立了船舶建造合同,约定由船厂为船东建造船舶,船东共分八期支付合同价款。第一期签约后立即支付,第二期至第四期分别在签约两个月、三个月及四个月之后支付。剩余的数额再分四期支付,第一期在签约六个月之后且船舶甲板已完成时支付;第二期在八个月之后且船舶已可试航时支付;第三期在十一个月之后且船舶已建造完毕时支付;第四期则在十三个月之后支付。船厂开始建造船舶,船东也按照约定支付了部分建造款。在第十个月时船厂破产了,当时船舶仍在船厂,尚未建造完毕。主机和部分结构还没有安装上船。船东支付的建造款已经超过未建造完毕的船舶及主机等的价值。在船舶的龙骨上已标有船东的名字。船东认为未建造完毕的船舶、主机和部分结构等均为自己的财产,船厂的受托人则认为这些都是船厂的财产。

8.121

王座法院认为船东可以获得未完成的船舶、主机和材料等。财税法院认为 Mucklow v Mangles 一案确立的船舶的所有权在建造完毕之前不发生转移是原

8.122

---

① (1828) 8 B & C 277 at 284.
② (1856) 6 E & B 355.

则，而所有权在此之前发生转移的则是例外。Jervis 法官说：①

> I agree with the Court below that the ship passed. That question is merely one of fact . . . , the property does not pass merely by its being manufactured, but only when it is the intention of the parties that it shall pass. And here I think the facts shew such an intention. I further concur with the details of the judgment below, so far as the ship is concerned.

8.123　虽然财税法院也认为船东可以获得未完成的船舶，但财税法院认为船东不能获得主机和材料。主机和材料的所有权并不随未完成船舶的所有权的转移而转移，Jervis 法官说：②

> But I do not think that, as the Court below seems to have held without much consideration, the unfixed materials destined for the ship did pass. They do not appear to have been circumstanced exactly as the rudder and cordage were in *Woods* v *Russell* (5 B & Ald 942), where they had become, it seems, a part of the ship. Here they are merely provided for the ship. If the circumstances in *Woods* v *Russell* were the same as here, I should doubt whether the decision in that case was right . . . . The question is, What is the ship? not, What is meant for the ship? I think those things pass which have been fitted to the ship, and have once formed part of her, as, for instance, a door hung upon hinges, although afterwards removed for convenience. I do not think the circumstance that materials have been fitted and intended for the ship makes them part of the ship.

8.124　*Wood* v *Bell* 一案确立了船舶所有权在船舶完成之前不发生转移这一原则，虽然当事人可以约定所有权在此前发生转移。另外，任何材料只有安装上船的才成为船舶的一部分，其所有权才随船舶所有权的转移而转移。这一案例以及 *Woods* v *Russell* 确立了船舶所有权转移时间的普通法原则，并得到了此后判例的援引和确认。例如在 *Seath & Co* v *Moore*③ 一案中，原告是船厂，被告是向船厂提供主机和其他用于船舶建造的机器的供应商的受托人。供应商曾向船厂作出如下承诺：

> Second. That, upon a payment being made on account of any such

---

① (1856) 6 E & B 355 at 361.
② Ibid.
③ (1886) LR 11 App Cas 350.

contract, the portions of the subject thereof, so far as constructed, and all materials laid down for the purpose of constructing the same, shall become, and be held as being, the absolute property of the said TB Seath & Co., subject only to our lien for payment of the price on any balance thereof that may remain due to us.

Third. In the event of our becoming bankrupt or insolvent, or failing from and cause whatsoever to proceed with due diligence in the execution of the work of any such contract, the said TB Seath & Co. shall have power and be entitled not only to take possession of the portion executed, and of all materials laid down and obtained by us for the construction thereof, but shall also be entitled, if deemed proper by them, with a view to the completion of the work of such contract, to enter upon, use, and occupy our premises, and thereto and thereat use our plant, tools, machinery, and other implements, for the purpose of so completing the work of such contract, and to cause the necessary work to be executed and completed by any person or persons whom they may seem fit to employ, and to pay to such person or persons such reasonable sum or sums as he or they shall think proper, which shall form a claim against us, and which we shall pay forthwith, or allow to be deducted from the price of the work of such contract, if any be due.

8.125 虽然该案并不是一个船舶建造合同案例，但是上议院认为适用于出售船舶的原则同样可以适用于任何正在制造中的产品。遵循 *Wood v Bell* 一案的判决，上议院认为船东对未完成的主机、机器等并不享有所有权。Lord Watson 认为除非材料装上了主机，否则所有权就不会发生转移，他说：①

> ... that materials provided by the builder and portions of the fabric, whether wholly or partially finished, although intended to be used in the execution of the contract, cannot be regarded as appropriated to the contract, or as "sold", unless they have been affixed to or in a reasonable sense made part of the corpus.

8.126 上议院的 Lord Blackburn 认为确定所有权转移的时间取决于对合同条款的解释，他说：②

> I do not examine the various English authorities cited during the

---

① (1886) LR 11 App Cas 350 at 381.
② (1886) LR 11 App Cas 350 at 370.

argument. It is, I think, a question of the construction of the contract in each case, at what stage the property shall pass; and a question of fact, in each case whether that stage has been reached.

当事人意愿的确定

8.127 虽然船舶所有权可以按照当事人的意愿发生转移,但当事人意愿的确定会涉及到对合同条款的解释。在 *Sir James Laing & Sons Limited* v *Barclay Curle & Co Limited*① 一案中,船舶建造合同约定由船厂为一家意大利船东建造一艘船,船东按节点分期支付合同价格。合同还约定船舶在通过试航后才可交接。船舶建造完毕后,绝大部分建造款均已支付,但船舶在试航前因意大利船东的债务而被扣押。船厂主张船舶被扣时所有权尚未转移。一审法院认为船舶所有权并没有转移至意大利船东。苏格兰最高民事法院也认为,按照1893年《货物买卖法》的规定,所有权应当依当事人在合同中表示的意愿转移,而通过对合同的解释,船舶的所有权应当在船舶交给船东之后才发生转移。苏格兰最高民事法院的这一判决得到了上议院的支持,Lord Robertson 说:②

> In the present case I find the contract to require no aid or supplement from the statutory rules, for it seems to me to provide from beginning to completion of this ship for the building of it by the shipbuilders with their materials, and transfers it to the purchasers only as a finished ship and at a stage not in fact yet reached. This is a simple view of the matter; but, in my judgment, it is the sound one. It treats the Sale of Goods Act as superseding the previous law; and if in some instance it may be found necessary to revive and reconstruct the old common law for purposes of illustration, I can only say that that occasion has not yet come.

8.128 对当事人意愿的判断并不是主观的,而应当是客观的。因此,对当事人意愿的客观判断未必与当事人的主观意愿相吻合。在 *Davy Offshore Ltd* v *Emerald Field Contracting Ltd*③ 一案中,原告被告之间的合同约定由原告向被告提供一个海上浮动生产设施,一个海上浮动储存装置,一个单点系泊系统以及其他各种辅助设施,并且由原告负责安装和调试。被告应当在合同生效日支付两笔款项,分

---

① (1908) SC(HL) 1.
② (1908) SC(HL) 1 at 2.
③ [1992] 2 Lloyd's Rep 142.

别是 900 万美元和 2,480 万美元。被告还应当向原告提供由巴克莱银行开立的金额为 9,400 万美元的信用证。原告应当在完工前向被告发出不多于 28 天但不少于 14 天的书面通知。完工后,原告应当向被告提供卖据和最终的节点证书。被告则应当签发完工证书,会签最终节点证书等,并将这些文件返还给原告。合同第18.1(a)条规定:

> Title to the Work and the Facilities ... shall be with Contractor until and shall be transferred to and vest in the Company immediately upon Completion and payment of the amount due from the Company at Completion as referred to in Clause 17.2. ... (c) At the time of transfer to and vesting of title pursuant to sub-clause (a) above, the Contractor shall deliver to the Company a duly executed legal bill of sale in respect of the FPF.

双方的争议是海上浮动生产设施所有权的转移时间。被告认为所有权应当在原告提供卖据之时或在原告提供卖据后非信用证付款的数额支付之时转移,被告并且认为所有权转移并不取决于完工证书或最终节点证书的签发。原告则认为最早的所有权发生转移的时间是他们收到信用证文件以及非信用证付款的数额支付之时转移。一审的 Hobhouse 法官认为所有权在银行接受文件之时,即银行认为文件符合信用证要求之时发生转移。

被告上诉,上诉法院认为海上浮动生产设施的所有权应当根据当事人的意图转移。由于被告要将卖据送还原告以便原告用于信用证的提示,因此双方不可能有所有权在卖据交到被告手上时转移的意愿。Staughton 法官认为这样与合同第 18.1(a) 条的规定不相吻合,他说:①

> In my judgment that provision makes no sense in the light of the other terms of the contract. It may be that the draftsman did not, when he was writing cl.18, have in mind the more detailed provisions which he later inserted in cl.36, under which the bill of sale was to be returned to Davy and used for presentation to the bank. Or was there to be a second bill of sale for the bank, in respect of the same property? There is high authority that provisions of a contract may be rejected if they cannot be reconciled with the remainder: *Glyn and others* v *Margetson & Co* [1893] AC 351 at p 357.

8.129

8.130

---

① [1992] 2 Lloyd's Rep 142 at 155.

8.131　至于海上浮动生产设施所有权发生转移的时间，Staughton 法官说：①

> In my judgment, the property does not pass under the prime contract until Davy are provided by Emerald with the documents which are required to operate the letter of credit. I would therefore dismiss the appeal on this issue, although I would make some alteration to the Judge's order where it also required presentation of the documents to the bank, and unconditional acceptance of them.

逐步转移的约定

8.132　有些船舶建造合同会约定船舶的所有权在建造过程中逐步由船厂转移至船东。就尚未使用的材料而言，此种约定有可能是无效的。在 *Reid* v *Macbeth and Gray*② 一案中，船厂和船东订立了船舶建造合同，约定由船厂在船东的监造下为船东建造一艘船舶。船舶建造合同的第 4 条规定：

> The vessel as she is constructed, and all her engines, boilers, and machinery, and all materials from time to time intended for her or them, whether in the building-yard, workshop, river, or elsewhere, shall immediately as the same proceeds become the property of the purchasers, and shall not be within the ownership, control, or disposition of the builders, but the builders shall at all times have a lien thereon for their unpaid purchase-money.

8.133　船级社的检验人在供应商的场地对将用于船舶建造的材料进行了检验，并在经过检验的钢板上标明了船号以及应当安装在船上的部位。船厂在这个时候遭遇破产。当时钢板尚未运至船厂，龙骨已经安放完毕，在船厂仍有大量的材料尚未安装，其中钢板是船厂向一家供货商订购的。钢板上均已标明了该船的船号，有的还注明了船舶上的特定位置。破产信托人和船东就钢板的所有权发生了争议，各自主张对钢板拥有所有权。船东依据上述合同条款以及《货物买卖法》第 17 条主张自己拥有所有权：

> (a) Where there is a contract for the sale of specific or ascertained goods the property in them is transferred to the buyer at such time as the parties to the contract intend it to be transferred.

---

① [1992] 2 Lloyd's Rep 142 at 156.
② (1904) AC 223.

(b) For the purpose of ascertaining the intention of the parties regard shall be had to the terms of the contract, the conduct of the parties and the circumstances of the case.

苏格兰最高民事法院外庭的 Lord Ordinary 认为合同约定的是一艘"完整"船舶的买卖,钢板不能视为船舶的一部分。而就钢板而言并不存在特定或确定货物的买卖,因此钢板并不是船东的财产。但是内庭的 Lord Trayner 法官则推翻了 Lord Ordinary 的命令。该案最后上诉至上议院,上议院的 Halsbury 伯爵认为合同约定的是船舶的出售,而不是材料的出售,而且材料未得到接受。Halsbury 伯爵说:① 8.134

> ... that there was no acceptance of these materials in any sense which can be relied upon, except in a sense which, as I have said, is inapplicable for the purpose, namely, the certificate of Lloyd's as to the goodness of the materials .... I am of opinion that there was no sale here at all of these materials as distinguished from a contract of sale of the ship, and that there was no acceptance of these materials in any sense which can be relied upon, except in a sense which, as I have said, is inapplicable for the purpose, namely, the certificate of Lloyd's as to the goodness of the materials, it seems to me, with all respect to the leaned judges who have decided the case in the Court below, that their decision was wrong and ought to be reversed; and I move your Lordships accordingly.

上议院的 Lord Davey 则对"as the same proceeds"的含义作出了解释,他认为:② 8.135

> I will only add a few words to what he has said as to the expression ... "as the same proceeds." I think "the same" must mean either as the ship proceeds or as the construction of the ship proceeds; but whether you put the one or the other of those meanings upon the words, it is clear, whatever else may be obscure in this forth clause, that the goods in question are only to become the property of the purchaser from time to time as progress is made in the construction of the ship ... it was only when the chattels in question were applied for the use of the ship, and became part of the structure of the ship ....

---

① (1904) AC 223 at 231.
② Ibid.

8.136　从上述判例中可以得出的结论是,用于船舶建造的材料在成为船舶组成部分之前,其所有权应当不发生转移,依然由船厂拥有。

"指定"的解释

8.137　在 *Atkinson v Bell*[①] 一案中法院认为由于没有对精纺机作出指定,因此精纺机的所有权不发生转移。*In re Blyth Shipbuilding & Drydocks Company Limited*[②] 一案涉及当事人关于船舶建造材料所有权的约定。船厂与意大利船东订立的船舶建造合同约定由船厂为船东建造一艘船舶,船东分期支付合同价格,第一期在合同签署后支付,第二期在铺龙骨时支付,第三期在结构成型后支付,第四期在船舶下水时支付,第五期在交船时支付。船舶建造合同的第 6 条又有如下规定:

> ... from and after payment by the purchasers to the builders of the first instalment on account of the purchase price the vessel and all materials and things appropriated for her should thenceforth, subject to the lien of the builders for unpaid purchase money including extras, become and remain the absolute property of the purchasers.

8.138　船舶建造合同的第 10 条则有如下内容:

> During the construction of the vessel and until it shall be delivered to the purchasers, the builders shall at their own expense insure the vessel and all material and things built into the vessel against all fire, launching, harbor and marine risks.

8.139　在船东支付了两期建造款后,由于船厂财务状况出现问题,法院为船厂指定了委托管理人并且同意船厂无须继续履行船舶建造合同。船舶当时尚未完成建造,船东和委托管理人就未完成的船舶以及材料的所有权归属问题产生了争议。由此产生的问题是已部分建成的船舶以及为建造该船舶准备的材料的所有权应当由船厂拥有还是船东拥有。

8.140　一审法院认为虽然合同的约定足以转让未完成船舶的所有权,但发生所有权转让的不包括尚未安装至船上的那部分材料,即使是已经得到船东检验和认可的材料。一审法院认为船东对已部分建成的船舶享有所有权,但对材料不享有所有权。Romer 法官说:[③]

---

① (1828) 8 Barnewall and Cresswell 277(KB).
② [1926] Ch 494.
③ (1925) 23 Ll L Rep 205 at 206.

I therefore come to the conclusion that the property in the uncompleted vessel has passed to the Italian company, and the reasoning that has led me to this conclusion also leads me to the conclusion that the property in the materials not actually built into the vessel has not so passed. For, until these materials were so built into the vessel, they were not to be paid for by the Italian company, and the only fact in any way tending to show that the parties intended the property in them to pass is the fact that they were inspected and passed by the surveyor of the Italian company. This circumstance, however, can have no weight in view of the fact that, according to the construction which I have put upon the contract, the parties have expressly agreed that the property in the uncompleted vessel should pass to the Italian company, but have made no express provision as to the passing of the property in the loose materials.

船东提起上诉，但上诉法院维持了一审法院的判决。Ernest Pollock 爵士对船舶建造合同第 6 条进行了解释，他说：① 8.141

With these authorities before me I feel that I am guided to give a construction to these words far narrower than at first sight I should myself have given. It seems to me that the materials and things must be appropriated in a much closer and more complete sense than by mere acceptance by the surveyor or by having been made in such a manner as that they could be fitted upon the vessel. I come ultimately to the conclusion after examining the cases that the words in question mean materials which have been fitted into the vessel, or if they have not been completely fixed upon the vessel are substantially in situ, so that the removal of them would involve a going back upon the work to be done upon the vessel.

Sargant 法官也对"指定"作出了解释，他说：② 8.142

I do not think that a material is appropriated for the purpose of passing property, by any intention, however definite, on the part of one of the parties to the contract, or by any process of approval of the quality of the material by the surveyor of another party. For appropriation I think there must be some definite act, such as the affixing of the property to the vessel itself, or some definite agreement between the parties which amounts to an assent to the property in the materials passing from the

---

① [1926] Ch 494 at 515.
② [1926] Ch 494 at 518.

builders to the purchasers.

《货物买卖法》规定的适用

8.143　　在 In re Blyth Shipbuilding & Drydocks Company Limited 一案审理时，1893 年《货物买卖法》已经实施了。该法第 16 条的规定是：

> Where there is a contract for the sale of unascertained, goods no property in the goods is transferred to the buyer unless and until the goods are ascertained.

8.144　　按照第 16 条的规定，在货物买卖合同中，货物所有权只有在货物确定之后才可能发生转移。但是该法第 17 条则有如下规定：①

> Unless a different intention appears, the following are ascertaining rules for ascertaining the intention of the parties as to the intention, time at which the property in the goods is to pass to the buyer.
>
> Rule 5. -(i) Where there is a contract for the sale of unascertained or future goods by description, and goods of that description and in a deliverable state are unconditionally appropriated to the contract, either by the seller with the assent of the buyer, or by the buyer with the assent of the seller, the property in the goods thereupon passes to the buyer. Such assent may be express or implied, and may be given either before or after the appropriation is made.

8.145　　按照第 17 条的规定，除非当事人另有约定，船舶的所有权似乎只能在船舶处于可交接状态后才会发生转移。在 Reid v Macbeth and Gray② 一案中，Lord Davey 认为船舶建造合同与其他货物买卖合同不同，船舶建造合同所买卖的是船舶，而不是建造船舶所需的材料。因此《货物买卖法》的规定不适用于船舶建造合同。他说：③

> My Lords, it seems to me that those sections have no application whatever to the case before your Lordships, for the simple reason . . ., that here there was no contract for purchase of these materials. The

---

①　s.18, r.5(i).
②　(1904) AC 223.
③　(1904) AC 223 at 232.

learned counsel and also the learned judges in the Court below seem to me to have proceeded on the supposition or hypothesis that this contract contained, not only a contract for the purchase of the ship, but a separate contract for the purchase of the materials also; and that seems to me to be a complete fallacy. There is only one contract – a contract for the purchase of the ship. There is no contract for the sale or purchase of these materials separatim; and unless you can find a contract for the sale of these chattels within the meaning of the Sale of Goods Act, it appears to me that the sections of that Act have no application whatever to the case.

所有权的回转

8.146　船舶所有权在船舶建造完成之前发生转移并不影响船东按照船舶建造合同规定享有的拒绝接受船舶的权利。一旦船东行使了拒绝接受船舶的权利,船舶的所有权即回转至船厂一方。在 Nelson v William Chalmers & Company Limited① 一案中,原告是船东,被告是船厂。船东与船厂订立了船舶建造合同,约定由船厂为船东建造一艘摩托艇。船舶建造合同的第 4 条规定:

> The contractors bind and oblige themselves to have the yacht completed in accordance with the specification, and to the satisfaction of the said designer, not later than twelve weeks from receipt of first building plans . . . .

8.147　船舶建造合同的第 6 条则有如下规定:

> The right of property in the yacht will pass from the contractors to the owner on payment of the first instalment of the price, subject to the contractors' lien for the balance of the price, and extras.

8.148　摩托艇建造完毕后,船东拒绝接船,理由是摩托艇的建造在很多方面都不符合合同要求。船厂认为在船东支付了第一期款后,摩托艇就已经是船东的财产了,因此船东无权拒绝接受摩托艇。法院拒绝了船厂的这一观点,Lord Dewar 认为只要船厂所交付的摩托艇不符合船舶建造合同的规定,船东就可以拒绝接受摩托艇,他说:②

---

① 1913 1 SLT 190.
② 1913 1 SLT 190 at 194.

> The contract is for a completed yacht to be built in terms of a specification to the satisfaction of the pursuer. Clause 6 is intended merely as a security. Under such a contract I do not think that the pursuer is bound to accept delivery unless the vessel is completed conform to the contract.

8.149　在 *McDougall v Aeromarine of Emsworth Ltd*① 一案中，船舶建造合同的第 8 条规定，船舶及建造人为建造而购买的所有材料、设备、配件和机器，无论是否在船厂、车间、水上或其他地方，在买方支付了第一期款后即成为买方的绝对的财产。但建造人就所有应付款项，无论是否按照合同的规定或修改开具了发票，对船舶、材料、设备、配件和机器享有留置权。法院认为，即使所有权随船舶或建造的进行以及设备的采购而转移至买方，买方依然有权拒绝接受尚未完成的船舶。一旦买方拒绝接受船舶，未完成船舶的所有权随即转移回建造人。高院的 Diplock 法官说：②

> ... The clause, which was no doubt designed for the protection of the purchaser in the event of the insolvency of the builder, thus seems to me to be quite inept for that purpose.
>
> It is not an unfamiliar conception in contracts for the sale of goods that the property should pass defeasibly .... I do not think that a clause providing for the transfer of property, whether qualified by the adjective "absolute" or not, in incomplete goods or their components, of itself, irrevocably deprives the buyer of any right to reject the goods when completed and to divest himself of his property therein ....

建造合同的规定

8.150　虽然按照成文法的规定船厂和船东可以约定船舶所有权转移的时间，③但在实践中，船舶建造合同都会规定船舶所有权在船舶交接时自船厂转移至船东。前面提到的 SAJ 格式便规定船舶的所有权在船厂和船东的船舶交接完成之时发生转移。④ Norwegian 格式也规定船舶所有权在船舶交接后转移。⑤ CSTC 格式的

---

① [1958] 2 Lloyd's Rep 345.
② [1958] 2 Lloyd's Rep 345 at 356.
③ Sale of Goods Act 1979, s.18.
④ Article VII.5.
⑤ Article VIII.4.

规定与上述两种格式略有不同:①

> Title to and risk of the VESSEL shall pass to the BUYER only upon delivery thereof. As stated above, it being expressly understood that, until such delivery is effected, title to the VESSEL, and her equipment, shall remain at all times with the SELLER and are at the entire risk of the SELLER.

虽然 CSTC 格式在上述规定中说的是船舶所有权在"交接"时转移至船东一方,但这里的"delivery"应当是指交接备忘录的签署和交换,因为在该条的前面有如下内容:② 8.151

> ... delivery of the VESSEL shall be effected forthwith by the concurrent delivery by each of the parties hereto, one to the other, of the Protocol of Delivery and Acceptance, acknowledging delivery of the VESSEL by the SELLER and acceptance thereof by the BUYER ....

而 NEWBUILDCON 格式则明确规定船舶所有权在船厂和船东签署并交换交接备忘录后转移至船东一方:③ 8.152

> Title and risk of loss of or damage to the Vessel shall rest with the Builder until exchange of the Protocols of Delivery and Acceptance is effected, immediately upon which title and risk shall pass to the Buyer.

所有权的保留

虽然船舶建造合同大都会规定船舶的所有权在船舶交接之时自船厂转移至船东一方,但是这并不妨碍船厂在船舶建造合同中对船舶所有权作出保留。例如 Norwegian 格式就有船厂保留船舶所有权的规定:④ 8.153

> The Builder may retain the Vessel until full payment has been made in accordance with the agreed payment terms ....

Norwegian 似乎是唯一有保留船舶所有权规定的标准格式。毫无疑问,船厂可以在船舶建造合同中作出此种保留。1979 年《货物买卖法》便允许卖方在合同 8.154

---

① Article VII.4.
② Article VII.2.
③ Clause 31, para.1.
④ Article III.3, para.5.

中约定货物所有权在约定的条件满足之时才发生转移:①

> Where there is a contract for the sale of specific goods or where goods are subsequently appropriated to the contract, the seller may, by the terms of the contract or appropriation, reserve the right of disposal of the goods until certain conditions are fulfilled; and in such a case, notwithstanding the delivery of the goods to the buyer, or to a carrier or other bailee or custodier for the purpose of transmission to the buyer, the property in the goods does not pass to the buyer until the conditions imposed by the seller are fulfilled.

8.155　但是，Norwegian 格式规定的所有权保留与 1979 年《货物买卖法》规定的所有权保留应当是不同的。前者的保留实际上是以继续占有船舶为前提的，而后者的保留则是在放弃了货物的实际占有情况下进行的。后者的保留仅仅适用于一般的货物，即使货物已经交给了买方，但货物所有权在约定条件满足之前不会转移至买方，买方在这种情况下处置货物的往往也是一种无权处分。

船厂的留置权

8.156　即使船厂在船舶建造合同中没有对船舶所有权作出保留，船厂在船舶交接时且船舶所有权转移至船东一方后依然有成文法规定的未收货款卖方的救济。船厂可以对船舶行使留置权从而确保获得船舶建造合同规定的建造款。1979 年《货物买卖法》的规定是:②

> Subject to this and any other Act, notwithstanding seller's rights. that the property in the goods may have passed to the buyer, the unpaid seller of goods, as such, has by implication of law –
> (a) a lien on the goods or right to retain them for the price while he is in possession of them;
> ......

8.157　在 *Woods* v *Russell* 一案中，船舶的所有权已经从船厂转移至了船东，但船东尚有建造款没有支付，Abbott 法官认为船厂依然享有留置权，他说:③

> The defendant had, at that time, paid half what the ship, when

---

① s.19(1).
② s.39(1).
③ (1822) 5 B & Ald 942 at 497.

complete, would be worth. Paton could not be injured by having the general property in the ship considered as vested in the defendant, because he would still have a lien upon the possession for the residue of the price . . . .

很显然,无论是普通法的留置权还是成文法的留置权,相同的前提是船厂继续占有并控制着船舶。然而,除非船舶所有权在交船之前就已转移至船东一方,在船舶建造过程中船厂一旦将船舶交给了船东也就放弃了对船舶的占有。船舶虽然是动产,但适用不动产的登记制度。船舶的登记对船舶所有权的归属会产生很大的影响,船东一旦将船舶登记在自己的名下,船厂保留的所有权其实已经失去了所有权固有的性质。船东一旦出售船舶,船厂享有的所谓所有权并不能使船厂成功主张船东的出售无效而重新获得船舶。这时,船厂实际上享有的其实只是一项债权而已。

8.158

船舶抵押

在航运市场低迷时,船东的财务状况可能会遇到困难。如果没有银行的支持,支付最后一期建造款都会有问题。不少船厂在船东有财务困难时一般会同意推迟收取最后一期款。如前所述,船厂对船舶所有权作出任何保留都不能保障船东欠款的偿还。作为一种保障,船厂应当要求船东对船舶设定以船厂为抵押权人的抵押。由于船东造船往往有银行的融资安排,银行都会要求对船舶设定以银行为抵押权人的抵押。在已经有抵押的情况下,船厂即使可以对船舶设定抵押,也只能是第二顺序的抵押权人。船厂的权利的实现必须以作为第一顺序抵押权人银行的权利的全部实现为条件。

8.159

所有权转移的准据法

船舶建造合同的准据法未必就是所有权转移问题的准据法,按照冲突法原则,动产所有权转移的有效性适用动产所在地国家的法律(*lex situs*)。按照动产所在地法律是有效的,转移在英国也就是有效的;按照动产所在地法律是无效的,转移在英国也是无效的:①

8.160

(1) A transfer of a tangible movable which is valid and effective by the

---

① Collins, et al, *Dicey and Morris on the Conflict of Laws*, 16th edn Sweet & Maxwell 2012, para.25R-001, Rule 144.

law of the country where the movable is at the time of the transfer is valid and effective in England.

(2) Subject to the Exception hereinafter mentioned, a transfer of a tangible movable which is invalid or ineffective by the law of the country where the movable is at the time of the transfer is invalid or ineffective in England.

8.161　普通法的地位与此相同,在 Re Anziani 一案中,高院的 Maugham 法官是这样说的:①

I do not think that anybody can doubt that with regard to the transfer of goods, the law applicable must be the law of the country where the movable is situate. Business could not be carried on if that were not so.

8.162　上诉法院的 Devlin 法官在 Bank Woor Handel en Scheepvaart NV v Slatford (No.2) 也持相同的意见,他说:②

There is little doubt that it is the *lex situs* which as a general rule governs the transfer of movables when effected contractually. The maxim *mobilia sequuntur personam* is the exception rather than the rule, and is probably to be confined to certain special classes of general assignments such as marriage settlements and devolutions on death and bankruptcy.

8.163　差不多 15 年以后同样是在上诉法院,Diplock 法官在 Hardwick Game Farm v Suffolk Agricultural Poultry Producers Association 一案中指出,管制动产转移的法律是动产所在地法。他说:③

The proper law governing the transfer of corporeal movable property is the *lex situs*. A contract made in England and governed by English law for the sale of specific goods situated in Germany, although it would be effective to pass the property in the goods at the moment the contract was made if the goods were situate in England, would not have that effect if under German law (as I believe to be the case) delivery of the goods was required in order to transfer the property in them. This can only be because the property passes at the place where the goods themselves are.

---

① [1930] 1 Ch 407 at 420.
② [1953] 1 QB 248 at 257.
③ [1969] 1 WLR 287 at 330.

中国法的规定

在我国船厂建造船舶的,船舶所有权转移的有效性应当适用中国法。针对动产交付,除非法律另有规定,动产的所有权随交付转移:① 8.164

> 动产物权的设立和转让,自交付时发生效力,但是法律另有规定的除外。

中国法也允许买卖合同中的卖方保留货物的所有权,在卖方收到买方支付的价款之前不发生转移:② 8.165

> 当事人可以在买卖合同中约定买受人未履行支付价款或者其他义务的,标的物的所有权属于出卖人。

本书第1章曾提及在我国对于船舶建造合同的性质有不同的观点,③若将船舶建造合同视为承揽合同的,似乎就不存在船舶所有权转移的问题,因为船舶在建造过程中始终是船东的财产,船厂只对船舶享有留置权:④ 8.166

> 定作人未向承揽人支付报酬或者材料费等价款的,承揽人对完成的工作成果享有留置权或者有权拒绝交付,但是当事人另有约定的除外。

从上述规定其实也能看出,将船舶建造合同视为承揽合同可能并不妥当。但是有一点应当是明确的,只要船舶建造合同规定了船舶所有权在船舶交接时发生转移,即使船舶建造合同被视为是承揽合同,船舶所有权在交船之前依然应当由船厂拥有。 8.167

VII 风险的转移

普通法原则

作为普通法的一个基本原则,风险随所有权转移而转移。在 *Martineau* v *Kitching* 一案中,王座法院的 Blackburn 法官说:⑤ 8.168

---

① 《中华人民共和国民法典》第二百二十四条。
② 《中华人民共和国民法典》第六百四十一条。
③ 见本书第1章第II节。
④ 《中华人民共和国民法典》第七百八十三条。
⑤ (1871-72) LR 7 QB 436 at 454.

As a general rule, *res perit domino*, the old civil law maxim, is a maxim of our law; and when you can shew that the property passed the risk of the loss, *prima facie*, is in the person in whom the property is. If, on the other hand, you go beyond that, and shew that the risk attached to the one person or the other, it is a very strong argument for shewing that the property was meant to be in him.

8.169　这一普通法原则被吸收进了成文法，1893 年《货物买卖法》便规定货物风险随货物所有权一起转移：①

Unless otherwise agreed, the goods remain at the seller's risk until the property therein is transferred to the buyer, but when the property therein is transferred to the buyer, the goods are at the buyer's risk whether delivery has been made or not.

8.170　1979 年《货物买卖法》的措辞虽稍有不同，但货物风险随货物所有权一起转移的原则却得到了完全的保留：②

Unless otherwise agreed, the goods remain at the seller's risk until the property in them is transferred to the buyer, but when the property in them is transferred to the buyer the goods are at the buyer's risk whether delivery has been made or not.

建造合同的规定

8.171　常用的船舶建造合同的标准格式似乎都规定船舶的风险随船舶所有权一起在交船时自船厂转移至船东。这里所称之"风险"是指船舶遭受灭失或损坏的风险。对此，NEWBUILDCON 格式予以了明确：③

Title and risk of loss of or damage to the Vessel shall rest with the Builder until exchange of the Protocols of Delivery and Acceptance is effected, immediately upon which title and risk shall pass to the Buyer.

8.172　和船舶所有权一样，船厂对船舶承担的风险也在双方签署并交换交接备忘录之时转移至船东一方。这一时刻通常也正是船厂所投保的建造人保险的保险期

---

① s.20, para.1. 中国法在这个问题上与英国成文法基本相同，《中华人民共和国民法典》第六百零四条规定："标的物毁损、灭失的风险，在标的物交付之前由出卖人承担，交付之后由买受人承担，但是法律另有规定或者当事人另有约定的除外"。
② s.20(1)。
③ Clause 31, para.1.

限届满之时。即使船舶建造合同没有规定船舶风险发生转移的时间,按照 1979 年《货物买卖法》的规定,船舶风险也依然随船舶所有权一起转移至船东一方。①根据成文法的规定,一旦船舶的所有权在船舶交接之前已经转移至船东一方的,除非船舶建造合同另有约定,即使船厂仍然实际占有并控制着船舶,船舶的风险也依然随船舶所有权转移至船东一方。

违约与风险的转移

按照 1979 年《货物买卖法》的规定,如果货物交付发生延迟,货物风险应当由造成货物交付迟延的一方承担:② 8.173

> But where delivery has been delayed through the fault of either buyer or seller the goods are at the risk of the party at fault as regards any loss which might not have occurred but for such fault.

按照上述规定,假设造成船舶交接延误的是船东的过失,双方约定推迟交船日期。在这种情况下,虽然船舶所有权依然会在船舶实际交接之时发生转移,但船舶风险似乎在应当交船之日就会转移至船东一方,尽管船东还没有实际占有和控制船舶。③ 船舶建造合同一般只会规定船舶风险随船舶所有权转移而转移,一旦船舶交接发生延误,无论是船厂的过失还是船东的错误造成了此种延误的发生,实践中的做法是船厂通常会延长建造人险的保险期限。④ 但是按照 1979 年《货物买卖法》的上述规定,一旦是船东原因造成船舶交接发生延误的,船厂的建造人险似乎就会有保险利益的问题,这是因为在延误期间船厂已经无需承担船舶风险了。 8.174

相反,假设船东在接受船舶之后有正当理由拒绝接受船舶的,船东应当可以退还船舶给船厂。这里同样会有船舶风险应当由谁承担的问题。1979 年《货物买卖法》似乎并没有针对这一情况作出规定。但是普通法的原则应当是由船厂承担船舶风险。*Head v Tattersall* 一案是涉及到买卖马匹的案件,在该案中买方在接受了马匹后按照合同约定退还了不符合合同规定的马匹,在讨论应当由哪一方 8.175

---

① s.20(1).
② s.20(2).
③ 中国法也有类似的规定,《中华人民共和国民法典》第六百零五条规定:"因买受人的原因致使标的物未按照约定的期限交付的,买受人应当自违反约定时起承担标的物毁损、灭失的风险"。
④ 船舶建造人险的保险期限的届满通常有两种,一种是在交船后届满,另一种则是在约定的日期届满。如果是后者,一旦船舶延期交接的日期在保险失效之后的,船厂就应当延长保险期限。关于建造人险请参见本书第 14 章。

承担马匹受损造成的后果时，Cleasby 法官认为马匹的卖方应当对马匹受伤承担责任，他说：①

> I think in such a case that the person who is eventually entitled to the property in the chattel ought to bear any loss arising from any depreciation in its value caused by an accident for which nobody is in fault. Here the [seller] is the person in whom the property is revested, and he must therefore bear the loss.

8.176　按照1979年《货物买卖法》的规定，如果在卖方交付货物后，买方有权拒绝接受货物的，则无需将货物退还卖方：②

> Unless otherwise agreed, where goods are delivered to the buyer, and he refuses to accept them, having the right to do so, he is not bound to return them to the seller, but it is sufficient if he intimates to the seller that he refuses to accept them.

8.177　但是在船舶建造中应当不会发生类似的情形。船厂向船东实际交付船舶时通常是船东已经明确接受了船舶，而且，即使船东认为自己依然有权拒绝接受船舶，也不应当存在是否需要退还的问题。但是，船东在接船后有权按照船舶建造合同或法律的规定将船舶退还给船厂的，船舶风险就应当又回到了船厂一方。船东在这种情形下对船厂的责任就是一个受托人或保管人的责任。

Ⅷ　提交船舶

"提交船舶"的概念

8.178　在交船中有可能发生的事情是船厂按照船舶建造合同的规定向船东交付船舶，但船东则由于各种原因没有接船。针对这种情况，SAJ 格式作出了所谓的"提交船舶"的规定：③

> If the BUYER fails to take delivery of the VESSEL after completion thereof according to this Contract and the Specifications without any justifiable reason, the BUILDER shall have the right to tender delivery

---

① (1871-72) LR 7 Ex 7 at 14.
② s.36.
③ Article Ⅶ.4.

of the VESSEL after compliance with all procedural requirements as above provided.

CSTC 格式也有类似的规定。① 这一规定是以船厂的交船符合船舶建造合同规定为前提的,而船东拒绝接受是没有任何正当理由为前提的。虽然"提交"船舶应发生在船东拒绝接受之后,但是这里的"提交"一词的含义似乎不太明确。通常"提交"是指债务人向债权人提交一定数额的钱或银行票据。在货物买卖中通常是买方向卖方提交,从而避免卖方以没有收到货款为由对货物实施留置或变卖等。"提交"应当是无条件的,虽然可以是"带抗议的"。在货物买卖中,"提交"还有另一个含义,即"交付":②   8.179

The term "tender" is also applied to goods when they are offered to a person in performance of a contract for their delivery.

在船舶建造中,"提交"应当是船厂单方面履行交船义务的行为,船厂"提交"船舶应当是船舶交接的开始,因为只有在船厂提交船舶的情况下才会有船东的"接受"。船厂"提交"船舶同时也是一个要求,即要求船东履行船舶建造合同规定的接船义务。然而,SAJ 格式中"提交船舶"应当指船厂在船东没有正当理由拒绝接船的情况下的"提交船舶"。毫无疑问,在船东拒绝接受船舶时,船厂继续向船东交付船舶应当是没有意义的。因此,这里的"提交船舶"应当具有罗马法中的提存(deposito)的意义,即在债权人迟延或拒绝接受债务人的适当给付情形下,债务人可以将标的物或金钱提存以免除债务。非债务人过错造成的标的物的意外灭失或损坏由债权人承担。③   8.180

船厂的责任

虽然这一规定是为了船厂利益而设,但若船厂在船东不接船的情况下将船舶进行提存非但无法保护船厂自己的利益,还有可能给船厂带来不必要的风险和责任。一旦船东拒绝接船,船厂也就不太可能收到最后一期建造款了。船厂在没有收取最后一期建造款的情况下依然交付船舶并不符合自己的利益。如果船厂视自己提交船舶的行为构成已向船东交付船舶,也就意味着船厂放弃了船舶的所有权,这可能给船厂处置船舶带来障碍和困难。即使船厂对船舶所有权作出了保   8.181

---

① Article VII.6. AWES 和 NEWBUILDCON 则没有类似的规定.
② Daniel Greenberg, *Jowitt's Dictionary of English Law*, 3rd edn Sweet & Maxwell 2010, p.2236.
③ 丁玫. 罗马法契约责任[M]. 北京:中国政法大学出版社,1998:225.

留，只要放弃了对船舶的占有和控制，船厂在处置船舶时就会遇到问题。在没有船东接船的情况下交船显然是无法转移船舶占有权的，船舶依然在船厂的实际控制之下。如果船厂视船舶已交付而放弃对船舶的占有和控制，船厂可能会面临更大的风险。如船舶因不可抗力事件或意外事故灭失或损坏的，船厂似乎解脱不了自己的责任。

8.182　根据1979年《货物买卖法》关于买方不接货情形的规定，买方未按照买卖合同约定接受货物的不仅应当对因此产生的货物灭失承担责任，而且还应当支付合理的货物保管的费用：①

> When the seller is ready and willing to deliver the goods, and requests the buyer to take delivery, and the buyer does not within a reasonable time after such request take delivery of the goods, he is liable to the seller for any loss occasioned by his neglect or refusal to take delivery, and also for a reasonable charge for the care and custody of the goods.

8.183　但是按照上述规定，卖方似乎并不能随意放弃对货物的占有。如果货物由于卖方在买方拒绝接受货物情况下放弃了占有而遭受灭失或损坏的，卖方是应当承担责任的。对此，1979年《货物买卖法》已经作出了如下规定：②

> Nothing in this section affects the duties or liabilities of either seller or buyer as a bailee or custodier of the goods of the other party.

8.184　虽然上述规定既适用于卖方，也适用于买方，但是在船东拒绝接受船舶的情形下，依然占有和控制船舶的无疑只能是船厂，因此船厂对船舶负有受托人或保管人的责任。

IX　船舶离厂

建造合同的规定

8.185　船东接船之前通常都已经为船舶办理了临时登记，并且也办理了船壳保险和保赔保险的手续，此外还应当为船舶配备了全套船员。在大多数情况下船舶的航次都已经安排妥当了，因此船舶交接完毕后，船舶便能立即离开船厂。在期限上，

---

① s.37(1).
② s.20(3).

SAJ 格式只给了船东三天的免费期限:①

> The BUYER shall take possession of the VESSEL immediately upon delivery and acceptance thereof and shall remove the VESSEL from the premises of the Shipyard within three(3)days after delivery and acceptance thereof is effected. If the BUYER shall not remove the VESSEL from the premises of the Shipyard within the aforesaid three(3)days, then, in such event the BUYER shall pay to the BUILDER the reasonable mooring charges of the VESSEL.

按照上述规定,船舶滞留在船厂时间超过三天的船东就应向船厂支付锚泊费用。对船厂而言,收取锚泊费用未必能解决船舶滞留码头影响其他船舶下水的问题。CSTC 格式的规定似乎考虑到这一影响,因为按照该格式的规定,船厂可以将船舶移走:② 8.186

> The BUYER shall take possession of the VESSEL immediately upon delivery and acceptance thereof, and shall remove the VESSEL from the premises of the BUILDER within seven(7)days after delivery and acceptance thereof is effected. If the BUYER shall not remove the VESSEL from the premises of the BUILDER within the aforesaid seven(7)days, then, in such event without prejudice to the SELLER's right to require the BUYER to remove the VESSEL immediately at any time thereafter, the BUYER shall pay to the SELLER the reasonable mooring charges of the VESSEL.

船舶滞留在船厂时间超过合同约定期限的,船厂一般会将船舶移至锚地,从而确保船厂的其他船舶可以按时下水。NEWBUILDCON 格式也针对船舶的离开作出了类似的规定:③ 8.187

> The Buyer shall remove the Vessel from the place of delivery within five (5)running days after Delivery and Acceptance as aforesaid. If the Buyer does not so remove the Vessel within the said period, the Buyer shall pay to the Builder reasonable mooring charges for the Vessel. The Builder shall also have the right to move the Vessel from the place of delivery to another safe place at its convenience at any time after the five(5)running days' period has expired provided the Buyer is notified accordingly.

---

① Article VII.6.
② Article VII.5.
③ Clause 32(b).

8.188　　　NEWBUILDCON格式的上述规定和CSTC格式的规定有明显的区别。按照CSTC格式的规定，约定期限届满时，船厂可以同意船舶继续留在船厂码头，但船东应当支付锚泊费用，船厂也可以要求船东将船舶驶离船厂的码头。然而按照NEWBUILDCON格式的规定，在约定期限届满时，除非船厂同意船舶继续留在船厂码头，否则船厂需要自己将船舶移走，而且还必须将船舶移至另一个安全的地点。也就是说，船厂要对新的船舶停泊地点的安全负责。另外，虽然NEWBUILDCON格式没有明确规定，但由于是船厂自己将船舶移走，这就意味着船厂不仅要为移动船舶配备船员，而且还要为船舶移动承担风险和责任。

合理期限

8.189　　　如果船舶建造合同没有约定船舶驶离船厂的期限，船东应当在合理的期限内将船舶驶离船厂。何谓合理的期限则是一个事实问题，应根据具体情况予以确定。在 *Penarth Dock Engineering Company Ltd v Pounds*① 一案中，合同买卖的是在码头上的一个浮船坞，合同没有关于买方应当在几天内移走浮船坞的规定，但是发票则有如下内容：

> Although it is desirous to remove the Pontoon as speedily as possible, no time limit to be imposed.

8.190　　　码头要求买方移走浮船坞，但买方没有理睬。码头要求买方支付损害赔偿，理由是买方违反了合同，在没有得到码头允许的情况下占用了码头的场地。但买方则认为移走浮船坞并没有时限。Lord Denning认为发票构成合同内容构成规定，买方应当尽快移走浮船坞，买方没有尽快移走浮船坞构成违约，因此应当承担码头的损失。Lord Denning说：②

> I agree that no time limit was imposed, so I start with that. I agree, too, that he ought to be allowed a reasonable time to find a purchaser and decide whether the dock was to be removed to a purchaser or dealt with as scrap where it was. I think I should be generous to him in saying that I will allow six months for those endeavours to be made and that decision to be reached . . . .

---

① [1963] 1 Lloyd's Rep 359.
② [1963] 1 Lloyd's Rep 359 at 361.

船舶留在船厂的安排

在航运市场不好时,船东接船往往意味着亏损的开始。因此有船东会设法推迟船舶交接的时间,从而尽可能避免船舶投入营运带来的亏损。船东和船厂可能就船东接船后继续将船舶留在船厂或船厂附近的锚地或码头的做法达成一致,包括对船舶的保险、锚泊费用等作出约定。具体而言主要有两种做法。第一种情形是船东支付了交船款,第二种情形则是船东没有支付交船款。这两种做法有着比较根本的区别。 8.191

船东已支付交船款

虽然已经支付了交船款,但由于市场原因船东无法将船舶投入营运。在这种情况下,船东将船舶继续留在船厂的好处是船舶的锚泊费用可能低于对船舶进行闲置的费用。由于已经收取了交船款,只要船东同意支付停泊费,船厂通常会同意让船舶继续停留在船厂。此种情形在实践中并不多见,除了船东造船的目的是通过转售获得利润,否则船东在支付了交船款可能不再愿意将船舶留在船厂。 8.192

船东未支付交船款

第二种情形是船东确认船舶建造已完毕且符合建造合同要求,但为了推迟接船与船厂达成让船舶继续留在船厂的协议。在这种情况下,船东并没有支付交船款。这样的安排对船东而言无疑是有利可图的,只要不实际接船,船龄始终为零。然而,船厂应当明白推迟交船不仅意味着无法收取交船款,更重要的是将继续承担交船前的所有风险。这种做法对船厂而言有百害而无一利。船厂可以考虑接受的是:船东可以不支付交船款,但应当完成船舶交接。一旦交接完毕,船舶继续留在船厂对船厂而言也是收取交船款的一种保障。 8.193

第 9 章 不可抗力

I 不可抗力概述

来源

9.1　不可抗力（force majeure）并不是英国法概念，①force majeure 是法语，是法国民法采用的概念，其含义是"超级力量"。按照《法国民法典》的规定，债务人若由于不可抗力而不履行其债务的，不承担损害赔偿责任。② 不可抗力的概念应当来自罗马法，而罗马法中的不可抗力是指行为人通常不能预见或虽能预见但也无法抗拒的外部事由，包括地震、海啸、火灾、海盗、敌人入侵等。正如上诉法院的 Cockburn 法官在 Nugent v Smith 一案中所评述的：③

> ... the Roman law made no distinction between inevitable accident arising from what in our law is termed the "act of God" and inevitable accident arising from other causes, but, on the contrary, afforded immunity to the carrier, without distinction, whenever the loss resulted from "*casus fortuitus*", or, as it is also called, "*damnum fatale*", or "*vis major*"- unforeseen and unavoidable accident.

9.2　因此，与英国法不同，罗马法的不可抗力既包括由于自然原因导致的不可抗力，同时也包括其他原因导致的不可抗力。继承了罗马法的法国法同样只强调行为人对不可抗力的无法预见性和无法抗拒性，也不区分不可抗力的原因。王座法院的 McCardie 法官在 Lebeaupin v Richard Crispin & Co 一案中对 force majeure 在法国法中的定义和范围进行了说明，他说：④

---

① 英国法把不可抗力条款视为当事人的约定，see Hugh Beale, *Chitty on Contracts*, 35th edn Sweet & Maxwell 2023, para.40－233.
② 第 1148 条。
③ (1876) 1 CPD 423 at 429.
④ (1920) 4 Ll L Rep 122 at 124.

This phrase "*force majeure*" has been introduced into many English commercial contracts within recent years. It is employed not only with increasing frequency, but without any attempt to define its meaning or any effort to coordinate the phrase to the other provisions of documents. It is a phrase employed in the Code de Commerce of France. Thus, for example, Art.230 of that Code provides: "*La responsabilité du capitaine ne cesse que par la preuve d'obstacles de force majeure*".... A broad statement on the matter appears in Giraud's French Commercial Law, 2nd edition, page 854, which says: -"*Force Majeure* - This term is used with reference to all circumstances independent of the will of man, and which it is not in his power to control, and such *force majeure* is sufficient to justify the non-execution of a contract. Thus war, inundation and epidemics are cases of *force majeure*; it has even been decided that a strike of workmen constitutes a case of *force majeure*."

英国法

英国法把不可避免的事件(*casus fortuitus*)分为两大类,一类是不涉及人为因素或其他因素而单由自然力引起的不可避免的事件,另一类则是全部或部分由于人为因素,无论是作为还是不作为,无论是懈怠行为还是不当行为,或任何与自然力无关的原因所引起的。① 英国法中的"天灾"(Acts of God)是指由于自然原因导致的不可抗力,即第一类事件。②

比较 force majeure 和"天灾",我们不难看出,两者的共同点是:无论是"天灾"事件还是 force majeure 事件均与主张免责的合同当事人的主观意志无关,也非合同当事人所能控制的。而两者的区别则是:"天灾"从其字面就可以看出是指也仅仅局限于因自然原因引起的合同履行不能,例如地震、海啸和恶劣天气等。然而 force majeure 除了自然原因外还包括其他非自然原因,例如战争、罢工等。因此 force majeure 的范围明显大于"天灾"。

在 Matsoukis v Priestman & Co 一案中,王座法院的 Bailhache 法官拒绝接受船东主张的不可抗力即为英国法中天灾的观点,并认为不可抗力的范围应当大于天灾的范围,他说:③

At the same time I cannot accept the argument that the words are

9.3

9.4

9.5

---

① *Forward* v *Pittard* 1 TR 27 per Lord Mansfield.
② *Nugent* v *Smith* (1876) 1 CPD 423 at 429.
③ [1915] 1 KB 681 at 686.

interchangeable with "*vis major*" or "act of God". I am not going to attempt to give any definition of the words "*force majeure*", but I am quite satisfied that I ought to give them a more extensive meaning than "act of God" or "*vis major*". The difficulty is to say how much more extensive.

9.6 　王座法院的 McCardie 法官在 *Lebeaupin* v *Richard Crispin & Co* 一案中根据先例对不可抗力在英国法中的范围给予总结和说明，他认为不可抗力包括：战争、罢工、机器故障、坏天气和暴风雨等，他说：①

This is a wide definition, but I think that it usefully, though loosely, suggests not only the meaning of the phrase as used on the Continent, but also the meaning of the phrase as often employed in English contracts. That "war" comes within the meaning of force majeure would seem to be the opinion of Lord Justice Swinfen Eady in *Zinc Corporation* v *Hirsch* (1916, 1 King's Bench, page 541, at page 555). That a strike of workmen comes within the phrase was the opinion of Mr. Justice Bailhache in *Matsoukis* v *Priestman* (1915, 1 King's Bench, page 681). That learned Judge was, if I may respectfully say so, clearly right when he said that the phrase *force majeure* was not interchangeable with *vis major* or "the Act of God." It goes beyond the latter phrases. Any direct legislative or administrative interference would, of course, come within the term, for example, an embargo. But even such a thing as a breakdown of machinery through accident was deemed by Mr. Justice Bailhache to come within the words *force majeure*. (See *Matsoukis* v *Priestman*, 1915, 1 King's Bench, page 681, at page 687.) This opinion is agreeable to the view of Mr. Justice Walton in *Yraza* v *Astral Shipping Company* (1903, 9 Commercial Cases, page 101), where he ruled that though a miscalculation of the Master and Engineer of a ship causing a ship to leave with insufficient coals whereby she was compelled to call at another port and thereby suffered delay and depreciation of cargo was not a case of *force majeure*, yet that it would have been a case of *force majeure* if the deficiency of coal had arisen from some accident or casualty. In *Matsoukis*' case (1915, 1 King's Bench, page 681), Mr. Justice Bailhache seems to have ruled that delay caused by bad weather was not within the *force majeure* clause. But he was there dealing with the particular facts, and I

---

① Ibid.

conceive that normal bad weather is one thing, whereas abnormal tempest, storm, or the like may be another thing, and might well fall within the *force majeure* clause . . . .

由于不是英国法的概念,因此不可抗力在英国法中并没有一个准确且统一的定义,Donaldson 法官在 *Thomas Borthwick（Glasgow）Ltd* v *Faure Fairclough Ltd* 一案中是这样说的:①

9.7

The precise meaning of this term, if it has one, has eluded the lawyers for years. Commercial men have no doubt as to its meaning. Unfortunately no two commercial men can be found to agree upon the same meaning, so perhaps in this, as in so many other matters, there is very little difference between the commercial and legal fraternity.

II 不可抗力的特征

从不同的判例中可以看出不可抗力事件通常具有如下特征。

9.8

实际发生

作为免除合同当事人义务的不可抗力应当是实际发生,而且已经造成了合同当事人无法履行合同的后果。若仅仅是对不可抗力事件的恐惧或担忧并不构成可以免除合同当事人合同义务,王座法院的 Sankey 法官在 *Hackney BC* v *Doré* 一案中所说的:②

9.9

I regret the introduction of foreign words into English statutes and Orders without any definition of them being given. In my view "force majeure" case means some physical or material restraint, and does not include a reasonable fear or apprehension of such a restraint. "Fear" is a term relative to the courage or embarrassment of the person who experiences it.

无法预见

不可抗力事件应当是无法预见的,如果不可抗力事件的发生在合同订立之时

9.10

---

① [1922] 1 Lloyd's Rep 16 at 28.
② [1922] 1 KB 431 at 437.

就预知的，合同当事人就不能主张免责。在 *Ciampa and Others* v *British India Steam Navigation Company Limited*① 一案中，合同约定的不可抗力事件包括"君主的限制"以及"任何船东无法控制的情形"。法国政府规定对挂靠过有瘟疫港口的船舶进行灭鼠措施。装有柠檬的船舶曾挂靠过有疫情的蒙巴萨，船东在这种情况下依然将船舶驶往马赛。船上的柠檬由于马赛港的灭鼠措施变质了。王座法院认为船东不能援引合同的不可抗力条款免责，王座法院的理由是当船舶驶往马赛时船东就已经知道船上的柠檬会因灭鼠措施而损坏。王座法院的 Rowlatt 法官说：②

> ... I think the facts which bring that law into operation must be facts which have supervened after the ship has started on the voyage in question. When facts exist which show conclusively that the ship was inevitably doomed before the commencement of the voyage to become subject to a restraint, I do not think that there is a "restraint of princes".

无法避免或克服

9.11　不可抗力事件应当是人力所无法避免或克服的，否则也就不再是不可抗力了。但是不可抗力的不可避免或克服并不是绝对的，正如上诉法院的 Cockburn 法官在 *Nugent* v *Smith* 一案中提到了不可抗力事件是否可以克服的问题，他说的是：③

> I do not think that because some one may have discovered some more efficient method of securing the goods which has not become generally known, or because it cannot be proved that if the skill and ingenuity of engineers or others were directed to the subject something more efficient might not be produced, that [he] can be made liable. I find no authority for saying that the *vis major* must be such as "no amount of human care or skill could have resisted", or the injury such as "no human ability could have prevented", and I think this construction of the rule erroneous.

---

① [1915] 2 KB 774.
② [1915] 2 KB 774 at 779.
③ (1876) 1 CPD 423 at 429 per Cockburn CJ.

导致履行不可能

构成不可抗力事件必须实际导致合同义务的无法履行,而不仅仅给合同义务的履行增加了麻烦或困难。对此,王座法院的 Branson 法官在 *Hackney BC v Doré* 一案中是这样说的:①

> In my view "*force majeure*" cannot be established by showing that the consequences of doing the act which would be suffered by the person relying upon the clause would be unpleasant, troublesome or perhaps disastrous. In order to succeed, the appellants must show that what the statute ordered them to do has become impossible; it is not enough for them to say that it has become inconvenient or unpleasant for them to do it. I agree that the appeal must be dismissed.

Ⅲ 不可抗力的后果

一旦发生合同约定的不可抗力事件,合同便有可能自动解除,或者一方或双方当事人可以解除合同,或者可以延期履行合同。

合同的解除

有时合同虽然有不可抗力条款,但同时又明确规定了一方的义务。即使该项义务是绝对的,只要没有相反的约定,负有该义务的一方依然可以凭不可抗力条款而免除其合同义务。在 *Pagnan SpA v Tradax Ocean Transportation SA*② 一案中,从泰国出口木薯至欧盟国家的买卖合同第 19 条规定:

> Prohibition – In case of prohibition of export ... or in case of any executive or legislative act done by or on behalf of the government of a country of origin ... restriction export ... only such restriction shall be deemed by both parties to apply to the contract ... to prevent fulfilment ... and to that extent this contract or any unfulfilled portion ... shall be cancelled.

买卖合同还规定:

---

① [1922] 1 KB 431 at 438.
② [1987] 2 Lloyd's Rep 342.

Any special terms and conditions contained herein and/or attached hereto shall be treated as if written on such Contract Form and shall prevail in so far as they may be inconsistent with the printed clauses of such Contract Form.

9.16　买卖合同在合同的特别条件中则规定：

Sellers to provide for export certificate enabling buyers to obtain import licence into EEC under tariff 07.06 with 6% import levy.

9.17　泰国政府对向欧盟国家的木薯出口实施了配额制度,在配额用完后便禁止向欧盟国家出口木薯。卖方在出运了部分木薯后由于没有了配额而无法继续履行买卖合同。买方主张卖方违约并要求损害赔偿,争议提交了仲裁。仲裁庭要求法院解决的问题是：一,合同规定的卖方应当获得出口证书的义务是卖方的一项绝对的义务还是"尽最大努力"的义务；二,如果卖方获得出口证书的义务是绝对的,合同特别条款是否优先于合同不可抗力条款的适用。高院认为：Sellers to provide for export certificate 一句的含义是卖方承诺获得或提供相关证书的义务,从文意来看此项义务构成卖方的绝对义务,而不仅仅是合理的恪尽职责的义务。如果卖方能够证明第19条适用,特别条件的规定并不优先于第19条的适用。一审法院最终判决卖方胜诉,买方提起了上诉。

9.18　上诉法院驳回了买方的起诉,上诉法院认为合同特别条件的规定并没有提及"尽最大努力"或者"恪尽职责",也没有使用任何类似的语言,因此卖方获得出口证书的义务是绝对的。如果出现第19条规定的情形,卖方可以免除其合同义务,而第19条的适用似乎并无此限制。在合同第19条与合同特别条件之间并不存在不一致的问题,泰国政府对出口的限制导致了买卖合同的解除。在卖方获得出口证书义务是否构成绝对义务问题上,上诉法院的 Bingham 法官说：①

> I find myself in full agreement with the learned Judge that this clause imposed more than an obligation to use best endeavours or due diligence. Accordingly, I agree that the clause imposed an absolute obligation on the sellers to provide for the export certificate, save in so far as any other clause of the contract might modify the sellers' obligation or relieve him from the consequence of breach.

---

① [1987] 2 Lloyd's Rep 342 at 348.

但是在买卖合同第 19 条与合同特别条件之间哪个规定应当优先适用的问题 9.19
上,Bingham 法官则认为:①

> The natural construction of this contract in my judgment is that the sellers were to provide for the export certificate, but, in case of prohibition of export or in case of any executive or legislative act done by, or on behalf of, the government of Thailand (as the country of origin and shipment) restricting export, the unfulfilled portion of the contract was to be cancelled. That construction does not deprive the special condition of effect. The obligation to provide for the export certificate remained on the sellers. If the certificate was not provided for as a result of oversight, error, mishap, bureaucratic inefficiency or delay, and probably also if the certificate was not provided for simply because the Thai authorities failed to issue it, the sellers would remain liable. But, if the sellers were unable to provide for the certificate because of any impediment falling within the carefully-defined ambit of cl.19, they were relieved of their contractual obligation because that is what cl.19 says and there is no indication whatever that cl.19 is not to apply to this as to all other contractual obligations.

上诉法院的 Woolf 法官认为:② 9.20

> The special condition does not go on to specify the time within which the export certificate had to be provided; nor does it expressly deal with what was to happen if there should occur a situation which made it difficult or impossible to obtain the export certificate. The contract did, however, contain what I will describe as "a standard force majeure" or "frustration clause"; that is cl.19. That clause comes into operation in the circumstances which it specifies, which are inter alia where there is a prohibition on export, a blockade or hostilities, or in the case of any executive or legislative act done by, or on behalf of, the Government of the country of origin; and it provides that in those circumstances the contract shall be cancelled to the extent that fulfilment is no longer possible.
>
> Clause 19, if allowed to operate, does not directly deal with the seller's obligations to obtain an export certificate, but it clearly can affect that obligation of the seller, since in some circumstances, if cl.19 operates,

---

① [1987] 2 Lloyd's Rep 342 at 351.
② [1987] 2 Lloyd's Rep 342 at 352.

the export certificate will no longer be required. However, this qualification does not mean that cl.19 is inconsistent with the special condition; on the contrary, cl.19 supplements the special condition and deals expressly with circumstances with which the special condition could have dealt but did not deal.

In my judgment the special condition and cl.19 cannot only march together side by side, but they can do so in step. Clause 19 does not cut down or detract from the benefits to the seller under the special condition. Mr. Johnson on behalf of the buyers seeks to elevate the special condition to a status where it amounts to a warranty, not only that an export certificate would be provided, but that the contract would be capable of being performed as was contemplated with the benefit of an import licence into the E. E. C. under tariff 07.06 with the benefit of the 6 per cent. import levy. This is not justified and in my judgment this case is clearly distinguishable from the sort of situation referred to by Mr. Justice Diplock (as he then was) in *Walton (Grain) Ltd v British Italian Trading Co* [1959] 1 Lloyd's Rep. 223 at p.236, and the case to which he refers of *Peter Cassidy Seed Co Ltd v IL Osuutukukkauppa* [1957] 1 Lloyd's Rep. 25; [1957] 1 W. L. R. 273. In the latter case Mr. Justice Devlin held that there was a collateral warranty where there had been an assurance given by the seller that the obtaining of the licence would be a pure formality.

9.21 有些船舶建造合同规定,在因不可抗力原因而无法继续建造的情况下,船东有权决定是否继续履行船舶建造合同。船舶建造合同之所以如此规定,其原因应当是船东希望掌握主动,以便根据当时的市场情况作出是否继续建造船舶的决定。

自动解除

9.22 只要合同作出约定,一旦发生导致一方无法履行或继续履行合同的不可抗力事件,合同可以自动解除而无须任何一方向对方发出通知。在 *Continental Grain Export Corp v STM Grain Ltd*[①] 一案中,买卖合同的第 23 条规定:

Should the fulfilment of this Contract be rendered impossible by prohibition of export ... or by any executive or legislative act done by

---

① [1979] 2 Lloyd's Rep 460.

or on behalf of the Government of the country of origin of the goods . . . this contract or any unfulfilled part thereof, to be cancelled. If required by Buyers, Sellers must provide documentary evidence to establish any claim for cancellation under this clause.

高院的 Robert Goff 法官认为,根据第 23 条的规定,合同的解除是自动的,卖方无需向买方发出任何通知,他说:① 9.23

Unlike cl. 21 of GAFTA 100, cl. 23 of FOSFA does not contain a provision requiring the sellers to advise the buyers without delay if shipment should prove impossible during the contract period by reason of one of the specified events . . . . I cannot see that cancellation under the clause is contingent upon the giving of notice or of the fulfilment by the sellers of his obligation to provide documentary evidence . . . .

The second point raised by . . . the buyers was whether cl. 23, if applicable, had the effect that the contract was automatically cancelled. The answer to that must, in my judgment, be in the affirmative, for the simple reason that that is what the clause provides.

在实践中也有船舶建造合同规定在船舶建造因不可抗力原因而无法完成的情况下,船舶建造合同即告解除。虽然在实践中,船厂依然会通知船东船舶建造合同的解除,但此种通知并不构成船厂解除合同的前提条件。 9.24

履行推迟

不可抗力事件除了会导致合同的解除外,也可能引起合同履行的推迟。船舶建造合同的标准格式一般都有关于在发生不可抗力事件后船厂可以顺延合同交船日的规定。SAJ 格式便有如下规定:② 9.25

If, at any time before the actual delivery, either the construction of the VESSEL or any performance required a prerequisite of delivery of the VESSEL is delayed due to Acts of God, . . . the Delivery Date shall be postponed for a period of time which shall not exceed the total accumulated time of all such delays.

由于不可抗力条款规定的是合同履行的延期而不是合同的解除,因此特定的 9.26

---

① [1979] 2 Lloyd's Rep 460 at 471.
② Article VIII.1.

事件是否构成不可抗力事件的要求也相对宽松一些。即使不可抗力事件影响的是其他船舶的建造，船厂似乎依然有机会主张不可抗力。在 *Matsoukis* v *Priestman & Co*① 一案中，船舶建造合同于1912年2月21日订立，被告同意为原告建造一艘船，并约定1913年2月28日之前交船。合同有下列除外条款：

> If the said steamer is not delivered entirely ready to purchaser at the above-mentioned time, the builders hereby agree to pay to the purchaser for liquidated damages, and not by way of penalty, the sum of 101 sterling for each day of delay and in deduction of the price stipulated in this contract, being excepted only the cause of *force majeure*, and/or strikes of workmen of the building yard where the vessel is being built, or the workshops where the machinery is being made, or at the works where steel is being manufactured for the steamer, or any works of any sub-contractor.

9.27　1912年的煤矿工人罢工于3月1日开始，4月8日结束。船厂的业务以及为船厂建造之前船舶提供材料的企业的业务均发生了全面的混乱。船厂的船舶建造因此产生了滞延，之前建造的船舶停在泊位上的时间延长了，导致船东的船舶的建造延误了7天。实际上船舶是在1913年8月22日交接的。为了获得船舶，船东在保留权利的情况下支付船舶建造合同价格的全额。

9.28　船东在接船后向船厂提出了索赔，要求船厂支付约定赔偿。船厂认为船厂的业务混乱导致之前船舶建造的延误是合同约定的不可抗力，是船厂无法控制的情形，因为罢工是船厂无法控制的。船东则认为不可抗力事件是指自然原因引起的事件，并不应当包括罢工。即使不可抗力事件包括罢工，在本案中同样也不应当包括罢工，因为船舶建造合同规定的罢工是特定的。如果双方的意图是包括煤矿工的罢工，船舶建造合同就应当予以明确。但是高院的Bailhache法官则认为，虽然罢工直接造成的是其他船舶的延误，但是同样构成不可抗力，他是这样说的：②

> ...I think I am justified in saying that did constitute a case of *force majeure*. Of course if I were to give the words the full meaning ... there would be no doubt about the matter, but giving them a more restricted meaning I think that the complete dislocation of business in the north of England as a consequence of the universal coal strike, which

---

① [1915] 1 KB 681.
② [1915] 1 KB 681 at 686.

operated directly on the ship in turn for building previously to the plaintiff's steamer, and only indirectly on the plaintiff's steamer, did come within the reasonable meaning of the words "*force majeure*".

Ⅳ 不可抗力条款

合同中关于不可抗力规定的条款称之为"不可抗力条款",它规定了在发生不可抗力事件时合同当事人的免责以及免责的条件等。船舶建造合同的标准格式都有不可抗力条款,虽然在格式中的位置不太一样,但其内容则基本一致。 9.29

SAJ 格式

SAJ 格式中的不可抗力条款规定的是:① 9.30

If, at any time before the actual delivery, either the construction of the VESSEL or any performance required a prerequisite of delivery of the VESSEL is delayed due to Acts of God, acts of princes or rulers, intervention of government authorities, war, blockade, revolution, insurrections, mobilization, civil commotion, riots, strikes, sabotages, lockouts, labour shortages, plague, epidemics, fire, flood, typhoons, hurricanes, storms or other weather conditions not included in normal planning, earthquakes, tidal waves, landslides, explosions, collisions, strandings, embargoes, delays in transportation, shortage of materials or equipment, or delay in delivery or inability to take delivery thereof, provided that such materials and equipment at the time of ordering could reasonably be expected by the BUILDER to be delivered in time, prolonged failure or restriction of energy sources including electric current and petroleum, mishaps of casting and/or forging; or by destruction of the Shipyard or works of the BUILDER or its subcontractors, or of the VESSEL or any part thereof by fire, flood, or other causes as above specified; or due to delays in the BUILDER's other commitments resulting from any such causes here in above described which in turn delay the construction of the VESSEL or the BUILDER's performance under this Contract; or due to other causes or accidents beyond control of the BUIDER, its subcontractors or supplier of the nature whether or not indicated by the foregoing words,

---

① Article Ⅷ.1.

irrespective of whether or not these events could be foreseen at the day of signing this Contract, the Delivery Date shall be postponed for a period of time which shall not exceed the total accumulated time of all such delays.

9.31 按照 SAJ 格式不可抗力条款的规定，不可抗力事件可以分为如下两大类，第一类是自然原因引起的不可抗力事件，这些事件包括：天灾、火灾、水灾、台风、飓风、暴风雨、地震、潮波、山崩以及其他不包括在正常预期中的天气状况等。第二类则是因人为因素造成或与人为因素有关的不可抗力事件，这些事件包括：政府的干预或限制、战争和暴乱等。发生不可抗力事件的后果是船舶建造合同规定的合同交船日按照不可抗力事件对船舶建造的实际影响进行顺延。

9.32 SAJ 格式的不可抗力条款使用的文字和行文似乎并不十分流畅，存在不必要的重复，而且还有并不十分合适的规定，例如关于锻造和铸造的事故的规定恐怕没有太大的实际意义。而且，将锻造和铸造事故视为不可抗力至少在当今船舶建造中已不再有适当的依据了。

NEWBUILDCON 格式

9.33 NEWBUILDCON 格式中关于不可抗力的规定与其他格式有着比较大的区别。NEWBUILDCON 格式并没有独立的"不可抗力"条款，格式起草人把不可抗力放入了可允许延误之内。格式的第 34 条是"可允许延误"，该条第 1 款规定了合同交船日可以推迟的两种情形，其中第一种便是不可抗力事件。其内容如下：

The Delivery Date shall be extended if any of the following events cause actual delay to the delivery of the Vessel:
(i) Force majeure events
 (1) acts of God;
 (2) any government requisition, control, intervention, requirement or interference;
 (3) threat or act or war, warlike operations, terrorism or the consequences thereof;
 (4) riots, civil commotions, blockades or embargoes;
 (5) epidemics;
 (6) earthquakes, landslides, floods, tidal waves or extraordinary weather conditions;
 (7) strike, lockouts or other industrial action, but only if of a

general nature and not limited solely to the Builder and/or the sub-contractors or their employees;

(8) fire, accident, explosion(whether in the Shipyard or elsewhere);
(9) any interruption to the supply of public utilities to the Builder;
(10) any other cause of a similar nature to the above beyond the control of the Builder or its Sub-contractors;
(11) delays to sea trials inaccordance with Clause 27(b)(Sea Trial – Weather Conditions).

第二种则是其他各种因素,包括船东供应品的延误或缺陷;修改引起的延误;船级社规范或船旗国要求的变更引起的延误;船舶遭受全损以及船舶建造的中止等。与 SAJ 格式相比,NEWBUILDCON 格式关于不可抗力事件的规定比较清晰,也比较简洁。NEWBUILDCON 格式根据性质对不可抗力事件进行了基本的分类,例如将地震、山崩、水灾和潮波列为同一组不可抗力事件,将骚乱、平民暴动、封锁和禁运列为了同一组不可抗力事件;放弃了 SAJ 格式采用的一些词语,例如:瘟疫、内战、革命、动员和破坏等;增加了一些新的不可抗力事件,例如:异常天气条件、事故、类似战争行动、恐怖行为和海上试航的延误等;对一些常用的不可抗力事件作出了限制,例如在罢工、停工及其他劳工行动前加了"具有一般性质且不限于船厂或其分包商的雇员",在火灾、事故和爆炸前加了"无论是发生在船厂还是其他地方";对一些常见的不可抗力事件的名称作出了调整,例如不再使用明显过时了的"君主的行为",而改用"政府控制",用"向船厂提供的公共设施的中断"替代了"能源供应的故障和限制"。另一个值得注意的地方是,NEWBUILDCON 格式为所有的不可抗力事件设定了一个前提,即"船厂为避免或减轻不可抗力事件对船舶交接带来的实际延误已尽其所有合理的努力"。①

9.34

AWES 格式

其他标准格式的不可抗力条款与上述 SAJ 格式和 NEWBUILDCON 格式基本相同。AWES 格式并没有独立的不可抗力条款,相关内容在格式第 6 条(交船)中,其内容大致与 SAJ 格式的不可抗力条款相同。值得注意的是 AWES 格式的不可抗力事件包括"意外损坏包括船舶损坏及为修复此种损坏而花费的时间"。"意外损坏"似乎并不局限于因自然原因引起的损坏,还应当包括船厂雇员

9.35

---

① Norwegian 格式也有类似的规定,该格式第 IX.1(c)条便规定:"The Builder is obliged to do its utmost to avoid or minimise the *Force Majeure* Delay".

的疏忽或过错导致的船舶的损坏。然而,因船厂的疏忽或过错造成的损坏应当不构成传统意义上的不可抗力事件。

Norwegian 格式

9.36　　Norwegian 格式有与 SAJ 格式相类似的独立的不可抗力条款,但是按照该条款的规定,罢工和停工并不包括发生在船厂的劳工滋扰。上诉法院的 Goddard 法官在 *Horn v Sunderland Corp* 一案中对"disturbance"作出了解释,他说:①

> Disturbance implies that something is taking place against the will of the person disturbed. If an owner is expelled from his house, the expense he is put to in removal is in no way connected with the value of his house. It is a loss which he has suffered, as it seems to me, by being expelled, whatever the value of the house may be.

9.37　　从程度上来看,劳工滋扰显然比不上罢工,Norwegian 格式的起草者应当是想将尚未构成罢工但确又给船厂的船舶建造带来困难和麻烦的情形排除在罢工之外。

条款的解释

9.38　　不可抗力条款的解释就是合同条款的解释,适用合同解释的一般原则。解释不仅局限于某一个字或词,而应当考虑这些字和词的前后文。正如王座法院的 McCardie 法官在 *Lebeaupin v Richard Crispin & Co* 一案中所说的:②

> I take it that a force majeure clause should be construed in each case with a close attention to the words which precede or follow it, and with a due regard to the nature and general terms of the contract. The effect of the clause may vary with each instrument.

9.39　　有不少不可抗力条款在列明了不可抗力事件后往往会加上"以及其他合同当事人无法控制的事项"。在这种情况下应当按照其自然的和真实的含义予以解释,而并不一定要受同类解释规则(*ejusdem generis*)的限制。在 *Chandris v Isbrandtsen-Moller Co Inc*③ 一案中,合同规定船舶不装"碳酸矿、爆炸物、武器或

---

① [1941] 2 KB 26 at 53.
② (1920) 4 Ll L Rep 122 at 125.
③ [1951] 1 KB 240.

弹药,以及其他危险货物",法院认为解释时不应适用"同类解释规则",上诉法院的 Devlin 法官说:①

> *Anderson* v *Anderson* is a decision of the Court of Appeal in relation to a post-nuptial settlement in which all three Lords Justices clearly laid it down that general words were *prima facie* to be considered as having their natural and larger meaning and not to be restricted to things *ejusdem generis* previously enumerated, unless there was something in the deed to show an intention so to restrict them.... *Anderson* v *Anderson* is a decision which, unless distinguishable on the ground that I am concerned with a commercial document rather than a settlement, is binding on me. Apart from its authority, if I may respectfully say so, I entirely agree with it.
>
> A rule of construction cannot be more than a guide to enable the court to arrive at the true meaning of the parties. The *ejusdem generis* rule means that there is implied into the language which the parties have used words of restriction which are not there. It cannot be right to approach a document with the presumption that there should be such an implication. To apply the rule automatically in that way would be to make it the master and not the servant of the purpose for which it was designed – namely to ascertain the meaning of the parties from the words they have used.

而且"beyond the control of the parties"不仅适用于未列明的事项,同时也适用于已经列明的事项。为此高院的 Nigel Teare 法官在 *Frontier International Shipping Corp* v *Swissmarine Corporation Inc and Another(The Cape Equinox)* 一案中说:② 9.40

> In my judgment, ... the words "beyond the control of the consignee" apply not only to "any other causes or accidents" but also to the specified events of strikes, lockouts and civil commotions.... I accept that the words "beyond the control of the consignee" are also capable, as a matter of language, of applying only to the unspecified causes but I do not consider that such a construction can have been the intention underlying cl.9.

---

① [1951] 1 KB 240 at 244.
② [2005] 1 Lloyd's Rep 390 at 392.

9.41　合同的不可抗力条款不应该有附加条件,一旦有了附加条件,不可抗力条款就有可能形同虚设。因为希望援引不可抗力条款的一方当事人只有在满足了附加条件后才能主张不可抗力条款规定的免责。在 *B & S Contracts and Design Ltd* v *Victor Green Publications Ltd*① 一案中,合同的不可抗力条款规定：

> Every effort will be made to carry out any contract based on an estimate, but the due performance of it is subject to variation or cancellation owing to an act of God, war, strikes, civil commotions, work to rule or go-slow or overtime bans, lock-out, fire, flood, drought or any other cause beyond our control, or owing to our inability to procure materials or articles except at increased prices due to any of the foregoing causes.

9.42　承包商因遣散费与工人产生了纠纷,工人停止了工作,承包商主张免责。但是法院认为承包商只有在尽了一切努力后才能主张不可抗力条款规定的免责。上诉法院的 Eveleigh 法官：②

> In those circumstances I have come to the conclusion that every effort was not made to perform this contract, and consequently reliance cannot be placed upon that force majeure clause. Having come to that conclusion there is no need for me to deal with other arguments that have been put forward by the defendants in this case, for example to the effect that the plaintiffs, by their conduct in employing workmen who were on the brink of dismissal, were bringing strike troubles upon themselves. In my judgment that does not arise.

举证之责

9.43　主张不可抗力免责的一方负有举证之责,这一点应当是明确的。正如高院的 Aikens 法官在 *Mamidoil-Jetoil Greek Petroleum Company SA and Another* v *Okta Crude Oil Refinery AD* 一案中所说的：③

> I also accept ... that it is for the party relying on the force majeure clause to bring itself within the terms of the clause as construed.

---

① [1984] ICR 419.
② [1984] ICR 419 at 425.
③ [2003] 1 Lloyd's Rep 1.

主张方不仅要证明不可抗力事件的发生,而且还要证明所发生的不可抗力事件实际上确实导致其无法履行合同规定的义务或无法按时履行合同义务。正如 Longmore 法官在 *Agrokor AG v Tradigrain SA* 一案中所说的:① 9.44

> ... it is clear ... (a) that it is for the sellers to prove that they are entitled to rely on [*force majeure* clause] or equivalent; and (b) that, in order to do so, the sellers must show not merely that there was a ban which restricted the export of wheat, but also that the ban had the effect of restricting the performance of the actual contracts ....

Chitty on Contracts 对希望援引合同中不可抗力条款一方的举证之责作了如下归纳:② 9.45

> It is for a party relying upon a force majeure clause to prove the facts bringing the case within the clause. He must therefore prove the occurrence of one of the events referred to in the clause and that he has been prevented, hindered or delayed (as the case may be) from performing the contract by reason of that event. He must further prove:
> (i) that his non-performance was due to circumstances beyond his control; and
> (ii) that there were no reasonable steps that he could have taken to avoid or mitigate the event or its consequences.

在船舶建造合同中可能利用不可抗力条款主张免责或延期履行的一方应当是船厂,因此船厂首先需要证明的是:实际上已经发生了船舶建造合同约定的不可抗力事件,而且由于不可抗力事件的发生,船厂无法履行或无法按时履行船舶建造合同。除此之外,船厂还要证明的是:导致船厂无法履行或延迟履行的情形是其无法控制的,而且船厂无法通过采取合理措施来避免或减轻不可抗力事件所带来的后果。 9.46

免责的条件

在发生不可抗力事件时,船厂并不一定可以主张合同交船日的顺延,船厂只有在满足一定条件的前提下才可以主张合同交船日的顺延。NEWBUILDCON 格式便明确规定了船厂凭不可抗力事件顺延合同交船日的条件:③ 9.47

---

① [2000] 1 Lloyd's Rep 497 at 500.
② Hugh Beale, *Chitty on Contracts*, 35th edn Sweet & Maxwell 2023, para.27 – 082.
③ Clause 34(a)(iii).

Provided that in respect of (i) and (ii) above:
(1) such events were not caused by the error, neglect, act or omission of the Builder or its Sub-contractors; and
(2) were not, or could not reasonably have been, foreseen by the Builder at the date of the Contract; and
(3) the Builder shall have complied with Sub-clause (b) hereunder; and
(4) the Builder shall have made all reasonable efforts to avoid and minimize the effects such events have on the delivery of the Vessel.

9.48 上述规定中的"provided that"应当构成条件,即船厂只有在满足了上述四个条件的前提下才可以凭不可抗力事件造成的延误主张顺延合同交船日。①

没有疏忽或过失

9.49 不可抗力事件的基本特征是人力不可控,因此援引合同不可抗力条款主张免责的一方不能有疏忽或过失,有疏忽或过失的当事人不能主张不可抗力免责。王座法院的 McCardie 法官在 *Lebeaupin v Richard Crispin & Co* 一案中说:②

... a man cannot rely upon his own act or negligence or omission or default as force majeure.

9.50 不可抗力事件的出现应当与主张免责一方的违约无关。在 *Hull Central Dry Dock & Engineering Works Ltd v Ohlson Steamship Ltd*③ 一案中,修船合同规定船厂应当在 40 天内完成船舶修理,超过 40 天的船厂应支付约定赔偿。合同有罢工免责的规定。船东增加了修理项目,但双方没有约定期限的延长。40 天期限届满时,修理尚未完成。第二天,工人因劳资纠纷开始罢工,结果修理在七个月后才完成。船东要求船厂支付约定赔偿,但船厂则援引不可抗力条款主张自己可以免责。王座法院的 Bailhache 法官认为船厂只有在没有违约的情况下才能主张不可抗力免责,他说:④

... the [repairers] cannot rely upon the strike interfering with their work if at the time the strike began, they had exceeded their contract time. They can only rely upon the strike clause as being an interference with the work given to them or contracted for if at the time of the strike they

---

① *Forward v Pittard* (1785) 1 TR 27.
② [1920] 2 KB 714.
③ (1924) 19 Ll L Rep 54.
④ (1924) 19 Ll L Rep 54 at 56.

had committed no breach of contract.

王座法院的 Roche 法官在 *Lindvig* v *Forth Shipbuilding & Engineering Co Ltd* 一案中也认为,对自己造成的延误不能主张不可抗力,他说:①

9.51

> For this reason Mr. Wright has said truly, in my judgment, that in so far as the defendants themselves brought about a delay, they cannot rely upon force majeure. It is abundantly clear in such a case it would not have been force majeure, but the defendants' own inability to carry out the contract. Therefore, I proceed to consider how far there was inability on the part of the defendant company to complete by October, 1920.

值得注意的是,按照 SAJ 格式的规定,无论什么时候发生的不可抗力事件,船厂似乎都可以顺延合同交船日:②

9.52

> If, at any time before the actual delivery, either the construction of the VESSEL or any performance required a prerequisite of delivery of the VESSEL is delayed due to Acts of God, ... the Delivery Date shall be postponed for a period of time which shall not exceed the total accumulated time of all such delays.

上述的"at any time before the actual delivery"似乎只能解释为在实际交船前的任何时候,因此即使在合同交船日之后发生的不可抗力事件,船厂也可以主张顺延合同交船日。

9.53

已采取合理措施

主张不可抗力免责的一方应当已采取了所有合理措施以避免不可抗力事件可能带来的影响,如果只是增加费用便能解决的问题,合同当事人则不能主张不可抗力免责。上诉法院的 Griffiths 法官在 *B & S Contracts and Design Ltd* v *Victor Green Publications Ltd* 一案中是这样说的:③

9.54

> ... clauses of this kind have to be construed upon the basis that those relying on them will have taken all reasonable efforts to avoid the effect of the matters set out in the clause which entitle them to vary or cancel

---

① (1921) 7 Ll L Rep 254 at 255.
② Article VIII.1.
③ [1984] ICR 419 at 426.

the contract . . . . Generally speaking, also, a mere difficulty of additional expense is not a sufficient ground to enable a party to invoke an exception clause . . . .

9.55　在 *Channel Island Ferries Ltd* v *Sealink UK Ltd*① 一案中，双方订立合同由被告以光船租赁的方式向原告提供两艘船，合同规定任何一方当事人均无需对"罢工、封锁以及无法控制的任何性质的事件"承担责任。合同签订后，被告的雇员和船员罢工，最终被告和工会达成协议承诺不以光船租赁的方式出租船舶。接着被告向原告主张不可抗力。高院驳回了被告的主张，上诉法院支持了高院的判决，上诉法院的 Ralph Gibson 法官认为主张不可抗力免责的一方应当能够证明无法采取合理措施避免不可抗力事件的发生，他说：②

> . . . the accepted construction of a *force majeure* clause of this nature . . . requires that the party claiming its protection proves that there were no reasonable steps which it could have taken to avoid being prevented from performing its obligation by the incident or event said to be within the clause.

损害确已发生

9.56　在 *Nichols* v *Marsland* 一案中，上诉法院的 Mellish 法官对合同当事人主张不可抗力免责的条件进行了总结，他认为，作为一个法律问题，合同当事人不仅应当证明造成损害的原因是天灾，而且还应当证明天灾确实造成了损害。Mellish 法官认为在有不可抗力事件且不可抗力事件造成了损害的情形下，合同当事人才无需承担责任，他说：③

> A defendant cannot, in our opinion, be properly said to have caused or allowed the [damage], if the act of God or the Queen's enemies was the real cause of [the damage] without any fault on the part of the defendant . . . . We are of opinion, therefore, that the defendant was entitled to excuse herself by proving that the [damage caused] through the act of God.

---

① [1988] 1 Lloyd's Rep 323.
② [1988] 1 Lloyd's Rep 323 at 329.
③ (1876) LR 2 Ex D 1 at 5.

V 不可抗力事件

天灾

天灾通常是指直接的、突然的、有破坏力的并且是无法阻止的自然力。天灾的一个基本特征是与人的因素无关,上诉法院的 Lord Mansfield 在 *Forward* v *Pittard* 一案中说:①

9.57

> It is laid down that he is liable for every accident, except by the act of God, or the King's enemies. Now, what is the act of God? I consider it to mean something in opposition to the act of man; for everything is the act of God that happens by His permission; everything, by His knowledge . . . .

上诉法院的 Mellish 法官在 *Nugent* v *Smith* 一案中也强调了天灾的自然因素,并指出自然因素是人力所不能阻止的,他说:②

9.58

> The "act of God" is . . . any accident as to which he can shew that it is due to natural causes directly and exclusively, without human intervention, and that it could not have been prevented by any amount of foresight and pains and care reasonably to be expected from him.

虽然天灾的特点是自然力导致了事件的发生,并没有人为因素的参与。但是并非自然力就一定构成天灾,③

9.59

> On the other hand, it must be admitted that it is not because an accident is occasioned by the agency of nature, and therefore by what may be termed the "act of God," that it necessarily follows that [one] is entitled to immunity. The rain which fertilizes the earth and the wind which enables the ship to navigate the ocean are as much within the term "act of God" as the rainfall which causes a river to burst its banks and carry destruction over a whole district, or the cyclone that drives a ship against a rock or sends it to the bottom. Yet [one] who by the rule is entitled to protection in the latter case, would clearly not be able to claim it in case of damage occurring in the former.

---

① (1785) 1 TR 27 at 33.
② (1876) 1 CPD 423 at 444.
③ (1876) 1 CPD 423 at 435.

地震等

9.60　天灾包括地震（earthquake）、海啸（tsunami）、山崩（landslide）和潮波（tidal wave）。其中,地震是地壳运动而产生的突然的剧烈振动。地震能引起火灾和水灾,还可能造成海啸、滑坡、崩塌和地裂等灾害。海啸往往是由于海底发生地震而造成的海面巨浪的产生。山崩是指山上的岩石瞬间发生快速滑落。暴雨、洪水或地震都有可能引起山崩。相反,山崩也有可能引起地震。潮波并不是指正常的由于太阳和月亮等天体的作用而产生的潮汐现象,而是指异常大的海浪,尤其是指因水下地震等引起的异常的大海浪。在这一点上潮波应当是海啸的另一种表述方式。上述自然情形构成不可抗力事件应当不会有太大的争议。如果地震等不可抗力事件影响了船舶建造,船厂自然可以主张免责。船厂和船东可能产生争议的应当是上述自然情形是否对船舶建造带来实际的影响。

台风等

9.61　台风（typhoon）、飓风（hurricane）、风暴（storm）以及大风暴（tempest）属于天灾范畴同样不太会引起争议。上诉法院 Cockburn 法官在 *Nugent v Smith* 一案中认为天灾包括风暴,他说:①

> That a storm at sea is included in the term "act of God", can admit of no doubt whatever. Storm and tempest have always been mentioned in dealing with this subject as among the instances of *vis major* coming under the denomination of "act of God".

9.62　上述四个自然情形实际上是相互类似且重叠的。台风和飓风其实是不同程度或不同地区的风暴而已,形成于印度洋和西太平洋热带地区的风暴一般被称为台风,英文中的"typhoon"本身就是来自中文的外来语;而在北大西洋及东太平洋,尤其是加勒比海地区形成的风暴则通常被称为飓风。上诉法院的 Shaw 法官在 *Young v Sun Alliance Ltd* 一案中分别对风暴和大风暴进行了分析和比较,他说:②

> ..."storm" meant "rain accompanied by strong wind"; "tempest" denoted an even more violent storm ....

---

① *Nugent v Smith* (1876) 1 CPD 423 at 436 per Cockburn CJ.
② [1977] 1 WLR 104 at 107.

9.63 　　台风是在船舶建造合同履行中较为常见的不可抗力事件,我国江、浙、闽和粤海边的船厂每年都会遭遇台风的侵袭,往往会受到不同程度的损害。虽然在台风多发地区每年夏季有台风来临并不是不能预料的,换言之,台风并不是不可预期的,但是台风会在什么时候来临以及台风可能对船舶建造带来什么影响则是很难甚至是无法预料的。而且台风显然是无法通过人力预防或避免的。台风是否会对船舶建造带来负面影响往往取决于船舶建造处于哪一阶段。如果船舶在船台上,或下了水在水中,那么船舶建造势必会受到台风的影响。如果船舶建造尚在分段制作阶段,虽然船舶建造依然会受到台风的影响,但此种影响与船舶在船台上或水中的影响大不相同。如果船舶建造尚未正式开工,船厂正处于设计和制图以及采购阶段,即使有台风,船厂也很难以发生不可抗力事件为由主张推迟船舶建造节点或合同交船日。

水灾

9.64 　　水灾(flood)通常指因洪水泛滥给人类社会造成的灾害,水灾应当属于天灾的范畴。在 *Young v Sun Alliance Ltd* 一案中,上诉法院的 Shaw 法官分别对暴风雨和洪水的定义进行了分析和比较,他说:①

> ... "flood" was not something which came about by seepage or by trickling or dripping from some natural source, but involved "an overflowing or irruption of a great body of water" as one of the definitions in the Shorter Oxford English Dictionary, 3rd ed. (1944), puts it. The slow movement of water, which can often be detected so that the loss threatened can be limited, is very different from the sudden onset of water where nothing effective can be done to prevent the loss, for it happens too quickly.

9.65 　　构成免责事项的水灾应当是无法预料的,即使洪水或水灾有预报,但其强度以及所造成的危害则往往是难以预料的。在 *Nichols v Marsland* 一案中,上诉法院的 Mellish 法官说:②

> ... not only that there was no negligence in the construction or the maintenance of the reservoirs, but that the flood was so great that it could not reasonably have been anticipated, although, if it had been

---

① [1977] 1 WLR 104 at 107.
② (1876) LR 2 Ex D 1 at 5.

anticipated, the effect might have been prevented; and this seems to us in substance a finding that the escape of the water was owing to the "act of God". However great the flood had been, if it had not been greater than floods that had happened before and might be expected to occur again, the defendant might not have made out that she was free from fault; but we think she ought not to be held liable because she did not prevent the effect of an extraordinary act of nature, which she could not anticipate.

9.66　水灾对船舶建造的影响可能是多方面的,已经下水的船舶可能会受到水灾的影响;即使在船台上的船舶,其建造同样会因水灾而受影响。另外,水灾甚至还有可能影响船厂的采购,例如供应商因水灾无法完成设备的制造,或者设备无法运抵船厂等。

坏天气

9.67　SAJ 格式的不可抗力条款列举的不可抗力事件还包括"其他不包括在正常预期中的天气状况"。此类"天气状况"应当是指"坏天气"。因坏天气导致船舶建造无法开始或继续的情形应当说并不多见。但是特定的坏天气是否构成不可抗力事件则是极有可能引起争议的问题。坏天气并不应解释为正常天气以外的坏天气状况,例如下雨或下雪天气,而是指相当坏的天气。上诉法院的 Cleasby 法官在 *Nugent v Smith* 一案中说:①

... I think, that the weather was of such a nature "more than ordinary bad weather," as to come within the meaning of "act of God".

9.68　比较意外的是,在 *Matsoukis v Priestman & Co*② 一案中,王座法院的 Bailhache 法官认为机器故障构成不可抗力,但是坏天气则不构成不可抗力。他认为一般坏天气是正常情况。③ 王座法院的 McCardie 法官在 *Lebeaupin v Richard Crispin & Co* 一案中对此予以了评论,他认为坏天气不构成不可抗力。他说:④

In *Matsoukis'* case (1915, 1 King's Bench, page 681), Mr. Justice Bailhache seems to have ruled that delay caused by bad weather was not

---

① (1876) 1 CPD 423 at 442 per Cockburn CJ.
② [1915] 1 KB 681.
③ [1915] 1 KB 681 at 687.
④ Ibid.

within the *force majeure* clause. But he was there dealing with the particular facts, and I conceive that normal bad weather is one thing, whereas abnormal tempest, storm, or the like may be another thing, and might well fall within the *force majeure* clause . . . .

9.69　虽然坏天气有可能构成不可抗力事件应当是明确的,问题在于程度,即天气坏到何种程度才构成不可抗力事件。这可能成为船东和船厂争议的焦点。一个比较可取的方式是在船舶建造合同的不可抗力条款中列明船厂可以主张延期的不可抗力事件,例如气温超过 36 摄氏度的,下暴雨或大雪连续超过五天的等等。即使在船舶建造合同没有类似约定的情况下,船厂依然有机会以高温为由主张不可抗力的成立,例如当地政府通知高温放假等。

异常天气

9.70　与 SAJ 格式的不可抗力条款不同,NEWBUILDCON 格式采用的是"异常天气状况"。虽然"异常"与"不在正常计划内"相比更强调天气状况的异常性,但鉴于上文的解释,两者应当没有很大的实际差异。NEWBUILDCON 格式还将影响试航的坏天气视为不可抗力事件,但该格式第 26(b)条已经规定,如果由于天气原因导致海上试航无法进行或继续,因此产生的延误属于可允许延误。因此是否将这一情形列为不可抗力事件可能并不会有所不同。相反,按照 NEWBUILDCON 格式第 27(b)条的规定,所谓影响试航的天气状况是指不符合规格书规定的试航天气状况。规格书规定的试航天气状况是双方约定的,但不符合这一状况的未必就构成坏天气。双方可以对此种情形作出约定,即浪费的时间是否属于可允许延误。将此种天气状况列为不可抗力事件恐怕并不十分妥当,因为此种天气状况只是不符合当事人的约定而已,并没有对船舶航行或试航造成实际影响。

火灾和爆炸

9.71　火灾(fire)也是一项免责事项,但是火灾应当是指已经起火的状态,仅仅发热并不构成火灾,王座法院的 Wright 法官在 *Tempus Shipping* v *Louis Dreyfus* 一案中对此予以了明确:①

Mere heating, which has not arrived at the stage of incandescence or

---

① [1930] 1 KB 699 at 706.

ignition, is not within the specific words "fire".

9.72 爆炸(explosion)与火灾有着比较密切的关系,爆炸有可能是因为火灾引起的,而爆炸则通常会导致火灾。高院的 Staughton 法官在 *Commonwealth Smelting Ltd v Guardian Royal Exchange Ltd* 一案中说:①

> It seems to me that the word "explosion" is used ... to denote the kind of catastrophe described in Webster, 1961, and Encyclopaedia Britannica: an event that is violent, noisy and are caused by a very rapid chemical or nuclear reaction, or the bursting out of gas or vapour under pressure.

9.73 火灾和爆炸有可能是属于天灾的范畴,例如地震可能引起火灾和爆炸,但火灾和爆炸未必一定就是天灾,人为因素同样会导致火灾和爆炸的发生。但是作为船舶建造合同的不可抗力事件,引起火灾的原因是否具有人为因素可能并不影响船厂主张不可抗力免责。火灾和爆炸同样是 NEWBUILDCON 格式规定的不可抗力事件,但是在 NEWBUILDCON 格式中,火灾和爆炸之间还有一个不可抗力事件,即"事故"。这里的"事故"似乎应当理解为是与火灾或爆炸有关的或类似的事故,否则将"事故"放在"火灾"和"爆炸"之间就没有什么意义了。

罢工和停工

9.74 罢工(strike)一般是指工人拒绝工作,王座法院的 Sankey 法官在 *William Brothers(Hull) Ltd v Naamlooze Vernootschap WH Berghuys Kolanhandel* 一案中对"罢工"一词进行了定义,他也认为"罢工"在本质上就是工人因有不满而拒绝工作,他说的是:②

> I think the true definition of the word "strike", which I do not say is exhaustive, is a general concerted refusal by workmen to work in consequence of an alleged grievance.

9.75 差不多60年以后,上诉法院的 Lord Denning 在 *Tramp Shipping Corporation v Greenwich Marine Inc(The New Horizon)* 一案中对 Sankey 法官的定义进行了修改,他强调了罢工的目的并且对工人为实现自己目的停止的工作的情形与工人因

---

① [1984] 2 Lloyd's Rep 608 at 612.
② (1915) 21 Com Cas 253 at 257.

外来原因停止工作的情形进行了区分。Lord Denning 说：①

> If I may amplify it a little, I think a strike is a concerted stoppage of work by men done with a view to improving their wages or conditions, or giving vent to a grievance or making a protest about something or other, or supporting or sympathizing with other workmen in such endeavour. It is distinct from a stoppage which is brought about by an external event such as a bomb scare or by apprehension of danger.

Lord Denning 接着对"罢工"进行了进一步的解释，他说：② 9.76

> Applying this test, I agree ... that when these men refused to work 24 hours, but only eight hours, there was a "strike". They did it so as to get an improvement in their terms and conditions of work. They were not in breach of contract. But it is none the less a strike. Many a strike takes place after a lawful notice; but it is still a strike. It was discontinuous. At work during the day-time, off work at night. But a strike need not be continuous. It can be discontinuous and the periods may be added up ....

另外，应当注意的是当船厂的建造工作已经出现延误的时候，即使发生了罢 9.77
工或类似事件，船厂也未必可以主张交船日的顺延，因为在罢工发生时船厂已经
违约了。正如王座法院的 Baihache 法官在 *Hull Central Dry Dock & Engineering Works Ltd v Ohlson Steamship Ltd* 一案中所说的：③

> It seems to me perfectly plain that the plaintiffs cannot rely upon the strike interfering with their work, if at the time the strike began they had exceeded their contract time. They can only rely upon the strike clause as being an interference with the work given them or contracted for if at the time of the strike they had committed no breach of contract. That is analogous to the well-known rules as to the demurrage of ships.

停工（lockout）是与罢工相对的概念，罢工是工人拒绝工作，而停工则是资方 9.78
拒绝或阻止工人工作。停工和罢工一样，都是劳资纠纷的结果。为此，上诉法院
的 Collins 法官在 *Richardsons & M Samuel & Co, Re* 一案中说：④

---

① [1975] 2 Lloyd's Rep 314 at 317.
② Ibid.
③ (1924) 19 Ll L Rep 54 at 56.
④ [1898] 1 QB 261 at 268.

> I only wish to add, on the question of strikes and lock-outs, apart from the general words, it would appear that a strike is something beyond the control of the person against whom the strike takes place, and that a lock-out is also something that is forced upon him.

9.79　停工是指全面的停工，因此雇主解雇一名或数名工人的情形并不构成停工。正如上诉法院人的 Gigby 法官在 *Richardsons & M Samuel & Co, Re* 一案中所说的：①

> I do not say that in other cases a dismissal of workmen might not be analogous to a lock-out; but, having regard to the particular circumstances of this case, where the charterers' agent in his own interest dismissed his men, the matter stands on a different footing, and is not analogous to a lock-out. The expressions "strike" and "lockout" seem to me to be something imposed on the agent, and not something which he has elected to do, and elected to do not unreasonably.

9.80　在实践中，停工发生的机会远远小于罢工发生的机会。无论是罢工还是停工，船厂都可以援引船舶建造合同的不可抗力条款主张免责。就船厂而言，两者的区别是：罢工是工人开始的，而停工则是船厂开始的。然而，值得注意的是，即使在工人开始罢工的情况下，船厂依然有义务采取合理措施继续履行船舶建造合同。在罢工的情况下，如果船厂能够履行不受罢工影响的那部分合同义务而没有履行的，船厂就会丧失以罢工为由主张免责的权利。上诉法院的 Lord Esher 在 *Bulman & Dickson v Fenwick & Co* 一案中说：②

> ...a strike would in itself not be sufficient to exonerate the charterers from doing the best they could to [perform], and would not entitle them to fold their arms and do nothing. If, notwithstanding the strike, they could by reasonable exertion have [performed] within the proper time, the strike would not have afforded them any defence.

9.81　此外，虽然罢工直接造成其他船舶的延误，但同样有可能构成不可抗力，正如高院的 Bailhache 法官在 *Matsoukis v Priestman & Co* 一案中所说的：③

> ...I think I am justified in saying that did constitute a case of *force*

---

①　[1898] 1 QB 261 at 267.
②　[1894] 1 QB 179 at 185.
③　[1915] 1 KB 681 at 686.

majeure. Of course if I were to give the words the full meaning, ... there would be no doubt about the matter, but giving them a more restricted meaning I think that the complete dislocation of business in the north of England as a consequence of the universal coal strike, which operated directly on the ship in turn for building previously to the plaintiff's steamer, and only indirectly on the plaintiff's steamer, did come within the reasonable meaning of the words "*force majeure*".

一般性质

9.82　NEWBUILDCON 格式对罢工进行了限定,即罢工应当具有一般的性质,而且罢工并不仅限于船厂或其分包商的雇员的罢工。如果罢工的一般性质就是指前文提及的为了特定目的而拒绝工作,那么增加"一般的性质"可能并没有太大的意义。至于构成不可抗力事件的罢工是否仅包括船厂雇员和分包商雇员的罢工,还是包括其他人的罢工的意义似乎不太明确。罢工作为不可抗力事件的前提条件是罢工实际上造成了影响,例如拖延了船舶建造的进程。至于罢工由谁发起或进行的并不影响罢工作为不可抗力事件的成立。"不限于船厂和分包商雇员"应当是指船厂和分包商雇员以外的罢工只要对船舶建造造成影响的同样构成不可抗力。

战争

9.83　战争(war)在英国法中似乎是一个没有司法定义的词语。以前曾有法官采用国际法上战争的定义,例如在 *Janson v Driefontein Consolidated Mines Ltd* 一案中,王座法院的 Mathew 法官便引用了国际法意义上的战争状态。① 但是在 *Kawasaki Kisen Kabukishi Kaisha of Kobe* v *Bantham Steamship Company Ltd (No 2)* 一案中,上诉法院的 Wilfrid Greene 法官则认为,法院如果采用国际法战争定义的话就可能难以适从,他说:②

> Where these principles of international law for this purpose are to be found I must confess that I remain in complete doubt, since the only source of these principles suggested to us was the writings of various writers on international law. It is to be observed, as indeed it was to be expected, that these writers do not speak with one voice, and it is

---

① [1900] 2 QB 339 at 343.
② [1939] 2 KB 544 at 557.

possible to extract from their pages definitions of "war" which not only differ from one another, but which are inconsistent with one another in important respects. I asked for any authority in which for the purpose of the municipal law of this country "war" is in any way defined. No such authority could be suggested.

9.84 而且当代国际法似乎已经不再使用"战争"的字样而改用"武力冲突"(armed conflicts)的表述。因此在讨论战争状态时一方或双方是否已经宣战也就不再重要了。2001 年的《新牛津英语大词典》也已将"war"解释为:

A state of armed conflict between different nations or states or different groups within a nation or state.

9.85 从上述意义来看,"战争"应当是包括"内战",即一国内部的战争。在 *Spinney's(1948) Ltd, Spinney's Centres Sal and Michel Doumet, Joseph Doumet and Distributors and Agencies Sal* v *Royal Insurance Co Ltd* 一案中,高院的 Mustill 法官对内战作出了如下描述:①

In these circumstances, I consider that the right course is to look directly at the words "civil war" to see what is their ordinary meaning – although not the metaphorical sense in which the expression is often used. In my judgment, the ordinary and the literal meaning of the words are the same: a civil war is a war which has the special characteristic of being civil – i. e. internal rather than external. This special characteristic means that certain features of an international war are absent. Nevertheless, a civil war is still a war. The words do not simply denote a violent internal conflict on a large scale.

9.86 高院的 Saville 法官在 *National Oil Co of Zimbabwe(Private) Ltd and Others* v *Nicholas Collwyn Sturge* 一案中也说:②

In the context of a commercial contract such as the policy under discussion, the expressions "civil war", "rebellion" and "insurrection" bear their ordinary "business" meaning. In this context "civil war" means a war with the special characteristic of being civil i.e., being internal rather than external....

---

① [1980] 1 Lloyd's Rep 406 at 429.
② [1991] 2 Lloyd's Rep 281 at 282.

另外，虽然上诉法院的 Wilfrid Greene 法官在 *Kawasaki Kisen Kabukishi Kaisha of Kobe* v *Bantham Steamship Company Ltd（No 2）*一案中不愿意对 war 字下定义，但他认为外交关系的继续保留并不意味着不存在战争状况，他说：①

9.87

> If my view is right that the fact that diplomatic relations had not been severed did not compel the arbitrator to find that no war had broken out....

在 *Pesquerias y Secaderos de Bacalao de Espana* v *Beer* 一案中，法院认为"战争"包括"内战"。上议院的 Lord Morton 说：②

9.88

> I desire to say quite plainly that in my view the word "war"... includes civil war unless the context makes it clear that a different meaning should be given to the word.... I can see no good reason for giving to the word "war" a meaning which excludes one type of war.

由于动员通常是指军队的动员，其目的是为战争做好准备，因此动员也应当属于战争范畴。战争对船舶建造的影响既包括直接的，也包括间接的。直接影响是指由于战争或战争行为直接导致船舶建造无法进行；而间接影响则是指由于船厂所在国与船东所在国发生战争，因此两国之间的民间交易就将是非法的。在这种情况下，虽然船舶建造并没有受到任何实际的影响，但继续向船东出售船舶则会由于两国之间的战争而变得非法。

9.89

类似战争行动等

NEWBUILDCON 格式除了将战争列为不可抗力事件外，还增加了"类似战争行动"，"恐怖主义活动或其后果"。"类似战争行动"并不是指直接的战争行为，而是指与战争有关的，但又不是直接的战争行动。在 *Clan Line Steamers Ltd* v *Liverpool & London War Risks Insurance Association Ltd* 一案中，高院的 Atkinson 法官综合了之前的判例后对类似战争行动下了定义，他说：③

9.90

> The conclusion at which I have arrived from a careful examination of the authorities is that a warlike operation is one which forms part of an actual or intended belligerent act or series of acts by combatant forces. It may be performed preparatory to the actual act or acts of belligerency,

---

① [1939] 2 KB 544 at 557.
② (1949) 82 Ll L Rep 501 at 514.
③ [1943] 1 KB 209 at 221.

or it may be performed after such act or acts, but there must be a connection sufficiently close between the act in question and the belligerent act or acts to enable a tribunal to say, with at least some modicum of Lord Dunedin's common sense, that it formed part of acts of belligerency. If military equipment is being taken in a ship to a place behind the fighting front from which the forces engaged, or about to be engaged on that front, may be supplied, that ship may beyond question be said to be taking part in warlike operation. If a ship is bringing home such equipment after it has been employed on a fighting front or has been lying available for and at the service of a fighting front, again beyond question, she is taking part in a military operation.

9.91　至于恐怖主义活动,英国 2000 年《恐怖主义法》(Terrorism Act 2000) 已经对恐怖主义活动作出了定义:①

(1) In this Act "terrorism" means the use or threat of action where-
(a) the action falls within subsection(2),
(b) the use or threat is designed to influence the government or an international governmental organisation or to intimidate the public or a section of the public, and
(c) the use of threat is made for the purpose of advancing a political, religious or ideological cause.

(2) Action falls within this subsection if it –
(a) involves serious violence against a person,
(b) involves serious damage to property,
(c) endangers a person's life, other than that of the person committing the action,
(d) creates a serious risk to the health or safety of the public or a section of the public, or
(e) is designed seriously to interfere with or seriously to disrupt an electronic system.

(3) The use or threat of action falling within subsection (2) which involves the sue of firearms or explosives is terrorism whether or not subsection(1)(b) is satisfied.

(4) In this section –
(a) "action" includes action outside the United Kingdom,

---

①　s.1 of Terrorism Act 2000 as amended by the Terrorism Act 2006 s.34.

(b) a reference to any person or to property is a reference to any person, or to property, wherever situated,

(c) a reference to the public includes a reference to thepublic of a country other than the United Kingdom, and

(d) "the government" means the government of the United Kingdom, of a Part of the United Kingdom or of a country other than the United Kingdom.

(5) In this Act a reference to action taken for the purposes of terrorism includes a reference to action taken for the benefit of a proscribed organisation.

在 Ocean Steamship Co Ltd v Liverpool & London War Risks Association Ltd 一案中,上诉法院的 Scott 法官对 consequences of hostilities and warlike operations 的含义作出了解释,他说:① 9.92

> It is so easy to slip unconsciously into treating the word"consequences" in the phrase "consequences of hostilities and warlike operations" not as itself a named peril, but as the loss or damage consequential on – i. e. , caused by – a named peril .... Once the true interpretation is recognised, namely, that the word "consequences", in the established phrase is descriptive of perils and therefore that every opening which arises out of hostilities or warlike operations and every act or thing done for those purposes constitutes a specific war peril "consequential" on the generic perils named, the causal nexus between peril and loss becomes clearer, just because the particular happening, or act, is nearer to the loss; the cause is more obviously "proximate", in the sense given to that word in the decided cases. If so, the above interpretation does seem to me to be helpful for the light it throws on the final inquiry, namely, whether the loss or damage claimed was proximately caused by an insured peril.

革命、叛乱等

革命(revolution)、叛乱(rebellion)、暴动(insurrection)、平民暴乱(civil commotion)以及骚乱(riot)应当是指事件,有些还存在重叠。其中,革命、叛乱和暴动具有相似性,并且均与"内战"存在关联性。革命、叛乱和暴动的一个共同 9.93

---

① [1946] KB 561 at 569.

点是均有推翻政府的意图,但并不一定意味着有与内战相似的武力冲突。高院的 Mustill 法官在解释"叛乱"时使用了牛津英语词典的解释:①

> As regards "rebellion" I adopt the definition in the Oxford English Dictionary (Murray) –
>
> > ... organised resistance to the ruler or government of one's country; insurrection, revolt.
>
> To this I would add that the purpose of the resistance must be to supplant the existing rulers or at least to deprive them of authority over part of their territory.

9.94　高院的 Saville 法官在 *National Oil Co of Zimbabwe (Private) Ltd and Others* v *Nicholas Collwyn Sturge* 一案中将"叛乱"与"暴动"进行了比较,他认为两者只是存在程度上的差异而已,Saville 法官说:②

> "Rebellion" and "insurrection" have somewhat similar meanings to each other. To my mind, each means an organised and violent internal uprising in a country with, as a main purpose, the object of trying to overthrow or supplant the government of that country, though "insurrection" denotes a lesser degree of organisation and size than "rebellion" ....

9.95　相比较而言,革命则是指规模和目标更为广泛的暴乱,与暴动和叛乱相比,革命所实现的是更高一级的成功,而且更为持久。③ 平民暴乱的含义较为狭窄。在 *Bolivia* v *Indemnity Mutual Marine Assurance Co* 一案中,上诉法院的 Pickford 法官认为平民暴乱介乎于骚乱和内战之间:④

> Before the point is reached at which a state of civil war can be said to exist, there are ... various stages. First there is, possibly, a riot, and this may be followed by what may be described as "civil commotion". I think this was the stage at which affairs had arrived in the present case. If the adventure of those who seized the goods had been more successful, it might have developed into a civil war.

---

① *Spinney's (1948) Ltd, Spinney's Centre Sal and Michel Doumet, Joseph Doumet and Distributors and Agencies Sal* v *Royal Insurance Co Ltd* [1980] 1 Lloyd's Rep 406 at 436.

② [1991] 2 Lloyd's Rep 281 at 282.

③ Jonathan Gilman et al, *Arnould: Law of Marine Insurance and Average* 20th edn Sweet & Maxwell 2021, para.24 – 21.

④ [1909] 1 KB 785 at 801.

平民暴乱通常是为一般的目的而开始的,未必形成叛乱。而且平民暴乱并不 9.96
一定带有推翻政府的目的,骚乱和动荡则是其比较重要的特征。在 *Levy* v
Assicurazioni Generali 一案中,枢密院的 Luxmoore 法官对"平民暴乱"进行了定
义,他说:①

> [Civil commotion] has been defined to mean an insurrection of the people for general purposes, though not amounting to rebellion; but it is probably not capable of any very precise definition. The element of turbulence or tumult is essential; an organised conspiracy to commit criminal acts, where there is no tumult or disturbance until after the acts, does not amount to civil commotion. It is not, however, necessary to show the existence of any outside organisation at whose instigation the acts were done.

高院的 Mustill 法官认为平民暴乱也应当按照其自然含义进行解释,平民暴 9.97
乱的程度显然超过没有领导的乱民,他说:②

> ... civil commotion connotes something considerably more serious than a mere leaderless mob.

他又认为平民暴乱并非一定是要针对政府的,他说:③ 9.98

> In these circumstances I find nothing in the authorities compelling the Court to hold that a civil commotion must involve a revolt against the government, although the disturbances must have sufficient cohesion to prevent them from being the work of a mindless mob.

"骚乱"在上述各项中应当是激烈程度最低的不可抗力事件。此外,破坏 9.99
(sabotage)也是 SAJ 格式不可抗力条款列明的事件之一。破坏是指为了政治或
军事目的故意毁灭或损坏或阻碍的行为。单纯的破坏比较难以想象,破坏多半是
伴随战争、革命和叛乱等不可抗力事件而发生的不可抗力事件,因此破坏其实可
以放入战争、革命和叛乱这两组不可抗力事件之内。

就船舶建造而言,如果船舶建造合同的不可抗力条款已经列明了上述各项不 9.100
可抗力事件,对各项事件进行仔细的区分可能也就没有太大意义了,因为上述从

---

① [1940] AC 791 at 800.
② *Spinney's*(1948) *Ltd, Spinney's Centre Sal and Michel Doumet, Joseph Doumet and Distributors and Agencies Sal* v *Royal Insurance Co Ltd* [1980] 1 Lloyd's Rep 406 at 437.
③ [1980] 1 Lloyd's Rep 406 at 438.

骚乱到内战的不可抗力事件的范围应当说相当广泛了。

君主或统治者行为

9.101　君主或统治者的行为以及政府的干预均指影响合同当事人的政府强制性措施。政府的限制可以是本国政府,也可以是他国政府,例如本国政府限制向某一或数个国家出口产品。在此意义上,政府的限制与禁运及封锁等不可抗力事件有明显的相似之处,①禁运和封锁应当是同义词。君主或统治者的行为的限制可以是直接的,也可以是间接的。直接的是指针对主张不可抗力免责的合同当事人,而间接的则是指针对他人但主张不可抗力免责的合同当事人也同样受到影响。

9.102　政府的限制有可能是带有强制性的行为,也可能只是一个通知而已,但政府的限制是否带具有强制性并不是限制成立的必要条件。在 Sanday & Co v British and Foreign Marine Insurance Co② 一案中,英德之间爆发战争,英国船东知道后终止了驶往汉堡的航行,将货物卸下了船并委付给了保险人,要求保险人作为推定全损予以赔偿。保险人则认为英德之间的宣战并没有直接限制船舶驶往汉堡,虽然因君主限制而产生的损失并非一定要求强制力的实施,但至少要有对强制力实施的担忧。船东终止航行只是由于不合法性,因此损失的近因是战争。三审法院均认为"君主限制"成立。上议院认为只要出现会使继续履行构成非法的情形就可以成立,并不需要有实际强制力的行使。上议院的 Loreburn 伯爵是这样认为的:③

> My Lords, I am not pressed by the circumstance that force was neither exerted nor present, for force is in reserve behind every State command. And it would be a strange law which deprived the assured, if otherwise entitled to his indemnity, upon the ground that he had not resisted, till the hand of power was laid upon him, an order which it was his duty to obey. If it were an order which he was not bound to obey, and which he might have successfully resisted either by violence or by process of law, a question might arise whether or not there had been in fact a restraint. But that is outside the present case, and I say nothing of it.

---

① 从 NEWBUILDCON 格式对禁运和封锁的编排来看,该格式的起草人似乎并没有将禁运和封锁列为政府的行为,因为在 NEWBUILDCON 格式中,禁运和封锁与骚乱、平民暴动列为同一组的不可抗力事件。
② [1916] 1 AC 650.
③ [1916] 1 AC 650 at 659.

君主或统治者的行为以及政府的干预在船舶建造中主要体现为船厂所在国与船东所在国的关系发生了剧烈变化，导致船厂无法向船东交船。此种政府的限制可能是两国开战的必然的结果，但是即使在两国依然保持外交关系情况下此种限制同样是可能的，例如两国间的贸易纷争等。 9.103

政府征用、控制和要求

NEWBUILDCON 格式中的不可抗力事件包括"政府征用、控制和要求"，但是可以说并没有增加新的不可抗力事件，因为 SAJ 格式中的君主或统治者的行为显然可以包括"政府征用""政府控制"以及"政府要求"。 9.104

瘟疫和流行病

瘟疫（plague）是由于致病性微生物，如细菌和病毒引起的传染病，伴随着高烧和神志昏迷的症状。瘟疫一般是发生自然灾害后因不良环境卫生而引起的。流行病（epidemic）则是指可以在较短时间内感染众多人口且得到广泛蔓延的传染病，如流行性感冒、脑膜炎和霍乱等。流行病可以只是在某地区发生，也可以是全球性的大流行。瘟疫和流行病的共同点是短时间内的快速传播，两者的差异则是瘟疫的后果比起流行病可能更为严重。2019 年影响全球的新冠疫情是一个相当典型的流行病例子。 9.105

瘟疫和流行病本身对船舶建造可能并没有实际影响，其传统影响主要体现在劳动力由于瘟疫和流行病而出现大量的缺乏，从这个意义上说，瘟疫和流行病是导致劳动力短缺的原因。只是劳动力短缺还可以由于其他原因而引起，例如迁移等。然而，新冠疫情实际上并没有导致劳动力的大量缺乏。新冠疫情对船舶建造的影响来自各国政府对旅行以及相关活动的限制或禁止，即劳动力虽在，但无法投入工作。不仅船厂的工人以及管理人员无法投入工作，船东的监造代表和参加试航的技术代表也无法投入工作。 9.106

停电

停电（power cut）是另一个在船舶建造中经常发生的不可抗力事件。停电对船舶建造的影响应当是比较明显的，因为没有电，船厂是无法工作的。然而在实践中，停电通常有两个基本特征：一是停电往往不是绝对的，即供电机关只是通知船厂限制用电，而实际上并没有截断电力的输送。即使停电也往往是工业用电的停止供应，而民用电通常是提供的；二是停电的时间一般都不是很长，例如一天或 9.107

9.108　SAJ格式的不可抗力条款有关于停电的规定,该条款规定的是能源供应的故障或限制。这里的能源应当包括电力供应。但是由于使用了"持续的"一词,构成不可抗力事件的电力供应故障似乎有一个时间限制,即只有在电力供应发生"持续"故障时船厂才能主张不可抗力免责。鉴于停电对船舶建造的影响,这里的"持续"不应当解释为是长期的,而应当是指瞬间停电以外的,对船舶建造带来影响的所有停电情形。

9.109　有些船舶建造合同明确约定停电为不可抗力事件之一,但即使船舶建造合同没有明确约定停电为不可抗力事件,并不意味着船厂就不能以停电为由主张合同交船日的顺延。船厂在主张因停电而顺延合同交船日时应当提供相应的证据,不仅应当证明停电事实的实际存在,而且还应当证明停电实际上导致了船舶建造的停止。与其他不可抗力事件一样,作为不可抗力事件的停电同样也是指对船舶建造造成实际延误的停电,因此船厂如果在停电时间内依然继续船舶建造的,通常就可能丧失主张顺延合同交船日的权利,至少会影响船厂原本可以主张的延期天数。

公共设施的中断

9.110　NEWBUILDCON格式规定的不可抗力事件"向船厂提供的公共设施的中断"应当是包括了"停电"的,而且这个停电并不受时间长短的限制。只要发生停电且停电导致船舶建造无法继续的,船厂就可以主张不可抗力免责。因此,在这个问题上,NEWBUILDCON格式的规定显然要比SAJ格式的规定更为可取。

运输迟延等

9.111　运输的迟延、交货的迟延以及提货不能是针对分包商或供应商的。该三项不可抗力事件虽然没有提及迟延及不能的原因,但是造成运输迟延、交货迟延以及提货不能的原因应当是不可抗力。如果运输迟延和交付迟延系供应商的过失或违约行为导致的,船厂无法主张不可抗力免责。此外,援引这三项不可抗力事件均有一个条件,即船厂在订货之时是可以合理地预期材料和设备会按期交付。换言之,如果船东可以证明船厂在订货之时就知道或可以知道运输和交货会有迟延,或船厂无法提货的,船厂同样不能主张不可抗力免责。

船厂或船舶的毁坏

根据 SAJ 格式不可抗力条款的规定,因火灾、水灾或其他列明不可抗力事件引起的船厂毁坏、船厂或分包商的厂房的毁坏、船舶或其任何部分的毁坏也构成不可抗力事件。这一不可抗力事件可能没有太大的实际意义,因为 SAJ 格式列明的不可抗力事件即使没有达到导致船厂或其厂房被毁坏的程度,船厂依然是可以主张不可抗力免责的。而且,运输的迟延、交货的迟延以及提货不能实际上也是针对分包商或供应商的,分包商或供应商的厂房遭受毁坏的后果应当是无法按时供货或船厂无法提货,而运输迟延、交货迟延以及提货不能本来就是约定的不可抗力事件。

9.112

碰撞和搁浅

碰撞(collision)曾是指两个物体之间的接触,碰撞通常包括两个可航行物体间的接触,正如 Grove 法官在 *Hough v Head* 一案中所说的:①

9.113

> "Collision" appears to me to contemplate the case of a vessel striking another ship or boat, or floating buoy, or other navigable matter – something navigated, and coming into contact with. It, so to speak, imposts, as it were, two things. It may be that one is active and the other is passive, but still, in one sense, they each strike the other. That does not apply to striking on the ground at the bottom.

碰撞也可以包括船舶和码头、泊位、冰以及残骸的触碰。在 *Union Marine Insurance Co v Borwick* 一案中,高院的 Mathew 法官认为,碰撞不仅包括船舶之间的碰撞,而且也包括船舶与码头、泊位以及防波堤等其他固定物体的触碰,他说:②

9.114

> I am of opinion that the words "pier", "breakwater", and "toe" all denote one and the same structure, and therefore that the expression "collision with piers ... or stages or similar structures" covers the present case. I cannot distinguish collision with from striking against. It has been contended on behalf of the defendant that in order to constitute a collision the upper works of the ship must strike some one of the things referred to in the clause in the contract, and that there were not

---

① (1885) 52 LT 861 at 864.
② [1895] 2 QB 279 at 281.

collisions in the present case, because it appears that it was the keels of these two vessels which struck against the toe of the breakwater. According to the view which I have expressed as to the meaning of the words, that argument must be unavailing; and I am therefore satisfied that this was a case of damage by collision with a pier or similar structure, within the meaning of the 3rd clause in the contract of reinsurance.

9.115　搁浅(stranding)与碰撞相关,指船舶由于风和浪的作用而被迫在岸边或礁石间或浅滩上搁置。搁浅是指非正常情况下的搁浅,换言之,如果搁浅是正常的,例如船舶由于低潮而搁浅,此种搁浅可能未必构成不可抗力事件。在 *Magnus* v *Buttemer*① 一案中,船舶在港内由于退潮而触底,而在涨潮时又重新起浮的,法院认为不构成搁浅。

9.116　就船舶建造而言,碰撞和搁浅通常是指船舶在试航过程中或在其他必需的航行中发生的事故,例如船舶有可能在试航中与他船发生碰撞,或者在锚地或港口交船前停泊期间发生搁浅。碰撞和搁浅的发生可能没有船厂的过错,但也有可能因船厂的过错所致。船厂是否有过错应当不影响碰撞或搁浅作为约定不可抗力事件的成立。

材料或设备短缺

9.117　材料或设备短缺是指船厂无法在市场上获得船舶建造所需的材料或设备。如果材料或设备在市场上可以采购到但价格昂贵的话,船厂不能主张不可抗力免责。正如上议院的 Lord Dunedin 在 *Tennants(Lancashire) Ltd* v *CS Wilson and Co Ltd* 一案中所说的:②

> I do not think price as price has anything to do with it. Price may be evidence, but it is only one of many kinds of evidence as to shortage. If the [sellers] had alleged nothing but advanced price they would have failed.

其他原因

9.118　SAJ 格式除了列明的不可抗力事件外,还规定由于船厂、分包商或供应商无

---

① (1852) 11 CB 876; 21 LJCP 119.
② [1917] AC 495 at 516.

法控制的原因或事故导致船舶建造延误的,船厂也可以主张合同交船日的顺延。导致船舶建造延误的不可抗力事件既包括不可抗力条款列明的不可抗力事件,也包括不可抗力条款没有列明的不可抗力事件。在 Fenton v Thorley & Co Ltd 一案中,上议院可能是第一次为"事故"下定义。Lord MacNaghten 说:①

> I come, therefore, to the conclusion that the expression "accident" is used in the popular and ordinary sense of the word as denoting an unlooked-for mishap or an untoward event which is not expected or designed.

上议院的 Lord Lindley 则进一步对"事故"进行了解释和说明,他说:② 9.119

> The word "accident" is not a technical legal term with a clearly defined meaning. Speaking generally, but with reference to legal liabilities, an accident means any unintended and unexpected occurrence which produces hurt or loss. But it is often used to denote any unintended and unexpected loss or hurt apart from its cause; and if the cause is not known the loss or hurt itself would certainly be called an accident. The word "accident" is also often used to denote both the cause and the effect, no attempt being made to discriminate between them. The great majority of what are called accidents are occasioned by carelessness; but for legal purposes it is often important to distinguish careless from other unintended and unexpected events.

Lord Greene 则认为"事故"包括"天灾",他在 J & J Makin Ltd v London & North Eastern Rly Co 一案中说:③ 9.120

> In ... ordinary language the word "accident" seems to me without any doubt to cover an act of God.

Scott Lithgow Ltd v Secretary of State for Defence④ 一案关系到 "beyond contractor's control" 的解释。在该案中,船厂与国防部订立船舶建造合同,由船厂为国防部建造两艘潜水艇。船舶建造合同第 20A.3 条规定: 9.121

> In the event of exceptional dislocation and delay arising during the construction of the vessel due to alterations, suspensions of work or any

---

① [1903] AC 443 at 448.
② [1903] AC 443 at 453.
③ [1943] KB 467 at 475.
④ 1989 SLT 236.

other cause beyond the contractor's control, the effect thereof shall be assessed by agreement between the Ministry and the Contractor, failing which the Ministry may pay for the vessel on an "actual cost" basis, subject to cost investigation by the Ministry, plus a fair and reasonable sum for profit.

9.122　潜艇所需的电缆由经国防部认可的制造商 BICC 提供,并由船厂安装至潜艇上。1974 年 9 月,一艘潜艇的电缆安装完毕后被发现有缺陷,于是约定更换所有电缆。上议院认为经国防部认可的电缆供应商的违约不能视为承包商控制范围之内的事件。上议院的 Lord Keith of Kinkel 说:①

> The terms of cl.20A.3 do not reveal any genus capable of restricting the broad meaning of the words "any other cause beyond the contractor's control". Scott Lithgow did not fail in their contractual obligation to deliver submarines fitted with sound cables. They suffered exceptional dislocation and delay in doing so because BICC delivered faulty cables. Whether or not that was a matter within the control of Scott Lithgow is a question of fact. *Prima facie* it is not within the power of a contracting party to prevent quality breaches of contract on the part of a supplier or sub-contractor such as lead to delay. The contractor has no means in the ordinary case of supervising the manufacturing procedures of his supplier. He specifies his requirements but has no means of securing that they are met and the circumstance that he may have a claim against the supplier for breach of contract is irrelevant to the question whether delay consequent on the breach was due to a cause within his control. If the contractor failed to stipulate a time for delivery, consequent delay would be his own responsibility, but if he did so stipulate and delivery was late the position would be different. In this case the contract provided for a wide variety of equipment to be purchased by Scott Lithgow from many nominated suppliers or subcontractors, including in some instances the Australian Navy. Failures by such suppliers or subcontractors, in breach of their contractual obligations to Scott Lithgow are not matters which, according to the ordinary use of language, can be regarded as within Scott Lithgow's control. I therefore conclude that the First Division were right to answer in the negative the third and fourth questions posed in the case stated.

---

① 1989 SLT 236 at 241.

与此不同的是,Norwegian 格式的不可抗力条款明确规定分包商交付主要部件或履行分包合同的延误只有在其原因是约定的不可抗力事件时才构成船舶建造合同的不可抗力事件。① 9.123

Ⅵ 不可抗力通知

绝大多数船舶建造合同都对主张不可抗力免责的船厂设定了通知的义务,即船厂只有按照合同规定发出了不可抗力通知的才可以主张不可抗力免责。 9.124

标准格式

SAJ 格式规定了船厂发出不可抗力通知的义务。② 9.125

Within seven(7)days from the date of commencement of the delay on account of which the BUILDER claims that it is entitled under this Contract to a postponement of the Delivery Date of the VESSEL, the BUILDER shall advise the BUYER by cable confirmed in writing of the date such delay commences and the reasons therefor. Likewise within seven(7)days after such delay ends, the BUILDER shall advise the BUYER in writing or by cable confirmed in writing of the date such delay ended, and also shall specify the period of time by which the Delivery Date is postponed by reason of such delay. Failure of the BUYER to acknowledge the BUILDER's notification of any claim for postponement of the Delivery Date within seven(7)days after receipt of such notification shall be deemed to be a waiver by the BUYER of its right to object to such postponement.

上述条文规定了两个通知,第一个是船厂在不可抗力事件发生后的七天内向船东发出书面通知,告知船东不可抗力事件造成延误的开始及其理由;第二个则是在不可抗力事件结束后的七天内向船东发出书面通知告知延误的结束,而且还应当说明合同交船日应当顺延的天数。AWES 格式没有独立的不可抗力条款,该格式的第 6 条是交船条款,该条款一共包括五个部分,分别是:交船的时间和地点、交船文件、约定赔偿和奖励、不可抗力和可允许延误。其中不可抗力部分也有 9.126

---

① Norwegian Article IX.1(a).
② Article VIII.2.

通知的规定:①

> Within ... days after the CONTRACTOR becoming aware of the extent of an event of force majeure the CONTRACTOR shall notify the PURCHASER in writing thereof indicating the extent of the delay so caused.

9.127　由于使用了"an event of force majeure",因此 AWES 格式第 6 条中的通知应当只能解释为仅仅是针对不可抗力事件的通知。

9.128　NEWBUILDCON 格式也规定了船厂的通知义务,但有所不同:②

> The Builder shall notify the Buyer within ten(10) running days of when the Builder becomes aware of the occurrence of any event of delay on account of which the Builder asserts that it may have the right to claim an extension of the Delivery Date. A failure to so notify shall bar the Builder form claiming an extension to the Delivery Date. The Builder shall also advise the Buyer in writing(A) within two(2) running days of the ending of any event notified under this Clause that the event has ended, and(B) as soon as reasonably possible after(A), the length of extension of the Delivery Date claimed by the Builder.

9.129　NEWBUILDCON 格式实际上规定了三个通知,首先,船厂应当在知道船舶建造发生延误后的十天内向船东发出书面通知;其次,船厂应当在不可抗力事件结束后的两天内向船东发出书面通知;最后,船厂还应当在发出第二个书面通知后的合理时间内向船东发出书面通知,说明主张顺延合同交船日的天数。NEWBUILDCON 格式虽然规定十天的期限从船厂知道发生延误后起算,但实质上和 SAJ 格式规定的自不可抗力事件发生后起算并没有什么区别。这里提及的"知道"应当理解为不仅包括实际知道,也包括应当知道但实际并不知道的情形。

9.130　另外值得注意的是,船厂在知道不可抗力事件已经导致船舶建造延误后的十天内若没有向船东发出书面通知的就将丧失顺延合同交船日的权利。对船厂而言这是一个比较严格的规定,因为向船东发出书面通知构成了船厂主张合同交船日顺延的前提条件。Norwegian 格式就有类似的规定:③

> Failure by the Builder to give such notices as aforesaid shall prevent the

---

① Article 6(d), para.2.
② Clause 34(b).
③ Norwegian Article IX.2(a).

Builder from subsequently claiming Force Majeure Delay on account of such circumstances.

将 Norwegian 格式与 NEWBUILDCON 格式进行比较可以发现，在采用 NEWBUILDCON 格式时，船厂只有在发出了两个通知的情况下才有可能主张不可抗力免责。而且，船厂只有在发生不可抗力事件而未向船东发出书面通知的情况下才会丧失主张不可抗力免责的权利。 9.131

从上述三个标准格式关于不可抗力通知的规定来看，所谓的不可抗力通知其实是不可抗力延误通知。无论是 SAJ 格式规定的第一个不可抗力通知还是 NEWBUILDCON 格式规定的第一个不可抗力通知实际上并不是针对不可抗力事件的，而是针对发生不可抗力事件引起的延误，即船厂应当在不可抗力事件实际造成了延误的情况下才发出通知。 9.132

前提条件

合同当事人可以约定不可抗力通知是否构成船厂主张顺延合同交船日的前提条件。一旦船舶建造合同明确规定船厂没有按照合同规定发出通知即丧失顺延合同交船日的权利，只要此种约定是明确的就应当是有效的。问题是船舶建造合同往往会规定船厂应当向船东发出不可抗力通知，但并没有规定船厂的通知是否构成其主张合同交船日顺延的前提条件。在这种情况下，不可抗力通知是否构成此种前提条件在很大程度上取决于对相关条款内容的解释。在 *Alfred C Toepfer v Peter Cremer*① 一案中，采用 GAFTA 格式的豆粕货物买卖合同第 22 条（不可抗力及罢工）规定： 9.133

> Sellers shall not be responsible for delay in shipment of the goods or any part thereof occasioned by any Act of God, ... or any cause comprehended in the term "*force majeure*". If delay in shipment is likely to occur for any of the above reasons, Shippers shall give notice to their Buyers by telegram, telex or teleprinter or by similar advice within 7 consecutive days of the occurrence, or not less than 21 consecutive days before the commencement of the contract period, whichever is later. The notice shall state the reason(s) for the anticipated delay. If after giving such notice an extension to the shipping period is required, then Shippers shall give further notice not later than 2

---

① [1975] 1 Lloyd's Rep 406.

business days after the last day of the contract period of shipment stating the port or ports of loading from which the goods were intended to be shipped, and shipments effected after the contract period shall be limited to the port or ports so nominated.

9.134 高院的 Donaldson 法官认为第 22 条规定的通知是卖方主张履行期顺延的前提条件,他说:①

> Clause 22 is different. Whilst it is true that it is triggered by the sellers' action in giving a preliminary notice of the likelihood of delay, the seller is under an obligation to give such a notice and did in fact do so in the present case. If after this first notice has been given "an extension to the shipping period is required", the seller has to give the second notice. In my view, "required" means "necessary." The clause is not intended to give the seller an option to play the market by defaulting earlier on a rising market and claiming extension of time on one that is falling.

9.135 上诉法院同样也认为卖方的通知构成卖方主张交货延期的前提条件,上诉法院的 Lord Denning 说:②

> This flooding was "force majeure", and on account of it the sellers were entitled under cl.22 of GAFTA Form 100 to an extension of time for shipment…. In order to get an extension, the shippers (who were the first sellers) had to give two notices to the first buyer. The first notice was a warning notice telling the first buyer that shipment of the goods had been delayed or was likely to be delayed; and giving the reasons for it. The second notice was an extension notice telling the buyer that, owing to the delay, the shipper needed an extension of the contract period and stating the port or ports from which the goods were intended to be shipped. This gave the shipper an extension of one calendar month….

9.136 在 *Tradax Export SA* v *Andre & Cie SA*③ 一案中,同样是豆粕货物买卖合同,同样采用 GAFTA 格式合同,第 22 条(不可抗力及罢工)条款的内容也与 *Alfred C Toepfer* v *Peter Cremer* 一案中的相同。审理该案的高院法官依然是 Donaldson 法

---

① [1975] 1 Lloyd's Rep 406 at 418.
② [1975] 2 Lloyd's Rep 118 at 121.
③ [1975] 2 Lloyd's Rep 516.

官，但是他认为虽然第 22 条规定卖方应当发出两个通知，但由于发出通知的时限是重叠的，因此只要内容符合要求，卖方只需发出一个通知即可。Donaldson 法官虽然提及了 Lord Denning 和 Scarman 法官在 *Alfred C Toepfer* v *Peter Cremer* 一案中的判决，但并没有遵循该判决，他说：①

> The clause is intended to be worked by commercial men in a commercial way. Of course the warning notice will usually be given some time before the effective notice and the time limit for the warning notice will usually expire before, and long before, that for the effective notice. It is equally clear that there is no point in a warning notice after the effective notice has been given and the words "if after giving such notice" at the beginning of the fourth sentence exclude this possibility. But can the clause really mean that the effective notice must be delayed in order that the warning notice may precede it? I really cannot believe this. In my judgment, where the two time limits overlap, as they do here, a rolled up notice can be given which identifies the *force majeure*, this being the function of the warning notice, and further identifies the intended ports of shipment, this being the function of the effective notice. That was done in the present case and in my judgment the sellers are not to be deprived of the protection of cl.22 on this ground.

上诉法院也认为在这种情况下，卖方发出一个通知就够了，上诉法院的 Lord Denning 说：② 9.137

> In this case the embargo was imposed on June 27. That makes July 4 the latest date for the shippers to give the first notice. The contract period for shipment expired on Saturday, June 30. Two business days thereafter makes July 3 the latest date for the shippers to give the second notice (see cl.24). And then to be passed down the string without delay (see cl.23, last section). In point of fact there was only one notice given in this case. A question was raised as to whether it is sufficient to give only one notice, when two notices are provided by the clause. I think it is sufficient to give a "rolled-up notice" when it is within the specified times and gives all the required information.

差不多两年以后在 *Bremer Handelsgesellslchaft MBH* v *Vanden Avenne Izegem* 9.138

---

① [1975] 2 Lloyd's Rep 516 at 531.
② [1976] 1 Lloyd's Rep 416 at 422.

PVBA① 一案中,约定适用的 GAFTA 的货物买卖合同的第 22 条(不可抗力、罢工等)也有类似的规定。高院的 Mocatta 法官根据 *Tradax Export SA v Andre & Cie SA* 一案的判决认为买卖合同第 22 条规定的通知是卖方享受不可抗力免责的前提条件。Mocatta 法官说:②

> This matter appears, though this is not altogether certain, to have been decided adversely to[seller's] case by the Court of Appeal in *Tradax* v *Andre*.

9.139　这一观点在上诉法院得到了维持。但是上议院推翻了上诉法院的判决,上议院认为通知是否构成前提条件应当根据约定的形式、约定与合同的关系、一般的法律考虑予以认定。上议院认为该条款是中间条款,Lord Wilberforce 是这样说的:③

> Whether this clause is a condition precedent or a contractual term of some other character must depend on(i) the form of the clause itself, (ii) the relation of the clause to the contract as a whole, (iii) general considerations of law. As to(i), the clause is not framed as a condition precedent. The "cancellation" effected by the first sentence is not expressed to be conditional upon the second sentence being complied with: it operates automatically upon the relevant event .... Moreover, the generality of the words "without delay" tells against the buyer's contention: if a condition were intended a definite time limit would be more likely to be set. Then, as to(ii), provisions elsewhere in the contract(form 100) suggest that the second sentence is not intended as a condition, though it is right to say that the form, wearing as it does the appearance of a collage of clauses separately drafted, lacks consistency in many respects. However, cl.10,11(line 102) and 20 suggest that if a condition were intended, other and stricter language would have been used. (iii) Automatic and invariable treatment of a clause such as this runs counter to the approach, which modern authorities recognise, of treating such a provision as having the force of a condition(giving rise to rescission or invalidity), or of a contractual term(giving rise to damages only) according to the nature and gravity of the breach. The clause is then categorised as an innominate term .... In my opinion the clause

---

① [1977] 1 Lloyd's Rep 133.
② [1977] 1 Lloyd's Rep 133 at 163.
③ [1978] 2 Lloyd's Rep 109 at 113.

may vary appropriately and should be regarded as such an intermediate term: to do so would recognise that while in many, possibly most, instances, breach of it can adequately be sanctioned by damages, cases may exist in which, in fairness to the buyer, it would be proper to treat the cancellation as not having effect. On the other hand, always so to treat it may often be unfair to the seller, and unnecessarily rigid.

上议院的 Lord Salmon 也认为将通知作为前提条件的应当有明确的文字予以表示,他说:①   9.140

Had it been intended as a condition precedent, I should have expected the clause to state the precise time within which the notice was to be served, and to have made plain by express language that unless the notice was served within that time, the sellers would lose their rights under the clause.

从上述对不同判例的分析可以得出的结论应当是:船舶建造合同中关于不可抗力通知的实际效力往往取决于相关内容的具体措辞。   9.141

通知的解释

如果船舶建造合同规定船厂向船东发出不可抗力通知是其主张顺延合同交船日的前提条件,船厂就应当按照合同的规定发出不可抗力通知,但是除非另有约定,不可抗力通知的形式则并非十分重要。在 *Finance for Shipping Limited v Appledore Shipbuilders Limited*② 一案中,原告是船东,被告是船厂,双方订立了四个船舶建造合同。四艘船的交船均发生了不同程度的延误,造成延误的原因是主机供应商制造和交付主机的延误,对此双方没有争议。船厂根据船舶建造合同第10(a)条的规定主张不可抗力,但是第10(c)条则有如下规定: 9.142

Within a reasonable time but not exceeding 21 days from the date of commencement of any delay on account of which the Builders claim an extension of the delivery date the Builders shall advise the Purchasers in writing of the date such delay commenced and the reason therefor. Likewise within a reasonable time but not exceeding 21 days after such delay ends the Builders shall advise the Purchasers in writing of the date such delay ended and shall also specify the maximum period of time by

---

① [1978] 2 Lloyd's Rep 109 at 128.
② [1982] Com LR 49.

which the delivery date is to be extended by reason of such delay. Failure on the part of the Builders to provide the Purchasers with the dates of the commencement or end of any delay as aforesaid within the time stipulated herein shall disentitle the Builders from any extension of the delivery date in respect of the event for which the extension shall be claimed.

9.143 船厂没有按照上述规定向船东发出不可抗力通知，但双方的书信往来则有提及延误和不可抗力等。1977年9月21日，船厂致函船东

Further to our telephone conversation this morning, I would confirm that there appears to be a strong possibility of a delay in the delivery of the main engine for AS 121 ship.

9.144 1977年10月12日，船厂再一次致函船东：

The contracts for the construction and sale of the above vessels, which were exchanged on 5th October 1977, require at Clause 10(c) that you are informed of any delays which may affect the delivery of the ships. In our earlier letter of 21st September you were informed of delays in delivery of the main engine for ship No AS 121 which Doxford Engines Ltd., brought to our notice on 14th September 1977. These delays have now been quantified by Doxford Engines Ltd., as being of 8 weeks duration. This letter is, therefore, to confirm under the terms of the contracts of 5th October, our notification in our letter of the force majeure occurrence and to advise you that the delay in completion caused by the occurrence will be four weeks in respect of each of the above five Vessels. We shall, of course, continue to make every effort to mitigate the effect of these delays upon our building programme.

9.145 同年10月14日船东复函称：

We thank you for your letter of 12th October, 1977, referring to delays which may affect the delivery of the ships, the contents of which is noted.

9.146 1978年2月17日，船东致函船厂：

We write formally to acknowledge receipt of your letters dated 12th and 19th October, 8th, 9th and 24th November 1977 and 4th January 1978 in regard to circumstances which you feel constitute force majeure under Clause 10(a) of the Contracts so as to extend the completion day for the ships. We write to you in our capacity as supervisors under the various Supervisory Agreements entered into with the new Purchasers of the ships. The position of the Purchasers is as follows ....

Whilst we fully appreciate that you must notify us of circumstances which you feel may cause delay, and we are most grateful for you so doing, we trust that you will so arrange the construction of the ships that delays which you foresee by reason of the events of which you notify us are kept to a minimum by for instance ensuring that the delays run concurrently. You will appreciate that neither of us is obliged to reach agreement at this stage on the question of whether the various circumstances listed in your letters mentioned above entitles you to defer the completion day without paying liquidated damages, and indeed it would be premature to enter into any such discussions until it becomes clear that this will in fact happen. We have asked our supervisory engineering staff to co-operate with you in every way to try and help you to maintain the contractual delivery dates, and we hope the writing of this letter, which is purely done as a matter of caution to reserve our rights will not upset the present goodwill which exists between us.

船厂主张船东已经知情并且已经放弃了不可抗力通知。但船东则认为其信函并不足以构成放弃。上诉法院的 Eveleigh 法官认为双方来往的信函表明船厂已经按照第 10(c) 条的规定发出了不可抗力通知, 他说: ①

Alternatively – and there are various ways of putting it – it can be said that both parties were treating these letters as valid notice under Clause 10 .... Another way of putting it is that the correspondence, on the fact of it, contained the clear message that the Plaintiffs did not insist on strict notice, notice strictly in accordance with the terms of Clause 10(c); or further each party, thinking that the delay meant delay as contended for by the Defendants, or perhaps not even thinking about it at all, mutually accepted that these letters did comply with Clause 10 and were accepted as such, and therefore the Plaintiffs cannot now insist that there should have been a compliance with Clause 10(c) in a manner different from that which they actually accepted as compliance in accordance with the contract – whether you call it waiver, whether you call it estoppel or whether you call it convention of estoppel does not seem to me to matter.

---

① [1982] Com LR 49, Official Transcript.

VII 合同解除

9.148　船舶建造合同因不可抗力而被解除主要有两个特征:第一个特征是可以解除合同的往往是船东,而不是船厂;第二个特征则是合同的解除往往是不可抗力事件造成的延误超过一定期限的后果。

船东的合同解约权

9.149　针对船东因不可抗力事件导致延误而享有的解约权,SAJ 格式作出了如下规定:①

> If the total accumulated time of all delays on account of the causes specified in Paragraph 1 of this Article, excluding delays of a nature which, under the terms of this Contract, permit postponement of the Delivery Date, amounts to Two Hundred and Ten (210) days or more, then, in such event, the BUYER may rescind this Contract in accordance with the provisions of Article X hereof.

9.150　上述规定提及两个"延误",这两个"延误"具有不同的含义,第一个延误是在"因本条第一段列明的原因导致的所有延误累计时间达到 210 天或更多的,船东可以按照第X条的规定解除本合同"中的"延误",此种延误应当是指所有因第VIII.1条规定的不可抗力事件引起的累计的延误时间;第二种延误则是在"除去其性质按照本合同规定可以推迟交船日的延误"中的"延误",该延误虽然像是对第一部分规定的延误天数的修正,但实际上并非如此。第二部分规定的按照合同规定可以推迟合同交船日的延误其实是包括第一部分因不可抗力事件引起的延误。换言之,经过第二种延误的修正后就不会存在第一种延误。因为 SAJ 格式第VIII.1条规定的延误正是船厂可以推迟交船日的延误。这应当是 SAJ 格式的一个比较大的错误,不幸的是,该错误在我国绝大多数船厂使用的船舶建造合同中都得到了重复。对上述规定进行有意义的解释可能是:上述规定中的第一种"延误"是 SAJ 格式第VIII.1条列明的不可抗力事件引起的延误,而第二种"延误"则是第一种延误之外的船厂可以按照合同规定推迟合同交船日的延误。因此上述规定可以理解为:如果仅仅由于不可抗力原因引起的

---

① Article VIII.4.

延误达到 210 天或更多时,船东可以按照第X条的规定解除合同。

NEWBUILDCON 格式也有关于不可抗力事件造成的延误超过一定时间船东有权解约的规定:①　　9.151

> Buyer's Termination
> The Buyer shall have the right to terminate this Contract forthwith upon giving notice in the event that:
>
> ……
>
> (iii) (1) the delivery of the Vessel is delayed by more than 180 days by virtue of events that fall within Clause 34(a)(i)(Permissible Delays-Force Majeure events); or
>
> ……

按照 NEWBUILDCON 格式的规定,船东在因不可抗力事件引起的延误超过 180 天时可以向船厂发出通知,解除船舶建造合同。与 SAJ 格式的规定不同的是,按照 NEWBUILDCON 格式的规定,船东因不可抗力事件造成延误而有权解约是明确的。　　9.152

CSTC 格式并没有直接规定船东有权在不可抗力事件造成的延误超过约定天数后可以选择解除船舶建造合同,但是该格式有如下规定:②　　9.153

> If the total accumulated time of all permissible delays and non-permissible delays aggregate to ＿＿＿＿ days or more, excluding delays due to arbitration as provided for in Article XIII hereof or due to default in performance by the BUYER, or due to delays in delivery of the BUYER's supplied items, and excluding delays due to causes which, under Article V, VI, XI and XII hereof, permit extension or postponement of the time for delivery of the VESSEL, then in such event, the BUYER may in accordance with the provisions set out herein cancel this Contract by serving upon the SELLER telexed notice of cancellation which shall be confirmed in writing and the provisions of Article X of this Contract shall apply ....

CSTC 格式的上述规定是将可允许延误和不可允许延误放在一起计算,一旦超过了约定的天数,无论是由一种延误造成的,还是由两种延误共同造成的,船东都可以解除船舶建造合同。因此,一旦不可抗力事件引起的延误超过约定天数　　9.154

---

① Clause 39(a).
② Article VIII.3.

9.155　与上述几个标准格式不同的是AWES格式和Norwegian格式均没有关于船东可以在不可抗力事件引起的延误超过一定天数后解除船舶建造合同的规定。

船东解约的后果

9.156　根据SAJ格式的规定，一旦不可抗力事件导致船舶建造延误超过210天时，船东可以根据第X条的规定解除船舶建造合同。SAJ格式第X条是关于船东解约的规定。按照第X.2条的规定，在船东按照合同规定解除合同时，船厂应当返还已经收到的船东支付的所有建造款。但是船厂无需支付利息，因为第X.2条有如下内容：

> ... however, that if the said rescission by the BUYER is made under the provisions of Paragraph 4 of Article VIII hereof, then in such event the BUILDER shall not be required to pay any interest.

9.157　虽然在实践中不可抗力事件造成210天以上延误的可能性并不是很大，但是要求船厂返还所有已经收到的预付款有可能是不公平的。因为船厂实际上是承担了本不应由其承担的不可抗力事件带来的后果。而不可抗力事件的发生是船东和船厂均无法控制或避免的，不可抗力事件的发生显然也不存在船厂的过错。在这种情况下仅赋予船东解除合同并可获得所有预付款返还的权利应当是没有理由的，船厂有可能会处于极为不利的地位。假设发生不可抗力事件之时船舶已经下水，换言之，船东支付的预付款有可能已经全部花完了，甚至船厂已经自行支付了一部分建造费用。一旦不可抗力事件导致船厂无法继续建造的时间超过了210天，船东按照合同规定选择解除合同，船厂就必须返还所有已经收到的预付款。由于预付款已经全部用于船舶建造，船厂就必须另行筹款返还船东的预付款。船厂实际上等于花钱建造了一艘自己并不想要的船舶。如果船舶的市场价没有发生太大的变化，船厂遭受的损害可能不会太大。但如果市场发生大幅度下跌，船厂就将蒙受巨大的损失。

9.158　在采用NEWBUILDCON格式情况下船厂面临的问题则更为糟糕。如前文所述，在不可抗力事件造成船舶建造延误超过180天时，船东可以解除合同。

9.159　按照NEWBUILDCON的规定，船厂不仅要返还所有已经收到的船东预付

款,而且还要向船东支付按照约定利率计算的利息。因为 NEWBUILDCON 格式对此作出了明确的规定:①

> If this Contract is terminated by the Buyer, the Builder shall refund all sums paid by the Buyer to the Builder under Clause 7(Contract Price) and Clause 15(Payment) hereof plus interest thereon at the rate stated in Box 30 per annum from the date of payment to the date of refund ....

这一结果和船东在因船厂自身原因或过错造成船舶建造延误超过 180 天解除合同的结果是相同的,这显然是不合理的。如果船舶建造合同采用 CSTC 格式,船厂同样需要支付利息,因为该格式有如下规定:② 9.160

> In the event of the SELLER is obligated to make refundment, the SELLER shall pay the BUYER interest in United States Dollars at the rate of _____ percent (___%) if the cancellation or rescission of the Contract is exercised by the BUYER for the delay of aggregate ____ _____ (___) days in accordance with the provision of Paragraph 3 of Article VIII ....

船东作出选择的义务

在船舶建造合同规定船东可以在不可抗力事件造成的延误累积到一定天数后解除合同的情形下,船东未必会作出解约的选择。一旦船东没有对是否解约作出选择,船厂就可能处于比较尴尬的地位。对此,SAJ 格式作出了如下规定:③ 9.161

> ... The BUILDER may, at any time after the accumulated time of the aforementioned delays justifying rescission by the BUYER, demand in writing that the BUYER shall make an election, in which case the BUYER shall, within twenty(20) days after such demand is received by the BUYER, either notify the BUILDER of its intention to rescind this Contract, or consent to a postponement of the Delivery Date to a specific future date; it being understood and agreed by the parties hereto that, if any further delay occurs on account of causes justifying rescission as specified in this Article, the BUYER shall have the same right of rescission upon the same terms as hereinabove provided.

---

① Clause 39(e).
② Article X.2.
③ Article VIII.4.

9.162　　　上述规定应当是针对不可抗力事件造成的延误导致船东有权解除船舶建造合同的情形,这一规定的意义应当是船厂可以根据船东的决定作出下一步的安排,即是否继续建造船舶等。由于上述规定使用的是"may",因此船厂要求船东确认是否解约并不是一项合同义务,而是一项权利。一旦收到船厂的书面要求,船东就应当在20天内作出是否解除合同的决定。

第 10 章 延误及延期

I 建造中的延误

概述

本章中的"延误"是指由于各种原因船舶无法在船舶建造合同规定期限内完成建造并交付的情形。延误又可以分为不同性质的两种:第一种延误是指船厂因各种原因不能在合同交船日交船但可以在合同解约日之前交船的情形;第二种延误则是指船厂因各种原因既不能在合同交船日交船也不能在合同解约日之前交船的情形。如果导致延误发生的原因是船厂的行为或过失,船厂应当按照船舶建造合同的规定承担约定赔偿或船东有权按照船舶建造合同的规定解除合同。如果延误的原因是船东的行为或过失,船厂则可以按照船舶建造合同的规定顺延合同交船日。① 10.1

导致船厂承担约定赔偿义务或船东享有解除船舶建造合同权利的延误是"不可允许延误",即由于船厂的原因或过失造成的延误。相反,船厂可以顺延合同交船日的延误则被称为"可允许延误",即非船厂原因或过失造成的延误。可允许延误通常既包括不可抗力事件造成的延误,也包括因船东的原因或过失造成的延误。"延期"是指在船舶交接发生延误时,合同交船日可以按照船舶建造合同规定而推迟或顺延的情形。 10.2

可允许延误的定义

船舶建造合同的标准格式似乎都有关于可允许延误的规定,SAJ 格式有如下规定:② 10.3

---

① 由于船舶建造合同的规定,船厂有可能由于非自身的行为或过失,例如不可抗力事件引起的延误而需承担支付约定赔偿或合同被船东解除的后果,见本书第 9 章的相关内容。
② Article VIII.3, Norwegian Article IX.3, AWES Article 6(e), NEWBUILDCON Definitions.

Delays on account of such causes as specified in Paragraph 1 of this Article and any other delays of a nature which under the terms of this Contract permits postponement of the Delivery Date shall be understood to be permissible delays and are to be distinguished from unauthorized delays on account of which the Contract Price is subject to adjustment as provided for in Article III hereof.

10.4 从上述规定来看,可允许延误包括不可抗力事件以及其他按照船舶建造合同的规定可以推迟合同交船日的所有延误。无论是哪一原因引起的延误,船厂都无需支付约定赔偿。CSTC 格式中的可允许延误的定义比较特殊,似乎仅仅是指因不可抗力事件引起的延误:①

Delays on account of such causes as provided for in Paragraph 1 of this Article but excluding any other extensions of a nature which under the terms of this Contract permit postponement of the Delivery Date, shall be understood to be (and are herein referred to as) permissible delays, and are to be distinguished from non-permissible delays on account of which the Contract Price of the VESSEL is subject to adjustment as provided for in Article III hereof.

10.5 CSTC 格式的措辞应当是在 SAJ 格式基础上形成的,但与 SAJ 格式不同,有些费解,尤其是"but excluding..."一句似乎将可允许延误局限于因不可抗力事件引起的延误。NEWBUILDCON 格式的规定与大多数标准格式不同,该格式不仅有可允许延误的定义,而且还有专门的可允许延误的条款。该格式将可允许延误分为两种,一种是因不可抗力事件引起的延误,另一种则是其他原因引起的延误,这些原因包括:船东供应品晚交或有缺陷;因船东提出的修改造成的延误;因船级社规范或主管当局要求改变而引起的延误;因船舶发生实际或推定全损;以及船厂因船东未按约定支付建造款而中止建造引起的延误。②

可允许延误的种类

10.6 下列各项通常是构成可允许延误的情形。

---

① Article VIII.4.
② Clause 34(a)(i) & (ii).

不可抗力事件

不可抗力事件是指合同当事人无法预料、无法避免、无法控制的事件,因此不可抗力事件造成的延误应当是可允许延误。所有船舶建造合同标准格式都有船厂可因不可抗力事件造成船舶建造和交付影响的延误主张顺延合同交船日的规定。①

10.7

审图延误

船东审图造成的延误是指船东未能在船舶建造合同约定的时间内完成船厂送审图纸的审核和批准。② 在船东的监造代表入驻船厂之前,船厂是向船东送审图纸的。船东审图的延误有可能导致船厂开工的延误乃至交船的延误,尤其是在基本图纸审核上的延误。因为在船东退审图纸之前,船厂显然是无法正式开工的。在建造过程中送审的图纸是否影响船舶建造进程则是一个事实问题,并非船东未能在约定时间内完成审图的就一定构成可允许延误。即使船东的审图确有延误,船厂也未必可以根据实际延误天数主张合同交船日的顺延。

10.8

监造代表的延误

按照绝大多数船舶建造合同的规定,船东有权在船厂开工后指派一名或数名监造代表驻厂对船舶建造进行监督。船东的监造代表参与船舶建造的整个过程,他们的行为有可能影响船舶建造的按期进行和完成。船东监造代表的延误可以分成三种情形:第一种是船东指派的监造代表未能在船厂开工后入驻船厂且影响船厂建造工作的开展;第二种是入驻船厂的船东监造代表在审图上的延误;第三种是船东监造代表在完成船舶检验和检查时的延误。但是船东指派监造代表驻船、审图以及检验和检查均为船东的权利,换言之,船东或其监造代表可以放弃权利。一旦船东或其监造代表放弃了审图或检验权利的,船厂不应等待,而应继续船舶的建造。但是船东或其监造代表是否放弃了相关的权利应当通过船东或其监造代表的语言和行为予以判断,船厂也可以要求船东或其监造代表作出表态。

10.9

---

① 关于不可抗力请参见本书第9章。
② 关于审图请参见本书第5章第Ⅱ节。

修改引起的延误

10.10　可能影响船舶建造进程和交船安排的修改既包括船东提出的修改请求,也包括因船级规范或主管当局要求变更而产生的修改。修改可以说是最为常见的有可能影响船舶建造进程或交船安排的事项。值得注意的是,在船舶建造合同约定修改合同价格以及合同交船日的更改以双方取得一致为条件时,船厂往往只有在约定的条件成就时才能主张合同交船日的顺延。

船东供应品引起的延误

10.11　船东供应品是指按照船舶建造合同的规定应当由船东负责向船厂提供,而由船厂负责安装或测试的设备、系统和装置等。由于船厂只有在船东供应品运抵船厂时才能进行安装和测试,因此船东供应品的延误就可能影响到整个船舶建造的进程和安排,由此产生的延误就是可允许延误。船东供应品引起的延误并不仅仅局限于交付晚于合同约定时间,而且还应当包括由于船东供应品的缺陷或问题导致的船厂的安装和测试无法在正常时间内完成的情形,因此产生的延误也应当构成可允许延误。

建造款支付延误

10.12　船东支付建造款的延误对船厂而言只是收款的延误,实际上并不当然导致船舶建造的延误。但大多数船舶建造合同都会规定船东支付建造款有延误的,船厂便可相应顺延合同交船日。有些船舶建造合同还规定船东支付建造款有延误的,合同交船日即自动顺延。虽然船东未按合同约定支付建造款构成违约,但除非有约定,否则船厂并不当然有权中止船舶建造。NEWBUILDCON 格式对此作出了明文规定:①

> Without prejudice to Sub-clause (b) above the Builder shall have the right to suspend work under this Contract if the Buyer fails to pay any instalment stated in Box 11 due for a period of fifteen (15) Banking Days until payment of such outstanding sums.

---

① Clause 39(c).

船东原因造成的延误

10.13 除了上述各项延误外,一旦船舶建造因船东的行为、原因或过失而导致延误的,船厂都有机会主张合同交船日的顺延。

完工和延误

10.14 完工通常是指工作的完成,而延误则是指未能在合同规定期限内完成约定的工作。即使已经完成的工作存在缺陷,需要额外的时间纠正缺陷,但这并不影响工作的完成。为弥补缺陷所需的额外时间并不导致工作无法在规定时间内完成。在 *Westminster Corp* v *J Jarvis and Son and Another* ①一案中,合同规定分包商工作有延误的,承包商可以顺延完工日。合同的 23(g)条有如下规定:

> Upon it becoming reasonably apparent that the progress of works is delayed, the contractor, shall forthwith give written notice, of the cause of the delay to the architect ... and if in the opinion of the architect ... the completion of the works is likely to be or has been delayed beyond the date for completion stated in the appendix to these conditions or beyond any extended time previously fixed under either this clause or clause 33(1)(c) ... (g) by delay on the part of nominated subcontractors ... which the contractor has taken all practicable steps to avoid or reduce ... then the architect ... shall ... make ... a fair and reasonable extension of time for completion of the works ....

10.15 雇主指定的分包商按时完成了工作,但是事后雇主发现分包商的工作有缺陷,于是分包商又开始了纠错的工作,结果导致了承包商工作的延误。高院认为承包商不可以推迟合同规定的完工日,理由是并不存在分包商的延误。高院的观点是:分包商的工作有缺陷可以弥补,如果分包商弥补了缺陷,就不存在违约。如果分包商弥补错误的时间超过了合同允许的时间,分包商才会因延误而导致违约。如果分包商在时间届满时停止弥补工作,分包商的违约行为是不完全履行,而不是延误。如果分包商不对错误进行弥补或分包商并不知道自己的工作有错误,分包商的违约行为是不适当履行,同样不是延误。Donaldson 法官是这样说的:②

---

① [1970] 1 WLR 637.
② [1969] 1 WLR 1448 at 1455.

> Delay on the part of the sub-contractor in the context of clause 23(g) can only occur whilst the sub-contractor is still in the process of performing or purporting to perform the sub-contract .... If a sub-contractor in the course of performance makes an error, as this sub-contractor did ..., he is entitled to remedy it if he can and the error, if fully remedied, constitutes no breach of contract. The process of correction may more than exhaust the contractual period of time available to him and thus lead to a breach of contract by delay, but it is the continuance of work after the expiration of the allotted span which constitutes the breach of contract. If, instead, he stops work when time runs out, leaving the sub-contract works admittedly incomplete, he commits a breach of contract, but it consists of partial non-performance, not delay. If he does not make good the error, either because he does not choose to do so or, as in this case, because he is unaware of it, and ceases to perform the contract at the end of the allotted period claiming that he has fully performed, he again commits a breach of contract. But this breach consists of disconform performance, which may or may not be properly also regarded as non-performance. It does not consist of or constitute delay. If thereafter he returns to remedy the work, he is no longer performing the contract – he is remedying his breach and mitigating the building owner's loss.

10.16 但是上诉法院则不同意 Donaldson 法官的理由,上诉法院推翻了高院的判决,认为承包商可以推迟合同规定的完工日,理由分包商完成工作存在延误。上诉法院的 Davis 法官说:①

> That, in my view, cannot possibly be right. Delay in this context may mean dilatoriness in the performance of the work, for example, where work has to be performed in stages and has to keep pace with the operations of the contractor or other subcontractors. But it must obviously also embrace lateness in the proper completion of the sub-contract works .... Then it is said that "delay" cannot include delay due to defective work. I find myself quite unable to accept this argument. If defective work causes delay, then delay it is. Both, of course, are breaches of contract; but if defective work causes delay, then, in my view, that falls within clause 23(g).

10.17 案件上诉至上议院时,上议院又推翻了上诉法院的判决,上议院认为只有当

---

① [1969] 1 WLR 1448 at 1456.

分包商工作的缺陷是在分包商的完工日之前发现的,且分包商未能在完工日或之前完成弥补缺陷工作的才构成延误。最后上议院维持了高院 Donaldson 法官的判决。上议院的 Lord Wilberforce 是这样说的:①

> It is not without its difficulties. Some of these were clearly demonstrated in the Court of Appeal; it is only necessary to point to the fact that, if the defects in the piles had been discovered before the sub-contract completion date and work had been at once put in hand to remedy them – thereby producing a similar period of delay in the completion of the main contract – the clause would, it seems, have applied, but it does not do so if the work was "complete" (though defective) on that same date so that the contractor could take over. One must set against this the advantage that, if the subcontract work is apparently completed and handed over, and some defects appear very much later, but before the contract date, as they might in a large contract, this would not, on the employer's construction, be a case of delay, though it might be so on the sub-contractor's.

共同延误

10.18 共同延误(concurrent delay)是建造合同中的概念,是指由于两个或两个以上的原因所产生的延误,在造成延误的原因中有些应当由雇主负责,有些则应当由承包商负责。

因果关系

10.19 因果关系(causation)是普通法的一项基本原则,按照这一原则的要求,索赔方只有在证明过失和损失之间存在有效的因果关系时才可以获得对其损失的赔偿。过失和损失是否存在有效的因果关系是一个事实问题,需要作出判断,而因果关系的判断始终是普通法中的一个相当复杂的问题。正如法官在 *Galoo Ltd and Others* v *Bright Grahame Murray* 一案中所指出的:②

> This argument depends upon the nature of the causation necessary to establish liability for breach of duty, whether in contract or in tort. There is no doubt that this is one of the most difficult areas of the law.

---

① [1970] 1 WLR 637 at 650.
② [1994] 1 WLR 1360 at 1369.

10.20　在该案中,原告是一家从事动物产品贸易的公司,被告包括曾为原告进行审计的会计师。原告已经破产了,但会计师的审计有错并没有被发现,于是原告继续其贸易,结果遭受了损失。如果会计师向原告提供的报告是正确的,原告可能就不会再继续贸易了。这里显然有两个原因,一个是会计师的疏忽,另一个则是导致亏损的贸易。对损失的发生,这两个原因都是必需的,但是会计师的疏忽本身并不足以导致贸易损失的发生。Glidewell 法官说:①

> ... if a breach of contract by a defendant is to be held to entitle the plaintiff to claim damages, it must first be held to have been an "effective" or "dominant" cause of his loss .... It is necessary to distinguish between a breach of contract which causes a loss to the plaintiff and one which merely gives the opportunity for him to sustain the loss, is helpful but still leaves the question to be answered "How does' the court decide whether the breach of duty was the cause of the loss or merely the occasion for the loss?"

> The answer in my judgment is supplied by the Australian decisions to which I have referred, which I hold to represent the law of England as well as of Australia, in relation to a breach of a duty imposed on a breach of contract. The answer in the end is "By the application of the court's common sense". Doing my best to apply this test, I have no doubt that the deputy judge arrived at a correct conclusion on this issue. The breach of duty by the defendants gave the opportunity to Galoo and Gamine to incur and to continue to incur trading losses; it did not cause those trading losses, in the sense in which the word "cause" is used in law.

10.21　在船舶建造合同中,共同延误也时有发生,例如在不可抗力事件导致船厂无法工作的同时,船厂实际上并没有人手进行工作,即使没有不可抗力事件,船厂实际上依然无法工作;又如,船厂因自己设计的错误而不得不返工,但与此同时船东的供应品晚到了。毫无疑问,因果关系在船舶建造合同中是一个相当关键的问题,但在延误和原因之间的因果关系往往不是那么清晰。相同或类似的原因在不同的案件中有可能出现截然不同的结果。

可以延期的原因

10.22　如果在造成延误的数个原因中有一个是船厂可以主张延期的原因,即使船厂

---

① [1994] 1 WLR 1360 at 1374.

应当对其他原因负责,船厂依然应当有机会顺延合同交船日。在 *Henry Boot Construction(UK) Ltd v Malmaison Hotel(Manchester) Ltd* 一案中,高院的 Dyson 法官说:①

> ... it is agreed that if there are two concurrent causes of delay, one of which is a Relevant Event, and the other is not, then the contractor is entitled to an extension of time for the period of delay caused by the Relevant Event notwithstanding the concurrent effect of the other event. Thus, to take a simple example, if no work is possible on a site for a week not only because of exceptionally inclement weather(a Relevant Event), but also because the contractor has a shortage of labour(not a Relevant Event), and if the failure to work during that week is likely to delay the Works beyond the Completion Date by one week, then if he considers it fair and reasonable to do so, the Architect is required to grant an extension of time of one week. He cannot refuse to do so on the grounds that the delay would have occurred in any event by reason of the shortage of labour.

违约方对违约负责

10.23　如果两个或数个原因有一个是一方的违约行为,按照 Devlin 法官在 *Heskell v Continental Express* 一案中所指出的,违约的一方应当承担责任:②

> It may be that the term "a cause" is, whether in tort or contract, not rightly used as a term of legal significance unless it denotes a cause of equal efficiency with one or more other causes. Whatever the true rule of causation may be I am satisfied that if a breach of contract is one of two causes, both co-operating and both of equal efficacy, as I find in this case, it is sufficient to carry judgment for damages.

10.24　*Heskell v Continental Express* 一案的判决在 *Great Eastern Hotel Company Ltd v John Laing Construction Ltd Laing Construction Plc* 一案中得到了引用,David Wilcon 法官说:③

> If a breach of contract is one of the causes both co-operating and of equal efficiency in causing loss to the Claimant the party responsible for

---

① (1999) 70 Con LR 32 see Ali D Haidar, *Global Claims in Construction*, Springer 2011, p.108.
② (1949/50) Ll L Rep 438 at 458.
③ [2005] EWHC 181 at [314].

breach is liable to the Claimant for that loss. The contract breaker is liable for as long as his breach was an "effective cause" of his loss .... The Court need not choose which cause was the more effective.

整体索赔

10.25 应当可以看出 Great Eastern Hotel Company Ltd v John Laing Construction Ltd Laing Construction Plc 一案的判决是基于不同的原因在造成延误上具有相同的作用。但是在很多情况下数个造成延误的原因之间并不一定可以确定哪一个原因是决定性原因(dominant cause)。在这种情况下,索赔人提出的索赔被称为"整体索赔"(global claim, total cost claim),即索赔人的索赔数额只是一个总体的数额,并没有确定特定原因和特定数额损失之间的直接的因果关系。Ramsey 法官在 London Underground Limited v Citylink Telecommunications Limited 一案中对整体索赔做了如下描述:①

The essence of a global claim is that, whilst the breaches and the relief claimed are specified, the question of causation linking the breaches and the relief claimed is based substantially on inference, usually derived from factual and expert evidence.

10.26 在整体索赔情况下,虽然索赔人依然必须证明原因与延误之间的因果关系,但要求则不再非常严格了。正如 Lord McFadyen 在 John Doyle Construction v Laing Management(Scotland) Ltd 一案中所说的:②

Ordinarily, in order to make a relevant claim for contractual loss and expense under a construction contract (or a common law claim for damages) the pursuer must aver (1) the occurrence of an event for which the defender bears legal responsibility, (2) that he has suffered loss or incurred expense, and (3) that the loss or expense was caused by the event. In some circumstances, relatively commonly in the context of construction contracts, a whole series of events occur which individually would form the basis of a claim for loss and expense. These events may interreact with each other in very complex ways, so that it becomes very difficult, if not impossible, to identify what loss and expense each event has caused. The emergence of such a difficulty does not, however,

---

① [2007] EWCH 1749 at [142].
② 2004 SC 713 at [35].

absolve the pursuer from the need to aver and prove the causal connections between the events and the loss and expense. However, if all the events are events for which the defender is legally responsible, it is unnecessary to insist on proof of which loss has been caused by each event. In such circumstances, it will suffice for the pursuer to aver and prove that he has suffered a global loss to the causation of which each of the events for which the defenders is responsible has contributed. Thus far, provided the pursuer is able to give adequate specification of the events, of the basis of the defender's responsibility for each of them, of the fact of the defender's involvement in causing his global loss, and of the method of computation of that loss, there is no difficulty in principle in permitting a claim to be advanced in that way.

虽然对索赔人而言,因果关系的要求不再十分严格,但是索赔人所主张的造成损失的原因则都必须是被告应当负责的原因,否则整体索赔就无法成立。对此,Lord McFadyen 在 *John Doyle Construction* v *Laing Management(Scotland) Ltd* 一案中引用了 Lord Ordinary 的判词:① 　10.27

The logic of a global claim demands, however, that all the events which contribute to causing the global loss be events for which the defender is liable. If the causal events include events for which the defender bears no liability, the effect of upholding the global claim is to impose on the defender a liability which, in part, is not legally his. That is unjustified. A global claim, as such, must therefore fail if any material contribution to the causation of the global loss is made by a factor or factors for which the defender bears no legal liability .... Advancing a claim for loss and expense in global form is therefore a risky enterprise. Failure to prove that a particular event for which the defender was liable played a part in causing the global loss will not have any adverse effect on the claim, provided the remaining events for which the defender was liable are proved to have caused the global loss. On the other hand, proof that an event played a material part in causing the global loss, combined with failure to prove that that event was one for which the defender was responsible, will undermine the logic of the global claim. Moreover, the defender may set out to prove that, in addition to the factors for which he is liable founded on by the pursuer, a material contribution to the causation of the global loss has been made by another

---

① 2004 SC 713 at 716.

factor or other factors for which he has no liability. If he succeeds in proving that, again the global claim will be undermined.

分摊

10.28　在索赔人提出整体索赔的情况下,法院或仲裁庭就必须根据具体情况在原因和延误之间作出分摊。简而言之,分摊就是确定造成延误的原因和延误之间关系的过程。由于造成延误的原因有两个或两个以上,因此分摊也就会变得复杂和困难。传统普通法中很少有关于分摊的判例,这可能是由于传统普通法强调因果关系的缘故。如果造成延误的原因有两个或两个以上,即使船东应当对其中一个原因负责,只要船厂无法证明船东的原因和延误之间的因果关系也就无法主张合同交船日的延期。直到本世纪初,这种情形才有所转变。在 *John Doyle Construction* v *Laing Management(Scotland) Ltd* 一案中,Lord McFadyen 提出了对损失进行分摊的观点,他说:①

> Where disruption to the contractor's work is involved, matters become more complex. Nevertheless, we are of opinion that apportionment will frequently be possible in such cases, according to the relative importance of the various causative events in producing the loss. Whether it is possible will clearly depend on the assessment made by the judge or arbiter, who must of course approach it on a wholly objective basis. It may be said that such an approach produces a somewhat rough and ready result. This procedure does not, however, seem to us to be fundamentally different in nature from that used in relation to contributory negligence or contribution among joint wrongdoers. Moreover, the alternative to such an approach is the strict view that, if a contractor sustains a loss caused partly by events for which the employer is responsible and partly by other events, he cannot recover anything because he cannot demonstrate that the whole of the loss is the responsibility of the employer. That would deny him a remedy even if the conduct of the employer or the architect is plainly culpable, as where an architect fails to produce instructions despite repeated requests and indications that work is being delayed. It seems to us that in such cases the contractor should be able to recover for part of his loss and expense, and we are not persuaded that the practical difficulties of carrying out the

---

① 2004 SC 713 at 721.

exercise should prevent him from doing so.

10.29 在 *City Inn* v *Shepherd Construction* 一案中,Lord Drummond Young 也认为在两个或两个以上原因造成延误且无法判断哪个延误具有决定性影响时,法院应当在不同的原因之间分摊延误,他说:①

> Where a contractor finished late partly because of a cause that was excusable under this provision and partly because of a cause that was not, it was the duty of the contracting officer to make, if at all feasible, a fair apportionment of the extent to which completion of the job was delayed by each of the two causes, and to grant an extension of time commensurate with his determination of the extent to which the failure to finish on time was attributable to the excusable one.

10.30 *City Inn Ltd* v *Shepherd Construction Ltd* 案中的合同是建造合同,由被告为原告在布里斯托建造一家酒店。最初的完工日期是 1999 年 1 月 25 日,后又改为 1999 年 2 月 22 日。发生延误的,被告应当每星期支付 30,000 英镑的约定赔偿。被告实际上是在 1999 年 4 月 12 日才完工的。造成这一延误的原因有很多,既包括被告无需负责的原因,也包括被告应当承担责任的原因。被告主张自己可以延期十一周,但原告则认为被告不能主张任何延期,理由是所有原因对被告完成工作没有影响。一审法院认为被告可以获得九周的延期。被告上诉,苏格兰最高民事法院内庭维持了 Lord Ordinary 的判决,Lord Drummond Young 说:②

> The Lord Ordinary observes (para.18): "While delay for which the contractor is responsible will not preclude an extension of time based on a relevant event, the critical question will frequently, perhaps usually, be how long an extension is justified by the relevant event. In practice the various causes of delay are likely to interact in a complex manner; shortages of labour will rarely be total; some work may be possible despite inclement weather; and the degree to which work is affected by each of these causes may vary from day to day. Other more complex situations can be imagined. What is required by cl.25 is that the architect should exercise his judgment to determine the extent to which completion has been delayed by relevant events. The architect must make a determination on a fair and reasonable basis." With those observations I find myself in complete agreement.

---

① [2010] CSIH 67 at 141.
② [2010] CSIH 67 at 152.

Ⅱ 关键路径

概述

10.31　关键路径(critical path)是一个项目管理的概念,指工程从开始到完成过程中由各种关键活动组成的序列,该序列的最长总工期决定了整个项目的最短完成时间。关键路径所需的工期决定了整个项目的工期。任何关键路径上的关键活动的延迟将直接影响项目的预期完成时间。高院的 Toulmin 在 *Mirant Asia-Pacific Construction(Hong Kong) Ltd v Ove Arup & Partners International Ltd* 一案中对关键路径做了如下描述:①

> The critical path can be defined as "the sequence of activities through a project network from start to finish, the sum of whose durations determines the overall Project duration".

10.32　根据关键路径的原理形成的项目管理的方式称之为关键路径法,简而言之,关键路径法是为完成工程找到最短工期的工具:②

> The critical path method is a tool that demonstrates the shortest possible path to completion at any stage by breaking down the interrelationship of the discrete elements that comprise the activities to be undertaken. It is a mathematical and logical tool that can be used to predict the duration it will take to complete a series of activities. A well constructed programme using the critical path method allows the parties to identify which parts of the projects, called activities, are critical.

10.33　关键路径法比较适合由一系列相对独立的"活动"组成的工程。如果一些活动只有在另一些活动完成之后才可以开始的,在这种情况下整个工程就会成为包括各种活动的一张网。所谓"活动"是指组成整个工程的每一项特定工作。虽然完成某一项特定工作的时间基本上是固定的,但是由于工作之间的先后关系,该工作开始的时间可能取决其他工作的完成时间。关键路径法适用于建筑工程,也适用于船舶建造。船舶建造可以说是比较典型的由一系列相对独立的活动组成的工程,例如分段的制造甚至可以在船厂之外的地方进行并完成,与在船厂的

---

① [2007] EWHC 918 at [121].
② Ali D Haidar, *Global Claims in Construction*, Springer 2011, p.102.

其他工作并不会发生冲突。然而,船舶在船台上的合拢则是以分段制造完成为前提的。

关键路径法已经得到了法院的接受,尤其是在比较复杂的工程中。高院的 Toulmin 法官在 *Mirant Asia-Pacific Construction (Hong Kong) Ltd v Ove Arup & Partners International Ltd* 一案中对关键路径做了如下描述:① 10.34

> As computers have become more sophisticated, the critical path analysis has been enabled to become more sophisticated. This has become an invaluable tool which enables a complex construction Project to be managed with better available information. The analysis will identify at a given date which important aspects of the Project are falling behind the programme, particularly if they are on or close to the critical path, what if any is the impact on other aspects of the programme and where additional resources need to be placed. It will also demonstrate where activities are ahead of what is planned and enable a decision to be taken on whether planned activities need to be rescheduled. It is also used as a tool for analysing, as at the given date, what has caused any delay that has occurred and what is the extent of that delay.

关键路径法并不能直接解决延误问题,充其量也只是专家证据的一种,正如高院的 Ramsey 法官在 *London Underground Ltd v Citylink Telecommunications Ltd* 一案中所指出的:② 10.35

> ... whilst analysis of critical delay by one of a number of well-known methods is often relied on and can assist in arriving at a conclusion of what is fair and reasonable, that analysis should not be seen as determining the answer to the question. It is at most an area of expert evidence which may assist the arbitrator or the court in arriving at the answer of what is a fair and reasonable extension of time in the circumstances.

关键路径法的局限性

关键路径法一般适用于所有活动都是相对确定的工程,如果组成整个工程的活动有不确定特征的,通过关键路径法得出的关键路径以及时间的计算就可能是 10.36

---

① [2007] EWHC 918 at [129], [130].
② [2007] CSOH 190 at [30].

不可靠的。首制船就往往是一个具有不确定因素的工程。由于是首制船,船厂在制定计划时有些建造活动以及完成这些建造活动所需的时间可能是不确定的。除非船厂的计划时间与实际完成那些活动的时间是吻合的,否则按照关键路径法得到的关键路径就是不可靠的。同样道理,由于关键路径法是以所有的组成整个工程的相关活动的具体信息为依据对关键路径进行计算的,因此一旦相关活动的具体信息有缺失,关键路径法计算出的完成工程所需的工期也就未必可靠。

10.37　此外,关键路径法作为一个程序,其准确性在很大程度上会受操作人员的影响。操作人员为了使某项工作具有关键性可以通过对活动期间及其与其他活动的逻辑关系的确定使其更具关键性。在有变更的情况下,操作人员也可以使变更具有影响整个工序的关键因素。此外,关键路径法也未必一定会得到法院的接受,例如在 Great Eastern Hotel Company Ltd v John Laing Construction Ltd 一案中,双方当事人的专家采用不同的方式对延误进行分析,从而得出了不同的结果。高院的 David Wilcox 法官说:①

> I reject [defendant's] evidence that the late design information either caused or contributed to the critical delay in the Project. His analysis was self confessedly incomplete. He did not have the time to approach the research of this aspect of the case in the complete and systematic way, furthermore, the impacted as planned analysis delay takes no account of the actual events which occurred on the Project and gives rise to an hypothetical answer when the timing of design release is compared against the original construction programme. Thus it would take no account of the fact that the design team would have been aware of significant construction delays to the original master programme, and would have been able to prioritise design and construction to fit this. Furthermore, [defendant] in his report compares the timing of the actual design releases against an original programme which was superseded by later versions of the procurement programme on which [defendant] showed later dates for the provision of the information required.

10.38　在 City Inn Ltd v Shepherd Construction Ltd 一案中,苏格兰最高民事法院上诉法院的 Lord Drummond Young 也拒绝接受采用竣工关键路径法的专家意见,他说:②

---

① [2005] EWHC 181 at [184].
② [2007] CSOH 190 at [30].

In my opinion the pursuers clearly went too far in suggesting that an expert could only give a meaningful opinion on the basis of an as-built critical path analysis .... I am of opinion that such an approach has serious dangers of its own. I further conclude ... that [expert's] own use of an as-built critical path analysis is flawed in a significant number of important respects. On that basis, I conclude that that approach to the issues in the present case is not helpful. The major difficulty, it seems to me, is that in the type of programme used to carry out a critical path analysis any significant error in the information that is fed into the programme is liable to invalidate the entire analysis.

关键路径在中国的应用

10.39　关键路径法在中国造船业的应用曾一度很不普及，原因可能是多方面的。多年来中国大部分船厂依然采用传统的方法对船舶建造制定计划并实施管理，而传统的造船方式一般不会采用关键路径这种项目管理方式。在确定主要节点时往往凭借以往情形和经验，并没有对所有相关活动进行计算后得出主要节点的时间。但这种情形已经有了比较明显的改变，采用关键路径法的船厂越来越多了。

10.40　关键路径法有各种不同的软件，操作也并不复杂。采用关键路径法的好处应当是比较明显的：首先，由于关键路径法的采用需要对整个建造项目作出仔细的分析，因此有利于船厂以及项目经理等对船舶建造有一个比较明确的理解和认识；其次，采用关键路径法有利于船厂确定延误的存在以及完成特定工作所需的额外时间；最后，关键路径法不仅与完成工程的时间有关，而且与完成工程的成本也有关，它可以帮助船厂计算和确定每项活动的成本。通过采用关键路径法，船厂还可以知道在什么活动上增加成本可以加快工程的进程，从而争取到更多的时间完成船舶建造。

影响关键路径的延误

10.41　关键路径法是基于对组成整个工程的所有活动均可以计算出完成复杂工程所需的时间，并且可以确定在所有活动中哪些活动是"关键的"，即必须按时完成的活动。在关键路径上的节点都是关键的，一旦这些关键的节点发生延误，整个工程就会受到影响。例如：在船舶下水的时间和试航的时间均已确定的情况下，一旦船舶下水时间发生了延误，按照原计划船舶试航日期也就会因此受到影响，并可能进一步影响到船舶交接的时间安排。相反，如果延误确实在船舶下水之前发生的，但由于船厂对计划进行了调整从而保证了船舶下水没有发生延误。在这种情况下，虽然发生了延误，但实际上并不存在关键路径的延误，因为船舶下水的时间并没有被耽误。除非另有其他延误，否则试航的时间也不会因此受影响。同样道理，加快任何活动未必就能缩短完成整个工程所需的时间，只有加快或提前关键路径上的关键活动才有可能缩短完成整个工程所需的时间。例如在船舶上船台这一节点的时间没有提前的情况下，任何分段的提前制作完成都无法提前船舶交船的时间。

10.42 　　从上述分析中可以看出，关键路径法以所有组成整个工程的活动为基础，即关键路径法对完成工程所需工期的判断是以每一项具体活动所需的时间为依据进行计算而获得的。而且关键路径法所使用的数据是可以更新的，例如在某一具体活动完成后就会产生一个完成该活动的实际时间，这个时间若与之前的计划时间有所不同的就有可能影响整个关键路径。延误通常是指未能在约定时间内完成约定工作。在采用关键路径法的船舶建造中，某项工作的延误未必一定会影响船舶节点的按期完成，即未必会影响船舶建造的关键路径。在这种情况下，即使存在延误，船厂也未必可以主张合同交船日的顺延，正如 Humphrey Lloyd 法官在 *Balfour Beatty Construction Ltd* v *The Mayor and Burgesses of the London Borough of Lambeth* 一案中所说的：①

> I accept the ... point that a delay in one location will not necessarily prevent work in another location, and would not necessarily cause a delay. Rather, the project must be reviewed in the round.

III　阻碍原则

概述

10.43 　　阻碍原则（prevention principle）是普通法中一项古老的原则，其本质含义是：当合同一方无法履行其合同义务是由于合同另一方的过错引起的，有过错的一方便不能要求对方履行。阻碍原则也被认为是任何人均不得因自己的错误而获益的另一种说法。Bull 法官在 *Perini Pacific Ltd* v *Greater Vancouver Sewerage and*

---

① 　[2002] EWHC 597 at [6.1].

Drainage District 一案中说:①

> Since the earliest times it has been clear that a party to a contract is exonerated from performance of a contract when that performance is prevented or rendered impossible by the wrongful act of the other party.

在 *Multiplex Constructions(UK) Ltd* v *Honeywell Control Systems Ltd* 一案中，Jackson 法官指出,阻碍原则适用于建造合同的意义是,一旦承包商因雇主的原因而无法在约定时间完成工作的,雇主不能要求承包商对此负责,他说:② 10.44

> In the field of construction law, one consequence of the prevention principle is that the employer cannot hold the contractor to a specified completion date, if the employer has by act or omission prevented the contractor from completing by that date. Instead, time becomes at large and the obligation to complete by the specified date is replaced by an implied obligation to complete within a reasonable time. The same principle applies as between main contractor and sub-contractor.

在实践中,绝大多数船舶建造合同都有关于船厂可以顺延合同交船日的规定。这种在合同中规定延期或在合同中加入延期条款从某种意义上可以说是阻碍原则的适用。 10.45

延误责任的承担

Holme v *Guppy*③ 应当是适用阻碍原则最早的案例,在该案中,按照建造合同的规定,原告应当在四个半月内完成建造工作,否则应支付每星期 40 英镑的约定赔偿。由于无法进入场地,原告在合同订立四个星期后才开始工作。结果迟了五个星期才完成工作,其中一个星期的延误是原告自己的工人的原因,而四个星期的延误则是由于被告雇员的原因。财税法院认为被告不能获得约定赔偿,Parke 法官说:④ 10.46

> On looking into the facts of the case, we think no deduction ought to be allowed to the defendants. It is clear, from the terms of the agreement, that the plaintiffs undertake that they will complete the work in a given four months and a half; and the particular time is extremely material, because they probably would not have entered into the contract unless

---

① (1966) 57 DLR(2d) 307 at 318.
② [2007] Bus LR Digest D109 at D110.
③ (1838) 3 M & W 387.
④ (1838) 3 M & W 387 at 389.

they had had those four months and a half, within which they could work a greater number of hours a day. Then it appears that they were disabled by the act of the defendants from the performance of that contract; and there are clear authorities, that if the party be prevented, by the refusal of the other contracting party, from completing the contract within the time limited, he is not liable in law for the default.

10.47　　在 *Dodd* v *Churton* 一案中，建造合同规定了完工日，承包商超过完工日完成工作的应当支付每星期 2 英镑的约定赔偿。雇主按照建造合同的规定增加了工作量，结果承包商未能在规定的完工日或之前完成工作。郡法院认为要求承包人完成额外工作意味着雇主已经放弃了要求承包商在完工日之后完成工作支付约定赔偿的权利。上诉法院的 Lord Esher 说：①

> The principle is laid down in *Comyns's Digest*, Condition L(6), that, where one party to a contract is prevented from performing it by the act of the other, he is not liable in law for that default; and, accordingly, a well recognised rule has been established in cases of this kind, beginning with *Holme* v *Guppy*, to the effect that, if the building owner has ordered extra work beyond that specified by the original contract which has necessarily increased the time requisite for finishing the work, he is thereby disentitled to claim the penalties for non-completion provided by the contract. The reason for that rule is that otherwise a most unreasonable burden would be imposed upon the contractor.

延误和约定赔偿

10.48　　在船舶建造合同有约定赔偿规定时，如果延误是由于船东的行为或原因引起的，船东就不再有权因为延误而要求船厂支付约定赔偿，因为约定赔偿是针对船厂的过失而设定的。在 *Peak Construction (Liverpool) Ltd* v *McKinney Foundations Ltd* 一案中，建造合同规定承包人应当在 24 个月之内完工，但结果延误了。延误的原因部分是雇主指定的分包人的过失，部分则是雇主自己的行为。上诉法院 Salmon 法官认为，即使造成延误的原因是雇主和承包商双方的过失，合同中关于约定赔偿的规定也不再适用，他说：②

> In my judgment, however, the plaintiffs are not entitled to anything at

---

①　[1897] 1 QB 562 at 566.
②　[1970] 1 BLR 111 at 121.

all under this head, because they were not liable to pay any liquidated damages for delay to the corporation. A clause giving the employer liquidated damages at so much a week or month which elapses between the date fixed for completion and the actual date of completion is usually coupled, as in the present case, with an extension of time clause. The liquidated damages clause contemplates a failure to complete on time due to the fault of the contractor. It is inserted by the employer for his own protection; for it enables him to recover a fixed sum as compensation for delay instead of facing the difficulty and expense of proving the actual damage which the delay may have caused him. If the failure to complete on time is due to the fault of both the employer and the contractor, in my view, the clause does not bite. I cannot see how, in the ordinary course, the employer can insist on compliance with a condition if it is partly his own fault that it cannot be fulfilled . . . .

在 *Astilleros Canarios SA* v *Cape Hatteras Shipping Co Inc*, The " Cape Hatteras"①一案中,修船合同规定船舶未能按时完成修理的,船厂应当每天向船东支付12,000美元。由于船东的行为导致船厂实际完成修理是在合同规定日期后92天。法院认为船东无权获得约定赔偿。Bull法官说:② 10.49

> Accordingly, the principle established by the authorities, that no liquidated damages for delay can be claimed if completion was in part delayed by conduct of the employer, is applicable in the present case. Had the parties wished to avoid that result, they could and should have inserted in the contract a term that the agreed date for completion should be extended in the event of delay caused by the defendants.

合法行为和原因

船厂顺延合同交船日并不一定要以船东的行为构成违约为前提,按照船舶建造合同的规定实施的行为一样可以导致船厂有权顺延合同交船日,例如要求船厂完成额外工作等。在 *Trollope & Colls Ltd* v *North West Metropolitan Regional Hospital Board* 一案中,上诉法院的Lord Denning说:③ 10.50

> It is well settled that in building contracts – and in other contracts too –

---

① [1982] 1 Lloyd's Rep 518.
② [1982] 1 Lloyd's Rep 518 at 526.
③ [1973] 1 WLR 601 at 607.

when there is a stipulation for work to be done in a limited time, if one party by his conduct – it may be quite legitimate conduct, such as ordering extra work – renders it impossible or impracticable for the other party to do his work within the stipulated time, then the one whose conduct caused the trouble can no longer insist upon strict adherence to the time stated. He cannot claim any penalties or liquidated damages for non-completion in that time. The time becomes at large. The work must be done within a reasonable time – that is, as a rule, the stipulated time plus a reasonable extension for the delay caused by his conduct.

船舶建造合同和阻碍原则

10.51 在 *Adyard Abu Dhabi v SD Marine Services*[1] 一案中，高院的 Hamblen 法官对阻碍原则的先例进行了分析，并将其归纳为如下三点：

(1) In a basic shipbuilding contract, which simply provides for a Builder to complete the construction of a vessel and to reach certain milestones within specific periods of time, the Builder is entitled to the whole of that period of time to complete the contract work.

(2) In the event that the Buyer interferes with the work so as to delay its completion in accordance with the agreed timetable, this amounts to an act of prevention and the Builder is no longer bound by the strict requirements of the contract as to time.

(3) The instruction of variations to the work can amount to an act of prevention.

10.52 船舶建造合同规定的时间限制是以船厂的工作内容不发生变化为前提的。如果由于船东的要求导致船厂的工作量发生了变化，船厂就不再受原合同规定的时间和期限的限制。船东造成船厂无法在约定期限内完成船舶建造的行为均为阻碍行为。阻碍行为可以分为违约的阻碍行为和合同的阻碍行为。违约的阻碍行为包括拒绝提供或批准图纸等；而合同的阻碍行为则包括船东根据船舶建造合同的规定要求船厂完成额外工作。无论发生哪一种阻碍行为，船厂都可以主张合同交船日的顺延。

---

[1] [2011] EWHC 848(Comm) at [242].

IV 延误通知

概述

凡是船舶建造合同中有延期条款的往往都会有关于延误通知的规定。在本书第 9 章中已有关于不可抗力通知的讨论,本章讨论的延误通知是指不可抗力以外的延误通知。合同一般会要求船厂在发生其认为可以顺延合同交船日的事件或情形时向船东发出书面通知,主张顺延合同交船日。不少船舶建造合同还明确规定延误通知是船厂主张顺延合同交船日的前提条件,船厂未能按照合同规定发出延误通知的就将丧失主张顺延合同交船日的权利。从普通法来看,此类通知的性质在大多数情况下取决于合同的性质以及对合同条款的解释,同样措辞的通知条款在不同的合同中可能会有不同的结果。

10.53

标准格式的规定

船舶建造合同标准格式都有关于延误通知的规定,但这些规定各不相同。

10.54

SAJ 格式

SAJ 格式第 VIII.1 条列明了船厂可以顺延合同交船日的不可抗力事件,第 VIII.2 条则规定了延误通知:

10.55

> Within seven (7) days from the date of commencement of the delay on account of which the BUILDER claims that it is entitled under this Contract to a postponement of the Delivery Date of the Vessel, the BUILDER shall advise the BUYER by cable confirmed in writing of the date such delay commences and the reasons therefor ....

从逻辑上看,上述规定应当是针对不可抗力事件的,因为第 VIII.2 条使用的是"the delay",即是指特定的延误,而特定的延误就应当是指第 VIII.1 条中提及的不可抗力事件造成的延误。但是第 VIII.2 条并没有在文字上明确延误通知仅仅适用于不可抗力,而且第 VIII 条实际上并不是单纯的不可抗力条款,而是"交船时间的延误及延期(不可抗力)"条款,延期显然并不仅仅局限于因不可抗力事件引起的延期。因此船东应当有机会主张延误通知不仅适用于不可抗力事件,同时也适用于其他的船厂可以顺延合同交船日的延误,包括因船东行为或过失导致

10.56

的延误。

10.57　然而,如果将第 VIII.2 条规定的通知解释为适用于所有船厂可以主张顺延合同交船日的延误则会产生其他问题。假设,船东的供应品提供不及时影响了船舶建造的进程并导致时间的浪费,在这种情况下要求船厂在延误开始和结束后分别通知船东近乎是荒谬的。如果船厂由于没有按照约定发出延误通知而丧失顺延合同交船日权利则有可能是对违约的一种鼓励。因为船东的违约非但没有受到惩罚,反而从中获益。又如,船舶建造合同规定船东支付建造款有延误的船厂可以顺延合同交船日,船厂未按规定发出通知便丧失顺延合同交船日的权利,这显然剥夺了船厂本应享有的船东违约的合同救济。因此不难得出结论,SAJ 格式起草者的本意应当是第 VIII.2 条规定的通知仅仅适用于不可抗力事件,而不适用于其他船厂认为可以顺延合同交船日的延误。

CSTC 格式

10.58　CSTC 格式应当是在 SAJ 格式的基础上制定的,但 CSTC 格式的起草者似乎并没有意识到 SAJ 格式中延误通知的问题,因为 CSTC 格式同样没有明确延误通知是否仅仅局限于不可抗力事件。相反,CSTC 格式将 SAJ 格式中的"the delay"改为了"any delay":①

> Within seven (7) days from the date of commencement of any delay on account of which the SELLER claims that it is entitled under this Contract to an extension of the time for delivery of the VESSEL ....

10.59　由于使用了"any delay",CSTC 格式也就更倾向于规定船厂不仅要针对因不可抗力事件引起的延误通知船东,而且要将其他船厂可以主张合同交船日顺延的延误通知船东。

NEWBUILDCON 格式

10.60　与 SAJ 格式和 CSTC 格式不同,NEWBUILDCON 格式起草者的本意就应当是要求船厂针对船厂认为所有可以顺延合同交船日的延误情形发出通知,这一点从该格式的规定就可以看出:②

> The Builder shall notify the Buyer within ten (10) running days of when

---

① Article VIII.2, para.1.
② Clause 34(b).

the Builder becomes aware of the occurrence of any event of delay on account of which the Builder asserts that it may have the right to claim an extension of the Delivery Date ....

10.61 按照 NEWBUILDCON 格式的规定,船厂的通知是针对任何造成延误的事件,这些事件包括:船东供应品的延误或有缺陷导致的延误,因船东提出修改要求而导致的延误,以及船东不按合同规定支付建造款导致的延误。这些事件不是船东的有意行为便是船东的违约行为。就船东的违约行为而言,要求船厂在船东违约后的十天内发出通知,若船厂未能按照约定发出通知的,船东则无需承担任何违约责任。这样的规定显然是不合理的,是否有效都可能是问题。

AWES 格式

10.62 AWES 格式在交船条款中的不可抗力部分规定了延误通知:①

Within ... days after the CONTRACTOR becoming aware of the extent of an event of force majeure the CONTRACTOR shall notify the PURCHASER in writing thereof indicating the extent of the delay so caused.

10.63 由于使用了"an event of force majeure",因此 AWES 格式第 6 条中的通知只能解释为是仅仅针对不可抗力事件的通知。

Norwegian 格式

10.64 Norwegian 格式关于不可抗力的内容排列与 SAJ 格式大致相同,但是关于通知的规定则有比较明显的区别:②

Within 10 days after the Builder becomes aware or should have become aware of any cause of delay as aforesaid, on account of which the Builder will claim that it is entitled under the Contract to postpone the Delivery Date, the Builder shall notify the Buyer in writing or by telefax, confirmed by registered mail, of the date such cause of delay commenced. Likewise, within 10 days after the date such cause of delay ended, the Builder shall notify the Buyer in writing or by telefax, confirmed by registered mail, of the date when such cause of delay ended.

---

① Article 6(d), para.2.
② Article IX.2(a).

10.65　虽然上述 Norwegian 格式使用了"任何原因的延误"（any cause of delay），但是"任何原因的延误"是受"上文所称之延误"（delay as aforesaid）限制的。因此，Norwegian 格式关于通知的规定也仅仅适用于不可抗力事件。

通知作为前提条件

10.66　如果船舶建造合同明确规定在发生任何影响船舶建造和交付的事件和情形时船厂均应书面通知船东并主张顺延合同交船日，并规定该书面通知构成顺延合同交船日的前提条件或规定船厂不发通知便不能主张顺延合同交船日的，除非另有相反约定，这一通知将构成船厂主张顺延合同交船日的前提条件。在 *Multiplex Constructions (UK) Ltd v Honeywell Control Systems Ltd (No 2)*①一案中，原告是重建温布利球场的承包商，原告委托被告负责大楼控制和通信所需的各种电气系统的设计、供应及安装。合同条件第 11 条包含下列规定：

> 11.1.3 It shall be a condition precedent to the Sub-Contractor's entitlement to any extension of time under clause 11, that he shall have served all necessary notices on the Contractor by the dates specified and provided all necessary supporting information including but not limited to causation and effect programmes, labour, plant and materials resource schedules and critical path analysis programmes and the like. In the event the Sub-Contractor fails to notify the Contractor by the dates specified and/or fails to provide any necessary supporting information then he shall waive his right, both under the Contract and at common law, in equity and/or to pursuant to statute to any entitlement to an extension of time under this clause 11.

10.67　原告曾向被告发出过三个修改工程安排的指示，最后一个通知的完工日期是 2006 年 3 月 31 日，但实际上工程未能在这一日期或之前完成。被告认为是原告的行为导致工程的耽误。法院则认为，如果原告根据合同规定发出的指示妨碍了被告按时完成工作，其行为便构成阻碍行为，被告可以主张完工日的推迟。但是被告并没有按照第 11.1.3 条的规定向原告发出通知，因此不能援引阻碍行为原则。Jackson 法官认为发出通知具有重要的意义，它不仅有利于对事件进行调查，而且也给予当事人撤销指示的机会。他说的是：②

---

① [2007] Bus LR Digest D109.
② [2007] Bus LR Digest D109 at D115.

Contractual terms requiring a contractor to give prompt notice of delay serve a valuable purpose; such notice enables matters to be investigated while they are still current. Furthermore, such notice sometimes gives the employer the opportunity to withdraw instructions when the financial consequences become apparent .... If the facts are that it was possible to comply with clause 11.1.3 but [contractor] simply failed to do so (whether or not deliberately), then those facts do not set time at large. [Contractor] is not entitled to the relief ....

10.68　阻碍原则的一个基本特征是,任何一方都不得因自己的过失主张权利。然而,如果船厂未能按照船舶建造合同规定发出延误通知而丧失主张顺延合同交船日的权利,船东不但可以获得约定赔偿甚至有机会解除船舶建造合同。如果导致延误的原因是船东的有意行为或过失,实际上船东还是利用自己的过失获得了利益。

前提条件的成立

10.69　如果船舶建造合同没有明确规定船厂发出通知是否构成其顺延合同交船日的前提条件,船厂向船东发出通知是否具有前提条件的性质便取决于对合同相关条款的解释。在 *Bremer Handelsgesellslchaft Schaft MBH v Vanden Avenne Izegem PVBA* 一案中,上议院的 Lord Salmon 认为,将通知作为前提条件的应当有关于发出通知时间的规定,他说:①

Had it been intended as a condition precedent, I should have expected the clause to state the precise time within which the notice was to be served, and to have made plain by express language that unless the notice was served within that time, the sellers would lose their rights under the clause.

10.70　Lord Wilberforce 则认为关于通知的条款应当视为中间条款,是否构成前提条件应根据违反的后果予以确定,他说的是:②

In my opinion the clause may vary appropriately and should be regarded as such an intermediate term: to do so would recognise that while in many, possibly most, instances, breach of it can adequately be sanctioned by damages, cases may exist in which, in fairness to the

---

① [1978] 2 Lloyd's Rep 109 at 128.
② [1978] 2 Lloyd's Rep 109 at 113.

buyer, it would be proper to treat the cancellation as not having effect. On the other hand, always so to treat it may often be unfair to the seller, and unnecessarily rigid.

10.71　*Bremer* v *Vanden* 一案是上议院的判决，因此可以得出普通法关于通知构成前提条件的要件，即合同所使用的文字不仅应当包括发通知的时间，还应当明确规定未发通知的即丧失权利。由于通知的性质取决于合同条款的解释，合同中没有明确是否具有前提条件性质的延误通知依然可以构成主张延期的前提条件。在 *Steria Limited* v *Sigma Wireless Communications Limited*① 一案中，被告是承包商，原告是分包商。分包合同第6.1条规定：

> The Sub-Contractor shall complete the Sub-Contract Works within the time for completion thereof specified in the Fifth Schedule hereto. If by reason of any circumstance which entitles the Contractor to an extension of time for the Completion of the Works under the Main Contract, or by reason of a variation to the Sub-Contract Works, or by reason of any breach by the Contractor the Sub-Contractor shall be delayed in the execution of the Sub-Contract Works, then in any such case provided the Sub-Contractor shall have given within a reasonable period written notice to the Contractor of the circumstances giving rise to the delay, the time for completion hereunder shall be extended by such period as may in all the circumstances be justified . . . .

10.72　分包合同第7.1条又规定：

> If the Sub-Contractor fails to complete the Sub-Contract Works or any part thereof within the time for completion or any extension thereof granted under Clause 6(Completion), there shall be deducted from the Sub-Contract Price, or the Sub-Contractor shall pay to the Contractor as and for liquidated damages . . . .

10.73　在分包商的通知是否构成其推迟完工日的前提条件问题上，承包商认为由于使用了"provided"，因此通知毫无疑问是分包商推迟完工日的前提条件。但是分包商则认为，如果通知是前提条件，分包合同就应当对此作出明确规定，而分包合同实际上并没有此种明确的规定。高院的 Stephen Davies 法官认为分包商的书面通知是其推迟完工日的前提条件，他说：②

---

① [2008] BLR 79.
② [2008] BLR 79 at 96.

... in my judgment the phrase 'provided that the sub-contractor shall have given within a reasonable period written notice to the contractor of the circumstances giving rise to the delay' is clear in its meaning. What the sub-contractor is required to do is give written notice within a reasonable period from when he is delayed .... I consider that a notification requirement may, and in this case does, operate as a condition precedent even though it does not contain an express warning as to the consequence of non-compliance. It is true that in many cases (see for example the contract in the Multiplex case itself) careful drafters will include such an express statement, in order to put the matter beyond doubt. It does not however follow, in my opinion, that a clause – such as the one used here – which makes it clear in ordinary language that the right to an extension of time is conditional on notification being given should not be treated as a condition precedent.

不利于制定人原则

所谓不利于制定人原则(*contra proferentum*)是指由一方当事人提供的合同条款有歧义的,应作对提供方不利的解释。在 *Multiplex Constructions (UK) Ltd* v *Honeywell Control Systems Ltd* 一案中,Jackson 法官说:①   10.74

In so far as the extension of time clause is ambiguous, it should be construed in favour of the contractor.

Jackson 法官对上述观点进行了如下补充,他说:②   10.75

It seems to me that, in so far as an extension of time clause is ambiguous, the court should lean in favour of a construction which permits the contractor to recover appropriate extensions of time in respect of events causing delay.

在 *Steria Limited* v *Sigma Wireless Communications Limited* 一案中,高院的 Stephen Davies 法官认为对通知条款是否构成前提条件若确有歧义的应当作不构成前提条件解释,他说:③   10.76

So far as the application of the *contra proferentum* rule is concerned, it

---

① [2007] Bus LR Digest D109 at D112.
② Ibid.
③ [2008] BLR 79 at 96.

seems to me that the correct question to ask is not whether the clause was put forward originally by Steria or by Sigma; the principle which applies here is that if there is genuine ambiguity as to whether or not notification is a condition precedent, then the notification should not be construed as being a condition precedent, since such a provision operates for the benefit of only one party, i.e. the employer, and operates to deprive the other party (the contractor) of rights which he would otherwise enjoy under the contract.

通知的内容

10.77　在 Steria Limited v Sigma Wireless Communications Limited① 一案中，被告是承包商，原告是分包商。分包合同第6.1条规定：

> If by reason of any circumstance which entitles the Contractor to an extension of time for the Completion of the Works under the Main Contract, or by reason of a variation to the Sub-Contract Works, or by reason of any breach by the Contractor the Sub-Contractor shall be delayed in the execution of the Sub-Contract Works, then in any such case provided the Sub-Contractor shall have given within a reasonable period written notice to the Contractor of the circumstances giving rise to the delay, the time for completion hereunder shall be extended by such period as may in all the circumstances be justified ....

10.78　分包商未能在规定时间内完成分包工作，承包商没有全额支付分包合同规定的价款，理由是可以凭分包合同规定的约定赔偿或一般的损害赔偿予以抵销。高院的 Stephen Davies 法官认为分包商若要主张延期就应当按照约定向承包商发出通知，而且他还认为虽然通知无需明确说明分包商根据第6.1条的规定要求延期或者对延误作出估计，但此类通知不仅应当描述发生的相关情况，而且还应当说明相关情况引起了延误。他说：②

> In my judgment it is necessary for Steria to notify Sigma first that identified relevant circumstances have occurred and second that those circumstances have caused a delay to the execution of the sub-contract works. In my judgment the latter is required, either by a process of purposive construction or by a process of necessary implication, because

---

① [2008] BLR 79.
② [2008] BLR 79 at 95.

otherwise it seems to me that the notice would not achieve its objective; a communication by Steria that, for example, CAMP East was delaying in approving the FDS, without also stating that in consequence the sub-contract works were being delayed, would not achieve the essential purpose of the notification requirement. I am unable however to accept Sigma's submission that the notice must go on to explain how and why the relevant circumstances have caused the delay. That would be to import a requirement for Steria to provide a level of detail in the notice which goes beyond the simple notification which is of the essence of the clause.

10.79 按照上述判决,船厂向船东发出的延误通知不仅要包括造成延误的事件或情况,而且还要说明此等事件或情况造成了延误。Stephen Davies 法官的观点应当是:通知的目的是让收到通知的一方知道已经有延误产生,因此仅仅讲述事件或情况的发生并不一定意味着已有延误产生。但是在船舶建造合同中,有时在特定情形发生时延误应当是必然的,例如船东没有在约定的时间内完成船厂送审的第一批图纸的审核。在这一特定情形下,由于船厂没有图纸而无法开工,因此延误的产生是无需解释或说明的,而且该延误的产生是由于船东的过失导致的。在这种情况下,船厂发出的通知即使没有明确说明船东未能在约定时间内完成审图已经造成延误,该通知也应当是一份合格的通知。

V 交船的延期

概述

10.80 船舶建造合同和建造合同等一样有延期条款或关于延期的规定。在没有延期条款的情况下,一旦船舶建造由于船东的原因或过失而无法在约定的期限内完成,船厂可以顺延合同交船日。这是因为船厂顺延合同交船日的权利来自于普通法中的阻碍原则,而不是依赖合同中的延期条款。在船厂可以按照阻碍原则顺延合同交船日的情况下,延期通常是不受时间限制的。在船舶建造合同有延期条款的情况下,船厂可以根据延期条款主张顺延合同交船日。如果船舶建造合同没有延期条款的,其实船厂依然可以主张合同交船日的顺延,只是依据不同而已。正如 Hamblen 法官 *Adyard Abu Dhabi v SD Marine Services* 一案

中所说的:①

> If, for example, a two-day variation was instruction the day before the sea trials date, and was a variation of a type which would need to be completed before sea trials, then, if there was an extension time clause, [shipyard] would be entitled to one day extension, or, if there was no such clause, [shipyard] could rely on the prevention principle.

延期条款的作用

10.81　船舶建造合同中的延期条款虽然会规定船厂可以主张延期的情形,但如前所述,船厂的权利并非来自合同而是普通法。因此,延期条款实际上是对阻碍原则适用的障碍,正如 Jackson 法官在 *Multiplex Constructions(UK) Ltd* v *Honeywell Control Systems Ltd* 一案中所说的:②

> It is in order to avoid the operation of the prevention principle that many construction contracts and sub-contracts include provisions for extension of time. Thus, it can be seen that extension of time clauses exist for the protection of both parties to a construction contract or sub-contract.

10.82　虽然船舶建造合同的延期条款会规定船厂的延期权利,但延期条款更多的是对船厂行使延期权利规定各种条件和限制。因此,与其说延期条款保护的是船厂的利益,更恰当地说延期条款保护的主要是船东的利益。正如 *Keating on Construction Contracts* 所写到的:③

> Extension of time clauses are regarded as primarily for the benefit of the employer because they enable the original completion date to be re-fixed where delay to the completion of the works has been caused by matters which are the employer's responsibility, thereby retaining the benefit of a clearly identified completion date and any related entitlement on the employer's part to liquidated and ascertained damages. Extension of time provisions should also, however, be viewed as benefitting the contractor in that they protect the contractor from a claim for general damages in respect of its failure to complete by the original contractual date for completion and provides certainty in the event of its culpable

---

① [2011] EWHC 848(Comm) at [295].
② [2007] Bus LR Digest D109 at D110.
③ Stephpen Furst et al, *Keating on Construction Contracts* 11th edn Sweet & Maxwell 2021, para.8-017.

delay.

上文提及的 Hamblen 法官在 *Adyard Abu Dhabi v SD Marine Services* 一案中对阻碍原则作出的归纳是以合同没有相反规定为前提的,如果船舶建造合同中有延期条款,情形则将有所不同。为此,Hamblen 法官说道:①

> However, as Jackson J stated in the *Multiplex* v *Honeywell* case, the prevention principle does not apply if the contract provides for an extension of time in respect of the relevant events. Where such a mechanism exists, if the relevant act of prevention falls within the scope of the extension of time clause, the contract completion dates are extended as appropriate and the Builder must complete the work by the new date, or pay liquidated damages (or accept any other contractual consequence of late completion).

由于船舶建造合同中的延期条款一般会针对各种延期情形作出是否可以延期以及延期几天的规定,因此一个明确的交船日始终存在,这就确保了船东可以在交船迟于合同交船日的情况下根据合同规定获得约定赔偿的权利。

标准格式的规定

总体上说,虽然船舶建造合同标准格式都有关于延期的规定甚至有延期条款,但就这些规定或条款的具体内容来看似乎都存在不同的问题。下文将针对标准格式的延期规定或延期条款进行一个简单的分析。

SAJ 格式

SAJ 格式的第 VIII 条是"交船时间的延误和延期(不可抗力)",因此该条款主要是针对因不可抗力事件引起的交船的延误和延期。该条共分四个部分:延误的原因、延误通知、可允许延误的定义以及过度延误解约权。除了因不可抗力事件引起的延误外,关于延期的规定在可允许延误的定义以及过度延误解约权两部分里有如下内容:②

> ... any other delays of a nature which under the terms of this Contract permits postponement of the Delivery Date shall be understood to be permissible delays ....

---

① [2011] EWHC 848(Comm) at [243].
② Article VIII.3.

10.87　上述规定提到的"the terms of this Contract"主要是指第 V 条"修改",第 VI 条"试航",以及第 XI 条"船东违约"中规定的船厂可以顺延合同交船日的情形。其中第 VI 条"试航"规定的船厂可以顺延合同交船日的情形,在本质上依然是不可抗力造成的。虽然上述规定似乎将船厂可以顺延合同交船日的情形局限于船舶建造合同有规定的情形,但一旦发生其他因船东行为、选择或过失导致的延误且影响船厂船舶建造及交船安排的,船厂应当可以凭阻碍原则顺延合同交船日。

Norwegian 格式

10.88　相比较之下,Norwegian 格式的延期条款的规定要好不少:①

> Delays on account of such causes as specified in this Article IX, Clause 1 and in Article VI hereof and any other delays caused by non fulfillment by the Buyer of the Buyer's obligation hereunder or any other delays of a nature which under the terms of this Contract permit postponement or extension of the Delivery Date shall constitute Permissible Delay and shall extend the Delivery Date for any net delay caused thereby.

10.89　从上述规定来看,可允许延误似乎可以分为三大类:第一类是船舶建造合同已有规定的延误,例如第 VI 条和第 IX 条规定的原因引起的延误;第二类是因船东未履行合同义务而引起的延误,这一类可允许延误应当是不受合同是否有规定的限制;第三类则是按照合同规定可以顺延合同交船日的其他可允许延误。第三类和第一类的共同之处是它们均以合同规定为依据顺延合同交船日,其实二者应当是相同的。虽然上述规定只提及第 IX 条"交船时间的延误和延期(不可抗力)"和第 VI 条"修改"两条涉及可允许延误的条款,但实际上 Norwegian 格式的其他条款也有关于可允许延误的规定,例如按照该格式第 VII 条"测试和试航"条款的规定,因不良天气导致试航延误的应视为可允许延误。② 根据上述规定,凡构成可允许延误的均可根据实际产生的延误顺延合同交船日。但是 Norwegian 格式实际上并没有给 net delay 下定义。因此在采用 Norwegian 格式时 net delay 有可能成为争议。

---

① Article IX.3.
② Article VII.2.

NEWBUILDCON 格式

NEWBUILDCON 格式明确规定了船厂依不可抗力事件顺延合同交船日的条件:①   10.90

> Provided that in respect of (i) and (ii) above:
> (1) such events were not caused by the error, neglect, act or omission of the Builder or its Sub-contractors; and
> (2) were not, or could not reasonably have been, foreseen by the Builder at the date of the Contract; and
> (3) the Builder shall have complied with Sub-clause (b) hereunder; and
> (4) the Builder shall have made all reasonable efforts to avoid and minimize the effects such events have on the delivery of the Vessel.

值得注意的是,上述规定中的(i)是指可允许延误中的不可抗力事件,而(ii)则是指其他包括因船东行为、原因和过失等情形,例如船东供应品晚到、船东提出修改请求等。该格式的起草人在设计上述四个条件时应当是仅仅针对不可抗力事件的,似乎并没有注意到这些条件同时也适用于船东行为、原因和过失造成的延误。因此不免显得有些奇怪,尤其是第四个条件,要求船厂采取所有合理措施来防止或减少因船东的过失或违约行为对船厂的船舶建造和交船安排的影响应当是不合理的。   10.91

对船舶建造的影响

船厂可以主张顺延合同交船日的必须是实际的延误,即在实际影响了船厂的船舶建造以及交船安排的延误。船厂只有在证明船舶建造及交船安排确实受到影响的情况下才可以主张顺延合同交船日。在 *Adyard Abu Dhabi v SD Marine Services* 一案中,船舶建造合同有关于延期的规定,并且还规定了船厂发出延误通知的义务。船厂没有按照规定发出延误通知的,法院认为船厂不能主张顺延合同交船日。Hamblen 法官说:②   10.92

> Even if no such notice is required, any extension of time under Article II, clause 3.3 depends on proof of actual delay. As with Article II, clause 3.2 one must look at what actually happened. Article II, clause

---

① Clause 34(a)(iii).
② [2011] EWHC 848 at [299].

3.3 requires consideration of the period of delay "caused by the Buyer's default or any Permissible Delay". If there is such delay then there shall be an extension of the period of time to sea trials "to the same extent". This requires a retrospective analysis, identifying the delay actually caused by the default or Permissible Delay and adding that period of delay to the original sea trials date.

船厂的举证之责

10.93　　只有在由于船东原因导致船舶建造和交船安排延误时,船厂才可以主张顺延合同交船日。因此船厂必须证明延误是由于船东的原因造成的。在 *Adyard Abu Dhabi* v *SD Marine Services*① 一案中,船厂和船东的争议是船东是否可以解除 2007 年 12 月 14 日订立的两个船舶建造合同。船号分别为 10 和 11,建造价则分别为 14,837,000 美元和 13,932,000 美元。规格书有如下规定:

> The Vessel shall be built to Lloyd's Regulations for ships, +100A1 TUG, LMC, UMS, IWS0. The Vessel must also satisfy the United Kingdom Maritime Coastguard Agency(MCA) requirements for a class VII Cargo Vessel and the IMO Code of Safety for Special Purpose Ships.... In addition the Vessel must satisfy the following regulations:
>
> ...
> IMO Codes/Resolutions
> SPS
> Special Purpose Ship Code

10.94　　船舶建造合同规定的试航日期分别为 2009 年 9 月 30 日与 11 月 30 日。船舶建造合同第 II.3.3 条规定:

> If the Builder fails to complete either of the stages contained in Clause 3.1(c)or(e) by the dates specified therein, then the Buyer may, at its option, rescind this Contract in accordance with the provisions of Article X hereof, provided always that, to the extent that any delays are caused by the Buyer's default or any Permissible Delay, that period shall be extended to the same extent.

10.95　　船舶在规定的试航日未能准备就绪,船东分别于 2009 年 10 月 7 日和 12 月 1

---

① [2011] EWHC 848(Comm).

日解除了船舶建造合同。船厂认为船东无权解除船舶建造合同,因为是船东的行为阻碍了船舶的试航,船厂有权顺延试航日期。船厂还认为试航的延误是由于英国的海事和海岸警备队颁布的新的设计项目以及船东在2009年6月至7月间提出了新的设计要求。船东则认为新的设计项目实际上是变更项目,并没有造成延误。但是双方的专家都认为船厂所主张构成变更的新设计项均属于IMO的特种船安全守则(IMO Code Safety for Special Purpose Ships)的范围。因此,延误是由于船厂自身的原因造成的。Homblen法官说:①

> It follows from my finding that [shipyard] failed to complete the stage referred to in Article II, clause 3.1(e)(Sea Trials) of the contracts by the dates specified in that clause(namely 30 September 2009 and 30 November 2009), and that the failure to have done so was not caused by any Permissible Delay or Buyer's Default. Accordingly, [shipowner] was entitled to rescind pursuant to Article II, clause 3.3 of the contracts.

VI 延误解约权

概述

大多数船舶建造合同都会有"解约日"(cancellation day)的规定,即规定船厂在解约日依然未能交船的,船东可以解除船舶建造合同。"解约日"又被称为"死亡日"(drop dead day)。解约日通常是合同交船日加上一个确定的期限后的第一天,这一期限的长短不一,常见的是180天或210天。由于合同交船日并不一定是一个固定的日期,因此解约也同样不是一个确定的日期。解约日需要根据合同交船日、约定期限的长短以及实际发生的可允许延误的天数进行计算得出。

10.96

不可抗力解约权

SAJ格式有如下内容的解约日规定:②

10.97

> ...if the delay in delivery of the VESSEL should continue for a period

---

① [2011] EWHC 848(Comm) at [301].
② Article III.1(c).

of hundred and eighty (180) days from the thirty-first (31st) day after the Delivery Date, then in such event, and after such period has expired, the BUYER may at its option rescind this Contract in accordance with the provisions of Article X hereof . . . .

10.98　船东按照这一条解除合同只需满足一个条件,即合同规定的解约日已到。这里的 210 天仅指由于船厂原因造成的延误,并不包含可允许延误。因此船东在计算自己是否可以解除船舶建造合的同时应当考虑是否存在任何可允许延误。如果在 210 天有可允许延误的,船东就不能在合同交船日 210 天后解约。有些船舶建造合同在规定解约日时并不区分可允许延误和不可允许延误,而是笼统规定一个期限,CSTC 格式就是一个例子。该格式对延误解约权作出了如下规定:①

> If the total accumulated time of all permissible delays and non-permissible delays aggregate to ＿＿＿＿ days or more, excluding delays due to arbitration as provided for in Article XIII hereof or due to default in performance by the BUYER, or due to delays in delivery of the BUYER's supplied items, and excluding delays due to causes which, under Article V, VI, XI and XII hereof, permit extension or postponement of the time for delivery of the VESSEL, then in such event, the BUYER may in accordance with the provisions set out herein cancel this Contract by serving upon the SELLER telexed notice of cancellation which shall be confirmed in writing and the provisions of Article X of this Contract shall apply . . . .

10.99　上述 CSTC 格式的规定不仅不以不可抗力事件造成的延误为前提,而且既包括可允许延误也包括不可允许延误。实际上,上述规定似乎得到了我国大多数船厂的采用。然而将可允许延误和不可允许延误放在一起计算对船厂来说无疑是相当不利的。不可抗力造成的延误本应是船厂可以据以顺延合同交船日的,因为不可抗力事件导致的延误构成可允许延误。把可允许延误和不可允许延误放在一起计算船东可以解除合同的期限就等于把可允许延误视为不可允许延误。虽然在把两种延误放在一起计算的情况下,期限会比仅计算不可允许延误的期限长一些,但这依然是不可取的。假设合同约定的船东可以解约的期限届满了,但其中有 80%甚至更高的比例实际上是不可抗力事件造成的延误,但船厂依然有可能面临船东解除船舶建造合同的选择。按照上述规定,关于船东解约权期限的计算还应有一些扣除,例如船东解约权期限的计算应当扣除"因第 XIII 条规定的仲裁

---

① Article VIII.3.

而引起的延误"。这里所说的仲裁应当是在船舶建造过程中开始的仲裁,CSTC格式第 XIII.7 条的规定是:

> ... However, if the construction of the VESSEL is affected by any arbitration or court proceedings, the SELLER shall then be permitted to extend the Delivery Date as defined in Article VII and the decision or the award shall include a finding as to what extent the SELLER shall be permitted to extend the Delivery Date.

10.100 按照上述规定,一旦船舶建造因仲裁程序或法院程序而受影响的,船厂可以顺延合同交船日。这一规定应当是有问题的。假设船舶建造因仲裁程序或法院程序发生延误,不论裁决或判决如何认定船厂都可以顺延合同交船日吗?这应当是不可能的。船厂只有在裁决或判决认为船厂有权顺延合同交船日的前提下才能顺延合同交船日。换言之,在裁决或判决认为船厂不能顺延合同交船日时,船厂不能凭借第一句顺延合同交船日的。

10.101 此外,船东解约日的计算不包括船舶建造合同第 V 条、第 VI 条、第 XI 条以及第 XII 条规定的可以顺延交船的原因引起的延误。CSTC 格式的第 V 条是修改条款,因此因船东提出的修改而产生的延误不能计算为船东解约权期限;第 VI 条是试航条款,因此因天气等原因导致试航推迟而产生的延误也应当予以扣除;第 XI 条是船东违约条款,而船东违约此前已经提及;第 XII 条则是保险条款,因此因船舶遭受部分损失而导致的延误也应当从船东解约权期限计算中予以扣除。在上述各条中规定的延误实际上都是可允许延误,船厂均可顺延合同交船日。因此将可允许延误和不可允许延误放在一起计算船东的解约期限应当是不合适的。

10.102 在 Harland & Wolf v Lakeport① 一案中,船舶建造合同第 4 条有如下规定:

> But if in any event the delay in delivery, inclusive of Force Majeure delays but exclusive of any delay for which the Buyer is responsible continues for a period of more than One Hundred and Fifty (150) days after the date of delivery set forth in this Agreement, then in such event the Buyer may, at its option, cancel this Agreement by serving upon the Builder written notice of cancellation.

10.103 按照这一规定,船东既可以因船厂原因造成的延误解除合同,也可以因不可

---

① [1974] 1 Lloyd's Rep 301.

抗力造成的延误解除合同。但是船舶建造合同第 10 条规定船厂可以因不可抗力事件导致延误时顺延合同交船日。因此船舶建造合同的条款之间应当是有矛盾的，Ackner 法官对第 4 条作出了下列评论：①

> To have coupled in one and the same sub-paragraph two entirely different causes of delay, the one being, in substance, beyond the parties' control and the other being due to the default of only one of the parties – the builder – and then to have provided for the same remedy to follow the delay produced by these contrasting causes, was unlikely to be productive of a commercially satisfying result. The parties having chosen not to differentiate between *force majeure* delay and the culpable delay of the builder, I approach the interpretation of the sub-clause substantially pre-conditioned against being surprised that it should, on the Arbitrator's interpretation or on the buyer's interpretation, produce odd results, for indeed, without rewriting the sub-clause, it cannot be made to function in a manner which is free from anomalies.

10.104　由于船东可以在不可抗力原因引起的延误超过 150 天时解除合同，这就意味着船厂有可能在没有任何过错的情况下承担船舶建造合同被解除的后果。Ackner 法官继续说：②

> I must confess that I initially found and still find great difficulty in envisaging the builder on being asked the question –"If there is delay of more than 150 days caused solely by force majeure, what rights would that give you?", replying, "Of course absolutely no rights – only the buyer would be able to cancel in such circumstances. We did not trouble to spell this out. It was too obvious".

解约的日期

10.105　除非另有约定，船东解除船舶建造合同的权利只有在合同规定的期限届满时才产生，即在船厂可以交船的最后一日的次日。除非另有约定，船东在该日期之前即使有理由相信船厂绝对不可能在约定的解约日之前交付，船东依然不能在解约日之前解除船舶建造合同。在 *Cheikh Boutros Selim El-Khoury and Other v Ceylon Shipping Lines Ltd (The Madeleine)* ③一案中，租约规定船东应当在上午

---

① [1974] 1 Lloyd's Rep 301 at 308.
② [1974] 1 Lloyd's Rep 301 at 309.
③ [1967] 2 Lloyd's Rep 224.

9:00 之后,下午 6:00 之前交船,第 22 条规定:

> Should the vessel not be delivered by 2nd day of May 1957 the Charterers to have the option of cancelling.

后来双方又将解约日推迟至 1957 年 5 月 10 日。在 5 月 10 日上午 08:00 点,租船人知道船舶不可能在当天驶抵交船港,于是通知船东拒绝接受船舶并且解除了租约。在 18:48,租船人又一次通知船东解约。船东开始了仲裁,主张租船人解约是错误的。仲裁员要求法院解决的法律问题是:租船人的解约是否构成对租约的毁约。租船人认为 5 月 10 日上午和下午发出的解约通知是有效的,因为船舶并没有在 5 月 10 日驶抵交船港。但是船东则认为自己都有权在 5 月 10 日向租船人交船。法院认为租船人的行为并没有构成毁约,Roskill 法官说:①

10.106

> In my judgment, both as a matter of construction of the charter-party and as a matter of authority, it is clear law that there is no contractual right to rescind a charter-party under the cancelling clause unless and until the date specified in that clause has been reached. In other words ..., there is no anticipatory right to cancel under the clause.

Scrutton on Charterparties and Bills of Lading 也写到:②

10.107

> A charterer is not entitled to cancel (semble under the clause as distinct from any right he may have to rescind at common law) before the cancelling date even though it is clear that the owner will be unable to tender the ship in time. But if the charterer gives notice of cancellation in such circumstances, and the owner accepts it without demur, this will amount to a cancellation by agreement. In deciding whether the charterer is entitled to cancel under a cancelling clause, it is for the charterer to establish the right he claims. He cannot cancel if in breach of contract he has nominated a port which the ship cannot reach by her cancelling date.

虽然上述判例和著作所涉及的并不是船舶建造合同而是租约,但是在解约人是否有预期权问题上应当是可以适用于船舶建造合同的。而所谓的普通法权利则应当是指普通法中的合同落空,也就是说除非船东可以合同落空为由,否则船

10.108

---

① [1967] 2 Lloyd's Rep 224 at 244.
② David Foxton et al, *Scrutton on Charterparties and Bills of Lading* 24th edn Sweet & Maxwell 2020, para. 9-009.

东不可以在约定的解约日到来之前解除船舶建造合同。

作出选择的义务

10.109　在按照船舶建造合同规定可以解除合同时,船东有可能会立即解除合同,也可能不会。在很大程度上,船东是否解除合同取决于当时航运市场的状况。即使船东没有解除合同的打算,也未必会马上告诉船厂。因此,船厂处在一个相当被动的地位:是继续全力以赴地完成已经延误交船的船舶的建造,还是放弃建造或把重点放在其他有可能无法在最后交船日之前交接的船。对此,SAJ格式对此作出了规定,即在船东可以解约但尚未解约时,船厂可以要求船东作出是否解约的决定:①

> The BUILDER may, at any time after the expiration of the aforementioned hundred and eighty (180) days of delay in delivery, if the BUYER has not served notice of rescission as provided in Article X hereof, demand in writing that the BUYER shall make an election, in which case the BUYER shall, within fifteen (15) days after such demand is received by the BUYER, notify the BUILDER of its intention either to rescind this Contract or to consent to the acceptance of the VESSEL at an agreed future date; it being understood by the parties hereto that, if the VESSEL is not delivered by such future date, the BUYER shall have the same right of rescission upon the same terms and conditions as hereinabove provided.

10.110　在有上述规定时,船厂实际上是以15天时间为代价决定自己是否还要继续船舶的建造。一旦船厂发出通知,要求船东作出是否解除合同的选择,船东就应当在15天内作出决定,这实际上已经成为船东的一项合同义务。考虑到合同交船日可能因可允许延误而顺延的性质,船东在不考虑任何可允许延误情况下计算出来的解约日到来时未必会立即作出解除合同的决定。因为一旦存在船厂可以顺延合同交船日的可允许延误,船东解除合同就将是错误的。在这种情况下,船厂发出的要求船东作出选择的通知也会给船东带来一定的压力。CSTC格式也有类似的规定,只是15天的期限在CSTC格式改为了30天。②

10.111　在实践中不少船舶建造合同把这一规定改为:船舶未能在最后交船日交付且船东没有解除合同的,船厂可以向船东提出新的交船日,船东应当在约定的期限

---

① Article III.1(c).
② Article VIII.3.

内回复,作出是解约还是接受新交船日的选择。一旦船东未能在约定期限内作出解约与否选择的,就应被视为接受了新的交船日。这样的话,船东若打算解约就有义务在规定的时间内作出明确的选择。NEWBUILDCON 格式便有如下规定:①

> The Builder may at any time after the right to terminate has occurred give notice requesting that the Buyer either agrees to a new delivery date or terminates this Contract. Such new delivery date shall be a reasonable estimate by the Builder of the date when the Vessel will be ready for delivery. Within fifteen(15) days of the Builder's request, the Buyer shall notify the Builder of its decision. If the Buyer does not terminate this Contract then the new delivery date shall be deemed to be the Delivery Date provided it does not occur later than thirty(30) days prior to the expiry of the Refund Guarantee (Clause 14(b)(Guarantees – Builder's Refund Guarantee)). Notwithstanding Clause 34(a)(i)(Permissible Delays – Force majeure events) and this Clause 39(a)(iii)(1), (2)or (3)but subject to Clause 34(a)(ii)(Permissible Delays – Other events), if the Vessel is not delivered by that date, the Buyer shall have the right to terminate this Contract. The Builder's right to request the Buyer to agree a new delivery date shall operate on each and every occasion the events stated in this Sub-clause(a)(iii) give rise to the Buyer's option to terminate.

另一种有可能出现的情况是,船厂在解约日依然未能交船,船东也没有宣布或通知船厂解除船舶建造合同。但是如果船厂在船东作出解约的意思表示之前完成了船舶的建造并向船东作出了交付,这时船东就有可能丧失解除船舶建造合同的权利而必须接船。因为除非另有约定,船东没有作出解约表示的应当视为是继续履行合同的表示。   10.112

解约权的丧失

由于船东的解约权是一项选择权,船东在按照船舶建造合同的规定可以解除合同时可以选择解约,也可以选择不解约。除非船东明确选择解约,否则就应当继续按照船舶建造合同的规定履行合同。在 *Harland & Wolff Ltd v Lakeport Navigation Co Panama SA*② 一案中,船舶建造合同规定交船延误超过合同规定交   10.113

---

① Clause 39(a)(iii).
② [1974] 1 Lloyd's Rep 301.

船日150天的,船东有权解除合同。合同第4(1)(d)条还规定,如果船东没有发出解除合同通知的,船厂可以在150天届满之时书面要求船东做出选择,这时船厂和船东应在30天内就解除合同或在新的交船日交接船舶进行洽谈并达成一致:

> ... the Builder and the Buyer shall negotiate and agree within thirty(30) days ... either to cancel, or to consent to deliver and accept the vessel at a future date under the conditions mutually agreed by the Buyer and the Builder in the course of negotiation ....

10.114　船厂的交船延期了,但船东始终表示愿意维持合同。在交船延迟超过150天时,船厂正式要求船东做出解除合同抑或通过谈判确定接受船舶条件的选择。船厂希望通过谈判提高合同价格从而弥补其遭受的损失。船东则认为只有在他决定解除合同时才可以重新洽谈合同条款。即使重谈合同条款也应当限于对船东有利的重谈。仲裁员认为船厂有权重新洽谈合同条款。法院支持了仲裁员的观点,Ackner法官说:①

> ... on the clear wording of the sub-clause the buyer, by communicating to the builder his intention not to exercise the option cannot deprive the latter of his right or discharge him from his obligation under the sub-clause to make the demand ... [Buyer] submits that it is necessary for the business efficacy of the sub-paragraph for there to be implied after the words "under the conditions mutually agreed" the words "but only in the buyers' favour". This would undoubtedly prevent the builder profiting from his own delay but, on the other hand, when the delay is due to force majeure, would deprive the builder of a very valuable right to impose cancellation upon the buyer who wishes to continue with the contract but refuses to pay reasonable increases in the price caused by the delays due to force majeure. Again the words of the clause are quite plain and to introduce the words suggested would not be to construe it, but to rewrite it.

---

① [1974] 1 Lloyd's Rep 301 at 309.

第11章 质量保证

Ⅰ 质保条款

概述

船舶建造合同一般都有质量保证条款(warranty of quality),这里 warranty 应当与 guarantee 是同义词,即船厂对船舶质量承担约定的保证责任。"保证"是 warranty 一词的最基本的含义,正如上诉法院的 Denning 法官在 *Oscar Chess Ltd v Williams* 一案中所说的:①

11.1

> I use the word "warranty" in its ordinary English meaning to denote a binding promise. Everyone knows what a man means when he says, "I guarantee it" or "I warrant it", or "I give you my word on it". He means that he binds himself to it. That is the meaning which it has borne in English law for three hundred years from the leading case of *Chandelor* v *Lopus* [(1603) Cro Jac 4] onwards.

船舶建造合同中的质保条款可以说是为船厂和船东双方的利益而制定的。对船厂而言,质保条款使其对质保期内出现的问题进行补救,这也是对自己履约缺陷的一种补救。对船东而言,质保条款带来的好处是在约定期限内船东可以要求船厂对船舶出现的问题进行弥补而无需承担费用。正如上诉法院的 May 法官在 *BHP Petroleum Ltd and Others* v *British Steel Plc and Dalmine SpA* 一案中所指出的:②

11.2

> Clauses of this kind do not limit or exclude liability. Typically they confer additional rights and obligations requiring the contractor or supplier to undertake additional work to rectify defects which appear

---

① [1957] 1 All ER 325 at 327.
② [2000] 2 Lloyd's Rep 277 at 288.

within a defined time after completion usually without additional payment. They may be seen as benefiting both parties. The employer is entitled to have the defects rectified without having to engage and pay another contractor to carry out the rectification: the contractor or supplier is entitled to carry out the rectification himself which may normally be expected to be less expensive for him than having to reimburse the cost to the employer of having it done by others. Without a clause of this kind, the contractor or supplier would normally have no right to do work after completion, although an employer faced with defects after completion would need to mitigate his loss, if he wished to claim damages, and mitigation would often lead to inviting the contractor or supplier to do the work.

产品责任

11.3 船厂根据船舶建造合同的质保条款承担的是"产品质量责任",与此相似的一个概念是"产品责任"(product liability)。虽然两者均涉及质量,但是"产品质量责任"和"产品责任"是两个不同的概念。产品责任是指产品的生产者和销售者等因产品存在问题或缺陷造成消费者人身或财产损失而应承担的责任,产品质量责任则是船厂应当对船舶质量存在问题或缺陷承担的责任。产品责任是针对不特定的消费者的责任,船厂的船舶质量保证则是针对特定的船舶建造合同相对方的责任。产品责任是一种侵权责任,甚至有可能构成刑事责任,船厂的质量保证则是一种合同责任。产品责任通常是严格责任,即责任的承担不以有过错为基础,船厂的质量保证是普通责任,责任的承担以有过错为基础。

质量保证

11.4 船厂的质量保证与"质量保证"(quality assurance)也是两个截然不同的概念。如前所述,船厂承担的船舶的质量保证是船舶建造合同规定的一项合同义务,违反这一义务的,船厂应承担法律责任。质量保证则通常是指企业为了保证产品的质量而建立的包括一系列有计划有组织地控制产品质量活动的管理体系。

II 船舶交接的意义

船厂义务的终止

如果船舶不符合船舶建造合同或规格书的规定,即使船舶已经交接且所有权也已经转移至船东一方,船厂依然需要承担船舶建造合同的违约责任,这是船厂的普通法义务。同时,按照 1979 年《货物买卖法》的规定,即使买卖合同没有规定,卖方依然负有成文法规定的默示保证,这些默示保证包括:卖方交付的货物必须符合买卖合同对货物的描述;①货物具有令人满意的质量;②货物适合其用途等。③ 就船舶建造合同而言,这些义务并不仅仅局限于船舶交接之前的合同期间,作为买方的船东在接船后发现船舶不符合合同规定的或违反成文法保证的,船东依然对船厂享有索赔的权利,这是船厂的成文法义务。④ 然而,合同当事人可以通过合同条款的约定排除普通法和成文法的适用,正如 Diplock 法官在 *Ashington Piggeries Ltd* v *Christopher Hill Ltd* 一案中所说的:⑤

11.5

> ... as a basic principle of the English law of contract that, subject to any limitations imposed by statute or by common-law rules of public policy, parties to contracts have freedom of choice not only as to what each will mutually promise to do but also as to what each is willing to accept as the consequences of the performance or non-performance of those promises so far as those consequences affect any other party to the contract.

上议院的 Lord Wilberforce 在 *Photo Production Ltd* v *Securicor Transport Ltd* 一案中也说:⑥

11.6

> ... there is everything to be said ... for leaving the parties free to apportion the risks as they think fit and for respecting their decisions.

1979 年《货物买卖法》以成文法的形式确认了合同当事人的这一权利:⑦

11.7

---

① s.13(1).
② s.14(2).
③ s.14(3).
④ 1979 年《货物买卖法》的规定实际上是将关于货物买卖的普通法原则进行了成文法化。
⑤ [1971] 1 Lloyd's Rep 245 at 275.
⑥ [1980] 1 Lloyd's Rep 545 at 549.
⑦ s.55(1).

Where a right, duty or liability would arise under a contract of sale of goods by implication of law, it may (subject to the Unfair Contract Terms Act 1977) be negatived or varied by express agreement, or by the course of dealing between the parties, or by such usage as binds both parties to the contract.

标准格式的规定

11.8　　SAJ格式规定船舶一旦交接完毕,船舶建造合同即告履行完毕,船厂除了质保外已不再承担任何船舶建造合同的义务:①

The guarantee contained as hereinabove in this Article replaces and excludes any other liability, guarantee, warranty and/or condition imposed or implied by the law, customary, statutory or otherwise, by reasons of the construction and sale of the VESSEL for and to the BUILDER.

11.9　　上述规定很清楚,船舶建造合同的质量保证排除了普通法、习惯、成文法或其他所有明示或默示规定的责任、保证、担保或条件。但是上述规定并不足以排除合同的明示规定,若要排除合同明示规定就需要使用更为明确的措辞。在 *Andrews Bros(Bournemouth) Ltd* v *Singer & Co Ltd*② 一案中,被告向原告出售一辆新车,汽车买卖合同第5条规定:

All cars sold by the company are subject to the terms of the warranty set out in Schedule No.3 of this agreement and all conditions, warranties and liabilities implied by statute, common law or otherwise are excluded.

11.10　　被告将一辆行驶过相当路程的汽车作为新车卖给了原告,被告的观点是,虽然没有向原告提供符合合同描述的汽车违反了成文法规定的义务,但是原告接受的合同已经明确排除了被告应当承担的责任。但是上诉法院的Scrutton法官则认为合同已经明确规定被告出售的是一辆新车,而实际上被告提供的并不是新车。他说:③

In my view there has been in this case a breach of an express term of the

---

① Article IX.4(c).
② [1934] 1 KB 17.
③ [1934] 1 KB 17 at 23.

contract. If a vendor desires to protect himself from liability in such a case he must do so by much clearer language than this, which, in my opinion, does not exempt the defendants from liability where they have failed to comply with the express term of the contract.

11.11 在 China Shipbuilding Corp v Nippon Yusen Kabukishi Kaisha & Anor① 一案中的质保条款第 IX.3(d)条有如下内容：

> The guarantee contained as hereinabove in this Article replaces and excludes any other liability, guarantee, warranty and/or condition imposed or implied by the law, customary, statutory or otherwise, by reason of the construction and sale of the Vessel by the Builder for and to the Buyer.

11.12 高院的 Thomas 法官也认为质保条款并没有排除合同明示条款的违约责任，他说：②

> It was common ground that art. IX.3(d) excluded the liability of the builder under any implied term (whether implied by operation of law or by statute) but did not exclude liability for breach of an express term of the contract ....

11.13 因此，除非使用相当明确的措辞，否则质保条款排除的只能是船厂的默示责任，而不是船舶建造合同明确规定的明示责任。AWES 格式也有类似规定：③

> On delivery of the VESSEL to the PURCHASER every responsibility for the safely and generally for the condition of the VESSEL is transferred to the PURCHASER, and thereafter all responsibilities on the part of the CONTRACTOR shall cease with the exception of the guarantee obligations provided for in Article 12 hereof.

11.14 就责任排除而言，AWES 格式的规定存在比较明显的欠缺。上述规定所使用的"all responsibilities"是否足以排除合同以外的责任，例如普通法或成文法的责任应当是不明确的。Norwegian 格式也有类似的规定：④

> Save as provided for below, and provided always that the deficiencies

---

① [2000] CLC 566.
② [2000] CLC 566 at 571.
③ Article 8(b), para.2.
④ Article X.1.

have been rectified within a reasonable time, the Builder shall have no responsibility for defects or the consequences thereof (including loss of profit and loss of time) discovered after the Delivery and Acceptance of the Vessel.

11.15 相比之下，NEWBUILDCON 格式的规定则比较详尽，该格式有下列两处规定涉及责任排除：①

Except to the extent expressly provided in Clause 35 (Builder's Guarantee), the Builder shall have no liability in contract, tort (including negligence), breach of statutory duty or otherwise for:

(i) any Defect discovered after delivery of the Vessel or
(ii) any loss, damage or expenses caused as a consequence of such Defect (which shall include, but not be limited to, loss of time, loss of profit or earnings or demurrage directly or indirectly incurred by the Buyer).

The guarantee contained in Clause 35 (Builder's Guarantee) replaces and excludes any other liability, guarantee, warranty and/or condition and/or innominate term imposed or implied by the law, customary, statutory or otherwise, by reason of the construction and sale of the Vessel by the Builder for and to the Buyer.

11.16 上述规定不仅排除了船厂对交船后发现的"缺陷"的责任，同时也排除了船厂对"缺陷"造成损失的责任。虽然从理论上说船东在接船后发现"缺陷"以外的问题依然可以向船厂主张权利，但实际上船东能够成功主张的可能性微乎其微，因为"缺陷"的范围应当是比较广的：②

"Defect" means any deficiencies or defects in the design, construction, material and/or workmanship on the part of the Builder or its subcontractors.

11.17 CSTC 格式则明确规定船东放弃了权利：③

The Guarantee provided in this Article and the obligation and the liabilities of the SELLER hereunder are exclusive and in lieu of and the BUYER hereby waives all other remedies, warranties, guarantees or

---

① Clauses 37(b), 37(d), Norwegian 格式和 CSTC 格式则没有关于排除船厂交船后责任的类似规定.
② NEWBUILDCON Definitions.
③ Article IX.4, para.3.

liabilities, express or implied, arising by law or otherwise (including without limitation any obligations of the SELLER with respect to fitness, merchantability and consequential damages) or whether or not occasioned by the SELLER's negligence . . . .

CSTC 格式起草者的用意应当是明确的,即船厂在按照船舶建造合同规定承担船舶质保情况下就不再承担任何其他责任了。上述规定还明确排除了成文法规定的货物合适性和令人满意质量的默示保证。① 11.18

合理性要求

与合同中责任排除条款一样,船舶建造合同中关于排除普通法和成文法责任的规定也必须是合理的,否则此种排除责任的规定就应当是无效的。这一原则在 *Edmund Murray Ltd* v *BSP International Foundations Ltd*② 一案中已经阐述的很明确。该案中的钻井平台购买合同采用标准格式,该标准格式的第 12 条是保证条款,其中第12.5条和第12.6条有如下内容: 11.19

12.5 The guarantee in this Condition 12 is in lieu of and excludes any other conditions, guarantees, liabilities or warranties expressed or implied statutory or otherwise and in no event shall the Sellers be liable for any loss, injury or damage howsoever caused or arising EXCEPT for death or personal injury arising from the proven negligence of the Sellers or one or more of the Sellers' employees in the course of his or their employment where this Contract is not an international supply contract.

12.6 The Sellers shall not be liable for loss of profit, or any other consequential or special loss or damage howsoever caused and (without prejudice to the foregoing generality) shall not be liable for any damage (whether or not consequential) arising from stoppage or breakdown of the goods or in any other way from the performance of the goods in operation or any damage to plant or any expenditure incurred on the goods or arising out of any suggestions which may be made by the Sellers for the use of any goods, whether supplied by the Sellers or not or arising from any layouts provided by the Sellers for any purpose.

---

① 但这一排除是否有效应当是不确定的。
② (1992) 33 Com LR 1, Official Transcript.

11.20　　作为 Official Referee① 高院的 Wilcox 法官认为上述两条符合 1977 年《不公平合同条款法》规定的合理原则,但是上诉法院则认为上述两条均未满足合理性的要求,上诉法院的 Neill 法官说:②

> If and in so far as, however, it is proved that any failure in performance was due to a breach of the obligation to provide a rig which complied with the specification or to provide a rig which was fit for the purpose for which EML ordered it I consider that Condition 12.5 would not satisfy the requirement of reasonableness.
>
> Condition 12.6 presents its own difficulty. On the face of it a term excluding consequential loss would appear to be fair and reasonable as between parties contracting at arm's length. But this condition goes further and provides (inter alia) that BSP shall not be liable "for any damage (whether or not consequential) arising from stoppage or breakdown of the goods or in any other way from the performance of the goods in operation". Here again, if the failure of performance is proved to be due to a breach of the obligation to provide a rig which complied with the specification or to provide a rig which was fit for the purpose for which EML required it I consider that this condition would not satisfy the requirement of reasonableness.

11.21　　Neill 法官认为虽然买方知道排除责任条款的存在,也可以对这些条款的性质咨询专业意见,而且钻井平台也是以低价出售的,但是排除责任条款按照 1977 年《不公平合同条款法》规定的标准依然是不合理的。③ 因为在钻井购买合同订立之时的相关情况包括:(1)钻井是特别订购的;(2)规格书包含了钻井平台应当满足的技术标准的明确细节;(3)买方已使卖方知道其订购钻井平台的目的。Neill 法官认为在这种情况下剥夺买方的权利是不公平和不合理的。他是这样说的:

---

① Official Referee(官方调查人,咨询官)是 1873 年《司法法》(Judicature Act 1873)所设置的司法官员,根据该法规定,高院的法官可以将需要较长时间查阅文件或账目的案件,或者涉及陪审团较难实施的科学或当地调查的案件交由 Official Referee 处理。Official Referee 被 1971 年《法院法》(Courts Act 1971)废除。按照该法第 25 条的规定,Official Referee 的职能由 Lord Chancellor(最高法院院长)指定的巡回法院法官(Circuit judges)行使。按照 1981 年《高级法院法》(Senior Courts Act 1981)第 68(1)(a)条的规定,王座法院的首席法官(Lord Chief Justice)可以在咨询了 Lord Chancellor 之后指定巡回法院法官、巡回法院代理法官或地区法官(Recorders)行使 Official Referee 的职能。
② (1992) 33 Com LR 1, Official Transcript.
③ Section 11: "... the term shall have been a fair and reasonable one to be included having regard to the circumstances which were, or ought reasonably to have been, known to or in the contemplation of the parties when the contract was made".

Against this background it cannot have been fair or reasonable in my judgment to take away from EML any right to seek compensation or redress for a breach of the express terms set out in the specification or for a breach of the implied obligation to supply a rig which was fit for the required purpose . . . .

11.22　船舶建造合同中关于排除交船后责任的规定应当是符合 1977 年《不公平合同条款法》规定的合理性，因为船舶建造合同不同于一般的货物买卖合同中买方通常不会参与卖方货物的生产或采购。在船舶建造合同中，船东实际上参与整个建造过程，并且有权对整个过程进行监督和检查。此外，在船舶完成试航后，船东依然有机会对船舶作出是否接受的决定。因此，船舶建造合同中排除交船后责任的规定应当是合理的，因此也是有效的。

合同要求的符合

11.23　船舶建造合同中的质保条款是解决交船后可能发生的船舶质量问题，与船厂履行船舶建造合同无关。船厂建造的船舶应当符合船舶建造合同和规格书规定的要求，质保条款并不能免除船厂确保船舶在交付时符合合同及规格书规定的质量状况的义务。在 *Cammell Laird & Co Ltd* v *Manganese Bronze and Brass Co Ltd* ①一案中，螺旋桨供应商向船厂提供的螺旋桨在安装后发出很大的噪声，船级社拒绝为船舶入级，船东也拒绝接受船舶。螺旋桨供应商认为鉴于其已提供了为期六个月的质量保证，因此螺旋桨的采购合同就不再有螺旋桨应当适合其用途的默示规定了（*expressum facit cessare tacitum*）。上诉法院的 Roche 法官则指出合同中的明示保证并不当然排除合同中的默示条件，他说：②

> I say that the answer to that is that which was given by the House of Lords in *Wallis, Son & Wells* v *Pratt & Haynes, sup.*, at p.394, and by the Court of Appeal in the case of *Baldry* v *Marshall* [1925] 1 KB 260. The answer to that, shortly, is that an express warranty does not necessarily oust, or make unnecessary, an implication of a condition. Another answer, I think, in the construction of this particular warranty, was that it related to an entirely different period of time. It was to be a guarantee which was to operate after delivery, and after the delivery of the ship to the owners.

---

① (1932) 43 Ll L Rep 466.
② (1932) 43 Ll L Rep 466 at 478.

III 质保范围

标准格式的规定

11.24　船舶建造合同一般都会明确规定船厂根据质保条款承担的质保范围,SAJ 格式规定的质保范围是:①

> Subject to the provisions hereinafter set forth, the BUILDER undertakes to remedy, free of charge to the BUYER, any defects in the VESSEL which are due to defective material and/or bad workmanship on the part of the BUILDER and/or its subcontractors, provide that the defects are discovered within a period of twelve (12) months after the date of delivery of the VESSEL and a notice thereof is duly given to the BUILDER as hereinabove provided.
>
> For the purpose of this Article, the VESSEL shall include her hull, machinery, equipment and gear, but excludes any arts for the VESSEL which have been supplied by or on behalf of the BUYER.

11.25　根据上述规定,船厂的质保责任主要有两个方面:一是因船厂或其分包商的材料缺陷造成的包括船壳、机械和设备等的缺陷;二是因船厂或其分包商的不良工艺造成的缺陷。SAJ 格式规定的质保责任范围比较小,AWES 格式和 CSTC 格式的规定与 SAJ 格式比较相似,船厂承担的质保责任范围同样局限于材料和工艺的缺陷。② Norwegian 格式规定的质保范围明显要比 SAJ 格式的范围大,该格式在 SAJ 格式的责任范围基础上又增加了因设计产生的缺陷:③

> The Builder undertakes to repair and rectify at its own cost and expense and free of charge to the Buyer, any defects – including latent defects or deficiencies – concerning the Vessel or parts thereof which are caused by faulty design, defective material and/or poor workmanship on the part of the Builder, its servants, employees or Subcontractors, but excluding defects arising after delivery due to normal wear and tear or improper handling of the Vessel or caused or aggravated by omission or improper

---

① Article IX.1.
② AWES Article 12(a), para.2; CSTC Article IX.1.
③ Article X.2, para.1.

use or maintenance of the Vessel on the part of the Buyer, its servants or agents and excluding Buyer's Supplies.

缺陷

与其他标准格式不同,NEWBUILDCON 格式的规定是:① 11.26

The Builder shall guarantee the Vessel against any Defects (see Definitions ...)

(i) discovered within the number of months stated in Box 20 (hereinafter "the Guarantee Period") after delivery of the Vessel in accordance with Clause 28(Delivery); and

(ii) notice thereof is given to the Builder as soon as reasonably possible after the discovery thereof and latest thirty (30) running days after the expiry of the Guarantee Period describing such Defects so far as reasonably practical

NEWBUILDCON 格式的定义条款对"缺陷"的范围作了如下规定: 11.27

"Defects" means any deficiencies or defects in the design, construction, material and/or workmanship on the part of the Builder or its subcontractors.

根据上述定义,"缺陷"是指船厂及其分包商在设计、建造、材料以及工艺上的不足或缺陷。可以说,NEWBUILDCON 格式规定的质保责任范围是各标准格式中最大的。上述定义只是明确了范围,至于什么是"缺陷",该格式实际上说的是"缺陷就是不足和缺陷",但没有说明什么是"不足"和"缺陷"。 11.28

英国普通法有"缺陷"的定义,在 *McGiffin* v *Palmer's Shipbuilding & Iron Co Ltd* 一案中,Stephen 法官对机械的缺陷下了定义,他说:② 11.29

A defect in the machinery would be the absence of some part of the machinery, or a crack, or anything of that kind.

在 *Yarmouth* v *France* 一案中,Lindley 法官则对缺陷做出了如下的描述:③ 11.30

I take defect to include anything which renders the plant etc. unfit for

---

① Clause 35(a).
② (1882) 10 QBD 5 at 9.
③ (1887) 19 QBD 647 at 658.

the use for which it is intended, when used in a reasonable way and with reasonable care: and, if a horse intended for drawing trolleys is from any cause unfit for such work, and a person is driving him with reasonable care, and is injured by reason of the unfitness of the horse for his work, such person may be properly said to be injured by reasons of a defect in plant.

11.31　"缺陷"又可以分为"明显的缺陷"（patent defect）和"隐藏的缺陷"（latent defect），前者是指显而易见的缺陷，往往通过肉眼就能够发现。后者则是指隐藏的或潜在的缺陷，通常无法通过肉眼发现。但就船舶建造合同中船厂的质量保证义务而言，缺陷的此种分类并没有太大的实际意义，因为质量保证条款并不仅仅针对在交船后发现的隐藏的缺陷，而是针对所有缺陷，既包括明显的缺陷，也包括隐藏的缺陷。

11.32　NEWBUILDCON 格式使用的"不足"（deficiency）与"缺陷"应当是不同的，"不足"应当是指"缺乏"或"缺少"。如果船厂提供的备件不符合船级社规范或规格书的要求应当构成的是"不足"，而不是"缺陷"；如果船厂提供的备件是完整的，某些备件存在质量问题就应当是"缺陷"，而不是"不足"。

缺陷导致的损坏

11.33　船厂的质保责任是否包括因质保缺陷引起的船舶损坏在标准格式中并不统一。按照 SAJ 格式和 AWES 格式的规定，船厂无需承担因质保缺陷引起的船舶损坏，但 Norwegian 格式，CSTC 格式以及 NEWBUILDCON 格式则都规定了船厂应当承担因质保缺陷引起的船舶损坏的责任，只是措辞和条件有所不同而已。按照 Norwegian 格式的规定，船厂在特定情形下应当承担质保缺陷造成的船舶的损坏：①

> ... the Builder shall have no other liability for any damage or loss caused as a consequence of the defect, except for repair or renewal of the Vessel's part/parts that have been damaged as a direct and immediate consequence of the defect without any intermediate cause, and provided such part or parts can be considered to form a part of the same equipment or same system ....

11.34　上述规定中的"direct"应当是指缺陷直接造成的，而"immediate"强调的应当

---

① Article X.3(a).

不是时间上的意义。按照 Atkinson 法官在 *Saint Line Limted* v *Richardsons, Westgarth & Co Limited* 一案中所说的,"immediate"并没有在"direct"的基础上增加任何其他的意义。Atkinson 法官是这样说的:①

> In Webster's Dictionary, the meaning of "immediate" is, "not separated by anything intervening", and it gives as a synonym the word "direct." It merely means "flowing directly from without intervening cause." I do not think "immediate" adds anything to the word "direct" and I do not think "consequential" adds anything to the word "indirect." What the clause does do is to protect the respondents from claims for special damages which would be recoverable only on proof of special circumstances and for damages contributed to by some supervening cause. I am satisfied that it does not protect them from the claims which are made in this case.

CSTC 格式的规定如下:② 11.35

> The SELLER shall be liable to the BUYER for defects and damages caused by any of the defects specified in Paragraph 1 of this Article provided that such liability of the SELLER shall be limited to damage occasioned within the guarantee period specified in Paragraph 1 above ....

上述规定中的"damages"可能是笔误,作为"损害"或"损坏",damage 通常只能是单数,damage 用作复数时不再是指"损害"或"损坏",而是指损害赔偿,即一定数量的金钱。NEWBUILDCON 格式规定的质保责任也包括因质保缺陷引起的损坏:③ 11.36

> The Builder shall make any necessary repairs or replacements to rectify any Guarantee Defects or damage to the Vessel caused as a direct and immediate consequence of such Guarantee Defects. Such repairs and replacements shall be made at the Shipyard at the Builder's cost and expense.

船厂承担的质保责任是仅仅针对有质保缺陷的部分进行修理或替换还是同时还包括针对因质保缺陷产生的船舶损坏进行修理或替换存在着极大的差别。 11.37

---

① [1940] 2 KB 99 at 104.
② Article IX.4, para.2.
③ Clause 35(b).

因此,这是船厂在订立船舶建造合同时应当注意的问题。

Ⅳ 质保期限

标准格式的规定

11.38　船厂承担的船舶质保期限一般为十二个月,自交船之日起算。前文提及的 SAJ 格式关于质保期限的规定,CSTC 格式也有类似的规定。① Norwegian 格式关于质保期限的规定如下:②

> The Builder's liability as stated herein shall terminate if the defects as aforesaid have not been discovered within the Guarantee Period (of 12 months or such other period as the Builder and Buyer may agree) unless otherwise provided for in the Contract.

11.39　AWES 格式和 NEWBUILDCON 格式均没有规定质保期限的长短,而是留给当事人自己约定。但船厂承担质保责任的期限自船东接船之日开始起算应当是明确的。在 China Shipbuilding Corporation v Nippon Yusen Kabukishi Kaisha and Another③ 一案中,船舶建造合同的质保条款第 IX.1 条规定的是自船东接受船舶之时起算:

> The Builder for a period of twelve months following acceptance by the Buyer of the vessel, guarantees the vessel her hull and machinery … which are manufactured, furnished or supplied by the Builder … against all defects in materials and/or workmanship on the part of the Builder ….

11.40　高院的 Thomas 法官认为"接受"是指船东接船,而不是船东在船舶试航后对船舶作出接受的表示。因此,质保期限应当从船东接船之日开始起算:④

> In my view, acceptance in the first line of art.IX meant acceptance of the vessel by the buyers on delivery by the builder, accompanied by the protocol of delivery and acceptance. This was the date from which the guarantee period was to run …. It is therefore clear that "acceptance"

---

① Article IX.1.
② Article X.2, para.2.
③ [2000] CLC 566.
④ [2000] CLC 566 at 575.

in art. IX had nothing to do with the state of the vessel after the completion of the trials or the operation of art.VI.

质保期限内的缺陷

船厂的质保责任以船舶建造合同规定的质保期限为条件,在质保期限届满后发现的任何缺陷,船厂均无需承担责任,在 *China Shipbuilding Corporation* v *Nippon Yusen Kabukishi Kaisha and Another*① 一案中,船舶建造合同的质保条款规定的质保期为 12 个月,合同第IX.3(a)条则有如下规定: 11.41

> The Builder shall have no obligation under this guarantee for any defect discovered after the expiration of the guarantee period specified hereinabove and for any defects whatsoever in the Vessel other than the defects specified in Section 1 of this Article. Nor shall the Builder in any circumstances be liable for any indirect consequential or special losses damages or expenses ... occasioned to the Buyer by reason of the defects specified in Section 1 of this Article or due to repairs done or other work done to remedy such defects ....

船东接受了船舶,双方签署了船舶交接备忘录。船东在质保期届满后发现了焊接缺陷。船东要求船厂赔偿焊接修理的费用以及船舶的贬值。法院支持了船厂的主张,高院的 Thomas 法官说:②   11.42

> In my judgment, the first part of the first sentence excluded liability under the guarantee for defects which were not discovered during the 12 months; that part therefore excluded defects which might have existed or occurred during the 12 month period but which were not discovered within that period. The second part of the first sentence excluded liability under the contract for any defects other than those specified in art.IX.1 .... The liability the yard accepted under art.IX.1 was limited to repair and replacement; this of necessity meant that there was no claim for diminution in value.

---

① [2000] CLC 566.
② [2000] CLC 566 at 573.

期限的延长

11.43　一旦船东在质保期内发现了属于船厂质保责任范围内的缺陷,船厂应当按照船舶建造合同的规定对此种缺陷进行修理或替换。船厂的质保责任同样适用于修理和替换,通常情况下船厂也会提供12个月的质保。这样整个船舶的质保期就可能会因此延长,超过合同规定的12个月。SAJ格式对此没有相关的条文,但是AWES格式则对此作出了如下规定:①

> Replacements and repairs pursuant to the CONTRACT's guarantee obligations shall be subject to guarantee in accordance with this article, provided that the guarantee period in regard to such replacements and repairs shall start at the date of completion thereof and provided that the total guarantee period shall never exceed a period of two years after delivery of the VESSEL.

11.44　应当注意的是,虽然按照上述规定船厂承担的质保责任期限从12个月变成最长不超过24个月,但船厂承担质保责任的期限实际上并没有延长。如果在12个月内没有发生任何质保修理或替换的,船厂在12个月期限届满时不再有任何质保的合同义务了。如果在12个月内发生质保修理或替换的,除了修理或替换的部分,船厂的质保责任依然会在12个月届满时终止。针对已进行修理或替换的部分,船厂自修理或替换完成之日开始承担12个月的质量保证。如果质保修理或替换是在质保期限开始后的两个月内发生的,船厂针对经过修理或替换部分的质保责任同样会在修理或替换后12个月终止;如果质保修理或替换是在质保期限开始后的第12个月发生的,船厂针对经过修理或替换部分的质保责任同样会在此后的12月届满时终止。由此可见,将12个月的质保期限延长至24个月是针对极端情形的,即在船舶建造合同规定的12个月的质保期限行将结束之时发生质保索赔。此种情况较为罕见,因此在实践中绝大多数的船舶建造合同会规定最长的质保期限不超过18个月:

> For repaired or replaced parts of the Vessel a further Guarantee Period of twelve(12) months shall apply from the date of the reparation or replacement. However, the Guarantee Period under no circumstances shall extend beyond eighteen(18) calendar months from the Delivery Date of the Vessel.

---

① Article 12(a), para.4.

Norwegian 格式针对质保期限延长作出了与绝大多数标准格式不同的规定, 11.45
这些规定比较有利于对船东利益的保护:①

The Guarantee Period will be extended in the following cases:

(a) After repair and rectification under this Article X has been carried out, there will be a further period of guarantee of Months for the repaired and rectified items. The further Guarantee Period shall, however, not be less than the original Guarantee Period for any such item. Such additional guarantee period will be granted on all remedial works notified by the Buyer to the Builder in the Guarantee Period, or any extension thereof. The Buyer shall, however, not be entitled to such additional guarantee for deficiencies caused by poor workmanship if the guarantee work has not been performed by the Builder or their Subcontractors.

(b) If as a result of guarantee works the Vessel has been lying idle in the Guarantee Period for an accumulated period of 30 days or more, the Guarantee Period shall be extended by the total number of days the Vessel has been lying idle, whether or not other work is carried out during such period.

Norwegian 格式根据两种情形规定了质保期限的延长。第一种情形是发生了 11.46
质保缺陷的修理或替换的情形。在这种情况下,船厂应当针对已修理或更换的部分提供不低于 12 个月的质保。但是不存在一个最长的质保期限的问题,只要在质保期限内或在延长的质保期限内发生质保修理或替换的,船厂就应当提供不少于 12 个月的质保。第二种情形虽然也是发生了质保缺陷的修理或替换的情形,但并不是针对已修理或更换部分的质保延期,而是针对因修理或替换导致的船舶的闲置。一旦船舶因质保修理或替换导致闲置超过 30 天的,船舶的质保期限就应当有相应的延长。

NEWBUILDCON 格式也有关于闲置时间计入质保期限的类似规定,②但与 11.47
Norwegian 格式的规定有所不同。Norwegian 格式规定的 30 天闲置时间是累计的,而 NEWBUILDCON 格式规定的 30 天闲置时间则是连续的。

---

① Article X.2, para.5.
② Clause 35(f).

V 质保通知

标准格式的规定

11.48　船厂承担质保责任是以收到船东的质量缺陷通知为前提的,例如 SAJ 格式便有如下规定:①

> The BUYER shall notify the BUILDER in writing, or by cable confirmed in writing, of any defects for which claim is made under this guarantee as promptly as possible after discovery thereof. The BUYER's written notice shall describe the nature and extent of the defects. The BUILDER shall have no obligation for any defects discovered prior to the expiry date of the said twelve(12) months period, unless notice of such defects is received by the BUILDER not later than thirty(30) days after such expiry date.

11.49　SAJ 格式不仅规定了缺陷通知的形式,即书面通知,而且还规定了缺陷通知的内容,即对缺陷的性质进行描述。此外,船东的缺陷通知还应在发现缺陷后尽可能"及时"发出。船东的缺陷通知应当是船厂履行质保义务的前提,由于船厂已不再实际控制船舶,因此除非船上有船厂派遣的质保工程师,否则没有船东的通知船厂就不会知道缺陷的存在。但是,关于及时的要求应当不构成船东提出质保索赔的前提条件。除非船东无故拖延时间,而且船厂能够证明船东的拖延确实给船厂带来了损失或额外费用,否则船厂不能以船东未及时发出缺陷通知为由拒绝履行自己的质量保证义务。

11.50　另外,上述规定提及船厂在质保期限届满后的30天内收到船东质量缺陷通知的依然应当承担质保责任,但这并不意味着船厂应当承担在质保期限届满后发现的缺陷,而仅仅是指在质保期限内发现的缺陷,但由于发现缺陷之时质保期限已快要届满,而船东的质量缺陷通知只能在质保期限届满后送至船厂。只要缺陷是在质保期限届满后发现的,无论船东是否在质保期限届满后的30天内通知了船厂,船厂均无需承担质保责任。

11.51　CSTC 格式的规定与 SAJ 格式的规定基本相同,NEWBUILDCON 格式的措

---

① Article IX.2, see also CSTC Article IX.2.

辞虽有不同,但基本上没有脱离 SAJ 格式的模式。① AWES 格式使用的文字则比较简单,只是规定船东应当在发现质保缺陷后的 30 天内发出通知。② 相比之下,Norwegian 格式针对质保期限延长作出的规定比较特别:③

> Any such defects shall be notified to the Builder as soon as possible after discovery and at the latest within 8 days after expiry of the Guarantee Period. Such notice shall include particulars of the deficiency in such detail as can reasonably be expected.
>
> If defects could only be discovered on dry docking the vessel, notice of such defect(s) need not be tendered before the Vessel is in the dock, but must be tendered before the Vessel leaves the dry-docking.

上述第一部分的规定与 SAJ 等格式没有太大的区别,只是把 30 天改为 8 天而已。第二部分的规定应当是 Norwegian 格式所独有的,这一规定针对船舶进坞发现缺陷的情形。按照这一规定,如果船舶的缺陷只有通过船舶进坞才能被发现的,船东无需在进坞前发通知,但应当在船舶出坞前发通知。如果缺陷只能通过进坞才可能被发现,在船舶进坞前发通知显然是不现实的。这里的问题应当是 12 个月的质保期限是否依然有效。如果 12 个月的质保期同样适用于进坞才能发现的缺陷,上述第二段的规定恐怕没有什么意义了,因为进坞也应当在质保期内进行。如果 12 个月的质保期不适用于进坞才能发现的缺陷,质保期的约定就此种缺陷而言也就不再有意义了,因为船东可以在质保期届满后向船厂发出有效的缺陷通知。另外还有一种解释,即 12 个月的质保期依然适用,但若船东在质保期届满后船舶进坞时发现缺陷的可以向船厂发缺陷通知,但船东必须证明在船舶进坞时发现的缺陷实际上在交船后的 12 个月内就已存在。船东要证明这一点可能是比较困难的。

11.52

质保义务的前提

在船舶建造合同明确规定了缺陷通知的情况下,船东就应当按照合同规定发出缺陷通知,否则船厂就可能无需承担合同的质保义务,例如在 *Aktiebolaget Gotaverken* v *Westminster Corporation of Monrovia and Another*④ 一案中,船舶改装

11.53

---

① Clause 35(a)(ii).
② Article 12(a), para.2.
③ Article X.2, para.3, 4.
④ [1971] 2 Lloyd's Rep 505.

合同的第 13 条规定：

> Claims on account of delay in delivery shall be given by the customer as soon as the customer has been informed of the delay, at the latest, however, at the delivery.
>
> Claims on account of asserted defects or deficiencies of material or workmanship shall always be given immediately after such defects or deficiencies have been discovered.
>
> Where the customer has not given notice prior to the departure of the ship from the shipyard, the shipyard shall be discharged from all liability for the delivery, save that such hidden defects or deficiencies of material or workmanship as the customer obviously could not detect or should not have detected prior to delivery, may be claimed within [six] months after the delivery.

11.54　船东在交船后的第一个载货航次中发现舱口盖的设计有缺陷，货物因此遭受水损。船东在其他船厂对舱口盖进行了修理，但是依然没有解决水密问题，船东于是又采购了油布。但是在交船后的 6 个月内，除了修理成本外，船东没有按照第 13 条的规定提出其他索赔。高院的 Donaldson 法官认为，针对明显的缺陷，船东应当在船舶离开船厂之时提出；而针对隐藏的缺陷，船东则应当在 6 个月内提出。Donaldson 法官说：①

> In my judgment, the third paragraph of this regulation bars claims for patent defects, if they are not made on or before the departure of the vessel from the yard and for latent defects at the end of six months thereafter. The three months in the print was extended to six months by the last clause of the contract. The second paragraph of the regulation, which provides that claims "shall always be given immediately after" discovery, places an obligation on owners, the breach of which sounds in damages, but does not bar a claim. If, for example, the owners know that the engine bed-plates are defective but allow the engines to be installed before saying anything, they may be liable in respect of the additional cost of remedial work. Furthermore, "immediately" is not to be construed as "instantaneously". What is or is not "immediately" is a question of fact for the arbitrators.

---

① [1971] 2 Lloyd's Rep 505 at 513.

VI 修理和替换

大多数船舶建造合同都规定船厂对发现的质保缺陷负有修理或替换的义务。但不同合同的不同规定实际上给船厂的质保责任带来了相当大的变化。　11.55

SAJ 格式

按照 SAJ 格式的规定，船厂的质保义务是在船厂对质保缺陷进行修理或替换：①　11.56

> The BUILDER shall remedy, at its expense, any defects, against which the VESSEL is guaranteed under this Article, by making all necessary repairs or replacements at the Shipyard.

由于船厂的质保义务是在船厂对质保责任范围的缺陷进行修理或更换并承担费用，这就意味着船东在发现质保缺陷时应当将船舶驶回船厂。这一规定显然是不利于船东的，而且可以说是不公平的。因为在很多情况下船舶往返船厂的费用会远远超过质保缺陷的修理或替换费用。于是，SAJ 格式对此作出了例外的规定：②　11.57

> However, if it is impractical to bring the VESSEL to the Shipyard, the BUYER may cause the necessary repairs or replacements to be made elsewhere which is deemed suitable for the purpose, provided that, in such event, the BUILDER may forward or supply replacement parts or materials to the VESSEL, unless forwarding or supplying thereof to the VESSEL would impair or delay the operation or working schedule of the VESSEL. In the event that the BUYER proposes to cause the necessary repairs or replacements to be made to the VESSEL, at any other shipyard or works than the Shipyard, the BUYER shall first, but in all events as soon as possible, give the BUILDER notice in writing or by cable confirmed in writing of the time and place such repairs will be made, and if the VESSEL is not thereby delayed, or her operation or working schedule is not thereby impaired, the BUILDER shall have the right to verify by its own representative(s) the nature and extents of the defects complained of. The BUILDER shall, in such case, promptly advise

---

① Article IX.3(a).
② Article IX.3(b).

the BUYER by cable, after such examination has been completed, of its acceptance or rejection of the defects as ones that are covered by the guarantee herein provided. Upon the BUILDER's acceptance of the defects as justifying remedy under this Article or upon award of the arbitration so determining, the BUILDER shall immediately pay to the BUYER for such repairs or replacements a sum equal to the reasonable cost of making the same repairs or replacements in the Shipyard.

11.58　除非船舶就在船厂附近，否则"不切实际"这一条件通常是可以满足的。一旦这一条件得到满足，船厂可以做的只能是为修理或替换提供配件或材料了，而且也必须是在不影响船舶营运情况下进行。虽然船厂可以派遣自己的代表对质保缺陷进行核实，但这同样要以不影响船舶营运为前提。值得一提的是上述规定的最后一句，即在船东自己实施质保修理或替换的情况下，船厂的义务是向船东支付在船厂实施相同修理或替换的合理成本。这一规定实际上推翻了同一条款中关于船东在将船舶驶往船厂不切实际时可以在其他地点实施质保缺陷的修理或替换的规定。对船厂而言，船东自己实施质保缺陷修理或替换在不增加成本的同时至少避免了船厂的时间支出。

AWES 格式

11.59　AWES 格式关于船厂质保义务的规定与 SAJ 格式的大致相同，也有关于例外的规定：①

> If the replacements or repair under this Article cannot be conveniently made at (one of) the CONTRACTOR's yard(s), the PURCHASER may have carried out elsewhere such repairs and/or replacements; in such a case the CONTRACTOR is discharged from this guarantee and shall reimburse the PURCHASER the documented expenses incurred by the PURCHASER, but such a reimbursement shall not exceed the estimated costs of carrying out the guarantee work at the CONTRACTOR's yard(s).

Norwegian 格式

11.60　Norwegian 格式针对船厂的质保责任作出了如下规定：②

---

① Article 12(a), para.5.
② Article IX.3.

The repair, replacements and/or rectifications shall be made at the Builder's yard. However, the Buyer may, after having notified the Builder in writing, cause the necessary repairs, replacements and/or rectifications to be carried out elsewhere. In such case, the Builder shall at its own costs be entitled to forward necessary replacement parts or materials.

The Builder's liability shall in such case be limited to pay the cost of repairs including travelling and forwarding expenses (unless paid by Subcontractors), but limited to the price of the work which the Builder would normally charge at its yard.

11.61 虽然规定修理和替换应当在船厂进行,但随后的一句实际上已经将是否在船厂进行质保修理或替换的权利交给了船东。船东只要给船厂发出通知就可以在其他地方对质保缺陷进行修理或替换。而且,船东决定在其他地方对质保缺陷进行修理或替换并不以将船舶驶回船厂不经济或不切实际为条件的。船东完全可以按照自己的意愿行事。但有意思的是,按照上述规定,无论船东花费了多少修理或替换费用,船厂只需按照自己船厂的标准支付修理或替换费用。

11.62 当船舶建造合同明确规定船东在委托第三人对质保缺陷进行修理或替换之前应当书面通知船厂,船东若擅自委托第三人对质保缺陷实施修理或替换,船厂应当只需承担自己对质保缺陷进行修理或替换而需产生的合理费用。在 *Pearce and High Limited v Baxter*① 一案中,原告是建筑商,为被告建造房屋,建造合同的第2.5条规定:

> Any defects, excessive shrinkages or other faults which appear within six months ... of the date of practical completion and are due to materials or workmanship not in accordance with the contract or frost occurring before practical completion shall be made good by the contractor entirely at his own cost unless the architect ... shall otherwise instruct.

11.63 上诉法院认为如果被告未按合同第2.5条的规定允许建筑商对被发现的缺陷进行补救,或者在发现缺陷后通知建筑商都将影响到其可以从建筑商那里获得赔偿的数额。Evans 法官说:②

---

① (1999) 1 TCLR 157.
② (1999) 1 TCLR 157 at 162.

The cost of employing a third party repairer is likely to be higher than the cost to the contractor of doing the work himself would have been. So the right to return in order to repair the defect is valuable to him. The question arises whether, if he is denied the right, the employer is entitled to employ another party and to recover the full cost of doing so as damages for the contractor's original breach. In my judgment, the contractor is not liable for the full cost of repairs in those circumstances. The employer cannot recover more than the amount that it would have cost the contractor himself to remedy the defects.

CSTC 格式

11.64　　CSTC 格式的规定与 SAJ 格式的规定不太相同,可能是考虑了来自船东的反对意见,CSTC 格式不再要求船东将发生质保缺陷的船舶驶回船厂进行修理或替换了:①

The SELLER shall remedy at its expense any defects, against which the VESSEL or any part of the equipment thereof is guaranteed under this Article by making all necessary repairs and/or replacement. Such repairs and/or replacement will be made by the SELLER.

However, if it is impractical to make the repair by the SELLER, and if forwarding by the SELLER of replacement parts and materials can not be accomplished without impairing or delaying the operation or working of the VESSEL, then, in any such event, the BUYER shall, cause the necessary repairs or replacements to be made elsewhere at the discretion of the BUYER provided that the BUYER shall first and in all events, will, as soon as possible, give the SELLER notice in writing, or by telex confirmed in writing of the time and place such repairs will be made and, if the VESSEL is not thereby delayed, or her operation or working is not thereby delayed, or her operation or working is not thereby impaired, the SELLER shall have the right to verify by its own representative(s) or that of Classification Society the nature and extent of the defects complained of. The SELLER shall, in such cases, promptly advise the BUYER, by telex, after such examination has been completed, of its acceptance or rejection of the defects as ones that are subject to the guarantee herein provided. In all minor cases, the

---

① Article IX.3, para.1 & 2.

Guarantee Engineer, as hereinafter provided for, will act for and on behalf of the SELLER.

11.65 由于CSTC格式没有对SAJ格式作出结构上的改动,因此SAJ格式中的"船舶驶回船厂不切实际"的规定就成了CSTC格式中的"船厂修理不切实际"。按照上述规定,船东在其他地方对船舶的质保缺陷进行修理或替换应当满足两个前提:第一是回船厂修理不切实际;第二是为了修理或替换运送部件或材料将影响或延误船舶的营运。这两个前提实际上都与时间有关,虽然让船舶驶回船厂往往是不切实际的,但船厂修理并不一定是指在船厂修理,船厂派遣自己的雇员或委托他人对质保缺陷实施修理或替换同样是船厂的修理,而这种修理则未必会在时间上给船舶的营运造成延误。

11.66 CSTC格式可能是第一个作出参照相关船厂报价确定船东产生的修理或替换费用规定的标准格式。在实际采用中往往还加上了中国船厂。①

In any circumstances as set out below, the SELLER shall immediately pay to the BUYER in United States Dollars by telegraphic transfer the actual cost for such repairs or replacements including forwarding charges, or at the average cost for making similar repairs or replacements including forwarding charges as quoted by a leading shipyard each in Japan, South Korea and Singapore, whichever is lower:

(a) upon the SELLER's acceptance of the defects as justifying remedy under this Article, or

(b) if the SELLER neither accepts nor rejects the defects as above provided, nor request arbitration within thirty (30) days after its receipt of the BUYER's notice of defects.

NEWBUILDCON 格式

11.67 NEWBUILDCON格式的规定有不少与其他标准格式不同之处:②

The Builder shall make any necessary repairs or replacements to rectify any Guarantee Defects or damage to the Vessel caused as a direct and immediate consequence of such Guarantee Defects. Such repairs and

---

① Article IX.3, para.3.
② Clause 35(b), (c), (d).

replacements shall be made at the Shipyard at the Builder's cost and expense.

11.68　首先，虽然船厂有机会在船厂对质保缺陷进行修理或替换，但是船厂所承担的质保责任不仅仅是对质保缺陷进行修理或替换，而且还包括对因质保缺陷而产生的损害进行修理或替换。这一区别应当是比较根本的，因为它扩大了船厂的质保责任的范围。

> The Buyer shall have the right to arrange for the necessary repairs to rectify any Guarantee Defects or damage to the Vessel caused as a direct and immediate consequence of such Guarantee Defects to be made elsewhere or obtain any necessary replacement parts and materials:
>
> (i) if it is impractical to bring the Vessel to the Shipyard; or
> (ii) if the Builder cannot supply necessary replacement parts and materials without impairing or delaying the operation or working of the Vessel.

11.69　其次，NEWBUILDCON 格式明确规定在其他地方对质保缺陷及其造成的损害进行修理或替换是船东的权利，此项权利的行使只需符合两个条件中的任何一个，即将船舶驶回船厂不切实际，或者船厂提供部件和材料将影响或延误船舶的营运或工作。这一规定的实际意义就是推翻了前面关于船厂可以在船厂进行修理和替换的规定。

> In the event that the Buyer makes the necessary repairs or replacements at any other shipyard or works other than the Shipyard, the Buyer shall first, but as soon as possible, give the Builder notice of the time and place such repairs will be made. The Builder shall have the right, without prejudice, to inspect through its own representative the nature and extent of the Guarantee Defects to be replaced or repaired. The Builder shall, in such case, promptly advise the Buyer in writing, after such examination has been completed, of its acceptance or rejection of such Guarantee Defects as ones that are covered by the guarantee.
>
> (i) The Builder shall pay the Buyer in the currency stated in Box 9 the reasonable cost and expenses of such repairs or replacements.
> (ii) Where applicable, the Buyer shall return replaced parts to the Builder at the Builder's request and cost and expense provided the Builder makes such request at the time of the replacement. In the event that they are the subject of a dispute under Clause 42 (Dispute

Resolution), the Builder shall hold the replaced parts available for inspection by the Buyer. Upon their replacement, the ownership of replaced parts shall revert to the Builder.

再次,当船东决定在其他地方对质保缺陷及其造成的损害进行修理或替换时,船厂似乎是不能反对的,而只能要求对将要被修理或替换的质保缺陷进行检查。有意思的是,虽然船东修理或替换的对象不仅包括质保缺陷,而且还包括质保缺陷造成的船舶损坏,但上述规定仅提及船厂可以检查质保缺陷的性质和程度。在船厂应当对质保缺陷造成损害进行修理或替换的情况下,船厂应当可以对由质保缺陷造成的损坏的性质和程度进行检查。　　11.70

最后,按照上述规定,船东在其他地方对质保缺陷进行了修理或替换后,船厂可以要求船东提供被替换了的部件并为此承担费用。但是规定船厂必须在替换之时提出此种要求似乎并不合理。既然是质保范围之内的,发生缺陷的部件应当是船厂制造或提供的,因此在船厂完成了替换后,被替换的部件就应当是船厂的财产,这一点其实已经在上述规定中得到了确认。因此,除非得到船厂的许可,船东应当无权随意处置被替换了的部件。从最后一句来看,似乎在发生争议时只有船厂才有义务保留被替换了的部件供船东检验。　　11.71

Ⅶ 间接损失

特征

按照 SAJ 格式的规定,船厂根据船舶建造合同承担质保责任有一个明显的特征,即船厂仅承担船舶缺陷产生的修理或替换,而不承担因缺陷导致的其他损失的赔偿责任。SAJ 格式的规定是:①　　11.72

> The BUILDER shall have no responsibility or liability for any other defects whatsoever in the VESSEL than the defects specified in Paragraph 1 of this Article. Nor the BUILDER shall in any circumstances be responsible or liable for any consequential or special losses, damages or expenses including, but not limited to, loss of time, loss of profit or earning or demurrage directly or indirectly occasioned to the BUYER be reason of the defects specified in Paragraph 1 of this

---

① Article Ⅸ.4(a).

Article or due to repairs or other works done to the VESSEL to remedy such defects.

11.73 根据上述规定，船厂承担的只是对质保缺陷进行修理或替换，而不承担其他责任。在 *China Shipbuilding Corp* v *Nippon Yusen Kabukishi Kaisha & Another* 一案中，船舶建造合同的质保条款包括如下内容：

> The Builder, for a period of twelve months following acceptance by the Buyer of the vessel, guarantees the vessel, her hull and machinery and all parts and equipments thereof which are manufactured, furnished or supplied by the Builder and/or its subcontractors under this contract against all defects in materials and/or workmanship on the part of the Builder and/or its subcontractor; provided, however, that the Builder's warranties under this contract do not extend nor apply to the Buyer's supplies(as defined hereinafter). The Builder's obligations under this Article are limited to the repair and replacement at its costs of all defects against which the Builder's guarantees are given under this Article.

11.74 高院的 Thomas 法官认为上述条款规定的船厂责任是修理和替换，而不包括其他责任，他说：①

> There was also argument before the arbitrators as to the claim for diminution in value; on the arbitrators' conclusion, the point did not arise, but they expressed the view that if, contrary to their conclusions, the claim for breach of art. I was covered by art. IX, the claim for diminution in value was excluded by the last sentence of art. IX.1. I agree with that view. The liability the yard accepted under art.IX.I was limited to repair and replacement; this of necessity meant that there was no claim for diminution in value.

结果性损失

11.75 这里的"结果性"（consequential）和"特别"（special）都应当做"间接"解释。"结果性损失"或"特别损失"通常是指那些非直接的或者遥远的损失，而不包括在正常情况下事件直接导致的自然结果。在 *Saint Line Limted* v *Richardsons, Westgarth & Co Limited* 一案中，Atkinson 法官说：②

---

① [2000] CLC 566 at 574.
② [1940] 2 KB 99 at 103.

The word "consequential" is not very illuminating, as all damage is in a sense consequential, but there is a definition in the Oxford English Dictionary to which both sides have appealed: "Of the nature, of a consequence, merely; not direct or immediate; eventual." It cites the definition of "consequential damages" from Wharton as: "losses or injuries which follow an act, but are not direct or immediate upon it." But, apart from that, I have the guidance of the Court of Appeal as to what is meant by "consequential." In *Millar's Machinery Company, Ld* v *David Way & Son*, where the Court was construing a clause of the same class as this, I find this that Maugham LJ said: "On the question of damages the word 'consequential' has come to mean 'not direct'." Roche LJ agreed "that the damages recovered by the defendants on the counterclaim were not merely 'consequential' but resulted directly and naturally from the plaintiffs' breach of contract." It is quite clear that the Court there took it for granted that the word "consequential" meant "merely consequential" and referred to something which was not the direct and natural result of the breach.

11.76 在 *Croudace Construction Ltd* v *Cawoods Concrete Products Ltd*① 一案中, 买卖合同的第 4 条规定:

No complaint of any kind can be entertained (except in special circumstances justifying delay) unless it is made within 24 hours after the time of supply of the material or goods of which complaint is made. Although we make every effort to supply materials or goods strictly to accord with the quality or specification ordered, if any materials or goods supplied by us should be defective or not of the correct quality or specification ordered our liability shall be limited to free replacement of any materials or goods shown to be unsatisfactory. We are not under any circumstances to be liable for any consequential loss or damage caused or arising by reason of late supply or any fault failure or defect in any material or goods supplied by us or by reason of the same not being of the quality or specification ordered or by any other matter whatsoever.

11.77 买方以卖方供货迟延为由要求卖方赔偿损失, 高院认为"consequential"一词并不包括任何"在正常情况下, 迟延交货直接造成和自然引起的损失", Parker 法官说:②

---

① [1978] 2 Lloyd's Rep 55.
② [1978] 2 Lloyd's Rep 55 at 58.

> It is in my judgment clear that the word "consequential" is, in the present context, used to describe or indicate a type of loss or damage which is in some way less direct or more remote than that loss or damage which is to remain recoverable despite the exclusion. This appears to me to follow from the ordinary use of the words and from the fact that it would be commercial nonsense to give it any other meaning.

11.78　上诉法院支持一审的判决,Lord Megaw 法官说:①

> Accordingly, taking the view that I do, that Mr. Justice Parker was right to hold that the word "consequential" does not cover any loss which directly and naturally results in the ordinary course of events from late delivery, I would dismiss the appeal.

事实问题的认定

11.79　但是什么是直接损失,什么是间接损失是一个事实问题。在 *Deepak Fertilisers and Petrochemicals Corporation* v *ICI Chemicals & Polymers Ltd and Others*② 一案中,原告在印度建造一座甲醇工厂,被告为之提供了技术。合同的第6.8条有如下内容:

> DAVY does not assume any liability except as expressly set out in the CONTRACT and in no event shall DAVY by reason of its performance or obligation under this CONTRACT be liable in tort or for loss [of] anticipated profits, catalyst, raw materials and products or for indirect or consequential damage.

11.80　1991年9月工厂建造完毕并开始测试,10月生产出第一批甲醇。但从一开始甲醇转化炉就无法在设计允许温度内工作,而且提高温度后问题依然存在。1992年10月30日,甲醇转化炉发生爆炸,工厂的所有生产因此全部停工。原告起诉要求被告赔偿损失。高院认为由于合同第6.8条的规定,被告无需承担所有列明的责任,包括利润损失。高院的 Rix 法官认为利润损失是间接损失。但是上诉法院则认为被告之所以无需承担原告的利润损失是因为合同条款明确予以了排除,而不是因为利润损失是间接损失,上诉法院并不接受 *Croudace Construction*

---

① [1978] 2 Lloyd's Rep 55 at 62.
② [1998] 2 Lloyd's Rep 139.

Ltd v Cawoods Concrete Products Ltd 一案的判决。上诉法院的 Stuart-Smith 法官说：①

> We are unable to accept that conclusion. The direct and natural result of the destruction of the plant was that Deepak was left without a methanol plant, the reconstruction of which would cost money and take time, losing for Deepak any methanol production in the meantime. Wasted overheads incurred during the reconstruction of the plant, as well as profits lost during that period, are no more remote as losses than the cost of reconstruction. Lost profits cannot be recovered because they are excluded in terms, not because they are too remote. We consider that this Court is bound by the decision in *Croudace* where a similar loss was not excluded by a similar exclusion and considered to be direct loss. Accordingly we cannot agree with the learned Judge's conclusion:
>
> > In essence, thereforc, loss of profits and overhead expenses thrown away are too closely related elements of the consequential loss which flows from a break in production.
>
> We have come to the conclusion that this was an error in law and that the finding of the Judge on this issue must be reversed.

建造合同规定

与上文提及的 SAJ 格式的规定相类似，AWES 格式也明确规定船厂及其分包商和供应商除了约定质保责任外既不承担直接损失，也不承担间接损失：②   11.81

> ... the CONTRACTOR's liability shall be limited to the above mentioned obligations as to extent and duration and the CONTRACTOR and/or its subcontractors and suppliers shall have no further liability whatsoever for any direct or indirect loss, damages or expense in any way deriving from or connected with the above defects ....

上述规定提及的损失不仅包括因质保缺陷引起的损失，而且还包括与质保缺陷有关的损失，而且这里的损失包括灭失、损坏以及费用。Norwegian 格式也规定船厂也应承担质保缺陷造成的船舶的损坏：③   11.82

---

① [1999] 1 Lloyd's Rep 387 at 403.
② Article 12(a), para.3.
③ Article X.3(a).

> ... the Builder shall have no other liability for any damage or loss caused as a consequence of the defect, except for repair or renewal of the Vessel's part/parts that have been damaged as a direct and immediate consequence of the defect without any intermediate cause, and provided such part or parts can be considered to form a part of the same equipment or same system . . . .

11.83　按照上述规定,船厂应当承担质保缺陷造成的损坏责任的前提是:(1)损失是质保缺陷直接造成的,没有任何其他因素促成此种损失的产生;(2)受损坏的部分是发现质保缺陷的设备或系统的组成部分。此外,Norwegian 格式虽然明确规定被替换的部件归船厂所有,但以船厂在合理期限内提出要求为条件:①

> The Builder shall have the ownership of replaced parts. The Buyer will return such parts to the Builder at Builder's request and at Builder's expense. If the Builder fails to present such request within a reasonable time, the Buyer has no responsibility for the replaced parts.

11.84　其实,在所有权已经明确的情况下,实际占有被替换部件的船东负有照管这些部件的责任。虽然船东有权要求船厂补偿其为保管这些部件所产生的所有费用,但在没有通知船厂的情况下,船东应当无权处置这些部件,否则应对相应的后果承担责任。

11.85　CSTC 格式关于船厂免责的规定有如下内容:②

> Upon delivery of the VESSEL to the BUYER, in accordance with the terms of the Contract, the SELLER shall thereby and thereupon be released of all responsibility and liability whatsoever and howsoever arising under or by virtue of this Contract (save in respect of those obligations to the BUYER expressly provided for in this Article IX) including without limitation, any responsibility or liability for defective workmanship, materials or equipment, design or in respect of any other defects whatsoever and any loss or damage resulting from any act, omission or default of the SELLER. Neither CSTC nor the BUILDER shall, in any circumstances, be liable for any consequential loss or special loss, or expenses arising from any cause whatsoever including, without limitation, loss of time, loss of profit or earnings or demurrage

---

① Article X.3(d).
② Article IX.4, para.3.

directly from any commitments of the BUYER in connection with the VESSEL.

  根据上述规定,船厂无需承担的责任可以分为两个部分,第一部分是船厂对有缺陷的工艺、材料或设备、设计或因船厂的行为或违约造成的灭失或损坏不承担责任,但这是以船厂按照合同规定承担质保责任即第 IX 条规定的责任为前提的。然而,实际上并不存在两种由于缺陷工艺、材料或设计引起的损失,船厂应当对其中一种负责,而对另一种不负责。只要是在质保期限内的,船厂不仅应当对工艺、材料或设计的缺陷负责,而且还要对质保缺陷造成的船舶损坏负责。第二部分才是通常意义上的免责范围。 11.86

第三人的修理或替换

  允许第三人对船厂承担质保的缺陷进行修理已成为船舶建造业的惯例了,然而,一旦修理或替换是由船厂以外的第三人实施的,船厂就无需为此种修理或替换提供质保了。对此,SAJ 格式就有如下规定:① 11.87

> The BUILDER shall not be responsible for any defects in any part of the VESSEL which may subsequent to delivery of the VESSEL have been replaced or in any way repaired by any other contractor ....

  当然,如果实施修理或替换的第三人是根据船厂的指示或请求行事的,船厂自然应当对修理或替换继续承担质保责任。NEWBUILDCON 格式则有如下规定:② 11.88

> The Builder shall not be responsible for any Defects in any part of the Vessel which may, subsequent to delivery of the Vessel, have been replaced or in any way repaired by any contractor, other than the Builder or its Sub-contractors ....

  上述规定的含义应当是明确的,但是在上述规定中使用"Defects"应当是有问题的,因为"Defects"是有特定含义的词。按照 NEWBUILDCON 格式定义条款的规定,"Defects"是指"船厂或其分包商的设计、建造、材料或工艺的缺陷或不足"。因此不应用有特定含义的 Defects 来描述由第三人进行修理或替换时产生"缺陷"。 11.89

---

① Article IX.4(b).
② Clause 37(c).

其他原因

11.90 　　这里的"其他原因"主要是指自然损耗以及船东自身的原因。自然损耗是必然的,不可避免的,因此船厂无需为此负责。此外,船东无疑应当为其自身原因造成的缺陷承担责任。这两种原因的一个共同特征是:均为船厂无法控制的原因。SAJ格式对作出了如下规定:①

> The BUILDER shall not be responsible ... for any defects which have been caused or aggravated by omission or improper use and maintenance of the VESSEL on the part of the BUYER, its servants or agents or by ordinary wear and tear or by any other circumstances whatsoever beyond the control of the BUILDER.

11.91 　　AWES格式也类似的规定:②

> ... the CONTRACTOR ... shall have no further liability whatsoever ... for defects due to normal wear and tear or overloading or due to corrosion of the materials or due to accidents, fire, improper loading or stowage of the VESSEL, mismanagement or negligence in the use and maintenance of the VESSEL.

11.92 　　NEWBUILDCON格式则有如下规定:③

> The Builder shall not be responsible ... for any such Defects which have been caused in whole or part by omission or improper use of maintenance of the Vessel on the part of the Buyer or by ordinary wear and tear.

11.93 　　同样,按照上述规定船厂无需对因船东的行为及自然损耗引起的缺陷负责,但"Defects"一词的使用应当是有问题的,正确的应当使用"defects"。

责任排除的效力

11.94 　　合同中排除责任的条款或规定应当是明确的,否则就有可能是无效的。正如上诉法院在 *J Gordon Alison & Co Ltd* v *Wallsend Shipway and Engineering Co Ltd*

---

① Article IX.4(b).
② Article 12(a), para.3.
③ Clause 37(c).

一案中所说的：①

> ... if a person was under a legal liability and wished to get rid of it he could only do so by using clear words.

合同条款的解释原则同样适用于排除责任条款的解释，排除责任的条款应当是相当明确且无歧义的。上议院的 Lord Wilberforce 在 *Ailsa Graig Fishing Co Ltd v Malvern Fishing Co Ltd(The Strathallan)* 一案中说：② 11.95

> Whether a clause limiting liability is effective or not is a question of construction of that clause in the context of the contract as a whole. If it is to exclude liability for negligence, it must be most clearly and unambiguously expressed, and in such a contract as this, must be construed *contra proferentem*. I do not think that there is any doubt so far.

按照 SAJ 格式的规定，船厂根据船舶建造合同承担质保责任有一个明显的特征，即船厂仅承担船舶缺陷产生的修理或替换，而不承担因缺陷导致的其他损失的赔偿责任。SAJ 格式的规定是：③ 11.96

> The BUILDER shall have no responsibility or liability for any other defects whatsoever in the VESSEL than the defects specified in Paragraph 1 of this Article. Nor the BUILDER shall in any circumstances be responsible or liable for any consequential or special losses, damages or expenses including, but not limited to, loss of time, loss of profit or earning or demurrage directly or indirectly occasioned to the BUYER be reason of the defects specified in Paragraph 1 of this Article or due to repairs or other works done to the VESSEL to remedy such defects.

船舶建造合同中关于排除船厂责任的规定应当明确，因为只有明确的措辞才会起到排除责任的效果。在 *BHP Petroleum Ltd and Others v British Steel Plc and Dalmine SpA*④ 一案中，原告和被告订立合同，约定由被告为原告在海上安装的天然气回注管系提供钢材。供应合同的第 14.5 条有下列规定： 11.97

---

① [1983] 1 WLR 964 at 966.
② (1927) 43 TLR 323 at 324.
③ Article IX.4(a).
④ [1999] 2 Lloyd's Rep 583.

Neither the Supplier nor the Purchaser shall bear any liability to the other ... for loss of production, loss of profits, loss of business or any other indirect losses or consequential damages arising during and/or as a result of the performance or non-performance of this Contract regardless of the cause thereof but not limited to the negligence of the party seeking to rely on this provision.

11.98 供应合同的第 17.5 条则有如下规定:

The Supplier shall immediately remedy, at the contracted point of delivery, at his expense any defect in the Work due to faulty design, materials or workmanship which shall appear within eighteen (18) months of the date stated in the Purchase Order or such longer period as may be provided in the Purchase Order, but not later than twenty-four months after delivery of the Work to the Purchaser ... at which time all liability of the Supplier relating to the Works shall terminate.... The Suppliers [sic] liability hereunder shall not exceed 15% ... of the Contract Price by Line Item – the payment of which shall fully discharge all liabilities of the Supplier ....

11.99 1994 年 2 月 11 日,管系送到了现场,焊接后管系在 4 月 30 日和 6 月 27 日之间铺设完毕。1996 年 4 月投入使用。1996 年 6 月,原告发现管系有裂缝,于是在 7 月通知了被告,并且取了样进行测试。原告认为裂缝是由于管子不符合规格要求导致的。法院需要解决的问题是:(1) 按照合同第 17.5 条的规定,被告在交付两年后即 1996 年 2 月 11 日后是否已无需承担责任了;(2) 如果对(1) 的答案是否定的,那么被告的责任是否以合同价格的 15% 为限。高院认为:(1) 中的合同第 17.5 条第一句包含了针对所有缺陷,包括没有在 24 个月内出现的缺陷的责任终止条款;(2) 中的合同第 17.5 条最后一句规定对所有责任,无论是否因疏忽引起,作出了合同价 15% 的限定。高院的 Rix 法官认为,合同第 17.5 条中的 "all liabilities" 是指所有责任,既包括合同的责任,也包括疏忽的责任。他说的是:①

> First, prima facie "all liability of the Supplier relating to the Work" is wider than liability merely under the rectification obligation contained in cl.17.5, whether that obligation is viewed as found in the first sentence of that clause or in the clause as a whole. If it had been intended to limit the cesser of liability merely to the additional obligation to remedy

---

① [1999] 2 Lloyd's Rep 583 at 591.

defects at the contracted point of delivery, then no words of exclusion would have been necessary at all .... "All liability of the Supplier relating to the Work" can be contrasted with the supplier's much more limited liability to remedy defects in the work which appear within 24 months, even if that liability is viewed as extending also to the additional obligations accepted in the rest of cl.17.5.

原告上诉但被驳回,上诉法院的 May 法官认为,虽然合同第 17.5 条起草得并不完美,但是其含义则是明确的,他说:①

11.100

> In my judgment, the meaning of cl.17.5 is as follows. The first part of the first sentence obliged and entitled British Steel to remedy, at their expense at the contracted point of delivery, defects in the Work due to faulty design, materials or workmanship which appeared within ... 18 months of the date stated in the Purchase Order .... The obligation to remedy defects so appearing did not depend on notice being given to British Steel requiring them to do the remedial work, as is common in other clauses of this general kind. The obligation depended on the defect appearing within the period, which would be a question of fact. The obligation to remedy a defect so appearing would not, by virtue of the subsequent limitation provision, cease if the remedial work were not accomplished until after the 18-month period had expired .... The words "at which time all liability of the Supplier relating to the Work shall terminate" mean what they clearly say. "All liability ... relating to the Work" embraces all liability arising out of the contract and its performance .... The words themselves are not apt to limit only the liability imposed on British Steel by cl.17.5 itself, which is limited in time anyway without them. Nor are these clear words to be tortured so as not to apply to exclude liabilities of British Steel which might be framed in negligence .... More importantly, perhaps, liability arising out of these and similar obligations to take due care would be liability "relating to the Work" which, by definition, included "all services ... to be provided by the Supplier under the contract".

从上述判例中可以看出,只要措辞明确,船厂不仅可以从时间上约定质保责任,而且也可以从数额上约定质保责任。

11.101

---

① [2000] 2 Lloyd's Rep 277 at 288.

排除责任的无效

11.102 合同中排除一方责任的条款并非始终有效,如果责任的产生是由于主张免责一方的违约行为,即使条款的措辞相当明确也一样无济于事。*Photo Productions Ltd v Securicor Transport Ltd*① 一案便是一例。在该案中,原告和被告订立合同,由被告为原告提供夜间巡逻的服务。合同的责任排除条款有如下内容:

> Under no circumstances shall the Company be responsible for any injurious act ... by any employee of the Company unless such act ... could have been foreseen and avoided by the exercise of due diligence on the part of the Company as his employer, nor in any event shall the Company be held responsible for:
>
> (a) any loss suffered by the customer through ... fire ... except insofar as such loss is solely attributable to the negligence of the Company's employees acting within the course of their employment ....

11.103 一天,被告的巡夜人员在原告的工厂内放火并导致工厂遭受严重损失。高院的 Mackenna 法官认为被告可以凭上述条款免除责任,上诉法院则作出了相反的判决。上诉法院认为合同的目的是保证工厂的安全,而纵火则是受雇的巡夜人员应当避免发生的事,因此被告不能援引合同中的责任排除条款。而且责任排除条款也没有包括故意毁坏的行为。然而上议院又推翻了上诉法院的判决,上议院认为在没有责任排除条款的情况下,被告承担的是绝对的责任。但是责任排除条款已经将这一绝对的责任修改为作为雇主的恪尽职责的责任了。Lord Diplock 是这样说的:②

> Applying these principles to the instant case; in the absence of the exclusion clause which Lord Wilberforce has cited, a primary obligation of Securicor under the contract, which would be implied by law, would be an absolute obligation to procure that the visits by the night patrol to the factory were conducted by natural persons who would exercise reasonable skill and care for the safety of the factory. That primary obligation is modified by the exclusion clause. Securicor's obligation to

---

① [1980] 1 Lloyd's Rep 545.
② [1980] 1 Lloyd's Rep 545 at 554.

do this is not to be absolute, but is limited to exercising due diligence in its capacity as employer of the natural persons by whom the visits are conducted, to procure that those persons shall exercise reasonable skill and care for the safety of the factory.

Ⅷ 质保的转让

转让的意义

船厂向船东提供的质保通常由两个部分组成,一部分是船厂自己提供的质保,例如船壳和船体结构等;另一部分则是船厂以分包商或供应商提供的质保为基础转而向船东提供的质保,例如船厂采购的主机和设备等。由于第二种质保实际上并不是船厂直接提供的,因此在实践中经常可以看见船厂将供应商提供的质保转让给船东。SAJ 格式没有关于质保转让的规定,但是 Norwegian 格式则有如下规定:①

> The Builder shall – upon the Buyer's request – assign to the Buyer any rights the Builder may have against any Subcontractors, including any right to pursue any claim under the relevant subcontract. This provision shall in no way alter or diminish the Builder's obligations under this Contract.
>
> The Builder shall endeavour to have provisions in the subcontracts whereby the Buyer may claim against the Subcontractor directly.

11.104

从上述规定来看,是否要求船厂转让质保应当是船东的权利。船东享有这一权利应当是符合船东的利益,而且也不会给船厂带来不利和不便。船厂应当做的是,在和分包商或供应商订立分包合同或采购合同时应确保分包商或供应商提供的质保是可以转让的。在船厂将质保转让给了船东的情况下,一旦发生应当由船厂的分包商或供应商负责的质保索赔,船东就可以和船厂的分包商或供应商直接接洽质保事宜。

11.105

非正常情况转让

NEWBUILDCON 格式也有关于质保转让的规定,但是该格式的规定似乎有

11.106

---

① Article X.4.

些费解：①

> Without prejudice to any other rights the Buyer may have under this Contract, following the expiry of the Guarantee Period or in the event that the Builder is in breach of its obligation to rectify Guarantee Defects in accordance with this Clause, the Builder shall at the Buyer's request assign(to the extent to which it may validly do so) to the Buyer, or as the Buyer may direct, the right, title and interest of the Builder in and to all guarantees or warranties given by the Sub-contractors or suppliers of any of the materials or equipment used in the construction of the Vessel.

11.107　上述规定实际上包含了船东要求船厂转让质保的两种情形，第一种情形是"质保期限届满"，第二种情形是船厂未能按照船舶建造合同的规定对质保责任范围内的缺陷进行修理或替换。第一种情形中的"质保期限"是有特定含义的，即该格式的方格部分规定的月份数为 12 个月。②然而在合同规定的质保期限届满之后转让质保似乎是没有意义的，因为船厂的质保义务已经终止了。即使船厂持有的分包商或供应商提供的质保期限超过船舶建造合同规定的质保期限，船厂的合同质保义务同样在质保期限届满时终止了。第二种船厂转让质保的情形是船厂违约，同样不是很清楚为何要在船厂违约时才转让质保。在正常情况下，由于真正提供质保的并不是船厂，而是船厂的分包商或供应商，因此船厂违约并不是较好的理由，如果船厂的违约是由于提供质保的分包商或供应商的违约所致，在这种情况下转让质保似乎同样也解决不了问题。

11.108　AWES 格式也有质保转让的规定，但似乎局限于分包商或供应商提供的质保的期限长于船厂提供的质保期限的质保：③

> In the event that the guarantee period provided by manufacturers or suppliers of various components of machinery, materials, equipment, appurtenances and outfit furnished to the CONTRACTOR and embodied in the VESSEL exceeds the aforesaid guarantee period, such extended guarantee rights are to be assigned and made available to the PURCHASER by the CONTRACTOR to the extent possible.

---

① Clause 35(g).
② 按照 NEWBUILDCON 格式方格 20 的规定，在没有规定质保期限时适用 12 月的质保期限。
③ Article 12(a), para.7.

换言之,如果分包商或供应商提供的质保的期限短于船厂提供的质保期限时似乎是不用转让的。然而,转让质保应当是船东的利益。 11.109

转售中的转让

Norwegian 格式不但针对船厂和船东之间的质保转让作出了规定,而且还针对因船东转手船舶可能产生的质保转让作出了规定:① 11.110

> If the Buyer sells the Vessel during the Guarantee Period and wishes to assign its rights hereunder, such assignment shall be subject to the Builder's consent, which shall not be unreasonably withheld or delay.

上述规定可能是多余的,因为一旦船厂将分包商或供应商提供的质保转让给了船东,船东是否可以将质保转让给买家似乎并不取决于船厂是否同意。 11.111

IX 质保工程师

概述

质保工程师是指船厂派遣的,在船舶交接后随船工作的工程师,其主要职责是负责保障船舶相关机械设备的正常工作。Mocatta 法官在 *Anglomar Shipping Co Ltd* v *Swan Hunter Shipbuilders Ltd and Swan Hunter Group Ltd*(*The London Lion*)一案中曾对质保工程师的职责作了如下描述:② 11.112

> The duty of this guarantee engineer was to act as the builders' representative aboard and give the purchaser and its employees full co-operation to enable them to obtain the most efficient use of the vessel's machinery and equipment.

船厂的权利

SAJ 格式针对船厂的权利作出了如下规定:③ 11.113

> The BUILDER shall have the right to appoint a Guarantee Engineer to serve on the VESSEL as its representative for such portion of the

---

① Article X.5.
② [1980] 2 Lloyd's Rep 456 at 463.
③ Article IX.5, para.1.

guarantee period as the BUILDER may decide. The BUYER and its employers shall give the Guarantee Engineer full cooperation in carrying out his duties as the representative of the BUILDER on board the VESSEL. The BUYER shall accord the Guarantee Engineer the treatment comparable to the VESSEL's Chief Engineer and shall provide him with accommodations and subsistence at no cost of the BUILDER and/or the Guarantee Engineer.

11.114 按照 SAJ 格式的规定,派遣质保工程师上船是船厂的权利,在 AWES 格式中派遣质保工程师同样是船厂的权利,船厂甚至可以派遣两名质保工程师随船航行。① 但是在 Norwegian 格式中,派遣质保工程师不仅仅是船厂的权利了,该格式规定:②

The Builder shall have the right and the Buyer may require the Builder to appoint a Guarantee Engineer to serve onboard the Vessel for such portion of the guarantee period as the Builder or Buyer may decide. The Buyer and its employees shall provided the Guarantee Engineer with full co-operation in carrying out his duties. The Buyer shall accord the Guarantee Engineer treatment and accommodation comparable to the Vessel's Chief Engineer, at no cost to the Builder ....

11.115 Norwegian 格式将船厂派遣质保工程师的权利和船东要求船厂派遣质保工程师的情形放在一起作出了规定。虽然规定的是船厂有权派遣而船东只是可以要求派遣,但这应当同样是船东的一项权利。

船厂的义务

11.116 NEWBUILDCON 格式的规定与上述 Norwegian 格式相反,按照该格式的规定,船东有权要求船厂派遣质保工程师上船:③

The Buyer shall have the right to require the Builder to, or the Builder may, appoint a Guarantee Engineer to attend onboard the Vessel for such portion of the Guarantee Period as the Buyer may reasonably require ....

11.117 鉴于船东的此项权利,船厂在船东行使这一权利时实际上是有义务派遣质保

---

① Article 12(b), para.1.
② Article X.6, para.1.
③ Clause 36(a).

工程师上船的。与此不同,CSTC 格式则是更为明确地将派遣质保工程师规定为船厂的一项合同义务了:①

> The BUILDER shall appoint one or two Guarantee Engineer(s) to serve the VESSEL as the BUILDER's representative(s) for a period of twelve(12) months from the delivery of the VESSEL. The BUYER, and its employees, shall give such Guarantee Engineer(s) full co-operation in carrying out his/their duties as the representative(s) of the BUILDER on board the VESSEL. The BUYER shall accord the Guarantee Engineer(s) the treatment comparable to the VESSEL's Chief Engineer, and shall provide him with accommodation and subsistence at no cost to the BUILDER and/or the Guarantee Engineer(s).

上述规定使用的"shall"应当明确表明派遣质保工程师是船厂的义务,而不是一项权利。而且,由于 CSTC 格式规定了质保工程师上船工作的期限为 12 个月,这似乎就意味着船厂在交船时就应当指派质保工程师上船了。然而,船厂在船舶建造合同中承担派遣质保工程师上船的义务可能没有太大的必要,尤其是在普通的商船建造中更没有必要。这不仅会给船厂带来人力资源的负担,而且也未必是船东所欢迎的。在实践中,除非是特殊船舶或者是首制船,船厂自己派遣或根据船东要求派遣质保工程师在船舶交接后随船工作的情形实际上并不十分常见。

11.118

费用

标准格式似乎都规定质保工程师的费用应当由船东负担,按照 SAJ 格式的规定,船东不仅需要支付质保工程师每月的工资,还要承担质保工程师回东京的机票费用:②

11.119

> The BUYER shall pay to the BUILDER the sum of .... per months as a compensation for a part of costs and charges to be borne by the BUILDER in connection with the Guarantee Engineer and also shall pay the expenses of repatriation in Tokyo, Japan, by air upon termination of his service.

按照 AWES 格式的规定,船东应当给予质保工程师不低于轮机长的地位,但是质保工程师的工资则由双方约定。③ Norwegian 格式则规定船东应当按照欧洲

11.120

---

① Article IX.5, para.1.
② Article IX.5, para.2.
③ Article 12(b), para.2.

轮机长的标准支付质保工程师的工资,并承担质保工程师回国的机票。① CSTC 格式规定的船东应当支付的费用比较具体,包括质保工程师每月的工资,回北京的遣返机票,通信费用,医疗费用等。此外,CSTC 格式还规定了船东对质保工程师的人身伤亡以及财产损坏或灭失的责任。②

船东的过失责任

11. 121　　Norwegian 格式和 CSTC 格式都规定了船东的过失责任,Norwegian 格式的规定如下:③

> The Guarantee Engineer shall, at all times and in all respects, be deemed to be the employee of the Builder. The Buyer shall be under no liability whatsoever to the Builder or to the Guarantee Engineer for personal injuries, including death, suffered by the Guarantee Engineer during the time when he is on board the vessel, unless such personal injuries, including death, were caused by gross negligence of the Buyer, or of any of its employees or agents. Nor shall the Buyer be under any liability whatsoever to the Guarantee Engineer for damage to or loss or destruction of property of the Guarantee Engineer, unless such damage, loss or destruction is caused by gross negligence of the Buyer, or of any of its employees or agents. The Guarantee Engineer shall if requested sign a Letter of Indemnity required by the Buyer.

11. 122　　上述规定类似于 Norwegian 格式关于船厂对船东监造代表责任的规定,④船东只有在有"重大过失"的情况下才需对质保工程师的人身伤亡和财产损失承担责任。CSTC 格式也有类似的规定,只是与 Norwegian 格式有所不同。Norwegian 格式是以船东不承担责任为原则,承担责任的情形作为例外处理;而 CSTC 格式则是从正面规定船东应当承担责任,只是以为"重大过失"为前提而已:⑤

> ... The BUYER, its successor(s) and/or assign(s), shall be liable to and indemnify the BUILDER, and/or the Guarantee Engineer(s) and/or the SELLER for personal injuries, including death and damages to, or loss or destruction of property of the Guarantee Engineer(s), if such death,

---

① Article X.6, para.1.
② Article IX.5, para.2.
③ Article X.6, para.2.
④ Article V.5.
⑤ Article X.5, para.2.

injuries, damages, loss and/or destruction were caused by gross negligence or willful misconduct of the BUYER, its successor(s) and/or assign(s) or its employees and/or agents.

11.123　CSTC 格式关于船东对质保工程师责任的规定与该格式关于船厂对船东监造代表责任的规定有着比较大的区别。船厂对船东监造代表的责任是以免责为原则,以"重大过失"或故意行为承担责任为例外。NEWBUILDCON 格式设有专门的责任条款,按照该格式的责任条款的规定,任何一方均需对自己的雇员承担雇主责任,除非人身伤亡或财产损失是由于一方的故意行为或明知有可能发生人身伤亡或财产损失的鲁莽行为造成的。①

11.124　值得注意的是,虽然船舶建造合同明确规定任何一方只有在其或其雇员等有"重大过失"或"故意行为"的情况下才需承担对方雇员的人身伤亡的责任,但这并不意味着任何一方无需对自己或自己雇员的疏忽承担责任。在 *EE Caledonia Ltd v Orbit Valve Co Europe*② 一案中,海上平台检修合同第 10(b) 条有下列规定:

> Company's and Contractor's Employees and Property. Each party hereto shall indemnify ... the other, provided that the other party has acted in good faith, from and against any claim, demand, cause of action, loss expense or liability ... arising by reason of any injury to or death of any employee ... of the indemnifying party, resulting from or in any way connected with the performance of this Order.

11.125　双方约定合同规定的服务应在 10 天内完成,在此期间检修承包人的服务工程师将居住在平台上。一天,当服务工程师结束工作后回到生活区时遭遇失火并不幸丧生。失火与服务工程师无关。服务工程师的家人向平台所有人提出了索赔,双方最终达成了和解,由平台所有人赔付了 642,627.67 英镑。于是平台所有人根据合同第 10(b) 条的规定要求检修承包人赔偿自己的损失。平台所有人承认是自己雇员的疏忽造成了失火。但是高院的 Hobhouse 法官认为虽然第 10(b) 条并没有明确规定,但是平台所有人不能因自己的疏忽向检修承包人主张赔偿。Hobhouse 法官说:③

> It is well established that indemnity will not lie in respect of loss due to a person's own negligence or that of his servants unless adequate and

---

① 见本书第 5 章第 III 节。
② [1993] 2 Lloyd's Rep 418.
③ [1993] 2 Lloyd's Rep 418 at 423.

clear words are used or unless the indemnity could have no reasonable meaning or application unless so applied . . . .

In art.10(b)there is no express reference to negligence; therefore there is no express provision that the right to an indemnity should cover a liability arising out of negligence of the party seeking the indemnity. However the words used are wide enough potentially to cover a liability arising from negligence. The words are "any claim . . . or liability". Clearly such liability could, and will often be, a liability which has arisen from the negligence of the party liable or of those for whom he is responsible. But the liability need not arise from such negligence. It could arise as a result of a breach of a statutory duty which has occurred without any negligence of the party liable or his servants. This could be the situation with regard to both the company and the contractor; both are subject to statutory duties which could give rise to civil liabilities for death or personal injury. The examples are not fanciful; in an environment such as an off-shore platform in an oil field where a strict statutory regime operates, the possibility of a strict liability arising is a real one and is directly within the contemplation of this contract.

第12章 船东的解约

I 概述

"解约"的表述

与解约有关的三个英文字是：cancellation，rescission 以及 termination。Cancel 作为动词其本意是"毁坏"（destroy, deface）或"涂抹"（obliterate），从而引申为"使其无效""解除"。Cancellation 作为名词指"毁坏"或"涂抹"的动作。Cancellation 可以是合同生效前的，也可以是合同生效后，因此可以译为"解除"或"撤销"。例如买卖合同中买方在"冷却期"（cooling-off period）内撤销合同的做法。① Cancellation 的一个基本特征是合同视为从未订立过。

12.1

Rescind 具有"取消"（cancel）和"废除"（abrogate）的意思，从而引申为"使无效"（make void），"废除"（repeal），"宣告无效"（annul）。Rescission 是 rescind 的名词，强调的是合同一方当事人的解约行为。发生违约时，rescission 通常被视为守约方的救济，即守约方无需继续履行合同义务。Rescission 也可以指合同当事人通过约定解约的行为，正如上议院的 Lord Porter 在 *Heyman v Darwins Ltd* 一案中所说的：②

12.2

> To say that the contract is rescinded or has come to an end or has ceased to exist may in individual cases convey the truth with sufficient accuracy, but the fuller expression that the injured party is thereby absolved from future performance of his obligations under the contract is a more exact description of the position. Strictly speaking, to say that on acceptance of the renunciation of a contract the contract is rescinded is incorrect. In such a case the injured party may accept the renunciation

---

① Consumer Credit Act 1974, ss 67–73, Consumer Protection(Distance Selling) Regulations 2000 rr 10–12.
② [1942] AC 356 at 399.

as a breach going to the root of the whole of the consideration. By that acceptance he is discharged from further performance and may bring an action for damages, but the contract itself is not rescinded.

12.3　但是在 *Johnson* v *Agnew* 一案中,上议院似乎认为 rescission 也可以是自始的解除,因为 Lord Wilberforce 说:①

> ... although the vendor is sometimes referred to in the above situation as "rescinding" the contract, this so-called "rescission" is quite different from rescission *ab initio*, such as may arise for example in cases of mistake, fraud or lack of consent. In those cases, the contract is treated in law as never having come into existence. In the case of an accepted repudiatory breach the contract has come into existence but has been put an end to or discharged. Whatever contrary indications may be disinterred from old authorities, it is now quite clear, under the general law of contract, that acceptance of a repudiatory breach does not bring about "rescission *ab initio*".

12.4　Terminate 的含义是"结束""终止"(to end)。Termination 作为名词即为"解除"。上议院的 Lord Radcliffe 在 *Bridge* v *Campbell Discount Co Ltd* 一案中认为 termination 既可以指依照约定的解除,也可以指基于一方毁约的解除,他说:②

> "Termination" is an ambiguous word, since it may refer to a termination by a right under the agreement or by a condition incorporated in it or by a deliberate breach by one party amounting to a repudiation of the whole contract.

12.5　在 *Stocznia Gdynia SA* v *Gearbulk Holdings Ltd* 一案中,上诉法院的 Moore-Bick 法官则认为 termination 可以是指双方均无责任的自始的所有权利义务的解除,也可以是指因合同落空而导致的解除,但最常见的则是指因基于一方违约的解除,他说的是:③

> The meaning of the word "terminate" depends on the context in which it is used. It is capable of meaning what is nowadays generally called rescission, that is, the discharge of all rights and obligations under the contract *ab initio* without liability on either side, and is also used in the

---

① [1980] AC 367 at 392.
② [1962] 1 All ER 355 at 394.
③ [2009] 1 Lloyd's Rep 461 at 466.

context of discharge by frustration, but it is most commonly used in commercial contracts in the context of a right given to one party to a contract to treat it as discharged by reason of a breach on the part of the other.

解约方式

本章讨论的内容是船东的解约。船东的解约有两种:其一是指船东按照船舶建造合同的规定解除合同,即船东解约的依据是合同规定;其二是指船东在船厂违约且该违约构成毁约时按照法律规定解除合同,即船东解约的依据是法律规定。由于第一种船东解约是基于建造合同的约定,一旦约定的情形出现了,船东就可以解约,至于船厂是否违约并不重要。在第二种船东解约情形下,船东的解约通常以船厂毁约为前提,因为只有船厂的毁约才赋予船东解除建造合同的权利。

12.6

标准格式

船舶建造合同标准格式的用词比较随意,且各不相同。SAJ 格式使用的是 rescission。Norwegian 格式使用的是 cancellation。CSTC 格式同时使用了 rescission 和 cancellation 两个字:①

12.7

> ... In the event the BUYER shall exercise its right of cancellation and/or rescission of this Contract under and pursuant to any of the provisions of this Contract specifically permitting the BUYER to do so ....

虽然同时使用了 rescission 和 cancellation,但是就"解除"而言并没有增加任何新的含义。在 AWES 格式和 NEWBUILDCON 格式中,"解除"的英文既没有用 cancellation,也没有使用 rescission,而是采用了"termination"一字:②

12.8

> If in accordance with any of the provisions of Article 5 or 6 the PURCHASER shall ... exercise the option of the PURCHASER to terminate this CONTRACTOR, ...

从上述分析来看,cancellation,rescission 以及 termination 都可以用于合同的解除。它们之间若有区别的话则可能是:cancellation 侧重的应当是合同实际生效之前的解除,而 rescission 则强调解除的自始性,即被解除的合同应视为从未订立

12.9

---

① Article X.1.
② AWES Article 11, NEWBUILDCON Clause 39.

过。而 Termination 作为解除,其所强调的应当是合同生效后一方因另一方的违约而实施的解除,即解除合同的一方不再受合同约束的意思表示。Cancellation 和 rescission 之间的区别应当是比较明显的,而在 rescission 和 termination 之间的差异可能不太明显。*Chitty on Contracts* 是这样区分两者特征的:①

> Since the decision of the House of Lords in *Johnson v Agnew* a much clearer and sharper distinction has been drawn between rescission of a contract abinitio and termination of the contract for subsequent breach. The former generally has retrospective effect, while the latter does not; indeed, termination usually affects only some of the obligations under the contract and it is strictly incorrect to speak of the contract ceasing to exist through termination. It is clear from *Johnson v Agnew* itself that rescission for fraud is rescission ab initio, and will therefore prima facie have retrospective effect, though it has already been submitted that such rescission will not deprive the representee of a right to damages for fraud, because that right arises in tort, and not out of the contract.

II 根据合同约定解约

12.10　船东按照合同约定解约是指船舶建造合同明确规定了船东可以解除合同的情形,一旦发生合同规定的情形,船东就可以解约。从常见的船舶建造合同标准格式的规定来看,船东按照合同规定解约的情形主要有以下几种。

不符合保证事项

12.11　本书第 4 章曾讨论过关于船厂在船舶建造合同作出各种船舶性能保证的做法。一旦船舶不符这些明示保证并且达到约定的船东可以解约程度,船东就享有解除合同的选择权。② 船东的解约权并不以约定的解约情形构成普通法的毁约为前提。在 *Admiralty Commissioners* v *Cox and King*③ 一案中,船舶建造合同规定船厂保证航速达到 40 节,并允许船东在航速达不到 40 节时解除合同。船舶的航速没有达到 40 节,船东解除了合同。虽然航速达不到 40 节的原因是船东提供的主机马力不够,但高院认为合同并没有规定船东有义务提供特定马力的主机,因

---

① Hugh Beale, *Chitty on Contracts*, 35th edn Sweet & Maxwell 2023, para.10-126.
② 关于船东因船舶不符合船厂保证的解约请参见第 4 章第 VI 节。
③ (1927) 27 Ll L Rep 223.

此船东可以解除合同,船东还可以获得建造款的返还。船厂上诉,但上诉法院驳回了上诉,Bankes 法官说:①

> The claim is with regard to the contract, although broken by the contractors, the contract subsisting for this purpose: they are entitled, under the conditions of the contract, to reject the boat which under the conditions had to become their property – to reject it, and to claim back the money; and they make those claims on the footing that so far as they are concerned the contract, so far as those remedies are concerned, is a subsisting contract.

船东只能在船舶建造合同明确规定的解约情形出现时才可以解除船舶建造合同,例如 SAJ 格式便对此作出了明确的规定:② 12.12

> ... under and pursuant to any of the provisions of this Contract specifically permitting the BUYER to do so ....

在船舶建造合同采用 SAJ 格式情况下,船东可以解约的情况主要有:(1)船舶航速低于保证航速超过 1 节的;③(2)船舶油耗超过保证油耗约定百分比的;④(3)船舶载重吨低于保证载重吨约定数值的;⑤CSTC 格式同样也规定上述三种船东有权解除合同的情形。⑥ AWES 格式,Norwegian 格式以及 NEWBUILDCON 格式则在此基础上增加了船东可以因船舶舱容不符合保证而解除合同的情形。⑦ 12.13

交船延迟

所有船舶建造合同标准格式都规定,船厂未能按照约定时间交船的,船东就可以在扣除了所有可以顺延合同交船日的可允许延误后选择解除合同,两者区别只是在于允许船厂在合同交船日之后交船期限的长短而已。Norwegian 格式和 NEWBUILDCON 格式规定船厂在合同交船日后 180 天依然没有交船的船东便可解除合同;⑧SAJ 格式规定的期限为 210 天;⑨AWES 格式规定的期限最长,达到 12.14

---

① (1927) 27 Ll L Rep 223 at 225.
② Article X.1.
③ Article III.2.
④ Article III.3.
⑤ Article III.4.
⑥ Article III.2, 3 & 4.
⑦ AWES Article 5(c), Norwegian Article IV.5, NEWBUILDCON Clause 11.
⑧ Norwegian Article IV.1(b), NEWBUILDCON Clauses 13 & 39(a)(iii).
⑨ Articles III.1, VIII.4.

360 天。①

担保人破产

12.15 将提供还款保函的第三人的破产作为船东解除船舶建造合同理由之一应当是 NEWBUILDCON 格式所特有的,该格式的规定是:②

> The Buyer shall have the right to terminate this Contract forthwith upon giving notice in the event that:
>
> (i) the guarantor providing the Refund Guarantee on behalf of the Builder in accordance with Clause 14(b)(Guarantees – Builder's Refund Guarantee) is deemed in solvent pursuant to Sub-clause(d) below unless the Builder provides a replacement Refund Guarantee acceptable to the Buyer within 30 days of the Buyer's notice requiring a replacement Refund Guarantee to be provided, during which period no further payments shall be made to the Builder by the Buyer and provided that notice of termination is given before an acceptable replacement Refund Guarantee is received by the Buyer ....

12.16 NEWBUILDCON 格式还对破产作出了如下说明:③

> A Party or the guarantor providing the Refund Guarantee shall be deemed insolvent if proceedings are commenced against the insolvent Party or the guarantor for winding up, dissolution orreorganization (otherwise than for the purpose of amalgamation or reconstruction), liquidation, the appointment of a receiver, trustee or similar officer, bankruptcy, suspension of payments or similar events.

12.17 上述规定应当理解为:一旦提供还款保函的第三人破产,船东可以向船厂发出通知解除船舶建造合同,除非船厂在收到船东通知后的 30 天内提供船东接受的替代还款保函。该格式只是规定:"在发生下列情形时,船东在发出通知后应享有解除本合同的权利",并没有关于船东如何解除合同以及船东的解除如何生效的规定。船东通知船厂要求后者提供替代还款保函似乎并不是一项合同义务,换言之,船东可以要求船厂提供替代还款保函,也可以不通知船厂而直接解除船舶建造合同。但是允许船东在还款担保人破产时直接解除船舶建造合同未必是合

---

① Articles 6(c), para.2.
② Article 39(a)(i).
③ Clause 39(d).

理的,还款担保人毕竟不是船舶建造合同的当事人。船东关心的是还款保函的可靠性,而在原担保人破产后船东就可以解约的条款对保函的可靠性应当是无济于事的。船厂应当有合理的时间提供替代还款保函,只有当船厂拒绝或无法提供替代还款保函时船东才可以解约。

NEWBUILDCON 格式没有将船厂破产列为违约而是选择将还款担保人的破产作为船厂的违约,这可能是起草人意识到船舶建造合同中关于船东解约权的规定可能会受船厂所在地法律的影响,船东是否可以以此为由解约可能会有问题。按照《中华人民共和国企业破产法》的规定,法院受理破产申请后,由法院指定的破产管理人有权决定是解除还是继续履行破产申请前成立的而债务人和对方当事人均未履行完毕的合同,并通知对方当事人。只有在破产管理人自破产申请受理之日起两个月内未通知对方当事人,或者自收到对方当事人催告之日起 30 日内未答复的,合同才可视为解除。如果破产管理人决定继续履行合同的,对方当事人应当履行。①

12.18

中止建造

NEWBUILDCON 格式有一个比较特别的规定,即船厂中止船舶建造时,船东就可以解除船舶建造合同:②

12.19

The Buyer shall have the right to terminate this Contract forthwith upon giving notice in the event that:

. . . .

(ii) the Builder fails to perform any work relating to the construction of the Vessel for a running period of at least the number of days stated in Box 22(i), excluding Permissible Delays, provided that thereafter the Buyer gives the Builder at least the number of days' written notice stated in Box 22(ii) of its intention to terminate this Contract under this Clause and within that period the Builder fails to remedy its breach and provided further that the notice of termination is given before the Builder has remedied its breach . . . .

允许船东在船厂没有进行任何工作达到一定天数的情况下解除船舶建造合同应当是与合同允许船厂在合同交船日后 180 天或 210 天内交船的规定相冲突

12.20

---

① 第十八条。
② Clause 39(a)(ii)。

的。在船舶建造合同规定了弃船日的情况下,只要船厂在弃船日之前交船,船东应当没有任何时间上的理由拒绝接船。上述规定允许船东在合同规定的弃船日,甚至是合同交船日到来之前解除船舶建造合同,这实际上剥夺了船厂按照合同本应享有的建造时间。虽不合理,但合同当事人可以作出此种约定。需要搞清楚的应当是"any work relating to the construction of the Vessel"的含义。设计是不是与船舶建造有关的工作,答案应当是肯定的;采购是不是与船舶建造有关的工作,答案也应当是肯定的。如果设计和采购都是与船舶建造有关的工作,为什么工作人员的替换或管理人员的调整就不是与船舶建造有关的工作呢?从上述规定来看,船厂没有工作并不是以有过错为基础的,即使船厂没有过错,船东依然可以解除船舶建造合同。船厂应当设法避免建造合同中有类似的约定。

未提供还款保函

12.21　　NEWBUILDCON 格式不仅规定船东可以在还款担保人破产时解除船舶建造合同,而且还规定船厂没有按照约定提供还款保函的,船东也可以解除船舶建造合同。① 严格说这两个船东可以解约的事项应当是相同的,即没有还款保函或还款保函不可靠。虽然船厂未能按照约定提供还款保函构成违约,但此种违约未必会给船东带来真实的风险。船厂的还款保函通常是在船东支付建造款之前提供的,船厂没有按照约定提供还款保函意味着船东也没有支付建造款,换言之,船东并没有面临无法收回预付款的风险。而且在正常情况下,解约并不会有助于船东保护自己的利益。相反,如果船东由于市场等原因不打算继续履行建造合同了,此种约定则为船东不履约提供了机会。

破产或重组

12.22　　Norwegian 格式有一条关于船厂破产的规定,该规定的内容如下:②

> If on or before Delivery and Acceptance of the Vessel the Builder is declared bankrupt, proposes or enters into a fund or a formal composition arrangement or moratorium or otherwise proves to be in such financial position that it is likely to be unable during the Guarantee Period to perform its guarantee obligations, the Buyer may demand that the Builder shall provide satisfactory security for the performance by the

---

① Clause 39(a)(ix).
② Article III.3, para.8.

Builder of such guarantee obligations, limited to ……. % of the Original Contract Price, or failing such guarantee, the Buyer is entitled to deposit the equivalent amount in an escrow account in the joint name of the Builder and the Buyer and to deduct this amount from the instalment to be paid on Delivery and Acceptance.

12.23　上述条文规定的并非船东在船厂破产或进行债务重组时可以解约,而是可以要求船厂提供履约担保。但上述规定可能缺乏操作性。在船厂已经破产或进入债务重组的情况下要求船厂提供履约担保应当没有太大的意义。船东希望得到的履行担保往往是由银行出具的,但在船厂破产后很难想象还会有银行愿意出具履约担保。而且船厂的履约实际上就是继续建造船舶,如果船东已经持有可靠的还款保函,进一步提供履约保函同样是没有意义的。船厂拒绝或无法继续船舶建造的,船东获得的依然是其已支付的建造款的返还及其利息。如果船厂已经进入破产程序,船厂可以选择继续并完成船舶建造,但进入破产程序的船厂已不再有义务继续履约了。是否继续履行合同应当是破产管理人如何考虑最大程度保护债权人的问题了。① 船东在船厂没有提供履约担保时将其所要求的履约担保金额存入船东与船厂的共同账户或第三人托管账户应当也没有什么意义。船东这样做的目的应当是设法避免自己支付的建造款成为船厂的破产财产,但这样做是否可以解决问题恐怕是不明确的。如果船东有机会支付尾款并接船,也就意味着船厂的破产管理人决定继续履行船舶建造合同。如果在船厂破产时船东已经支付了交船前的各期建造款,船东实际上也不再有任何其他支付义务了,在共同账户或托管账户存入任何数额的款项恐怕也都没有意义。如果在船厂破产时船东尚有交船前应支付的建造款未支付的,船东似乎没有任何理由将建造款汇入共同账户或托管账户,这样做实际上会构成船东未按约定支付交船前的各期建造款的违约。最后,将船厂"proposes or enters into a fund"作为破产之一似乎并不妥当,实际上"proposes or enters into a fund"本身就缺乏明确的含义。另外,"托管账户"通常是指由当事人以外的第三人根据当事人的指示持有的账户,而"共同账户"则是由两个或两个以上当事人共同持有的账户。因此,托管账户不可能由当事人共同持有,而共同账户则不可能交由第三人持有。

---

① 《中华人民共和国企业破产法》第二十五条。

Ⅲ 根据法律规定解约

12.24 船东除了按照船舶建造合同的规定解约外,还可以按照法律规定解约。船东按照法律规定可以解约的情形通常是船厂的行为构成毁约,例如船厂在船舶建造合同生效后拒绝建造船舶,或者在完成船舶建造后拒绝向船东交船等,即使合同没有明文规定船东依然可以凭法律规定解约。

违反默示保证

12.25 英国成文法针对卖方规定的默示保证比较严厉,船东拒绝接受船舶不以船厂有疏忽为前提,船厂也不因造成违约的缺陷来自于分包商而免责。根据1979年《货物买卖法》的规定,买卖合同中主要的默示保证包括船舶具有令人满意的质量以及船舶符合合理的用途。① 在船舶建造中,满足上述两个默示保证应当是必然的,因为船厂的船舶建造只有在符合船级符号并通过船级社代表的检验后才有可能交船。如果船厂提供了船舶的完整证书,船东应当是无法以船厂未满足两个默示保证为由而拒绝接船的。

船舶不适航

12.26 船厂建造的船舶应当是适航的,尤其是在船厂负责设计的情况下更是如此。如果船舶在交接时是不适航的,船东应当有权拒绝接受船舶。在 *Samuel White & Co Ltd v Coombes, Marshall & Co Ltd*② 一案中,船舶建造合同规定:

> ... to build, launch and complete subject to the provisions of the contract and in accordance with the plans and specifications signed by the parties.

12.27 高院的 Bailhache 法官说:③

> Now, it appears in this case that the plans were prepared by the builders' naval architect, in consultation, it is true, with the original building owners' surveyor, but prepared by the builders. In my opinion, when plans are prepared in that way there is an implied

---

① 关于默示保证请参见本书第 1 章第 Ⅴ 节。
② (1922) 13 Ll L Rep 122.
③ (1922) 13 Ll L Rep 122 at 124.

condition that these plans if carried out will provide a seaworthy ship.

12.28 在 McDougall v Aeromarine of Emsworth① 一案中,船舶建造合同有如下规定:

> The builders will lay down, construct, launch and fit out the craft to be identified by the builders' reference number in accordance with the detailed specification and drawings annexed hereto each separate sheet bearing the signature of both parties to this agreement.

12.29 实际上船舶建造合同并没有附上详细的规格书和图纸,但是高院认为船厂有义务保证按图施工后的船舶是适航的,Diplock 法官说:②

> ... and I find ... when the vessel was tendered for delivery, it was not seaworthy or of merchantable quality or fit for the purpose of use as a cruising or racing yacht. I find also that the plaintiff was not unreasonable in being dissatisfied with her construction.

船厂毁约

12.30 毁约(repudiation)是一种违约,构成毁约的违约被称为 repudiatory breach。毁约是指合同一方当事人以言语或行为表明自己不履行合同义务的意图或明示宣布自己不再履行合同义务。正如 Greene 法官在 Toller v Law Accident Insurance Society Ltd 一案中所指出的:③

> Repudiation of a contract may mean that, having admittedly made a contract, you decide to breach it and break it in such a way that you intend not to proceed with it. Another use of the word "repudiation" is where you say: "There never was a contract at all between us." If it turns out there was a contract, the act of one party denying the existence of it is to repudiate it; but supposing it turns out he was right and there never was a contract, then "repudiation" is used in a different sense from that in which it would be used when an existing contract is broken by a refusal to perform.

12.31 合同一方毁约,另一方可以接受毁约并解除合同。解除合同是一种选择权,

---

① [1958] 2 Lloyd's Rep 345.
② [1958] 2 Lloyd's Rep 345 at 353.
③ [1936] 2 All ER 952 at 956.

即守约的一方可以选择接受毁约并解除合同,也可以选择拒绝接受毁约并要求对方继续履行合同。上议院的 Lord Sumner 在 *Hirji Mulji* v *Cheong Yue Steamship Company* 一案中这样说道:①

> Rescission(except by mutual consent or by a competent Court) is the right of one party, arising upon conduct by the other, by which he intimates his intention to abide by the contract no longer. It is a right to treat the contract as at an end if he chooses, and to claim damages for its total breach, but it is a right in his option ....

12.32　即使船舶建造合同没有约定船东的解约权,但除非有相反约定,一旦船厂的违约行为构成毁约,船东就可以解约。船东解约权来自普通法。例如船厂明确以语言或行为表示不会建造船舶,或者将已经建造完毕的船舶转手给他人等。违约行为是否构成毁约取决于是否存在拒绝履行的意图,而且应当从整体来看。Lord Wilberforce 在 *Woodar Investment Development Ltd* v *Wimpey Construction(UK) Ltd* 一案中说的是:②

> ... in considering whether there has been a repudiation by one party, it is necessary to look at his conduct as a whole. Does this indicate an intention to abandon or to refuse performance of the contract? ... So far from repudiating the contract [defendants] were relying on it in invoking one of the its provisions, to which both parties had given their consent and, unless the invocation of that provision was totally abusive or lacking in good faith ..., the fact that it has proved to be wrong in law cannot turn it into a repudiation.

12.33　如果船舶建造合同约定船厂应当向船东提供还款保函,船厂没有按照约定提供还款保函就有可能构成毁约。在 *Covington Marine Corp and Others* v *Xiamen Shipbuilding Industry Co Ltd*③ 一案中,船舶建造合同规定船厂应当提供还款保函。船厂没有按照约定提供约定的保函,相反却和其他船东签订了船舶建造合同。高院认为船厂已经构成了毁约性违约,船东可以接受这一违约并解除船舶建造合同。Langley 法官说:④

> [Shipyard] accepted that if I reached the conclusions which I have so

---

① [1926] AC 497 at 509.
② [1980] 1 WLR 277 at 280.
③ [2006] 1 Lloyd's Rep 745.
④ [2006] 1 Lloyd's Rep 745 at 758.

far, then it must follow that the builder was in repudiatory breach of the Covington and Washington contracts. Those breaches were accepted as bringing the contracts to an end before the expiry of the three and six month periods for the fulfilment of sub-paras(ii) to(v) of article 21.

但是,即使船厂的行为已经构成违约,但只要没有构成毁约,船东就不能解除船舶建造合同,否则就有可能构成毁约。在 *Wuhan Ocean Economic & Technical Cooperation Co Ltd and Another* v *Schiffahrts-Gesellschaft "Hansa Murica" mbH & Co KG*① 一案中,船厂和船东在船舶建造合同的补充协议中约定推迟合同交船日,由于新的合同交船日已经超过了原有的还款保函的有效期,船厂承诺对原有的还款保函进行延期。原有的还款保函的有效期到 6 月 30 日届满,在 6 月 28 日船东解除了船舶建造合同,理由是船厂的行为已经构成了毁约。仲裁庭认为船东有权解除船舶建造合同,因为船厂在 6 月 28 日依然没有延期还款保函已经构成了毁约。但是高院则认为,虽然船厂没有办理还款保函延期构成了违约,但并不构成毁约,因此船东在 6 月 28 日解除合同是错误的。Cooke 法官说:②

12.34

> The arbitrators erred in law. They set out the right test for repudiatory breach but they cannot have applied it if their earlier conclusion about the triggering effect of an arbitration, whenever commenced, as set out in para.51 of their Reasons, is taken into account. A correct application of the test for repudiatory breach in these circumstances would lead inevitably to one answer only and this is part of the second stage of reasoning to which Mustill J(as he then was) referred in *The Chrysalis* at page 507. Furthermore, even if they did apply the right test, once they had decided as they did, correctly, in para.51, their conclusion is one that no reasonable arbitrators could reach. Their conclusion that the failure to extend the Refund Guarantee by 28 June 2010, two days before the expiry date of the existing guarantee, was a repudiatory breach, cannot be right as a matter of law.

实际履行

在一般合同中,一方违约且构成毁约的,另一方可以接受对方的毁约并解除

12.35

---

① [2013] 1 Lloyd's Rep 273.
② [2013] 1 Lloyd's Rep 273 at 284.

合同,也可以拒绝接受对方的毁约而选择要求对方继续履行合同。要求对方继续履行合同的也就是要求对方实际履行。实际履行是一项衡平法的救济,其特征是法院命令被告实际履行其合同义务。实际履行作为一种衡平法的救济是因为在某些情况下法律所能提供的救济未必充分,它是作为一种有别于金钱赔偿救济手段的救济方式得到法院的采用。但是否适用实际履行这一救济方式并无明确的规定,而由法院自由裁量。

12.36　1979 年《货物买卖法》也明确规定了实际履行这一来自衡平法的救济:①

> In any action for breach of contract to deliver specific or ascertained goods the court may, if it thinks fit, on the plaintiff's application, by its judgment or decree direct that the contract shall be performed specifically, without giving the defendant the option of retaining the goods on payment of damages.

12.37　然而,建造合同不适用实际履行这一救济方式是一项原则,而适用则是一种例外。② 正如 *Chitty on Contracts* 所指出的:③

> The general rule is that a contract to erect a building cannot be specifically enforced against the builder. There seem to be three reasons for this rule. First, damages may be an adequate remedy if another builder can be engaged to do the work. Secondly, the contract may be too vague to be specifically enforced if it fails to describe the work to be done under it with sufficient certainty. And thirdly, specific enforcement of the contract may require more supervision than the court is willing to provide. But where the first two reasons do not apply, the third has not been allowed to prevail.

12.38　船舶建造合同虽然是买卖合同的一种,但其毕竟具有不少建造合同的特征,法院同样也很少会在船舶建造合同争议中适用实际履行,实际上船舶建造合同还有自己所特有的不适合适用实际履行的原因。正如高院的 Hirst 法官在 *Gyllenhammar & Partners International Ltd and Others* v *Sour Brodogradevna Industrija* 一案中所指出的:④

> Here I need say no more than that the voluminous specification shows

---

① s.52(1).
② *Wolverhampton Corp* v *Emmons* [1901] 1 QB 515.
③ Hugh Beale, *Chitty on Contracts*, 35th edn Sweet & Maxwell 2023, para.31－044.
④ [1989] 2 Lloyd's Rep 403 at 422.

that this is a very complex contract requiring extensive co-operation between the parties on a number of matters, in particular modifications, optional variations, and, perhaps most important of all, matters of detail (some by no means unimportant) left undefined in the specification. In my judgment these factors, coupled with the consideration that the work would take place in a foreign yard outside the Court's jurisdiction, would tell strongly against an order for specific performance being in principle appropriate in the present case.

IV 解约的后果

解约的不可逆转

12.39　按照船舶建造合同的规定,在船东可以解除合同时,船东既可以选择要求船厂继续履行合同,也可以选择解除合同。但是除非得到船厂的同意,一旦船东解除了船舶建造合同就不能再要求船厂履行合同了。相反,在船东要求船厂继续履行的情况下,船东解除合同的权利并未因此丧失。除非船厂已经按照约定继续履行合同了,否则船东依然可以选择解除合同。对此,Lord Wilberforce 在 Johnson v Agnew 一案中说得非常清楚:①

> It is easy to see that a party who has chosen to put an end to a contract by accepting the other party's repudiation cannot afterwards seek specific performance. This is simply because the contract has gone – what is dead is dead. But it is no more difficult to agree that a party, who has chosen to seek specific performance, may quite well thereafter, if specific performance fails to be realised, say, "Very well, then, the contract should be regarded as terminated."

建造款返还

12.40　本书第 4 章曾对预付款和定金予以了分析和区别。② 由于船舶建造合同已经有了明确的规定,即使船东支付的款项具有定金的性质,一旦船厂违约且导致船东有权解除船舶建造合同时,船厂依然应当按照双方的约定返还已经收到的建

---

① [1980] AC 367 at 398.
② 关于预付款和定金请参见本书第 4 章第 II 节。

造款。SAJ 格式规定：①

> Thereupon the BUILDER shall promptly refund to the BUYER the full amount of all sums paid by the BUYER to the BUILDER on account of the VESSEL, unless the BUILDER proceeds to the arbitration under the provisions of Article XIII hereof.
>
> In such event, the BUILDER shall pay the BUYER interest at the rate of .... Percent (........%) per annum on the amount required herein to be refunded to the BUYER, computed from the respective dates on which such sums were paid by the BUYER to the BUILDER to the date of remittance by transfer of such refund to the BUYER by the BUILDER, provided, however, that if the said rescission by the BUYER is made under the provisions of Paragraph 4 of Article VIII hereof, then in such event the BUILDER shall not be required to pay any interest.

12.41　其他标准格式也有类似的规定。② 虽然船厂通常会向船东提供由第三人出具的还款保函，但是首先负有还款义务的依然是船厂。只有在船厂未能按照约定返还船东支付的款项时，出具还款保函的第三人才负有支付的义务。

利息

12.42　作为原则，船厂在返还船东支付的预付款时应当支付相应的利息。但是利息并不是始终应当支付的。在有些情况下，船厂按照船舶建造合同的约定虽然有义务返还船东已经支付的预付款，但没有义务支付利息。按照 SAJ 格式的规定，如果船东因为不可抗力事件造成的延误超过 210 天而解除船舶建造合同的，船厂虽然应当返还预付款，但无需支付利息。③

12.43　CSTC 格式对船厂返还款项的利息作出了比较详细的规定：④

> ... In the event of the SELLER is obligated to make refundment, the SELLER shall pay the BUYER interest in United States Dollars at the rate of _____ percent (____%) if the cancellation or rescission of the Contract is exercised by the BUYER for the delay of aggregate _____ (____) days in accordance with the provision of Paragraph 3 of Article

---

① Article X.2.
② AWES Article 11, CSTC Article X.2, Norwegian Article XII.1, para.2, NEWBUILDCON Clause 39(e).
③ Article X.2, para.2.
④ Article X.2.

VIII or/by the events described in Article III.1(c), 2(c), 3(c)or 4(c) hereof, however in the event of total loss as described in Article XII of this Contract, then, no interest will be refunded on the amount required herein to be refunded to the BUYER, computed from the respective dates when such sums were received by Bank of China, New York Branch or any such other bank account as nominated by the SELLER pursuant to Article II.4(c), 4(c)or 4(d) from the BUYER to the date of remittance by telegraphic transfer of such refund to the BUYER by the SELLER.

12.44 按照上述规定,船东以交船延误超过约定期限以及船舶性能不符合保证性能且达到约定程度为由解除合同的,船厂在返还船东已经支付的预付款外还应当按照约定利率支付利息。如果船东因船舶遭受全损而解除了合同,船厂只需返还船东已经支付的预付款,而无需支付任何利息。但按照NEWBUILDCON格式的规定,在发生船舶全损情况下,如果双方无法就船舶的建造达成一致的,船东就可以解除船舶建造合同,而船厂则应立即返还船东已经支付的预付款及其利息。① 而按照AWES格式和Norwegian格式的规定,在船舶遭受全损的情况下,船东并不享有解除船舶建造合同的权利,但是可以获得保险赔偿。②

其他费用返还

12.45 在船舶建造中,虽然船东的主要义务是按照合同的约定支付各期建造款,但实际上除了建造款外,船东还可能需要支付其他费用,例如因船东提出修改而产生的费用等。在船东按照船舶建造合同规定解约时,船厂除了应当返还各期已经收到的建造款外是否还应返还其他已经收到的款项是一个合同解释的问题。按照SAJ格式和CSTC格式的规定,船厂应当返还的不仅包括船东支付的各期建造款,而且还应当包括船东支付的所有其他款项。因为SAJ格式和CSTC格式都规定"full amount of all sums"。③ 因此,在船东解除船舶建造合同后船厂不仅应当返还船东已经支付的各期建造款,同时也要返还船东已经支付的其他所有款项。Norwegian格式虽然使用的是"payment of all sums",但是却有一个限定,即"under Article III hereof..."。而该格式的第III条规定的实际上就是各期建造款,因此按照Norwegian格式的规定,船厂似乎只需返还各期建造款及其利息。

---

① Clause 38(b)(ii)(2).
② AWES Article 9; NEWBUILDCON Clause 38(b)(ii).
③ SAJ Article X.2, para.1, CSTC Article X.2.

AWES 格式规定的是：①

> ... the CONTRACTOR shall be liable to repay to the PURCHASER the amount of all monies paid by the PURCHASER for or on account of the CONTRACT price of the VESSEL together with interest at the rate of ...... percent annum ....

12.46　很显然，"the amount of all monies paid"本身足以包括除各期建造款以外船东所支付的所有款项，但是"for or on account of the CONTRACT price"似乎把"all monies"局限于合同价格，而合同价格则仅仅是指各期建造款而已。因此，在使用 AWES 格式的情况下，船厂应当返还的款项也仅限于船东已经支付的各期建造款。NEWBUILDCON 格式关于返还预付款的规定如下：②

> If this Contract is terminated by the Buyer, the Builder shall refund all sums paid by the Buyer to the Builder under Clause 7(Contract Price) and Clause 15(Payments) hereof plus interest thereon at the rate stated in Box 30 per annum from the date of payment to the date of refund ....

12.47　NEWBUILDCON 格式的第 7 条规定的是合同价格，而第 15 条则规定各期建造款的支付以及修改等费用的支付，因此在适用 NEWBUILDCON 格式时，船厂应当返还的款项不仅包括船东支付的各期建造款，而且还包括修改费用以及其他所有费用。

船东供应品返还

12.48　在船舶建造合同标准格式中似乎只有 Norwegian 格式和 NEWBUILDCON 规定了船东除了返还预付款外还应当归还船东提供的设备等。其中 Norwegian 格式的规定如下：③

> Upon cancellation the Builder shall refund all sums paid by Buyer to the Builder under Article III hereof, including interest thereon at the rate of ...... %(per cent) per annum from the date of payment to the date of refund. The Builder shall also return Buyer's Supplies, or if they cannot be returned the Builder shall pay to the Buyer an amount equal to the Buyer's costs for such equipment.

---

① Article 11.
② Clause 39(e).
③ Article XII.1, para.3.

12.49 按照Norwegian格式的规定，当船东依据建造合同约定解约时，船厂不仅要返还已经收到的所有款项，而且还应当返还船东提供的设备等。这里所说的不能返还应当是指已经安装上船舶的设备。如果船舶试航所用的燃油也是由船东提供的，船厂也应当作价支付。① 其实，即使船舶建造合同没有要求船厂归还船东提供的设备，船厂应当依然有义务返还，因为船东对自己向船厂提供的设备拥有所有权。上述规定对船厂的影响是：一旦船东提供的设备等已经安装上船，船厂就要支付现金，这等于是船厂向船东购买了那些设备等物品。

处置船舶的权利

12.50 船东解除船舶建造合同意味着对船舶的放弃。一旦解除了合同，船东就不能对船舶主张任何权利。除非另有约定，船舶在交船前始终系船厂的财产，随着不再有交付船舶的义务，船厂可以处置船舶应当是不言而喻的。船厂处置船舶的前提是对船舶享有所有权，船舶的所有权只有在交船时才转移至船东一边。一旦船东解除了船舶建造合同，船厂如何处置船舶往往不再是法律问题，而是一个商业问题了。如果在船东解约时船舶已经下水了，船厂通常会完成船舶的建造，因为一艘有船级和证书的船舶的市场价格无疑会高于没有船级和证书的船舶的市场价格。如果船舶处于其他建造阶段时发生船东解约的，船厂是否继续完成船舶建造就取决于当时的市场以及船厂已经产生的建造成本等。不难想象，船东选择解约往往是基于市场的决策，因此对船厂来说，处置船舶绝不会是轻而易举或甚至有利可图的。

船舶建造的继续

12.51 有些船舶建造合同会规定在船东解除合同后有权继续在船厂完成船舶的建造，虽然这种约定通常是有效的，但实际操作则可能会遇到问题。如果船厂在船东解除合同后破产或船东因为船厂破产而解除合同的，这一约定就未必是可以执行的。在 *Merchants' Trading Company v Banner*② 一案中，船舶改造合同规定：

---

① See also NEWBUILDCON Clause 39(e).
② (1871) LR 12 Eq 18.

... it is hereby agreed and declared by and between the said parties hereto that ... in case the [shipyard] shall refuse, neglect, or fail to carry on and complete the said steam-vessel according to the true intent and meaning of these presents ... it shall and may be lawful for the said company, its successors or assigns, with workmen or others, to enter and go into the yard or dock of the [shipyard] the said vessel shall be building or be in progress of construction, and either to take away the said steam-vessel, or parts thereof, and the said engines, boilers, and machinery, or parts thereof, or to employ workmen to finish the same, without any molestation or hindrance whatsoever from the [shipyard], their executors, administrators, or assigns, or the workmen or other persons employed by them, and without making any allowance for the use of the said dockyard, machinery, or premises.

12.52 船厂在船舶被分割成两段时破产了,船东要求进入船厂继续船舶的改造,但是船厂的破产管理人拒绝船东进入船厂。衡平法院拒绝执行船舶改造合同的约定,法院把这一情形视为不存在破产的实际履行要求,Romilly 法官说:①

There is a stipulation that if [shipbuilders] refuse or neglect to perform the contract ... there is a power to the Plaintiff to take possession and complete the vessel .... It is merely a power to enter ... and it appears to me to be a contract which the Court cannot possibly perform .... At all events, I am of opinion that I cannot do it by specific performance ....

12.53 但是在 *BMBF(No 12) Ltd* v *Harland & Wolff Shipbuilding & Heavy Industries Limited*② 一案中,船舶建造合同的第 15.2 条规定,在船厂违约时,船东可以解除合同并获得已支付建造款的返还,也可以按照合同规定在船厂或其他地方完成船舶的建造。船厂在建造完毕后交船,但船东拒绝接船,理由是船舶尚未处于可交船状态。船东向船厂发出了占有船舶并自行继续建造的通知,并向法院申请禁令命令船厂执行该通知。仲裁庭、高院以及上诉法院均认为船东可以占有船舶并完成建造,上诉法院的 Potter 法官是这样说的:③

In my view, the contractual remedies provided for, as cl.15.2 clearly states, contemplate alternative remedies of EITHER cancellation on the

---

① (1871) LR 12 Eq 18 at 23.
② [2001] 2 Lloyd's Rep 227.
③ [2001] 2 Lloyd's Rep 227 at 241.

one hand, in which case, upon repayment in full of the owner's expenditure plus interest, the property in the uncompleted vessel, (previously in the owner), vests in the builder without any preservation of any right in the owner to liquidated damages . . . ; OR completion in accordance with the contract save that the owner carries out the works necessary to complete the vessel in accordance with the contract.

V 责任的解除

船厂在船东解除船舶建造合同后返还了已收到的所有建造款并支付了利息后是否依然还有其他义务或责任可以分为两种情况予以讨论：一种情况是船东按照船舶建造合同的规定解约；另一种情况则是船东按照普通法的规定解约。

12.54

按合同约定解约

在 *Stocznia Gdynia SA* v *Gearbulk Holdings Ltd*① 一案中，原告船厂和被告船东订立建造三艘散货船的船舶建造合同。三个合同采用了相同的条款，均规定船厂在 2003 年 8 月 15 日依然无法交付第一艘船的，船东便可解除合同。船舶建造合同均规定了解约的后果，包括船厂返还已经收到的各期建造款并支付利息，船厂的这一义务由一份银行出具的还款保函作为担保。另外，合同的第 10.7 条有如下规定：

12.55

> Upon termination of this Contract by the Purchaser in accordance with the provisions of Article 10 or any other provision of this Contract expressly entitling the Purchaser to terminate this Contract, the Seller shall forthwith repay to the Purchaser all sums previously paid to the Seller under this Contract, together with interest accrued thereon calculated at the rate of 1 month LIBOR per annum from the respective date(s) of payment of such sums until date of refund . . . .
>
> It is however further expressly understood and agreed upon by the Parties hereto that, if the Purchaser terminates this Contract under this Article, the Purchaser shall not be entitled to any liquidated damages under Articles 10.1, 10.2, 10.3 or 10.4 hereof.

但是在第 10 条开始处有如下文字：

12.56

---

① [2009] 1 Lloyd's Rep 461.

> The Purchaser shall not be entitled to claim any other compensation and the Seller shall not be liable for any other compensation for damages sustained by reason of events set out in this Article and/or direct consequences of such events other than liquidated damages specified in this Article.

12.57　三艘船的船号分别是24,25和26。针对船号为24的船,船厂只是割了一些钢板,在2003年1月起就不再有任何其他工作;而针对船号为25和26的两艘船,船厂则没有进行过任何工作。双方曾在2003年6月至10月进行洽谈但没有结果,于是船东在2003年11月7日解除了24号船的船舶建造合同,接着要求还款保函银行还款并支付利息。2004年8月4日和11月30日,船东又分别解除了第25号船和第26号船的船舶建造合同,并要求还款保函银行还款并支付利息。在船东解约后,双方就船东在获得还款后是否还可以向船厂索赔交易损失的问题上发生了争议。船厂认为由于船东是根据合同规定解约的,因此其救济只能是获得已支付款项的返还。仲裁员认为船厂不能也不愿履行合同,因此构成了毁约。仲裁员还认为船舶建造合同第10条并没有排除任何法律规定的权利。船厂对仲裁员的裁决提出了上诉,法院需要解决的问题是:(1)第10条是否排除了所有的解约权利;(2)第10条是否排除了所有损害赔偿的索赔;(3)船东根据合同规定解约是否就不可以根据普通法解约。

12.58　高院的Burton法官认为:(1)第10条并没有排除船东根据普通法接受毁约的权利;(2)第10条并不能排除其所不适用的普通法中毁约的赔偿;(3)船东根据合同规定解除了合同就不能再根据普通法解除合同。Burton法官还对裁决进行了修改:①

> Gearbulk Holdings Ltd is precluded from claiming damages at common law for the repudiation of the three contracts by virtue of it having affirmed them and recovered monies together with interest from the Refund Guarantor in accordance with the provisions of the contracts.

12.59　船东就(3)提起上诉,而船厂则就(1)和(2)提起了上诉。上诉法院推翻了一审的判决,恢复了仲裁员的裁决。上诉法院的Moore-Bick法官认为合同当事人在订立合同时都知道一旦对方违约,法律将赋予自己获得交易损失赔偿的权利,他说的是:②

---

① [2009] 1 Lloyd's Rep 461 at 465.
② [2009] 1 Lloyd's Rep 461 at 469.

For reasons given earlier, any person approaching negotiations with a view to entering into a legally binding contract (and certainly experienced businessmen such as the parties to these contracts) is to be taken to know that the law gives him a right to recover damages for loss of his bargain if the other party commits a breach which deprives him of substantially the whole benefit that it was intended that he should obtain from it. That, of course, is a valuable right, even more valuable, perhaps, than the right of set-off .... The court is unlikely to be satisfied that a party to a contract has abandoned valuable rights arising by operation of law unless the terms of the contract make it sufficiently clear that that was intended. The more valuable the right, the clearer the language will need to be.

Moore-Bick 法官认为第 10 条并没有排除船东根据普通法规定可以获得赔偿的权利,他说:① 　　12.60

If the contract is terminated, the vessel will not be delivered and the delivery instalment will not become payable. Consistently with that, no provision is made for the payment of liquidated damages in respect of the termination of the contract (although it could have been) and there is nothing elsewhere in the Article which touches on the question. The second paragraph of Article 10.7 points in the same direction: if the contract is terminated liquidated damages are not payable, the implication being that Gearbulk is entitled to recover any losses in the usual way. For these reasons, which are in substance the same as those of the arbitrator and the judge, I agree that Article 10 does not exclude Gearbulk's right to recover damages at common law for the loss of its bargain.

从上述案例可以看出,船东的普通法权利是否已通过船舶建造合同予以排除是一个合同解释问题。几乎所有船舶建造合同标准格式都有关于在船厂返还了船东已经支付的建造款后就无需承担任何责任的规定,其中 SAJ 格式的规定如下:② 　　12.61

Upon such refund by the BUILDER to the BUYER, all obligations, duties and liabilities of each of the parties hereto to the other under this Contract shall be forthwith completely discharged.

---

① [2009] 1 Lloyd's Rep 461 at 467.
② Article X.3.

12.62　将 SAJ 格式的上述规定与 *Stocznia Gdynia SA v Gearbulk Holdings Ltd* 一案中的规定比较，似乎 SAJ 格式的上述规定并没有强调在船东解约时船厂无需支付约定赔偿，但是"under this Contract"则把"obligations, duties and liabilities"局限于船舶建造合同，换言之，上述规定并没有明确排除船东根据普通法可以享有的权利。CSTC 格式的规定与 SAJ 格式的规定措辞几乎一样，因此也没有明确排除船厂按照普通法应当承担的责任。Norwegian 格式的相关规定是：①

> Save for the Builder's obligation to refund amounts as set out above, the Builder shall have no liability for any other loss suffered by the Buyer caused by a cancellation pursuant to this Article XII, clause 1, first paragraph.

12.63　相比较而言，Norwegian 格式的规定可能比 SAJ 格式的规定更为明确一些，因为它排除了船厂针对船东根据船舶建造合同解约所遭受损失的赔偿责任。

按法律规定解约

12.64　NEWBUILDCON 格式有专门的责任以及责任排除条款，该条款不仅针对船东解约作出了规定，而且也针对船厂的解约作出了规定：②

> In the event of termination in accordance with the provisions of Clause 39(Suspension and Termination), neither Party shall have any liability to the other whatsoever or howsoever arising except as expressly provided in that Clause.
>
> In the event, however, that a Party fails to perform the Contract, or unequivocally indicates its intention not to perform it, in a way which thereby permits the other Party to treat the Contract as at an end other than under the terms of the Contract, any such claim that the other party may have shall not be limited or excluded by the terms of this Contract.

12.65　上述规定第一段针对的是船厂或者船东按照船舶建造合同的明确规定解约的情形。在这种情形下，违约一方应当按照第 39 条的规定承担责任，除此之外就无需承担任何其他责任了。这里的其他责任应当是明确的，即包括所有责任，因为第一段使用了"all liabilities""whatsoever"以及"howsoever"。而就船厂在船东解除合同时的责任而言，该格式的第 39 条规定的仅仅是返还船东已经支付的所

---

① Article XII.1, para.4.
② Clause 37(e).

有款项及其利息。但是上述规定第二段所针对的并不是根据船舶建造合同规定解除合同的情形,而是按照普通法规定解除合同的情形。在这种情形下,违约一方应当承担的责任就没有任何限制或排除。值得一提的是,按照普通法解约的前提是一方当事人的违约构成毁约。

如前所述,构成毁约应当是船厂明确表示不再履行船舶建造合同了。只有在这种情况下,船东才可以解除合同。NEWBUILDCON 格式使用的是"unequivocally indicate"。Unequivocally 的含义是"明确无误"或"不含糊其词",而 indicate 的意思应当是"提出""建议"或"暗示",indicate 不是直截了当且一清二楚的表示,而是具有"旁敲侧击"或"暗示"的意思。将 unequivocally 与 indicate 组成搭配应当是比较有意思的。船东若凭船厂的"暗示不再履行合同"或"婉转表达不再履约"解约恐怕会面临解约错误且构成和毁约的风险。

12.66

VI 减损义务

法律义务

减少损失(mitigation)简而言之是指合同的一方当事人在对方违约时,为了避免或减少因对方违约可能产生的损失而采取的行动。减少损失是一项普通法的基本原则,也是守约一方的法律义务。*Chitty on Contracts* 指出了这一原则的特征:①

12.67

> There are three rules often referred to under the comprehensive heading of "mitigation": they will be considered in turn. First, the claimant cannot recover damages for any part of his loss consequent upon the defendant's breach of contract which the claimant could have avoided by taking reasonable steps. Secondly, if the claimant in fact avoids or mitigates his loss consequent upon the defendant's breach, he cannot recover for such avoided loss, even though the steps he took were more than could be reasonably required of him under the first rule. Thirdly, where the claimant incurs loss or expense in the course of taking reasonable steps to mitigate the loss resulting from the defendant's breach, the claimant may recover this further loss or expense from the defendant.

---

① Hugh Beale, *Chitty on Contracts*, 33th edn Sweet & Maxwell 2019, para.26-087.

12.68　*Chitty on Contracts* 认为设定减损义务的目的是为了避免资源的浪费：①

> The purpose of the rules on mitigation is to prevent the waste of resources in society, since they are obviously limited. Wherever the innocent party, following the defendant's breach, is able to find substitute performance from a third party, the mitigation rules give him a strong incentive to accept the substitute. The rules inevitably give some incentive to the defendant deliberately to breach his contractual undertaking whenever he finds a better opportunity for the resources he intended to use in performing the contract: if he makes a higher profit on a new contract, he may be better off even after paying damages to compensate the original promise (because these damages may be relatively low whenever substitute performance is readily available).

合同义务

12.69　在 Sembawang Corp Ltd v Pacific Ocean Shipping Corp (No 3)②一案中，船舶改装合同约定由船厂为船东将一艘散货船改装为铺管船。船舶改装合同的第37.2条有如下规定：

> In the event of termination under paragraph 1 above, the BUILDER and the OWNERS shall have the following rights, obligations and duties: -
>
> (a) the Owners shall have the right to complete the WORK itself or with the assistance of THIRD PARTIES . . . ; and
>
> (b) the BUILDER shall be liable for the costs and expenses incurred by the OWNERS in the completion of the WORK. The OWNER has the duty to mitigate costs . . . .

12.70　船东按照改装合同的规定解除了合同，当时在新加坡有两家规模比较大的船厂，一家是吉宝船厂，另一家则是裕廊船厂。但是船东既没有找吉宝船厂，也没有找裕廊船厂继续完成船舶的改装，而是与一家英国船厂签订了合同，继续完成船舶的改装，因此产生了巨额费用。双方的争议之一是应当如何解释船舶改装合同第37.2(b)条，以及船东是否违反了该条中的"duty"。船厂认为由于写入了合同，船东减损的义务就是一项合同义务。由于船东的这义务没有任何限制，因此是一

---

① Hugh Beale, *Chitty on Contracts*, 35th edn Sweet & Maxwell 2023, para.30-098.
② [2004] App LR 11.

项绝对的义务。船东则认为第 37.2(b) 条规定的义务就是一般的法律规定的索赔人的义务,该义务并不是绝对的,而且船东已经履行了该义务。在合同解释问题上,仲裁庭接受了船东的解释。仲裁庭成员一致认为合同规定的减损义务并不比法律规定的减损义务更重。仲裁庭多数成员认为船东没有违反减损义务。高院支持了多数仲裁员的裁决,Gross 法官说:①

> ... I am wholly unable to accept that the arbitrators erred in their construction of the key words of Art. 37.2(b). In my judgment, the arbitrators were plainly right to conclude, as in this instance they did unanimously, that the duty resting on owners required them to take reasonable steps to mitigate the costs of completing the Work ....

Gross 法官的理由是:首先,当事人是将"duty to mitigate"作为法律术语使用的,法律术语应当具有法律赋予的含义;其次,"absolute duty"与合同所用的措辞其实相距甚远;最后,第 37 条并没有表明船东的义务与普通法规定的义务有所不同。

12.71

---

① [2004] App LR 11 [18].

第 13 章 船东的违约

I 违约的构成

违约的定义

13.1 英文中的"breach"一般是指对义务的违反或是对法律的违背,包括对合同的违反。① 与 Breach 相对应的中文应当是"违约",由于有了"约"字,"违约"通常是指对合同约定的违反,即一方当事人违反合同义务。在 Jarvis v Moy Davies Smith Vandervell and Company 一案中,上诉法院的 Greer 法官在比较违约和侵权时说:②

> The distinction in the modern view, for this purpose, between contract and tort may be put thus: where the breach of duty alleged arises out of a liability independently of the personal obligation undertaken by contract, it is tort, and it may be tort even though there may happen to be a contract between the parties, if the duty in fact arises independently of that contract. Breach of contract occurs where that which is complained of is a breach of duty arising out of the obligations undertaken by the contract.

13.2 违约既可以是拒绝履行合同义务,也可以是不按照约定履行合同义务。英国法对此并没有予以区分。当合同一方违反了一项合同义务后即会产生另一项义务,即向合同相对方支付损害赔偿的义务,然而就合同相对方而言,在特定情况下不仅可以获得损害赔偿,而且还有权决定是否解除合同而不再继续履行。导致对方有权解除合同的违约就是毁约。Anson's Law of Contract 一书是这样说的:③

---

① Daniel Greenberg, *Jowitt's Dictionary of English Law* 3rd edn Sweet & Maxwell 2010, p.289.
② [1936] 1 KB 399 at 405.
③ J. Beatson, et al, *Anson's Law of Contract* 30th edn Oxford University Press 2016, p.533.

If one of the parties to a contract breaches an obligation which the contract imposes, that party is in breach of contract. The breach may consist in the non-performance of the relevant obligation, or its performance in a manner or at a time which fails to comply with the requirements of the contract. English law does not generally distinguish between these different forms of breach of contract, but applies the same remedial regime to them all, and as soon as the party is in breach a new obligation will in every case arise by operation of law – an obligation to pay damages to the other party in respect of any loss or damage sustained by the breach.

船东的支付义务

如前所述,船东在船舶建造合同中最为重要的义务是按照约定支付各期建造款。① 船东若不按约定支付各期建造款便构成违约,船厂可以按照1979年《货物买卖法》的规定对船东提起诉讼,要求支付到期建造款:②

13.3

Where, under a contract of sale, the price is payable on a day certain irrespective of delivery and the buyer wrongfully neglects or refuses to pay such price, the seller may maintain an action for the price, although the property in the goods has not passed and the goods have not been appropriated to the contract.

有时船舶建造合同还会规定船东按照约定支付建造款的义务不受双方争议的影响,例如SAJ格式便有如下内容:③

13.4

No payment under this Contract shall be delayed or withheld by the BUYER on account of any dispute or disagreement of whatever nature arising between the parties hereto.

违约后果的约定

按照契约自由原则,当事人可以在合同中约定构成违约的事项,也可以约定发生特定违约事项的后果。在实践中,大多数船舶建造合同都有船东违约的条

13.5

---

① 但有不少船舶建造合同规定船东支付第一期建造款是船舶建造合同的生效条件,在这种情况下,船东支付第一期建造款就不再是履行合同义务了。
② s.49(2).
③ Article II.4, para.2.

款,而且都给船东的违约下了定义。SAJ 格式便有如下规定:①

> The BUYER shall be deemed to be in default of performance of its obligations under this Contract in the following cases:
>
> (a) If the BUYER fails to pay any of the First, Second and Third Installments to the BUILDER within three(3)days after such Installment becomes due and payable under the provisions of Article II hereof; or
>
> (b) If the BUYER fails to pay the Fourth Installment to the BUILDER concurrently with the delivery of the VESSEL by the BUILDER to the BUYER as provided in Article II hereof; or
>
> (c) If the BUYER fails to take delivery of the VESSEL, when the VESSEL is duly tendered for delivery by the BUILDER under the provisions of Article VII hereof.

13.6　一旦当事人对违约作出了约定,除非该约定因违法而无效,否则当事人约定的违约是否构成法律规定的违约已不再重要。按照上述规定,船东的违约主要有三个方面:第一是没有按照船舶建造合同的约定支付第一期、第二期以及第三期建造款;第二是没有在接船时支付第四期建造款;第三是在船厂按照船舶建造合同规定交付船舶时没有接船。在船舶建造合同中,船东的义务相对于船厂是比较简单的,船东最根本的义务就是按照约定支付建造款。虽然 SAJ 格式将船东的违约分为三个方面,但实际上就是按照约定支付建造款的义务。把第四期,即最后一期建造款的支付区别于前面三期建造款的支付可能并没有太大的意义,因为同样是船东没有按照约定支付建造款。在实践中,船厂通常在船东的第四期款已经汇入自己指定的银行后才交船的,因此发生船东接了船但却未支付第四期款情形的可能性相当小。同样道理,很难想象船东会在支付了第四期建造款后拒绝接船。

13.7　CSTC 格式的规定与 SAJ 格式的规定基本相同,但由于 CSTC 格式把船厂收到船东支付的第一期建造款作为船舶建造合同生效的条件之一,因此关于迟延支付的规定并不包括第一期建造款。② NEWBUILDCON 格式约定的船东违约情形有以下几种:③

---

① Article XI.1.
② Article XI.1.
③ Clause 39(b).

(i) The guarantor providing the Instalment Guarantee or Performance Guarantee on behalf of the Buyer under Clause 14(a)(Buyer's Instalment/Performance Guarantee) is deemed insolvent pursuant to Sub-clause(d) below, unless the Buyer can provide a replacement Performance Guarantee acceptable to the Builder within 30 days and provided that notice of termination is given before an acceptable Buyer's Instalment or Performance Guarantee is received by the Builder, or
(ii) The Buyer fails to pay any sums due under this Contract for a period of twenty-one(21) Banking Days provided that the Builder thereafter gives the Buyer at least 5 Banking Days notice of its intention to terminate under this Clause, and within that period the Buyer fails to remedy the breach and provided that notice of termination is given before the Buyer pays the outstanding sums due, or
(iii) The Buyer fails to take delivery of the Vessel tendered in accordance with this Contract, or
(iv) The Buyer is in breach of Clause 14(Guarantees).

13.8 第一种情形是在针对船东承诺提供履约保函的,提供履约保函的担保人破产构成船东的违约。在实践中船东提供履约保函的情形并不多见。第四种情形同样是针对船东承诺提供履约保函的。一旦船东未能按照约定提供履约保函的即构成违约。

II 利息和费用

违约利息

13.9 如果船东支付建造款有迟延的就应当支付利息并应支付因迟延支付而产生的费用。实际上,船东因迟延支付建造款而须支付利息并不需要船舶建造合同予以明确规定。1979年《货物买卖法》便有如下规定:①

> Nothing in this Act affects the right of the buyer or the seller to recover interest or special damages in any case where by law interest or special damages may be recoverable, or to recover money paid where the consideration for the payment of it has failed.

---

① s.54.

13.10　传统上,利息是由衡平法院判决的。衡平法院认为当事人支付利息并不是为了惩罚,而是针对遗嘱执行人或受托人或任何基于信用的人对金钱的滥用或谋取私利的情形判决利息。正如 Lord Denning 在 *Wallersteiner* v *Moir(No 2)* 一案中所总结的,他说:①

> Those judgments show that, in equity, interest is never awarded by way of punishment. Equity awards it whenever money is misused by an executor or a trustee or anyone else in a fiduciary position – who has misapplied the money and made use of it himself for his own benefit .... The reason is because a person in a fiduciary position is not allowed to make a profit out of his trust: and, if he does, he is liable to account for that profit or interest in lieu thereof. In addition, in equity interest is awarded whenever a wrongdoer deprives a company of money which it needs for use in its business. It is plain that the company should be compensated for the loss thereby occasioned to it. Mere replacement of the money – years later – is by no means adequate compensation, especially in days of inflation.

13.11　按照普通法规定,法院只有在被告拒绝履行金钱支付义务时才会判决被告承担利息,而根据合同约定应当进行的支付,除非当事人另有约定或者存在习惯做法,法院通常不会判决利息。在 *Page* v *Newman* 一案中,被告向原告借钱并立了字据。原告要求被告支付利息,但是法院认为双方并没有约定利息。因此 Lord Tenterden 认为原告不能获得利息,他说:②

> I think that we ought not to depart from the long-established rule, that interest is not due on money secured by a written instrument, unless it appears on the face of the instrument that interest was intended to be paid, or unless it be implied from the usage of trade, as in the case of mercantile instruments.

13.12　普通法不判决利息的做法实际上也受到了法官的批评,在 *Sempra Metals Ltd (formerly Metallgesellschaft Ltd)* v *Inland Revenue Commissioners and another* 一案中,上议院的 Lord Hope 就说:③

> The common law's unwillingness to presume interest losses where

---

① [1975] QB 373 at 388.
② (1829) 9 B&C 378 at 381.
③ [2008] AC 561 at 601.

payment is delayed is, I readily accept, unrealistic. This is especially so at times when inflation abounds and prevailing rates of interest are high. To require proof of loss in each case may seem unduly formalistic. The common law can bear this reproach. If a party chooses not to prove his interest losses the remedy provided by the law is to be found in the statutory provisions .... For these reasons I consider the court has a common law jurisdiction to award interest, simple and compound, as damages on claims for non-payment of debts as well as on other claims for breach of contract and in tort.

13.13 在同一个案件中，Lord Scott 也认为原则上利息应当获得赔偿，他说：①

... interest losses caused by a breach of contract or by a tortious wrong should be held to be in principle recoverable, but subject to proof of loss, remoteness of damage rules, obligations to mitigate damage and any other relevant rules relating to the recovery of alleged losses.

13.14 但是普通法并不假设迟延支付本身会造成损害，因此当事人在可以对利息作出约定的情况下而不在合同中作出约定的则表明当事人有可能放弃利息的意图。对此，Lord Hope 是这样说的：②

The common law does not assume that delay in payment of a debt will of itself cause damage. Loss must be proved.

支付利息的约定

13.15 常见的船舶建造合同标准格式都有船东违约利息适用的利率，例如 SAJ 格式就有如下规定：③

If the BUYER is in default to payment as to any Installment as provided in Paragraph(a)and(b)of this Article, the BUYER shall pay interest on such Installment at the rate of .... percent (.......%) per annum from the due date thereof to the date of payment to the BUILDER of the full amount including interest; in case the BUYER shall fail to take delivery of the VESSEL as provided in Paragraph 1(c) of this Article, the BUYER shall be deemed in default of payment of the

---

① [2008] AC 561 at 609.
② [2008] AC 561 at 601.
③ Article XI.2, para.1.

> Fourth Installment and shall pay interest thereon at the same rate as aforesaid from and including the day on which the VESSEL is tendered for delivery by the BUILDER.

13.16 船东没有按照船舶建造合同规定支付建造款的应当按照约定的利率支付利息。但船东应当支付利息的情形似乎也仅限于建造款而已,因为 SAJ 格式第 IX 条(a)和(b)规定的就是建造款。换言之,如果船东支付其他款项有迟延的,例如船东没有按时支付因自己提出修改而产生的费用应当是无需支付利息的。

13.17 船东应当支付利息的期限是自应付建造款"到期日"起至实际支付日。① 到期日是指船东应当支付建造款的日期。然而船舶建造合同规定的到期日通常是一个期间,如"5 个银行工作日"或"7 个银行工作日"等,船东在这种情况下可以在约定期限内的任何一天支付建造款,均不构成迟延支付。船东只有在到期日之后支付建造款才构成迟延支付,才有支付利息的义务。如果 SAJ 格式规定的船东应当支付利息的期限包括到期日的,也就意味着船东必须为自己在到期日没有支付建造款而须支付利息,而在到期日支付建造款并不构成迟延支付,因此船东应当支付利息的期限是自合同约定的船东支付建造款的期限届满后的第一天起至船东实际支付建造款的那一天止。

13.18 SAJ 格式将船东在船厂交付船舶时拒绝接船视为船东违反了支付最后一期建造款的义务。虽然船东在支付了最后一期建造款后不太可能会拒绝接船,但是将拒绝接船视为违反付款义务可能没有太大的意义。因为,船东一旦在支付了最后一期建造款后依然拒绝接船的,船厂实际上是不能主张船东迟延支付的。如果船东拒绝接船且没有支付最后一期建造款的,船东没有按照约定支付建造款的事实已经发生,船厂根本无需将船东拒绝接船的行为视为违反了支付建造款的义务。②

13.19 AWES 格式关于利息的规定比较简单:③

> Should the PURCHASER be in default in payment of any CONTRACT instalment and/or other amounts due under this CONTRACT, then the PURCHASER shall pay to the CONTRACTOR – as from the due date – interest thereon at the rate of .... percent per annum over ....

---

① 几乎所有船舶建造合同标准格式规定的迟延支付利息均从到期日开始计算。
② CSTC 格式也有类似的规定,见 Article XI.3(a)。
③ Article 10, para.1.

13.20　与 SAJ 格式不同的是,由于 AWES 格式使用了"other amounts due under this CONTRACT",因此关于迟延支付利息的规定不仅适用于船东未能按照船舶建造合同规定的时间支付各期建造款的情形,而且还适用于船东未能按照约定向船厂支付所有其他款项的情形。NEWBUILDCON 格式并没有针对船东的支付义务作出关于迟延支付利息的规定,但该格式有一专门规定利息的条款,从该条款的规定来看,在使用 NEWBUILDCON 格式时,利息应当适用于所有应付而未按时支付的款项。该条款的内容是:①

> If either Party fails to pay any sum due in accordance with the terms of this Contract, the other Party shall have the right to charge interest from the due date at the rate stated in Box 30 on such outstanding sums(see also Clause 39(Suspension and Termination)).

13.21　在利息期的计算上,CSTC 格式的规定似乎比较特殊:②

> If the BUYER is in default of payment as to any instalment as provided in Paragraph 1(a)and/or 1(b)of this Article, the BUYER shall pay interest on such instalment at the rate of ＿＿＿ percent(＿＿%) per annum for a period of 15 days from the due date thereof and thereafter at the rate of ＿＿＿ percent(＿＿%) per annum until the date of the payment of the full amount, including all aforesaid interest.

13.22　与 SAJ 格式相同,CSTC 格式规定的利息也应当仅针对各期建造款的。利息的计算分为两个期间并适用不同的利率。第一个期间是到期日起的 15 天,适用一个利率。第二个期间是自第 16 天起至船东实际支付之日,适用不同的利率。按照 CSTC 格式的规定,船东迟延支付建造款超过 15 天的,船厂就可以解除船舶建造合同,③因此自第 16 天起,船厂既可以选择解约,也可以选择适用不同的利率收取利息。

违约费用

13.23　在船东没有按照合同规定的期限支付建造款时,船东不仅应当支付迟延支付的利息,而且还应当承担船厂因其迟延支付而产生的各项费用。为此 SAJ 格式规

---

① Clause 18.
② Article XI.3(a).
③ Article XI.4(b).

定的是:①

> In any event of default by the BUYER, the BUYER shall also pay all charges and expenses incurred by the BUILDER in consequence of such default.

13.24 如果船东迟延支付的是第一期或第二期建造款,因此产生的费用可能并不会很多。如果船东迟延支付的是最后一期建造款,因此产生的费用则会比较多一些,这些费用大致包括:安排交船的费用、约定交船日后的船舶看管以及保险费用等。

III 顺延和中止

概述

13.25 虽然船东未按约定支付款项构成违约,但除非双方另有约定,船厂并不能因此当然顺延合同交船日或中止船舶建造。"顺延"(extension)和"中止"(suspension)并不是普通法规定的权利。船厂顺延合同交船日或中止船舶建造实际上都是拒绝履行合同的行为,同样有可能构成违约甚至毁约。正如 Staughton 法官在 *Channel Tunnel Group Ltd and France Manche SA v Balfour Beatty Construction Ltd and Others* 一案中所指出的:②

> It is well established that if one party is in serious breach, the other can treat the contract as altogether at an end, but there is not yet any established doctrine of English law that the other party may suspend performance, keeping the contract alive. It is said that there is authority, at any rate in the Commonwealth, which would support such a doctrine.

13.26 根据普通法原则,只有当一方的违约行为构成毁约时,另一方才可以选择解除合同而不再继续履行。因此,在船舶建造合同中船厂顺延合同交船日和中止船舶建造的权利是以合同有约定为前提的。

---

① Article XI.2, para.2, see also CSTC Article XI.3(b).
② [1992] 2 Lloyd's Rep 7 at 11.

合同交船日顺延

有些船舶建造合同规定,船东延迟支付时,船厂可以顺延合同交船日,有些则没有此种规定。SAJ 格式允许船厂顺延合同交船日,而且还是自动顺延。该格式的规定是:①

13.27

> If any default by the BUYER occurs as provided hereinbefore, the Delivery Date shall be automatically postponed for a period of continuance of such default by the BUYER.

AWES 格式也有类似的规定:②

13.28

> The CONTRACTOR shall be entitled to one day's postponement of the Delivery Date of the VESSEL for each day of delay in excess of two days in the payment of the aforesaid sums ....

上述 SAJ 格式和 AWES 格式规定的不同之处应当是比较明显的。按照 SAJ 格式的规定,船东迟延支付款项的,合同交船日便会自动顺延。然而按照 AWES 格式的规定,顺延合同交船日只是船厂的一项选择权而已。而作为选择权,只有在作出选择时才生效。如果船厂未作出选择,将被视为放弃顺延合同交船日的权利。此外,按照 AWES 格式的规定,只有当船东迟延支付超过两天时,船厂才可以从第三天起顺延合同交船日。CSTC 格式同样将顺延合同交船日视为船厂的一项选择权。③

13.29

NEWBUILDCON 格式并没有直接规定在船东迟延支付款项时船厂可以顺延合同交船日,而只是规定船东迟延支付款项的,船厂可以中止船舶建造。④ 而在该格式的"可允许延误"条款中则规定了船厂中止船舶建造的可以顺延合同交船日的有关细则:⑤

13.30

> The Delivery Date shall be extended if any of the following events cause actual delay to the delivery of the Vessel:
>
> ......
>
> (5) Suspension of work pursuant to Clause 39 (c) (Suspension and

---

① Article XI.3(a).
② Article 10, para.2.
③ Article XI.4(a).
④ Clause 39(c).
⑤ Clause 34(a)(ii).

Termination – Suspension of Work)。

13.31　值得注意的是,船厂顺延合同交船日是以船东的违约实际造成交船延误为条件的。船东延迟支付建造款有可能导致交船的延误,但未必一定会导致交船的延误。

中止建造的权利

13.32　如前所述,中止建造并不是船厂的普通法权利,而是合同约定的权利。因此,只有在船舶建造合同有约定时船厂才能按照约定中止船舶建造。SAJ 格式并没有关于船东中止船舶建造权利的规定,但 AWES 格式则有此规定:①

> ... if the delay exceeds 15 days as from the due date the CONTRACTOR shall have the option to suspend the CONTRACTOR's obligations under this CONTRACT until payment of such sums and interest thereon has been received by the CONTRACTOR.

13.33　NEWBUILDCON 格式规定,船东没有按照船舶建造合同规定支付建造款的,船厂可以中止船舶建造:②

> Without prejudice to Sub-clause (b) above the Builder shall have the right to suspend work under this Contract if the Buyer fails to pay any instalment stated in Box 11 due for a period of fifteen (15) Banking Days until payment of such outstanding sums.

13.34　通过比较不难看出两者的区别。NEWBUILDCON 格式把 AWES 格式规定的 15 天改成了 15 个银行工作日,因此实际上是延长了船厂可以中止船舶建造的期限。AWES 格式与 SAJ 格式相同,没有规定船东支付的时间期限,而是规定船东应当在到期日支付。③ 因此按照 AWES 格式的规定,一旦船东未能在款项到期日起的 15 天内支付的,船厂就可以中止船舶建造。然而按照 NEWBUILDCON 格式支付条款的规定,船东可以在款项支付日到期后的 5 个银行工作日内支付,因此只有当船东在到期日后的 20 个银行工作日内依然没有支付款项的,船厂才可以中止船舶建造。

13.35　Norwegian 格式也有关于船厂中止船舶建造的规定。按照该格式的规定,船

---

① Article 10, para.2.
② Clause 39(c).
③ Article 7(c), para.2.

东未能按照船舶建造合同的规定支付建造款的，船厂应当向船东发出通知，要求船东支付：①

> If the Buyer fails to make payments provided for in Article III clause 3,② the Builder shall by written notice or by telefax confirmed by registered mail to the Buyer request payment of the unpaid amount. If the amount has not been paid within 7 Banking Days from receipt of such notice, the Builder may postpone the commencement of or stop the work on the Vessel and enforce payment of the claim, the net loss of time caused thereby being Permissible Delay under the Contract.

Norwegian 格式规定船东应当在特定日期后的一定银行工作日内支付各期建造款，具体天数由当事人约定填入。上述规定提及的船东未能按第Ⅲ.3条的规定支付款项应当是指船东在约定的银行工作日内没有支付的情形。因此上述规定中的7个银行工作日也就是在双方约定的船东应当支付款项的银行工作日之后才起算的7个银行工作日，换言之，只有当船东在这两个期限内依然没有支付约定款项时，船厂才可以中止船舶建造。 13.36

中止建造和合同交船日顺延

上文提及的 NEWBUILDCON 格式和 Norwegian 格式都有关于船厂在船东未按约定支付建造款时可以中止建造的规定。这里讨论的问题是：船东未按约定支付建造款，船厂没有中止建造，但是否可以主张顺延合同交船日？如果船厂按照合同规定在船东未按约定时间支付建造款时中止了船舶建造，在采用 Norwegian 格式的情况下，只要确有时间损失，船厂应当可以主张合同交船日的顺延的。在采用 NEWBUILDCON 格式情况下，如果船东支付延迟确实导致交船的延误，船厂也应当有机会主张顺延合同交船日。但是，如果船厂在船东未按约定时间支付建造款时并没有中止船舶建造而是选择继续建造船舶，在这种情况下船厂是否依然可以主张合同交船日的顺延则可能是有问题的。Norwegian 格式规定的是"时间净损失"，可视为可允许延误，但若船厂实际上在该期间是继续建造的，所谓的"时间净损失"就不存在了，故而船厂未必可以主张合同交船日的顺延。在采用 NEWBUILDCON 格式时，船厂同样未必可以在实际建造船舶的情况下主张合同 13.37

---

① Article XII.2(a).
② Norwegian 格式的原文是"Article IV, Clause 3"，但该条 Article IV, Clause 3 是关于油耗过度的规定，而 Article III, Clause 3 则是关于支付条件和方式的规定，因此"Article IV, Clause"有可能是"Article III, Clause 3"的笔误。

交船日的顺延,因为在这种情况下船舶建造可能并没有发生延误。而且,"可允许延误"的定义是:"船舶建造或交付的延误",即"可允许延误"应当是以船舶建造或交付实际上遭受延误为前提的。

Ⅳ 船厂的解约

支付的违约

13.38 　　船东在船舶建造合同中的根本义务就是按照约定支付建造款。普通法原则是合同中关于支付时间的规定并不构成合同的条件条款,①因此除非船东迟延支付款项构成毁约或者合同有明确约定,船厂并不能因船东未按约定支付建造款而享有解约的权利。几乎所有的船舶建造合同标准格式都规定,船东未按合同约定支付建造款超过一定期限的,船厂可以解除船舶建造合同,SAJ 格式的规定是:②

> If any default by the BUYER continues for a period of fifteen (15) days, the BUILDER may, as its option, rescind this Contract by giving notice of such effect to the BUYER by cable confirmed in writing. Upon receipt by the BUYER of such notice of rescission, this Contract shall forthwith become null and void and any of the BUYER Supplies shall become the sole property of the BUILDER.

13.39 　　根据 SAJ 格式的规定,在建造款到期后的三天内船东依然没有支付的就构成违约。③ 按照 SAJ 格式的规定,船东应当在收到船厂的通知后支付。④ 根据普通法,在当事人没有约定履行期限时应当适用合理期限,Cockburn 法官在 *Alexiadi v Robinson* 一案中是这样说的:⑤

> Under ordinary circumstances, when a man is called upon by a contract to do an act, and no time is specified, he is allowed a reasonable time for doing it; and what is a reasonable time may depend on all the circumstances of the case.

---

① 请参见本书第 4 章第 Ⅱ 节。
② Article XI.3(b).
③ Article XI.1(a).
④ Article II.4.
⑤ (1846) 9 QB 713 at 724.

合理期限有多长是一个事实问题,应根据具体事实和情况予以判断,但由于 SAJ 格式实际上规定船东在款项到期后的三天内依然未支付的即构成违约,因此合理期限也就不再有适用的意义了。一旦船东在建造款到期后没有支付超过 18 天,船厂就有权解除合同。相比之下,AWES 格式规定的船厂行使解约权之前必须等待的时间则要长很多,该格式的规定是:①

13.40

> If the aforesaid delay exceeds 30 calendar days from the due date, the CONTRACTOR, even if it has elected to suspend the work as aforesaid, may have the right to terminate the CONTRACT by giving notice in writing, which may be by telefax if confirmed by letter, to the PURCHASER about such termination. In this event the CONTRACTOR shall be entitled to recover damages from the PURCHASER in respect of any loss that the CONTRACTOR has suffered by reason of the PURCHASER's default.

AWES 格式与 SAJ 格式一样,也没有规定船东支付的时间期限,而只是规定船东应当在到期日支付。因此在适用 AWES 格式的情况下,一旦船东在到期日后的 30 天内依然没有支付建造款的,船厂就可以选择解除船舶建造合同。两个标准格式只是在期限长短上不同而已。而且,船厂解除合同的权利并不受其中止船舶建造决定的影响。换言之,船东迟延支付超过 15 天的,船厂可以中止或暂缓船舶的建造。一旦船东迟延支付超过 30 天的,船厂就可以选择解除船舶建造合同。②

13.41

违约通知和解约通知

除非双方另有约定,合同一方违约并使对方有权解除合同的,对方可以解除合同而无需发出违约通知或解约通知。但不少船舶建造合同标准格式都有关于违约通知的规定,例如 CSTC 格式规定:③

13.42

> If the BUYER is in default of payment or in performance of its obligations as provided hereinabove, the SELLER shall notify the BUYER to that effect by telex after the date of occurrence of the default as per Paragraph 1 of this Article and the BUYER shall forthwith

---

① Article 10, para.3.
② 按照 Norwegian 格式的规定,船东迟延支付超过 21 天的,船厂便可以解除船舶建造合同,见 Article XII.2(b)。
③ Article XI.2.

acknowledge by telex to the SELLER that such notification has been received. In case the BUYER does not give the aforesaid telex acknowledgment to the SELLER within three(3)calendar days it shall be deemed that such notification has been duly received by the BUYER.

13.43　由于船厂有义务在解约前向船东发出违约通知,上述规定应当理解为船厂在发出违约通知之前是不能解约的。CSTC 格式同时又有如下规定:①

If any such default as defined in Paragraph 1(a)or 1(b)or 1(c)of this Article committed by the BUYER continues for a period of fifteen(15) days, then, the SELLER shall have all following rights and remedies:

(1) The SELLER may, at its option, cancel or rescind this Contract, provided the SELLER has notified the BUYER of such default pursuant to Paragraph 2 of this Article, by giving notice of such effect to the BUYER by telex confirmed in writing ....

13.44　在解约问题上,CSTC 格式实际上分别规定了两个通知,即违约通知和解约通知。上述"has notified the BUYER of such default"是指上文提及的违约通知,而"by giving notice of such effect"则应是指解约通知。换言之,船东违约的,船厂应当先发出违约通知。如果船东未能在违约后的 15 天内纠正违约,船厂才可以发出解约通知并解除建造合同。按照 CSTC 格式的规定,船厂发出的违约通知似乎还需要船东确认收到,船东没有确认的则在船厂发出违约通知三天后视为收到。规定违约通知需要对方确认收到恐怕是没有什么意义,因为船东在违约后的15 天内没有纠正违约的,船厂就可以解约了。

13.45　SAJ 格式没有要求船厂在解约之前应当发出违约通知,而只是规定了解约通知,按照 SAJ 格式的规定,船厂的解约通知在船东收到之时生效:②

... Upon receipt by the BUYER of such notice of rescission, this Contract shall forthwith become null and void ....

13.46　NEWBUILDCON 格式关于通知的规定与众不同,该格式的规定是:③

The Buyer fails to pay any sums due under this Contract for a period of twenty-one(21) Banking Days provided that the Builder thereafter gives the Buyer at least 5 Banking Days notice of its intention to terminate

---

① Article XI.4(b)(i).
② Article XI.3(b), para.1, see also AWES Article 10, para.3.
③ Clause 39(b)(ii).

under this Clause, and within that period the Buyer fails to remedy the breach and provided that notice of termination is given before the Buyer pays the outstanding sums due, or . . . .

13.47　船东在款项到期后的 21 个银行工作日未支付似乎依然没有构成违约,至少船厂是不能解约的。船厂打算解约的还应当在 21 个银行工作日后再给船东 5 个银行工作日。只有当船东依然没有在该 5 个银行工作日内支付的,船厂才可以解约。NEWBUILDCON 格式实际上对船东支付约定建造款都规定了期限,例如除了第一期和最后一期款外的其他各期建造款都应当在到期日后的 4 个银行工作日内支付。① 但上述规定使得船东付款期限都不再有意义了。

船厂权利的排除

13.48　与其他船舶建造合同标准格式不同,Norwegian 格式有关于船厂解约权排除的规定:②

Notwithstanding the above, if there is a dispute in respect of the Buyer's payment obligation, the Builder has no right to postpone the commencement or stop the work or cancel the Contract, if the Buyer provides security acceptable to the Builder for the disputed unpaid amount.

13.49　按照上述规定,一旦双方对船东是否迟延支付款项产生争议,船厂既不可以推迟或停止船舶的建造,也不可以解除船舶建造合同,但是船东应当就争议数额提供船厂接受的担保。就船东的支付义务而言,由于船舶建造合同已经明确规定了支付的时间以及具体数额,实际上不太可能发生争议。而就上述关于担保的规定来看,似乎仅仅是指关于船东应当支付的数额的争议。然而就支付数额而言,除了最后一期建造款由于有可能涉及修改等原因而出现数额的增减,其他各期建造款的数额在船舶建造合同订立之时就已经确定了,因此双方就数额发生争议的可能性应当不是太大。船舶建造合同大多采用固定价格的方式,而且与海工设备的建造不同,在商船建造中出现的修改可能涉及的金额一般不会太大,因此船东为有争议数额提供担保恐怕没有太大的意义。

---

① Clause 15(a)(iii).
② Article XII.2, para.3.

因破产而解约

13.50　Norwegian 格式第 XII 条是违约规定,共有三款:(1)船厂的违约以及与此相对应的船东解约;(2)船东的违约以及双方关于支付的争议;(3)关于合同一方破产对船舶建造合同的影响。Norwegian 格式关于破产解约的规定如下:①

> If proceedings are commenced by or against the Buyer or Builder for winding up, dissolution or reorganisation (except in case of merger) or for the appointment of a receiver, trustee or similar officer, or if bankruptcy is opened, the party who is not subject to such proceedings shall have the right to cancel this Contract.
>
> Upon such cancellation, the Builder shall refund all sums paid by Buyer to the Builder under Article III hereof, including interest thereon at the rate of ....%(per cent) annum from the date of payment to the date of refund. The Builder shall also return Buyer's Supplies, or if they cannot be returned, the Builder shall pay to the Buyer an amount equal to the Buyer's costs for such equipment.
>
> Save as for the Builder's obligation to make refund as set out above, neither the Builder nor the Buyer shall have any liability for losses suffered by the other party caused by the cancellation pursuant to this Article XII, clause 3.

13.51　第一段提及的歇业、解散、重组、指定接管人或受托人以及破产程序开始等既可以针对船东也可以针对船厂,如果是船厂发生上述情形,船东就有权解约;如果是船东发生上述情形,船厂也可以解约。第二段的规定似乎有问题,按第二段的规定,一旦建造合同被解除,船厂就应当向船东返还所有已收到款项并按照约定利率支付利息,而且船厂还要向船东归还船东供应品,若无法归还的则应支付船东的采购成本。由于第一段提及的解约的当事方并不是确定的,因此第二段中的"此种解约"既有可能是指船厂的解约,也有可能是指船东的解约。如果船东由于船厂违约而解约的,船厂理应返还所有预付款及其利息;但若是船厂由于船东破产而解约的,解约后依然要返还预付款及其利息显然是没有丝毫依据的。

---

① Article XII.3.

V 解约的结果

建造款的保留

13.52 在船厂解除船舶建造合同时船东可能已经支付了几期建造款,这就会产生船东已付建造款的归属问题。虽然大多数船舶建造合同都会规定船东支付的建造款具有预付款性质,但在船东违约时应当没有理由要求船厂返还已经支付的建造款。只有在船厂违约而船东解除合同时才存在预付款返还的问题。SAJ 格式明确规定船厂在船东违约情况下有权保留船东已支付的建造款:①

> In the event of such rescission of this Contract, the BUILDER shall be entitled to retain any Installment or Installments theretofore paid by the BUYER to the BUILDER on account of this Contract.

13.53 AWES 格式和 Norwegian 格式没有类似的规定,但是 CSTC 格式的规定则与 SAJ 格式的规定基本相同。② NEWBUILDCON 格式也有类似的规定:③

> If this Contract is terminated by the Builder, the Builder shall have the right to retain the Buyer' Supplies together with any instalments paid by the Buyer ....

到期款的支付

13.54 船厂在按照约定解约时可以获得已到期但船东尚未支付的款项,这是因为船厂针对已到期建造款的权利已经产生,即使船厂解除了船舶建造合同也同样可以获得已到期的建造款。正如 Dixon 法官在 *McDonald v Dennys Lascelles Ltd* 一案中所指出的:④

> When a party to a simple contract, upon a breach by the other contracting party of a condition of the contract, elects to treat the contract as no longer binding upon him, the contract is not rescinded as from the beginning. Both parties are discharged from further

---

① Article XI.3(b), para.2.
② CSTC Article XI.4(b)(ii).
③ Clause 39(f).
④ (1933) 48 CLR 457 at 476.

performance of the contract, but rights are not divested or discharged which have already been unconditionally acquired. Rights and obligations which arise from the partial execution of the contract and causes of action which have accrued from its breach alike continue unaffected.

13.55　按照1997年《货物买卖法》的规定,如果合同约定的支付日期是确定的,一旦买方未按照约定支付货款,卖方有权对买方提起诉讼,要求买方支付约定的货款。而船舶的所有权在交船之前归船厂所有这一事实并不影响船厂要求船东支付约定价款的权利。该法的规定如下:①

Where, under a contract of sale, the price is payable on a day certain irrespective of delivery and the buyer wrongfully neglects or refuses to pay such price, the seller may maintain an action for the price, although the property in the goods has not passed and the goods have not been appropriated to the contract.

13.56　在 *Workman, Clark & Co Ltd v Lloyd Brazilero*② 一案中,船东向船厂订造新船,建造合同规定了建造款分期支付。船东主张1893年《货物买卖法》第49条第2款规定不适用于货款分期支付的买卖合同(1979年《货物买卖法》第49条内容和1893年《货物买卖法》相同)。但是上诉法院则认为第49条第2款适用于货款分期支付的买卖合同,无论货物所有权是否转移。上诉法院的 Farwell 法官说:③

But, if any such difficulty could now arise, I think that it is met by s.49 of the Sale of Goods Act, 1893. The terms of that section appear to me to apply to the sale of goods for a price to be paid by instalments ....

13.57　虽然船舶建造合同规定支付建造款的时间为安放龙骨之日,但安放龙骨之日是可以根据建造进程确定的事件,因此依然符合1893年《货物买卖法》第49条第2款规定的确定日支付。

13.58　在 *Hyundai Heavy Industries Co Ltd v Papadopoulos and Others*④ 一案中,船东没有按照船舶建造合同的约定支付建造款,船厂解除了合同并根据船东提供的付款保函索赔。上议院的 Dilhorne 子爵对船厂可以获得已经到期款项的权利作出

---

① s.49(2).
② [1908] 1 KB 968.
③ [1908] 1 KB 968 at 978.
④ [1980] 2 Lloyd's Rep 1.

了说明,他引用了 *Hudson on Building Contract* 一书的观点:①

> Where the contractor has become entitled to an instalment payment, he will not normally forfeit his right to such payment by a subsequent abandonment of repudiation of the contract, but will be entitled to sue for any unpaid instalment if he has satisfied the conditions for it to become due, subject, of course, to the employer's right to counterclaim for damages for breach of contract.

尚未到期的款项

13.59　除非船舶建造合同另有规定,船厂在解约后没有权利获得尚未到期的建造款。同样是在 *Hyundai Heavy Industries Co Ltd* v *Papadopoulos and Others* 一案中,上议院的 Lord Fraser 强调船厂不能获得尚未到期的建造款。他认为在船厂解除合同后,船东就不再有支付建造款的义务了,船东的义务是支付损害赔偿。他是这样说的:②

> ... nobody has suggested that future instalments (that is, instalments which have not fallen due for payment by the date of cancelation of the contact) are payable. It is, I think, clear that they cease to be payable as instalments, and are replaced by the buyer's obligation to pay any deficiency brought out in the final accounting.

13.60　在实践中,有的船舶建造合同会规定船厂在因船东违约而解除合同后有权宣布所有尚未到期的建造款立即到期,船东应当立刻支付所有各期建造款。CSTC格式便有类似的规定:③

> (Applicable to any BUYER's default defined in 1(a) of this Article) The SELLER shall, without prejudice to the SELLER's right to recover from the BUYER the 5th instalment, interest, costs and/or expenses by applying the proceeds to be obtained by sale of the VESSEL in accordance with the provisions set out in this Contract, have the right to declare all unpaid 2nd, 3rd and 4th instalments to be forthwith due and payable, and upon such declaration, the SELLER shall have the right to immediately demand the payment of the aggregate amount of all unpaid

---

① [1980] 2 Lloyd's Rep 1 at 4.
② [1980] 2 Lloyd's Rep 1 at 13.
③ Article XI.4(b)(iii).

2nd, 3rd, and 4th instalments from the Guarantor in accordance with the terms and conditions of the guarantee issued by the Guarantor.

13.61　虽然船舶建造合同中的此类规定似乎不会被法院认定为无效,但这一规定可能并不会给船厂带来太多的实际意义。首先,在船东的付款有银行保函担保的情况下,船厂应当没有必要提前收取所有未到期建造款。第二,船厂是否可以要求提供付款保函的银行提前支付建造款似乎也是一个问题,因为船舶建造合同的规定并不当然约束提供付款保函的银行。第三,船厂是否需要建造款可能取决于船舶建造已完成的阶段以及船厂处置船舶的意图。如果船厂已经收了两期建造款但刚开始采购,分段的制作尚未开始,而船厂也没有将船舶建造完毕的意图,这时船厂可能并不需要船东支付其他建造款。如果船舶已经下水并且已经完成了大部分舾装工作,船厂也已经收取了所有交船前的各期建造款,在这种情况下,除非市场价格出现剧烈的下跌,否则船厂依然无需船东支付交船款。船的价值以及已经收到的四期建造款应远远超过了船舶建造合同的合同价格,即使船东支付了交船款,船厂也要将其作为多余款项退还给船东。第四,船厂若要求船东立刻支付所有到期和未到期的建造款应当意味着船厂将继续并完成船舶的建造,这未必符合船厂的利益,尤其是在船舶建造刚开始阶段。最后,值得注意的是,在船东违约不支付约定建造款的情况下,船东按照船厂的要求支付所有尚未到期的建造款的可能性显然是不大的。船东不支付建造款通常出于两个原因:一是船东遇到了财务困难,确实拿不出钱;二是市场原因,虽然船东有钱,但鉴于合同价格和当时市场价格的巨大差距,船东选择放弃已经支付的款项以避免更大损失的发生。无论是哪一种情况,船东似乎都不会因为船厂的要求而支付所有未到期的建造款。正如 Roskill 法官在 *Hyundai Shipbuilding & Heavy Industries Co Ltd* v *Pournaras* 一案中所说的:[①]

> It is, of course, notorious, and has been notorious for some years, that there are in this world too many ships chasing too few cargoes; it is equally notorious that all too many ships, have, immediately they come from the builder's yard, been unable to find any remunerative employment. That being the state of the market, it is not surprising that those who in more optimistic days entered into contracts for the sale and delivery of ships to be constructed by yards all over the world should seek, if they can, to escape from the bonds either of the shipbuilding

---

① [1978] 2 Lloyd's Rep 502 at 504.

contracts they originally made or from the contracts of guarantee which were entered into collaterally with the shipbuilding contracts as part of the transaction with the shipbuilders concerned.... The yards have found that there has been default on the contracts sometimes, as here, before any construction has taken place, or after only minimal construction has taken place, or after construction is complete....

船东供应品的归属

SAJ 格式没有船厂解约后如何处置船东供应品的规定,而按照 CSTC 格式的规定,船厂解除船舶建造合同后船东供应品即成为船厂的财产:①   13.62

> ... Upon receipt by the BUYER of such telex notice of cancellation or rescission, all of the BUYER's Supplies shall forthwith become the sole property of the SELLER, and the VESSEL and all its equipment and machinery shall be at the sole disposal of the SELLER for sale or otherwise....

在船舶建造合同中约定船东供应品在船厂解约后归船厂所有的意义可能是船厂不再有返还船东供应品的义务了,因为船东供应品在本质上是船东的财产。虽然当事人可以在合同中按照各自的意图作出约定,但在船舶建造合同中约定船东在违约时丧失自己采购的供应品的所有权应当没有太好的依据。船东违约的自应对自己的违约行为承担后果,但船东并不会因此丧失依法享有的权利。NEWBUILDCON 格式关于船东供应品的规定与 CSTC 格式不同:②   13.63

> If this Contract is terminated by the Builder, the Builder shall have the right to retain the Buyer's Supplies together with any instalments paid by the Buyer....

按上述规定,船厂解除船舶建造合同后有权保留船东供应品,但保留是否意味着船东供应品所有权的转移似乎是不明确的。   13.64

船舶的处置

在船厂因船东违约解除船舶建造合同后,船厂处置在建船舶的权利应当是不言而喻的。这是因为船舶在交船前始终是船厂的财产,而船东的违约意味着船厂   13.65

---

① Article XI.4(b)(i).
② Clause 39(f).

已不再有向船东交付船舶的合同义务了。然而，按照 AWES 格式的规定，船厂处置船舶似乎还需要船东的授权，该格式规定的是：①

> In the event of termination of the CONTRACT as above provided, the CONTRACTOR is herewith irrevocably authorized by the PURCHASER to sell the VESSEL before or after having completed her without prejudice to any other CONTRACTOR's rights.

13.66　由于船舶的所有权在交船之前始终归船厂拥有，因此船厂处置在建船舶并不需要船东的授权。之所以 AWES 格式会有船东授权船厂出售船舶的规定可能是因为在 AWES 格式中船厂承诺不处置船舶或对船舶设定抵押权：②

> During construction the VESSEL shall be the CONTRACTOR's property and the CONTRACTOR undertakes not to dispose of the VESSEL and not to allow any mortgage or lien being registered on the VESSEL except with the PURCHASER's prior written consent.

13.67　上述规定的前提是船东接船，只有在船东接船的情况下，船厂在上述规定中作出的承诺才是有意义的。若船东违约，就会丧失要求接船的权利，船舶的处置和抵押也就不再与船东有关了。

船厂的选择

13.68　在船厂因船东未按约定支付建造款而解约的情况下，虽然船舶建造的完成程度不同，但船舶通常尚未建造完毕。因此船厂会面临如何处置尚未建造完毕船舶的问题，即是继续建造直至完成后再出售船舶，还是出售尚未完成的船舶。船厂的选择应当是出于商业的考虑，而不是出于法律的考虑。船厂作出完成或不完成船舶建造的决定通常取决以下几个因素：第一，船舶建造已经完成的节点。原则上，船舶建造越接近完成，船厂选择建造完毕后再出售船舶不仅成功的机会更大，而且价格也更优。相反，船舶建造越接近开始阶段，除非船舶的未来市场看好，船厂选择完成建造再出售的可能性相对比较小。因为建造所需的时间有可能带来诸多不确定因素。第二，当时的市场情况。如果市场的船价高于船舶建造合同价格的且市场趋势是船价看涨的，船厂应当倾向于完成建造后再出售船舶。相反，如果当时的市场不好且有继续走低的趋势，船厂则可能为了避免损失的扩大而倾

---

① Article 10, para.4.
② Article 8(b), para.1.

向于处置未完成的船舶。第三,船舶的特征。船舶的特征同样会影响船厂作出是否继续建造的决定。船舶越具有标准性、通用性的,船厂选择完成建造的可能性就越大,因为处置标准性和通用性强的船舶相对而言会比较容易。相反,船舶个性越强的,船厂则越倾向于选择处置未完成的船舶。例如钻井平台或浮式生产储存卸货装置等,由于这些设施往往是根据特定海上油气田的特征设计建造的,缺乏通用性,因此船厂会倾向于处置尚未完成的船舶。第四,完成建造所需的资金。完成船舶建造所需资金越少的,船厂选择完成建造后再出售的可能性就越大,因为以较小成本为代价实现船舶处置较大的价值回报无疑是值得的。相反,完成船舶建造所需资金越多的,船厂则会更倾向于不完成建造便出售船舶。因为这样做无疑有利于避免风险或损失的进一步扩大。

船舶建造合同一般都会有关于船厂可以选择是否完成建造的规定,例如 SAJ 格式便有如下规定:① 13.69

> In the event of rescission of this Contract as above provided, the BUILDER shall have full right and power either to complete or not to complete the VESSEL as it deems fit, and to sell the VESSEL at a public or private sale on such terms and conditions as the BUILDER thinks fit without being answerable for any loss or damage.

从上述规定来看,船厂既可以选择完成船舶的建造后再出售,也可以选择将在建船舶出售。而且,船厂既可以采用公开拍卖的方式出售船舶,也可以通过私下的交易出售船舶,而无需承担损失。CSTC 格式也有几乎相同的规定,但是该格式增加了一句,即船厂出售船舶的应当以书面方式通知船东。② NEWBUILDCON 格式也规定船厂可以决定是否完成船舶建造。③ 13.70

完成建造后出售

船厂是否完成船舶建造会影响船厂损失的计算方式。按照 SAJ 格式的规定,如果船厂选择完成船舶建造后再出售船舶的,出售所得应当按照如下规定进行分配:④ 13.71

> In the event of the sale of the VESSEL in its completed state, the

---

① Article XI.4(a).
② Article XI.5(a).
③ Clause 39(f).
④ Article XI.4(b).

proceeds of the sale received by the BUILDER shall be applied firstly to payment of all expenses attending such sale and otherwise incurred by the BUILDER as a result of the BUYER's default, and then to payment of all unpaid Installments of the Contract Price and interest on such Installment at the rate of .... percent (....... %) per annum from the respective due dates thereof to the date of application.

13.72 　出售船舶所得首先用于支付因出售船舶而产生的费用,因为在船舶建造合同得到正常履行的情况下,船舶是在船厂交付给船东的,因而无需支出出售船舶的费用。此项费用是由于船东的违约而产生的,它主要包括为出售船舶而支付的检验费用、佣金、法律费用以及其他杂费。出售所得其次应用于支付船东按照船舶建造合同规定应当支付但尚未支付的建造款及其利息。AWES 格式和 Norwegian 格式均没有类似的规定,但 CSTC 格式以及 NEWBUILDCON 格式则有与上述规定基本相同的规定。① 上述规定的意义在于将船厂置于船舶建造合同得到正常履行后的状态,这也是船厂与船东订立船舶建造合同的目的。

未完成建造的出售

13.73 　如果船厂决定不再继续船舶建造,而将未完成的船舶进行变卖的,损失的计算方式便会有所不同。SAJ 格式的规定是:②

In the event of sale of the VESSEL in its incompleted state, the proceeds of sale received by the BUILDER shall be applied firstly to all expenses attending such sale and otherwise incurred by the BUILDER as a result of the BUYER's default, and then to payment of all costs of construction of the VESSEL less the Installments so retained by the BUILDER and compensation to the BUILDER for a reasonable loss of profit due to the rescission of this Contract.

13.74 　船厂出售未完成船舶的所得首先应当用于支付因变卖船舶而产生的费用,与船厂选择完成建造后再将船舶出售相同,此种费用同样不是船厂履行船舶建造合同会产生的正常费用。如果尚有剩余的则应当用以支付扣除已支付款项后的建造成本和利润。由于船舶是在尚未完成建造的情况下出售的,船厂并没有产生完成船舶建造所需的全部成本,因此船厂获得全部合同价格就应当是不公平的。这是船厂不完成全部建造而出售船舶的损失计算方式不同于完成全部建造再出售

---

① CSTC Article XI.5(b); NEWBUILDCON Clause 39(f)(i).
② Article XI.4(c).

船舶的损失计算方式的原因。由于船厂可以在已发生成本得到全部补偿的基础上再获得合理的利润,因此船厂实际上也将处于船舶建造合同得到正常履行情况下的地位。

13.75 在船厂选择出售尚未完成的船舶问题上,NEWBUILDCON 格式的规定与 SAJ 格式的规定有所不同:①

> In the event of the sale of the Vessel in its incomplete from the proceeds of sale received by the Builder shall be applied in the following order:
>
> (1) to payment of all expenses incurred by the Builder in respect of the sale and otherwise incurred by the Builder as a result of the Buyer's default;
> (2) to payment of all unpaid instalments of the Contract Price to the extent due but not yet paid at the date of termination and interest on such instalments at the rate of interest stated in Box 30 from the respective due dates thereof to the date of application;
> (3) to payment of all costs of part construction of the Vessel less any paid instalments and less any sums credited under(2)above;
> (4) to payment of the Builder's reasonable net loss of profit caused by the Buyer's default.

13.76 按照 NEWBUILDCON 格式的规定,船厂出售未完成船舶的所得应当按照下列顺序进行分配:第一,用以支付因出售或变卖船舶而产生的费用;第二,用以支付在船厂解约时所有已到期但尚未支付的建造款及其利息;第三,用以支付扣减船厂已经收到的建造款以及上述第二项建造款后的所有用于船舶建造已完成部分的成本;第四,用于支付船厂因船东违约而损失的净利润。不难看出,船东应当承担的是船厂在解约时已完成船舶建造的成本加上合理利润。

出售船舶的义务

13.77 除非船舶建造合同另有约定,船厂并没有出售船舶的义务。在 *Stocznia Gdanska SA v Latvian Shipping Co Latreefer Inc and Others*② 一案中,船舶建造合同有类似 SAJ 格式关于船东违约的条款,第5.05(2)条有如下规定:

> [1] If the Purchaser defaults in the payment of any amount due to the Seller under sub-clauses(b)or(c)or(d)of Clause 5.02 for twenty-one

---

① Clause 39(f)(ii).
② [1998] 1 Lloyd's Rep 609.

(21) days after the date when such payment has fallen due the Seller shall be entitled to rescind the Contract.

[2] In the event of such rescission by the Seller of this Contract due to the Purchaser's default as provided for in this Clause, the Seller shall be entitled to retain and apply the instalments already paid by the Purchaser to the recovery of the Seller's loss and damage and at the same time the Seller shall have the full right and power either to complete or not to complete the Vessel and to sell the Vessel at a public or private sale on such terms and conditions as the Seller deems reasonable provided that the Seller is always obliged to mitigate all losses and damages due to any such Purchaser's default.

13.78 根据上述规定,船东有权以公开或私下的方式出售已完成的或尚未完成的船舶。船东在支付了第一期建造款后出现了财务困难,最终船厂解除了合同。上诉法院认为第 5.05(2)条实际上规定了船厂出售船舶的义务。上诉法院的 Staughton 法官也认为船厂应当出售船舶,他说:①

It is not said that the yard also have power not to sell the vessel, in those very words. I am inclined to think that the wording of the clause does require the yard to sell the vessel; and it certainly does where the obligation to mitigate requires there to be a sale. In any case, it is not to be supposed that the yard will in practice wish to retain unsold a partly completed vessel, or one that has been completed, for some such purpose as showing it to visitors.

13.79 虽然普通法并不要求船厂出售船舶,但是 Staughton 法官认为合同第5.05条已经排除了船厂按照普通法可以享有的权利。他说:②

It does not provide an option, which the yard may ignore if they choose. Otherwise there would be no point in laying down the detailed procedure which the clause contains. As I have already said, I think that on a true interpretation of the clause a sale is mandatory; and it certainly is when mitigation requires there to be a sale. The owners then obtain an indefeasible right to such share of the proceeds as the clause confers on them. The common law rights of the yard are displaced by the regime of cl.5.05.

---

① [1996] 2 Lloyd's Rep 132 at 137.
② [1996] 2 Lloyd's Rep 132 at 138.

13.80 但是上议院则认为合同第5.05(2)条并没有规定船厂出售船舶的义务,Lord Goff 说:①

> The Court of Appeal expressed the opinion that this provision imposed on the seller an obligation to sell the completed or uncompleted vessel. But this is not what cl.5.05(2) says; and there may be circumstances in which there is no buyer available, or in which the seller's duty to mitigate requires a different course to be taken. At all events the article contemplates that, if a sale takes place, it may occur either when the vessel has or has not been completed, and makes provision for the application of the proceeds of sale (after deducting the reasonable costs and expenses of the sale) in either circumstance.

13.81 Lord Goff 认为出售船舶是船厂获得损害赔偿的一种方式,他说:②

> ... in addition it was, in my opinion, open to the yard to argue that, on a true construction of cl. 5.05, the yard's right to recover damages (recognized in cl.5.05(2)) may in certain circumstances refer to damages on the measure recoverable at common law. Such an argument could, for example, be advanced on the basis that (a) the yard's "full right and power" to sell the vessel under cl.5.05(2) was (contrary to the opinion expressed by Lord Justice Staughton) no more than a power of sale and as such not mandatory ....

13.82 按照 NEWBUILDCON 格式的规定,船厂出售船舶似乎既是权利,同时又是一项合同义务,该格式的规定是:③

> ... the Builder ... shall have the right and power either to complete or not to complete the Vessel as it deems fit but in any event shall sell the Vessel (either in its complete or incomplete form), including those Buyer's Supplies which are installed or have been utilised on board the Vessel, at the best price reasonably obtainable at a public or private sale on reasonable terms and conditions.

13.83 实际上船厂是否出售或变卖尚未完成的船舶在很大程度上取决于船厂因船东的违约而遭受的损失的程度,以及在船东违约时船舶建造已经完成的进度。在 *Stocznia Gdanska SA v Latvian Shipping Co Latreefer Inc and Others* 一案中,船东在

---

① [1998] 1 Lloyd's Rep 609 at 617.
② [1998] 1 Lloyd's Rep 609 at 621.
③ Clause 39(f).

支付了第一期建造款后便没有能力继续按照船舶建造合同的规定支付其余各期建造款了。不难想象,当时船舶的建造应当刚刚开始,船厂并没有为船舶建造产生较大数额的成本。如果船东已经支付的那一期建造款已足以弥补船厂已经产生的损失,船厂似乎就不再有出售或变卖在建船舶的动力了。如果船舶已下水,或者已经完成了大部分舾装,船厂不出售船舶的可能性就不会太大。因为在这种情况下,船东已经支付的建造款应当很难弥补船厂为船舶建造已经产生的成本。

13.84 　　船厂没有出售或变卖在建船舶义务并不意味着船厂依然可以拥有在建船舶的所有权。如果船东已经支付的建造款足以补偿船厂业已产生的损失(包括利润损失)及费用,船厂是否可以出售在建船舶并拥有出售所得可能会有问题。对船厂而言,在自己不再有任何实际损失的前提下拥有出售在建船所得有可能构成不当得利。但若在建船持续产生保管和维护费用船东也不对船舶进行处理,船厂应当是可以处置在建船的。船厂处置的依据并非所有权,而是减损义务。

余额的处置

13.85 　　余额是指船厂按照建造合同规定对船舶出售所得进行分配的剩余部分。由于船厂按照合同规定获得各项款项后就已经处于船舶建造合同得到正常履行后的地位,继续保留剩余的款项即为不当得利,理应退还给船东。SAJ 格式对此作出了如下规定:①

> In either of the above events of sale, if the proceeds of sale exceeds the total of amounts to which such proceeds are to be applied as aforesaid, the BUILDER shall promptly pay the excess to the BUYER without interest, provided, however, that the amount of such payment to the BUYER shall in no event exceed the total amount of Installments already paid by the BUYER and the cost of the BUYER's Supplies, if any.

13.86 　　按照上述规定,船东可以获得的剩余款项的数额不应超过船东已经实际支付的所有建造款的总额以及船东供应品的成本。除非市场出现大幅度上升,否则出现此种情形的可能性不大。虽然这是船舶建造合同的规定,但是如果船东不能获得超过自己实际支付和产生数额的剩余款项,这就意味着船厂会因为船东的违约而获得船舶建造合同得到正常履行情况下所无法获得的利益。船厂获得此种额外的利益同

---

① Article XI.4(d).

样缺乏正当的理由。至于船厂退还出售船舶所得余款时无需支付利息的规定似乎是多余的,因为这一切是船东的违约行为造成的。但是若船厂没有及时退还余额则可能需要支付利息。NEWBUILDCON 格式在这个问题上作出了如下规定:①

> In either of the above events if the proceeds of sale exceed the sums to which such proceeds are to be applied as aforesaid the Builder shall promptly pay any such excess to the Buyer without interest thereon, provided that the amount of such payment to the Buyer shall in no event exceed the total amount of instalments paid by the Buyer. The Builder shall at the same time either permit the Buyer to remove the Buyer's Supplies which are not installed or utilised onboard the Vessel(if any) from the Shipyard for the cost and expense of the Buyer, or give credit to the Buyer for the full value thereof.

NEWBUILDCON 格式的规定与 SAJ 格式的规定基本相似,即船东不能获得超过自己已实际支付数额的出售船舶所得的余款。但是船厂应当允许船东撤走尚未安装上船的船东供应品或者按照其价值支付。 13.87

额外支付义务

船厂出售船舶后的所得有可能足以弥补自己因船东违约而遭受的损失,但也有可能由于市场等原因,出售船舶的所得不足以弥补船厂遭受的损失。当出售所得不足以弥补船厂损失时,船东依然有义务承担船厂的损失。SAJ 格式对此作出了规定:② 13.88

> If the proceeds of sale are insufficient to pay such total amounts payable as aforesaid, the BUYER shall promptly pay the deficiency to the BUILDER upon request.

而 NEWBUILDCON 格式则允许船厂首先变卖尚未装上船的船东供应品,③依然不足以弥补船厂遭受的损失的,船东应当承担不足部分及其利息。该格式的规定是:④ 13.89

> If the proceeds of sale are still insufficient to pay the Builder the total amounts due from the Buyer as aforesaid, the Buyer shall pay to the

---

① Clause 39(f)(iii).
② Article XI.4(e).
③ Clause 39(f)(iv).
④ Clause 39(f)(v).

Builder the amount of such deficiency, plus interest at the rate stated in Box 30 to cover periods whenever payments from the Buyer became overdue.

担保人的义务

13.90　在船东的付款义务有付款保函担保的情况下,船东违约的,船厂可以要求付款担保人按照船舶建造合同的规定支付建造款。即使船厂已经解除了船舶建造合同,付款担保人的义务并不因此受到影响。在 *Hyundai Shipbuilding and Heavy Industries Co Ltd v Pournarus and Others*① 一案中,船东的支付义务由被告担保,保函包括以下内容:

> ... In consideration of your entering into the shipbuilding contract ... the [defendant] hereby irrevocably and unconditionally guarantees the payment in accordance with the terms of the contract of all sums due or to become due by the buyer to you under the contract and in case the buyer is in default of any such payment the [defendant] will forthwith make the payment in default on behalf of the buyer ....

13.91　船东没有足额支付第一期建造款,船厂解除了合同并且对提供保函的担保人提起了诉讼,要求担保人支付已到期的建造款。担保人则认为船东支付建造款的义务在船厂解除船舶建造合同之时就已经终止,因此作为担保人也不再负有支付建造款的义务。船厂只能主张丧失合同机会的损害赔偿。但是这一观点分别被一审法院、上诉法院以及上议院驳回。上诉法院的 Roskill 法官说:②

> To my mind, the fact that these contracts came to an end ... did not free the buyers from their respective obligations to pay the various instalments, liability for which had already accrued and accordingly ... the guarantors' several liabilities for those instalments under the respective guarantees remained wholly unaffected.

13.92　在 *Hyundai Heavy Industries Co v Papadopoulos and Others*③ 一案中,上议院的 Lord Fraser 也认为只要已经到期,船厂的解约并没有解除船东支付建造款的责任。他说:④

---

① [1978] 2 Lloyd's Rep 502.
② [1978] 2 Lloyd's Rep 502 at 507.
③ [1980] 2 Lloyd's Rep 1.
④ [1980] 2 Lloyd's Rep 1 at 15.

For these reasons I am of opinion that the cancellation of the contract did not release the buyer from his liability for the second instalment, the due date for payment of which had passed before cancellation. That remained, and still remains, a debt due by the buyer to the builder.

上议院的 Dilhorne 子爵甚至认为即使船厂丧失了针对船东的权利，也并不因此丧失针对担保人的权利：① 13.93

If the terms of the guarantee are such, as they clearly are in this case, as to guarantee payment of that instalment on the due date, the builder had an accrued right to payment by the guarantors. It was conceded that the builder had had an accrued right to payment of that sum by the buyer and by the guarantors. In my view the fact, if it was the fact, that the builder lost his right as against the buyer on cancellation, would not deprive the builder of his accrued right against the guarantors.

---

① [1980] 2 Lloyd's Rep 1 at 7.

第14章 保 险

I 建造风险

概述

14.1　保险在船舶建造合同中相当重要。在船舶建造合同中,船舶的所有权通常是在船舶交给船东时才发生转移,由于船厂对交船前的船舶拥有所有权,所以船舶的风险也自然而然地由船厂承担(*res perit domino*)。1979年《货物买卖法》便有如下规定:①

> Unless otherwise agreed, the goods remain at the seller's risk until the property in them is transferred to the buyer, but when the property in them is transferred to the buyer the goods are at the buyer's risk whether delivery has been made or not.

14.2　绝大多数船舶建造合同都会规定,船舶的风险在交船之前由船厂承担,例如Norwegian格式便有如下规定:②

> Until Delivery and Acceptance, the Builder bears the risk of loss of or damage to the Vessel materials, parts, machinery, boilers and equipment.

14.3　在建造期间,船舶可能面临各种自然的和人为的风险,这些风险不仅有可能导致船舶的灭失或损坏,而且还可能导致作为船舶所有人的船厂承担责任或产生费用。

---

① s.20(2).
② Article XI.2(a).

建造人保险

船厂按照船舶建造合同规定投保的是建造人保险,建造人保险是专门适用于船舶建造的财产保险,属于海上保险的一种。建造人保险所针对的是处于建造过程中的船舶及其材料和设备等。当在建船舶或其材料和设备等因承保风险而遭受灭失或损坏的,保险人将以保险金额为限向被保险人支付保险赔偿金,从而使船厂可以对遭受灭失或损害的船舶进行重建或修理。因此,建造人保险的标的物不仅包括在建船舶,而且还包括用于建造的材料、附属物、设备以及装置等。建造人保险实际上不仅承保了船舶建造过程中的风险,即工程险;而且也承保了船舶在下水和试航过程中的风险,这些风险又类似于一般的船舶险。

14.4

在 *Commonwealth Construction Company Limited* v *Imperial Oil Ltd* 一案中,加拿大最高法院的 de Grandpré 法官对建造人保险的作用作出了如下描述:①

14.5

> Whatever its label, its function is to provide to the owner the promise that the contractors will have the funds to rebuild in case of loss, and to the contractors, the protection against the crippling cost of starting afresh in such an event, the whole without resort to litigation in case of negligence by anyone connected with the construction, a risk accepted by the insurers at the outset. This purpose recognizes the importance of keeping to a minimum the difficulties that are bound to be created by the large number of participants in a major construction project, the complexity of which needs no demonstration.

协会建造人保险条款

协会条款(institute clauses)是指由伦敦保险人协会制定的适用于各种不同保险的保险条款,协会建造人保险条款便是其中之一。该保险协会条款在造船业得到相当广泛的采用。由于协会建造人保险条款是在协会船舶条款的基础上制定的,因此两者有不少条款是相同的。最早的协会建造人保险条款于1963年5月1日制定,经过1972年12月1日的修订,增加了基于1971年的协会碰撞责任条款碰撞责任险。与其他协会条款一样,协会建造人保险条款也适用英国法以及英国的习惯做法。目前在船舶建造中得到广泛使用

14.6

---

① [1976] 6 WWR 219 at [35].

的则是 1988 年 6 月 1 日制定的协会建造人保险条款。可以说，协会建造人保险条款为船舶建造中的保险设定了行业标准，虽然具体的保单会有不同于协会条款的内容，但在整体上船舶建造保险都是在协会条款的框架下进行的。

保险利益

14.7　　保险利益(insurable interest)是所有保险合同有效的前提，被保险人必须对保险标的物享有保险利益。根据 1906 年《海上保险法》(Marine Insurance Act 1906)的规定，如果被保险人没有保险利益，保险合同就将被视为是赌博合同而告无效：①

> (1) Every contract of marine insurance by way of gaming or wagering is void.
> (2) A contract of marine insurance is deemed to be a gaming or wagering contract –
>> (a) Where the assured has not an insurable interest as defined by this Act, and the contract is entered into with no expectation of acquiring such an interest; or

14.8　　被保险人没有保险利益的保险合同是无效的，但是成文法规定的被保险人享有保险利益的时间并不是在投保时，而是在事故发生之时，即被保险人在投保时并不需要对保险标的物享有保险利益，但在事故发生时必须有保险利益，否则不能获得保险人的保险赔偿。②

> The assured must be interested in the subject-matter insured at the time of the loss though he need not be interested when the insurance is effected....

合同义务

14.9　　船舶建造合同一般都会规定船厂负有为船舶建造进行投保的义务，例如 SAJ 格式就有如下规定：③

---

① s.4.
② s.6(1).
③ Article XII.1, para.1, see also CSTC Article XII.1, para.1.

> From the time of keel-laying of the VESSEL until the same is completed, delivered to and accepted by the BUYER, the BUILDER shall, at its own cost and expense, keep the VESSEL and all machinery, materials, equipment, appurtenances and outfit, delivered to the Shipyard for the VESSEL or built into, or installed in or upon the VESSEL, including the BUYER's Supplies, fully insured with Japanese insurance companies under coverage corresponding to the Japanese BUILDER's Risks Insurance Clause.

14.10　按照上述规定,船厂的投保义务始于龙骨的安放,即分段上船台之时,止于船舶交接。虽然 SAJ 格式规定船厂的投保义务始于分段上船台之时,但是船厂的建造责任实际上在此之前就已经开始了。在分段上船台之前船厂同样面临着各种风险,因此在实践中船厂往往在此之前就已经投保。①

Ⅱ　保险单

保险标的物

14.11　按照上述 SAJ 格式的规定,作为建造人保险的标的物应当包括:在建船舶、机器、材料、设备、附属物、装备以及船东供应品等。但除了在建船舶外的其他机器设备等以运抵船厂的时间为开始承保的时间。虽然保险人通常也只对运抵船厂的机器设备等进行承保,但建造人保险可以承保在供应商处的正处于建造中的机器,包括自机器生产地至船厂的运输。② 船厂的采购属于船厂的合同义务范围,所有关于质量以及交货期的风险均由船厂承担,但有的船舶建造合同则规定船厂应对船东供应品以外的自己采购的机器设备的运输进行投保,例如 Norwegian 格式就有如下规定:③

> The insurance shall comprise necessary fire and transport insurance of material and equipment which the Builder procures from Subcontractors. Except as otherwise agreed the Builder is not obliged to insure the transport of Buyer's Supplies.

---

① SAJ 格式规定船厂应当在日本的保险公司投保建造人险并适用日本的建造人险保险条款,在实践中,船东一般都会在本国选择保险公司投保建造人险,但大多数保险都适用协会建造人保险条款。
② See Institute Clauses for Builders' Risks, Section 1(B).
③ Article XI.2(b), see also CSTC Article XII.1, para.2.

14.12　由于建造人保险的标的物并不局限于在建船舶，还可以包括材料和设备等其他物件，因此保险标的物及其范围应当在保单中明确记载。这也是 1906 年《海上保险法》的要求：①

The subject-matter insured must be designated in a marine policy with reasonable certainty.

保险价值

14.13　保险价值是保险人承担保险责任的最高限额。若以是否约定保险标的物价值为标准，保单可以分为两种，即定值保单和不定值保单。不定值保单是不记载保险标的物价值的保单，而定值保单则是保险标的物价值已经确定的保单：②

A valued policy is a policy which specifies the agreed value of the subject-matter insured.

14.14　虽然保单约定的保险标的物的价值未必与其市场价值相吻合，但除非有欺诈行为，否则保单约定价值即为最终的，对双方均有约束力：③

Subject to the provisions of this Act, and in the absence of fraud, the value fixed by the policy is, as between the insurer and assured, conclusive of the insurable value of the subject intended to e insured, whether the loss be total or partial.

14.15　从船舶建造合同标准格式来看，船厂安排的建造人保险应当采用定值保单，因为几乎所有标准格式都有关于保险价值的规定。SAJ 格式规定船厂应当投保的金额不低于船东支付的建造款与包括船东供应品价格之和，④而 Norwegian 格式则在 SAJ 格式的基础上增加了利息：⑤

The insured amount shall as a minimum cover the aggregate of the instalments paid by the Buyer pursuant to Article III from time to time together with interest thereon and the value of any Buyer' Supplies.

---

① s.26(1).
② Marine Insurance Act 1906, s.27(2).
③ Marine Insurance Act 1906, s.27(3).
④ Article XII.1, para.2, see also CSTC Article XII.1, para.2.
⑤ Article XI.2(b), para.2.

然而 NEWBUILDCON 格式不仅规定建造人保险的保险金额应当不低于船东支付的建造款以及船东供应品价值的总额,而且还规定船东可以要求船厂提高保险金额:①

> If specifically requested by the Buyer, the Builder shall increase the amount insured under the policy to cover the rebuilding costs of the Vessel or such other amount as the Buyer may request. Any additional premium charged for this shall be paid by the Buyer.

建造人保险的保险价值一般可以通过两种方式予以确定,一种是船舶建造合同的合同价再加上船东供应品价值,另一种则是船厂建造船舶的成本、利润再加上船东供应品价值。由于航运市场的变动,两者之间有可能出现相当大的差距。上述提及的船东已经支付的建造款总额与船东供应品的价值之和实际上远远低于合同价格与船东供应品价值之和,因为船东已经支付的建造款并不包括交船时应当支付的那一期建造款。如果船厂以这一数额投保建造人保险,除非船厂的全部建造成本低于扣除最后一期款后的全部建造款,否则保险赔偿显然是无法支付船厂重新建造船舶的实际成本。在航运市场低迷时,按照合同价格与船舶供应品价值的总额确定建造人保险的保险价值会遇到问题。因为在市场低迷时期的合同价格低于实际建造成本的情形并不少见。根据实际建造成本与船东供应品价值的总额确定建造人保险的保险价值可能遇到的问题是,在市场上扬期间,船厂的利润水平同样会出现上升的趋势。根据实际建造成本确定保险金额虽然有可能解决完成或重新建造船舶所需的费用,但船厂本应获得的利润则不复存在了。

与其他定值保单不同,在建造人保险中船厂有权对写入保单的保险价值进行调整。协会建造人保险条款关于保险价值的规定是:②

> Whereas the value stated herein is provisional, it is agreed that the final contract price, or the total building cost plus ....% whichever is the greater, of the subject-matter of this insurance shall be the insured value.

从上述规定可以看出,在保单已经载明保险价值的情况下,最终的保险价值仍然可以根据船舶建造合同的最终价格,即考虑了所有价格变动因素后的实际价格,或者船厂为建造船舶而支付的实际总成本再加上一个作为利润的百分比予以

---

① Clause 38(a).
② cl.1.1.

确定,两者以金额高者为建造人保险的保险价值。如果最终的保险价值超过原先保险价值数额,船厂应当对超出部分另行支付保费,①但最终的保险价值以原先保险价值的125%为限。② 如果最终的保险价值低于原先保险价值数额,保险人则应当调整保险价值并退还减少部分数额的保费。③

被保险人

14.20　　"建造人保险"是一个有可能会造成误解的名称,因为并不是只有建造人才可以成为建造人保险的被保险人,实际上与建造物有关的所有人,甚至连为建造进行融资的银行等都可以成为建造人保险的被保险人。船舶建造合同往往会对建造保险的被保险人作出规定,例如 SAJ 格式便规定船厂是建造人保险的被保险人:④

> The policy referred to hereinabove shall be taken out in the name of the BUILDER and all losses under such policy shall be payable to the BUILDER.

14.21　　在船厂是唯一被保险人的情况下,所有保险赔偿均应支付给船厂也就顺理成章了。但是在实践中,船东也可能希望成为建造人保险中的被保险人,而 Norwegian 格式则明确规定船东应当是建造人保险的共同被保险人:⑤

> The insurance policies shall be taken out in the joint names of the Builder and the Buyer.

14.22　　船东成为建造人保险的共同被保险人并不会给船厂带来很大的影响,而成为共同被保险人其实对保费负有支付的合同义务。虽然 NEWBUILDCON 已明确规定船东无需支付保费,⑥但这一规定仅仅局限于船厂和船东的船舶建造合同中,对保险人并无约束力。船东依然对保险人负有支付保费的义务。按照1906年《海上保险法》的规定,支付保费是保险人签发保单的对流条件:⑦

> Unless otherwise agreed, the duty of the assured or his agent to pay the

---

① cl.1.2.1.
② cl.1.3.
③ cl.1.2.2.
④ Article XII.1, para.3, see also CSTC Article XII.1, para.2.
⑤ Article XI.2(c)(i), see also NEWBUILDCON Clause 38(a), para.1.
⑥ Clause 38(a), para.1.
⑦ s.52.

premium, and the duty of the insurer to issue the policy to the assured or his agent, are concurrent conditions, and the insurer is not bound to issue the policy until payment or tender of the premium.

被保险人的名称

作为保险合同的被保险人,其名称并不一定要在保险合同中载明。在 Stone Vickers Ltd v Appledore Ferguson Shipbuilders Ltd[①] 一案中,船厂为国家环境研究署建造一艘远洋考察船。按照船舶建造合同的规定,规格书中列明的机器等均应由指定的供应商供应,而原告则是提供螺旋桨的指定供应商。船厂承诺投保建造人保险,保险适用的是协会建造人保险条款,协会罢工条款,以及协会战争条款等。1982 年 4 月,船厂和螺旋桨供应商订立了螺旋桨的采购合同。船厂投保的建造人保险的一般条件包括以下内容:

14.23

> Agreed include Associated and Subsidiary Companies and/or Sub-Contractors as additional Co-assured for their respective rights and interests. Without recourse against any Co-assured.
>
> It is further agreed that, in respect of additional (Co-) Assured named or referred to herein, this Policy will discharge any liability that it would bear if each of the Assured named or referred to herein was separately insured and in the event of any act or omission on the part of one Assured in respect of which Underwriters exercise their right to void the Policy the remaining Assured (including those named in the first paragraph of this Clause) for whom this Policy remains in full force shall not be prejudiced thereby.

保险合同的一般条件又有如下规定:

14.24

> It is agreed to couple the names of Assured's customers as Joint Assured hereunder if the Assured are requested to give them this protection, but for the purposes of this Insurance, such customers remain as Third Parties to the Assured and any legal liabilities of the Assured towards them or theirs are recoverable hereunder.

1984 年 6 月船舶试航时发现螺旋桨有噪音,在对螺旋桨进行了调整后再一次进行了试航,噪音明显得到改善。螺旋桨供应商要求船厂赔偿螺旋桨,但船厂

14.25

---

① [1991] 2 Lloyd's Rep 288.

认为供应商供应的螺旋桨易于发出噪声违反了采购合同的质量和设计要求。螺旋桨供应商认为船厂已经得到保险人的赔偿，保险人已代位并以螺旋桨供应商的名义正在向另一个被保险人追偿，保险人的做法因而违反了保险合同的规定。法院需要解决的问题是是否可以就保险人已经赔偿的损失向螺旋桨供应商追偿。高院的代理法官 Colman 认为保险一般条件区分了保单列明的额外被保险人和额外的共同被保险人或保单提及的被保险人。保单列明的额外被保险人可以是根据第一条宣布的船厂的客户。"Referred to"应当是指种类，而不是名称，"关联和附属公司以及/或分包商"应当有权获得保单的利益。只要是提及的种类之一的，一旦有保险利益就可以成为共同被保险人，即使没有通知过保险人也无妨。Colman 代理法官说：①

> Therefore declarations under this policy can in my judgment be effective to include sub-contractors even if they are not identified by such declarations. Consequently the omission from the declaration in this case of the name of SV as "Assured" does not lead to the conclusion that SV in its capacity as sub-contractor is not capable of being a Co-assured entitled to cover.

14.26　但是在 *Talbot Underwriting Ltd* v *Nausch Hogan & Murray Inc* (*The Jascon 5*)②一案中，一艘在中国建造的海洋铺管船被拖至新加坡的三巴旺船厂完成装配、调试和测试等工作，船东 CPL 是 Sea Trucks 集团的成员。船舶建造合同第 15.7.1 条规定船厂应当投保每次事故不低于 500 万美元赔偿的船舶修理人保险，但船厂没有投保。合同第 15.12 条规定船东应当安排建造人保险，并且规定船厂应列为共同被保险人，而保险人应放弃针对船厂的追偿。2003 年 5 月船东的保险经纪人与保险人就船舶安排了建造人一切险保单，该保单本应列明船厂为共同被保险人，保险经纪人已获得船厂的授权。但保单只把 Sea Trucks 集团列为被保险人并且写明：

> ... and/or Subsidiary, Affiliates, Associated and Interrelated Companies and/or Joint Ventures as may be required as their respective rights and interest may appear ....

14.27　此外，保单还规定：

---

①　[1991] 2 Lloyd's Rep 288 at 297.
②　[2006] 1 CLC 1138.

Including Assured, interest of Mortgagees (and Notices of Assignment in respect thereof), Loss Payees, Additional Assureds and Waivers of Subrogation as may be required.

14.28 经纪人一直到 2003 年 10 月 14 日才告诉保险人船厂要求成为共同被保险人的意图。当天船舶在重新起浮时有几个处所包括发电机房均进了水。船厂根据保单向保险人提出了索赔，但保险人拒绝理赔，理由是船厂并不是保单的被保险人。2004 年 4 月 28 日，船厂与船东签订了和解协议，船东同意支付 85 万美元。接着船东又从经纪人和保险人处获得了赔偿。2004 年 7 月 26 日，船东、Sea Trucks 以及船厂与保险人签订了转让协议，将针对经纪人未能以船厂名义获得保险的索赔权转让给了保险人。转让协议还规定：

> Except as provided herein, [the Insurers] hereby waive and fully and finally settle all existing rights, benefits, interests and claims they may have under the BAR Policy and/or by way of subrogation against CPL and ST and SSPL [Sembawang] save that any outstanding premiums ... remain due and owing ....

14.29 保险人于是开始了针对经纪人的诉讼，但经纪人认为保险人拒绝向船厂赔付是错误的。法院需要解决的首要问题包括：船厂是不是建造人险保单的共同被保险人。高院的 Cooke 法官认为建造人保险并不是为了船厂利益投保的保险，船厂既不是关联公司，也不是合资企业，而且船厂也不是附加被保险人，因此船厂不是建造人险保单的共同被保险人。船厂上诉，但被上诉法院驳回。上诉法院的 Moore-Bick 法官认为船厂并不是建造人险保单的被保险人。他说：①

> On this view of the matter the parties presumably had some "Additional Assureds" clause in mind, but, although they have had ample opportunity to do so, [brokers] have not attempted either in their statement of case or in argument to identify any specific form of wording that might fall within that description, much less one that would automatically entitle Sembawang to claim as an assured under the policy without any prior notification to the insurers. In those circumstances I am satisfied that on the true construction of the contract Sembawang was not one of the assured.

---

① [2006] 1 CLC 1138 at 1150.

保险期限

14.30　建造人保险应当是定期保险，即保险人在确定的期间内承保约定的保险标的物的保险。按照 1906 年《海上保险法》的规定，定期保险是：①

> ... where the contract is to insure the subject-matter for a definite period of time the policy is called a "time policy".

14.31　在定期保险中，保险人责任的开始和结束可以用两个日期决定，例如 2002 年 1 月 12 日至 2004 年 6 月 12 日；但也可以用两个可以确定日期的事件决定，例如船舶建造开工至船舶交接。如果采用具体日期，应当明确时间的计算标准，例如采用北京时间或者格林尼治时间。如果采用事件确定保险期限，则应采用可以确定具体时间的事件，例如船舶下水等。

期限的开始

14.32　按照 SAJ 格式的规定，船厂投保的建造人保险应当"自船舶铺龙骨时"开始，②但以铺龙骨作为保险人责任的开始其实并不十分适当。这是因为现代造船实际上已不再有严格意义上的"铺龙骨"了。而且在船舶分段开始合拢之时，船厂通常已经完成了大部分采购，至少钢板已大部分运抵船厂。在此之前船厂采购的钢板等其他材料因建造人保险所承保的风险而遭受的损失是无法获得保险赔偿的。因此，保险责任在铺龙骨时才开始显然是比较迟的。CSTC 格式关于保险期限的规定与 SAJ 格式的规定基本相同，只是 CSTC 格式规定的船厂开始投保的时间是"船舶第一个分段铺龙骨之时"。③ 虽然这一规定的含义实质上与 SAJ 格式的规定相同，但"第一个分段铺龙骨"的说法可能不够严谨。就一个分段而言，即使该分段是龙骨分段，应当很难不存在所谓的"铺龙骨"。相比之下，NEWBUILDCON 格式规定的保险期限开始的时间应当比较合理：④

> From the time of first steel cutting or equivalent (or delivery of the Buyer's Supplies, whichever is earlier) until the Vessel is completed, delivered to the accepted by the Buyer ....

---

① s.25(1).
② Article XII.1, para.1, 以前建造人保险的承保期限大多从船舶铺龙骨开始起算。
③ Article XII.1, para.1.
④ Clause 38(a), para.1.

14.33　从上述规定来看,NEWBUILDCON 格式规定的保险期限开始的时间其实并非一特定的时间,而是与船厂的投保义务相关的事件发生的时间。与铺龙骨相比,开工作为建造人保险开始承保的时间无疑是比较合理的。通常情况下,船厂往往会选择在其所采购的钢板运抵船厂的时候开工,在此之前船厂往往还没有投保的义务。然而按照 NEWBUILDCON 格式的规定,如果开工是在船东供应品运抵船厂之前发生的,开工就是建造人保险的保险人承担责任的开始时间点,如果船东供应品先于开工运抵船厂,保险人的责任则自船东供应品运抵船厂之时开始。

期限的结束

14.34　在保险期限结束时间上,船舶建造合同标准格式的规定似乎比较一致,即船舶交付给船东之时。SAJ 格式规定的是:"... until the same is completed, delivered to and accepted by the BUYER";①AWES 格式的规定是:"... up to the date of delivery ...".② 在实践中,不少船厂投保的建造人保险的保险期限的结束往往是用一个具体的日期规定的。这个日期有的保单采用的是船舶建造合同的合同交船日,有些保单则采用合同交船日后的 30 天,60 天,90 天或更长的时间。

14.35　船舶在合同交船日交付的情形可以说是比较罕见的,有时船厂会在合同交船日之前交船,但更多时候船厂是在合同交船日之后交船。以确定的日期作为保险期限的开始之日应当还是可以接受的,该日期可以是船舶建造合同的开工之日,也可以是船舶建造合同的生效之日。但采用确定的日期作为建造人保险的保险期限结束之日并不妥当,因为在投保之时,船厂未必能准确计算出船舶的实际交船之日。在整个建造过程中船厂有可能会遭遇各种影响船舶实际交船日的事件或因素。如果船舶实际交船日是在建造人保险的保险期限届满之后,一旦船厂由于疏忽而没有事先和保险人就保险期限的延长达成协议就将承担所有的风险,而且还将构成船舶建造合同的违约。因此,比较好的做法是以实际交船作为保险期限结束的时间。即使船舶的实际交船日由于各种事件或因素被拖延至合同交船日之后,船舶依然能够得到承保。

---

① Article XII.1, para.1; see also CSTC Article XII.1, para.1; NEWBUILDCON Clause 38(a), para.1.
② Article 9, para.1.

期限的延伸

14.36 建造人保险的保险期限可以通过船厂和保险人的约定予以延长,甚至延长至船舶交付以后的期限,即建造人保险转化为船舶质保责任的保险。但是保险人承保船厂质保责任的船舶应当是建造人保险的标的物。在 *Heesens Yacht Builders BV v Cox Syndicate Management Ltd Munich Re Capital Ltd(The Red Sapphire)*①一案中,一家荷兰船厂建造了两艘船,船舶建造合同有质保条款。第一艘船于1997年10月开始建造,1999年8月1日交付,1999年10月11日船东提出了质保索赔;第二艘船于2000年3月17日开始建造,2001年9月8日交付,2002年4月26日船东也提出了质保索赔。保险人签发的第一份建造人险保单为期12个月,自1998年7月1日起算。船厂在1998年7月28日向保险人提供4艘船的清单,包括已经开始建造的和将要开始建造的。1998年9月4日保险经纪人通知保险人延长保险期限从而使承包范围包括船厂的质保责任。1998年9月22日保险人同意延长保险,批单载明:

> Vessel/yachts as per building risks policy . . . . Twelve months, risk attaching as per guarantee clause.

14.37 1999年6月,保单自1999年7月1日续保18个月,保险条款写明:

> Section A – Construction Risks . . . Section B – Guarantee Risks

14.38 此后,保单又于2000年12月延长了12个月,自2001年1月1日起算,2001年12月又延长了12个月,自2002年1月1日起算。船厂认为保险人应对在保单期内交付的船舶负责,因此第一艘船的索赔符合1999年保单的要求,而第二艘的索赔则符合2001年保单的要求。但是保险人认为自己仅对在保单期内开始建造的船舶的质保责任负责,因此第一艘船的索赔并不在1999年保单的承保范围之内,因为该船的建造在1999年保单开始生效之前就已经开始了。高院接受了船厂的观点,认为1999年的保单承保了第一艘船的质保责任。但是上诉法院的Rix法官则推翻了一审判决,他认为1999年的保单并没有包括第一艘船,他说:②

> What vessels are covered by the policy for construction risks? The answer is: those whose construction commence during the policy period.

---

① [2006] 2 Lloyd's Rep 35.
② [2006] 2 Lloyd's Rep 35 at 40.

It is those vessels which are covered during construction, during their delivery voyage ....

Ⅲ 承保风险

一切险承保风险

保险的承保范围通常是指保险人承保的风险范围,如果对保险的承保范围的描述使用了"all risks of loss of or damage to",该保险就应当是"一切险"保险,建造人保险也属于"一切险"保险。"一切险"保险的一个基本特征是保险人承保的范围是全部风险,而不是列明的风险。正如 Walton 法官在 *Schloss Brothers* v *Stevens* 一案中所说的:①

14.39

> I have to read this policy as I think it would be reasonably understood by any merchant or insurance broker, and doing so I come to the conclusion that the words "all risks by land and by water", etc, must be read literally as meaning all risks whatsoever. I think they are intended to cover all losses by any accidental cause of any kind occurring during the transit.

当然,"一切险"并非没有任何限制,Lord Sumner 在 *British and Foreign Marine Insurance Co* v *Gaunt* 一案中指出,"一切险"既不包括内在缺陷,也不包括自然损耗,他说:②

14.40

> There are, of course, limits to "all risks". They are risks and risks insured against. Accordingly the expression does not cover inherent vice or mere wear and tear or British capture. It covers a risk, not a certainty; it is something which happens to the subject-matter from without, not the natural behavior of that subject-matter, being what it is, in the circumstances under which it is carried. Nor is it a loss which the assured brings about by his own act, for then he has not merely exposed the goods to the chance of injury, he has injured them himself.

因此,"一切险"承保的应当是除外责任以外的所有因意外因素导致的风险。风险具有偶然性,既有可能发生也有可能不发生。保险标的物固有的或内在的特

14.41

---

① [1906] 2 KB 665 at 673.
② [1921] 2 AC 41 at 57.

征引起的损失不具有偶然性,因此不是保险承保的对象。自然损耗是必然发生的,因此也不是风险,同样不是保险承保的内容。毫无疑问,被保险人自己造成或引起的损失也不是保险承保的范围。

14.42　根据协会建造人保险条款的规定,建造人保险的承保范围是:①

Subject always to its terms, conditions and exclusions this insurance is against all risks of loss of or damage to the subject-matter insured caused and discovered during the period of this insurance including the cost of repairing replacing or renewing any defective part condemned solely in consequence of the discovery therein during the period of this insurance of a latent defect. In no case shall this insurance cover the cost of renewing faulty welds.

14.43　具体来说,建造人保险的承保风险是:导致船舶及设备等在保险期内产生并发现的灭失和损坏的所有风险,包括在保险期内发现的潜在缺陷引起的修理、替换、换新缺陷部分等的费用。

延迟交船

14.44　建造人保险的承保范围包括延迟交船:②

Held covered at a premium to be arranged in the event of delivery to Owners being delayed beyond the provisional period(s) mentioned above, but in no case shall any additional period of cover extend beyond 30 days from completion of Builders' Trials.

14.45　虽然名称是"延迟交船",但保险人承保的其实并不是船厂延迟交船,而是在船厂延迟交船情况下继续承保之前承保的各项风险。船厂不仅要为此另行支付保费,而且保险人同意承保的期限以船舶完成试航后的 30 天为限。船厂也可以针对因交船迟延而引起的风险在商业保险市场进行交船迟延或交船不能风险的投保。在船东因船厂交船迟延或交船不能而按照船舶建造合同规定或法律规定解除合同时,保险人将按照约定赔偿船厂因此遭受的损失。此种交船迟延或交船不能的保险通常与建造人保险一起提供。但是保险人在提供此类保险之前要对船厂的以往交船情况进行审核,通常只会向拥有良好交船记录的船厂提供此类保险。

---

① Institute Clauses for Builders' Risks, cl.5.1.
② Institute Clauses for Builders' Risks, cl.3.

潜在缺陷

"潜在缺陷"通常是指虽实际存在,但一般的检查却不能发现的缺陷,就海上货物运输而言,关于"潜在缺陷"的经典解释是上议院的 Lord Keith 在 *Riverstone Meat Co Pty Ltd v Lancashire Shipping Co Ltd(The Muncaster Castle)* 一案中作出的,他认为潜在缺陷是船东或合格的专家通过克尽职责仍不能发现的缺陷。他说:①

14.46

> [The carrier] will be protected against latent defects, in the strict sense, in work done on his ship, that is to say, defects not due to any negligent workmanship of repairers or others employed by the repairers, and, as I see it, against defects making for unseaworthiness in the ship, however caused, before it became his ship, if these could not be discovered by him, or competent experts employed by him, by the exercise of due diligence.

Lord Keith 将工艺上的疏忽区别于潜在缺陷的,但是在 *Baxall Securities Ltd & Anr v Sheard Walshaw Partnership & Ors* 一案中,上诉法院的 David Steel 法官也对"潜在缺陷"作出了解释,虽然他的解释与 Lord Keith 是相同的,但是 Steel 法官认为潜在缺陷既包括工艺缺陷也包括设计缺陷,他说:②

14.47

> The concept of a latent defect is not a difficult one. It means a concealed flaw. What is a flaw? It is the actual defect in the workmanship or design, not the danger presented by the defect. To what extent must it be hidden? In my judgment, it must be a defect that would not be discovered following the nature of inspection that the defendant might reasonably anticipate the article would be subjected to.

然而就建造人保险而言,潜在缺陷是否包括工艺或设计可能并不是问题,因为无论是工艺上的缺陷还是设计上的缺陷在建造人保险中均为承保风险,而不是除外风险。

14.48

设计缺陷

根据协会建造人保险条款的规定,建造人保险的承保风险包括船舶及设备等

14.49

---

① [1961] AC 807 at 872.
② [2002] PNLR 24 at [45].

在保险期内产生并发现的因设计缺陷而引起的灭失和损坏,但是不包括修理、修改、替换或换新的成本或费用,也不包括对设计进行改良或调整的成本或费用:①

> Notwithstanding anything to the contrary which may be contained in the Policy or the clauses attached thereto, this insurance includes loss of or damage to the subject matter insured caused and discovered during the period of this insurance arising from faulty design of any part or parts thereof but in no case shall this insurance extend to cover the cost or expense of repairing, modifying, replacing or renewing such part or parts, nor any cost or expense incurred by reason of betterment or alteration in design.

14.50 设计中的缺陷有可能通过一般的检验或检测而被发现,但检验和检测未必一定可以发现设计缺陷,因此设计缺陷有可能构成潜在缺陷。正如 Colman 法官在 *Stone Vickers Ltd* v *Appledore Ferguson Shipbuilders Ltd* 一案中所说的:②

> It would be otherwise if, for example, in the case of trials a design defect in the tailshaft caused damage to some other part of the vessel. The cost of repairing the damage and of re-running the trials would be recoverable, but not the cost of remedying the design defect itself.

14.51 保险人之所以只承担由缺陷设计导致的灭失和损坏而不承担对有缺陷设计进行改良或调整的成本或费用可能是因为对设计进行任何改良或调整实际上已不再与作为保险标的物的船舶和设备等有必然的联系了。如果试航由于设计缺陷而失败,保险人就无需承担再一次试航的费用,对此,Colmen 法官是这样说的:③

> If the only reason why trials are unsuccessful and have to be re-run is that a part has been found to have design defects, the additional expenses cannot be recovered under this clause because effect must be given to the words in the faulty design clause and cl.6 –

> ... nor any cost or expense incurred by reason of betterment or alteration in design.

---

① cl.8.
② [1991] 2 Lloyd's Rep 288.
③ [1991] 2 Lloyd's Rep 288 at 304.

焊接缺陷

根据协会建造人保险条款的规定,建造人保险的承保风险并不包括焊接缺陷:①   14.52

In no case shall this insurance cover the cost of renewing faulty welds.

焊接中的缺陷并不是潜在缺陷,因为焊接缺陷是可以通过适当的检测而被发现的缺陷。建造人保险对因焊接中的缺陷而产生的重新焊接的费用不承担责任。   14.53

船舶下水的费用

船舶下水由于各种原因有可能失败,一旦船舶下水失败,建造人保险将承担为完成下水而产生的所有费用:②   14.54

In case of failure of launch, the Underwriters to bear all subsequent expenses incurred is completing launch.

应当注意的是保险人承诺支付的是"以后的费用",即下水失败后为再次下水而产生的所有费用。换言之,保险人并不承担已经失败的那次下水的相关费用,因为在正常的船舶建造中,船厂至少应当承担一次下水的所有费用,此项费用是船厂完成船舶建造的必不可少的成本。   14.55

污染风险

建造人保险的污染风险是特定的,是指政府当局为了防止或减小污染危险或污染危险的威胁而采取行动所造成船舶的灭失或损坏,但是导致政府当局采取行动的原因则必须是保险人承保的船舶损失,而且政府当局的行动还不应当是由被保险人、船东或船舶管理人未能恪尽职责防止或减小污染危险或污染危险的威胁而引起的:③   14.56

This insurance covers loss of or damage to the Vessel caused by any governmental authority acting under the powers vested in it to prevent or mitigate a pollution hazard, or threat thereof, resulting directly from damage to the Vessel for which the Underwriters are liable under this

---

① cl.5.1.
② cl.5.2.
③ cl.7.

insurance, provided such act of governmental authority has not resulted from want of due diligence by the Assured, the Owners, or Managers of the Vessel or any of them to prevent or mitigate such hazard or threat. Master, Officers, Crew or Pilots not to be considered Owners within the meaning of this Clause 7 should they hold shares in the Vessel.

14.57　虽然在船舶建造中依然存在着污染的风险,但与修船和拆船相比,污染的风险明显要小很多。值得注意的是,建造人保险所承保的污染风险并不局限于油污,而是任何污染。

航行风险

14.58　航行风险是指船舶在航行中可能遭遇的风险,而航行可以是在一个港口之内的,也可以是在两个港口之间的;航行既可以是利用船舶本身的动力进行航行,也可以是通过拖带完成的航行:①

> With leave to proceed to and from any wet or dry docks, harbours, ways, cradles and pontoons within the port or place of construction and to proceed under own power, loaded or in ballast, as often as required, for fitting out, docking, trials or delivery, within a distance by water of 250 nautical miles of the port or place of construction, or held covered at a premium to be arranged in the event of such distance being exceeded.
>
> Any movement of the Vessel in tow outside the port or place of construction held covered at a premium to be arranged, provided previous notice be given to the Underwriters.

14.59　就在建船舶而言,试航显然是一种航行,即使船舶在船厂码头之间移动同样也是一种航行。上述规定提到的"许可"应当是指船舶在港内的移位是得到相关当局许可的,而不是指船舶每次在港内的移位都需要得到保险人的许可。相反,由于保险条款明确规定了250海里的限制,因此如果船舶试航超过250海里,则应在试航之前征得保险人的许可。通常情况下250海里的距离就试航而言应当是足够的,但是对于那些不是在海边的船厂,例如长江内的船厂,由于试航必须在海上进行,船舶首先要离开船厂驶往沿海港口、泊位或锚地,然后再进行船舶的海上试航。在这种情况下,从船厂至试航船舶行驶的最远点之间的距离有可能超过

---

① cl.9.

250海里,此时船厂应当事先征得保险人的许可。

碰撞风险

碰撞是建造人保险承保的风险,协会建造人保险条款有如下规定:① 14.60

The Underwriters agree to indemnify the Assured for any sum or sums paid by the Assured to any other person or persons by reason of the Assured becoming legally liable by way of damages for

(1) Loss of or damage to any other vessel or property on any other vessel
(2) Delay to or loss of use of any such other vessel or property thereon
(3) General average of, salvage of, or salvage under contract of, any such other vessel or property thereon, where such payment by the Assured is in consequence of the Vessel hereby insured coming into collision with any other vessel.

碰撞风险主要是指船舶在进行试航或者移位期间可能面临的风险。虽然在船厂里的船舶,尤其是下了水的船舶也同样面临碰撞的风险,但实际发生碰撞的概率应当说并不很大。建造人保险所承保的碰撞风险主要包括:船厂应当承担的其他船舶或船上财产的灭失或损坏的责任;其他船舶或船上财产因无法使用而导致的时间损失;共同海损;其他船舶或船上财产的救助(包括以合同为基础的救助和不以合同为基础的救助)。 14.61

保险人承保的碰撞责任是有前提的,这些前提包括:当船舶与他船发生碰撞且互有过失时,除非一船或两船的责任可以限制,保险的赔偿以交叉责任原则(cross liabilities)②为依据进行计算;③而且保险人的责任总额以被保险船舶的保险价值按比例应当承担的数额为限。④ 保险人还同意承担船厂为抗辩或限制责 14.62

---

① cl.17.1.
② 简而言之,交叉责任原则是船舶碰撞中计算损害赔偿的一种方式,是针对单一责任(single liabilities)原则而言的。按照单一责任原则,在互有过失碰撞中经过对各自的责任和损失进行计算后由承担较大责任一方向另一方支付损害赔偿。在 *Stoomvart Maatschappij Nederland* v *P and O Steam Navigation Co (The Khedive)* (1882) 7 App Cas 795 一案中,上议院认为就船舶碰撞而言,单一责任原则是正确的方式。然而在采用单一责任原则计算损失时产生了船东和船壳保险人之间的问题。由于按照单一责任原则收到损害赔偿的一方实际上并没有支付过任何数额,因而就无法根据本船保单的碰撞责任条款获得赔偿。因此从1890年 *The London Steamship Owners' Insurance Co* v *Grampian Steamship Co (The Balnacraig)* 24 QBD 32 一案后,互有过失碰撞的损害赔偿开始按照交叉责任原则计算。按照交叉责任原则计算损失时,没有支付的一方同样会被视为已经支付实际上由对方扣除的数额,其船壳保险人也同样按照保单规定支付。交叉责任原则在解决船东和船壳保险人问题的同时并没有违反普通法认定的在碰撞责任中的单一责任原则。
③ cl.17.2.1.
④ cl.17.2.2.

任而产生的或必须支付的法律费用,但法律费用的产生以事先得到保险人书面同意为限。①

保赔保险风险

14.63　　保障和赔偿保险简称"保赔保险"(P&I insurance)是海上保险的一种形式,但却和传统海上保险有着明显的差别。保赔保险中的"保障"是指作为保赔保险保险人的保赔协会在被保险人,即保赔协会会员的船东遇到事故或其他情形时提供保赔协会的服务;而保赔保险中的"赔偿"则是指保赔协会在船东遭受损失时提供赔偿。一般的海上保险,例如船壳保险和建造人保险都属于商业保险的范畴,而保赔保险则具有互助保险的特征。保赔保险针对的是船东对第三人的法律责任,而第三人则是船东以外的任何人。根据协会建造人保险条款的规定,保险人向船厂不仅提供责任的保赔保险,而且还提供费用的保赔保险。其中,关于责任的承保风险是:②

> The Underwriters agree to indemnify the Assured for any sum or sums paid by the Assured to any other person or persons by reason of the Assured becoming legally liable, as Owner of the Vessel, for anyclaim, demand, damages and/or expenses, where such liability is in consequence of any of the following matter or things and arises from an accident or occurrence during the period of this insurance:
>
> (1) loss of or damage to any fixed or movable object or property or other thing or interest whatsoever, other than the vessel, arising from any cause whatsoever in so far as such loss or damage is not covered by Clause 17.
> (2) any attempted or actual raising, removal or destruction of any fixed or movable object to property or other thing, including the wreck of the Vessel, or any neglect or failure to raise, remover, or destroy the same.
> (3) liability assumed by the Assured under contracts of customary towage for the purpose of entering or leaving port or maneuvering within the port.
> (4) loss of life, personal injury, illness or payments made for life salvage.

---

① cl.17.3.
② cl.19.1.

保赔保险的特征是保赔协会承担的是船厂实际支付的数额,即船厂必须首先支付,然后才能获得保赔协会的补偿,这就是所谓的"先付原则"。只有在船厂依法应当向第三人支付赔偿且已实际支付了赔偿的情况下,保赔协会才会向船厂进行赔偿。① 在建造人保险中,保险人向船厂提供的保赔保险所承保的风险主要包括:(1)建造人保险承保的碰撞责任所不包括的,船舶以外的固定或移动物体或财产等遭受的灭失或损坏;(2)船厂试图或实际打捞或移动或毁坏任何固定或移动的物体或财产包括打捞在建船舶的残骸的行为,或者打捞固定或移动物体或财产的疏忽;(3)船厂根据拖带合同规定应当承担的责任;(4)人身伤亡、疾病或为拯救生命而进行的救助的费用。

14.64

建造人保险的保赔保险提供的费用保险的承保范围是:②

14.65

The Underwriters agree to indemnify the Assured for any of the following arising from an accident or occurrence during the period of this insurance:

(1) the additional cost of fuel, insurance, wages, stores, provisions and port charges reasonably incurred solely for the purpose of landing from the Vessel sick or injured persons or stowaways, refugees, or persons saved at sea.
(2) Additional expenses brought about by the outbreak of infectious disease on board the Vessel or ashore.
(3) Fines imposed on the Vessel, on the Assured, or on any Master Officer crew member or agent of the Vessel who is reimbursed by the Assured, for any act or neglect or breach of any statute or regulation relating to the operation of the Vessel, provided that the Underwriters shall not be liable to indemnify the Assured for any fines which result from any act neglect failure or default of the Assured their agents or servants other than Master Officer or crew member.
(4) The expenses of the removal of the wreck of the Vessel from any place owned, leased or occupied by the Assured.
(5) Legal costs incurred by the Assured, or which the Assured may be compelled to pay, in avoiding, minimizing or contesting liability with the prior written consent of the Underwriters.

---

① 一个例外是在发生油污损害时,受损的第三人可以直接向保赔协会主张索赔,即所谓的"直接诉讼"(direct action)。
② cl.19.2.

14.66　上述费用是指因发生建造人保险所承保的风险而产生的各种费用,这些费用包括:与人员有关的费用,例如因船厂人员生病或受伤,传染病的爆发等引起的相关费用;与政府有关的费用,例如因违法操纵或作业而遭受的罚款;与船舶有关的费用,例如残骸的清除费用;以及与法律有关的费用,例如律师费用等。就船舶建造而言,上述费用的产生有的与船舶的试航有关,有的则与在船厂的建造有关。

共同海损和救助

14.67　按照协会建造人保险条款的规定,建造人保险的保险人承保与共同海损和救助相关的费用:①

> This insurance covers the Vessel's proportion of salvage, salvage charges and/or general average, reduced in respect of any under-insurance, but in case of general average sacrifice of the Vessel the Assured may recover in respect of the whole loss without first enforcing their right of contribution from other parties.

14.68　"救助费用"是指在没有订立合同的情况下实施救助的救助人依法可以获得的救助报酬。1906年《海上保险法》是这样解释救助费用的:②

> "Salvage charges" means the charges recoverable under maritime law by a salvor independently of contract. They do not include the expenses of service in the nature of salvage rendered by the assured or his agents, or any person employed for hire by them for the purpose of averting a peril insured against. Such expenses, where properly incurred, may be recovered as particular charges or as a general average loss, according to the circumstances under which they were incurred.

14.69　因此保险人承担的既包括救助报酬,也包括救助费用,即使救助是在救助方和被救助方之间没有救助合同的情况下进行的。而"共同海损"一词从其实际使用来看似乎比较随意,并不始终表达同一种含义,而是在不同情况下表达着不同的含义。Arnould's Law of Marine Insurance and Average 一书是这样描述"general average"一词的:③

---

① cl.13.1.
② s.65(2).
③ Jonathon Gilman et al, *Arnould: Law of Marine Insurance and Average* 20th edn Sweet & Maxwell 2021, para.26-01.

The term "general average" is used indiscriminately, sometimes to denote the kind of loss which gives a claim to general average contribution, and sometimes to denote such contribution itself; in order to avoid confusion, it would have been better to use the term "general average loss" when speaking of the former, and "general average contribution" when speaking of the latter.

14.70 共同海损既可以是指共同海损损失,也可以是指共同海损分摊。共同海损损失是指为了共同利益而产生或遭受的损失,共同海损分摊则是指受益方对共同海损损失的承担。1906年《海上保险法》为"共同海损损失"下了如下定义:①

A general average loss is a loss caused by or directly consequential on a general average act. It includes a general average expenditure as well as a general average sacrifice.

14.71 而关于"共同海损分摊",1906年《海上保险法》则有如下规定:②

Where there is a general average loss, the party on whom it falls is entitled, subject to the conditions imposed by maritime law, to a rateable contribution from the other parties interested, and such contribution is called a general average contribution.

14.72 按照协会建造人保险条款的规定,无论是船舶遭受的共同海损损失还是船舶应当支付的共同海损分摊,建造人保险的保险人都将承担责任。但是保险人承担赔偿责任的前提是产生共同海损的原因应当是建造人保险所承保的风险:③

No claim under this Clause 13 shall in any case be allowed where the loss was not incurred to avoid or in connection with the avoidance of a peril insured against.

承保风险的约定

14.73 前文讨论的是建造人保险的标准承保风险,即以协会建造人保险条款的规定为依据的承保风险。但是在实践中船厂和保险人可以通过协商对承保风险的范围作出调整或更改。

---

① s.66(1).
② s.66(3).
③ cl.13.4.

Ⅳ 除外责任

14.74　除外责任是指保险人不承担的责任。除外责任可以是法律规定的，也可以是当事人约定的。

法定除外责任

14.75　1906年《海上保险法》规定了保险人无需承担责任的事项，这些事项包括：①

(1) Subject to the provisions of this Act, and unless the policy otherwise provides, the insurer is liable for any loss proximately caused by a peril insured against, but, subject as aforesaid, he is not liable for any loss which is not proximately caused by a peril insured against.

(2) In particular –

(a) The insurer is not liable for any loss attributable to the wilful misconduct of the assured, but, unless the policy otherwise provides, he is liable for any loss proximately caused by a peril insured against, even though the loss would not have happened but for the misconduct or negligence of the master or crew;

(b) Unless the policy otherwise provides, the insurer on ship or goods is not liable for any loss proximately caused by delay, although the delay be caused by a peril insured against;

(c) Unless the policy otherwise provides, the insurer is not liable for ordinary wear and tear, ordinary leakage and breakage, inherent vice or nature of the subject-matter insured, or for any loss proximately caused by rats or vermin, or for any injury to machinery not proximately caused by maritime perils.

14.76　上述1906年《海上保险法》的条文规定了三项保险人无需承担赔偿责任的事项。首先，保险人无需对因被保险人自身的故意不当行为造成的损失承担赔偿责任，但是保险人应当对由于承保风险造成的损失负责，即使不存在被保险人的故意不当行为就不会产生的损失，保险人依然应当负责；其次，保险人无需对因延误造成的损失承担赔偿责任，即使延误本身是由于保险所承保的风险引起的；最后，保险人无需对因船舶或设备等的自然损耗、正常破碎以及固有缺陷或特性等原因

---

① s.55.

造成的损失承担赔偿责任。

法律规定的除外责任即使没有写进保险合同,保险人依然无需承担。当事人可以在保险合同中排除上述法律条文的适用,即在合同中约定保险人应当承担成文法排除的保险责任。当事人可以在保险合同中约定保险人应当对由于内在缺陷造成的损失承担赔偿责任,但此种约定必须是明确的,否则就有可能是无效的。并非所有除外责任都可以通过合同条款予以排除,例如除非是由于承保风险引起的损失,即使保险合同另有约定,保险人依然无需承担因被保险人自己的故意行为造成的损失。

14.77

固有缺陷和潜在缺陷

区分固有缺陷(inherent vice)和潜在缺陷的意义在于前者是保险人无需承担责任的风险,而后者则是保险人应当承保的风险。固有缺陷是指作为物之特征或特性而内在的或固有的一种问题或缺陷,在 *Soya Gmbh Mainz Kommanditgesellschaft v White* 一案中,上议院的 Lord Diplock 认为固有缺陷造成的损失是指在正常情况下由于自身原因而发生的损失,他说:①

14.78

> This phrase (generally shortened to "inherent vice") where it is used in s.55(2)(c) refers to a peril by which a loss is proximately caused; it is not descriptive of the loss itself. It means the risk of deterioration of the goods shipped as a result of their natural behaviour in the ordinary course of the contemplated voyage without the intervention of any fortuitous external accident or casualty. Prima facie, this risk is excluded from a policy of marine insurance unless the policy otherwise provides, either expressly or by necessary implication . . . .

在实践中区分固有缺陷和潜在缺陷未必是一件简单的事情,在很多情况下两者的差异可能是相当细微的。但普通法似乎确立了这样一个原则,即在有潜在缺陷情况下保险人不能以固有缺陷为由拒绝理赔。在 *Prudent Tankers Ltd SA v The Dominion Insurance Co Ltd (The Caribbean Sea)*②一案中,船舶保险合同有如下规定:

14.79

> Subject to the conditions of this Policy, this insurance also covers loss of or damage to the vessel directly caused by the following . . . . Any latent

---

① [1983] 1 Lloyd's Rep 122 at 126.
② [1980] 1 Lloyd's Rep 338.

defect in the machinery or hull .... Negligence of Masters Officers Crew or Pilots; provided such loss or damage has not resulted from want of due diligence by the Assured, the Owners or Managers of the vessel or any of them ....

14.80　　1977 年 5 月 20 日,船舶在通过马拉开波湖的航道时突然出现左倾,不久又恢复正常。船厂的判断是船舶触底,但没有查询船舶是否受损,直到船舶于 23 日驶抵巴尔博亚时才签署了海事声明。5 月 27 日,船舶在太平洋行驶。虽然当时天气和海况并不恶劣,但船舶由于机舱进水而沉没。船东向保险人提出索赔,理由是 5 月 20 日的触底损坏了右舷主通海阀的接口,导致 5 月 27 日的机舱进水;或者是由于连接船板和接口的环焊焊缝出现疲劳裂缝而导致的;也可能是缘板底端出现的疲劳裂缝而导致的,因此损失是由于船体的潜在缺陷导致的。保险人拒绝承担责任,理由是船舶是由于不适航而沉没的;如果是右舷的主通海阀的问题导致损失,损失就是由于船体或机器的正常损坏引起的,因此不是承保风险造成的。高院的 Goff 法官认为船东只有在能够证明船舶的沉没是直接由于船体的潜在缺陷造成的情况下才可以得到保险赔偿,他认为疲劳裂缝构成潜在缺陷,因此船东可以获得保险赔偿。Goff 法官说:①

> I have therefore to consider whether the policy, by covering the assured against loss of or damage to the vessel directly caused by any latent defect in the machinery or hull, does provide otherwise. It is to be observed that s.55(2)(c) likewise excludes liability for inherent vice or nature of the subject matter insured; that provision is clearly inconsistent with the cover under the Inchmaree clause, and so inapplicable to a policy containing the clause.

约定除外责任

14.81　　除了成文法规定以外,保险合同的当事人也可以在合同中约定保险人无需承担保险赔偿责任的风险或损失。② 约定的方式包括保险合同的规定,保险条款的规定等。

---

① [1980] 1 Lloyd's Rep 338 at 347.
② 此种约定以不违反 1977 年《不公平合同条款法》为条件。

地震和火山爆发

协会建造人保险条款规定保险人无需承担地震或火山爆发引起的灭失、损坏、责任和费用等：①   14.82

> In no case shall this insurance cover loss damage liability or expense caused by earthquake or volcanic eruption. This exclusion applies to all claims including claims under Clauses 13, 17, 19 and 20.

地震和火山爆发是建造人保险的除外责任，而就船舶建造合同而言，地震和火山爆发都属于不可抗力事件，即"天灾"，尤其是地震在绝大多数船舶建造合同中都是列明的不可抗力事件。但是在船舶建造合同中，不可抗力事件的发生只是允许船厂按照实际发生的延误顺延合同交船日，船厂依然要承担地震或火山爆发带来的损失。因为除非另有规定，船舶在交付给船东之前的所有权归船厂享有，风险也同样由船厂承担。如果地震和火山爆发造成的船舶的灭失和损坏等不属于建造人保险的承保范围，船厂就应当对此承担责任。   14.83

碰撞

按照协会建造人保险条款的规定，保险人既承保碰撞及碰撞责任，同时又规定碰撞责任中的除外责任。协会条款的规定是：②   14.84

> Provided always that this Clause 17 shall in no case extend to any sum which the Assured shall pay for or in respect of:
> (1) removal or disposal of obstructions, wrecks, cargoes or any other thing whatsoever;
> (2) any real or personal property or thing whatsoever except other vessels or property on other vessels;
> (3) the cargo or other property on, or the engagements of, the insured Vessel;
> (4) loss of life, personal injury or illness;
> (5) pollution or contamination of any real or personal property or thing whatsoever(except other vessels with which the insured Vessel is in collision or property on such other vessels).

---

① Institute Clauses for Builders' Risk, cl.6.
② Institute Clauses for Builders' Risk, cl.17.4.

14.85　上述除外责任是针对碰撞责任的,虽然保险人承诺赔偿被保险人的碰撞责任,但是保险人的赔偿并不包括:(1)障碍物、残骸、货物或任何其他物品的清除或处置;(2)其他船舶或其上财产以外的任何不动产或个人财产或物品;(3)承保船舶上的或与承保船舶有关的货物或其他财产;(4)人身伤亡或疾病;(5)任何不动产或个人财产或物品的污染或沾污(与承保船舶发生碰撞的船舶或在该船上的财产除外)。如前所述,就建造人保险而言,碰撞的发生和碰撞责任的产生主要在船舶的试航期间,以及为在海上试航而必须完成的内河航行期间。虽然在建船舶在下水后同样有可能与其他船舶发生碰撞,但此种风险基本上是理论上的风险。

保赔保险

14.86　与碰撞责任相类似,协会建造人保险条款不仅规定保险人保赔保险的承保范围,同时也规定了保险人保赔保险的除外责任,该条款的规定如下:①

> Notwithstanding the provisions of Clause 19.1 and 19.2, this Clause 19 does not cover any liability cost or expense arising in respect of:
>
> (1) any direct or indirect payment of the Assured under workmen's compensation or employers' liability acts and any other statutory or common law, general maritime law or other liability whatsoever in respect of accidents to or illness of workmen or any other persons employed in any capacity whatsoever by the Assured or others in on or about or in connection with the Vessel or her cargo materials or repairs;
>
> (2) liability assumed by the Assured under agreement expressed or implied in respect of death or illness of or injury to any person employed under a contract of service or apprenticeship by the other party to such agreement;
>
> (3) punitive or exemplary damages, however described;
>
> (4) cargo or other property carried, to be carried or which has been carried on board the Vessel but this Clause 19.3.4 shall not exclude any claim in respect of the extra cost of removing cargo from the wreck of the Vessel;
>
> (5) loss of or damage to property, owned by builders or repairers or for which they are responsible, which is on board the Vessel;
>
> (6) liability arising under a contract or indemnity in respect of

---

① cl.19.3.

(7) cash, negotiable instruments, precious metals or stones, valuables or objects of a rare or precious nature, belonging to persons on board the Vessel, or non-essential personal effects of any Master, Officer or crew member;

(8) fuel, insurance, wages, stores, provisions and port charges arising from delay to the Vessel while awaiting a substitute for any Master, Officer or crew member;

(9) fines or penalties arising from overloading or illegal fishing;

(10) pollution or contamination of any real or personal property or thing whatsoever.

14.87 就建造人保险而言,上述针对保赔保险的除外责任主要包括:(1)船厂根据雇佣合同或雇主责任法就雇员的人身伤亡或疾病支付的任何款项;(2)船厂按照合同约定应对人身伤亡或疾病而承担的责任;(3)任何惩罚性赔偿,所谓惩罚性赔偿是指不以金钱赔偿为目的而以惩罚为目的超出实际损害的赔偿,违反合同义务的通常不能适用惩罚性赔偿;①(4)承保船装载的货物或其他财产;(5)承保船上船厂拥有或负责的财产的灭失或损坏;②(6)承保船上船厂拥有或负责的集装箱、设备、燃油或其他财产的合同责任;(7)承保船上人员的现金、可流通票据、贵金属或宝石、贵重物品、稀有或珍贵物品;(8)燃油、保险、工资、备用品、物料以及因承保船替换船长和船员的延误而产生的港口使费;(9)因超载或非法捕鱼而产生的罚金或罚款;(10)任何不动产或个人财产或物件的污染或沾污。在这些除外风险中,在船舶建造中出现的可能性相对比较大是第1项至第7项。

战争

14.88 战争风险通常不与其他风险一起承保,而是由船厂和保险人在另行磋商并由船厂支付保费的情况下才会予以承保:③

In no case shall this insurance cover loss damage liability or expense caused by:

(1) war civil war revolution rebellion insurrection, or civil strife arising

---

① See *Kenny v Preen* [1963] 1 QB 499.
② 这一除外风险应当包括船东供应品,虽然船东供应品并不是船厂的财产,但一旦运抵船厂,船厂就应当对船东供应品负责,包括办理保险。
③ cl.21.

    therefrom, or any hostile act by or against a belligerent power;

    (2) capture seizure arrest restraint or detainment (barratry and piracy excepted), and the consequences thereof or any attempt thereat;

    (3) derelict mines torpedoes bombs or other derelict weapons of war.

14.89　上述风险中有一些已经在本书第 9 章中有过介绍。① 在实际船舶建造中，上述风险发生的可能性应当说并不大，但是由于船舶在交付给船东之前的风险是由船厂承担的，因此这些风险也就是船厂的风险了。

罢工

14.90　与战争风险相类似，罢工风险通常也不会和其他一般风险一起承保，而往往和战争风险一起承保：②

    In no case shall this insurance cover loss damage liability or expense caused by:

    (1) strikers, locked-out workmen, or persons taking part in labour disturbances, riots or civil commotion;

    (2) any terrorist or any person acting form a political motive.

14.91　实际上，罢工风险不仅包括罢工以及与罢工相关的事件，而且还包括与罢工并没有直接关系的恐怖分子活动和带有政治动机的行为。

恶意行为

14.92　恶意行为 (malicious acts) 应当是一个刑法的用词，指没有正当理由的故意恶意行为。在 *Bromage v Prosser* 一案中，Bayley 法官说：③

    Malice in common acceptation means ill-will against a person, but in its legal sense it means a wrongful act done intentionally without just cause or excuse.

14.93　而在 *Allen v Flood* 一案中，枢密院的 Hawkins 法官则认为恶意的动机才是恶意行为的关键，他说：④

    If I rightly estimate the effect of the plaintiffs' evidence, I do not think

---

① 关于战争请参见本书第 9 章第 V 节。
② cl.22.
③ (1825) 4 B & C 247 at 255.
④ [1898] AC 1 at 18.

anything falling within the ordinary popular acceptation of "malice," such as spite or ill-will, is at all essential to the maintenance of this present action, although, if it be so, there is evidence of its existence; a wrongful motive, however, is, in my opinion, essential.

14.94 作为建造人保险的除外责任,协会条款仅规定了两种恶意行为,分别是爆炸和使用武器:①

In no case shall this insurance cover loss damage liability or expense arising from:

(1) the detonation of an explosive;
(2) any weapon of war and caused by any person acting maliciously or from a political motive.

14.95 因此,爆炸和使用战争武器产生的灭失、损坏、责任和费用均不是保险人应当承担保险责任的风险。

核风险

14.96 核风险除外应当是所有保险合同的标准条款,核风险除外的是:核废料和核燃料;核装置或和部件;以及核武器,保险人不仅不承担因核风险造成的灭失和损坏,同时也不承担因此产生的责任和费用:②

In no case shall this insurance cover loss damage liability or expense directly or indirectly caused by or contributed to by or arising from

(1) ionising radiations from or contamination by radioactivity from any nuclear waste from the combustion of nuclear fuel
(2) the radioactive, toxic, explosive or other hazardous properties of any explosive nuclear assembly or nuclear component thereof
(3) any weapon of waremploying atomic or nuclear fission and/or fusion or other like reaction or radioactive force or matter.

14.97 除了成文法规定以外,保险合同的当事人也可以在合同中约定保险人无需承担保险赔偿责任的风险或损失。③ 约定的方式包括保险合同的规定,保险条款的规定等。

---

① cl.23.
② cl.24.
③ 此种约定以不违反 1977 年《不公平合同条款法》为条件。

除外责任的承保安排

14.98　作为保险合同当事人的船厂和保险人不仅可以约定保单的承保范围，也可以约定除外责任的排除，即将除外责任转化为保单承保责任。船厂要求保险人承保除外责任往往是因为船舶建造合同的要求，例如 SAJ 格式就有如下规定：①

> If the BUYER so requests, the BUILDER shall at the BUYER's cost procure insurance on the VESSEL and all parts, materials, machinery and equipment intended therefore against risks of earthquake, strike, war peril or other risks not heretofore provided and shall make all arrangements to that end. The cost of such insurance shall be reimbursed to the BUILDER by the BUYER upon delivery of the VESSEL.

14.99　AWES 格式也有类似规定，除非船东另有要求，船厂可以决定是否投保战争险，但似乎无论出于何种原因投保战争险，保险费用均应由船东承担：②

> ... If considered necessary by the CONTRACTOR or if required by the PURCHASER was risks insurance for not less than the CONTRACT price to be effected by the CONTRACTOR at PURCHASER's account up to the date of delivery to the extent that such insurance is obtainable on the .... insurance market.

14.100　而 NEWBUILDCON 格式则明确规定船厂应当投保包括战争险和罢工险的建造人保险：③

> ... Such Builder's Risk Insurance shall:
>
> (ii) be on terms no less wide than Institute Clauses for Builder's Risk terms(1/6/88) including Institute War and Institute Strike Clauses; and

14.101　是否投保战争险、罢工险或其他风险其实并不是船东是否有要求的问题，也不是合同义务的问题，而是船厂自身利益的问题。就拿船舶建造合同常见的不可抗力事件为例，即使船厂无需为实际发生的不可抗力事件造成的损失承担责任，船厂似乎也没有理由不针对那些不可抗力事件进行投保。更何况，根据常见的船

---

① Article XII.1, para.4.
② Article 9, para.1.
③ Clause 38(a)(ii).

舶建造合同标准格式的规定,在发生不可抗力事件时船厂似乎并不一定能够享受免责。因此,适当的做法是针对所有可能发生的风险以及船舶建造合同约定的风险进行投保,例如地震和火山爆发、船厂对船东供应品的责任等进行投保。这样才能确保船厂的利益不会因为意外事件的发生而遭受损失。

V 船舶的损失

部分损失

14.102　部分损失就是全部损失以外的损失,即除非构成全部损失,否则就是部分损失。1906年《海上保险法》的规定是:①

A loss may be either total or partial. Any loss other than a total loss, as hereinafter defined, is a partial loss.

全损

14.103　全部损失或全损是指保险标的物的灭失。全损可以是实际全损,也可以是推定全损。

实际全损

14.104　按照1906年《海上保险法》的规定,实际全损是:②

Where the subject-matter insured is destroyed, or so damaged as to cease to be a thing of the kind insured, or where the assured is irretrievably deprived thereof, there is an actual total loss.

14.105　从上述规定可以看出,实际全损应当包括三种情形:第一种情形是指保险标的物全部毁坏;第二种情形是指虽然保险标的物尚未遭到全部毁坏,但其受损程度已使其不再具有投保时的物理状态;第三种情形是指被保险人对保险标的物的占有已被不可挽回地剥夺。就船舶而言,第一和第二种情形之间的差异似乎仅仅是程度而已。两者的共同之处是作为标的物投保的船舶已不再是船舶了,正如

---

① s.56(1).
② s.57(1).

Abbott 法官早在 *Cambridge* v *Anderton* 一案中所指出的:①

> If the subject matter of insurance remained a ship, it was not a total loss, but if it were reduced to a mere congeries of planks, the vessel was a mere wreck, the name which you may think fit to apply to it cannot alter the nature of the thing.

14.106　法院曾认为船舶一旦沉没即构成实际全损,在 *Sailing Ship Blairmore Co Ltd* v *Macredie* 一案中,上议院的 Halsbury 伯爵便认为船舶一旦沉没即构成实际全损,他说:②

> I myself should say a ship was totally lost when she goes to the bottom of the sea, though modern mechanical skill may bring her up again; and I think, in construing a contract now for many years a common contract, no one could doubt that that contract was intended by the parties to contemplate the loss of a ship as comprehending the case of her being sunk.

14.107　但是在 *Captain JA Cates Tug and Wharfage Co Ltd* v *Franklin Insurance Co* 一案中,船舶虽然已经沉没,但枢密院的 Sumner 子爵则认为并不因此构成实际全损,他并且对 Halsbury 伯爵的观点予以了说明。他说:③

> What Lord Halsbury said [in the *Blairmore* case] was not necessary to the decision, nor was it part of the reasoning on which the decision of the House was based, and it expresses only his opinion at that time on the particular fact which the case presented – namely, that this ship had been sunk in a squall in 60 fathoms, while laid up in ballast in San Francisco Bay in the year 1896. The physical possibility of raising a sunken ship depends not only on the place where she lies, her size and injuries, and the available facilities for salvage work, but also on the existing state of the salvors' art, which, since 1896, has made very considerable advances. Lord Halsbury's remark must not be taken as meaning that any ship is an actual total loss whenever she is under water, nor even when she is submerged in such circumstances as to present to salvors a problem of some difficulty.

---

① (1824) 2 B & C 691 at 692.
② [1898] AC 593 at 598.
③ [1927] AC 698 at 704.

Potter 法官在 *Fraser Shipping Ltd v Colton and Others* 一案中对第三种情形的实际全损作出了说明,他认为船舶是否"已被不可挽回地剥夺"取决于是否还能到达,而船舶是否还能到达则又取决于船舶本身是否可以获救。他说的是:①

14.108

> As to the definition of actual total loss, whether the plaintiff were "irretrievably deprived" of the vessel *prima facie* depends upon whether, by reason of the vessel's situation, it was wholly out of the power of the plaintiffs or the underwriters to procure its arrival. It seems to me that this, in turn, depends upon whether the vessel could have been physically salved or not. The undisputed evidence in this respect was to the effect that it was feasible to salvage the vessel subject to accessibility and cost.

船舶被不可挽回地剥夺的情形与船舶的实际状况无关,而是指船东已不可能重新获得船舶了,若能重新获得船舶的,即使非常困难也依然不构成"已被不可挽回地剥夺"。在 *George Cohen, Sons and Co v Standard Marine Insurance Co Ltd*② 一案中,一艘军舰在被拖船拖带时在荷兰沿海失事,拖船离开了失事地点。军舰面临着漂移的危险。法院虽然认为该军舰已经构成推定全损,但法院认为船东并没有被不可挽回地剥夺该军舰。因为该军舰实际上依然存在,Roche 法官说:③

14.109

> It is not contended that this ship was destroyed. She is there still. It is not and could not be contended that she is so damaged as to cease to be a thing of the kind insured, but it is suggested that the assured is irretrievably deprived thereof, and that, accordingly, she is an actual total loss …. My reasons for deciding that the plaintiffs have not been irretrievably deprived thereof are as follows …. I am of opinion that this vessel physically could be got off. It would be a matter of great elaboration and difficulty, but, at all events, putting the matter at the highest, I am not satisfied that she could not. On the whole, I think that she could … in these circumstances, there has been no irretrievable deprivation which a court can find by reason of physical impossibility.

由此可见,第三种情形应当适用于在航行中的船舶,而在建造人保险中的船舶除了试航,在整个保险期间内并不会离开船厂,因此第三种情形的实际全损出现在建造人保险中的可能性应当不是太大。

14.110

---

① [1997] 1 Lloyd's Rep 586 at 591.
② (1925) 21 Ll L Rep 30.
③ (1925) 21 Ll L Rep 30 at 33.

推定全损

14.111　推定全损,顾名思义,应当是指保险标的物尚未遭受实际全损但被视为实际全损的情形。1906年《海上保险法》为推定全损下了如下定义:①

(1) Subject to any express provision in the policy, there is a constructive total loss where the subject-matter insured is reasonably abandoned on account of its actual total loss appearing to be unavoidable, or because it could not be preserved from actual total loss without an expenditure which would exceed its value when the expenditure had been incurred.

(2) In particular, there is a constructive total loss –

(i) Where the assured is deprived of the possession of his ship or goods by a peril insured against, the (a) it is unlikely that he can recover the ship or goods, as the case may be, or (b) the cost of recovering the ship or goods, as the case may be, would exceed their value when recovered; or

(ii) In the case of damage to a ship, where she is so damaged by a peril insured against that the cost of repairing the damage would exceed the value of the ship when repaired.

In estimating the cost of repairs, no deduction is to be made in respect of general average contributions to those repairs payable by other interests, but account is to be taken of the expense of future salvage operations and of any future general average contributions to which the ship would be liable if repaired; or

(iii) In the case of damage to goods, where the cost of repairing the damage and forwarding the goods to their destination would exceed their value on arrival.

14.112　上述规定的第一项似乎是推定全损的定义,而第二项则是推定全损的各种情形。第二项中的情形似乎与第一项中的定义并不完全吻合。实际上第一项和第二项共同组成了推定全损的定义,上议院的 Lord Wright 在 *Robertson* v *Petros M Nomikos Ltd* 一案中是这样说的:②

---

① s.60.
② [1939] AC 371 at 382.

The objective definition of a constructive total loss is found in the preceding section of the Act [s.60]. Some difficulty has been found in interpreting that section, because it consists of two parts. Sub-section 2 is purely objective; it gives the two cases of constructive total loss of ship, the first being deprivation of possession, the second the cost of repairs. This is completely consistent with s.61. But s.60(1) is said to be inconsistent, because it makes the constructive total loss depend on the condition that the subject matter is reasonably abandoned for either of the reasons stated. This, I think, does not qualify the definition in sub-s.2. The two sub-sections contain two separate definitions, applicable to different conditions of circumstances.

14.113 在 Rickards v Forestal Land, Timber and Railways Co Ltd 一案中,上议院的 Lord Wright 也认为,第 60 条的两部分均为定义,适用于不同的事实状况。第二部分是对第一部分的补充,而不是说明。他说:①

Some aspects of the section [s.60] have been recently discussed in this House in Robertson v Petros M Nomikos. In particular, the difficulty of fitting together the two sub-sections of s.60 and reading them together with s.61 was there considered. I think the view which this House arrived at was that the two sub-sections contain two separate definitions, which may be applied to different conditions of fact. Thus, an assured can base his claim on the terms of sub-s(2), which give an objective criterion in each case, ship, goods, or freight, not only more precise than, but substantially different from, that in sub-s(1). Sub-section (2), as compared with sub-s(1), is thus additional, and not merely illustrative.

14.114 在发生推定全损时,被保险人可以将船舶遭受的损失视为部分损失,也可以委付船舶从而将船舶遭受的损失视为实际全损。对此,1906 年《海上保险法》是这样规定的:②

Where there is a constructive total loss the assured may either treat the loss as a partial loss, or abandon the subject-matter insured to the insurer and treat the loss as if it were an actual total loss.

14.115 建造人保险是一种定值保险,即保险合同明确约定了船舶的价值。但是按照

---

① [1941] 3 All ER 62 at 79.
② s.61.

1906年《海上保险法》的规定,除非另有约定,在确定推定全损是否成立时保单确定的价值并不具有决定性意义。① 换言之,船舶推定全损的金额可以高于也可以低于保单确定的价值。就建造人保险的保险人而言,是否成立推定全损意味着保险人是否应当支付保险金额全额甚至更多。② 因此是否成立推定全损及如何成立推定全损直接关系到保险人的利益,协会建造人保险条款对此作出了如下规定:③

> In ascertaining whether the subject-matter insured is a constructive total loss, the insured value shall be taken as the repaired value and nothing in respect of the damaged or break-up value shall be taken into account.
>
> No claim for constructive total loss based upon the cost of recovery and/or repair shall be recoverable hereunder unless such cost would exceed the insured value. In making this determination, only the cost relating to a single accident or sequence of damages arising from the same accident shall be taken into account.

14.116　所谓的"保险价值"是指船厂和保险人约定的保险人承担保险合同责任的最大限额;而"修复后价值"是指遭受损坏的船舶在修复后的市场价格。保险人承诺赔偿的是保险价值,而无论修复后的船舶在市场上有多大的价值。

协议全损

14.117　协议全损是指保险人和被保险人在特殊情况下通过协商约定对尚未构成全损的情形适用关于全损的规定。协议全损通常是符合保险人和被保险人各自利益的损害赔偿方式,例如船东接受低于保险金额的赔偿但保留受损船舶所有权的做法就是一种协议全损。协议全损的一个特征是虽然被保险人没有或不能提出实际或推定全损的索赔,但对船舶进行修复则又不切实际。

索赔通知

14.118　一旦发生船厂可以凭建造人保险向保险人提出灭失、损坏、责任或费用索赔的,船厂应当及时并且在自己开始修理之前通知保险人:④

---

① s.27(4).
② 如果发生施救的,保险人承担的赔偿责任就可能超过保险合同规定的保险金额。
③ cl.12.
④ cl.14.

In the event of loss damage liability or expense which may result in a claim under this insurance, prompt notice shall be given to the Underwriters prior to repair and, if the subject-matter is under construction abroad, to the nearest Lloyd's Agent so that a surveyor may be appointed to represent the Underwriters should they so desire.

14.119　什么是"及时"应当是一个事实问题,而且在不同情况下"及时"可能会有不同的时间长短。按照 1967 年《统一国际买卖法》(Uniform Laws on International Sales Act, 1967)的规定,"及时"应当是指可以实施该行为那一刻起的尽可能短的时间内:①

Whereunder the present Law an act is required to be performed "promptly", it shall be performed within as short a period as possible, in the circumstances, from the moment when the act could reasonably be performed.

14.120　虽然协会条款并没有规定船厂没有发出通知就不能提出索赔,但是索赔通知显然值得船厂重视。无故拖延且造成保险人利益受损的,保险人应当有机会主张自己不再有赔偿的义务。

VI 船厂的施救义务

施救义务概述

14.121　虽然保险人承保了各项风险,但这并不意味着船厂可以不再为船舶及设备等的灭失或损坏担心,可以任由各种风险对船舶及设备等造成灭失或损坏。船厂依然负有避免损失、防止损失扩大的合同义务,此项义务也被称为是"施救义务"。虽然共同海损和救助实际上也是对船舶的一种施救,但它们并不是施救义务。在 Aitchison v Lohre 一案中,上议院的 Lord Blackburn 是这样描述施救义务的:②

... I think that general average and salvage do not come within either the words or the object of the suing and labouring clause, and that there is no authority for saying that they do. The words of the clause are that

---

① Art.11.
② (1879) 4 App Cas 755 at 764.

in case of any misfortune it shall be lawful "for the assured, their factors, servants, and assigns, to sue, labour, and travel for, in, and about the defence, safeguard, and recovery of" the subject of insurance, "without prejudice to this insurance, to the charges whereof we the insurers will contribute". And the object of this is to encourage and induce the assured to exert themselves, and therefore the insurers bind themselves to pay in proportion any expense incurred, whenever such expense is reasonably incurred for the preservation of the thing from loss, in consequence of the efforts of the assured or their agents.

14.122 几乎所有的海上保险合同中都有"施救条款"。协会建造人保险条款的施救条款有如下内容:①

In case of any loss or misfortune it is the duty of the Assured and their servants and agents to take such measures as may be reasonable for the purpose of averting or minimizing a loss which would be recoverable under this insurance.

14.123 即使保险合同没有关于施救义务的规定,被保险人依然是有这一义务的,因为1906年《海上保险法》就有如下规定:②

It is the duty of the assured and his agents, in all cases, to take such measures as maybe reasonable for the purpose of averting or minimising a loss.

14.124 这是一项直接关系到被保险人是否可以获得保险赔偿的义务,如果被保险人或其代理人采取措施就可以避免或减小损失但被保险人或其代理人没有采取措施的,保险人就可以拒绝赔偿。Colman 法官在 *National Oilwell(UK) Ltd* v *Davy Offshore Ltd* 是这样说的:③

It goes no further than the fairly obvious proposition that if after the advent of an insured peril or when the advent of an insured peril was obviously imminent the assured or his agent failed to act to avert or minimize loss in circumstances where any prudent uninsured would have done so, the chain of causation between the insured peril and the loss will be broken. Clearly, if the insured peril is not the proximate cause

---

① cl.20.1.
② s.78(4).
③ [1993] 2 Lloyd's Rep 582 at 618.

of the loss, the assured cannot recover. Accordingly, in my view, s.78(4)probably had the limited function of stating that the assured must not fail to take such obvious steps to avert or minimize the loss as any prudent uninsured could be expected to take. The consequence of his failure to do so would be that he would be unable to establish that the loss was proximately caused by an insured peril. It could instead be proximately caused by his own fault.

施救费用的承担

被保险人的施救义务实际上是符合保险人利益的,因此保险人同意分摊被保险人因施救而产生的合理的费用:① 14.125

Subject to the provisions below and to Clause 10 the Underwriters will contribute to charges properly and reasonably incurred by the Assured their servants or agents for such measures. General average, salvage charge(except as provided for in Clause 20.4) collision defence or attach costs and costs incurred by the Assured in avoiding, minimizing or contesting liability covered by Clause 19 are not recoverable under this Clause 20.

保险人承担的施救费用有三个特征:(1)这些费用是在发生损失或不幸之时所采取的措施而产生的费用;(2)这些费用是为避免或减小损失而采取合理措施的费用;(3)这些费用是被保险人或其代理人产生的费用。只有当费用符合上述三个特征,保险人才会同意分担这些费用。 14.126

施救费用超过施救所得

被保险人采取措施未必就一定成功,即使成功了施救费用也可能大于施救所得。但是只要施救的措施是合理的,保险人就应当参与施救费用的分担:② 14.127

When a claim for total loss of the subject-matter insured is admitted under this insurance and expenses have been reasonably incurred in saving or attempting to save the subject-matter insured and other property and there are no proceeds, or the expenses exceed the proceeds, then this insurance shall bear its pro rata share of such

---

① cl.20.2.
② cl.20.4.

proportion of the expenses, or of the expenses in excess of the proceeds, as the case may be, as may reasonably be regarded as having been incurred in respect of the subject-matter insured.

14.128　保险人承担的施救费用并不计算入保险赔偿数额中,而是独立的赔偿。但保险人支付施救费用的责任以保险金额为限,换言之,在有施救情况下,保险人有可能赔付两个保险金额:①

The sum recoverable under this Clause 20 shall be in addition to the loss otherwise recoverable under this insurance but shall in no circumstances exceed the amount insured under this insurance in respect of the Vessel.

VII　保险赔偿的应用

14.129　由于发生全损和部分损失的保险赔偿是不同的,因此船舶建造合同通常会针对部分损失和全损两种情形作出保险赔款应用的规定。

部分损失

14.130　除了比较极端的例子外,当在建船舶遭受部分损失时,船厂通常是可以对受损船舶进行修理的。因此 SAJ 格式便规定在发生部分损失时船厂应当利用保险赔偿对在建船舶进行修理:②

In the event the VESSEL shall be damaged by any insured cause whatsoever prior to acceptance thereof by the BUYER and in the further event that such damage shall not constitute an actual or a constructive total loss of the VESSEL, the BUILDER shall apply the amount recovered under the insurance policy referred to in Paragraph 1 of this Article to the repair of such damage satisfactory to the Classification Society, and the BUYER shall accept the VESSEL under the Contract if completed in accordance with this Contract and Specifications.

14.131　按照上述规定,船舶在交船前遭受部分损失的,只要船厂对受损船舶进行的修理符合船级社的要求,船东是有义务接船的。对此 AWES 格式作出了更为明

---

① cl.20.5.
② Article XII.2(a), see also CSTC Article XII.2(a), Norwegian Article XI.2(c)(iii), NEWBUILDCON Clause 38(b)(i).

确的规定：①

> In the event of the VESSEL and/or such parts materials etc. as aforesaid sustaining damage, including war damage, before delivery of the VESSEL then any monies received in respect of any insurance effected under this Article shall be applied by the CONTRACTOR in making good such damages with all due dispatch during ordinary working hours in a reasonable and workmanlike manner and the PURCHASER shall not on account of any such damage or any repair thereof be entitled to object to the VESSEL or to make any claim for alleged consequential loss or depreciation.

按照常见的船舶建造合同标准格式的规定，当在建船舶遭受建造人保险承保的部分损失时，船厂的义务是利用保险赔偿继续并完成船舶的建造，而船东的义务则是在船厂按照合同完成船舶建造后接船。当然，这并不影响船厂和船东就是否继续建造以及保险赔偿的分配等另行达成协议。 14.132

全损

一旦在建船舶遭受全损，即使是推定全损依然与在建船舶遭受部分损失有着明显的不同。如果是实际全损，例如在建船舶发生爆炸而遭受严重毁坏或者因沉没且无法打捞，这时是否应当重新开始船舶的建造往往是船厂和船东必须通过协商决定的事。在建船舶遭受推定全损的情况下，决定继续建造的双方将面临建造成本可能高于建造完成后船舶的市场价值的问题。因此在船舶遭受全损的情况下，船厂继续或重新建造船舶便不再是一项合同义务了。船舶建造合同标准格式均规定，在这种情况下船厂和船东应通过协商决定是否继续或重新船舶建造。其中 SAJ 格式的规定是：② 14.133

> However, in the event that the VESSEL is determined to be an actual or constructive total loss, the BUILDER shall by the mutual agreement between the parties hereto, either:
>
> (i) Proceed in accordance with the terms of this Contract, in which case the amount recovered under said insurance policy shall be applied to the reconstruction of the Vessel's damage, provided the parties hereto shall have first agreed in writing as to such reasonable

---

① Article 9, para.2.
② Article XII.2(b).

postponement of the Delivery Date and adjustment of other terms of this Contract including the Contract Price as may be necessary for the completion of such reconstruction; or

(ii) Refund immediately to the Buyer the amount of all Installments paid to the Builder under this Contract without any interest, whereupon this Contract shall be deemed to be rescinded and all rights, duties, liabilities and obligations of each of the parties to the other shall terminate forthwith.

If the parties hereto fail to reach such agreement within two(2)months after the Vessel is determined to be an actual or constructive total loss, the provisions of Sub-paragraph(b)(ii)as above shall apply.

14.134　按照上述规定,船厂和船东可以通过协商决定是否重新建造船舶。如果双方决定重新开始建造船舶,就应当先就交船期推迟以及合同条款包括合同价格的调整达成书面协议。如果双方决定不再建造船舶,船厂应当向船东返还所有已经收到的建造款,但无需为此支付利息。船舶建造合同则应视为被当事人协议解除。在这种情况下,收取建造人保险赔偿的是船厂,船厂利用保险赔偿向船东返还其已支付的建造款。船厂返还建造款和获得保险赔偿是相互独立的,即船厂返还建造款并不以其收到保险赔偿为前提条件。如果双方在船舶遭受全损后的两个月内依然没有或无法就是否重新建造达成一致,船舶建造合同则被视为已解除,船厂应当立即返还已经收到的所有建造款。

14.135　CSTC 格式的内容大致与 SAJ 格式的内容相同,但是按照 CSTC 格式的规定,在船舶发生全损且双方约定继续建造的情形下,船厂不能要求增加合同价格。该格式的规定是:①

By the mutual agreement between the parties hereto, proceed in accordance with terms of this Contract, in which case the amount recovered under said insurance policy shall be applied to the reconstruction and/or repair of the VESSEL's damage and/or reinstallation of BUYER's supplies without additional expenses to the BUYER, provided the parties hereto shall have first agreed in writing as to such reasonable extension of the Delivery Date and adjustment of other terms of this Contract including the Contract Price as may be necessary for the completion of such reconstruction . . . .

---

① Article XII.2(b)(i).

NEWBUILDCON 格式关于继续建造的规定基本与 SAJ 格式的规定相同,但是关于终止船舶建造合同的规定则有所不同。当双方在合理期间内依然未能就船舶建造合同的修改达成一致的情况下,船厂不仅要返还船东已经支付的建造款,而且还要支付利息。该格式的规定如下:①

14.136

> If the Builder and Buyer are unable to agree within a reasonable time on an extension to the Delivery Date and/or any other necessary amendment to the Contract as provided for in Sub-clause(b)(ii)(1)the Builder shall:
> (i) promptly refund to the Buyer the full amount of sums paid by the Buyer to the Builder together with interest thereon at a rate per annum as stated in Box 30 from the date of payment to the date of refund; and
> (ii) make payment to the Buyer of the insured value of the Buyer's Supplies or alternatively, at the Builder's cost, deliver the Buyer's Supplies to the Buyer in undamaged condition.

虽然要求船厂在船舶遭受实际或推定全损的情况下返还船东已经支付的建造款是合理的,但要求船厂支付利息应当是没有太好的理由。船舶遭受全损的原因是建造人保险承保的风险,并不是船厂的过错,更何况不能继续履行船舶建造合同对船厂而言往往是一种损失。船厂返还建造款的义务是独立于建造人保险的,即无论是否有保险,船厂在这种情况下都应当返还建造款及其利息。但是要求船厂在这种情况下支付利息似乎意味着船厂无论是否违约均需承担违约责任。在实践中,船厂虽然有可能约定高于实际价值的保险金额,但保险人通常不会计算利息。而且,规定船厂有义务将船东供应品运送回船东处所似乎同样是没有太好的依据。

14.137

在这个问题上,Norwegian 格式的规定似乎比较特别,该格式并不是按照船舶是否遭受全损来决定船厂是否依然有义务继续或重新建造船舶的,而是规定两种船厂不再有继续或重新建造船舶的义务,该格式的规定是:②

14.138

> If prior to its delivery the Vessel sustains such heavy damages that the Builder has no obligation to rebuild the Vessel, or if the parties and the insurance company agree on total/constructive/compromised total loss then the proceeds under the insurance shall be paid as follows:

---

① Clause 38(b)(ii)(2).
② Article XI.2(c)(iv).

(a) The Buyer will recover direct from the insurance company an amount equal to the instalments paid together with interests in accordance with the terms of the contract.
The Buyer will further collect directly from the insurance company any extra proceeds recoverable under an insurance policy taken out for Buyer's account in accordance with Article XI clause 2(b) above.
The Buyer shall further collect payment for Buyer's Supplies covered by the insurance policies.
(b) The remaining part of the insurance proceeds shall be paid to the Builder.
(c) Notwithstanding the above should the parties agree to continue with the Contract and rebuild the Vessel, the proceeds of the insurance policies shall be paid to the Builder as set out in this Article XI clause 2(c)(iii) above. Such contract will include a possible revised Delivery Date.

14.139　　Norwegian 格式规定了船厂不再有义务重新建造船舶的两种情形：第一种是船舶遭受的损坏已经达到船厂不再有重新建造船舶义务的程度，第二种是船厂和船东与保险人就船舶的实际全损或推定全损或协议全损达成了协议。这两种情形是不同的，即第一种情形不包括第二种情形中提及的船舶遭受实际全损或推定全损或协议全损的情形。尽管如此，第一种情形依然是不明确的，即船舶遭受何种损坏才会使船厂不再有义务重新建造船舶是不确定的。所谓的"heavy damage"应当是没有明确定义的，因此船厂是否有义务重新建造船舶就有可能会发生争议。在船舶遭受全损的情况下，实际全损是可以认定的，并不需要船厂和船东与保险人达成协议。按照上述规定，船东不仅可以直接从保险人处得到其已支付的所有建造款及其利息，而且还可以直接从保险人处获得船厂采购的材料和设备以及船东供应的设备的赔偿。且不说建造人保险的保险人是否会按照建造款和利息等支付保险赔偿，船东可以获得的仅仅是保险人对船东供应品作出的赔偿，而船厂采购的材料和设备应当已经包含在保险人支付的建造款赔偿之内。[1] 即使两者是分开的，船东同样没有权利获得船厂自己支出的用于采购材料和设备的资金。船东在获得的其所支付的所有预付款及其利息后再享有船厂的资金显然构成了不当得利。[2]

---

[1] 按照 Norwegian 格式的规定，船厂投保的金额应当是各期建造款、利息以及船东供应品的总额，见 Article XI.2(b), para.2.
[2] See also AWES Article 9, para.3.

另外，作为"损害"或"损坏"的英文应当是"damage"，而"damage"的复数 14.140
"damages"似乎已不再是指"损害"或"损坏"，而应当是指"损害赔偿"，即为一赔
偿数额。虽然"damage"有时也用来指"damages"，但"damages"应当不能用来指
"damage"。正如上诉法院的 Fletcher Moulton 法官在 Swansea Corpn v Harpur 一
案中所说的：①

> The word "damages" and "damage" in law have been more than one
> meaning, and great care has to be exercised in examining the context in
> which they severally appear. "Damage" may mean injury; "damage",
> and "damages" especially, may mean sums paid under the order of the
> Court for compensation for a breach of contract or a wrong.

在 Hall Brothers SS Co Ltd v Young 一案中，上诉法院的 Greene 法官则对 14.141
"damages"作出他的解释，他说：②

> "Damages" to an English lawyer imports this idea, that the sums
> payable by way of damages are sums which fall to be paid by reason of
> some breach of duty or obligation, whether that duty or obligation is
> imposed by contract, by the general law, or legislation.

合同交船日的调整

在船舶遭受全损或部分损失后，如果船厂和船东约定继续建造船舶，双方通 14.142
常会重新订立船舶建造合同或者对当时的船舶建造合同进行修改。修改的内容
主要包括两个方面，一是合同价格，二是合同交船日。从船舶建造合同标准格式
的规定来看，似乎在船舶遭受全损的情况下，船厂可以顺延合同交船日，但是在船
舶遭受部分损失情况下，标准格式则没有类似的规定。但是只要遭受损失而使船
厂无法在合同约定的期限内完成船舶建造的，船厂应当有权顺延合同交船日。

Ⅷ 保险义务的终止

船厂对船舶建造进行投保的义务于船舶交付给船东之时终止，SAJ 格式规定 14.143
如下：③

---

① [1912] 3 KB 493 at 505.
② [1939] 1 KB 748 at 756.
③ Article XII.3.

> The BUILDER's obligation to insure the VESSEL hereunder shall cease and terminate forthwith upon delivery thereof and acceptance by the BUYER.

14.144 　在其他常见的船舶建造合同标准格式中,似乎只有以 SAJ 格式为基础订立的 CSTC 格式才有类似的规定,①而其他标准格式则没有类似的规定。上述规定可以说没有太大的实际意义,因为实际上 SAJ 格式已经规定船厂投保的建造人保险始于分段上船台止于船舶交接。②

---

① Article XII.3.
② Article XII.1, para.1.

第 15 章　争议和仲裁

I　仲裁概述

解决争议的方式

15.1　仲裁简而言之是当事人自愿采用的解决争议的一种方式。早在 1858 年，上诉法院的 John Romilly 法官在 *Collins v Collins* 一案中就曾对仲裁作出过解释，他说：①

> An arbitration is a reference to the decision of one or more persons, either with or without an umpire, of some matter or matters in difference between the parties.

15.2　在 *Re Carus-Wilson and Greene's Arbitration* 一案中，上诉法院的 Lord Esher 从司法特征对仲裁进行了说明，并且将仲裁区别于其他类似的争议解决形式。他说：②

> If it appears from the terms of the agreement by which a matter is submitted to a person's decision, that the intention of the parties was that he should hold an inquiry in the nature of a judicial inquiry, and hear the respective cases of the parties, and decide upon evidence laid before him, then the case is one of an arbitration. The intention in such cases is that there shall be a judicial inquiry worked out in a judicial manner. On the other hand, there are cases in which a person is appointed to ascertain some matter for the purpose of preventing differences from arising, not of settling them when they have arisen, and where the case is not one of arbitration but of a mere valuation. There may be cases of an intermediate kind, where, though a person is

---

① (1858) 26 Beav 306 at 312.
② (1886) 18 QBD 7 at 9.

appointed to settle disputes that have arisen, still it is not intended that he shall be bound to hear evidence or arguments. In such cases it may be often difficult to say whether he is intended to be an arbitrator or to exercise some function other than that of an arbitrator. Such cases must be determined each according to its particular circumstances.

15.3　1996 年英国《仲裁法》(Arbitration Act 1996)并没有为仲裁下定义,但是从该法关于仲裁目的的规定可以看出仲裁的本质:①

... the object of arbitration is to obtain the fair resolution of disputes by an impartial tribunal without unnecessary delay or expense;

仲裁的优点

15.4　作为解决争议的一种方式,仲裁经常受到称赞。比较常见的说法是:仲裁具有私密性、经济性和自主性等。*Arbitration Law* 一书是这样说的:②

The advantages of arbitration are readily apparent. First, arbitration allows the parties to keep private the details of their dispute. Secondly, as the parties can choose their own rules of procedure, there is greater scope for minimizing acrimony, keeping costs low and electing the times and places at which hearings may be held. Thirdly, the ability of the parties to chose their own "judge" permits the choice of an expert in the field who may have knowledge or skills not possessed by the ordinary courts and who is more able to view the dispute in its commercial setting. Finally, it is possible for the arbitrator to establish a rapport with the parties and thus to obtain greater insights than might otherwise be possible.

15.5　然而,在实践中,上述各项优点中除了当事人可以按照自己的意愿指定仲裁员外,似乎并不很常见或者很明显。虽然私密性曾经是商人们所重视的,但随着商业活动的全球化,仲裁的私密性似乎已不再是当事人选择仲裁作为解决争议手段考虑的因素了。而且,大量的仲裁程序和仲裁裁决的报道与引用以及上诉至法院的仲裁案的法律报告实际上是对传统的仲裁私密性的否定。仲裁的经济性同样是值得商榷的。仲裁之所以经济是因为在仲裁开始推广时,采用仲裁解决的案件的涉案金额一般都不是太大而且争议相对也不太复杂。由于担任仲裁员的往

---

① s.1(a).
② Robert Merkin, *Arbitration Law* LLP 2004, para.1.2.

往是商人,因此省去了通过诉讼解决争议而必须产生的费用。但是随着越来越多的涉及法律问题的复杂争议通过仲裁方式解决,越来越多的王室大律师参与仲裁,仲裁的经济性已不复存在。而且,由于在仲裁中败诉的一方依然有上诉的机会,因此从仲裁开始到法院诉讼结束的整个过程的费用甚至会高过争议一开始就通过法院诉讼解决所需的费用。

从当前的情形来看,仲裁的优点似乎主要体现在两个方面:第一,当事人可以按照自己的意愿选择仲裁员始终是仲裁作为解决争议手段的一个明显的优势;由于至少可以选择自己的仲裁员,当事人就有机会根据争议的特征挑选合适的仲裁员;第二,仲裁之所以可以在国际商事中得到如此规模的适用的一个重要原因是仲裁裁决的可执行性。除非在两国间有司法协助协定,否则一国法院的判决并不能在另一国得到执行;而仲裁裁决则可以通过1958年《关于承认及执行外国仲裁裁决公约》(简称"《纽约公约》")在缔约国得到承认和执行。 15.6

英国1996年《仲裁法》

在英国,最早的仲裁立法应当是1698年的立法。该法经过修订并一直适用至1854年《普通法程序法》(Common Law Procedure Act 1854)颁布。1889年《仲裁法》使之前关于仲裁的法律得到了编纂,而其本身又得到了1934年《仲裁法》的补充。1950年《仲裁法》是在之前仲裁法基础上编纂而成的,其中包括1833年《民事程序法》(Civil Procedure Act 1833),并且形成了英国仲裁法的基本框架。1975年《仲裁法》主要涉及非国内仲裁,并规定英国法院应当中止违反非国内合同中仲裁条款的规定而开始的诉讼。1979年《仲裁法》则对传统的法院对仲裁的司法控制进行了大幅度的修改,取消了法院以"陈述案例"的方式行使审核权的做法,取而代之的是对法院的审核权予以了限制,减少了当事人对仲裁裁决提起上诉的机会。现行的仲裁法是1996年《仲裁法》,该法取代了之前所有的仲裁法律。 15.7

从某种意义上可以说1996年《仲裁法》是受1985年12月11日生效的《联合国国际贸易法委员会国际商事仲裁示范法》(简称"《示范法》")催生而成的。《示范法》的颁布应当是划时代的,在此之前,国际上最重要的仲裁文件就应当是《纽约公约》了。《纽约公约》问世之初并没有得到太多的肯定,于是联合国国际贸易法委员会起草了《示范法》。《示范法》与《纽约公约》的不同之处在于其在参考了主要贸易国的仲裁实践基础上,试图在世界范围内为国际商事仲裁确立基本 15.8

的原则和规则,为仲裁法在国际范围内的统一开了先例。英国在经过慎重考虑后最终决定不采纳《示范法》,而是开始对英国仲裁法进行修订。1996年《仲裁法》正是在这样的背景下制定的。

仲裁协议

15.9 　　仲裁协议是仲裁得以开始和进行的基础,是仲裁庭管辖权的依据。仲裁协议是仲裁和诉讼之间的一个根本的区别,虽然当事人可以订立管辖权条款,但诉讼的开始并不一定以存在管辖权条款为前提。但仲裁则不同,简单地说,没有仲裁协议就没有仲裁。英国成文法关于仲裁协议的定义似乎也经历了一个发展的过程。1950年《仲裁法》关于仲裁协议的定义是:①

　　... "arbitration agreement" means a written agreement to submit present or future differences to arbitration, whether an arbitrator is named therein or not.

15.10 　　1975年《仲裁法》关于仲裁协议的定义是:②

　　... "arbitration agreement" means an agreement in writing(including an agreement contained in an exchange of letters or telegrams) to submit to arbitration present or future differences capable of settlement by arbitration ....

15.11 　　1950年《仲裁法》是一部关于英国国内仲裁的立法。虽然1950年《仲裁法》已经有了关于法院根据仲裁协议终止诉讼程序的规定,但依然是针对国内的仲裁。③ 1975年《仲裁法》对1950年《仲裁法》关于中止诉讼程序的规定进行了较大的修改,并且明确规定该法关于中止诉讼程序的规定仅适用于非国内仲裁协议。④ 关于仲裁协议的定义也正是在这一基础上修改的。1975年的定义对1950年的定义进行了修改,其原因主要是《纽约公约》对仲裁协议作出了定义。《纽约公约》特别对"书面协议"(agreement in writing)作出了规定:⑤

　　The term "agreement in writing" shall include an arbitral clause in a

---

① s.32.
② s.7(1).
③ Arbitration Act 1950, s.4(1).
④ Arbitration Act 1975, s.1(2).
⑤ Article II.2.

contract or an arbitration agreement, signed by the parties or contained in an exchange of letters or telegrams.

15.12 1996年《仲裁法》关于仲裁协议的定义似乎并不是在之前成文法定义的基础上修改而得的,而且这一定义已不再有国内或非国内仲裁的适用限制了。1996年《仲裁法》关于仲裁协议的定义是:①

… "arbitration agreement" means an agreement to submit to arbitration present or future disputes(whether they are contractual or not).

The reference in an agreement to a written form of arbitration clause or to a document containing an arbitration clause constitutes an arbitration agreement if the reference is such as to make that clause part of the agreement.

15.13 如果拿1996年《仲裁法》仲裁协议的定义与《示范法》仲裁协议的定义相比较,不难看出两者的共同之处。《示范法》为仲裁协议下的定义是:②

Anarbitration agreement is an agreement by the parties to submit to arbitration all or certain disputes which have arisen or which may arise between them in respect of a defined legal relationship whether contractual or not. An arbitration agreement may be in the form of an arbitration clause in a contract or in the form of a separate agreement.

15.14 仲裁协议大致可以分为两类,一类是在争议发生前订立的仲裁协议,另一类则是在争议发生后订立的仲裁协议。第一类仲裁协议在绝大多数情况下体现为合同中的仲裁条款,几乎所有的船舶建造合同标准格式都有仲裁条款。仲裁协议是仲裁程序开始的前提和基础,同时也是仲裁员管辖权的依据。

争议和分歧

15.15 仲裁的开始除了在仲裁当事人之间存在仲裁协议外还必须有争议或分歧的存在。"争议"并不是指互不相让的状态,而是指争议的内容,正如Evans法官在 *The Dawlish* 一案中所说的:③

---

① s.32(1).
② Article 7(1).
③ [1910] P 339 at 342.

On one side it is said that the word "dispute" means "contention", and that therefore it arises where the contention is made. On the other hand it is said that "dispute" means the matter or question in dispute .... Putting it in one word, in my view "dispute" ... means, not disputation, but matter in dispute.

15.16 然而在 Halki Shipping Corp v Sopex Oils Ltd 一案中，上诉法院的 Swinton Thomas 法官则为争议举出了例子，他说：①

In my view, ... there is a dispute once money is claimed unless and until the defendants admit that the sum is due and payable .... In my judgment if a party has refused to pay a sum which is claimed or has denied that it is owing then in the ordinary use of the English language there is a dispute between the parties.

15.17 "分歧"（difference）在普通法里有时被视为与"争议"相同，而有时则被认为与"争议"不同。与"争议"相比，"分歧"强调的并不是相互间的冲突，而是相互间未能达成一致。在 May and Butcher Limited v The King 一案中，Dundin 子爵认为：②

In no proper meaning of the word can this be described as a dispute arising between the parties; it is a failure to agree, which is a very different thing from a dispute.

15.18 而在 F & G Sykes (Wessex) Ltd v Fine Fare Ltd 一案中，上诉法院的 Danckwerts 法官也同样认为分歧不同于争议，他说：③

The word "differences" seems to me to be particularly apt for a case where the parties have not agreed .... But it seems to me that the word "difference" is particularly apt to describe that situation. At the beginning of this arbitration clause there is the provision providing for differences of the kind with which the parties are faced. Then the following words "the meaning of or effect of this Agreement", more particularly the effect of the agreement, is a matter to be dealt with. Then the performance by either party of their obligation is a matter to be dealt with. Then finally there is the reference to "matters incidental

---

① [1998] 1 WLR 726 at 761.
② [1934] 2 KB 17 at 22.
③ [1967] 1 Lloyd's Rep 53.

thereto". All those seem to me to be sufficiently wide to cover a difference of the kind which has arisen in this case.

1996年《仲裁法》不再区分"争议"和"分歧"的差异,仅采用"争议",但又明确定"争议"包括"分歧"。① 因此无论"争议"在普通法中作何解释,它的范围已被大大地扩大了。 15.19

开始仲裁的前提

如果在当事人之间不存在争议或分歧,就无法开始仲裁。在 *Collins* v *Collins*② 一案中,按照当事人订立的转让酿酒厂合同的规定,转让价款由买卖双方各自指定一人,并由该两人共同指定一名公断人确定。合同还规定: 15.20

... that they should choose an umpire before entering upon the valuation.

但是当事人指定的人无法就公断人的人选达成一致,于是当事人请求法院指定仲裁员。法院认为实际上并不存在仲裁,因为在当事人之间并不存在任何分歧。John Romilly 法官说:③ 15.21

... I fully concur in the observation, that fixing the price of a property may be "arbitration". But I do not think that in this particular case, the fixing of the price of the property is an arbitration, in the proper sense of the term. An arbitration is a reference to the decision of one or more persons, either with or without an umpire, of some matter or matters in difference between the parties .... If nothing has been said respecting the price by the vendor and purchaser between themselves, it can hardly be said that there is any difference between them. It might be that if the purchaser knew the price required by the seller, there would be no difference, and that he would be willing to give it. It may well be that if the vendor knew the price which the purchaser would give, there would be no difference, and that he would accept it. It may well be that the decision of a particular valuer appointed might fix the price and might be equally satisfactory to both; so that it can hardly be said that there is a difference between them.

---

① s.82(1).
② (1858) 26 Beav 306.
③ (1858) 26 Beav 306 at 311.

15.22　在 *Vosper Thorncyroft Ltd v Ministry of Defence*① 一案中,船厂为国防部建造护卫舰,船舶建造合同规定,因技术规范修改造成建造延误的,双方应通过协议确定延误的影响,无法达成协议的,船东可以支付船舶的实际成本及其公平合理的利润。合同的仲裁条款规定:

> Any dispute or difference between the parties .... Whether in regard to the carrying out of the work under the contract or as to the construction or meaning of the contract ... shall be referred to the Controller of the Navy who may enter upon the reference ....

15.23　由于技术规范的修改,船舶建造发生了延误,国防部支付了 200 万英镑,但船厂主张国防部还应当支付 400 万英镑。国防部认为支付另外 400 万英镑应以双方达成协议为前提,由于没有协议,因此国防部没有支付义务。而双方无法达成协议并不是仲裁条款所提及的争议,因此不能通过仲裁解决。但是法院则认为双方的争议应当通过仲裁解决,Ackner 法官说:②

> ... the arbitration clauseis in wide terms. It refers not only to "disputes" but also "differences". Again it is common ground that the parties have agreed to differ. It is their very difference which has brought them before the Commercial Court. Given the existence of agreed machinery for settling their differences, it seems to me essential for the business efficacy of this proviso to imply a term, that in default of agreement, the effect of the exceptional dislocation and delay be determined by arbitration pursuant to and under the arbitration clause.

II　仲裁适用的法律

概述

15.24　国际商事仲裁往往会涉及各种不同的法律,既包括实体法,也包括程序法;既有与一方有关的法律,也有与双方均有关系的法律。*Redfern and Hunter on International Arbitration* 一书将仲裁涉及的法律进行了如下归纳:③

---

① [1976] 1 Lloyd's Rep 58.
② [1976] 1 Lloyd's Rep 58 at 61.
③ Nigel Blackaby, et al, *Redfern and Hunter on International Arbitration* 7th edn Sweet & Maxwell 2022, para.3.05.

(1) the law governing the arbitration agreement and the performance of that agreement;
(2) the law governing the existence and proceedings of the arbitral tribunal(the *lex arbitri*);
(3) the law, or the relevant legal rules, governing the substantive issues in dispute (generally described as the "applicable law", the "governing law", "the proper law of the contract", or "the substantive law");
(4) other applicable rules and non-binding guidelines and recommendations; and
(5) the law governing recognition and enforcement of the award(which may, in practice, prove to be not one law, but two or more, if recognition and enforcement is sought in more than one country in which the losing party has, or is thought to have, assets).

上述(1)是仲裁协议准据法,由于仲裁协议不仅体现为合同的一个条款,而且也可以体现为当事人在争议发生以后订立的协议,因此仲裁协议可以有自己的准据法;(2)是关于仲裁程序的法律,仲裁程序法通常是仲裁地法;(3)是合同准据法,合同准据法是仲裁庭审理争议并作出裁决要依据的法律;(4)是其他适用的规则和并无约束力的指南和建议等;(5)是关于仲裁裁决的承认和执行的法律。上议院的 Lord Mustill 在 *Channel Tunnel Group Ltd and Another* v *Balfour Beatty Construction Ltd. and Others* 一案中对仲裁涉及各种法律的情形给予了很好的说明,他说:①

15.25

> In all these instances one or more national laws may be relevant because they are expressly or impliedly chosen by the parties to govern the various aspects of their relationship. As such, they govern the arbitral process from within. But national laws may also apply *ab extra*, when the jurisdiction of the national court is invoked independently of any prior consent by the parties. An obvious case exists where the claimant, in face of an arbitration agreement, brings an action before a national court which must apply its own local law to decide whether the action should be stayed, or otherwise interfered with. Equally obvious is the case of the national court which becomes involved when the successful party applies to it for enforcement of the arbitrator's award.

---

① [1933] AC 334 at 358.

15.26　下面对仲裁可能涉及的主要法律做一简单的介绍,这些法律是:合同准据法、仲裁协议准据法以及仲裁程序法。

合同准据法

15.27　合同准据法是指确定合同效力、解释合同当事人权利义务所依据的法律,在 *Philipson-Stow* v *Inland Revenue Comrs* 一案中,上诉法院的 Lord Evershed 是这样解释准据法的:①

> The words "proper law" are well understood when applied to a contract. In such a context they mean the law which the contracting parties intend to govern their contractual obligations, wherever performed ....

15.28　在 *Amin Rasheed Shipping Corp* v *Kuwait Insurance Co (The Al Wahab)* 一案中,上议院的 Lord Diplock 认为准据法是关于合同解释及效力,履行方式及违约后果的法律:②

> ... the law that governs the interpretation and the validity of the contract and the mode of performance and the consequences of breaches of the contract.

15.29　由于合同准据法是确定合同当事人权利义务等实体问题的法律,因此合同准据法是实体法。

准据法的约定

15.30　准据法是指船舶建造合同的准据法,在实践中船舶建造合同通常会有关于合同准据法的规定,例如 SAJ 格式规定的准据法是船舶所在地法:③

> The parties hereto agree that the validity and interpretation of the Contract and of each Article and part thereof shall be governed by the laws of the country where the VESSEL is built.

AWES 格式由当事人决定合同准据法,④Norwegian 格式规定的准据法是挪威法,⑤NEWBUILDCON 格式规定的合同准据法是英国法,但当事人可以选择其

15.31

---

① [1959] 3 All ER 879 at 883.
② [1983] 3 WLR 241 at 260.
③ Article XX.1.
④ Article 15(a), para.2.
⑤ Article XIX.1.

他法律作为合同准据法。① CSTC 格式规定的准据法也是英国法。②

没有准据法约定

船舶建造合同没有约定合同准据法的情形比较少见。当事人没有对准据法作出约定或选择意图不明确时,按照普通法的规定与合同有最密切联系的法律就是该合同的准据法。在 Compagnie Tunisienne de Navigation SA v Compagnie d' Armement Maritime SA 一案中,上议院的 Lord Reid 说:③

15.32

> In the absence of any positive indication of intention in the contract the law will determine the proper law by deciding with what country or system of law the contract has the closest connection.

当事人虽然没有约定合同准据法,但若约定了仲裁地的,除非另有相反的约定或合理的推定,该仲裁地的法律就应当被视为是当事人约定的合同准据法。在 Compagnie Tunisienne de Navigation SA v Compagnie d' Armement Maritime SA 一案中,上议院的 Lord Diplock 是这样说的:④

15.33

> Where the only express choice of law in a contract is that of curial law, resulting from the inclusion in the contract of a provision for arbitration in a particular country, an intention of the parties to exercise their right also to choose the proper law of the contract and, if so, the proper law which they have chosen, can only be deduced fey implication from what they have expressly agreed and the circumstances in and in relation to which their agreement was made. The fact that they have expressly chosen to submit their disputes under the contract to a particular arbitral forum of itself gives rise to a strong inference that they intended that their mutual rights and obligations under the contract should be determined by reference to the domestic law of the country in which the arbitration takes place, since this is the law with which arbitrators sitting there may be supposed to be most familiar.

---

① Clause 41.
② Article XIII.1, para.1.
③ [1970] 3 WLR 389 at 583.
④ [1970] 3 WLR 389 at 604.

仲裁协议准据法

15.34　　仲裁协议是当事人订立的约定将争议提交仲裁的协议。仲裁协议可以体现在当事人在争议发生后订立的独立的协议中,但更多的则体现在当事人在争议发生前订立的合同的仲裁条款中。如果当事人在争议发生后再订立协议将争议提交仲裁的,有可能会约定仲裁协议的准据法。但是合同中的仲裁条款则通常都没有关于仲裁条款准据法的约定。

15.35　　仲裁条款只是合同条款之一,如果当事人约定了合同准据法的,该准据法也应当成为仲裁条款的准据法。正如 Saille 法官在 *Union of India* v *McDonnell Douglas Corporation* 一案中所指出的:①

> An arbitration clause in a commercial contract like the present one is an agreement inside an agreement. The parties make their commercial bargain, i. e. exchange promises in relation to the subject matter of the transaction, but in addition agree on a private tribunal to resolve any issues that may arise between them. The parties may make an express choice of the law to govern their commercial bargain and that choice may also be made of the law to govern their agreement to arbitrate. In the present case it is my view that by art.11 the parties have chosen the law of India not only to govern the rights and obligations arising out of their commercial bargain but also the rights and obligations arising out of their agreement to arbitrate. In legal terms, therefore, the proper law of both the commercial bargain and the arbitration agreement is the law of India.

15.36　　在 *Sonatrach Petroleum Corporation(BVI)* v *Ferrell International Limited* 一案中,Colman 法官也持相同的观点,他说:②

> Where the substantive contract contains an express choice of law, but the agreement to arbitrate contains no separate express choice of law, the latter agreement will normally be governed by the body of law expressly chosen to govern the substantive contract. Where, however, there is no such express choice of law in either the substantive agreement or the arbitration agreement, but the venue of the arbitration is identified, it will normally, but not invariably, be concluded that the arbitration agreement and the substantive contract are both governed by

---

① [1993] 2 Lloyd's Rep 48 at 49.
② [2002] 2 All ER 627 at 883.

the law of that place.

因此仲裁协议可以有自己的准据法,仲裁协议的准据法可以和合同准据法相同,也可以是合同准据法以外的法律。但若当事人没有约定仲裁协议的准据法时通常适用合同准据法。 15.37

仲裁程序法

仲裁程序法是指仲裁程序适用的法律,包括仲裁庭的组成方式、仲裁员关于临时措施等的权力以及仲裁裁决的效力等。仲裁程序法对仲裁进行的方式乃至是否可以对仲裁裁决提起上诉等都会有相当大的影响,因此仲裁程序的进行将因所适用的仲裁程序法的不同而不同。仲裁法是程序法,例如英国的 1996 年《仲裁法》。在 Paul Smith Ltd v H & S International Holding Inc 一案中,高院的 Steyn 法官把仲裁程序法描述成是在仲裁协议和当事人意愿之外设定仲裁程序标准的规则,他说的是:① 15.38

> What then is the law governing the arbitration? It is ... a body of rules which sets a standard external to the arbitration agreement, and the wishes of the parties, for the conduct of the arbitration. The law governing the arbitration comprises the rules governing interim measures (eg Court orders for the preservation or storage of goods), the rules empowering the exercise by the Court of supportive measures to assist an arbitration which has run into difficulties (eg filling a vacancy in the composition of the arbitral tribunal if there is no other mechanism) and the rules providing for the exercise by the Court of its supervisory jurisdiction over arbitrations (eg removing an arbitrator for misconduct).

仲裁法的拉丁文是 *lex arbitri*,而仲裁地法的拉丁文则是 *lex loci arbitri*。仲裁法未必一定是仲裁地法。从仲裁自主原则出发,当事人可以选择仲裁地法为仲裁程序适用的法律,也可以选择仲裁地法以外的法律作为仲裁程序适用的法律。如果仲裁地法适用于仲裁程序,仲裁程序应当不会有任何影响。但如果仲裁地法以外的法律适用于仲裁程序,就可能出现一国法院适用外国程序法的情形。鉴于主权原则,一国法院没有适用外国程序法的义务。 15.39

---

① [1991] 2 Lloyd's Rep 127 at 130.

仲裁本座

15.40　英国 1996 年《仲裁法》采用了"仲裁本座"(seat of arbitration)的概念：[1]

> In this Part "the seat of the arbitration" means the juridical seat of the arbitration designated –
>
> (a) by the parties to the arbitration agreement, or
> (b) by any arbitral or other institution or person vested by the parties with powers in that regard, or
> (c) by the arbitral tribunal if so authorised by the parties,
>
> or determined, in the absence of any such designation, having regard to the parties' agreement and all the relevant circumstances.

15.41　"仲裁本座"本是普通法中的概念，只是 1996 年《仲裁法》第一次用在成文法中而已。之前的《仲裁法》使用的是"仲裁地"(place of arbitration)，但两者的区别应当是比较明显的。前者模糊了地域的概念，强调的则是司法概念；后者则仅仅强调地域概念。在采用"仲裁本座"概念情况下，仲裁实际开庭乃至作出仲裁裁决的地点与仲裁所属地不同的并不影响仲裁本座的成立，仲裁本座法院的管辖权也随之确立。在某种意义上，这也确立了仲裁地法即为仲裁法这一原则在成文法中的地位。Aikens 法官在 *Dubai Islamic Bank PJSC* v *Paymentech Merchant Services Inc* 一案中是这么说的：[2]

> Although English Courts were familiar with the concept of the "seat" of an arbitration before the 1996 Act was passed, the use of the concept in an English statute concerning arbitration is new. It is clear from s.2(1) of the Act that the concept is used in order to define which arbitrations will be subject to the statutory regime in Part One of the 1996 Act. Part One of the Act gives the English Court important powers in relation to arbitration proceedings which will be exercisable at different stages of an arbitration. Therefore, in general, only those arbitrations that have their "seat" in England and Wales should be subject to the exercise of the Court's powers in Part One of the Act. The Act uses the concept of the "seat" as the test for the exercise of Part One powers rather than the choice of procedural law made by the parties in their arbitration agreement.

---

[1] s.3.
[2] [2001] 1 Lloyd's Rep 65 at 71.

仲裁程序法的约定

所有船舶建造合同标准格式都没有仲裁条款准据法的规定。在仲裁程序法的约定上,NEWBUILDCON 格式不仅规定英国 1996 年《仲裁法》或其修订为仲裁程序的适用法,而且还规定了仲裁应当适用的规则。虽然伦敦海事仲裁员协会是一个仲裁机构而且也有自己的仲裁规则,但是按照伦敦海事仲裁员协会的仲裁规则进行的仲裁并不是机构仲裁,而是临时仲裁。因为伦敦海事仲裁员协会并不对当事人的仲裁程序进行管理或监督。Norwegian 格式虽然没有规定适用于仲裁程序的法律,但却规定当事人未按照约定指定仲裁员的,由船厂所在地上诉法院的法官指定,①AWES 格式留出空格要求当事人填入约定的仲裁程序法。② 除非船舶建造合同关于合同准据法的约定违法,否则当事人的约定便是有效的。相比较之下,NEWBUILDCON 格式的仲裁条款是比较典型的伦敦仲裁条款:③

15.42

> ... any dispute arising out of or in connection with this Contract shall be referred to arbitration in London in accordance with the Arbitration Act 1996 or any statutory modification or re-enactment thereof save to the extent necessary to give effect to the provisions of this Clause.
>
> The arbitration shall be conducted in accordance with the London Maritime Arbitrators Association (LMAA) Terms current at the time when the arbitration proceedings are commenced.

如果合同没有关于适用于仲裁程序的法律的约定,在通常情况下适用于仲裁的应当是仲裁地法。这一原则应当来自于程序法适用法院地法(lex fori)的冲突法原则。Dicey, Morris and Collins on the Conflict of Laws 这样写道:④

15.43

> The principle that procedure is governed by the *lex fori* is of general application and universally admitted .... [T]he maxim that procedure is governed by the *lex fori* means in effect that it is governed by the ordinary law of England without any reference to any foreign law whatever. Thus the English court will always apply its own rules of procedure, and will, moreover, refuse to apply any foreign rule which in its view is procedural. In deciding whether a foreign rule is

---

① Article XIX.2.
② Article 15(c), para.2.
③ Clause 42(c), paras.1 & 2.
④ Collins, et al, *Dicey and Morris on the Conflict of Laws* 16th edn Sweet & Maxwell 2012, para.4-002.

procedural, the court refers to the foreign law in order to determine whether the rule is of such a nature as to be procedural in the English sense.

15.44 在 Whitworth Street Estates(Manchester) Ltd v James Miller & Partners Ltd 一案中,上议院的大多数法官认为当事人没有约定仲裁程序法的,仲裁程序应当适用仲裁地法。上议院的 Lord Hodson 是这样说的:①

Here the parties did not, in the first place, choose the law which should govern the arbitration proceedings but they subsequently accepted a Scottish arbiter in Scottish arbitration proceedings. This agreement involved no variation of the original contract for it is not inconsistent with the terms of that agreement that arbitration, if any, should take place in Scotland and be governed by Scottish procedure.

15.45 但是 Lord Reid 和 Lord Wilberforce 则持不同意见,他们认为在合同没有约定仲裁程序法时应当根据合同准据法确定仲裁程序法, Lord Wilberforce 说:②

The arbitration clause itself is silent, and I would agree that in the normal case, where the contract itself is governed by English law, any arbitration would be held under English procedure. Moreover, the mere fact that the arbitrator was to sit either partly or exclusively in another part of the United Kingdom, or, for that matter, abroad, would not lead to a different result: the place might be chosen for many reasons of convenience or be purely accidental; a choice so made should not affect the parties' rights.

15.46 在 Union of India v McDonnell Douglas Corporation 一案中,高院的 Saville 法官也说:③

If the parties do not make an express choice of procedural law to govern their arbitration, then the Court will consider whether they have made an implicit choice. In this circumstance the fact that the parties have agreed to a place for the arbitration is a very strong pointer that implicitly they must have chosen the laws of that place to govern the procedures of the arbitration. The reason for this is essentially one of common sense. By choosing a country in which to arbitrate the parties have, *ex hypothesi*,

---

① [1970] AC 583 at 607.
② [1970] AC 583 at 616.
③ [1993] 2 Lloyd's Rep 48 at 50.

created a close connection between the arbitration and that country and it is reasonable to assume from their choice that they attached some importance to the relevant laws of that country, ie those laws which would be relevant to an arbitration conducted in that country.

III 仲裁的开始

争议范围

15.47　当事人之间的仲裁协议不仅是仲裁程序开始的依据,同时也确定了仲裁庭应当审理的争议范围。SAJ格式的仲裁条款有如下规定:①

> In the event of any dispute between the parties hereto as to any matter arising out of or relating to this Contract or any stipulations herein or with respect which can not be settled by the parties themselves, such dispute shall be submitted to and settled by arbitration held in Tokyo, Japan, by the Japan Shipping Exchange, Inc. (hereinafter called "Exchange") in accordance with the provisions of the Rules of Maritime Arbitration of the Exchange, except as hereinafter otherwise specifically provided.

15.48　按照上述规定,船舶建造合同当事人提交仲裁的争议是"任何因合同或合同条文引起的或与合同或合同条文有关的争议"。在 *H E Daniel Ltd* v *Carmel Exporters & Importers Ltd* 一案中,Pilcher法官认为"any dispute arising out of the contract"包括除了合同是否存在以外的所有争议,他说:②

> The parties have agreed to submit all their disputes to arbitration. The words "any dispute arising out of the contract" cover every dispute except a dispute as to whether there was ever a contract at all, because if there was no contract there was no arbitration clause.

15.49　应当注意的是,由于上述条文规定提交仲裁的争议是双方无法通过协商解决的争议,因此任何一方在将争议提交仲裁之前应当先设法通过协商来解决争议,

---

① Article XIII.1, para.1, see also CSTC Article XIII.1, para.1.
② [1953] 2 Lloyd's Rep 103 at 111,关于仲裁条款独立于合同的"分离原则"(doctrine of separability)是在1993年的 *Harbour Assurance Co (UK) Ltd* v *Kansa General International Insurance Co Ltd* [1993] 1 Lloyd's Rep 455 一案中得到确立的。

只有在协商无法解决争议时才可以将争议提交仲裁。

"关于合同的"

15.50　　合同的争议和仲裁条款在描述争议时大多会使用"arising out of""in relation to""in connection with""under"等,不少仲裁条款还会将它们放在一起使用。因此有必要搞清楚这些用词的区别或差异。按照 *The New Oxford Dictionary of English* 的解释,"arising out of"的含义是 occurring as a result of;"in relation to"则是 in the context of 或者 in connection with 之意;而"in connection with"就是 with reference to 或者 concerning 之意,而"with reference to"或"in reference to"则又做 in relation to 解;"under"则可做 as provided for by the rules of 解。仅就字典的解释,似乎在这些常见的用词之间并没有太明显的区别。在 *Heyman v Darwins Ltd* 一案中,上诉法院的 Lord Porter 认为"under"与"arising out of"是有区别的,因为他说:①

> Are these disputes under the contract – I use the word "under" advisedly, since expressions such as "arising out of" or "concerning" have a wider meaning? I think they are.

15.51　　但是 Lord Porter 并没有指出两者的区别。Lord Porter 的观点在 *E B Aaby's Rederi AS v The Union of India（The Evje）* 一案中受到了挑战,上议院的 Dilhorne 子爵则不认为两者有区别,他说:②

> In *Heyman v Darwins Ltd* [1942] AC 356 Lord Porter said that the words "arising out of a contract" have a wider meaning than the words "under a contract", a view which was repeated by Lord Justice Sellers in *Government of Gibraltar v Kenney* [1956] 2 QB 410. Although the words are different, I must confess my inability to discern any difference in their content.

机构仲裁和临时仲裁

15.52　　按照仲裁庭的组成方式以及仲裁程序管理方式的不同,仲裁可以分为机构仲裁和临时仲裁。机构仲裁简而言之是指由常设仲裁机构管理的仲裁。Redfern

---

① (1942) 72 Ll L Rep 65 at 89.
② [1974] 2 Lloyd's Rep 57 at 66.

and Hunter on International Arbitration 一书有一个简洁的机构仲裁的定义：①

> An 'institutional' arbitration is one that is administered by a specialist arbitral institution under its own rules of arbitration.

15.53 与机构仲裁相对应的是临时仲裁，临时仲裁是指为特定争议而成立的仲裁庭对争议进行仲裁并作出裁决的仲裁，Arbitration Law 一书是这样说的：②

> Ad hoc arbitration, by contract, does not involve reference to a specific arbitral body but rather is concerned either with arbitration on one-off terms or arbitration subject to standard rules as adopted by the parties.

15.54 Redfern and Hunter on International Arbitration 一书是这样描述临时仲裁的：③

> Parties to an ad hoc arbitration may establish their own rules of procedure (so long as these rules treat the parties with equality and allow each party a reasonable opportunity of presenting its case). Alternatively, and more usually, the parties may agree that the arbitration will be conducted without involving an arbitral institution, but according to an established set of rules, such as those of UNCITRAL, which provide a sensible framework within which the tribunal and the parties may add any detailed provisions as they wish – for example rules providing for the submission of pre-trial briefs or the agreement of expert reports.

15.55 "ad hoc"在拉丁文中的本义是"为此"，即为了特定的争议。将"ad hoc arbitration"译为"临时仲裁"未必准确，因为所谓的临时应当是针对机构仲裁的常设特征而言的，但实际上即使在机构仲裁中，虽然仲裁机构是常设的，但审理争议的仲裁庭同样也是"临时的"。

15.56 仲裁机构一般都会有自己的仲裁规则，这些仲裁规则适用于在该机构进行的仲裁。在机构仲裁中，虽然也有仲裁庭，而且争议的审理也是由仲裁庭进行。但是作出裁决的其实并不是仲裁庭，而是仲裁机构。与此不同，临时仲裁在整个仲

---

① Nigel Blackaby, et al, *Redfern and Hunter on International Arbitration* 7th edn Sweet & Maxwell 2022, para.1.155.
② Robert Merkin, *Arbitration Law* LLP 2004, para.1.47.
③ Nigel Blackaby, et al, *Redfern and Hunter on International Arbitration* 7th edn Sweet & Maxwell 2022, para.1.152.

裁过程中不受任何机构的管理或约束,作出裁决的是仲裁庭。英国法实际上并没有把仲裁分成"临时的"和"机构的",因为仲裁庭是独立的,任何机构都不能影响仲裁庭独立审理争议。英国也有仲裁机构,例如著名的伦敦海事仲裁员协会,但是这一机构并不是机构仲裁意义上的机构。伦敦海事仲裁员协会除了根据当事人的请求为当事人指定仲裁员外,并不参与任何的仲裁程序。

15.57　按照 SAJ 格式的规定,船舶建造合同当事人应当将争议提交在东京的日本航运交易所按照该交易所的仲裁规则进行仲裁,日本航运交易所是一个常设的仲裁机构。但在实践中将船舶建造合同争议提交日本航运交易所仲裁解决的并不很多。船舶建造合同最常见的仲裁地是伦敦,适用伦敦海事仲裁委员会的仲裁规则。

"一事不再理"原则

15.58　"一事不再理"(*res judicata*)的拉丁文原意是"已审的事件",这一原则的基本含义是合同的相同当事人不能就同一问题进行第二次诉讼,也不能就其他本可在诉讼中一起解决的问题再次开始诉讼。正如上议院的 Lord Guest 在 *Carl-ZeissiStiftung v Rayner & Keeler Ltd(No.2)* 一案中所说的:①

> As originally categorized, *res judicata* was known as "estoppels by record". But as it is now quite immaterial whether the judicial decision is pronounced by a tribunal which is required to keep a written record of its decisions, this nomenclature has disappeared and it may be convenient to describe *res judicata* in its true and original form as "cause of action estoppels". This has long been recognised as operating as a complete bar if the necessary conditions are present. Within recent years the principle has developed so as to extend to what is now described as "issue estoppels", that is to say where in a judicial decision between the same parties some issue which was in controversy between the parties and was incidental to the main decision has been decided, then that may create an estoppels *per rem judicatam*.

15.59　在 *Conquer v Boot* ② 一案中,被告同意为原告盖一座平房。在平房盖完后,原告在 1926 年 8 月以质量有问题为由在郡法院对被告提起诉讼并获得了赔偿。1927 年 6 月原告以被告使用的材料不当为由再一次在郡法院起诉被告,虽然被

---

① [1967] 1 AC 857 at 933.
② [1928] 2 KB 336.

告提出了一事不再理的原则作为抗辩,但郡法院依然支持了原告的诉讼请求。被告于是向高院提起了上诉,高院接受了被告的上诉并推翻了郡法院的判决。高院的 Sankey 法官说:①

> The cause of action here is: (1) the contract to complete in a good and workmanlike manner a bungalow, and (2) the breach of it. I do not think that every breach of it – every particular brick or particular room that is faulty – gives rise to a separate cause of action. I am of opinion that the cause of action here was the contract and the breach of it, both of which had been assigned in the original action. I do not think it is possible to say that every one of these breaches is a separate cause of action.

但是一事不再理原则似乎应当由主张一方提出的,而不是由仲裁庭或法院主动适用的。换言之,当事人是可以放弃一事不再理原则的主张。*H E Daniel Ltd v Carmel Exporters & Importers Ltd*② 一案应当是此种情形的一个例子。在该案中,货物买卖合同的仲裁条款规定: 15.60

> Any dispute arising out of this contract shall be settled by arbitration in London according to the Rules of the General Produce Brokers' Association of London.

买方在对货物进行了检验后发现货物与样品不符,双方于是就货物的质量问题开始了仲裁,仲裁庭最终裁定买方胜诉。接着买方又开始了关于货物不符合合同描述的仲裁,卖方以一事不再理为由拒绝参加仲裁。经纪人协会为卖方指定了仲裁员,最终仲裁庭作出了买方胜诉的裁决。卖方拒绝执行裁决,于是买方便开始了执行裁决的诉讼。买方认为虽然源于同一个合同,但买方在两个仲裁中享有两个不同的诉因,买方在第一个仲裁中的诉因是卖方未能履行其关于货物质量的承诺;而在第二个仲裁中买方的诉因则是卖方未能履行其关于货物符合合同描述的承诺。虽然卖方可以在第二个仲裁中提出"一事不再理"的抗辩,但是他们没有这么做,因此应当履行第二个仲裁裁决。卖方则认为买方始终只有一个诉因,即卖方交付的货物是否符合合同规定的质量和描述。高院的 Pilcher 法官也认为该案应当适用一事不再理的原则,Pilcher 法官是这样说的:③ 15.61

---

① [1928] 2 KB 336 at 342.
② [1953] 2 Lloyd's Rep 103.
③ [1953] 2 Lloyd's Rep 103 at 111.

> For the purpose of this judgment I am prepared to assume that if the defendants had taken steps to have the award in the second arbitration stated in the form of a special case raising the point which they now put forward, they might well have been held entitled to succeed under the decision in Conquer v Boot.

15.62　但是 Pilcher 法官又认为由于卖方没有采取任何措施而听由第二次仲裁进行，卖方就应当履行第二个仲裁裁决，他说：①

> The defendants had an opportunity of ensuring that the point of law which they were raising should be considered by the Court. They failed to take this opportunity and now find themselves faced with a final award which cannot be impugned on any of the ordinary grounds. Having allowed the matter to proceed in this way, the award of the arbitrators in the second arbitration is, in my view, conclusive against them.

电子邮件

15.63　在当今实践中，船厂和船东联系的最为常见的方式应当是电子邮件。然而一方的电子邮件未必一定会送到对方的收件人手中，但只要电子邮件的地址是正确的，通过电子邮件进行通知等就是有效的，至于收件人是否真正看见已不再重要了。在 Bernuth Lines Limited v High Seas Shipping Ltd② 一案中，期租租约中的仲裁条款规定：

> All disputes arising out of this contract shall be arbitrated at London and, unless the parties agree forthwith on a single arbitrator be referred to the final arbitrament of two arbitrators carrying on business in London who shall be members of the Baltic Mercantile & Shipping Exchange and engaged in Shipping, one to be appointed by each of the parties, with power to such arbitrators to appoint an umpire . . . .

15.64　双方发生了争议，船东通过电子邮件要求租船人支付租金并要求租船人指定独任仲裁员。船东使用的邮件地址并不是之前和租船人邮件来往所使用的邮件地址，而是从租船人的网站上获取的。仲裁开始后租船人并没有参加仲裁，而仲裁庭使用的也是那个邮件地址。仲裁庭作出裁决后将结果寄给了租船人，随后收

---

① Ibid.
② [2006] 1 Lloyd's Rep 537.

到了租船人律师的函,表示租船人在收到裁决之前并不知道有仲裁,所有通过邮件发出的通知可能都发送到租船人的班轮货运部了,并且有可能被忽视了。高院的 Christopher Clarke 法官说:①

> If the e-mails never reached the relevant managerial and legal staff, that is an internal failing which does not affect the validity of service and for which Bernuth has only itself to blame. Having put info@ bernuth. com into the current Lloyd's Maritime Directory as their only e-mail address, they can scarcely be surprised to find that an e-mail inviting them to agree to the appointment of an arbitrator in a maritime matter was sent to that address.

仲裁开始的时间

15.65　仲裁的开始具有保护时效的作用,因此确定仲裁开始的时间是有意义的。临时仲裁的开始通常是打算开始仲裁的一方指定仲裁员。1996 年《仲裁法》规定,当事人可以按照自己的意愿约定仲裁开始的具体时间。在当事人没有约定仲裁开始时间的情况下,仲裁开始的时间因具体情况的不同而不同。如果仲裁协议载明仲裁员姓名或已确定仲裁员的,仲裁程序自一方当事人向对方当事人发出要求对方向该仲裁员提交争议的书面通知之时开始;②如果仲裁员需要当事人指定的,仲裁程序自一方当事人向对方当事人发出要求对方指定或通知仲裁员的书面通知之时开始;③如果仲裁员需要由当事人以外的人指定的,仲裁程序自一方当事人向该人发出要求指定仲裁员的书面通知之时开始。④ 实践中最为常见的仲裁程序开始的时间应当是打算开始仲裁的一方当事人指定自己的仲裁员后以书面方式通知对方并要求对方指定仲裁员之时。

开始仲裁的时限

15.66　船舶建造合同有时会对开始仲裁规定时限,除非仲裁在规定时限内开始,否则就不能仲裁。类似的条款是否构成前提条件在很大程度上取决于对条款的解释以及交易的特征。正如 Tindal 法官在 *Stavers v Curling and Another* 一案中所

---

① [2006] 1 Lloyd's Rep 537 at 542.
② s.14(3).
③ s.14(4).
④ s.14(5).

说的：①

> The rule has been established by a long series of decisions in modern times, that the question whether covenants are to be held dependent or independent of each other, is to be determined by the intention and meaning of the parties as it appears on the instrument, and by the application of common sense to each particular case; to which intention, when once discovered, all technical forms of expression must give way ....

15.67　在 *Metalimex Foreign Trade Corpn* v *Eugenie Maritime Co*② 一案中，租约第 42 条是仲裁条款，该条款规定：

> Arbitration to be in London, Owners and Charterers each to appoint one Arbitrator and the two thus chosen shall nominate an Umpire. Any claim arising under this Charter Party has to be made in writing within 6 months after final discharge.

15.68　租船人在卸完货以后的六个月内没有提出过任何索赔，McNair 法官认为除非在规定的期间内提出索赔，否则租船人就丧失了索赔的权利。他说：③

> It is said in terms that: "Any claim arising out of this charter-party is to be made in writing within six months after final discharge." That seems to be precisely equivalent, to my mind, though stated in a positive form, to what might be equally stated without any change of meaning in a negative form, as meaning: "No claim arising under this charter-party shall be admissible unless made in writing within six months after final discharge." If those words were used, I should have thought that it was clear beyond controversy that the clause operated as a bar if the claim were not made in writing.

15.69　在 *Tradax Internacional SA* v *Cerrahogullari TaS*(*The M Eregli*)④ 一案中，租约的仲裁条款有如下规定：

> All disputes ... arising out of this contract shall unless the parties agree forthwith on a single arbitrator, be referred to the final arbitrament of

---

① (1836) 3 Bing NC 355 at 368.
② [1962] 1 Lloyd's Rep 378.
③ [1962] 1 Lloyd's Rep 378 at 385
④ [1981] 2 Lloyd's Rep 169.

> two arbitrators carrying on business in London ... one to be appointed by each of the parties with power to such arbitrators to appoint an umpire. Any claim must be made in writing and claimants' arbitrator appointed within nine months of final discharge and where this provision is not complied with the claim shall be deemed to be waived and absolutely barred ....

15.70 高院的 Kerr 法官也认为,如果索赔人没有在规定的时限内开始仲裁就将丧失索赔的权利,除非索赔人能够获得延期:①

> Where there is a claim which is subject to a time limit in an arbitration clause, the claimant must operate the arbitration clause unless there is no dispute because the other party has admitted liability. If he fails to abide by the clause, then he can only recover if he succeeds in obtaining an extension of time under s.27.

15.71 如果一方当事人指定仲裁员晚于规定时限,另一方当事人指定仲裁员的行为并不构成放弃,即该当事人依然可以主张对方当事人指定仲裁员超过规定时限。在 *T H Skogland & Son* v *W H Muller & Co (London) Ltd*② 一案中,租约规定争议应提交仲裁解决,申请人的仲裁员应当在卸货后的三个月内指定。实际上申请人是在卸货后三个月以后才指定仲裁员的,但被申请人此后也指定了仲裁员。法院的 Roche 法官认为,被申请人指定仲裁员的行为并不构成对申请人应当在三个月内指定仲裁员要求的放弃,他说:③

> ... the fact that the defendants appointed their arbitrator and said nothing about the point does not in my view constitute or is evidence of waiver; it is not an action inconsistent with the defendants' right to insist on this point, as it seems to me, for one entirely sufficient reason, that the appointment of an arbitrator was one step in the appointment of a tribunal which could decide and, if it thought fit, reject, or, if it thought fit, approve this point which I am deciding; and in those circumstances it seems to me impossible to hold that such an act amounted to, or was evidence of, waiver of this point. That is my decision on the facts of the case.

---

① [1981] 2 Lloyd's Rep 169 at 175.
② (1926) 24 Ll L Rep 322.
③ (1926) 24 Ll L Rep 322 at 324.

时限的延长

15.72　并非所有指定仲裁员的延误都会导致开始仲裁一方丧失索赔权，按照 1996 年《仲裁法》的规定，法院在符合下列情形时应当延长开始仲裁的时限：①

> The court shall make an order only if satisfied –
> (a) that the circumstances are such as were outside the reasonable contemplation of the parties when they agreed the provision in question, and that it would be just to extend the time, or
> (b) that the conduct of one party makes it unjust to hold the other party to the strict terms of the provision in question.

仲裁开始的方式

15.73　除非当事人另有约定，按照 1996 年《仲裁法》的规定，开始仲裁的一方只需指定自己的仲裁员并通知对方即可。但是 CSTC 格式似乎给开始仲裁的一方规定了形式上的要求：②

> ... Any demand for arbitration by either party hereto shall state the name of the arbitrator appointed by such party and shall also state specifically the question or questions as to which such party is demanding arbitration ....

15.74　由于上述规定十分明确，一旦开始仲裁的一方没有列明所有提交仲裁的问题就有可能导致仲裁尚未有效开始的后果。

法院的参与

15.75　通常情况下，法院不会主动参与仲裁程序，只有在一方或双方当事人向法院作出了申请，法院才会考虑是否参与仲裁程序。1996 年《仲裁法》是一部主张仲裁自主的法律，明确规定法院参与仲裁程序的目的是支持仲裁。该法对法院参与仲裁的情形予以了限制，只有在法律明文规定的情形发生时，法院才能参与仲裁程序，这些情形主要包括：取证、证据保全、保护相关财物、变卖货物以及发出禁令等其他紧急措施等，这些情形都具有一个特征，即仲裁庭由于各种原因很难满足

---

① s.12(3).
② Article XIII.1, para.1.

当事人请求的情形。① 法院的参与应当是对仲裁的支持而不是干涉。在 *Stellar Shipping Company LLP v Cosco(Dalian) Shipyard Company Limited*② 一案中,船东和船厂因船舶建造合同产生了争议,船舶当时已经建造完毕,随时可以交船。船东单方面向法院申请了禁令,禁止船厂出售船舶。船东的依据是 1996 年《仲裁法》第 44(3)条的规定:

> If the case is one of urgency, the court may, on the application of a party or proposed party to the arbitral proceedings, make such orders as it thinks necessary for the purpose of preserving evidence or assets.

法院根据船东的申请作出了禁止船厂出售船舶的禁令。于是船厂向法院申请撤销该禁令。船东认为禁令应当维持,理由主要有三个:一是虽然船舶建造合同规定双方的争议应当提交伦敦仲裁解决,但由于事态紧急,如果法院不发出禁令,船舶将被船厂出售给第三人;二是船舶是特殊的且几乎是唯一的,一旦船舶被出售,船厂的赔偿就将是不充分的。高院的 Steel 法官撤销了禁令,并认为禁令的撤销并不会给船东带来任何损失,他说:③ 15.76

> It is common ground that there is a serious issue to be tried. So the first question is, would damages be an adequate remedy and in that regard I suppose the initial point is whether the sellers are in a financial position to meet a claim for damages. This is not admitted, although no positive case is advanced. But in my judgment, on any realistic basis it must be accepted that the sellers are a well funded state enterprise with a substantial income and significant assets. The buyer's potential claim for losses accruing by reason of having to engage other vessels and perhaps more modest vessels to carry out their trade is going to be a relatively small claim. China is a signatory to the New York Convention. I conclude the sellers are probably able to meet any legitimate claim which may be advanced in the arbitration.
>
> Against all that background I conclude that damages are an adequate remedy to the buyer and, that even if this was a case in which urgency was established, injunctive relief would not be appropriate.

---

① s.44.
② [2011] EWHC 1278(Comm).
③ [2011] EWHC 1278(Comm) at [38].

IV 仲裁庭的组成

仲裁员的指定

15.77 当事人可以约定仲裁庭的组成方式,包括仲裁员的人数及其指定方式。在指定仲裁员的问题上,由于 SAJ 格式规定的是机构仲裁,因此打算将争议提交仲裁解决的一方应当向仲裁机构提交指定仲裁员的通知以及仲裁申请:①

> Either party desiring to submit such dispute to the arbitration of the Exchange shall file with the Exchange the written Application for Arbitration, the Statement of Claim and the notice of appointment of an arbitrator accompanied by written acceptance of such arbitrator appointed by such party.

15.78 鉴于绝大多数船舶建造合同的争议均通过在伦敦仲裁的方式解决,因此 NEWBUILDCON 格式关于指定仲裁员的规定比较符合实际情况:②

> The reference shall be to three arbitrators. A Party wishing to refer a dispute to arbitration shall appoint its arbitrator and send notice of such appointment in writing to the other Party requiring the other Party to appoint its own arbitrator within fourteen (14) calendar days of that notice and stating that it will appoint its arbitrator as sole arbitrator unless the other Party appoints its own arbitrator and gives notice that it has done so within the fourteen (14) days specified. If the other Party does not appoint its own arbitrator and give notice that it has done so within the fourteen (14) days specified, the Party referring a dispute to arbitration may, without the requirement of any further prior notice to the other Party, appoint its arbitrator as sole arbitrator and shall advise the other Party accordingly. The award of a sole arbitrator shall be binding on both Parties as if he had been appointed by agreement.

15.79 通常的做法是由三名仲裁员组成仲裁庭对船舶建造合同的争议进行仲裁,先由合同双方各自指定一名仲裁员,再由被指定的两名仲裁员共同指定第三名仲裁员。根据上述规定,一方在指定了自己的仲裁员并通知了对方后 14 天内对方依

---

① Article XIII.1, para.2.
② Clause 42(c), para.3.

然没有指定自己仲裁员并发出通知的,已指定仲裁员的一方就可以指定自己的仲裁员为独任仲裁员。这一规定对开始仲裁的一方是比较有利的。按照 1996 年《仲裁法》的规定,在对方拒绝或未能在 14 天内指定仲裁员时,已经指定仲裁员的一方应当通知对方并建议指定自己的仲裁员为独任仲裁员。只有在对方仍未能在 7 天内指定仲裁员并发出通知时,已指定仲裁员的一方才可以指定自己的仲裁员为独任仲裁员。①

Norwegian 格式关于指定仲裁的规定比较特殊:② 15.80

> Any dispute between the parties concerning the Contract shall be settled with final and binding effect for both parties by Arbitration in ...., Norway. The parties will jointly appoint three arbitrators of which at least one shall be a lawyer admitted to practice in Norway. If the parties fail to agree on the choice of arbitrations within 14 days from presentation by either party of a written demand for arbitration, each party shall appoint one arbitrator, and the two so appointed shall appoint a third arbitrator who shall act as the chairman of the arbitration panel. If a party fails to appoint an arbitrator within 14 days after he has been requested to do so by the other party, the Chief Justice of the Appeal Court in the district where the Builder has its venue shall at the request of either party appoint the arbitrator(s).

实际上争议的双方通常不太可能共同指定三位仲裁员,而且规定仲裁员中至少有一名律师似乎也没有太大的必要。就当事人而言,是否指定律师担任仲裁员往往取决于争议的性质。 15.81

仲裁庭组成的时间

在仲裁员按照当事人的约定全部指定完毕后,仲裁庭即告组成。只有符合当事人的仲裁条款规定的仲裁庭才可以审理争议。SAJ 格式在这个问题上的规定是:③ 15.82

> The three (3) arbitrators thus appointed shall constitute the board of arbitration (hereinafter called the "Arbitration Board") for the settlement of such dispute.

---

① s.17(2).
② Article XIX.2.
③ Article XIII.1, para.5, see also CSTC Article XIII.1, para.1.

15.83　在实际做法中,有时获得当事人指定的两名仲裁员可以在指定第三名仲裁员之前开始仲裁程序,这样无疑有利于节省不必要的开支。但两名仲裁员在开始仲裁程序之前应当得到当事人双方的同意,因为当事人约定的是由三名仲裁员组成仲裁庭对争议进行仲裁,两名仲裁员并不能组成仲裁庭,由两名仲裁员审理案件不符合当事人仲裁条款的规定。如果得到了当事人的同意,两名仲裁员就可以开始仲裁程序,但是一旦两名仲裁员就任何问题无法达成一致或者在开庭之前则应当共同指定第三名仲裁员。

独任仲裁员

15.84　可能是由于船舶建造合同争议涉及的金额一般都比较大,且大都会涉及比较复杂的事实问题,因此当事人约定将相互间的争议交由独任仲裁员仲裁的情形并不多见。即使出现了仲裁庭由一名仲裁员组成的情形也多半是由于一方没有按照约定的时间指定仲裁员而导致的。SAJ格式的规定如下:①

> In the event, however, that the said other party should fail to appoint a second arbitrator as aforesaid within twenty (20) days following receipt of the documents concerned from the Exchange, it is agreed that the said other party shall thereby be deemed to have accepted and appointed as its own arbitrator the one appointed by the party demanding arbitration, and the arbitration shall proceed forthwith before this sole arbitrator who alone, in such event, shall constitute the Arbitration Board.

小额仲裁

15.85　NEWBUILDCON格式有关于小额仲裁的规定:②

> In cases where neither the claim nor any counterclaim exceeds the sum of US＄100,000 (or such other sum as the Parties may agree) the arbitration shall be concluded in accordance with the LMAA Small Claims Procedure current at the time when the arbitration proceedings arecommenced.

15.86　双方的争议符合船舶建造合同中关于小额仲裁规定的,按照约定的小额仲裁程序开始仲裁就成为开始仲裁一方的合同义务。伦敦海事仲裁员协会的小额索

---

① Article XIII.1, para.6, see also CSTC Article XIII.1, para.2.
② Clause 42(c), para.5.

赔程序是伦敦海事仲裁员协会为金额较小的索赔专门设计的仲裁程序,目前最新的版本是2021年版。小额索赔程序并没有绝对数额的规定,适用小额程序的数额是当事人约定的。只要有当事人的约定,再大的数额都可以适用小额索赔程序。当事人约定的数额仅仅是指双方争议的数额,而不包括利息和费用。如果开始仲裁的一方根据其索赔数额按照小额索赔程序开始仲裁程序,但对方却提出了一个超过约定数额的反索赔,任何一方当事人均可要求仲裁庭适用伦敦海事仲裁员协会的正常程序。

小额索赔程序具有如下几个的基本特征:第一,争议由独任仲裁员作出裁决,双方可以共同指定一位独任仲裁员组成仲裁庭,双方无法就独任仲裁员达成一致的则由协会的主席指定;第二,任何一方均不得对裁决提起上诉;第三,双方向仲裁庭递交的索赔、答辩和反索赔文件都受到字数的限制;第四,在仲裁中没有文件披露阶段,但仲裁员有权命令当事人提供相关文件;第五,仲裁员应当在一个月内作出裁决。在没有开庭的情况下,一个月期限自仲裁员收到所有文件后起算,在有开庭的情况下则自开庭结束开始起算。NEWBUILDCON格式规定的小额的数额是100,000美元,但船东和船厂通常不太会为了这一数额的争议开始仲裁。 15.87

V 技术争议的解决

概述

按照SAJ格式的规定,当船舶建造合同的当事人就船舶建造、机器和设备或材料和工艺的质量发生争议时应当将争议提交船级社解决:① 15.88

> Notwithstanding the proceeding provisions of this Paragraph, it is recognized that in the event of any dispute or difference of opinion arising in regard to the construction of the VESSEL, her machinery or equipment, or concerning the quality of materials or workmanship thereof or thereon, such dispute may be referred to the Classification Society upon mutual agreement of the parties hereon as far as the Classification Society agrees to determine such dispute. The decision of the Classification Society shall be final and binding upon the parties thereto.

---

① Article XIII.1, para.8, see also CSTC Article XIII.2.

15.89　AWES 格式也有关于技术争议解决方式的规定：①

> ... should any dispute arise between the parties in regard to the construction of the Vessel, engines materials or workmanship it shall forthwith be referred to an expert nominated by agreement between the parties hereto or failing such agreement by the ＿＿＿＿＿ and his decision shall be final and binding upon both parties hereto.

15.90　NEWBUILDCON 格式不仅有关于船级社解决技术争议的规定，而且还有关于专家解决争议的规定：②

> Any dispute concerning the Vessel's compliance or non compliance with the rules, regulations and requirements of the Classification Society or other Regulatory Authorities shall be referred to the Classification Society or other Regulatory Authorities, as the case may be, the final decision of which shall be final and binding upon the Parties hereto. All other disputes shall be referred to expert determination or arbitration in accordance with Sub-clause(b)through(e).
>
> ... in the event that a dispute arises under this Contract either Party may require by notice in writing to the other Party that such dispute be referred to an independent third party(an "Expert") as the Parties jointly nominate in writing ....

15.91　上述争议的一个基本特征是涉及技术问题。这些涉及技术问题的争议可以分为两大类，一类是与船级社规范、条例和要求等有关的技术争议，另一类是与船级社规范、条例和要求等无关的技术争议。就第一类争议而言，对船级社规范条例以及要求等作出解释本应是船级社的职责，并不是应当事人的要求以第三人身份对争议作出的决定。而就第二类争议而言，船级社通常不会接受当事人的邀请或指定对相关的技术问题予以解决，因为船级社不愿意介入船厂和船东的纠纷。而且，船级社与船厂实际上还签订了一个监造协议，即船级社是船厂的合同相对方。从严格意义上说，鉴于利益冲突，船级社并不适合充当船厂和船东的技术争议的仲裁人。实践中，船级社对船厂与船东的争议充当仲裁人的情形并不多见。

---

① Article 15(b).
② Clause 42(a)&(b).

专家裁定

专家裁定是一种替代性争议解决方法,是对诉讼和仲裁的补充。专家是指拥有与争议相关的专业知识、技术和经验的人。作为争议解决的方式之一,专家裁定的优点是程序相对简单,可以快速解决问题,而且成本也比较低。涉及技术问题的争议通过专家裁定通常能较好地解决问题,涉及法律问题的争议则很难通过专家裁定解决。 15.92

NEWBUILDCON 格式有一项比较特别的专家裁定条款,非常详细地规定了专家裁定的程序:① 15.93

> Unless Sub-clause(a) applies or Sub-clauses(c) to(e) apply, in the event that a dispute arises under this Contract either Party may require by notice in writing to the other Party that such dispute be referred to an independent third party(an "Expert") as the Parties jointly nominate in writing, subject to the following procedure:
>
> (i) if the Parties fail to nominate an Expert within seven(7) days of the date of the notice referred to in this Sub-clause(b), the dispute shall be resolved in accordance with Sub-clauses(c) to(e) below;
>
> (ii) the Expert shall act as an expert and not as an arbitrator and his decision shall be final and binding upon the Parties;
>
> (iii) the Expert's determination shall be conducted in accordance with the following rules, unless otherwise agreed by the Parties:
>
> > (1) the Parties may make written representations within seven(7) days of the Expert's appointment and shall copy in full such written representations to the other Party within such time period;
> >
> > (2) the Parties shall have a further seven(7) days to make written comments on each other's representations and shall copy in full such written comments to the other Party within such time period;
> >
> > (3) the Expert may call for such other documents and written evidence from the Parties as the Expert may reasonably require and the Parties shall provide such documents and

---

① NEWBUILDCON Clause 42(b).

written evidence within the period specified by the Expert. The Parties shall copy, in full, such documents and written evidence to the other Party within such time period provided that if either Party claims any such information is confidential to it then, provided in the reasonable opinion of the Expert that Party has properly claimed the same as confidential, the Expert shall not disclose the same to the other Party or to any third party;

(4) the Expert shall decide whether or not to take oral representations from or on behalf of either Party, but if he does so he shall give the other Party the opportunity to be present;

(5) the Expert shall have regard to all representations and evidence before him when making his decision, which shall be in writing, and give full reasons for his decision; and

(6) the Expert shall use all reasonable endeavours to publish his decision within twenty-eight(28) days of his appointment.

(iv) Unless the Parties agree otherwise, each Party shall bear its own costs of a reference to the Expert, and fees and expenses of the Expert shall be borne equally between the Parties.

(v) Without prejudice to the rest of this Sub-clause(b)the Parties shall consider on an ongoing basis whether or not it would be suitable to refer any dispute to an Expert or to enter into mediation in accordance with Sub-clause(e).

15.94 虽然通过专家解决当事人之间关于技术问题的争议不失为解决争议的一种方式，但是专家利用自己的专业知识解决当事人之间的技术问题或争议与通过仲裁解决当事人相互间的问题或争议具有不同的性质。仲裁具有明显的司法性质，而专家解决争议则不具有司法性质。在 *MacDonald Estates Plc* v *National Car Parks Ltd* 一案中，苏格兰最高法院内庭的 Lord Hodge 对仲裁与专家裁定这两个解决争议的方法进行了区分，他说：①

> Expert determination, in particular, can be broadly distinguished from arbitration in not being judicial in character. What expert determination involves in any particular case will depend on the parties' agreement, and may differ according to the context. Nevertheless, although the use

---

① 2010 SC 250 at 261.

of the word "expert" is not conclusive, phrases such as "acting as an expert and not as an arbiter" denote a concept which is clear in its general effect. A person who sits in a judicial or quasi-judicial capacity, as an arbiter ordinarily does, decides matters on the basis of submissions and evidence put before him, whereas an expert, subject to the provisions of his remit, is entitled to carry out his own investigations and come to his own conclusion regardless of any submissions or evidence adduced by the parties themselves.

专家对建造合同技术争议的决定基于其专业知识和技能,既不需要任何实体法的指引,也不需要任何程序法的帮助。正是由于这一基本特征,专家解决争议不具有任何司法性质。专家对争议作出的决定与仲裁裁决不同,专家的决定对当事人并不当然具有约束力,而是完全取决于当事人的约定,或者说专家决定对当事人的约束力是以当事人的约定为前提的。在 *Campbell* v *Edwards* 一案中,上诉法院的 Lord Denning 说:①   15.95

> It is simply the law of contract. If two persons agree that the price of property should be fixed by a valuer on whom they agree, and he gives that valuation honestly and in good faith, they are bound by it. Even if he has made a mistake they are still bound by it. The reason is because they have agreed to be bound by it. If there were fraud or collusion, of course, it would be very different.

由于不具有司法性,专家决定与仲裁裁决相比有两个比较明显的特征:一是在当事人对专家的决定不服时无法提起上诉;二是在当事人拒绝履行专家决定时无法通过法院予以执行。②   15.96

VI 调解

概述

调解,简单地说是指争议双方在第三人的协助下解决相互间争议的过程。与仲裁相比,调解不具有约束力,调解始终由当事人控制,当事人随时可以停止调   15.97

---

① [1976] 1 WLR 403 at 407.
② 虽然专家作出的决定可能无法通过一国的法院得到执行,但是当事人同意受专家决定约束的约定则应当有可能得到法院的执行。

解。调解通常是以不公开的方式进行的。*Mediation of Construction Disputes* 一书为调解下了如下定义：①

> Mediation is a more structured form of assisted negotiation. It is a voluntary (unless required by contract), flexible process within a framework of joint and private meetings where the mediator helps the parties clarify the key issues and construct their own settlement.

15.98　从上述定义中可以看出，调解的最大特征是其不具有约束力，而且即使调解成功，调解结果并不是调解人的决定而是争议当事人在自愿基础上达成的和解协议。Conciliation 是与 mediation 相似的概念，conciliation 在中文中同样用"调解"来表示。按照《联合国国际贸易法委员会国际商事调解示范法》（UNCITRAL Model Law on International Commercial Conciliation）的规定，conciliation 还可以包括 mediation：②

> For the purposes of this Law, "conciliation" means a process, whether referred to by the expression conciliation, mediation or an expression of similar import, whereby parties request a third person or persons ("the conciliator") to assist them in their attempt to reach an amicable settlement of their dispute arising out of or relating to a contractual or other legal relationship. The conciliator does not have the authority to impose upon the parties a solution to the dispute.

建造合同争议的调解

15.99　NEWBUILDCON 格式可能是唯一一个有关于调解规定的船舶建造合同标准格式，该格式的规定是：③

> Notwithstanding Sub-clauses (c) and (d) above, the Parties may agree at any time to refer to mediation any difference and/or dispute arising out of or in connection with this Contract.

15.100　NEWBUILDCON 格式还进一步规定了调解的具体程序，从该规定来看，调解并不是双方正式开始仲裁之前的程序，而是在仲裁开始后的程序。在仲裁中，一方有调解意愿的可以向对方发出调解通知。收到调解通知的一方可以同意进行调解，也可以拒绝进行调解。同意调解的双方应当就调解人的人选达成一致，双

---

① David Richbell, *Mediation of Construction Disputes* Blackwell Publishing 2008, para.2.1.3
② UNCITRAL Model Law on International Commercial Conciliation, Article 1(3).
③ Clause 42(e), para.1.

方无法就调解人人选达成一致的则由仲裁庭或仲裁庭指定的人指定。① 收到调解通知的一方拒绝调解的,要求调解的一方可以通知仲裁庭,而仲裁庭则应在裁决费用时对拒绝调解的事实予以考虑:②

> If the other Party does not agree to mediate, that fact may be brought to the attention of the Tribunal and may be taken into account by the Tribunal when allocating the costs of the arbitration as between the Parties.

15.101　这一规定的含义应当是不同意调解的一方在仲裁中应当承担更多的费用,但这一规定似乎并不十分妥当。假设不同意调解的一方最终在仲裁中获胜,其可以获得补偿的费用并不能由于其曾拒绝调解而有所减少。实际上拒绝调解本身并没有导致仲裁费用的增加,相反是减少了整个解决争议的费用,因为调解同样会有费用产生。如果不同意调解的一方最终在仲裁中败诉,其应当承担的费用也不能由于其曾拒绝调解而有所增加。因为就仲裁本身而言,拒绝调解并不当然导致仲裁费用的增加。在仲裁中类似的方式是,一方提出愿意支付的数额,对方拒绝且在仲裁中没有获得赔偿或所获赔偿不超过该数额的,对方应当支付仲裁费用,因为仲裁费用本可以避免。然而调解则不同,调解是自愿的,只有在双方都自愿的情形下才可以开始调解程序。要求当事人因拒绝调解而在费用上承担额外的责任实际上是对调解自愿性的否定。

15.102　鉴于调解不具有约束力的特征,在船舶建造合同中得到采用的情形实际上并不多。但是在一些涉及数额巨大且事实复杂的争议中,调解或许是一个值得争议双方考虑的选择。如果双方指定的调解人与已经开始的仲裁程序中仲裁庭成员具有相类似法律或专业背景的,该调解人的决定应当有助于当事人对争议以及对自己在争议中的地位有一个更好的理解,甚至双方在调解结束后就有可能达成和解协议了。

VII　仲裁裁决

概述

15.103　裁决,简而言之,是仲裁庭作出的对仲裁当事人有约束力的决定争议结果的

---

① Clause 42(e), para.2, (i) & (ii).
② Clause 42(e), para.2(iii).

文件。虽然裁决未必一定解决当事人提交的所有争议或问题，但是作为裁决的一个基本条件是就裁决所处理的事情而言都是"终局的"，因此所有裁决都是最终的裁决。Arbitration Law 一书是这样形容仲裁裁决的：①

> A final award, as the name indicates, is an award by the arbitrators which determines all of the issues in dispute between the parties. Such an award is, subject to any challenge in the courts, final and binding on parties and on any person claiming through or under them ....

15.104　除非当事人另有限制，仲裁庭可以针对不同的问题作出数个裁决，仲裁庭的裁决可以针对影响整个索赔的问题作出裁决，也可以针对索赔或反索赔的一部分作出裁决。② 在当事人授权情况下，仲裁庭可以作出临时裁决，即将仲裁庭在最后裁决中的一部分内容提前作出裁决；③仲裁庭也可以根据当事人的请求作出约定裁决，即以裁决的形式记录当事人已经达成的协议。④

裁决通知

15.105　按照 SAJ 格式的规定，仲裁庭作出的裁决应当以书面方式通知船东和船厂，该格式的规定是：⑤

> The award shall immediately be given to the BUYER and the BUILDER in writing or by cable confirmed in writing.

15.106　上述规定似乎比较奇怪。船舶建造合同是船东和船厂之间的合同，仲裁员并不是该合同的当事人，因此船舶建造合同的任何规定并不能约束仲裁员。如果希望仲裁庭快速作出仲裁裁决，当事人可以在开始仲裁时或开始仲裁后向仲裁庭提出。即使是指仲裁庭作出裁决后的立即，仲裁庭通常只有在收到了仲裁报酬后才有义务向当事人提供仲裁裁决。在收到报酬之前，仲裁庭对裁决享有留置权。如果当事人支付了仲裁员的报酬，仲裁庭没有理由拒绝提供裁决。在实践中，一旦收到报酬后，仲裁庭通常会通过电子邮件立即向双方当事人提供仲裁裁决，然后再通过邮寄提供纸质的仲裁裁决。

---

① Robert Merkin, *Arbitration Law* LLP 2004, para.18.3.
② Arbitration Act 1996, s.47.
③ Arbitration Act 1996, s.39.
④ Arbitration Act 1996, s.51.
⑤ Article XIII.2, see also CSTC Article XIII.3.

仲裁费用

15.107 因仲裁而产生的费用大致可以分为四种:(1)仲裁员的报酬和费用,此项费用包括仲裁员一般按照时间收取的报酬以及仲裁员因参与仲裁而产生的使费,例如复印费,差旅费等;(2)与仲裁机构有关的费用,例如由仲裁机构指定仲裁员的费用;(3)当事人因仲裁产生的法律费用和其他费用,例如聘请律师的法律费用、指定专家的费用、开庭的场地费、速记费以及当事人自身的差旅费等;(4)其他与仲裁有关的费用。① 除非当事人另有约定,仲裁员可以对仲裁费用的争议作出裁决。仲裁费用承担的原则是败诉一方承担双方的费用,即所谓的"costs follow events"。②

15.108 SAJ 格式并没有规定被诉方承担仲裁费用,而是规定仲裁裁决应当包括费用承担的内容:③

> The Arbitration Board shall determine which party shall bear the expenses of the arbitration or the portion of such expenses which each party shall bear.

15.109 仲裁员在决定费用的分摊时不仅会考虑仲裁当事人的胜诉和败诉,还会考虑双方争议的问题及其相应花费的费用。在 *Matheson & Co Ltd* v *A Tabah & Sons* 一案中,高院的 Megaw 法官指出,仲裁员裁定仲裁费用所应遵循的原则与法官裁定诉讼费用所遵循的原则是相同的,他说:④

> Where a party is successful, by which I understand to be meant that he obtains judgment for a sum of money, in the ordinary way, he is entitled to recover the costs which he has incurred in the proceedings which have been necessary for him to obtain an order for the payment of that sum to which he is entitled. But that is subject of course to exceptions and provisos in relation to particular cases. If, for example, the claim has been grossly exaggerated and the award is for a much smaller sum than the award claimed, that is a factor which the Court is entitled to take into consideration in depriving a successful claimant of his costs or of part of them. There are all kinds of other matters which

---

① Arbitration Act 1996, s.59.
② Arbitration Act 1996, s.61(1).
③ Article XIII.3, see also CSTC Article XIII.4.
④ [1963] 2 Lloyd's Rep 270 at 273.

may also properly be considered in the exercise of the Court's discretion. They would include the conduct of the parties in the course of the hearing, they would include questions whether one particular facet of the claim failed on which a large amount of time had been spent and so forth.

15.110　虽然在仲裁中获胜的一方有权获得费用的补偿,但仅仅是有权而已,实际上获胜的一方承担的费用完全有可能多于败诉的一方。在 *Kastor Navigation Co Ltd v AGF MAT*① 一案中,法院根据各个争议计算出各方应当分摊的费用,结果获胜一方不仅需要承担自己的费用,而且还要承担对方费用的 70%。虽然一方在整体上获胜,但并没有在所有有争议的问题上均获胜,其所获胜的问题仅涉及少量时间和费用,而未获胜的问题则涉及大量的时间和费用。上诉法院认为按照具体问题的胜败结果计算费用并没有错,Rix 法官说:②

> These factors might have justified an order that the insurers should pay all or a very substantial part of the owners' costs. But this is not to say that the Judge was wrong to take into account the fact that the owners had been wholly unsuccessful on the actual total loss claim and that this had occupied most of the time at trial and generated much of the cost before it. They had started with this claim and pursued it without ever having a sustainable case on causation. They made the choice to pursue it at trial when they need not have done. This is obviously a factor which pulls the other way. On its own it obviously justified the order which the Judge made.

15.111　按照普通法的规定,当事人可以决定如何分摊仲裁费用。在 *Fitzsimmons* v *Lord Mostyn* 一案中,上议院的 Halsbury 伯爵说:③

> ... I do not think, where there are plain words used in an instrument of this sort, you can give a different interpretation according to the state of the facts to which they are applied. If these were costs at all − other questions might of course arise where it was suggested that they were not included within the costs − but if these were costs at all, and therefore the words apply to them, it appears to me that we have nothing to do with the merits of the two parties, whether they were reasonable or

---

① [2004] 2 Lloyd's Rep 119.
② [2004] 2 Lloyd's Rep 119 at 149.
③ [1904] AC 46 at 48.

unreasonable towards each other; the only question is what is the true construction of these words.

但是 1996 年《仲裁法》似乎对普通法的这种规定作出了限制：①   15.112

An agreement which has the effect that a party is to pay the whole or part of the costs of the arbitration in any event is only valid if made after the dispute in question has arisen.

根据上述成文法的规定，当事人只有在争议发生后才可按照他们的意愿约定仲裁费用的分担。在订立合同时作出的关于费用分担的约定则是无效的。   15.113

合同交船日的改变

SAJ 格式有关于因仲裁引起的合同交船日改变的规定，该规定的内容是：②   15.114

In the event of reference to arbitration of any dispute arising out of matters occurring prior to delivery of the VESSEL, the award may include any postponement of the Delivery Date which the Arbitration Board may deem appropriate.

作出这一规定的目的应当是确保船厂顺延合同交船日的权利，而且上述规定提及的仲裁并不涉及船舶建造合同解除的争议。CSTC 格式似乎在此基础上更进了一步，作出了如下规定：③   15.115

In the event of reference to arbitration of any dispute arising out of matters occurring prior to delivery of the VESSEL, the SELLER shall not be entitled to extend the Delivery Date as defined in Article VII hereof and the BUYER shall not be entitled to postpone its acceptance of the VESSEL as declared by the SELLER. However, if the construction of the VESSEL is affected by any arbitration or court proceeding, the SELLER shall then be permitted to extend the Delivery Date as defined in Article VII and the decision or the award shall include a finding as to what extent the SELLER shall be permitted to extend the Delivery Date.

上述规定无疑区分了在交船前进行仲裁的两种情形：一种是船舶建造并没有因为仲裁的进行而受影响；另一种则是仲裁的进行影响了船舶的建造。在前一种   15.116

---

① s.60.
② Article XIII.5.
③ Article XIII.7.

情况下,船厂不得主张合同交船日的顺延,船东也不得推迟接受船舶;而在后一种情况下,船厂则可以顺延合同交船日。但是规定在第一种情况下不得顺延合同交船日或推迟接船似乎是没有意义的。因为第一种情况本来就不存在任何可以顺延或推迟的理由。

VIII 仲裁裁决的上诉

上诉的权利

15.117　如前所述,仲裁裁决的终局性和对仲裁当事人的约束力是指当事人必须执行仲裁裁决。除非明确约定放弃对裁决提起上诉的权利,当事人依然有机会对仲裁裁决提起上诉。1996年《仲裁法》明确规定了仲裁当事人对仲裁裁决提起上诉的权利:①

> Unless otherwise agreed by the parties, a party to arbitral proceedings may (upon notice to the other parties and to the tribunal) appeal to the court on a question of law arising out of an award made in the proceedings.

15.118　当事人对裁决提起上诉的方式有两个:一个是得到所有仲裁当事人的同意;另一个则是得到法院的同意。② 除非双方对仲裁裁决均不满意,否则败诉一方显然很难得到胜诉一方的同意而开始上诉。另外,即使当事人没有约定不可以上诉,只要当事人约定仲裁裁决无需说明理由,任何一方就不得针对裁决提起上诉,因为当事人的约定已经构成对法院管辖权的排除。③

法律问题

15.119　1996年《仲裁法》规定,当事人只能对仲裁裁决中的法律问题提起上诉。不仅只能针对法律问题,而且只能针对英国法的法律问题才能提起上诉。在 *Egmatra AG v Marco Trading Corporation*④ 一案中,合同的仲裁条款规定在伦敦仲裁,适用瑞士法律。仲裁庭作出裁决后,一方当事人不服仲裁裁决,于是根据

---

① s.69(1).
② s.69(2).
③ s.69(1).
④ [1999] 1 Lloyd's Rep 862.

1996 年《仲裁法》第 69 条的规定向高院申请上诉许可。高院 Tuckey 法官认为第 69 条允许的是针对英国法的法律问题的上诉,而不是其他法律:①

> Swiss law is foreign law. It seems to me that in their application of that foreign law the arbitrators were not dealing with a question of the law of England and Wales. Section 69 only permits appeals on questions of law. These are defined by s.2(1) of the Act as a question of the law of England and Wales. The rejection point raises no such questions. So I think that this is a complete answer to this part of the application.

15.120　法律问题和事实问题并非始终是可以明确区分的,但是关于仲裁庭作出裁决的证据是否充分并不是法律问题。在 *Demco Investments & Commercial SA v Se Banken Forsakring Holding Aktiebolag*② 一案中,原告向被告出售一家公司,双方的争议涉及该公司是否有误售退休金的问题。仲裁员认为误售成立,原告应当赔偿被告损失。原告向法院申请上诉许可,理由包括仲裁员掌握的证据不充分。高院的 Cooke 法官拒绝同意原告的申请,他说:③

> The arbitrators' approach, as set out in paras.10.49 and 10.50 of the Award involves no error of law and the criticism made does not give rise to any question of law for the purpose of the 1996 Act. The criticism amounts to saying that there was insufficient evidence before the arbitrators for them to reach the conclusion of mis-selling in the sample cases in which they did arrive at that conclusion. Not only is it not open to the sellers to contest the finding of fact thus involved by saying that there was no evidence to support it, but it is clear that there was evidence upon which they could properly and reasonably reach that conclusion.

允许上诉的理由

15.121　1996 年《仲裁法》明确列出了法院允许仲裁当事人对仲裁裁决提起上诉的理由,这些理由是:④

> Leave to appeal shall be given only if the court is satisfied –

---

① [1999] 1 Lloyd's Rep 862 at 865.
② [2005] 2 Lloyd's Rep 650.
③ [2005] 2 Lloyd's Rep 650 at 656.
④ s.69(3).

(a) that the determination of the question will substantially affect the rights of one or more of the parties,
(b) that the question is one which the tribunal was asked to determine,
(c) that, on the basis of the findings of fact in the award –
   (i) the decision of the tribunal on the question is obviously wrong, or
   (ii) the question is one of general public importance and the decision of the tribunal is at least open to serious doubt, and
(d) that, despite the agreement of the parties to resolve the matter by arbitration, it is just and proper in all the circumstances for the court to determine the question.

15.122　在上述各项理由中最值得提及的应当是第三项理由，即仲裁庭的决定有明显的错误，所涉及的问题具有普遍公共重要性且仲裁庭的决定至少存在重大的疑问。

明显的错误

15.123　明显的错误也是法院同意上诉的一个理由。① 所谓明显的错误应当是明确无误的，而不是模棱两可的，即有可能错但未必一定错。正如 Tuckey 法官在 *Egmatra AG v Marco Trading Corporation* 一案中所说的：②

> The test to be applied is clear. It is not enough to say maybe they were wrong or even that there is only a possibility that they were right. The Court has to be satisfied that the arbitrators were obviously wrong on a question of law.

普遍公共重要性

15.124　普遍公共重要性是指裁决中的法律问题不仅影响到仲裁当事人的利益，而且还可能影响到以后的相关当事人的利益。③ 普遍公共重要性强调的是裁决中的法律问题对其他当事人以及法律的影响，而不是案件中当事人的影响。如果裁决中的法律问题仅仅适用于仲裁当事人，法院通常不会同意上诉。"普遍公共重要性"与上述"明显的错误"是法院决定允许仲裁当事人对仲裁裁决提起上诉必须

---

① s.69(3)(c)(i).
② [1999] 1 Lloyd's Rep 862 at 864.
③ s.69(3)(c)(ii).

满足的条件,但按照1996年《仲裁法》的规定,两个条件中只要有一个得到满足的,法院便可允许针对仲裁裁决的上诉。但是在适用"普遍公共重要性"的情况下,法院应当满足的条件是仲裁庭的决定至少存在重大疑问。

Pioneer Shipping Ltd v B T P Tioxide Ltd(The Nema, No 2)①是一个关于租约 15.125 的案件,该案涉及标准格式中一条特殊条款的适用问题。高院允许仲裁当事人上诉并且更改了仲裁员关于合同落空问题的裁决。上诉法院则维持了仲裁员关于合同落空问题的裁决,但是上诉法院认为高院不应当允许针对仲裁裁决的上诉,因为争议的意义仅限于仲裁当事人。上议院驳回了上诉,Lord Diplock 对法院是否应当允许上诉的问题作出指导性的判决,首先他指出了法院不应当允许上诉的情形,他说:②

> Where, as in the instant case, a question of law involved is the construction of a "one-off" clause the application of which to the particular facts of the case is an issue in the arbitration, leave should not normally be given unless it is apparent to the judge upon a mere perusal of the reasoned award itself without the benefit of adversarial argument, that the meaning ascribed to the clause by the arbitrator is obviously wrong. But if on such perusal it appears to the judge that it is possible that argument might persuade him, despite first impression to the contrary, that the arbitrator might be right, he should not grant leave; the parties should be left to accept, for better or for worse, the decision of the tribunal that they had chosen to decide the matter in the first instance.

接着 Lord Diplock 又分析了法院应当允许上诉的情形,他说:③ 15.126

> ... rather less strict criteria are in my view appropriate where questions of construction of contracts in standard terms are concerned. That there should be as high a degree of legal certainty as it is practicable to obtain as to how such terms apply upon the occurrence of events of a kind that it is not unlikely may reproduce themselves in similar transactions between other parties engaged in the same trade, is a public interest that is recognised by the Act particularly in section 4. So, if the decision of the question of construction in the circumstances of the particular case

---

① [1982] AC 724.
② [1982] AC 724 at 742.
③ [1982] AC 724 at 743.

would add significantly to the clarity and certainty of English commercial law it would be proper to give leave in a case sufficiently substantial to escape the ban imposed by the first part of section 1(4) bearing in mind always that a superabundance of citable judicial decisions arising out of slightly different facts is calculated to hinder rather than to promote clarity in settled principles of commercial law. But leave should not be given even in such a case, unless the judge considered that a strong *prima facie* case had been made out that the arbitrator had been wrong in his construction; and when the events to which the standard clause fell to be applied in the particular arbitration were themselves "one-off" events, stricter criteria should be applied on the same lines as those that I have suggested as appropriate to "one-off" clauses.

15.127　　上述案件发生在 1996 年《仲裁法》之前,所提及的法律是指 1979 年《仲裁法》。1996 年《仲裁法》关于普遍公共重要性的规定是在此案判决的基础上形成的,但是 1996 年《仲裁法》设定的法院应当允许上诉的条件似乎比 *The Nema*, *No 2* 一案设定的条件更为宽松一些,因为只要存在重大疑问即可同意上诉。在 *Antaios Compania Naviera SA* v *Salen Rederierna AB* (*The Antaios*)① 一案中,Lord Diplock 根据存在不同观点的判决又对高院是否应当接受当事人的上诉申请作出了指导性的规定,他说:②

My Lords, I think that your Lordships should take this opportunity of affirming that the guideline given in *The Nema* [1982] A.C. 724, 743 that even in a case that turns on the construction of a standard term, "leave should not be given ... unless the judge considered that a strong *prima facie* case had been made out that the arbitrator had been wrong in his construction," applies even though there may be dicta in other reported cases at first instance which suggest that upon some question of the construction of that standard term there may among commercial judges be two schools of thought. I am confining myself to conflicting dicta not decisions. If there are conflicting decisions, the judge should A give leave to appeal to the High Court, and whatever judge hears the appeal should in accordance with the decision that he favours give leave to appeal from his decision to the Court of Appeal with the appropriate certificate under section 1(7) as to the general public importance of the

---

① [1983] 1 AC 191.
② [1983] 1 AC 191 at 203.

question to which it relates; for only thus can be attained that desirable degree of certainty in English commercial law which section 1(4)of the Act of 1979 was designed to preserve.

15.128 当前普通法应当是 Lord Diplock 在 *The Antaios* 一案中的判决,而不是在 *The Nema*, *No 2* 一案中判决。正如上诉法院的 Lord Phillips 在 *CMA CGM SA v Beteiligungs-Kommanditgesellschaft MS "Northern Pioneer" Schiffahrtsgesellschaft mbH & Co and Others* 一案中所说的:①

> The criterion for granting permission to appeal in s.69(3)(c)(ii)is that the question should be one of general public importance and that the decision of the arbitrators should be at least open to serious doubt. These words impose a test which is broader than Lord Diplock's requirement that permission to appeal should not be given "unless the judge considered that a strong prima facie case had been made out that the arbitrator had been wrong in his construction". Section 69(3)(c)(ii)is consonant with the approach of Sir John Donaldson in *The Antaios*.

上诉的放弃

15.129 仲裁当事人是否可以就仲裁裁决向法院提起上诉应当是仲裁地法律和仲裁规则的问题,但仲裁当事人可以约定放弃针对仲裁裁决的上诉。仲裁当事人可以书面方式约定放弃上诉。如果建造合同双方约定适用国际争议解决中心的仲裁规则(ICDR International Arbitration Rules),任何一方都不能针对仲裁裁决提起上诉,因为该规则规定当事人放弃任何形式的上诉。②

---

① [2003] 1 Lloyd's Rep 212 at 225.
② Article 30.1.

第 16 章　转让和变更

I　转让

概述

16.1　普通法将物分为两种,即诉讼之物(things in action, choses in action)和占有之物(things in possession),前者是指只有通过诉讼才能获得的财产权利,①而后者则是通过占有才能获得的财产权利。合同权利在普通法中属于诉讼之物。按照普通法的规定,合同权利只有得到合同双方当事人同意的情况下才可以转让。② 但是衡平法允许合同权利转让,且不论该合同权利是普通法的还是衡平法的。③ 除了上述两种转让以外还有根据成文法的转让,即根据特定的成文法的规定进行的合同权利的转让,例如根据 1992 年《海上货物运输法》转让的提单或根据 1906 年《海上保险法》转让的海上保险保单等。但无论是普通法转让还是衡平法转让,除非征得合同权利人的同意,合同义务均不得转让,对此 Collins 法官在 *Tolhurst* v *Associated Portland Cement Manufacturers (1900) Ltd* 一案中说的很明确:④

> It is, I think, quite clear that neither at law nor in equity could the burden of a contract be shifted off the shoulders of a contractor on to those of another without the consent of the contractee. A debtor cannot relieve himself of his liability to his creditor by assigning the burden of the obligation to some one else; this can only be brought about by the consent of all three, and involves the release of the original debtor....

---

① *Langham* v *Nenny*(1797) 30 ER 1109.
② 中文的"转让"若用英文予以表述似乎是 transfer,而不是 assignment。
③ Hugh Beale, *Chitty on Contracts*, 35th edn Sweet & Maxwell 2023, paras.23 - 001, 23 - 002.
④ [1902] 2 KB 660 at 668.

16.2 　　衡平法的转让相当简单,甚至连一个正式的通知都不是必需的。① 需要做的只是让债务人知道合同权利已经转让,如果是以通知方式告诉债务人的,该通知也无需符合任何特殊的形式要求。Lord Macnaghten 在 *William Brandt's Sons & Co v Dunlop Rubber Co* 一案中说的是:②

> To constitute a good equitable assignment of a debt, all that is necessary is that debtor should be given to understand that the debt has been made over by the creditor to some thirdperson, and if debtor disregards such notice he does so at his peril.

诉权的转让

16.3 　　普通法和衡平法的一个共同之处是,虽然诉权可以随财产权利一起转让,但诉权本身则是不可以转让的,Scrutton 法官是这样说的:③

> But there came a point on which both Courts would have agreed; to assign a bare right of action, a bare power to bring an action was not permitted in either Court; and the reason was as pointed out by Warrington LJ that both Courts treated such an assignment as offending against the law of maintenance or champerty or both.

16.4 　　在 *Trendtex Trading Corp* v *Credit Suisse* 一案中,上诉法院的 Lord Denning 似乎认为除了具有人身特征的诉权不能转让外,其他诉权都是可以转让的,他是这样说的:④

> The old saying that you cannot assign a "bare right to litigate" is gone. The correct proposition is that you cannot assign a personal right to litigate, that is, which is in its nature personal to you yourself. But you can assign an impersonal right to litigate, that is, which is in its nature, a proprietary right: provided that the circumstances are such as reasonably to warrant it.

16.5 　　但是上议院则有不同的看法,上议院依然认为诉权本身是不能转让的,上议院的 Lord Roskill 说:⑤

---

① *Gorringe* v *Irwell India Rubber Works*(1886) 34 Ch D 128.
② [1905] AC 454 at 461.
③ Ibid.
④ [1980] QB 629 at 657.
⑤ [1982] AC 679 at 703.

My Lords, I am afraid that, with respect, I cannot agree with the learned Master of the Rolls [1980] QB 629, 657 when he said in the instant case that "The old saying that you cannot assign a 'bare right to litigate' is gone." I venture to think that that still remains a fundamental principle of our law. But it is today true to say that in English law an assignee who can show that he has a genuine commercial interest in the enforcement of the claim of another and to that extent takes an assignment of that claim to himself is entitled to enforce that assignment unless by the terms of that assignment he falls foul of our law of champerty, which, as has often been said, is a branch of our law of maintenance.

转让的限制

16.6　根据契约自由原则,合同当事人可以在合同中约定禁止转让合同权利或者为转让设定条件,例如一方只有得到另一方的许可方可转让合同权利。在合同中约定禁止或限制转让显然有实在的理由,正如 Lord Browne-Wilkinson 在 *Linden Gardens Trust Ltd* v *Lenesta Sludge Disposal Ltd* 一案中所指出的:①

The reason for including the contractual prohibition viewed from the contractor's point of view must be that the contractor wishes to ensure that he deals, and deals only, with the particular employer with whom he has chosen to enter into a contract. Building contracts are pregnant with disputes: some employers are much more reasonable than others in dealing with such disputes.

16.7　在合同对转让作出禁止或限制的情况下,当事人是否可以转让合同权利往往是合同解释的问题。在 *Linden Gardens Trust Ltd* v *Lenesta Sludge Disposal Ltd*② 一案中,合同第17(1)条规定:

The employer shall not without written consent of the contractor assign this contract.

16.8　上议院的 LordBrowne-Wilkinson 认为合同第17(1)条禁止了雇主转让合同利益,他说:③

---

① [1994] 1 AC 85 at 105.
② [1994] 1 AC 85.
③ [1994] 1 AC 85 at 103.

Although it is true that the phrase "assign this contract" is not strictly accurate, lawyers frequently use those words inaccurately to describe an assignment of the benefit of a contract since every lawyer knows that the burden of a contract cannot be assigned .... Accordingly, in my view clause 17(1)of the contract prohibited the assignment by the employer of the benefit of the contract.

由于违反合同规定的转让显然是无效的,因此 Lord Browne-Wilkinson 继续说:①

Therefore in my judgment an assignment of contractual rights in breach of a prohibition against such assignment is ineffective to vest the contractual rights in the assignee. It follows that the claim by Linden Gardens fails and the Linden Garden action must be dismissed.

船舶建造合同权利的转让

虽然很多年前曾有船东使用自有资金建造船舶的做法,但在当今船舶建造中几乎已不再有使用自有资金建造船舶的做法了,绝大多数船东都是通过融资方式建造船舶的。在有融资安排的船舶建造中,提供融资的银行通常会要求船东转让其在船舶建造合同中的权利作为还款保障。因此船舶建造合同关于合同权利转让的规定将会直接影响到船东的融资安排。船舶建造合同的标准格式几乎都有关于合同权利转让的规定,但不尽相同。其中,SAJ 格式有如下规定:②

Neither of the parties hereto shall assign this Contract to a third party unless prior consent of the other party is given in writing.

In case of assignment by the BUYER, such assignment shall further be subject to approval of the Japanese Government, and the BUYER shall remain liable under this Contract ....

很显然,SAJ 格式的规定不利于船东的融资安排。虽然第一段使用的是"转让合同"这一表述,但正确的理解是:"转让合同"是指转让合同的权利,而不包括合同的义务。如果我们将 assign 理解为仅指权利的转让,按照第一段的规定,无论是船东还是船厂转让合同权利义务的都需事先得到对方的书面同意。在船舶

---

① [1994] 1 AC 85 at 109.
② Article XIV para.1&2.

建造合同中，船厂最主要的权利就是收取建造款或其他应付款项。如果船厂转让这一权利，对船东来说只是收款账号上的区别。如果船东转让其建造合同的权利，虽然会导致船厂履行对象的改变，但履行义务的内容并不会因为转让而发生变化。从第二段来看，关于船东转让合同权利必须以获得日本政府批准为条件的规定体现了 SAJ 格式的历史特征，应当不再有现实意义了。而船东依然承担建造合同义务的规定则没有太大的意义，即使没有这一规定，船东依然需要承担建造合同的义务，因为其所转让的仅仅是合同的权利而已，不涉及合同的义务。CSTC 格式关于转让的规定基本上与 SAJ 格式的规定相同：①

> Neither of the parties hereto shall assign this Contract to any other individual, firm, company or corporation unless prior consent of the other party is given in writing.

16.12 　AWES 格式关于转让的规定则与 SAJ 格式有所不同，该格式的规定是：②

> Neither party shall be entitled to transfer its rights unless prior written approval has been obtained from the other party, which shall not be unreasonably withheld. Both parties shall have the right to study all documents relevant to such transfer and to renegotiate such terms and conditions as it requires.

16.13 　虽然 AWES 格式第 18 条的名称是"转让"，但在条文中使用的却是"转移"。这里的"转移"有可能是"转让"的误用。根据 *The New Oxford Dictionary of English* 的解释，"transfer"作为动词是指"make over the possession of (property, a right, or a responsibility) to someone else"；而作为名词则是指"conveyance of property, especially stocks and shares, from one person to another"。"转移"若作"转让"解，其不仅包含权利的转移，同时也包含义务的转移，因此"转移"和"转让"是两个具有不同含义的词。但从上述规定的最后一句来看，"转移"则又不像是"转让"的误用，因为最后一句规定双方均有权对所有与转移相关的文件进行研究，并对转移的条件重新进行谈判。但就转让而言，似乎并没有研究和谈判的必要，因为转让的前提是义务不发生变化，只是履行对象发生了变化而已。

16.14 　虽然 AWES 格式规定转让合同需要得到对方事先的书面同意，但由于增加了"which shall not be unreasonably withheld"一句，性质则有较大的不同。按照

---

① Article XIV.
② Article 18, para.1, see also Norwegian Article XIII.

SAJ 格式的规定,只要一方不同意,另一方就不能转让船舶建造合同的权利;而按照 AWES 格式的规定,虽然一方可以拒绝另一方转让合同权利的要求,但必须给出合理的理由。如果一方不合理地拒绝了另一方的转让请求,另一方的转让是否有效在普通法中似乎并没有明确的答案。在 Hendry v Chartsearch Ltd① 一案中,合同有如下规定:

> Interface shall not be entitled to assign or otherwise transfer this Agreement in whole or in part or to sub-contract any of obligations hereafter without the prior written consent of the [defendant] which shall not be unreasonably withheld.

实际上一方在得到被告的同意之前就将合同权利进行了转让,事后被告拒绝同意转让。一方认为由于被告拒绝转让是不合理的,因此转让就应当是有效的。法院认为被告有权拒绝同意,但并没有对转让是否有效的问题作出判决,上诉法院 Evans 法官说:②

16.15

> The third issue, namely, whether the assignment was invalid or ineffective on the ground that no prior request was made, even though consent could not reasonably have been refused, therefore does not arise. Although I have read the judgment of Millett LJ in draft, I prefer to leave open the question whether the established law concerning leases necessarily applies to assignments of contractual rights.

转让的区分

NEWBUILDCON 格式对船厂的转让和船东的转让予以了区分,该格式关于船厂转让的规定是:③

16.16

> The Builder shall have the right to assign the benefits of this Contract to the Builder's financiers for the purpose of securing the Builder's financing.

NEWBUILDCON 格式关于船东转让的规定是:④

16.17

> (i) The Buyer shall have the right to assign the benefits of this Contract

---

① [1998] CLC 1382.
② [1998] CLC 1382 at 1392.
③ Clause 45(a).
④ Clause 45(b).

to the Buyer's financiers for the purpose of securing the Buyer's financing.

(ii) The Buyer shall have the right, subject to the Builder's consent which shall not be unreasonably withheld, to assign, transfer or novate this Contract to any other third party.

16.18 区分船厂的转让和船东的转让应当是有意义的,因为两者的转让无论从需求还是特征来看都不相同。在船舶建造合同中,船厂承担的义务是建造船舶,船厂的合同权利则是收取合同价款。就合同价款的收取而言,除了收款账号的变更外,船厂转让合同对船东来讲几乎是没有影响的。相反,船东转让合同给船厂带来的影响则可能是比较大的,例如船舶监造的方式以及变更请求等。按照上述规定,船东有权将合同转让给融资人而无需征得船厂的同意;如果船东将合同转让给融资人以外的第三人,则需征得船厂的同意。上述第二段分别使用了"assign" "transfer"以及"novate",关于 transfer 前文已有解释,而关于 novate 则下文有专门的讨论。

转让的通知

16.19 船东转让船舶建造合同权利的通常会以书面的方式通知船厂,其实这也是融资文件所要求的。在转让通知中,船东会告诉船厂自己已经将船舶建造合同的权利进行了转让,并会列明除非得到受让人指示否则船东不会行使的权利,例如对船舶建造合同进行任何变更、解约、放弃权利和再一次转让等等。下面是常见的船东发出的转让通知的内容:

We may not without the prior consent of the Assignee:

(a) agree to any variation of the Contract or any substantial variation of the specification of the Ship including agreeing any extras, additions or alterations the cost of which will alter the fixed price of the Ship by an amount greater than five per cent of the said fixed price or release you from any of your obligations under the Contract or waive any breach of your obligations thereunder or consent to any such act or omission by you as would otherwise constitute such breach; and

(b) either exercise or fail to exercise any right which we may have to reject the Ship or cancel or rescind or otherwise terminate the Contract provided always that any suchrejection of the Ship or cancellation, rescission or other termination of the Contract by us after such consent is given shall be without responsibility on the part of the Assignee who shall be under no liability whatsoever to the extent that such rejection, rescission, cancellation or termination is thereafter adjudged to constitute a repudiation or other breach of the Contract by us.

16.20　在收到上述转让通知的情况下,船厂应当意识到这一通知对自己可能带来的影响。在船东发出转让通知之前,船东可以提出变更的请求,船厂也可以和船东就变更引起的费用和时间达成协议。虽然转让通知未必一定构成对船舶建造合同条款的改变,但转让通知毫无疑问会改变船厂履行合同的方式,即关于价值超过合同固定价格5%的变更不应当和船东达成协议,而应当和受让人达成协议。船东除了向船厂发出转让通知外,一般还会要求船厂签署一份转让确认书。转让确认书的签署意味着船厂对受让人单方面作出了承诺。下面是常见的转让确认的部分内容:

In accordance with authority and instructions given to us by the Buyer which cannot be revoked or varied without your consent, and in consideration of your making finance available to the Buyer to assist in payment of part of the purchase price of the Ship, we hereby undertake:

(a) to hold the Ship and the builder's certificate and any other documents of title to the Ship to your order and disposal free from any claim which we may have against the Buyer;
(b) to pay to you all sums which we may become due to pay to the Buyer under the Contract including sums arising from an arbitration award;
(c) that should default be made by the Buyer in the due payment of any instalment or instalments of the purchase price or should the Buyer commit anyother default by reason whereof we claim a right to determine the Contract we shall forthwith give you notice in writing of such default; and
(d) that before exercising any option or right accruing to us on any such default, we shall first give you the option to be exercised within 30 days of you, or your nominee, making good the default and assuming all the Buyer's liabilities under the Contract.

16.21　从上述船厂向船舶建造合同受让人作出的承诺来看,只要与船东的通知不冲突,(a)和(b)应当没有什么问题。但是(c)和(d)则不同,它们实际上改变了船舶建造合同条款的内容。按照船舶建造合同的规定,一旦船东的行为构成违约且船厂可以根据约定解除合同的，船厂就可以选择解除合同。但是在船厂向受让人作出上述承诺后，即使船东违约，船厂也不能按照船舶建造合同的约定解约，而必须通知受让人并允许受让人在30天内作出补救。只有当受让人拒绝补救或在30天内没有补救时，船厂才可以解除船舶建造合同。转让通知或转让承诺更改船舶建造合同内容的，船厂可以接受，但没有义务接受。船厂可以要求在自己的履约义务不发生任何变化的情况下接受船东的转让。船厂可以这样做的理由应当是明显的，即合同条款的更改必须得到所有合同当事人的同意。

船东的履约责任

16.22　如前所述，船东转让的其实只是船舶建造合同的权利而已，并不包括任何义务。船东转让合同义务意味着将由第三人来代替船东履行船舶建造合同的义务，此种转让只有在征得船厂同意的情况下才有可能发生。而且除非合同另有规定，船厂拒绝此种转让并不以理由是否合理为条件，这是因为船厂有权按照自己的喜好决定和谁订立合同。AWES格式规定在合同发生转让的情况下，原来的合同当事人应当与新的合同当事人对合同的履行承担连带责任：①

> ... The original party shall guarantee performance and shall jointly and severally with the new party be liable under the terms of the CONTRACT.

16.23　然而，就船舶建造合同的义务而言，其性质以及履行主体并不会因为发生合同权利的转让而发生任何变化。如果船东转让了船舶建造合同的权利，他依然对合同的义务承担履行义务，例如转让合同权利后船东依然负有按照约定支付建造款的合同义务。

转让的费用

16.24　合同权利发生转让可能产生费用，除非合同另有规定，因转让产生的费用应当由要求转让的一方承担。AWES格式可能是唯一有关于转让费用规定的船舶建造合同标准格式，该格式的规定是：②

> All costs of any kind whatsoever, including legal and other costs in relation to such assignment shall be borne and paid for by the new party to the CONTRACT.

---

① Article 18, para.2.
② Article 18, para.2.

按照 AWES 格式的规定，承担转让费用的应当是受让人，但在实践中承担转让费用的往往是船东。但除非另有规定，船厂不应当承担因转让产生的任何费用。

索赔权的保留

在我国船舶建造实践中，可能是由于银行的要求，船东在转让船舶建造合同以及还款保函时通常会保留索赔的权利，即只有船东才可以向船厂或提供还款保函的银行提出索赔。但是很难想象船东在向其融资人转让船舶建造合同以及还款保函时可以作出类似的保留，因为这样的保留意味着受让船舶建造合同和还款保函的融资人实际上已经丧失了行使此种权利的机会。而且，在衡平法转让中，受让人都应当享有针对债务人的诉权。在 Three Rivers DC v Bank of England 一案中，上诉法院的 Peter Gilbson 法官对转让后的诉权进行了解释，他认为衡平法转让中的受让人实际上就是对被转让物享有权利的一方，他可以对债务人提起诉讼。Peter Gilbson 法官说：①

> These authorities, in my judgment, clearly establish that the equitable assignee can be regarded realistically as the person entitled to the assigned chose and is able to sue the debtor on that chose, but that save in special circumstances the court will require him to join the assignor as a procedural requirement so that the assignor might be bound and the debtor protected. If, unusually, the assignor sues, he will not be allowed to maintain the action in the absence of the assignee.

从上述案例的判决中可以看出，合同权利的受让人对债务人应当享有诉权。因此在船舶建造合同中，受让还款保函的一方应当对提供还款保函的银行享有诉权。其实，提供还款保函的银行要求保函受益人不得转让索赔权可能并没有一个太好的理由。还款保函显然是可以转让的，可转让性正是还款保函价值之所在。在当今普遍通过融资建造船舶的情形下，如果还款保函不可转让，船舶建造合同可能就无法订立了。在还款保函可以转让的前提下不同意转让还款保函的索赔权其实还是否定了还款保函的可转让性。就提供还款保函的银行而言，是否同意还款保函受益人转让索赔权对其并没有太大的影响。无论是谁行使还款保函的索赔权，其行使方式、形式要求以及责任限额等均不会发生变化，都是提供还款保函的银行在一开始就同意接受的条件和风险。

16.25

16.26

16.27

---

① [1966] QB 292 at 313.

II 针对受让人的抵销

概述

16.28　在一方没有将自己合同权利转让给他人时,其所针对合同另一方的权利都会受另一方的反索赔或抵销等的限制。在船舶建造合同中,船厂面对船东的任何权利都可以主张抵销,例如船厂可以因船东没有按照约定支付变更费用而主张针对船东有权收取的约定赔偿的抵销。问题是,如果船东将自己的合同权利转让给第三人,船厂是否依然可以针对受让人主张抵销。从普通法的案例来看这个问题有一个发展过程。在 *Watson v Mid Wales Railway Co* 一案中,民事法庭的 Bovill 法官认为转让以后在原当事人之间产生的,与受让人主张的权利无关的债务不能针对受让人主张抵销,他说:①

> No case has been cited to us where equity has allowed against the assignee of an equitable chose in action a set-off of a debt arising between the original parties subsequently to the notice of assignment, out of matters not connected with the debt claimed, nor in any way referring to it.

16.29　但是在 *Newfoundland v Newfoundland Railway Co* 一案中,上议院的态度则不同,他们认为只要与转让有关,非约定赔偿可以和受让人的权利进行抵销。枢密院的 Lord Hobhouse 先是解释了不能抵销可能出现的"令人遗憾"的情形:②

> It would be a lamentable thing if it were found to be the law that a party to a contract may assign a portion of it, perhaps a beneficial portion, so that the assignee shall take the benefit, wholly discharged of any counter-claim by the other party in respect of the rest of the contract, which may be burdensome.

16.30　接着,Lord Hobhouse 明确指出非约定赔偿可以抵销受让人的权利,他说:③

> Unliquidated damages may now be set off as between the original

---

① (1866-67) LR 2 CP 593 at 598.
② (1888) 13 App Cas 199 at 212.
③ (1888) 13 App Cas 199 at 213.

parties, and also against an assignee if flowing out of and inseparably connected with the dealings and transactions which also give rise to the subject of the assignment.

关联性

在 *Muscat v Smith*① 一案中,被告是一栋破旧房屋的租户,1995 年当地政府发出了失修通知。业主于是开始了房屋的修缮工作,从而给被告带来了不便。被告开始停止租金的支付。1999 年房屋尚未修缮完毕,业主将房屋出售给了原告,价格为 128 周的租金。原告要求占有房屋,被告则针对业主的失修违约主张租金的抵销。郡法院认为原告应自购买房屋时起承担失修违约造成的损失,但被告无论是按照普通法还是衡平法均无权主张抵销。被告上诉,上诉法院认为被告的反索赔是由于第三人将权利转让给原告而引起的,因此被告可以主张非约定赔偿的衡平法的抵销。上诉法院的 Sedley 法官说:②

16.31

> If the law were as the judge below held it to be, it would be asymmetrical and anomalous. It would distinguish on no just basis between the tenant who, faced with serious breaches of his landlord's repairing covenant, could find the money and obtain the necessary access to do the works and the tenant who, in the same situation, was forced by lack of means or want of access to put up with the consequences of disrepair. To treat rental payments withheld by the tenant as expended in the first case on rent but in the second case as simply retained on account of damages, although seemingly inconsequential, would have radical consequences for the tenant's finances, and frequently too for his security of tenure, if the reversion is assigned.

船舶建造合同约定

NEWBUILDCON 格式可能是唯一有关于抵销规定的船舶建造合同标准格式,该格式的规定是:③

16.32

The Buyer shall not have the right to retain or set-off any amount against

---

① [2003] 1 WLR 2853.
② [2003] 1 WLR 2853 at 2861.
③ Clause 17.

any payment due to the Builder under this Contract except in relation to the Final Instalment as specifically provided in this Contract(see Clause 15(Payments) and Clause 30(Final Instalment)).

16.33　从上述规定来看,船东实际上并没有放弃主张抵销的权利,而只是放弃了在交船前主张抵销的权利。然而在正常情况下,船东按照船舶建造合同规定应当支付的最后一期交船款的数额通常会远远大于在船舶建造过程中有可能产生的船厂应当向船东支付的数额。

Ⅲ 合同变更

概述

16.34　合同变更(novation)是指合同一方或多方当事人由非合同第三人取代的情形。在 *Scarf* v *Jardine* 一案中,上议院的 Lord Selborne 说:①

> In the Court of first instance the case was treated really as one of what is called "novation," which as I understand it means this – the term being derived from the Civil Law – that there being a contract in existence, some new contract is substituted for it, either between the same parties (for that might be) or between different parties; the consideration mutually being the discharge of the old contract.

16.35　在 *The Tychy(No.2)* 一案中,高院的 David Steel 法官在分析关于合同变更案例基础上对合同变更的特征作了比较详细的说明,他说:②

> As might be expected, there was no dispute as to the relevant legal principles. They can be summarized as follows: –(a)Novation involves the creation of a new contract where an existing party is replaced by a new party. (b) Thus, novation requires the consent of all parties, including in particular the party which is thereby accepting a new person as his debtor or as his counterpart under an executory contract. (c)The consent may be apparent from express words or inferred from conduct. (d) The consent must be clearly established on the evidence as being only consistent with the intent of achieving a novation ....

---

① (1882) 7 App Cas 345 at 351.
② [2001] 1 Lloyd's Rep 10 at 24.

就合同变更而言,可以是合同当事人的变更,也可以是合同内容的变更,也可 16.36
以两者兼而有之。在通常情况下,novation 是特指合同当事人的变更,至于合同
内容的变更一般会使用 variation 一词予以表达。① 如前所述,普通法并不允许合
同当事人单方面转让合同权利,要在普通法中转让合同的话,合同变更便成为唯
一的选择。但所谓的合同当事人变更实际上就是原来合同的解除和新合同的订
立,因此对价也同样是必需的。正如 *Chitty on Contracts* 一书所说:②

> Novation takes place where there being a contract in existence, some
> new contract is substituted for it, either between the same parties ... or
> between different parties; the consideration mutually being the discharge
> of the old contract.

与合同转让相比,合同变更应当具有如下两个明显的特征:第一,合同变更导 16.37
致合同权利和合同义务一起发生转移,被新当事人替代的原合同当事人无需继续
承担其原有的合同义务,其合同义务均由新合同当事人负责履行,而合同转让仅
涉及合同权利的转让,合同义务人依然保持不变;第二,合同变更需要得到所有当
事人的同意,而合同转让并不以义务人同意为前提条件。

合同变更的必要性

前文曾介绍过船东转让船舶建造合同的必要性,其实船舶建造合同的变更往 16.38
往是船东通过融资安排建造船舶而引起的。船舶融资有各种不同的形式,例如在
所谓的表外融资(off-sheet financing)安排中,由于作为借款人的船东在名义上已
不再与真正的融资受益人有法律上的关系,因此就有必要对已经订立的船舶建造
合同进行当事人的变更,由作为借款人的船东成为船舶建造合同中的船东,并在
此基础上再转让船舶建造合同。

虽然在所谓的表外融资安排中,融资银行希望自己对作为借款人的船东享有 16.39
实际的控制,其目的是为了保证资产的安全。但是一旦成为船舶建造合同的船东
后就自然而然地承担了支付建造款以及其他款项的合同义务。一旦真正的融资
受益人违约,虽然融资银行可以根据融资协议的规定采取各种措施保护自己的利
益,但融资银行控制的船东并没有解除合同的理由。而这显然是融资银行不愿意
看见的,因此有时融资银行还会要求船厂同意在约定的情形发生时,船舶建造合

---

① Hugh Beale, *Chitty on Contracts*, 35th edn Sweet & Maxwell 2023, para.26 – 034.
② Hugh Beale, *Chitty on Contracts*, 35th edn Sweet & Maxwell 2023, para.23 – 089.

同原来的船东即自动替换回船东,融资银行控制的船东则无需承担任何合同义务。

合同变更协议

16.40　约定变更合同当事人的通常会签署一份称之为合同变更协议的文件,该文件会明确规定各方当事人在合同变更后各自的权利义务。在船舶建造合同中,合同变更前关于船舶所有权归属的约定并不影响合同的变更。在 *Rasbora Ltd v JCL Marine Ltd* 一案中,高院的 Lawson 法官正是这样认为的,他说的是:①

> The fact that under the terms of the original contract at the early stage of its construction [vessel] became the buyers property in my judgment does not affect the substitution I have mentioned. I regard this as the clearest possible case of a true novation.

船厂的权利

16.41　与船舶建造合同的转让不同,合同变更对船厂来讲意味着与船东以外的人订立合同,而且鉴于融资银行的特殊安排,成为船舶建造合同主体的新当事人通常是船厂闻所未闻的。除非船舶建造合同另有约定,船厂可以拒绝变更合同当事人的请求。如前所述,合同变更和合同转让的根本区别之一是合同变更只有在得到所有当事人同意的情况下才可能发生,之所以需要所有当事人的同意是因为合同变更实际上是原合同解除和新合同成立两个过程的结合。就新合同订立而言,需要所有当事人的同意正是契约自由的体现。因此船厂可以拒绝合同变更且无需提供特殊的理由。当然,船厂也可以在确保自己的利益不受影响的情况下同意协助船东的融资安排,例如原船东和新船东应当对合同义务承担连带责任。正因为如此,在实践中能看见合同变更协议规定原船东始终对船舶建造合同的适当履行负责,或原船东作为担保人保证新船东切实履行船舶建造合同。

---

① [1977] 1 Lloyd's Rep 645 at 650.

第17章 税收和规费

I 船厂所在国税收和规费

概述

税收通常是指一国政府向该国公民、企业以及其他组织或机构强制征收的款项。"税收"似乎并不是一个专门的法律用语,*The New Oxford Dictionary of English* 对 tax 的解释是:

> A compulsory contribution to state revenue, levied by the government on workers' income and business profits, or added to the cost of some goods, services, and transactions.

17.1

从上述定义应当能够看出税收的几个基本特征,即:政府强制收取的;既针对个人的收入,也针对经营的利润,而且还针对货物、服务以及交易的成本。而 duty 一字在作为税收解时则往往是指关税。*The New Oxford Dictionary of English* 对 duty 的解释是:

17.2

> A payment levied on the import, export, manufacture, or sale of goods.

就船舶建造而言,通常有可能涉及的税类大致有:船厂营业税、利润税、增值税、设备进口税、船舶出口税以及合同印花税等。

17.3

税收和规费的分担

绝大多数船舶建造合同都会对与船舶建造相关税收的承担作出约定,通常的规定是船厂承担船厂所在国针对船舶建造合同及其履行所征收的所有税款,但针

17.4

对船东供应品征收的税款除外。SAJ 格式的规定如下：①

> This BUILDER shall bear and pay all taxes and duties imposed in Japan in connection with execution and/or performance of this Contract, excluding any taxes and duties imposed in Japan upon the BUYER's Supplies.

17.5　AWES 格式也有类似的规定：②

> All taxes, duties, stamps and fees levied by the Authorities in .... and connected to this CONTRACT are to be borne by the CONTRACTOR.

17.6　上述规定中的 stamps 是指印花税，即 stamp duties。印花税是政府收取的各种税收之一，其基本特征是针对书面文件收取且由纳税人按规定自行购买并粘贴税票的一种税收，例如签订船舶建造合同应当支付的印花税。在我国应当缴纳印花税的主体并不局限于中国公民和法人，在中国境内设立或领受相关合同和凭证的中国或外国公民和法人也同样有缴纳印花税的义务。以船舶建造合同为例，在我国，船厂和船东都是印花税的纳税人。鉴于上述 AWES 格式明确了印花税由船厂支付，因此缴纳印花税不仅是船厂的法定义务，同时也是船厂的合同义务。SAJ 格式没有关于印花税的规定，但通常均由船厂支付印花税。

17.7　而"费用"则应当是指各项规费。规费是指通常由政府部门收取的各种费用，例如一般应当由船厂缴纳的工程排污费、社会保障费等。这些规费有的是由于船舶建造而产生的，例如工程排污费；有的则是船厂应当负责的，例如船厂职工的公积金和养老金等。CSTC 格式关于税收的规定与其他船舶建造合同标准格式似乎有所不同，该格式的规定是：③

> All costs for taxes including stamp duties, if any, incurred in connection with this Contract in the People's Republic of China shall be borne by the SELLER. Any taxes and/or duties imposed upon those items or services procured by the SELLER in the People's Republic of China or elsewhere for the construction of the VESSEL shall be borne by the SELLER.

17.8　按照上述规定，船厂应当承担两种税收：一种是在中国境内发生的针对船舶

---

① Article XV.1, see also Norwegian Article XIV.1.
② Article 13, para.1, see also NEWBUILDCON Clause 13, para.2.
③ Article XV.1.

建造合同的税收；另一种则是在中国境外发生的针对船舶建造的税收。很难想象船厂所在国以外的国家会对在中国的船厂征收与船舶建造有关的税收，因此船厂在船舶建造合同中承诺承担此类税收应当是没有什么意义的。

出口退税

出口退税是一国鼓励本国货物出口的一项措施，其基本含义是对出口货物退还其在国内应缴纳的各种税负，例如产品税、增值税、营业税和特别消费税等。我国对船用设备产品的进口征收关税，但对于用于出口船的进口船用设备产品则实行退税。退税以船厂收到船舶建造合同价款为前提，换言之，船厂只有在船舶出口的情况下才可以享受退税的优惠。船舶出口退税税率在17%左右。 17.9

II 其他税收和规费

船东的责任

按照绝大多数船舶建造合同标准格式的规定，船东应当承担在船厂所在国以外地方产生的与船舶建造合同有关的税款，例如 SAJ 格式便有如下规定：① 17.10

> This BUYER shall bear and pay all taxes and duties imposed outside Japan in connection with execution and/or performance of this Contract, except for taxes and duties imposed upon those items to be procured by the BUILDER for construction of the VESSEL.

AWES 格式的规定更为简单：② 17.11

> Any taxes, duties, stamps and fees outside are to be borne by the PURCHASER.

上述规定应当和 AWES 格式同一条内的前一句一起理解，因为在前一句中应当有一个地点或国家，因此这里的 outside 也就是指另一句中载明的国家以外的地方。在 NEWBUILDCON 格式规定：③ 17.12

---

① Article XV.2, see also Norwegian Article XIV.2.
② Article 13, para.2.
③ Clause 16(b).

The Buyer shall bear and pay all taxes, duties, stamps, dues and fees imposed outside the place stated in Box 2 in connection with the execution and/or performance of this Contract, except for taxes, duties, stamps, dues and fees imposed upon those items and services procured by the Builder for construction of the Vessel.

17.13　　上述 NEWBUILDCON 格式规定中的"地点"应当是"国家",实际上在方格 2 中本应填入船厂的名称、地址等外还应当填入船厂所在地的国家。就税收而言,"地点"和"国家"应当是不同的,因为大多国家都有地方税和国家税之分,例如在我国就有国税和地税的区分。如果船厂在上海而船东同意承担上海以外的税负,这就意味着船东有可能要承担中国的税负了。

关于税负的约定

17.14　　CSTC 格式下面的规定也应当是比较特别的:①

The SELLER shall indemnify the BUYER for, and hold it harmless against, any duties imposed in the People's Republic of China upon materials and equipment which under the terms of this Contract and/or the Specifications will, or may be, supplied by the BUYER from the abroad for installation in the VESSEL as well as any duties imposed in the People's Republic of China upon running stores, provisions and supplies furnished by the BUYER from abroad to be stocked on board the VESSEL and also from the payment of export duties, if any, to be imposed upon the VESSEL as a hole or upon any of its parts or equipment.

Any tax or duty other than those described hereinabove, if any, shall be borne by the BUYER.

17.15　　按照上述规定,船厂应当承担中国政府针对船东根据船舶建造合同规定从国外提供的用于船舶建造的材料、设备以及用于船上的备用品、伙食以及其他供应品征收的税款。虽然中国政府通常并不对船上的备用品、伙食以及供应品征收关税,但船厂主动承诺赔偿船东因此产生的费用并没有太好的理由。如果说船厂同意承担最终将安装在船上的设备的进口税是因为船厂能够得到退税,同意承担船上备用品等的进口税则没有合理的理由,因为这些物品最终将随船舶一起离开船厂。上述规定的最后一段也可能有问题,该段只是说第一段提及的税负以外的所

---

① Article XV.2.

有税负均应由船东承担,它既没有明确是什么税负,也没有提及是向谁征收的。按照上述规定,任何向船厂征收的且第一段没有包含的税款都应当由船东来承担。

17.16 实际上,在船舶建造合同中对税收的承担作出约定没有太大的意义,因为政府通常是针对应当纳税的人进行征税,而就应当纳税的人而言,纳税是一种法定义务,纳税人并不能通过其与他人的合同约定免除自己的纳税义务。在船舶建造合同中对税收作出约定的意义应当是一方当事人替另一方当事人承担或缴纳发生在该方当事人所在国的但针对另一方当事人的税款,然后再由负有纳税义务的一方返还相关税款。在船舶建造合同有类似规定时,船厂或船东为对方垫付税款就成为了一项合同义务,而偿还对方为自己垫付的税款同样也成为一项合同义务。对此,NEWBUILDCON 格式已经作出了相应的规定:①

> If either Party pays any taxes, duties, stamps, dues and fees for which the other Party is responsible under this Clause, the other Party shall reimburse the paying Party within fifteen (15) Banking Days of receipt of notice to that effect, together with evidence of the amount paid.

---

① Clause 16(c).

第18章 专利、商标和版权

I 知识产权

概述

18.1　知识产权是一种无形的权利,通常包括专利、设计、商标、版权以及与此相关的权利。世界知识产权组织给知识产权下了如下定义:①

> Intellectual property, very broadly, means the legal rights which result from intellectual activity in the industrial, scientific, literary and artistic fields. Countries have laws to protect intellectual property for two main reasons. One is to give statutory expression to the moral and economic rights of creators in their creations and the rights of the public in access to those creations. The second is to promote, as a deliberate act of Government policy, creativity and the dissemination and application of its results and to encourage fair trading which would contribute to economic and social development.

18.2　与知识产权相关的另一个词应当是"工业产权",世界知识产权组织关于工业产权的定义是:②

> Industrial property shall be understood in the broadest sense and shall apply not only to industry and commerce proper, but likewise to agricultural and extractive industries and to all manufactured or natural products, for example, wines, grain, tobacco leaf, fruit, cattle, minerals, mineral waters, beer, flowers, and flour.

18.3　虽然工业产权同样也是一种无形的权利,包括专利、工业设计、商标和服务标

---

① *WIPO Intellectual Property Handbook* WIPO Publication No. 489(E), 2nd edn 2004, reprint 2008, p.3.
② Paris Convention for the Protection of Industrial Property, as amended 1979, Article 1(3).

志等权利,但工业产权与知识产权还是有区别的,两者的区别应当是知识产权通常包括著作权和版权,而工业产权则不包括著作权和版权。世界知识产权组织将知识产权分为两个分支,即版权和工业产权。①

专利

专利作为一项权利是指专利权人对自己的发明创造享有的排他性专有权利。专利通常是一种技术,一种受到法律保护的专有技术。Patent 一字的本意是"明显的"或"易辨别的",而"公开"正是专利的一个基本特征。公开是指技术发明人将其技术公之于众,公众可以随意获得关于专利技术的信息。专利权是诉讼权利之一,在 *British Mutoscope & Biograph Co Ltd* v *Homer* 一案中,财税法庭的 Farwell 法官说:②

18.4

> ... a patent right is a privilege granted by the Crown in the exercise of its prerogative to a first inventor, and is ... an incorporeal chattel. I should be disposed to classify it myself as a chose in action .... I refer to the common form of a patent: "Know ye therefore, that we ... do by these presents ... give and grant unto the said patentee our especial licence, full power, sole privilege, and authority, that the said patentee by himself, his agents, or licensees, and no others, may ... make, use, exercise, and vend the said invention ... and that the said patentee shall have and enjoy the whole profit and advantage from time to time accruing by reason of the said invention ...."

从 1977 年《专利法》(Patents Act 1977) 关于获得专利权要求的规定可以看出专利的特征:③

18.5

A patent may be granted only for an invention in Patentable respect of which the following conditions are satisfied, that is to say -

(a) the invention is new;
(b) it involves an inventive step;
(c) it is capable of industrial application;
(d) the grant of a patent for it is not excluded by subsections (2) and (3) below;

---

① *Understanding Industrial Property* WIPO Publication No.895(E), 2nd edn 2004, reprint 2008, p.3.
② [1901] 1 Ch 671 at 675.
③ s.1(1).

and references in this Act to a patentable invention shall be construed accordingly.

商标

18.6 商标就是一种标志,用来区别商品或服务的标志。商标可以是注册的商标,也可以是未经注册的商标。1994 年《商标法》(Trade Marks Act 1994) 给商标下的定义是:①

> In this Act a "trade mark" means any sign capable of being represented graphically which is capable of distinguishing goods or services of one undertaking from those of other undertakings.
>
> A trade mark may, in particular, consist of words (including personal names), designs, letters, numerals or the shape of goods or their packaging.

18.7 在 *Smith-Kline & French Laboratories Ltd* v *Sterling-Winthrop Group Ltd* 一案中,上议院的 Lord Diplock 介绍了商标的起源及发展,以及随之而来的功能上的变化,他说:②

> Trade marks in their origin were marks that were applied to goods by their maker so that a buyer by visual examination of the goods could tell who made them. Makers' marks on silver and gold plate afford some of the earliest examples. With the growth of advertising, representations of trade marks have become widely used in advertisements so as to familiarise buyers with the mark, but the application of trade marks to the actual goods or to the packages containing them still constitutes their basic function. The mark may be applied by the maker to whatever visible part of the goods he chooses as suitable. If he habitually places it in a particular position on the goods, its distinctiveness in fact as indicating that the goods are of his manufacture may be associated with the position in which it appears upon the goods and in the case of markings of a kind which are not intrinsically uncommon their distinctiveness as a trade mark may depend upon the position in which the markings appear upon the goods; as, for example, bands of colour or a raised moulded pattern round the neck of a bottle containing the

---

① s.1(1).
② [1975] 2 All ER 578 at 583.

manufacturer's product.

商号

商号即企业的字号或名称，是企业特定的标志。商号与商标不尽相同。商标强调的是其与特定商品或服务之间的关系，而商号则着重其与生产或经营者之间的联系。　　18.8

II 船舶建造中的知识产权

专利

在船舶建造中不可避免地会涉及到专利和商标及其使用，不仅船厂的设计和建造会涉及到专利或商标，船厂的采购同样有可能涉及到专利或商标。但相对而言商标及其使用在船舶建造中似乎并不是经常引起索赔或争议的原因，而专利及其使用引起索赔或争议的可能性则会大一些。船舶建造合同标准格式的规定也大多是针对专利作出的。从我国知识产权局公布的统计数据来看，与船舶建造有关的专利申请主要集中在船舶或其他水上船只和船用设备，船只下水、进出干坞，船舶的推进装置或操舵装置以及船上辅助设备等方面。在所有船舶建造涉及的知识产权中，有的是船厂自己拥有的，例如船舶建造工艺等；有的则是他人拥有的，例如设备供应商拥有的专利。　　18.9

SAJ 格式有如下规定:① 　　18.10

Machinery and equipment of the VESSEL may bear the patent number, trademarks or trade names of the manufactures.

其他格式如 CSTC 格式和 Norwegian 格式都有类似的规定,②但这一规定实际上只是一个说明而已，即说明船舶上的机器和设备有可能有专利号、制造商的商标或商号。　　18.11

船厂的合同义务

船舶建造中的设计、建造以及设备都有可能涉及专利和商标，而在接船后船　　18.12

---

① Article XVI.1, para.1.
② CSTC Article XVI, para.1, Norwegian Article XV, para.1.

东即成为了这些专利和商标的实际使用人,因此船东就有可能面对关于专利或商标的索赔。为了保证船东享有使用船舶及其设备的权利的完整性,船厂通常会在船舶建造合同中作出保证船东使用船舶的权利不受影响之类的承诺。类似的承诺因此也就成了船厂的合同义务了。其中 SAJ 格式作出了如下规定:①

> The BUILDER shall defend and save harmless the BUYER from patent liability or claims of patent infringement of any nature or kind, including costs and expenses for, or on account of any patented or patentable invention made or used in the performance of this Contract and also including costs and expenses of litigation, if any.

18.13 船厂承诺的是:一旦发生任何与专利有关的索赔,船厂将承担相关的责任和费用。由于使用了 defend 一字,在发生诉讼的情况下,船厂应当代表船东进行诉讼。AWES 格式的规定有些许不同:②

> The CONTRACTOR shall indemnify the PURCHASER against any infringement of patent rights by or in connection with the construction at the Shipyard, of the VESSEL, but not such liability shall lie with the CONTRACTOR with regard to components and/or equipment and/or design supplied by the PURCHASER.

18.14 AWES 格式的规定与 SAJ 格式的规定有一个比较明显的区别,即按照 AWES 格式的规定,船厂承担的是赔偿的责任。而赔偿是指对由于他人行为造成的损失进行弥补:③

> To indemnify is to make good a loss which one person has suffered in consequence of the act or default of another; and the operation of making good the loss is called indemnification.

18.15 因此,在采用 AWES 格式的情况下,船厂并没有义务代替船东参与关于专利索赔或争议的诉讼,而是在船东因专利索赔或争议遭受损失后再作出赔偿。显然,就船东利益而言,SAJ 似乎较为有利一些。Norwegian 格式的规定基本上与 SAJ 格式的规定相同,只是在专利的基础上增加了商标、版权以及其他知识产权而已。④

---

① Article XVI.1, para.2, see also CSTC Article XVI, para.1.
② Article 14, para.1.
③ Daniel Greenburg, *Jowitt's Dictionary of English Law*, 3rd edn Sweet & Maxwell, Vol 1, p.1164.
④ Article XV, para.2.

责任范围及期限

船厂承担赔偿责任的对象应当是船厂向船东交付的船舶及其所有设备、装置、系统等,但船东供应品除外。SAJ 格式就有如下规定:①   18.16

The BUILDER's warranty hereunder does not extend to the BUYER's Supplies.

CSTC 格式的规定与 SAJ 格式的内容基本一致,但是 CSTC 格式没有使用 warranty,而是使用了 indemnity,可以说 indemnity 较 warranty 更为恰当:②   18.17

The SELLER's indemnity hereunder does not extend to equipment or parts supplied by the BUYER to the BUILDER, if any.

在责任期限问题上,唯独 CSTC 格式作出了规定。实际上 CSTC 格式是在 SAJ 格式规定的基础上又增加了新的内容:③   18.18

Nothing contained herein shall be construed as transferring any patent or trademark rights or copyright in equipment covered by this Contract, and all such rights are hereby expressly reserved to the true and lawful owners thereof. Notwithstanding any provisions contained herein to the contrary, the SELLER's obligation under this Article should not be terminated by the passage of any specified period of time.

"SELLER's obligation under this Article"一句其实与上述规定无甚关联,因为上述规定实际上只是一种说明,即相关的知识产权并不因船舶建造合同而发生转让。上述规定只是 CSTC 格式第 XVI 条中的一段,其中第一段有船厂赔偿船东损失的规定,因此"obligation under this Article"是指船厂负有的赔偿义务。船厂明确承诺其合同义务不受任何时间限制的做法有可能导致无法以时效为由抗辩任何索赔。船厂在船舶建造合同中作出如此承诺似乎没有太好的理由。   18.19

---

① Article XVI.1, para.4, see also Norwegian Article XV, para.4.
② Article XVI, para.3.
③ Article XVI, para.2.

Ⅲ 知识产权的保护

18.20　船舶建造涉及的知识产权以权利主体的特征为标准可以分为两大类,一类是船厂以外的第三人拥有的知识产权,另一类则是船厂拥有的知识产权。

第三人的知识产权

18.21　毋庸置疑,只有知识产权的权利人才可以转让自己的权利。船厂在船舶建造过程中虽然涉及知识产权的使用,但通常不会购买或受让他人的知识产权。因此,绝大多数船舶建造合同都会规定,任何合同条款均不得解释为转让第三人的知识产权。例如:SAJ 格式便有如下规定:[1]

> Nothing contained herein shall be construed as transferring any patent or trademark rights or copyright in equipment covered by this Contract, and all such rights are hereby expressly reserved to the true and lawful owners thereof.

18.22　从上述规定可以看得出,所谓的知识产权是针对设备的,而设备通常是船厂通过采购或分包获得的。设备的知识产权通常归供应设备的制造商拥有。船厂在船舶建造过程中充其量也只是使用制造商的知识产权,而不可能拥有这些知识产权,因此船厂也就不可能成为向船东转让知识产权的一方。Norwegian 格式的相应内容与 SAJ 格式的规定基本相同,只是在"all such rights"后面增加了"including the design of the Vessel"[2]。

船厂的知识产权

18.23　船厂自己也可能拥有知识产权,但船厂同样也不愿意通过船舶建造将自己的知识产权转让给船东。因此,除非有明确的相反规定,属于船厂的知识产权同样也不会随着船舶所有权的转移而发生转移。SAJ 格式规定:[3]

> The BUILDER retains all rights with respect to the Specification, and plans and working drawings, technical descriptions, calculations, test results and other data, information and documents concerning the design

---

[1] Article XVI.1, para.3, see also AWES Article 14, para.2.
[2] Article XV, para.3.
[3] Article XVI.2.

and construction of the VESSEL and the BUYER undertakes therefore not to disclose the same or divulge any information contained therein to any third parties, without the prior written consent of the BUILDER, excepting where it is necessary for usual operation, repair and maintenance of the VESSEL.

船厂的知识产权主要包括规格书、图纸、技术文件、计算、测试结果以及其他数据等。船东承诺在没有征得船厂同意的情况下不向任何第三方透露,但为船舶营运、修理和保养的除外。从上述规定来看,似乎船东将船舶进行转售都应当事先得到船厂的同意。AWES 格式与 SAJ 格式的规定基本一致:①

18.24

The CONTRACTOR retains all rights to the Specifications, plans and working drawings, technical descriptions, calculations, test results and other data information and documents concerning the design and construction of the VESSEL and the PURCHASER undertakes therefore not to bring them to the knowledge of third parties, without the prior written consent of the CONTRACTOR except if and to the extent necessary in the normal operation or repair of the VESSEL.

船舶的处置

按照上述规定,在知识产权保护上,第三人的知识产权和船厂的知识产权应当是不同的。就第三人知识产权保护而言,船厂只是明确声明在船厂和船东之间不存在任何知识产权的转让;而就船厂知识产权的保护而言,船舶建造合同则规定了船东不得泄露的义务。按照 SAJ 格式的规定,这一义务具体到船东承诺在事先没有获得船厂书面许可的情况下不向任何第三人透露或泄露规格书和图纸等的任何信息。这一义务实际上意味着船东在接船后出售船舶都有可能需要事先得到船厂的书面同意,因为船东出售船舶将无可避免地要向买方提供规格书和图纸等文件,而且船东向第三方披露信息未必最终导致船舶出售的成功。虽然绝大多数船舶建造合同都有类似的规定,但几乎可以肯定的是船东出售船舶必须征得船厂书面同意并不是双方的真实意图。

18.25

NEWBUILDCON 格式

NEWBUILDCON 格式关于知识产权保护的规定与其他的标准格式的规定有

18.26

---

① Article 8(a).

较大的区别,该格式打破了传统的按照权利人特征确定知识产权保护方式的做法,采用针对权利而不是权利人的方式对知识产权保护作出了规定。该格式有如下规定:①

> Where they are owned and supplied by a Party, that Party shall retain all copyright, trade mark, patent or similar rights (hereinafter called "Intellectual Property Rights") with respect to the Specification, Plans and Drawings, technical descriptions, calculations, test results and other data, and information and documents concerning the design and construction of the Vessel. The other Party undertakes not to disclose the same or divulge any information contained therein to any third parties without the prior written consent of the first Party, except where it is necessary for usual operation, repair and maintenance of the Vessel and to subsequent owners.

18.27　针对权利而不是权利人规定知识产权保护显然是比较合理的,在实践中提供规格书和图纸的并不始终是船厂,在不少情况下提供规格书和图纸的是船东而不是船厂。针对权利作出规定就无需考虑权利人了。而且 NEWBUILDCON 格式针对船东出售船舶的情形作出了规定,即把船东出售船舶作为不得披露相关信息的例外,无需征得船厂的同意。即使与规格书和图纸等相关的知识产权归船厂所有,船东出售船舶也不构成对船厂知识产权的侵犯。NEWBUILDCON 格式除了针对与船舶设计建造相关的知识产权保护作出了规定外,还针对与船舶建造中采购相关的知识产权保护作出了如下规定:②

> Each Party shall ensure that any manufacture and/or supply according to specifications, drawings, models or other instructions supplied by it shall not infringe any Intellectual Property Rights of third parties. Should claims nevertheless be made against the other Party in respect of Intellectual Property Rights arising out of or in any way related to the performance of the Contract, the first Party shall keep the other Party indemnified against the cost of such claims, including any legal costs in connection therewith.

18.28　在不少船舶建造中,提供设备或其他装置和物品的不仅有船厂,而且还有船东,由船东提供的即为船东供应品。根据上述规定,凡是提供设备或其他装置和

---

① Clause 40(a).
② Clause 40(b).

物品的均应保证其供应不侵犯任何第三人的知识产权,一旦另一方因违反知识产权而遭受索赔的,供应方应当赔偿另一方的损失,包括法律费用。

另外,NEWBUILDCON格式还针对"保密信息"作出了如下规定:①   18.29

> For the purpose of this Sub-clause(c), "Information" means technical information relating to the Vessel designated by one Party as confidential, except information which corresponds in substance to information which:
>
> (i) was developed by and in possession of the other Party prior to first receipt from the first Party; and/or
> (ii) at the date hereof or hereafter, through no wrongful act or failure to act on the part of the other Party, enters the public domain.
>
> Where it is necessary during the performance of this Contract for the first Party to make Information available to the other Party, the other Party shall hold all such Information in confidence and not disclose it to any third parties or use it for any purpose other than as provided herein without the prior written consent of the first Party, which shall not be unreasonably withheld.

这类似于合同中保密条款的规定在船舶建造合同中的意义似乎并不十分明确。首先,这里的"Information"在第40条的(a)和(b)中并没有出现过,而且虽然第一个字母采用了大写,但在格式的定义条款中并没有定义;其次,第40(c)条实际上是对"Information"作出了定义和解释,而"For the purpose of this Sub-clause(c)"一句似乎又将"Information"的定义和解释仅仅适用于第40(c)条,仅仅适用于解释可能会使解释不再有太大的意义了;最后,所谓的保密应当是针对技术诀窍的,而第40条涉及的是版权、商标和专利,这些知识产权并不是通过保密而得到保护的。   18.30

---

① Clause 40(c).

第 19 章　船东供应品

I　原因

19.1　　虽然在船舶建造中,船舶所需的设备一般都会由船厂负责采购并连同船舶一起交付给船东,但也会出现船舶所需的部分设备或装置由船东提供的情形。所谓的"船东供应品"是指由船东提供的最终将安装在船上的设备、装置和系统等。船东提供部分设备可能是因为船厂无法采购到或无法以优惠的价格采购到船东提供的设备,或者船东提供的设备是其专有的,船厂无法在市场上获得。在普通商船建造中,由船东负责提供某些设备的做法实际上并不多见,这可能是因为船东的采购和船厂的采购并没有实质性的区别。船东往往会指定特定的制造商或供应商,并且指定特定的品牌和产地,然后要求船厂进行实际采购。船东按照船舶建造合同规定提供相关设备的做法实际上承担了相当大的风险。这些风险不仅包括将船东供应品运输至船厂码头的运输风险,而且也包括了船东供应品的质量风险,因为除非另有约定,船东供应品的质量风险均应由船东承担。

19.2　　鉴于船东供应品是船东自行采购并向船厂提供的设备,合同价格不包括船东供应品的价格应当是比较适当的做法。但有些船舶建造合同,尤其是海工设备建造合同的合同价格则会包括船东供应品价格,即由船东按照约定的方式和数额支付合同价款,而船厂则负责支付船东供应品的价款。在船舶建造合同价格包括船东供应品的情况下,船厂需要提供的还款保函的金额也将随之提高,一旦船东有机会解除合同的,船厂就有可能遭受额外的损失。

Ⅱ 船东的责任

建造合同规定

在船舶设备由船东提供的情况下,建造合同通常会对此作出约定。此种约定的目的是分清船厂和船东针对船东供应品的合同责任,例如 SAJ 格式就有如下规定:①   19.3

> The BUYER shall, at its own risk, cost and expense, supply and deliver to the BUILDER all of the items to be furnished by the BUYER as specified in the Specifications (herein called the "BUYER's Supplies") at warehouse or other storage of the Shipyard in the proper condition ready for installation in or on the VESSEL, in accordance with the time schedule designated by the BUILDER.

其他船舶建造合同标准格式也有类似的规定。② 船东除了应当按照合同规定提供船东供应品外,还应当向船厂提供安装船东供应品所需的文件和必要的协助。对此 SAJ 格式作出了如下规定:③   19.4

> In order to facilitate installation by the BUILDER of the BUYER's Supplies in or on the VESSEL, the BUYER shall furnish the BUILDER with necessary specifications, plans, drawings, instruction books, manuals, test reports and certificates required by the rules and regulations. The BUYER, if so requested by the BUILDER, shall, without any charge to the BUILDER, cause the representatives of the manufacturers of the BUYER's Supplies to assist the BUILDER in installation thereof in or on the VESSEL and/or to carry out installation thereof by themselves or to make necessary adjustments thereof at the Shipyard.

船东应当提供与船东供应品有关的规格书、图纸、手册、测试报告和证书等船厂安装船东供应品所必需的文件,除此之外,船东还应当在船厂提出要求时指派制造商代表协助船厂安装船东供应品或指派制造商代表在船厂安装或调   19.5

---

① Article XVII.1(a).
② CSTC Article V.4, para.1, Norwegian Article XVI.1(a), NEWBUILDCON Clause 21(a)(i).
③ Article XVII.1(b).

试船东供应品。在这个问题上 Norwegian 格式的规定似乎有些不同，该格式规定的是：①

> In order to facilitate installation by the Builder of the Buyer's Supplies in or on the Vessel, the Buyer shall furnish the Builder with necessary specifications, plans, drawings, instruction books, manuals, test reports and certificates required by all applicable rules and regulations. If so reasonably requested by the Builder, the Buyer shall without any charge to the Builder, provided always that such installation is not Builder's responsibility pursuant to the Specifications, cause the representatives of the manufacturers of the Buyer's Supplies to assist the Builder in installation thereof in or on the Vessel and/or to carry out installation thereof by themselves or to make necessary adjustments at the Builder's yard.

19.6　上述规定与 SAJ 格式不同，它似乎包含了两种情形，即船厂负责安装船东供应品的情形以及供应商负责按照船东供应品的情形。在第一种情形下，为了方便船厂的安装，船东应当提供相关的规格书、图纸和手册等文件。在第二种情形下，船厂应安排供应商完成船东供应品的安装。但是上述规定的第二句比较费解。如果负有安装义务的是船东，船东应当自行安装船东供应品，既无需船厂发出合理的请求，也不存在所谓的协助船厂完成船东供应品的安装。

船厂的拒绝

19.7　SAJ 格式还规定了船厂有权拒绝船东供应品的情形，该规定的内容如下：②

> Any and all of the BUYER's Supplies shall be subject to the BUILDER's reasonable right of rejection, as and if they are found to be unsuitable or in improper condition for installation. However, if so requested by the BUYER, the BUILDER may repair or adjust the BUYER's Supplies without prejudice to the BUILDER's other rights hereunder and without being responsible for any consequences therefrom. In such case, the BUYER shall reimburse the BUILDER for all costs and expenses incurred by the BUILDER in such repair or adjustment and the Delivery Date shall be automatically postponed for a period of time necessary for such repair or replacement.

---

① Article XVI.1(b).
② Article XVII.1(c).

如果船东供应品不适合安装在船上，船厂拒绝船东供应品显然是合理的，而船东则可以要求船厂对船东供应品进行修理或调整。在这种情况下，船东应补偿船厂因修理或调整船东供应品而产生的成本和费用，船厂还可以顺延合同交船日。Norwegian 格式和 NEWBUILDCON 格式也有类似的规定，① 其中NEWBUILDCON 格式在不适合安装的基础上还增加了船东供应品不符合船级社或船旗国主管当局规定或要求的情形。如果船东供应品不符合船级社或船旗国主管当局的规定或要求，即使船厂安装了，船级社也不会颁发相关的证书。在这种情况下，修理和调整就未必能够解决问题了。

19.8

除非无法安装，船厂通常不会也没有理由拒绝安装船东供应品。在船东要求船厂对船东供应品进行修理或调整后再安装的，船厂可以对船东供应品进行修理和调整，但此种修理和调整是否构成船厂的合同义务则取决于对船舶建造合同的解释。从 SAJ 格式的规定来看，修理和调整似乎并不构成船厂的合同义务，因为所使用的是"may"，即船厂可以作出是否修理和调整的决定。船厂在决定是否对船东供应品进行修理或调整时应当谨慎。船东供应品通常也是相关制造商或供应商提供的，如果船东供应品不适合安装在船上，问题有可能出在船东一方，也可能出在制造商或供应商一方。船厂在这种情况下若贸然对船东供应品进行修理或调整有可能会使问题更加复杂。而且，制造商和供应商一般都会提供质保，船厂的修理和调整也会影响船东供应品的质保。

19.9

提供迟延

船舶建造合同通常会规定船东应当提供船东供应品的时间，这个时间一般是根据船舶建造的进程、船东供应品应当安装的节点以及船东供应品的制造商或供应商的情况予以确定的。不少船舶建造合同都会规定，船东未能在约定时间提供船东供应品的，合同交船日自动顺延。此外，船东还应当赔偿船厂因此遭受的损失。SAJ 格式的规定如下：②

19.10

> Should the BUYER fail to deliver any of the BUYER's Supplies within the time designated, the Delivery Date shall be automatically extended for a period of such delay in delivery. In such event, the BUYER shall be responsible for and pay to the BUILDER all losses and damages incurred by the BUILDER by reason of such delay in delivery of the

---

① Norwegian Article XVI.1(c), NEWBUILDCON Clause 21(a)(iii).
② Article XVII.1(d), para.1.

> BUYER's Supplies and such payment shall be made upon delivery of the VESSEL.

19.11 　　由于明确规定船东供应品延迟交付的,合同交船日自动顺延,因此船东供应品延迟交付对船舶建造是否真正构成延误也就不再重要了。无论船东供应品的交付延误了几天,合同交船日就将自动顺延几天。CSTC 格式似乎对 SAJ 格式作出了修改,CSTC 格式的规定如下:①

> Should the BUYER fail to deliver to the BUILDER such items within the time specified, the delivery of the VESSEL shall automatically be extended for a period of such delay, provided such delay in delivery of the BUYER's supplied items shall affect the delivery of the VESSEL. In such event, the BUYER shall pay to the SELLER all losses and damages sustained by the SELLER due to such delay in the delivery of the BUYER's supplied items and such payment shall be made upon delivery of the VESSEL.

19.12 　　按照上述规定,船东供应品交付延误的,合同交船日并不自动顺延。只有在船东供应品交付延迟实际上影响了交船的,合同交船日才可以顺延。另外,"In such event"的所指也发生了变化。如果没有"provided ..."一句,"such event"就是指船东未能在约定时间交付船东供应品的情形。而在有"provided ..."一句的情况下,"such event"则应指船东未能在约定时间交付船东供应品且影响交船的情形。很明显,CSTC 格式的规定给船厂顺延合同交船日增加了难度。

继续建造的权利

19.13 　　如果船东供应品没有按期运抵船厂,船厂通常会继续等待,但船厂显然无法长期等待。因为一艘船的等待,尤其是在船台上的等待实际上意味着所有船舶的延误。因此 SAJ 格式作出了如下规定:②

> If delay in delivery of any of the BUYER's Supplies exceeds thirty (30) days, then, the BUILDER shall be entitled to proceed with construction of the VESSEL without installation thereof in or on the VESSEL, without prejudice to the BUILDER's other rights as hereinabove provided, and the BUYER shall accept and take delivery of the VESSEL so constructed.

---

① Article V.4, para.2.
② Article XVII.1(d), para.2.

船厂同意等待的期限为30天,在30天内船东供应品依然没有运抵船厂的,船厂就可以继续建造而无需安装船东供应品,而船东则不能以船厂没有安装船东供应品为由拒绝接受船舶。CSTC格式也有类似的规定。① 当然,如果船东供应品涉及船舶的船级,船厂恐怕还是应当继续等待,否则即使船舶建造完毕也未必可以获得约定的船级符号。Norwegian格式虽也有类似的规定,但该格式增加了关于不可抗力的内容:② 19.14

> If delay in the delivery of any of the Buyer's Supplies exceeds thirty (30) days, then the Builder shall be entitled to proceed with construction of the Vessel without installation thereof in or on the Vessel as hereinabove provided, and the Buyer shall accept and take delivery of the Vessel so constructed, unless such delay is caused by Force Majeure in which case the provisions of Article XVI.1(d) shall apply.

按照上述规定,如果船东供应品交付迟延的原因是不可抗力的话,船厂可以不安装船东供应品而继续船舶的建造。这并不影响船厂顺延合同交船日。NEWBUILDCON格式也给船厂继续建造船舶设定了条件,该格式的规定是:③ 19.15

> If delay in delivery of any of the Buyer's Supplies in accordance with Subclause(a)(i)exceeds thirty(30)days and will cause actual delay to the delivery of the Vessel, the Builder shall have the right to proceed with the construction of the Vessel without Installation of the delayed items. The Buyer shall accept and take delivery of the Vessel so constructed.

根据NEWBUILDCON格式的规定,船东供应品交付延迟超过30天的,船厂不能拒绝安装船东供应品而继续船舶的建造。只有在船东供应品交付延迟实际上造成交船延误的情况下,船厂才可以不再等待而继续船舶的建造。假设船东供应品按照约定应当在船舶下水后运抵船厂,船舶下水了,而且船舶试航日期也已经确定了。即使船东供应品运抵船厂的时间比约定的时间晚了30天,只要船舶试航的日期没有受此影响,船厂似乎就不能不安装船东供应品而继续船舶的建造。 19.16

责任抑或权利

不少船舶建造合同标准格式都把船东提供船东供应品视为一项义务或责任, 19.17

---

① Article V.4, para.3.
② Article XVI.1(e).
③ Clause 21(a)(iv).

例如 SAJ 格式和 Norwegian 格式都把船东提供船东供应品规定为"买方的责任"。但从合同条款的具体内容来看，提供船东供应品似乎并不是一项合同义务，而更像是一项合同权利，一项选择权。除非是船舶船级必不可少的供应品，船东可以按照合同规定选择提供船东供应品，也可以选择不提供船东供应品。船东选择不提供船东供应品的，船厂的合同义务不受船东供应品的任何影响。如果提供船东供应品是船东的合同责任或义务，船东不提供船东供应品就应当承担违约责任。但事实上船东不提供船东供应品并不构成违约，只要船东在应当提供船东供应品的时间内宣布不再提供船东供应品，船厂并不因此享有任何索赔的权利。

Ⅲ 船厂的责任

保管和安装义务

19.18　　船东交付船东供应品的时间和船厂安装船东供应品的时间未必正好吻合，因此在船东供应品运抵船厂后，船厂需要对其进行妥善的保管。船厂的保管责任应当始于船东供应品运抵船厂，止于船东接船之时。就船厂妥善保管船东供应品而言，SAJ 格式作出了如下规定：①

> The BUILDER shall be responsible for storing and handling with reasonable care of the BUYER's Supplies after delivery thereof at the Shipyard, and shall, at its own cost and expense, install them in or on the VESSEL, unless otherwise provided herein or agreed by the parties hereto, provided, always, that the BUILDER shall not be responsible for quality, efficiency and/or performance of any of the BUYER's Supplies.

19.19　　船厂的义务包括合理谨慎地储存和处理船东供应品。上述规定中关于船厂应当负责船东供应品的安装并承担费用的内容应当是指按照船舶建造合同约定应由船厂完成的安装。如果船东供应品的安装应由制造商或供应商完成，相关费用也应当由制造商或供应商承担。CSTC 格式和 NEWBUILDCON 格式似乎没有区分应当由船厂负责安装的船东供应品和应当由制造商或供应商负责安装的船东供应品的情形。② Norwegian 格式的规定则考虑了承担船东供应品安装义务的

---

① Article XVII.2.
② CSTC Article V.4, para.4, NEWBUILDCON Clause 21(b)(i).

有可能并不是船厂的情形,该格式的规定是:①

> The Builder shall be responsible for storing and handling with due diligence the Buyer's Supplies after delivery thereof at the Builder's yard, and shall, at its own cost and expense, install them in or on the Vessel, unless otherwise provided herein or agreed by the parties hereto, provided always, that the Builder shall not be responsible for the quality, efficiency and/or performance of any of the Buyer's Supplies.

上述规定中"unless otherwise..."应当能够解决船厂按照约定不负责船东供应品安装的情形。   19.20

船东供应品的质量

按照绝大多数船舶建造合同标准格式的规定,虽然船厂应当对船东供应品的储存、保管以及安装承担合同责任,但鉴于船东供应品是船东自行采购的且没有任何船厂的参与,因此船厂无需为船东供应品的质量、效率以及运作等承担责任。   19.21

联合检验

CSTC格式作出了联合检验的规定,该格式的规定是:②   19.22

> Upon arrival of such shipment of the BUYE's supplied items, both parties shall undertake an joint unpacking inspection. If any damages are found to be not suitable for installation, the BUILDER shall be entitled to refuse to accept the BUYER's supplied items.

联合检验的目的应当是让双方有一个共同见证船东供应品表面状况及质量的机会。这种检验无论是对船厂还是对船东都应当是有益的,因为它有助于明确并固定船东供应品在运抵船厂时的状况。此外,"joint"前面不应当是"an",而应当是"a","damages"则应当是"damage"。   19.23

船舶建造人险

船舶建造合同都有关于船厂应当投保建造人保险的规定,而建造人保险的标   19.24

---

① Article XVI.2.
② Article V.4, para.5.

的物通常可以包括船东供应品。船厂在安排船东供应品保险时应当做好衔接工作,例如船东供应品运抵船厂的时间和具体地点与船东供应品保险的起保时间和地点应当一致。如果船东供应品的运输是由船厂承担风险的,船厂则应加保船东供应品的运输风险。

第 20 章 通　知

I　概述

商业合同中一般都有通知条款,其意义在于确定了双方沟通的方式。大多数船舶建造合同也有通知条款,规定通知应当如何制作、如何发出以及如何视为收悉等。没有按照约定发出的通知就可能存在效力问题。所谓"通知"还应当包括"要求","索赔"以及其他文件。如果合同一方以合同通知条款约定方式以外的方式发出通知或进行联系的,对方可以要求重新以约定的方式发出通知或进行联系,甚至不予理会。如果通知是一方当事人享有权利的前提条件,这时通知是否符合合同规定就至关重要了,对方有可能会对通知的有效性提出质疑。在实践中,船舶建造合同的洽谈很少会停留在通知条款上,船东或船厂没有严格按照通知条款规定发出通知的情形时有出现。此外,通知的形式要求是可以放弃的,而且放弃也并非一定是直接的,也可以是推定的。 20.1

II　地址

收件人

SAJ 格式规定:① 20.2

Any and all notices and communications in connection with this Contract shall be addressed as follows:

To the BUYER:

....

---

① Article XVIII.1.

Cable Address: ....
Telex No.: ....

To the BUILDER:

....
Cable Address: ....
Telex No.: ....

20.3 如果填入的仅仅是地址，与船舶建造合同有关的所有通知或通信均应发送至该列明的地址；如果填入的不仅仅是地址，而且包括收件人姓名，则所有通知均应发送至该列明收件人。合同载明的收件人一旦有变化，发生变化的一方应及时通知对方。此种通知同样应当符合通知条款规定的要求。合同也可以指定一个部门作为收件人，例如船厂的经营部或船东的新造船部等。在这种情况下，只要通知被送至指定部门，该部门是否有人确实看见该通知就不再是发件人所关心的了。

20.4 按照上述规定，船厂和船东的联系方式是电报和电传，但在当今世界的船舶建造业乃至航运业已经很少有人还在使用电报和电传了。在船舶建造中使用最为广泛的应当是电子邮件。Norwegian 格式通知条款的内容与 SAJ 格式的内容基本一致，但作为通信方式的电报和电传被改为电话、传真和电子邮件。① AWES 格式通知条款规定的通信方式也是传真和电子邮件。② 有意思的是，AWES 格式的通知条款要求当事人根据技术问题以及法律和财务问题分别填入相关的联系地址和联系人。③ 但这一要求不构成严格的合同义务，换言之，如果一方将应当发送至法律收件人的信函发送至了财务收件人，另一方应当不能将该信函视为没有发送。

形式要求

20.5 似乎只有 NEWBUILDCON 格式对通知的形式做出了规定：④

All notices given by either Party or their agents to the other Party or their agents in accordance with the provisions of this Contract shall be in writing and shall, unless specifically provided in this Contract to the contrary, be sent to the address for that other Party as set out in Box 2

---

① Norwegian Article XVII.1.
② AWES Article 20.
③ Ibid.
④ Clause 43(a).

or Box 3 as appropriate or to such other address as the other Party may designate in writing.

20.6　按照上述规定,双方向对方发出的通知必须是书面的,因此通过电话发出的通知便是无效的。CSTC 格式虽然没有规定双方的通知必须采用书面形式,但却规定双方更改通信地址的通知应当是书面的,而且还必须采用挂号信的方式:①

> Any change of address shall be communicated in writing by registered mail by the party making such change to the other party and in the event of failure to give such notice of change, communications addressed to the party at their last known address shall be deemed sufficient.

20.7　挂号信的使用应当是越来越少了,取而代之的可能是快递方式。如果是通过快递方式送递的,即使实际收件人不是合同载明收件人并不影响通知已经被送递至合同载明的收件人。另外,无论是挂号信还是快递,发件人均应当保留能够证明已经发出通知的证据。

通知的生效

20.8　CSTC 格式以及 NEWBUILDCON 格式都有关于通知如何生效的规定,这些规定显然对日期的计算具有相当重要的意义。其中 CSTC 格式有如下内容:②

> Any and all notices, requests, demands, instructions, advice and communications in connection with this Contract shall be deemed to be given at, and shall become effective from, the time when the same is delivered to the address of the party to be served, provided, however, that registered airmail shall be deemed to be delivered ten(10) days after the date of dispatch, express courier service shall be deemed to be delivered five(5) days after the date of dispatch, and telex acknowledged by the answerbacks shall be deemed to be delivered upon dispatch.

20.9　上述规定仅针对采用挂号信、快递以及电传方式发出的通知,挂号信在发出日的 10 天后视为送到,快递则在发出日的 5 天后视为送到,而电传则在发出时即视为送到。虽然 CSTC 格式的通知条款包括传真方式,但并没有针对这种方式作出生效时间的规定。由于没有规定电子邮件作为通知的方式,因此也没有关于电子邮件生效时间的规定。相比较之下,NEWBUILDCON 格式关于通知生效的规

---

① Article XVII, para.3.
② Article XVII, para.4.

定明显比较合适,该格式的规定是:①

> And notice given under this Contract shall take effect on receipt by the other party and shall be deemed to have been received:
>
> (i) if posted, on the seventh(7th) day after posting;
> (ii) if sent by facsimile or electronically, on the day of transmission;
> (iii) if delivered by hand, on the day of delivery.
>
> And in each case proof of posting, transmission or handing in shall be proof that notice has been given.

20.10　上述规定并没有包括通过电子邮件发通知的情形,而实际上电子邮件可以说是船舶建造中最为常见的通信方式。相反,除了双方高层的联系或者已经产生争议后的联系外,采用信函方式通信的基本没有了。其中"by hand"应当是指通过快递发出,但规定在发出的当日就视为对方已经收到似乎有些不切实际。因为在国际船舶建造中,船厂和船东往往是在不同国家的实体,快递在发出的当天送到收件人应当是不可能的。

联合卖方的通知

20.11　CSTC格式是唯一由船厂和贸易公司作为共同卖方的船舶建造合同标准格式,该格式对此作出了如下规定:②

> Any notices and communications sent by CSTC or the BUILDER alone to the BUYER shall be deemed as having being sent by both CSTC and the BUILDER.

20.12　CSTC格式与其他船舶建造合同标准格式的不同之处是:"卖方"实际上既包括船厂,也包括贸易公司。上述规定强调的是无论船厂还是贸易公司向船东发出的通知或函件等均可视为是由船厂和贸易公司同时发出的,换言之,船厂和贸易公司对各自发出的通知和函件等承担连带责任。虽然上文没有提及船东向船厂或贸易公司发出通知或函件的情形,但应当可以肯定的是,无论船东是向船厂还是贸易公司发出通知或函件均可视为已同时向贸易公司和船厂发出了通知或函件。在CSTC格式的开始部分就已经明确规定船厂和贸易公司是作为共同卖方签署船舶建造合同的。

---

① Clause 43(c).
② Article XVII, para.2.

Ⅲ 语言

英语应当是国际船舶建造业中得到最广泛采用的语言,因此船舶建造合同标准格式也无一例外地规定通知和通信应当采用英语,例如 SAJ 格式就有如下规定:① 20.13

Any and all notices and communications in connection with this Contract shall be written in the English language.

CSTC 格式在规定通知、通信、规格书和图纸均应采用英语的同时还规定合同一方没有将英语文件译成其他语言的义务:② 20.14

Any and all notices, communications, Specifications and drawings in connection with this Contract shall be written in the English language and each party hereto shall have no obligation to translate them into any other language.

除非另有约定,采用英语订立的合同就已经意味着合同的语言是英语。 20.15

---

① Article XVIII.2, see also Norwegian Article XVII.2.
② Article XVII, para.5.

第 21 章　合同的生效

I　合同的条件

概述

21.1　本书第 2 章有关于合同条件的讨论,①所谓"条件"是指合同条款的一种分类,即合同的条件条款。合同条件条款是相对于合同保证条款的概念。而本章讨论的条件是指一个事件。正如 *Chitty on Contracts* 所写到的:②

> The word "condition" may refer either to an event, or to a *term* of a contract (as in the phrase "conditions of sale"). Where "condition" refers to an event, that event may be one of the following.
> (1) It may refer to an occurrence which neither party undertakes to bring about. Where, for example, a contract requires A to work for B, andB to pay A ￡50, "if it rains tomorrow", the obligations of both parties are contingent on the happening of the specified event. This may therefore be described as a *contingent* condition.
> (2) It may refer to the performance by one party of his undertaking. Where, for example, A agrees to work for B at a weekly wage payable at the end of the week, the contract is immediately binding on both parties, but B is not liable to pay until A has performed his promise to work. Such performance is a condition of B's liability, and, as A has promised to render it, the condition may be described as *promissory*.
> (3) An intermediate situation arises in the case of a unilateral contract, in which performance by the promisor becomes due on the performanceby the promise of the stipulated act (such as walking to

---

① 请参见本书第 2 章第 X 节。
② Hugh Beale, *Chitty on Contracts*, 35th edn Sweet & Maxwell 2023, para.4-196.

York) or abstention (such as not smoking for a year), which is in the control of the promisee. Since it follows from the nature of such a contract that the promisee has not promised to render the stipulated performance, the condition on which his entitlement depends is properly classified as contingent. It differs from (1) because the condition there is contingent on some event which is neither party's control, while the condition in (3) is contingent on an event within the promisee's control.

作为合同条款的条件具有承诺的性质,因此可以称为"承诺性条件",而作为事件的条件则具有偶然性,因此可以称为"偶然性条件"。本章讨论的是偶然性条件。　21.2

条件的分类

偶然性条件又可以分为先决条件和解除条件。先决条件是指合同的生效以双方约定事件的发生为前提条件的;而解除条件则是指合同在生效以后因双方约定事件的发生而告无效。*Chitty on Contracts* 是这样写的:①　21.3

> Contingent conditions may be precedent or subsequent. A condition is precedent if it provides that the contract is not to be binding until the specified event occurs. It is subsequent if it provides that a previously binding contract is to determine on the occurrence of the specified event: e. g. where A contracts to pay an allowance to B until B marries. A provision entitling a party to terminate a contract on the occurrence or non-occurrence of a specified event would likewise amount to, or give rise, to a condition subsequent.

在合同有先决条件的情况下,除非约定的条件得到满足,否则合同当事人没有履行合同的义务。虽然合同当事人没有义务促使或保证约定条件得到满足,但合同当事人不能故意阻止约定条件得到满足。合同的成立以当事人达成协议为基础,即合同在要约得到接受之时成立。除非当事人另有约定,合同成立后即对当事人具有约束力。由于绝大多数商业合同都采用书面形式且双方通常会签署合同,因此在大多数合同中当事人都会约定合同在双方签署后生效。在合同中规定先决条件或解除条件是合同当事人对合同生效或效力的一种限制。大多数船舶建造合同都有生效条款,该条款通常会列明船舶建造合同生效的条件,在这种　21.4

---

① Hugh Beale, *Chitty on Contracts*, 35th edn Sweet & Maxwell 2023, para.4－197.

情况下,船舶建造合同只有在约定的生效条件满足时才生效。

II 合同的生效

SAJ 格式

21.5　　SAJ 格式规定的合同生效条件相当简单:①

> This Contract shall become effective as from the date of execution hereof by the BUYER and the BUILDER.

21.6　　按照上述规定,一旦船厂和船东完成了签署,合同即自双方签署之日起生效。因此,没有双方签署的船舶建造合同就不是生效的合同。

CSTC 格式

21.7　　CSTC 格式也规定了合同的生效条件:②

> This Contract shall become effective upon fulfillment of all the following conditions:
>
> (1) due execution of this Contract and the Specifications; and
> (2) receipt by the SELLER of the first instalment in accordance with Paragraph 3(a) and 4(a) of Article II of this Contract; and
> (3) receipt by the SELLER of a Letter of Guarantee in the form annexed hereto as Exhibit B issued by a first class international bank acceptable to Bank of China and the SELLER in accordance with Article II Paragraph 6 hereof;
> (4) receipt by the BUYER of a Refund Guarantee in the form annexed hereto as Exhibit A issued by Bank of China, Head Office Banking Department in accordance with Article II Paragraph 7 hereof;
> (5) approval by the Board of Director of the BUYER and the Board of Director of China State Shipbuilding Corporation.
>
> If, due to whatever reasons, any one or more of the above conditions fail to be fulfilled by then this contract shall be made null and void, having no effect whatsoever.

---

① Article XIX, para.1.
② Article XVIII.

在合同中规定生效条件有时是出于合同当事人无法控制的原因,例如政府的相关许可等,也可能是由于签署合同的人尚无完全的授权,因此会约定合同的生效"以董事会批准为准"。船舶建造合同中的一个情形是无论是船厂还是船东都希望将合同生效条件掌握在自己手中,这可能是瞬息万变的航运市场使然。但是生效条件过多的话,问题已不再是控制而是合同是否会生效了。虽然合同在船厂收到第一期建造款后才生效对船厂而言比较容易控制,但是否支付第一期建造款实际上是由船东控制的,相反在船东支付第一期建造款之前船厂其实应当首先提供还款保函,而船东在收到还款保函依然没有支付第一期建造款的义务。况且,在有董事会批准这一生效条件情况下,其他的生效条件未必会有太大的意义。CSTC 格式支付条款中关于第一期建造款的支付则有如下规定:①

21.8

> The sum of United States Dollars ＿＿＿＿＿＿＿ (US $ ＿＿＿＿),representing ＿＿＿ percent(＿＿%) of the Contract Price shall become due and payable and be paid by the BUYER on or before this Contract becoming effective and provided that the SELLER shall have submitted to the BUYER the Refund Guarantee in the form annexed hereto as Exhibit "A" issued by Bank of China, Head Office, Banking Department, Beijing, the People's Republic of China, and provided further that the SELLER shall have RECEIVED the first class international Bank's Letter of Guarantee in accordance with Paragraph 6 of this Article.

按照 CSTC 格式的生效条款的规定,船舶建造合同只有当包括船东支付第一期建造款在内的列明五项条件均得到满足时才告生效,但是按照上述规定,船东在收到船厂提供的还款保函后就有义务支付第一期建造款,而且船东支付第一期建造款的义务似乎并不受船舶建造合同是否生效的限制。因此产生的问题是,为船东设定义务的条款在整个船舶建造合同生效之前是否已经对船东产生约束力了。如果有的话,此种约束力的依据又何在;如果没有的话,这一规定又有何意义。即使该规定在整个合同生效之前就已经对船东有约束力了,船东似乎依然可以要求船厂先提供还款保函。一旦船厂向船东提供了还款保函,显然是希望合同生效的,但那时控制合同生效的已不再是船厂,而是船东了。即使已经收到还款保函,但只要船东不支付第一期建造款,建造合同就不会生效。

21.9

---

① Article II.3(a).

NEWBUILDCON 格式

21.10　相比较而言，NEWBUILDCON 格式规定的船舶建造合同生效条件比较合理。首先该格式允许当事人对合同生效条件作出约定，若双方没有约定的合同生效日的，方格 1 中的日期便是合同生效日：①

> This Contract shall become effective when the conditions stated in Box 25 have been satisfied. If no conditions are stated in Box 25 then the effective date of the Contract shall be the date stated in Box 1 ....

Ⅲ 合同的失效

21.11　合同失效是指一个有效的合同因发生双方约定的事件而不再继续有效的情形。SAJ 格式不仅规定船舶建造合同的生效条件，而且还规定了船舶建造合同失效的条件。该格式关于失效条件的规定如下：②

> However, in the event that Export Licence and Construction Permit for the VESSEL shall not have been issued by the Japanese Government with .... (..........) days from the date of this Contract, then, in such case, this Contract shall automatically become null and void, unless otherwise mutually agreed in writing between the parties hereto, and both parties hereto shall be immediately and completely discharged from all of their obligations to each other under this Contract as though this Contract had never been entered into at all.

21.12　按照上述规定，除非双方另有约定，一旦船厂无法在约定的时间内获得船舶出口许可的，合同即告自动失效。

Ⅳ 当事人的行为

因自己过错主张利益

21.13　如果合同生效条件的不成就或失效条件的成就是由于合同一方的过错或懈

---

① Clause 44(a).
② Article XIX, para.2.

急造成的,合同可能并不会因此不生效或失效。在 *New Zealand Shipping Co Ltd* v *Societe des Ateliers et Chantiers de France*① 一案中,原告是船东,被告是船厂。船厂和船东订立船舶建造合同。合同第 5 条有如下规定:

> The said steamer unless the construction thereof shall be delayed by fire, strike, or lock-out of workmen, or any other unpreventable cause beyond the control of the Builders (in which case a fair proportionate extension of time 1918 shall be allowed), shall be completed ready for trial by the 30th October, 1914, and delivered afloat as usual in the port of Dunkirk free of dock and other dues as soon as such trial has been completed to the satisfaction of the Purchasers or their representatives.

合同第 7 条又规定: 21.14

> In the event of the said vessel not being completed and ready for trial on or before 30th October, 1914 ... the Builders undertake to pay the Purchasers as liquidated damages the sum of 10*l*. per working day for each working day during which such delivery may be delayed beyond the 30th October, 1914, unless such delay is due to any of the causes specified in clause 5 hereof ....

而合同的第 12 条则有下列规定: 21.15

> In case the Builders become bankrupt or insolvent or shall fail or be unable to deliver the steamer within eight months from the date agreed by this contract, thereupon this contract shall become void and all money paid by the Purchasers shall be repaid to them with interest accrued thereupon at 5 per cent .... Except only in the event of France becoming engaged in a European war, then the above limit of eight months shall be extended equal to the duration of the said war, but in no case to exceed eighteen months in all.

船厂和船东后来将 1914 年 10 月改为了 1915 年 1 月 30 日。1914 年 8 月 2 日,法国加入了欧洲战争。18 个月后船舶的建造依然没有完成。船厂认为船舶建造合同在 1916 年 7 月 30 日即告无效,而船东则认为宣告合同无效是他们的选择权。仲裁庭认为船舶建造合同在 1916 年 7 月 30 日即告无效。高院和上诉法院均认为仲裁庭的裁决是正确的。枢密院的 Lord Kinlay 说:② 21.16

---

① [1919] AC 1.
② [1919] AC 1 at 6 & 8.

> It is a principle of law that no one can in such case take advantage of the existence of a state of things which he himself produced.
>
> The decisions on the point are uniform, and are really illustrations of the very old principle laid down by Lord Coke(Co Litt 206b) that a man shall not be allowed to take advantage of a condition which he himself brought about. In the present case the builder was in no way responsible for the non-completion within eighteen months, and there is no reason why clause 12 should not be interpreted according to the natural meaning of the words so as to render the contract void.

21.17　枢密院的 Lord Atkinson 也认为合同当事人不能以自己的行为来影响合同的效力,他说:①

> The application to contracts such as these of the principle that a man shall not be permitted to take advantage of his own wrong thus necessarily leaves to the blameless party an option whether he will or will not insist on the stipulation that the contract shall be void on the happening of the named event. To deprive him of that option would be but to effectuate the purpose of the blameable party. When this option is left to the blameless party, it is said that the contract is voidable, but that is only another way of saying that the blameable party cannot himself have the contract made void, cannot force the other party to do so, and cannot deprive the latter of his right to do so. Of course, the parties may expressly or impliedly stipulate that the contract shall be voidable at the option of either party to it.

21.18　在发生约定事件时,因自己的过错造成事件发生的一方不能主张合同无效,只有另一方才能主张合同无效。Lord Wrenbury 是这样说的:②

> The rule is that in a contract "void" is to be read "voidable," if the result of reading it as "void" would be to enable a party to avail himself of his own wrong to defeat his contract. It may be stated either in the form that if one party is in default it is "void as against him," or that if one party is in default it is "voidable at the option of the other party." The two amount to the same thing. But the contract is not "void" in favour of or "voidable at the option of" the party in default. He cannot say that it is void, and has no option of avoiding it in his own wrong.

---

① [1919] AC 1 at 9.
② [1919] AC 1 at 15.

> Here the contract is, in my opinion, voidable at the option of either party provided always that he is not seeking to avoid it in his own wrong.

合同当事人不能因自己的错误行为而获益这一原则似乎并不仅仅是一个解释原则，而且也是法律原则。在 *Cheall* v *Association of Professional Executive Clerical and Computer Staff(APEX)* 一案中，上议院对 *New Zealand Shipping* 案予以了进一步的说明，上议院认为负有义务应当是指对合同另一方负有义务，如果是对第三人负有义务则不构成上述原则的适用。Lord Diplock 说：① 21.19

> [In] the *New Zealand Shipping* case [1919] AC 1 ... reference was made by all their Lordships to the well known rule of construction that, except in the unlikely case that the contract contains clear express provisions to the contrary, it is to be presumed that it was not the intention of the parties that either party should be entitled to rely upon his own breaches of his primary obligations as bringing the contract to an end, i.e. as terminating any further primary obligations on his part then remaining unperformed. This rule of construction, which is paralleled by the rule of law that a contracting party cannot rely upon an event brought about by his own breach of contract as having terminated a contract by frustration, is often expressed in broad language as: "A man cannot be permitted to take advantage of his own wrong." But this may be misleading if it is adopted without defining the breach of duty to which the pejorative word "wrong" is intended to refer and the person to whom the duty is owed.... To attract the principle, whether it be one of construction or one of law, that a party to a contract is not permitted to take advantage of his own breach of duty, the duty must be one that is owed to the other party under that contract; breach of a duty whether contractual or non-contractual owed to a stranger to the contract does not suffice.

解释问题

普通法有一项原则，即任何人均不得利用自己的过错主张利益。但是合同当事人应当可以通过合同约定排除这一原则的适用，是否确已排除这一原则的适用在很大程度上取决于对合同相关条款的解释。在 *Gyllenhammar & Partners* 21.20

---

① [1983] 2 AC 180.

International Ltd v Sour Brodogradevna Split[①] 一案中,1986 年 6 月 12 日,船东和船厂订立了一个船舶建造合同,由船厂为船东建造一艘 42,000/48,000 载重吨的散货船,价格为 15,125,000 美元,船号为 358。同日,船厂给予船东再建造一艘姐妹船的选择权。1988 年 4 月 12 日,船东行使了选择权,和船厂又订立一个船舶建造合同,规定由船厂为船东再建造一艘 42,000/48,000 的散货船,合同价格依然是 15,125,000 美元,船号为 365。该船舶建造合同的第 23 条规定:

This Contract is subject to:

(a) The Builder declaring by telex to the Buyer and the Bank that the Letter of Guarantee, as provided for in Article 15(2) of the Contract, has been obtained and airmailed to the Bank at 9 King Street, London EC2V 6EA(telex 8812511) and that a copy thereof has been faxed to the Bank(fax no. 7268930).

(b) The Builder declaring by telex to the Buyer and the Bank that all necessary permissions and approvals have been obtained.

(c) The payment by the Buyer of the first instalment of per Article 5(a) of the Contract. If(a)and(b)above are not obtained within thirty(30) days of the date of this Contract, or if the first instalment as per Article 5(a)is not paid within ten(10) days of its due date this Contract, unless otherwise mutually agreed, shall become null and void.

21.21　合同订立后市场开始上扬,1987 年同类船舶的市场价已从 1,600 万至 1,700 万美元上涨至 2,100 万美元了。在规定的 30 天期限届满前,船厂告诉船东无法在期限内获得必要的许可和批准,要求将期限延长 30 天,船东同意延长 30 天。1988 年 5 月 30 日,船厂通过电传通知船东,银行担保和必要的许可和批准均未获得,因此船号为 365 的船舶建造合同无效。船东起诉,要求实际履行或者赔偿损失。船厂认为,按照第 23 条的规定,一旦约定情形在规定时间内没有发生的,无论自己是否有过失合同均自动无效。但船东则认为获得银行担保是船厂的义务,船厂的行为构成了对其主要义务的违反,因此不能援引第 23 条的规定。如果船厂没有尽全力,同样不能援引第 23 条的规定。船东的依据便是任何人不得以自己的违约行为免除继续履行合同的义务。船东认为在第 23 条中应当存在默示规定,即船厂应当尽全力获得银行担保和许可。高院的 Hirst 法官认为当事人不能

---

① [1989] 2 Lloyd's Rep 403.

凭自己的违约行为获利是以没有明示约定为前提的,而第 23 条的(a)和(c)似乎只能是在违反约定的情况下才可能发生的,他说:①

> It follows that the defendants are entitled to succeed, because, as is common ground, sub-cl.(a) was not satisfied since the telex was not sent, and the letter of guarantee had not been obtained; and sub-cl.(b) was not satisfied seeing that the telex was not sent, and, for the reasons given below, the necessary permissions and approvals of the National Bank of Yugoslavia and the National Bank of Croatia had not been obtained. Nor had the approval of the yard's commercial bankers been obtained if, contrary to my view expressed below, that falls within the ambit of sub-cl.(b).

Hirst 法官认为 *New Zealand* 一案确立的原则只是解释的原则而已,因此当事人可以通过明确的约定予以排除。他说:② 21.22

> I also derive support from the passage quoted above from Lord Justice Donaldson dissenting judgment in the *Cheall* case in the Court of Appeal, which underlines the point that the *New Zealand* rule is no more than a principle of construction which can be displaced by the express terms of the clause itself.

主观意志

在 *Fast Ferries One SA* v *Ferries Australia Pty Ltd* ③ 一案中,船舶建造合同的第9.1.2条有如下规定: 21.23

> Failure of Debis to provide finance necessary for the Purchaser to acquire the vessel on delivery, despite the Purchaser having met all conditions specified in the commitment letter will not constitute a default on the part of the Purchaser. For such instance the deposit paid … will be refunded to the Purchaser and the contract will be deemed to be cancelled.

而合同的第 27 条则规定如下先决条件: 21.24

> This agreement is conditional upon Debis agreeing to provide finance for

---

① [1989] 2 Lloyd's Rep 403 at 416.
② Ibid.
③ [2000] 1 Lloyd's Rep 534.

the vessel on terms and conditions which are satisfactory to the purchaser and builder.

The above condition shall be met before the 28th February 1995 for this agreement to become effective.

21.25 船东支付了定金后便开始与融资人以及船厂就融资问题进行谈判，但最终没有获得融资。船东要求船厂返还定金但遭到船厂的拒绝，理由是船东并未采取 all reasonable steps and exercise best endeavours 争取到融资，因而构成违约。但是法院并没有支持船厂的观点，法院认为双方约定的合同生效条件是船厂和船东满意，而满意是主观的。高院的 David Steel 法官是这样说的：①

> ... it is important to bear in mind that the contract had been conditional on the provision of finance by Debis on terms that were satisfactory to both parties. The assessment of what were to be regarded as satisfactory terms was by definition to be an entirely subjective matter from each party's perspective. They had reached the stage where they were both satisfied with the terms of the somewhat ineptly titled commitment letter. In short the parties were agreed on the "finance terms": the only outstanding matter was the need for credit committee approval which was perceived as being no more than a formality. While a term could readily be implied that neither party would prevent approval being given on the terms offered (eg by withdrawing the application), there is no basis (let alone necessity) for implying any term to the effect that either party was under an obligation to accept different finance terms.

---

① [2000] 1 Lloyd's Rep 534 at 541.

第 22 章 解　释

Ⅰ　概述

合同解释,简而言之,是指法院确定书面合同中的文字应当具有的法律含义的过程。对书面合同进行解释的目的是从中找出合同当事人的共同意图。对书面合同进行解释应当是客观的,而不是主观的,换言之,法院需要找出的并不是当事人的真实意图或者理解,而是一个具有合同当事人在缔约时应当具备的背景知识的合理的第三人应当有的理解。①

22.1

缔约的情形

合同的解释是在合同订立之后进行的,在法院对合同进行解释时的相关情形有可能和合同订立时的相关情形有所不同,因此法院应当根据合同订立时的情形对合同进行解释。正如上议院的 Lord Dunedin 在 *Charrington & Co Ltd* v *Wooder* 一案中所说的:②

22.2

> Now, in order to construe a contract the Court is always entitled to be so far instructed by evidence as to be able to place itself in thought in the same position as the parties to the contract were placed, in fact, when they made it — or, as it is sometimes phrased, to be informed as to the surrounding circumstances. As Lord Davey says in the case of *Bank of New Zealand* v *Simpson* ([1900] AC 183), quoting from a decision of Lord Blackburn's, "The general rule seems to be that all facts are admissible(to proof) which tend to shew the sense the words bear with reference to the surrounding circumstances of and concerning which the words were used."

---

① Hugh Beale, *Chitty on Contracts*, 35rd edn Sweet & Maxwell 2023, para.16 – 047.
② [1914] AC 71 at 82.

22.3　法院应当考虑的缔约当时的情形包括一方或双方当事人均未予以考虑或重视的事实,上议院的 Lord Wilberforce 在 *Reardon Smith Line Ltd* v *Yngvar Hansen-Tangen* 一案中是这样说的:①

> I think that all of their Lordships are saying, in different words, the same thing — what the court must do must be to place itself in thought in the same factual matrix as that in which the parties were. All of these opinions seem to me implicitly to recognise that, in the search for the relevant background, there may be facts which form part of the circumstances in which the parties contract in which one, or both, may take no particular interest, their minds being addressed to or concentrated on other facts so that if asked they would assert that they did not have these facts in the forefront of their mind, but that will not prevent those facts from forming part of an objective setting in which the contract is to be construed.

解释的原则

22.4　在 *Investors Compensation Scheme Ltd* v *West Bromwich Building Society* 一案中,上议院的 Lord Hoffmann 对之前的先例做了总结归纳,更为清晰地提出了合同解释的原则,他说:②

> I think I should preface my explanation of my reasons with some general remarks about the principles by which contractual documents are nowadays construed. I do not think that the fundamental change which has overtaken this branch of the law, particularly as a result of the speeches of Lord Wilberforce in *Prenn* v *Simmonds* [1971] 1 WLR 1381, 1384-1386 and *Reardon Smith Line Ltd* v *Yngvar Hansen-Tangen* [1976] 1 WLR 989, is always sufficiently appreciated. The result has been, subject to one important exception, to assimilate the way in which such documents are interpreted by judges to the common sense principles by which any serious utterance would be interpreted in ordinary life. Almost all the old intellectual baggage of "legal" interpretation has been discarded. The principles may be summarised as follows:
>
> (1) Interpretation is the ascertainment of the meaning which the document would convey to a reasonable person having all the

---

① [1976] 1 WLR 989 at 997.
② [1998] 1 WLR 896 at 912.

background knowledge which would reasonably have been available to the parties in the situation in which they were at the time of the contract.

(2) The background was famously referred to buy Lord Wilberforce as the "matrix of fact", but this phrase is, if anything, an understated description of what the background may include. Subject to the requirement that it should have been reasonably available to the parties and to the exception to be mentioned next, it includes absolutely anything which would have affected the way in which the language of the document would have been understood by a reasonable man.

(3) The law excludes from the admissible background the previous negotiations of the parties and their declarations of subjective intent. They are admissible only in an action for rectification. The law makes this distinction for reasons of practical policy and, in this respect only, legal interpretation differs from the way we would interpret utterances in ordinary life. The boundaries of this exception are in some respects unclear. But this is not the occasion on which to explore them.

(4) The meaning which a document(or any other utterance) would convey to a reasonable man is not the same thing as the meaning of its words. The meaning of words is a matter of dictionaries and grammars; the meaning of the document is what the parties using those words against the relevant background would reasonably have been understood to mean. The background may not merely enable the reasonable man to choose between the possible meanings of words which are ambiguous but even(as occasionally happens in ordinary life) to conclude that the parties must, for whatever reason, have used the wrong words or syntax: see *Mannai Investments Co Ltd* v *Eagle Star Life Assurance Co Ltd* [1997] AC 749.

(5) The "rule" that words should be given their "natural and ordinary meaning" reflects the common sense proposition that we do not easily accept that people have made linguistic mistakes, particularly in formal documents. On the other hand, if one would nevertheless conclude from the background that something must have gone wrong with the language, the law does not require judges to attribute to the parties an intention which they plainly could not have had.

Lord Hoffmann 归纳的解释原则是:(1)解释是确定文件向合理的第三人传

达意思;(2)解释应当考虑所有背景事实;(3)当事人间之前的磋商等不予考虑;(4)文字的含义并不取决于其本身的含义,而是在考虑了背景事实后向合理第三人传达的含义;(5)文字应当具有自然和正常的意义。

II 文件间的关系

概述

22.5　书面合同可能仅由一份文件组成,也可能会由不同文件组成。在组成合同的文件有两份或两份以上的情况下,一旦发生歧义或冲突就会产生以哪一份文件为准的问题。这也是法院在解释合同时应当考虑的问题,当事人也可以对不同文件的适用优先作出约定。

建造合同特征

22.6　船舶建造合同是一个比较典型的例子,船舶建造合同的文件通常包括合同文本、规格书、图纸和厂商表等。如果存在修改项目,船厂和船东之间的来往邮件和签署的文件同样成为船舶建造合同的组成部分。大多数船舶建造合同都会对不同文件的适用优先作出规定,例如SAJ格式便针对这一问题作出了如下规定:①

> All general language or requirements embodied in the Specifications are intended to amplify, explain and implement the requirements of this Contract. However, in the event that any language or requirements so embodied permit of an interpretation inconsistent with any provisions of this Contract, then, in each and every such event, the applicable provisions of this Contract shall prevail and govern. The Specifications and Plan are also intended to explain each other, and anything shown on the Plan and not stipulation in the Specifications or stipulated in the Specifications and not shown on the Plan shall be deemed and considered as if embodied in both. In the event of conflict between the Specifications and Plan, the Specifications shall prevail and govern.

22.7　规格书实际上是对合同文本的规定进行补充、解释和细化。合同文本与规格书发生冲突或有歧义的,以合同内容为准。规格书和总布置图之间的关系则是相

---

① Article XX.2, see also AWES Article 1(a).

互解释的关系,总布置图中有而规格书中没有的内容或者规格书中有而总布置图中没有的内容应当视为规格书和总布置图中都有。当规格书和总布置图发生冲突或有歧义时以规格书为准。① Norwegian 格式也有类似规定:②

> In the event of inconsistency between this Standard Form Shipbuilding Contract and the Specifications and/or the Drawings, this Standard Form Shipbuilding Contract shall prevail. In the event of inconsistency between the Specifications and the Drawings, the Specifications shall prevail. In case of inconsistency between any of the Drawings, the later in date shall prevail.

按照 Norwegian 格式的规定,虽然规格书和图纸发生冲突同样以规格书为准,但不再把规格书或图纸所有的内容视为图纸或规格书也有。因此,一旦规格书和图纸发生冲突的,适用的应当是规格书。在规定不同文件的效力以及适用优先问题上,NEWBUILDCON 格式的规定比较全面,该格式的第一部分有如下内容: 22.8

> This Contract consists of Part I including additional clauses, if any agreed and stated in Box 34, and Part II as well as any Annexes agreed and attached hereto and shall be performed subject to the conditions contained herein. In the event of a conflict of conditions the provisions of Part I shall prevail over those of Part II to the extent of such conflict, but not further.
>
> The Specification, Maker's List, Plans, and/or Drawings hereafter approved by the Buyer shall form part of this Contract, but in the event of conflict between the provisions of this Contract and the Specification, Maker's List, Plans and/or drawings, the provisions of this Contract shall prevail. In the event of inconsistency between the Specification and Maker's List, on the one hand and the Plans and/or Drawings on the other, the Specifications/Maker's List shall prevail. In the case of inconsistency between any of the Plans and/or Drawings, the later in date shall prevail.

NEWBUILDCON 格式的第一部分或方格部分的内容主要包括当事人情况、船舶描述、建造不符合基本性能保证的合同价格调整、延迟交船的合同价格调整、 22.9

---

① 如果总布置图中有的内容应视为规格书中也有,相反亦然,在总布置图和规格书之间应当不会再发生冲突。
② Article II.1.

付款保函和还款保函、中止和终止的规定、管辖权及争议解决条款、生效条款、选择权以及合同担保人等。双方另外约定的补充条款也视为第一部分的内容。NEWBUILDCON 格式第二部分则是其他条款。第一部分和第二部分内容发生冲突或有歧义的，以第一部分的内容为准。

22.10　　规格书、厂商表、总布置图及其他图纸经船东同意的则成为合同的一部分。如果合同文本的内容与规格书、厂商表、总布置图及其他图纸发生冲突或有歧义的，以合同文本的内容为准。规格书、厂商表与总布置图和其他图纸发生冲突或有歧义的，以规格书和厂商表为准。如果总布置图和其他图纸发生冲突或有歧义的，以日期在后的图纸为准。

Ⅲ　整体协议

概述

22.11　　在合同中加入整体协议条款（entire agreement clause）的目的是确保合同包含了当事人的所有权利和义务，任何一方当事人都不得以合同规定以外的东西主张权利。SAJ 格式规定：①

> This Contract contains the entire agreement and understanding between the parties hereto and supersedes all prior negotiations, representations, undertakings and agreements on any subject matter of this Contract.

22.12　　NEWBUILDCON 格式也规定：②

> This Contract constitutes the entire agreement between the Parties and no promise, understanding, representation, warranty or statement by either Party to the date of this Contract stated in Box 1 shall affect this Contract. Any modification of this Contract shall not be of any effect unless in writing signed by or on behalf of the Parties.

22.13　　船厂和船东在约定整体协议条款时应注意"合同"的范围，即整体协议提及的"合同"包括哪些文件。从 SAJ 格式的规定来看，"Contract"一字虽然第一字母采用了大写，但并没有特定的含义。从 SAJ 格式的上下文来看，"Contract"应当是指合同文本，不包括规格书、图纸和厂商表等。因此船厂和船东达成的整体协

---

① Article XX.3.
② Clause 47.

议应当以合同文本的内容为限。而 NEWBUILDCON 格式中的"Contract"则有特定含义,它既包括合同文本的第一部分以及补充条款,也包括合同文本的第二部分以及由规格书和厂商表组成的附录和图纸。因此,该格式的整体协议条款中的"Contract"所包含的内容远大于 SAJ 格式整体协议中的"Contract"。

缔约前的承诺

在 Ravennavi SpA v New Century Shipbuilding Co Ltd① 一案中,船厂和船东订立了选择权协议,船东可以选择继续建造两艘原油油轮和成品油油轮,分别于 2007 年 10 月 31 日和 12 月 31 日交船。选择权协议同时规定只要有可能,船厂就会尽量提前交船。船东宣布建造两艘选择船,交船日为 2007 年的 10 月和 12 月,双方签署了包含一整体协议条款的船舶建造合同。几个月后,船东发现船厂正在与其他船东磋商更早交船日的船舶建造。船东起诉,主张船厂违反了选择权协议规定的提前交船的义务。法院认为,选择权协议确实设立了在有可能时提前交船期的持续性义务,但是该义务在船厂和船东订立包含整体协议条款的船舶建造合同时就消失了。船东上诉,上诉法院认为一旦船舶建造合同订立后,双方应当以合同约定而不是选择权协议内容为准。Moore-Bick 法官说:

22.14

> ... It was the parties' intention that the Yard should offer the Buyer an earlier date for delivery if one became available prior to the exercise of the option, but that once the option had been exercised the delivery date would be fixed once and for all (subject, of course, to any subsequent renegotiation) and would appear as such in Article VII.1 of the formal contract.

误述

误述是指虚假的陈述。实际上陈述可以有不同的种类和性质,例如事实陈述、观点陈述、意图陈述或者是评论性的陈述。按照传统的原则,只有虚假的事实陈述才会构成误述。观点陈述即使被证明是没有依据也不构成误述,而意图陈述即使没有付诸实施也不构成误述,因为这些陈述均不构成关于事实的陈述。②

22.15

在 1967 年《误述法》(Misrepresentation Act 1967)颁布之前,普通法的原则

22.16

---

① [2007] 1 CLC 176.
② Hugh Beale, *Chitty on Contracts*, 35th edn Sweet & Maxwell 2023, para.10 - 007.

是：合同一方因对方的误述而与之订立合同的有权解除合同，但通常没有权利主张损害赔偿，除非误述构成欺诈性误述，或特定情况下的疏忽性误述，或者误述已具有合同效力。① 在 1967 年《误述法》颁布之后，只要在相同情况下可以针对欺诈性误述主张损害赔偿的，受误述影响而订立合同的一方就可以针对所有疏忽性误述主张损害赔偿。1967 年《误述法》有如下规定：②

> Where a person has entered into a contract after a misrepresentation has been made to him, and
> (a) the misrepresentation has become a term of the contract; or
> (b) the contract has been performed;
> or both, then, if otherwise he would be entitled to rescind the contract without alleging fraud, he shall be so entitled, subject to the provisions of this Act, notwithstanding the matters mentioned in paragraphs (a) and (b) of this section.

22.17　虽然合同中的整体协议条款具有排除当事人之间其他约定的效力，但整体协议并不能排除误述的适用，即因对方误述而订立合同的一方当事人可以误述为由解除合同。在 AXA Sun Life Services Plc v Campbell Martin Ltd③ 一案中，合同的第 24 条是整体协议条款，该条款规定：

> This Agreement and the Schedules and documents referred to herein constitute the entire agreement and understanding between you and us in relation to the subject matter thereof. Without prejudice to any variation as provided in clause 1.1, this Agreement shall supersede any prior promises, agreements, representations, undertakings or implications whether made orally or in writing between you and us relating to the subject matter of this Agreement but this will not affect any obligations in any such prior agreement which are expressed to continue after termination.

22.18　上诉法院的 Stanley Burnton 法官认为当事人可以在整体协议条款中排除误述，但是否有效排除则是条款的解释问题。他说：④

> I have no doubt that clause 24 does not exclude or supersede misrepresentations as to matters that are not the subject of the terms of the Agreement. Notwithstanding the words "This Agreement …

---

① Hugh Beale, *Chitty on Contracts*, 35th edn Sweet & Maxwell 2023, para.10 – 001.
② s.1.
③ [2011] 1 CLC 312.
④ [2011] 1 CLC 312 at 324.

constitute the entire agreement and understanding between us in relation to the subject matter thereof" and "this Agreement shall supersede any prior ... representations ... between you and us relating to the subject matter of this Agreement" I do not think that the clause is sufficiently clear for this purpose. Indeed, I have difficulty in seeing how a written agreement can "supersede" a representation that does not relate to the terms of the agreement. Thus I think that a representation by AXA such as "We are the largest insurance company in the country", if false and relied upon, is not superseded by the clause.

而上诉法院的 Rix 法官则认为整体协议条款关系到合同当事人同意的事宜, 而误述则是合同当事人没有同意的事宜,因此整体协议条款与误述无关。他是这样说的:① 22.19

> I would be inclined, subject to authority, to regard clause 24 as being concerned only with matters of agreement, and not with misrepresentation at all. The essence of agreement is that it is concerned with matters which the parties have agreed. The essence of misrepresentation, however, is that it is not concerned with what the parties have agreed, but rather with inaccurate statements (innocently, negligently or fraudulently inaccurate statements) which have been made by one party to the other, have been relied on by the representee in entering into their agreement, and which may give the representee rights to rescind that agreement and/or claim tortious or quasi-tortious damages by reason of loss arising out of entering into the agreement ..., I would thus provisionally conclude that misrepresentation and the exclusion of misrepresentation or liability for it are simply not the business of the clause at all.

按照 1967 年《误述法》的规定,即使当事人在合同中约定排除误述救济的适用,此种约定也同样是无效的:② 22.20

> If any agreement (whether made before or after the commencement of this Act) contains a provision which would exclude or restrict –
>
> (a) any liability to which a party to a contract may be subject by reason of any misrepresentation made by him before the contract was made; or

---

① [2011] 1 CLC 312 at 333.

② s.3.

(b) any remedy available to another party to the contract by reason of such a misrepresentation;

that provision shall be of no effect except to the extent(if any) that, in any proceedings arising out of the contract, the court or arbitrator may allow reliance on it as being fair and reasonable in the circumstances of the case.

第 23 章　选择权

I　选择权概述

一般选择权

23.1　选择权(option),顾名思义,是一项权利,一项作出选择的权利,正如上议院的 Lord Devlin 在 *Reardon Smith Line Ltd* v *Ministry of Agriculture, Fisheries and Food* 一案中所指出的:①

> My Lords, "option" in its widest interpretation means simply choice or freedom of choice. An obligation in a contract can frequently be performed in a large number of ways and the party under obligation can choose any one of ways that he likes .... There is, however, a narrower sense in which the word can be used, and that is to confer a right of choice specially granted to the holder of the option and to be used solely for his own benefit. It is in this sense, I think, that the word is generally used in the business world.

23.2　*Chitty on Contracts* 通过将"选择权"与"优先购买权"进行比较对"选择权"作出了如下解释:②

> An *option* has at least some of the characteristics of an offer in that it can become a contract of sale when the purchaser accepts it by exercising the option; and it cannot have this effect where it fails to specify the price. A *right of pre-emption*, on the other hand, is not itself an offer but an undertaking to make an offer in certain specified future circumstances. An agreement conferring such a right is, therefore, not void for uncertainty merely because it fails to specify the

---

① [1963] AC 691 at 729.
② Hugh Beale, *Chitty on Contracts*, 33rd edn Sweet & Maxwell 2019, para.2 - 135.

price. It obliges the landowner to offer the land to the purchaser at a price at which he is in fact prepared to sell; and if the purchaser accepts that offer there is no uncertainty as to price. This is so even though the parties have described the right as an "option" when its true legal nature is that of a right of preemption.

标准格式中的选择权

23.3　船舶建造中的选择权是指船东在已经订造船舶的前提下选择以相同价格和船型要求船厂另行建造一艘或多艘船舶的权利。选择权可以采用船舶建造合同条款的形式，也可以采用独立的协议的形式。关于选择权的约定是以船东和船厂订立船舶建造合同为前提的，换言之，没有船舶建造合同的存在，就没有船东选择权的行使。NEWBUILDCON 格式可能是唯一有选择权条款的船舶建造合同标准格式，该格式规定：①

The Buyer shall have the option for the construction by the Builder of additional vessels as stated in Box 27 at the contract price and delivery dates stated in Box 28, but otherwise on the same terms and conditions as this Contract with logical amendments. Such option must be declared by the Buyer to the Builder within the number of months stated in Box 29 following the Effective date of this Contract referred to in Clause 44 (Effective date of Contract).

II　船舶建造选择权

要约的特征

23.4　船厂在船舶建造合同中或在单独的协议中同意船东享有选择权的做法具有要约的某些特性。这是船厂向船东发出的一个要约，只要船东作出的要求建造船舶的选择符合选择权协议的规定，船舶建造合同就将在船东和船厂之间成立。选择权约定或选择权协议的一个明显特征是双方已经对价格作出了约定，没有约定价格而留待双方另行磋商的也就丧失了选择权的意义。在船舶建造中，没有约定船舶价格的选择权协议实质上对船厂是没有约束力的，因此也就不再是一种选择

---

① Clause 46.

权。船厂同意给船东选择权的要约虽然会过期,但船厂不能撤销。船厂一旦撤销选择权要约就意味着违反了选择权协议或选择权承诺。同意给船东选择权的船厂负有其选择权要约在得到接受后履行合同的义务。

Halsbury's Laws of England 把选择权合同解释为给予选择权一方受选择权合同的约束,在享有选择权的一方作出选择后与其订立合同:① 23.5

> A contract of option is one whereby the grantor of the option offers to enter into what may be called a "major" contract with a second person and makes a separate contract to keep his offer open. Usually, but not necessarily, the person to whom the grantor of the option binds himself to keep the offer open is that second person, who may be conveniently referred to as the "option-holder". The contract of option may make it possible for the rights of the option-holder to be assigned.

单方的选择

虽然选择权协议既可以是单方的,也可以是双方的,但是船舶建造实践中的选择权始终是单方的,即只有船东有权选择按照约定的价格和技术规范与船厂另行订立船舶建造合同。在选择权协议中享有权利的是船东,负有义务的则是船厂。船东是主动的,船厂是被动的。拥有选择权对船东而言意味着一种机会,船东可以根据市场情况决定是否选择订立新的船舶建造合同。正如 Hoffmann 法官在 *Spiro v Glencrown Properties Ltd* 一案说的,给予选择权的一方并没有给接受方设定任何义务,而是为自己设定了义务,一旦接受方作出了选择,就与其订立合同。他说的是:② 23.6

> The granting of the option imposes no obligation on the purchaser and an obligation on the vendor which is contingent on the exercise of the option. When the option is exercised, vendor and purchaser come under obligations to perform as if they had concluded an ordinary contract of sale. And the analogy of an irrevocable offer is, as I have said, a useful way of describing the position of the purchaser between the grant and exercise of the option.

---

① *Halsbury's Laws of England*, 5th edn-Contract Vol 22(2019) para.41.
② [1991] Ch 531 at 543.

III 选择权的给予

原因

23.7　　船厂同意给船东选择权多半出于开拓业务的目的,但无论从哪个角度说,选择权协议对船厂来说始终是一种义务或负担。一旦与船东订立了选择权协议,在约定的船东行使选择权的期间内,船厂就很难另行接单。因为一旦船东作出了选择,建造船舶就成为船厂的合同义务了。船厂给予船东选择权多半是由于市场不景气的缘故,船厂希望能获得更多的订单。但是选择权协议的订立必定会给船厂带来限制。在市场处于平稳的状态时,选择权协议未必会给船厂带来太大的风险,但当市场开始上扬,尤其是快速上扬时,船厂就会比较被动。由于市场上扬,船东行使选择权的可能性就大大增加。与此同时,船厂在市场上接单也会变得容易,而且价格一定会高于已经订立船舶建造合同的合同价格。在这种情况下,即使船厂愿意自行在市场上接单,但鉴于选择权协议,船厂自由接单的机会无疑会受到限制。相反,如果选择权协议订立后,市场开始下滑,几乎可以肯定的是船东不会行使选择权。因此,选择权协议对船厂来说实际上并不会带来真正的利益。

影响

23.8　　在实践中,通常是船东要求船厂给予自己建造船舶的选择权,这本是船东对未来市场的一种投机。如前所述,此种投机既无需船东承担任何风险,也无需船东支付任何费用,因此船东享有选择权永远是一件好事。相对而言,船厂给船东选择权则永远是一种负担和风险。为了不至于使自己处于过于被动的地位,船厂在同意和船东订立选择权协议或同意给予船东选择权时应当考虑以下几点:第一,船东行使选择权的时间限制;船东可以行使选择权的时间期限越长对船厂就越不利,因此船厂应当注意在给船东选择权的同时应当在行使选择权的时间上予以限制;第二,如果船东可以选择数艘船舶的,船厂应当约定船东必须同时对所有船舶作出选择;第三,在选择权协议中不应规定具体的选择船的交船日期或期间,相反应当规定交船日期按照船厂当时的实际情况予以约定;第四,船厂应设定可以控制合同生效的条件。

IV 选择权的行使

如果选择权协议规定了船东行使选择权必须满足的前提条件,船东作出的选择只有在满足了规定的前提条件时才是有效的。在 *Haugland Tankers AS v RMK Marine Gemi Yapim Sanayii ve Deniz Tasimaciligi Iisletmesi AS* [①]一案中,船东和船厂订立了船舶建造合同,由船厂为船东建造一艘成品油轮,船号是 63。双方还签署了一个选择权协议,赋予船东以相同的合同条件向船厂购买一艘与 63 号油轮相同船舶的选择权。选择权协议包含如下内容:

23.9

> 2. Upon the exercise by the BUYER of the Option as per clause 4 below the SELLER shall enter into a Shipbuilding Contract (the Option Contract) for the Option Vessel.
>
> 4. The Option shall be declared by the BUYER by the service of notice latest within 6 months after effectiveness of Contract for Hull No 63. Simultaneously, the BUYER shall be required to pay one percent(1%) (Commitment Fee) of the Contract Price to the SELLER. In case the remaining fourteen percent(14%) of the Contract Price as the remaining part of the first instalment which shall become due upon notice of construction of the Vessel is not paid by BUYER, then the SELLER shall have the right to retain the commitment fee of 1% and this Option Agreement shall become null and void.
>
> 6. The execution of the new Shipbuilding Contract, pursuant to this Option Agreement, shall take place on or before April 10, 2004.

此后,双方又订立了选择权协议的补充协议,对船东行使选择权作出了新的规定:

23.10

> The Optional Vessel to be declared by Buyer within 6 months after the first instalment for the firm Vessel is received by Builder, and the Builder shall commence production within 9 months after declaration of the Option Vessel by Buyer and shall deliver the Option Vessel 16 months after commencement of its production.

63 号油轮的第一期款是在 2004 年 6 月 16 日支付的,船东在 2004 年 12 月 2

23.11

[①] [2005] 1 CLC 271.

日作出了购买相同船舶的选择,并要求船厂提供选择船的建造合同文本。但是船东并未按照第 4 条的规定支付 1% 的承诺费。6 个月的期限届满后,船厂主张由于船东没有支付承诺费,因此船东的选择是无效的。船东则认为从整个选择权协议来看,承诺费应当在协议生效之时且在船厂提供了还款保函之后支付。法院认为按照第 4 条的规定,支付承诺费是船东作出选择的前提条件,船东应当在作出选择之时支付承诺费。高院的 Langley 法官说:①

> ... in my judgment, ... simultaneous payment was a condition precedent to or a requirement for the proper exercise of the Option. The matter is one largely of impression but, insofar as analysis is available:
>
> (i) The entire and short agreement is an "Option Agreement" and so likely to address only matters material to its exercise and the resulting Option Contract should it be exercised.
> (ii) Clause 2 refers to "the exercise" of the Option "as per clause 4". Whilst it is true that Clause 4 contains, in the third and subsequent sentences, matters which do not relate to the exercise of the Option but to the consequences of payment of the Commitment Fee and circumstances in which the Option Agreement will be "null and void", the first two sentences do not use the word "exercise" but refer to the claimant "declaring" the Option and paying the fee.
> (iii) The word "simultaneously" is much stronger than, say, "upon giving notice". The notice and payment must be given and made at the same time and so, I think, usually as part of a single process in this case of exercising the Option.
> (iv) The language of "Commitment Fee" suggests that payment of the Fee is part of what is required to secure the commitment of the defendant to the bilateral contract which would come into existence upon exercise of the Option.

---

① [2005] 1 CLC 271 at 279.

第 24 章 其他规定

I 设计和图纸费用

24.1 船舶建造合同的价格为固定价格,除非另有约定,① 合同价格通常包括完成船舶建造所需的所有成本和费用。SAJ 格式中的"合同价格"并没有定义,但是该合同价格不包括船东供应品。② 另外,SAJ 格式还特别规定合同价格包括设计和供应图纸的费用:③

> It is hereby mutually confirmed that the Contract Price includes the expenses amounting to ¥........................ for design and supply of drawings as the technical services required to be rendered by the BUILDER under this Contract.

24.2 SAJ 格式是唯一明文规定合同价格包括设计和图纸费用的船舶建造合同标准格式。在船舶建造合同约定船厂负有设计义务时,即使没有上述规定,船厂依然应当承担设计和图纸的费用。

II 第三人权利

24.3 这里的"第三人"相对于合同当事人而言,是指合同当事人以外的任何人。普通法中的合同相对性原则的基本含义是合同既不能赋予第三人权利,也不能为第三人设定义务。合同相对性受到很多的批评并最终导致 1999 年《合同(第三人权利)法》(Contracts(Rights of Third Parties) Act 1999)的颁布。该法创立了普通法合同相对性原则的一个例外。该法的目的是确保第三人可以执行合同当事人

---

① 例如因船东提出修改请求或船级社规范或船旗国要求变化引起的合同价格的调整。
② Article II.1.
③ Article XXI.

的意图。按照该法规定,只要合同有规定,第三人就可以以自己的名义执行合同的条款:①

> Subject to the provisions of this Act, a person who is not a party to a contract (a "third party") may in his own right enforce a term of the contract if –
> (a) the contract expressly provides that he may, or
> (b) subject to subsection (2), the term purports to confer a benefit on him.

24.4 由于1999年《合同(第三人权利)法》允许合同当事人约定第三人不得执行合同或其任何条款,②因此在该法实施以后,越来越多的合同出现了限制第三人权利的条款,其目的是为了排除第三人执行合同的相关条文。在船舶建造合同标准格式中,NEWBUILDCON格式便有第三人权利条款,该条款规定:③

> Unless expressly identified in this Contract, no third parties shall have the right to enforce any term of this Contract.

Ⅲ 当事人住所地

24.5 AWES格式有专门的住所地条款,该条款的内容是:④

> For all the purposes of this CONTRACT the PURCHASER elects its legal domicile at its registered office in .... and the CONTRACTOR at its registered office in ....

24.6 英文中的domicil或domicile应当来自拉丁文中的 *domicilium*,通常指一个人的永久住所。在 *Whicker* v *Hume* 一案中,上议院的Lord Cranworth对domicile作出了如下解释:⑤

> By domicile we mean home, the permanent home; and if you do not understand your permanent home, I am afraid that no illustration drawn from foreign writers or foreign languages will very much help you to it.

---

① s.1(1).
② s.1(2).
③ Clause 48.
④ Article 17.
⑤ (1858) 7 HL Cas 124 at 160.

I think the best I have ever heard is one which describes the home as the place(I believe there is one definition in which the "*lares*" [household gods] are alluded to) "*under non sit discessurus sie nihil avocet; unde cum profectus est, peregrinari videtur*" [from which you cannot be separated if nothing removes you; when you depart from them you are seen as a stranger]. I think that is the best *illustration*, and I use that word rather than *definition*, to describe what I mean.

确定法人住所的意义在于确定权利义务所适用的法律,例如当事人的业务活动范围及其实施某一特定行为的有效性等问题通常应根据其住所地法予以确定。按照 AWES 格式的规定,船东和船厂的住所地均为其注册地。然而在船舶建造合同已经列明了合同当事人注册地的情况下,除非住所地和注册地不同,否则合同中关于当事人住所地的条款也就不再有额外的意义了。实际上,AWES 格式的开头部分已经有船厂和船东的注册地的记载。 24.7

IV 责任限制

在船舶建造实践中,除了约定船厂应当承担的约定赔偿的最高限额外,很少有船舶建造合同会约定船厂应当承担的最高责任限额。① AWES 格式应当是一个例外,该格式有如下规定:② 24.8

The liability of the CONTRACTOR shall be limited to the remedies provided for the PURCHASER in this CONTRACT and there shall be no further liability whatsoever for any direct or indirect losses, damages or expenses deriving from the obligations of the CONTRACTOR under this CONTRACT.

从上述规定来看,合同限制的实际上并不是船厂应当承担责任的数额,而是责任种类,即船厂仅承担船舶建造合同规定的责任。除此之外,船厂无需承担任何其他责任。但是,船厂是否应当承担合同约定责任以外的责任在很大程度上取决于对合同规定的解释。 24.9

---

① 然而在海工设备建造合同中则通常会有关于船厂应当承担的最大责任的规定,见本书第 25 章第 I 节。
② Article 19.

第25章 海工装备建造

Ⅰ 概述

海洋工程

25.1 《中国大百科全书》把海洋工程定义为应用海洋基础科学和有关技术学科开发利用海洋所形成的一门综合技术科学,也是指开发利用海洋的各种建筑物或其他工程设施和技术措施。海洋开发利用则是指:海洋资源开发(包括生物资源、矿产资源、海水资源等),海洋空间利用(包括沿海滩涂利用、海洋运输、海上机场、海上工厂、海底隧道等)以及海洋能利用(潮汐发电、波浪发电、温差发电等)。[①]

25.2 按海洋开发利用的海域,海洋工程可以分为海岸工程、近海工程和深海工程,但三者其实有所重叠。海岸工程主要是指海岸防护工程、围海工程、海港工程、河口治理工程、海上疏浚工程、沿海渔业设施工程、环境保护设施工程等。近海工程主要是指在大陆架较浅水域的海上平台、人工岛等的建设工程,和在大陆架较深水域的建设工程。近海工程又称离岸工程。深海工程则主要是指深海潜水器和遥控海底采矿等工程。

25.3 本章讨论的内容与海洋工程中的近海工程有关。近海工程的主要标志是油气田的开发。近海工程的装备主要以浮式结构为主,例如钻井船、浮船式平台、半潜式平台等适用于水深较大的大陆架海域石油和天然气勘探开采。"海工"应当是"近海工程"的简称。

---

① 中国大百科全书(第二版)[M].北京:中国大百科全书出版社,2009:9-88.

海工装备

"海工装备"是"海洋工程装备"的简称,但什么是"海工装备"并没有统一的定义。海工装备种类繁多,通常是指海洋资源相关装备尤其是海洋油气资源勘探、开采、加工、储运、管理等方面的工程装备和辅助装备。 25.4

海工装备可以分为三大类:海洋油气资源开发装备;其他海洋资源开发装备;海洋浮体结构物。其中海洋油气开发装备主要有平台(包括钻井平台和生产平台)、①油气外输系统以及辅助船(浮式生产储油船、卸油船、起重船、铺管船、海底挖沟埋管船、潜水作业船等)。平台的分类似乎也没有形成统一形式,有的将平台分为固定式的和移动式的,有的则将平台分为固定式的、顺应式的以及浮动式的。固定式平台是最早的海上作业平台形式,1947年出现于美国的墨西哥湾。固定式平台固定于海底,作业水深一般只有数十米。顺应式平台的出现解决了作业水深的问题。浮动式平台则不受作业地域的限制,基本上可以在任何水域进行作业。 25.5

不同的平台有不同的结构,使用的水深和环境也各不相同。按照上述平台的分类,固定式平台(fixed platform)包括主要用于原油和天然气钻探,萃取和储存的重力式平台(concrete/gravity platform)和通常在水深比较浅区域作业的导管架式平台(jacket platform);顺应式平台(compliant platform)的特征是平台可控性比较的平台,包括用于油气生产的顺应塔式平台(compliant tower platform)、拉索塔平台(guyed tower platform)和铰接塔平台(articulated tower platform);浮动式平台(floating platform)是与海底没有连接的海上浮动平台,包括可以上下升降的自升式钻井平台(jack-up drilling platform)、②可以在水深超过300米海域作业的张力腿平台(tension leg platform, TLP)、可以在水深超过500米海域作业的半潜式平台(semi-submersible platform)、可以满足生产,加工和储存功能的生产储油装置(floating production storage & offloading, FPSO)③和主要从事钻探的钻井船(drilling vessel)等。④ 25.6

---

① 有的平台用于钻井,有的用于生产,有的平台则兼具钻井和生产两种功能。
② 自升式平台由于依靠桩腿支撑,因而又被称为桩腿式平台。自升式平台又可以分为桩靴式平台(leg jack-up platform)和沉垫式平台(cushion platform)。
③ 基于天然液化气船建造或改装的浮式生产储卸装置具有天然气液化功能,因而也被称为天然气浮式生产储卸装置(LNG-FPSO)。浮式生产储卸装置同时具有钻井功能,称之为复式钻井生产储卸装置(floating drilling production storage and off-loading, FDPSO)。
④ 虽然钻井船严格意义上并非平台,但钻井船具有钻井平台的功能,因而也被视为是浮动平台的一种。

25.7　海上支持船(offshore support vessel，OSV)是为海上油气作业提供全面支持和服务船舶的统称。海上支持船提供的支持包括操锚、拖航就位、物资运输、守护、消防和污染处理等。有人将海上支持船分为起重船、工作船和供应船三类。起重船主要用于大件的装卸和安装，由于起重船上有吊机，因而又被称为浮吊船(floating crane)。工作船(anchor handling towing supply vessel，AHTS)在海上油气作业中起着非常重要的作用。工作船一般不受航区限制且有较优良的配置，能够为海上油气作业提供广泛的支持服务，包括提供物资、操锚、救助、守候甚至清污等服务。① 与工作船相比，供应船(platform supply vessel，PSV)强调的并非其工作的功能，而是供应即运输的功能，其主要功能是完成海上平台的供应。其他的与海上油气作业相关的船舶还包括：负责由平台向外运送油气穿梭油船；从事海底管道铺设的铺管船；为海上作业人员提供居住设施的居住船以及用于海上风机运输和安装的风电安装船等。②

海工装备建造合同的特征

25.8　与一般的船舶建造合同相比，海工装备建造合同不仅建造标的物不同，而且在工作界面、风险划分、责任承担以及条款设置等方面都具有其特殊性，这些特殊性可以简单归纳如下。

合同价格

25.9　一般的船舶建造合同价格大小取决于所建造的船舶种类，如果建造的是灵便型散货船或1,000标准箱左右的集装箱支线船，合同价格通常不会很高，也就数千万美元左右。但如果船厂建造的载重吨超过四五十万吨的散货船、超大型油轮、液化天然气船、20,000标准箱以上的集装箱船或者大型现代化先进游轮，合同价格上亿或数亿美元就很平常了。与此相同，海工装备建造合同的合同价格大小也取决于所建造的海上装备特征，如果船厂建造的是不到一百米的海上供应船，价格一般也就两千万美元左右，但若建造的是钻井平台、大型海上风电安装船，合同金额通常就比较大，数亿美元的合同价格也屡见不鲜。

---

① 鉴于其功能，工作船又被称为操锚供应拖船，不仅可以对平台进行拖航、起抛锚、动力定位和供应物资，而且还可以用作紧急救援船。

② 关于海工装备，请参见 Gunther Clauss, et al. *Offshore Structures* Springer 1992；James Wilson, *Dynamics of Offshore*, John Wiley & Sons 2003；Subrata Chakrabarti, *Handbook of Offshore Engineering* Elsevier 2005；Srinivasan Chandrasekaran, *Dynamic Analysis and Design of Offshore Structures*, 2nd ed. Springer 2018 以及《海洋工程装备》(马延德主编，清华大学出版社，2013 年)。

值得船厂注意的是，在海工装备建造中设备的采购通常占据了合同金额比较大的比例。合同金额包括所有采购金额显然会使合同金额变得很大，但合同金额在这种情况下变大除了统计意义上的价值外与船厂的实际利益应当是没有关系的。相反，一旦船东以船厂违约或过错为由解约，船厂就等于自己买下了所有采购设备，而这些设备在绝大多数情况下对船厂而言恐怕是没有价值的。如果船厂可以把自己采购的设备换成船东采购的设备，船厂的合同利益并不会因此受损，但即使合同被船东解除，船厂的损失至少不会莫名增加。 25.10

设计

虽然海工装备也有通用性比较大的，例如海上供应船，但更多的海工装备，尤其是钻井平台等，由于作业区域不同而各具独特的功能和特征。为了实现其特定功能，海工装备一般不会采用标准设计，而是有针对性地专门设计。绝大多数船厂未必有能力满足船东的这一设计要求，即使船厂具有专业的设计能力，船东可能更倾向于委托或指定自己有偏爱的或之前已有过合作的设计公司完成设计工作。正是由于这一类原因，在海工设备建造中船厂负责全部设计的情形并不多见，比较常见的是船厂负责详细设计和施工设计。在不少海工装备建造合同中船厂仅负责施工设计。 25.11

在建造合同的设计责任划分中一般有两种情形，一种情形是由船东负责概念设计或概念设计和基本设计，船厂负责详细设计和施工设计；另一种情形是由船厂负责所有设计，但其中的概念设计和基本设计由船厂委托船东指定的设计公司完成。

在第一种情形中，船东和船厂都应当对自己负责的设计承担责任，但在第二种情形中，虽然部分设计是由船东指定的设计公司完成的，但由于船厂在建造合同中承担了全部设计责任，因此应当向船东承担设计公司过错或迟延的责任。如果建造合同的安排采用第二种情形，除非船厂对船东指定的设计公司有比较充分的了解，否则应当设法在合同中针对船东指定的设计公司的过失与疏忽作出相应的保留，从而避免承担与己无关之过失或疏忽的责任。 25.12

采购

在海工装备建造中的设备采购不仅金额比较大，而且具有科技含量高的特征，但是对船厂而言基本上没有选择的范围。在一般的船舶建造中，船东和船厂通常会约定可以接受的供应商，船厂可以在约定供应商中选择一家或数家进行采 25.13

购。然而在海工装备建造中，可以按照技术规格书要求提供设备的供应商并不多，有些设备在全球范围内只有寥寥几家供应商。由于供应商实际处于垄断或半垄断的地位，船厂的采购基本上没有买家优势。船厂在采购中不仅没有压价的机会，而且还不得不接受供应商比较苛刻的采购条件。

保函

25.14　在海工装备建造中，船厂需要针对船东的预付款提供还款保函，基本上不存在例外情形。除了还款保函外，船东往往还要求船厂提供质保保函和履约保函。而且这些保函一般都是银行保函，而非公司保函。然而在海工装备建造合同中很少能看见船东提供预付款付款保函的情形。在海工装备建造中如果船东同意提供付款保函对船厂来说显然是有利的，因为付款保函能基本确保船厂会履行合同。付款保函解决的是船东付款能力的问题，而船东是否有付款能力或切实履行合同的意愿则未必只能通过付款保函予以证明。如果在船厂下单的是一家很有实力且有良好市场声誉的油气公司，船厂是不是持有付款保函可能也就不再重要了。相反，如果船厂有理由怀疑船东的支付能力或其切实履行合同的意愿，现实告诉我们在这种情况下船厂获得船东的可靠付款保函应当是不可能的。因此船厂面临的是可以获得付款保函多半是没什么意义的，而确实需要付款保函的则往往是得不到的。

25.15　在船东不提供付款保函且船厂有理由怀疑船东付款能力或切实履行合同意愿的情况下，船厂还是有其他方式尽可能避免船东的信用风险，例如船厂可以通过合同价格支付期数以及首付款的数额来避免风险。假设合同价格为两亿美元，船东分八期支付。只要第一第二两期建造款达到一定的比例，例如20%，船东不履行合同的可能性就会比较小，因为那意味着船东将丧失四千万美元。船东持续支付预付款，船厂收到的预付款的数额逐渐变大，船厂承受的风险也将进一步变小。

付款期数及比例

25.16　在海工装备建造中，建造款往往通过很多期分期支付，多的甚至超过十期，而且大多是以建造进程完成百分比为节点进行支付。但有的海工装备建造合同会约定合同款分两期支付，第一期通常由船东在收到船厂的还款保函后支付，第二期则是在交船时支付。如果两期款的比例相差很大，例如第一期为合同款的10%或甚至5%，第二期为合同款的90%或95%以及加减账。遇到此种情况，船厂应当意识到船东很有可能是在赌市场。几乎可以肯定的是,船东在船厂下单之时手上是没有合同的,即船东既没有船舶的买家或租家,也没有可以自行运行的合同。一旦没有着落,船东很有可能便会弃船而走。

船厂接下此种订单就意味着陪船东一起赌市场,但与船东不同的是,船东有可能赌输市场,也可能赌赢市场,但船厂则只会赌输市场而不可能赌赢市场。由于船东的首付非常少,船厂就必须依靠自己的资金或融资才有可能完成海工装备的建造。在装备建造完毕时,几乎所有的建造成本都是船厂付出的。如果船东按照约定接受装备的交付,谢天谢地,船厂心中的石头才算落地。但这并不是船厂赌赢了市场,因为这本来就是合同得到履行的正常结果。相反,如果因各种原因船东放弃首付款不再接收装备的交付,船厂就将面临非常可怕的局面。船东拒绝接受是其赌输市场的结果,与此同时也意味着船厂无法另行处置海工装备,至少不可能通过处置而收回成本。 25.17

船厂如果决定接单就应当与船东共进退,即在承担船东赌输市场结果的同时也为自己留有赌赢市场的机会。船东是有止损机制的,即放弃首付款。船厂也应当有自己的止损机制,例如船厂可以在约定情形出现时停止建造或推迟建造,或者船东应当提前支付等。船东按照约定接船意味着赌赢了市场,船厂应当与船东分享赌赢市场带来的利润或利益。 25.18

更改

虽然在性质上相同,在船舶建造中的变更(modification)来到了海工设备建造中成了"更改"(variation)或"更改指示"(charge order)。在一般的船舶建造合同中,变更所针对的可以说是例外情形,因为在合同履行过程中变更并不多见,即使有变更也是比较小且基本不影响船舶基本功能和运行的变更。然而在海工装备建造中,由于设计的复杂性、独特性以及创新特征,更改已不再是例外,而成了常态。几乎不存在没有更改的情形,有时在建造开始之时海工装备的某些功能或特征甚至有可能尚未最终确定。更改势必涉及额外成本的产生,而且更改涉及的金额往往很大,有时甚至有可能超过合同价格。这也是海工装备建造的一个特点。 25.19

由于数额比较大,合同应当对更改价格的确定和支付作出约定。在一般的船舶建造合同中,变更的价格通常由船东在接船时与尾款一并支付,但若在海工装备建造中也采用此种支付方式对船厂而言显然是不公平的,船厂不得不为更改而垫资。如果船东按照合同约定在交付前支付的预付款比例不太高时尤为如此。 25.20

适当的做法应当是船厂与船东就更改价格的支付另行作出约定，例如一部分在变更工作开始之前支付，另一部分则在变更工作完成之后的确定时间内支付，或者在船东支付下一期建造款时一并支付。

责任限制

25.21　在一般船舶建造合同中责任限制通常是指约定赔偿的最高限额，例如船厂推迟交船的每天应支付 1 万美元的约定赔偿，但最高不超过 180 万美元；又如实际航速低于保证航速每十分之一节船厂支付 2 万美元的约定赔偿，但最高不超过 20 万美元等等。此类责任限制的规定有一个特征，即当船厂应当支付约定最高赔偿限额之时也就是船东可以解约之时。在海工装备建造合同中也会有类似的约定赔偿的内容，但通常还会有另一种责任限制，例如海工装备建造合同会规定船厂的赔偿责任不超过合同价的 50%。船厂应当注意的是后一种责任限制。

25.22　在一般船舶建造合同中，船东针对船厂违约的合同救济是收取约定赔偿或解除建造合同。船东收取约定赔偿通常是以接船为前提的，换言之，船东收取约定赔偿就不能解约。反之，除非另有约定，如果船东选择解约也就不能获得约定赔偿。海工装备建造合同中的责任限制同样也是针对船厂的违约，但与船东的解约不再有关系了。船东既可以选择解约并主张赔偿，也可以选择不解约而要求船厂赔偿。

船东提供设备

25.23　在一般的船舶建造合同中，船东有时会提供自己的供应品，即"船东供应品"，在海工装备建造中，船东供应品通常称为"船东提供设备"（owner furnished equipment, OFE）。船东提供设备比较多也是海工装备建造的一大特点。船东供应品一般是比较小的设备或部件，而船东提供设备则是比较大型且重要的设备。海工装备建造中的船东供应品通常有可能是因为船东有自己的采购渠道或者对相关设备有特殊的要求。船东负责船东提供设备的采购并负责将设备运至船厂，船厂在收到船东提供设备后负责卸载、检验和保管。

25.24　有时海工装备建造合同会约定船厂负责船东提供设备的采购，相关款项计入海工装备建造合同的合同总价，船东则会事先将相关设备购置款汇入船厂指定的账号。在此种安排中，船厂很可能承担了一个额外的风险。一旦发生船东可以解约的情形，船东的解约便有可能导致船厂不得不偿还船东提供设备的购置款项，而在船东解约后，船东提供设备对船厂而言多半是没有利用价值的。

船东的解约权

海工装备建造中的另一特征是船东可以按照合同的约定随时解除合同或中止船厂的建造工作。合同中有此类约定应当是海上油气开发的特征所决定的。承包商需要有海工装备才有可能完成海上油气项目，但承包商拥有所有项目需要的海工装备应当是不可能的，即使有可能在财力上也是无法接受的。因此承包商合理的做法应当是在获得作业合同后再建造作业所需的海工装备，但一个已经拥有相关装备的承包商获得作业合同的机会显然远大于其他没有相关装备的承包商。这就驱使四处寻找作业合同的承包商选择在获得作业合同前就订造相关的海工装备，从而增加自己在招标中的竞争力。如果一切如其所愿，海工装备的建造自然不会受到影响。然而一旦出现意外，例如原来的油气项目因各种原因而被放弃，继续建造海工装备对承包商而言也就不再有意义了。在这种情况下，承包商就可以利用约定的解约权尽快解除建造合同，从而尽可能减少因意外情况带来的损失。

25.25

LOGIC 标准格式

LOGIC 是 Leading Oil and Gas Industry Competitiveness 的缩写，即"引领油气行业竞争"。作为一个公司，LOGIC 由英国油气行业特别小组（UK Oil & Gas Industry Task Force，OGITF）成立于 1999 年，旨在引领行业的竞争。LOGIC 是一家非盈利组织，其董事会由发起组织的人员担任。指派董事会的组织是：英国石油天然气公司（Oil & Gas UK，OGUK）的前身英国海上作业人员协会（UK Offshore Operators Association，UKOOA）、海上承包商协会（Offshore Contractors Association，OCA）、国际钻井承包商协会（International Association of Drilling Contractors，IADC）、能源工业理事会（Energy Industries Council，EIC）以及国际海洋承包商协会（International Marine Contractors Association，IMCA）。标准格式是指 Standard Contracts for the UK Offshore Oil and Gas Industry，但有不同的格式。

25.26

LOGIC 标准格式第一版发布于 1997 年，当时被称为 CRINE 合同。CRINE 是 Cost Reduction in the New Era 的缩写，成立于 20 世纪 90 年代初并于 1999 年当 LOGIC 成立时并入了 LOGIC，其宗旨是降低油气田开发的资本成本。CRINE 逐渐形成了网络并得到了英国油气勘探和生产行业的支持，从而增加了提高全球参与者竞争的目的，包括为行业制定样板合同文件。LOGIC 格式在海上油气合

25.27

同得到了比较广泛的采纳,其中海上建造版在海工装备建造中得到了青睐,包括水下建造、铺管和海上结构安装。

25.28 合同标准格式带来的好处是:合同当事人只需就重要的和关键的条款进行深入的磋商,针对并不十分重要或程序性条款可以采用标准格式,从而节省洽谈的时间。参与标准格式起草的都是具有丰富经验的专业人士,他们的起草考虑当事方的地位及需求等,有利于减少争议的发生,因而为标准格式带来了附加值。但标准格式同样也有不利之处,例如标准格式往往会忽视合同及其当事人的个性。由于针对特定利益或问题,标准格式的措辞有可能不够明确或肯定。当事方在标准格式中做出的选择有可能带来不同的后果。正如 LOGIC 格式所述及的:①

> The purpose of the model General Conditions of Contract is to provide a commonly known and understood foundation around which the Company and the Contractor can build their particular requirements.
>
> This eliminates much of the effort historically spent reviewing, qualifying and reviewing qualifications to the many different sets of general conditions offered by the industry. That time is now available to focus on developing specific terms directly beneficial to the work to be done.
>
> The model General Conditions are supported by a model Form of Agreement which includes a schedule of other sections to the contract. These facilities allow the Company to shape the total contract to match the Scope of Work.
>
> Provision is made in the model Form of Agreement for Special Conditions of Contract. This enables the Company, in negotiation with the Contractor, to adapt the General Conditions as necessary to suit their specific requirements and purpose.

25.29 LOGIC 前后制定了各种带有辅助性指南的合同一般条件格式,这些格式包括:海上建造、建造、钻井服务、设计、移动钻井机、厂房和设备主要部件的供应、货物购买、中小企业服务、中小企业分包合同服务以及海上拖运。

---

① General Conditions of Contract for Marine Construction Contracts, Edition 3, May 2021, Guidance Notes.

II 中止建造与解约

概述

绝大多数海工装备建造合同都会约定船东可以随时解除合同或中止建造。船东解除合同或中止建造是一种选择权,此种选择权的行使有两种情形,一是在船厂违约时行使;另一是按照船东自己的意愿行使,不以船厂违约或有过错为前提。船东只要发出书面通知就可以按照自己的意愿解除合同或者中止船厂的建造。

25.30

两种不同的解约或中止建造有不同的结果。如果解约或中止是基于船东自己的意愿,船东通常应按照合同的约定根据解约时或中止时实际已完成的建造支付对价。如果解约或中止建造是基于船厂违约的,船东可以根据合同的约定享有救济或行使权利。船东不仅可以享有合同约定的救济,除非已排除,船东还可以享有法律规定的救济。与一般船舶建造合同不同的是,在船东解约时往往还有接受未完成建造装备并主张约定赔偿的选择权。

25.31

决定的效力

船东的突然解约显然不是船厂希望看见的,此种解约不仅会给船厂带来损失,而且会对船东的建造合同造成困扰和麻烦。但只要合同有了明确的约定,即使会对一方造成明显的不公平,约定的效力并不会因此受影响。在 *BP Exploration Operating Company Limited* v *Dolphin Drilling Limited* 一案中,①双方于 2008 年 9 月签署了框架协议,约定由原告向被告租入了一台半潜式钻井平台,被告负责平台的作业,日租金为 410,000 美元。2009 年 3 月双方又在 1997 年的第一版 LOGIC 格式基础上签署了租船合同。按照约定,钻井作业开始日不早于 2010 年 1 月 1 日不晚于 2010 年 3 月 31 日。合同明确约定,原告只需发出通知就可以按自己的意愿解约。

25.32

22. TERMINATION

22.1 The COMPANY shall have the right by giving notice to terminate all or any part of the WORK or the CONTRACT at such time or times

---

① [2010] 2 Lloyd's Rep 192.

as the COMPANY may consider necessary for any or all of the following reasons:

(a) to suit the convenience of the COMPANY;

……

25.33 由于全球性金融危机，钻井平台日租金下降至 410,000 美元以下。原告在开始日之前解除了合同并主张自己可以按照合同约定解约。原告认为自己只需向被告支付解约前已完成的工作。被告则认为原告在开始日之前无权解约。法院认为只要合同的措辞是明确的，即使给一方带来不利，法院也应当按照当事人的约定解释合同。高院的 David Steel 法官说：①

> It may be severe in the circumstances that have arisen but in my judgment Dolphin has fallen a long way short of establishing that something had gone wrong with the language let alone establishing otherwise what a reasonable person would regard the parties as having meant by the terms of section II.22.

中止建造

25.34 按照 LOGIC 格式的规定，船东在两种情形下可以发出通知随时中止全部或部分建造工作：②

> The COMPANY shall have the right, by notice to the CONTRACTOR, to suspend the WORK or any part thereof to the extent detailed in the notice, for any of the following reasons:
>
> (a) subject only to Clause 15.3, in the event of some default on the part of the CONTRACTOR; or
> (b) in the event that suspension is necessary for the proper execution or safety of the WORK, or persons; or to suit the convenience of the COMPANY.

25.35 第一种中止建造的情形是船厂违约，第二种中止建造的情形则是为了适当地完成建造或者为了海工装备或人员的安全或者依照船东的意愿。虽然"为了适当地完成建造"和"为了海工装备或人员的安全"并非有明确含义的情形，但由于船

---

① [2010] 2 Lloyd's Rep 192 [32].
② LOGIC Standard Contracts for the UK Offshore Oil and Gas Industries, General Conditions of Contract for Marine Construction Edition 3, May 2021, cl.15.1.

东可以凭自己意愿中止建造,因此进一步分析"为了适当地完成建造"和"为了海工装备或人员的安全"的确切含义恐怕不再有太大的意义。

如果船东因船厂违约而中止建造,船东应当首先发出违约通知,只有当船厂不采取任何积极措施纠正其违约时,船东才能选择中止建造。① 船厂除了应按照船东指示中止建造外,还应当承担船东因船厂违约而产生的额外成本。② 一旦建造中止之后,双方应当在七天内就中止期间的各种事宜进行磋商并作出约定。③ 这里的磋商可以分为因船厂违约导致中止的磋商和因船东意愿主动中止的磋商。前者相对比较简单,原则上船厂应当对因自己违约造成的损失、成本和费用承担责任。后者则可能比较复杂一点,LOGIC 格式针对这一情形作出规定:④

25.36

> If the period of any suspension not arising as a result of default on the part of the CONTRACTOR exceeds the period stated in Appendix 1 to Section I - Form of Agreement the CONTRACTOR may serve a notice on the COMPANY requiring permission within fourteen (14) days from the receipt of such notice to proceed with the WORK or that part thereof subject to suspension. If within the said fourteen (14) days the COMPANY does not grant such permission the CONTRACTOR, by a further notice, may (but is not bound to) elect to treat the suspension as either:
>
> (a) where it affects part only of the WORK, an omission of such part under Clause 13; or
>
> (b) where it affects the whole of the WORK, termination in accordance with Clause 29.1(a).

所谓中止意味着建造会得到恢复,否则便构成下文讨论的解约了。在建造中止期间,船东可以通知船厂恢复建造,船厂也可以向船东申请恢复建造。船东表示继续中止建造或在收到船厂要求恢复建造申请后 14 天内没有回复,船厂可以根据当时的具体情况作出自己的选择。如果中止建造仅对部分海工装备的建造造成影响的,船厂可将船东的中止视为合同约定的更改,即船厂可以主张新的交

25.37

---

① LOGIC Standard Contracts for the UK Offshore Oil and Gas Industries, General Conditions of Contract for Marine Construction Edition 3, May 2021, cl.15.3.
② LOGIC Standard Contracts for the UK Offshore Oil and Gas Industries, General Conditions of Contract for Marine Construction Edition 3, May 2021, cl.15.5.
③ LOGIC Standard Contracts for the UK Offshore Oil and Gas Industries, General Conditions of Contract for Marine Construction Edition 3, May 2021, cl.15.5.
④ LOGIC Standard Contracts for the UK Offshore Oil and Gas Industries, General Conditions of Contract for Marine Construction Edition 3, May 2021, cl.15.8.

付日期和额外的建造成本。如果中止对整个海工装备的建造造成影响的,船厂则可以将船东的中止视为船东依照自身意愿的解约。

解除合同

25.38　按照 LOGIC 格式的规定,船东只需发出通知就可以随时解约:①

> The COMPANY shall have the right by giving notice to terminate all or any part of the WORK or the CONTRACT at such time or times as the COMPANY may consider necessary for any or all of the following reasons:
>
> (a) to suit the convenience of the COMPANY; or
> (b) subject only to Clause 29.2 in the event of any default on the part of the CONTRACTOR; or
> (c) in respect of the CONTRACTOR, in the event:
> > (i) an order is made, or a meeting is called to pass a resolution, for the winding up(except for the purposes of amalgamation or reconstruction), administration, appointment of a receiver or similar procedure;
> > (ii) a receiver, administrative receiver, administrator, provisional liquidator, liquidator or similar official is appointed or notice of the proposed appointment of any of the foregoing is given to any party;
> > (iii) a voluntary arrangement or scheme of arrangement is proposed, or negotiations are commenced, or a composition, compromise, assignment or arrangement, is entered into with one or more of its creditors with a view to rescheduling any of its indebtedness (because of actual or anticipated financial difficulties); or
> > (iv) any equivalent act or thing is done or suffered under any applicable or analogous law in any jurisdiction.

25.39　按照上文规定,船东既可以整体解除合同,也可以就任何部分解除合同。船东的解约理由同样有三种情形:(1)船东可以凭自己的意愿解约;(2)船东可以凭船厂的违约解约;(3)船东也可以凭船厂的其他原因解约,这些原因包括船厂停业、进入破产管理、指定接管人或进入类似程序,船厂指定了接管人、管理接管人、破产管理人、临时清盘人、清盘人或类似官员或发出了上述指定的通知,船厂提出

---

① LOGIC Standard Contracts for the UK Offshore Oil and Gas Industries, General Conditions of Contract for Marine Construction Edition 3, May 2021, cl.29.1.

了自愿偿债安排或协议偿债安排或者已经与一个或数个债权人为了对债务重新调整就破产和解或破产安排或转让及其实施开始了谈判,在任何地方按照任何法律开始了相同的行动。

25.40　　船东可以在解约通知中规定解约生效的日期,如果解约通知没有规定生效日期的则应被视为立即生效。船厂在收到船东解约通知后应当根据通知的要求立即停止相关的建造工作;允许船东或其代表接管或移走建造中的装备或任何部分;按照船东的意愿向船东或其代表转让所有或相关的权利、利益、责任和与建造中装备有关的分包合同。船厂还应当在船东解约后的30天内向船东送交所有技术信息、图纸、规格书、计算、程序等文件和材料。①

25.41　　上述三种解约理由中的第二种情形和第三种情形对船厂而言应当既可以理解,也可以接受,因为是船厂自身的原因导致船东解约的,而且船东以船厂违约为由解约还应当首先发出违约通知,只有当船厂未能采取积极行动纠正违约时船东才可以解约。② 如果船东的解约理由是第一种情形,虽然船厂可以就船东解约时已经完成的建造工作收取报酬,但是这样的解约很有可能给船厂带来麻烦:③

> In the event of termination under Clause 29.1(a) the CONTRACTOR shall be entitled to payment as set out in Section III – Remuneration for the part of the WORK performed in accordance with the CONTRACT together with such other payments and fees as may be set out in that Section or, in the absence of such provisions, such reasonable costs as agreed between the PARTIES at the time of termination.

25.42　　如果船东以船厂违约或船厂原因为由解约的,船厂要承担责任:④

> In the event of termination of all of the WORK or the CONTRACT in accordance with Clause 29.1(b) or Clause 29.1(c) the following conditions shall apply:
>
> (a) the CONTRACTOR shall cease to be entitled to receive any money or monies on account of the CONTRACT until the expiration of the

---

① LOGIC Standard Contracts for the UK Offshore Oil and Gas Industries, General Conditions of Contract for Marine Construction Edition 3, May 2021, cl.29.3.
② LOGIC Standard Contracts for the UK Offshore Oil and Gas Industries, General Conditions of Contract for Marine Construction Edition 3, May 2021, cl.29.2.
③ LOGIC Standard Contracts for the UK Offshore Oil and Gas Industries, General Conditions of Contract for Marine Construction Edition 3, May 2021, cl.29.4.
④ LOGIC Standard Contracts for the UK Offshore Oil and Gas Industries, General Conditions of Contract for Marine Construction Edition 3, May 2021, cl.29.6.

Defects Correction Period specified in Clause 28 (assuming that the COMPLETION DATE in respect of the whole of the WORK would have been the date specified in the SCHEDULE OF KEY DATES) and thereafter until the costs of COMPLETION and all other costs arising as a result of the CONTRACTOR's default or other events giving rise to the termination have been finally ascertained;

(b) thereafter and subject to any deductions that may be made under the provisions of the CONTRACT the CONTRACTOR shall be entitled to payment only as set out in Section III – Remuneration for the part of the WORK completed in accordance with the CONTRACT up to the date of termination; and

(c) any additional costs reasonably incurred by the COMPANY as a direct result of the CONTRACTOR's default or other events giving rise to termination shall be recoverable from the CONTRACTOR.

25.43　按照上述规定，除非船厂纠正了自己的违约，否则就不能依据合同获得任何建造款；船厂有机会就船东解约前已经完成的建造工作获得报酬；船厂还应当承担船东因船厂违约或其他原因而产生的额外成本。

25.44　船厂未必可以找到较好的理由拒绝接受船东依其意愿解约的权利，但船厂应当可以针对船东行使此项权利设定一些条件，例如船东依其意愿解约的应当提前发出一个月的事先通知，由船厂根据当时的具体情况停止部分或全部建造工作。此外，船东不仅要针对解约时已经完成的建造支付报酬，还应当对船厂因船东的解约而遭受的损失或额外产生的成本或费用等承担合理的补偿。

Ⅲ　更改

船东的权利

25.45　与船舶建造做法不同，在海工装备建造中，更改是船东的权利：①

The COMPANY has the right, subject to the CONTRACTOR's other existing contractual commitments, to issue instructions to the CONTRACTOR at any time to do any of the following:

(i) make any revision to the WORK which may include additions,

---

① LOGIC Standard Contracts for the UK Offshore Oil and Gas Industries, General Conditions of Contract for Marine Construction Edition 3, May 2021, cl.13.1(a).

omissions, substitutions and changes in quality, form, character, kind, position, dimension, level or line and changes in any method of construction specified by the COMPANY;
(ii) revise elements of the WORK already completed in accordance with the CONTRACT;
(iii) after commencement of the WORK, accelerate the WORK or any part thereof in order to recover all or part of any delay in respect of which the CONTRACTOR would otherwise have been entitled to a revision to the SCHEDULE OF KEY DATES in accordance with Clause 13.5;
(iv) reprogramme the WORK and reschedule its resource within the limits of practicality in order to complete the WORK or any part thereof in accordance with any amendment to the SCHEDULE OF KEY DATES the COMPANY may require.

......

船东可以在任何时候发出更改的指示，船东可以发出任何更改指示，无论是针对已经完成的建造还是尚未开始的建造。船东既可以要求船厂加快建造速度，也可以要求船厂放慢建造速度。应当注意的是，船东的更改指示并不一定要采取书面形式。①   25.46

船厂提出更改的程序

船厂虽然也可以提出更改，但适用不同的程序。船厂认为有更改的应当在相关工作开始实施之前以书面的形式向船东提出，要求船东发出更改指示。船厂应当详细说明构成更改的情形，包括相关的日期以及船厂依赖的合同相关条文：②   25.47

If the CONTRACTOR considers that an occurrence has taken place for which it is entitled to receive a VARIATION, the CONTRACTOR, before proceeding with any work affected by such occurrence, shall request without delay in writing that the COMPANY issue a VARIATION. Any such request shall include details of the occurrence including any relevant dates and the Clause or Clauses of the CONTRACT under which the CONTRACTOR considers itself to be

---

① LOGIC Standard Contracts for the UK Offshore Oil and Gas Industries, General Conditions of Contract for Marine Construction Edition 3, May 2021, cl.13.1.
② LOGIC Standard Contracts for the UK Offshore Oil and Gas Industries, General Conditions of Contract for Marine Construction Edition 3, May 2021, cl.13.3(a).

entitled to a VARIATION . . . .

25.48　如果船厂未能按照约定向船东提出更改请求或未能提供相关的估算，船厂就可能因此丧失要求加账或调整交付日期的权利：①

> If the CONTRACTOR fails to submit requests for VARIATIONS in accordance with Clause 13.3(a) when it considers or should reasonably have considered that an occurrence has taken place for which it is entitled to receive a VARIATION and/or fails to provide supporting estimates in accordance with Clause 13.4, the CONTRACTOR shall, at the sole discretion of the COMPANY, forfeit any right to receive such VARIATIONS and any rights concerning adjustment to the CONTRACT PRICE and/or SCHEDULE OF KEY DATES.

25.49　由上可见，更改的发生可以有两种情形，一种是船东要求船厂按照其要求作出更改，另一种则是船厂向船东主张更改的发生并主张自己的权利。船东可以随时向船厂发出更改的指示且不受特定形式的限制，船东实际向船厂发出的可能是一项具体工作的指示，有可能并不提及是否系一更改指示。这时船厂应及时按照约定向船东提出更改的请求，否则就有可能在完成了更改工作后既得不到报酬，又无法顺延交付日期。

加账和交付日期的顺延

25.50　除非涉及工作量比较小，更改通常会导致额外费用的产生和建造进程的调整。LOGIC 格式对合同价格及其关键日期的调整也作出了比较明确的规定：②

> Adjustments to the CONTRACT PRICE and SCHEDULE OF KEY DATES relating to any VARIATION shall be made as follows:
>
> Wherever possible the effect(if any) of a VARIATION on CONTRACT PRICE and SCHEDULE OF KEY DATES shall be agreed before the instruction is issued or before work starts, using the estimates prepared by the CONTRACTOR in accordance with Clause 13.4.
>
> Failing agreement on the basis of the CONTRACTOR's estimate, the COMPANY shall determine the effects of VARIATIONS in accordance

---

① LOGIC Standard Contracts for the UK Offshore Oil and Gas Industries, General Conditions of Contract for Marine Construction Edition 3, May 2021, cl.13.3(b).
② LOGIC Standard Contracts for the UK Offshore Oil and Gas Industries, General Conditions of Contract for Marine Construction Edition 3, May 2021, cl.13.5.

with the following principles:

(a) where work is of a similar nature and carried out under similar conditions to work priced in the CONTRACT it shall be valued at the appropriate rates and prices included in the CONTRACT.
In the event that rates and prices for delay and/or adjustments to the SCHEDULE OF KEY DATES are included in Section III – Remuneration, then such rates and prices shall be used where appropriate;

(b) where work is not of a similar nature or is not carried out under similar conditions to work priced in the CONTRACT or there are no appropriate rates or prices in the CONTRACT then a fair valuation shall be made;

(c) with respect to effect on the SCHEDULE OF KEY DATES a fair and reasonable adjustment shall be made taking into account all relevant factors including any acceleration instructed under Clause 13.1(a).

Except insofar as the CONTRACTOR can demonstrate that adjustments (including nil adjustments) to the CONTRACT PRICE and/or SCHEDULE OF KEY DATES determined for a VARIATION are incorrect due to factors which could not have been foreseen by the CONTRACTOR at the time of such determination, any such adjustments shall not be subject to renegotiation and shall be deemed to include any cumulative effect of the VARIATION and the determined effect of any and all other previously authorised VARIATIONS on the CONTRACT PRICE and the SCHEDULE OF KEY DATES.

Should factors arise which could not have been foreseen as described, no alteration shall be made to any agreed VARIATION but a new VARIATION shall be issued to deal with any additional effects of such factors.

25.51 船东只有在船厂能够证明因船东的原因导致建造延误或产生额外成本的情况下才会同意更改的成立：①

The COMPANY shall authorise a VARIATION if the CONTRACTOR can show that it has suffered delay and/or incurred cost as a direct result of any of the following:

---

① LOGIC Standard Contracts for the UK Offshore Oil and Gas Industries, General Conditions of Contract for Marine Construction Edition 3, May 2021, cl.13.5.

(a) failure of the COMPANY to comply with relevant CONTRACT provisions in respect of drawings and/or specifications and/or other information;
(b) failure of the COMPANY to comply with relevant CONTRACT provisions in respect of Section X – Materials, Services and Facilities to be provided by the COMPANY;
(c) information supplied by the COMPANY for which the COMPANY is liable under the terms of the CONTRACT and which is incorrect, provided the CONTRACTOR has complied with its obligations under Clause 7.1;
(d) subject to any restrictions specified in Appendix 1 to Section I – Form of Agreement, failure by the COMPANY to provide free and unrestricted access for the CONTRACTOR to any part of the WORKSITE.

无法达成一致的情形

25.52　更改未必始终能在双方之间达成一致,经常发生的情形是由于双方对合同或规格书的理解有差异而无法就特定工作是否构成更改达成一致。按照 LOGIC 格式的规定,双方无法就更改达成一致的,船厂应当保留或制作相关的记录并及时以书面方式通知船东自己有关合同价格及建造进程调整的主张。船东可以要求船厂做好并保留相关记录并在每月月底将具体情况通报船东。船厂如果未通知船东自己的主张或未能提供相关记录的则可能丧失主张合同价格及建造进程调整的主张。①

更改费用的支付

25.53　LOGIC 格式并没有就更改费用的支付作出专门的规定。由于更改涉及的金额有可能比较大,因此在建造合同中对更改费用的支付作出约定无疑是恰当的。除非另有约定,在双方就更改价格达成一致的情况下,船东就应当负有支付的义务。船东希望在支付尾款时一并支付更改费用无疑是可以理解的,因为这实际上意味着是船厂提供的无息贷款。船厂希望及时收到更改费用同样是可以理解的,因为这样会减轻船厂的融资压力。一个比较合理的方法是:双方在建造合同中针对更改费用约定一个数额,例如 1,000,000 美元,一旦更改费用超过 1,000,000

---

① LOGIC Standard Contracts for the UK Offshore Oil and Gas Industries, General Conditions of Contract for Marine Construction Edition 3, May 2021, cl.13.7.

美元的,船东就应当在收到船厂发票后的 30 天内支付;如果更改费用低于一百万美元的,船东可以随下一期建造款一并支付。

IV 相互赔偿条款

概述

25.54　相互赔偿条款(mutual indemnity clause)是赔偿条款的一种。赔偿条款的作用是在发生约定情形时将合同一方的风险转移至合同另一方,相互赔偿条款则是合同双方相互转移风险和承担赔偿责任的约定。赔偿与担保不同,赔偿设定的义务是第一性的义务,而担保设立的义务则是第二性义务。赔偿是指提供补偿;担保则可以是提供补偿,也可以是代为履行合同,但均以主债务人拒绝或无法履行义务为前提。赔偿条款通常包含两种方式承担责任,一是第三方针对被赔偿人的索赔,另一则是被赔偿人与受益人之间的索赔。

25.55　相互赔偿条款在海上油气合同中非常常见,大型的油气公司都有自己设计制定的相互赔偿条款。相互赔偿条款又被称为相互免赔条款(knock-for-knock clause),在 *Smit International (Deutschland) GmbH v Josef Mobius, Bau-Gesellschaft(GmbH &Co)* 一案中,高等法院的 Morison 法官把相互赔偿条款称为是对风险和责任进行的粗糙但可行的分配:①

> The knock for knock agreement . . . was a crude but workable allocation of risk and responsibility

25.56　在 *Caledonia North Sea Limited* v *British Telecommunications Plc (Scotland) and Others* 一案中,上议院的 Lord Bingham 把相互赔偿条款描述为是结合了海上作业特征的市场惯例:②

> . . . a market practice has developed to take account of the peculiar features of offshore operations.

身份与过错

25.57　如前所述,相互赔偿条款的目的是在合同当事人之间转移风险和责任。此类

---

① [2001] CLC 1545.
② [2002] UKHL 4 at [7].

条款通常使用的是 indemnify 或 hold harmless 字样等。在 *Farstad Supply AS v Enviroco Limited and another (Scotland)* 一案中，① 租船合同的第33.5条有如下规定：

> Subject to Clause 33.1, the Owner shall defend, indemnify and hold harmless the Charterer, its Affiliates and Customers from and against any and all claims, demands, liabilities, proceedings and causes of action resulting from loss or damage in relation to the Vessel (including total loss) or property of the Owner, including personal property of Owner's Personnel or of anyone for whom the Owner may be responsible on the Vessel, irrespective of the cause of loss or damage, including where such loss or damage is caused by, or contributed to, by the negligence of the Charterer, its Affiliates or Customers.

25.58　英国最高法院的 Lord Clarke 认为上述条款已经排除了租船人对船东承担的因租船人疏忽导致船舶损坏的责任。Lord Clarke 认为 indemnify 和 hold harmless 具有相同的含义，他说：②

> The word 'indemnify' can sometimes mean indemnify a third party. As ever, all will depend upon the context. Here the context is plain. The expression 'defend, indemnify and hold harmless' is used in both senses and is wide enough to include the exclusion of liability for loss incurred by the owner or charterer as the case may be ....

25.59　相互赔偿条款的基本特征是在发生财产损坏和人员伤亡时业主与承包商相互赔偿对方遭受的损失和面临的责任。其结果是合同各方在不考虑原因和过错的前提下对自己一方遭受的财产损失和人员伤亡承担赔偿责任包括费用。这是合同对风险予以划分的做法，基于索赔人或财产所有人的身份而不是过错。因此相互赔偿的约定有悖于传统的风险划分方式和普通法原则。

约定范围的措辞

25.60　相互赔偿条款通常会约定负责的一方应当确保另一方不会因第三方的索赔遭受损失，包括在第三方起诉时为对方进行抗辩和赔偿。相互赔偿条款通常涉及两种损失，一是财产损失，即由一方承担另一方遭受的财产损失的赔偿责任；一是

---

① [2010] UKSC 18.
② [2010] UKSC 18 at [27].

人身伤亡,即承担由对方过错造成的本方的人身伤亡。相互赔偿条款通常会约定各自承担各自雇员、代理人、管理人遭受的人身伤亡和财产损失的赔偿责任。

相互赔偿条款涉及的责任及赔偿范围取决于该条款的措辞,相互之间的责任承担和赔偿以条款约定为前提。在 *Westerngeco Ltd v ATP Oil & Gas* 一案中,①原告是提供油气开发服务的承包商,被告是海洋油气开发公司。双方订立了合同,由原告为被告提供地震勘测作业。合同是在 LOGIC 标准格式基础上形成的,被告承诺赔偿被告因原告的疏忽而导致的第三方的财产损失。第 19 条有如下内容:

25.61

19. Indemnities

19.1 The Contractor shall be responsible for and shall save, indemnify, defend and hold harmless the Company Group from and against all claims, losses, damages, costs (including legal costs), expenses and liabilities in respect of:

...

(c) ... loss of or damage to the property of any third party to the extent that any such injury, loss or damage is caused by the negligence ... of the Contractor Group.

...

19.8 The parties agree that Contractor Group's liability under this Contract shall not exceed the aggregate amount of payments received by Contractor for the Work and Company shall save, indemnify, defend and hold harmless Contractor for any amounts in excess thereof.

作业内容包括从船上传输地震电缆,原告以光租的方式租用了一艘名为 *Western Regent* 的船舶。由于原告的疏忽船舶与井口的标识浮标发生了碰撞,导致了第三方的损失。第三方对原告提起索赔后,原告要求被告根据第19.8条的约定给予赔偿。原告认为其对第三方因疏忽造成的损失构成第19.8条中的"liability under this Contract",因此被告应当承担超过原告已收款项部分的索赔。但被告认为"liability under this Contract"仅限于原告的合同责任。法院认为"liability under this Contract"首先是指法律责任,而不是其他责任;其次,它是指针对特定对象即被告的法律责任,而不是针对非合同的或无法获得合同利益的一方;最后,

25.62

---

① [2006] 2 Lloyd's Rep 535.

它是指一种支付责任,即超过原告已收款项部分的支付责任。"Any amounts"只能是指"liability under this contract"。按照第19.1(c)条的约定,在双方之间,原告应单独对碰撞造成的第三方财产损失的所有索赔、灭失、损坏、成本、费用以及责任负责。因此原告的责任并不构成第19.8条提及的"liability under this Contract",被告无需承担超过已收款总额的赔偿。高院的 Aikens 法官是这样说的:①

> I have concluded that the responsibility of the contractor for all claims, losses, damages and so forth, in respect of the damage to the property of Total, does not constitute a "liability under this contract" within clause 19.8. This is for the obvious reason that, by the terms of clause 19.1(c), the responsibility for that matter rests solely with the contractor. Total had sued the contractor for the damage done to its property as a result of the collision. As between the contractor and the company, the contractor is responsible for those claims, damages, costs and expenses. The company is not. Therefore, there is no legal liability on the contractor to pay anything over to the company in respect of those claims, damages, costs and expenses. That being so, there is nothing in respect of which the company is obliged to indemnify the contractor, if there were an excess above the aggregate payments received by the contractor for the work done under the contract.

偏袒与任意

25.63　由于相互赔偿条款是针对身份而非过错作出风险和责任的转移或划分,因此出现不合理甚至有明显利益倾向性的情形几乎是注定的。然而,法院在解释相互赔偿条款时并不会因为存在不合理性或利益倾向性而认定相互赔偿条款无效。Chartbrook Ltd v Persimmon Homes②一案虽不是与海上油气开发相关的判例,但该案关于合同解释的判词具有着相当大的意义。在该案中,原告是业主,被告是开发商。双方缔约由被告为原告获得土地开发许可,再开始进行住宅和商业开发,然后再以长期租赁方式出售。原告同意按照被告的意思出租,由被告收入租金后再向原告支付约定的金额。双方因"额外住宅支付"的数额产生了争议。"额外住宅支付"在合同中有定义,但与双方在缔约前的约定并不一致。原告起诉要求被告支付未付部分的额外住宅支付。被告认为缔约前双方磋商一致的真

---

① [2006] 2 Lloyd's Rep 535 at [28].
② [2009] UKHL 38.

实意图未能在合同中体现并以此为由要求法院予以纠正。高院认为原告对合同的解释是对的,而被告提出的合同的纠正不能接受,尤其是在合同已有明确定义的情况下更是如此。高院的判决得到了上诉法院多数意见的支持。被告将争议上诉至上议院,上议院接受了被告的上诉并推翻了上诉法院的判决。

上议院并没有将缔约前磋商内容接受为证据,而是根据合同解释原则做出了判决。上议院认为:合同中"额外住宅支付"的定义存在歧义且有缺陷,虽然法院不能随意主张正式文件中存在语言错误,但若一个了解相同背景情况的合理人士对相关文字的理解表明有错的话,法院可以通过解释纠正错误。相比之下,被告对"额外住宅支付"的解释更为合理。上议院的 Lord Hoffmann 是这样说的:① 25.64

> It is of course true that the fact that a contract may appear to be unduly favourable to one of the parties is not a sufficient reason for supposing that it does not mean what it says. The reasonable addressee of the instrument has not been privy to the negotiations and cannot tell whether a provision favourable to one side was not in exchange for some concession elsewhere or simply a bad bargain. But the striking feature of this case is not merely that the provisions as interpreted by the judge and the Court of Appeal are favourable to Chartbrook. It is that they make the structure and language of the various provisions... appear arbitrary and irrational, when it is possible for the concepts employed by the parties... to be combined in a rational way.

从上述 Lord Hoffmann 的判词中可以得出的是:如果相互赔偿条款存在利益的偏袒,法院对条款的解释应当不会因此受到影响,但若存在任意和非理性的话,情形则可能就不同了。然而,任意和非理性并非显而易见。 25.65

明确的约定

在相互赔偿条款有明确约定的情况下,除非存在错误,否则法院通常会根据当事人的约定对条款进行解释。在 *Transocean Drilling UK Ltd v Providence Resources plc* 一案中,②原告是一座名为 *GSF Arctic III* 半潜钻井平台的船东,与被告订立了在爱尔兰南部沿海外开钻一口评估井的合同。合同是在 LOGIC 格式基础上订立的。合同第18条是关于相互赔偿的条款,按照第18.1条的约定,双方 25.66

---

① [2009] UKHL 38 [20].
② [2016] EWCA Civ 372.

各自承担自己一方的财产损失和雇员的人身伤亡损失以及因各自疏忽导致的第三方的类似损失。按照第18.2条的约定,被告接受自己一方的财产及雇员人身伤亡以及第三方损失的赔偿责任;按照第18.3条和第18.4条的约定,被告接受因污染及源自钻井架船体的污染以外的责任;按照第18.5条的约定,被告承担发生在孔内的或转盘以下的原告财产或设备损坏的赔偿责任,除非损坏系因自然损耗或原告疏忽所致;按照第18.8条的约定,排除和赔偿的适用既不因受赔偿一方的原因、疏忽、失职或其他错误的影响,也不因依法律规定而产生索赔的影响。合同第20条是关于间接损失的条款:

20. CONSEQUENTIAL LOSS

For the purposes of this Clause 20 the expression "Consequential Loss" shall mean:

(ⅰ) any indirect or consequential loss or damages under English law, and/or

(ⅱ) to the extent not covered by (ⅰ) above, loss or deferment of production, loss of product, loss of use (including, without limitation, loss of use or the cost of use of property, equipment, materials and services including without limitation, those provided by contractors or subcontractors of every tier or by third parties), loss of business and business interruption, loss of revenue (which for the avoidance of doubt shall not include payments due to CONTRACTOR by way of remuneration under this CONTRACT), loss of profit or anticipated profit, loss and/or deferral of drilling rights and/or loss, restriction or forfeiture of licence, concession or field interests

25.67 钻井作业由于防喷器部分失调导致钻井作业中止,一个多月以后才恢复作业。延误在当事方之间就原告在"争议期间"可以获得报酬以及被告因作业时间延长可以获得的"分摊成本"赔偿等问题产生了争议。争议的关键问题在于延误是否因原告违约而产生。一审法院认为由于防喷器在钻井架交付时已经有残渣堆积,因此钻井架并未处于合同约定的良好工作状态。法院认为残渣堆积导致了27小时的时间损失,而船员未能适当关紧堵塞器则导致了10小时的延误。一审法院采用针对"除外条款"的严格解释规则认为分摊成本的浪费并不构成间接损失。虽然原告合同排除了赔偿损失的责任,根据作不利于提供者解释原则,被告依然可以获得延误期间的成本补偿。原告仅就这一问题提起了上诉。上诉需要解决的问题并不复杂,即被告因原告的违约而遭受的分摊成本的浪费是否构成双方在第 20 条约定的间接损失。上诉法院推翻了高等法院的判决,认为责任互免条款有效地排除了承包商承担浪费成本的赔偿责任。虽然 *Chartbrook Ltd v Persimmon Homes* 一案的判决被提及,但由于并不存在错误,上诉法院根据当事方所用文字本义对第 20 条进行了解释。上诉法院的 Moore-Bick 法官说:①

> I fully accept that where the language of an exclusion clause leaves room for doubt as to its meaning, the principle applied in these cases may provide a valuable tool for ascertaining its correct meaning and in some cases it may lead to the conclusion that a restricted meaning must be given to the clause in question in order to achieve the parties' common objective. But it does not in my view provide sufficient justification for overriding the parties' intention where that has been clearly expressed. The principle of freedom of contract, which is still fundamental to our commercial law, requires the court to respect and give effect to the parties' agreement. One of the striking features of this contract, to which I have already adverted, is the extent to which the parties have agreed to accept responsibility for losses that might otherwise have been recoverable as damages for breach of contract. If, as a result of incorporating several different provisions of that kind, the parties have effectively agreed to exclude any liability for damages for any breaches, it is difficult to see why the court should not give effect to their agreement.

25.68 如果我们再回到 *Transocean Drilling UK Ltd v Providence Resources plc* 一案,"明确的约定"应当还是无法推翻"任意"或"非理性"的。换言之,约定无论如何清晰,只要存在"任意"或"非理性",约定的效力也应当是有问题的。

整体的解释

25.69 赔偿条款的解释取决于赔偿条款的措辞以及当事人在合同中表现出来的意图。在 *Wood v Capita Insurance Services Limited*② 一案中,卖方向买方出售其公司的股权,双方为此签署了股权买卖协议。卖方原来是公司的执行董事并在股权买卖完成后依然担任公司的执行董事,但此后被买方解聘。卖方就解聘提起诉讼,要求买方赔偿,而买方则凭买卖协议的赔偿条款提起反诉,要求卖方赔偿自己的损失。买卖协议的第 7.11 条是赔偿条款,有如下内容:

---

① [2016] EWCA Civ 372 [17].
② [2017] UKSC 24.

The Sellers undertake to pay to the Buyer an amount equal to the amount which would be required to indemnify the Buyer and each member of the Buyer's Group against all actions, proceedings, losses, claims, damages, costs, charges, expenses and liabilities suffered or incurred, and all fines, compensation or remedial action or payments imposed on or required to be made by the Company following and arising out of claims or complaints registered with the FSA, the Financial Services Ombudsman or any other Authority against the Company, the Sellers or any Relevant Person and which relate to the period prior to the Completion Date pertaining to any mis-selling or suspected mis-selling of any insurance or insurance related product or service.

25.70 虽然按上述条款的内容，卖方显然已经明确地对卖方作出了赔偿的承诺，但从合同整体来看，情形则有所不同。例如买卖协议第 8 条规定了卖方的责任限制，即卖方根据买卖协议承担的责任最大不超过股权买卖价格，这一责任限制适用于根据第7.11条提出的索赔。买卖协议附件五的第 3 段则对索赔规定了时间限制，按照该段的规定，根据第7.11条提出的索赔应当在两年内提出。一审法院认为卖方应当按照第7.11条的规定赔偿买方的损失，但上诉法院则认为卖方无需赔偿买方。上诉法院的观点得到了上议院的肯定。

25.71 上议院认为第7.11条的起草不够精准，其含义有含糊之处。第7.11条应当与整个合同一起予以解释。第7.11条是对附件四列明保证的补充，而附件四的保证责任受附件五规定时限的限制，即公司应当在股权买卖完成日后的两年内提出。第7.11条的赔偿范围应按受时间限制的保证规定予以评估。上议院最终驳回了买方的上诉。上议院的 Lord Hodge 说：①

> Business common sense suggests that Capita had an interest in obtaining as broad an indemnity against the adverse consequences of mis-selling as it could obtain. But the sellers had given warranties of compliance with regulatory requirements, which covered such mis-selling, subject to the agreed limits of quantum and time. The sellers were exposed to a potential liability under those warranties for the two years after the Completion Date, during which Capita could learn of the Company's sales practices. One may readily infer that they had an interest in minimising their further exposure to liability after that time had elapsed. Business common sense is useful to ascertain the purpose of a provision

---

① [2017] UKSC 24 at [28].

and how it might operate in practice. But in the tug o' war of commercial negotiation, business common sense can rarely assist the court in ascertaining on which side of the line the centre line marking on the tug o' war rope lay, when the negotiations ended. I therefore turn to examining the clause in more detail before returning to the commercial context.

重大疏忽和故意不当行为

25.72　相互赔偿条款中一般都有关于重大疏忽和故意不当行为的内容,传统上,大多数相互赔偿条款都将重大疏忽和故意不当行为排除在相互赔偿范围之外。① 但逐渐形成的做法是将重大疏忽和故意不当行为也包括了相互赔偿条款的范围之内。虽然普通法认为免责条款并不能免除一方"不顾其所负义务的故意"的违约,但普通法并没有阻止合同对一方的故意作为或不作为的责任进行排除或限制。② 在 Suisse Atlantique Societe d'Armement SA v NV Rotterdamsche Kolen Centrale 一案中,上议院的 Lord Wilberforce 是这样说的:③

> The "deliberate" character of a breach cannot, in my opinion, of itself give to a breach of contract a "fundamental" character, in either sense of that word. Some deliberate breaches ... may be, on construction, within an exceptions clause(for example, a deliberate delay for one day in loading). This is not to say that "deliberateness" may not be a relevant factor: depending on what the party in breach 'deliberately' intended to do, it may be possible to say that the parties never contemplated that such a breach would be excused or limited.

25.73　故意不当行为(wilful misconduct)一般是指行为人明知错误而依然实施的行为,或指行为人不考虑对错也不考虑后果而鲁莽实施的行为。在 Lewis v Great Western Railway 一案中,上诉法院的 Bramwell 法官认为故意不当行为包括明知故犯的情形,也包括不计后果的情形,他是这样说的:④

> ... misconduct to which the will is a party, something opposed to accident or negligence; the misconduct, not the conduct, must be

---

① 关于重大疏忽与一般疏忽的区别,请参见本书第 5 章第 Ⅲ 节的内容。
② Hugh Beale, *Chitty on Contracts*, 35ᵗʰ edn Sweet & Maxwell 2023, para.18‑019.
③ [1967] 1 AC 361 at 435.
④ (1877) 3 QBD 195 at 206.

wilful. It has been said, and, I think, correctly, that, perhaps one condition of "wilful misconduct" must be that the person guilty of it should know that mischief will result from it. But to my mind there might be other "wilful misconduct." I think it would be wilful misconduct if a man did an act not knowing whether mischief would or would not result from it. I do not mean when in a state of ignorance, but after being told, "Now this may or may not be a right thing to do." He might say, "Well I do not know which is right, and I do not care: I will do this." I am much inclined to think that that would be "wilful misconduct", because he acted under the supposition that it might be mischievous, and with an indifference to his duty to ascertain whether it was mischievous or not. I think that would be wilful misconduct.

25.74 在 Graham v Belfast and Northern Counties Ry Co 一案中, Johnson 法官给故意不当行为下了如下定义: ①

Wilful misconduct in such a special condition means misconduct to which the will is party as contradistinguished from accident, and is far beyond any negligence, even gross or culpable negligence, and involves that a person wilfully misconducts himself who knows and appreciates that it is wrong conduct on his part in the existing circumstances to do, or to fail or omit to do (as the case may be), a particular thing, and yet intentionally does or fails or omits to do it, or persists in the act, failure, or omission regardless of consequences . . . .

25.75 在 Forder v Great Western Railway 一案中, Alverstone 法官认为故意不当行为包括明知故犯的情形, 也包括不计后果的情形, 他认为在上述 Johnson 法官的定义基础上还应当增加: ②

or acts with reckless carelessness, not caring what the results of his carelessness may be.

25.76 在 Horabin v British Overseas Airways Corporation 一案中, Barry 法官给故意不当行为下了如下定义: ③

In order to . . . establish wilful misconduct, the plaintiff must satisfy you, not beyond reasonable doubt, but satisfy you that the person who

---

① [1901] 2 IR 13, see *Forder* v *Great Western Railway* [1905] 2 KB 532 at 535.
② [1905] 2 KB 532 at 536.
③ [1952] 2 Lloyd's Rep 450 at 459.

did the act knew that he was doing something wrong, and knew it at the time, and yet did it just the same, or alternatively that the person who did the act did it quite recklessly not caring whether he was doing the right thing or the wrong thing, quite regardless of the effect of what he was doing upon the safety of the aircraft and the passengers for which and for whom he was responsible.

不公平合同条款

作为成文法,1977年《不公平合同条款法》显然是适用于海工装备建造合同中的相互赔偿条款的。《不公平合同条款法》针对人身伤亡有如下规定:①   25.77

(1) A person cannot by reference to any contract term or to a notice given to persons generally or to particular persons exclude or restrict his liability for death or personal injury resulting from negligence.
(2) In the case of other loss or damage, a person cannot so exclude or restrict his liability for negligence except in so far as the term or notice satisfies the requirement of reasonableness.
(3) Where a contract term or notice purports to exclude or restrict liability for negligence a person's agreement to or awareness of it is not of itself to be taken as indicating his voluntary acceptance of any risk.

按照上述的规定,对有疏忽的一方而言,相互赔偿条款中关于人身伤亡风险和责任转移的约定恐怕是无效的。如果涉及的是财产的损失或责任,相互赔偿条款中关于风险和责任转移的约定是否有效取决于此种约定是否满足合理性的要求。   25.78

LOGIC 格式

LOGIC 格式有专门的赔偿条款,其中第21.1条是针对承包商的:②   25.79

The CONTRACTOR shall be responsible for and shall save, indemnify, defend and hold harmless the COMPANY GROUP from and against all claims, losses, damages, costs (including legal costs) expenses and liabilities in respect of:

(a) loss of or damage to property of the CONTRACTOR GROUP

---

① Unfair Contract Terms Act 1977, s.2.
② LOGIC Standard Contracts for the UK Offshore Oil and Gas Industries, General Conditions of Contract for Marine Construction Edition 3, May 2021, cl.21.1.

whether owned, hired, leased or otherwise provided by the CONTRACTOR GROUP arising from, relating to or in connection with the performance or non-performance of the CONTRACT; and

(b) personal injury including death or disease to any personnel of the CONTRACTOR GROUP arising from, relating to or in connection with the performance or non-performance of the CONTRACT; and

(c) subject to any other express provisions of the CONTRACT, personal injury including death or disease or loss of or damage to the property of any third party to the extent that any such injury, loss or damage is caused by the negligence or breach of duty (whether statutory or otherwise) of the CONTRACTOR GROUP. For the purposes of this Clause 21.1(c) "third party" means any party which is not a member of the COMPANY GROUP or CONTRACTOR GROUP.

25.80　承包商应当承担责任的有三种情形：第一种是承包商因履行或不履行合同而遭受的财产的灭失和损坏；第二种是承包商因履行或不履行合同而遭受的人身伤亡；第三种则是第三方因承包商的疏忽或失职而遭受的人身伤亡或财产的灭失和损坏。上述三种承包商承担责任的情形均基于承包商自身行为。①

保赔保险

25.81　传统的保赔保险的基本原则是会员不能通过合同或其他方式主动承担依法不应承担或按照适用法可以排除或限制的赔偿责任，但由于相互赔偿条款在海上油气业已成为通用做法，保赔协会同意在会员没有放弃适用法规定的限制责任权利的条件下批准赔偿相互赔偿协议产生的责任。国际保赔协会集团规定的相互赔偿的定义如下：②

Knock for knock: a provision stipulating(1)that each party to a contract shall be similarly responsible for loss of or damage to, and/or death of or injury to, any of its own property or personnel, and/or the property or personnel of its contractors and/or of its or their subcontractors and/or of other third parties, and(2)that such responsibility shall be without recourse to the other party and arise notwithstanding any fault or neglect of any party and(3)that each party shall, in respect of those losses, damages or other liabilities for which it has assumed responsibility,

---

① LOGIC 格式第 21.2 条是针对业主的赔偿。
② Pooling Agreement 2020-Appendix V-11. Contracts and Indemnities.

correspondingly indemnify the other party against any liability that that party shall incur in relation thereto.

25.82 　从上述要求来看，合同中的责任和赔偿条款应当是平衡且互惠的，否则会员就无法得到保赔协会的赔偿。

V 健康、安全与环境条款

概述

25.83 　健康、安全与环境条款也是海工装备建造合同中常见的条款，通常被简称为 SH&E 条款。海工装备建造合同中的健康安全与环境条款是指船东向船厂提出并为船厂设定了健康安全与环境管理上的要求，这些要求既包括管理体系，也包括合同履行。在实践中基本上不存在双方对健康安全与环境条款进行磋商和修改的情形。对船厂来说，健康安全与环境条款并不是一个简简单单的合同承诺，而是符合建造合同要求的健康、安全与环境管理体系的实施和执行。

25.84 　健康、安全与环境问题是可持续发展势必面临的问题，健康、安全与环境问题主要涉及工作环境、劳动保护、急救、职业病、人身伤亡、污染以及环境保护等。虽然健康、安全与环境被视为一个整体，但在实践中，健康、安全与环境通常分为"健康、安全"和"环境"两个部分分别对待。国际标准组织也分别制定了健康、安全与环境有关的国际标准，即环境健康管理体系（Environmental Management System, ISO 14001）和职业健康与安全管理体系"（Occupational Health and Safety Management Systems, ISO 45001）。大多数国家都有健康、安全与环境的专职部门并制定了相关的标准和法律。

ISO 14001

25.85 　ISO 14001 是国际标准组织制定的关于环境保护管理体系的国际标准，最新版本是 2015 年颁布的 ISO 14001:2015。ISO 14001 旨在协助企业通过有效利用资源和减少浪费保护并改善环境。保护环境以及防止对环境造成负面影响已成为企业、公司或组织所面临的挑战。建立并实施环境管理体系有助于企业、公司或组织减少有可能导致环境责任的事故，获得较低成本的保险，从而实现材料及能源投入的节省。环境管理体系由确定企业、公司或组织环境问题的政策、流程、计划、做法及记录组成。虽然不同的企业、公司或组织应当有适合自身特征的环境管理体系，但 ISO 14001 规定的要求为环境管理体系的建立提供了框架和指南。

25.86　　ISO 14001 涵盖了环境管理体系的七项要求：组织环境、领导力、计划、支持、运行、执行评估以及改进。组织环境要求对自己的组织及其环境有清晰的了解，只有了解自己的组织及其环境才有可能有效地建立并实施环境管理体系。具体的要求包括识别组织内部和外部问题，识别有兴趣的当事方及其期望值，确定环境管理体系的范围并制定环境管理体系所需的流程。领导力要求组织的最高管理层在实施环境管理体系中发挥作用，最高管理层应当通过制定并宣传环保政策以及在组织内设定岗位和职责的方式展现出其对实施环境管理体系的承诺。计划要求对环境管理体系的功能进行计划，对体系的风险和机会进行评估，对改善环境的目标进行识别并制定措施予以实现。支持要求所有资源包括关于权限、意识、沟通和文件控制等方面均为环境管理体系的实施提供支持。运行要求涉及组织流程所需的环境控制等各个方面的实施，包括对潜在紧急情况的识别以及应对计划。执行评估要求确保对环境管理体系是否运行正常实施监控，包括对流程进行监控和衡量，对环保合规、内部审计以及管理审核进行评估。改进要求组织确保环境管理体系不断改善，包括对流程不符点进行评估并对流程采取矫正行动。①

ISO 45001

25.87　　工伤事故以及与工作活动有关的致命疾病是可以并且应当予以避免的。ISO
25.88　　45001 是国际化标准组织制定的关于职业健康与安全管理体系的国际标准。职业健康与安全的英文缩写为"OH & S"。ISO 45001 是在 OHSAS 18001 基础上制定的，OHSAS 18001 是职业健康与安全管理体系（Occupational Health and Safety Management Systems）的简称。由于 OHSAS 18001 是英国的标准，因而又称为 BS OHSAS 18001。任何组织都必须对自己的工人或其他人员的职业健康与安全负责，职业健康与安全管理体系旨在防止工人遭受与工作相关的受伤和健康损害，提供安全健康的工作场所。组织应当采取有效的预防和保护措施以消除危险降低职业健康与安全风险。职业健康与安全管理体系的实施有助于组织管理职业健康与安全风险，改善组织的职业健康与安全的效能，从而帮助组织满足法律规

---

① See ISO 14001: 2015 Environmental Management Systems-Requirements with Guidance for Use.

定及其他方面的要求。①

中国的健康、安全与环境

  中国政府对企业、公司和组织关于健康、安全与环境方面的要求均已成为国家标准，关于健康和安全方面的国家标准有《职业安全卫生管理体系试行标准》、《体力劳动强度分级》、《企业职工伤亡事故分类》、《机械设备防护罩安全要求》、《防护屏安全要求》、《安全标志》、《生产过程安全卫生要求总则》、《常用危险化学品的分类和标志》、《安全标志使用导则》、《重大危险源辨别》等；关于环境保护的有《环境影响评价技术导则-生态影响》和《建设项目环境影响技术评估导则》等。

25.89

  这些标准的制定依据是我国的相关立法，这些法律包括1982年的《中华人民共和国海洋环境保护法》、1987年的《中华人民共和国大气污染防治法》、1989年的《中华人民共和国环境保护法》、1996年的《中华人民共和国环境噪声污染防治法》、1998年的《中华人民共和国消防法》、2001年的《中华人民共和国职业病防治法》、2002年的《中华人民共和国安全生产法》、2003年的《中华人民共和国环境影响评估法》和《中华人民共和国放射性污染防治法》、2007年的《中华人民共和国卫生防疫法》和2008年的《中华人民共和国水污染防治法》等。

25.90

法定责任和合同责任

  健康、安全与环境管理体系包含为实现健康、安全与环境目标所需的政策、措施及程序等。健康、安全与环境管理体系的建立与实施有助于雇员了解具体的要求。对船厂而言，建立并实施健康安全与环境管理体系实际上是一项法定义务，即使没有海工装备建造合同的约定，船厂也必须按照相关法律或条例的规定切实建立并实施健康、安全与环境管理体系。对船东而言，要求船厂建立并实施健康、安全与环境管理体系可能是船东的法定义务或体系要求。在这种情况下，建立并实施健康、安全与环境管理体系既是船厂的法定义务，同时也是船厂的合同义务。

25.91

  健康、安全与环境管理体系是ISO 14001与ISO 45001的结合，即职业健康安全管理体系与环境管理体系的结合。英文缩写为HS&E。健康、安全与环境管理体系有助于雇员了解具体的要求。健康、安全与环境管理体系一般包含：文件的

25.92

---

① See ISO 45001: 2018 Occupational Health and Safety Management Systems-Requirements with Guidance for Use.

控制和分发、安全检查清单、风险评估、应急计划、培训及记录、内部审计、合规清单、人员配备、衡量标准、定期会议及交流、定期管理审核等。ISO 45001 在核心内容和定义上与国际标准组织的其他国际标准是相同的,包括 ISO 9001 和 ISO 14001。如果船厂已经建立并实施了 ISO 9001 的话,将 ISO 14001 和 ISO 45001 融合进已有的 ISO 9001 体系并非难事,因为三者系基于相同的框架制定的。

25.93　　船东为了方便自己的健康、安全与环境管理体系的实施有可能要求船厂适用船东的管理体系,或者是按照船东管理体系的要求对船厂的健康、安全与环境管理体系进行审核和审计。虽然健康、安全与环境管理体系在本质上通常不会有很大的差别,但不同体系的流程和工作方式等往往各不相同,适用不同的体系有可能导致与自身体系发生冲突的情形。船厂在同意实施船东的管理体系时应当确保这样做并不会给自己管理体系的实施带来障碍或造成麻烦,尤其是按照船东的管理体系要求对船厂的管理体系进行审核和审计。

LOGIC 格式

25.94　　LOGIC 格式的第 39 条是健康安全与环境条款,该条并没有针对健康、安全与环境管理体系作出具体的规定,而是要求船厂实施最高标准的健康、安全与环境管理体系:①

> The COMPANY places prime importance on health, safety and environment (hereinafter "HS & E") issues and requires that the CONTRACTOR GROUP subscribes to and actively pursues the highest standards of HS & E performance.

25.95　　要求船厂高度重视健康、安全与环境问题无疑是可行的,但要求船厂积极实施最高标准的健康、安全环境要求恐怕难以适从。关于健康、安全与环境的标准似乎并没有最高标准和最低标准之分,而且健康、安全与环境管理体系实质上也不存在好坏与高低的区别。如果海工装备建造合同采用 LOGIC 格式的第 39 条,船厂可以做到适用于船东的健康、安全与环境管理体系相同或相类似的管理体系就应当符合"最高标准"的要求。

25.96　　按照 LOGIC 格式的要求,船厂应当与船东建立两个健康安全与环境管理体

---

① LOGIC Standard Contracts for the UK Offshore Oil and Gas Industries-General Conditions of Contract for Marine Construction, Edition 3, May 2021, cl.39.1.

系的连接并制作连接两个管理体系的文件:①

> The CONTRACTOR shall take full responsibility for the adequacy, stability and safety of all its operations and methods necessary for the performance of the WORK and shall keep strictly to the provisions of Section VI – Health, Safety and Environment. The CONTRACTOR shall collaborate with the COMPANY in establishing HS & E interface arrangements and the production of a HS & E interface document.

25.97 连接两个相互独立的管理体系有可能涉及各自管理体系本身的修改,因此船厂应当注意的是自己的体系与船东体系衔接的问题。船厂需要考虑的问题是此种衔接是否会影响自己的健康、安全与环境管理体系,而且其他船东也可能会要求与船厂的健康、安全与环境管理体系建立相同的连接,若与数个船东的健康安全与环境管理体系建立的衔接,船东就可能有义务满足所有健康、安全与环境管理体系的要求,否则船东就可以解约:②

> Failure to meet the requirements of Section VI – Health, Safety and Environment or to satisfy the COMPANY's reasonable requirements with regard to the control of HS&E risks in any material respect will be regarded as due cause for the COMPANY giving notice to terminate all or any part of the WORK or the CONTRACT in accordance with Clause 29.1(b).

25.98 应急响应体系是健康、安全与环境管理体系的组成部分,是专门针对意外事故发生的安排。一个有效的应急响应体系能把事故可能带来的损害降到最低。设立应急响应体系还应当设专人负责对应急响应体系的定期检查,包括对设施的检查和对文件的检查。LOGIC 格式对此就有明确要求:③

> The CONTRACTOR shall co-operate with the COMPANY in providing an appropriate response to any emergency occurring at the WORKSITE and shall immediately take such action as may be necessary to protect life and make safe property where such is in imminent peril.

---

① LOGIC Standard Contracts for the UK Offshore Oil and Gas Industries-General Conditions of Contract for Marine Construction, Edition 3, May 2021, cl.39.1.
② LOGIC Standard Contracts for the UK Offshore Oil and Gas Industries-General Conditions of Contract for Marine Construction Edition 3, May 2021, cl.39.3.
③ LOGIC Standard Contracts for the UK Offshore Oil and Gas Industries-General Conditions of Contract for Marine Construction Edition 3, May 2021, cl.39.4.

VI 反腐败条款

概述

25.99　　反腐败条款也是海工装备建造合同中常见的条款，几乎所有海工装备建造合同都会有反腐败条款。反腐败条款是针对合同双方的，要求合同双方包括其董事、管理人员、雇员、代理人或顾问等未曾也不会违反适用的反腐败法律和法规，向任何政府部门、合同相对方、相关第三方等的政府官员、董事、管理人员、雇员、代理人或顾问直接或间接提供资金、礼品或其他任何有价物品、服务，或从事任何贿赂行为。在海工装备建造中，无论建造合同是否有反腐败条款，相关的反腐败法律同样适用，船东和船厂均负有遵守各自反腐败法律规定的义务。

国际商会规则

25.100　　国际商会于 1977 年公布了《反勒索及行贿行为规则》，并分别于 1996 年，1999 年，2005 年以及 2010 年进行了修订。2011 年的《国际商会反腐败规则》（ICC Rules on Combating Corruption）是目前的最新版本，按照国际商会的解释，腐败包括：贿赂、勒索或索取、影响力交易以及洗钱。国际商会还给这四种情形下了定义：[①]

> Bribery is the offering, promising, giving, authorizing or accepting of any undue pecuniary or other advantage to, by or for any of the persons listed above or for anyone else in order to obtain or retain a business or other improper advantage, e.g. in connection with public or private procurement contract awards, regulatory permits, taxation, customs, judicial and legislative proceedings.
>
> Bribery often includes(i) kicking back a portion of a contract payment to government or party officials or to employees of the other contracting party, their close relatives, friends or Business Partners or (ii) using intermediaries such as agents, subcontractors, consultants or other Third Parties, to channel payments to government or party officials, or to employees of the other contracting party, their relatives, friends or Business Partners.

---

① ICC Rules on Combating Corruption 2011, Part I Anti-Corruption Rules, art.1.

Extortion or Solicitation is the demanding of a bribe, whether or not coupled with a threat if the demand is refused. Enterprises will oppose any attempt of extortion or solicitation and are encouraged to report such attempts through available formal or informal reporting mechanisms, unless such reporting is deemed to be counter-productive under the circumstances.

Trading in Influence is the offering or solicitation of an undue advantage in order to exert an improper, real, or supposed influence with a view of obtaining from a public official an undue advantage for the original instigator of the act or for any other person.

Laundering the proceeds of the corrupt practices mentioned above is the concealing or disguising the illicit origin, source, location, disposition, movement or ownership of property, knowing that such property is the proceeds of crime.

《国际商会反腐败规则》由三部分内容组成:(1)规则;(2)企业应当制定的政策;(3)执行反腐败规则的有效因素。《国际商会反腐败规则》供合同当事方自愿适用。国际商会还根据三部分内容分别制定了可供选择的三种反腐败条款。

经合组织公约

1996年经合组织制定通过了《经合组织国际商务交易反对贿赂外国公职人员公约》(OECD Convention on Combating Bribery of Foreign Public Officials in International Business Transactions),简称为《经合组织反贿赂公约》(OECD Anti-Bribery Convention)"。《经合组织反贿赂公约》的特征是针对外国公职人员的贿赂并要求成员国在国内通过立法将贿赂规定为刑事犯罪:①

1. Each Party shall take such measures as may be necessary to establish that it is a criminal offence under its law for any person intentionally to offer, promise or give any undue pecuniary or other advantage, whether directly or through intermediaries, to a foreign public official, for that official or for a third party, in order that the official act or refrain from acting in relation to the performance of official duties, in order to obtain or retain business or other improper advantage in the conduct of international business.

2. Each Party shall take any measures necessary to establish that

---

① Art.1.

complicity in, including incitement, aiding and abetting, or authorisation of an act of bribery of a foreign public official shall be a criminal offence. Attempt and conspiracy to bribe a foreign public official shall be criminal offences to the same extent as attempt and conspiracy to bribe a public official of that Party.

25.103　《经合组织反贿赂公约》不仅要求成员国制定相关的法律,而且还规定了反贿赂和腐败的法人责任:①

Each Party shall take such measures as may be necessary, in accordance with its legal principles, to establish the liability of legal persons for the bribery of a foreign public official.

25.104　《经合组织反贿赂公约》不仅供经合组织成员国签署加入,而且也对其他国家开放。② 《经合组织反贿赂公约》于1999年2月15日生效,目前已有四十四个成员国。③ 反贿赂是《经合组织反贿赂公约》成员国的条约义务,成员国的企业均受此约束。

联合国公约

25.105　2003年联合国大会通过了《联合国反腐败公约》(United Nations Convention against Corruption),④该公约的宗旨是:⑤

(一)促进和加强各项措施,以便更加高效而有力地预防和打击腐败;
(二)促进、便利和支持预防和打击腐败方面的国际合作和技术援

---

① Art.2. 考虑成员国法律有可能没有针对法人的刑事责任,第3.2条还规定:"In the event that, under the legal system of a Party, criminal responsibility is not applicable to legal persons, that Party shall ensure that legal persons shall be subject to effective, proportionate and dissuasive non-criminal sanctions, including monetary sanctions, for bribery of foreign public officials".
② Art.13.
③ 《经合组织反贿赂公约》的成员国是:阿根廷、澳大利亚、奥地利、比利时、巴西、保加利亚、加拿大、智利、哥伦比亚、哥斯达黎加、捷克、丹麦、爱沙尼亚、芬兰、法国、德国、希腊、匈牙利、冰岛、爱尔兰、以色列、意大利、日本、韩国、拉脱维亚、立陶宛、卢森堡、墨西哥、荷兰、新西兰、挪威、秘鲁、波兰、葡萄牙、俄罗斯、斯洛伐克、斯洛文尼亚、南非、西班牙、瑞典、瑞士、土耳其、英国和美国,其中阿根廷、巴西、保加利亚、秘鲁、俄罗斯和南非是非经合组织成员。
④ 2005年10月27日,中国第十届全国人民代表大会常务委员会第十八次会议决定批准《联合国反腐败公约》并同时声明,中国不受该公约第六十六条第二款的约束。按照第六十六条第二款的规定:两个或者两个以上缔约国对于本公约的解释或者适用发生任何争端,在合理时间内不能通过谈判解决的,应当按其中一方请求交付仲裁。如果自请求交付仲裁之日起六个月内这些缔约国不能就仲裁安排达成协议,则其中任何一方均可以依照《国际法院规约》请求将争端提交国际法院。我国保留的是将争议提交国际法院解决。
⑤ 《联合国反腐败公约》第一条。

助,包括了资产追回方面;

(三)提倡廉正、问责制和对公共事务和公共财产的妥善管理。

25.106 《联合国反腐败公约》要求各缔约国设立机构或安排人员专门负责打击腐败的工作。① 此外,《联合国反腐败公约》不仅规定了缔约国国家机关在反腐败工作上的合作,包括举报和提供信息,②还规定了各缔约国在反腐败工作上的国际合作,例如各缔约国在刑事案件中的相互合作;适当情况下在民事和行政案件调查和诉讼中相互协助。③

腐败行为

25.107 《联合国反腐败公约》列出的腐败行为包括:贿赂本国公职人员、贿赂外国公职人员或者国际公共组织官员、公职人员贪污、挪用或者以其他类似方式侵犯财产、影响力交易、滥用职权、资产非法增加、私营部门内的贿赂、私营部门内的侵吞财产、对犯罪所得的洗钱行为、窝赃以及妨害司法。

25.108 贿赂本国公职人员是指:(一)直接或间接向公职人员许诺给予、提议给予或者实际给予该公职人员本人或者其他人员或实体不正当好处,以使该公职人员在执行公务时作为或者不作为;(二)公职人员为其本人或者其他人员或实体直接或间接索取或者收受不正当好处,以作为其在执行公务时作为或者不作为的条件。公职人员系指:(1)无论是经任命还是经选举而在缔约国中担任立法、行政、行政管理或者司法职务的任何人员,无论长期或者临时,计酬或者不计酬,也无论该人的资历如何;(2)依照缔约国本国法律的定义和在该缔约国相关法律领域中的适用情况,履行公共职能,包括为公共机构或者公营企业履行公共职能或者提供公共服务的任何其他人员;(3)缔约国本国法律中界定为"公职人员"的任何其他人员。"公职人员"还可以指依照缔约国本国法律的定义和在该缔约国相关法律领域中的适用情况,履行公共职能或者提供公共服务的任何人员。

25.109 贿赂外国公职人员或者国际公共组织官员是指:(一)直接或间接向外国公职人员或者国际公共组织官员许诺给予、提议给予或者实际给予该公职人员本人或者其他人员或实体不正当好处,以使该公职人员或者该官员在执行公务时作为或者不作为,以便获得或者保留与进行国际商务有关的商业或者其他不正当好

---

① 《联合国反腐败公约》第三十六条。
② 《联合国反腐败公约》第三十八条。
③ 《联合国反腐败公约》第四十三条。

处;(二)外国公职人员或者国际公共组织官员直接或间接为其本人或者其他人员或实体索取或者收受不正当好处,以作为其在执行公务时作为或者不作为的条件。"外国公职人员"系指外国无论是经任命还是经选举而担任立法、行政、行政管理或者司法职务的任何人员,以及为外国,包括为公共机构或者公营企业行使公共职能的任何人员;"国际公共组织官员"系指国际公务员或者经此种组织授权代表该组织行事的任何人员。

25.110　公职人员贪污、挪用或者以其他类似方式侵犯财产是指公职人员为其本人的利益或者其他人员或实体的利益,贪污、挪用或者以其他类似方式侵犯其因职务而受托的任何财产、公共资金、私人资金、公共证券、私人证券或者其他任何贵重物品。

25.111　影响力交易是指:(一)直接或间接向公职人员或者其他任何人员许诺给予、提议给予或者实际给予任何不正当好处,以使其滥用本人的实际影响力或者被认为具有的影响力,为该行为的受益人或者其他任何人从缔约国的行政部门或者公共机关获得不正当好处;(二)公职人员或者其他任何人员为其本人或者他人直接或间接索取或者收受任何不正当好处,以作为该公职人员或者该其他人员滥用本人的实际影响力或者被认为具有的影响力,从缔约国的行政部门或者公共机关获得任何不正当好处的条件。

25.112　滥用职权是指公职人员在履行职务时违反法律,实施或者不实施一项行为,以为其本人或者其他人员或实体获得不正当好处。

25.113　资产非法增加是指公职人员的资产显著增加,而本人无法对其收入的合法性作出合理解释。

25.114　私营部门内的贿赂是指:(一)直接或间接向以任何身份领导私营部门实体或者为该实体工作的任何人许诺给予、提议给予或者实际给予该人本人或者他人不正当好处,以使该人违背职责作为或者不作为;(二)以任何身份领导私营部门实体或者为该实体工作的任何人为其本人或者他人直接或间接索取或者收受不正当好处,以作为其违背职责作为或者不作为的条件。

25.115　私营部门内的侵吞财产是指以任何身份领导私营部门实体或者在该实体中工作的人员侵吞其因职务而受托的任何财产、私人资金、私人证券或者其他任何贵重物品。

25.116　对犯罪所得的洗钱行为是指:(一)明知财产为犯罪所得,为隐瞒或者掩饰该财产的非法来源,或者为协助任何参与实施上游犯罪者逃避其行为的法律后果而转换或者转移该财产;明知财产为犯罪所得而隐瞒或者掩饰该财产的真实性质、来源、所在地、处分、转移、所有权或者有关的权利;(二)在符合本国法律制度基本概念的情况下,在得到财产时,明知其为犯罪所得而仍获取、占有或者使用;对本条所确立的任何犯罪的参与、协同或者共谋实施、实施未遂以及协助、教唆、便利和参谋实施。

25.117　　窝赃是指行为所涉及的人员虽未参与根据本公约确立的任何犯罪,但在这些犯罪实施后,明知财产是根据本公约确立的任何犯罪的结果而窝藏或者继续保留这些财产。

25.118　　妨害司法是指:(一)在涉及根据本公约确立的犯罪的诉讼中使用暴力、威胁或者恐吓,或者许诺给予、提议给予或者实际给予不正当好处,以诱使提供虚假证言或者干扰证言或证据的提供;(二)使用暴力、威胁或恐吓,干扰审判或执法人员针对根据本公约所确立的犯罪执行公务。本项规定概不影响缔约国就保护其他类别公职人员进行立法的权利。①

LOGIC 格式

25.119　　LOGIC 格式也有反贿赂反腐败条款。② 在海工装备建造合同采用 LOGIC 格式情况下,虽然反贿赂反腐败条款是合同条款,但反贿赂反腐败的义务则在合同成立之前就已存在。因此反贿赂反腐败义务是缔约前的义务,在合同中则是以保证的形式出现的:③

> Each PARTY warrants and represents that in negotiating and concluding the CONTRACT it has complied, and in performing its obligations under the CONTRACT it has complied and shall comply, with all APPLICABLE ANTI-BRIBERY LAWS.

25.120　　反贿赂反腐败对船厂而言并不仅仅是一个合同承诺而已,而是必须付诸实践的义务。船厂必须建立符合适用法律要求的反贿赂反腐败的程序:④

> The CONTRACTOR warrants that it has an ABC PROGRAMME setting out adequate procedures to comply with APPLICABLE ANTI-

---

① 见《联合国反腐败公约》第三章。
② LOGIC Standard Contracts for the UK Offshore Oil and Gas Industries, General Conditions of Contract for Marine Construction Edition 3, May 2021, cl.33.
③ LOGIC Standard Contracts for the UK Offshore Oil and Gas Industries, General Conditions of Contract for Marine Construction Edition 3, May 2021, cl.33.1.
④ LOGIC Standard Contracts for the UK Offshore Oil and Gas Industries, General Conditions of Contract for Marine Construction Edition 3, May 2021, cl.33.2.

BRIBERY LAWS and that it will comply with such ABC PROGRAMME in respect of the CONTRACT.

25.121　船厂不仅必须建立反腐败程序,船东只要事先通知船厂就可以派人对船厂的反贿赂和腐败机制及其运行进行审查。①

In addition and subject to Clause 30, on provision of no less than thirty (30) days' formal notice, the COMPANY or its duly authorised representatives shall have the right to audit, at its own cost, the existence, content and implementation of the CONTRACTOR's ABC PROGRAMME, but such right shall not include access to documents that are legally privileged or were created for the purpose of an on-going internal investigation.

25.122　船厂没有按照约定履行其反贿赂反腐败义务将会有严重的后果。按照LOGIC 格式的规定,一旦业主有合理理由怀疑承包商已违反贿赂反腐败义务的,业主就可以停止付款:②

Subject to the remaining provisions of this Clause 33.5, if the COMPANY has a reasonable belief that the CONTRACTOR has breached Clause 33.1, the COMPANY may give formal notice of its intention to suspend payments under the CONTRACT to the CONTRACTOR giving the basis of such reasonable belief. If within seven (7) days of receipt of such formal notice the CONTRACTOR neither responds with information reasonably satisfactory to the COMPANY to refute such belief nor commences and continues with action reasonably satisfactory to the COMPANY to remedy such suspected breach of Clause 33.1, the COMPANY may, by the provision of formal notice, suspend with immediate effect any payments due under Section III – Remuneration without liability.

25.123　如果业主的合理怀疑在发出中止付款通知后的 30 天内依然存在,业主可以发出通知解除合同。③ 一旦业主解约,合同将视为因承包商违约被解除。在此种情况下,虽然承包商可以得到解约前已完成工作的报酬,但无权获得任何与贿赂

---

① LOGIC Standard Contracts for the UK Offshore Oil and Gas Industries, General Conditions of Contract for Marine Construction Edition 3, May 2021, cl.33.3.
② LOGIC Standard Contracts for the UK Offshore Oil and Gas Industries, General Conditions of Contract for Marine Construction Edition 3, May 2021, cl.33.5(a).
③ LOGIC Standard Contracts for the UK Offshore Oil and Gas Industries, General Conditions of Contract for Marine Construction Edition 3, May 2021, cl.33.5(d)(ii).

腐败相关的款项。如果业主能证明承包商确实存在贿赂或腐败情形的,业主还可以要求承包商赔偿其因此产生的额外成本。只要业主在发出解约通知时确有理由怀疑承包商违反了反贿赂反腐败法律,即使证据表明承包商实际上并没有违反任何反贿赂反腐败法律,业主的解约也不构成违约。但是承包商可以获得业主以承包商违反反贿赂反腐败法律为由扣留的所有款项。[1]

船厂的地位

25.124　按照 LOGIC 格式的规定,船东仅凭自己的合理怀疑就可以解约,无需任何证据。而且,即使事实证明船东解约错误也无需承担任何违约责任。LOGIC 格式的这一规定对船厂来说应当是不公平的。合理怀疑可以是主观的,而且往往是主观的。换言之,船东可以凭主观意愿解除合同。更重要的是,船东无需对自己的错误承担违约责任。虽然按照 LOGIC 格式第 29.1(a) 条的规定,船东是可以按照自己的意愿解除合同,但两种解约的后果显然不同。船东按照第 29.1(a) 条的规定解约,船东应当根据船厂已完成的工作支付报酬,但船东以船厂违反反贿赂反腐败法律解约,船东则无需支付建造款,即使是船厂已经完成的工作也不例外。即使船厂最终证明并没有违反反腐败法律,船东虽然应当针对船厂已完成的工作支付报酬,但似乎并没有支付利息的义务。

---

[1] LOGIC Standard Contracts for the UK Offshore Oil and Gas Industries, General Conditions of Contract for Marine Construction Edition 3, May 2021, cl.33.6.

案例

A C Controls Limited v British Broadcasting Corporation [2002] EWHC 3132 ...... 2.111
Adams v Lindsell (1818) 1 B & Ald 681 ...... 2.73
Admiralty Commissioners v Cox and King (1927) 27 Ll L Rep 223 ...... 4.140, 12.11
Adyard Abu Dhabi v SD Marine Services [2011] EWHC848 ...... 5.31, 6.44, 6.68 10.51, 10.83, 10.92, 10.93
Afovos Shipping Co SA v Pagnan [1983] 1 All ER 499 ...... 12.20
Agrokor AG v Tradigrain SA [2000] 1 Lloyd's Rep 497 ...... 9.44
Ailsa Graig Fishing Co Ltd v Malvern Fishing Co Ltd (The Strathallan)(1927) 43 TLR 323 ...... 11.95
Aitchison v Lohre (1879) 4 App Cas 755 ...... 14.121
Aktiebolaget Gotaverken v Westminster Corporation of Monrovia and Another [1971] 2 Lloyd's Rep 505 ...... 5.28, 5.155, 11.53
Alexander Thorn v The Mayor and Commonalty of London (1876) 1 App Cas 120 ...... 5.37
Alexander v Rayson [1936] 1 KB 169 ...... 6.78
Alexiadi v Robinson (1846) 9 QB 713 ...... 13.39
Alfred C Toepfer v Peter Cremer [1975] 1 Lloyd's Rep 406; [1975] 2 Lloyd's Rep 118 ...... 9.133, 9.136
Allan v Leo Lines Ltd [1957] 1 Lloyd's Rep 127 ...... 2.219
Alldridge (Builders) Ltd v Grandactual Limited (1996) 55 Con LR 91 ...... 2.114
Allen v Flood[1898] AC 1 ...... 14.93
Alpha Trading Ltd v Dunnshaw-Patten Ltd [1981] 1 Lloyd's Rep 122 ...... 2.221
Amin Rasheed Shipping Corp v Kuwait Insurance Co (The Al Wahab) [1983] 3

WLR 241 ·· 15.28
Anangel Atlas Compania Naviera SA and Others v Ishikawajima-Harima Heavy
　　Industries Co Ltd (No.2) [1990] 2 Lloyd's Rep 526 ················ 2.98, 2.169
Anderson v Anderson [1895] 1 QB 749 ·· 9.39
Andrews Bros (Bournemouth) Ltd v Singer & Co Ltd [1934] 1 KB 17
　　·· 1.92, 11.9
Anglomar Shipping Co Ltd v Swan Hunter Shipbuilders Ltd and Swan Hunter
　　Group Ltd (The London Lion) [1980] 2 Lloyd's Rep 456 ················ 11.112
Anns v Merton London Borough Council [1978] AC 72 ····················· 3.53
Antaios Compania Naviera SA v Salen Rederierna AB (The Antaios)
　　[1983] 1 AC 191 ·· 15.127, 15.119
Ashington Piggeries Ltd v Christopher Hill Ltd [1971] 1 Lloyd's Rep 245
　　··· 1.68, 1.194, 11.5
Astilleros Canarios SA v Cape Hatteras Shipping Co Inc andHammerton Shipping
　　Co SA (The Cape Hatteras) [1982] 1 Lloyd's Rep 518 ············ 4.114, 10.49
Astley v Weldon2 B & P 346 ·· 4.102
Astro AMO Compania Naviera SA v Elf Union SA and First National City
　　Bank (The Zographia M) [1976] 2 Lloyd's Rep 382 ···················· 4.36
Athens Cape Naviera SA v Deutsche Dampfschiffahrtsgesellschaft "Hansa"
Aktiengesellschaft and Another (The Barenbels) [1985] 1 Lloyd's Rep 528
　　··· 1.84
Atkinson v Bell (1828) 8 B & C 277 ································ 8.119, 8.136
Atlas Maritime Co SA v Avalon Maritime Ltd (The Coral Rose) [1991] 1 Lloyd's
　　Rep. 563 ··· 2.198
Australian Steamship Proprietary Ltd v John Lewis & Sons Ltd (1933) 47 Ll L
　　Rep 132 ··· 4.85
AXA Sun Life Services Plc v Campbell Martin Ltd [2011] 1 CLC 312 ····· 22.17
Azimut-Benetti Spa v Healey [2011] 1 Lloyd's Rep 473 ······················ 4.120
B & S Contracts and Design Ltd v Victor Green Publications Ltd [1984] ICR 419
　　··· 9.41, 9.54
Baldry v Marshall [1925] 1 KB 260 ··· 11.23
Balfour Beatty Building Ltd v Chestermount Properties Ltd (1933) 9 Const LR 117

.... 6.34

Balfour Beatty Construction Ltd v The Mayorand Burgesses of the London Borough of Lambeth [2002] EWHC 597 .... 10.42

Balmoral Group Ltd v Borealis (UK) Ltd [2006] 2 CLC 220 .... 1.116

Bank of Baroda v Patel [1995] 1 Lloyd's Rep 391 .... 4.205

Bank woor Handel en Scheepvaart NV v Slatford (No 2) [1953] 1 QB 248
.... 8.123

Baring v Corrie (1818) 2 B & Ald 137 .... 2.207

Baxall Securities Ltd & Anr v Sheard Walshaw Partnership & Ors [2002] PNLR 24
.... 14.47

Beal v South Devon Rly (1864) 3 H & C 337 .... 5.117

Berezovsky and Another v Edmiston & Co Ltd and Another (The Darius) [2011] 1 Lloyd's Rep 419 .... 2.218

Bell Electric Ltd v Aweco Appliance Systems GmbH & Co KG [2002] CLC 1246
.... 2.209

Bernuth Lines Limited v High Seas Shipping Ltd [2006] 1 Lloyd's Rep 537
.... 15.63

BHP Petroleum Ltd and Others v British Steel Plc and Dalmine SpA [1999] 2 Lloyd's Rep 583; [2000] 2 Lloyd's Rep 277
.... 11.2, 11.97, 11.98

Blackpool and Fylde Aero Club Ltd v Blackpool Borough Council [1990] 1 WLR 1195 .... 2.124

BMBF (No 12) Ltd v Harland & Wolff Shipbuilding & Heavy Industries Limited [2001] 2 Lloyd's Rep 227 .... 12.53

BOC Group plc v Cention LLC & Anor [1999] CLC 497 .... 4.78

Bolivia v Indemnity Mutual Marine Assurance Co [1909] 1 KB 785 .... 9.95

BP Exploration Operating Company Limited v Dolphin Drilling Limited [2010] 2 Lloyd's Rep 192 .... 25.32

Bramhill v Edwards [2004] 2 Lloyd's Rep 653 .... 1.110

Bremer Handelsgesellslchaft mbH v Vanden Avenne-Izegem PVBA [1977] 1 Lloyd's Rep 133; [1978] 2 Lloyd's Rep 109 .... 9.138, 10.69

Brinkibon Ltd v Stahag Stahl Und Stahlwarenhandels GmbH [1983] 2 AC 34

.... 2.86
Bristol and West Building Society v Mothew [1998] 1 Ch 1 .... 2.213
Bristol Tramways & Carriage Co Ltd v Fiat Motors Ltd [1910] 2 KB 831
.... 1.145 – 1.147
Britain Steamship Co Ltd v Lithgows Ltd (1933) 45 Ll L Rep 89; 1975 SC 110
.... 1.95, 1.148
British and Foreign Marine Insurance Co v Gaunt [1921] 2 AC 41 .... 14.40
British Mutoscope & Biograph Co Ltd v Homer [1901] 1 Ch 671 .... 18.4
British Steel Corporation v Cleveland Bridge and Engineering Co Ltd [1984]
  1 All ER 504 .... 2.26, 2.27, 2.31, 2.61
Brogden v Metropolitan Railway Co (1877) 2 App Cas 666 .... 2.38
Bromagev Prosser (1825) 4 B & C 247 .... 14.92
Bronester v Priddle [1961] 3 All ER 471 .... 4.41, 12.3
Brunswick Construction Ltd v Nowlan 21 BLR 27 .... 5.40
BS Brown and Son Ltd v Craiks Ltd [1970] 1 WLR 750 .... 1.120
BTP Tioxide Ltd v Armada Marine SA (The Nema No 2) [1982] AC 724
.... 15.127
Bulman & Dickson v Fenwick & Co [1894] 1 QB 179 .... 9.88
Butler Machine Tool Co Ltd v Ex-Cell-O Corporation (England) Ltd [1979]
  1 WLR 401 .... 2.101
Byrne & Co v Leon Van Tienhoven & Co (1880) 5 CPD 344 .... 2.62, 2.38
Caja de Ahorros del Mediterraneo & Ors v Gold Coast Ltd [2002] CLC 397
.... 4.169
Caledonia North Sea Limited v British Telecommunications Plc (Scotland) and
  Others [2002] UKHL 4 .... 25.56
Cambridge v Anderton (1824) 2 B & C 691 .... 14.105
Cammell Laird & Co Ltd v Manganese Bronze and Brass Co Ltd (1932) 43
  Ll Rep 466; (1933) 45 Ll L Rep 89; [1934] AC 402
.... 1.111, 1.112, 1.113, 1.135 – 144, 11.23
Campbell v Edwards [1976] 1 WLR 403 .... 15.95
Captain JA Cates Tug and Wharfage Co Ltd v Franklin Insurance Co [1927] AC 698
.... 14.107

Carl-ZeissiStiftung v Rayner & Keeler Ltd (No. 2) [1967] 1 AC 857 ········· 15.58
Cehave MV v Bremer Handelgesellschaft mbh (The Hansa Nord) [1975]
　2 Lloyd's Rep 445 ·· 2.183
Cellulose Acetate Silk Co v Widnes Foundry [1933] AC 20 ·········· 4.109
Cenargo Ltd v Empresa Nacional Bazan de Construcciones Navales Militarres SA
　[2002] CLC 1151 ·································· 4.96, 4.118, 5.78
Chandelor v Lopus (1603) Cro Jac 4 ································ 11.1
Chandris v Isbrandtsen-Moller Co Inc [1951] 1 KB 240 ············· 9.39
Channel Island Ferries Ltd v Sealink UK Ltd [1988] 1 Lloyd's Rep 323 ······ 9.55
Channel Tunnel Group Ltd and Another v Balfour Beatty Construction Ltd and
　Others [1933] AC 334 ··· 15.25
Charrington & Co Ltd v Wooder [1914] AC 71 ······················ 22.2
Chartbrook Ltd v Persimmon Homes [2009] UKHL 38 ·········· 25.63, 25.67
Cheall v Association of Professional Executive Clerical and Computer Staff
　(APEX) [1983] 2 AC 180 ······································ 21.19
Cheikh Boutros Selim El-Khoury and Other v Ceylon Shipping Lines Ltd
　(The Madeleine) [1967] 2 Lloyd's Rep 224 ······················ 10.105
Chemco Leasing SpA v Rediffusion Plc [1987] FTLR 201 ············ 4.223
China Shipbuilding Corporation v Nippon Yusen Kabukishi Kaisha and another
　(Seta Maru, Saikyo and Suma) [2000] 1 Lloyd's Rep 367;
　[2000] CLC 566 ···························· 7.75, 11.11, 11.39, 11.41, 11.73
Christie & Vesey Ltd v Maatschappij Tot Exploitatie Van Schepen en Andere
　Zaken Helvetia NVmmm [1960] 1 Lloyd's Rep 540 ················ 8.2
Christie, Owen and Davies Ltd v Stockton [1953] 1 WLR 1353 ········ 2.147
Ciampa and OthersvBritish India Steam Navigation Company Limited [1915]
　2 KB 774 ·· 9.10
City Inn Ltd v Shepherd Construction Ltd [2003] BLR 468; [2010] CSIH 67
　································· 6.40, 10.29, 10.30, 10.38
Clan Line Steamers Ltd v Liverpool & London War Risks Insurance Association
　Ltd [1943] 1 KB 209 ··· 9.90
Clydebank Engineering & Shipbuilding Co Ltd v Don Jose Ramos Izquierdo y
　Castaneda [1905] AC 6 ······················ 4.86, 4.90, 4.99, 4.107, 4.112

CMA CGM SA v Beteiligungs-Kommanditgesellschaft MS "Northern Pioneer"
  Schiffahrtsgesellschaft mbH & Co and Others [2003] 1 Lloyd's Rep 212
  .... 15.128
Collins v Collins (1858) 26 Beav 306 .... 15.1, 15.20
Commonwealth Construction Company Limited v Imperial Oil Ltd [1976] 6
  WWR 219 .... 14.5
Commonwealth Smelting Ltd v Guardian Royal Exchange Ltd [1984] 2 Lloyd's
  Rep 608 .... 9.72
Compagnie Commerciale Sucres et Denrees v C Czarnikow Ltd [1990]
  1 WLR 1337 .... 8.21
Compagnie Tunisienne de Navigation SA v Compagnie d'Armement Maritime SA
  [1970] 3 WLR 389 .... 15.33
Confetti Records v Warner Music UK [2003] EWCH 1274 .... 2.146
Conquer v Boot [1928] 2 KB 336 .... 15.59
Continental Grain Export Corp v STM Grain Ltd [1979] 2 Lloyd's Rep 460
  .... 9.22
Continental Illinois National Bank & Trust Company of Chicago v Papanicolaou
  [1986] 2 Lloyd's Rep 441 .... 4.68
Cooden Engineering Co v Stanford [1953] 1 QB 86 .... 4.97
Couchman v Hill [1947] KB 554 .... 1.71, 1.72, 1.73, 1.78
Courtney & Fairbairn Ltd v Tolaini Brothers (Hotels) Ltd. and Another [1975]
  1 WLR 297 .... 2.155
Covington Marine Corp and Others v Xiamen Shipbuilding Industry Co Ltd
  [2006] 1 Lloyd's Rep 745 .... 12.33
Covington Marine Corporation v Xiamen Shipbuilding Industry Co Ltd [2006]
  1 CLC 624 .... 2.41
Croudace Construction Ltd v Cawoods Concrete Products Ltd [1978] 2 Lloyd's
  Rep 55 .... 11.76, 11.80
Currie v Misa (1875) LR 10 Ex 153 .... 2.162
David Baxter Edward Thomas, Peter Sandford Gander v BPE Solicitors [2010]
  EWHC 306 .... 2.88
Davis Contractors Ltd v Fareham Urban District Council [1956] AC 696 ...... 4.4

Davy Offshore Ltd v Emerald Field Contracting Ltd [1992] 2 Lloyd's Rep 142 .... 8.128

Deepak Fertilisers and Petrochemicals Corporation v ICI Chemicals & Polymers Ltd and Others [1999] 1 Lloyd's Rep 387 .... 11.79

Demco Investments & Commercial SA v Se Banken Forsakring Holding Aktiebolag [2005] 2 Lloyd's Rep 650 .... 15.120

Dixon Kerly Ltd v Robinson [1965] 2 Lloyd's Rep 404 .... 5.35

Docker v Hyams [1969] 1 Lloyd's Rep 487 .... 7.87

Dodd v Churton [1897] 1 QB 562 .... 6.33, 10.47

Dubai Islamic Bank PJSC v Paymentech Merchant Services Inc [2001] 1 Lloyd's Rep 65 .... 15.41

Dunlop Pneumatic Tyre Company Ltd v New Garage Motor Company Ltd [1915] AC 79 .... 4.110

E B Aaby's Rederi AS v The Union of India (The Evje) [1974] 2 Lloyd's Rep 57 .... 15.51

Edmund Murray Ltd v BSP International Foundations Ltd (1992) 33 Com LR 1 .... 11.19

Edward Owen Engineering Ltd v Barclays Bank International Ltd & Umma Bank [1978] 1 QB 159 .... 4.216

Edwards v Skyways Ltd [1964] 1 WLR 349 .... 2.49

EE Caledonia Ltd v Orbit Valve Co Europe [1993] 2 Lloyd's Rep 418 .... 5.110, 11.124

Egerton v Bronlow (1853) 4 HL Cas 1 .... 4.8

Egmatra AG v Marco Trading Corporation [1999] 1 Lloyd's Rep 862 .... 15.119, 15.123

Entores Ltd v Miles Far East Corp [1955] 2 QB 327 .... 2.78

ERDC Group Limited v Brunel University [2006] EWHC 687 (TCC) 2.113, 6.28

F & G Sykes (Wessex) Ltd v Fine Fare Ltd [1967] 1 Lloyd's Rep 853 .... 15.18

Fast Ferries One SA v Ferries Australia Pty Ltd [2000] 1 Lloyd's Rep 534 .... 21.23

Felkin v Lord Herbert (1861) 30 LJ Ch 798 .... 8.104

Fenton v Thorley & Co Ltd [1903] AC 443 .... 9.118
Fibrosa Spolka Ackyjna v Fairbairn Lawson Combe Barbour Ltd [1943] AC 32
 .... 2.163
Finance for Shipping Limited v Appledore Shipbuilders Limited [1982] Com LR 49
 .... 9.142
Finnegan v Allen [1943] 1 KB 425 .... 2.180
Fitzsimmons v Lord Mostyn [1904] AC 46 .... 15.111
Forder v Great Western Railway [1905] 2 KB 532 .... 25.75
Forward v Pittard (1785) 1 TR 27 .... 9.57
Fraser Shipping Ltd v Colton and Others [1997] 1 Lloyd's Rep 586. ...... 14.108
Frederick Leyand & Co Ltd (J Russell & Co) v Compania Panamena Europea
 Navegacion Ltada (1943) 76 Ll L Rep 113; [1934] Ch 431 .... 4.64
Frontier International Shipping Corp v Swissmarine Corporation Inc and Another
 (The Cape Equinox) [2005] 1 Lloyd's Rep 390 .... 9.41
G Percy Trentham Ltd v Archital Luxfer Ltd [1993] 1 Lloyd's Rep 25
 .... 2.40, 2.91
Galoo Ltd and Others v Bright Grahame Murray [1994] 1 WLR 1360 ...... 10.19
George Cohen, Sons and Co v Standard Marine Insurance Co Ltd (1925)
 21 Ll L Rep 30 .... 14.109
George Moundreas & Co SA v Navimpex Centrala Navala [1985] 2 Lloyd's
 Rep 515 .... 2.222
Gibson v Manchester City Council [1978] 1 WLR 520; [1979] 1 WLR 294
 .... 2.51
Gilbert Ash (Northern) Ltd v Modern Engineering (Bristol) Ltd [1974] AC 689
 .... 4.66, 4.75
Gill & Duffus SA v Rionda Futures Ltd [1994] 2 Lloyd's Rep 67 .... 2.165
Gold Coast Ltd v Caja de Ahorros del Mediterraneo & Others
 [2002] 1 Lloyd's Rep 617 .... 4.177, 4.196
Guiness Mahon & Co Ltd v Kensington & Chelsea Royal BC [1999] QB 215
 .... 2.163
Government of Gibraltar v Kenney [1956] 2 QB 410 .... 15.51
Graham v Belfast and Northern Counties Ry Co [1901] 2 IR 13

Great Eastern Hotel Company Ltd v John Laing Construction Ltd Laing
   Construction Plc [2005] EWHC 181 ·························· 10.24, 10.25, 10.37
Grill v General Iron Screw Collier Co (1866) LR 1 CP 600 ················ 5.118
Gyllenhammar & Partners International Ltd and Others v Sour Brodogradevna
   Industrija [1989] 2 Lloyd's Rep 403 ······························· 12.38
H E Daniel Ltd v Carmel Exporters & Importers Ltd [1953] 2 Lloyd's Rep 103
   ·· 15.48, 15.60
Hackney BC v Doré [1922] 1 KB 431 ·························· 9.9, 9.12
Halki Shipping Corp v Sopex Oils Ltd [1998] 1 WLR 726 ··············· 15.16
Hall Brothers SS Co Ltd v Young [1939] 1 KB 748 ······················ 14.41
Hancock Shipping Co Ltd v Deacon & Trysail (Private) Ltd and Another
   (The Casper Trader)[1991] 2 Lloyd's Rep 550 ·················· 5.127
Hardwick Game Farm v Suffolk Agricultural Poultry Producers Association
   [1969] 1 WLR 287 ··· 8.124
Harland & Wolff Ltd v Lakeport Navigation Co Panama SA [1974] 1 Lloyd's
   Rep 301 ··· 8.29, 10.102, 10.113
Harlingdon and Leinster Enterprises Ltd v Christopher Hull Fine Art Ltd
   [1991] 1 QB 564 ·································· 1.75, 1.76, 1.77, 178
Harrison v Holland & Hannen & Cubitts Ltd [1921] 3 KB 297 ············ 4.43
Hartley v Hymans [1920] 3 KB 475 ·· 8.20
Harvela Investments Ltd v Royal Trust Co of Canada (CI) Ltd [1986] AC 207
   ··· 2.122
Harvey v Facey [1893] AC 552 ··· 2.44
Haugland Tankers AS v RMK Marine Gemi Yapim Sanayii ve Deniz
   Tasimaciligi Iisletmesi AS [2005] 1 CLC 271 ···························· 23.9
Head v Tattersall (1871-72) LR 7 Ex 7 ···································· 8.175
Heald v O'Connor [1971] 1 WLR 497 ····································· 4.171
Heesens Yacht Builders BV v Cox Syndicate Management Ltd Munich Re
   Capital Ltd(The Red Sapphire)[2006] 2 Lloyd's Rep 35 ················ 14.36
Heilbut, Symons & Co v Buckleton [1913] AC 30 ························ 2.184
Hendry v Chartsearch Ltd [1998] CLC 1382 ······························· 16.14
Henry Boot Construction (UK) Ltd v Malmaison Hotel (Manchester) Ltd

(1999) 70 Con LR 32 …………………………………………………… 10.22
Henthorn v Fraser [1892] 2 Ch 27 …………………………………… 2.75
Heskell v Continental Express (1949/50) Ll L Rep 438 …………… 10.23, 10.24
Heyman v Darwins Ltd [1942] AC 356; (1942) 72 Ll L Rep 65
   …………………………………………………………………… 12.2, 15.50
Hill v Haines [2008] 1 Ch 416 ………………………………………… 2.167
Hinton v Dibber (1842) 2 QB 646 …………………………………… 5.117
Hirji Mulji v Cheong Yue Steamship Company [1926] AC 497 …… 12.31
Hobson v Bartram & Sons Ltd (1950) 83 Ll L Rep 313 …………… 5.112
Holme v Brunskill (1878) 3 QBD 495 ……………………………… 4.203
Holme v Guppy (1838) 3 M & W 387 …………………… 4.13, 10.46, 10.47
Hong Kong and Shanghai Banking Corp v Kloeckner & Co AG [1990] 2 QB 514
   …………………………………………………………………………… 4.67
Hongkong Fir Shipping Co Ltd v Kawasaki Kisen Kaisha Ltd [1962] 2 QB 26
   …………………………………………………………………………… 2.182
Horabin v British Overseas Airways Corporation [1952] 2 Lloyd's Rep 450
   …………………………………………………………………………… 25.76
Horn v Sunderland Corp [1941] 2 KB 26 …………………………… 9.36
Hough v Head (1885) 52 LT 861 …………………………………… 9.113
Household Fire Insurance Co v Grant [1879] 4 Ex D 216 ………… 2.76
Howe v Smith (1884) 27 Ch D 89 …………………………………… 4.42
Hull Central Dry Dock & Engineering Works Ltd v Ohlson Steamship Ltd
   (1924) 19 Ll L Rep 54 ……………………………… 6.38, 9.50, 9.77
Hurstanger v Wilson [2007] 1 WLR 2351 …………………………… 2.214
Hyde v Wrench (1840) 3 Beavan 334 ………………………………… 2.96
Hyundai Heavy Industries Co Ltd v Papadopoulos and Other
   [1980] 2 Lloyd's Rep 1 ………… 1.16, 13.58, 13.59, 13.61, 13.90, 13.92
In re Blyth Shipbuilding & Drydocks Company Limited (1925) 23 Ll L Rep 205;
   [1926] Ch 494 ……………………………………………… 8.137, 8.143
In Re Wait [1927] 1 Ch 606 …………………………………… 1.63, 1.65
Investors Compensation Scheme Ltd v West Bromwich Building Society [1998]
   1 WLR 896 …………………………………………………………… 22.4

J Gordon Alison & Co Ltd v Wallsend Shipway and Engineering Co Ltd [1983]
  1 WLR 964 ·· 11.94
J & J Makin Ltd v London & North Eastern Rly Co [1945] 1 KB 467 ······ 9.120
Janson v Driefontein Consolidated Mines Ltd [1900] 2 QB 339 ·············· 9.83
Jarvis v Moy Davies Smith Vandervell and Company [1936] 1 KB 399 ······ 13.1
Jayaar Impex Ltd v Toaken Group Ltd [1996] 2 Lloyd's Rep 437 ············ 2.93
John Doyle Construction v Laing Management (Scotland) Ltd 2004 SC 713
  ··· 10.26, 10.27, 10.28
Johnson v Agnew [1980] AC 367 ·· 12.3, 12.39
Kastor Navigation Co Ltd v AGF MAT [2004] 2 Lloyd's Rep 119 ········· 15.110
Kawasaki Kisen Kabukishi Kaisha of Kobe v Bantham Steamship Company Ltd
  (No 2) [1939] 2 KB 544 ··· 9.83, 9.87
Kingston-upon-Hull (Governors) v Petch (1854) 10 Ex 610 ················ 2.144
Kleinwort Benson Ltd v Malaysian Mining Berhad [1988] 1 WLR 799 ······ 4.220
Langham v Nenny (1797) 30 ER 1109 ··· 16.1
Lauritzen v. Larsen (1953) 345 US 571 ······································ 3.110
Law v Redditch Local Board [1892] 1 QB 127 ································· 4.88
Leaf v International Galleries [1950] 2 KB 86 ································· 1.78
Lebeaupin v Richard Crispin & Co (1920) 4 Ll L Rep 122
  ··· 9.2, 9.6, 9.38, 9.49, 9.68
Levy v Assicurazioni Generali [1940] AC 791 ································· 9.96
Linden Gardens Trust Ltd v Lenesta Sludge Disposal Ltd [1994] 1 AC 85
  ··· 16.7, 16.8
Lindvig v Forth Shipbuilding & Engineering Company Ltd (1921) Ll L Rep 253
  ·· 8.24, 9.51
Little v Courage Ltd (1995) 70 R&CR 469 ···································· 2.160
Lloyds Bank Ltd v Bundy [1975] QB 326 ····································· 2.168
Lloyds Bank Ltd v Marcan [1973] 2 All ER 359 ······························· 5.124
The London Steamship Owners' Insurance Co v Grampian Steamship Co
  (The Balnacraig) [1890] 24 QBD 32 ·· 14.62
London Underground Limited v Citylink Telecommunications Limited [2007]
  EWCH 1749; [2007] CSOH 190 ·································· 10.25, 10.35

Lord Elphinstone v The Monkland Iron and Coal Company Limited and
Liquidators [1886] 11 App Cas 332 ················· 4.100
MacDonald Estates Plc v National Car Parks Ltd 2010 SC 250 ············ 15.94
Magnus v Buttemer (1852) 11 CB876; 21 LJCP 119 ················· 9.115
Mamidoil-Jetoil Greek Petroleum Company SA and Another v Okta Crude Oil
Refinery AD [2003] 1 Lloyd's Rep 1 ················· 9.43
Mannai Investments Co Ltd v Eagle Star Life Assurance Co Ltd [1997] AC 749
················· 22.4
Marc Rich & Co AG and Others v Bishop Rock Marine Co Ltd, Bethmarine Co
Ltd and Nippon Kaiji Kyoki (The Nicholas H) [1992] 2 Lloyd's Rep 481
················· 3.50
Mardorf Peach & Co Ltd v Attica Sea Carriers Corporation of Liberia
(The Laconia) [1977] 1 Lloyd's Rep 315 ················· 4.37
Mariola Marine Corporation v Lloyd's Register of Shipping (The Morning Watch)
[1990] 1 Lloyd's Rep. 547 QB ················· 3.48
Marston Construction Co Ltd v Kigass Ltd (1989) 15 Con LR 116 ············ 2.29
Martindale v Smith [1841] 1 QB 389 ················· 2.187
Martineau v Kitching (1871-72) LR 7 QB 436 ················· 8.168
Matheson & Co Ltd v A Tabah & Sons [1963] 2 Lloyd's Rep 270 ········ 15.109
Matsoukis v Priestman & Co [1915] 1 KB 481 ············· 9.5, 9.26, 9.68
May and Butcher Limited v The King [1934] 2 KB 17 ············· 2.59, 15.17
McDonald v DennysLascelles Ltd (1933) 48 CLR 457 ················· 13.54
McDougall v Aeromarine of Emsworth Ltd [1958] 2 Lloyd's Rep 345
················· 1.15, 1.114, 7.42, 7.94, 8.26, 8.149, 12.28
McGiffin v Palmer's Shipbuilding & Iron Co Ltd (1882) 10 QBD 5 ········ 11.29
Merchants' Trading Company v Banner (1871) LR 12 Eq 18 ················· 12.51
Metalimex Foreign Trade Corpn v Eugenie Maritime Co [1962] 1 Lloyd's Rep 378
················· 15.67
Midland Bank Trust Co Ltd v Green [1981] AC 513 ················· 2.163
Milford v Hughe (1846) 16 Meeson and Welsby 174 ················· 2.204
Millar's Machinery Co v David Way & Son (1934) 40 Com Cas 204 ······ 11.75
Mirant Asia-Pacific Construction (Hong Kong) Ltd v Ove Arup & Partners

International Ltd [2007] EWHC 918 ··· 10.31, 10.34

Mitsubishi Corporation v Aristidis I Alafouzos [1988] 1 Lloyd's Rep 191
·· 4.10, 4.217

Mucklow v Mangles [1808] 1 Taunt 318 ······················· 8.114, 8.118, 8.119

Multiplex Constructions (UK) Ltd v Honeywell Control Systems Ltd [2007]
Bus LR Digest D109 ································· 10.44, 10.66, 10.74, 10.81

Muscat Dhows between Great Britain and France (Hague Court Reports 1916, p.93)
·· 3.109

Muscat v Smith [2003] 1 WLR 2853 ·· 16.31

National Oil Co of Zimbabwe (Private) Ltd and Others v Nicholas Collwyn Sturge
[1991] 2 Lloyd's Rep 281 ··· 9.86, 9.94

National Oilwell (UK) Ltd v Davy Offshore Ltd [1993] 2 Lloyd's Rep 582
·· 14.124

Nelson v William Chalmers & Co Ltd 1913 SC 441 ··············· 5.154, 8.146

New Zealand Shipping Co Ltd v Societe des Ateliers et Chantiers de France
[1919] AC 1 ··· 21.13, 21.19, 21.22

Newfoundland v Newfoundland Railway Co (1888) 13 App Cas 199 ········ 16.29

Niblett Ltd v Confectioners' Materials Co Ltd [1921] 3 KB 387 ······ 1.85, 1.88

Nichols v Marsland (1876) LR 2 Ex D 1 ································· 9.56, 9.65

North Ocean Shipping Co Ltd v Hyundai Construction Co Ltd and Hyundai
Shipbuilding and Heavy Industries Co Ltd [1979] 1 Lloyd's Rep 89 ······ 4.159

Nugent v Smith (1876) 1 CPD 423 ························· 9.1, 9.11, 9.58, 9.61

Ocean Steamship Co Ltd v Liverpool & London War Risks Association Ltd
[1946] KB 561 ··· 9.92

Okura & Co Ltd v Navara Shipping Corporation SA [1981] 1 Lloyd's Rep 561;
[1982] 2 Lloyd's Rep 537 ··· 2.137

Oresundsvarvet Aktiebolag v Marcos Diamantis Lemos (The Angelic Star)
[1988] 1 Lloyd's Rep 122 ··· 4.94

Oscar Chess Ltd v Williams [1957] 1 All ER 325 ···································· 11.1

Page v Newman (1829) 9 B&C 378 ·· 13.11

Pagnan SpA v Tradax Ocean Transportation SA [1987] 2 Lloyd's Rep 342
·· 9.14

Parkin v Thorold (1852) 16 Beav 59 ·········· 2.186
Paton & Sons v Payne & Co (1897) 35 SLR 112 ·········· 8.20
Paul Smith Ltd v H & S International Holding Inc [1991] 2 Lloyd's Rep 127
    ·········· 15.38
Peak Construction (Liverpool) Ltd v McKinney Foundations Ltd [1970]
    1 BLR 111 ·········· 10.48
Pearce and High Limited v Baxter (1999) 1 TCLR 157 ·········· 11.62
Penarth Dock Engineering Company Ltd v Pounds [1963] 1 Lloyd's Rep 359
    ·········· 8.189
Pentecost v London District Auditor [1951] 2 KB 759 ·········· 5.119
Perini Pacific Ltd v Greater Vancouver Sewerage and Drainage District (1966)
    57 DLR (2d) 307 ·········· 10.43
Pesquerias y Secaderos de Bacalao de Espanav Beer (1949) 82 Ll L Rep 501
    ·········· 9.88
Peter Lind & Co Ltd v Mersey Docks & Harbour Board [1972] 2 Lloyd's Rep 234
    ·········· 2.68
Philips Hong Kong Ltd v The Attorney-General of Hong Kong [1993] HKLR 269
    ·········· 4.92
Philipson-Stow v Inland Revenue Comrs [1959] 3 All ER 879 ·········· 15.27
Photo Production Ltd v Securicor Transport Ltd [1980] 1 Lloyd's Rep 545
    ·········· 11.6, 11.102
Pigot's Case (1614) 11 Co Rep 26 ·········· 4.201
Pioneer Shipping Ltd v B T P Tioxide Ltd (The Nema, No 2) [1982]AC 724
    ·········· 15.125, 15.126, 15.119
Prenn v Simmonds [1971] 1 WLR 1381 ·········· 22.4
Prudent Tankers Ltd SA v The Dominion Insurance Co Ltd (The Caribbean Sea)
    [1980] 1 Lloyd's Rep 338 ·········· 14.79
Raiffeisen Zentralbank Osterreich AG v Crossseas Shipping Ltd & Ors [2000]
    1 WLR 1135 ·········· 4.202
Raineri v Miles [1981] AC 1050 ·········· 4.30, 8.32
Rainy Sky SA and Others v Kookmin Bank [2011] 1 Lloyd's Rep 233; [2012]
    1 Lloyd's Rep 34 ·········· 4.178

Rasbora Ltd v JCL Marine Ltd [1977] 1 Lloyd's Rep 645 ·················· 1.107, 1.129 – 133, 16.40

Ravennavi SpA v New Century Shipbuilding Co Ltd [2007] 1 CLC 176 ··· 22.14

RD Harbottle (Mercantile) Ltd v National Westminster Bank Ltd [1978] 1 QB 146 ·················· 4.215

Re Altantic Computer Plc (in administration) [1995] BCC 696 ············ 4.228

Re Anziani [1930] 1 Ch 407 ·················· 8.161

Re Bankruptcy Notice (No 171 of 1934) (1943) 76 Ll L Rep 113 ············ 4.65

Re Carus-Wilson and Greene's Arbitration (1886) 18 QBD 7 ············ 15.2

Reardon Smith Line Ltd v Ministry of Agriculture, Fisheries and Food [1963] AC 691 ·················· 23.1

Reardon Smith Line Ltd v Yngvar Hansen-Tangen [1976] 1 WLR 989; [1976] 2 Lloyd's Rep 60 ·················· 1.53, 1.73, 3.7, 3.8, 22.3, 22.4

Red Sea Tankers Ltd and Others v Paopachristidis and Others [1997] 2 Lloyd's Rep 547 ·················· 5.121

Reed (Albert E) & Co Ltd v London and Rochester Trading Co Ltd [1954] 2 Lloyd's Rep 463 ·················· 5.125

Regalian Properties plc v London Docklands Development Corp [1995] 1 WLR 212 ·················· 2.24

Reid v Macbeth & Gray [1904] AC 223 ············ 1.12, 1.14, 8.132, 8.145

Republic of India v India Steamship Co Ltd (The Indian Endurance and The Indian Grace)(No 2) [1989] AC 878 ·················· 5.84

Reversionary and General Securities Co Ltd v Hall [1908] 1 Ch 383 ············ 4.9

Richardsons v Sylvester (1873 – 74) LR 9 QB 34 ·················· 2.130

Richardsons & M Samuel & Co, Re [1898] 1 QB 261 ·················· 9.78

Rickards v Forestal Land, Timber and Railways Co Ltd [1941] 3 All ER 62 ·················· 14.113

Riverstone Meat Co Pty Ltd v Lancashire Shipping Co Ltd (The Muncaster Castle) [1961] AC 807 ·················· 14.46

Robertson v Petros M Nomikos Ltd [1939] AC 371 ·················· 14.112

Rogers v Parish (Scarborough) Ltd [1987] QB 933 ·················· 1.117, 1.118

Rose and Frank Co v J R Grompton & Bros. Ltd [1923] 2 QB 261 ············ 2.48

Routledge v Grant (1828) 4 Bing 653 ··· 2.61
RTS Flexible Systems Ltd. v Molkerei Alois Müller GMBH & Co. K. G.
　(UK Productions)[2010] 1 WLR 753 ·································· 2.33
Sailing Ship Blairmore Co Ltd v Macredie [1898] AC 593 ················ 14.106
Saint Line Limted v Richardsons, Westgarth & Co Limited [1940] 2 KB 99
　··· 11.34, 11.75
Samuel White & Co Ltd v Coombes, Marshall & Co Ltd (1922) 13 Ll. L.
　Rep. 122 ·· 12.26
Sanday & Co v British and Foreign Marine Insurance Co [1916] 1 AC 650
　·· 9.102
Sandeman Coprimar SA v Transitos y Transportes Integrales SL [2003] 2 CLC 551
　·· 2.166
Scandinavian Trading Tranker Co AB v Flota Petrolera Ecuatoriana (The Scaptrade)
　[1981] 2 Lloyd's Rep 425 ·· 2.159
Scarf v Jardine (1882) 7 App Cas 345 ···································· 16.34
Schenkers Ltd v Overland Shoes Ltd [1998] 1 Lloyd's Rep 498 ············· 4.82
Schloss Brothers v Steven [1906] 2 KB 665 ······························ 14.39
Scott Lithgow Ltd v Secretary of State for Defence 1989 SLT 236 ········· 9.121
Scott v Brown Doering McNab & Co [1892] 2 QB 724 ·················· 6.76
Seath & Co v Moore (1886) LR 11 App Cas 350 ························ 8.124
Sembawang Corp Ltd v Pacific Ocean Shipping Corp (No 3)[2004] App LR 11
　·· 12.69
Sempra Metals Ltd (formerly Metallgesellschaft Ltd) v Inland Revenue
　Commissioners and another [2008] AC 561 ··························· 13.12
Serck Controls Limited v Drake & Schull Engineering Limited 73 Con LR 100
　··· 6.27
Shanghai Shipyard Co Ltd v Reignwood International Investment (Group)
　Company Limited [2021] EWCA Civ 1147 ····················· 4.217-4.219
Sir James Laing & Sons Limited v Barclay Curle & Co Limited (1908) SC (HL) 1
　·· 8.127
Slater and Others v Finning Ltd [1997] AC 473 ················· 1.149-1.150
Smit International (Deutschland) GmbH v Josef Mobius, Bau-Gesellschaft

(GmbH & Co) [2001] CLC 1545 ························· 25.39
Smith v Hughes [1871] LR6 QB 597 ························ 2.39
Smith-Kline & French Laboratories Ltd v Sterling-Winthrop Group Ltd [1975]
   2 All ER 578 ·· 18.7
Sonatrach Petroleum Corporation (BVI) v Ferrell International Limited [2002]
   2 All ER 627 ·· 15.36
Soya Gmbh Mainz Kommanditgesellschaftv White [1983] 1 Lloyd's Rep 122
   ··· 14.78
Spencer and Others v Harding and Others (1870) LR 5 CP 561 ············ 2.121
Spinney's (1948) Ltd, Spinney's Centre Sal and Michel Doumet, Joseph
   Doumet and Distributors and Agencies Sal v Royal Insurance Co Ltd
   [1980] 1 Lloyd's Rep 406 ························· 9.85, 9.93(n), 9.97(n)
Spiro v Glencrown Properties Ltd [1991] Ch 531 ························ 23.6
Stavers v Curling and Another (1836) 3 Bing NC 355 ··················· 15.66
Stellar Shipping Company LLP v Cosco (Dalian) Shipyard Company Limited
   [2011] EWHC 1278 ··· 15.75
Steria Limited v Sigma Wireless Communications Limited
   [2008] BLR 79 ································ 4.71, 10.76, 10.77, 10.105
Stevenson v Rogers [1999] QB 1028 ························· 1.102, 1.103
Stewart Gill Ltd v Horatio Myer & Co Ltd [1992] QB 600 ················ 4.80
Stocznia Gdanska SA v Latvian Shipping Co [1996] 2 Lloyd's Rep 132;
   [1998] 1 WLR 574; [1998] 1 Lloyd's Rep 609
   ··························· 1.17, 1.18, 2.171, 3.10, 4.61, 13.77, 13.83
Stocznia Gdynia SA v Gearbulk Holdings Ltd [2009] 1 Lloyd's Rep 461
   ·· 12.5, 12.55, 12.62
Stone Vickers Ltd vAppledore Ferguson Shipbuilders Ltd [1991] 2 Lloyd's
   Rep 288 ··· 14.23, 14.50
Stoomvart Maatschappij Nederland v P and O Steam Navigation Co (The Khedive)
   (1882) 7 App Cas 795 ······································ 14.62
Suisse Atlantique Societe d'Armement SA v NV Rotterdamsche Kolen Centrale
   [1966] 1 Lloyd's Rep 529 ····································· 4.87
Suisse Atlantique Societe d'Armement SA v NV Rotterdamsche Kolen Centrale

[1967] 1 AC 361 ··· 25.72
Sunnyside Nursing Home v Builders Contract Management (1986) 2 Const LJ 240
　 ·· 5.41
Swansea Corpn v Harpur [1912] 3 KB 493 ································ 14.141
T & J Harrison and Others v Knowles & Foster [1918] 1 KB 608 ······ 1.69, 1.70
T H Skogland & Son v W H Muller & Co (London) Ltd (1926) 24 Ll L Rep 322
　 ··· 15.71
Tekdata Interconnections Ltd v Amphenol Ltd [2009] 2 CLC 866 ············ 2.100
Talbot Underwriting Ltd v Nausch Hogan & Murray Inc (The Jascon 5)
　[2006] 1 CLC 1138 ··· 14.26
Tempus Shipping v Louis Dreyfus [1930] 1 KB 699 ······························· 9.71
Tennants (Lancashire) Ltd v CS Wilson and Co Ltd [1917] AC 495 ········ 9.117
The Amoco Cadiz [1984] 2 Lloyd's Rep 304 ······································· 5.42
The Dawlish [1910] P 339 ·· 15.15
The Tychy (No.2)[2001] 1 Lloyd's Rep 10 ······································· 16.35
Thomas Borthwick (Glasgow) Ltd v Faure Fairclough Ltd [1922] 1 Lloyd's
　Rep 16 ·· 9.7
Three Rivers DC v Bank of England [1966] QB 292 ···························· 16.26
Tolhurst v Associated Portland Cement Manufacturers (1900) Ltd [1902] 2 KB 660
　 ·· 16.1
Toller v Law Accident Insurance Society Ltd [1936] 2 All ER 952 ········· 12.30
Tradax Export SA v Andre & Cie SA [1976] 1 Lloyd's Rep 416 ············ 9.136
Tradax Internacional SA v Cerrahogullari TaS (The M Eregli) [1981] 2 Lloyd's
　Rep 169 ·· 15.69
Tradigrain SA and Others v Intertek Testing Services (ITS) Canada Limited
　and Others [2007] EWCA Civ 154 ··· 5.120
Tramp Shipping Corporation v Greenwich Marine Inc (The New Horizon)
　[1975] 2 Lloyd's Rep 314 ··· 9.75
Transocean Drilling UK Ltd v Providence Resources plc [2016] EWCA Civ 372
　 ··· 25.66
Trendtex Trading Corp v Credit Suisse[1980] QB 629; [1982] AC 679 ······ 16.4
Trollope & Colls Ltd v North West Metropolitan Regional Hospital Board [1973]

1 WLR 601 .... 10.50
TS & S Global Limited v John Fithian-Franks, Anthony Charles Hayes, Frank
 David Simpson, Robert Edward Poskitt, Ian Fifthian-Franks [2007] EWHC
 1401 .... 4.172
Union Marine Insurance Co v Borwick [1895] 2 QB 279 .... 9.114
Union of India v McDonnell Douglas Corporation [1993] 2 Lloyd's Rep 48
 .... 15.35, 15.46
United Scientific Holdings Ltd v Burnley BC [1978] AC 904 .... 2.188
Vosper Thornycroft Ltd v Ministry of Defence [1976] 1 Lloyd's Rep 58
 .... 6.25, 15.22
Vossloh Aktiengesellschaft v Alpha Trains (UK) Limited [2011] 2 All ER 307
 .... 4.165
Wackerbarth v Masson (1812) 3 Camp 270 .... 8.50
Walford and Others v Miles and Another [1992] 2 AC 128 .... 2.158
Wallersteiner v Moir (No 2) [1975] QB 373 .... 13.10
Wallis, Son & Wells v Pratt & Haynes [1911] AC 394 ...... 2.176, 2.177, 11.23
Walton (Grain) Ltd v British Italian Trading Co [1959] 1 Lloyd's Rep 233
 .... 9.20
Watson v Mid Wales Railway Co (1866-67) LR 2 CP 593 .... 16.28
Westerngeco Ltd v ATP Oil & Gas [2006] 2 Lloyd's Rep 535 .... 25.61
Westminster Corporation v J Jarvis and Son and Another [1969] 1 WLR 1448;
 [1970] 1 WLR 637 .... 8.9, 10.14
Whicker v Hume (1858) 7 HL Cas 124 .... 24.6
Whittle Movers Ltd v Hollywood Express Ltd [2009] 2 CLC 771 ...... 2.29, 2.35
Whitworth Street Estates (Manchester) Ltd v James Miller & Partners Ltd
 [1970] AC 583 .... 15.44
Wickman Machine Tool Sales Ltd v L Schuler AG [1972] 2 WLR 840 ...... 2.178
William Brandt's Sons & Co v Dunlop Rubber Co [1905] AC 454 1(1915) 21
 Com Cas 2536. 3 William Brothers (Hull) Ltd v Naamlooze Vernootschap
 WH Berghuys Kolanhandel (1915) 21 Com Cas 253 .... 9.74
William Lacey (Hounslow) Ltd v Davis [1957] 1 WLR 932 .... 2.131
Williams v Roffey Bros & Nicholls (Contractors) Ltd [1991] 1 QB 1

.... 1.8, 4.161
Wilson Smithett & Cape (Sugar) Ltd v Bangladesh Sugar and Food
　Industries Corporation [1986] 1 Lloyd's Rep 378 ································ 2.117
Wolverhampton Corp v Emmons [1901] 1 QB 515 ································ 12.37
Wood v Bell (1856) 6 E&B 355 ································ 8.121, 8.124, 8.125
Wood v Capita Insurance Services Limited [2017] UKSC 24 ················ 25.69
Woodar Investment Development Ltd v Wimpey Construction UK Ltd
　[1980] 1 WLR 277 ··· 12.32
Woods v Russell (1822) 5 B & Ald 942 ····························· 8.116, 8.118
Workman Clark & Co Ltd v Lloyd Brazileno [1908] 1 KB 968 ······ 4.15, 13.56
Wuhan Ocean Economic & Technical Cooperation Co Ltd and Another v
　Schiffahrts-Yarmouth v France (1887) 19 QBD 647 ························ 11.30
Young v Sun Alliance Ltd [1977] 1 WLR 104 ························ 9.62, 9.64
Yraza v Astral Shipping Company (1904) 20 TLR 153 ······················· 9.6
Zinc Corporation v Hirsch [1916] 1 KB 541 ································· 9.6

英国成文法

Arbitration Act, 1889, 1934 ············ 15.7
Arbitration Act, 1950 ············ 15.7, 15.9
   s. 4(1) ································ 15.11
Arbitration Act, 1975 ················ 15.7
   s. 1(2) ································ 15.10
   s. 7(1) ································ 15.10
Arbitration Act, 1979 ········ 15.7, 15.127
Arbitration Act 1996
   ········ 15.3 15.7, 15.8, 15.38, 15.65,
            15.119, 15.124, 15.127
   s. 1(a) ································ 15.3
   s. 3 ·································· 15.40
   s. 5 ································· 15.120
   s. 12(3) ····························· 15.72
   s. 14(1) ····························· 15.65
   s. 14(2) ····························· 15.65
   s. 14(3) ····························· 15.65
   s. 14(4) ····························· 12.65
   s. 17(2) ····························· 15.79
   s. 32(1) ····························· 15.11
   s. 39 ································ 15.104
   s. 44 ································· 15.75
   s. 47 ································ 15.104
   s. 51 ································ 15.104
   s. 59 ································ 15.107
   s. 60 ································ 15.112
   s. 61(1) ····························· 15.107
   s. 69(2) ····························· 15.118

   s. 69(3) ····························· 15.121
   s. 69(3)(c) ············· 15.121, 15.124
   s. 82 ································· 15.19
Bills of Sale Act (1878) Amendment Act, 1882
   s. 9 ·································· 2.134
Civil Procedure Act, 1833 ·············· 15.7
The Commercial Agents (Council Directive)
   Regulations, 1993r. 2(1) ············ 2.208
Common Law Procedure Act 1854 ······ 15.7
Consumer Credit Act, 1974
   s. 65 ································· 2.134
Contracts (Rights of Third Parties) Act 1999
   s. 1(1) ································ 24.3
   s. 1(2) ································ 24.4
CourtsAct, 1971 ······················· 11.19
Electronic Communications Act, 2000
   s. 8(1) ······························· 2.152
Judicature Act, 1873
   s. 25 ································· 11.19
Law of Property Act, 1925
   s. 52 ································· 2.134
   s. 40 ································· 2.134
Marine Insurance Act, 1906 ············ 14.66
   s. 4 ··································· 14.7
   s. 6(1) ································ 14.8
   s. 25(1) ······························ 14.32
   s. 26(1) ······························ 14.12
   s. 27(4) ····························· 14.115

s. 52	14.22
s. 55	14.75
s. 56(1)	14.102
s. 57(1)	14.104
s. 60	14.111
s. 61	14.114
s. 65(1)	14.68
s. 66(1)	14.70
s. 66(3)	14.71
s. 78(4)	14.123

Merchant Shipping Act, 1995
s. 9	3.110

Misrepresentation Act, 1967
s. 1	22.16
s. 3	22.20

Patents Act, 1977
s. 1(1)	18.5

Sale and Supply of Goods Act, 1994
s. 1	1.3, 1.109

Sale of Goods Act, 1893
………… 1.36, 1.109, 1.125, 8.127
s. 1(1)	1.136
s. 10	8.27
s. 10(1)	8.18
s. 14	1.106, 1.137
s. 14(1)	1.139–1.140
s. 14(2)	1.125, 1.131
s. 16	8.144
s. 17	8.144
s. 18, r. 5(1)	8.144
s. 20(1)	8.170
s. 49(2)	13.56, 13.57
s. 61(2)	8.19

Sale of Goods Act 1979
………… 1.36–1.45, 1.50–1.52, 1.54–1.57, 1.59–1.61, 1.63–1.65, 1.75, 1.80–1.81, 1.83–1.87, 1.89–1.91, 1.93, 1.98–1.102, 1.104, 1.106, 1.109, 1.115–1.117, 1.120–1.123, 1.126, 1.128, 1.131, 1.134–1.137, 8.4, 8.154, 8.155, 12.31
s. 1(1)	1.36
s. 2(1)	1.41
s. 2(3)	1.63
s. 2(4)	1.44
s. 2(5)	1.43
s. 2(6)	1.45
s. 3	1.38
s. 4(1)	2.135
s. 5(1)	1.57, 1.60
s. 5(2)	1.64
s. 5(3)	1.40
s. 6(1)	8.3, 8.4
s. 7	1.38
s. 10(2)	4.30
s. 11	8.51
s. 12	1.40, 1.81
s. 12(1)	1.63, 1.83, 1.86
s. 12(2)	1.84–1.86
s. 12(5A)	1.83, 1.86
s. 13(1)	1.65, 1.75, 1.89, 1.93, 11.5
s. 13(1A)	1.91
s. 13(2)	1.90
s. 14	1.102, 1.109, 1.117
s. 14(1)	1.98, 1.100
s. 14(2)	1.75, 1.99, 1.100–1.102, 1.109, 1.115, 1.135, 11.5
s. 14(2A)	1.109, 1.120
s. 14(2B)	1.115–1.116, 1.117

s. 14(2C) ·············· 1.122-1.123	s. 54 ·················· 1.38, 13.9
s. 14(2D) ·················· 1.121	s. 55(1) ················ 1.39, 11.7
s. 14(2E) ·················· 1.121	s. 61(1)
s. 14(2F) ·················· 1.121	········ 1.42, 1.51, 2.181, 8.3, 8.107
s. 14(3) ·········· 1.134, 1.150, 11.5	s. 61(5) ······················· 8.6
s. 14(5) ···················· 1.104	s. 62(2) ······················ 1.37
s. 14(6) ···················· 1.128	Sale of Goods (Amendment) Act, 1994
s. 15(1) ····················· 1.40	····················· 1.36, 1.115
s. 16 ············· 1.40, 1.56, 1.61	Sale of Goods (Amendment) Act, 1995
s. 17 ······················· 1.61	····························· 1.36
s. 17(1) ····················· 1.55	Senior CourtsAct, 1981
s. 18, r. 5(1) ················ 8.143	s. 68(1)(a) ···················· 11.20
s. 18, r. 1 ···················· 1.56	Statute of Westminster, 1931 ······· 1.33
s. 19(1) ···················· 8.155	Trade Marks Act, 1994
s. 20(1) ·············· 8.170, 8.172	s. 1(1) ······················ 18.6
s. 20(2) ···················· 8.173	Terrorism Act 2000 ············· 9.91
s. 20(3) ···················· 8.183	Unsolicited Goods and Services (Amendment)
s. 27 ······················· 8.6	Act, 1975,
s. 28 ······················ 8.52	s. 1 ························ 2.134
s. 29(2) ····················· 8.49	Unfair Contract Terms Act 1977
s. 34 ······················ 7.48	············ 1.39-1.40, 1.86, 4.81,
s. 35(2) ····················· 7.38	4.83, 11.20, 11.21
s. 36 ······················ 8.176	s. 2 ···················· 3.58, 5.109
s. 37(1) ····················· 8.182	s. 6(1) ······················ 1.40
s. 39(1) ····················· 8.156	s. 11 ······················ 11.20
s. 49(2) ·············· 13.3, 13.55	Uniform Laws of International Sales Act 1967
s. 52 ······················ 1.56	s. 11 ······················ 14.119
s. 52(1) ·············· 1.55, 13.9	

其他法律

法国法

《法国民法典》
  第1148条 ·················· 9.1

美国法

Merchant Marine Act, 1936
  s. 501 ·················· 1.158

中国法

《建造中船舶抵押权登记暂行办法》
  第3条 ·················· 3.117
  第4条 ·················· 3.117
《中华人民共和国船舶登记条例》
  第2条 ·················· 7.65
  第13条 ·················· 3.111
  第15条 ·················· 7.65
  第20条 ·················· 8.107
《〈中华人民共和国船舶登记条例〉若干问题的说明》
  第8条 ·················· 8.107
《中华人民共和国船舶最低安全配员规则》
  第12条 ·················· 7.66

《中华人民共和国海商法》
  第4条 ·················· 3.63
  第13条 ·················· 3.83
  第14条第1款 ·················· 8.85
《中华人民共和国海上交通安全法》
  第5条 ·················· 7.64
《中华人民共和国民法典》
  第595条 ·················· 1.24
  第770条 ·················· 1.24
  第788条 ·················· 1.24, 1.28
  第783条 ·················· 1.30
  第787条 ·················· 1.30
  第808条 ·················· 1.31, 8.166
  第799条 ·················· 1.31
  第595条 ·················· 1.32
  第279条 ·················· 1.28
  第287条 ·················· 1.28
《中华人民共和国企业破产法》
  第18条 ·················· 12.23
  第25条 ·················· 12.23
《中华人民共和国无线电管理条例》
  第14条 ·················· 7.66

国际公约及文件

1958 年《承认及执行外国仲裁裁决公约》
………………………… 15.6, 15.8
　第Ⅱ.2 条 ……………………… 15.11
1958 年《公海公约》
　第 5(1)条 ……………………… 3.101
1966 年《国际载重线公约》…… 3.104, 3.124
　第 4(1)条 ………………………… 3.99
1969 年《国际船舶吨位丈量公约》
………………………… 3.104, 3.124
　第 3(1)条 ………………………… 3.99
　附录 1,规则第 2(2)条 …………… 3.16
　附录 1,规则第 2(3)条 …………… 3.16
　附录 1,规则第 3 条 ……………… 3.18
　附录 1,规则第 4 条 ……………… 3.18
1972 年《国际海上避碰规则公约》
………………………… 3.104, 3.124
1973 年《国际防止船舶造成污染公约》
………………………… 3.104, 3.124
1974 年《国际海上人命安全公约》(SOLAS)
…… 3.26, 3.27, 3.104, 3.124, 6.72
　第Ⅰ章
　B 部分,规则第 12(a)条 ………… 3.27
　B 部分,规则第 13 条 …………… 3.39
　第Ⅱ-1 章
　A 部分,规则和第 1.2 条 ………… 4.20
　A 部分,规则第 3.14 条 ………… 3.26
　A 部分,规则第 3.15 条 ………… 3.26
　A-1 部分,规则第 3-1 条 ……… 3.104
　A-1 部分,规则第 3-2 条
………………… 6.72, 6.74, 6.75, 6.79
1979 年《保护工业产权巴黎公约》
　第 1(3)条 ………………………… 18.2
1982 年《联合国海洋法公约》
　第 90 条 ………………………… 3.98
　第 91(1)条 …………… 3.102, 3.109
　第 92 条 ………………………… 3.100
　第 94 条 ………………………… 3.106
2009 年《香港国际安全及环境无害化拆船公约》
　第 5 条 ………………………… 3.132
　附录,第 1 章,规则第 1.4 条 …… 3.133
《船舶专用海水压载舱及散货船双层舷侧处所保护涂层性能标准规则》(PSPC)
……… 3.134, 6.71, 6.72, 6.73, 6.79
《共同结构规范》(CSR) …… 3.84, 6.19,
　　　　　　　　　　　　6.73, 6.74, 6.75
《国际海事组织拆船指南》 ………… 3.130
《国际商会见索即付保函统一规则》(URDG 758)
………………… 4.175, 4.176, 4.177
《联合国国际商事仲裁示范法》……… 15.8
　第 7(1)条 ……………………… 15.13
《散货船共同结构规范》
　第 1.1.1 条 ……………………… 3.46
　第 1.1.2 条 ……………………… 3.46
《有害物质清单制定编制指南》 …… 3.128

标准格式

AWES 格式 ············ 1.156, 3.133, 3.144,
　　　　　　　　　　5.75, 8.90, 9.35, 9.155,
　　　　　　　　　　11.33, 12.44, 12.45
Art. 1(a) ································ 5.21
Art. 1(c) ································ 3.113
Art. 1(e) ······················ 1.156, 3.144
Art. 2(a)
　······ 5.131, 5.134, 5.140, 5.143, 5.146
Art. 2(b) ································
3.150, 3.153, 5.22, 5.48, 5.49, 5.59, 5.70
Art. 3(a) ······················· 6.8, 6.16
Art. 3(b) ····················· 1.156, 6.54
Art. 3(c) ···························· 6.66
Art. 3(d) ···························· 6.89
Art. 4(a) ···························· 7.16
Art. 4(b) ···························· 7.34
Art. 4(c) ·········· 7.12, 7.45, 7.53, 7.57
Art. 4(d) ·········· 7.69, 7.81, 7.85, 7.99
Art. 4(e) ···························· 7.74
Art. 5(a) ·························· 4.136
Art. 5(c) ···················· 4.154, 12.13
Art. 6 ······························· 9.127
Art. 6(a) ················ 8.14, 8.47, 8.67
Art. 6(b) ···························· 8.82
Art. 6(c) ············ 4.132, 4.124, 12.14
Art. 6(d) ······················ 9.126, 10.62
Art. 7(c) ·············· 4.3, 4.54, 13.34

Art. 7(d) ······················ 6.31, 6.90
Art. 7(e) ·························· 4.115
Art. 7(f) ··························· 4.72
Art. 8(a) ·························· 18.25
Art. 8(b) ············ 8.100, 8.110, 11.13
Art. 9 ······· 14.34, 14.99, 14.131, 14.139
Art. 10
······ 13.19, .13.28, 13.32, 13.45, 13.65
Art. 11 ··············· 12.13, 12.41, 12.45
Art. 12(a)
　······ 11.43, 11.51, 11.59, 11.81, 11.108
Art. 12(b) ················ 11.113, 11.120
Art. 13 ························ 17.5, 17.11
Art. 14 ···························· 18.21
Art. 15(a) ·························· 15.31
Art. 15(b) ···················· 5.72, 15.89
Art. 17 ······························ 24.6
Art. 18 ··· 16.12, .16.13, 16.22, 16.24,
Art. 19 ······························ 24.8
Art. 20 ····························· 20.4
CMAC 格式 ·················· 1.169-1.171
Art. 30 ···························· 1.171
Art. 30(2) ························· 1.170
CSTC 格式······ 1.167, 1.168, 2.193, 3.145,
　　7.24, 7.26, 7.36, 7.52, 8.56, 8.58, 8.59,
　　11.18, 11.25, 11.33, 11.65, 12.45
Art. I.2 ···························· 3.64

Art. I. 6 ················ 3.65	Art. VIII. 3 ········ 9.139, 10.98, 10.110
Art. I. 8 ················ 3.113	Art. IX. 1 ················ 11.24, 11.39
Art. II ················· 1.167	Art. IX. 2 ···················· 11.48
Art. II. 3	Art. IX. 3 ············ 10.3, 11.64
4.14, 4.16, 4.17, 4.24, 4.55, 4.59, 4.127	Art. IX. 4 ········ 11.17, 11.36, 11.85
Art. II. 3(a) ················ 21.8	Art. IX. 5 ······ 11.117, 11.118, .11.120
Art. II. 4(e) ················ 8.55	Art. X ·················· 1.167
Art. II. 5 ················ 4.48	Art. X. 1 ·················· 12.12
Art. II. 6 ················ 4.211	Art. X. 2 ········ 9.145, 12.40, 12.43
Art. II. 7 ················ 4.189	Art. X. 6 ·················· 11.119
Art. III. 1(e) ·············· 4.130	Art. XI ··················· 10.87
Art. III. 2 ················ 12.13	Art. XI. 1 ·················· 13.7
Art. III. 3 ················ 12.13	Art. XI. 2 ·················· 13.23
Art. III. 4 ················ 12.13	Art. XI. 3(a) ············ 13.18, 13.21
Art. IV. 2 ·············· 5.52, 5.88	Art. XI. 4(a) ················ 13.29
Art. IV. 3 ················ 5.136	Art. XI. 4(b) ················ 13.22
Art. IV. 6 ················ 5.129	Art. XI. 4(b)(i) ············ 13.43, 13.53
Art. V ················ 1.167, 10.98	Art. XI. 4(b)(ii) ··············· 13.53
Art. V. 1 ············ 6.14, 6.17, 6.52	Art. XI. 4(b)(iii) ··············· 13.60
Art. V. 4 ········ 19.11, 19.14, 19.19, 19.22	Art. XI. 5(a) ··············· 13.70
Art. VI ··················· 10.98	Art. XI. 5(b) ··············· 13.72
Art. VI. 1 ··················· 7.21	Art. XII ···················· 10.98
Art. VI. 2(a) ·············· 7.39, 7.45	Art. XII. 1 ················ 14.32
Art. VI. 2(b) ················ 7.52	Art. XII. 2(b)(i) ············· 14.135
Art. VI. 3(a) ················ 7.38	Art. XII. 3 ·················· 14.144
Art. VI. 4(a) ················ 7.69	Art. XIII ··················· 1.167
Art. VI. 4(d) ················ 7.69	Art. XIII. 1 ············· 15.31, 15.73
Art. VI. 6 ·················· 7.74	Art. XIII. 2 ················· 3.46
Art. VII. 1 ··············· 8.13, 8.37	Art. XIII. 7 ············ 10.99, 15.115
Art. VII. 2 ················ 8.151	Art. XIV ··················· 16.11
Art. VII. 4 ················ 8.150	Art. XV. 1 ················· 17.7
Art. VII. 5 ················ 8.150	Art. XV. 2 ················ 17.14
Art. VII. 6 ················ 8.185	Art. XVI
Art. VIII. 2 ················ 10.58	············ 18.11, 18.17, 18.18, 18.19

Art. XVII
　　20.6,20.8,20.9,20.11,20.12,20.14
Art. XVIII　……………… 4.190,4.212,21.7
MARAD 格式 ………………… 1.158-1.163
NEWBUILDCON 格式
　　………… 1.164-1.166,1.169,3.4,3.28,
　　3.29,3.30,3.63,3.93,4.23,4.26,4.28,
　　4.193,7.91,8.66,8.82,8.87,8.88,8.90,
　　8.91,8.94,9.33,9.70,9.73,9.82,9.90,
　　9.104,9.110,11.26,11.27,11.123,
　　　　　　　　　　　　12.21,22.8
BOX 4(A) …………………………… 3.17
cl. 1(a) …………………… 3.30,4.155
cl. 2(a) ……………………………… 3.5
cl. 2(b) ………… 3.28,4.151,4.138,4.147
cl. 3(a) …………………………… 3.93
cl. 3(b) …………………………… 3.63
cl. 4 ……………………………… 3.129
cl. 5 ……………………………… 3.134
cl. 6 ……………………………… 3.137
cl. 8 ……………………………… 4.138
cl. 9 ……………………………… 4.145
cl. 9(b) …………………………… 4.103
cl. 10 ……………………………… 4.151
cl. 11 ………………………… 4.154,12.14
cl. 12 ……………………………… 4.104
cl. 13 ………………………… 4.126,12.14
cl. 14(a) ………………………… 4.213
cl. 14(b) ………………………… 4.193
cl. 14(c) ………………………… 4.192
cl. 15(a)
　　………… 4.24,4.28,4.40,4.53,4.57
cl. 15(b)(i) ……………………… 6.88
cl. 15(d) ………………………… 4.35

cl. 15(d)(ii) ……………………… 4.26
cl. 16(b) ………………………… 17.12
cl. 16(c) ………………………… 17.16
cl. 17 ……………………… 4.73,16.32
cl. 18 …………………………… 13.20
cl. 19 …………………………… 1.165
cl. 20(b) ……………… 5.26,5.50,5.63
cl. 20(c) ………………………… 5.60
cl. 20(d) ………………………… 5.76
cl. 20(e) ………………………… 5.67
cl. 20(f) ………………………… 5.82
cl. 21(a)(i) ……………………… 19.3
cl. 21(a)(iii) …………………… 19.8
cl. 21(a)(iv) …………………… 19.15
cl. 21(b)(i) …………………… 19.19
cl. 22(a) ……………………… 5.93,5.97
cl. 22(c) ………………………… 5.132
cl. 22(d) ………………………… 5.133
cl. 23(d) ………………………… 5.152
cl. 24 …………………… 1.165,6.12
cl. 24(e) ………………………… 5.77
cl. 25 …………………………… 6.56,6.58
cl. 26(b) ………………………… 6.67
cl. 26(c) ………………………… 6.62
cl. 27(a) ……………………… 7.16,7.18
cl. 27(b) ………………………… 7.36
cl. 27(c)(i) …………………… 7.40,7.53
cl. 27(c)(ii) …………………… 7.45
cl. 27(c)(iii) ………………… 7.61,7.63
cl. 27(d)(i) …………………… 7.69
cl. 27(d)(iii) ………………… 7.70
cl. 28 ……………………… 8.82,8.39,8.46
cl. 30 …………………………… 8.57
cl. 30(b) ………………………… 8.65

cl. 31	8.171
cl. 32(b)	8.187
cl. 34(a)(i)	10.5
cl. 34(a)(ii)	10.5
cl. 34(a)(iii)	10.90
cl. 34(b)	1.165, 9.128, 10.60
cl. 35(a)	11.26, 11.44
cl. 35(b)	11.36, 11.67
cl. 35(c)	11.67
cl. 35(d)	11.67
cl. 35(f)	11.47
cl. 35(g)	11.106
cl. 36(a)	11.116
cl. 37(b)	11.15
cl. 37(c)	11.92
cl. 37(d)	11.15
cl. 37(e)	12.64
cl. 37(f)	5.122
cl. 37(g)	5.122
cl. 38(a)	14.16, 14.22, 14.32, 14.34
cl. 38(a)(ii)	14.101
cl. 38(b)(ii)	12.44
cl. 38(b)(ii)(2)	14.136
cl. 39	12.8
cl. 39(a)	9.151
cl. 39(a)(i)	12.15
cl. 39(a)(iii)	8.43, 10.111, 12.14
cl. 39(b)(ii)	13.46
cl. 39(c)	10.12, 13.29, 13.33
cl. 39(d)	12.16
cl. 39(e)	9.159, 12.46, 12.49
cl. 39(f)	13.53, 13.63, 13.70
cl. 39(i)	13.72
cl. 39(ii)	13.75
cl. 39(iii)	13.88
cl. 39(iv)	13.88
cl. 39(v)	13.89
cl. 40(a)	18.26
cl. 40(b)	18.27
cl. 40(c)	18.29
cl. 41	15.31
cl. 42	5.76
cl. 42(a)	15.90
cl. 42(b)	7.100, 15.90, 15.93
cl. 42(c)	15.42, 15.78, 15.85
cl. 42(e)	15.93, 15.94
cl. 43(a)	20.5
cl. 43(c)	20.9
cl. 44(a)	4.194, 21.10
cl. 45(a)	16.16
cl. 45(b)	16.17
cl. 47	22.12
cl. 48	24.4
Annex A	4.191, 4.208
Norwegian 格式	1.157, 8.59, 8.72, 8.73, 8.82, 8.90, 8.95, 8.150, 8.155, 9.36, 9.37, 9.123, 9.131, 11.33, 11.46, 11.47, 11.52, 11.115, 12.44, 12.45, 19.17
Art. I	3.140
Art. II. 1	3.5, 5.24, 22.7, 4.39
Art. II. 2	3.28, 3.32
Art. II. 4	3.147
Art. II. 5	3.114
Art. III. 3	4.28, 4.52, 4.143, 13.35
Art. III. 3	4.52, 4.455, 8.59, 8.153, 12.13, 12.22
Art. IV	4.111
Art. IV. 1(b)	12.14

Art. IV. 2	4.136
Art. IV. 5	4.153, 12.13
Art. V. 1(a)	5.51
Art. V. 1(b)	5.61
Art. V. 1(c)	5.74
Art. V. 1(e)	5.81
Art. V. 1(d)	5.52, 5.68
Art. V. 2	5.91, 5.95
Art. V. 3	5.143
Art. V. 4	5.102
Art. V. 5	5.108, 11.222
Art. V. 6	5.100
Art. VI. 1	6.11, 6.18, 6.20, 6.21, 6.56
Art. VI. 2	6.63
Art. VI. 3	6.84
Art. VII. 1	7.16, 7.17
Art. VII. 2	10.89
Art. VII. 3	7.45, 7.53
Art. VII. 4(a)	7.69
Art. VII. 4(d)	7.85
Art. VII. 4(e)	7.100
Art. VII. 5	7.74
Art. VIII. 1	6.63, 8.45
Art. VIII. 2	8.38, 8.39, 8.41, 8.71
Art. VIII. 4	8.150
Art. IX. 2(a)	9.130, 10.64
Art. IX. 3	10.88, 11.60
Art. X. 1	11.15
Art. X. 1	11.25, 12.7
Art. X. 2	11.25, 11.38, 11.45
Art. X. 3	11.33, 11.82, 11.83
Art. X. 4	11.104
Art. X. 5	11.110
Art. X. 6	5.77, 1.114, 11.120, 11.121
Art. XI. 1	8.112
Art. XI. 2(a)	14.2
Art. XI. 2(b)	14.11, 14.15, 14.140
Art. XI. 2(c)(i)	14.21
Art. XI. 2(c)(iv)	14.138
Art. XI. 3(b)	13.52
Art. XII. 1	12.48, 12.62, 14.9
Art. XII. 2(a)	13.35
Art. XII. 2	13.48
Art. XII. 3	13.50
Art. XV	18.11, 18.15, 18.22
Art. XVI. 1(b)	19.5
Art. XVI. 1(c)	19.8
Art. XVI. 1(e)	19.14
Art. XVI. 2	19.19
Art. XVII. 1	20.4
Art. XIX. 1	15.29
Art. XIX. 2	15.42, 15.80

SAJ 格式

1.153–1.155, 1.156, 1.164, 1.167, 1.168, 3.5, 3.25, 3.27, 3.26, 3.62. 3.65, 3.94, 3.144, 4.6, 4.17, 4.28, 4.72, 4.103, 5.16, 5.48, 5.56, 8.82, 8.87, 8.180, 9.31, 9.32, 9.34–9.36, 9.67, 9.67, 9.70, 9.99, 9.104, 9.108, 9.110, 9.112, 9.118, 11.25, 13.32, 13.40, 15.57, 19.19

Art. I. 1	3.3
Art. I. 2	3.15, 3.23, 3.29
Art. I. 3	3.90, 3.91, 3.126, 6.59
Art. I. 4	1.154, 3.143
Art. I. 5	3.111
Art. II. 1	4.2, 6.47, 24.1
Art. II. 3	4.16

Art. II. 3(d) ·················· 6.24	Art. VI. 6 ·················· 7.63
Art. II. 4	Art. VII. 1 ············ 8.13, 8.44
········· 3.147, 4.25, 4.54, 13.5, 13.39	Art. VII. 2 ·················· 8.69
Art. II. 4(d) ·················· 8.54	Art. VII. 3 ·················· 8.88
Art. II. 5 ·················· 4.48	Art. VII. 4 ············ 8.54, 8.178
Art. III ·················· 4.101	Art. VII. 5 ·················· 8.103
Art. III. 1 ·················· 12.14	Art. VII. 6 ·················· 8.185
Art. III. 1(a) ·················· 4.125	Art. VIII ·················· 10.110
Art. III. 1(c) ············ 10.97, 10.109	Art. VIII. 1
Art. III. 1(d) ·················· 4.129	········· 1.154, 5.157, 9.25, 9.30, 9.52
Art. III. 2 ············ 4.135, 12.13	Art. VIII. 2 ·················· 10.58
Art. III. 3 ······ 4.17, 4.28, 4.123, 12.13	Art. VIII. 3 ············ 10.3, 10.110
Art. III. 4 ············ 4.149, 12.13	Art. VIII. 4
Art. IV. 1(a) ·················· 5.15	········· 8.150, 9.149, 9.161, 12.14
Art. IV. 1(b) ·················· 5.55	Art. IX. 1 ·················· 11.24
Art. IV. 1(c) ·················· 5.65	Art. IX. 2 ·················· 11.48
Art. IV. 2 ·················· 5.88	Art. IX. 3(a) ·················· 11.56
Art. IV. 3 ············ 5.136, 5.151	Art. IX. 3(b) ·················· 11.57
Art. IV. 4 ·················· 5.101	Art. IX. 4(a) ············ 11.72, 11.96
Art. IV. 5 ·················· 4.153,	Art. IX. 4(b) ············ 11.87, 11.90
Art. IV. 6 ············ 5.99, 5.129	Art. IX. 4(c) ·················· 11.8
Art. V. 1	Art. IX. 5 ············ 11.113, 11.119
········· 6.6, 6.12, 6.14, 6.17, 6.48, 6.52	Art. X. 1 ············ 4.38, 12.7, 12.12
Art. V. 2 ············ 5.95, 6.60	Art. X. 2 ······ 11.25, 11.38, 12.40,
Art. VI. 1 ············ 7.14, 7.36	12.42, 12.43, 12.45
Art. VI. 2 ············ 6.63, 7.31, 7.33	Art. X. 3 ·················· 12.61
Art. VI. 3 ·················· 6.82	Art. XI. 1 ············ 13.5, 13.9
Art. VI. 3(a) ············ 7.38, 7.56	Art. XI. 1(a) ·················· 13.39
Art. VI. 3(b) ·················· 7.58	Art. XI. 2 ············ 13.15, 13.23
Art. VI. 4(a) ·················· 7.68	Art. XI. 3(a) ·················· 13.27
Art. VI. 4(b) ············ 7.79, 7.91	Art. XI. 3(b) ······ 13.38, 13.45, 13.52
Art. VI. 4(c) ············ 7.71, 7.82	Art. XI. 4(b) ·················· 13.71
Art. VI. 4(e) ·················· 7.99	Art. XI. 4 (c) ·················· 13.73
Art. VI. 5 ·················· 7.73	Art. XI. 4(d) ·················· 13.85

Art. XI. 4(e) ……………… 13. 88	……………… 18. 10, 18. 12, 18. 16, 18. 21
Art. XII. 1 ………… 14. 9, 14. 15, 14. 20, 14. 32, 14. 34, 14. 98	Art. XVI. 2 ……………………… 18. 23
	Art. XVII. 1(a) ……………………… 19. 4
Art. XII. 2(a) ……………………… 14. 130	Art. XVII. 1(b) ……………………… 19. 5
Art. XII. 2(b) ……………………… 14. 132	Art. XVII. 1(c) ……………………… 19. 5
Art. XII. 3 ……………………… 14. 143	Art. XVII. 1(d) …………… 19. 10, 19. 13
Art. XIII. 1 ……… 15. 47, 15. 77, 15. 82, 15. 84, 15. 88	Art. XVII. 2 ……………………… 19. 18
	Art. XVIII. 1 ……………………… 20. 2
Art. XIII. 2 ……………………… 15. 105	Art. XVIII. 2 ……………………… 20. 13
Art. XIII. 3 ……………………… 15. 108	Art. XIX. 1 ……………………… 15. 30
Art. XIII. 5 ……………………… 15. 114	Art. XIX ………………… 21. 5, 21. 11
Art. XIV(1) …………… 16. 10, 16. 11	Art. XX. 2 ……………………… 22. 6
Art. XV. 1 ……………………… 17. 4	Art. XX. 3 ……………………… 22. 11
Art. XV. 2 ……………………… 17. 10	Art. XXI ………………… 15. 30, 24. 1
Art. XVI. 1	

参考文献

1. BLACKABY N, PARASIDES C, REDFERN A, et al. *Redfern & Hunteron Law and Practice of International Commercial Arbitration*[M]. 6th ed. Oxford: Oxford University Press, 2015.
2. HAIDAR A D. *Global Claims in Construction*[M]. Berlin: Springer, 2011.
3. BURROWS A. *A Restatement of the English Law of Contract*[M]. Oxford: Oxford University Press, 2016.
4. *Benjamin' Sale of Personal Property*[M]. 8th ed. London: Sweet & Maxwell, 2010.
5. *Dicey, Morris & Collins, on the Conflict of Laws*[M]. 16th ed. London: Sweet & Maxwell, 2023.
6. GREENBERG D. *Jowitt's Dictionary of English Law*[M]. 3rd ed. London: Sweet & Maxwell, 2010.
7. FOXTON D, BERRY SMITH C, et al. *Scrutton on Charterparties and Bills of Lading*[M]. 24th ed. London: Sweet & Maxwell, 2020.
8. RICHBELL D. *Mediation of Construction Disputes*[M]. Oxford: Blackwell Publishing, 2008.
9. MARTIN E A. *Oxford Dictionary of Law*[M]. 5th ed. Oxford: Oxford University Press, 2002.
10. TUPPER E C. *Introduction to Naval Architecture*[M]. 5th ed. Oxford: Butterworth-Heinemann, 2013.
11. TREITEL G H. *The Law of Contract*[M]. 11th ed. London: Sweet & Maxwell, 2003.
12. AFFAKI G, GOODE R. *Guide to ICC Uniform Rules for Demand Guarantees URDG* 758[M]. Paris: International Chamber of Commerce, 2011.
13. CLAUSS G, LEHMANN E, ÖSTERGAARD. *Offshore Structures*[M]. Berlin:

Springer, 1992.

14. HALVEY. *Halsbury's Laws of England: Contract Volume* 22 [M]. 5th ed. London: Butterworths Law, 1994.
15. BEALE H. *Chitty on Contracts*[M]. 31st ed. London: Sweet & Maxwell, 2012.
16. BEALE H. *Chitty on Contracts*[M]. 35th ed. London: Sweet & Maxwell, 2023.
17. BEATSON J, BURROWS A, CARTWRIGHT J. *Anson's Law of Contract*[M]. 30th ed. Oxford: Oxford University Press, 2016
18. EYRES J, BRUCE G J. *Ship Construction* [M]. 7th ed. Amsterdam: Elsevier, 2012.
19. WILSON J. *Dynamics of Offshore* [M]. New York: John Wiley & Sons, 2003.
20. GILMAN J, BLANCHARD C, TEMPLEMAN M. *Arnould: Law of Marine Insurance and Average*[M]. 20th ed. London: Sweet & Maxwell, 2021.
21. BASEDOW J, WURMNEST W. *Third-Party Liability of Classification Societies – A comparative perspective*[M]. Berlin: Springer, 2005.
22. LAGONI N. *The Liabilities of Classification Societies* [M]. Berlin: Springer, 2007.
23. READY N P. *Ship Registration* [M]. London: Lloyd's of London Press Ltd, 1991.
24. WATTS P. *Bowstead & Reynolds on Agency* [M]. 21st ed. London: Sweet & Maxwell, 2018.
25. FURMSTON M. *Powell-Smith & Furmston's Building Contract Casebook*[M]. 4th ed. Oxford: Blackwell Publishing, 2006.
26. MERKIN R. *Arbitration Law* [M]. London: Informa Law, 2004.
27. KAROBKIN R. *Negotiation – Theory and Strategy* [M]. Amsterdam: Wolters Kluwer, 2009.
28. CURTIS S, GAUNT I, CECIL W. *The Law of Shipbuilding Contracts*[M]. 5th ed. London: Informa Law, 2020.
29. CHANDRASEKARAN S. *Dynamic Analysis and Design of Offshore Structures* [M]. 2nd ed. Berlin: Springer, 2018.
30. CHAKRABARTI S. *Handbook of Offshore Engineering* [M]. Amsterdam: Elsevier, 2005.
31. LAMB T. *Ship Design and Construction*[M]. Jersey City: The Society of Naval

Architects and Marine Engineers, 2003.

32. WIPO. *Understanding Industrial Property* [M]. 2nd ed. Geneva: WIPO Publication, 2004.

33. WIPO. *WIPO Intellectual Property Handbook: Policy, Law and Use* [M]. 2nd ed. Geneva: WIPO Publication, 2004.

34. 马延德.海洋工程装备[M].北京:清华大学出版社,2013.

35. 丁玫.罗马法契约责任[M].北京:中国政法大学出版社,1998.

36. 詹宁斯,瓦茨.奥本海国际法:第一卷:第二分册[M].9版.王铁崖,李适时,汤宗舜,等,译.北京:中国大百科全书出版社,1998.

37. 《中国大百科全书》总编辑委员会.中国大百科全书.法学(修订版)[M].北京:中国大百科全书出版社,2006.

38. 《中国大百科全书》编委会.中国大百科全书[M].2版.北京:中国大百科全书出版社,2009.

39. 林源民.关于"上海格式"的若干意见[M]//上海海事大学海商法研究中心.海大法律评论.上海:上海浦江教育出版社,2011:28-43.

40. 罗国强.造船合同法律规制与中国《海商法》的修改[J].学术论坛,2008(2):88-92.

41. 单红军,于诗卉.非单一性:船舶建造合同法律属性之特征[J].中国海商法年刊,2010(4):81-85.

42. 张敏,刘征宇.买卖性造船合同下的所有权安排[J].中国海商法年刊,2006(1):328-336.

43. 周平.论建造中船舶的物权问题[J].海商法研究,2000(1):30.

索引

安慰函
 不受约束的表示 ········ 4.228-4.229
 承担义务的意愿 ········ 4.226-4.227
 船舶建造合同 ················ 4.230
 措辞 ···························· 4.223
 概念 ···························· 4.222

保险赔偿的应用
 部分损失 ······················ 14.130

变更
 必要性 ················· 16.38-16.39
 船厂权利 ······················ 16.41
 概述 ················· 16.34-16.37
 协议 ···························· 16.40
 转售船东 ······················ 2.199

不可抗力
 来源 ······················ 9.1-9.2
 特征 ···························· 9.8
  履行不可能 ················ 9.12
  实际发生 ···················· 9.9
  无法避免 ··················· 9.11
  无法预见 ··················· 9.10
 英国法 ···················· 9.3-9.7

不可抗力后果 ···················· 9.13
 当事人解除合同 ········ 9.11-9.21
  船东的解约权 ········ 9.148-9.155
  解约后果 ············ 9.156-9.160
  选择的义务 ·········· 9.161-9.162

 合同自动解除 ············ 9.12-9.24
 履行推迟 ················ 9.25-9.28

不可抗力事件
 罢工、停工 ············ 9.74-9.81
 一般性质 ························ 9.82
 材料设备短缺 ·················· 9.117
 船舶毁坏 ······················ 9.112
 船厂毁坏 ······················ 9.112
 革命、叛乱 ············ 9.93-9.100
 火灾、爆炸 ············ 9.67-9.70
 君主行为 ·············· 9.71-9.73
  政府征用 ··················· 9.104
 其他原因 ············ 9.114-9.118
 碰撞、搁浅 ·········· 9.118-9.123
 天灾 ·················· 9.57-9.59
  地震、海啸 ················· 9.60
  坏天气 ·············· 9.67-9.69
  水灾 ················ 9.64-9.66
  台风、飓风 ·········· 9.61-9.53
  异常天气 ············ 9.70-9.106
 停电 ················ 9.107-9.109
  公共设施 ··················· 9.110
 瘟疫、流行病 ·················· 9.105
 运输迟延 ······················ 9.111
 战争 ················· 9.83-9.89
  恐怖主义 ··················· 9.91
  类似战争行为 ········ 9.90-9.92

不可抗力条款 ……………… 9.124
　　AWES 格式 ……………… 9.35
　　NEWBUILDCON 个格式 …… 9.33-9.34
　　Norwegian 格式 …………… 9.36-9.37
　　SAJ 格式 ………………… 9.30-9.32
　　解释 ……………………… 9.38-9..42
　　举证之责 ………………… 9.43-9.46
　　免责条件 ………………… 9.47-9.48
　　　合理措施 ……………… 9.54-9.55
　　　疏忽或过失 …………… 9.44-9.47
不可抗力通知 ……………… 9.124
　　标准格式规定 …………… 9.125-9.132
　　解释 ……………………… 9.142-9.147
　　前提条件 ………………… 9.133-9.141
承保风险
　　保赔风险 ………………… 14.63-14.66
　　船东供应品 ……………… 19.24
　　共损和救助 ……………… 14.67-14.72
　　焊接缺陷 ………………… 14.52
　　航行风险 ………………… 14.58-14.59
　　碰撞风险 ………………… 14.60-14.62
　　潜在缺陷 ………………… 14.46-14.48
　　设计缺陷 ………………… 14.49-14.51
　　污染风险 ………………… 14.56-14.57
　　下水费用 ………………… 14.54-14.55
　　延迟交船 ………………… 14.44-14.45
　　一切险 …………………… 14.39-14.43
　　一切险承保风险 ………… 14.39
除外责任
　　除外责任承保 …………… 14.98-14.101
　　法定除外责任 …………… 14.75-14.77
　　固有和潜在缺陷 ………… 14.78-14.80
　　约定除外责任 …………… 14.81
　　　罢工 …………………… 14.90-14.91

保赔保险 …………………… 14.86-14.87
地震和火山爆发 …………… 14.82-14.83
恶意行为 …………………… 14.92-14.95
核风险 ……………………… 14.96-14.97
碰撞 ………………………… 14.84-14.85
战争 ………………………… 14.88-14.89
船舶
　　入级 ……………………… 3.36
　　首制船 …………………… 2.5,2.24,7.11
　　留置权 …………………… 8.109
船舶登记 …………………… 3.97
　　办理 ……………………… 3.111-3.115
　　船舶抵押登记 …………… 1.109
　　船舶国籍 ………………… 3.98-3.107,7.64-7.65
　　船舶临时登记 …………… 1.109,7.64-7.66
　　船旗 ……………………… 3.100
　　船旗国职责 ……………… 3.103-3.106
　　法律效力 ………………… 3.107-3.108
　　条件 ……………………… 3.109-3.110
　　在建船舶登记
　　　英国法 ………………… 3.118-3.119
　　　在建船舶抵押登记 …… 3.120,8.85
　　　中国法 ………………… 3.116-3.117
船舶描述 …………………… 1.69-1.96,3.8
　　船舶尺寸和吨位 ………… 3.14-3.17
　　船舶特征 ………………… 3.20-3.24,3.29,3.91
　　船号 ……………………… 3.1-3.5,3.7-3.10
　　　特定性 ………………… 3.6-3.8
　　　唯一性 ………………… 3.10-3.13
　　航速 ……………………… 4.108,4.118,4.122,4.136
　　货舱容积 ………………… 4.153
　　油耗 ……… 4.103,4.108,4.118,4.143,4.147
　　载重吨
　　　……… 4.85,4.108,4.122,4.149-4.151

索引

船舶检验 ················· 5.136
　船东代表的检验 ············ 5.137-5.140
　　重复检验 ················ 5.149-5.150
　　通知缺陷的义务 ··········· 5.151-5.152
　　争议的解决 ·············· 5.157
　船级社的检验 ············· 5.159-5.161
船舶建造
　厂商表 ·················· 2.12-2.14
　船级社监造 ··············· 3.122
　规格书 ·················· 2.114,2.171
　海工装备建造 ············· 25.8-25.118
　建造标准 ················ 3.32-3.34,3.122
　建造进程报告 ············· 5.162-5.164
　交船 ··················· 4.17-4.18,4.23-4.25
　开工 ··················· 4.18-4.19
　码头试验 ················ 7.2,4.20-4.21
　上船台 ·················· 4.24,4.60,4.128
　试航 ··················· 7.1
　下水 ··················· 4.18,4.22,4.24,4.58
船舶建造合同标准格式 ········ 1.152
　AWES格式 ··············· 1.156
　CMAC ·················· 1.169-1.171
　CSTC格式 ··············· 1.167-1.168
　LOGIC格式 ·············· 25.26-25.29
　MARAD格式 ············· 1.158-1.163
　NEWBUILDCON格式 ······· 1.164-1.166
　Norwegian格式 ··········· 1.157
　SAJ格式 ················ 1.153-1.155
　作用 ··················· 1.172-1.174
船舶建造合同当事人 ········· 2.201
　船厂 ··················· 2.201,2.202
　船东 ··················· 2.196
　　登记船东 ··············· 2.196
　　最终受益人 ············· 2.197-2.198
　　联合建造人 ············· 2.193
　　质保受让人 ············· 2.202
　　指定买方 ··············· 2.199
　　转售船东 ··············· 2.201
船舶建造合同
　第三人权利 ·············· 24.3-24.5
　对价 ··················· 2.161
　　合同变更的对价 ··········· 2.169
　　合同解除后的对价
　　　················ 2.103-2.104,2.170-2.172
　海工装备建造 ············· 25.8
　　保函 ·················· 25.14-25.15
　　采购 ·················· 25.13
　　船东的解约权 ············ 25.25
　　船东提供设备 ············ 25.23-25.24
　　付款期数及比例 ·········· 25.16-25.18
　　更改 ·················· 25.19-25.20
　　合同价格 ··············· 25.9-25.10
　　设计 ·················· 25.11-25.12
　　责任限制 ··············· 25.21-25.22
　合同文件 ················ 22.5
　合同形式 ················ 2.133
　质量默示保证 ············· 1.97,1.134
　用途默示保证 ············· 1.134-1.137
　日期 ··················· 3.46,6.63,6.64,6.74
　特征 ··················· 1.156,1.168
　性质 ··················· 1.11,1.30-1.31
　英国法 ·················· 1.12-1.20
　英国法的适用 ············· 1.32-1.34
　　历史原因 ··············· 1.33
　　法律原因 ··············· 1.34
　　语言原因 ··············· 1.35
　责任限制 ················ 24.9
　中国法 ·················· 1.21,1.24-1.26
　　承揽合同 ··············· 1.27

混合合同 …………………………… 1.26	交船款支付 …………………… 4.47,8.51
建设工程合同 ………………………… 1.28	标准格式 ……………………………… 8.54
买卖合同 …………………………… 1.29	特殊性 ………………………………… 8.52
住所 …………………………… 24.6-24.7	支付安排 ……………………………… 8.61
船舶建造合同洽谈 …………………… 2.1	支付争议 ……………………………… 8.63
合同价格 ……………………………… 4.1	交船文件 ……………………………… 8.83
固定价格 …………………………… 4.2-4.5	交接备忘录 …………………………… 8.82
货币选择 …………………………… 4.6-4.7	接受和接船 …………………………… 8.185
两种货币计价 …………………………… 4.7	可交接状态 ………………………… 8.8-8.10
虚假合同价格 ……………………… 4.8-4.11	日期
公共政策 ………………………… 4.8-4.11	不确定交船日 ……………… 8.34-8.236
技术洽谈 …………………………… 2.4-2.5	性质 ………………………………… 8.18
合理报酬 ………………………… 2.27,2.131	约定 ………………………………… 8.17
恢复原状 ……………………………… 2.27	违约构成 ……………………………… 8.32
"如果"合同 …………………………… 2.122	所有权转移
商务洽谈 ………………………… 2.15-2.17	成文法的适用 ………………………… 8.3
问题单 ………………………………… 2.65	船厂拥有所有权惯例 …… 8.108-8.111
船舶交接 ……………………………… 8.5	抵押 …………………………… 8.112-8.159
船舶交接程序 …………………… 8.55-8.56	中国法 ………………………… 8.164-8.167
船舶离厂 ……………………………… 8.185	准据法 ………………………… 8.160-8.163
船舶建造合同规定 …………… 8.185-8.186	时间 …………………………………… 8.113
船舶留厂的安排 ……………………… 8.191	船舶完成后转移 ……………………… 8.114
合理期限 …………………………… 8.189	合同规定 ……………………………… 8.150
船厂留置权 ………………………… 8.156	随意愿转移 …………………………… 8.121
船厂义务终止 ………………………… 11.5	意愿的确定 …………………………… 8.127
地点 ………………………… 8.44,8.188	同意船东登记 ………………… 8.117-8.118
风险转移	指定前不转移 ………………………… 8.119
船舶建造合同规定 …………… 8.171-8.172	指定的解释 …………………… 8.137-8.139
普通法原则 …………………… 8.168-8.170	意义 ………………………… 8.103,8.105
违约 …………………………………… 8.173	约定 ………………………… 8.121,8.132
概述	所有权保留 …………………… 8.153-8.155
意义 …………………………… 8.1-8.4	所有权回转 …………………………… 8.146
合同规定 ……………… 8.29,11.18,11.81	提交船舶
合理性要求 …………………………… 11.19	概念 …………………………… 8.178-8.180
合同交船日前交船 ……………… 8.38-8.39	船厂的责任 …………………………… 8.181

索引

船舶设计
- 船东设计 …………………… 5.31
- 第三人设计 ………………… 5.34
  - 船厂的责任 …………… 5.35
  - 明显缺陷 ……………… 5.40
- 海工装备建造 ……………… 25.8
- 合同规定
  - AWES 格式 …………… 5.21
  - NEWBUILDCON 格式 …… 5.26
  - Norwegian 格式 ……… 5.24
  - SAJ 格式 ……………… 5.16
- 设计和图纸费用 …………… 24.1
- 设计和工艺 ………………… 5.28

船舶损失
- 部分损失 …………………… 14.102
- 全损 ………………………… 14.103
  - 实际全损 ……………… 14.104
  - 推定全损 ……………… 14.111
  - 协议全损 ……………… 14.117

船厂的保证
- 建造保证 …………………… 4.155
- 交船日 ……………………… 4.130
- 航速 ………………… 3.14, 4.135-4.139
- 货舱容积 …………………… 4.153
- 油耗 ………………………… 3.24, 4.143
- 载重吨 ……………………… 3.24, 4.149

船厂解约 ………………… 13.51
- 船舶处置
  - 出售的选择 …………… 13.68
    - 完成后出售 ………… 13.71
    - 未完成出售 ………… 13.73
  - 出售的义务 …………… 13.77
  - 权利 …………………… 13.82
  - 余额及处置 …………… 13.85

- 船东额外支付义务 ………… 13.88
- 船东供应品归属 …………… 13.62
- 担保人义务 ………………… 13.90
- 付款义务 …………………… 13.3
- 建造款的保留 ……………… 13.52
- 解约权 ……………………… 13.40
  - 船舶建造合同规定 …… 13.3
- 利息和费用
  - 费用 …………………… 13.23
  - 利息 …………………… 13.9
  - 利息的约定 …………… 13.15
- 权利的排除 ………………… 13.48
- 顺延和中止
  - 船厂的权利 …………… 13.32
  - 概述 …………………… 13.25
  - 合同交船日顺延 ……… 13.26
  - 中止与顺延 …………… 13.37
- 违约构成
  - 定义 …………………… 13.1
- 违约后果约定 ……………… 13.5
- 违约通知 …………………… 13.42
- 未到期款项 ………………… 13.59
- 已到期款项 ………………… 13.54

船东供应品
- 船厂继续建造的权利 ……… 19.13
- 船厂拒收权 ………………… 19.7
- 船厂责任
  - 保管和安装 …………… 19.18
  - 船舶建造人险 ………… 19.24
  - 船东供应品质量 ……… 19.21
  - 联合检验 ……………… 19.22
- 船东责任
  - 船舶建造合同规定 …… 19.3
  - 责任或权利 …………… 19.17
- 概述

合同价格 ………………………… 19.2
原因 ……………………………… 19.1
船东提供设备 ……………… 25.23-25.24
延迟提供 ………………………… 19.10

船东解约

不可抗力解约权 ………………… 10.97
概述 ……………………………… 10.96
根据法律解约
 船厂毁约 ……………………… 12.30
 船舶不适航 …………………… 12.26
 违反默示条件 ………………… 12.25
根据合同解约
 船厂破产或重组 ……………… 12.22
 船厂中止建造 ………………… 12.19
 船舶不符合保证 ……………… 12.10
 还款担保人破产 ……………… 12.15
 交船延迟 ……………………… 12.14
 未提供还款保函 ……………… 12.21
海工装备建造合同
 ……………………… 25.25,25.38-25.44
 概述 …………………………… 25.30
 决定的效力 …………………… 25.32
 LOGIC 格式 …………………… 25.26
合同的解除 ……………………… 12.9
减损义务
 法律义务 ……………………… 12.67
 合同义务 ……………………… 12.69
解约的不可逆转性 ……………… 12.39
解约权丧失 ……………………… 10.113
解约期限的计算 ………………… 10.99
实际履行
 普通法义务 …………………… 12.35
 成文法义务 …………………… 12.36
 选择的义务 …………………… 10.109
 责任的解除 …………………… 12.54

根据法律解约 …………………… 12.64
根据合同解约 …………………… 12.55

船级社

船级规范的符合 ………………… 3.90
船舶入级
 概述 …………………………… 3.36
 入级符合 ……………………… 3.90
 意义 …………………………… 3.68
国际船级社协会 ………………… 3.42
 成员船级社 …………………… 3.43
 共同结构规范 ………………… 3.45
 技术问题决定权 ……………… 3.60
免责条款 ………………………… 3.56
双重船级 ………………………… 3.96
性质 ……………………………… 3.58
争议解决 ………………… 5.70,6.13
作用和服务 ……………………… 3.37
 法定检验 ……………………… 3.39
 入级检验 ……………………… 3.41

船级社监造

保护涂层 ………………………… 3.134
和船厂的关系 …………………… 3.122
共同结构规范 …………… 3.46,3.82
监造的必要性 …………………… 3.123
监造费用 ………………………… 3.122
监造协议 ………………………… 3.125
有害物质清单 …………………… 3.129
原产地 …………………………… 3.137
责任限制 ………………………… 3.56

对价 ……………………………… 2.161
定义 ……………………………… 2.161
合同变更的对价 ………………… 2.169
合同解除后的对价 ……………… 2.170
合适性 …………………………… 2.167

利益的获得 …………………… 21.65

反腐败条款
　船厂的地位 …………………… 25.123
　腐败行为 ……………………… 25.106
　概述 …………………………… 25.98
　国际商会规则 ………………… 25.98
　经合组织公约 ………… 25.101-25.103
　联合国公约 …………………… 25.104
　LOGIC 格式 …………… 25.118-25.122

分包
　船厂的权利 …………………… 3.143
　分包商地位 …………………… 3.152
　谨慎之责 ……………………… 3.155
　责任限制 ……………………… 3.157

抵销
　标准格式规定 ………………… 4.71
　概念 …………………………… 4.65
　明确规定 ……………………… 4.75
　排除的效力 …………………… 4.80
　权利的排除 …………………… 4.66

付款保函 …………………… 4.207
　标准格式的规定 ……………… 4.211
　海工装备建造 ………… 25.14-25.15
　母公司保函 …………………… 4.210
　无条件性 ……………………… 4.215
　性质 …………………………… 4.08
　准据法 ………………………… 4.220
　作用 …………………………… 4.208

更改
　费用的支付 …………………… 25.53
　更改的程序 …………… 25.47-25.49
　海工装备建造 ………… 25.19-25.20
　船东的权利 …………… 25.45-25.46
　加帐及交付顺延 ……… 25.50-25.51

无法达成一致 ………………… 25.52

关键路径
　概述 …………………………… 10.31
　局限性 ………………… 10.36-10.38
　关键路径延误 ………… 10.41-10.42
　在我国的应用 ………… 10.39-10.40

合同
　定义 …………………………… 1.1-1.7
　陈述
　　欺诈性陈述 ………………… 2.130
　成立
　　意思表示一致 ……………… 2.37
　　客观标准 …………………… 2.39
　　"以合同为准" ……………… 2.144
　解释
　　概述 ………………………… 22.1
　　原则 ………………………… 22.4
　合同生效条件
　　概述 ………………………… 21.1-21.2
　　解除条件 …………………… 21.3
　合同条款
　　保证 ………………… 2.174, 2.180
　　陈述成为合同条款 ………… 2.184
　　履行时间规定 ……………… 2.186
　　条件 ………………………… 2.174
　　中间条款 …………………… 2.182
　合同形式
　　船舶建造合同 ……………… 2.152
　　电子方式订立 ……………… 2.152
　　买卖合同 …………………… 2.135
　　以合同为准 ………………… 2.144
　洽谈合同的协议
　　不可执行性 ………………… 2.155
　　尽最大努力 ………………… 2.159
　要约

定义	2.43
交易的邀请	2.50
要约的撤回	2.61

合同价格 4.1
海工装备建造	25.9-25.10
价格重谈	4.157
加价的对价	4.159
加价的机会	4.158
减价的机会	4.163
价格调整	4.122
交船日	4.123
航速	4.135
货舱容积	4.153
油耗	4.143
载重吨	4.149
种类	
固定价格	4.2,4.4

合同解释
缔约当时情形	22.2-22.3
概述	22.1
合同文件之间的关系	
船舶建造合同特征	22.6-22.10
概述	22.5
原则	22.4
整体协议	
NEWBUILDCON 格式	22.12-22.13
缔约前承诺	22.14
概述	22.5
误述	22.15-22.20

合同文件
厂商表	2.12
规格书	2.6
图纸	2.9
中横剖面图	2.11

总布置图	2.10

合同生效条件
NEWBUILDCON 格式	21.10
当事人行为	
过错	21.15-21.19
合同解释	21.20-21.22
主观意志	21.23-21.24
概述	21.1-21.2
解除条件	21.11-21.12
条件分类	21.3-21.4

还款保函 4.164
保证合同	4.165
标准格式的规定	4.189
担保人责任解除	4.201
海工装备建造	25.14-25.15
性质	4.170
法院的解释	4.179
见索即付	4.175
主债务人	4.171
有效期	4.185
仲裁条款	4.195
转让	4.187

货物买卖法
1893 年《货物买卖法》	1.36
1979 年《货物买卖法》	1.36
1994 年《货物买卖法》	1.36
成文法的适用	1.39
对价	
确定货物	1.55
区分	1.56
特定货物	1.50
未来货物	1.60
区分	1.61
船舶建造合同	1.79

索引

未确定货物 ·························· 1.54
 区分 ································· 1.56
现有货物 ···························· 1.59
 区分 ································· 1.61

技术争议及解决
 概述 ······························· 15.88
 审图争议的解决 ················ 5.70
 特征 ······················· 15.88-15.90

建造人保险
 船厂义务的终止 ············· 14.143
 概述
  保险利益 ························ 14.7
  船厂的风险 ···················· 14.89
  合同义务 ························ 14.9
  建造人保险 ···················· 14.4
  协会条款 ························ 14.6
 合同交船日调整 ············· 14.142
 索赔通知 ······················ 14.118

健康安全与环境条款
 法定责任和合同责任 ··· 25.90-25.92
 概述 ······················ 25.83-25.84
 ISO 14001 ············· 25.85-25.86
 ISO 45001 ······················ 25.87
 LOGIC 格式 ············ 25.93-25.97
 中国做法 ················ 25.88-25.89

建造人保险保单
 保险价值 ······················· 14.13
 保险期限 ······················· 14.30
  结束 ···························· 14.34
  开始 ···························· 14.32
  延伸 ···························· 14.36
 被保险人 ······················· 14.20
  名称 ···························· 14.23
  标的物 ························· 14.13

监造代表
 船厂的协助 ···················· 5.101
 船东的雇主责任 ·············· 5.106
  NEWBUILDCON 格式 ······ 5.122
  船厂的过失 ···················· 5.116
  非船厂雇员 ···················· 5.112
  免责的约定 ···················· 5.109
 更换 ······························ 5129
 和船厂的关系 ················· 5.104
 和船级社的联系 ·············· 5.134
 授权 ······························ 5.94
 指派 ······························ 5.88
 职责 ······························ 5.99

交船文件
 IMO 有害物质清单 ············· 8.96
 测试报告 ························ 8.85
 建造人证书 ····················· 8.90
 交接备忘录 ····················· 8.82
 卖据 ······························ 8.95
 其他文件 ······················ 8.100
 商业发票 ························ 8.93
 设备和备件清单 ················ 8.86
 授权委托书 ··················· 8.102
 图纸 ······························ 8.92
 无登记证书 ····················· 8.94
 无负担保证 ····················· 8.91
 消耗品清单 ····················· 8.87
 证书 ······························ 8.88

解释
 不可抗力条款解释 ············· 9.38
 不可抗力通知解释 ············ 9.142
 船舶建造合同特征 ······ 22.6-22.10
 缔约当时情形 ············ 22.2-22.3
 概述 ······························ 22.1

合同解释 ·················· 21.20-21.22
原则 ······················ 22.4
整体协议
 NEWBUILDCON 格式 ······ 22.8-22.10
 缔约前承诺 ··············· 22.14
 概述 ····················· 22.11
 误述 ··············· 22.15-22.20
指定的解释 ················· 8.137

接受
沉默 ······················· 2.93
定义 ······················· 2.66
反要约 ····················· 2.95
格式之战 ··················· 2.101
明确和肯定 ················· 2.68
生效时间 ··················· 2.72
 电子邮件 ················· 2.88
 对生效的质疑 ············· 2.76
 瞬间通信 ················· 2.77
行为接受 ··················· 2.91

解约的后果
船厂处置船舶的权利 ········· 12.50
船厂继续建造 ··············· 12.51
船东供应品的 ··············· 12.48
海工装备建造 ········ 25.38-25.44
还款保函执行 ··············· 12.33
建造款的返还 ··············· 12.40
利息的支付 ················· 12.42
其他费用的返还 ············· 12.45
仲裁的开始 ················· 12.34

可允许延误
定义 ···················· 10.3-10.5
计算 ······················ 10.36
例子
 不可抗力 ············ 10.7,10.97

船东供应品 ······· 7.68,10.11,10.61,
       19.10,19.12-19.13
船东原因 ········ 8.17,10.13,10.93
检验 ······················ 5.71
监造 ······················ 10.9
审图 ······················ 10.8
试航 ············· 7.33-7.37,9.33,9.70
修改 ············ 6.36-6.36,6.44,10.10
支付 ······················ 10.13
种类 ······················ 10.6

买卖合同
出售 ······················· 1.42
出售协议 ··················· 1.43
 区分 ····················· 1.47
 船舶建造合同 ············· 1.79
定义 ······················· 1.39
绝对的买卖 ················· 1.65
凭描述买卖 ················· 1.66
 船舶描述 ················· 1.69
 对描述的依赖 ············· 1.75
 描述的性质 ··············· 1.67
 种类 ····················· 1.66
有条件的买卖 ··············· 1.63

默示保证 ···················· 1.80
符合描述保证 ··············· 1.89
 不符合描述 ··············· 1.93
 船舶的描述 ··············· 1.95
 默示条款的理解 ··········· 1.92
 条件条款 ················· 1.91
 样品买卖 ················· 1.127
所有权保证 ················· 1.81
 不受干扰的占有 ··········· 1.84
 船舶建造合同 ············· 1.87
 享有权利的时间 ··········· 1.82
适合用途保证 ··············· 1.134

船舶建造 …………………… 1.151
　质量保证 ………………………… 1.97
　　令人满意质量 ………………… 1.109
　　　安全 ……………………… 1.119
　　　出售目的 ………………… 1.116
　　　船舶建造 ………………… 1.104
　　　例外 ……………………… 1.122
　　　外观和外表 ……………… 1.117
　　　考虑的因素 ……………… 1.120
　　　责任排除效力 …………… 1.129
　　可销售质量 ……………………… 1.106
　　买者自负 ………………………… 1.98
　　业务经营 ………………………… 1.101
试航
　参加试航人员 …………………… 7.44
　　厂商的代表 …………………… 7.54
　　船厂的代表 …………………… 7.45
　　船东的代表 …………………… 7.48
　　船级社代表 …………………… 7.53
　船舶不符合合同
　　争议 ………………………… 7.99
　船东的接受与拒绝 ……………… 7.68
　　船东的表态 …………………… 7.68
　　接受船舶的意义 ……………… 7.73
　　权利的放弃 …………………… 7.71
　船东解约的权利 ………………… 7.94
　船东拒绝船舶的权利 …………… 7.82
　　错误拒绝 …………………… 7.101
　　客观理由 …………………… 7.87
　概述 ……………………………… 7.1
　海试 ……………………………… 7.1
　　船厂的试航 …………………… 7.11
　　其他通知 ……………………… 7.28
　试航成本分摊 …………………… 7.56
　　消耗品处置 …………………… 7.62

试航的进行
　试航的方式 ……………………… 7.38
　试航通知 ………………………… 7.14
　　船厂的义务 …………………… 7.15
　　数个通知 ……………………… 7.21
　试航的延期
　　船东代表缺席 ………………… 7.11
　　船东代表的签证 ……………… 7.26
　天气状况
　　对试航的影响 ………………… 7.29
　　船厂的决定 …………………… 7.31
　性能的含义 ……………………… 7.42
施救
　费用超过结果 ………………… 14.127
　概述 …………………………… 14.121
　施救费用 ……………………… 14.125
税收和规费
　出口退税 ……………………… 17.9
　分担 ……………………… 17.4-17.8
　概述 ……………………… 17.1-17.3
　合同约定 ……………… 17.14-17.16
调解
　概述 …………………………… 15.97
　船舶建造合同的规定 ………… 15.99
　通知
　不可抗力通知 ………………… 9.124
　裁决通知 ……………………… 15.105
　电子邮件 ……………………… 15.63
　付款通知 ……………………… 4.51
　解约通知 ……………………… 13.42
　其他通知 ……………………… 7.28
　缺陷通知 ……………………… 5.152
　试航通知 ……………………… 7.14
　索赔通知 ……………………… 14.118

通知条款
 概述 …………………………………… 20.1
 地址 …………………………………… 20.2-20.3
 联合卖方的通知 ……………………… 20.11
 通知的生效 …………………………… 20.8
 通知的形式要求 ……………………… 20.5-20.7
 语言 …………………………………… 20.13-20.15
违约通知 ………………………………… 13.42
延误通知
 AWES 格式 …………………………… 10.62
 CSTC 格式 …………………………… 10.58
 NEWBUILDCON 格式 ……………… 10.60
 Norwegian 格式 ……………………… 10.64
 SAJ 格式 ……………………………… 10.55
 前提条件 ……………………………… 10.66
质保通知 ………………………………… 14.18
转让通知 ………………………………… 16.19

图纸审核 ………………………………… 5.43
 船东审图 ……………………………… 5.47
  额外时间 …………………………… 5.52
  船东代表审图 ……………………… 5.54
 船东审图意见 ………………………… 5.57
  不构成修改 ………………………… 5.59
  不明确 ……………………………… 5.61
 船级社审图 …………………………… 5.54
 船级社审图延误 ……………………… 5.45
 审图争议 ……………………………… 5.70
 视为批准 ……………………………… 5.65
 图纸 …………………………………… 2.9
 意义 …………………………………… 5.49

相互赔偿条款
 保赔保险 ……………………………… 25.81-25.82
 不公平合同条款 ……………………… 25.77-25.78
 措辞 …………………………………… 25.60-25.62
 概述 …………………………………… 25.54-25.56

 LOGIC 格式 …………………………… 25.79-25.80
 明确约定 ……………………………… 25.66-25.68
 偏袒与任意 …………………………… 25.63-25.65
 身份与过错 …………………………… 25.57-25.59
 整体解释 ……………………………… 25.69-25.71
 重大过失与故意不当行为
 ………………………………………… 25.72-25.76

新建船经纪人 …………………………… 2.203
 法律地位 ……………………………… 2.204
 商业代理人 …………………………… 2.208
 唯一经纪人 …………………………… 2.212
 业务素质 ……………………………… 2.215
 佣金 …………………………………… 2.217
  船厂违约 …………………………… 2.221
  获得佣金的权利 …………………… 2.218

修改
 材料替代 ……………………………… 6.81
 船厂的修改 …………………………… 6.52
 船东的修改
  标准格式规定 ……………………… 6.6-6.11
  原因 ………………………………… 6.3-6.5
  概述 ………………………………… 6.1-6.2
 工作量减少 …………………………… 6.45
 合同交船日顺延 ……………………… 6.35
  不能顺延到情形 …………………… 6.38
  实际延误 …………………………… 6.36
  顺延的条件 ………………………… 6.40
 修改的约定 …………………………… 6.14-6.15
 修改费用 ……………………………… 6.20
  船厂的权利 ………………………… 6.25
  合理报酬 …………………………… 6.27
  支付 ………………………………… 6.30
 修改的争议 …………………………… 6.50
 修改与约定赔偿 ……………………… 6.33
 船级规范等变更

船厂的义务和权利 ……………	6.60
船厂履行合同的义务 ……………	6.67
概述 …………………………	6.58
修改费用 ………………………	6.88
合同倒签 ………………………	6.71
PSPC 规则 …………………	6.72
公共政策 …………………	6.76
性质 ………………………	6.74
影响 ………………………	6.79

要约

包含主要条款 …………………	2.59
创立法律关系 …………………	2.48
定义 ………………………	2.43
交易的邀请 …………………	2.50
要约的撤回 …………………	2.61

选择权

标准格式中的选择权 …………	23.3
单方的选择 …………………	23.6
选择权的给予	
影响 …………………	23.8
原因 …………………	23.7
要约的特征 …………………	23.4-23.5
一般选择权 …………………	23.1-23.2
行使 ………………………	23.9-23.10

延期

标准格式规定	
NEWBUILDCON 格式 ………	10.60
Norwegian 格式 …………	10.64
SAJ 格式 …………………	10.55
船厂举证之责 …………………	10.85
概述 ………………………	10.93
计算 ………………………	8.63
延期条款作用 …………………	10.45
影响船舶建造 …………………	10.66

延误

概述 ………………………	10.1-10.3
共同延误 …………………	10.18
可延期原因 …………………	10.22
违约 ………………………	10.23-10.24
因果关系 …………………	10.21
可允许延误定义 …………………	10.4-10.5
可允许延误种类 …………………	10.6-10.10
通知	
AWES 格式 …………………	10.62
CSTC 格式 …………………	10.58
NEWBUILDCON 格式 ………	10.60
Norwegian 格式 …………	10.64
SAJ 格式 …………………	10.55
标准格式规定 …………………	10.54
不利制定人原则 …………………	10.74
概述 ………………………	10.53
规定不明确 …………………	10.54
内容 ………………………	10.77
前提条件 …………………	10.66
完工和延误 …………………	10.14
整体索赔 …………………	10.25
分摊 ………………………	10.28

阻碍原则

船舶建造合同 …………………	10.51
概述 ………………………	10.53
合法行为 …………………	10.54
延误责任 …………………	6.33, 10.46
约定赔偿 …………………	10.48

意向书 ………………… 2.110

性质 ………………………	2.111
要约性质 …………………	2.113
约束力 …………………	2.117

约定赔偿

惩罚 ………………………	4.88

惩罚的例子	4.89
船舶建造合同	4.115
船东支付的约定赔偿	4.120
当事人之间的约定	4.105
过错	4.113
数额	
确定数额的时间	4.110
实际损失超过数额	4.109
约定数额的名称	4.107
特征	4.84
支付	4.115

招标
合理报酬	2.131
没有约束力	2.114
欺诈性陈述	2.130
性质	2.111
招标和要约	2.120
招标人谨慎行事	2.124

支付	4.12
海工装备建造	25.16-25.18
节点	
交船	4.18
开工	4.18
签约	4.18
上船台	4.18
下水	4.18
建造款	4.18
建造款的性质	12.40
预付款与定金	4.38,12.42
交船款的支付	4.47,8.51
标准格式	8.54
船舶抵押	8.159
特殊性	8.52
支付安排	8.61
支付争议	8.63

提前支付	4.48
支付方式	
分期支付	4.15
电汇支付	4.25
支付时间	4.30
法律规定	4.30
银行工作日	4.33
支付条件	4.51
付款通知	4.54
还款保函	4.52
节点证书	4.59
真实的节点	4.61
监造代表会签	4.64

争议和仲裁
"一事不再理"原则	15.8-15.62
争议和分歧	15.15-15.19
仲裁裁决	
裁决通知	15.105
概述	15.103
仲裁概述	
解决争议方式	15.1-15.3
英国仲裁法	15.7-15.8
优点	15.4-15.6
仲裁开始的前提	15.20-15.22
仲裁协议	15.9-15.13
仲裁程序的开始	
机构仲裁和临时仲裁	15.52-15.57
开始的方式	15.73-15.74
开始的时间	15.68
仲裁费用	15.107-15.112
仲裁适用的法律	
概述	15.24-15.25
合同准据法	15.27-5.29
仲裁程序法	15.38-15.39
仲裁协议准据法	15.34-15.37

仲裁庭
  独任仲裁员 ·················· 15.84
  小额仲裁 ····················· 15.85
  仲裁员的指定 ·············· 15.77
  组成的时间 ·················· 15.82
  专家裁定 ············· 15.92-15.96

知识产权
NEWBUILDCON 格式 ······ 18.26-18.29
保护 ····································· 18.20
船舶处置 ······························ 18.25
船舶建造专利 ················ 18.9-18.11
  船厂义务 ··················· 18.12-18.15
  范围及期限 ················ 18.16-18.19
船厂知识产权 ··············· 18.23-18.24
第三人知识产权 ············ 18.21-18.22
概述 ······························· 18.1-18.3
商标 ································ 18.6-18.7
商号 ···································· 18.8
专利 ······························· 18.4-18.5
"不受干扰地占有" ··················· 1.74

质量保证
概述 ······························· 11.1-11.3
缺陷
  定义 ································ 11.26
  缺陷导致的损坏 ··················· 11.37
  质保期限内的缺陷 ················ 11.41
其他缺陷 ······························ 11.90
间接损失
  特征 ································ 11.72
  结果性损失含义 ··················· 11.75
  事实问题 ··························· 11.79
  责任排除的效力 ··················· 11.94
  责任排除无效 ····················· 11.102
  合同规定 ··························· 11.81
修理和替换 ··························· 11.55

AWES 格式 ·························· 11.59
CSTC 格式 ·························· 11.64
NEWBUILDCON 格式 ············· 11.67
Norwegian 格式 ···················· 11.60
SAJ 格式 ····························· 11.56
第三人修理和替换 ·················· 11.87
质保范围 ······················ 11.24-11.25
质保工程师
  船厂的义务 ························ 11.116
  船厂的权利 ························ 11.113
  船东的过失责任 ··················· 11.121
  费用 ································ 11.119
质保期限 ······················ 11.38-11.40
  期限的延长 ················· 11.43-11.47
质保条款 ····················· 11.4, 11.24
质保通知 ······················ 11.48-11.52
  前提 ································ 11.53
质保转让
  期限届满后的转让 ················ 11.107
  意义 ································ 11.104
  转售中的转让 ····················· 11.110

仲裁裁决的上诉
法律问题 ····························· 15.119
上诉的放弃 ·························· 15.129
上诉的权利 ·························· 15.117
允许上诉的理由 ····················· 15.121
  明显错误 ··························· 15.123
  普遍重要性 ························ 15.124

仲裁程序的开始
法院的参与 ···························· 15.75
电子邮件 ······························ 15.63
"关于合同" ··························· 15.50
机构仲裁和临时仲裁 ········· 15.52-15.55
开始的方式 ···························· 15.73
开始的时间 ···························· 15.65

时间计算 …………………………… 12.65
时间限制 …………………………… 15.66
时限的延长 ………………………… 15.72
争议范围 …………………… 15.47-15.48

仲裁适用的法律
概述 ………………………………… 15.24
合同准据法 ………………………… 15.27
 合同无约定 ……………… 15.32-15.33
 合同有约定 ………………………15.30
仲裁程序法 ………………… 15.38-15.39
 合同没约定 ……………… 15.43-15.46
 合同有约定 ………………………15.42
 仲裁所属地 ……………… 15.40-15.41
仲裁协议准据法 …………… 15.34-15.37

中止建造
海工装备建造 ……………… 25.34-25.37

转让
船舶建造合同 ……………… 16.11-16.16
船东的履约责任 …………… 16.22-16.23
抵销
 船舶建造合同规定 ……… 16.32-16.33
 概述 ………………………………16.28
 关联性 ……………………………16.31
概述 ………………………………16.1-16.2
诉权转让 …………………… 16.3-16.5
索赔权保留 ………………… 16.26-16.27
转让费用 …………………… 16.24-16.25
转让区分 …………………… 16.16-16.18
转让通知 …………………… 16.19-16.21
转让限制 …………………… 16.6-16.9